1 MONTH OF
FREE
READING

at

www.ForgottenBooks.com

By purchasing this book you are eligible for one month membership to ForgottenBooks.com, giving you unlimited access to our entire collection of over 1,000,000 titles via our web site and mobile apps.

To claim your free month visit:
www.forgottenbooks.com/free1028830

ISBN 978-0-331-21264-8
PIBN 11028830

MESSAGE

FROM THE

PRESIDENT OF THE UNITED STATES

TO THE

TWO HOUSES OF CONGRESS

AT THE COMMENCEMENT OF THE

FIRST SESSION OF THE FORTY-SEVENTH CONGRESS,

WITH THE

REPORTS OF THE HEADS OF DEPARTMENTS

AND

SELECTIONS FROM ACCOMPANYING DOCUMENTS.

EDITED BY

BEN: PERLEY POORE.

WASHINGTON:
GOVERNMENT PRINTING OFFICE.
1881.

A. 8081

Prepared in accordance with the provisions of the Revised Statutes, approved June 23, 1874.

SEC. 75. The Joint Committee on Public Printing shall appoint a competent person, who shall edit such portion of the documents accompanying the annual reports of the Departments as they may deem suitable for popular distribution, and prepare an alphabetical index thereto.

* * * * * * *

SEC. 196. The head of each Department, except the Department of Justice, shall furnish to the Congressional Printer copies of the documents usually accompanying his annual report on or before the first day of November in each year, and a copy of his annual report on or before the third Monday of November in each year.

* * * * * * *

SEC. 3798. Of the documents named in this section there shall be printed and bound, in addition to the usual number for Congress, the following numbers of copies, namely:

* * * * * * *

Second. Of the President's message, the annual reports of the Executive Departments, and the abridgment of accompanying documents, unless otherwise ordered by either house, ten thousand copies for the use of the members of the Senate and twenty-five thousand copies for the use of the members of the House of Representatives.

2

MESSAGE

OF

THE PRESIDENT OF THE UNITED STATES.

To the Senate and
  House of Representatives
    of the United States:

An appalling calamity has befallen the American people since their
chosen representatives last met in the halls where you are now assembled. We might else recall with unalloyed content the rare prosperity
with which throughout the year the nation has been blessed. Its harvests have been ·plenteous; its varied industries have thriven; the
health of its people has been preserved; it has maintained with foreign
governments the undisturbed relations of amity and peace. For these
manifestations of His favor, we owe to Him who holds our destiny in
His hands the tribute of our grateful devotion.

To that mysterious exercise of His will, which has taken from us the
loved and illustrious citizen who was but lately the head of the nation,
we bow in sorrow and submission.

The memory of his exalted character, of his noble achievements, and
of his patriotic life will be treasured forever as a sacred possession of
the whole people.

The announcement of his death drew from foreign governments and
peoples tributes of sympathy and sorrow which history will record as
signal tokens of the kinship of nations and the federation of mankind.

The feeling of good-will between our own government and that of Great
Britain was never more marked than at present. In recognition of this
pleasing fact, I directed, on the occasion of the late centennial celebration at Yorktown, that a salute be given to the British flag.

Save for the correspondence to which I shall refer hereafter in relation
to the proposed canal across the Isthmus of Panama, little has occurred
worthy of mention in the diplomatic relations of the two countries.

Early in the year the Fortune Bay claims were satisfactorily settled
by the British Government paying in full the sum of £15,000, most of
which has been already distributed. As the terms of the settlement
included compensation for injuries suffered by our fishermen at Aspee
Bay, there has been retained from the gross award a sum which is
deemed adequate for those claims.

The participation of Americans in the exhibitions at Melbourne and
Sydney will be approvingly mentioned in the reports of the two exhibi-

tions, soon to be presented to Congress. They will disclose the readiness of our countrymen to make successful competition in distant fields of enterprise.

Negotiations for an International Copyright Convention are in hopeful progress.

The surrender of Sitting Bull and his forces upon the Canadian frontier has allayed apprehension, although bodies of British Indians still cross the border in quest of sustenance. Upon this subject a correspondence has been opened, which promises an adequate understanding. Our troops have orders to avoid meanwhile all collisions with alien Indians.

The presence at the Yorktown celebration of representatives of the French Republic and descendants of Lafayette and of his gallant compatriots who were our allies in the Revolution, has served to strengthen the spirit of good-will which has always existed between the two nations.

You will be furnished with the proceedings of the Bi-metallic Conference held during the summer at the city of Paris. No accord was reached, but a valuable interchange of views was had, and the conference will next year be renewed.

At the Electrical Exhibition and Congress also held at Paris, this country was creditably represented by eminent specialists who, in the absence of an appropriation, generously lent their efficient aid at the instance of the State Department. While our exhibitors in this almost distinctively American field of achievement have won several valuable awards, I recommend that Congress provide for the repayment of the personal expenses incurred, in the public interest, by the honorary commissioners and delegates.

No new questions respecting the status of our naturalized citizens in Germany have arisen during the year, and the causes of complaint, especially in Alsace and Lorraine, have practically ceased through the liberal action of the Imperial Government in accepting our often-expressed views on the subject. The application of the treaty of 1868 to the lately acquired Rhenish provinces has received very earnest attention, and a definite and lasting agreement on this point is confidently expected. The participation of the descendants of Baron von Steuben in the Yorktown festivities, and their subsequent reception by their American kinsmen, strikingly evinced the ties of good-will which unite the German people and our own.

Our intercourse with Spain has been friendly. An agreement concluded in February last fixes a term for the labors of the Spanish and American Claims Commission. The Spanish Government has been requested to pay the late awards of that commission, and will, it is believed, accede to the request as promptly and courteously as on former occasions.

By recent legislation onerous fines have been imposed upon American shipping in Spanish and colonial ports for slight irregularities in manifests. One case of hardship is specially worthy of attention. The bark "Masonic," bound for Japan, entered Manila in distress, and is there sought to be confiscated under Spanish revenue laws for an alleged shortage in her trans-shipped cargo. Though efforts for her relief have thus far proved unavailing, it is expected that the whole matter will be adjusted in a friendly spirit.

The Senate resolutions of condolence on the assassination of the Czar Alexander II were appropriately communicated to the Russian Government, which in turn has expressed its sympathy in our late national bereavement. It is desirable that our cordial relations with Russia should be strengthened by proper engagements, assuring to peaceable Americans who visit the Empire the consideration which is due to them as citizens of a friendly state. This is especially needful with respect to American Israelites, whose classification with the native Hebrews has evoked energetic remonstrances from this government.

A supplementary consular agreement with Italy has been sanctioned and proclaimed, which puts at rest conflicts of jurisdiction in the case of crimes on shipboard.

Several important international conferences have been held in Italy during the year. At the Geographical Congress of Venice, the Beneficence Congress of Milan, and the Hygienic Congress of Turin, this country was represented by delegates from branches of the public service, or by private citizens duly accredited in an honorary capacity. It is hoped that Congress will give such prominence to the results of their participation as they may seem to deserve.

The abolition of all discriminating duties against such colonial productions of the Dutch East Indies as are imported hither from Holland has been already considered by Congress. I trust that at the present session the matter may be favorably concluded.

The insecurity of life and property in many parts of Turkey has given rise to correspondence with the Porte, looking particularly to the better protection of American missionaries in the empire. The condemned murderer of the eminent missionary Dr. Justin W. Parsons has not yet been executed, although this government has repeatedly demanded that exemplary justice be done.

The Swiss Government has again solicited the good offices of our diplomatic and consular agents for the protection of its citizens in countries where it is not itself represented. This request has, within proper limits, been granted.

Our agents in Switzerland have been instructed to protest against the conduct of the authorities of certain communes in permitting the emigration to this country of criminals and other objectionable persons. Several such persons, through the cooperation of the Commissioners of Emigration at New York, have been sent back by the steamers which brought them. A continuance of this course may prove a more effectual remedy than diplomatic remonstrance.

Treaties of commerce and navigation, and for the regulation of consular privileges, have been concluded with Roumania and Servia since
their admission into the family of European states.

As is natural with contiguous States having like institutions and like
aims of advancement and development, the friendship of the United
States and Mexico has been constantly maintained. This government
has lost no occasion of encouraging the Mexican Government to a beneficial realization of the mutual advantages which will result from more
intimate commercial intercourse, and from the opening of the rich interior of Mexico to railway enterprise. I deem it important that means
be provided to restrain the lawlessness unfortunately so common on the
frontier, and to suppress the forays of the reservation Indians on either
side of the Rio Grande.

The neighboring states of Central America have preserved internal
peace, and their outward relations toward us have been those of intimate friendship. There are encouraging signs of their growing disposition to subordinate their local interests to those which are common to
them by reason of their geographical relations.

The boundary dispute between Guatemala and Mexico has afforded
this government an opportunity to exercise its good offices for preventing a rupture between those states, and for procuring a peaceable solution of the question. I cherish strong hope that in view of our relations
of amity with both countries our friendly counsels may prevail.

A special envoy of Guatemala has brought to me the condolences of
his government and people on the death of President Garfield.

The Costa Rican Government lately framed an engagement with
Colombia for settling by arbitration the boundary question between
those countries, providing that the post of arbitrator should be offered successively to the King of the Belgians, the King of Spain,
and the President of the Argentine Confederation. The King of the
Belgians has declined to act, but I am not as yet advised of the action
of the King of Spain. As we have certain interests in the disputed territory which are protected by our treaty engagements with one of the
parties, it is important that the arbitration should not, without our
consent, affect our rights, and this government has accordingly thought
proper to make its views known to the parties to the agreement, as well
as to intimate them to the Belgian and Spanish Governments.

The questions growing out of the proposed interoceanic water-way
across the Isthmus of Panama are of grave national importance. This
government has not been unmindful of the solemn obligations imposed
upon it by its compact of 1846 with Colombia, as the independent and
sovereign mistress of the territory crossed by the canal, and has sought
to render them effective by fresh engagements with the Colombian Republic looking to their practical execution. The negotiations to this
end, after they had reached what appeared to be a mutually satisfactory

solution here, were met in Colombia by a disavowal of the powers which its envoy had assumed, and by a proposal for renewed negotiation on a modified basis.

Meanwhile this government learned that Colombia had proposed to the European powers to join in a guarantee of the neutrality of the proposed Panama Canal—a guarantee which would be in direct contravention of our obligation as the sole guarantor of the integrity of Colombian territory and of the neutrality of the canal itself. My lamented predecessor felt it his duty to place before the European powers the reasons which make the prior guarantee of the United States indispensable, and for which the interjection of any foreign guarantee might be regarded as a superfluous and unfriendly act.

Foreseeing the probable reliance of the British Government on the provisions of the Clayton-Bulwer treaty of 1850, as affording room for a share in the guarantees which the United States covenanted with Colombia four years before, I have not hesitated to supplement the action of my predecessor by proposing to Her Majesty's Government the modification of that instrument and the abrogation of such clauses thereof as do not comport with the obligations of the United States toward Colombia, or with the vital needs of the two friendly parties to the compact.

This government sees with great concern the continuance of the hostile relations between Chili, Bolivia, and Peru. An early peace between these republics is much to be desired, not only that they may themselves be spared further misery and bloodshed, but because their continued antagonism threatens consequences which are, in my judgment, dangerous to the interests of republican government on this continent, and calculated to destroy the best elements of our free and peaceful civilization.

As in the present excited condition of popular feeling in these countries there has been serious misapprehension of the position of the United States, and as separate diplomatic intercourse with each through independent ministers is sometimes subject, owing to the want of prompt reciprocal communication, to temporary misunderstanding, I have deemed it judicious, at the present time, to send a special envoy, accredited to all and each of them, and furnished with general instructions, which will, I trust, enable him to bring these powers into friendly relations.

The government of Venezuela maintains its attitude of warm friendship, and continues with great regularity its payment of the monthly quota of the diplomatic debt. Without suggesting the direction in which Congress should act, I ask its attention to the pending questions affecting the distribution of the sums thus far received.

The relations between Venezuela and France, growing out of the same debt, have been for some time past in an unsatisfactory state, and this government, as the neighbor and one of the largest creditors of Venezuela, has interposed its influence with the French Government with the view of producing a friendly and honorable adjustment.

I regret that the commercial interests between the United States and Brazil, from which great advantages were hoped a year ago, have suffered from the withdrawal of the American lines of communication between the Brazilian ports and our own.

Through the efforts of our minister resident at Buenos Ayres and the United States minister at Santiago, a treaty has been concluded between the Argentine Republic and Chili, disposing of the long-pending Patagonian boundary question. It is a matter of congratulation that our government has been afforded the opportunity of successfully exerting its good influence for the prevention of disagreements between these republics of the American continent.

I am glad to inform you that the treaties lately negotiated with China have been duly ratified on both sides, and the exchange made at Peking. Legislation is necessary to carry their provisions into effect. The prompt and friendly spirit with which the Chinese Government, at the request of the United States, conceded the modification of existing treaties, should secure careful regard for the interests and susceptibilities of that government in the enactment of any laws relating to Chinese immigration.

Those clauses of the treaties which forbid the participation of citizens or vessels of the United States in the opium trade will doubtless receive your approval. They will attest the sincere interest which our people and government feel in the commendable efforts of the Chinese Government to put a stop to this demoralizing and destructive traffic.

In relation both to China and Japan, some changes are desirable in our present system of consular jurisdiction. I hope at some future time to lay before you a scheme for its improvement in the entire East.

The intimacy between our own country and Japan, the most advanced of the eastern nations, continues to be cordial. I am advised that the Emperor contemplates the establishment of full constitutional government and that he has already summoned a parliamentary congress for the purpose of effecting the change. Such a remarkable step toward complete assimilation with the western system cannot fail to bring Japan into closer and more beneficial relationship with ourselves as the chief Pacific power.

A question has arisen in relation to the exercise in that country of the judicial functions conferred upon our ministers and consuls. The indictment, trial, and conviction in the consular court at Yokohama of John Ross, a merchant-seaman on board an American vessel, have made it necessary for the government to institute a careful examination into the nature and methods of this jurisdiction.

It appeared that Ross was regularly shipped under the flag of the United States, but was by birth a British subject. My predecessor felt it his duty to maintain the position that, during his service as a regularly shipped seaman on board an American merchant vessel, Ross was subject to the laws of that service and to the jurisdiction of the United States consular authorities.

I renew the recommendation which has been heretofore urged by the Executive upon the attention of Congress, that after the reduction of such amount as may be found due to American citizens, the balance of the indemnity funds heretofore obtained from China and Japan, and which are now in the hands of the State Department, be returned to the governments of those countries.

The King of Hawaii, in the course of his homeward return after a journey around the world, has lately visited this country. While our relations with that kingdom are friendly, this government has viewed with concern the efforts to seek replenishment of the diminishing population of the islands from outward sources, to a degree which may impair the native sovereignty and independence, in which the United States was among the first to testify a lively interest.

Relations of unimpaired amity have been maintained throughout the year with the respective Governments of Austria-Hungary, Belgium, Denmark, Hayti, Paraguay and Uruguay, Portugal, and Sweden and Norway. This may also be said of Greece and Ecuador, although our relations with those states have for some years been severed by the withdrawal of appropriations for diplomatic representatives at Athens and Quito. It seems expedient to restore those missions, even on a reduced scale, and I decidedly recommend such a course with respect to Ecuador, which is likely, within the near future, to play an important part among the nations of the Southern Pacific.

At its last extra session the Senate called for the text of the Geneva Convention for the relief of the wounded in war. I trust that this action foreshadows such interest in the subject as will result in the adhesion of the United States to that humane and commendable engagement.

I invite your attention to the propriety of adopting the new Code of International Rules for the Prevention of Collisions on the high seas, and of conforming the domestic legislation of the United States thereto, so that no confusion may arise from the application of conflicting rules in the case of vessels of different nationalities meeting in tidal waters. These international rules differ but slightly from our own. They have been adopted by the Navy Department for the governance of the war ships of the United States on the high seas and in foreign waters; and, through the action of the State Department in disseminating the rules, and in acquainting shipmasters with the option of conforming to them without the jurisdictional waters of the United States, they are now very generally known and obeyed.

The State Department still continues to publish to the country the trade and manufacturing reports received from its officers abroad. The success of this course warrants its continuance, and such appro priation as may be required to meet the rapidly-increasing demand for these publications. With special reference to the Atlanta Cotton Exposition, the October number of the reports was devoted to a valuable collection of papers on the cotton-goods trade of the world.

The International Sanitary Conference, for which, in 1879, Congress made provision, assembled in this city early in January last, and its sessions were prolonged until March. Although it reached no specific conclusions affecting the future action of the participant powers, the interchange of views proved to be most valuable. The full protocols of the sessions have been already presented to the Senate.

As pertinent to this general subject I call your attention to the operations of the National Board of Health. Established by act of Congress approved March 3, 1879, its sphere of duty was enlarged by the act of June 2 in the same year. By the last-named act the board was required to institute such measures as might be deemed necessary for preventing the introduction of contagious or infectious diseases from foreign countries into the United States or from one State into another.

The execution of the rules and regulations prepared by the board and approved by my predecessor has done much to arrest the progress of epidemic disease, and has thus rendered substantial service to the nation.

The International Sanitary Conference, to which I have referred, adopted a form of a bill of health to be used by all vessels seeking to enter the ports of the countries whose representatives participated in its deliberatons. This form has since been prescribed by the National Board of Health and incorporated with its rules and regulations, which have been approved by me in pursuance of law.

The health of the people is of supreme importance. All measures looking to their protection against the spread of contagious diseases, and to the increase of our sanitary knowledge for such purposes, deserve attention of Congress.

The report of the Secretary of the Treasury presents in detail a highly satisfactory exhibit of the state of the finances and the condition of the various branches of the public service administered by that department.

The ordinary revenues from all sources for the fiscal year ending June 30, 1881, were:

From customs	$198,159,676 02
From internal revenue.............................	135,264,385 51
From sales of public lands........................	2,201,863 17
From tax on circulation and deposits of national banks	8,116,115 72
From repayment of interest by Pacific Railway Companies...	810,833 80
From sinking fund for Pacific Railway Companies...	805,180 54
From customs fees, fines, penalties, &c........	1,225,514 86
From fees—consular, letters patent, and lands	2,244,983 98

From proceeds of sales of government property $262,174 00

From profits on coinage 3,468,485 61

From revenues of the District of Columbia.......... 2,016,199 23

From miscellaneous sources 6,206,880 13

Total ordinary receipts...................·..... 360,782,292 57

The ordinary expenditures for the same period were:

For civil expenses $17,941,177 19

For foreign intercourse............................. 1,093,954 92

For Indians 6,514,161 09

For pensions 50,059,279 62

For the military establishment, including river and
harbor improvements and arsenals................ 40,466,460 55

For the naval establishment, including vessels, machinery, and improvements at navy-yards 15,686,671 66

For miscellaneous expenditures, including public
buildings, light-houses, and collecting the revenue.. 41,837,280 57

For expenditures on account of the District of Columbia 3,543,912 03

For interest on the public debt...................... 82,508,741 18

For premium on bonds purchased 1,061,248 78

Total ordinary expenditures 200,712,887 59

Leaving a surplus revenue of 100,069,404 98

Which was applied as follows:

To the redemption of—

Bonds for the sinking fund $74,371,200 00

Fractional currency for the sinking fund............ 109,001 05

Loan of February, 1861 .... 7,418,000 00

Ten-forties of 1864................................. 2,016,150 00

Five-twenties of 1862............................... 18,300 00

Five-twenties of 1864 .... 3,400 00

Five-twenties of 1865........... .... 37,300 00

Consols of 1865................................... 143,150 00

Consols of 1867 .... 959,150 00

Consols of 1868................................... 337,400 00

Texan indemnity stock....... .... 1,000 00

Old demand, compound-interest, and other notes..... 18,330 00

And to the increase of cash in the Treasury.......... 14,637,023 93

100,069,404 98

The requirements of the sinking fund for the year amounted to $90,786,064.02, which sum included a balance of $49,817,128.78, not provided for during the previous fiscal year. The sum of $74,480,201.05 was applied to this fund, which left a deficit of $16,305,873.47. The increase of the revenues for 1881 over those of the previous year was $29,352,901.10. It is estimated that the receipts during the present fiscal year will reach $400,000,000, and the expenditures $270,000,000, leaving a surplus of $130,000,000 applicable to the sinking fund and the redemption of the public debt.

I approve the recommendation of the Secretary of the Treasury, that provision be made for the early retirement of silver certificates, and that the act requiring their issue be repealed. They were issued in pursuance of the policy of the government to maintain silver at or near the gold standard, and were accordingly made receivable for all customs, taxes, and public dues. About sixty-six millions of them are now outstanding. They form an unnecessary addition to the paper currency, a sufficient amount of which may be readily supplied by the national banks.

In accordance with the act of February 28, 1878, the Treasury Department has, monthly, caused at least two millions in value of silver bullion to be coined into standard silver dollars. One hundred and two millions of these dollars have been already coined, while only about thirty-four millions are in circulation.

For the reasons which he specifies, I concur in the Secretary's recommendation that the provision for coinage of a fixed amount each month be repealed, and that hereafter only so much be coined as shall be necessary to supply the demand.

The Secretary advises that the issue of gold certificates should not for the present be resumed, and suggests that the national banks may properly be forbidden by law to retire their currency except upon reasonable notice of their intention so to do. Such legislation would seem to be justified by the recent action of certain banks on the occasion referred to in the Secretary's report.

Of the fifteen millions of fractional currency still outstanding, only about eighty thousand has been redeemed the past year. The suggestion that this amount may properly be dropped from future statements of the public debt seems worthy of approval.

So, also, does the suggestion of the Secretary as to the advisability of relieving the calendar of the United States courts in the southern district of New York, by the transfer to another tribunal of the numerous suits there pending against collectors.

The revenue from customs for the past fiscal year was $198,159,676.02, an increase of $11,637,611.42 over that of the year preceding. $138,098,562.39 of this amount was collected at the port of New York, leaving $50,251,113.63 as the amount collected at all the other ports of the country. Of this sum, $47,977,137.63 was collected on sugar, melado, and molasses; $37,285,624.78 on wool and its manufactures; $21,462,534.34 on iron and steel, and manufactures thereof; $19,038,665.51 on manufactures of silk;

$10,825,115.21 on manufactures of cotton; and $6,469,643.04 on wines and spirits; making a total revenue from these sources, of $133,058,720.81.

The expenses of collection for the past year were $6,419,345.20, an increase over the preceding year of $387,410.04. Notwithstanding the increase in the revenue from customs over the preceding year, the gross value of the imports, including free goods, decreased over twenty-five millions of dollars. The most marked decrease was in the value of unmanufactured wool, $14,023,682, and in that of scrap and pig iron, $12,810,671. The value of imported sugar, on the other hand showed an increase of $7,457,474; of steel rails, $4,345,521; of barley, $2,154,204; and of steel in bars, ingots, &c., $1,620,046.

Contrasted with the imports during the last fiscal year, the exports were as follows:

Domestic merchandise	$883,925,947
Foreign merchandise	18,451,399
Total	902,377,346
Imports of merchandise..............................	642,664,628
Excess of exports over imports of merchandise	259,712,718
Aggregate of exports and imports	1,545,041,974

Compared with the previous year, there was an increase of $66,738,688 in the value of exports of merchandise, and a decrease of $25,290,118 in the value of imports. The annual average of the excess of imports of merchandise over exports thereof, for ten years previous to June 30, 1873, was $104,706,922; but for the last six years there has been an excess of exports over imports of merchandise amounting to $1,180,668,105, an annual average of $196,778,017. The specie value of the exports of domestic merchandise was $376,616,473 in 1870, and $883,925,947 in 1881, an increase of $507,309,474, or 135 per cent. The value of imports was $435,958,408 in 1870, and $642,664,628 in 1881, an increase of $206,706,220, or 47 per cent.

During each year from 1862 to 1879, inclusive, the exports of specie exceeded the imports. The largest excess of such exports over imports was reached during the year 1864, when it amounted to $92,280,929. But during the year ended June 30, 1880, the imports of coin and bullion exceeded the exports by $75,891,391; and during the last fiscal year the excess of imports over exports was $91,168,650.

In the last annual report of the Secretary of the Treasury the attention of Congress was called to the fact that $469,651,050 in five per centum bonds and $203,573,750 in six per centum bonds would become redeemable during the year, and Congress was asked to authorize the refunding of these bonds at a lower rate of interest. The bill for such refunding having failed to become a law, the Secretary of the

Treasury, in April last, notified the holders of the $195,690,400 six per centum bonds then outstanding, that the bonds would be paid at par on the first day of July following, or that they might be "continued" at the pleasure of the government, to bear interest at the rate of three and one-half per centum per annum.

Under this notice $178,055,150 of the six per centum bonds were continued at the lower rate, and $17,635,250 were redeemed.

In the month of May a like notice was given respecting the redemption or continuance of the $439,841,350 of five per centum bonds then outstanding, and of these, $401,504,900 were continued at three and one-half per centum per annum, and $38,336,450 redeemed.

The six per centum bonds of the loan of February 8, 1861, and of the Oregon war debt, amounting together to $14,125,800, having matured during the year, the Secretary of the Treasury gave notice of his intention to redeem the same, and such as have been presented have been paid from the surplus revenues. There have also been redeemed at par $16,179,100 of the three and one-half per centum "continued" bonds, making a total of bonds redeemed, or which have ceased to bear interest during the year, of $123,969,650.

The reduction of the annual interest on the public debt through these transactions is as follows:

By reduction of interest to three and one-half per cent.. $10,473,952 25
By redemption of bonds..................................   6,352,340 00

    Total.. 16,826,292 25

The three and one-half per centum bonds, being payable at the pleasure of the government, are available for the investment of surplus revenue without the payment of premiums.

Unless these bonds can be funded at a much lower rate of interest than they now bear, I agree with the Secretary of the Treasury that no legislation respecting them is desirable.

It is a matter for congratulation that the business of the country has been so prosperous during the past year as to yield by taxation a large surplus of income to the government. If the revenue laws remain unchanged this surplus must, year by year, increase, on account of the reduction of the public debt and its burden of interest, and because of the rapid increase of our population. In 1860, just prior to the institution of our internal-revenue system, our population but slightly exceeded 30,000,000; by the census of 1880 it is now found to exceed 50,000,000. It is estimated that even if the annual receipts and expenditures should continue as at present the entire debt could be paid in ten years.

In view, however, of the heavy load of taxation which our people have already borne, we may well consider whether it is not the part of wisdom to reduce the revenues, even if we delay a little the payment of the debt.

It seems to me that the time has arrived when the people may justly demand some relief from their present onerous burden, and that by due economy in the various branches of the public service, this may readily be afforded.

I therefore concur with the Secretary in recommending the abolition of all internal-revenue taxes, except those upon tobacco in its various forms, and upon distilled spirits and fermented liquors ; and except also the special tax upon the manufacturers of, and dealers in, such articles. The retention of the latter tax is desirable as affording the officers or the government a proper supervision of these articles for the prevention of fraud. I agree with the Secretary of the Treasury, that the law imposing a stamp tax upon matches, proprietary articles, playing cards, checks, and drafts, may with propriety be repealed, and the law also by which banks and bankers are assessed upon their capital and deposits. There seems to be a general sentiment in favor of this course.

In the present condition of our revenues the tax upon deposits is especially unjust. It was never imposed in this country until it was demanded by the necessities of war, and was never exacted, I believe, in any other country, even in its greatest exigencies. Banks are required to secure their circulation by pledging with the Treasurer of the United States bonds of the general government. The interest upon these bonds, which at the time when the tax was imposed was 6 per cent., is now, in most instances, 3½ per cent. Besides, the entire circulation was originally limited by law and no increase was allowable. When the existing banks had practically a monopoly of the business, there was force in the suggestion, that for the franchise to the favored grantees the government might very properly exact a tax on circulation ; but for years the system has been free, and the amount of circulation regulated by the public demand.

The retention of this tax has been suggested as a means of reimbursing the government for the expense of printing and furnishing the circulating notes. If the tax should be repealed it would certainly seem proper to require the national banks to pay the amount of such expense to the Comptroller of the Currency.

It is perhaps doubtful whether the immediate reduction of the rate of taxation upon liquors and tobacco is advisable, especially in view of the drain upon the Treasury which must attend the payment of arrears of pensions. A comparison, however, of the amount of taxes collected under the varying rates of taxation which have at different times prevailed, suggests the intimation that some reduction may soon be made without material diminution of the revenue.

The tariff laws also need revision ; but, that a due regard may be paid to the conflicting interests of our citizens, important changes should be made with caution. If a careful revision cannot be made at this session, a commission such as was lately approved by the Senate and is now recommended by the Secretary of the Treasury would doubtless lighten the labors of Congress whenever this subject shall be brought to its consideration.

The accompanying report of the Secretary of War will make known to you the operations of that department for the past year.

He suggests measures for promoting the efficiency of the Army without adding to the number of its officers, and recommends the legislation necessary to increase the number of enlisted men to thirty thousand, the maximum allowed by law.

This he deems necessary to maintain quietude on our ever-shifting frontier; to preserve peace and suppress disorder and marauding in new settlements; to protect settlers and their property against Indians, and Indians against the encroachments of intruders; and to enable peaceable immigrants to establish homes in the most remote parts of our country.

The Army is now necessarily scattered over such a vast extent of territory that, whenever an outbreak occurs, reinforcements must be hurried from many quarters, over great distances, and always at heavy cost for transportation of men, horses, wagons, and supplies.

I concur in the recommendations of the Secretary for increasing the Army to the strength of thirty thousand enlisted men.

It appears by the Secretary's report that in the absence of disturbances on the frontier the troops have been actively employed in collecting the Indians hitherto hostile, and locating them on their proper reservations; that Sitting Bull and his adherents are now prisoners at Fort Randall; that the Utes have been moved to their new reservation in Utah; that during the recent outbreak of the Apaches it was necessary to reinforce the garrisons in Arizona by troops withdrawn from New Mexico; and that some of the Apaches are now held prisoners for trial, while some have escaped, and the majority of the tribe are now on their reservation.

There is need of legislation to prevent intrusion upon the lands set apart for the Indians. A large military force, at great expense, is now required to patrol the boundary line between Kansas and the Indian Territory. The only punishment that can at present be inflicted is the forcible removal of the intruder and the imposition of a pecuniary fine, which, in most cases, it is impossible to collect. There should be a penalty by imprisonment in such cases.

The separate organization of the Signal Service is urged by the Secretary of War, and a full statement of the advantages of such permanent organization is presented in the report of the Chief Signal Officer. A detailed account of the useful work performed by the Signal Corps and the Weather Bureau, is also given in that report.

I ask attention to the statements of the Secretary of War regarding the requisitions frequently made by the Indian Bureau upon the Subsistence Department of the Army for the casual support of bands and tribes of Indians whose appropriations are exhausted. The War Department should not be left, by reason of inadequate provision for the Indian Bureau, to contribute for the maintenance of Indians.

The report of the Chief of Engineers furnishes a detailed account of the operations for the improvement of rivers and harbors.

I commend to your attention the suggestions contained in this report in regard to the condition of our fortifications, especially our coast defenses, and recommend an increase of the strength of the Engineer Battalion, by which the efficiency of our torpedo system would be improved.

I also call your attention to the remarks upon the improvement of the South Pass of the Mississippi River, the proposed free bridge over the Potomac River at Georgetown, the importance of completing at an early day the north wing of the War Department building, and other recommendations of the Secretary of War which appear in his report.

The actual expenditures of that department for the fiscal year ending June 30, 1881, were $42,122,201.39. The appropriations for the year 1882 were $44,889,725.42. The estimates for 1883 are $44,541,276.91.

The report of the Secretary of the Navy exhibits the condition of that branch of the service, and presents valuable suggestions for its improvement. I call your especial attention also to the appended report of the Advisory Board, which he convened to devise suitable measures for increasing the efficiency of the Navy, and particularly to report as to the character and number of vessels necessary to place it upon a footing commensurate with the necessities of the government.

I cannot too strongly urge upon you my conviction that every consideration of national safety, economy, and honor imperatively demands a thorough rehabilitation of our Navy.

With a full appreciation of the fact that compliance with the suggestions of the head of that department and of the Advisory Board must involve a large expenditure of the public moneys, I earnestly recommend such appropriations as will accomplish an end which seems to me so desirable.

Nothing can be more inconsistent with true public economy than withholding the means necessary to accomplish the objects intrusted by the Constitution to the national legislature. One of those objects, and one which is of paramount importance, is declared by our fundamental law to be the provision for the "common defense." Surely nothing is more essential to the defense of the United States and of all our people than the efficiency of our Navy.

We have for many years maintained with foreign governments the relations of honorable peace, and that such relations may be permanent is desired by every patriotic citizen of the Republic.

But if we heed the teachings of history we shall not forget that in the life of every nation emergencies may arise when a resort to arms can alone save it from dishonor.

2 Ab

No danger from abroad now threatens this people, nor have we any cause to distrust the friendly professions of other governments.

But for avoiding as well as for repelling dangers that may threaten us in the future, we must be prepared to enforce any policy which we think wise to adopt.

We must be ready to defend our harbors against aggression, to protect, by the distribution of our ships of war over the highways of commerce, the varied interests of our foreign trade, and the persons and property of our citizens abroad, to maintain everywhere the honor of our flag, and the distinguished position which we may rightfully claim among the nations of the world.

The report of the Postmaster-General is a gratifying exhibit of the growth and efficiency of the postal service.

The receipts from postage and other ordinary sources during the past fiscal year were $36,489,816.58. The receipts from the money-order business were $295,581.39, making a total of $36,785,397.97. The expenditure for the fiscal year was $39,251,736.46. The deficit supplied out of the general Treasury was $2,481,129.35, or $6\frac{1}{5}$ per cent. of the amount expended. The receipts were $3,469,918.63 in excess of those of the previous year, and $4,575,397.97 in excess of the estimate made two years ago, before the present period of business prosperity had fairly begun.

The whole number of letters mailed in this country in the last fiscal year exceeded one thousand millions.

The registry system is reported to be in excellent condition, having been remodeled during the past four years, with good results. The amount of registration fees collected during the last fiscal year was $712,882.20, an increase over the fiscal year ending June 30, 1877, of $345,443.40.

The entire number of letters and packages registered during the year was 8,338,919, of which only 2,061 were lost or destroyed in transit.

The operations of the money-order system are multiplying yearly under the impulse of immigration, of the rapid development of the newer States and Territories, and the consequent demand for additional means of intercommunication and exchange.

During the past year, 338 additional money-order offices have been established, making a total of 5,499 in operation at the date of this report.

During the year the domestic money orders aggregated in value $105,075,769.35.

A modification of the system is suggested, reducing the fees for money orders not exceeding $5 from ten cents to five cents, and making the maximum limit $100 in place of $50.

Legislation for the disposition of unclaimed money orders in the possession of the Post-Office Department is recommended, in view of the fact that their total value now exceeds one million dollars.

The attention of Congress is again invited to the subject of establishing a system of savings depositories in connection with the Post-Office Department.

The statistics of mail transportation show that during the past year railroad routes have been increased in length 6,249 miles, and in cost $1,114,382, while steamboat routes have been decreased in length 2,182 miles, and in cost $134,054. The so-called star routes have been decreased in length 3,949 miles, and in cost $364,144.

Nearly all of the more expensive routes have been superseded by railroad service. The cost of the star service must therefore rapidly decrease in the Western States and Territories.

The Postmaster-General, however, calls attention to the constantly increasing cost of the railway mail service as a serious difficulty in the way of making the department self-sustaining.

Our postal intercourse with foreign countries has kept pace with the growth of the domestic service. Within the past year several countries and colonies have declared their adhesion to the Postal Union. It now includes all those which have an organized postal service, except Bolivia, Costa Rica, New Zealand, and the British colonies in Australia.

As has been already stated, great reductions have recently been made in the expense of the star-route service. The investigations of the Department of Justice and the Post-Office Department have resulted in the presentation of indictments against persons formerly connected with that service, accusing them of offenses against the United States. I have enjoined upon the officials who are charged with the conduct of the cases on the part of the government and upon the eminent counsel who, before my accession to the Presidency, were called to their assistance, the duty of prosecuting with the utmost vigor of the law all persons who may be found chargeable with frauds upon the postal service.

The Acting Attorney-General calls attention to the necessity of modifying the present system of the courts of the United States—a necessity due to the large increase of business, especially in the Supreme Court. Litigation in our Federal tribunals became greatly expanded after the close of the late war. So long as that expansion might be attributable to the abnormal condition in which the community found itself immediately after the return of peace, prudence required that no change be made in the constitution of our judicial tribunals.

But it has now become apparent that an immense increase of litigation has directly resulted from the wonderful growth and development of the country. There is no ground for belief that the business of the United States courts will ever be less in volume than at present. Indeed, that it is likely to be much greater is generally recognized by the bench and bar.

In view of the fact that Congress has already given much consideration to this subject, I make no suggestion as to detail, but express the hope that your deliberations may result in such legislation as will give early relief to our overburdened courts.

The Acting Attorney-General also calls attention to the disturbance of the public tranquility during the past year in the Territory of Arizona. A band of armed desperadoes, known as "Cow Boys," probably numbering from fifty to one hundred men, have been engaged for months in committing acts of lawlessness and brutality which the local authorities have been unable to repress. The depredations of these "Cow Boys" have also extended into Mexico, which the marauders reach from the Arizona frontier. With every disposition to meet the exigencies of the case, I am embarrassed by lack of authority to deal with them effectually. The punishment of crimes committed within Arizona should ordinarily, of course, be left to the Territorial authorities. But it is worthy consideration whether acts which necessarily tend to embroil the United States with neighboring governments should not be declared crimes against the United States. Some of the incursions alluded to may perhaps be within the scope of the law (Revised Statutes, section 5286) forbidding "military expeditions or enterprises" against friendly states; but in view of the speedy assembling of your body, I have preferred to await such legislation as in your wisdom the occasion may seem to demand.

It may, perhaps, be thought proper to provide that the setting on foot within our own territory, of brigandage and armed marauding expeditions against friendly nations and their citizens, shall be punishable as an offense against the United States.

I will add that in the event of a request from the Territorial government for protection by the United States against "domestic violence," this government would be powerless to render assistance.

The act of 1795, chapter 36, passed at a time when Territorial governments received little attention from Congress, enforced this duty of the United States only as to the State governments. But the act of 1807, chapter 39, applied also to Territories. This law seems to have remained in force until the revision of the statutes, when the provision for the Territories was dropped. I am not advised whether this alteration was intentional or accidental, but, as it seems to me that the Territories should be offered the protection which is accorded to the States by the Constitution, I suggest legislation to that end.

It seems to me, too, that whatever views may prevail as to the policy of recent legislation by which the Army has ceased to be a part of the *posse comitatus*, an exception might well be made for permitting the military to assist the civil Territorial authorities in enforcing the laws of the United States. This use of the Army would not seem to be within the alleged evil against which that legislation was aimed. From sparseness of population and other circumstances it is often quite impracticable to summon a civil posse in places where officers of justice require assistance, and where a military force is within easy reach.

The report of the Secretary of the Interior, with accompanying documents, presents an elaborate account of the business of that department. A summary of it would be too extended for this place. I ask your careful attention to the report itself.

Prominent among the matters which challenge the attention of Congress at its present session is the management of our Indian affairs. While this question has been a cause of trouble and embarrassment from the infancy of the government, it is but recently that any effort has been made for its solution, at once serious, determined, consistent, and promising success.

It has been easier to resort to convenient makeshifts for tiding over temporary difficulties than to grapple with the great permanent problem, and, accordingly, the easier course has almost invariably been pursued.

It was natural, at a time when the national territory seemed almost illimitable and contained many millions of acres far outside the bounds of civilized settlements, that a policy should have been initiated which more than aught else has been the fruitful source of our Indian complications.

I refer of course to the policy of dealing with the various Indian tribes as separate nationalities, of relegating them by treaty stipulations to the occupancy of immense reservations in the West, and of encouraging them to live a savage life, undisturbed by any earnest and well-directed efforts to bring them under the influences of civilization.

The unsatisfactory results which have sprung from this policy are becoming apparent to all.

As the white settlements have crowded the borders of the reservations, the Indians, sometimes contentedly and sometimes against their will, have been transferred to other hunting-grounds, from which they have again been dislodged whenever their new-found homes have been desired by the adventurous settlers.

These removals, and the frontier collisions by which they have often been preceded, have led to frequent and disastrous conflicts between the races.

It is profitless to discuss here which of them has been chiefly responsible for the disturbances whose recital occupies so large a space upon the pages of our history.

We have to deal with the appalling fact that though thousands of lives have been sacrificed, and hundreds of millions of dollars expended in the attempt to solve the Indian problem, it has until within the past few years seemed scarcely nearer a solution than it was half a century ago. But the government has of late been cautiously but steadily feeling its way to the adoption of a policy which has already produced gratifying results, and which, in my judgment, is likely, if Congress and the Executive accord in its support, to relieve us ere long from the difficulties which have hitherto beset us.

For the success of the efforts now making to introduce among the Indians the customs and pursuits of civilized life, and gradually to absorb them into the mass of our citizens, sharing their rights and holden to their responsibilities, there is imperative need for legislative action.

My suggestions in that regard will be chiefly such as have been already called to the attention of Congress, and have received to some extent its consideration:

First. I recommend the passage of an act making the laws of the various States and Territories applicable to the Indian reservations within their borders, and extending the laws of the State of Arkansas to the portion of the Indian Territory not occupied by the five civilized tribes.

The Indian should receive the protection of the law. He should be allowed to maintain in court his rights of person and property. He has repeatedly begged for this privilege. Its exercise would be very valuable to him in his progress toward civilization.

Second. Of even greater importance is a measure which has been frequently recommended by my predecessors in office, and in furtherance of which several bills have been from time to time introduced in both Houses of Congress. The enactment of a general law permitting the allotment in severalty, to such Indians, at least, as desire it, of a reasonable quantity of land secured to them by patent, and for their own protection made inalienable for twenty or twenty-five years, is demanded for their present welfare and their permanent advancement.

In return for such considerate action on the part of the government, there is reason to believe that the Indians in large numbers would be persuaded to sever their tribal relations and to engage at once in agricultural pursuits. Many of them realize the fact that their hunting days are over, and that it is now for their best interests to conform their manner of life to the new order of things. By no greater inducement than the assurance of permanent title to the soil can they be led to engage in the occupation of tilling it.

The well-attested reports of their increasing interest in husbandry justify the hope and belief that the enactment of such a statute as I recommend would be at once attended with gratifying results. A resort to the allotment system would have a direct and powerful influence in dissolving the tribal bond, which is so prominent a feature of savage life, and which tends so strongly to perpetuate it.

Third. I advise a liberal appropriation for the support of Indian schools, because of my confident belief that such a course is consistent with the wisest economy.

Even among the most uncultivated Indian tribes there is reported to be a general and urgent desire on the part of the chiefs and older members for the education of their children. It is unfortunate, in view of this fact, that during the past year the means which have been at the command of the Interior Department for the purpose of Indian instruction have proved to be utterly inadequate. The success of the schools which are in operation at Hampton, Carlisle, and Forest Grove should not only encourage a more generous provision for the support of those institutions, but should prompt the establishment of others of a similar character.

They are doubtless much more potent for good than the day schools upon the reservation, as the pupils are altogether separated from the surroundings of savage life, and brought into constant contact with civilization.

There are many other phases of this subject which are of great interest, but which cannot be included within the becoming limits of this communication; they are discussed ably in the reports of the Secretary of the Interior and the Commissioner of Indian Affairs.

For many years the Executive, in his annual message to Congress, has urged the necessity of stringent legislation for the suppression of polygamy in the Territories, and especially in the Territory of Utah. The existing statute for the punishment of this odious crime, so revolting to the moral and religious sense of Christendom, has been persistently and contemptuously violated ever since its enactment. Indeed, in spite of commendable efforts on the part of the authorities who represent the United States in that Territory, the law has in very rare instances been enforced, and, for a cause to which reference will presently be made, is practically a dead letter.

The fact that adherents of the Mormon church, which rests upon polygamy as its corner-stone, have recently been peopling in large numbers Idaho, Arizona, and other of our Western Territories, is well calculated to excite the liveliest interest and apprehension. It imposes upon Congress and the Executive the duty of arraying against this barbarous system all the power which, under the Constitution and the law, they can wield for its destruction.

Reference has been already made to the obstacles which the United States officers have encountered in their efforts to punish violations of law. Prominent among these obstacles is the difficulty of procuring legal evidence sufficient to warrant a conviction even in the case of the most notorious offenders.

Your attention is called to a recent opinion of the Supreme Court of the United States, explaining its judgment of reversal in the case of Miles, who had been convicted of bigamy in Utah. The court refers to the fact that the secrecy attending the celebration of marriages in that Territory makes the proof of polygamy very difficult; and the propriety is suggested of modifying the law of evidence which now makes a wife incompetent to testify against her husband.

This suggestion is approved. I recommend also the passage of an act providing that in the Territories of the United States the fact that a woman has been married to a person charged with bigamy shall not disqualify her as a witness upon his trial for that offense. I further recommend legislation by which any person solemnizing a marriage in any of the Territories shall be required, under stringent penalties for neglect or refusal, to file a certificate of such marriage in the supreme court of the Territory.

Doubtless Congress may devise other practicable measures for obviating the difficulties which have hitherto attended the efforts to suppress this iniquity. I assure you of my determined purpose to co-operate with you in any lawful and discreet measures which may be proposed to that end.

Although our system of government does not contemplate that the nation should provide or support a system for the education of our people, no measures calculated to promote that general intelligence and virtue upon which the perpetuity of our institutions so greatly depends, have ever been regarded with indifference by Congress or the Executive.

A large portion of the public domain has been, from time to time, devoted to the promotion of education.

There is now a special reason why, by setting apart the proceeds of its sales of public lands, or by some other course, the government should aid the work of education. Many who now exercise the right of suffrage are unable to read the ballot which they cast. Upon many who had just emerged from a condition of slavery, were suddenly devolved the responsibilities of citizenship in that portion of the country most impoverished by war. I have been pleased to learn from the report of the Commissioner of Education that there has lately been a commendable increase of interest and effort for their instruction; but all that can be done by local legislation and private generosity should be supplemented by such aid as can be constitutionally afforded by the national government.

I would suggest that if any fund be dedicated to this purpose it may be wisely distributed in the different States according to the ratio of illiteracy, as by this means those localities which are most in need of such assistance will reap its special benefits.

The report of the Commissioner of Agriculture exhibits the results of the experiments in which that department has been engaged during the past year, and makes important suggestions in reference to the agricultural development of the country.

The steady increase of our population, and the consequent addition to the number of those engaging in the pursuit of husbandry, are giving to this Department a growing dignity and importance. The Commissioner's suggestions touching its capacity for greater usefulness deserve attention, as it more and more commends itself to the interests which it was created to promote.

It appears from the report of the Commissioner of Pension that, since 1860, 789,063 original pension claims have been filed; 450,949 of these have been allowed and inscribed on the pension-roll ; 72,539 have been rejected and abandoned, being 13+ per cent. of the whole number of claims settled.

There are now pending for settlement 265,575 original pension claims, 227,040 of which were filed prior to July 1, 1880. These, when allowed, will involve the payment of arrears from the date of discharge in case of an invalid, ahd from date of death or termination of a prior right in all other cases.

From all the data obtainable it is estimated that 15 per cent. of the number of claims now pending will be rejected or abandoned. This would show the probable rejection of 34,040 cases, and the probable admission of about 193,000 claims, all of which involve the payment of arrears of pension.

With the present force employed, the number of adjudications remaining the same and no new business intervening, this number of claims (193,000) could be acted upon in a period of six years; and taking January 1, 1884, as a near period from which to estimate in each case an average amount of arrears, it is found that every case allowed would require, for the first payment upon it, the sum of $1,350. Multiplying this amount by the whole number of probable admissions gives $250,000,000 as the sum required for first payments. This represents the sum which must be paid upon claims which were filed before July 1, 1880, and are now pending, and entitled to the benefits of the arrears act. From this amount ($250,000,000) may be deducted from ten to fifteen millions, for cases where, the claimant dying, there is no person who, under the law, would be entitled to succeed to the pension, leaving $235,000,000 as the probable amount to be paid.

In these estimates, no account has been taken of the 38,500 cases filed since June 30, 1880, and now pending, which must receive attention as current business, but which do not involve the payment of any arrears beyond the date of filing the claim. Of this number it is estimated that 86 per cent. will be allowed.

As has been stated, with the present force of the Pension Bureau, 675 clerks, it is estimated that it will take six years to dispose of the claims now pending.

It is stated by the Commissioner of Pensions that by an addition of 250 clerks (increasing the adjudicating force rather than the mechanical) double the amount of work could be accomplished, so that these cases could be acted upon within three years.

Aside from the considerations of justice which may be urged for a speedy settlement of the claims now on the files of the Pension Office, it is no less important on the score of economy, inasmuch as fully one-third of the clerical force of the office is now wholly occupied in giving attention to correspondence with the thousands of claimants whose cases have been on the files for the past eighteen years. The fact that a sum so enormous must be expended by the Government to meet de-

mands for arrears of pensions, is an admonition to Congress and the
Executive to give cautious consideration to any similar project in the
future. The great temptation to the presentation of fictitious claims
afforded by the fact that the average sum obtained upon each application is $1,300, leads me to suggest the propriety of making some special
appropriation for the prevention of fraud.

I advise appropriations for such internal improvements as the wisdom of Congress may deem to be of public importance. The necessity
of improving the navigation of the Mississippi River justifies a special
allusion to that subject. I suggest the adoption of some measure for the
removal of obstructions which now impede the navigation of that great
channel of commerce.

In my letter accepting the nomination for the Vice-Presidency, I
stated that in my judgment "no man should be the incumbent of an
office, the duties of which he is for any cause unfit to perform; who is
lacking in the ability, fidelity, or integrity which a proper administration of such office demands. This sentiment would doubtless meet with
general acquiescence, but opinion has been widely divided upon the wisdom and practicability of the various reformatory schemes which have
been suggested and of certain proposed regulations governing appointments to public office.

"The efficiency of such regulations has been distrusted, mainly because
they have seemed to exalt mere educational and abstract tests above
general business capacity and even special fitness for the particular work
in hand. It seems to me that the rules which should be applied to the
management of the public service, may properly conform in the main to
such as regulate the conduct of successful private business:

"Original appointments should be based upon ascertained fitness.

"The tenure of office should be stable.

"Positions of responsibility should, so far as practicable, be filled by
the promotion of worthy and efficient officers.

"The investigation of all complaints and the punishment of all official
misconduct should be prompt and thorough."

The views expressed in the foregoing letter are those which will
govern my administration of the Executive Office. They are doubtless shared by all intelligent and patriotic citizens, however divergent
in their opinions as to the best methods of putting them into practical
operation.

For example, the assertion that "original appointments should be
based upon ascertained fitness" is not open to dispute.

But the question how in practice such fitness can be most effectually
ascertained, is one which has for years excited interest and discussion.
The measure, which, with slight variations in its details, has lately been
urged upon the attention of Congress and the Executive, has as its principal feature the scheme of competitive examination. Save for certain
exceptions, which need not here be specified, this plan would allow ad-

mission to the service only in its lowest grade, and would accordingly demand that all vacancies in higher positions should be filled by promotion alone. In these particulars it is in conformity with the existing civil-service system of Great Britain. And indeed the success which has attended that system in the country of its birth is the strongest argument which has been urged for its adoption here.

The fact should not, however, be overlooked that there are certain features of the English system which have not generally been received with favor in this country, even among the foremost advocates of civil-service reform.

Among them are:

1. A tenure of office which is substantially a life-tenure.

2. A limitation of the maximum age at which an applicant can enter the service, whereby all men in middle life or older, are, with some exceptions, rigidly excluded.

3. A retiring allowance upon going out of office.

These three elements are as important factors of the problem as any of the others. To eliminate them from the English system would effect a most radical change in its theory and practice.

The avowed purpose of that system is to induce the educated young men of the country to devote their lives to public employment by an assurance that having once entered upon it they need never leave it, and that after voluntary retirement they shall be the recipients of an annual pension. That this system as an entirety has proved very successful in Great Britain seems to be generally conceded even by those who once opposed its adoption.

To a statute which should incorporate all its essential features, I should feel bound to give my approval. But whether it would be for the best interests of the public to fix upon an expedient for immediate and extensive application, which embraces certain features of the English system but excludes or ignores others of equal importance, may be seriously doubted, even by those who are impressed, as I am myself, with the grave importance of correcting the evils which inhere in the present methods of appointment.

If, for example, the English rule which shuts out persons above the age of twenty-five years from a large number of public employments is not to be made an essential part of our own system, it is questionable whether the attainment of the highest number of marks at a competitive examination should be the criterion by which all applications for appointment should be put to test. And under similar conditions, it may also be questioned, whether admission to the service should be strictly limited to its lowest ranks.

There are very many characteristics which go to make a model civil servant. Prominent among them are probity, industry, good sense, good habits, good temper, patience, order, courtesy, tact, self-reliance, manly deference to superior officers and manly consideration for inferiors. The absence of these traits is not supplied by wide knowledge of books or by promptitude in answering questions, or by any other quality likely to be brought to light by competitive examination.

To make success in such a contest, therefore, an indispensable condition of public employment, would very likely result in the practical exclusion of the older applicants, even though they might possess qualifications far superior to their younger and more brilliant competitors.

These suggestions must not be regarded as evincing any spirit of opposition to the competitive plan, which has been to some extent successfully employed already, and which may hereafter vindicate the claim of its most earnest supporters. But it ought to be seriously considered whether the application of the same educational standard to persons of mature years and to young men fresh from school and college would not be likely to exalt mere intellectual proficiency above other qualities of equal or greater importance.

Another feature of the proposed system is the selection by promotion of all officers of the government above the lowest grade, except such as would fairly be regarded as exponents of the policy of the Executive and the principles of the dominant party.

To afford encouragement to faithful public servants by exciting in their minds the hope of promotion, if they are found to merit it, is much to be desired.

But would it be wise to adopt a rule so rigid as to permit no other mode of supplying the intermediate walks of the service?

There are many persons who fill subordinate positions with great credit, but lack those qualities which are requisite for higher posts of duty; and, besides, the modes of thought and action of one whose service in a governmental bureau has been long continued are often so cramped by routine procedure as almost to disqualify him from instituting changes required by the public interests. An infusion of new blood, from time to time, into the middle ranks of the service might be very beneficial in its results.

The subject under discussion is one of grave importance. The evils which are complained of cannot be eradicated at once; the work must be gradual.

The present English system is a growth of years, and was not created by a single stroke of executive or legislative action.

Its beginnings are found in an order in council, promulgated in 1855, and it was after patient and cautious scrutiny of its workings that fifteen years later it took its present shape.

Five years after the issuance of the order in council, and at a time when resort had been had to competitive examinations as an experiment much more extensively than has yet been the case in this country, a select committee of the House of Commons made a report to that house, which, declaring its approval of the competitive plan, deprecated, nevertheless, any precipitancy in its general adoption as likely to endanger its ultimate success.

During this tentative period the results of the two methods of pass examination and competitive examination were closely watched and compared. It may be that before we confine ourselves upon this important question within the stringent bounds of statutory enactment, we may profitably await the result of further inquiry and experiment.

The submission of a portion of the nominations to a central board of examiners selected solely for testing the qualifications of applicants may, perhaps, without resort to the competitive test, put an end to the mischiefs which attend the present system of appointment, and it may be feasible to vest in such a board a wide discretion to ascertain the characteristics and attainments of candidates in those particulars which I have already referred to as being no less important than mere intellectual attainment.

If Congress should deem it advisable at the present session to establish competitive tests for admission to the service, no doubts such as have been suggested shall deter me from giving the measure my earnest support.

And I urgently recommend, should there be a failure to pass any other act upon this subject, that an appropriation of $25,000 per year may be made for the enforcement of section 1753 of the Revised Statutes.

With the aid thus afforded me, I shall strive to execute the provisions of that law according to its letter and spirit.

I am unwilling, in justice to the present civil servants of the government, to dismiss this subject without declaring my dissent from the severe and almost indiscriminate censure with which they have been recently assailed. That they are as a class indolent, inefficient, and corrupt, is a statement which has been often made and widely credited. But when the extent, variety, delicacy, and importance of their duties are considered, the great majority of the employés of the government are in my judgment deserving of high commendation.

The continuing decline of the merchant marine of the United States is greatly to be deplored. In view of the fact that we furnish so large a proportion of the freights of the commercial world and that our shipments are steadily and rapidly increasing, it is cause of surprise that not only is our navigation interest diminishing, but it is less than when our exports and imports were not half so large as now, either in bulk or value. There must be some peculiar hinderance to the development of this interest, or the enterprise and energy of American mechanics and capitalists would have kept this country at least abreast of our rivals in the friendly contest for ocean supremacy. The substitution of iron for wood and of steam for sail have wrought great revolutions in the carrying trade of the world; but these changes could not have been adverse to America if we had given to our navigation interests a portion of the aid and protection which have been so wisely bestowed upon our manufactures. I commend the whole subject to the wisdom of Congress, with the suggestion that no question of greater magnitude or farther-reaching importance can engage their attention.

In 1875 the Supreme Court of the United States declared unconstitutional the statutes of certain States which imposed upon ship-owners or consignees a tax of one dollar and a half for each passenger arriving from a foreign country, or, in lieu thereof, required a bond to indemnify the State and local authorities against expense for the future relief or support of such passenger. Since this decision the expense attending the care and supervision of immigrants has fallen on the States at whose ports they have landed. As a large majority of such immigrants, immediately upon their arrival, proceed to the inland States and the Territories to seek permanent homes, it is manifestly unjust to impose upon the State whose shores they first reach, the burden which it now bears. For this reason, and because of the national importance of the subject, I recommend legislation regarding the supervision and transitory care of immigrants at the ports of debarkation.

I regret to state that the people of Alaska have reason to complain that they are as yet unprovided with any form of government by which life or property can be protected. While the extent of its population does not justify the application of the costly machinery of Territorial administration, there is immediate necessity for constituting such a form of government as will promote the education of the people and secure the administration of justice.

The Senate, at its last session, passed a bill providing for the construction of a building for the Library of Congress, but it failed to become a law. The provision of suitable protection for this great collection of books, and for the copyright department connected with it, has become a subject of national importance and should receive prompt attention.

The report of the Commissioners of the District of Columbia, herewith transmitted, will inform you fully of the condition of the affairs of the District.

They urge the vital importance of legislation for the reclamation and improvement of the marshes and for the establishment of the harbor lines along the Potomac River front.

It is represented that in their present condition these marshes seriously affect the health of the residents of the adjacent parts of the city; and that they greatly mar the general aspect of the park in which stands the Washington Monument. This improvement would add to that park and to the park south of the Executive Mansion a large area of valuable land, and would transform what is now believed to be a dangerous nuisance into an attractive landscape extending to the river front.

They recommend the removal of the steam railway lines from the surface of the streets of the city, and the location of the necessary depots in such places as may be convenient for the public accommodation; and they call attention to the deficiency of the water supply, which seriously affects the material prosperity of the city and the health and comfort of its inhabitants.

I commend these subjects to your favorable consideration.

The importance of timely legislation with respect to the ascertainment and declaration of the vote for Presidential electors was sharply called to the attention of the people more than four years ago.

It is to be hoped that some well-defined measure may be devised before another national election, which will render unnecessary a resort to any expedient of a temporary character, for the determination of questions upon contested returns.

Questions which concern the very existence of the government and the liberties of the people were suggested by the prolonged illness of the late President, and his consequent incapacity to perform the functions of his office.

It is provided by the second article of the Constitution, in the fifth clause of its first section, that "in case of the removal of the President from office, or of his death, resignation, or inability to discharge the powers and duties of said office, the same shall devolve on the Vice-President."

What is the intendment of the Constitution in its specification of "inability to discharge the powers and duties of said office," as one of the contingencies which calls the Vice-President to the exercise of Presidential functions?

Is the inability limited in its nature to long-continued intellectual incapacity, or has it a broader import?

What must be its extent and duration?

How must its existence be established?

Has the President, whose inability is the subject of inquiry, any voice in determining whether or not it exists, or is the decision of that momentous and delicate question confided to the Vice-President, or is it contemplated by the Constitution that Congress should provide by law precisely what should constitute inability, and how and by what tribunal or authority it should be ascertained?

If the inability proves to be temporary in its nature, and during its continuance the Vice-President lawfully exercises the functions of the Executive, by what tenure does he hold his office?

Does he continue as President for the remainder of the four years' term?

Or would the elected President, if his inability should cease in the interval, be empowered to resume his office?

And if having such lawful authority he should exercise it, would the Vice-President be thereupon empowered to resume his powers and duties as such?

I cannot doubt that these important questions will receive your early and thoughtful consideration.

Deeply impressed with the gravity of the responsibilities which have so unexpectedly devolved upon me, it will be my constant purpose to co-operate with you in such measures as will promote the glory of the country and the prosperity of its people.

CHESTER A. ARTHUR.

WASHINGTON, *December* 6, 1881.

REPORT

OF

THE SECRETARY OF THE TREASURY.

TREASURY DEPARTMENT,
Washington, D. C., December 5, 1881.

SIR: I have the honor to submit the following report:

The ordinary revenues from all sources for the fiscal year ended June 30, 1881, were—

From customs......................................	$198,159,676 02
From internal revenue.............................	135,264,385 51
From sales of public lands........................	2,201,863 17
From tax on circulation and deposits of national banks...	8,116,115 72
From repayment of interest by Pacific Railway Companies...	810,833 80
From sinking-fund for Pacific Railway Companies..	805,180 54
From customs' fees, fines, penalties, &c.............	1,225,514 86
From fees—consular, letters-patent, and lands......	2,244,983 98
From proceeds of sales of Government property....	262,174 00
From profits on coinage...........................	3,468,485 61
From revenues of the District of Columbia.........	2,016,199 23
From miscellaneous sources........................	6,206,880 13
Total ordinary receipts.....................	360,782,292 57

The ordinary expenditures for the same period were—

For civil expenses................................	$17,941,177 19
For foreign intercourse............................	1,093,954 92
For Indians.......................................	6,514,161 09
For pensions......................................	50,059,279 62
For the military establishment, including river and harbor improvements, and arsenals...............	40,466,460 55
For the naval establishment, including vessels, machinery, and improvements at navy-yards.........	15,686,671 66
For miscellaneous expenditures, including public buildings, light-houses, and collecting the revenue.	41,837,280 57
For expenditures on account of the District of Columbia..	3,543,912 03
For interest on the public debt....................	82,508,741 18
For premium on bonds purchased..................	1,061,248 78
Total ordinary expenditures..................	260,712,887 59
Leaving a surplus revenue of......................	$100,069,404 98

Which was applied as follows:

To the redemption of—

Bonds for the sinking-fund........................	74,371,200 00
Fractional currency for the sinking-fund...........	109,001 05
Loan of February, 1861...........................	7,418,000 00

3 Ab

Ten-forties of 1864	$2,016,150	00
Five-twenties of 1862	18,300	00
Five-twenties of 1864	3,400	00
Five-twenties of 1865	37,300	00
Consols of 1865	143,150	00
Consols of 1867	959,150	00
Consols of 1868	337,400	00
Texan indemnity stock	1,000	00
Old demand, compound-interest, and other notes	18,330	00
And to the increase of cash in the Treasury	14,637,023	93
	100,069,404	98

The requirements of the sinking-fund for the last fiscal year, including a balance of $49,817,128.78, not provided for up to the close of the previous year, amounted to $90,786,064.02. There was applied thereto from the redemption of bonds and fractional currency, as shown in the above statement, the sum of $74,480,201.05, leaving a deficit of $16,305,873.47. It is estimated that the requirements of the fund for the present fiscal year, including the balance from last year, will amount to $59,634,856.50. The amount of bonds redeemed during the months of July, August, September, and October of the present year is in excess of the requirements of the sinking-fund for the entire year by the sum of $6,176,593.50. The surplus revenues, however, which may hereafter accrue during the year, will be applied to the purchase or redemption of the public debt, as contemplated in section 2 of the act approved March 3, 1881, (21 Stats., p. 457.)

Compared with the previous fiscal year, the receipts for 1881 have increased $29,352,901.10, in the following items: In customs revenue, $11,637,611.42; in internal revenue, $11,255,011.59; in sales of public lands, $1,185,356.57; in tax on circulation and deposits of national banks, $1,101,144.28; in proceeds of sales of Indian lands, $1,055,202.40; in deposits by individuals for surveying public lands, $1,329,588.85; in fees on letters-patent, $50,415.84; in profits on coinage, $676,298.83; in revenues of the District of Columbia, $206,729.53; and in miscellaneous items, $855,541.79. There was a decrease of $2,097,219.51, as follows: In repayment of interest by Pacific Railway Companies, $896,533.38; in interest and premium on Indian trust-fund stocks, $631,595.76; in registers' and receivers' fees, $154,798.29; and in unenumerated items, $414,292.08; making a net increase in the receipts, from all sources, of $27,255,681.59.

The expenditures show a decrease over the previous year of $21,700,800.39, as follows: In the Interior Department, (pensions,) $6,717,894.82; in premium on bonds purchased, $1,734,071.64; and in the interest on public debt, $13,248,833.93. There was an increase of $14,770,730.20, as follows: In the War Department, $2,349,544.33; in the Navy Department, $2,149,686.92; in the Interior Department, (Indians,) $568,704; and in the civil and miscellaneous, $9,702,794.95— making a net decrease in the expenditures of $6,930,070.19.

FISCAL YEAR 1882.

For the present fiscal year the revenue, actual and estimated, is as follows:

Source.	For the quarter ended September 30, 1881. Actual.	For the remaining three quarters of the year. Estimated.
From customs....................................	$59,184,469 15	$155,815,530 85
From internal revenue	37,575,562 22	117,424,497 78
From sales of public lands	948,368 19	1,551,631 81
From tax on circulation and deposits of national banks......................................	4,307,988 86	3,692,011 14
From repayment of interest by Pacific Railway Companies	59,999 49	1,440,000 51
From customs' fees, fines, penalties, &c	421,811 62	928,186 38
From fees—consular, letters-patent, and lands....	639,189 08	1,810,819 92
From proceeds of sales of Government property...	66,363 58	183,636 42
From profits on coinage..........................	809,317 80	2,440,682 20
From revenues of the District of Columbia.......	158,445 95	1,641,554 05
From miscellaneous sources......................	4,009,596 15	4,890,403 85
Total receipts...........................	108,181,043 09	291,818,936 91

The expenditures for the same period, actual and estimated, are—

Source.	For the quarter ended September 30, 1881. Actual.	For the remaining three quarters of the year. Estimated.
For civil and miscellaneous expenses, including public buildings, light-houses, and collecting the revenue...................................	$12,252,053 71	$47,247,946 29
For Indians...................................	2,011,984 70	4,288,015 30
For pensions..................................	17,220,122 12	52,779,877 88
For military establishment, including fortifications, river and harbor improvements, and arsenals	13,517,184 11	30,982,815 89
For naval establishment, including vessels and machinery, and improvements at navy-yards...	4,646,969 78	10,853,030 22
For expenditures on account of the District of Columbia...................................	1,131,476 04	2,368,523 96
For interest on the public debt.	24,271,948 93	46,428,051 07
Total ordinary expenditures	75,051,739 39	194,948,260 61

Total receipts, actual and estimated	$400,000,000 00
Total expenditures, actual and estimated...........	270,000,000 00
	130,000,000 00
Estimated amount due the sinking-fund............	59,634,856 50
Leaving a balance of	70,365,143 50

FISCAL YEAR 1883.

The revenues of the fiscal year ending June 30, 1883, estimated upon the basis of existing laws, will be—

From customs......	$215,000,000 00
From internal revenue...........................	155,000,000 00
From sales of public lands	2,500,000 00
From tax on circulation and deposits of national banks...	8,000,000 00
From repayment of interest by Pacific Railway Companies...	1,500,000 00
From customs' fees, fines, penalties, &c	1,350,000 00
From fees—consular, letters-patent, and lands	2,450,000 00
From proceeds of sales of Government property.....	250,000 00
From profits on coinage...........................	3,250,000 00
From revenues of the District of Columbia	1,800,000 00
From miscellaneous sources.......................	8,900,000 00
Total estimated ordinary receipts............	400,000,000 00

The estimates of expenditures for the same period, received from the several Executive Departments, are as follows:

Legislative	$2,993,455 92
Executive	16,291,367 73
Judicial	403,200 00
Foreign intercourse	1,315,055 00
Military establishment...........................	29,509,524 17
Naval establishment..............................	17,249,148 46
Indian affairs	5,841,713 91
Pensions	100,000,000 00

Public works:

Treasury Department.............	$3,282,000 00	
War Department................	11,479,506 03	
Navy Department................	2,829,938 00	
Interior Department..........	386,900 00	
Post-Office Department...........	8,000 00	
Department of Agriculture........	43,730 00	
Department of Justice...........	1,500 00	
		18,031,574 03
Postal service...............................		920,077 95
Miscellaneous....................................		18,141,851 95
District of Columbia.............................		3,562,599 31

Permanent annual appropriations:

Interest on the public debt........	$65,000,000 00	
Sinking-fund	45,611,714 22	
Refunding—customs, internal reve-		
nue, lands, &c	7,514,100 00	
Collecting revenues from customs..	5,500,000 00	
Miscellaneous....................	2,577,125 00	
		$126,202,939 22

Total estimated expenditures, including sink-ing-fund.................................	340,462,507 65
Or, an estimated surplus of	$59,537,492 35

Excluding the sinking-fund, the estimated expenditures will be $294,850,793.43, showing a surplus of $105,149,206.57.

The foregoing estimates of expenditures for the fiscal year 1883 are $56,069,257.60 in excess of those submitted last year, as follows:

Increase—

Legislative	$389,285 05	
Executive proper...................	11,736 00	
Department of State...............	53,520 00	
Treasury Department	1,699,332 69	
War Department	914,221 37	
Navy Department..................	4,132,634 40	
Interior Department...............	51,586,130 04	
Department of Agriculture..........	160,260 00	
		$58,947,119 55

Decrease—

Post-Office Department.............	2,648,261 95	
Department of Justice..............	229,600 00	
		2,877,861 95

Net increase.............................	56,069,257 60

The estimates of this Department are submitted as made up by the officers in charge of the public duties to which they respectively pertain, and while exceeding those of last year by the sum of $1,699,332.69, they are in excess of the appropriations made for the Department at the last session of Congress only to the extent of $608.55.

PUBLIC MONEYS.

The monetary transactions of the Government have been conducted through the offices of the United States Treasurer, nine assistant treasurers, one depositary, and one hundred and thirty-two national-bank depositaries.

The receipts of the Government, amounting during the fiscal year, as shown by warrants, to $474,532,826.57, were deposited as follows:

In independent-treasury offices $343,800,718 83
In national-bank depositaries 130,732,107 74

The quarterly examinations of independent-treasury offices required by law have been duly made, and in addition thereto the offices have been subjected to special examinations by officers of this Department. As far as known there have been no losses to the Government by public officers engaged either in the receipt, safe-keeping, or disbursement of the public moneys.

By act of Congress, approved March 3, 1857, public disbursing officers were required to place all funds intrusted to them for disbursement, on deposit with a public depositary, and to draw for them only in favor of the persons to whom payment was to be made. The provisions of this law remained unchanged until the act of June 14, 1866, reproduced as section 3620, Revised Statutes, was passed, removing the restrictions as to the method of drawing checks. By an act approved February 27, 1877, that section was so amended as to re-enact the provisions of the act of March 3, 1857, concerning disbursing officers' checks, which the Department had found impracticable to enforce. The attention of Congress has been called to this matter in the annual reports of the Secretary for years 1857, 1858, and 1878, fully explaining the impracticability of enforcing the law according to the letter as it now stands, and it is recommended that it be so amended that payment may be made and checks drawn under regulations prescribed by the Secretary of the Treasury.

NATIONAL BANKS.

The report of the Comptroller of the Currency contains full information in reference to the affairs of the national banks. It shows that on October 1 of the present year there were a greater number of banks in operation than at any previous time, the number being 2,132. Their returns show that they had on that day an aggregate capital of $463,821,985; surplus, $128,140,617; individual deposits, $1,070,997,531; loans, $1,169,022,303; and specie, $114,334,736. The aggregate circulation, $360,344,250, as well as the amount of loans and individual deposits, was much larger than at any time since the organization of the system.

The corporate existence of 396 banks will expire previously to February 25, 1883. The Comptroller recommends that an act be passed authorizing any national bank, at any time within two years prior to the expiration of its corporate existence, to extend its period of succession by amending its articles of association by the votes of shareholders owning two-thirds of the capital of the association, if such association, upon an examination of its affairs, shall be found to be in a satisfactory condition. The law provides that the Comptroller shall issue his certificate authorizing any banking association to commence business, if it shall conform in all respects to the legal requirements. The banks may, therefore, under the present law, continue their existence, and, in the absence of prohibitory legislation, many of them undoubtedly will, on the expiration of their corporate existence, organize new associations, and obtain from the Comptroller authority to continue business. The passage, however, of an act directly authorizing an extension of the corporate existence of the banks, would in many instances save much labor, and avoid the distribution of the present large surplus fund among the shareholders, which would result from liquidation. The passage of a bill authorizing such a renewal of their charters is recommended.

The Comptroller gives official information in tabulated form of the proportion of coin, paper money, and checks used by the national banks, in their business, in each State and principal city. Returns have been obtained from the banks showing their total receipts upon two different dates. The total receipts of 1,966 banks on June 30, last, were $284,714,016, and of 2,132 banks on September 17, $295,233,779. Upon this latter date the receipts were composed of $4,078,044 in gold coin, $500,302 in silver coin, and $13,026,571 in paper money, the remainder, amounting to $277,628,862, being in checks and drafts, including $6,593,337 of clearing-house certificates. The proportion of paper-money and coin was 5.9 per cent., and of checks and drafts 94.1 per cent. The receipts of 48 banks in the city of New York were $165,000,000, and the total percentage of coin and paper money was 1.2 per cent. only, and of checks and drafts 98.8 per cent. The receipts of 237 banks in sixteen reserve cities, including New York, were $243,115,594, and the proportion of checks and drafts was 96.7 per cent. The banks elsewhere reported receipts amounting to $52,118,185, in which the proportion of checks and drafts was 81.7 per cent. These returns show how small an amount of money actually enters into large transactions, and how much its use has been superseded by the machinery of banking, with its modern system of checks, bills of exchange, and clearing-houses.

Full statistics are given in regard to the taxation of the banks, from which it seems that the amount of taxes paid, both by the National and State banks, to the Federal Government during the last year, has been greater than in any previous year, the total amount collected being $8,493,552 from the former, and $3,762,208 from the latter. The taxes collected by the States have also increased, and the amounts assessed are alleged to be disproportioned to the amount collected upon other moneyed capital. In another part of this report suggestion is made as to a reduction of the taxes upon these institutions.

United States five and six per cent. bonds, amounting to $245,601,050, held by the national banks, have been extended with interest at 3½ per cent., and it is estimated that the net interest at the current market value, upon all the bonds held by them, does not exceed that rate.

RESERVE.

Previously to the resumption of specie-payments, a reserve was accumulated in the Treasury by the sale of $95,500,000 of bonds, and by the retention of an additional amount of about $40,000,000 from surplus revenues. The policy pursued by this Department, as repeatedly announced to Congress, has been to retain as reserve for the redemption of United States notes, about 40 per cent. of the notes outstanding, and in addition thereto to have sufficient money in the Treasury to meet all other demand obligations outstanding. This policy has been adhered to as rigidly as practicable. The reserve has never fallen below 36 per cent., nor been above 45 per cent. of outstanding notes. The silver certificates issued are payable only in silver coin, and the gold received for these certificates is now available for resumption purposes. There is now in the Treasurer's cash about $25,000,000 of fractional silver coin having only a limited legal-tender value, and not available for resumption purposes. The remainder of this reserve consists chiefly of gold coin. It is generally conceded that, for safe banking, a reserve of 40 per cent. to meet current obligations is necessary. The Government, by the issue of its notes, payable on demand, and its obligation to meet them when presented, is in a position analogous to that of banking, and should therefore act upon principles found to be sound and safe in that business.

SILVER CERTIFICATES.

The Department has issued silver certificates at the several subtreasury offices, upon a deposit of gold coin in like amount with the assistant treasurer at New York, and through this means certificates have been issued for nearly all the silver held by the Treasury. These certificates amount to about $66,000,000, and are now outstanding.

About $34,000,000 of silver dollars are now in circulation. The total result of this silver coinage is to increase the currency of the country to the extent of about $100,000,000, and to require the Treasurer of the United States to hold the silver coin in which the certificates are payable. On November 1, 1881, the Department held in its cash about $7,000,000 of the certificates, and about $250,000 of the coin for which certificates had not been issued.

The act of February 28, 1878, requiring the issue of silver certificates upon the deposit of standard silver dollars was a part of the policy of the Government to maintain the standard of the silver dollar at or near the value of the standard gold dollar. The same act provided that such certificates should be receivable "for customs, taxes, and all public dues."

The liberal purchase of bullion and coinage of silver dollars by this Government, and the receipt of them by it for public dues, has failed to raise the price of silver bullion to any great extent in the markets of the world.

As is said elsewhere herein, the circulation of some sixty-six millions of silver certificates seems an inexpedient addition to the paper currency. They are made a legal-tender for the purposes named, yet have for their basis about eighty-eight per cent. only of their nominal value. There is no promise from the Government to make good the difference between their actual and nominal value.

There need be no apprehension of a too limited paper circulation. The national banks are ready to issue their notes in such quantity as the laws of trade demand, and as security therefor the Government will hold an equivalent in its own bonds.

The embarrassments which are certain to follow from the endeavor to maintain several standards of value, in the form of paper currency, are too obvious to need discussion.

It is recommended, therefore, that measures be taken for a repeal of the act requiring the issue of such certificates, and the early retirement of them from circulation.

GOLD CERTIFICATES.

Immediately preceding resumption, the issue of certificates upon deposits of gold was discontinued. It was feared that parties might present legal-tender notes based upon a 40 per cent. reserve, obtain the gold therefor, and immediately deposit it for the certificates for which, by law, the Department was required to hold 100 per cent. Though often requested, the Department has ever since refused to make any further issue of these certificates. By consent of the Comptroller of the Currency, these certificates are allowed to form a part of the lawful reserve of national banks, much of which reserve is now in gold coin. Should the certificates be issued, they would at once take the place of this coin, and the Treasury would hold the coin instead of the banks. In view of any possible demand for the redemption in coin of legal-tender notes, the issue of these certificates is very objectionable.

RETIREMENT OF NATIONAL-BANK NOTES.

Under existing law, any national bank can at any time, upon a deposit of legal-tender notes or coin with the Treasurer of the United States, withdraw the bonds held as security therefor, and leave the Treasury to redeem an equal amount of its notes. This privilege was given to the banks, evidently for the purpose of securing a proper elasticity of the currency; and in view of the rapid payment of the public debt, it would seem that this privilege is necessary for the purpose of facilitating the redemption of bonds held by the banks; but should many of the banks, through apprehension of adverse legislation, or from any other cause, desire to retire their circulation, the deposit of such an amount of money with the Treasurer might cause a serious and sudden contraction of the currency and grave embarrassments in business. That the apprehension of such action is not groundless is shown by what took place on the passage of the three per cent. refunding bill by Congress at its last session. If it is thought advisable Congress can enact that national banks be prohibited from retiring their currency, except on a previous notice of intention so to do; the length of that notice to be fixed by law.

LEGAL-TENDER NOTES.

This Department has little to add to what has been said in former reports from it on the subject of the notes known as legal-tender notes. That they are convenient and safe for the community is without doubt. That it is for the profit of the Government to continue them is also without doubt. Yet there is one consideration that should have notice, and that is, whether the Government can continue to claim for them the quality of being a legal-tender for debts. This Department understands that the constitutionality of making them a solvent of contracts was found in the exigencies of the Government raised by the civil war. Whether now, that that war has sometime since ceased, and the Government has resumed payment of its debts in gold and silver coin, notes of the United States shall be maintained as currency with the legal-tender quality, is a question worthy of attention.

FRACTIONAL PAPER CURRENCY.

Of the $15,000,000 of fractional paper currency outstanding, only about $80,000 has been redeemed this year, and this amount is likely to grow less each succeeding year. It is suggested that Congress authorize the Department to drop this amount from any statement of public debt hereafter issued, and make a permanent appropriation for the redemption of such small amount of notes as may hereafter be presented. In this connection, attention is called to the fact that of the public debt that matured before the year 1860, there remains outstanding and unpaid the sum of about $100,000. It is suggested that authority may well be given to treat this amount in the same manner.

PAYMENT OF UNITED STATES BONDS IN GOLD.

The gold dollar at the standard weight of 25.8 grains is by law the unit of value, while the standard silver dollar by this standard is now worth about eighty-eight cents.

Although the act of July 14, 1870, provides for the issue of United States bonds, "redeemable in coin of the present standard value," whereby were included both gold and silver coin of that value, yet as by the act of February 12, 1873, the further coinage of silver dollars was prohibited, and the Revised Statutes declared gold coin only to be legal tender for sums exceeding five dollars, equity, if not strict construction of law, requires that the holders of such bonds should receive payment thereof in gold or its equivalent.

By act of February 28, 1878, silver dollars of the standard weight and fineness were again made a legal tender at the nominal value for all debts and dues, public and private, except where otherwise expressly stipulated in the contract.

Between the adoption of the Revised Statutes, June 22, 1874, and 1878, silver coin was not a tender in payment of United States bonds, and it might fairly be regarded, especially by foreign holders who had acquired bonds during this interval, as a breach of faith, if bond-creditors were compelled to receive payment in a coin worth in the markets of the world but eighty-eight per cent. of our own standard of value.

This Government is abundantly able to discharge all its obligations at home and abroad in money which is everywhere accepted as a true standard of value.

STANDARD SILVER DOLLARS.

As required by the act of February 28, 1878, the Department has caused to be coined into standard silver dollars each month, at least $2,000,000 in value of bullion of that metal.

Constant efforts have been made to give circulation to this coin, the expense of transferring it to all points where it was called for having been paid by the Government.

Only about thirty-four millions are now in circulation, leaving more than sixty-six millions in the vaults, and there is no apparent reason why its circulation should rapidly increase.

The silver question is involved in some embarrassments. The monetary conference, to which a commission was sent the past year, after elaborate discussion, reached no conclusion, except to adjourn to meet again for a further discussion next April. Whether a renewal at the present time of the consideration of the subject by it is likely to lead to any practical or acceptable results, seems doubtful. That most of the European nations have a deep interest in a proper adjustment of the ratio between gold and silver coinage, if not deeper than the United States, admits of no doubt. We furnish the world with the largest portion of both gold and silver, and our exports command the best money of the world, as they ever should do and will, unless we bind ourselves to accept of a poorer. We need not appear anywhere as supplicants when we clearly may be the controllers. Some of the European nations, whose concurrent action is necessary to any result that is sought, do not yet appear ready to accept bi-metalism, and when ready they may ask for a ratio that it will be inconvenient for us to adopt, and reduce the ratio of silver below the standard of our coinage, while the market or intrinsic value of silver indicates the propriety of a considerably increased ratio. That an agreement of the principal nations of Europe with us, for the larger use of silver coinage would furnish a larger market for silver, and to that extent increase its value, is certain, but the excess of it over the supply for that purpose would only command the price of a commodity on the market. Therefore, the fixing of any ratio is a matter of extreme delicacy to be fully considered.

The most potential means of bringing about any concert of action among different nations, would appear to be for the United States to suspend, for the present, the further coinage of silver dollars. This is the decided opinion, in both France and America, of the highest authorities on bi-metalism, and of those who wish to bring silver into general use and raise its value; and it is believed that a cessation of coinage would, at a very early day, bring about a satisfactory consideration of the whole subject among the chief commercial nations.

The silver question, obviously, is one that demands the early attention of our law-makers, or the subject may drift beyond our control unless control is retained at a great sacrifice. A continuance of the monthly addition to our silver coinage will soon leave us no choice but that of an exclusive silver coinage, and tend to reduce us to a place in the commercial world among the minor and less civilized nations.

It may be assumed that a people as enterprising and progressive as that of the United States, holding a leading position among nations, will not consent to the total abandonment of the use of gold as one of the metals to be employed as money, and we cannot consent to be placed in the very awkward position of paying for all that we buy abroad upon a gold standard, and selling all that we have to sell on a silver standard.

It is, therefore, recommended that the provision for the coinage of a fixed amount each month be repealed, and the Secretary be authorized to coin only so much as will be necessary to supply the demand.

The effect of storing large amounts of silver coin in the Treasury vaults, with the present law requiring the issue of silver certificates, is to furnish a paper currency not payable in gold or its equivalent. This policy is open to most of the objections that can be urged against the increase of United States notes or of gold certificates, and to the additional objection that it furnishes a currency depreciated, from the very nature of the basis on which it rests—that is, silver coin of a debased value as compared with gold coin.

There is no objection to supplying fully a demand for silver dollars for actual use at home and in some few foreign markets, but so long as generally, in the markets of the world, they are of less value than the gold dollar, which is our legal standard of value, they must be regarded as subsidiary coin. It is believed that the amount in circulation will be steadily increased, but not so fast as to require, for some months, or perhaps years, any addition to the amount already coined.

In answer to inquiry, it is well to say that what are the profits on the coinage is shown from year to year by the report of the Register of the Treasury. The receipt of them into the Treasury is acknowledged in the item of miscellaneous receipts, and they are put to the same uses as any other receipts into the Treasury, that is, to the payment of the expenses or debts of Government.

CUSTOMS.

The revenue from customs for the past fiscal year was $198,159,676.02, an increase of $11,637,611.42 over that of the preceding year.

Of the amount collected, $138,908,562.39 was collected at the port of New York, leaving $59,251,113.63 as the amount collected at all the other ports of the country.

Of the total amount, $47,977,137.63 was collected on sugar, melade, and molasses; $27,285,624.78 on wool and its manufactures; $21,462,534.34 on iron and steel, and manufactures thereof; $19,038,665.81 on manufactures of silk; $10,825,115.21 on manufactures of cotton; and $6,469,643.04 on wines and spirits; making a total revenue from the articles specified, of $133,058,720.81.

The expenses of collection for the past year were $6,419,345.20, an increase over the preceding year of $387,410.04. While there was an increase in the revenue from customs over the preceding year of over eleven and a half millions of dollars, the gross value of the imports, including free goods, decreased over twenty-five millions of dollars. The most marked decrease was in the value of unmanufactured wool, $14,023,682, and in that of scrap and pig-iron, $12,810,671. There was, on the other hand, an increase in the value of sugar imported, of $7,427,474; on steel-rails, of $4,345,521; on barley, $2,154,204; and on steel in ingots, bars, &c., $1,620,046.

The exports, as contrasted with the imports during the last fiscal year, (1881,) are as follows:

Exports of domestic merchandise...................	$883,925,947
Exports of foreign merchandise.....................	18,451,399
Total..	902,377,346
Imports of merchandise............................	642,664,628
Excess of exports over imports of merchandise.......	259,712,718
Aggregate of exports and imports..................	1,545,041,974

Compared with the previous year, there was an increase of $66,738,688 in the value of exports of merchandise, and a decrease of $25,290,118 in the value of imports. The annual average of the excess of imports of merchandise over exports thereof, for ten years previous to June 30, 1873, was $104,706,922; but for the last six years there has been an excess of exports over imports of merchandise amounting to $1,180,668,105— an annual average of $196,778,017. The specie value of the exports of domestic merchandise has increased from $376,616,473 in 1870, to $883,925,947 in 1881, an increase of $507,309,474, or 135 per cent. The imports of merchandise have increased from $435,958,408 in 1870, to $642,664,628 in 1881, an increase of $206,706,220, or 47 per cent.

During each year from 1862 to 1879, inclusive, the exports of specie exceeded the imports thereof. The largest excess of such exports over imports was reached during the year 1864, when it amounted to $92,280,929. But during the year ended June 30, 1880, the imports of coin and bullion exceeded the exports thereof by $75,891,391; and during the last fiscal year the excess of imports over exports was $91,168,650.

A revision of the tariff seems necessary to meet the condition of many branches of trade. That condition has materially changed since the enactment of the tariff of 1864, which formed the basis of the present tariff as to most of the articles imported. The specific duties imposed by that act, for instance, on iron and steel in their various forms, had then a proper relation to the *ad valorem* duties imposed on the articles manufactured from those metals; but by a large reduction in the values, especially of the cruder forms of iron and steel, the specific duty imposed thereon now amounts, in many cases, to an *ad valorem* duty of over 100 per cent.; while the *ad valorem* duties on manufactured articles have not been changed. The growing demands of trade have led, also, to the importation of iron and steel in forms and under designations not enumerated in the tariff, and the great disproportion between the specific and *ad valorem* duties is a constant stimulus to importers to try to bring the merchandise under the *ad valorem* rate. This produces uncertainty, appeals from the action of collectors, and litigation, which prove embarrassing to business interests as well as to the Government; and what is instanced as the case with iron and steel will be found to be the case with other articles. An equalization of the tariff, and a simplification of some of its details, are needed. How far such revision shall involve a reduction of the tariff is a question for Congress to decide.

In what manner that revision shall be initiated is also within the province of Congress to determine. The method of a commission which has been proposed has some features that commend it. A commission made up of leading representatives of the manufactures, agriculture, and commerce of the country—experts in the subject-matters dealt with by a tariff—sitting as a board without hampering formalities, and intent upon one subject to the consideration of which the members would bring requisite and ready knowledge and experience, should be able to frame a tariff law that would equalize its burdens and its benefits, and give a reasonable degree of satisfaction to the varied interests affected by it. It is sometimes objected that to wait for the passage of a law creating a commission, and for the organization of it, and for the result of its deliberations, would delay the action of Congress too long. It is to be considered whether there might not be such limitations of time put upon the life of the commission as would preclude such a result. It is conceded that the interests that a tariff affects are so numerous and so diverse that extensive and minute knowledge is needed to treat the subject fairly and comprehensively. Is it not, therefore, worthy of consideration whether the country cannot afford the proper length of time for a skilful, judicious, and complete framing of a bill? Should exigencies exist or arise calling for immediate legislation upon particular matters, they could be treated specifically for the time, while awaiting the complete and comprehensive system.

Attention is invited to the report of this Department for 1880, in regard to a repeal of the discriminating duties imposed by section 2501 of the Revised Statutes, especially on tea and coffee produced iu the possessions of the Netherlands, and the recommendation therein contained is renewed.

REDUCTION OF TAXES.

It is a matter of gratulation that the business of the country so thrives as to endure the onerous taxation that is upon it, and yet grow in volume, and apparently in profits, and yield to the Government a surplus over its needs. The result upon the public revenue is to embarrass this Department in disposing of the surplus in lawful way, and with regard to economy. While it is asserted that there is stringency in the money market, and that the business community is in straits, the call of this Department for millions of bonds is slowly heeded, and its offer to purchase bonds is not in full accepted. There is another way in which to dispose of the surplus, namely, to enter the markets and buy bonds at the current rates. Calculations of experts show that, at the premium that now rules upon the four and four-and-a-half per cent. bonds, this could not be done without a loss to the Treasury, which it is of doubtful propriety to make. And it is almost certain that an announcement of a purpose so to do would enhance the market value of those bonds. Meanwhile the daily receipts from the community by the Treasury continue, the surplus over its needs increases, and money lies idle. It seems that the plan most just, for giving relief, is to reduce taxation, and thereby diminish receipts and surplus.

The rapid reduction of the public debt and the increase of the surplus in the Treasury present the question to Congress whether there should not be a reduction in the taxation now put upon the people. It is estimated that, if the present ratio of receipt and expenditure is kept up, the public debt, now existing, may be paid in the next ten years. In view of the large sum that has been paid by the present generation upon that debt, and of the heavy taxation that now bears upon the industries and business of the country, it seems just and proper that another generation should meet a portion of the debt, and that the burdens now laid upon the country should be lightened. It is to be considered, too, whether the seeming affluence of the Treasury does not provoke to expenditure larger in amount than a wise economy would permit, and upon objects that would not meet with favor in a pinched or moderate condition of the Federal Exchequer. In some quarters there is already talk of an overflowing Treasury, and projects are put forth for lavish expenditure, not only to the furtherance of public works of doubtful legitimacy and expediency, but in aid of enterprises no more than *quasi* public in character. Can a Government be justly said to have an overflowing Treasury when there is an outstanding debt against it greater than it could pay if lawfully presented, and when its means of payment in the future must be taken from its denizens by burdensome taxation? And is it a beneficial exercise of governmental power to raise money by taxation in greater sums than the lawful demands upon the Government require, when those demands are of themselves a heavy burden upon the industry and business of the country?

Other considerations have been presented; such as that if the public debt be fully paid and all Government bonds retired, the best and safest basis for the national-bank system will be gone, and that a desirable mode of investment for savings banks, trust companies, and fiduciary representatives will be taken away, and that the return of the large sums paid to the holders of bonds, to seek reinvestment through other channels, will disturb the business of the country. It is doubtful whether, in a government like ours, not designed for a paternal one, these will be held as sufficient reasons for keeping on foot a large public debt, requiring for the management of it, and for the collection of the revenue to meet the interest upon it, many officials and large expense.

It is proper to say that there is a formidable matter to be weighed on the other hand. The Commissioner of Pensions, it is understood, makes known the need of large sums to meet the arrearages of pensions on claims allowed and likely to be allowed by him. He puts the figures at $235,000,000. Besides this, he has furnished to this Department an estimate, based upon the facts found in the records of his office, which gives these data:

Number of claims filed to November 1, 1881 .... 789, 063

Number of claims admitted to November 1, 1881 .... 450, 949
Number of claims pending to November 1, 1881 .... 265, 575
Number of claims rejected and abandoned to November 1, 1881 . 72, 539

789, 063

4 Ab

Number of claims pending entitled to benefits of arrears acts. 227, 040
Number of claims pending NOT entitled to benefits of arrears
  acts.. 35, 596
Number of old war claims (not entitled) pending 1, 631
Number of 1812 war claims (not entitled) pending...........   1, 308
                                                              ─────────
                                                               265, 575

He estimates that the average value on the first day of January, 1884, of each claimed allowed out of the class of 227,040, above shown, will be $1,350, and that the probable allowances out of that class will be 193,000.

This Department is not aware of any other matter that will materially increase the needful expenditures of the Government.

It is, then, for Congress to determine whether there shall be a reduction of the revenues derived from taxation. If it shall, it will be important to know how it may be effected. A statement of the receipts from internal revenue shows them to be $135,264,385.51 for the year that ended June 30, 1881, and that was in excess of the preceding year by $11,255,011.59; a large part of this was from spirits, tobacco, and fermented liquors. The tax on those articles is a tax on appetite or indulgences, legitimate subjects of taxation when taxation is needful. A reduction of that tax is not recommended. Other objects from which internal revenue is derived are the stamps on bank-checks and matches. The former is a tax on business, somewhat irritating and hampering in its nature. The latter is a tax on an article of hourly and necessary consumption by all classes. It is urged by some that the abolition of the stamp-tax on matches would not reduce the price of the article to the consumer. That contention does not seem well founded, when the cost of the stamp is in so large a ratio to the cost of the article stamped, and when the economy of purchasing stamps in large quantities gives to capital an advantage in the manufacture of the article. There is also the duty derived from proprietary stamps. An abolition of the revenue from these three sources would be an equal lessening of burdens. The tax on the deposits in national banks and upon their capital, in the judgment of the Department, may, with propriety and justice, be lessened, if not entirely removed, whenever it is determined that the public revenue exceeds the public needs. The tax on circulation is different in its nature. It is a tax on a franchise of profit to the favored grantee, and upon a subject, in the furnishing of which to the national banks, the Government is at an expense. There seems to be a reason that, while taxation is the means of meeting governmental expenses, this tax should not be among the first to be taken off. There are other minor sources of internal revenue that might be given up, keeping that from spirits, fermented liquors, and tobacco.

The other source of revenue where a reduction may be made is the customs. It already appears that the revenue from customs for the year ended June 30, 1881, was $198,159,676.02, being an increase of $11,637,611.42 over the preceding year.

While it is a principle that taxation for the expenses of Government, to be just, should bear on all alike and equally, it must also be one that when the aggregate of taxation is to be lessened, the reduction should be made in such ways that all will be relieved alike and equally. Hence, it is assumed that if Congress does determine on a decrease of the revenue, it will seek that end, as well through a revision of the existing tariff laws as through an abolition or abatement of the internal revenue. This Department does not venture, at this time, to point out wherein the wisdom of Congress may find places in the tariff laws for its exercise in revision and reduction. In another part of this report somewhat is said upon the mode of making a revision of those laws. If the mode of a commission to experts should be adopted, and delay in the final adoption of a revised tariff law should be anticipated, it may be well for Congress to consider what is to be done in the meantime with the surplus revenue that is likely to accrue unless prevented by the payment of arrearages of pensions.

TRIAL OF CUSTOMS CASES.

On the 1st of July, 1881, 2,376 suits against collectors of customs, nearly all for the refund of customs duties, were pending in the United States courts of New York. The delay in the trial of these cases heightens the expense of the litigation, and puts off the final determination of the rights in controversy, and also increases the number of the suits that are brought. It sometimes happens that before a test case can be brought to trial and decided in the Supreme Court, importers are compelled to commence hundreds of suits in order to preserve their rights. If these cases are put up on the calendar, it is done at the expense and inconvenience of private litigants. The only remedy appears to be the establishment of a new tribunal for the trial of customs cases, or their transfer to some existing tribunal like the Court of Claims. The Department has issued a circular to experts, asking their views as to the best mode of meeting this difficulty, and it may submit, in a special communication to Congress, some more definite views upon the subject.

CLAIMS.

The claims against the Government, presented to this Department, often involve important disputed questions of law or fact, which require for their correct decision the taking of depositions and the cross-examination of witnesses, and sometimes of the parties themselves. For this no provision is made by law. Authority from Congress to refer any such claims as the Secretary may think proper to the Court of Claims, would give to the claimants and to the Government a proper judicial trial and judgment; which would not only do justice to the parties but prevent re-examinations which are now urged upon every change of Departmental officers.

It is believed that a proper statute of limitations upon claims would promote the substantial ends of justice. The reasons for such a statute in the case of claims against the Government, such as the death of witnesses, and the loss of paper evidence, and the policy of putting an end to controversies, are obvious and too familiar to need more than a suggestion. On the other hand, in the prosecution of demands by the United States, great hardships to private parties are often occasioned. This is especially the case where those sued are sureties and there has been neglect and delay on the part of the governmental agents in adjusting accounts and making demand for alleged balances.

SUGAR.

The duties collected upon sugar, molasses, and melado during the past fiscal year amount to $47,977,137, or nearly one-quarter of the whole amount of our revenues from customs. The difficulties attending the collection of these duties have largely occupied the attention of committees of Congress during several past sessions. The Dutch standard of color, as applied to the apparent color of imported sugars, is no longer a test of their saccharine strength or value for refining purposes. Imputing this fact to artificial coloring used for the purpose of affecting the rate of duties, this Department has claimed the right to look beyond the apparent color, and to classify the invoices according to the true color which they would show without that artificial treatment. The importers, claiming sometimes that their sugars are not in any sense artificially colored, and sometimes that they have the right to have them classified by their color, according to the Dutch standard, whether artificially colored before being imported or not, have brought many suits to recover duties alleged to have been illegally exacted. A test suit, recently tried in New York, is pending in the Supreme Court, and is expected to give some aid in the true construction of the law upon the point whether the Department has a right to regard anything but the apparent color of the sugar at the time of importation. Whatever may be the decision of this question, the fact remains that, either by artificially coloring or by changes in the process of manufacturing, sugars of the highest saccharine strength and value have been for some years imported, which appear to be of the lowest grade of color, and are, therefore, claimed to be entitled to entry at the lowest rate of duties.

The amount in controversy in the suits referred to, claimed by the importers to have been overpaid upon sugars imported during the last fiscal year, by reason of classification above their apparent color, is $708,810.99, while the amount of duties collected by the classification of sugars at the increased rate during the same year is $1,857,324.10; so that the Government has gained during that time, by the higher classification of sugar, $1,148,513.11, as to which there is no controversy.

The Dutch standard was adopted undoubtedly upon the theory that color substantially represented value, and the intention, no doubt, was to impose duties upon sugar substantially *ad valorem*. The attention of Congress is earnestly invited to the subject, so that while the producers of sugar in this country are fairly treated, importers may be relieved from the embarrassments attending the present method of classification.

INTERNAL REVENUE.

From the various sources of taxation under the internal-revenue laws, the receipts for the fiscal year ended June 30, 1881, were as follows:

From spirits	$67,153,974 88
From tobacco	42,854,991 31
From fermented liquors	13,700,241 21
From banks and bankers	3,762,208 07
From adhesive stamps	7,375,255 72
From penalties	231,078 21
From collections not otherwise provided for	152,162 90
Total	135,229,912 30

The increase of the revenue from spirits during the last fiscal year was $5,968,466.09; the increase from tobacco in its various forms of manufacture for the same period, $3,984,851.23; the increase from fermented liquors was $870,438.37; the increase of revenue from taxes on banks and Bankers was $411,222.79; the total increase of internal revenue from all sources was $11,019,454.50.

CONTINUANCE OF SIX PER CENT. AND FIVE PER CENT. BONDS AT
3¼ PER CENT.

In the last annual report the attention of Congress was invited to
a portion of the interest-bearing debt becoming redeemable on or before
July 1, 1881, as follows:

Title of loan.	Rate.	Redeemable.	Amount.
Loan July and August, 1861	6 per cent .	June 30, 1881	$145,786,500
Loan of 1863, (1881's)	6 per cent .	June 30, 1881	57,787,250
Funded Loan of 1881	5 per cent .	May 1, 1881	469,651,050

Recommendation was made for authority to refund into Treasury
notes or bonds bearing a lower rate of interest such portion of these
bonds as should remain unredeemed at maturity.

Congress adjourned on the 3d of March, the bill for refunding these
amounts having failed to become a law.   On March 1 there remained
outstanding of these bonds the following amounts:

Title of loan.	Rate.	Redeemable.	Amount.
Loan of July and August, 1861	6 per cent .	June 30, 1881	$144,339,900
Loan of 1863	6 per cent .	June 30, 1881	57,216,100
Funded Loan of 1881....................	5 per cent .	May 1, 1881	469,320,650

Included in these amounts were $29,479,300 of five per cent. bonds
which had been purchased, or called for redemption but not matured,
and $5,887,950 of six per cent. bonds in process of redemption for the
sinking-fund, leaving to be provided for, of the five per cent. bonds,
$439,841,350, and of the six per cent. bonds, $196,378,600.

The financial condition of the Government at that time, and the
policy pursued by my immediate predecessor in dealing with these
bonds, are set forth in his letter of August 8, 1881, to the American
Bankers' Association, as follows:

•   •   •   •   •   •   •

"It may be stated, however, that when I entered upon the duties of
my present position, in March last, I found that of the bonded indebtedness of the Government there were of five per cent. bonds, redeemable at the option of the Government after May 1, 1881, the amount of
$469,320,650, of which the amount of $146,101,900 was represented by
coupon bonds; and of six per cent. bonds redeemable at the option of
the Government after July 1, 1881, the amount of $202,266,550, of
which $45,391,000 were represented by coupon bonds.

"Only the coupons for the quarterly interest falling due on May 1,

the Department gave notice that the coupon five per cent. bonds of the loan of July 14, 1870, and January 20, 1871, would be paid on August 12, 1881, with a like privilege of continuing the bonds at 3½ per cent. to such of the holders as might present them for that purpose on or before July 1, 1881; and at the same time the Treasury offered to receive, for continuance, in like manner, any of the uncalled registered bonds of that loan to an amount not exceeding $250,000,000, the remainder of the loan being reserved with a view of its payment from the surplus revenues.

"The continued three-and-a-half per cent. bonds having a market price slightly above par, the five per cents in question were rapidly presented, and it became necessary to extend somewhat the limit fixed for the amount of registered bonds to be accepted for continuance.

"On July 1, a notice for the payment, on October 1, 1881, of the registered fives not continued was given, and the resources of the Treasury will be ample to meet their payment.
*   *   *   *   *   *   *

"By this plan the Department has been not only relieved from the embarrassment of providing for the payment of the coupon interest, but has reduced all the six and five per cent. loans of the Government to a loan payable at the option of the Government, and bearing interest at only 3½ per cent. per annum; and this, with the trifling expense to the Government of preparing the new registered bonds, and of paying the actual expenses of the London agency, at which only three persons have been employed for a few weeks, issuing about $44,500,000 of the continued bonds."
*   *   *   *   *   *   *

It will be observed that at no time were calls made for bonds in excess of the ability of the Department to meet the payments therefor had the bonds called been presented for redemption instead of for continuance.

In conducting these operations, expenses were incurred for paper and for printing the new bonds to an amount estimated not to exceed $6,000, and there was paid for all other expenses, including those of the London agency, $4,499.08.

Under this arrangement, in addition to the six per cent. bonds continued, as stated in the letter, there were continued of the five per cent. bonds $401,504,900; of which amount $108,494,500 were coupon bonds, leaving to be paid from the surplus revenue $10,151,950 of coupon bonds, with interest to August 12, 1881, and $23,184,500 of registered bonds, with interest to October 1, 1881, which transactions were not completed when the above letter was written.

The annual saving in interest through the continuance of these bonds is as follows:

On the 6 per cent. bonds, continued at 3½ per cent......	$4,451,378 75
On the 5 per cent. bonds, continued at 3½ per cent......	6,022,573 50
Total..	10,473,952 25

REDEMPTIONS.

It was also stated in the last annual report that there would become payable on December 31, 1880, the loan of February 8, 1861, amounting to $13,414,000, and on July 1, 1881, the Oregon-War Debt, amounting to $711,800, both of which loans bore interest at the rate of 6 per cent. Previous to the maturity of these loans public notice was given to the holders that the bonds would be paid at the respective dates of maturity, and that interest would cease thereafter. All the bonds presented have been paid from the surplus revenues of the Government.

In addition to these amounts there have been purchased or called for redemption, and interest has ceased upon, during the year ending November 1, 1880, bonds in the following amounts:

Bonds bearing interest at 6 per cent.................	$25,518,600
Bonds bearing interest at 5 per cent.................	68,146,150
Bonds bearing interest at 3½ per cent., (continued sixes) .	16,179,100
Total..	109,843,850

making a total of bonds redeemed, or on which interest ceased during the year, of $123,969,650.

The following statement shows the changes in the interest-bearing debt, and the saving of interest thereon, by the continuance and payment of bonds during the year ending November 1, 1881:

Amount.	Rate.	Disposition.	Yearly saving.
$178,055,150	6 per cent .	Continued at 3½ per cent...............	$4,451,378 75
401,504,900	5 per cent .	Continued at 3½ per cent...............	6,022,573 50
39,644,400	6 per cent .	Redeemed or interest ceased............	2,378,664 00
68,146,150	5 per cent .	Redeemed or interest ceased............	3,407,307 50
16,179,100	3½ per cent.	Redeemed or interest ceased............	566,268 50
		Total annual saving in interest................	16,826,192 25

making the annual interest-charge on the debt, November 1, 1881, $60,962,245.25.

On the 1st of November there remained outstanding of bonds bearing 3½ per cent. interest, payable at the pleasure of the Government after proper notice, $563,380,950, included in which were $12,035,500 called bonds not matured. If the excess of revenues over expenditures should continue as during the past year, its application to the payment of these bonds can be made at the discretion of the Secretary, and to that extent the Government will be relieved from the necessity of paying any premium in the consequent redemption of its bonded debt.

It is not improbable that the subject of the funding of the public debt in bonds bearing a rate of interest less than that of any yet issued will be considered by Congress during the present session. When that subject is taken up, it is respectfully suggested that it should be borne in mind that the bonds now outstanding, known as the extended sixes and fives, on interest at the rate of $3\frac{1}{2}$ per cent., possess a quality seldom found in a debt against a Government. That quality is in the power that the Government has to call them in for payment at any time, or to postpone payment of them for years. This is a valuable privilege to the Government, and it is to be considered whether it will be wise to give it up. The possession of it enables the Government to accommodate the payment of that portion of the public debt to the varying state of the public means. It would be difficult, probably, to market a loan at a low rate of interest which should be redeemable at the pleasure of the Government. Indeed, one of the requisites of a loan proposed at a low rate is, that it be issued for a long term, and made irredeemable until the expiration thereof. The reason is on the surface. A debt at a low rate is not likely to be sought for, save by those wishing permanent investments, as public institutions, trustees, guardians, and other fiduciary holders of funds, or wealthy persons with whom safety, stability, permanence, and regularity of income are of more importance than a high rate of return. It is also to be considered that the gain that would accrue to the Government from a small reduction of the rate of interest is, to some extent, lost in the expenses necessarily attendant on the making of a new loan. It is a part of the information that the Department has from men engaged in financial operations that a new loan at 3 per cent. would be taken up if it was by its condition irredeemable save at a long term. Emphasis is put by them on this condition. None have placed the term at less than ten years. Most have put it at twenty. Some have suggested a term of forty years, with an option in the Government to pay at the end of ten.

For these reasons this Department makes no recommendation of legislation for the refunding of the bonds now outstanding bearing interest at $3\frac{1}{2}$ per centum. It does recommend that if a new loan at a lower rate is offered, there be given to the bonds a long term of payment.

PACIFIC-RAILROAD SINKING-FUND.

The third section of the act approved May 7, 1878, provides—

"That there shall be established in the Treasury of the United States a sinking-fund, which shall be invested by the Secretary of the

Treasury in bonds of the United States; and the semi-annual income. thereof shall be in like manner from time to time invested, and the same shall accumulate and be disposed of as hereinafter mentioned And in making such investments the Secretary shall prefer the five per centum bonds of the United States, unless, for good reason appearing to him, and which he shall report to Congress, he shall at any time deem it advisable to invest in other bonds of the United States. All the bonds belonging to said fund shall, as fast as they shall be obtained, be so stamped as to show that they belong to said fund, and that they are not good in the hands of other holders than the Secretary of the Treasury until they shall have been endorsed by him, and publicly disposed of pursuant to this act."

The Secretary of the Treasury has, upon several occasions, recommended to Congress a modification of the terms of this act, so as to permit the investment of the fund in the first-mortgage thirty-year bonds of the Union Pacific Railroad Company, and of the Central Pacific Railroad Company, authorized by section 10 of the act of Congress of July 2, 1864, chapter 216, and section 1 of the act of Congress of March 3, 1865, chapter 88, or in any interest-bearing bonds of the United States.

The ninth section of the sinking-fund act referred to provides that all sums required to be paid into the fund are made a lien upon all the property and franchises of the roads, "subject to any lawfully prior and permanent mortgage, lien, or claim thereon." These bonds being thus payable from the sinking-fund, they would seem to be the best investment which now offers, and especially so in view of the low rate of interest now realized from investment in United States bonds. Should Congress, however, not deem it desirable to authorize such investment, the Secretary would suggest that the amounts withheld from the respective railroad companies on account of the fund, should be credited semi-annually on the books of the Treasury Department, with interest at the rate of 5 per centum per annum. This method of treating the matter will obviate the necessity of purchasing bonds, which frequently cannot be done without the payment of a large premium, and will realize to the companies a rate corresponding more nearly with that which they would receive were the amounts invested in first-mortgage bonds of their respective roads.

CONTINUED TRUST-FUND BONDS.

Included in the amount of five per cent. bonds, continued at 3½ per cent., are $451,350 held by the Secretary of the Treasury as part of the sinking-fund for the Pacific Railroads, under the act of May 7, 1878, and $52,000 held in trust for the South Carolina school-fund, act of March 3,

1873. The continuance of these bonds at 3½ per cent. was deemed a better investment than their sale and reinvestment in other United States bonds.

BUREAU OF ENGRAVING AND PRINTING.

During the year the Bureau of Engraving and Printing has added to its valuable stock of machinery five new steam-power plate-printing presses. These presses have now been in operation several months, with satisfactory results, and it is confidently expected that the slow and laborious process of plate-printing on hand-presses will, to a great extent, be superseded by the use of the more rapid and economical power-press.

DISTINCTIVE PAPER.

The use of the silk-threaded, fibre paper for the printing of notes, certificates, checks, and other obligations, including registered bonds, has been continued during the year with results such as warrant the further use of it. Since July 1, 1881, all pension-checks for the Department of the Interior have been printed upon this paper. Tables accompanying the report will show the disposition made of the 22,231,000 sheets manufactured for the Department since its adoption in 1879.

The distinctive features of the paper, combined with its superior quality, have afforded complete protection to the securities of the Government, the paper not having been successfully counterfeited.

There have also been received since July 1, 1880, 37,880,518 sheets of distinctive paper for printing United States internal-revenue stamps.

COUNT, EXAMINATION, AND DESTRUCTION OF REDEEMED SECURITIES.

During the fiscal year there have been received by this office for final count and destruction redeemed United States legal-tender notes, national currency, and miscellaneous securities amounting to $310,139,416.14. The United States legal-tender notes, national currency, United States bonds, and other obligations mutilated in process of printing, and over-due coupons and unissued notes received for destruction, amounted to $49,412,119.82—making an aggregate of securities counted, cancelled, and destroyed during the fiscal year of $359,551,535.96, the details of which are set forth in the tables accompanying the report.

EXPORTS AND IMPORTS OF CATTLE.

The number of living horned cattle exported, chiefly to England, in the year ended June 30, 1881, was 185,707, valued at $14,304,103, being an excess over the previous year of 2,951 in number, and $959,906 in value, and almost $6,000,000 in value above the year 1879.

* These shipments to England might be vastly increased, should the order of the Privy Council of Great Britain be rescinded, which requires that all American cattle be slaughtered within ten days after arrival at the port of entry. This order was made to prevent the introduction into that country, from this, of the disease known as pleuro-pneumonia. The demand in England for imported meat is so imperative that it is not doubted that this order will be rescinded whenever the British government is satisfied that our cattle may be sold, driven through, and fattened in that country without danger from the disease mentioned.

The rescission of the order would allow the exportation from this country of store-cattle in great numbers to be fed and fattened on English soil, while at present only animals fitted for immediate slaughter can be exported there.

At the last session of Congress a small appropriation was made to be expended under the direction of the Secretary of the Treasury to investigate the question as to the existence of the disease in this country, preparatory to the protection of the great routes of transportation of cattle from the West to the sea-coast for exportation. A commission of three persons has been appointed to make the investigation, and a report to the Secretary will be submitted to Congress early in the session.

It may be assumed that this report will show that contagious pleuro-pneumonia has never existed in this country west of the Allegheny Mountains, while it undoubtedly does exist in certain portions of New York, Pennsylvania, Connecticut, Delaware, and Maryland. It is believed that its introduction into the great cattle-ranches of the West would be a national calamity, and the attention of Congress is earnestly called to the subject, so that proper measures may be adopted to prevent its introduction into healthy districts, and to cause its extirpation in such as are infected. The attention of Congress is also called to the necessity of more direct legislation authorizing quarantining of imported cattle and for providing places for the quarantine thereof, and for the expenses attendant thereon.

LIFE-SAVING SERVICE.

The annual report of the Life-Saving Service shows excellent results of the operations of this beneficent institution.

The number of stations in commission during the year was one hundred and eighty-three. The reports of the district officers show that two hundred and fifty disasters to vessels occurred within the field of station operations. There were eighteen hundred and eighty persons on board these vessels, of whom eighteen hundred and fifty-four were

saved, twenty-six only being lost. Four hundred and seven ship-
wrecked persons were succored at the stations, to whom one thousand
and sixty days' relief in the aggregate was afforded. The estimated
value of property involved in these disasters was $4,054,752, of which
$2,828,680 was saved, and $1,226,072 lost. The number of vessels
totally lost was sixty-six.

Of the new stations authorized by law, three on Lake Huron have
been completed, and are now in commission, and two others at Cape
Fear, North Carolina, and one at Bolinas Bay, California, will be in
operation during the winter.

The service has been greatly embarrassed by the resignation of a
number of keepers of stations on account of insufficient pay. Others
have only been induced to remain in the hope of an increase in their
compensation by Congress at its present session. The professional experience of these men makes their services valuable. In many cases
men of equal qualification could not be found to fill their places, and
some vacancies have occurred which it has been impossible to fill at
all. The district officers represent that the resignations next season
will be general unless the rate of pay, which is now only $400 per an-
num, is raised. It is obvious that this service should not be allowed
to retrograde, and the attention of Congress is earnestly invited to the
necessity of making such provision as will retain the requisite professional capacity in these important positions.

It is also necessary to make provision for increasing the compensation of the district superintendents, which is too low, being but $1,000
per annum, except in the two largest districts, where it is only $1,500.
These officers give large bonds, ranging from $20,000 to $50,000 in
amount, and are charged with grave duties which occupy all their
time, and the proper discharge of which involves the efficient conduct
of the service in their respective districts.

The general superintendent, in his annual report, urges other measures for the improvement of the service which merit attention.

PUBLIC BUILDINGS.

The appropriations for the construction of public buildings during
the past fiscal year were such as to permit the prosecution of work
during the year without interruption, and the Supervising Architect
reports the progress on the various works as generally satisfactory.

REVENUE MARINE.

The vessels of this service now number 36, comprising 5 sailing-
vessels and 31 propelled wholly or in part by steam. There are employed, at the present time, to man this fleet 198 officers and 794 men.

The Revenue Marine has been actively employed, during the past year, in protecting the customs revenue and assisting distressed vessels, as will appear by the following exhibit:

Aggregate number of miles cruised   282,027
Number of vessels boarded and examined.............   29,101
Number of vessels seized or reported for violating the law.   3,163
Number of vessels wrecked or in distress assisted.....   148
Number of persons rescued from drowning..........   141
Estimated value of vessels and their cargoes imperilled
    assisted $2,766,882 00
Expenses of the service for the year $346,791 99

The Revenue Marine has rendered important aid to other branches of the public service, especially to the Light-House Establishment, the Commission of Fish and Fisheries, and the Life-Saving Service. The revenue-steamer "Perry," in September, performed valuable and timely service in conveying supplies to the sufferers by forest fires in Michigan.

Under the law providing for the use of revenue-vessels for protecting the interests of the Government on the seal islands and sea-otter hunting-grounds, and enforcing the provisions of law in Alaska generally, the revenue-steamers "Corwin" and "Rush," under competent commanders, have cruised extensively during the past season in the waters washing our most northerly possessions. The "Corwin," under Captain Hooper, has plied principally in the extreme north, following the illicit traffickers in breech-loading arms and liquors into their retreats in the Arctic Ocean, while continuing the search begun last year for the missing whalers, "Mount Wollaston" and "Vigilant" and the Arctic-exploring steamer "Jeannette." In pursuing this search, Captain Hooper landed upon and thoroughly explored Herald Island in July, and in August landed with an exploring party upon the southeast coast of Wrangel Land. Captain Hooper expresses the conclusion, based upon his cruising of the past two seasons, that the missing whalers referred to are hopelessly lost, and that the "Jeannette," in 1879, passed to the northward without stopping at any place in the Arctic Ocean, and that her movements in the extreme polar regions have been subsequently largely controlled by the movements of the ice; that this vessel is not likely to return by the way of Behring Sea; and that, if any action is taken for her relief, it should be done promptly, and a vessel dispatched to the Arctic waters, on the eastern coast of this continent, carrying sledge parties to prosecute the search for the people of the exploring steamer. I commend the subject to the attention of Congress.

The cruising of the "Rush" has been effectual in guarding the waters of Southern Alaska and the Aleutian chain from the incursions of vessels unlawfully engaged in the killing of seals and other fur-bearing animals.

The presence of one or more vessels in Alaskan waters named is deemed necessary for the protection of the Government interests there, but the revenue-cutters now available are not adapted for the long voyages required in the work. It is accordingly recommended that provision be made for the construction of a revenue-vessel specially adapted for Alaskan service.

In the last annual report recommendation was made for an appropriation for two new vessels, at a cost of $75,000 each, to take the place of two upon the Atlantic coast that were in need of extensive repairs. Congress, however, provided for one only. The reasons then existing for the appropriation apply with still stronger force at the present time, the vessel to be replaced having become almost entirely unseaworthy. The recommendation is therefore renewed. It is also recommended that an appropriation be made for the construction of a new hull and the alteration of the steam-machinery of the revenue-steamer "Perry," now stationed on Lake Erie, a board of survey having reported the vessel as unfit for duty in her present condition. To make these repairs and construct the new vessel, the sum of $150,000 has been included in the estimates.

The service is seriously embarrassed by the large and constantly increasing number of officers who, through old age or physical disability, have become unequal to the performance of duty. The number of officers in the Revenue Marine is limited by law to one of each grade for a vessel, and the active list is reduced by so many as are unfit for duty, there being no provision for retiring the disabled. The active list is still further reduced by details made for duty in connection with the Life-Saving Service, under the act of June 18, 1876. The work of the service consequently devolves on a smaller number of officers than the law contemplates, or safety and efficient management justify. Besides, the retention of the permanently incapacitated bars the way to promotion of the junior officers, thus removing from the service a valuable incentive to improvement. To remedy these evils a system for the retirement of officers, who have in the line of duty become permanently disabled, is desirable. It has also been urged that provision be made for extending the benefits of the pension laws to the officers and seamen of the Revenue Marine. Under existing statutes they are entitled to a pension only when they have been wounded or otherwise disabled in the line of duty while co-operating with the Navy. In view of the constant activity required of them, in time of peace as well as of war, and of the hazard involved in their service, their cruising being mostly upon the shallow waters and dangerous courses near the coast, subjecting them during the inclement winter season to extreme hardships and dangers, their claim to pensions seems to be well founded.

Upon these grounds the attention of Congress is invited to the recommendations heretofore made by my predecessors in office, for the establishment of a retired list, and the extension of the pension laws to the Revenue-Marine Service.

ALASKA.

The experience of the past year has shown more strongly than ever the necessity of establishing some simple form of government for the protection of persons and property in the Territory of Alaska; and it is recommended that Congress, at the approaching session, take action on the subject.

The Alaska Commercial Company has taken, during the past year, the full number of seals allowed under its lease, namely, one hundred thousand.

MARINE-HOSPITAL SERVICE.

The Supervising Surgeon-General reports that during the past year 32,613 patients received relief from the Marine-Hospital Service, of whom 12,449 were treated in the hospitals, and 20,164 at the different dispensaries; that 309,596 days' relief in hospital were furnished, and a considerable amount expended for surgical appliances for out-patients. Seventeen incurable patients have been furnished transportation to their own homes. The officers of the service have examined 4,384 pilots for color-blindness, and have made physical examinations of 57 seamen of the Light-House and Merchant Services, and 44 officers, cadets, and applicants for appointment as cadets, and 305 seamen of the Revenue-Marine Service.

Section 4569 of the Revised Statutes requires certain vessels to carry a medicine-chest, but as it does not specify what should be contained therein, a book prepared by the Supervising Surgeon-General, giving the necessary information, has been published by the Department, and is now issued to those concerned.

The receipts from all sources were $386,059.81, and the net expenditures $400,404.46. It is believed that the receipts will be largely increased during the present fiscal year, as a result of the special investigations now in progress.

Notwithstanding the great increase in the number of patients, the expenditures are not greater than last year, and the *per capita* cost has been reduced from $16.18, as stated in the last report, to $12.27.

The hospitals are generally in better condition now than at any pre-

5 Ab

vious time. The temporary hospital at Bedloe's Island, at the port of New York, has received such furniture and appliances as were necessary, but little has been done in the way of repairing the buildings, or enlarging them to meet the needs of the service, Congress having as yet given no authority for their transfer from the War to the Treasury Department. It seems that the city of New York, with its extensive commerce, and large numbers of men engaged in the merchant-marine service, should have a more permanent arrangement for the care of sick and disabled seamen than that which is now provided.

The attention of Congress is again invited to the necessity for some legislation concerning the unclaimed effects of seamen dying in marine hospitals. There is now in the Treasury as a special deposit, to the credit of the Secretary, $2,125.51 from this source. It is recommended that Congress authorize the sale of such unclaimed effects, and that the proceeds, together with the unclaimed money now on hand, be placed to the credit of the marine-hospital fund.

The recommendations of my predecessors, and of the Supervising Surgeon-General, concerning statutory provision for the appointment of medical officers, for the compulsory physical examination of seamen, as preliminary to shipment, the establishment of a "Snug Harbor," and a re-enactment of the law providing for the investment of surplus funds, are concurred in, and respectfully commended to the favorable consideration of Congress.

STEAMBOAT INSPECTION.

The following table shows the operations of this office during the past year:

Table showing the number of steam-vessels inspected, their aggregate tonnage, and the officers licensed for the several divisions of navigation, during the fiscal year ended June 30, 1881.

Divisions.	Steamers.	Tonnage.	Officers licensed.
Pacific coast............................	287	102,712.60	1,061
Atlantic coast...........................	2,154	552,393.76	7,065
Western rivers	909	190,033.36	4,334
Northern lakes..........................	1,058	269,086.67	3,437
Gulf coast...............................	371	89,776.71	1,881
Total...............................	4,779	1,204,003.10	17,798

Recapitulation.

Total number of vessels inspected......................	4,779
Total tonnage of vessels inspected.....................	1,204,003.10
Total number of officers licensed......................	17,798

Showing an increase over the preceding year as follows:

Increase in number of vessels..........................	243
Increase in tonnage	82,195.05
Increase in number of licensed officers..................	1,137

Receipts.

Receipts from inspection of steam-vessels...............	$167,629 21
Receipts from sales of licenses.........................	139,925 00
Total..	307,554 21

Expenditures.

Salaries of inspectors and clerks........................	$180,931 18
Travelling and miscellaneous expenses..................	37,651 08
Total..	218,582 26
Total receipts from all sources	$307,554 21
Total expenditures	218,582 26
Balance of receipts unexpended	88,971 95

The total number of accidents to steam-vessels during the year, resulting in loss of life, was:

Explosions	19
Fire..	3
Collisions..	7
Snags, wrecks, and sinking............................	8
Total.............	37

Total number of lives lost by accidents from various causes during the fiscal year ended June 30, 1881.

Explosions	43
Fire..	11
Collisions..	30
Snags, wrecks, and sinking............................	150
Accidental drowning..................................	29
Miscellaneous casualties..............................	5
Total lives lost......................................	268

Under the head of "snags, wrecks, and sinking" are included the disasters to the steamers "City of Very Cruz" and "Alpena," wrecked by hurricanes, whereby 128 lives were lost. These vessels were fully equipped according to law, and the accidents were from causes wholly beyond any precautions that could have been taken by the Steamboat-Inspection Service.

The Supervising Inspector-General, in his annual report, suggests several amendments to the steamboat laws, and calls special attention to the increasing accumulation of funds exacted by way of tax upon licensed officers for the support of this service, showing a surplus in the past year of $88,971.95, and an aggregate surplus now in the Treasury of $649,320.35.

These subjects are commended to the consideration of Congress.

COMMERCE AND NAVIGATION.

The total tonnage of vessels of the United States at the close of the fiscal year 1881, as shown by the records of the Register of the Treasury, was 4,057,734 tons; of this amount 1,335,586 tons were comprised in 2,326 vessels registered for the foreign trade, and 2,722,148 tons in 21,739 vessels enrolled and licensed for the coasting trade and fisheries. There has been a decrease of 17,224 tons in vessels employed in the foreign trade, and an increase of 6,924 tons in such as were engaged in the domestic trade.

The following table exhibits the number of vessels built and documented during the last fiscal year, with their tonnage:

	Number.	Tons.
Sailing-vessels	493	81,209
Steam-vessels	444	118,070
Canal-boats	57	10,189
Barges	114	70,988
Total	1,108	280,456

As the larger part of the canal-boats and barges now built in the country are not documented, it is presumed that the above numbers represent but a small proportion of the vessels of those classes which were built.

TRADE IN AMERICAN AND FOREIGN BOTTOMS.

The total tonnage of vessels entered from foreign countries was 15,251,329 tons during 1880, and 15,630,541 tons during the year ended June 30, 1881, showing an increase of 379,212 tons, or about two and one-half per cent. The American tonnage entered in the foreign trade exhibits a decrease of 221,020 tons, or seven per cent., while the foreign tonnage shows an increase of 600,232 tons, or about five per cent. The tonnage in these cases is computed on the basis of the number of entries of vessels and not on the number of vessels, and is limited to the seaboard ports.

Of the merchandise brought in at seaboard, lake, and river ports during the year, an amount of the value of $133,631,146 was imported in American vessels, and $491,840,269 in foreign. Of the exports of merchandise, an amount of the value of $116,955,324 was shipped in American, and $777,162,714 in foreign vessels. Of the combined imports and exports of merchandise, 16 per cent. only of the total value was conveyed in American vessels; and the amount of transportation to and from our ports in our own vessels has fallen off one per cent. in the fiscal year 1881 as compared with that of 1880.

COAST AND GEODETIC SURVEY.

The work of the survey of the coast, and the geodetic operations in the interior, have been advanced during the year as effectively as the means appropriated would permit.

On the Atlantic slope, or Eastern Division, the work has been in progress on the coasts of Maine, Connecticut, New York, New Jersey, Pennsylvania, Delaware, Maryland, Virginia, Florida, Louisiana, and Mississippi, including the Mississippi river to Memphis; the coast of Texas; and in the interior of the States of New Hampshire, Vermont, New York, Pennsylvania, New Jersey, Ohio, Kentucky, Tennessee, Indiana, Illinois, Missouri, and Wisconsin. On the Pacific slope, or Western Division, the detailed survey has been in progress in important parts of the coasts of California, Oregon, and Washington Territory. The extension of the triangulation of the interior has been in progress in California, Nevada, and Colorado. Surveys and examinations of important localities have also been made in Alaska Territory.

The publication of maps and charts, the Coast Pilot, and tide-tables has kept pace with the progress of field operations.

The officer in charge of the survey asks attention to the increasing demands for information which that work is intended to supply, corresponding with the steady development of the country. With a view to the most advantageous employment of the parties engaged in the widely-separated localities in which the work is now in progress, he recommends an increase of appropriations over the amounts granted for the past few years. This recommendation only proposes to raise the appropriation to an amount from which it was reduced at a time of great commercial depression. It is for Congress to determine whether the importance of the work calls for the increase in appropriation.

DISTRICT OF COLUMBIA.

The net expenditures on account of the District of Columbia for the fiscal year 1881 were $3,543,912.03. The revenues deposited in the Treasury for the same period were $2,016,199.23.

From July 1, 1880, to July 1, 1881, the bonded indebtedness has been reduced by operation of the sinking-fund $254,573.33, and the annual interest-charge upon the District debt has been reduced $12,816.66. Since the offices of the commissioners of the sinking-fund of the District of Columbia were abolished and their duties and powers transferred to the Treasurer of the United States by the act Congress of June 11, 1878, the principal of the funded debt has been reduced $938,900, and the annual interest-charge has been reduced $55,792.62.

NATIONAL BOARD OF HEALTH.

During the past year the board has continued its investigations into matters affecting the public health, and has collected much valuable information bearing upon sanitary questions. Under the provisions of the act approved June 2, 1879, entitled "An act to prevent the introduction of contagious and infectious diseases into the United States," the board has completed a temporary refuge station at Ship Island, Mississippi, maintained a service of inspection on the Mississippi river, a temporary refuge station on Blackbeard Island, off the coast of Georgia, and a hospital-boat at Norfolk, Virginia, in readiness for use in case of emergency. Happily no epidemic of yellow-fever has invaded the country during the past year; and that the board has rendered efficient service in compassing this result, and established the utility of its refuge stations, is abundantly shown in the number of infected vessels effectually treated during the past summer. Eight vessels with yellow-fever patients on board have been sent by local health authorities to its stations—four to the station on Ship Island and four to the station on Blackbeard Island; and it is a matter of congratulation that no cases of fever occurred on board either of the vessels after they were released, or in any of the ports at which they subsequently touched. But for this timely assistance on the part of the Government a serious epidemic might have occurred, involving far greater loss to the country than the expenses incurred by the board.

The total expenditures of the board during the past year were $164,989.46. As required by law, the expenditures have been made upon estimates submitted by the board and approved by the Secretary of the Treasury; and while a liberal construction has been placed upon the laws in providing the board with funds for carrying out the purposes of the several acts defining its duties, a strict accountability has been maintained by the accounting officers of the Department in relation to its disbursements.

In view of the want of proper facilities on the part of local health authorities on the South Atlantic and Gulf coasts for effectually protecting the country against the introduction of contagious or infectious diseases, the attention of Congress is respectfully called to the subject of providing the additional temporary refuge stations suggested by the board in its annual report.

The several reports of the heads of offices and bureaus are herewith respectfully transmitted.

CHAS. J. FOLGER,

Secretary.

To the SPEAKER OF THE HOUSE OF REPRESENTATIVES.

TABLES ACCOMPANYING THE REPORT.

TABLE A.—*STATEMENT of the NET RECEIPTS (by warrants) during the fiscal year ended June 30, 1881.*

CUSTOMS.

Quarter ended September 30, 1880	$56,395,143 44
Quarter ended December 31, 1880	42,241,041 09
Quarter ended March 31, 1881	48,747,010 97
Quarter ended June 30, 1881	50,776,480 52
	$198,159,676 02

SALES OF PUBLIC LANDS.

Quarter ended September 30, 1880	434,590 66
Quarter ended December 31, 1880	608,936 86
Quarter ended March 31, 1881	542,486 28
Quarter ended June 30, 1881	615,849 37
	2,201,863 17

INTERNAL REVENUE.

Quarter ended September 30, 1880	32,496,422 38
Quarter ended December 31, 1880	34,605,802 77
Quarter ended March 31, 1881	30,020,086 29
Quarter ended June 30, 1881	38,052,074 07
	135,264,385 51

TAX ON CIRCULATION, DEPOSITS, ETC., OF NATIONAL BANKS.

Quarter ended September 30, 1880	3,933,346 37
Quarter ended December 31, 1880	5,523 94
Quarter ended March 31, 1881	4,164,281 83
Quarter ended June 30, 1881	12,963 58
	8,116,115 72

REPAYMENT OF INTEREST BY PACIFIC RAILROAD COMPANIES.

Quarter ended September 30, 1880	211,402 76
Quarter ended December 31, 1880	225,752 17
Quarter ended March 31, 1881	192,412 26
Quarter ended June 30, 1881	181,266 61
	810,833 80

CUSTOMS FEES, FINES, PENALTIES, AND FORFEITURES.

Quarter ended September 30, 1880	351,870 95
Quarter ended December 31, 1880	377,395 06
Quarter ended March 31, 1881	375,009 37
Quarter ended June 30, 1881	428,793 69
	1,533,069 07

FEES, CONSULAR, LETTERS PATENT, AND LAND.

Quarter ended September 30, 1880	542,064 23
Quarter ended December 31, 1880	472,682 72
Quarter ended March 31, 1881	563,753 04
Quarter ended June 30, 1881	666,483 99
	2,244,983 98

PROCEEDS OF SALES OF GOVERNMENT PROPERTY.

Quarter ended September 30, 1880	56,311 23
Quarter ended December 31, 1880	78,139 93
Quarter ended March 31, 1881	52,429 94
Quarter ended June 30, 1881	75,292 90
	262,174 00

PROFITS ON COINAGE.

Quarter ended September 30, 1880	983,882 46
Quarter ended December 31, 1880	447,691 45
Quarter ended March 31, 1881	1,050,392 44
Quarter ended June 30, 1881	984,519 26
	3,468,485 61

REVENUES OF DISTRICT OF COLUMBIA.

Quarter ended September 30, 1880	265,872 65
Quarter ended December 31, 1880	1,095,117 68
Quarter ended March 31, 1881	318,666 89
Quarter ended June 30, 1881	336,542 01
	2,016,199 23

MISCELLANEOUS.

Quarter ended September 30, 1880	2,216,332 79
Quarter ended December 31, 1880	1,446,260 71
Quarter ended March 31, 1881	1,148,039 58
Quarter ended June 30, 1881	1,893,873 38
	6,704,506 46

Total ordinary receipts	360,782,292 57
Cash in Treasury June 30, 1880	203,838,419 53
Total	564,620,712 10

TABLE B.—*STATEMENT of the NET DISBURSEMENTS (by warrants) during the fiscal year ended June 30, 1881.*

CIVIL.

Congress	$5, 082, 046 11	
Executive	6, 878, 442 70	
Judiciary	4, 347, 531 15	
Government of Territories	224, 288 58	
Subtreasuries	333, 609 22	
Public land offices	678, 559 25	
Inspection of steam vessels	218, 582 28	
Mint and assay offices	178, 117 90	
Total civil		**$17, 941, 177 19**

FOREIGN INTERCOURSE.

Diplomatic salaries	278, 432 90	
Consular salaries	428, 594 19	
Contingencies of consulates	164, 949 93	
Rescuing American seamen from shipwreck	5, 946 59	
American and Spanish Claims Commission	8, 691 56	
Contingent expenses of foreign missions	48, 180 58	
Shipping and discharging seamen	3, 659 93	
Prisons for American convicts	19, 010 03	
Expenses under the neutrality act	3, 100 00	
American and Chinese Commission	29, 769 73	
American and French Commission	34, 120 32	
International Bimetallic Commission	37, 043 16	
Publication of commercial and consular reports	12, 079 78	
Contingent and miscellaneous	25, 376 22	
Total foreign intercourse		**1, 093, 954 92**

MISCELLANEOUS.

Mint establishment	1, 091, 349 03
Coast Survey	556, 369 33
Light-House Establishment	1, 997, 694 64
Building and repairs of light-houses	644, 974 35
Refunding excess of deposits for unascertained duties	3, 083, 254 24
Revenue-cutter service	839, 914 77
Life-saving service	469, 018 60
Custom-houses, court-houses, post-offices, &c	2, 919, 185 80
Furniture, fuel, &c., for public buildings under Treasury Department	736, 005 93
Repairs and preservation of buildings under Treasury Department	198, 698 16
Collecting customs revenue	6, 383, 288 10
Debenture and drawbacks under customs laws	1, 722, 192 86
Marine-Hospital Establishment	400, 404 47
Compensation in lieu of moieties	32, 509 73
Assessing and collecting internal revenue	4, 327, 793 24
Punishing violations of internal-revenue laws	67, 416 30
Internal-revenue stamps, papers and dies	476, 323 15
Refunding duties erroneously or illegally collected	29, 191 97
Internal-revenue allowances and drawbacks	35, 654 27
Redemption of internal-revenue stamps	27, 775 78
Deficiencies of revenue of Post-Office Department	3, 895, 638 66
Expenses national currency	166, 578 14
Suppressing counterfeiting and fraud	75, 286 57
Contingent expenses, Independent Treasury	72, 378 03
Survey of public lands	236, 266 37
Repayment for lands erroneously sold	39, 174 46
Five per cent. fund, &c., to States	264, 907 88
Payments under relief acts	94, 308 70
Postage	141, 111 12
Purchase and management of Louisville and Portland Canal	422, 970 00
Vaults, safes, and locks for public buildings	49, 243 82
Indemnity for swamp lands	16, 003 19
Propagation, &c., of food fishes	137, 190 91
Collecting statistics relating to commerce	8, 796 93
Geological survey of Territories	149, 395 62
Deposits by individuals for surveys of public lands	861, 086 94
Sinking fund of Pacific Railroads	972, 803 84
Education of the blind	5, 275 00
Transportation of United States securities	11, 129 38
National Board of Health	192, 634 15
Expenses of Tenth Census	3, 564, 432 31
Improvement of Yellowstone National Park	14, 969 76
Payment of judgments, Court of Claims	310, 459 36
Mail transportation, Pacific Railroads	1, 092, 103 46
Department of Agriculture	218, 222 53
Patent Office	96, 099 48
Expenses of Bureau of Engraving and Printing	379, 550 23
Smithsonian Institution	121, 583 88
Completion of Washington Monument	170, 147 85
Public buildings and grounds in Washington	260, 032 32
Annual repairs of the Capitol	59, 700 00
Improving and lighting Capitol grounds	92, 950 97
State, War, and Navy Departments' building	301, 231 02
Columbian Institute for Deaf and Dumb	61, 000 00
Government Hospital for the Insane	174, 224 49
Freedmen's Hospital	41, 800 00

TABLE B.—*STATEMENT of the NET DISBURSEMENTS (by warrants) during the fiscal year ended June 30, 1881*—Continued.

MISCELLANEOUS—Continued.

Howard University	$10,000 00
Support and treatment of transient paupers	15,000 00
Redemption of District of Columbia securities	17,130 60
Refunding taxes, District of Columbia	5,147 86
Water fund, District of Columbia	110,110 65
Employment of the poor in the District of Columbia	20,299 92
Repairing Pennsylvania avenue, act July 19, 1876	1,522 85
Expenses of District of Columbia	3,341,612 20
Washington Aqueduct	8,890 13
Charitable institutions	198,408 70
Statue of Gen. Daniel Morgan	20,000 00
Transportation of silver coin	21,749 51
Reproducing plats of surveys of public lands	31,500 00
Rocky Mountain locusts	25,009 80
Survey private land claims	28,041 32
Claims for swamp lands	11,756 55
Depredations on public timber	32,865 03
Miscellaneous	102,458 59
Total miscellaneous	$45,381,192 60

INTERIOR DEPARTMENT.

Indians	6,514,161 09
Pensions	50,059,279 62
Total Interior Department	56,573,440 71

MILITARY ESTABLISHMENT.

Pay Department	12,542,798 48
Commissary Department	2,233,239 76
Quartermaster's Department	10,353,028 90
Medical Department	741,330 34
Ordnance Department	1,522,962 42
Military Academy	93,589 18
Improving rivers and harbors	8,518,673 78
Survey of Territories west of the one hundredth meridian	15,000 00
Contingencies	36,547 75
Expenses of recruiting	71,198 41
Signal Service	385,447 91
Expenses of military convicts	65,344 50
Publishing the official records of the rebellion	70,995 22
Support of National Home for Disabled Volunteers	1,033,560 83
Support of Soldiers' Home	87,242 92
Horses and other property lost in service	107,791 13
Payments under relief acts	79,702 42
Construction of military posts, roads, &c	309,474 31
Fortifications	245,786 27
Miscellaneous	96,721 94
National cemeteries	182,196 71
Fifty per cent. arrears of Army transportation due certain railroads	66,513 40
Construction of military telegraphs	74,963 15
Bounty to soldiers, act July 28, 1866	88,192 58
Transportation, Army and supplies, Pacific Railroads	139,223 08
Survey of Northern and Northwestern lakes	64,758 04
Bounty to volunteers	328,634 70
Refunding to States expenses incurred	156,187 45
Claims for quartermasters' stores	359,780 11
Claims of loyal citizens	344,259 36
Total military establishment	40,466,460 55

NAVAL ESTABLISHMENT.

Pay and contingencies of the Navy	7,230,183 81
Marine Corps	778,546 65
Naval Academy	187,111 37
Navigation	217,032 76
Ordnance	309,744 30
Equipment and Recruiting	927,225 09
Yards and Docks	1,154,403 88
Medicine and Surgery	102,366 96
Construction and Repair	978,706 70
Provisions and Clothing	1,877,284 70
Steam Engineering	1,111,208 72
Miscellaneous	752,856 12
Total Naval establishment	15,686,671 66
Interest on the public debt	82,508,741 18
Total net ordinary expenditures	259,651,638 81
Premium on redemption of loans	1,061,248 78
Redemption of the public debt	51,401,801 05
Total expenditures	312,114,688 64
Cash in Treasury June 30, 1881	252,506,023 46
Total	564,620,712 10

TABLE C.—*STATEMENT of the ISSUE and REDEMPTION of LOANS and TREASURY NOTES (by warrants) for the fiscal year ended June 30, 1881.*

	Issues.	Redemptions.	Excess of issues.	Excess of redemptions.
Texan indemnity stock, act of September 9, 1850	....	$1, 000 00	....	$1, 000 00
Loan of February, 1861, act of February 8, 1861	....	15, 193, 000 00	....	15, 193, 000 00
Oregon war debt, act of March 2, 1861.	....	54, 250 00	....	54, 250 00
Seven-thirties of 1861, act of July 17, 1861...	....	200 00	....	200 00
Loan of July and August, 1861, acts of July 17 and August 5, 1861	....	16, 712, 450 00	....	16, 712, 450 00
Old demand notes, acts of July 17 and August 5, 1861, and July 12, 1862...	....	440 00	....	440 00
Five-twenties of 1862, act of February 25, 1862	....	21, 300 00	....	21, 300 00
Legal-tender notes, acts of February 25 and July 11, 1862, January 7 and March 3, 1863	$54, 545, 334 00	54, 545, 334 00	....	....
Fractional currency, acts of July 17, 1862, March 3, 1863, and June 30, 1864.....	....	109, 001 05	....	109, 001 05
Coin certificates, act of March 3, 1863.	....	2, 221, 680 00	....	2, 221, 680 00
One year notes of 1863, act of March 3, 1863	....	2, 000 00	....	2, 000 00
Two year notes of 1863, act of March 3, 186"	....	500 00	....	500 00
Compound interest notes, acts of March 3, 1863, and June 30, 1864....	....	12, 340 00	....	12, 340 00
Loan of 1863, act of March 3, 1863, and June 30, 1864.	....	7, 057, 100 00	....	7, 057, 100 00
Ten-forties of 1864, act of March 3, 1864......................	....	2, 016, 150 00	....	2, 016, 150 00
Five-twenties of March, 1864, act of March 3, 1864	....	....	....	....
Five-twenties of June, 1864, act of June 30, 1864	....	3, 400 00	....	2, 400 00
Seven-thirties of 1864 and 1865, acts of June 30, 1864, and March 3, 1865..	....	2, 750 00	....	2, 750 00
Five-twenties of 1865, act of March 3, 1865	....	37, 300 00	....	37, 300 00
Consols of 1865, act of March 3, 1865..	....	143, 150 00	....	143, 150 00
Consols of 1867, act of March 3, 1865..	....	959, 150 00	....	959, 150 00
Consols of 1868, act of March 3, 1865..	....	337, 400 00	....	337, 400 00
Funded loan of 1881, acts of July 14, 1870, January 20, 1871, and January 14, 1875	....	42, 769, 400 00	....	42, 769, 400 00
Funded loan of 1907, acts of July 14, 1870, January 20, 1871, and January 14, 1875	678, 200 00	....	$678, 200 00	....
Certificates of deposit, act of June 8, 1872	17, 615, 000 00	20, 155, 000 00	....	2, 540, 000 00
Silver certificates, act of February 28, 1878.................	40, 912, 000 00	2, 119, 740 00	38, 792, 260 00	....
Refunding certificates, act of February 26, 1879	....	678, 200 00	....	678, 200 00
Total	113, 750, 534 00	165, 152, 335 05	39, 470, 460 00	90, 872, 261 05
Excess of redemptions.................	....	....	....	90, 872, 261 05
Excess of issues	....	....	....	39, 470, 460 00
Net excess of redemptions charged in receipts and expenditures.......	....	....	... .	51, 401, 801 05

TABLE D.—*STATEMENT of the NET RECEIPTS and DISBURSEMENTS (by warrants) for the quarter ended September 30, 1881.*

RECEIPTS.

Customs	$59,184,469 15
Sales of public lands	948,368 19
Internal revenue	37,575,502 22
Tax on circulation, deposits, &c., of national banks	4,307,988 86
Repayment of interest by Pacific Railroad Companies	59,999 49
Customs fees, fines, penalties, and forfeitures	421,811 62
Consular, letters patent, homestead, &c., fees	639,180 08
Proceeds of sales of government property	66,363 58
Profits on coinage	809,317 80
Miscellaneous	4,168,042 10
Total net ordinary receipts	108,181,043 09
Balance in the Treasury June 30, 1881	252,506,023 46
Total	360,687,066 55

DISBURSEMENTS.

Customs	4,369,836 80
Internal revenue	1,040,393 53
Diplomatic service	336,582 76
Judiciary	674,005 13
Interior (civil)	1,428,375 23
Treasury proper	5,395,156 04
Quarterly salaries	133,280 24
Total civil and miscellaneous	13,383,529 75
Indians	2,011,984 70
Pensions	17,220,122 12
Military Establishment	13,517,184 11
Naval Establishment	4,646,969 78
Interest on public debt	24,271,948 93
	75,051,739 39
Redemption of the public debt	34,318,332 30
Balance in Treasury, September 30, 1881	251,316,994 86
Total	360,687,066 55

PAPERS

REPORT OF THE SECRETARY OF THE TREASURY.

REPORT OF THE COMMISSIONER OF INTERNAL REVENUE.

TREASURY DEPARTMENT,
OFFICE OF INTERNAL REVENUE,
Washington, November 25, 1881.

SIR: The receipts of internal revenue for the fiscal year 1879 were
$113,449,621.38; for the fiscal year 1880, $123,981,916.10; for the fiscal
year ended June 30, 1881, $135,229,912.30, and the receipts for the first
four months of the present fiscal year have been $50,876,970.11, being
$7,061,722.85 in excess of the receipts for the corresponding months of
the last fiscal year. If this increase should be maintained during the
remaining eight months of the fiscal year, the receipts for 1882 will be
fully $157,000,000.

Following is a statement of the receipts of internal-revenue taxes from
the various objects of taxation during the past two fiscal years:

	1880.	1881.	Increase.	Decrease.
SPIRITS.				
Spirits from fruit	$905,201 75	$1,531,075 83	$625,874 08	....
Spirits from grain, molasses, &c	55,013,917 43	60,683,051 73	5,669,134 30	....
Rectifiers	172,004 60	170,145 99	....	$1,858 61
Liquor dealers	4,578,810 57	4,741,111 89	162,301 32	....
Miscellaneous	515,574 44	28,589 44	....	486,985 00
Total of spirits	61,185,508 79	67,153,974 88	5,968,466 09	....
TOBACCO.				
Cigars	14,206,819 49	16,095,724 78	1,888,905 29	....
Cigarettes	715,269 39	992,981 22	277,711 83	....
Snuff	634,609 34	689,183 03	54,573 69	....
Tobacco, chewing and smoking	21,170,154 40	22,833,287 60	1,663,133 20	....
Dealers in leaf tobacco	88,329 10	76,996 76	....	11,332 34
Dealers in manufactured tobacco	1,864,422 41	1,976,071 55	111,649 14	....
Manufacturers of tobacco and cigars	153,132 71	151,442 57	....	1,690 14
Peddlers of tobacco	28,700 45	26,258 13	....	2,442 32
Miscellaneous	8,702 79	13,045 67	4,342 88	....
Total of tobacco	38,870,140 08	42,854,991 31	3,984,851 23	....
FERMENTED LIQUORS.				
Ale, beer, lager, and porter	12,346,077 26	13,237,700 63	891,623 37	....
Brewers' special tax	201,395 97	195,308 52	....	6,087 45
Dealers in malt liquors	282,329 61	267,232 06	....	15,097 55
Total of fermented liquors	12,829,802 84	13,700,241 21	870,438 37	....
BANKS AND BANKERS.				
Bank deposits	2,510,775 43	2,946,906 64	436,131 21	....
Bank capital	811,436 48	811,006 35	....	430 13
Bank circulation	28,773 37	4,295 08	....	24,478 29
Total of banks and bankers	3,350,985 28	3,762,208 07	411,222 79	....

	1880.	1881.	Increase.	Decrease.
MISCELLANEOUS.				
Bank checks	$2,162,310 00	$2,253,411 20	$91,101 20	
Friction matches	3,237,546 00	3,278,580 62	41,034 62	
Patent medicines, perfumery, cosmetics, &c.	1,733,840 30	1,843,263 90	109,423 60	
Penalties	383,755 08	231,078 21		$152,676 87
Collections not otherwise provided for	228,027 73	152,162 90		75,864 83
Total of miscellaneous	7,745,479 11	7,758,496 83	13,017 72	
Aggregate receipts	123,981,916 10	135,229,912 30	11,247,996 20	

The quantities of spirits, cigars, cigarettes, snuff, tobacco, and beer upon which taxes were paid during this period, were as follows:

Spirits from fruit, 1880—1,005,781 gallons; 1881—1,701,206 gallons; increase, 695,425.
Spirits from grain, &c., 1880—51,126,634 gallons; 1881—57,426,000 gallons; increase, 6,299,366.
Number of cigars, 1880—2,367,803,248; 1881—2,682,620,797; increase, 314,817,549.
Number of cigarettes, 1880—408,708,366, 1881—567,396,963; increase, 158,687,617.
Pounds of snuff, 1880—3,966,308; 1881—4,307,394; increase, 341,086.
Pounds of tobacco, 1880—132,309,526; 1881—142,706,011; increase, 10,396,485.
Barrels of ale, beer, &c., 1880—13,347,110; 1881—14,311,028; increase, 963,918.

REDUCTION OF INTERNAL TAXES.

The large increase in the receipts of the government and the great reduction in the interest and principal of the public debt are causing discussion as to the propriety of reducing the income of the government by lowering some of the taxes and dropping others altogether.

Attention is called to the recent action of the National Distillers' Association, in favor of applying to Congress for a reduction of the tax on distilled spirits. These tax-payers seem to think that the time has come when a portion of the tax from their productions can be taken off, that tax now amounting to 300 per cent. upon fine whiskies and 600 per cent. upon ordinary spirits.

Whenever the wants of the government will allow a reduction of internal taxation, my opinion is that it will be wise to confine these taxes to distilled spirits, malt liquors, tobacco and its products, and to special taxes upon manufacturers and dealers in these articles, and to fix the taxes at such rates as will yield the amount of revenue necessary to be raised from these sources.

AMOUNTS COLLECTED, BY DISTRICTS, AND COST OF COLLECTION.

Immediately after the close of the past fiscal year an examination was made of the accounts of the collectors of internal revenue, and it was found that they had accounted for all the public moneys which came to their hands. I am gratified to be able to state that during the past five fiscal years $602,310,797.30 have been collected, and that the entire amount has been paid into the Treasury without any loss to the government by defalcation.

The cost of collection for the past fiscal year, distributed among the different items of appropriation, was as follows:

For salaries and expenses of collectors, including pay of deputy collectors, clerks, &c	$1,898,103 43
For salaries and expenses of revenue agents, surveyors of distilleries, gaugers, storekeepers, and miscellaneous expenses	2,365,000 00
For stamps, paper, and dies	473,803 07
For expenses of detecting and punishing violations of internal revenue laws	63,789 98
For salaries of officers, clerks, and employés in the office of Commissioner of Internal Revenue	253,330 00
Total	5,054,026 48

The entire expense for the past five years has been $21,979,002, being three and sixty-four one hundredths per cent. upon the amount collected; and in the disbursement of this money there has been no loss to the government. This satisfactory result is due to the intelligence, capacity, and fidelity of the officers and employés of the Internal Revenue Service, to whom I desire to convey my appreciation of their laudable efforts to reach and maintain the highest standard of excellence.

Following is a statement showing the aggregate collections in each collection district during the fiscal year 1881, with the names of the several collectors:

Collection districts.	Names of collectors.	Aggregate collections.
First Alabama	Louis H. Mayer	$9,143 28
Do	Albion L. Morgan	46,287 09
Second Alabama	James T. Rapier	75,221 02
Arizona	Thomas Cordis	38,008 21
Arkansas	Edward Wheeler	132,086 94
First California	William Higby	3,277,931 88
Fourth California	Amos L. Frost	335,458 96
Colorado	James S. Wolfe	215,051 06
First Connecticut	Joseph Selden	283,883 46
Second Connecticut	David F. Hollister	295,806 56
Dakota	John L. Pennington	48,603 66
Delaware	James McIntire	311,066 76
Florida	Dennis Eagan	254,889 51
Second Georgia	Andrew Clarke	206,405 74
Third Georgia	Edward C. Wade	97,727 74
Idaho	Austin Savage	13,806 60
Do	Ronello W. Berry	11,993 57
First Illinois	Joel D. Harvey	9,905,157 60
Second Illinois	Lucien B. Crooker	247,243 80
Third Illinois	Alfred M. Jones	483,092 53
Do	A. H. Hershey	41,704 54
Do	Albert Woodcock	41,608 57
Fourth Illinois	John Tillson	1,203,221 51
Fifth Illinois	Howard Knowles	11,425,131 77
Seventh Illinois	John W. Hill	67,684 77
Eighth Illinois	Jonathan Merriam	1,407,226 90
Thirteenth Illinois	Jonathan C. Willis	962,409 34
First Indiana	James C. Veatch	261,752 57
Fourth Indiana	Will Cumback	3,399,731 14
Sixth Indiana	Frederick Baggs	1,094,927 90
Seventh Indiana	Deles W. Minshall	2,253,760 27
Tenth Indiana	George Moon	174,925 19
Eleventh Indiana	John F. Wildman	96,156 41
Second Iowa	Sewall S. Farwell	167,240 11
Do	John W. Green	88,090 39
Third Iowa	James E. Simpson	281,317 63
Fourth Iowa	John Connell	168,046 03
Fifth Iowa	Lampson P. Sherman	219,081 92
Kansas	John C. Carpenter	239,527 33
Second Kentucky	William A. Stuart	672,159 61
Fifth Kentucky	James F. Buckner	2,277,152 73
Do	William S. Wilson	1,212,519 39
Sixth Kentucky	Winfield S. Holden	2,064,451 74
Do	John W. Finnell	1,120,760 29
Seventh Kentucky	Armsted M Swope	1,009,848 31
Eighth Kentucky	William J Landram	216,081 51
Ninth Kentucky	John E Blaine	145,579 68
Louisiana	Morris Marks	760,618 92
Maine	Franklin J. Rollins	82,457 05
Third Maryland	Robert M. Proud	2,334,864 27
Fourth Maryland	Daniel C. Bruce	25,011 83
Do	Webster Bruce	123,587 37
Third Massachusetts	Charles W. Slack	1,454,636 28
Fifth Massachusetts	Charles C. Dame	857,447 12
Tenth Massachusetts	Edward R. Tinker	367,597 80
First Michigan	Luther S. Trowbridge	1,223,504 44
Third Michigan	Harvey B Rowlson	249,175 12
Fourth Michigan	Sluman S Bailey	137,251 82
Sixth Michigan	Charles V. De Land	177,343 89
First Minnesota	Andrew C Smith	116,126 82
Second Minnesota	William Bickel	329,013 51
Mississippi	James Hill	96,122 19
First Missouri	Isaac H. Sturgeon	5,543,333 70
Second Missouri	Alonzo B Carroll	66,451 05
Fourth Missouri	Rynd E. Lawder	886,170 56
Fifth Missouri	David H. Budlong	145,571 72

Collection districts.	Names of collectors.	Aggregate collections.
Sixth Missouri	Robert T. Van Horn'	$286, 623 16
Do	Philip Doppler	40, 199 20
Montana	Thomas P. Fuller	44, 881 67
Nebraska	Lorenzo Crounse	962, 004 86
Nevada	Frederick C. Lord	53, 431 41
New Hampshire	Andrew H. Young	809, 720 94
First New Jersey	William P. Tatem	288, 810 32
Third New Jersey	Culver Barcalow	320, 683 57
Fifth New Jersey	Robert B. Hathorn	4, 256, 182 43
New Mexico	Gustavus A. Smith	47, 465 80
First New York	Rodney C. Ward	2, 959, 673 22
Second New York	Marshall B. Blake	3, 377, 850 78
Third New York	Max Weber	5, 757, 541 95
Eleventh New York	Moses D. Stivers	208, 236 50
Twelfth New York	Jason M. Johnson	545, 007 54
Fourteenth New York	Ralph T. Lathrop	600, 482 13
Fifteenth New York	Thomas Stevenson	294, 733 58
Twenty-first New York	James C. P. Kincaid	326, 846 08
Twenty-fourth New York	John B. Strong	494, 109 45
Twenty-sixth New York	Benjamin De Voe	316, 088 22
Twenty-eighth New York	Burt Van Horn	974, 838 32
Thirtieth New York	Frederick Buell	1, 377, 990 99
Second North Carolina	Elihu A. White	74, 432 35
Fourth North Carolina	Isaac J. Young	850, 967 45
Fifth North Carolina	William H. Wheeler	1, 015, 329 53
Do	George B. Everitt	36, 255 94
Sixth North Carolina	John J. Mott	496, 456 08
First Ohio	Amor Smith, jr	12, 538, 346 58
Third Ohio	Robert Williams, jr	1, 806, 871 17
Fourth Ohio	Robert P. Kennedy	512, 582 86
Sixth Ohio	James Pursell	352, 210 02
Seventh Ohio	Charles C. Walcutt	594, 593 31
Tenth Ohio	Clark Waggoner	1, 089, 868 12
Eleventh Ohio	Benjamin F. Coates	1, 398, 257 92
Fifteenth Ohio	Jewett Palmer	195, 871 89
Eighteenth Ohio	Worthy S. Streator	806, 588 83
Oregon	John C. Cartwright	85, 004 14
First Pennsylvania	James Ashworth	2, 678, 845 82
Eighth Pennsylvania	Joseph T. Valentine	632, 634 45
Ninth Pennsylvania	Thomas A. Wiley	1, 278, 820 81
Twelfth Pennsylvania	Edward H. Chase	370, 256 14
Fourteenth Pennsylvania	Charles J. Bruner	212, 580 65
Sixteenth Pennsylvania	Edward Soull	211, 588 05
Nineteenth Pennsylvania	Charles M. Lynch	137, 258 54
Twentieth Pennsylvania	James C Brown	94, 909 77
Twenty-second Pennsylvania	Thomas W Davis	1, 408, 472 82
Twenty-third Pennsylvania	John M Sullivan	653, 836 95
Rhode Island	Elisha H. Rhodes	200, 079 27
South Carolina	Ellery M. Brayton	135, 907 16
Second Tennessee	James M Melton	110, 174 68
Fifth Tennessee	William M Woodcock	922, 014 14
Eighth Tennessee	Robert F Patterson	114, 574 82
First Texas	William H Sinclair	101, 043 60
Third Texas	Benjamin C. Ludlow	80, 784 41
Fourth Texas	Adam G Malloy	29, 178 09
Do	Theodore Hitchcox	37, 629 51
Utah	Ovando J. Hollister	43, 116 79
Vermont	Charles S Dana	53, 145 83
Second Virginia	James D Brady	943, 416 96
Third Virginia	O H Russell	2, 076, 473 46
Fourth Virginia	William L Fernald	1, 053, 260 58
Fifth Virginia	J. Henry Rives	1, 763, 176 49
Sixth Virginia	Beverly B Botts	236, 778 26
Washington	James R Harden	32, 763 73
First West Virginia	Isaac H Duval	340, 708 62
Second West Virginia	George W Brown	104, 507 00
Do	Francis H Pierpont	7, 205 71
First Wisconsin	Irving M Bean	2, 373, 693 87
Second Wisconsin	Henry Harnden	169, 982 52
Third Wisconsin	Charles A Galloway	229, 859 40
Sixth Wisconsin	Hiram E. Kelley	136, 559 22
Wyoming	Edgar P. Snow	18, 551 18
Total from collectors		127, 851, 634 66
Cash receipts from sale of adhesive stamps		7, 375, 255 72
From salaries (repealed tax)		3, 021 93
Total receipts from all sources		135, 229, 912 30

I estimate the expenses of the Internal Revenue Service for the fiscal year ending June 30, 1883, as follows:

For salaries and expenses of collectors	$2,100,000
For salaries and expenses of thirty-five revenue agents, for surveyors, for fees and expenses of gaugers, for salaries of storekeepers, and for miscellaneous expenses	2,400,000
For dies, paper, and stamps	500,000
For detecting and bringing to trial and punishment persons guilty of violating the internal revenue laws, including payment for information and detection	75,000
For salaries of officers, clerks, and employés in the office of the Commissioner of Internal Revenue	255,080
Total	5,330,080

ENFORCEMENT OF THE LAWS.

I am glad to be able to report that there is a commendable disposition on the part of the great body of tax-payers to yield a ready obedience to the laws, and that the taxes are collected with the least possible friction. In the collection districts where frauds in the manufacture and sale of spirits and tobacco have been rife, and where resistance to authority has prevailed, there has been a manifest improvement in public sentiment. While it is shown by a table on page 22 that during the past sixteen months 859 illicit distilleries have been seized, and 1,510 illicit distillers arrested, I am enabled to report that illicit distilling has, by the active operations of the past five years, been reduced to a minimum, and the illicit manufacture of tobacco has for the most part been abandoned. The business of "blockading," so called, that is, the sale of illicit whisky and tobacco from peddlers' wagons, has almost been suppressed. Bands of illicit distillers combined together in defiance of law have been broken up, and forcible resistance to the officers of the government, though it has not entirely ceased, is of much less frequent occurrence than heretofore. The practice so long in vogue of law-breakers resorting to the processes of the State courts as a means of revenging themselves upon the officers of the government for the enforcement of the laws of the United States has been to a great extent discontinued. Cordial relations now exist in most cases between the officers of the United States charged with the enforcement of the internal revenue laws, and the officers of the State governments. This satisfactory condition of things has been brought about by a just, firm, and conciliatory enforcement of the laws. As a result, a strong public sentiment has set in against frauds upon the revenues of the government and in favor of sustaining its authority. Respectable citizens who in times past, though opposed to these frauds, were not disposed to give information and aid in their suppression, for fear of injury to their persons or property, now take a bold stand against them, and in some districts good citizens have formed committees to co-operate with the officers of the government in the suppression of the illicit manufacture and traffic in whisky. By maintaining a careful supervision over those districts where frauds have hitherto prevailed, and having them regularly policed by deputy collectors, I believe that a relapse into the former condition of fraud, lawlessness, and bloodshed will be prevented.

The extraordinary expenses incident to the suppression of frauds upon the revenue in the illicit manufacture and sale of whisky and tobacco during the past five years, in the districts of second Alabama, Arkansas, second Georgia, third Georgia, fourth North Carolina, fifth North Carolina, sixth North Carolina, South Carolina, second Tennessee, fifth Tennessee, eighth Tennessee, and fifth Virginia, where frauds on the revenue have most prevailed, have been about $285,000. The net gains are the establishment of the supremacy of the laws, and their comparatively peaceful observance and enforcement, and an increase in the collection of internal revenue taxes in the districts named, as follows:

1879 over 1878, an increase of...	$628,283
1880 over 1878, an increase of...	735,418
1881 over 1878, an increase of...	1,220,285
Total increase..	2,583,986

PROTECTION OF REVENUE OFFICERS.

I again recommend additional legislation for the protection of the lives and persons of officers of the United States from the unlawful assaults of those who resist their authority. There should be a law for the trial and punishment in the courts of the United States of persons who kill or make assaults with intent to kill officers of the United States while engaged in the performance of their lawful duties. At this time the only offenses cognizable in the courts of the United States for acts of this character are obstructing and conspiring to obstruct the enforcement of the law, the punishment for which is entirely inadequate to the many heinous crimes against the lives and persons of officers of the government which have been committed within the past few years.

PENSIONS TO WIDOWS AND ORPHANS OF OFFICERS KILLED.

The struggle maintained for the past five years for the suppression of illicit distilling has resulted in the killing of 28 and the wounding of 64 officers and employés.

Amongst the number who lost their lives while enforcing the laws of the United States against illicit distillers was Lieutenant McIntire, of the Second United States Infantry, who was killed in Georgia February 9, 1877. By reason of his being an officer of the United States Army his widow has been awarded a pension of $15 a month (the highest rate allowed by law) and $2 a month for each of her five children. This is eminently just and proper.

On the 9th of August, 1878, Deputy Collector Cooper, of Knoxville, Tenn., whilst co-operating with other officers in putting down armed resistance to the law, was shot and instantly killed, and on the 20th of July last Deputy Collector Thomas L. Brayton, of South Carolina, was killed by an illicit distiller, under circumstances of peculiar atrocity. Each of these officers left a wife and children bereft of their natural means of support. Deputy Collectors Cooper and Brayton, equally with Lieutenant McIntire, lost their lives in the service of the government and in the effort to enforce its laws against armed resistance, but being in the civil instead of in the military service of the government, the law makes no provision for the relief of their widows and orphans. This distinction is not just, and I respectfully suggest the propriety of legislation authorizing suitable pensions to be awarded to the widows and dependent families of officers and employés killed in the enforcement of the law, and directing proper provisions to be made for officers and employés wounded or disabled in the service.

6 Ab

FIXED SALARIES FOR U. S. MARSHALS AND DISTRICT ATTORNEYS.

Wherever the rights of a citizen in person or property are involved it is better that an officer shall err by doing too little than by doing too much. The best and most satisfactory work of an officer is performed from a sense of duty. Where the pecuniary interests of the officer are promoted by the oppression of the citizen there is great danger of abuse, and a system of laws which makes it the interest of an officer to thus misuse his authority is wrong in principle, and will, by the permanent temptation to evil, breed abuses even in long established and well ordered communities under the most careful system of administration. In new and remote settlements this practice, at times, will be little better than brigandage.

I regard the system of fees and allowances to marshals and district attorneys as open to this objection. Their maximum compensation is fixed by law and the orders of the Attorney-General, but the amount actually received depends almost wholly upon the institution and prosecution of cases in court. While these officers are paid out of the Treasury in respect to cases in which the United States is a party, the compensation thus paid is for fees made, expenses incurred, and services rendered in connection with criminal and civil cases instituted in behalf of the United States. The district attorney is made the judge of the propriety of commencing a criminal prosecution against a citizen on account of which he and the marshal will receive pay from the government whether the party be guilty or innocent. These officers may prefer complaints against citizens, cause United States commissioners to issue warrants, may arrest and examine the parties before the commissioner and the district attorney, marshal, guard, witnesses, and the commissioner will all get their fees from the government even though the party arrested be discharged.

Instances have been brought to my attention where numerous prosecutions have been instituted for the most trivial violations of law, and the arrested parties taken long distances and subjected to great inconvenience and expense, not in the interest of the government, but apparently for no other reason than to make costs. I have consulted with a number of prominent district attorneys and marshals, and they all concurred with me in condemning the system under which they are compensated for their services as one calculated to encourage abuses. It is not to be wondered at that abuses have grown up under such a system. The wonder is that the abuses are not greater. A remedy will be found by fixing by law the salaries of district attorneys and marshals, and paying them as other officers from the Treasury, and authorizing the Attorney-General to fix the salaries and traveling expenses of deputy marshals in the same manner that the salaries and traveling expenses of deputy collectors of internal revenue are now fixed. This plan would relieve these officers from all temptation to institute prosecutions for petty and trivial violations of the revenue laws where no frauds were committed or intended.

THE CIVIL SERVICE.

The improvement of the civil service is a subject which has received much public attention, and will probably be considered by Congress during the coming session. I venture to offer a few suggestions which, I trust, will not be regarded as out of place in this report.

There is unquestionably on every hand an earnest desire to have the offices filled by persons who are honest, capable, and diligent, and to have the business between the government and the people transacted promptly, acceptably, and in a thorough, business-like manner. The chief point of discussion seems to be in respect to the manner of making appointments to and removals from office. It is insisted by some that the best civil service will be found in making it absolutely non-partisan; that is to say, that political considerations shall not enter into the question of applications for appointment to office, nor into the exercise of the powers of appointment and removal.

It would seem axiomatic that the tenure of office and the powers of appointment and removal should agree with the genius of the government and the spirit of the people from whom all powers emanate.

Our governments, State and National, are founded upon the elective system. Originally, the constitutions of many of the States made provision for the legislatures to choose the judiciary. The growth of the spirit of self-government in process of time changed most of these constitutions, so that to-day, in nearly all the States of the Union, the judges are elected by the people for a fixed term of years. The wide diffusion of education and knowledge amongst the people, the ease of obtaining information of public affairs through the press, the constant participation in the affairs of government at the ballot-box and otherwise, and the important and stirring political events of the past twenty years have so wrought upon the people of this country that they now take more interest in public affairs than ever before, and the great mass of educated and intelligent men competent to hold office are identified with one or the other of the political parties of the country. In fact, it has come to be expected that every citizen of standing, and worthy of consideration, will have definite political opinions and affiliations. This being the case, it is obvious that there are not existing in the country men suitable for holding the public offices who are free from political convictions; so that, in point of fact, in selecting officers it is necessary to choose from one or the other of the political parties of the country.

To give the country a government of the people, the principles influencing the exercise of the power of appointment should be in harmony with the principles controlling the people in making choice of officers through the elective franchise.

If this proposition be sound, it remains to be ascertained by what rule the people are governed when they come to cast their ballots for elective officers. In respect to the great majority of people, the rule may be safely stated thus: The elector demands that the candidate shall be honest and capable, and that he shall agree with him in his political opinions. We give expression to our political convictions at the polls by electing men to make and to enforce the laws who agree with us politically. The principle of agreement in political opinions is the great test of voting for candidates from President to constable.

It is argued that the inferior officers and clerks employed by the government at the capital and throughout the country can perform their duties satisfactorily, notwithstanding their opinions differ from the dominant political party, and the conclusion is drawn that therefore changes should not be made in these positions where the persons are found to be honest, capable, and diligent. To me it seems entirely improbable that such a rule will be adopted with the concurrence of the people, considering the fact that the political complexion of the country will be changed only after a great struggle and elaborate discussion. Such a change necessarily implies a deliberate opinion on the part of the people that the party proclaimed as dominant is better fitted to administer the government than the party it is to supersede. The electors who bring the party into power and the chief men who take office as the result of the election will no doubt entertain the opinion that men equally honest and capable can be selected from their own party to fill the various offices of the government, and they will no doubt insist that to insure a successful administration it is absolutely necessary to make many changes. In fact the struggle at the polls was to change the policy of the government by changing its officers.

Between the position on the one hand that no changes shall be made, and on the other hand that all shall be changed, there would seem to be a ground, at once reasonable and just, upon which all might stand. It occurs to me that if the leading and confidential positions in each department and bureau were subject to change at any time, for reasons satisfactory to the head of the department, and all the clerkships and other employments were for terms of four years, greater stability would be given to the service, sudden and sweeping changes would be avoided, and as these terms would be constantly expiring, the entire body of the public service would be within the easy reach of public opinion.

FIXITY OF TENURE.

Fixity of tenure is recognized as a wise limitation upon the power of choosing officers by ballot. So, upon principle, the same limitation may be applied to the appointing power, with acceptability to the people, but it is inconsistent with the genius of our government, and contrary to the public sentiment of the people to have the great body of the officers and employés of the executive branch of the government to hold their positions by a life tenure, or during good behavior. Such a system would create a privileged class removed from the influences of popular sentiment, which in this country is a constantly operating force favorable to honest, efficient administration. It would repress the laudable and honorable ambition of other citizens to serve the government in official positions and would manifestly tend to weaken the hold that our system of popular government has upon the minds of the people.

I am of opinion that the highest type of civil administration can be found by giving increased certainty to the official tenure by which offices are now held, but leaving them within the easy control of public sentiment, so that the whole official body can be kept abreast with the progressive opinions of the people.

One of the most important changes to be made in the present system is to provide by law for a fixed tenure for subordinate officers and clerks appointed by the various heads of departments. Where an applicant for appointment, whose indorsements as to character, standing, and habits are satisfactory, has passed a suitable examination, as now provided for by law, the appointment should be on trial, say, for a period of twelve months. At the end of this time if the appointee has been diligent in the performance of duty and has shown an aptitude for the service, he should be appointed for a term of three years, and be eligible for reappointment.

PROMOTIONS, REMOVALS, AND RETIREMENTS.

The promotions from grade to grade are necessarily slow. With the great majority of clerks, therefore, in all the departments the hope of promotion does not constitute a very powerful motive to excel. It would greatly tend to secure efficiency in the service to provide that the regular pay of 10 per cent. of the clerks in each bureau might be increased at the beginning of each fiscal year, say, 5 per cent. for marked capacity, fidelity, and zeal in the discharge of duty, this increase to be made upon the certificate of the head of division, the chief clerk, and the head of the bureau. Promotions should be made strictly upon merit, after a suitable examination, and upon the recommendation of the head of the proper bureau.

The removals of clerks and employés should be for dishonesty, incapacity, neglect of duty, insubordination, intemperance, immorality, or inability, such disqualifications to be ascertained under suitable regulations prescribed by the head of the proper department.

Heads of divisions and persons occupying confidential relations to the heads of departments and bureaus should be subject to change for reasons satisfactory to the head of the department.

Persons retiring from the service upon resignation or expiration of term, without fault, should be given an honorable discharge. The removal from the service of persons rendered unfit by the infirmities of years, or from other causes disconnected from misconduct, is at all times an unpleasant duty to perform, especially when such officers or clerks have rendered valuable services through a number of years and from their meager salaries have been unable to lay by a competency for old age. To mitigate the hardship of such cases and to insure a proper recognition of faithful service I would suggest the propriety of providing by law that all subordinate officers, clerks, and employés retired, without fault, by resignation, expiration of term, or inability after a service of four years, shall be entitled to receive one month's pay for each year and *pro rata* for each fraction of a year of service rendered, such retiring pay to be computed at the rate of pay the person has received from time to time.

RECAPITULATION.

The adoption of this system would embody the following ideas:

1. The establishment of a term of office of four years for subordinate officers, clerks, and employés.

2. Requiring all applicants for appointment to be well indorsed as to character, and to stand a proper examination as to attainments.

3. A temporary appointment for one year, on trial.

4. If found worthy, the temporary officer or clerk to be appointed for three years, the balance of a regular term of four years.

5. The officer or clerk to be eligible for reappointment.

6. As a stimulus to the exercise of marked capacity, fidelity, and zeal in the service, the pay of 10 per cent. of the clerks of each bureau to be increased 5 per cent. upon proper certificates at the commencement of each fiscal year.

7. Promotions to be upon merit, ascertained by examination and certified to by the head of the bureau.

8. Causes for removal to be dishonesty, incapacity, neglect of duty, insubordination, intemperance, immorality, or inability.

9. Persons retiring, without fault, to receive an honorable discharge.

10. Subordinate officers, clerks, and employés, retired, without fault, after a service of four years, to receive retiring pay, equal to one month's pay for each year and *pro rata* for each fraction of a year of service.

The principles suggested could readily be applied to the entire civil service of the country.

In respect to the question of retiring pay, I am satisfied that the great majority of the persons to whom it would apply are solely dependent upon their salaries for the support of themselves and families. Inquiry in the Internal Revenue Office shows the fact that the average number of persons dependent upon the salaries of clerks and employés is as follows: Salaries of $1,800, $1,600, $1,400, $1,200, and $720, the average is four persons to each salary; salaries of $1,000, three persons; salaries of $900, two persons; and salaries of $660, five persons to each salary. It is obvious from this statement that persons drawing salaries of $1,800 and less, will have but little left at the end of the year after supporting their families. It will be readily understood that, with a knowledge of such facts, the head of a bureau will be disposed to hesitate to recommend the discharge of persons who, after serving the government a number of years with fidelity, have become incapacitated for a proper performance of duty by old age. They thus become pensioners on the government and are retained to the injury of the service. The proposed provision for retiring pay, if adopted, would, as before stated, mitigate the hardship of discharging such persons from the service, and would, in my opinion, be a satisfactory solution of a difficult and delicate problem.

TERM OF OFFICE OF COLLECTORS.

In my annual report for the year ended June 30, 1877, I used the following language on the subject of tenure of office of collectors:

I call your attention to the fact that the law creating the office of collector of internal revenue fixes no tenure to the office. In my opinion it is altogether desirable that the term of this office should be fixed at four years. It often occurs that when a collector has served for a longer period than four years, constant efforts are being made for his removal; and many officers, however well they may have discharged their duties, feel, after a four years' service, uncertain as to the length of time they will be retained in office. Where an officer is appointed for a term of four years he has a right to expect that if he performs his duty diligently and faithfully he will not be disturbed until his term expires, and this feeling of security I regard as an important element in maintaining a good public service. From my limited observation in public life, I have come to the conclusion that when it can reasonably be done there should be a fixed tenure of all officers of the government. I have the honor to recommend that a law be passed fixing the tenure of office of all collectors of internal revenue hereafter appointed at a term of four years.

I now renew my recommendation in the hope that this subject will receive the early and earnest attention which it demands. It is an anomaly in the creation of important executive offices to omit fixing four years as the official term. By sections 769, 779, 2613, and 3830, United States Revised Statutes, the term of office of district attorneys, marshals, collectors of customs, naval officers, surveyors, and postmasters is fixed at four years. The original act, from which some of these sections are taken, was approved September 24, 1789, and the rule thus early adopted has, I believe, been maintained by subsequent legislation, with the exception of the act of July 1, 1862, creating the office of collector of internal revenue.

ADDITIONAL TAXES DUE FROM BANKS.

Last March certain facts came to the knowledge of the collector of internal revenue at Chicago which led him to believe that one of the banks of that city had failed to make full returns of its capital and deposits for taxation. At the collector's request I sent a competent revenue agent to make an examination of the books of the bank, which was done under the supervision of the collector, and it was found that a large amount of taxes was due the government. The books of all the banks in the city of Chicago making returns to this office were also examined, and in most cases it was found that errors had been made in rendering their returns, though in a number of instances the amounts involved were not large. In the case of certain foreign banks doing business in that city, large amounts of taxes were found due on capital brought into the United States and actually employed in the business of banking.

The result of the examination in Chicago seemed to make it necessary to scrutinize the returns of the bankers of other cities. I therefore detailed a number of revenue agents to report to the collectors of internal revenue in the cities of Baltimore, Philadelphia, New York, and Boston, and the books of many of the banks were examined. A number of new and interesting questions of law arose upon the application of the statute to the varied and intricate business operations of bankers. It was found that while the returns of some banks had been accurate to the last cent the returns of others had been made with deductions as to both capital and deposits which in the opinion of this office were not admissible under the law.

Many bankers have submitted their books for examination without the necessity of invoking legal proceedings, and have shown a willingness that their entire liability for taxation shall be ascertained. Many other bankers have agreed to carefully examine their books and make full statements under the decisions recently rendered by this office of such additional taxes as they may be liable for, such statements to be subject to the verification of officers of internal revenue. Other bankers, questioning the right of internal-revenue officers to examine their books, have refused to either produce them or to answer interrogatories in regard to their liability for additional taxes. There has been already ascertained to be due the sum of $722,705 from seventy banks in the cities of Chicago, New York, Baltimore, Boston, and Philadelphia, a considerable portion of which has been collected and paid into the Treasury. The other collectors have been instructed to examine the banks of their respective districts in regard to their liability for additional taxes. I am satisfied that large additional sums are due the government from this source.

Considerable irritation has been felt by many of the bankers in respect to the enforcement of the one hundred per cent. penalty imposed for rendering a "false or fraudulent return," it being contended that the penalty was intended to be enforced only when the return made was wilfully false. A case in which this question was involved was recently tried before the United States circuit court for the southern district of New York, "The German Savings Bank *vs.* Joseph Archbold, collector," and the court decided that it is not a prerequisite to the addition of the penalty that the return shall be wilfully false, but that if the return is not in fact true the Commissioner is authorized to affix the penalty. The exact language of the statute (R. S., section 3182) is " authorized *and required.*"

This case has been appealed to the United States Supreme Court, and at my request the Attorney-General has had it advanced on the docket, and it is set down for argument on the 20th of January next. Pending the decision of the Supreme Court upon this point I have consented in several important cases that the collection of the one hundred per cent. penalty already assessed shall be held in abeyance to await the decision of the court.

INDIVIDUAL STAMP FOR CIGARS.

The collecting the tax on cigars by placing the stamp on each cigar, instead of on the boxes as now provided by law, would afford the highest proof of the payment of the tax, and would prevent the fraudulent refilling of stamped boxes which is believed to be a great means of loss to the government. Various patented stamps and devices have received the consideration of this office, the use of which at present seemed to be impracticable by reason of the great expense of some, and the difficulty 'n the preparation and handling of all of them. The frequent consideration of this subject, however, has brought me to the conclusion that the system of stamping each cigar with a stamp prepared for general use, without reference to the number packed in the box, can be introduced at an increase of nearly double the cost for paper and printing. To compensate the cigar manufacturer for the expense of putting the stamp on each cigar, a deduction of 5 per cent. might be made upon the stamps purchased which would cover the cost of applying the stamps to the cigars. The material objection to the adoption of this plan would be the repacking of imported cigars. Such a system would in my opinion materially add to the revenue of the government, and I recommend that the subject receive the careful consideration of Congress.

FRAUDS IN THE MANUFACTURE OF VINEGAR.

I again recommend the passage of a law either to prohibit the manufacture of vinegar by the alcoholic vaporizing process, provided for in section 5 of the act of March 1, 1879, or requiring the supervision of a storekeeper at each vinegar factory using the vaporizing process, the compensation of such storekeeper to be repaid to the government by the vinegar manufacturer. Experience has shown that the act above referred to opens the door to great frauds, and I am clearly of the opinion that early legislation should be had upon this subject.

APPARENT OVERPRODUCTION OF SPIRITS.

In my last annual report under this heading I made the following statement:

I take the liberty of calling especial attention of distillers and the trade to the fact that on the 1st July, 1879, there were on hand in distillery warehouses 19,212,000 gallons of spirits, which was an increase of about 5,000,000 of gallons over the stock on hand at the same period of the previous year, and that on the 1st day of November, 1880, the amount of spirits on hand was 32,640,000, being an increase of 13,400,000 gallons over the amount on hand on the 1st of July, 1879. The steady increase in the number and capacity of distilleries in operation, suggests the probability of the continued enlargement of the stock on hand. It has occurred to me that this business was on the eve of being overdone, and that in the event of a recurrence of the agitation for a reduction of the tax, the holders of these spirits would be in danger of loss.

The amount of distilled spirits in distillery warehouses on the 1st day of November, 1881, was 67,442,186 gallons, an increase of 34,330,150 gallons over last year. On page 98 will be found a table showing the stock on hand by districts. The great bulk of these spirits is held in the State of Kentucky, and they are chiefly what are known as " sour mash " whiskies. The amount in warehouses on July 1, 1881, produced in the year 1879, was 3,138,360 gallons, the tax upon which will fall due during the year 1882. It would seem probable that the high price of grain and this immense stock on hand will cause a reduction in the product during the ensuing year, and the probability of the distillers and owners of this stock having serious trouble in meeting their obligations to the government for the taxes as they fall due, will thereby be greatly diminished.

DISTILLERIES OF 100 BUSHELS AND UNDER.

Prior to January, 1881, all distilleries of the capacity of sixty bushels a day and under were in charge of but one officer, who performed the joint duties of storekeeper and gauger, and all distilleries above the capacity of sixty bushels were in charge of storekeepers and gaugers as distinct officers. After consideration, I came to the conclusion that it was desirable, as an economic measure, to raise the rate of capacity of distilleries at which a storekeeper and gauger combined in one officer could be employed from 60 to 100 bushels per day. On my recommendation to the honorable Secretary it was accordingly ordered that in all distilleries of the capacity of 100 bushels per day and under, a combined storekeeper and gauger should be employed. The saving thus effected cannot be exactly computed, but is believed to be in the neighborhood of $22,000 per annum.

REDUCTION OF PAY OF STOREKEEPER AND GAUGERS.

In April last I directed that the daily compensation of officers holding the combined office of storekeeeper and gauger, and assigned to duty at distilleries having a daily capacity of not exceeding twenty bushels of grain, should be reduced from $4 dollars to $3 dollars per diem. This change seemed to be demanded by reason of the disparity between the amount of labor required of these officers and the pay received.

Accordingly notice of the change in rate of pay, to take effect on the first of the month succeeding, was sent out to 634 officers assigned to the same number of distilleries having the daily capacity above stated, and situated in 46 collection districts, resulting in an immediate saving of $634 daily, and a total saving during the remainder of the fiscal year of nearly $26,000.

Notwithstanding these measures of economy there was a deficiency in the appropriation for the pay of storekeepers and gaugers and miscellaneous expenses for the last fiscal year, of $65,000. I have the honor to recommend that this sum be appropriated at the earliest day practicable, so that these officers shall receive pay for their services.

APPOINTMENTS OF STOREKEEPERS, GAUGERS, &C.

On the 16th of July last the system of appointing storekeepers, gaugers and other subordinate officers of the Internal Revenue Service, established by circular of date of June 30, 1880, was changed by the following order:

TREASURY DEPARTMENT, OFFICE OF THE SECRETARY,
Washington, D. C., July 16, 1881.

To Collectors of Internal Revenue:

Hereafter, in recommending persons for appointment to the office of storekeeper, gauger, storekeeper and gauger, or inspector of tobacco, snuff, and cigars, collectors of internal revenue will require each person recommended to make an application in writing, addressed to the Secretary of the Treasury, stating his age, legal residence, place of nativity, service in the Army or Navy, if any, names of relatives, if any, in the government service, and in what capacity employed; experience in the duties of the office for which he applies; business in which engaged at date of application, and interest which he proposes to retain therein should he be appointed.

The application must be accompanied by testimonials as to character for sobriety, industry, and business habits of the applicant, and will be inclosed in a letter addressed by the collector of the district to the Secretary of the Treasury, and forwarded to the Commissioner of Internal Revenue, stating the necessity for the appointment, and his personal knowledge as to the fitness of the applicant for the position.

If the appointment will involve the dismissal of any person in the service, that fact should be stated by the collector, as well as the reasons why, in his opinion, the dismissal should be made.

Correspondence relative to the removals and resignations of incumbents should be addressed to the Secretary of the Treasury through the Commissioner of Internal Revenue.

All papers relating to the appointment and removal of such officers (including copies of reports of revenue agents) will be forwarded by the Commissioner of Internal Revenue, with his recommendation in each case indorsed thereon, to the Secretary of the Treasury for action.

WILLIAM WINDOM,
Secretary.

The system established by this circular works admirably. A beneficial effect upon the service was felt immediately after its adoption, and it is now found quite practicable to hold these officers to a proper accountability, and to establish amongst them a spirit of emulation similar to that which prevails in other branches of the service.

GENERAL CONDITION OF THE SERVICE.

The condition of the service continues to improve, ard the spirit of emulation engendered by frequent inspections of officers, and reports upon the various districts is unabated. Thorough discipline is enforced in every branch, and every officer is held responsible for the faithful performance of his duties.

EXAMINATION OF COLLECTORS' OFFICES.

The frequent examination of the accounts of collectors has been continued during the past year with most gratifying results. Increased pride in the service is everywhere manifest, and complete uniformity in the method of keeping accounts prevails throughout the country. The standard of excellence reached is very commendable and reflects great credit upon the collectors and their subordinates.

Experience has shown that the most trusted persons having custody of public or private funds may yield to the temptation of converting those funds to their individual use. The sense of wrong-doing prevents the perpetration of such acts by the majority of persons, but the constant danger of detection and exposure by careful examinations of accounts, made at irregular intervals, doubtless exerts a wholesome check over those who might otherwise, perhaps, prove derelict.

MISCELLANEOUS EXPENSES.

In compliance with the provisions of the act of March 3, 1881, making appropriation for internal revenue, I submit the following detailed statement of the miscellaneous expenses for the service:

Express on public money to depositories	$6,655 37
Stationery for internal-revenue officers	13,925 36
Internal-revenue Record for internal-revenue officers	2,409 35
Telegraphing	1,312 13
Compensation of United States attorneys in internal-revenue cases under sections 827 and 838, Revised Statutes	7,948 50
Locks for distilleries	4,509 10
Hydrometers for use in gauging spirits	10,200 95
Gauging-rods for standard-test gauging, &c	217 00
Expenses of seizures and sales by collectors	709 05
Steel dies for numbering stills for fruit spirits	18 15
Traveling expenses of clerks under special orders of the department	930 44
Rent of offices leased by the Secretary of the Treasury in New York City for the collector of the second district	5,291 67
Total	54,127 87

*   *   *   *   *

MANUFACTURE OF PAPER.

During the fiscal year there has been manufactured by Messrs. S. D. Warren & Co., of Boston, under the contract entered into May 24, 1880, 600,000 pounds of paper for internal-revenue stamps. The prices paid were for vegetable-sized paper 11¼ cents per pound, and for animal-sized paper 12½ cents per pound. An additional order has been given to the above-named parties for 261,000 pounds under the same contract and at same rates for the year ending June 30, 1882. The paper furnished has been satisfactory as to quality, and orders have been promptly executed.

PRODUCTION OF STAMPS.

During the last fiscal year all internal-revenue stamps have been produced by the Bureau of Engraving and Printing, except stamps imprinted upon bank checks, which are supplied by the Graphic Company of New York City, and stamps upon foil wrappers for tobacco, which are printed by John J. Crooke & Co., of the aforesaid city, both under the superintendence of this office.

NUMBER AND VALUE OF STAMPS ISSUED.

During the fiscal year stamps were received by this office from the printers, and issued to collectors, agents, and purchasers as follows, viz:

Kind.	Number.	Value.
Stamps for distilled spirits, tax-paid	1, 367, 400	$71, 084, 790 00
Stamps for distilled spirits, other than tax-paid........................	4, 798, 800	20, 600 00
Stamps for distilled spirits, aggregate	6, 165, 200	71, 105, 390 00
Stamps for tobacco and snuff.................................	246, 163, 720	28, 993, 066 12
Stamps for cigars and cigarettes	78, 070, 733	17, 033, 956 50
Stamps for fermented liquors and brewers' permits..................	49, 618, 420	14, 630, 225 00
Stamps for special taxes	729, 570	9, 606, 850 00
Stamps for documents and proprietary articles........................	331, 712, 680	4, 165, 206 75
Total..	712, 460, 323	145, 534, 694 37

All stamps delivered to this office by the Bureau of Engraving and Printing were, on their receipt, counted, and their issue, as above, involved the preparation of 45,340 packages. 42,774 of which were forwarded to their destination by registered mail and 2,566 were forwarded by express. The handling of this large number of stamps has been accomplished without loss, either while in the hands of the printers, in the custody of this office, or in the course of transmission. The officers of the Washington City post-office are entitled to the thanks of this office for the prompt and faithful manner in which this large amount of registered matter has been handled.

REDEMPTION OF STAMPS.

I renew the recommendation made in my last report, that that portion of section 17 of the act of March 1, 1879, which prohibits the redemption of stamps unless the same are presented within three years after their purchase from the government or a government agent for the sale of stamps, be repealed.

MATCH STAMPS SOLD.

Amount of stamps sold to match manufacturers during the following fiscal years, commissions not deducted :

1876	$2,849,524 00
1877	2,982,275 00
1878	3,064,574 00
1879	3,357,251 00
1880	3,561,300 00
1881	3,606,437 62

SUITS ON MATCH BONDS.

Of the thirteen suits referred to in my last annual report as pending against stamp agents and match manufacturers, on bonds, for the recovery of $117,413.01 due on the sale of stamps for the past five years, there are ten remaining undisposed of, amounting to $107,877.20.

There have been 24 persons, principals and sureties on match manufacturers' bonds, proceeded against criminally for attempting to defraud the government, five of whom have been convicted and are now in the penitentiary.

ABSTRACT OF SEIZURES.

Seizures of property for violation of internal-revenue laws during the fiscal year ended June 30, 1881, were as follows :

30,714 gallons of distilled spirits, valued at	$25,624 37
30,299 pounds of tobacco, valued at	6,288 69
902,377 cigars, valued at	9,127 58
Miscellaneous property, valued at	118,534 69
Total	159,575 33

ABSTRACT OF REPORTS OF DISTRICT ATTORNEYS.

The reports of district attorneys for the fiscal year 1881 of internal-revenue suits commenced, pending, and disposed of show that there were pending July 1, 1880, 7,417 suits, of which 6,053 were criminal actions, 1,064 civil actions, and 300 proceedings *in rem.* During the fiscal year 1881, there were commenced 3,859 suits, 3,519 of which were criminal suits, 279 civil suits, and 61 actions *in rem.* Of the total of 3,859 suits thus pending, 862 have been decided in favor of the United States, with all costs paid, and 1,378 are reported as decided in favor of the government but neither judgment nor costs paid; 158 suits were settled by compromise; 540 suits were decided against the United States; 1,371 suits were dismissed, and 6,623 suits were pending July 1, 1881. Sentence has been suspended during good behavior in 331 criminal cases.

* * * * * * *

COLLECTIONS FROM RAILROADS.

The sum of $91,669.66, unpaid taxes accrued under former laws, has been collected during the year from ten different railroad companies, making an aggregate amount collected from this source in five years of $585,810.77.

CO-OPERATION OF OFFICERS OF JUSTICE.

I take great pleasure in tendering the thanks of this office to the district attorneys and marshals, and their assistants and deputies, for the promptness and regularity with which their reports have been made and the correspondence with this office has been attended to, and especially for their valuable aid in securing the enforcement of the laws. The clerks of courts are also entitled to thanks for the promptness with which they have made their reports.

RECEIPTS FROM TOBACCO.

The total amount of collections from tobacco for the fiscal year ended June 30, 1881, was $42,854,991.31. This amount includes the collections of internal-revenue taxes imposed upon imported manufactured tobacco, snuff, and cigars, and the special taxes paid by manufacturers of tobacco, snuff, and cigars, and by dealers in leaf and manufactured tobacco, and is more than the receipts from the same source for the fiscal year ended June 30, 1880, by $3,984,851.23.

TOBACCO AND SNUFF.

Manufactured tobacco, at 16 cents per pound	$22,832,310 13
Manufactured tobacco at 24 cents per pound	977 47
Snuff, taxed at 16 cents per pound	689,183 03
Total for the year ended June 30, 1881	23,522,470 63
Total for the year ended June 30, 1880	21,804,763 74
Increase of collections on tobacco and snuff	1,717,706 89

Of this increase, $1,663,133.20 was on chewing and smoking tobacco and $54,573.69 on snuff.

CIGARS AND CIGARETTES.

Cigars taxed at $6 per thousand	$16,095,724 78
Cigarettes taxed at $1.75 per thousand	992,927 22
Cigarettes taxed at $6 per thousand	54 00
Total collections for year ended June 30, 1881	17,088,706 00
Total collections for year ended June 30, 1880	14,922,088 85
Increase in collections from cigars and cigarettes	2,166,617 12

OTHER COLLECTIONS.

Export stamps, year ended June 30, 1881	$6,852 40
Export stamps, year ended June 30, 1880	6,622 40
Increase in sale of export stamps	230 00
Dealers in manufactured tobacco, year ended June 30, 1881	1,976,071 55
Dealers in manufactured tobacco, year ended June 30, 1880	1,864,422 41
Increase in collections from dealers in manufactured tobacco	111,649 14
Special taxes, manufacturers of tobacco and cigars, in 1881	151,442 57
Special taxes, manufacturers of tobacco and cigars, in 1880	153,132 71
Decrease in special taxes, manufacturers of tobacco and cigars	1,690 14
Special taxes, peddlers of tobacco, year ended June 30, 1881	26,258 13
Special taxes, peddlers of tobacco, year ended June 30, 1880	28,700 45
Decrease in collections from peddlers of tobacco	2,442 32
Dealers in leaf tobacco, year ended June 30, 1881	83,190 03
Dealers in leaf tobacco, year ended June 30, 1880	90,409 49
Decrease in collections from dealers in leaf tobacco	7,219 46

PRODUCTION OF MANUFACTURED TOBACCO, CIGARS, ETC.

Adding to the several quantities of tobacco, snuff, and cigars removed for consumption during the fiscal year ended June 30, 1881, as computed from the amount of revenue derived therefrom, the quantities removed in bond for export, we have the following results, which show the entire production for the last fiscal year:

	Pounds.
Tobacco taxed at 16 cents per pound	142,701,938
Tobacco taxed at 24 cents per pound	4,073
Snuff taxed at 16 cents per pound	4,307,394
Total quantity removed for consumption	147,013,405
Tobacco and snuff removed for exportation	10,686,471
Total production of tobacco and snuff, 1881	157,699,876
Total production for year ended June 30, 1880	146,082,885
Increase of production	11,616,991

PRODUCTION OF CIGARS AND CIGARETTES.

	Number.
Cigars, cheroots, &c., taxed at $6 per thousand	2,682,620,797
Cigarettes taxed at $1.75 per thousand	567,386,983
Cigarettes taxed at $6 per thousand	9,000
Cigars and cigarettes removed for export	40,388,135
Total product for fiscal year 1881	3,290,404,915
Total product for fiscal year 1880	2,820,159,820
Increase during fiscal year 1881 of	470,245,095

Cigarettes weighing over three pounds per thousand have been generally reported by the manufacturers as cigars; hence the above number, 9,000, does not represent the entire number of cigarettes of this class.

IMPORTED CIGARS.

The cigars imported during the fiscal year ended June 30, 1881, as given by the Bureau of Statistics—

	Pounds.
Aggregate in quantity	618,503
Of this quantity there were exported	77,252
Leaving to be withdrawn for consumption	541,251
Allowing 13½ pounds to the thousand as the weight of imported cigars, the number would be	40,092,67
Number withdrawn, 1880	45,264,667
Decrease during fiscal year 1881 was	5,172,000

COMPARATIVE STATEMENT OF COLLECTIONS FROM TOBACCO.

The largest collection of revenue from manufactured tobacco and snuff made in any one fiscal year was made during the fiscal year ended June 30, 1877, to wit, $28,148,767.90. The rates of tax then were, for all kinds of manufactured chewing and smoking tobacco, 24 cents per pound, and for snuff, 32 cents per pound. Of the former, 112,722,055 pounds were removed for consumption, and of the latter, 3,424,048 pounds.

During the last fiscal year the total quantity of manufactured tobacco, including snuff, removed for consumption was 147,013,405 pounds, being

34,291,350 pounds more than for the year 1877. By reason of the reduced and uniform rate of tax, the collections upon tobacco and snuff
for the last fiscal year fell below those of 1877 by the sum of $4,626,297.27.

The collections from cigars, cheroots, and cigarettes for the fiscal year
ended June 30, 1877, were $11,061,278.15, whilst for the last fiscal year
they aggregated $17,088,706, showing an increase of $6,027,427.85.

The total receipts from tobacco in all its sources for the fiscal year
ended June 30, 1877, were $41,106,546.92. This is the largest amount
collected on tobacco in any one year prior to the last, which shows an
increase over the year 1877 of $1,748,444.39.

It is easy to see from the foregoing statement and figures that the
large and increased collections for the last fiscal year are due mainly to
the remarkable increase in the production and consumption of cigars
and cigarettes, the rates of tax on which have remained undisturbed
since March, 1875.

COMPARATIVE PERCENTAGE OF INCREASE.

The increase in the quantity of tobacco and snuff removed for consumption during the last fiscal year over that of the fiscal year ended
June 30, 1877, is found to be 26¾ per cent., while the increase of cigars
has been over 49 per cent., and of cigarettes over 280 per cent.

TOBACCO PRODUCT FOR THE LAST FIVE YEARS.

The following shows the annual product of manufactured tobacco,
snuff, and cigars, for the last five fiscal years:

Tobacco—including snuff.

	Pounds.
1877	127,481,149
1878	119,406,588
1879	131,433,409
1880	146,082,885
1881	161,631,108

Cigars—including cigarettes.

	Number.
1877	1,958,391,488
1878	2,092,356,362
1879	2,276,534,081
1880	2,820,159,820
1881	3,307,650,345

NUMBER OF MANUFACTURERS AND DEALERS IN TOBACCO.

The following exhibit shows the number of manufacturers of tobacco,
snuff, and cigars; of dealers and peddlers of manufactured tobacco,
and of dealers in leaf tobacco who paid special tax as such during the
last fiscal year:

Manufacturers of tobacco and snuff	917
Manufacturers of cigars and cigarettes	14,228
Dealers in manufactured tobacco	395,215
Peddlers of manufactured tobacco	1,424
Dealers in leaf tobacco	3,993
Total persons who paid special taxes	415,777

LEAF TOBACCO.

The annexed tables show that during the calendar year 1880, the number of pounds of leaf tobacco consumed in the manufacture of tobacco, snuff, cigars, cheroots, and cigarettes, was as follows:

	Pounds.
Manufactured into tobacco and snuff......................................	145,911,394
Made into cigars, cheroots, and cigarettes..............................	61,183,358
Total leaf manufactured in 1880.......................................	207,094,752
Deduct imported leaf used...	6,764,530
Total domestic leaf used in 1880.....................................	200,330,222

The tabular statements made in the report of the Bureau of Statistics for the fiscal year ended June 30, 1881, show that the number of pounds of leaf tobacco exported during that year was 227,026,605.

STATEMENT showing the NUMBER of CIGARS MANUFACTURED in the UNITED STATES during the calendar year 1880, and the QUANTITY of LEAF TOBACCO used in their MANUFACTURE, together with the NUMBER of ACCOUNTS REPORTED on FORM 144.

State.	Number of accounts.	Pounds of tobacco.	Number of cigars.
Alabama	33	37,693	1,294,500
Arizona	4	5,675	249,425
Arkansas	18	27,826	1,240,210
California	363	2,749,459	116,136,114
Colorado	27	32,812	1,353,363
Connecticut	315	574,183	24,678,317
Dakota	13	12,675	558,050
Delaware	51	116,704	5,133,967
Florida	109	1,059,188	42,439,735
Georgia	32	69,319	2,788,890
Illinois	1,021	3,152,501	132,622,258
Indiana	458	1,079,723	44,544,037
Iowa	301	681,857	29,282,209
Kansas	110	272,531	11,337,680
Kentucky	246	728,518	31,410,607
Louisiana	176	733,734	29,047,595
Maine	52	104,807	4,498,343
Maryland	784	1,826,180	72,902,969
Massachusetts	523	1,507,434	65,661,726
Michigan	539	1,761,213	72,567,520
Minnesota	99	335,734	14,101,857
Mississippi	3	2,154	47,600
Missouri	580	1,252,896	54,640,795
Nebraska	65	144,815	5,786,656
Nevada	2	515	16,150
New Hampshire	40	64,981	3,056,915
New Jersey	732	1,174,218	50,090,475
New Mexico	1	873	33,350
New York	3,908	21,959,781	821,351,885
North Carolina	27	38,725	1,959,789
Ohio	1,678	5,570,213	243,367,539
Oregon	10	19,866	784,250
Pennsylvania	4,008	10,778,611	480,273,088
Rhode Island	80	173,180	7,813,695
South Carolina	17	28,324	1,130,030
Tennessee	33	45,086	1,909,106
Texas	56	117,324	4,917,172
Utah	2	6,433	215,150
Vermont	23	59,749	2,260,815
Virginia	141	613,994	19,378,344
Washington Territory	3	5,416	193,760
West Virginia	121	661,634	34,049,955
Wisconsin	384	1,503,471	62,899,096
Wyoming	1	232	9,200

Cigarettes reported.

	Number.
California	4,854,170
Florida	363,317
Illinois	1,953,690
Louisiana	8,661,210
Maryland	53,488,965
Massachusetts	5,994,735
Missouri	33,000
New Hampshire	229,500
New Jersey	11,015,800
New York	384,072,082
North Carolina	2,347,206
Ohio	6,519,440
Pennsylvania	2,230,390
Texas	158,900
Virginia	52,259,440

RECAPITULATION.

Total number of accounts reported	17,373
Total number of cigars manufactured	2,509,653,197
Total number of cigarettes manufactured	532,718,995
Total number of pounds tobacco used	61,183,358

*   *   *   *   *   *   *

SPIRITS WITHDRAWN FROM DISTILLERY WAREHOUSES UPON PAYMENT OF TAX.

	Gallons.
The quantity of spirits withdrawn from distillery warehouses upon payment of tax was, in 1881	67,372,575
And was in 1880	61,100,362
Increase	6,272,213

This increase is distributed, except as to the kind known as high wines, as follows:

	Gallons.
Bourbon whisky	787,050
Rye whisky	440,641
Alcohol	1,788,825
Rum	35,158
Gin	71,888
Pure, neutral, or cologne spirits	2,846,819
Miscellaneous	1,575,990
Total increase	7,546,371
Decrease in withdrawals of high wines	1,274,158
Net increase in withdrawals, tax-paid	6,272,213

LOSS OF SPIRITS BY LEAKAGE IN WAREHOUSE.

The quantity of spirits, 811,466 gallons, reported in the preceding table as lost by leakage or evaporation in warehouse is that portion of the actual leakage in warehouse which has occurred during the year and which has been allowed in accordance with the provisions of section 17 of the act of May 28, 1880. It is noted that in most cases the quantity allowed by the law has covered the entire loss, so that the above quantity is believed to indicate almost the entire loss in warehouse on the spirits withdrawn during the year, except in cases of casualty, and may be safely used as a factor in computing probable losses on spirits in distillery warehouses.

7 Ab

LOSS OF SPIRITS BY CASUALTIES.

During the fiscal year 1881 there were reported as lost by fire and other casualties, while stored in warehouse, 108,008 taxable gallons of spirits, or about seventy-three thousandths of one per cent. of the entire quantity of spirits (149,092,019 gallons) handled in the several distillery warehouses in the United States during that period. The loss so reported is distributed among the several kinds of spirits as follows:

	Gallons.
Whisky	417
Rye whisky	83,642
Alcohol	86
Gin	208
Miscellaneous	23,655
Total	108,008

Of the 83,642 gallons of rye whisky above reported, 73,785 gallons were reported destroyed by one fire in the twenty-second district of Pennsylvania; and of the 23,655 gallons miscellaneous spirits, 23,612 gallons were reported as lost in Southern districts, and mainly in warehouses located in remote parts of the districts where the supervision of revenue officers is necessarily limited.

*   *   *   *   *

SPIRITS WITHDRAWN FROM WAREHOUSE FOR SCIENTIFIC PURPOSES, AND FOR USE OF THE UNITED STATES.

The quantity of alcohol withdrawn free of tax from distillery warehouses for the use of colleges and other institutions of learning in the preservation of specimens of natural history in their several museums, or for use in their chemical laboratories, and of spirits of various kinds for use of the United States, amounted during the year to 24,902 gallons, an increase of 353 gallons over the quantity withdrawn during the previous year.

DISTILLED SPIRITS ALLOWED FOR LOSS BY LEAKAGE OR EVAPORATION IN WAREHOUSES.

The quantity of distilled spirits allowed under the provisions of section 17 of the act of May 28, 1880, for loss by leakages or evaporation in warehouses during June, 1880 (the only month of the fiscal year in which the act was in force), was 75,834 gallons.

The quantity allowed during the fiscal year 1881 was 811,466 gallons.

SPIRITS REMAINING IN WAREHOUSES AT THE CLOSE OF THE YEAR.

In my report for the year ended June 30, 1879, it was shown that the quantity (19,212,470 gallons) in warehouses June 30, 1879, exceeded the quantity in warehouse at the close of any preceding fiscal year. This quantity, however, was much exceeded by the quantity (31,363,869 gallons) remaining in warehouse June 30, 1880, which latter quantity is more than doubled by the quantity (64,646,111 gallons) in warehouse June 30, 1881.

The following table shows the quantity remaining in distillery warehouses at the close of each of the thirteen fiscal years during which spirits have been stored in such warehouses:

	Gallons.
Quantity remaining June 30, 1869	16,685,166
Quantity remaining June 30, 1870	11,671,886
Quantity remaining June 30, 1871	6,741,360
Quantity remaining June 30, 1872	10,103,882
Quantity remaining June 30, 1873	14,650,118
Quantity remaining June 30, 1874	15,575,224

Gallons.

Quantity remaining June 30, 1875	13, 179, 596
Quantity remaining June 30, 1876	12, 595, 850
Quantity remaining June 30, 1877	13, 091, 773
Quantity remaining June 30, 1878	14, 088, 773
Quantity remaining June 30, 1879	19, 212, 470
Quantity remaining June 30, 1880	31, 363, 869
Quantity remaining June 30, 1881	64, 648, 111

It is understood from leading distillers that since the extension of the bonded period the business of selling spirits in bond has largely increased, and that the greater portion of goods now in bond is owned by dealers in various parts of the country who have assumed to the distiller the payment of the taxes as they fall due.

It is evident that the causes adverted to in my last year's report as leading to this great increase in the stock of spirits remaining in distillery warehouses, and as indicating the growing ability on the part of distillers to discharge their obligations to the government, have been in full operation the past fiscal year.

The case of the sixth district of North Carolina was then cited as illustrating the great increase in the number of the legally authorized distilleries in sections of the country recently infested by illicit distillers. The same district can be again used as illustrating this fact, the number of distillery warehouses in that district having increased from 229 July 1, 1880, to 253 June 30, 1881.

In my last year's report reference was made to the building and successful operation of the largest distillery in the United States. I have now to report that this distillery has been enlarged and continued in successful operation during the year, that another having a capacity greater than the original capacity of the largest distillery has been built and operated during this year, and that others of its class have been greatly enlarged and fitted up with the latest improvements, thus enabling them to materially reduce the cost of production and to improve the character of their products. By the use of the latest improved purifying, refining, and redistilling apparatus, and the employment of experts, fine grades of alcohol, and pure, neutral, or cologne spirits are produced in distilleries ready for use in the arts and sciences without additional manipulation.

The decrease in the production and withdrawal of high wines, and the increase in the production and withdrawal of all other and finer kinds of spirits, are facts satisfactorily showing continued improvement in the methods of producing distilled spirits.

Nearly nine-tenths of the spirits remaining in warehouse June 30, 1881 (58,102,094 gallons out of 64,648,111 gallons), were bourbon and rye whiskies, and the increase in the quantity in warehouse that day over that in warehouse June 30, 1880, was mainly the increase in these two varieties.

There was an increase in all varieties, as follows:

Increased quantity in warehouse, of—

Gallons.

Bourbon whisky	24, 751, 479
Rye whisky	6, 039, 477
Alcohol	256, 919
Rum	105, 083
Gin	53, 351
High wines	208, 016
Pure, neutral, or cologne spirits	1, 122
Miscellaneous	1, 868, 795
Total increase	33, 284, 242

TRANSFER OF SPIRITS TO MANUFACTURING WAREHOUSES.

In my report for the fiscal year ended June 30, 1880, attention was called to the law then recently enacted (May 28, 1880, section 14) enlarging the provisions of the internal-revenue act of March 1, 1879, as to transfers of spirits from distillery warehouses to warehouses known as manufacturing warehouses, and established at ports of entry for the manufacture of medicines, preparations, compositions, perfumeries, cosmetics, cordials, and other liquors for export.

As stated in my previous report the act of May 28, 1880, enlarged the scope of the act of March 1, 1879, so as to provide for the withdrawal of every kind of spirits from distillery warehouses, the article theretofore withdrawn having been limited to alcohol.

The following varieties of spirits appear to have been withdrawn under this new provision of the law, viz:

	Gallons.
Bourbon whisky	966
Rye whisky	913
Pure, neutral, or cologne spirits	13,468
Total	15,347
Add alcohol withdrawn:	190,481
Total all kinds withdrawn	205,828

This quantity is 13,384 gallons less than the quantity withdrawn for transfer to manufacturing warehouses during the year ended June 30, 1880.

SPIRITS AND TOBACCO REMOVED IN BOND FOR EXPORT.

The following statement shows the quantity and percentage of production of distilled spirits and manufactured tobacco (including snuff) removed in bond for export during each fiscal year since the passage of the act of June 6, 1872:

Year.	Distilled spirits.		Year.	Manufactured tobacco.	
	Taxable (proof) gallons exported.	Percentage of production.		Pounds of tobacco exported.	Percentage of production.
1873	2,358,630	3.45+	1873	10,110,045	8.59+
1874	4,060,160	5.90+	1874	10,800,927	9.11+
1875	587,413	0.96+	1875	9,179,316	7.13+
1876	1,308,900	2.25+	1876	9,434,485	7.87+
1877	2,529,528	4.22+	1877	11,335,046	8.88+
1878	5,499,252	9.80+	1878	10,581,744	8.89+
1879	14,837,581	20.63+	1879	11,034,951	8.62+
1880	16,765,666	18.55+	1880	9,808,409	6.71+
1881	15,921,482	13.52+	1881	10,686,132	6.61+
Total	63,868,612		Total	92,971,055	

SPIRITS WITHDRAWN FOR EXPORT DURING FOUR MONTHS ENDED
OCTOBER 31, 1877 TO 1881.

*STATEMENT, by DISTRICTS, of the QUANTITY, in TAXABLE GALLONS, of
SPIRITS WITHDRAWN for EXPORT during the four months ended October 31, in
the years 1877, 1878, 1879, 1880, and 1881.*

Districts.	Taxable gallons.				
	1877.	1878.	1879.	1880.	1881.
First California				180	441
First Illinois	165, 376	1, 043, 630	513, 097	265, 050	94, 309
Third Illinois	43, 088	98, 711	128, 505	252, 527	52, 036
Fifth Illinois	218, 411	1, 334, 489	1, 486, 534	1, 453, 923	879, 486
Eighth Illinois			214, 380	812, 937	183, 299
First Indiana		▼	25, 913	68, 200	
Fourth Indiana	6, 327	52, 352		13, 362	
Seventh Indiana			394, 839	192, 441	53, 511
Second Iowa				117, 732	125, 267
Fifth Iowa				196, 729	167, 792
Fifth Kentucky		1, 064			
Sixth Kentucky	1, 022	2, 493		1, 367	
Seventh Kentucky		1, 096		139	2, 747
Eighth Kentucky		1, 053			
Third Maryland	7, 687				
Third Massachusetts	26, 233	147, 642	84, 062	106, 216	67, 068
Fifth Massachusetts	289, 365	357, 900	369, 840	263, 078	227, 407
First Missouri		200, 494			
Nebraska	5, 980		20, 134	98, 261	16, 098
First New York		7, 888		7, 909	
First Ohio	21, 497	53, 906	17, 436	126, 351	28, 515
Third Ohio				48, 953	80, 637
Sixth Ohio	2, 470			1, 938	
Twenty-third Pennsylvania					293
First Wisconsin			4, 404		
Total	787, 471	3, 302, 706	3, 209, 144	4, 024, 292	1, 979, 505

PRODUCTION AND MOVEMENT OF SPIRITS DURING THE FIRST FOUR
MONTHS OF THE PRESENT FISCAL YEAR.

The preceding tables show the production and movement of distilled
spirits during the first four months of the present fiscal year.

They show that the production is 1,889,623 gallons greater than for
the corresponding period last year, the withdrawals for exportation
are 2,044,787 gallons less, the withdrawals upon payment of the tax
2,314,957 gallons greater, and that the increased receipts from the
gallon tax amount to $2,083,461.30.

Months.	Produced.	Withdrawn for export.	Withdrawn tax-paid.	Amount of tax paid.
	Gallons.	*Gallons.*	*Gallons.*	
July, 1881	7, 362, 663	1, 112, 827	5, 147, 956	$4, 633, 160 40
August, 1881	6, 181, 880	535, 605	5, 942, 148	5, 347, 933 20
September, 1881	7, 159, 695	149, 419	6, 622, 649	5, 960, 384 10
October, 1881	9, 563, 572	181, 654	7, 207, 932	6, 487, 138 80
Total	30, 267, 810	1, 979, 505	24, 920, 685	22, 428, 616 50

Increase over 1880.	Production.	*Withdrawn for export.	Withdrawn tax-paid.	Amount of tax paid.
	Gallons.	*Gallons.*	*Gallons.*	
In July	232, 588	86, 575	159, 739	$142, 765 10
In August	453, 919	238, 027	519, 767	467, 790 30
In September	331, 264	644, 492	755, 234	679, 710 60
In October	871, 852	1, 035, 693	880, 217	792, 195 30
Total	1, 889, 623	2, 044, 787	2, 314, 957	2, 083, 461 30

*Decrease.

EXPORTATION OF MANUFACTURED TOBACCO AND SNUFF IN BOND.

1. *Removed and unaccounted for July 1, 1880.*

	Pounds.	Pounds.
Tobacco, at 20 cents per pound tax	29,002	
Bonds in the hands of United States district attorneys	17,094	
Tobacco, at 24 cents, removed under exportation bonds	533,212	
Tobacco, at 24 cents, removed under transportation bonds	207,660¾	
Tobacco, at 16 cents, removed under exportation bonds	3,946,809½	
Tobacco, at 16 cents, removed under transportation bonds	307,926¼	
		5,041,704½

2. *Removed during the year ended June 30, 1881.*

Tobacco and snuff, at 16 cents per pound tax	10,686,132¼	
Tobacco and snuff, at 16 cents per pound tax (excess)	339	
		10,686,471¼
		15,728,175¾

3. *Exported and during the year accounted for.*

Tobacco, at 20 cents per pound tax	29,002	
Tobacco, at 24 cents per pound tax	580,200	
Tobacco and snuff, at 16 cents per pound tax	14,007,644 13/16	
Tobacco, at 24 cents per pound tax (tax paid on deficiencies)	386	
Tobacco and snuff, at 16 cents per pound tax (tax paid on deficiencies)	470	
		14,617,702 13/16

4. *Remaining unaccounted for June 30, 1881.*

Bonds in the hands of United States district attorneys	17,094	
Tobacco, at 24 cents, removed under exportation bonds	33,974	
Tobacco, at 24 cents, removed under transportation bonds	126,312 3/16	
Tobacco and snuff, at 16 cents, removed under exportation bonds	830,576 9/16	
Tobacco and snuff, at 16 cents, removed under transportation bonds	102,515 3/16	
		1,110,472 15/16
		15,728,175¾

The quantity removed from manufactories for exportation during the fiscal year ended June 30, 1881, is 879,421.25 pounds greater than that removed during the fiscal year ended June 30, 1880, while the quantity unaccounted for at the close of the year 1881 is 3,931,231.375 pounds less than at the close of the year 1880.

The great diminution in the balance unaccounted for is clearly due to the operation of the act of June 9, 1880, amendatory of section 3385 of the Revised Statutes, to which attention was called in my last annual report. The increase in exportations may also, it is believed, be fairly attributed to the same cause.

In this connection I would call attention to the following paragraph which appeared in my last year's report, and renew the recommendation contained therein:

It, however, appears that in striking out a portion of section 3385, Revised Statutes, and substituting for the portion stricken out the amendatory provisions of the new law, the language of that part of section 3385 relied upon as authorizing the exportation of tobacco, snuff, and cigars by railroad cars and other land conveyances was, through inadvertence, not restored. I see no good reasons why the exportation of these articles under section 3385, as amended, should be confined to vessels, and I would therefore recommend that as early as possible in the next session of Congress the law be amended so as to clearly provide for the exportation of tobacco, snuff, and cigars by railroad or other land conveyances.

EXPORTATION OF CIGARS AND CIGARETTES IN BOND.

1. *Removed and unaccounted for July 1, 1880.*

	Number.	Number.
Cigars, at $6 per M tax	1,123,600	
Cigarettes, at $1.75 per M tax	20,356,280	
		21,479,880

2. *Removed during the year ended June 30, 1881.*

Cigars, at $6 per M tax	2,726,075	
Cigarettes, at $1.75 per M tax	37,662,060	
		40,388,135
		61,868,015

3. *Exported and accounted for during the year ended June 30, 1881.*

Cigars, at $6 per M tax	3,768,225	
Cigarettes, at $1.75 per M tax	53,865,340	
		57,633,565

4. *Remaining unaccounted for June 30, 1881.*

Cigars, at $6 per M	81,450	
Cigarettes, at $1.75 per M	4,153,000	
		4,234,450
		61,868,015

DATE OF BONDS REMAINING UNACCOUNTED FOR JUNE 30, 1881.

The years in which the bonds were given for the exportation of the tobacco, snuff, cigars, and cigarettes remaining unaccounted for by the evidence required by law for their cancellation on June 30, 1881, are as follows, viz:

Year.	Tobacco.	Snuff.	Cigars.	Cigarettes.
	Pounds.	*Pounds.*	*Number.*	*Number.*
1872	17,004			
1873				
1874				
1875	2,066			
1876	48,584½			
1877	16,080			
1878	51,925½			
1879	99,740			32,000
1880	94,810		10,500	6,000
1881	780,372½		70,950	4,115,000
Total	,110,472½		81,450	4,153,000

OPERATIONS AT SPECIAL BONDED WAREHOUSES FOR STORAGE OF GRAPE BRANDY.

The following statement shows the quantity of grape brandy placed in special bonded warehouses, withdrawn therefrom, and remaining therein at the beginning and close of the fiscal year ended June 30, 1881, in taxable gallons:

	Gallons.	Gallons.	Gallons.
Remaining in warehouse July 1, 1880:			
First district of California	63,157		
Fourth district of California	60,456		
		123,613	
Removed for exportation and unaccounted for July 1, 1880:			
First district of California		439	
			124,052
Produced and bonded during the year:			
First district of California	125,521		
Fourth district of California	114,603		
		240,124	
Received in first district from fourth district of California		20,345	
			260,469
			384,521
Exported and accounted for during the year:			
First district of California		689	
Removed tax-paid during the year:			
First district of California	69,238		
Fourth district of California	72,231		
		141,469	
Loss by regauge act of May 28, 1880:			
First district of California	2,686		
Fourth district of California	1,961		
		4,647	
Loss allowed for casualty:			
Fourth district of California		47	
Removed from fourth district to first district of California		20,345	
			167,197
Removed for exportation and unaccounted for June 30, 1881:			
First district of California		675	
Remaining in warehouse June 30, 1881:			
First district of California	136,174		
Fourth district of California	80,475		
		216,649	
			217,324
			384,521

The amount produced and bonded during the fiscal year ended June 30, 1881, was 111,038 gallons more than in the previous year, while the amount removed tax-paid was 29,749 gallons larger than in 1880.

Of the quantity in warehouse June 30, 1881, 136,174 gallons were in the following-named warehouses in the first district of California:

	Gallons.
No. 1. Bode & Danforth, at San Francisco	104,264
No. 2. Juan Bernard, at Los Angeles	19,179
No. 3. G. C. Carlon, at Stockton	12,731

and 80,475 gallons were in the following-named warehouses in the fourth district of California:

		Gallons.
No. 1. George Lichthardt, at Sacramento	....	37,766
No. 2. J. F. Boyce, at Santa Rosa	....	13,894
No. 3. H. J. Lewelling, at Saint Helena	....	23,885
No. 4. John Tivnen, at Sonoma	....	4,930

STATEMENT of DRAWBACK of INTERNAL REVENUE TAXES allowed on EX-PORTED MERCHANDISE during the fiscal year 1881.

Port.	Number of claims.	Proprietary articles.	Tobacco.	Snuff.	Cigars.	Fermented liquors.	Stills.	Distilled spirits.	Total.
Baltimore	6	$195 70	$2,265 42	$26 08	....	....	....	....	$2,487 20
Boston	25	543 04	568 72	....	....	$186 83	$20 00	....	1,318 59
Milwaukee	6	....	....	....	....	157 25	....	....	157 25
New York	632	25,169 92	683 70	....	$166 68	784 30	200 00	$455 40	27,460 00
Philadelphia	18	1,544 91	....	....	....	....	....	66 60	1,611 51
Rochester	1	24 63	....	....	....	....	....	....	24 63
San Francisco	31	86 40	5,078 76	....	1,065 75	....	....	639 90	6,870 81
Suspension Bridge	2	25 92	....	....	....	....	....	....	25 92
Saint Louis	25	854 47	....	....	....	....	....	....	854 47
Troy	3	38 88	....	....	....	....	....	....	38 88
Total	749	28,483 87	8,596 60	26 08	1,232 43	1,128 38	220 00	1,161 90	40,849 26
Allowed, 1880	872	35,153 86	22,314 02	....	1,094 97	2,205 42	80 00	*888 00	61,736 27

* Machinery exported, 1868.

In connection with the foregoing statement I have to renew the recommendation made in my last annual report, that section 3244 Revised Statutes be so amended as to include distilling-worms belonging to stills manufactured for export, which, like stills, are subject to a tax of $20 each. Also that an appropriation be made for the payment of drawback on articles exported under said section 3244 Revised Statutes, as also on distilled spirits exported under section 3329 Revised Statutes.

While a number of claims covering both stills and distilled spirits have been allowed by this office during the preceding two years, the claimants in these cases are unable to recover the amounts due them, in consequence of a failure on the part of Congress to make the necessary appropriation.

*   *   *   *   *   *   *

STATEMENT of AVERAGE CAPITAL and DEPOSITS of SAVINGS BANKS and the CAPITAL of BANKS and BANKERS other than NATIONAL BANKS invested in UNITED STATES BONDS, compiled from the returns of said BANKS and BANK-ERS, for the years ended May, 1877, 1878, 1879, 1880, and 1881.

	1877.	1878.	1879.	1880.	1881.
Capital of savings banks	$362,095	$601,872	$429,791	$507,876	$812,768
Capital of banks and bankers	33,027,476	36,425,306	40,013,376	40,371,865	35,099,939
Deposits of savings banks	102,859,674	121,855,622	154,847,346	182,580,893	194,886,529
Total	136,249,205	158,882,800	195,290,513	223,460,634	230,799,236

ASSESSMENTS.

The following table shows the assessments made by the Commissioner of Internal Revenue during the fiscal years ended June 30, 1880, and

June 30, 1881, respectively, and the increase or decrease on each article or occupation:

Article or occupation.	Amount assessed during fiscal year ended—		Fiscal year ended June 30, 1881.	
	June 30, 1880.	June 30, 1881.	Increase over 1880.	Decrease from 1880.
Tax on deficiencies in production of distilled spirits	$73,158 63	$48,494 36		$24,664 27
Tax on excess of materials used in the production of distilled spirits	2,829 97	3,547 10	$717 13	
Tax on deposits and capital of banks and bankers and of savings institutions other than national banks	3,247,998 90	3,955,183 20	707,184 30	
Tax on circulation of banks and others	461,597 82	10,788 02		450,809 80
Tax on distilled spirits fraudulently removed or seized	53,312 18	40,396 42		12,915 76
Tax on fermented liquors removed from brewery unstamped	877 75	854 96		22 79
Tax on tobacco, snuff, and cigars removed from factory unstamped	88,584 85	46,385 27		42,199 58
Tax on proprietary articles removed unstamped	1,529 86	5,132 29	3,602 43	
Assessed penalties	93,265 14	143,862 78	50,597 64	
Legacies and successions	135,532 80	63,859 39		71,673 41
Unassessed and unassessable penalties, interest, taxes previously abated, conscience money, and deficiencies in bonded accounts which have been collected, interest tax on distilled spirits, also, fines, penalties, and forfeitures, and costs paid to collectors by order of court or by order of Secretary, and unassessable taxes recovered; also, amount of penalties and interest received for validating unstamped instruments (Form 58)	555,315 50	275,524 93		279,790 57
Special taxes (licenses)	59,776 56	60,411 50	635 03	
Tax on income and dividends	40,614 60	14,903 33		25,711 27
Total	4,814,394 56	4,669,343 64		145,050 92

The foregoing table shows that a decrease has occurred in the assessments of the following taxes, as compared with the year ended June 30, 1880, viz:

On deficiencies in the production of distilled spirits.
On the circulation of banks.
On distilled spirits fraudulently removed or seized.
On fermented liquors removed from breweries unstamped.
On tobacco, snuff, and cigars sold or removed.
On legacies and successions.
On specific penalties, interest, taxes collected through suits.
On incomes and dividends.

The decrease on all the items named, except those relating to legacies and successions, incomes, and dividends, which are due under repealed laws, indicates a better observance and a clearer understanding of the requirements of the laws. The reduction of the assessed taxes on deficiencies in the production of distilled spirits, especially, indicates that the distillers are conducting their operations in a more business-like manner.

The reduction in the amount assessed on circulation, which has been principally the 10 per cent. tax on notes issued by manufacturing establishments and used in circulation in their vicinities, indicates that a rigid enforcement of the law levying such a tax has practically driven out of circulation all currency and money other than the standard coin or notes issued by the United States or secured by United States bonds.

The following statement shows the amount of assessments in each of the several States and Territories of the United States during the fiscal year ended June 30, 1881:

Alabama	$41,758 97	Montana	$6,682 15
Arizona	4,468 64	Nebraska	19,116 90
Arkansas	7,556 63	Nevada	8,894 81
California	376,647 78	New Hampshire	18,275 56
Colorado	27,785 92	New Jersey	35,132 49
Connecticut	54,036 26	New Mexico	2,318 72
Dakota	4,434 39	New York	1,250,662 63
Delaware	10,195 14	North Carolina	52,179 68
Florida	5,230 00	Ohio	221,468 83
Georgia	51,187 56	Oregon	12,656 95
Idaho	475 12	Pennsylvania	519,381 63
Illinois	424,346 70	Rhode Island	50,352 09
Indiana	105,362 36	South Carolina	23,684 64
Iowa	127,528 50	Tennessee	53,243 34
Kansas	40,638 98	Texas	64,025 79
Kentucky	152,227 56	Utah	9,352 27
Louisiana	50,629 33	Vermont	13,389 42
Maine	4,742 59	Virginia	70,801 10
Maryland	73,771 06	Washington	5,312 75
Massachusetts	90,393 05	West Virginia	29,455 78
Michigan	103,851 90	Wisconsin	96,239 39
Minnesota	48,551 73	Wyoming	3,060 07
Mississippi	24,960 47		
Missouri	272,876 01	Total	4,669,343 64

RECEIPTS FOR FIRST FOUR MONTHS OF PRESENT FISCAL YEAR.

The following table shows the receipts from the several sources of revenue for the first four months of the current fiscal year. The receipts for the corresponding period in the last fiscal year, and a comparison of the receipts for the two periods, are also given:

Sources of revenue.	Receipts from July 1, 1880, to October 31, 1880.	Receipts from July 1, 1881, to October 31, 1881.	Increase.	Decrease.
SPIRITS.				
Spirits distilled from apples, peaches, or grapes..	$388,749 22	$446,518 75	$57,769 53	....
Spirits distilled from materials other than apples, peaches, or grapes	20,362,974 86	22,377,909 70	2,014,934 84	....
Wine made in imitation of champagne, &c				
Rectifiers (special tax)	9,250 00	10,420 87	1,170 87	....
Dealers, retail liquor (special tax)	355,990 96	356,536 20	545 24	....
Dealers, wholesale liquor (special tax)	22,866 77	27,112 59	4,245 82	....
Manufacturers of stills, and stills and worms manufactured (special tax)	3,390 84	2,716 68	....	$674 16
Stamps for distilled spirits intended for export ..	4,666 10	2,413 00	....	2,253 10
Miscellaneous	681 77		....	681 77
Total	21,148,570 52	23,223,627 79	2,075,057 27	....
TOBACCO.				
Cigars and cheroots	5,537,551 40	6,407,041 55	869,490 15	....
Cigarettes	349,366 77	345,293 97	....	4,072 80
Manufacturers of cigars (special tax)	6,607 04	7,055 65	448 61	....
Snuff of all descriptions	241,926 28	290,149 25	48,222 97	....
Tobacco, manufactured, of all descriptions	7,819,825 79	10,248,892 01	2,429,066 22	....
Stamps for tobacco, snuff, and cigars intended for export	2,432 30	1,984 60	....	447 70
Dealers in leaf tobacco, not over 25,000 pounds (special tax)	256 64	1,015 46	758 82	....
Dealers in leaf tobacco (special tax)	4,595 16	6,460 18	1,865 02	....
Retail dealers in leaf tobacco (special tax)		583 34	583 34	....
Dealers in manufactured tobacco (special tax) ..	173,953 33	185,394 23	11,440 90	....
Manufacturers of tobacco (special tax)	555 85	485 85	....	70 00
Peddlers of tobacco (special tax)	3,565 75	2,913 36	....	652 39
Total	14,140,636 31	17,497,269 45	3,356,633 14	....

Sources of revenue.	Receipts from July 1, 1880, to October 31, 1880.	Receipts from July 1, 1881, to October 31, 1881.	Increase.	Decrease
FERMENTED LIQUORS.				
Fermented liquors, tax of $1 per barrel on........	$5, 051, 656 12	$6, 032, 944 21	$981, 288 09	....
Brewers (special tax)	6, 133 47	7, 116 95	983 48	....
Dealers in malt liquors (special tax)	39, 449 42	42, 829 99	3, 380 57	....
Total...........................	5, 097, 239 01	6, 082, 891 15	985, 652 14	....
BANKS AND BANKERS.				
Bank deposits	508, 913 60	712, 543 34	203, 629 74	....
Savings-bank deposits	8, 379 70	36, 235 25	27, 855 55	....
Bank capital	180, 010 46	359, 801 64	179, 791 18	....
Savings-bank capital..........................	6, 710 69	7, 194 88	484 19	....
Bank circulation..............................	544 32	2, 406 74	1, 862 42	....
Notes of persons, State banks, towns, cities, &c., paid out				
Total...........................	704, 558 77	1, 118, 181 85	413, 623 08	....
MISCELLANEOUS.				
Adhesive stamps	2, 598, 907 31	2, 867, 726 36	268, 819 05	....
Penalties	89, 528 04	52, 360 24	....	$37, 167 80
Collections not otherwise herein provided for	35, 807 30	34, 913 27	....	894 03
Total...........................	2, 724, 242 65	2, 954, 999 87	230, 757 22	....
Aggregate receipts	43, 815, 247 26	50, 876, 970 11	7, 061, 722 85	....

TABULAR STATEMENTS FOR THE APPENDIX.*

I submit herewith, to accompany the bound volume, tabular statements, as follows:

TABLE A.—Showing the receipts from each specific source of revenue, and the amounts refunded in each collection district, State, and Territory of the United States, for the fiscal year enped June 30, 1881.

TABLE B.—A statement of the number and value of special-tax stamps, of stamps for distilled spirits, fermented liquors, tobacco, snuff, cigars, and cigarettes issued; of the number and value of internal-revenue stamps ordered monthly from the American Bank Note Company and the New York Graphic Company; and the monthly receipts from the sale of stamps, and the commissions allowed thereon, for the fiscal year ended June 30, 1881.

TABLE C.—Comparative statement showing the percentages of receipts from the several general sources of revenue in each State and Territory of the United States to the aggregate receipts from the same sources, by fiscal years, from July 1, 1863, to June 30, 1881.

TABLE D.—Comparative statement showing the aggregate receipts from all sources, in each collection district, State, and Territory of the United States, by fiscal years, from September 1, 1862, to June 30, 1881, with appendix showing differences between reported and true collections.

TABLE E.—Showing the receipts from each specific source of internal revenue, by fiscal years, from September 1, 1862, to June 30, 1881.

TABLE F.—Exhibiting the ratio of receipts in the United States from specific sonrces of revenue to the aggregate receipts from all sources, by fiscal years, from July 1, 1863, to June 30, 1881.

TABLE G.—Statement of the returns of distilled spirits, manufactured tobacco, snuff, cigars, and cigarettes, under the several acts of legislation, and under the various rates of taxation, by fiscal years, from September 1, 1862, to June 30, 1881.

TABLE H.—Statement of the receipts from special taxes in each collection district, State, and Territory for the special-tax year ended April 30, 1881.

* These statements are omitted for want of space, but they are printed in the bound volumes of the Commissioner's report.

TABLE I.—Abstract of reports of district attorneys concerning suits and prosecutions under the internal-revenue laws during the fiscal year ended June 30, 1881.

TABLE K.—Abstract of seizures of property for violation of internal-revenue laws during the fiscal year ended June 30, 1881.

Very respectfully,

GREEN B. RAUM,
Commissioner.

Hon. CHAS. J. FOLGER,
Secretary of Treasury.

REPORT OF THE COMPTROLLER OF THE CURRENCY.

TREASURY DEPARTMENT,
OFFICE OF THE COMPTROLLER OF THE CURRENCY,
Washington, December 3, 1881.

I have the honor to submit for the consideration of Congress the nineteenth annual report of the Comptroller of the Currency, in compliance with section 333 of the Revised Statutes of the United States.

Eighty-six national banks were organized during the year ending November 1 last, with an aggregate authorized capital of $9,651,050, to which $5,233,580 in circulating notes have been issued. This is the largest number of banks organized in any year since 1872. Twenty-six banks with an aggregate capital of $2,020,000, and circulation of $1,245,530, have voluntarily discontinued business during the year. National banks are located in every State of the Union except Mississippi and in every Territory except Arizona, the total number in operation on October 1 last being 2,132. This is the greatest number of banks that has ever been in operation at any one time. The total number of national banks organized from the establishment of the national-banking system, February 25, 1863, to November 1 of the present year is 2,581.

From the establishment of the system to November 1 last, 340 banks have gone into voluntary liquidation by the vote of shareholders owning two-thirds of their respective capitals, and 86 have been placed in the hands of receivers for the purpose of closing up their affairs. The total amount of claims proved by the creditors of these insolvent banks is $25,966,602, and the amount of dividends paid to creditors is $18,561,698.

The estimated losses to creditors from the failures of national banks, during the eighteen years since the passage of the act, is $6,240,000, and the average annual loss has therefore been about $346,000, in the business of corporations having an average capital of about $450,000,000, and deposits averaging about $800,000,000. Twenty-one of these insolvent banks have paid their creditors in full, and forty of them have paid more than 75 per cent. each. The individual liabilities of shareholders of insolvent banks has been enforced in fifty-three instances, and about $2,700,000 has been collected from this source. During the past year dividends have been declared in favor of the creditors of insolvent national banks, amounting to $929,059, and the affairs of twelve such banks have been finally closed, nine of which have paid their creditors in full.

There were no failures of national banks during the period from June 19, 1880, to November 1 of the present year. Since that date the Mechanics' National Bank of Newark, and the Pacific National Bank of Boston, to which reference will be made hereafter, have suspended, and the former bank has been placed in the hands of a receiver.

The following table exhibits the resources and liabilities of the national banks, at the close of business on the 1st day of October, 1881, the returns from New York City, from Boston, Philadelphia and Baltimore, from the other reserve cities, and from the remaining banks of the country, being tabulated separately:

	New York City.	Boston, Philadelphia, and Baltimore.	Other reserve cities.*	Country banks.	Aggregate.
	48 banks.	102 banks.	87 banks.	1,895 banks.	2,132 banks.
RESOURCES.					
Loans and discounts............	$246,757,659	$211,814,653	$134,406,496	$576,043,493	$1,169,022,303
Overdrafts	143,733	55,507	386,397	4,188,143	4,773,780
Bonds for circulation	22,991,590	57,290,800	27,847,100	255,206,100	363,335,500
Bonds for deposits	320,000	325,000	3,848,000	10,247,000	15,540,000
U. S. bonds on hand............	7,854,050	2,518,050	8,302,000	24,298,350	40,972,450
Other stocks and bonds	13,413,587	7,385,371	4,614,456	36,482,409	61,895,702
Due from reserve agents		20,866,093	19,767,054	92,325,036	132,958,183
Due from other national banks.	19,917,055	14,143,191	10,479,467	33,965,733	78,505,446
Due from other banks and bankers	3,278,155	1,496,037	3,775,495	10,757,140	19,306,827
Real estate, furniture, and fixtures	10,760,838	6,739,161	4,598,197	25,235,915	47,339,111
Current expenses...............	1,089,101	792,083	844,553	4,006,199	6,731,936
Premiums	1,061,797	247,164	360,495	2,469,130	4,138,586
Checks and other cash items ..	2,513,144	1,337,655	1,048,504	9,932,577	14,831,879
Exchanges for clearing-house..	146,597,213	27,198,422	14,502,607	894,013	189,222,256
Bills of other national banks ..	1,580,588	1,802,778	2,019,871	12,329,475	17,732,712
Fractional currency	37,954	40,426	54,971	240,585	373,946
Specie	51,524,768	17,584,343	17,256,624	27,969,001	114,334,736
Legal-tender notes.............	8,983,371	6,934,070	10,767,998	26,478,002	53,158,441
U. S. certificates of deposit....	1,915,000	2,150,000	2,055,000	620,000	6,740,000
Five per cent. redemption fund.	1,016,807	2,543,414	1,194,348	11,361,183	16,115,752
Due from U. S. Treasurer......	395,180	218,485	136,165	607,014	1,356,844
Totals ...., ...	542,651,490	383,783,603	266,350,800	1,165,601,498	2,358,387,391
LIABILITIES.					
Capital stock....................	51,150,000	79,396,330	40,401,500	292,872,155	463,821,985
Surplus fund	19,947,316	21,954,102	12,206,793	74,030,407	128,140,618
Undivided profits	12,832,315	6,287,274	5,779,776	31,472,826	56,372,191
National bank notes outstanding	20,112,590	50,632,029	23,513,195	225,942,155	320,199,969
State bank notes outstanding..	47,472	35,614		161,932	245,018
Dividends unpaid	246,228	1,356,702	172,542	2,060,455	3,835,927
Individual deposits.............	295,692,013	163,432,337	120,094,419	491,776,762	1,070,997,531
U. S. deposits...................	437,422	366,243	2,262,560	5,410,465	8,476,690
Deposits of U. S. disbursing officers	89,934	107,140	844,813	2,589,916	3,631,803
Due to national banks.........	104,089,161	45,522,222	34,048,738	22,201,825	205,862,946
Due to other banks and bankers	38,007,039	13,926,472	24,885,452	12,226,508	89,047,471
Notes and bills rediscounted ..			364,393	2,726,772	3,091,165
Bills payable		764,138	1,774,619	2,125,320	4,664,077
Totals	542,651,490	383,783,603	266,350,800	1,165,601,498	2,358,387,391

*The reserve cities, in addition to New York, Boston, Philadelphia, and Baltimore, are Albany, Pittsburgh, Washington, New Orleans, Louisville, Cincinnati, Cleveland, Chicago, Detroit, Milwaukee, Saint Louis, and San Francisco.

The following table exhibits, in the order of their capital the sixteen States having an amount of capital in excess of $5,000,000, together with the amount of circulation, loans and discounts, and individual deposits of each, on October 1, 1881:

States.	Capital.	Circulation.	Loans and discounts.	Individual deposits.
Massachusetts	$96,177,500	$71,267,089	$205,248,480	$125,198,324
New York	85,780,160	47,946,726	330,257,556	372,853,780
Pennsylvania	56,518,340	42,429,247	139,860,386	138,046,152
Ohio	29,389,000	21,468,480	66,518,608	60,960,874
Connecticut	25,539,630	17,966,332	43,475,312	25,761,281
Rhode Island	20,065,000	14,718,956	28,496,882	11,317,338
Illinois	15,199,600	8,165,189	61,555,705	72,972,402
Maryland	13,603,030	8,605,433	30,205,683	26,117,350
Indiana	13,093,500	8,767,700	21,899,023	23,206,436
New Jersey	12,960,000	10,386,784	29,233,480	28,250,618
Kentucky	10,435,100	8,885,111	17,774,891	9,145,739
Maine	10,385,000	8,211,247	17,305,908	9,325,083
Michigan	9,435,600	5,614,979	24,329,000	23,127,184
Vermont	8,151,000	6,442,899	10,899,272	5,191,352
Iowa	5,950,000	4,414,103	13,456,065	15,770,134
New Hampshire	5,830,000	5,158,159	7,518,017	4,292,687

COMPARATIVE STATEMENTS OF THE NATIONAL BANKS FOR ELEVEN YEARS.

The following table exhibits the resources and liabilities of the national banks for eleven years, at nearly corresponding dates, from 1871 to 1881, inclusive:

	Oct 2, 1871.	Oct. 3, 1872.	Sept.12, 1873.	Oct. 2, 1874.	Oct. 1, 1875.	Oct. 2, 1876.	Oct. 1, 1877.	Oct. 1, 1878.	Oct. 2, 1879.	Oct. 1, 1880.	Oct. 1, 1881.
	1,767 banks.	1,919 banks.	1,976 banks.	2,004 banks.	2,087 banks.	2,089 banks.	2,080 banks.	2,053 banks.	2,048 banks.	2,090 banks.	2,132 banks.
RESOURCES.	Millions.	Millions.	Millions	Millions	Millions.	Millions.	Millions	Millions.	Millions.	Millions.	Millions.
Loans	831 6	877 2	944 2	954 4	984 7	931 3	891 9	834 0	878 5	1,041 0	1,178 8
Bonds for circulation	364 5	382 0	388 3	383 3	370 3	337 2	336 8	347 6	357 3	357 8	363 3
Other U. S. bonds	45 8	27 6	23 6	28 0	28 1	47 8	45 0	94 7	71 2	43 6	56 5
Stocks, bonds, &c.	24 5	23 5	23 7	27 8	33 5	34 4	34 5	36 9	39 7	48 9	61 9
Due from banks	143 2	128 2	149 5	134 8	144 7	146 9	129 9	138 9	167 3	213 5	230 8
Real estate	30 1	32 3	34 7	38 1	42 4	43 1	45 2	46 7	47 8	48 0	47 3
Specie	13 2	10 2	19 9	21 2	8 1	21 4	22 7	30 7	42 2	109 3	114 3
Legal-tender notes	107 0	102 1	92 4	80 0	76 5	84 2	66 9	64 4	69 2	56 6	53 2
Nat'l-bank notes	14 3	15 8	16 1	18 5	18 5	15 9	15 6	16 9	16 7	18 2	17 7
C. H. exchanges	115 2	125 0	100 3	109 7	87 9	100 0	74 5	82 4	113 0	121 1	189 2
U. S. cert. of deposit		6 7	20 6	42 8	48 8	29 2	33 4	32 7	26 8	7 7	6 7
Due from U. S. Treas				20 3	19 0	16 7	16 0	16 5	17 0	17 1	17 5
Other resources	41 2	25 2	17 3	18 3	19 1	19 1	28 7	24 9	22 1	23 0	26 2
Totals	1,730 6	1,755 8	1,830 6	1,877 2	1,882 2	1,827 2	1,741 1	1,767 8	1,868 8	2,105 8	2,358 4
LIABILITIES.											
Capital stock	458 3	479 6	491 0	493 8	504 8	499 8	479 5	466 2	454 1	457 6	463 8
Surplus fund	101 1	110 3	120 3	129 0	134 4	132 2	122 8	116 0	114 8	120 5	128 1
Undivided profits	42 0	46 6	54 5	51 5	53 0	46 4	44 5	44 9	41 3	46 1	56 4
Circulation	317 4	335 1	340 3	334 2	319 1	292 2	291 9	301 9	313 8	317 3	320 2
Due to depositors	611 4	628 9	640 0	683 8	679 4	666 2	630 4	668 4	736 9	887 9	1,083 1
Due to banks	171 9	143 8	173 0	175 8	170 7	170 8	161 0	165 1	201 2	267 9	294 9
Other liabilities	8 5	11 5	11 5	9 1	11 8	10 6	10 4	7 9	6 7	8 5	11 9
Totals	1,730 6	1,755 8	1,830 6	1,877 2	1,882 2	1,827 2	1,741 1	1,767 3	1,868 8	2,105 8	2,358 4

The following table shows, at corresponding dates for three years, the increase of loans, deposits, circulation, capital and surplus, the amount of United States bonds on hand, and the movement of money in the national banks of the country, arranged in three groups—viz, those in the New England and Middle States, those in the Western and Northwestern States, including Kentucky and Missouri, and those in the remaining States and Territories:

NEW ENGLAND AND MIDDLE STATES.

	Oct. 1, 1881.	Oct. 1, 1880.	Oct. 2, 1879.
	No. of banks, 1,202.	No. of banks, 1,187.	No. of banks, 1,168.
Loans and discounts..................................	$843,092,901	$773,916,399	$654,037,648
United States bonds on hand........................	27,373,650	21,076,400	41,983,650
Capital..	335,009,700	333,363,300	331,646,630
Surplus...	96,046,995	90,827,648	86,749,498
Net deposits..	749,303,734	689,694,705	548,757,240
Circulation..	233,132,972	229,826,416	227,824,388
Specie..	82,209,124	89,074,603	32,977,600
Legal-tenders and United States certificates..........	33,828,596	36,485,314	66,097,350

WESTERN AND NORTHWESTERN STATES.

	Oct. 1, 1881.	Oct. 1, 1880.	Oct. 2, 1879.
	No. of banks, 748.	No. of banks, 729.	No. of banks, 715.
Loans and discounts..................................	$204,703,034	$212,796,017	$179,161,250
United States bonds on hand........................	11,502,450	6,578,500	9,551,100
Capital..	99,760,000	95,597,500	94,013,150
Surplus...	25,708,991	24,191,511	23,034,727
Net deposits..	295,520,514	227,904,373	179,119,124
Circulation..	66,442,810	66,957,403	66,376,624
Specie..	23,985,587	15,118,278	6,229,429
Legal-tenders and United States certificates...........	21,170,992	23,491,204	24,465,934

SOUTHERN AND PACIFIC STATES AND TERRITORIES.

	Oct. 1, 1881.	Oct. 1, 1880.	Oct. 2, 1879.
	No. of banks, 182.	No. of banks, 174.	No. of banks, 165.
Loans and discounts	$66,000,148	$54,464,852	$45,304,199
United States bonds on hand.........................	2,096,350	1,138,500	1,407,350
Capital..	20,043,285	28,593,185	28,408,185
Surplus...	6,384,632	5,499,424	5,002,303
Net deposits..	60,804,503	50,342,345	41,008,042
Circulation..	20,624,287	20,566,217	19,585,330
Specie	6,477,845	3,988,508	2,966,703
Legal-tenders and United States certificates..........	4,891,016	4,415,410	5,392,678

Similar tables in reference to a number of the States in different sections of the country are given in the Appendix.

EXTENSION OF THE CORPORATE EXISTENCE OF NATIONAL BANKS.

Section 11 of the National Bank Act of February 25, 1863, provided that—

Every association formed pursuant to the provisions of this act may make and use a common seal, and shall have succession by the name designated in its articles of association and for the period limited therein, not, however, exceeding twenty years from the passage of this act.

Section 8 of the act of June 3, 1864, provides that each association—

Shall have power to adopt a corporate seal, and shall have succession by the name designated in its organization certificate, for the period of twenty years from its organization, unless sooner dissolved according to the provisions of its articles of association, or by the act of its shareholders owning two-thirds of its stock, or unless the franchise shall be forfeited by a violation of this act.

The act last named, as well as that which preceded it, contains the following provision:

Copies of such [organization] certificate, duly certified by the Comptroller, and authenticated by his seal of office, shall be legal and sufficient evidence in all courts and places within the United States, or the jurisdiction of the government thereof, of the existence of such association, and of every other matter or thing which could be proved by the production of the original certificate.

Section 5136 of the Revised Statutes of the United States provides that—

Upon duly making and filing articles of association and an organization certificate the association shall become, as from the date of the execution of its organization certificate, a body corporate, and as such and in the name designated in the organization certificate, it shall have power, first, to adopt and use a corporate seal; second, to have succession for the period of twenty years from its organization, unless it is sooner dissolved according to the provisions of its articles of association, or by the act of its shareholders owning two-thirds of its stock, or unless its franchise becomes forfeited by some violation of law.

From these sections it appears that the period of existence of an association, as a body corporate, commences from the date of its organization certificate, and not from that of the certificate of the Comptroller, authorizing the association to commence business, as provided for in section 5169 of the Revised Statutes. The corporate existence of the national bank first organized will, under this limitation of law, expire on January 1, 1882, and that of the second bank on April 11 following. From the date last named to February 25, 1883, the number of banks whose corporate existence will terminate is 393, having a capital of nearly 92 millions, and circulation of nearly 68 millions, as follows:

Date.	No. of banks.	Capital.	Circulation.
1882.			
In May	11	$3, 900, 000	$1, 781, 500
In June	16	4, 205, 000	3, 452, 500
In July	24	4, 385, 000	3, 591, 500
In August	10	1, 205, 000	863, 000
In September	11	3, 582, 500	1, 577, 500
In October	5	550, 000	404, 100
In November	5	850, 000	770, 000
In December	5	570, 000	505, 000
1883.			
In January	9	1, 250, 000	1, 080, 000
On February 25	297	71, 538, 450	53, 740, 810
Totals	393	91, 965, 950	67, 855, 910

The number of national banks organized under the act of June 3, 1864, the term of whose corporate existence will cease during each year prior to 1891, is 1,080, with capital and circulation as follows:

Years.	No. of banks.	Capital.	Circulation.
1884	248	$80, 034, 390	$62, 740, 950
1885	728	186, 161, 775	119, 266, 745
1886	19	2, 560, 300	1, 780, 000
1887	6	1, 100, 000	976, 500
1888	10	950, 000	692, 100
1889	4	650, 000	567, 000
1890	65	9, 415, 500	6, 557, 790
Totals	1, 080	280, 871, 965	192, 581, 085

Bills will undoubtedly be brought before Congress during its present session for the extension of the charters of those banks whose corporate existence is soon to expire.

The principal reason urged by those who favor a discontinuance of the national banking system is, that money can be saved by authorizing the government to furnish circulation to the country; in other words, that the profit to the banks upon their circulation is excessive. Sixteen years ago the banks had on deposit, as security for circulation, 276 millions of dollars in United States bonds, of which amount nearly 200 millions was in six per cents and 76 millions in five per cents. The banks now hold 32 millions of four and a half per cents; 92 millions of four per cents; 241 millions of three and a half per cents, converted from five and six per cents; and also 3¼ millions of Pacific railroad sixes. The remaining five per cent. bonds held by them, amounting in all to $758,900, have ceased to bear interest. The average premium borne by the four per cent. bonds during the last six months has been about sixteen per cent., and at this price they net to the holders less than three and a half per cent. interest. During the same period the three and a half per cents also have, for a considerable portion of the time, been worth a premium in the market of from one to two per cent., so that the banks do not at the present time, and it is probable that they will not, for a long time to come, receive an annual average rate of interest as great as three and a half per cent. upon the United States bonds deposited by them as security for their circulating notes. Until the year 1877 the banks continued to receive interest upon the par value of their bonds at the rate of either five or six per cent., while the net interest now received, as already stated, does not exceed three and one-half per cent. On ten per cent. of the amount of bonds thus deposited by the banks, amounting to 39 millions, they receive no circulation; and from this portion of their bond deposit they derive no benefit or advantage not possessed by any other class of bondholders. They pay a tax of one per cent. upon the amount of their circulating notes outstanding; keep on deposit with the Treasurer an amount of lawful money equal to five per cent. of their issues, as a permanent redemption fund; and also reimburse to the United States the expense of redeeming their notes at the Treasury. The actual net profit upon circulation, based upon a 4 and a 3½ per cent. bond, and with rates of interest on bank loans varying from five to ten per cent., is estimated to be as shown in the following table:

Class of bonds deposited.	5 per cent.	6 per cent.	7 per cent.	8 per cent.	9 per cent.	10 per cent.
	Per ct.	Per ct.	Per ct.	Per ct.	Per ct.	Per ct.
4 per cent. bonds, at 16 per cent. premium	1.49	1.19	.88	.58	.27	.03
3½ per cent. bonds, at 1 per cent. premium	1.74	1.50	1.43	1.28	1.12	.98

The profit upon circulation is seen to be greatest where the rate of interest for the loan of money is least; and this arises from the fact, already stated, that the bank receives in circulating notes ten per cent. less in amount than it deposits in bonds. Thus, if the bonds deposited are three and one-half per cents, and the commercial rate of interest is ten per cent., there is a loss to the bank of six and one-half per cent. upon the ten per cent. margin of bonds deposited. If the commercial value is six per cent. only, then the loss upon the margin mentioned is two and one-half per cent., instead of six and one-half per cent., as in the previous case.

The profit on circulation varies, therefore, from one and one-eighth per cent., where the interest on loans is nine per cent., to one and one-half per cent. where the rate of interest is six per cent.

The proportion of taxation, National and State, imposed upon the banks has been shown to be much greater than that upon any other moneyed capital, being in the aggregate equal to an average rate of four per cent. upon the amount of their issues. The amount of interest received by the banks upon the United States bonds held by them has in late years gradually decreased, and the profit upon circulation has thereby been reduced almost to the minimum. Such profit cannot now, at least, be said to be excessive.

But if the National Bank Act has conferred upon the associations organized thereunder the right to issue circulating notes, it has placed them all under the operation of a uniform system, and has surrounded them with numerous restrictions, among which are the following:

The capital stock must be fully paid in, and a portion of this capital, not less in any case than $50,000, must be invested in United States bonds and deposited with the Treasurer. If the capital stock of an association becomes impaired at any time, it must be promptly restored. Their circulating notes must be redeemed at par, not only at the place of issue, but at the Treasury of the United States.

The banks must lend on personal security only, and not upon that of real estate, and only ten per cent. of their capital may be loaned upon accommodation notes, or other than actual business paper, to any one person, company, firm or corporation. They cannot lend money on their own circulating notes, or upon shares of their own stock, and must take the notes of every other national bank in payment of debts due to them. The rate of interest charged must not be greater than the rate provided by the laws of the several States in which they are located. They must pay taxes or duties to the government upon their capital stock, deposits and circulation, and to the States they must pay such taxes as are imposed on other moneyed capital. They are required to keep on hand as a reserve, in coin or other lawful money, a certain proportion of their deposits. There must be no preference of creditors in cases of insolvency.

Shareholders are held individually responsible for all contracts, debts and engagements of the association, to the extent of the par value of their stock, in addition to the amount invested in such shares. The banks are required, before the declaration of any dividend, semi-annually to increase their surplus fund by an amount equal to one tenth of their net earnings for the preceding six months, until it shall equal twenty per cent. of their capital. Losses and bad debts must be charged to profit and loss account before dividends are paid. In other words, dividends must be earned before they are declared. Full statements, accompanied by schedules, of their resources and liabilities must be made to the Comptroller several times in each year, and must also be published at the expense of the association making the same. Other statements, showing their semi-annual profits, losses, and dividends, must also be returned, and statements in reference to the business of any association making the same may be required at any time, a penalty of $100 per day being prescribed for each day's delay to comply with the call therefor. The banks are subject to personal examinations, and if a bank becomes insolvent a receiver may be at once appointed. If the directors knowingly violate, or permit to be violated, any of the provisions of the act, all the rights and privileges of the bank are thereby forfeited; and the directors are held personally and individually responsible for all damages sustained by any person in consequence of such violation.

It is recommended that an act be passed during the present session, authorizing any national bank, with the approval of the Comptroller, at any time within two years prior to the date of the expiration of its corporate existence, to extend its period of succession for twenty years, by amending its articles of association. The bill may provide that such amendments must be authorized by the votes of shareholders owning not less than two-thirds of the capital of the association, the amendment to be certified to the Comptroller of the Currency, by the president or cashier, verified by the seal of the association, and not to be valid until the Comptroller's approval thereof shall have been obtained, and he shall have given to the association a certificate authorizing it to continue its business under such extension. Responsibility for the extension of the corporate existence of the banks will thus, in a measure, rest with the Comptroller; and he can require such an examination of its affairs to be made, prior to granting the extension, as may seem to him proper, in order to ascertain if the capital stock is intact, and all the assets of the bank in a satisfactory condition.

It is unquestionably true that many national banks would greatly prefer the abolishment of the national system, if it were accompanied by a repeal of the provision of law imposing a tax of ten per cent. upon State bank circulation; and there is little reason to doubt that such repeal would speedily follow the abrogation of the National Bank Act. The laws in many of the States authorize the issue of State bank notes, based upon the deposit of State bonds as security therefor. The repeal of the tax law referred to would result in re-establishing the State bank systems in many parts of the country, the issues of which would be far more profitable to the banks themselves than is the circulation now issued under the national system; while in other sections circulating notes, put forth without any security whatever, would prevail as formerly. The notes of these various systems would be redeemable, not at any common center, as at present, but at the chief city of each State or section of country issuing the same; and the price of exchange would thereby be enhanced to rates certainly not less than the cost of transporting gold from the places of redemption to the commercial center of the country. In many parts of the country these rates would necessarily be oppressive, resulting in great loss to the people, which loss would steadily increase with the growth of business.

As another consequence of the abolition of the present system, the large surplus which the national banks have now accumulated, amounting to $128,140,618, and which adds greatly to their strength and safety, would doubtless be divided among their shareholders; while many of the safeguards and restrictions of the present law, which experience has shown to be valuable, will be either abolished or so changed by the varying legislation of the several States, as to be practically of little value in comparison with the present homogeneous system.

If, on the other hand, the corporate existence of the national banks shall be extended, all the advantages of the existing system will be preserved, subject to such amendments as may be hereafter found necessary; while the circulation of the banks, which is the principal objection urged against the system, will, under existing laws, diminish in volume as the public debt shall be reduced.

The whole number of national banks in operation on October 1 last was 2,148. Of this number 393 were associations having a capital of $50,000 each; 164 had a capital of over $50,000 and less than $100,000, and the capital of 829 banks ranged from $100,000 to $150,000 each. The minimum amount of bonds required to be deposited by banks of the capital named is one-third of their capital, but not less in any case than $30,000. The minimum amount required by all other banks is $50,000, and the least amount of bonds which, under existing laws, may be deposited by the 2,148 banks now in operation, is about $82,400,000. It is probable that from 100 to 150 millions of United States bonds would be sufficient to supply the minimum amount necessary to be deposited with the Treasurer by all the banks which may be established during the next twenty years. It is therefore evident that the national banking system may be continued without change in this respect for many years, even if the bonded debt of the United States shall, during that time, continue to be reduced as rapidly as it has in the past year. The discussion of the question as to the kind of circulating notes which will be substituted for the national-bank notes, if the latter are retired, is postponed for the present, as it is impossible to forsee the events which may occur to affect that question within the next few years.

If, for any reason, the legislation herein proposed shall not be favorably considered by Congress, the banks can still, under the present laws, renew their existence if they so desire; and in the absence of prohibitory legislation many of them undoubtedly will, on the expiration of their present charters, organize new associations, with nearly the same stockholders as before, and will then apply for and obtain from the Comptroller certificates authorizing them to continue business for twenty years from the respective dates of their new organization certificates. Such a course of procedure will be perfectly legal, and, indeed, under the existing laws, the Comptroller has no discretionary power in the matter, but must necessarily sanction the organization, or reorganization, of such associations as shall have conformed in all respects to the legal requirements.

The passage, however, of a general act directly authorizing an extension of the corporate existence of associations whose charters are about to expire would, in many instances, relieve the banks from embarrassment. As the law now stands, if the shareholders of an association are all agreed, the process of reorganization is simple; but if any of the shareholders object to such reorganization, they are entitled to a complete liquidation of the bank's affairs, and to a *pro rata* distribution of all its assets, including its surplus fund. In many instances executors and administrators of estates hold national-bank stock in trust; and while they might prefer to retain their interests in the associations which issued the stock, they would perhaps have no authority to subscribe for stock in the new organizations. While, therefore, the legislation asked for is not absolutely essential, yet its passage at an early day would be a great convenience to many of the national banks, and especially so to the class last referred to.

SUBSTITUTES FOR MONEY.

For a long period in their early history, bills of exchange were in fact what their name implied—namely, bills drawn in one country to be paid in another. The common law of England, which inflexibly forbade the assignment of debt, was a bar to their early introduction into that country; but they eventually forced themselves into use there, through the facilities which they afforded in the conduct of trade with other nations. It was long before the transfer of inland debts was sanctioned in England; but the practice at length prevailed, being first adopted in the intercourse between London and York, and London and Bristol. By the gradual striking off of one limitation after another, bills of exchange,* after the lapse of several centuries, became what they now are, simply an order from one person to another to pay a definite sum of money. The convenience of trade gradually overpowered the narrow restrictions of the common law, until it became lawful to transfer an obligation from one person to another, in the form of a bill of exchange, while at the same time it remained unlawful to do so in other forms, such as by a simple acknowledgment of the debt by the debtor.

About the end of the sixteenth century the merchants of Amsterdam and Hamburg, and of some other places, began to use instruments of credit among themselves; and, as their intercourse increased, these instruments naturally assumed the form of an acknowledgment of the debt by the debtor, with a promise to pay to the bearer, on demand, or at a specified time. Such instruments are now called promissory notes. They first began to be used by the goldsmiths, who originated the modern system of banking soon after 1640. They were then called goldsmiths' notes, but they were not recognized by law. The first promissory notes issued in England, under the sanction of law, were those of the Bank of England, in 1694, and which were technically bills obligatory, or bills of credit. By the act founding the bank its notes were declared to be assignable by indorsement, although this privilege was not then extended to other promissory notes. But by an act passed in 1704, promissory notes of every kind, including those of private bankers and merchants, as well as of the Bank of England, were all placed on the same footing as inland bills of exchange; that is to say, they were all made transferable, by indorsement on each separately. With respect, however, to the Bank of England notes, as these were always payable on demand, the practice of indorsing soon fell into disuse, and they passed from hand to hand like money. In the case also of the notes of private bankers of great repute, the indorsement was often omitted.

Until near the year 1772, this method of making exchanges by the issue of promissory notes, made payable to bearer on demand, was generally adhered to by bankers. But about that time the practice in this respect became changed. When the bankers made discounts for their customers, or received deposits from them, instead of giving as before promissory notes or deposit receipts, they wrote down the amount to the credit of their customers on their books. They then gave them books containing a number of printed forms. These forms were called checks, and were really bills of exchange drawn upon the banker, payable to the bearer on demand.

Prior to the period when checks were introduced, the issue of promissory notes by the London bankers was very extensive; but the method of doing business by the use of checks was found by them to be so convenient, and it possessed so many practical advantages over that by way of notes, that issues of the latter were soon generally discontinued, and that of checks adopted in their stead. The bankers, however, were never forbidden to issue such notes until the bank act of 1844.

For many years the English courts held that a check is binding on the banker, having assets of the drawer, without acceptance; but more recently these earlier decisions have been overruled, and it is now the established doctrine of the highest English tribunals that a check is not binding upon a bank until accepted, notwithstanding the fact that the bank has assets of the drawer. In a case in which the First National Bank of New Orleans was defendant, where certain holders of its drafts on a Liverpool bank attempted to recover from the latter bank the amount of the drafts out of an ample balance to the credit of the New

---

* Much of the information regarding bills of exchange is gleaned from Macleod's ⁊ and Practice of Banking.

Orleans bank after its failure, the House of Lords affirmed the decision of the Lord Chancellor, and held that the drafts were not even equitable assignments of any part of the drawer's funds.[*]

PROPORTION OF BANK CHECKS, BANK NOTES, AND COIN USED IN LONDON, FROM DATA PREPARED BY SIR JOHN LUBBOCK.

The first information given to the public as to the amount and proportion of checks, bank notes, and coin used in the business of banking, was by Sir John Lubbock, an eminent scientist and banker, and president of the London Institute of Bankers, and was based upon the business of his own bank during the last few days of 1864. His statement, given below, is copied from a paper read by him before the London Statistical Society, in June, 1865, entitled "Country Clearing," and published in the journal of that society for September, 1865, to whose tables I have added the proportions of checks, bank notes, and coin:

In order to give the proportion of the transactions of bankers which passes through the clearing house to that which does not, I took the amount of £23,000,000, which passed through our hands during the last few days of last year, and found that it was made up as follows:

Clearing..	£16,346,000	70.8 per cent.
Cheques and bills, which did not pass through the clearing...	5,394,000	23.4 "
Bank notes...	1,137,000	4.9 "
Coin...	139,000	0.6 "
Country notes..	79,000	0.3 "
Total..	23,095,000	100.0 "

It would appear from this that out of each £1,000,000, rather more than £700,000 passes through the clearing. The second amount given above, £5,394,000, includes, of course, the transfers made in our own books from the account of one customer to that of another. These amounted to £3,603,000, the remainder, £1,791,000, representing the cheques and bills on banks which did not clear.

In order to ascertain the proportion of payments made in bank notes and coin, in town, I have taken an amount, £17,000,000, paid in by our London customers. This was made up as follows:

Cheques and bills on clearing bankers..................	£13,000,000	77.4 per cent.
Cheques and bills on ourselves.........................	1,600,000	9.5 "
Cheques and bills on other bankers.....................	1,400,000	8.3 "
Bank of England notes..................................	674,470	4.0 "
Country bank notes.....................................	9,570	0.1 "
Coin..	117,960	0.7 "
Total..	16,802,000	100.0 "

The above amount of bank notes, small as it is, must, I think, be still farther reduced. All the clearing bankers have accounts at the Bank of England, and, as we require notes to supply our till, we draw them from the Bank of England, crediting the bank in our books. Out of the above amount of £674,470, £266,000 were notes thus drawn by us from the bank to replenish our till, and did not represent an amount paid in by our customers to their credit. This amount must, therefore, I think, be deducted from both sides of the account. On the other hand we must add the amount of notes paid in for collection and discount, and loans on security, which pass through a different set of books and which represented a sum of £2,460,686.

Making these alterations we find that out of £19,000,000 credited to our town customers, £408,000 consisted of bank notes, £79,000 of country bank notes, and £118,000 of coin:

Cheques and bills......................................	£18,395,000	96.8 per cent.
Bank notes...	408,000	2.2 "
Country notes..	79,000	0.4 "
Coin...	118,000	0.6 "
Total..	19,000,000	100.0 "

---

[*] House of Lords, p. 352, June 17–19, 1873.

In an article on bank notes, published in the Journal of the Institute of Bankers, London, for March, 1880, Mr. John B. Martin gives a table showing the percentage of bank notes, coin and checks used in banking transactions, which was compiled by him from several sources. This table is given below:

	Robarts, Lubbock & Co.		Morrison, Dillon & Co.		Manchester and Salford Bank and another local bank.			Martin & Co.	
	Received 1864, London.	Received 1864, general.	Received.	Paid.	1859.	1864.	1872.	Received 1878-'79.	Paid 1878-'79.
	Per cent.	Per cent.	Per cent.	Per ct.	Per ct.	Per ct.	Per ct.	Per cent.	P. ct.
Bills and cheques ...	96.8	94.1	90	97	47	56	68	96.5	96.9
Notes	2.6	5.3	7	2	} 53	38	27	2.6	2.1
Coin	.6	.6	3	1		4	5	.9	1.0
	100	100	100	100	100	100	100	100	100

The first two columns of percentages are obtained from the data contained in the table previously given, and show the ratio of checks, notes, and coin received by the firm of Robarts, Lubbock & Co., in payments made to them during the last few days of 1864; the first column showing the percentages of the items named above, in the receipts from London bankers alone, and the second, the percentages in the receipts from all sources.　The next two columns are derived from an analysis of the receipts and payments of the firm of Messrs. Morrison, Dillon & Co. The next three columns show, for the years 1859, 1864, and 1872, respectively, the percentages of checks and cash derived from an estimate made of the total transactions of the Manchester and Salford Bank, and published in the Journal of the Statistical Society for March, 1873, at page 86. In reference to these transactions of the Manchester banks, it is stated that the amount of cash shown is very remarkable, and that it is believed the proportion of coin in it very largely exceeds that of England, taken as a whole, because the statement proceeds from a great wage-paying district.　The last two columns of the table show the results of an analysis of the receipts and payments of Martin & Co.　To obtain these percentages, the transactions of Mr. Martin's own firm were observed for six working days in each month, from the 20th to the 26th, for a period of several months, covering the latter part of 1878 and the first part of 1879.

In each instance in this table, it is to be observed, the transactions are those of one bank or firm only, and in making up the aggregate, from which the percentages are calculated, the business for several days has been taken; differing in these respects from the returns hereafter given from the national banks in this country, which are results obtained from combining the transactions upon one day, and for the most part of the same day, of a large number of banks doing business in widely different sections of the country.

PROPORTION OF BANK CHECKS USED, FROM DATA PRESENTED BY PRESIDENT GARFIELD.

The first information ever given upon this subject in this country was compiled by the late President Garfield, who was well known as a careful investigator of economic subjects.

In his speech on resumption, delivered in the House of Representatives on November 16, 1877, he said:

In 1871, when I was chairman of the Committee on Banking and Currency, I asked the Comptroller of the Currency to issue an order, naming fifty-two banks which were to make an analysis of their receipts. I selected three groups. The first was the city banks. The second consisted of banks in cities of the size of Toledo and Dayton, in the State of Ohio. In the third group, if I may coin a word, I selected the "countriest" banks, the smallest that could be found, at points away from railroads and telegraphs. The order was that those banks should analyze all their receipts for six consecutive days, putting into one list all that can be called cash—either coin, greenbacks, bank notes or coupons, and into the other list all drafts, checks, or commercial bills. What was the result? During those six days $157,000,000 were received over the counters of the fifty-two banks; and of that amount, $19,370,000—12 per cent. only—in cash, and eighty-eight per cent., that vast amount representing every grade of business, was in checks, drafts, and commercial bills.

RECEIPTS IN MONEY AND CHECKS OF ALL THE NATIONAL BANKS.

In order to obtain the fullest possible information on this subject the Comptroller recently issued two circular letters to the national banks, asking for classified returns of their receipts and payments at different dates. The first circular requested a return to be made for June 30, which date marked the close of the fiscal year; and the second one asked for a return on September 17, which was the middle of the third month following. It was believed that a comparison of returns made for dates so dissimilar would be a substantial test of their accuracy, and would present a fair average of their operations for the current year. Returns for June 30, were received from 1,966 of the 2,106 national banks then in operation, and in response to the request for statements for the date of September 17, returns were received from 2,132 banks, being all of the banks in operation at that date. A few of these later returns, about fifty in number, were for a day subsequent to September 17, but their relative number being small they have been tabulated as being of that date

The total receipts of the 1,966 banks, on June 30 last, were 284 millions of dollars ($284,714,017). Of this amount there was less than two millions ($1,864,105) in gold coin, about half a million ($440,997) in silver coin, and eleven and one-half millions ($11,554,747) in paper money; the remainder, amounting to 270 millions ($270,854,165), being in checks and drafts, including nine millions ($9,582,500) of clearing-house certificates. The gold coin equaled 0.65 of one per cent. of the total receipts; the silver coin was 0.16 of one per cent.; the paper money 4.6 per cent.; while the checks and drafts constituted 91.77 per cent. of the whole amount; or, including the clearing-house certificates, they were equal to 95.13 per cent. In other words, the total percentage of coin and paper money received was 4.87 per cent. only, while that of checks and drafts was 95.13.

The receipts of all of the national banks, 2,132 in number, on September 17, were $295,233,779. Of this sum $4,078,044 consisted of gold coin, $500,301 of silver coin, and $13,026,570 of paper money. The remainder, amounting to $277,628,862, consisted of checks and drafts, and $6,592,337 of clearing-house certificates. The gold coin equaled 1.38 per cent. of the total receipts; the silver coin 0.17 of one per cent.; the paper money 4.36 per cent., and the checks and drafts 91.85 per cent., while the checks, drafts and clearing-house certificates, together, were equal to 94.09 per cent. of the whole. On September 17, therefore, the total percentage of cash was 5.91 per cent. only.

TOTAL RECEIPTS OF MONEY AND CHECKS BY THE BANKS IN NEW YORK CITY AND IN FIFTEEN OTHER PRINCIPAL CITIES, AND BY THE REMAINING BANKS.

The receipts of the forty-eight national banks in New York City, on June 30, were 167 millions ($167,437,759), of which less than one-half million ($460,993.67) was in gold coin, $15,996.95 in silver coin, and $1,706,604.06 in paper money; the remaining 165 millions ($165,254,164) being in checks and drafts, including nearly four millions ($3,835,500) of clearing-house certificates.

The banks in New York City, on September 17, reported receipts amounting to $165,193,347, of which $805,588 was in gold coin, $7,857 in silver coin, and $1,071,315 in paper money, the remainder, $163,-308,587, being in checks and drafts, including $3,792,000 of clearing-house certificates.

The receipts of the 187 banks in the fifteen reserve cities, exclusive of New York, on June 30, were seventy-seven millions ($77,100,705), of which $581,070 was in gold, $114,485 in silver, $3,631,710 in paper money, and seventy-two millions ($72,773,450) in checks and drafts, including $5,747,000 of gold clearing-house certificates.

On September 17 the receipts of 189 banks in fifteen reserve cities, exclusive of New York, were $77,922,246, of which $1,448,415 was in gold, $138,248 in silver, $4,486,045 in paper money, and $71,849,538 in checks and drafts, including $2,734,378 in clearing-house certificates.

The total receipts of the banks outside of the cities, 1,731 in number, on June 30, were forty millions ($40,175,542), of which $822,041 was in gold coin, $310,516 in silver coin, six millions ($6,216,433) in paper money, and nearly thirty-three millions ($32,826,552) in checks and drafts.

On September 17 these banks, 1,895 in number, received $52,118,185, of which $1,724,040 was in gold coin, $354,197 in silver coin, $7,469,210 in paper currency, and $42,570,738 in checks and drafts.

TOTAL RECEIPTS AND PROPORTIONS OF GOLD COIN, SILVER COIN, PAPER MONEY, AND CHECKS AND DRAFTS.

In the following tables are shown, both for June 30 and for September 17, the proportions of gold coin, silver coin, paper money, and checks and drafts, including clearing-house certificates, to the total receipts, in New York City, in the other reserve cities, and in banks elsewhere, separately, and also the same proportions for the United States:

JUNE 30, 1881.

Localities.	Number of banks.	Receipts.	Proportions.			
			Gold coin.	Silver coin.	Paper currency.	Checks, drafts, &c.
			Per cent	Per cent.	Per cent.	Per cent.
New York City	48	$167,437,759	0 27	0.01	1 02	98.70
Other reserve cities	187	77,100,715	0.76	0.15	4.71	94.38
Banks elsewhere	1,731	40,175,542	2.04	0.77	15.47	81.72
United States	1,966	284,714,016	0.65	0.16	4.06	95.13

SEPTEMBER 17, 1881.

New York City	48	$165,193,347	0.54	0.01	0.65	98.80
Other reserve cities	189	77,922,247	1.86	0.18	5.61	92.35
Banks elsewhere	1,895	52,118,185	3.31	0.08	14.27	81.74
United States	2,132	295,233,779	1.38	0.17	4.36	94.09

On June 30 the proportion of gold coin to the whole receipts in New York City was 0.27 of one per cent.; of silver coin, 0.01 of one per cent.; of paper money, 1.02 per cent.; and of checks and drafts, including clearing-house certificates, 98.7 per cent.

The percentage of gold coin received in the fifteen other cities was 0.76; of silver coin, 0.15; of paper currency, 4.71; and of checks and drafts, 94.38. The percentage of gold coin received by the banks not included in these cities was 2.05; of silver coin, 0.77; of paper currency, 15.47; and of checks and drafts, 81.71.

Taking all the banks together, the relative proportion of gold coin received was 0.65, of silver coin 0.16, of paper currency 4.06, and of checks and drafts 95.13 per cent.

On September 17 the proportion of gold coin to the whole receipts in New York City was 0.545 of one per cent., and of silver coin, 0.005 of one per cent.; of paper money, 0.65 of one per cent., and of checks and drafts, including clearing-house certificates, 98.8 per cent.

The percentage of gold coin received in 15 other cities was 1.86; of silver coin, 0.18; of paper currency, 5.61; and of checks and drafts, 92.35. The percentage of gold coin by the remaining banks in the country was 3.31; of silver coin, 0.68; of paper currency, 14.27; and of checks and drafts, 81.74. The receipts of the 2,132 banks together show a relative proportion of gold coin, 1.38; of silver coin, 0.17; of paper currency, 4.36; and of checks and drafts, 94.09.

CHECKS AND DRAFTS IN THE PRINCIPAL CITIES.

The following table shows, for June 30 and September 17, the number of banks, the total receipts, and the ratio to such total of the checks and drafts received, in New York City and in fifteen of the other principal cities:

Cities.	June 30, 1881.			September 17, 1881.		
	No. of banks.	Receipts.	Proportion of checks, drafts, &c.	No. of banks.	Receipts.	Proportion of checks, drafts, &c.
			Per cent.			*Per cent.*
New York City	48	$167, 437, 759	98. 7	48	$165, 193, 347	98. 8
Boston.......................	54	33, 088, 080	96. 5	54	24, 094, 061	93. 7
Albany	7	1, 417, 704	93. 8	7	1, 480, 315	96. 5
Philadelphia.......	32	18, 061, 565	96. 0	32	17, 880, 648	96. 4
Pittsburgh	22	2, 149, 067	90. 4	22	3, 126, 749	86. 2
Baltimore	16	3, 875, 253	92. 9	16	4, 425, 113	92. 9
Washington	5	206, 601	60. 0	5	226, 783	45. 8
New Orleans................	7	1, 206, 759	89. 8	7	1, 620, 771	80. 2
Louisville	8	712, 330	92. 8	8	775, 804	83. 4
Cincinnati	8	2, 965, 355	88. 0	10	3, 876, 785	90. 0
Cleveland...................	6	1, 751, 037	94. 0	6	2, 618, 064	95. 1
Chicago.....................	9	8, 141, 189	92. 0	9	13, 026, 835	90. 8
Detroit	4	806, 211	87. 5	4	1, 219, 481	93. 5
Milwaukee	3	417, 244	88. 3	3	670, 172	94. 9
Saint Louis	5	1, 940, 053	82. 3	5	2, 627, 045	81. 5
San Francisco	1	332, 265	91. 8	1	298, 121	77. 4
Total, excluding New York City	187	77, 100, 715	94. 4	189	77, 922, 247	92. 3
Total, including New York City	235	244, 538, 474	97. 3	237	243, 115, 594	96. 7
Banks elsewhere.....	1, 731	40, 175, 542	81. 7	1, 895	52, 118, 185	81. 7
United States........	1, 966	284, 714, 016	95. 1	2, 132	295, 233, 779	94. 1

The table below exhibits the total receipts, on June 30 and September 17, of the 48 banks in New York City, the 54 in Boston, the 32 in Philadelphia, and the 9 in Chicago, and the proportion which the receipts in each city, and the aggregate of all of them, bear to the receipts of all the banks in the United States on the same dates. It also shows the receipts, and proportion to the whole, of the banks in twelve other cities, and the same as to the remaining banks of the country:

Banks in four principal cities, and elsewhere.	June 30, 1881.			September 17, 1881.		
	Number of banks.	Amount.	Per centage to total receipts.	Number of banks.	Amount.	Percentage to total receipts.
New York City	48	$167,427,759	58.81	48	$165,193,347	55.95
Boston	54	33,088,080	11.62	54	24,004,061	8.16
Philadelphia	32	18,061,565	6.34	32	17,830,648	6.04
Chicago	9	8,141,189	2.86	9	13,026,835	4.41
Totals...............	143	226,728,593	79.63	143	220,144,891	74.56
Twelve other cities	92	17,809,881	6.26	94	22,970,703	7.78
Totals of cities.......	235	244,538,474	85.89	237	243,115,594	82.34
All other banks	1,731	40,175,542	14.11	1,895	52,118,185	17.66
United States	1,966	284,714,016	100	2,132	295,233,779	100

From an examination of this table it will be seen that the receipts of the 48 banks in New York City on June 30 were nearly three-fifths (58.81 per cent.) of the whole, and on September 17 about 56 per cent. This fact shows how closely connected is the business of all the national banks with the great commercial center of the country, nearly every bank and banker in the Union having deposits, subject to sight-drafts, at that point. The receipts of the Boston banks on June 30 were nearly 12 per cent. of the whole, and were 8 per cent. on September 17; while those of Philadelphia were about 6 per cent. at the latter date, and of the banks in Chicago about 4.5 per cent. The receipts in these four great cities comprised nearly four-fifths of the total receipts on June 30, and nearly three-fourths of the total on September 17; while the receipts of the sixteen reserve cities on June 30 were more than 85 per cent., and on September 17 more than 82 per cent., of the whole amount. The receipts of 1,731 banks located in the districts outside of these cities on June 30 were but 14.11 per cent., and of the 1,895 banks on September 17 but 17.66 per cent., of the whole.

TOTAL RECEIPTS AND PROPORTIONS OF CHECKS AND DRAFTS IN STATES AND TERRITORIES.

The table next given shows, for the same dates, the receipts of the banks in each State and Territory, exclusive of those located in the cities named in the previous table, with similar percentages. Attention is called to the remarkable coincidence shown in this table, in the percentage of checks and drafts for the two dates named, it being 81.7 per cent. in each instance. The percentages of the cities for the same dates, as given in the next preceding table, also correspond very nearly, the small difference between them being principally due to the change in the city of Boston from 96.5, on June 30, to 93.7 per cent.

on September 17. The slight variation in the average ratios for the two dates is evidence of the general accuracy of the returns:

States and Territories.	June 30, 1881.			September 17, 1881.		
	No. of banks.	Receipts.	Proportion of checks, drafts, &c.	No. of banks.	Receipts.	Proportion of checks drafts, &c.
			Per cent.			Per cent.
Maine	67	$1,167,284	82.3	69	$1,016,012	79.8
New Hampshire	45	509,594	75.3	47	500,315	75.7
Vermont	41	405,256	79.2	47	407,423	74.3
Massachusetts	182	4,346,968	83.5	190	4,047,688	81.8
Rhode Island	58	1,235,886	87.9	62	1,486,144	90.5
Connecticut	79	2,532,108	87.4	85	3,536,106	88.1
New York	226	5,059,233	83.1	243	5,634,586	83.2
New Jersey	62	3,907,471	92.0	67	4,412,620	91.0
Pennsylvania	179	3,934,436	84.8	191	5,718,088	84.9
Delaware	14	318,628	86.3	14	381,077	89.0
Maryland	20	278,008	83.7	23	252,470	77.8
District of Columbia	1	27,983	64.0	1	44,699	76.4
Virginia	18	1,518,480	89.5	18	1,439,571	87.2
West Virginia	16	112,415	65.0	17	180,627	72.4
North Carolina	12	344,720	83.0	15	391,965	78.3
South Carolina	9	395,441	85.9	13	728,573	80.4
Georgia	11	281,995	69.5	12	738,926	77.3
Florida	2	23,026	23.7	2	40,739	77.8
Alabama	8	100,177	72.0	9	293,226	85.7
Texas	14	292,786	67.8	15	832,923	76.8
Arkansas	2	53,220	66.2	2	51,183	76.7
Kentucky	37	446,275	76.7	42	688,190	87.0
Tennessee	21	702,408	63.0	25	893,058	73.8
Ohio	142	2,825,066	80.0	161	3,150,787	78.1
Indiana	80	1,321,819	74.6	93	2,092,531	72.7
Illinois	120	1,411,907	70.6	130	3,832,447	80.0
Michigan	70	968,890	73.5	76	1,423,241	77.1
Wisconsin	30	543,935	80.8	31	545,019	64.3
Iowa	68	975,956	68.2	76	1,552,481	71.4
Minnesota	25	1,227,770	80.8	27	1,784,146	78.1
Missouri	13	163,481	67.3	17	566,861	82.3
Kansas	10	421,744	78.1	13	395,885	65.6
Nebraska	11	511,723	76.0	13	815,481	80.1
Colorado	13	1,185,387	81.1	17	1,533,504	85.1
Nevada	1	6,543	53.8	1	7,550	8.2
California	8	235,384	48.2	10	260,637	52.5
Oregon	1	165,420	71.8	1	174,526	72.6
Dakota	5	48,474	68.6	8	257,442	64.3
Idaho				1	17,921	51.2
Montana	2	19,662	88.6	3	75,716	58.1
New Mexico	4	117,306	83.5	4	119,972	79.8
Utah	1	92,969	49.8	1	112,764	80.5
Washington	1	15,526	37.4	2	38,242	30.0
Wyoming	2	6,782	33.6	3	144,796	87.8
Totals	1,731	40,175,542	81.7	1,895	52,118,185	81.7

PROPORTION OF RECEIPTS WHICH REPRESENT LEGITIMATE BUSINESS.

If all of these receipts represented legitimate business, the means for merchandising and for manufacturing would be most abundant. It would be an interesting subject for investigation to determine what proportion of the checks received by the banks in New York City, on any given day, represent operations at the Stock Exchange, and what proportions of these operations represent legitimate and what speculative transactions. In taking as a basis for such an estimate the posted sales of the Stock Exchange, a difficulty arises from the fact that these sales on any one day do not by any means include all the transactions at the board. In the opinion of the most experienced brokers, not more than one-third of the purchases and sales are recorded in the printed list. Even in the case of those recorded, the number of shares bought or sold, assumedly at par, is not an indication of the money value of the transactions as they appear in the bank clearings, on account of the different par value of the various shares dealt in. The par is usually one hundred dollars per share, but the average price of sales would not probably exceed sixty dollars per share.

The checks received by the banks in New York City, including both State and National, on the 30th of June, 1881, and which were cleared on the following day, amounted to 141 millions. Of this amount, 113 millions were cleared by twenty-three banks, all of which have relations to a greater or less extent with brokers. From an examination of the clearings of each of these twenty-three banks, it was found that the total of certified checks on that day amounted to about 80 millions, of which it is probable that at least 90 per cent., or 72 millions, represented stock transactions. About ten per cent. of this amount should be allowed for the daily payment and reborrowing of loans by brokers, which is accomplished by means of certified checks. It is therefore estimated by those who are conversant with these subjects, that of the 141 millions of exchanges, about 65 millions represent stock exchange transactions.

There are really no data upon which a conclusion can be obtained as to what proportion of these large stock transactions are speculative, and what legitimate, or for investment. It is estimated, however, by those who have had long experience in the business, that not more than five per cent. of all purchases and sales at the stock board are for investment account. Assuming that these estimates are reasonable, it would follow that about 60 millions of the 141 millions of clearings upon June 30, or about three-sevenths of the whole, represent the speculative transactions of the stock board, and that 81 millions, or four-sevenths, represent legitimate business transactions.

PROPORTION OF CHECKS WHICH PASS THROUGH THE CLEARING HOUSE.

The checks, drafts and certificates received by the national banks in New York City on June 30 amounted, as has been seen, to $165,233,164. The gold clearing-house certificates amounted to $3,814,500, which were received by the banks in payment of balances due them on the morning of June 30. The remainder consisted of checks and drafts alone. The clearing-house statement shows that on the morning of July 1 $126,937,110 of the before-mentioned checks and drafts were paid through the clearing-house. The remaining $34,381,554, which did not pass through the clearing-house, consisted probably of checks, which had been used in payments made by one depositor to another, in the same bank, and were consequently settled by simple transfers of accounts on the books of such banks. On Saturday, September 17, the total amount received by the banks in checks, drafts, and certificates was $163,208,586; of which $3,792,000 were in gold clearing-house certificates, received by the banks in payment of the balances due them at the clearing-house on the same day, leaving $159,416,586 of checks and drafts received. Of this latter sum, $139,881,760 consisted of checks, &c., which were paid through the clearing-house on the morning of Monday, September 19 (the next business day), by the same banks, as shown by the clearing-house statements of that day. Of the checks and drafts received by the national banks of New York City on September 17, about 20 millions were settled without passing through the clearing-house; and, as was remarked in reference to similar checks and drafts shown by the statement of June 30, they were probably settled by transfers of accounts on the books of the banks on which they were drawn.

It was about eighty years after the first issue of promissory notes by the Bank of England that the London clearing-house was established, and the organization of the New York clearing-house dates eighty years still later, in 1853; so that it may be said that the clearing arrangement now in use in this country, and so familiar to all bankers, has been in operation but twenty-eight years. The assistant treasurer in New York has been a member of the clearing-house but three years, and the large payments to the clearing-house banks, averaging two and a quarter tons of gold coin daily during the past year, which would be about thirty-six tons daily if paid in silver, are transferred in bags, or upon drays from the Treasury to the banks. If these balances could be paid in gold certificates instead of coin, the system of bank machinery in New York would be complete.

Checks, certificates of deposit, and drafts, or bills of exchange, which are now used so largely as substitutes for money, are the most important and useful parts of the machinery of the bank. The issue of circulating notes is not an essential feature of banking, for there are many banks in this country, chiefly incorporated under State laws, which do not issue such notes. But checks and drafts are almost as indispensable to the successful conduct of the business of banking as capital or deposits.

USE OF CHECKS IN FRANCE, ENGLAND, SCOTLAND, AND IRELAND, AND IN THE UNITED STATES.

In England, banks and bankers are numerous, and large numbers of such instruments of exchange are used, particularly in the principal cities. In France, on the other hand, their use is much more infrequent, for except the Bank of France, with its 90 branches, there are no incorporated banks in that country, and thirteen of these branches were conducted in 1880 at a loss of more than $30,000.

Victor Bonnet, a well-known French writer, says:

The use of deposits, bank accounts, and checks is still in its infancy in this country. They are very little used, even in the great cities, while in the rest of France they are completely unknown. It is, however, to be hoped that they will be more employed hereafter, and that here, as in England and the United States, payments will be more generally made through the medium of bankers, and by transfers in accounts current. If this should be the case, we shall economize both in the use of specie and of bank notes; for it is to be observed that the use of bank notes does not reach its fullest development, except in countries where the keeping of bank accounts is unusual, as is evident by comparing France in this respect with England. M. Pinard, manager of the Comptoir d'Escompte, testified before the commission of inquiry, that the greatest efforts had been made by that institution to induce French merchants and shopkeepers to adopt English habits in respect to the use of checks and the keeping of bank accounts, but in vain; their prejudices were invincible; it was no use reasoning with them, they would not do it, because they would not.

It would seem, however, from the following extract from the report of the Bank of France for 1880, that an effort is being made to overcome this prejudice:

Since the end of the operations of 1879, we have endeavored to give new advantages to those who had current accounts with us, and we have granted them facilities for transfer from one place to another, free of cost, for all sums proceeding from discount operations, or the encashment of documents on demand. We have desired to proceed further with this plan, and we have just completed this first arrangement by giving to all those who had current accounts with us, without exception, the means of disposing by open cheques of the whole of the sums which stand to their credit. These cheques, which are subject to a commission when they represent a simple deposit of funds, will, on the contrary, be delivered gratuitously when they are drawn against the proceeds of discounts or drafts on demand encashed by the bank, and they will be made payable in all our establishments indifferently. The cheques will thus become a powerful and very convenient means of exchange, which will simplify all transactions, and which will probably reduce, in considerable proportion, the need for the note circulation. In addition to this we have authorized the use of cheques within the town itself for the withdrawal of funds which do not require the displacement of capital. We are certain that when the use of cheques is thoroughly understood it will be of great service to commerce.

There are now in this country 6,796 banks and bankers located in all its principal cities and villages, and the number of checks and drafts in daily use by our own people is consequently larger, in fact, far greater, than anywhere else in the world. In some countries a charge is made to the depositor for keeping his account. In others, bank accounts are refused unless the depositor comes well introduced and it is believed that his account will be of considerable pecuniary benefit to the bank. In this country the bank is in many instances a convenience to the depositor, rather than the depositor of benefit to the bank; for the latter keeps the cash account of the depositor, and pays out amounts upon his order, and at his request returns to him his checks properly indorsed, which are then held by the depositor as vouchers or receipts for the payment of his debts.

It is evident that the amount of coin and paper currency used in any country depends largely upon the number of banks and bankers it contains, and upon the method of doing business; and no theory is more absurd than that which has been so frequently urged during the currency discussions of the past few years, that the amount of money required is in proportion to population. Tables showing the per capita of coin and currency in use in any country are curious and interesting, but almost valueless in determining the amount of paper money required. Through the machinery of the bank, with its system of checks, bills of exchange and clearing-houses, large amounts of business may be settled without the use of coin or circulating notes. Coin and currency are but the small change used in trade. Checks and drafts are substitutes for money, and in every case, if these were not used, the latter would be required. Yet, notwithstanding the almost exclusive use of these substitutes for money in large business transactions, all payments, great and small, depend for their integrity upon a true measure of value, and that measure is a piece of gold coin of standard weight and fineness. All other coins, not subsidiary and intrinsically worth less than the general standard recognized at commercial centers, and all kinds of paper money which are not immediately redeemable in gold coin, are not only not needed, but are worse than useless, for they disturb values.

The London Bankers' Magazine for November, which has just been eceived, contains an abstract of a paper recently read by Mr. Pownall before the London Bankers' Institute, from which the following table has been compiled. The percentages of the receipts in the city of New York on September 17 have also been added to the table:

Localities.	Coin.	Notes.	Checks.
	Per cent.	Per cent.	Per cent.
New York	.55	.65	98.80
London	.73	2.04	97.23
Edinburgh	.55	12.67	86.78
Dublin	1.57	8.53	89.90
Country banks in 261 places	15.20	11.94	72.86

It will be seen that the proportion of checks and drafts used in London does not vary greatly from that of the same items shown in the receipts of the banks in New York City. The proportions used in the banking business of the country districts is less, as in the United States it is less in the banks outside the cities; but the use of checks and drafts in the country districts in the United States is nearly nine per cent. greater han in the corresponding districts in England.

Through the courtesy of Mr. E. Dayrell Reed, secretary of the Institute of Bankers, London, the Comptroller acknowledges the receipt of a "rough proof" of an important paper read by Mr. George H. Pownall before the Institute, on October 19 last, on "The proportional use of credit documents and metallic money in English banks," and regrets that it was received too late for use in the preparation of this part of the report. The paper is elaborate, and gives, in addition to the table already quoted, many others; among which are tables showing the proportion of gold coin, silver coin, bank notes and checks used by banks located in agricultural places, in the metropolitan area, and in the cotton, woolen, iron, pottery, and silk manufacturing districts.   The entire paper will greatly interest the economic student; but under the circumstances the Comptroller is compelled to content himself with the following extracts:

There is a certain grim satire in these figures, when one thinks of the libraries filled with blue books full of weighty arguments, all curiously wrought out, to help in the settlement of the great note question.   It is clear that the cheque and the clearing system are the main lines upon which banking is destined to run.   Dead theories respecting notes and the right of issue belong to the generation to which they were living verities.   To us the living fact is the substitution of a new instrument of credit. For the present generation the improvement of the cheque and the clearing system, the mechanical details of office organization, those details of bookkeeping which save time, are, from the enormous number of documents passing through the hands of bankers, of more weight than the most learned treatise on notes and note makers.

Banking statistics, gathered with due patience, would play a great part in industrial statistics.   They represent trading totals, they rise and fall with prices, they expand with commercial prosperity, they contract in the day of bad trade.   Systematically collected, they would furnish constant lessons.   From no other source could we gain so much and so valuable information as to trading currents as from bankers. In their books the trading world is photographed.   It has been calculated that 97 per cent. of the transactions of British wholesale commerce pass through the hands of the bankers of the United Kingdom.   The sources of that commerce and its distribution must in the broadest way be marked in the totals of the banking world.   The cottons of Lancashire, the woolens of Yorkshire, the shipping of Liverpool, the commerce and finance of London, are all represented there.

The tendency of this generation is to seek to place its theories upon an exact basis. How much would the social and trading life of England be illustrated if we could mark out, though only at intervals, or even for a single day, the magnitude of our great industries as they are represented in the books of bankers.

The conversion of the mode of settlement of claims from payment by coin and notes into payment by cheque and clearing is not merely a local, or even a national, movement.   The American statistics, so opportunely published, demonstrate the wide-reaching influence of the causes working in that direction.

Wherever the English race has planted itself and founded a community, there the tendency towards a common financial organization has shown itself.   We see this at home, we see this in America, it is repeated in Australia.   There is, therefore, in despite of much diversity, much that is common to all these systems.

In the Appendix will be found tables giving the amounts and ratios of gold and silver coin and paper money, as well as that of checks and drafts, in each of the cities, States, and Territories of the Union.

TRANSACTIONS OF THE NEW YORK CLEARING HOUSE.

The New York Clearing House Association is composed of forty-five national and twelve State banks, and the assistant treasurer of the United States at New York.

Through the courtesy of Mr. W. A. Camp, its manager, a statement of the transactions during the year ending October 1, 1881, has been obtained, which shows that the total exchanges were more than $48,000,000,000, while the balances paid in money were less than $1,800,000,000.   The daily average balances paid were nearly $6,000,000, or about 3.5 per cent. of the amount of the settlements.   The balances paid in money during the year consisted of $1,394,966,000 in clearing house certificates of the Bank of America, legal-tenders amounting to over $8,633,161, and $372,419,000 in gold coin, weighing 686¼ tons.   If,

9 Ab

iustead of gold coin, silver had been used, the weight would have been nearly 11,000 tons. The largest transactions for any one day were on the 28th of November, and amounted to $295,821,422.37. The total transactions for the year exceed that of any previous year, by $11,643,-269,121.43. The following table shows the yearly transactions of the New York clearing house for the twenty-eight years since its organization in 1853, and the amounts and ratios of currency required for the payment of daily balances:

Years.	No. of banks.	*Capital.	Exchanges.	Balances paid in money.	Average daily exchanges.	Average daily balances paid in mony.	Ratios.
							Pr. ct.
1854	50	$47,044,900	$5,750,455,987	$297,411,494	$19,104,505	$988,078	5.2
1855	48	48,884,180	5,362,912,098	289,694,137	17,412,052	940,566	5.4
1856	50	52,883,700	6,906,213,328	334,714,489	22,278,108	1,079,734	4.8
1857	50	64,420,200	8,333,226,718	365,313,902	26,968,371	1,182,246	4.4
1858	46	67,146,018	4,756,664,386	314,238,911	15,393,736	1,016,954	6.6
1859	47	67,921,714	6,448,005,956	363,984,683	20,867,833	1,177,944	5.6
1860	50	69,907,435	7,231,143,057	380,693,438	23,401,757	1,232,018	5.3
1861 ..×.....	50	68,900,605	5,915,742,758	353,383,944	19,269,520	1,151,088	6.0
1862	50	68,375,820	6,871,443,591	415,530,331	22,237,682	1,344,758	6.0
1863	50	68,972,508	14,867,597,849	677,626,483	48,428,658	2,207,252	4.6
1864	49	68,546,763	24,097,196,656	885,719,205	77,984,455	2,866,405	3.7
1865	55	80,363,013	26,032,384,342	1,035,765,108	84,796,040	3,373,828	4.0
1866	58	82,370,200	28,717,146,914	1,066,135,106	93,541,195	3,472,753	3.7
1867	58	81,770,200	28,675,159,472	1,144,963,451	93,501,167	3,717,414	4.0
1868	59	82,270,200	28,484,288,637	1,125,455,237	92,182,164	3,642,250	4.0
1869	59	82,720,200	37,407,028,987	1,120,318,308	121,451,393	3,637,397	3.0
1870	61	83,620,200	27,804,539,406	1,036,484,822	90,274,479	3,365,210	3.7
1871	62	84,420,200	29,300,986,682	1,209,721,029	95,133,074	3,927,666	4.1
1872	61	84,420,200	32,636,997,404	1,213,293,827	105,964,277	3,939,266	3.7
1873	59	83,370,200	33,972,773,943	1,152,372,108	111,022,137	3,765,922	3.4
1874	59	81,635,200	20,850,681,063	971,231,281	68,139,484	3,173,958	4.7
1875	59	80,435,200	23,042,276,858	1,104,346,845	75,301,558	3,608,977	4.8
1876	59	81,781,200	19,874,815,361	1,009,532,037	64,738,812	3,298,361	5.1
1877	58	71,045,200	20,876,555,937	1,015,256,483	68,447,724	3,328,710	4.9
1878	57	63,611,500	19,922,733,947	951,970,454	65,106,074	3,111,015	4.8
1879	59	60,890,200	24,558,196,689	1,321,119,298	79,977,839	4,303,320	5.4
1880	57	60,475,200	37,182,128,021	1,516,538,631	121,510,224	4,956,009	4.1
1881	60	61,162,700	48,565,818,212	1,776,018,162	165,055,201	5,821,010	3.5
....		†71,403,743	‡584,440,115,759	‡24,448,833,204	68,181,783	†2,843,647	4.2

The total amount of transactions for the twenty-eight years given in the table is $584,440,115,759, and the annual average is $20,872,861,277.

The clearing-house transactions of the assistant treasurer of the United States at New York, for the year ending November 1, 1881, were as follows:

Exchanges received from clearing-house $358,193,774
Exchanges delivered to clearing-house 92,748,620

Balances paid to clearing-house... 270,966,495
Balances received from clearing-house 5,521,341

Showing that the amount paid by the assistant treasurer to the clearing-house was in excess of the amount received by him 265,445,154

A table compiled from statements made by the New York clearing-house, giving the clearings and balances weekly for the months of September, October, and November, of the year from 1872 to 1880, will be found in the appendix, and may be valuable for purposes of comparison.

DISTRIBUTION OF COIN AND PAPER CURRENCY.

The reports for 1879 and 1880 gave valuable tables of the amount of coin and paper money in the country on January 1, 1879 (the date of resumption), and on November 1 in 1879 and 1880.

---

* The capital is for various dates, the amount at a uniform date in each year not being obtainable.

† Yearly averages for twenty-eight years.   ‡ Totals for twenty-eight years.

The imports of gold in excess of exports, from the date of resumption to November 1, 1881, have been $197,434,114, and the estimated gold production of the mines is $104,150,000. The amount received from these two sources during the year ending November 1, 1881, has been $114,749,390.

The stock of standard silver dollars is also increasing at the rate of about two millions three hundred thousand monthly, the amount coined during the year having been $27,824,955. Tables are again given herewith showing the amount of coin and currency in the country on January 1, 1879, and on November 1, 1879, 1880 and 1881:

	January 1, 1879.	November 1, 1879.	November 1, 1880.	November 1, 1881.
Gold coin*	$278,310,126	$355,681,532	$453,882,692	$562,568,971
Silver coin*	106,572,908	126,009,537	156,320,911	186,037,365
Legal-tender notes	346,681,016	346,681,016	346,681,016	346,681,016
National bank notes	323,791,674	337,181,418	343,524,107	360,344,250
Totals	1,055,356,619	1,165,553,503	1,302,718,726	1,455,631,602

The amount of legal-tender notes has remained the same since May 31, 1878, in accordance with law. The increase of national-bank notes during the year ending November 1 last was $16,510,143. This, together with the increase of the gold coin, $108,686,279, and of silver coin, $27,716,454, makes a total increase of coin and bank notes of $152,912,876. The statement below gives the amount of coin and currency in the Treasury at the same dates as in the previous tables, and the amount in the national banks on the dates of their returns nearest thereto—viz, January 1 and October 2, 1879, and October 1, 1880 and 1881, respectively. The amounts given for the State banks, trust companies and savings banks, are for the nearest comparative dates of their official reports:

	January 1, 1879.	November 1, 1879	November 1, 1880.	November 1, 1881.
GOLD.				
In the Treasury, less certificates	$112,703,342	$156,907,986	$133,679,349	$167,781,909
In national banks, including certificates	35,039,201	37,187,238	102,851,032	107,222,169
In State banks, including certificates	10,937,812	12,171,292	17,102,130	19,901,491
Total gold	158,680,355	206,266,516	253,632,511	294,905,569
SILVER.				
In the Treasury, standard silver dollars	17,249,740	32,115,073	47,156,588	66,576,378
In the Treasury, bullion	9,121,417	3,824,631	6,185,000	3,424,575
In the Treasury, fractional coin	6,048,194	17,854,327	24,645,561	25,944,687
In national banks	6,460,557	4,986,492	6,495,477	7,112,567
Total silver	38,879,908	58,780,823	84,172,626	103,098,207
CURRENCY.				
In the Treasury, less certificates	44,425,655	21,711,376	18,221,826	22,774,830
In national banks, including certificates	126,491,720	118,546,369	86,439,925	77,630,917
In State banks, including certificates	25,944,485	25,555,280	25,828,794	27,391,317
In savings banks	14,513,779	15,880,921	17,072,680	11,782,243
Total currency	211,375,639	181,693,946	147,563,225	139,579,307
Grand totals	408,935,902	446,741,285	485,668,362	537,583,083

*Estimate of Director of the Mint, which includes bullion in process of coinage.

If the amount of coin and currency in the Treasury and in the banks be deducted from the total amount estimated to be in the country, the remainder will be the amount then in the hands of the people outside of these depositories, as follows:

	January 1, 1879.	November 1, 1879.	November 1, 1880.	November 1, 1881.
Gold	$119,629,771	$149,415,016	$200,250,181	$267,663,462
Silver	67,693,895	67,228,714	73,848,285	82,939,158
Currency	459,097,051	502,168,488	542,951,898	567,445,950
Totals	646,420,717	718,812,218	817,050,364	918,048,519

The gold in the Treasury, including bullion in process of coinage, has increased during the year $34,102,560, and in the banks $7,170,498. The paper currency in the Treasury has increased $4,553,004, and in the banks it has decreased $13,727,914. The increase of gold, outside of the Treasury and the banks, is $67,413,221, and of paper currency $241,494,061.

In the foregoing tables the silver certificates issued by the Treasury have not been included, but the standard silver dollars kept to redeem them on presentation form a portion of the silver coin in the Treasury. The silver certificates in the hands of the people and the banks, at dates corresponding with those given in the preceding tables, were as follows:

January 1, 1879.   November 1, 1879.   November 1, 1880.   November 1, 1881.
$413,360. $1,604,370. $19,780,240. $58,838,770.

It will be seen that the amount of these certificates in circulation has increased $39,058,530 during the past year. Of the $58,838,770 circulating on November 1, 1881, a large portion are constantly in the hands of the people, being paid out by the banks in preference to gold coin or legal-tender notes.

The total amount of silver dollars coined up to November 1, 1881, was $100,672,705, of which, as stated in one of the foregoing tables, $66,576,378 was then in the Treasury, although an amount equal to $58,838,769 was represented by certificates in the hands of the people and the banks, leaving only $7,737,609 actually belonging to the Treasury. Of the $100,672,705 coined, $34,096,327 were therefore circulating in the form of coin and $58,838,769 in the form of certificates. The remainder of the silver, $85,364,660, is in subsidiary and trade dollars and bullion, of which $29,409,262 is in the Treasury, and $55,955,398 is in use in place of the previous fractional paper currency, which, on March 23, 1874, was at its highest point, and amounted to $49,566,760. The increase since the date of resumption of gold and silver coin and paper currency outside of the Treasury and the banks, is thus estimated to be $271,627,802, and the increase during the year ending November 1, $100,998,254. Or, if the amount of silver certificates in circulation be added, the total increase in the circulating medium since resumption would be $330,053,217, and during the past year, $140,056,782.

AMOUNT OF INTEREST-BEARING FUNDED DEBT OF THE UNITED STATES AND THE AMOUNT HELD BY THE NATIONAL BANKS.

The report for 1880 contained tables exhibiting a classification of the interest-bearing bonded debt of the United States, and of the bonds held by the national banks, for a series of years. These tables are again presented, and now exhibit also the amount of the outstanding bonds of the government, and the amount held by the banks, on November 1 the present year.

The operations of the Secretary of the Treasury, in continuing the 5 and 6 per cent. bonds which matured during the year 1881, give them increasing interest. On March 1, 1881, 5 per cent. bonds amounting to $469,320,650 were outstanding, redeemable at the option of the government after May 1, 1881, and 6 per cent. bonds amounting to $202,266,550 were then outstanding similarly redeemable after July 1, 1881. The refunding bill, authorizing the sale of 3 per cent. bonds, with the proceeds of which, if sold, the maturing bonds would have been paid, did not receive the signature of the President, and failed to become a law. On April 11, the whole amount of 6 per cent. bonds were called for payment on July 1, 1881; but to the holders of all the 6 per cent. loans (except the Oregon war debt, amounting to $688,200) permission was given to have their bonds continued, at the pleasure of the government, with interest at 3½ per cent. per annum, provided they should so request and the bonds should be received by the Treasury for that purpose on or before May 10, 1881, which time was afterwards extended to May 20. Of these bonds there were presented for continuance the amount of $178,055,150, and the remainder, amounting to $24,211,400, has, since March 1, 1881, been either paid from the surplus revenues or has ceased to bear interest.

On May 12, a like privilege (for continuance at 3½ per cent.) was given to the holders of the five per cent. bonds, if presented on or before July 1, 1881; and on the latter date notice was given for the payment on October 1, 1881, of the registered fives not continued. The total amount of five per cent. bonds continued under this arrangement was $401,504,900, and of 6 per cent. bonds $178,055,150. The remaining 5 and 6 per cent. bonds outstanding March 1, 1881, amounting to $92,027,150, were paid upon presentation, or now remain outstanding without interest. There has also been paid during the year ending November 1, $123,969,650 of interest-bearing bonds, making a saving in interest of $6,352,240. The total interest saved during the year, by continuance and payment of the bonds, was $16,826,192.

The following table exhibits the classification of the unmatured, interest-bearing, bonded debt of the United States* on August 31, 1865, when the public debt reached its maximum, and on the 1st day of July in each year thereafter, together with the amount outstanding on November 1 of the present year:

Date.	6 per cent. bonds.	5 per cent. bonds.	4½ per cent. bonds.	4 per cent. bonds.	Total.
August 31, 1865	$906,518,091	$199,792,100			$1,108,310,191
July 1, 1866	1,008,348,469	198,526,435			1,206,916,904
July 1, 1867	1,421,110,719	198,533,435			1,619,644,154
July 1, 1868	1,841,521,800	221,588,400			2,063,110,200
July 1, 1869	1,886,341,300	221,589,300			2,107,930,600
July 1, 1870	1,764,932,300	221,589,300			1,986,521,600
July 1, 1871	1,613,897,300	274,236,450			1,888,133,750
July 1, 1872	1,374,883,300	414,567,300			1,789,451,100
July 1, 1873	1,281,298,650	414,567,300			1,695,865,950
July 1, 1874	1,213,624,700	510,628,050			1,724,252,750
July 1, 1875	1,100,865,550	607,132,750			1,707,998,300
July 1, 1876	984,999,650	711,685,800			1,696,685,450
July 1, 1877	854,621,850	703,266,650	$140,000,000		1,696,888,500
July 1, 1878	738,819,000	703,206,650	240,000,000	$98,850,000	1,780,735,650
July 1, 1879	310,932,500	646,905,500	250,000,000	679,878,110	1,887,716,110
July 1, 1880	235,780,400	484,864,900	250,000,000	739,347,800	1,709,993,100
July 1, 1881	196,378,600	439,841,350	250,000,000	739,347,800	1,625,567,750
	Continued at 3½ per cent.	Continued at 3½ per cent.			
November 1, 1881	161,876,050	401,504,900	250,000,000	739,347,800	1,552,728,750

* The Navy pension fund, amounting to $14,000,000 in 3 per cents., the interest upon which is applied to the payment of naval pensions exclusively, is not included in the table.

These operations of the Secretary during the present year have largely reduced the amount of interest receivable by the national banks upon the bonds held by them.

During the year 1871, and previous thereto, a large portion of the bonds bore interest at the rate of 6 per cent.; and until the year 1877 all of the bonds bore interest at either five or six per cent. At the present time, more than 65 per cent. of the amount pledged for circulation consists of bonds bearing interest at the low rate of 3½ per cent., and nearly 35 per cent. of them bear interest at the rate of 4 and 4½ per cent. This will be seen from the following table, which exhibits the amounts and classes of United States bonds owned by the banks, including those pledged as security for circulation and for public deposits, on the first day of July in each year since 1865, and upon Novmeber 1 of the present year:

Date.	United States bonds held as security for circulation.					U. S. bonds held for other purposes at nearest date.	Grand total.
	6 per cent. bonds.	5 per cent. bonds.	4½ per cent. bonds.	4 per cent. bonds.	Total.		
July 1, 1865.....	$170, 382, 500	$65, 576, 600	....	....	$235, 959, 100	$155, 785, 750	$391, 744, 850
July 1, 1866.....	241, 083, 500	86, 226, 850	....	....	827, 310, 850	121, 152, 950	448, 463, 800
July 1, 1867.....	251, 430, 400	89, 177, 100	....	....	340, 607, 500	84, 002, 650	424, 610, 150
July 1, 1868.....	250, 726, 950	90, 768, 950	....	....	341, 495, 900	80, 922, 500	422, 418, 400
July 1, 1869.....	255, 190, 850	87, 661, 250	....	....	342, 851, 600	55, 102, 000	397, 953, 600
July 1, 1870.....	247, 355, 350	94, 923, 200	....	....	342, 278, 550	43, 980, 600	386, 259, 150
July 1, 1871.....	220, 497, 750	139, 947, 800	....	....	350, 885, 550	39, 450, 800	790, 336, 350
July 1, 1872.....	173, 251, 450	207, 189, 250	....	....	380, 440, 700	31, 868, 200	412, 308, 900
July 1, 1873.....	160, 923, 500	229, 487, 050	....	....	390, 410, 550	25, 724, 400	416, 134, 950
July 1, 1874.....	154, 370, 700	236, 800, 500	....	....	891, 171, 200	25, 347, 100	416, 518, 300
July 1, 1875.....	136, 955, 100	232, 359, 400	....	....	876, 314, 500	26, 900, 200	403, 214, 700
July 1, 1876.....	109, 313, 450	232, 081, 300	....	....	341, 394, 750	45, 170, 300	386, 565, 050
July 1, 1877.....	87, 690, 800	206, 651, 050	$44, 872, 250	....	338, 713, 600	47, 315, 050	886, 028, 650
July 1, 1878.....	82, 421, 200	199, 514, 550	48, 448, 650	$19, 162, 000	349, 546, 400	68, 850, 900	418, 397, 300
July 1, 1879.....	56, 042, 800	144, 616, 300	35, 196, 550	118, 538, 950	354, 254, 600	76, 603, 520	430, 858, 120
July 1, 1880.....	58, 056, 150	139, 758, 650	37, 760, 950	126, 076, 300	361, 652, 050	42, 831, 300	404, 483, 350
July 1, 1881.....	61, 901, 800 Continued at 3½ per cent.	500		98, 687, 700	360, 488, 400	63, 849, 950	424, 338, 350
	53, 741, 600	187, 634, 550 at 3½ per cent.					
Nov. 1, 1881.....	53, 741, 600	187, 634, 550	81, 961, 650	92, 005, 800	369, 608, 500	56, 512, 450	426, 120, 950

The banks also held $3,486,000 of Pacific Railroad 6 per cents., and $738,900 of 5 per cents., upon which interest had ceased, which latter amount has since been reduced to $229,000.

AMOUNT OF UNITED STATES BONDS HELD BY COMMERCIAL BANKS, .TRUST COMPANIES, AND SAVINGS BANKS ORGANIZED UNDER STATE LAWS.

The amount of United States bonds held by banks organized under State laws is ascertained from such reports as have been received by the Comptroller, through the courtesy of State officers who have responded to his request for copies of their official returns at the latest dates. From such returns it is found that these institutions held, at different dates during the year 1881, the following amount of United States bonds:

Held by State banks in twenty-one States............................... $12, 048, 452
Held by trust companies in five States.................................... 15, 631, 573
Held by savings banks in fifteen States 210, 845, 514

Total 238, 525, 539

The amount held by geographical divisions in 1880 and 1881 was as follows:

Geographical divisions.	1880.	1881.
Eastern States	$45, 230, 098	$40, 468, 340
Middle States	157, 563, 757	176, 873, 889
Southern States	958, 470	1, 078, 460
Western States	2, 672, 342	5, 736, 518
Pacific States	7, 240, 835	14, 874, 382
Totals	213, 665, 402	288, 525, 589

This amount is $3,201,340 less than that returned to the Commissioner of Internal Revenue, who receives semi-annual reports, for purposes of taxation, not only from banks organized under State laws, but also from private bankers, giving their average capital and deposits, and the amount of such capital invested in United States bonds. From these returns the following table has been compiled, showing, by geographical divisions, the average amount of capital invested in United States bonds for the six months ending May 31, in the years 1879, 1880, and 1881:

Geographical divisions.	Capital invested in United States bonds.		
	By State banks, private bankers, and trust companies.	By savings banks.	Total.
May 31, 1879:			
New England States	$3, 669, 967	34, 941, 378	38, 611, 345
Middle States	25, 686, 469	123, 818, 148	149, 504, 617
Southern States	3, 593, 179	86, 021	3, 679, 200
Western States	8, 326, 402	2, 164, 668	10, 491, 070
Pacific States and Territories	5, 015, 948	1, 372, 845	6, 388, 793
United States	46, 291, 965	162, 383, 060	208, 675, 025
May 31, 1880:			
New England States	3, 737, 093	37, 693, 200	41, 430, 293
Middle States	20, 564, 834	146, 301, 155	166, 865, 989
Southern States	2, 541, 991	1, 000	2, 542, 991
Western States	8, 137, 554	2, 474, 557	10, 612, 111
Pacific States and Territories	3, 883, 816	2, 717, 904	6, 601, 720
United States	38, 865, 288	189, 187, 816	228, 053, 104
May 31, 1881:			
New England States	2, 985, 496	36, 640, 795	39, 626, 291
Middle States	21, 908, 703	168, 617, 049	190, 525, 752
Southern States	1, 707, 702	21, 689	1, 729, 391
Western States	6, 714, 948	2, 689, 447	9, 404, 895
Pacific States and Territories	5, 004, 313	6, 911, 198	11, 915, 511
United States	38, 321, 162	214, 880, 178	253, 201, 340

The above table gives the average amount of capital invested in United States bonds, from which should be deducted the amount of premium paid at the time of purchase, which cannot be ascertained.
The amount of United States bonds held by the national banks on October 1, 1881, was $426,120,950, and the average amount held by the other banks and bankers of the country, during the six months ending May 31 last, was $253,201,340. The total amount held by all the banks and bankers during the last two years is thus shown to be considerably

more than one-third of the whole interest-bearing funded debt of the United States, as follows:

	1880.	1881.
National banks	$403,369,350	$426,120,950
Savings banks	189,187,816	214,880,178
State banks and trust companies	24,498,604	21,650,668
Private bankers	14,366,684	16,670,494
Totals	631,422,454	679,822,290

LOANS AND RATES OF INTEREST.

The following table gives the classification of the loans of the banks in the city of New York, in Boston, Philadelphia, and Baltimore, and in the other reserve cities, at corresponding dates in each of the last three years:

OCTOBER 2, 1879.

Classification.	New York City.	Boston, Philadelphia, and Baltimore.	Other reserve cities.	Country banks.	Aggregate.
	47 banks.	99 banks.	82 banks.	1,820 banks.	2,048 banks.
On U. S. bonds on demand	$8,286,525	$2,017,226	$4,360,523		$14,664,274
On other stocks, bonds, &c., on demand	78,062,085	22,605,795	11,445,079		112,112,959
On single-name paper without other security	22,491,926	13,136,911	7,150,239		42,779,076
All other loans	97,011,366	118,267,128	65,023,494	$435,154,810	705,456,798
Totals	195,851,902	156,027,060	87,979,335	435,154,810	875,613,107

OCTOBER 1, 1880.

Classification.	47 banks.	101 banks.	83 banks.	1,859 banks.	2,090 banks.
On U. S. bonds on demand	$3,915,077	$525,445	$1,378,168		$5,818,690
On other stocks, bonds, &c., on demand	92,630,962	30,838,692	16,558,260		140,027,934
On single-name paper without other security	27,755,152	22,542,776	10,402,295		60,700,223
All other loans	114,127,290	137,405,246	75,687,334	$503,294,724	830,514,594
Totals	238,428,501	191,312,159	104,026,057	503,294,724	1,037,061,441

OCTOBER 1, 1881.

Classification.	48 banks.	102 banks.	87 banks.	1,895 banks.	2,132 banks.
On U. S. bonds on demand	$2,589,928	$415,164	$468,496	$2,661,256	$6,084,844
On other stocks, bonds, &c., on demand	97,249,162	39,251,526	24,227,158	35,423,896	196,151,742
On single-name paper without other security	26,935,878	34,465,661	12,904,338	73,114,405	147,420,282
All other loans	120,032,691	137,682,302	96,806,506	464,843,937	819,365,436
Totals	246,757,659	211,814,653	134,406,498	576,043,494	1,169,022,304

7.3 per cent. less than at the corresponding dates in 1875, and 5.2 per cent. less than in 1877. The opportunities for using money in this group of banks are not in proportion to the increase of deposits, and their balances in other banks have by no means diminished.

It will surprise those whose attention has not heretofore been called to the subject to find how closely the means of the banks in the commercial cities have been employed during the last eleven years, notwithstanding the variations in rates of interest, and particularly during the last two years, when money has been so abundant and the deposits have so rapidly increased. It will be seen that prior to 1876, with the exception of a single year, the loans in New York exceeded the net deposits, while since that time, though there has been considerable variation, the net deposits have been somewhat in excess of the loans at the dates given. In the other principal cities, which continually keep large amounts of money in New York subject to demand, and thus diminish their own net deposits, as given in the above table, the loans have always largely exceeded their deposits. The same remark is true of the banks in the country districts which have in New York, as well as in other cities, large amounts of money on deposits subject to call. The capital of this class of banks is also much larger as compared with their deposits than is that of the banks in the large cities, and their loans therefore relatively greater.

The same comments apply with equal force to the ratios shown by the returns for October 1 of the present year, as may be seen from the following table:

Dates.	New York City.	Other reserve cities.	States and Territories.	United States.
	Per cent.	Per cent.	Per cent.	Per cent.
October 1, 1881	72.6	70.8	66.4	68.9
October 1, 1880	70.8	67.7	65.7	67.3
October 2, 1879	70.8	65.4	63.9	65.7

The ratios of cash to net deposits for the same dates were as follows:

Dates.	New York City.	Other reserve cities.	States and Territories.	United States.
	Per cent.	Per cent.	Per cent.	Per cent.
October 1, 1881	22.9	16.8	10.8	15.5
October 1, 1880	26.4	18.5	12.1	17.9
October 2, 1879	24.7	19.4	12.7	18.9

In reference to reserves the Comptroller last year remarked as follows:

The amount of legal cash reserve required of the banks in New York City is 25 per cent. of their deposits, of the banks in the other reserve cities one-half of this ratio, and of the banks in the country districts 6 per cent. of their deposits.

The banks in the interior, if we consider their large deposits elsewhere, are as a rule found to be much stronger in available means than the banks in New York City; while the reverse of this should always be true when such large balances, amounting to more than 100 millions of the funds of other banks, are constantly on deposit in the latter city subject to demand.

The amount of legal reserve required to be held by the banks was largely reduced by the act of June 20, 1874, the provision requiring reserve on circulation having been repealed, and the percentage held in the larger cities has been greatly diminished during the past few years. The sudden and enormous increase of individual and bank deposits in the commercial centers should be accompanied, not only by the reserve required by law, but by a much greater percentage of coin and a much smaller expansion of loans, if the banks would check unhealthy speculation, and keep themselves in condition for an adverse balance of trade and for the legitimate demands of the depositors and correspondents who confide in them.

On October 1 of the present year the aggregate reserve held by the New York City banks, including the five per cent. redemption fund,

have increased largely in each group of banks, while the *cash*
: in each are being gradually reduced. It is evident that these
: **consist**, to a much greater extent than usual, of the avails of
aced to the credit of dealers. This exhibit shows that the banks
dly expanding; and there are many indications that this rapid
is not the result of legitimate business, but of venturesome
:ion, largely consequent upon the importation of coin and in-
issues of silver certificates and bank notes. The increase in
unt of United States bonds held by the banks has been 13 mil-
ring the last year, but it is 15 millions less than at a correspond-
a in 1879. This is somewhat surprising, when it is considered
per cent. bonds can be purchased at about par, and that the rate
est paid on deposits in New York City is from two to three per
ly.
ttention of Congress has previously been called to section 5200
evised Statutes, which places restrictions upon loans, and to the
y of enforcing its provisions. In cities where large amounts of
are received and stored, it is represented that it is impossible
oanks to transact this class of business, if restricted to loans for
unt not exceeding in any instance one-tenth of their capital. It
hat the limitation does not apply to loans upon produce in transit,
he drafts are drawn on existing values; but if produce is stored
of being shipped, large loans cannot be made except in violation
In such case the Comptroller has no means of enforcing the law,
iy bringing a suit for forfeiture of charter, and this course might
i great embarrassment to business, as well as loss to many inno-
ckholders of the banks. It is evident that the law should be so
il as to exclude from the limitation mentioned legitimate loans
oduce or warehouse receipts, as well as loans upon United States

: loans are also continually being made upon other stocks and
ind these loans are largely made to stock-brokers, the result
: assist and promote speculative operations upon the stock board.
vision of law mentioned is valuable, so far as it affects banks out-

RATES OF INTEREST IN NEW YORK CITY, AND IN THE BANK OF ENGLAND AND THE BANK OF FRANCE.

The average rate of interest in New York City for each of the fiscal years from 1874 to 1881, as ascertained from data derived from the Journal of Commerce and The Commercial and Financial Chronicle, was as follows:

1874, call loans, 3.8 per cent. ; commercial paper, 6.4 per cent.
1875, call loans, 3.0 per cent.; commercial paper, 5.6 per cent.
1876, call loans, 3.3 per cent. ; commercial paper, 5.3 per cent.
1877, call loans, 3.0 per cent.; commercial paper, 5.2 per cent.
1878, call loans, 4.4 per cent.; commercial paper, 5.1 per cent.
1879, call loans, 4.4 per cent.; commercial paper, 4.4 per cent.
1880, call loans, 4.9 per cent.; commercial paper, 5.3 per cent.
1881, call loans, 3.8 per cent.; commercial paper, 5.0 per cent.

The average rate of discount of the Bank of England for the same years was as follows:

During the calendar year ending December 31, 1874, 3.69 per cent.
During the calendar year ending December 31, 1875, 3.23 per cent.
During the calendar year ending December 31, 1876, 2.61 per cent.
During the calendar year ending December 31, 1877, 2.91 per cent.
During the calendar year ending December 31, 1878, 3.78 per cent.
During the calendar year ending December 31, 1879, 2.50 per cent.
During the calendar year ending December 31, 1880, 2.76 per cent.
During the fiscal year ending June 30, 1881, 2.74 per cent.

The rate of interest in the city of New York on December 2, as derived from the Daily Bulletin, was, on call loans, from 4 to 6 per cent., and on commercial paper from 6 to 7 per cent.

During the present year the rate of discount of the Bank of England has been changed six times, as follows: On January 13, increased from 3 to 3½ per cent.; February 17 reduced to 3 per cent., and on April 28 further reduced to 2½ per cent.; on August 18 increased to 3½ per cent.; August 25 to 4 per cent.; and again increased on October 6 to 5 per cent.

The rate of the Bank of France has been changed but twice during the present year, and in each instance there was an increase, as follows: On August 25 from 3½ to 4 per cent., and on October 20 from 4 to 5 per cent., which is the rate at the present time. The bank rates of discount for the week ending November 12 were, in Berlin, 5½ per cent., Amsterdam, 4 per cent., Brussels, 5¼ per cent., Vienna, 4 per cent., and St. Petersburg 6 per cent.[*]

DUTIES OF DIRECTORS AND EXAMINERS.

The recent failure of The Mechanics' National Bank of Newark has called the attention of the public directly to the duties of bank directors and of examiners of national banks.

Section 5147 of the Revised Statutes provides that each director, when appointed or elected, shall take an oath that he will, so far as the duty devolves on him, diligently and honestly administer the affairs of such association, and will not knowingly violate or permit to be violated any of the provisions of this act. Section 5136 also provides that the association shall have power to prescribe, by its board of directors, by-laws not inconsistent with law, regulating the manner in which its stock shall be transferred, its directors elected or appointed, its officers appointed, its property transferred, its general business conducted, and the privileges granted to it by law exercised and enjoyed.

---

[*] The Economist, London, November 12, 1881.

In accordance with the provisions of this last named section, by-laws are generally adopted by national banks soon after their organization, which usually contain, among other provisions, sections similar to the following:

There shall be a standing committee, to be known as the "Exchange Committee," appointed by the board, every six months, to continue to act until succeeded, who shall have power to discount and purchase notes and bills and other evidence of debts, and to buy and sell bills of exchange, and who shall, at each regular meeting, make a report of the notes and bills discounted and purchased by them since their last previous report.

There shall be appointed by the board every three months a committee, whose duty it shall be to examine into the affairs of the bank, to count its cash, and to compare its assets and liabilities with the balances on the general ledger for the purpose of ascertaining that the books are correctly kept and the condition of the bank corresponds therewith, and that the bank is in a sound and solvent condition; the result of which examination shall be reported to the board at its next regular meeting.

The object of these by-laws is, first, to keep the board of directors continuously informed what notes and bills are discounted, and to furnish them with a detailed account thereof; and secondly to establish a check by the directors upon the cashier, teller and bookkeeper of the bank, to whose immediate custody and control the assets and accounts of the bank are committed. A method is thus provided by which the diligent and continuous administration of the directors, which is required by their oaths, shall be performed.

It is thus seen that both the laws of the United States and the by-laws adopted by the directors themselves, under the law, in clear terms define their duties. The men employed by them in the banks are under their supervision, the law providing—

That the bank shall have power to elect or appoint directors, and by this board of directors to appoint a president, vice-president, cashier, and other officers, define their duties, require bonds of them and fix the penalty thereof, dismiss such officers or any of them at pleasure, and appoint others to fill their places.

The duties of the board of directors are plainly defined, and however innocent they may be of any intention of wrong, they are responsible for the safety of funds committed to their care. If it can be shown that any of them had notice of illegal transactions, it is a serious question whether they are not legally bound to make good the loss which may occur; and it is a question whether they are not also liable for losses which may occur from neglect of duty, even without notice. If this is not the just and proper construction of the present law, then it becomes a subject for the consideration of Congress, whether additional legislation upon this point is not required. The National Bank Act is full of restrictions, to which reference has already been made in another portion of this report, such as those requiring an adequate reserve; the enforced accumulation of the surplus; the method of increasing and reducing the capital stock and its prompt restoration if impaired; the prohibition against making loans on real estate and on the security of their own shares of stock, or of accommodation or other loans than business paper in excess of one-tenth of the capital of the bank; the prohibition against the declaration of dividends unless earned; against certifying checks without the necessary deposit; and many other similar provisions. These restrictions are intended to protect these institutions, by imposing upon them general rules, which experience has shown may be properly done by the government *without its thereby becoming the guardian of the bank, or of the moneys of its depositors or stockholders, or being in any way responsible for the management of its funds.* It is the duty of the examiner to ascertain whether the officers of the bank and its directors are complying with the requirements of the law and whether they are in any way violating any of its provisions, to the end that in such case they may be enforced by the proper authority.

The stockholders elect the directors, who are usually men not only of high character and well known in the community where the bank is located, but are generally also large stockholders in the bank, and having therefore each a personal interest in its prosperity and good management. The depositors confide in the bank because they believe the directors will manage its affairs honestly and diligently, and will employ honest and faithful servants for that purpose. They know that the bank is organized under laws which contain wholesome restrictions, and that it is the duty of the Comptroller, so far as he can through his corps of examiners, to inform himself of the condition of the bank, and to require that its business shall be conducted in conformity with law.

The examiner can have but a limited knowledge of the habits and character of those employed in the bank. If the teller is making false entries, and daily abstracting the funds of the bank; if the bookkeeper is keeping false accounts and rendering untrue statements; if the cashier is placing forged paper among the bills receivable and upon the register book, and transmitting such paper to distant places where it is purported to be payable, it is not possible for an examiner, in a day or two, to unravel this evil work, which may have continued for months, and obtain a correct balance sheet. A full and complete examination of the bank necessitates not only counting the cash, proving the bills receivable and stock ledger, comparing the individual deposit accounts with the general ledger, and ascertaining if the business of the bank is conducted in accordance with law; but, also, the thorough examination of all accounts, the verifying of accounts-current, and ascertaining by telegraph or letter the correctness of such verification, the calling in of every depositor's book, and correspondence with every bank or banker doing business with the bank.

Examinations should be periodically made by a competent committee, selected from the board. The directors have abundant means at their command, and if they have any reason to suspect dishonesty or fraud, it is their business to investigate thoroughly, and they should employ experts to assist them in so doing. The national bank examiners have, in fact, been frequently called upon by the directors of both national and State banks for this purpose; and if it is the intent of the law that the national banks shall be thus searchingly examined, it should be so amended as to make this intent clear, and should also make provision for the necessary compensation for such service. The small compensation now provided does not contemplate a yearly auditing of all the accounts of a bank by the examiner, as the pay is entirely inadequate for such a work—the amount allowed for the examination of banks of like capital being the same, without reference to the difference in the volume of their business. The inspection by an examiner of a small bank is usually completed in a day; of larger banks, through the aid of an assistant, in two or three days. But a thorough analyzing and scrutiny of everything would require one or two weeks; and if fraud were suspected it might continue for months without entirely satisfactory results.

The reports of the bank, as made to the Comptroller five times in each year, are each published in a newspaper where the bank is located, and every stockholder has, therefore, an opportunity to scrutinize these statements, and to make inquiry of the directors in reference to the affairs of the association.

The detection of embezzlement may occur as an incident, but it is not the principal object, of the system of bank examinations. It is peculiarly the business of the directors, who are daily or weekly in session, to keep themselves informed of the habits and characters of their employés, to see that their time is given to the service of the bank, and that they are not engaged in speculations, and thus, by continuous watchfulness, to prevent defalcations on the part of their servants; while it is the business of the examiner to detect frauds so far as in his power, and in his occasional visits to see that the directors are loaning the funds, and, with the other officers, managing the affairs of the bank strictly according to the provisions of the law. The examiner's visits are usually made about once a year, while the directors are at hand at all times. Faithful performance of the duties of each gives assurance of almost absolute safety. Lax performance of duty on the part of either invites disaster. The directory must continuously look after its own servants. The examiner looks after the acts of the directors.

The report of the examiner is confidential. It is for the use of the Comptroller's office only, and is in no sense a certificate of the good condition of the bank. In many instances the capital stock of a bank has thus been found to be impaired, and the deficiency has been made good without the knowledge of the general public. In other instances banks have been obliged to pass their usual dividends, using their earnings to liquidate all bad and doubtful debts—the number of banks passing dividends during the present year being 175; in 1880, 230; in 1879, 304; and in 1878, 343.

Hundreds of instances have occurred annually, and many are occurring daily, wherein the banks, under the reports of the examiner, are notified of violations of the act and are brought under the discipline of the law. The betterment of the condition of the banks, and the enforcement of the requirements of the law, are part of the continual and ordinary supervision exercised by this Office. It is a supervision and labor not seen or known of by the general public, whose attention is only excited when some sudden or unexpected failure occurs; and this simply illustrates the fact that, with the best endeavors, and the most careful supervision by this Office, such disasters may happen in the many contingencies of administering difficult and extensive duties, if directors neglect to exercise that continuous vigilance for which they were elected, and which they have sworn to perform.

The Mechanics' National Bank of Newark was placed in the hands of the receiver on November 2 last. It had a capital of $500,000, a surplus of $488,000, and deposits of over $2,500,000. The capital and surplus are lost, through the criminal conduct of the cashier, and the stockholders are personally liable for an amount equal to the capital stock. The depositors will, it is estimated, receive at the outcome from fifty to sixty per cent. of their claims, depending upon the amount collected from the stockholders and that received from the estate for whose benefit the funds of the bank are alleged to have been abstracted, which estate is also now in the hands of a receiver appointed by the courts. This bank was many times examined by skilled accountants of great experience, but it cannot be denied that some of them were misled by the criminal cashier, who, through his apparently high character and standing, so long deceived not only the directors, but every one with whom he had business relations. The examination of August 14, 1879, was conducted by two experienced experts, but was, as I am informed, rendered useless by a forged telegram purporting to be from the correspondent of the bank in New York. The examiner, on August 16, 1880, verified the accounts of correspondents, as he was specially instructed to do in a letter from the Comptroller in June previous; but he also was deceived by a forged letter from the New York correspondent, skillfully planned for this purpose, addressed to the examiner, received through the mail, and bearing the New York post-mark. Either of these examinations would have disclosed the robbery of the cashier, if the examiners had not been deceived by forgeries which would have been likely to mislead the most thorough expert.

It is, however, far from correct to represent that similar defalcations in national banks have not been previously discovered. The greatest defalcation in the history of the government, of eleven hundred thousand dollars, in the office of the assistant treasurer of New Orleans, which had certainly existed, in whole or in part, for more than a year, was discovered nearly fifteen years ago by an officer of this bureau, which discovery also resulted in the disclosure of a large deficiency in the First National Bank of New Orleans, and the placing of that bank in the hands of a receiver. Since that time many of the other banks which have failed have been placed in the hands of receivers through the vigilance of bank examiners; and in many other instances officers of solvent and insolvent banks have, through the same means, been indicted and convicted for criminal acts. The bank examiners in New York City and Boston are nominated by the clearing-houses of those cities, and many other examiners now employed are men of the highest character, who have for years rendered excellent service. It is of the greatest importance that all men employed in this branch of the public service shall be well-trained and fitted for their work. It is not claimed that every examiner employed is a first-class expert—the compensation authorized is not sufficient for that purpose in many small districts. If State lines can be disregarded in the appointment of examiners, and men be selected for these positions upon merit alone, and kept well employed, a corps of skilled examiners would soon be engaged in this work, who would reflect the highest credit upon this branch of the public service. The records of this office show, however, that only one among all the examiners ever appointed has been found guilty of wrongdoing, while in no branch of the government service have men performed more faithful duty than those who have been engaged in the examinations of the national banks.

Such disasters do not exhibit the weakness of the banking system, but rather the weakness and wickedness of human nature. The system is strong, and carefully and elaborately guarded. Private companies and individuals are continuously suffering from embezzlements and forgeries. It is scarcely to be expected, if a robber or a forger is placed in control of all of its assets, that a national bank can be saved from disaster by the occasional visits of an examiner. Some additional legislation will be required; but there is not so much necessity for additional restrictions as there is for increased care upon the part of examiners, and increased diligence and sagacity on the part of directors who are in charge of great trusts.

The Pacific National Bank of Boston suspended on November 18 ultimo. The last report of the examination of this bank gave what seemed to be a thorough exhibit of its affairs. A long communication was addressed by the Comptroller to the directors of the bank on February 19 last informing them of such irregularities as then existed in the conduct of its business. They were specially informed that the irregular and illegal practice of loaning the credit of the bank by the issue of certificates must be discontinued. In reply to this communication a letter from the president of the association was received on February 28, explaining the irregularities referred to.   In regard to the issuing of the certificates he said that "never in a single instance has any stipulation been made by us in regard to any certificate issued to any party.   They are issued in regular form, and are payable at any moment upon presentation."   To this it was replied by the Comptroller on March 3 that—

The examiner distinctly stated in his recent report that "loans are sometimes made by the issuing of demand certificates, and parties obtaining loans in this way indorse the certificates and pledge them as collateral, or stipulating the time of payment for them, have them regularly discounted, and thus raise money indirectly from other parties and banks."   If this statement be correct, the bank is lending its credit, which it is not authorized by law to do, and the practice must, as stated in my letter of the 19th ultimo, be discontinued.

That this information was brought to the attention of the directors is evident from a letter received since the date of suspension, on the 25th instant, from the person who made the examination, which says:

Had your letter, which you wrote after my last examination, which was read by Mr. Kenyon, the president, to the board, as you requested, been heeded, the present condition of things would have been avoided.

Such a letter, in any properly-conducted bank, addressed by the Comptroller to a board of directors composed, as was the case in this instance, of prominent merchants and business men, should have been sufficient to correct the abuse and save the bank from the disaster which has occurred.

This examiner also informs me that during the examination, and subsequent thereto, he called special attention of the directors to the hazardous manner of doing business, and urged them to follow closely the business and examine loans made by him and the way in which his business was conducted, and was promised by more than one director that close attention would be given to the whole matter.   The directors had full information in reference to the irregular and illegal methods of business which have since caused its ruin.

Statutes should certainly be so amended as to make it a criminal offense for an officer of a bank clandestinely to make loans, either by the use of certificates, as in this case, or otherwise.

RETIREMENT OF NATIONAL-BANK NOTES AND WITHDRAWAL OF BONDS HELD AS SECURITY THEREFOR.

The only legislation in reference to the national banks during the last session of Congress was contained in section 5 of "the funding act of 1881," which was as follows:

SEC. 5.   From and after the first day of July, eighteen hundred and eighty-one, the three per centum bonds authorized by the first section of this act shall be the only bonds receivable as security for national-bank circulation, or as security for the safe-keeping and prompt payment of the public money deposited with such banks; but when any such bonds deposited for the purposes aforesaid shall be designated for purchase or redemption by the Secretary of the Treasury, the banking association depositing the same shall have the right to substitute other issues of the bonds of the United States in lieu thereof: Provided, That no bond upon which interest has ceased shall be accepted or shall be continued on deposit as security for circulation or for the safe-keeping of the public money; and in case bonds so deposited shall not be withdrawn, as provided by law, within thirty days after interest has ceased thereon, the banking association depositing the same shall be subject to the liabilities and proceedings on the part of the Comptroller provided for in section 5234 of the Revised Statutes of the United States: And provided further, That section four of the act of June twentieth, eighteen hundred and seventy-four, entitled "An act fixing the amount of United States notes, providing for a redistribution of the national-bank currency, and for other purposes," be, and the same is hereby, repealed; and sections 5159 and 5160 of the Revised Statutes of the United States be, and the same are hereby, re-enacted.

This act was vetoed by the President.

The number of national banks, which deposited legal tender notes for the purpose of obtaining possession of their bonds, in anticipation of the passage of this bill, was 141. These banks were located in twenty-four States, and the amount of legal tender notes deposited by them was $18,764,434, as follows:

States and cities.	No. of banks.	Amount.	States and cities.	No. of banks.	Amount.
Philadelphia	6	$2,590,800	New York City	9	$2,843,849
Pennsylvania	14	2,083,300	New York	23	1,934,608
Boston	4	1,034,100	New Jersey	5	837,000
Massachusetts	2	81,000	Indiana	10	1,080,000
Connecticut	10	1,675,400	Missouri	3	164,745
Montana	1	36,000	Virginia	1	45,000
District of Columbia	1	72,000	Ohio	19	1,402,639
Rhode Island	2	385,200	Minnesota	3	135,000
Nebraska	2	171,900	Kentucky	1	310,900
Kansas	2	81,000	Michigan	1	27,000
Illinois	10	845,000	Iowa	4	100,460
Maine	2	135,000	Vermont	3	463,580
North Carolina	1	135,000	Wisconsin	1	21,150
Maryland	1	72,000			
			Totals	141	18,764,434

Only about one-third of the bonds which were thus released were subsequently redeposited, and for some months thereafter the total amount of bonds redeposited by the 141 banks which reduced their circulation was less than 7 millions. The Third National Bank of New York, which withdrew $840,000 of bonds, soon thereafter disposed of the same to the Government, and has not since made any deposit whatever. The same statement may be made in reference to eight other large banks, which withdrew bonds amounting to over two millions of dollars, and also to many other smaller banks—thus showing that they withdrew their bonds because they desired control of them, and not for the purpose of arbitrarily reducing circulation. The Comptroller has been unable to obtain any evidence that there was a combination on the part of the banks to deposit legal-tender notes and withdraw bonds for the purpose of deranging the money market.

Since the adjournment of Congress, only $2,394,545 of legal-tender notes have been deposited under the act of June 20, 1874, for the purpose of retiring circulation, and these notes have been redeemed without any expense whatever to the Government of the United States—the cost thereof having been paid from the five per cent. redemption fund. The bonds now held are chiefly 3½ and 4 per cents, there being 241 millions of the former and 92 millions of the latter. The amount of interest received from an investment in either class of these bonds is nearly the same, and there is but little disposition to deposit legal-tender notes for the purpose of withdrawing them. Some banks take occasion to withdraw their 4 per cents, for the purpose of realizing the large premium of 16 per cent., which they now bear, as this premium can be used for the purpose of liquidating any losses which may occur in their business. The 3½ per cent. bonds are being frequently called by the Secretary, and the banks may therefore have occasion to withdraw them after interest has ceased, and it is important that they continue to have this privilege, upon a deposit of lawful money as now provided by law.

The amount of loans of the national banks in New York City on October 1, 1881, was 246 millions, and 97 millions of this amount was payable on demand; the total amount of loans of all the banks was 1,169 millions, of which 196 millions was demand loans. It is probable that the proportion of demand loans held by the State banks is fully as great. Any proceeding which would tend to bring on a panic, or derange the money market in New York, would, first of all, affect the

...ring in the Treasury for that purpose large amounts of coin...

awful money, then section 4 of the act of June 20, 1874, may
nded as to require those desiring to withdraw bonds to give
ible notice of their intention to do so, before completing the
)n.

)onds deposited to secure the circulation of the national banks
for payment by the government, it is necessary that the banks
thdraw them for redemption. This they can do, either by sub-
other bonds or by depositing, under section 4 of the act of
1874, lawful money, to retire the circulation secured by the
ich they desire to withdraw. The most convenient method
anks is to avail themselves of the provision of section 4 re-
as in many cases they desire permanently to withdraw bonds,
ubstitution. Prior to May 23 last, the Treasurer of the United
d his predecessors in office, had, as a matter of convenience both
iks and the government, permitted the redemption of called
the following method: The banks sent a power of attorney,
ig the Comptroller to withdraw the bonds, and the Treasurer
nited States to assign them to the Secretary of the Treas-
demption on account of the bank, as much of the proceeds as
necessary being used to retire the circulation secured by the
[he bonds were never out of the hands of the officers of the
Department. The banks were thus relieved from the necessity
nding in the money to retire their circulation, and the Govern-
enabled to get in its called bonds with more promptitude. On
lowever, the Treasurer declined longer to allow this method of
al and redemption, alleging that the proceeds of these bonds
i, and not legal-tender notes, and that section 4 of the act of
'equires deposits for the retirement of circulation to be made
)nder notes only.

)e 1 the Comptroller addressed a letter to the Secretary of
sury, in which he stated the position taken by the Treasurer,
it he declined to receive gold coin, which is a legal tender in
of all debts, and insisted upon a deposit of United States notes,

$9,000 in lawful money, and to take up the bonds deposited for security of circulating notes; and that these words, as here used, possess their ordinary signification is apparent from the phraseology of concomitant and other provisions of law, and from considerations touching the general subject.

He also quoted a decision of his predecessor on a similar point, in confirmation thereof.   On the same date that this decision was rendered by the Attorney-General, the Secretary of the Treasury addressed another letter to him, in which two additional questions in reference to this matter were asked: First, whether, under section 3 of the act approved June 20, 1874, chapter 343, a national banking association may deposit any lawful money other than United States notes for redemption of its circulating notes; and, second, whether the holders of the notes of any solvent national banking association may demand of the Treasurer, under the provision of sections 3 and 4 of that act, redemption of such notes in United States notes?

On June 30, 1881, the Attorney-General replied, and, as to the first question, decided that a bank may deposit coin for the purpose mentioned in the 3d section as above quoted. In answer to the second question, he said:

I think the Treasurer, while having the privilege, under sections 3 and 4 of said act, to redeem bank circulation in United States notes, has the right to pay them in coin. The government notes are promises to pay dollars, and for such promises the thing promised may properly be substituted by the promiser, and that the act of June 20, 1874, chapter 343, was not intended to repeal or affect the general provisions of the law (Revised Statutes, section 3585, et seq.) making the coin of the United States legal tenders in all payments.

This decision removed all the distinctions which had been previously insisted upon by the Treasurer of the United States, as to the kind of lawful money that might be received or paid in these transactions.

NUMBER, CAPITAL AND DEPOSITS OF NATIONAL BANKS, STATE AND SAVINGS-BANKS, AND PRIVATE BANKERS.

The capital of the 2,115 national banks in operation on June 30, 1881, as will be seen by a table in the Appendix, was $460,227,835, not including surplus, which fund at that date amounted to more than 126 millions of dollars; while the average capital of all the State banks, private bankers and savings banks, for the six months ending May 31, 1880, was but $210,738,203. The latter amount is but little more than one-third of the combined capital and surplus of the national banks.

The following table exhibits in a concise form, by geographical divisions, the total average capital and deposits of all State and savings-banks and private bankers in the country, for the six months ending May 31, 1881:

Geographical divisions.	State banks and trust companies.			Private bankers.			Savings banks with capital.			Savings banks without capital.	
	No.	Capital.	Deposits.	No.	Capital	Deposits.	No.	Capital.	Deposits.	No.	Deposits.
		Mill's	Mill's		Mill's	Mill's		Mill's	Mill's		Mill's
New England States...	41	7.26	20.97	80	4.70	5.16	1	.02	.19	424	402.86
Middle States	218	39.28	189.78	938	55.40	94.11	7	.61	4.68	174	428.40
Southern States	240	24.71	42.43	258	5.59	17.32	6	.44	.84	3	1.24
Western States and Territories................	479	41.94	132.44	1,762	27.64	125.26	22	3.15	31.90	28	29.86
United States......	978	113.19	385.62	3,038	93.33	241.85	36	4.22	37.61	629	862.36

STATE BANKS AND TRUST COMPANIES.

From these returns the following abstract has been compiled, showing the resources and liabilities of State banks and trust companies for the last two years, the number reporting in 1880 being 650, and in 1881 683:

	1880.	1881.
RESOURCES.		
Loans and discounts	$381,496,731	$352,725,986
Overdrafts	597,699	1,407,695
United States bonds	26,252,182	27,686,025
Other stocks, bonds, &c.	35,661,792	42,330,957
Due from banks	40,340,345	54,982,829
Real estate	19,489,086	21,896,772
Other assets	7,374,037	11,941,741
Expenses	972,492	1,136,427
Cash items	11,176,502	16,900,762
Specie	6,905,977	17,925,638
Legal tenders, bank-notes, &c.	51,500,226	27,391,317
Total	481,774,159	575,509,139
LIABILITIES.		
Capital stock	109,318,451	112,111,325
Circulation	283,308	274,941
Surplus fund	25,008,431	27,857,976
Undivided profits	10,774,731	12,237,330
Dividends unpaid	486,094	576,413
Deposits	296,759,619	373,032,632
Due to banks	18,613,336	19,105,064
Other liabilities	18,530,189	30,303,368
Total	481,774,159	575,509,139

The foregoing table was prepared from returns from five New England States, exclusive of Maine, which has but one State bank in operation; from four Middle States, not including Delaware; and from all the Western States excepting Illinois, Kansas, and Nebraska. The only Southern States represented therein are South Carolina, Georgia, Louisiana, Texas, and Kentucky. The only Pacific State is California. There is but one State bank in New Hampshire, six in Vermont, and none in Massachusetts. There are, however, five trust and loan companies in the latter State, and ten in Connecticut.

SAVINGS BANKS.

The following table exhibits the aggregate resources and liabilities of 629 savings banks in 1880 and in 1881:

	1880.	1881.
RESOURCES.		
Loans on real estate	$315,273,232	$307,096,158
Loans on personal and collateral security	70,175,090	93,817,641
United States bonds	187,413,220	210,845,514
State, municipal, and other bonds and stocks	150,440,350	156,818,942
Railroad bonds and stocks	20,705,378	27,068,048
Bank stock	32,225,923	33,349,283
Real estate	39,038,502	41,967,674
Other assets	27,053,452	37,408,162
Expenses	216,423	135,572
Due from banks	22,063,091	40,603,641
Cash	17,072,680	13,756,106
Total	881,677,350	967,790,662
LIABILITIES.		
Deposits	819,106,973	891,961,142
Surplus fund	51,226,472	60,289,905
Undivided profits	4,740,861	10,325,800
Other liabilities	6,603,044	5,213,815
Total	881,677,350	967,790,662

The table below exhibits the capital and net deposits of the national banks on June 30, 1881, together with the aggregate average capital and deposits of all classes of banks other than national, for the six months ending May 31, 1881:

Geographical divisions.	State banks, savings-banks, private bankers, &c.			National banks.			Total.		
	No.	Capital.	Deposits.	No.	Capital.	Net deposits.	No.	Capital.	Deposits.
		Millions.	Millions.		Millions.	Millions.		Millions.	Millions.
New England States	546	12.0	429.2	552	165.9	208.6	1,098	177.9	637.8
Middle States	1,337	95.8	717.0	664	171.7	599.7	2,001	267.0	1,316.7
Southern States	507	30.7	61.8	184	31.1	59.5	691	61.8	121.3
Western States and Territories	2,291	72.7	319.4	715	91.5	272.1	3,006	164.2	591.5
United States	4,681	210.7	1,527.4	2,115	460.2	1,139.9	6,796	670.9	2,667.3

From this table it will be seen that the total number of banks and bankers in the country at the date named was 6,796, with a total banking capital of $670,966,043, and total deposits of $2,667,343,595.

In the Appendix will be found similar tables for various periods, from 1875 to 1881, where will also be found other tables giving the assets and liabilities of State institutions during the past year, so far as they could be obtained from the official reports of the several State officers.

A table arranged by States and principal cities, giving the number, capital and deposits, and the tax thereon, of all banking institutions other than national, for the six months ending May 31, 1881, and for previous years, will also be found in the Appendix.

The following table exhibits, for corresponding dates nearest to May 31 in each of the last six years, the aggregate amounts of the capital and deposits of each of the classes of banks given in the foregoing table:

Years.	National banks.			State banks, private bankers, &c.			Savings banks with capital.			Savings banks without capital.		Total.		
	No.	Capital.	Deposits.	No.	Capital.	Deposits.	No.	Capital.	Deposits.	No.	Deposits.	No.	Capital.	Deposits.
		Mil's	Mil's		Mil's	Mil's		Mil's	Mil's		Mil's		Mil's	Mil's
1876	2,091	504.4	718.5	3,803	214.0	480.0	26	5.0	37.2	691	844.6	6,611	719.4	2,075.3
1877	2,078	481.0	768.2	3,799	218.6	470.5	26	4.9	38.2	676	843.2	6,579	704.5	2,120.1
1878	2,056	470.4	677.2	3,709	202.3	413.3	28	3.2	26.2	668	803.3	6,456	675.8	1,920.0
1879	2,048	455.3	713.4	3,639	197.0	397.0	29	4.2	36.1	644	747.1	6,360	656.5	1,893.5
1880	2,076	455.9	900.8	3,798	190.1	501.5	29	4.0	34.6	629	783.0	6,532	650.0	2,219.9
1881	2,115	400.2	1,139.9	4,016	206.5	627.5	36	4.2	37.6	629	862.3	6,796	670.9	2,667.3

PRIVATE BANKERS.

In the Appendix will be found a table giving by geographical divisions, and by States, Territories and principal cities, the number of State banks, savings banks, trust and loan companies and private bankers of the country, together with the amount of their capital and deposits, and the amount invested by them in United States bonds. The first official information of this character ever published in regard to the private bankers of the country was contained in a table in the Comptroller's report for 1880. From the table in the Appendix, mentioned above, the following information in reference to the private bankers in sixteen of the principal cities has been separated, it being thought that it will prove of special interest:

Cities.	Number of banks.	Capital.	Deposits.	Invested in U. S. bonds.
Boston	47	$4,065,097	$2,570,068	$1,003,347
New York City	508	45,482,515	45,414,376	9,670,751
Albany	3	550,000	1,611,470	351,000
Philadelphia	52	1,800,614	6,174,785	224,208
Pittsburgh	7	563,910	2,025,477	20,374
Baltimore	19	773,657	2,389,032	195,384
Washington	6	364,000	3,747,703	287,029
New Orleans	5	32,000		
Louisville	3	178,000	728,464	
Cincinnati	8	812,167	3,863,817	280,295
Cleveland	4	55,000	963,938	8,997
Chicago	24	2,004,197	10,455,063	172,569
Detroit	7	161,256	945,669	7,333
Milwaukee	4	64,667	530,047	350
Saint Louis	11	261,302	304,978	44,405
San Francisco	9	1,275,918	8,271,680	104,074
Totals	717	58,534,300	89,996,545	12,370,012

The following table gives similar information for the thirty-one States and Territories, exclusive of the cities in the above table, having an amount of capital in excess of $100,000. In this table the number of private bankers is 2,255; the aggregate amount of capital, $34,169,435; and of deposits, $148,178,652, the average capital being $15,152, and the average deposits $65,711:

States and Territories.	Number of banks.	Capital.	Deposits.	Invested in U. S. bonds.
Illinois	310	$4,183,346	$21,656,149	$1,245,738
Pennsylvania	172	4,140,679	19,978,585	288,461
Ohio	213	4,119,220	19,931,774	656,222
Indiana	106	3,130,268	11,870,104	571,960
Iowa	276	2,975,737	10,388,843	67,287
Texas	107	2,560,951	7,033,240	14,000
New York	163	1,551,347	12,699,067	364,263
Michigan	137	1,213,796	5,218,413	74,464
Missouri	81	1,120,244	6,843,267	134,142
Kansas	135	1,001,172	4,076,393	32,600
Wisconsin	79	848,746	4,901,883	111,960
Minnesota	89	670,227	2,772,507	45,848
Nebraska	86	673,300	2,053,586	14,070
Alabama	21	564,085	1,372,342	800
Colorado	51	547,827	2,705,441	15,000
Montana	14	512,706	904,498	
Georgia	30	478,910	1,308,131	7,000
Oregon	12	436,500	973,519	250,000
California	22	387,709	1,022,592	
Virginia	18	369,792	2,102,077	25,000
Kentucky	23	308,731	1,936,815	80,000
Rhode Island	7	358,181	462,268	32,613
Mississippi	11	314,579	833,326	48,290
Nevada	9	292,851	657,530	100,000
Washington	9	284,050	657,015	
South Carolina	8	229,956	53,921	
Dakota	57	216,263	484,345	
Connecticut	12	168,500	1,359,079	8,063
Utah	10	137,225	1,484,710	
Louisiana	3	140,329	35,812	30,000
Wyoming	4	135,208	421,310	
Totals	2,255	34,169,435	148,178,652	4,227,815

The remaining fifteen States and Territories, not enumerated in the above table, contain 66 private bankers, with an aggregate capital of $620,120, and aggregate deposits of $3,670,357. Massachusetts has only three private bankers, outside the city of Boston, with an aggregate capital of $50,000, and aggregate deposits of $539,028. Maryland has but two private bankers, outside of the city of Baltimore. The State

e has but seven private bankers, North Carolina four, New re four, New Jersey five, Delaware and Vermont only one each, ix, and Arizona five. The average amount of capital held by hese 66 private bankers is $9,244, and of deposits $57,127.

tal number of private bankers in the foregoing cities is 717, with gate capital of $58,534,300, and aggregate deposits of $89,996,545 erage capital being $81,637, and the average deposits $125,518. 0 per cent. of these private banks are located in New York resenting nearly four-fifths of the aggregate capital and more half of the aggregate deposits. The average amount of capi- deposits of each private banker in the city of New York is 50,000; and the bankers in that city also held $9,670,751 of States bonds, which is more than one-half of the amount of ds held by all of the private bankers of the country.

llowing table shows, by geographical divisions, the number of bankers in the United States, with the aggregate amount of ital, deposits, and investments in United States bonds, for the hs ended May 31, 1881:

Geographical divisions.	Number of banks.	Capital.	Deposits.	Invested in U. S. bonds.
d States	80	$4,696,782	$5,162,708	$1,067,652
...	918	55,397,130	94,104,980	11,401,808
...tes	258	5,588,828	17,323,504	263,780
...tes and Territories	1,762	27,639,115	125,254,362	3,937,254
...States	3,038	93,323,855	241,845,554	16,670,494

ble below is a recapitulation of the foregoing, showing by groups egates for the bankers in the sixteen principal cities, in the e States and Territories having a private banking capital in f $100,000, and in the fifteen remaining States and Territories:

RECAPITULATION

	Number of banks.	Capital.	Deposits.	Invested in U. S. bonds.
...es	717	$58,534,300	483,996,545	$12,370,012
...tes and Territories	2,255	34,169,435	148,178,652	4,227,815
...tates and Territories	66	620,120	3,670,357	72,607
...States	3,038	93,323,855	241,845,554	16,670,494

STATE BANKS, SAVINGS BANKS, AND TRUST COMPANIES.

t of Congress of February 19, 1873, section 333 of the Revised requires the Comptroller to obtain from authentic sources, and to Congress, statements exhibiting under appropriate heads the and liabilities of such banks and savings banks as are organ- er the laws of the several States and Territories. In compliance act he has presented annually in the appendices to his reports rces and liabilities of these corporations, so far as it has been to obtain them.

zh the courtesy of State officers, returns of State banks, sav- ks, and trust and loan companies have during the past year ived from twenty-three States. Many of the States and Ter- including Illinois, Nebraska, Dakota, Oregon, Virginia, and e, do not require periodical returns of the condition of the dif- esses of banks organized under their laws.

The table below exhibits the capital and net deposits of the national banks on June 30, 1881, together with the aggregate average capital and deposits of all classes of banks other than national, for the six months ending May 31, 1881:

Geographical divisions.	State banks, savings-banks, private bankers, &c.		National banks.			Total.		
	No.	Capital.	Deposits.	No.	Capital.	Net deposits.	No.	Capital.	Deposits.
		Millions.	*Millions.*		*Millions.*	*Millions.*		*Millions.*	*Millions.*
New England States	546	12.0	429.2	552	165.9	208.6	1,098	177.9	637.8
Middle States	1,337	95.3	717.0	664	171.7	599.7	2,001	267.0	1,316.7
Southern States	507	30.7	61.8	184	31.1	59.5	691	61.8	121.3
Western States and Territories	2,291	72.7	319.4	715	91.5	272.1	3,006	164.2	591.5
United States	4,681	210.7	1,527.4	2,115	460.2	1,139.9	6,796	670.9	2,667.3

From this table it will be seen that the total number of banks and bankers in the country at the date named was 6,796, with a total banking capital of $670,966,043, and total deposits of $2,667,343,595.

In the Appendix will be found similar tables for various periods, from 1875 to 1881, where will also be found other tables giving the assets and liabilities of State institutions during the past year, so far as they could be obtained from the official reports of the several State officers.   •

A table arranged by States and principal cities, giving the number, capital and deposits, and the tax thereon, of all banking institutions other than national, for the six months ending May 31, 1881, and for previous years, will also be found in the Appendix.

The following table exhibits, for corresponding dates nearest to May 31 in each of the last six years, the aggregate amounts of the capital and deposits of each of the classes of banks given in the foregoing table:

Years.	National banks.		State banks, private bankers, &c.		Savings banks with capital.		Savings banks without capital.		Total.	
	No.	Capital	Deposits	No.	Capital	Deposits	No.	Capital	Deposits	No.	Deposits	No.	Capital	Deposits
		Mil's	*Mil's*		*Mil's*	*Mil's*		*Mil's*	*Mil's*		*Mil's*		*Mil's*	*Mil's*
1876	2,091	508.4	712.5	3,803	214.0	480.0	26	5.0	37.2	691	844.6	6,611	719.4	2,075.3
1877	2,078	481.0	768.2	3,799	218.6	470.5	26	4.9	38.2	676	848.2	6,579	704.5	2,120.1
1878	2,056	470.4	677.2	3,709	202.2	413.3	28	3.2	26.2	668	803.5	6,456	675.8	1,920.0
1879	2,048	455.3	713.4	3,639	197.0	397.0	29	4.2	36.1	644	747.1	6,360	656.5	1,893.5
1880	2,076	455.9	900.8	3,798	190.1	501.5	29	4.0	34.6	629	783.0	6,532	650.0	2,219.9
1881	2,115	460.2	1,139.9	4,016	206.5	527.5	36	4.2	37.6	629	862.3	6,796	670.9	2,667.3

PRIVATE BANKERS.

In the Appendix will be found a table giving by geographical divisions, and by States, Territories and principal cities, the number of State banks, savings banks, trust and loan companies and private bankers of the country, together with the amount of their capital and deposits, and the amount invested by them in United States bonds. The first official information of this character ever published in regard to the private bankers of the country was contained in a table in the Comptroller's report for 1880. From the table in the Appendix, mentioned above, the following information in reference to the private bankers in sixteen of the principal cities has been separated, it being thought that it will prove of special interest:

Cities.	Number of banks.	Capital.	Deposits.	Invested in U. S. bonds.
Boston	47	$4, 095, 097	$2, 570, 068	$1, 003, 347
New York City	508	45, 482, 515	45, 414, 376	9, 070, 751
Albany	3	550, 000	1, 611, 470	351, 000
Philadelphia	52	1, 800, 614	6, 174, 785	224, 208
Pittsburgh	7	563, 910	2, 025, 477	20, 374
Baltimore	19	773, 657	2, 389, 032	195, 384
Washington	6	364, 000	3, 747, 703	287, 029
New Orleans	5	32, 000		
Louisville	3	178, 000	728, 464	
Cincinnati	8	812, 167	3, 863, 817	280, 295
Cleveland	4	55, 000	963, 938	8, 967
Chicago	24	2, 004, 197	10, 455, 063	172, 549
Detroit	7	161, 256	945, 669	7, 333
Milwaukee	4	64, 667	530, 047	350
Saint Louis	11	261, 302	304, 976	44, 405
San Francisco	9	1, 275, 918	8, 271, 060	104, 074
Totals	717	58, 534, 300	89, 996, 545	12, 370, 012

The following table gives similar information for the thirty-one States and Territories, exclusive of the cities in the above table, having an amount of capital in excess of $100,000. In this table the number of private bankers is 2,255; the aggregate amount of capital, $34,169,435; and of deposits, $148,178,652, the average capital being $15,152, and the average deposits $65,711:

States and Territories.	Number of banks.	Capital.	Deposits.	Invested in U. S. bonds.
Illinois	310	$4, 183, 346	$21, 656, 149	$1, 245, 738
Pennsylvania	172	4, 140, 679	19, 978, 585	268, 401
Ohio	213	4, 119, 220	19, 931, 774	656, 222
Indiana	106	3, 130, 268	11, 870, 164	571, 960
Iowa	276	2, 975, 737	10, 388, 843	67, 287
Texas	107	2, 560, 951	7, 033, 240	14, 000
New York	163	1, 551, 347	12, 699, 067	364, 263
Michigan	137	1, 213, 796	5, 218, 413	74, 464
Missouri	81	1, 120, 244	6, 843, 207	134, 142
Kansas	135	1, 001, 172	4, 076, 393	32, 800
Wisconsin	79	848, 746	4, 901, 883	111, 960
Minnesota	89	670, 227	2, 772, 507	45, 848
Nebraska	86	675, 300	2, 053, 586	14, 070
Alabama	21	564, 085	1, 372, 342	800
Colorado	51	547, 827	2, 705, 441	15, 000
Montana	14	512, 706	904, 498	
Georgia	30	478, 910	1, 308, 131	7, 000
Oregon	12	436, 500	973, 519	250, 000
California	22	387, 709	1, 022, 592	
Virginia	18	369, 792	2, 102, 077	25, 000
Kentucky	23	368, 731	1, 936, 815	80, 000
Rhode Island	7	358, 181	462, 268	32, 613
Mississippi	11	314, 579	833, 326	48, 200
Nevada	9	292, 851	617, 530	100, 000
Washington	9	284, 050	657, 015	
South Carolina	8	229, 956	53, 921	
Dakota	37	216, 263	484, 345	
Connecticut	12	168, 500	1, 359, 079	8, 063
Utah	10	157, 225	1, 484, 710	
Louisiana	3	140, 329	35, 812	30, 000
Wyoming	4	135, 208	421, 310	
Totals	2, 255	34, 169, 435	148, 178, 652	4, 227, 815

The remaining fifteen States and Territories, not enumerated in the above table, contain 66 private bankers, with an aggregate capital of $620,120, and aggregate deposits of $3,670,357. Massachusetts has only three private bankers, outside the city of Boston, with an aggregate capital of $50,000, and aggregate deposits of $539,028. Maryland has but two private bankers, outside of the city of Baltimore. The State

) has but seven private bankers, North Carolina four, New
 are four, New Jersey five, Delaware and Vermont only one each,
ix, and Arizona five. The average amount of capital held by
hese 66 private bankers is $9,244, and of deposits $57,127.
tal number of private bankers in the foregoing cities is 717, with
gate capital of $58,534,300, and aggregate deposits of $89,996,545
erage capital being $81,637, and the average deposits $125,518.
0 per cent. of these private banks are located in New York
resenting nearly four-fifths of the aggregate capital and more
-half of the aggregate deposits. The average amount of capi-
deposits of each private banker in the city of New York is
30,000; and the bankers in that city also held $9,670,751 of
States bonds, which is more than one-half of the amount of
ds held by all of the private bankers of the country.
llowing table shows, by geographical divisions, the number of
bankers in the United States, with the aggregate amount of
ital, deposits, and investments in United States bonds, for the
hs ended May 31, 1881:

Geographical divisions.	Number of banks.	Capital.	Deposits.	Invested in U. S. bonds.
d States	80	$4,698,782	$5,162,706	$1,067,652
s	9 ix	55,397,130	94,104,980	11,401,808
ites	258	5,588,828	17,323,504	263,780
tes and Territories	1,762	27,639,115	125,254,362	3,937,254
l States	3,608	93,323,855	241,845,564	16,670,494

ble below is a recapitulation of the foregoing, showing by groups
egates for the bankers in the sixteen principal cities, in the
e States and Territories having a private banking capital in
f $100,000, and in the fifteen remaining States and Territories:

RECAPITULATION

	Number of banks.	Capital.	Deposits.	Invested in U. S. bonds.
les	717	$58,534,300	489,996,545	$12,370,012
ties and Territories	2,255	34,169,435	148,178,652	4,227,815
tates and Territories	(9)	620,120	3,670,357	72,667
l States	3,008	93,323,855	241,845,554	16,670,494

TATE BANKS, SAVINGS BANKS, AND TRUST COMPANIES.

t of Congress of February 19, 1873, section 333 of the Revised
. requires the Comptroller to obtain from authentic sources, and
to Congress, statements exhibiting under appropriate heads the
s and liabilities of such banks and savings banks as are organ-
er the laws of the several States and Territories. In compliance
s act he has presented annually in the appendices to his reports
irces and liabilities of these corporations, so far as it has been
to obtain them.
zh the courtesy of State officers, returns of State banks, sav-
ks, and trust and loan companies have during the past year
ived from twenty-three States. Many of the States and Ter-
including Illinois, Nebraska, Dakota, Oregon, Virginia, and
e, do not require periodical returns of the condition of the dif-
isses of banks organized under their laws.

STATE BANKS AND TRUST COMPANIES.

From these returns the following abstract has been compiled, showing the resources and liabilities of State banks and trust companies for the last two years, the number reporting in 1880 being 650, and in 1881 683:

	1880.	1881.
RESOURCES.		
Loans and discounts	$381,496,731	$352,725,986
Overdrafts	597,699	1,407,695
United States bonds	26,252,182	27,680,025
Other stocks, bonds, &c.	35,661,792	42,330,957
Due from banks	40,340,345	54,662,829
Real estate	19,489,086	21,396,772
Other assets	7,374,037	11,941,741
Expenses	979,492	1,136,427
Cash items	11,176,502	16,900,762
Specie	6,905,977	17,925,628
Legal tenders, bank-notes, &c.	51,500,226	27,391,317
Total	481,774,159	575,500,139
LIABILITIES.		
Capital stock	109,318,451	112,111,325
Circulation	283,308	274,941
Surplus fund	25,006,431	27,857,976
Undivided profits	10,774,731	12,237,320
Dividends unpaid	486,094	576,413
Deposits	298,759,619	373,032,632
Due to banks	18,613,336	19,105,664
Other liabilities	18,530,189	30,303,868
Total	481,774,159	575,500,139

The foregoing table was prepared from returns from five New England States, exclusive of Maine, which has but one State bank in operation; from four Middle States, not including Delaware; and from all the Western States excepting Illinois, Kansas, and Nebraska. The only Southern States represented therein are South Carolina, Georgia, Louisiana, Texas, and Kentucky. The only Pacific State is California. There is but one State bank in New Hampshire, six in Vermont, and none in Massachusetts. There are, however, five trust and loan companies in the latter State, and ten in Connecticut.

SAVINGS BANKS.

The following table exhibits the aggregate resources and liabilities of 629 savings banks in 1880 and in 1881:

	1880.	1881.
RESOURCES.		
Loans on real estate	$315,273,232	$307,096,158
Loans on personal and collateral security	70,175,090	93,817,641
United States bonds	187,413,220	210,845,514
State, municipal, and other bonds and stocks	150,440,359	159,819,942
Railroad bonds and stocks	20,705,378	27,069,048
Bank stock	32,225,923	33,348,283
Real estate	39,038,502	41,967,674
Other assets	27,053,452	37,468,162
Expenses	216,423	135,572
Due from banks	22,063,091	40,603,641
Cash	17,072,680	13,758,106
Total	881,677,350	967,790,682
LIABILITIES.		
Deposits	819,106,973	891,961,142
Surplus fund	51,226,472	60,289,905
Undivided profits	4,740,861	10,325,800
Other liabilities	6,603,044	5,213,815
Total	881,677,350	967,790,682

The foregoing table includes the returns from the six New England States, from four Middle States, not including Delaware, from the State of California, and from three other States and the District of Columbia. The aggregate of loans in the New England States is $230,239,027, and of deposits $403,304,135. In the Middle States the aggregate of loans is $130,204,828, and of deposits $424,212,944.

Some of the largest savings banks in the city of Philadelphia, organized under old charters, are not required to make reports to any State officer. Returns received directly from four of these banks, having deposits amounting to $26,895,295, are included in the returns for the State of Pennsylvania.

The savings-bank deposits given in the foregoing table for 1881, based on reports made to the State authorities, are $891,961,142, and the deposits of the State banks and trust companies were $373,032,632. These deposits do not include bank deposits. The deposits of the national banks on October 1, 1881, exclusive of those due to banks, were $1,086,942,470. These deposits of the national banks bear to those of the savings banks the proportion, nearly, of 55 to 45, to those of the State banks and trust companies the proportion of 74 to 26, and to the combined deposits of both the proportion of 46 to 54.

The total population of New England, according to the census of 1880, is 4,010,529, and the number of open deposit accounts in the savings banks is 1,227,899; which is equal to 30.6 accounts to each one hundred of the entire population. The average amount of each account is $328.45; and if the total deposits were divided among the entire population, the average sum of $100.56 could be given to each individual.

The deposits of the savings banks in the State of New York were $353,629,657, while the population is 5,082,871; showing that an equal distribution of the savings-bank deposits among the entire population of the State would give $69.57 to each individual.

Tables showing the aggregate resources and liabilities of State banks, trust companies and savings banks, in each State from which returns have been received from the State authorities, appear in the appendix.

SECURITY FOR CIRCULATING NOTES.

During the past year there has been much change in the classes of United States bonds which the national banks have on deposit to secure their circulation, owing to the redemption or continuation of the five and six per cent. bonds of 1881. The classes and amount of these bonds held by the Treasurer on the 1st day of November, 1881, are exhibited in the following table:

Class of bonds.	Authorizing act.	Rate of interest.	Amount.
Ten-forties of 1864 (interest ceased).	March 3, 1864...............................	5 per cent.	$50,000
Funded loan of 1881 (interest ceased).	July 14, 1870, and January 20, 1871....	5 ..do	708,900
Funded loan of 1891....................	.......do..............do.................	4½..do	31,981,650
Funded loan of 1907....................	.......do..............do.................	4 ..do	92,005,800
Loan of July and August, 1861, continued.	July 17 and August 5, 1861.............	3½..do	36,040,650
Loan of 1863, continued (81s)........	March 3, 1863..............................	3½..do	17,700,950
Funded loan of 1881, continued......	July 14, 1870, and January 20, 1871 ...	3½..do	187,634,550
Pacific Railway bonds...................	July 1, 1862, and July 2, 1864..........	6 ..do	3,486,000
Total...............................	....	....	369,608,500

The total amount of bonds held for the purpose of securing circulation on October 1, 1865, was $276,260,550, of which $199,397,950 was in 6 per cent. and $76,852,600 in 5 per cent. bonds. On November 1, 1880, the banks held $56,605,150 of six per cents, and $147,079,750 of 5 per cents.

On November 1, 1881, all of these bonds had been called, and, with the exception of $758,900, on which interest had ceased, had been redeemed, or extended at the rate of 3½ per cent. The banks now hold $31,981,650 of 4½ per cents, and $92,005,800 of 4 per cent. bonds. They hold also $3,486,000 of Pacific Railroad bonds, and $758,900 called bonds on which interest has ceased. The remainder, $245,601,050, consists of bonds bearing interest at the rate of 3½ per cent. The average rate of interest now paid by the United States upon the bonds deposited as security for circulating notes is about 3.7 per cent. upon their par value. The amount of interest paid is equal to about 3½ per cent. only of the current market value of the bonds.

SPECIE IN BANK AND IN THE TREASURY OF THE UNITED STATES, AND ESTIMATED AMOUNT IN THE COUNTRY—SPECIE IN THE BANK OF ENGLAND, AND IN THE BANK OF FRANCE.

The following table exhibits the amounts of specie held by the national banks at the dates of their reports for the last eight years, the coin and coin certificates held by the New York City banks being stated separately:

Dates.	Held by national banks in New York City.				Held by other national banks.	Aggregate.
	Coin.	U. S. gold certificates.	Clearing-house certificates.	Total.		
Oct. 3, 1872..	$920,767 37	$5,454,580	....	$6,375,347 37	$3,854,409 42	$10,229,756 79
Dec. 27, 1872 ..	1,306,091 05	12,471,940	....	13,778,031 05	5,269,305 40	19,047,336 45
Feb. 28, 1873..	1,958,769 86	11,539,780	....	13,498,541 86	4,279,123 67	17,777,673 53
Apr. 25, 1873..	1,344,950 93	11,743,320	....	13,088,250 93	3,780,557 81	16,868,808 74
June 13, 1873..	1,442,097 71	22,139,080	....	23,581,177 71	4,368,909 01	27,950,086 72
Sept. 12, 1873..	1,063,210 55	13,522,600	....	14,585,810 55	5,282,658 90	19,868,469 45
Dec. 26, 1873..	1,376,170 50	18,325,760	....	19,701,930 50	7,205,107 08	26,907,037 58
Feb. 27, 1874..	1,167,820 09	23,518,640	....	24,686,460 09	8,679,403 49	33,365,863 58
May 1, 1874..	1,530,282 10	23,454,660	....	24,984,942 10	7,585,027 16	32,569,969 26
June 26, 1874..	1,842,525 00	13,671,660	....	15,514,185 00	6,812,022 27	22,326,207 27
Oct. 2, 1874..	1,291,786 56	13,114,480	....	14,406,266 56	6,844,678 67	21,240,945 23
Dec. 31, 1874..	1,443,215 42	14,410,940	....	15,854,155 42	6,582,605 62	22,436,761 04
Mar. 1, 1875..	1,084,555 54	10,622,160	....	11,706,715 54	4,960,390 63	16,667,106 17
May 1, 1875..	930,105 76	5,753,220	....	6,683,325 76	3,937,035 88	10,620,361 64
June 30, 1875..	1,023,015 86	12,642,180	....	13,665,195 86	5,294,386 44	18,959,582 30
Oct. 1, 1875..	753,904 90	4,201,720	....	4,955,624 90	3,094,704 83	8,050,329 73
Dec. 17, 1875..	860,436 72	12,532,810	....	13,402,246 72	3,668,659 18	17,070,905 90
Mar. 10, 1876..	3,261,131 36	19,086,920	....	22,348,051 36	6,729,294 49	29,077,345 85
May 12, 1876..	832,313 70	15,183,760	....	16,015,073 70	5,698,529 06	21,714,594 26
June 30, 1876..	1,214,522 92	16,872,780	....	18,087,302 92	7,131,167 00	25,218,469 92
Oct. 2, 1876	1,120,814 34	13,446,760	....	14,576,574 34	6,785,079 69	21,361,654 03
Dec 22, 1876	1,434,701 83	21,602,900	....	23,037,601 83	9,962,046 06	32,999,647 89
Jan 20, 1877..	1,000,284 94	33,629,660	....	35,298,944 94	14,410,322 61	46,709,267 55
Apr 14, 1877..	1,970,725 59	13,859,180	....	15,829,905 59	11,240,132 19	27,070,037 78
June 22, 1877..	1,423,258 17	10,424,320	....	12,847,406 47	9,588,417 89	21,335,996 06
Oct. 1, 1877..	1,538,486 47	11,409,920	....	21,074,828,20	9,710 413 84	22,658,820 31
Dec. 28, 1877..	1,935,746 20	19,119,080	....	37,412,017 44	17,280,140 58	54,722,058 02
Mar. 15, 1878..	5,429,797 44	35,003,720	....	28,085,732 06	17,938,021 00	46,023,756 06
May 1, 1878..	2,688,692 06	23,397,610	....	13,860,205 22	15,391,264 55	29,251,409 77
June 29, 1878	1,805,705 22	11,854,500	....	13,284,602 83	17,394,004 16	30,688,606 59
Oct. 1, 1878	1,779,792 43	11,514,810	....	16,286,479 01	18,068,771 35	34,355,250 36
Dec. 6, 1878..	4,009,299 01	12,277,180	....	18,161,092 49	23,338,664 83	41,499,757 32
Apr. 4, 1879..	5,312,966 90	12,220,040	....	17,533,966 90	23,614,656 51	41,148,643 41
June 14, 1879..	6,058,472 34	13,291,270	....	19,349,742 34	23,983,545 10	43,333,287 44
Oct. 2, 1879..	7,218,967 09	12,130,900	....	19,349,867 09	22,823,873 54	42,173,731 23
Dec. 12, 1879..	20,096,249 04	8,309,140	$21,599,000 00	50,031,390 64	28,981,651 95	79,013,041 59
Feb. 21, 1880..	12,232,541 44	7,461,650	35,877,900 00	55,572,191 44	23,869,860 31	89,442,051 75
Apr. 23, 1880..	12,795,720 49	6,914,250	25,458,000 00	44,967,970 49	41,461,761 72	86,429,732 21
June 11, 1880..	16,642,226 10	7,810,200	33,817,000 00	57,829,426 10	41,677,078 86	99,506,505 26
Oct. 1, 1880..	16,104,855 28	7,489,700	36,189,000 00	59,783,555 38	49,562,954 11	109,346,509 49
Dec. 31, 1880..	19,773,850 01	6,709,900	28,246,000 00	54,729,779 01	52,443,141 91	107,172,900 92
Mar. 11, 1881..	15,924,683 90	4,825,260	30,809,041 00	51,758,985 00	53,797,211 36	105,156,195 26
May 6, 1881	26,242,108 60	4,825,900	34,176,000 00	65,044,008 60	57,584,553 48	122,624,562 08
June 30, 1881..	20,822,790 87	4,513,400	41,859,000 00	67,191,199 87	61,441,746 63	128,618,927 50
Oct. 1, 1881..	15,317,168 04	4,486,600	31,721,000 00	51,524,768 04	62,809,968 08	114,334,736 12

is the Bank of America, by which bank certificates of deposit were
issued on October 14, 1879. The amount of such certificates out-
ling on November 1, 1879, was $9,155,000, on January 1, 1880,
10,000, and on June 1 following, $39,550,000. The amount held by
ational banks in New York City on June 30, 1881, was $41,858,000;
n October 1, $31,721,000.

e clearing-houses of Boston, Philadelphia and Baltimore have
lized similar depositories, in order to utilize their gold coin, and
ve the risk and inconvenience of handling and transporting it.
total amount of such certificates held by the national banks in
York on October 1 was $31,721,000; by those in Philadelphia,
5,000; in Boston, $4,949,000; and in Baltimore, $1,095,000; total,
90,000.

e national banks held silver coin amounting, on October 1, 1877, to
0,703, and on October 1, 1878, to $5,392,628. On October 2, 1879,
mount held was $4,986,493, and on October 1, 1880, it was
5,477, including $1,165,120 in silver treasury certificates. On Octo-
of the present year, the official reports of the State banks in New
nd, New York, New Jersey, Pennsylvania, Maryland, Louisiana,
Indiana, Iowa, Wisconsin, Missouri, and Minnesota, show
these banks then held specie amounting to $9,019,500, of which
anks in New York City held $4,985,820. The official returns from
tate banks of California do not give separately the amount of coin
by them; but the bank commissioners of that State estimate that
e total cash reported, amounting to $11,276,000, $10,846,672 con-
l of coin. The amount of coin held by State banks in the States
e mentioned, including California, was, therefore, $19,866,172.

e Director of the Mint, in his report for 1880, estimates the
nt of coin in the country on June 30, 1880, at $501,555,711, of which
958,691 was gold and $142,597,020 was silver. His estimate for
scal year ending June 30, 1881, is as follows:

t of coin in the country June 30, 1880	$501,555,711
ld coinage for the year	78,293,087
ver coinage for the year	27,649,660

and $9,610,858 of silver, making the stock of coin in the country at the latter date $649,563,851, of which $468,493,227 was gold and $181,070,624 was silver.

The amount of bullion in the mint and in the New York assay office on November 1 is stated to have been $94,075,744 of gold and $4,966,741 of silver, making in all $99,042,485; which, added to the estimated amount of coin stated above, gives $748,606,336, of which amount $562,568,971 was gold and $186,037,365 was silver.

The following table shows the amount of gold and silver, including the amount held to protect gold and silver certificates, and the percentage of each, in the Treasury of the United States, on September 30 of each year from 1876 to 1881, and on November 1, 1881:

Period.	Silver.			Gold coin and bullion.	Total coin and bullion.	Per cent. of—	
	Standard dollars.	Other coin and bullion.	Total silver.			Silver.	Gold.
September 30, 1876.	....	$6,029,367	$6,029,367	$55,423,059	$61,452,426	9.8	90.2
September 30, 1877.	....	7,425,454	7,425,454	107,039,529	114,464,983	6.5	93.5
September 30, 1878.	$12,155,205	15,777,937	27,933,142	136,036,302	163,969,444	17.0	83.0
September 30, 1879.	31,806,774	21,173,023	52,979,797	169,827,571	222,807,368	23.8	76.2
September 30, 1880.	47,784,744	30,878,286	78,663,030	135,641,450	214,304,480	36.7	63.3
September 30, 1881.	66,092,687	28,945,297	96,037,984	174,361,343	269,399,307	35.3	64.7
November 1, 1881...	66,576,378	29,409,262	95,985,640	172,989,829	268,975,469	35.7	64.3

The bullion in the Bank of England for each year from 1870 to 1881 is shown in the following table, the pound sterling being estimated at five dollars:

1870	$103,900,000	1876	$143,500,000
1871	117,950,000	1877	126,850,000
1872	112,900,000	1878	119,200,000
1873	113,500,000	1879 *	150,942,930
1874	111,450,000	1880 †	141,637,000
1875	119,600,000	1881 †	115,221,870

Below is a similar table, giving the amount of gold and silver, and the percentage of each, in the Bank of France, on December 31 of each year ‡ from 1870 to 1880, and on November 10, 1881, five francs being estimated at one dollar:

Years.	Silver coin and bullion.	Gold coin and bullion.	Total.	Per cent. of	
				Silver.	Gold.
December 31, 1870	$13,700,000	$85,740,000	$99,440,000	13.8	86.2
December 31, 1871	16,240,000	110,680,000	126,920,000	12.8	87.2
December 31, 1872	26,520,000	131,740,000	158,260,000	16.8	83.2
December 31, 1873	31,260,000	122,260,000	153,520,000	20.4	79.6
December 31, 1874	62,640,000	204,220,000	266,860,000	23.5	76.5
December 31, 1875	101,000,000	234,860,000	335,860,000	30.1	69.9
December 31, 1876	127,720,000	306,080,000	433,800,000	29.4	70.6
December 31, 1877	173,080,000	235,420,000	408,500,000	42.4	57.6
December 31, 1878	211,620,000	196,720,000	408,340,000	51.8	48.2
December 31, 1879	245,520,000	148,320,000	893,840,000	62.3	37.7
December 31, 1880	244,360,000	110,480,000	354,840,000	68.9	31.1
November 10, 1881.	236,895,452	124,440,284	361,335,736	65.6	34.4

* London Economist, November 8, 1879.
† London Bankers' Magazine, October, 1880 and 1881.
‡ The Bulletin de Statistique, as quoted in the Bankers' Magazine, New York, vol. xiii, page 740; except the items for 1879,'80 and '81, which were obtained from the London Banker's Magazine for August, 1880, page 661, and September, 1881, page 710, and the last item from The London Economist, November 12, 1881.

NATIONAL-BANK FAILURES AND DIVIDENDS TO CREDITORS.

During the year ending November 1, 1881, no national banks have failed; but since that date, the Mechanic's National Bank of Newark, N. J., and the Pacific National Bank of Boston, Mass., have suspended, and the former bank has been placed in the hands of a receiver. The affairs of twelve banks which failed prior to November 1, 1880, have, during the year, been finally closed, and final dividends have been paid to creditors. These banks with the total dividends paid, are given below:

Total dividends.

Bethel, Conn., First National Bank.........................100 per cent. and interest.
Brattleboro', Vt., First National Bank.................100 per cent. and interest in full.
Delphi, Ind., First National Bank...................100 per cent. and interest in full.
Duluth, Minn., First National Bank................100 per cent. and interest in full.
Fort Scott, Kans., Merchant's National Bank ....60 per cent.
Franklin, Ind., First National Bank ....100 per cent. and interest in full.
Kansas City, Mo., First National Bank...100 per cent.
New Orleans, La., Crescent City National Bank.......................84.83 per cent.
Poultney, Vt., National Bank.........................100 per cent. and interest in full.
Saratoga, N. Y., Commercial National Bank........100 per cent. and interest in full.
Warrensburg, Mo., First National Bank.............100 per cent. and interest in full.
Winchester, Ill., First National Bank.....................................63.6 per cent.

Attention is called to the fact that nine of the twelve foregoing insolvent national banks, whose affairs have been closed during the past year, have paid in full the principal of the claims proved against them, and that eight of the nine have paid principal and interest, seven of them paying interest in full.

The following banks whose affairs are still in the hands of receivers paid dividends during the past year, as follows, the total dividends paid by them up to November 1 being also given:

Bozeman, Mont., First National Bank, 15 per cent.; total, 85 per cent.
Butler, Pa., First National Bank, 10 per cent.; total, 40 per cent.
Charlottesville, Va., Charlottesville National Bank, 5 per cent.; total, 55 per cent.
Chicago, Ill., City National Bank, 7 per cent.; total, 77 per cent.
Chicago, Ill., Third National Bank, 10 per cent.; total, 100 per cent.
Chicago, Ill., German National Bank, 25 per cent.; total, 80 per cent.
Fishkill, N. Y., National Bank, 15 per cent.; total 100 per cent.
Georgetown, Colo., Miners' National Bank, 30 per cent.; total, 65 per cent.
Helena, Mont., Peoples' National Bank, 15 per cent.; total, 30 per cent.
Lock Haven, Pa., Lock Haven National Bank, 10 per cent.; total, 90 per cent
Meadville, Pa., First National Bank, 35 per cent.; total, 100 per cent.
Newark, N. J., First National Bank, 10 per cent.; total, 90 per cent.
Norfolk, Va., First National Bank, 4 per cent.; total, 49 per cent.
Saint Louis, Mo., National Bank of State of Missouri, 5 per cent.; total 95 per cent.
Scranton, Pa., Second National Bank, 25 per cent.; total, 25 per cent.
Washington, D. C., German-American National Bank, 20 per cent.; total, 40 per cent.

It will be noticed that three of the above banks have already paid the principal of their claims to creditors, and it is believed that they will also pay interest, either in part or in full. Of the banks given which have not paid 100 per cent., it is expected that many will do so, and they will perhaps pay interest, in addition.

The total amount of dividends paid by the Comptroller to the creditors of insolvent national banks during the year ending November 1, 1881, was $929,059.16. The total dividends paid to creditors of the 86 banks placed in the hands of receivers prior to November 1 amount to $18,561,698, upon approved claims amounting to $25,966,602. The dividends paid equal about 70 per cent. of the proved claims. Assessments amounting to $7,601,750 have been made upon the shareholders of insolvent national banks, for the purpose of enforcing their individual liability, of which about $3,000,000 has been collected, and nearly $400,000 of it within the past year.

A table showing the national banks which have been placed in the hands of receivers, the amount of their capital, of claims proved, and the rates of dividends paid, and, also, one showing the amount of circulation of such banks issued, redeemed, and outstanding, will be found in the Appendix.

TAXATION OF NATIONAL BANKS.

The Comptroller again respectfully repeats his recommendation for the repeal of the law imposing a tax upon bank capital and deposits, and the two-cent stamp upon bank checks.

The receipts of internal revenue show an increase of $10,447,763 for the fiscal year 1880, and a still further increase of $11,447,906 for 1881, the total increase during the whole period being more than twenty-one and a half millions. The increase of the receipts of the government from customs, internal revenue, and other sources during the year 1880 was $59,699,426, and for the two years named it was nearly 87 millions ($86,955,108). The expenditures of the government during the last fiscal year were less than for either of the two previous years, and the surplus revenue during the same period was more than 100 millions. The receipts for the four months ending November 1 last show a still further increase, and it is probable that the surplus revenue for the present year will be much greater than for any one that has preceded it. The whole amount of internal revenue collected by the Commissioner during the last fiscal year was $135,229,912, all of which, with the exception of $11,520,704, was derived from the tax on spirits, beer, and tobacco.

The amount paid by the national banks to the Treasurer of the United States, for taxes on capital and deposits, during the year ending June 30, 1881, was $5,372,178.22, and the amount paid by banks, other than national, to the Commissioner of Internal Revenue, under the law taxing bank capital and deposits, was $3,757,912. The value of the two-cent check stamps issued during the fiscal year was $2,366,081. The total amount of bank taxes which it is recommended should be abated is $11,496,171, which amount is much less than the annual increase of the internal revenue during the past two years. The receipts from taxes are largely increasing, while the expenditures of the government are largely decreasing, through the reduction of the public debt and of the interest thereon. The reason that has heretofore been urged against the abrogation of these laws—namely, that the amount produced was necessary for the support of the government and for the payment of the public debt—has long since lost its force. Their repeal has already been recommended, both by the Secretary of the Treasury and the Commissioner of Internal Revenue.

While in many of the States there may be a necessity for taxing banking capital and deposits, for purposes of revenue, this reason for retaining a war tax, in the case of the United States Government, has passed away. The rates of interest for money are gradually lessening, and the State taxes which the banks are compelled to pay are as much as should be imposed upon these great agencies for developing the manufacturing and commercial interests of the country. The Comptroller herewith presents tables which give, as far as can be ascertained, the amount of the banking capital of the country, the amount of United States and State taxes, and the rate of taxation paid by the national banks in every State and principal city in the Union for the year 1880.

The following table shows the amount of United States and State taxes, and the rate of taxation paid by the national banks, in every State and principal city of the Union for the year 1880:

States and Territories	Capital.*	Amount of taxes.			Ratios to capital.		
		United States.	State.	Total.	United States.	State.	Total.
					Per ct.	Per ct.	Per ct.
Maine	$10,435,000	$124,884	$228,263	$353,147	1.2	2.3	3.4
New Hampshire	5,827,830	70,524	97,720	168,243	1.2	1.7	2.9
Vermont	8,355,083	93,745	141,678	235,423	1.1	1.8	2.9
Massachusetts	44,995,010	569,299	819,380	1,388,688	1.3	1.8	3.1
Boston	30,500,000	811,080	943,219	1,756,299	1.6	1.9	3.5
Rhode Island	20,009,800	210,778	255,850	466,628	1.0	1.3	2.3
Connecticut	25,556,933	308,612	400,797	709,409	1.2	1.6	2.8
New England States.	165,680,256	2,190,921	2,886,916	5,077,837	1.3	1.8	3.1
New York	32,847,771	561,912	590,085	1,151,997	1.7	1.9	3.6
New York City	50,650,000	1,580,926	1,459,209	3,040,135	2.1	2.0	6.0
Albany	1,800,000	55,398	57,124	112,522	3.1	3.2	6.3
New Jersey	14,147,917	225,397	241,937	467,334	1.7	1.9	3.6
Pennsylvania	28,969,856	465,380	182,124	647,504	1.6	0.7	2.3
Philadelphia	17,189,580	403,834	115,377	521,211	2.4	0.7	3.1
Pittsburgh	9,850,000	161,365	72,288	233,653	1.7	0.7	2.4
Delaware	1,761,677	28,573	7,423	35,906	1.6	0.4	2.0
Maryland	2,308,815	37,263	31,538	68,801	1.6	1.4	3.0
Baltimore	10,890,330	133,847	162,505	316,332	1.4	1.5	2.9
District of Columbia	252,000	4,837	3,910	8,747	1.9	1.6	3.5
Washington	1,125,000	16,513	4,428	20,941	1.5	0.4	1.9
Middle States	170,781,946	3,697,245	2,927,948	6,625,193	2.2	1.8	4.0
Virginia	2,866,000	55,892	51,270	107,162	2.0	2.0	4.0
West Virginia	1,780,795	25,033	26,835	51,868	1.4	1.7	3.1
North Carolina	2,501,000	34,459	32,477	66,936	1.4	1.4	2.8
South Carolina	2,324,900	32,299	55,185	87,484	1.4	2.5	3.9
Georgia	2,201,506	31,418	36,776	68,194	1.4	1.7	3.1
Florida	75,000	1,195	1,975	3,170	1.6	2.0	3.6
Alabama	1,518,000	20,054	32,734	52,808	1.3	2.2	3.5
New Orleans	2,875,000	56,992	4,851	61,843	2.0	0.2	2.2
Texas	1,267,042	19,248	17,548	36,796	1.5	2.0	3.5
Arkansas	205,000	3,546	2,750	6,296	1.7	1.3	3.0
Kentucky	7,151,135	92,417	41,088	133,505	1.3	0.6	1.9
Louisville	3,008,500	49,664	18,608	68,272	1.7	0.6	2.3
Tennessee	3,055,300	57,396	80,975	138,371	1.9	2.7	4.6
Southern States	30,829,178	479,618	403,092	882,705	1.6	1.4	3.0
Ohio	18,699,746	296,403	325,047	621,450	1.6	1.9	3.5
Cincinnati	4,225,000	96,157	94,722	190,879	2.3	2.3	4.6
Cleveland	3,700,000	54,013	60,362	114,375	1.4	1.6	3.0
Indiana	13,236,452	213,089	272,963	486,952	1.6	2.2	3.8
Illinois	10,714,600	199,573	180,842	380,415	1.9	1.8	3.7
Chicago	4,250,000	203,049	107,447	310,496	4.8	2.5	7.3
Michigan	7,384,851	114,968	115,216	230,184	1.6	1.7	3.3
Detroit	2,100,000	46,326	36,446	82,772	2.2	1.7	3.9
Wisconsin	2,425,000	48,903	43,332	92,235	2.0	1.9	3.9
Milwaukee	650,000	26,048	19,409	45,457	4.0	3.0	7.0
Iowa	5,793,813	103,810	121,676	225,486	1.8	2.1	3.9
Minnesota	4,901,552	76,613	81,289	157,902	1.6	1.8	3.4
Missouri	1,416,667	25,024	25,673	50,697	1.8	2.3	4.1
Saint Louis	2,650,000	62,407	64,089	126,496	2.4	2.5	4.9
Kansas	865,694	19,903	13,899	33,802	2.3	2.2	4.5
Nebraska	854,121	28,071	20,381	48,452	3.3	·25	5 8
Colorado	1,070,000	51,853	28,645	80,498	4.0	2.8	y y
Nevada	30,874	340	184	524	1.1	0.4	1.5
California†	1,680,073	23,955	16,369	40,324	1.4	1.0	2.4
San Francisco†	1,500,000	17,325	102	17,427	1.2	0.0	1.2
Oregon	250,000	8,660	3,688	12,348	3.5	1.5	5.0
Dakota	376,722	7,587	5,430	13,017	2.0	1.7	3.7
Idaho	100,000	1,564	3,111	4,675	1.6	3.1	4.7
Montana	200,000	6,622	2,078	8,700	3.3	2.1	5.4
New Mexico	400,000	6,857	8,655	15,512	1.7	2.2	3.9
Utah	200,000	4,513	3,350	7,863	2.3	1.7	4.0
Washington	150,000	2,622	1,440	4,062	1.7	1.0	2.7
Wyoming	150,000	3,160	3,021	6,190	2.1	2.0	4.1
Western States and Territories	89,975,165	1,750,324	1,658,866	3,409,190	1.9	2.0	3.9
Totals	457,266,545	8,118,103	7,876,822	15,994,925	1.8	1.8	3.6

* The capital of the banks that reported State, county, and municipal taxes on stock and real estate is $444,774,085.

† California banks pay no State taxes on capital, except on such as is invested in real estate.

Like tables for the years 1867 and 1869, and for the years 1874 to 1879, inclusive, may be found in the Appendix.

In order that the great inequality of the percentage of the United States and State taxes to the capital of national banks in the different geographical divisions of the country may be seen, tables have been prepared for the years 1879 and 1880, in which the capital stock invested and the percentage thereto of taxes paid is given, as follows:

1879.

Geographical divisions.	Capital.	Amount of taxes.			Ratios to capital.		
		United States.	State.	Total.	United States.	State.	Total.
New England States.....	$165, 032. 512	$1, 942, 209	$2, 532, 004	$4, 474, 213	1.2	1.5	2 7
Middle States	170, 431, 205	3, 190, 113	2, 936, 269	6, 126, 382	1.9	1.7	3.6
Southern States...........	30, 555, 018	425, 097	383, 927	809, 924	1.4	1.3	2.7
Western States and Terr's.	90, 949, 769	1, 457, 812	1, 751, 032	3, 208, 844	1.6	2.0	3.6
United States	456, 968, 504	7, 016, 131	7, 603, 232	14, 619, 363	1.5	1.7	3.2

1880.

New England States.....	$165, 680, 236	$2, 190, 921	$2, 886, 916	$5, 077, 837	1.3	1.8	3.1
Middle States............	170, 731, 946	3, 697, 245	2, 927, 948	6, 625, 193	2.2	1.8	4.0
Southern States.........	30, 829, 178	479, 613	403, 092	882, 705	1.6	1.4	3.0
Western States and Terr's.	89, 975, 165	1, 750, 324	1, 658, 866	3, 409, 190	1.9	2.0	3.9
United States......	457, 266, 545	8, 118, 103	7, 876, 822	15, 904, 925	1.8	1.8	3.6

The inequality in the percentages in United States taxes, which appears in the foregoing tables, arises from the fact that, while the United States tax is imposed on the three items of circulation, deposits, and capital, the percentages given in the tables are those of the total tax, derived from these three sources, to capital only. Where deposits and circulation are large in proportion to capital, the percentage of United States tax in the table is therefore greater; where the deposits and circulation are proportionately smaller, the percentage is less. The inequality in State taxes originates in an actual difference in the rates. The table below shows for the years 1878, 1879, and 1880 the great inequality in the rates in State taxation paid in the principal States in the country.

Cities.	1878.			1879.			1880.		
	United States.	State.	Total.	United States.	State.	Total.	United States.	State.	Total.
	Per ct.	Per. ct.	Per ct.	Per ct.	Per ct.	Per ct.	Per ct.	Per ct.	Per ct.
Boston	1.3	1.3	2.6	1.3	1.3	2.6	1.6	1.9	3.5
New York..............	2.2	2.9	5.1	2.6	2.9	5.5	3.1	2.9	6.6
Albany.................	2.8	2.8	5.6	2.9	2.5	5.4	3.1	3.2	6.3
Philadelphia	2.0	0.7	2.7	2.1	0.7	2.8	2.4	0.7	3.1
Pittsburgh	1.3	0.5	1.8	1.4	0.6	2.0	1.7	0.7	2.4
Baltimore	1.2	1.8	3.0	1.2	1.3	2.5	1.4	1.5	2.9
Washington	1.4	0.6	2.0	1.4	0.4	1.8	1.5	0.4	1.9
New Orleans	1.5	1.0	2.5	1.7	0.5	2.2	2.0	0.2	2.2
Louisville.............	1.4	0.5	1.9	1.5	0.6	2.1	1.7	0.6	2.3
Cincinnati	1.5	2.7	4.2	1.9	2.4	4.3	2.3	2.3	4.6
Cleveland.............	1.1	2.0	3.1	1.3	2.0	3.3	1.4	1.6	3.0
Chicago...............	2.5	2.6	5.1	3.4	2.4	5.8	4.8	2.5	7.3
Detroit.	1.7	1.5	3.2	1.8	2.2	4.0	2.2	1.7	3.9
Milwaukee	2.4	2.6	5.0	2.8	2.5	5.3	4.0	3.0	7.0
Saint Louis	1.6	2.4	4.0	1.8	2.1	3.9	2.4	2.5	4.9
Saint Paul	1.3	1.5	2.8	1.5	1.5	3.0	1.7	1.8	3.5

The tables already given indicate the necessity of some precise rule of State taxation. The States in which the rates of taxation were most excessive during the years 1878, 1879, and 1880 are given in the following table:

States.	1878.			1879.			1880.		
	United States.	State.	Total.	United States.	State.	Total.	United States.	State.	Total.
	Per ct.	Per ct.	Per ct.	Per ct.	Per ct.	Per ct.	Per ct.	Per ct.	Per ct
New York	2.0	2.6	4.6	1.5	2.0	3.5	1.7	1.9	3.6
New Jersey	1.4	1.8	3.2	1.5	1.8	3.3	1.7	1.9	3.6
Ohio	1.3	2.2	3.5	1.4	2.0	3.4	1.6	1.9	3.5
Indiana	1.3	2.1	3.4	1.4	2.1	3.5	1.6	2.2	3.8
Illinois	1.7	2.1	3.8	1.5	1.8	3.3	1.9	1.8	3.7
Wisconsin	1.7	2.2	3.9	1.6	1.8	3.4	2.0	1.9	3.9
Kansas	1.6	2.6	4.2	2.1	2.7	4.8	2.3	2.2	4.5
Nebraska	2.3	2.6	4.9	2.6	2.6	5.2	3.3	2.5	5.8
South Carolina	1.0	2.1	3.1	1.2	2.0	3.2	1.4	2.5	2.9
Tennessee	1.6	2.1	3.7	1.7	1.8	3.5	1.9	2.7	4.6

The national banks, under present law, pay to the United States a tax of one per cent. upon the amount of their notes in circulation, one-half of one per cent. upon the amount of their deposits, and the same rate upon the average amount of capital beyond the amount invested in United States bonds. These taxes are paid semi-annually by the national banks to Treasurer the of the United States.

The following table shows the amount annually paid under this law, from the commencement of the national banking system to July 1, 1881, showing an aggregate of taxes paid to the United States, by national banks, of $108,855,021.90:

Years.	On circulation.	On deposits.	On capital.	Total.
1864	$53,193 32	$95,911 87	$18,432 07	$167,537 26
1865	733,247 59	1,087,530 86	133,251 15	1,954,029 60
1866	2,106,785 30	2,633,102 77	406,947 74	5,146,835 81
1867	2,868,636 78	2,650,180 09	321,881 36	5,840,698 23
1868	2,946,343 07	2,564,143 44	306,781 67	5,817,268 18
1869	2,957,416 73	2,614,553 58	312,918 68	5,884,888 99
1870	2,949,744 18	2,614,767 61	375,962 26	5,940,474 00
1871	2,987,021 69	2,802,840 85	385,292 13	6,175,154 67
1872	3,193,570 03	3,130,984 37	389,356 27	6,703,910 67
1873	3,353,186 13	3,196,569 29	454,891 51	7,004,646 93
1874	3,404,483 11	3,209,907 72	469,048 02	7,083,498 85
1875	3,283,450 89	3,514,265 39	507,417 76	7,305,134 04
1876	3,091,795 76	3,505,129 64	632,296 16	7,229,221 56
1877	2,900,957 53	3,451,965 38	660,784 90	7,013,707 81
1878	2,948,047 08	3,273,111 74	560,296 83	6,781,455 65
1879	3,009,647 16	3,309,668 90	401,920 61	6,721,236 67
1880	3,153,635 63	4,058,710 61	379,424 19	7,591,770 43
1881	3,121,374 33	4,940,945 12	431,233 10	8,493,552 55
Aggregates	49,062,536 26	52,644,349 23	7,148,196 41	108,855,021 90

The amount of tax paid upon circulation alone is $49,062,536, while the whole cost to the government of the national system, since its establishment in 1863, has been but $5,148,649.01.

The banks, other than national, pay taxes to the United States on account of their circulation, deposits and capital, at the same rates as are paid by the national banks; but these taxes, instead of being paid to the Treasurer, are collected by the Commissioner of Internal Revenue.

The table below exhibits the taxes which have been paid by these banks for the years from 1864 to 1881, inclusive. The amounts given

11 Ab

under the head of tax on circulation have, for a number of years, been principally derived from the tax of ten per cent. upon State bank circulation paid out. The whole amount of tax paid by these banks is $61,540,471.63 :

Years.	On circulation.	On deposits.	On capital.	Totals.
1864	$2,056,996 30	$780,723 59		$2,837,719 82
1865	1,993,681 84	2,043,841 08	$903,387 08	4,940,870 90
1866	990,278 11	2,099,635 83	374,074 11	3,463,988 05
1867	214,208 75	1,355,395 98	476,887 73	2,046,562 46
1868	28,669 88	1,438,512 77	399,562 90	1,866,745 55
1869	16,565 05	1,734,417 63	445,071 49	2,196,054 17
1870	15,419 94	2,177,576 46	827,087 21	3,020,083 61
1871	22,781 92	2,702,196 84	919,262 77	3,644,241 53
1872	8,919 82	3,643,251 71	976,057 61	4,628,229 14
1873	24,778 62	3,009,302 79	736,950 05	3,771,031 46
1874	16,738 26	2,453,544 26	916,878 15	3,387,160 67
1875	22,746 27	2,972,260 27	1,102,241 58	4,097,248 12
1876	17,947 67	2,999,530 75	989,219 61	4,006,698 63
1877	5,430 16	2,896,637 93	927,661 94	3,829,729 23
1878	1,118 72	2,593,687 29	897,225 84	3,492,031 85
1879	13,903 29	2,354,911 74	830,068 56	3,198,883 59
1880	28,773 37	2,510,775 43	811,436 48	3,350,985 28
1881	4,295 08	2,946,906 64	811,006 35	3,762,208 07
Aggregates	5,483,323 05	42,713,108 92	13,344,039 66	61,540,471 63

From returns heretofore received, the following condensed table has been prepared, which shows the taxes, both National and State, paid by the national banks during each year from 1866 to 1880, inclusive, and their ratios to capital:

Years.	Capital stock.	Amount of taxes.			Ratio of tax to capital.		
		United States.	State.	Total.	United States.	State.	Total.
					Per ct.	Per ct.	Per ct.
1866	$410,593,435	$7,940,451	$8,069,938	$16,019,389	1.9	2.0	2.9
1867	422,804,666	9,525,607	8,813,127	18,338,734	2.2	2.1	4.3
1868	420,143,491	9,465,652	8,757,656	18,223,308	2.2	2.1	4.3
1869	419,619,860	10,061,244	7,297,096	17,378,340	2.4	1.7	4.1
1870	429,314,641	10,190,682	7,465,675	17,656,357	2.4	1.7	4.1
1871	451,994,133	10,649,895	7,860,078	18,509,973	2.4	1.7	4.1
1872	472,956,958	6,703,910	8,343,772	15,047,682	1.4	1.8	3.2
1873	488,778,418	7,004,646	8,499,748	15,504,394	1.4	1.8	3.2
1874	493,751,679	7,256,083	9,620,326	16,876,409	1.5	2.0	3.5
1875	503,687,911	7,317,531	10,058,122	17,375,653	1.5	2.0	3.5
1876	501,788,079	7,076,087	9,701,732	16,777,819	1.4	2.0	3.4
1877	485,250,694	6,902,573	8,829,304	15,731,877	1.4	1.9	3.3
1878	471,061,238	6,727,232	8,056,533	14,783,765	1.4	1.7	3.1
1879	456,968,504	7,016,131	7,603,232	14,619,363	1.5	1.7	3.2
1880	457,266,545	8,118,103	7,876,822	15,994,925	1.8	1.8	3.6

These statistics show that during the fifteen years covered by the table the average amount annually paid by the national banks to the States and to the United States was $16,589,199, or more than 3½ per cent. upon their capital stock; during the last year given, the total amount paid was $15,994,925, or more than 4 per cent. upon the amount of the average circulation of the banks then in operation.

STATE TAXATION OF NATIONAL BANKS.

The United States Supreme Court, in the case of The People ex rel. Williams vs. Weaver, at the October term in 1879, decided that the States have no right to assess the shares of national banks located within their borders, for purposes of taxation, at a greater rate or valuation than other moneyed capital in the hands of individuals is assessed; and that an individual in New York, holding bank shares, has the same right to deduct his just debts from the amount of his bank shares as he would have to deduct them from his personal property, including his

just debts from the assessed valuation of such shares, while under the general statutes of the State that right was granted to the owners of other moneyed capital. Justice Harlan, of the United States Supreme Court, recently decided in this suit that the law of Indiana "enforces in certain cases a rule of taxation inconsistent with the principle of equality underlying the legislation of Congress, and conformity to which is essential to the validity of State taxation of national bank shares." He decides that every shareholder of a national bank, who, at the time of assessment, had debts, and no credits from which he could deduct the same, except national bank shares, from which the State laws did not permit him to make such deduction, is entitled, through the bank, to an injunction against the tax assessed upon the shares.

As it is in the power of the States, under the present law of Congress, so to legislate that through unequal valuations bank shares may be discriminated against as compared with other moneyed capital in the hands of corporations or individuals, a necessity appears to exist that, in order to avoid protracted and expensive litigation, Congress shall so amend the present law that there can be no doubt as to the precise amount of taxation which may be imposed by the States on national bank shares.

In my last annual report a suggestion was made in reference to the amendment of section 5219, Revised Statutes of the United States. It is now again recommended that the section named shall be amended to read as follows:

But the legislature of each State may determine and direct the manner and place of taxing the shares of national banking associations located within the State, subject to the following restrictions, namely: That the maximum rate of tax shall not exceed —— per cent.; that the rate, and the valuation upon which such rate is calculated shall not exceed the least rate and valuation to which other moneyed capital, in the hands of individuals, or of corporations of any class, in such State is subjected, and that the shares of any national banking association, owned by a non-resident of any State, shall be taxed in the State or town in which the bank is located, and not elsewhere.

If such an amendment becomes a law it will, in a great measure, prevent the various forms of discrimination which have been exercised in the imposition and collection of taxes upon national-bank shares, under State authority. The Supreme Court of the United States has decided that, without the permission of Congress, the States would have no right to impose any taxes whatever upon national banks, and that in enacting the law under which the States now exercise this right, Congress was conferring a power on the States which they would not otherwise have had. This court also decided that it was the evident intention of Congress to protect the banks from anything beyond their equal share of the public burdens. Congress has therefore the power wholly to rescind the right granted to the States to tax national banking associations. This, however, is not asked or desired. But, inasmuch as it has been the tendency of legislation in different States to disregard, or render inoperative, the provisions of the act of Congress permitting and restricting State taxation of national bank shares, it is certainly not too much to expect that Congress will regard it as due to themselves to pass such amendments as will carry out the intention of their original act, clearly defined and sustained as it has been by the decisions of the Supreme Court of the United States.

LOSSES, SURPLUS, EARNINGS AND DIVIDENDS OF THE NATIONAL BANKS.

During the year ending September 1, 1881, the national banks charged off losses amounting to $12,691,349.75. Of this, $5,889,761.19 was charged off during the six months ending March 1, 1881, and $6,801,588.56 during the similar period ending September 1, 1881. The following table shows the number of banks that charged off these losses, and the amount so charged off by them, in each State and reserve city throughout the United States, for the two semi-annual periods ending March 1 and September 1, 1881, respectively. The total losses charged off in each of the four preceding years have been added to the table. Full tables for the five previous years may be found in the Appendix:

States and Territories.	March 1, 1881.		September 1, 1881.		Aggregate.
	No. of banks.	Losses.	No. of banks.	Losses.	
Maine	37	$77,806 40	39	$81,689 17	$159,495 57
New Hampshire	24	99,725 43	29	123,014 54	222,739 96
Vermont	23	126,093 71	29	155,990 86	282,084 57
Massachusetts	96	240,971 17	108	439,978 14	680,949 31
Boston	35	280,815 43	34	420,239 30	701,054 73
Rhode Island	27	566,227 60	25	247,484 81	813,712 41
Connecticut	43	193,035 40	54	238,940 77	431,976 17
New York	128	441,955 39	136	579,084 66	1,020,900 05
New York City	36	989,797 57	38	1,331,205 05	2,321,002 62
Albany	6	40,960 64	6	46,262 49	87,223 13
New Jersey	47	211,657 61	49	217,217 23	428,874 84
Pennsylvania	120	398,222 91	121	356,224 18	754,447 09
Philadelphia	27	175,251 05	26	230,998 11	406,249 16
Pittsburgh	16	152,358 84	18	105,729 25	258,088 09
Delaware	6	21,076 98	4	513 49	21,590 42
Maryland	11	15,713 42	10	36,429 10	52,142 52
Baltimore	9	51,336 66	10	47,843 10	99,179 76
District of Columbia	1	436 60	1	109 45	546 05
Washington	5	49,435 34	5	23,543 63	72,978 97
Virginia	13	53,809 45	13	58,828 98	112,688 43
West Virginia	10	24,596 12	9	8,851 42	33,447 54
North Carolina	7	30,522 29	9	89,067 00	119,589 29
South Carolina	7	63,772 53	8	138,042 71	201,815 24
Georgia	6	10,544 64	8	55,418 00	65,962 64
Florida	1	1,070 16	1	2,155 64	3,225 80
Alabama	3	10,270 81	5	56,027 38	66,298 19
New Orleans	6	15,187 27	7	59,782 98	74,920 25
Texas	9	39,264 53	11	71,519 97	110,784 50
Arkansas	2	5,925 23			5,925 23
Kentucky	24	51,289 88	25	59,876 67	111,116 50
Louisville	8	35,232 24	8	122,638 43	157,870 67
Tennessee	16	48,222 31	15	75,024 21	118,246 52
Ohio	86	189,875 45	91	215,348 17	405,223 62
Cincinnati	4	37,435 88	5	39,178 05	76,613 93
Cleveland	6	98,097 39	5	45,975 31	144,072 70
Indiana	52	197,852 79	51	200,483 52	397,336 31
Illinois	71	185,954 89	69	110,410 73	296,365 62
Chicago	8	49,189 62	8	36,201 75	85,391 37
Michigan	47	143,548 67	46	97,721 86	241,270 58
Detroit	3	28,208 26	3	10,599 86	38,808 12
Wisconsin	10	14,595 30	12	21,397 92	35,993 22
Milwaukee	3	15,556 79	2	21,091 99	36,648 78
Iowa	35	75,411 39	42	89,239 76	164,651 15
Minnesota	23	101,230 17	19	68,889 50	170,119 67
Missouri	7	20,294 95	7	16,410 92	36,705 87
Saint Louis	3	17,215 69	5	85,684 03	102,899 72
Kansas	7	21,534 68	8	23,210 21	44,744 89
Nebraska	4	10,805 98	5	39,662 66	50,468 64
Colorado	12	70,390 95	9	119,889 14	190,280 09
Nevada	1	123 30	1	338 59	461 89
California	6	26,939 94	5	30,925 82	57,865 76
San Francisco	1	10,425 43	1	3,226 83	13,652 26
Oregon	1	21,799 20	1	22,411 26	44,210 46
Dakota	4	17,050 20	2	18,017 29	35,067 49
Montana	2	4,277 20	2	5,254 94	7,532 14
New Mexico	3	12,284 79	1	1,858 45	14,143 24
Utah	1	776 50	1	2,542 40	3,318 90
Washington			1	2,893 13	2,893 13
Wyoming	2	1,900 18	2	43 75	1,943 93
Totals for 1881	1,210	5,889,761 19	1,269	6,801,588 56	12,691,349 75
Add for 1880	1,380	7,563,886 04	1,321	7,142,519 96	14,706,406 00
Add for 1879	1,421	10,238,324 98	1,442	11,487,330 17	21,725,655 15
Add for 1878	1,304	10,903,145 04	1,430	13,563,654 85	24,466,799 89
Add for 1877	980	8,175,960 56	1,108	11,757,627 43	19,933,587 99
Aggregate losses for five years		42,771,077 81		50,752,720 97	93,523,798 78

In order to compare the losses experienced by national banks located in the different sections of the United States, the following table is given, which shows the total losses charged off in each geographical division of the country during the last five years. The number of banks reporting losses is also given:

Six months ending—	New England States.		Middle States.		Southern States.		Western States and Territories.		United States.	
	No.	Amount.	No.	Amount.	No.	Amount.	No.	Amount.	No.	Amount.
March 1, 1877	289	$2,465,328	314	$3,462,684	80	$478,252	297	$1,769,697	980	$8,175,961
September 1, 1877 .	312	4,825,040	353	3,945,806	86	511,841	357	2,474,940	1,108	11,757,627
Total, 1877	.....	7,290,368	....	7,408,490	....	990,093	....	4,244,637	.....	19,933,588
March 1, 1878	327	3,344,012	417	4,506,813	124	672,032	436	2,380,288	1,304	10,903,145
September 1, 1878 .	399	4,016,814	449	5,502,770	140	1,225,602	442	2,818,469	1,430	13,563,655
Total, 1878	.....	7,360,826	....	10,009,583	....	1,897,634	....	5,198,757	.....	24,466,800
March 1, 1879	379	3,612,128	459	3,592,950	125	696,646	458	2,336,600	1,421	10,238,234
September 1, 1879 .	384	3,388,394	463	4,360,440	139	1,235,784	456	2,502,712	1,442	11,487,230
Total, 1879 ...	...	7,000,522	..	7,953,390	....	1,932,430	....	4,839,312	.....	21,725,654
March 1, 1880	362	2,236,928	446	3,152,317	121	530,769	431	1,643,872	1,360	7,562,896
September 1, 1880 .	320	1,866,658	440	2,817,870	124	787,046	431	1,670,946	1,321	7,142,520
Total, 1880 ..	.....	4,103,586	....	5,970,187	....	1,317,815	.....	3,314,818	.....	14,706,406
March 1, 1881	285	1,584,675	412	2,548,203	112	384,607	401	1,372,276	1,210	5,889,761
September 1, 1881 .	818	1,707,338	428	2,975,110	119	797,233	404	1,321,908	1,209	6,801,589
Total, 1881 ...	.....	3,292,013	....	5,523,313	....	1,181,840	.....	2,694,184	.....	12,691,250
Total for five years........	.....	29,047,315	....	36,864,963	....	7,319,812	.....	20,291,708	.....	92,523,798

Of the losses given in the foregoing tables, a portion is on account of the depreciation in the premium on United States bonds held by the banks. The amount of premium thus charged off during the past year was $2,271,339.50; and, during the last four and a half years, it amounted to $13,107,099. The total losses, shown in the above table, extending over a period of five years, are equal to 24.5 per cent. of the entire capital of the banks, and 19.1 per cent. of their combined capital and surplus.

In order further to illustrate this subject, several of the principal cities of the United States have been selected, and the losses sustained during the past five years by the national banks located in each are given in the following table:

Cities.	1877.	1878.	1879.	1880.	1881.	Total.
New York......	$4,247,941 66	$5,147,319 98	$3,135,557 37	$2,054,381 52	$3,321,002 63	$16,906,202 15
Boston	2,192,053 81	2,490,197 46	2,655,390 58	1,110,831 72	701,054 73	9,149,528 30
Philadelphia....	333,248 47	561,876 30	491,558 36	399,943 74	406,249 16	2,192,876 03
Pittsburgh	289,466 59	419,036 51	333,022 99	258,128 15	258,088 09	1,557,742 33
Baltimore......	200,597 74	368,915 99	204,507 00	211,329 01	99,179 76	1,174,529 50
New Orleans...	286,259 47	338,496 90	272,889 87	118,080 28	74,920 35	1,090,646 87

The losses charged off by the banks during the last year are about $2,000,000 less than those experienced during the previous year. A part of the losses charged off, as shown by the preceding tables, consisted of bad debts as defined in the law—viz, debts on which interest was due and unpaid for a period of six months, and which were neither secured nor in process of collection. The bad debts so charged off consisted of other stocks and bonds on which interest had ceased, as well as of bills receivable. Since the resumption of specie payments, the value of a portion of these bad assets has been realized; and it is estimated that in this way about 25 per cent. of these losses has since been recovered.

DIVIDENDS AND EARNINGS.

From the semi-annual returns made by the banks to this Office, tables have been prepared, showing the dividends and profits, and the ratios of each to capital, and to capital and surplus combined. The following table shows the capital, surplus, dividends, and total earnings of all the national banks, for each half year, from March 1, 1869, to September 1, 1881, with the ratios, as before specified:

Period of six months, ending—	No. of banks.	Capital.	Surplus.	Total dividends.	Total net earnings.	RATIOS.		
						Dividends to capital.	Dividends to capital and surplus.	Earnings to capital and surplus.
						Per cent.	*Per cent.*	*Per cent.*
Sept. 1, 1869	1,481	$401,650,892	$82,105,848	$21,767,831	$29,221,184	5.42	4.50	6.04
Mar. 1, 1870	1,571	416,366,991	86,118,210	21,479,095	28,996,934	5.16	4.27	5.77
Sept. 1, 1870	1,601	425,317,104	91,630,620	21,080,343	26,813,885	4.96	4.08	5.19
Mar. 1, 1871	1,665	428,699,165	94,672,401	22,205,150	27,248,102	5.18	4.24	5.21
Sept. 1, 1871	1,693	445,999,264	98,286,591	22,125,279	27,315,311	4.96	4.07	5.02
Mar. 1, 1872	1,750	450,693,706	99,431,243	22,850,826	27,502,539	5.07	4.16	5.00
Sept. 1, 1872	1,852	465,676,023	105,181,942	23,827,269	30,572,891	5.12	4.17	5.36
Mar. 1, 1873	1,912	475,918,683	114,257,288	24,826,061	31,926,478	5.22	4.21	5.41
Sept. 1, 1873	1,955	488,100,951	118,113,848	24,825,029	35,122,000	5.09	4.09	5.46
Mar. 1, 1874	1,967	489,510,322	122,440,850	23,529,928	29,544,120	4.81	3.84	4.82
Sept. 1, 1874	1,971	489,938,284	125,364,039	24,929,307	30,936,811	5.09	4.03	4.96
Mar. 1, 1875	2,007	493,568,831	131,560,637	24,750,610	29,136,007	5.01	3.96	4.66
Sept. 1, 1875	2,047	497,864,833	134,122,649	24,317,785	28,800,317	4.88	3.85	4.56
Mar. 1, 1876	2,076	504,209,491	134,467,595	24,811,581	23,097,921	4.92	3.88	3.62
Sept. 1, 1876	2,081	500,482,271	132,251,078	22,563,820	20,546,231	4.50	3.57	3.25
Mar. 1, 1877	2,080	496,651,580	130,872,165	21,803,969	19,592,002	4.39	3.47	3.12
Sept. 1, 1877	2,072	480,324,860	124,340,254	22,117,116	15,274,028	4.54	3.62	2.50
Mar. 1, 1878	2,074	475,609,731	122,373,561	18,982,390	16,946,496	3.99	3.17	2.82
Sept. 1, 1878	2,047	470,231,896	118,687,134	17,959,223	13,658,803	3.81	3.04	2.31
Mar. 1, 1879	2,043	464,413,996	116,744,135	17,541,054	14,676,660	3.78	3.02	2.53
Sept. 1, 1879	2,045	455,192,056	115,149,351	17,401,867	16,875,200	3.82	3.05	2.96
Mar. 1, 1880	2,046	454,080,090	117,226,501	18,121,273	21,152,784	3.99	3.17	3.70
Sept. 1, 1880	2,072	454,215,062	120,145,649	18,290,200	24,032,250	4.03	3.18	4.18
Mar. 1, 1881	2,087	456,844,865	122,481,788	18,877,517	24,452,021	4.13	3.20	4.22
Sept. 1, 1881	2,100	458,934,485	127,238,394	19,499,604	29,170,816	4.25	3.33	4.98

In the following table is given, by geographical divisions, the number of national banks, with their capital, which paid no dividends to their stockholders during the two semi-annual periods of 1881, to which the totals for each semi-annual period in the four preceding years have been added:

Geographical divisions.	Six months ending—				Average for the year	
	March 1, 1881.		September 1, 1881.			
	No. of banks.	Capital.	No. of banks.	Capital.	No. of banks.	Capital.
New England States	12	$1,881,000	8	$1,925,000	10	$1,903,000
Middle States	62	8,746,630	57	6,842,400	60	7,794,515
Southern States	18	2,109,900	19	1,875,150	18	1,992,525
Western States and Territories	83	7,584,000	87	7,745,000	85	7,664,500
Totals for 1881	175	20,321,530	171	18,387,550	173	19,354,540
Totals for 1880	226	30,407,200	233	26,334,150	230	28,370,675
Totals for 1879	309	53,843,700	299	44,576,300	304	49,210,000
Totals for 1878	328	48,797,900	357	58,736,950	343	53,767,425
Totals for 1877	245	40,452,000	288	41,166,200	266	40,809,100
Average for each year	257	38,764,466	269	37,840,230	263	38,302,348

The percentage to capital of dividends paid, and of dividends and earnings to combined capital and surplus, is given by similar divisions for the years 1879, 1880 and 1881, in the following table:

Geographical divisions.	1879.			1880.			1881.		
	Dividends to capital.	Dividends to capital and surplus.	Earnings to capital and surplus.	Dividends to capital.	Dividends to capital and surplus.	Earnings to capital and surplus.	Dividends to capital.	Dividends to capital and surplus.	Earnings to capital and surplus.
	Per ct.	Per ct.	Per ct.	Per ct.	Per ct.	Per ct.	Per ct.	Per ct.	Per ct.
New England States........	6.4	5.2	4.2	6.8	5.5	6.4	7.2	5.8	7.3
Middle States ..	7.9	6.1	5.8	8.4	6.5	8.6	8.5	6.4	9.4
Southern States	7.0	6.0	5.4	7.8	6.7	7.6	8.3	6.9	11.3
Western States and Territories	9.4	7.5	7.1	9.5	7.6	9.3	10.4	8.1	11.6
United States..	7.6	6.1	5.5	8.0	6.4	7.9	8.4	6.6	9.2

SURPLUS.

Under the law requiring the national banks to carry to surplus fund, before declaring dividends, a certain proportion of their earnings, the national banks of the country have accumulated a fund, in addition to their capital, which now amounts to $128,140,618. This surplus is not infringed upon, except in case of extraordinary losses, such as cannot be paid from the current earnings of the banks, and consequently forms, with the capital, the working fund of the banks. In the following table the gradual accumulation of this fund, from the commencement of the system to the present time, is shown, as nearly as possible, by semi-annual periods. The increase or decrease for each period is also given:

Dates.	Amount.	Semi-annual increase or decrease.	Dates.	Amount.	Semi-annual increase or decrease.
		Increase.			Increase.
July 4, 1864............	$1,129,910	....	June 13, 1873	$116,847,455	$5,437,206
January 2, 1865.......	8,663,311	$7,533,401	December 26, 1873....	120,961,268	4,113,813
July 3, 1865........	31,303,566	22,640,255	June 26, 1874........	126,230,308	5,275,040
January 1, 1866	43,000,371	11,696,805	December 31, 1874 ...	130,485,641	4,246,333
July 2, 1866........	50,151,992	7,151,621	June 30, 1875........	133,169,095	2,683,454
January 7, 1867	59,962,875	9,840,883			Decrease.
July 1, 1867.......	63,232,811	3,239,936	December 17, 1875 ...	133,085,422	$83,673
January 6, 1868	70,586,126	7,253,315	June 30, 1876	131,897,197	1,188,225
July 6, 1868.......	75,840,119	5,253,993	December 22, 1876 ...	131,390,665	506,532
January 4, 1869	81,169,937	5,329,818	June 22, 1877........	124,714,073	6,676,592
June 12, 1869.......	82,218,576	1,048,339	December 28, 1877...	121,568,455	3,145,618
January 22, 1870	90,174,281	7,955,705	June 29, 1878	118,178,531	3,389,924
June 9, 1870.......	91,689,834	1,515,553	January 1, 1879	116,200,804	1,977,667
December 28, 1870 ...	94,705,749	3,015,906	June 14, 1879.........	114,821,370	1,879,488
June 10, 1871........	98,322,204	3,616,464			Increase.
December 16, 1871....	101,573,154	3,250,950	December 12, 1879...	116,429,032	$1,107,656
June 10, 1872	105,181,943	3,608,789	June 11, 1880	118,102,014	2,672,982
December 27, 1872....	111,410,249	6,228,306	December 31, 1880 ..	121,824,629	3,722,615
			June 30, 1881	126,679,518	4,854,889

From December, 1875, to June, 1879 there was a constant decrease in this fund. In all other cases a gradual increase is to be noted.

UNITED STATES LEGAL-TENDER NOTES AND NATIONAL-BANK CIRCULATION.

The acts of February 25, 1862, July 11, 1862, and March 3, 1863, each authorized the issue of 150 millions of dollars of legal-tender notes, making an aggregate of 450 millions of dollars. On January 30, 1864, the amount of such notes outstanding was $449,338,902, which was the highest amount outstanding at any one time. The act of June 30, 1864,

In the following table is shown by States the amount of circulation issued and retired during the year ending November 1, 1881, and the total amount issued and retired since June 20, 1874:

States and Territories.	Circulation issued.	Circulation retired.		Total.
		Act of June 20, 1874.	Liquidating banks.	
Maine	$45,000	$68,145	$23,863	$92,008
New Hampshire	10,300		5,644	5,684
Vermont	200,700	165,471	38,759	204,230
Massachusetts	8,635,840	1,586,655	8,232	1,594,887
Rhode Island	1,586,240	290,219	1,672	291,891
Connecticut	1,912,360	819,721	2,265	821,986
New York	7,198,370	4,683,765	186,681	4,870,446
New Jersey	1,186,170	310,419	110,952	421,371
Pennsylvania	5,300,690	1,511,536	93,377	1,604,913
Delaware	45,000			
Maryland	700,000	24,240	2,243	26,483
District of Columbia	500	16,655	13,013	29,668
Virginia	258,300	70,935	32,800	103,755
West Virginia		40,805	13,014	53,819
North Carolina		51,144	13,445	64,569
South Carolina	81,000	93,258		93,258
Georgia	22,480	8,541	12,354	20,896
Florida				
Alabama		34,710	8,859	43,569
Mississippi			70	70
Louisiana	338,000	55,982	12,620	68,602
Texas	121,500		6,970	6,970
Arkansas		16,442	60	16,542
Kentucky	809,950	163,376	31,238	194,614
Tennessee	201,600	9,997	23,545	33,542
Missouri	876,100	129,056	92,372	221,428
Ohio	2,549,380	460,751	116,122	576,873
Indiana	600,970	750,020	122,329	872,349
Illinois	897,560	344,914	130,484	475,348
Michigan	311,400	225,460	49,023	274,483
Wisconsin	472,500	85,784	51,457	137,241
Iowa	447,300	81,222	66,051	147,273
Minnesota	147,600	94,733	47,092	141,825
Kansas	121,480	38,401	43,429	81,730
Nebraska	198,900	40,682	2,032	42,714
Nevada			160	160
Oregon				
Colorado	149,400		10,468	10,468
Utah			3,835	3,835
Idaho				
Montana	126,000	9,934	25,483	35,417
Wyoming	27,000			
New Mexico				
Dakota	117,000			
Washington	90,000	20,365		20,365
California	135,000			
Surrendered to this office and retired				410,873
Totals	30,979,630	12,303,246	1,402,013	14,116,134
Previously retired, under act of June 20, 1874	91,748,275	71,135,348	16,194,067	87,329,415
Previously surrendered, under same act				11,794,880
Grand totals	122,727,905	83,438,594	17,596,080	114,240,429

The amount of circulation issued to national banks for the year ending November 1, 1881, was $30,979,630, including $5,233,580 issued to banks organized during the year. The amount retired during the year was $14,075,054, and the actual increase for the same period was therefore $16,904,576, making the total on November 1, $359,422,738, which is the largest amount outstanding at any one time.

During the year ending November 1, 1881, lawful money to the amount of $23,847,844 was deposited with the Treasurer to retire circulation, of which amount $1,554,790 was deposited by banks in liquidation. The amount previously deposited under the act of June 20, 1874, was $85,684,998; by banks in liquidation, $18,390,555, to which is to be added a balance of $3,813,675, remaining from deposits made by liquidating banks prior to the passage of that act. Deducting from the total the amount of circulating notes redeemed and destroyed without reissue, $101,034,675, there remained in the hands of the Treasurer on November 1, 1881, $30,702,596 of lawful money for the redemption and retirement of bank circulation.

CIRCULATING NOTES OF THE BANK OF FRANCE AND IMPERIAL BANK OF GERMANY, BY DENOMINATIONS—NATIONAL-BANK AND LEGAL-TENDER NOTES, BY DENOMINATIONS.

The following table* exhibits by denominations the circulation of the Imperial Bank of Germany, on January 1, 1881, in thalers and marks, which are here converted into our currency:

		Thalers.				Marks.	
Number of pieces.	Denominations.	Value of each piece in dollars.	Amount in dollars. (Thaler=75 cents.)	Number of pieces.	Denominations.	Value of each piece in dollars.	Amount in dollars. (Mark=25 cents.)
81	500 thalers.	375 00	30,375	260,582	1,000 marks.	250	65,145,500
2,246	100 thalers.	75 00	168,450	217,449	500 marks.	125	27,181,125
1,664½	50 thalers.	37 50	63,394	4,848,362½	100 marks.	25	108,709,562
8,726	25 thalers.	18 75	163,612	....	....	....	....
9,036½	10 thalers.	7 50	67,699	....	....	....	....
21,770	....	....	493,530	4,826,413½	....	....	201,036,187

The circulation of the Imperial Bank of Germany, on January 1, 1879, was $165,933,942; its circulation on January 1, 1880, was $198,201,144; showing an increase of $32,267,202 during that year.

The following table† gives the circulation of the Bank of France and its branches, with the number of pieces, and the denominations in francs and in dollars, on January 27, 1881:

Number of pieces.	Denominations.	Value of each piece in dollars.	Amount in francs.	Amount in dollars. (Franc = 20 cts.)
5	5,000 francs.	1,000	25,000	5,000
1,370,596	1,000 francs.	200	1,370,596,000	274,119,200
712,243	500 francs.	100	356,121,500	71,224,300
2,889	200 francs.	40	577,800	115,560
7,555,345	100 francs.	20	755,534,500	151,106,900
671,119	50 francs.	10	33,555,950	6,711,190
25,587	25 francs.	5	639,675	127,935
282,999	20 francs.	4	5,659,980	1,131,996
189,095	5 francs.	1	945,475	189,095
1,224	Forms out of date.	....	425,900	85,180
10,811,102	....	....	2,524,081,780	504,816,356

The amount of circulation of the Bank of France on January 29, 1880, was 2,321,474,365 francs, or, say, $464,294,873, showing an increase between that time and January 27, 1881, the date of the foregoing table, of 202,607,415 francs, or $40,521,483.

* London Bankers' Magazine for September, 1881, page 706.   † Ibid., page 719.

It will be seen that the Imperial Bank of Germany issues no notes of a less denomination than $7.50, and that the Bank of France issues less than two millions of dollars in notes of a less denomination than five dollars. The Bank of England issues no notes of less than twenty-five dollars, and the Banks of Ireland and Scotland none of less than five dollars.

The amount of circulation in this country in denominations of five dollars and under, on November 1, 1880, was $214,326,838. In the foreign countries named a large amount of silver and gold coin of the lower denominations enters into general circulation. It will be impossible to keep in circulation here any large amount of small gold coins or silver dollars, unless the coinage of the latter is restricted and the small notes withdrawn.

In accordance with law, no national-bank notes of denominations less than five dollars have been issued since the 1st of January, 1879. Since that date the amount of ones and twos has been reduced $5,867,465, and during the same period the amount of legal-tender notes of these denominations has been increased $7,903,621. During the last year the amount of national-bank notes of these denominations has decreased $1,648,440. The total increase, therefore, of the amount of one and two dollar bills outstanding, in national-bank and legal-tender notes, is $6,255,181.

The following table shows, by denominations, the amount of national-bank and legal-tender notes outstanding on November 1, 1881, and the aggregate amounts of both kinds of notes at the same date in 1879 and 1880:

Denominations.	1881.			1880.	1879.
	National-bank notes.	Legal-tender notes.	Aggregate.	Aggregate.	Aggregate.
Ones	$1,329,112	$24,464,059	$25,793,171	$24,247,362	$22,897,502
Twos	522,170	23,732,196	24,254,366	23,036,578	21,090,983
Fives	100,480,080	67,899,982	168,380,062	167,042,896	159,522,853
Tens	121,308,840	75,408,831	196,717,671	189,655,588	181,447,558
Twenties	81,116,500	70,806,003	151,922,503	147,719,887	141,445,932
Fifties	23,284,200	23,157,575	46,441,775	45,777,475	46,177,945
One hundreds	29,951,000	33,239,370	63,190,370	59,958,600	58,332,780
Five hundreds	732,000	14,217,500	14,949,500	16,765,500	23,088,600
One thousands	201,000	12,065,500	12,266,500	14,640,500	23,111,580
Five thousands	....	2,430,000	2,430,000	2,430,000	3,250,000
Ten thousands	....	260,000	260,000	260,000	2,500,000
Add for unredeemed fragments of national-bank notes	+16,586	....	+16,586	+15,129	+13,586
Deduct for legal-tender notes destroyed in Chicago fire....	....	−1,000,000	−1,000,000	−1,000,000	−1,000,000
Totals.....................	358,941,488	346,681,016	705,622,504	688,744,467	681,815,526

The written signatures of the officers of the banks are necessary as an additional precaution against counterfeiting. It is recommended that a bill for preventing the lithographing or printing of the signatures of officers of banks, now required by law to be written on the notes, be passed by Congress, imposing a penalty of twenty dollars for a violation thereof.

REDEMPTIONS.

Section 3 of the act of June 20, 1874, provides that every national bank "shall at all times keep and have on deposit in the Treasury of the

United States, in lawful money of the United States, a sum equal to five per centum of its circulation, to be held and used for the redemption of such circulation." Since the passage of this act the banks have, as a rule, maintained their redemption fund, and their circulating notes have been promptly redeemed at the Treasury, without expense to the government.

The following table exhibits the amount of national-bank notes received for redemption monthly, by the Comptroller of the Currency, for the year ending October 31, 1881, and the amount received for the same period at the redemption agency of the Treasury, together with the total amount received since the passage of the act of June 20, 1874 :

Months.	Received by the Comptroller.					Received at redemption agency.
	From national banks for reissue or surrender.	From redemption agency for reissue.	Notes of national banks in liquidation.	Under act of June 20, 1874.	Total.	
1880.						
November	$11,600	$2,596,200	$78,305	$558,194	$3,244,290	$3,369,417
December	42,700	2,824,500	146,741	225,647	3,239,588	4,151,971
1881.						
January	77,624	3,218,900	203,374	656,677	4,156,575	5,550,743
February	29,905	4,005,600	189,613	751,995	4,927,113	4,498,501
March	55,230	3,251,400	125,155	858,932	4,290,717	4,804,393
April	24,460	3,071,800	143,025	2,231,988	5,471,213	6,860,425
May	3,205	4,659,300	98,066	1,540,498	6,301,069	8,035,983
June	14,900	6,220,800	310,635	2,239,566	8,785,901	7,151,961
July	50	3,149,800	57,214	647,235	3,854,299	4,988,307
August	20,850	3,467,500	99,885	1,184,073	4,772,308	4,540,053
September	58,710	2,178,700	69,233	624,066	2,930,709	3,622,833
October	67,720	3,789,600	155,472	740,834	4,753,626	4,945,668
Totals	406,894	42,434,100	1,626,718	12,259,705	56,727,417	62,510,255
Received from June 20, 1874, to October 31, 1880	12,667,195	387,314,155	16,069,075	71,345,508	487,395,933	1,038,013,014
Grand totals..	13,074,089	429,748,255	17,695,793	83,605,213	544,123,350	1,100,523,269

From the passage of the act of June 20, 1874, to October 31, 1881, there was received at the redemption agency of the Treasury $1,100,523,269 of national-bank currency. During the year ending October 31, 1881, there was received $62,510,225; of which amount $23,923,000, or about 38 per cent., was received from banks in New York City, and $5,679,000, or about 9 per cent., was received from banks in the city of Boston. The amount received from Philadelphia was $5,169,000; from Baltimore, $723,000; Pittsburgh, $624,000; Cincinnati, $1,023,000; Chicago, $2,777,000; Saint Louis, $732,000; Providence, $1,415,000. The amount of circulating notes fit for circulation returned by the redemption agency to the banks of issue during the year was $4,536,200.

The total amount received by the Comptroller of the Currency for destruction, from the redemption agency and from the national banks direct, was $56,727,417. Of this amount, $5,836,203 were issues of banks in the city of New York, $5,819,519 of Boston, $2,275,055 of Philadelphia, $912,700 of Baltimore, $971,483 of Pittsburgh, $409,300 of Cincinnati, $138,330 of Chicago, $105,800 of Saint Louis, $1,786,791 of Providence, and of each of the other principal cities less than $400,000.

The following table exhibits the number and amount of national-bank notes, of each denomination, which have been issued and redeemed since the organization of the system, and the number and amount outstanding on November 1, 1881:

Denominations	Number.			Amount.		
	Issued	Redeemed.	Outstand-ing.	Issued.	Redeemed.	Outstand-ing.
Ones	23, 167, 677	21, 838, 565	1, 329, 112	$23, 167, 677	$21, 838, 565	$1, 329, 112
Twos	7, 747, 519	7, 486, 434	261, 085	15, 495, 048	14, 972, 868	522, 170
Fives	73, 612, 504	53, 516, 484	20, 096, 016	368, 062, 520	267, 582, 440	100, 480, 080
Tens	29, 477, 519	17, 346, 635	12, 130, 884	294, 775, 190	173, 466, 350	121, 308, 840
Twenties	8, 940, 817	4, 884, 992	4, 055, 825	178, 816, 340	97, 699, 840	81, 116, 500
Fifties	1, 357, 574	801, 890	465, 644	67, 878, 700	44, 504, 500	23, 294, 200
One hundreds	950, 712	660, 202	290, 510	95, 971, 800	66, 020, 200	29, 951, 000
Five hundreds	21, 959	20, 495	1, 464	10, 979, 500	10, 247, 500	732, 000
One thousands	7 144	6, 943	201	7, 144, 000	6, 843, 000	301, 000
Portions of notes lost or destroyed					−16, 586	+16, 586
Totals	145, 292, 425	106, 652, 644	38, 639, 781	1, 062, 290, 165	703, 348, 677	358, 941, 488

A table showing the numbers and denominations of national-bank notes issued and redeemed, and the number of each denomination outstanding on November 1 for the last thirteen years, will be found in the Appendix.

The following table shows the amount of national bank notes received at this office and destroyed yearly since the establishment of the system:

Prior to November 1, 1865......................................	$175, 490
During the year ending October 31, 1866	1, 050, 382
During the year ending October 31, 1867......................................	3, 401, 423
During the year ending October 31, 1868......................................	4, 602, 425
During the year ending October 31, 1869......................................	8, 603, 729
During the year ending October 31, 1870......................................	14, 305, 690
During the year ending October 31, 1871......................................	24, 344, 047
During the year ending October 31, 1872......................................	30, 211, 720
During the year ending October 31, 1873......................................	36, 433, 171
During the year ending October 31, 1874......................................	49, 939, 741
During the year ending October 31, 1875......................................	137, 497, 686
During the year ending October 31, 1876......................................	98, 672, 716
During the year ending October 31, 1877......................................	76, 918, 983
During the year ending October 31, 1878......................................	57, 381, 249
During the year ending October 31, 1879......................................	41, 101, 880
During the year ending October 31, 1880......................................	35, 539, 690
During the year ending October 31, 1881......................................	54, 941, 130
Additional amount of notes of national banks in liquidation	28, 027, 215
Total	703, 348, 676

The amount of one and two dollar notes outstanding is but one-half of one per cent. of the whole circulation of the banks, the fives constitute 28 per cent., the tens 33.8 per cent., the twenties 22.6 per cent., while the fifties and over are only 15.1 per cent. of the entire circulation. While the amount of ones and twos of the national-bank circulation is steadily diminishing, the legal-tender notes of these denominations are as steadily increasing. Of the entire amount of national-bank and legal-tender notes outstanding, nearly 7.1 per cent. consists of one and two dollar notes, more than 30.9 per cent. of ones, twos, and fives, more than 58.8 per cent. is in notes of a less denomination than twenty dollars, while about 80.4 per cent. is in notes of a lower denomination than fifty dollars. Of the entire issue, about 19.4 per cent. is in denominations of fifties, one hundreds, five hundreds, and one thousands. There are also outstanding 486 legal-tender notes of the denomination of five thousand, and 26 notes of the denomination of ten thousand.

RESERVE.

The following table exhibits the amount of net deposits, and the reserve required thereon by the act of June 20, 1874, together with the amount and classification of reserve held by the national banks in New York City, in the other reserve cities, and by the remaining banks, at the dates of their reports in October of each year from 1875 to 1881:

NEW YORK CITY.

	Number of banks	Net deposits	Reserve required	Reserve held		Classification of reserve.			
				Amount.	Ratio to deposits.	Specie.	Other lawful money.	Due from agents.	Redemption fund.
		Millions.	Millions.	Millions.	Per cent.	Millions.	Millions.	Millions.	Millions.
October 1, 1875.	48	292.3	50.6	60.5	29.9	5.0	54.4	....	1.1
October 2, 1876.	47	197.9	49.5	60.7	30.7	14.6	45.3	....	0.8
October 1, 1877.	47	174.9	43.7	48.1	27.5	13.0	34.3	....	0.8
October 1, 1878.	47	189.8	47.4	50.9	26.8	13.3	36.5	....	1.1
October 2, 1879.	47	210.2	52.6	53.1	25.3	19.4	32.6	....	1.1
October 1, 1880.	47	263.1	67.0	70.6	26.4	58.7	11.0	....	0.9
October 1, 1881.	48	266.8	67.2	62.5	23.3	50.6	10.9	....	1.0

OTHER RESERVE CITIES.

	Number of banks	Net deposits	Reserve required	Reserve held		Classification of reserve.			
				Amount.	Ratio to deposits.	Specie.	Other lawful money.	Due from agents.	Redemption fund.
October 1, 1875.	188	223.9	56.0	74.5	33.3	1.5	37.1	33.3	2.6
October 2, 1876.	189	217.0	54.2	76.1	35.1	4.0	37.1	32.0	3.0
October 1, 1877.	188	204.1	51.0	67.3	33.0	5.6	34.3	24.4	3.0
October 1, 1878.	184	199.9	50.0	71.1	35.6	5.6	29.4	29.1	3.2
October 2, 1879.	181	228.8	57.2	83.5	36.5	11.3	33.0	35.7	3.5
October 1, 1880.	184	289.4	72.4	105.2	36.3	28.3	25.0	48.2	3.7
October 1, 1881.	189	335.4	83.9	100.8	30.0	34.6	21.9	40.6	3.7

STATES AND TERRITORIES.

	Number of banks	Net deposits	Reserve required	Reserve held		Classification of reserve.			
				Amount.	Ratio to deposits.	Specie.	Other lawful money.	Due from agents.	Redemption fund.
October 1, 1875.	1,851	307.9	46.3	100.1	32.5	1.6	33.7	58.3	11.5
October 2, 1876.	1,853	291.7	43.8	99.9	34.3	2.7	31.0	55.4	10.8
October 1, 1877.	1,845	290.1	43.6	95.4	32.0	4.3	31.6	48.9	10.7
October 1, 1878.	1,822	289.1	43.4	106.1	36.7	8.0	31.1	56.0	11.0
October 2, 1879.	1,820	329.9	49.5	124.3	37.7	11.5	30.2	71.3	11.2
October 1, 1880.	1,850	410.5	61.6	147.2	35.8	21.2	28.3	86.4	11.2
October 1, 1881.	1,895	507.2	76.1	158.3	31.2	37.5	27.1	92.4	11.4

SUMMARY.

	Number of banks	Net deposits	Reserve required	Reserve held		Classification of reserve.			
				Amount.	Ratio to deposits.	Specie.	Other lawful money.	Due from agents.	Redemption fund.
October 1, 1875	2,087	734.1	152.2	235.1	32.0	8.1	125.2	85.6	16.2
October 2, 1876.	2,089	706.6	147.5	236.7	33.5	21.3	113.4	87.4	14.6
October 1, 1877.	2,080	669.1	138.3	210.8	31.5	22.8	100.2	73.3	14.5
October 1, 1878.	2,053	678.8	140.8	228.1	33.6	30.7	97.0	85.1	15.3
October 2, 1879.	2,048	768.9	159.3	260.9	33.9	42.2	95.9	107.0	15.8
October 1, 1880.	2,090	968.0	201.0	323.0	33.4	106.2	64.3	134.6	15.9
October 1, 1881.	2,132	1,111.6	227.2	321.6	28.9	112.7	56.9	133.0	16.1

The following table, compiled from returns made to the clearing-house by the national banks in New York City, exhibits the movement of their reserve, weekly, during October, for the last eight years:

Week ending—	Specie.	Legal tenders.	Total.	Ratio of reserve to—	
				Circulation and deposits.	Deposits.
				Per cent.	Per cent.
October 4, 1873	$9,240,300	$9,251,900	$18,492,200	11.6	14.0
October 11, 1873	10,508,900	8,049,300	18,556,200	11.6	14.1
October 18, 1873	11,650,100	5,179,800	16,829,900	10.7	13.0
October 25, 1873	11,433,500	7,187,300	18,620,800	12.2	14.8
October 3, 1874	15,373,400	53,297,600	68,671,000	30.0	33.9
October 10, 1874	14,517,700	52,152,000	66,669,701	29.6	31.3
October 17, 1874	12,691,400	51,855,100	64,546,500	29.0	32.7
October 24, 1874	11,457,700	49,893,900	61,351,800	28.8	31.7
October 31, 1874	10,324,900	50,773,000	61,097,900	27.9	31.6
October 2, 1875	5,438,900	56,181,500	61,620,400	28.1	30.6
October 9, 1875	5,716,200	51,342,300	57,058,500	28.5	28.9
October 16, 1875	5,528,500	48,582,700	54,111,200	25.4	27.7
October 23, 1875	5,745,000	47,300,900	53,035,900	25.3	27.7
October 30, 1875	8,975,600	45,762,800	54,738,400	26.5	29.0
October 7, 1876	17,682,600	45,535,600	63,218,200	30.5	32.4
October 14, 1876	16,233,800	43,004,600	59,238,200	28.8	31.1
October 21, 1876	15,577,500	41,421,700	56,909,200	27.8	30.0
October 28, 1876	14,011,600	41,645,600	55,657,200	28.0	30.3
October 6, 1877	14,665,600	36,168,300	50,833,900	27.0	28.5
October 13, 1877	14,726,500	35,178,900	49,905,400	26.7	28.7
October 20, 1877	14,087,400	35,101,700	49,189,100	26.5	29.0
October 27, 1877	15,209,000	34,367,800	49,576,800	26.8	28.4
October 5, 1878	16,995,800	34,304,900	53,300,700	25.7	28.4
October 12, 1878	12,184,600	37,645,100	49,889,700	24.4	27.0
October 19, 1878	13,531,400	36,576,000	50,107,400	24.7	27.2
October 26, 1878	17,384,200	35,690,500	53,074,700	25.8	28.3
October 4, 1879	18,979,600	34,368,000	53,347,600	23.2	25.8
October 11, 1879	20,901,800	32,820,500	53,722,100	23.4	25.8
October 18, 1879	24,686,500	29,305,200	53,991,700	22.5	24.1
October 25, 1879	25,636,000	26,713,900	52,349,900	23.0	25.3
October 2, 1880	59,823,700	11,129,100	70,952,800	25.5	26.4
October 9, 1880	62,521,300	10,785,000	73,306,300	25.4	27.3
October 16, 1880	62,760,600	10,939,200	73,699,800	25.5	27.1
October 23, 1880	60,888,200	10,988,200	71,876,400	24.9	26.6
October 30, 1880	61,471,600	10,925,000	72,396,600	25.0	26.7
October 1, 1881	54,954,600	12,150,400	67,105,000	23.1	24.8
October 8, 1881	53,287,900	12,153,800	65,441,700	23.2	24.9
October 15, 1881	51,008,300	12,452,700	63,461,000	23.2	25.6
October 22, 1881	54,016,200	12,496,500	66,512,700	24.6	26.8
October 29, 1881	55,961,200	12,947,900	68,909,100	25.6	27.4

*APPENDIX.

Tables will be found in the appendix, exhibiting the reserve of the national banks as shown by their reports, from October 2, 1874, to October 1, 1881; the reserve by States and principal cities for October 1, 1881; and in the States and Territories, in New York City, and in the other reserve cities, separately, at three dates in each year, from 1878 to 1881.

Special attention is called to the synopsis of judicial decisions contained in the appendix, to the numerous and carefully prepared tables in both report and appendix, and to the index of subjects and list of tables to be found at the close of the appendix. At the end of the full volume of more than seven hundred pages is an alphabetical list of the cities and villages in which the national banks are situated.

In concluding this report the Comptroller gratefully acknowledges the zeal and efficiency of the officers and clerks associated with him in the discharge of official duties.

JOHN JAY KNOX,
Comptroller of the Currency

Hon. JOSEPH WARREN KEIFER,
Speaker of the House of Representatives.

* The appendix, which is omitted for want of space, may be found in the bound volumes of the Comptroller's report.

REPORT OF THE DIRECTOR OF THE MINT.

TREASURY DEPARTMENT,
BUREAU OF THE MINT,
November 1, 1881.

SIR: I have the honor to present my third and the ninth annual report from this bureau, showing the operations of the mints and assay offices of the United States for the fiscal year ending June 30, 1881.

The influx of gold from foreign countries, noticed in my last report, continued during the year, giving a net import of $5,836,058, American gold coin, and of $91,715,012 foreign coin and bullion.

This has not only largely increased the work of this bureau but the business and operations of the New York assay office, where $91,499,168.61 of foreign gold was received, and of the Philadelphia mint, to which it was sent for coinage. Besides this heavy import, the American mines have maintained [within a few thousand dollars], a gold production equaling that of the preceding year.

DEPOSITS AND PURCHASES.

The bullion and coin received and operated upon during the year, at all the mints and assay offices, including redeposits, contained $193,371,101.01 of gold and $32,854,421.45 of silver, a total of $226,225,522.46, exceeding in value the receipts of any previous year by more than $50,000,000.

The reports and accounts submitted to this bureau show, during the year, deposits of gold of domestic production, $35,815,036.55; of plate, jewelry, and worn coin, $1,784,207.90; and of foreign coin and bullion, $93,233,858; being a total of $130,833,102.45, and thirty-two millions in excess of the gold deposits of last year.

The silver bullion deposits and purchases, including partings from gold, amounted at the coining value to $30,791,146.66, of which $28,477,059.31 consisted of domestic bullion, $2,046,576.80 of foreign coin and bullion, and $267,510.05 of plate, jewelry, and American coin. The following table shows the amount and character of the deposits:

	Gold.	Silver.	Total.
Domestic production	$35,815,036 55	$28,477,059 21	$64,292,095 76
United States coin	440,776 97	7,307 40	448,084 37
Foreign bullion	37,771,472 26	1,312,144 58	39,083,616 84
Foreign coin	55,462,345 74	734,482 22	56,196,817 96
Old jewelry, plate, &c	1,343,43? 93	260,203 25	1,603,634 18
Total	130,833,102 45	30,791,146 66	181,634,249 11

A portion of these deposits were manufactured at the institutions receiving them into bars, which were again deposited or transferred to other institutions for treatment or coinage. The redeposits for this purpose amounted to $62,537,998.56 in gold, and to $2,063,271.79 in silver.

COINAGE.

At the commencement of the fiscal year the coinage mints and assay offices held $40,724,337.91 of uncoined gold bullion. The deposits of the year, amounting to $130,833,102.45, increased the stock of bullion available for coinage to $171,557,440.36.

The value of the total gold coinage of the year was $78,733,864, and of the gold bullion uncoined at its close, $86,548,696.96, a portion of the deposits having been paid in fine bars.

The silver coinage amounted to $27,649,966.75, of which $27,637,955 were silver dollars, and $12,011.75 proof silver coins of other denominations.

The coinage of gold into smaller denominations than heretofore executed was continued, only $15,345,520 in double eagles having been struck, while the eagles and half eagles amounted to $63,371,230.

Nearly all of the gold produced on the Pacific coast was deposited and coined at the San Francisco Mint, while the principal part of the gold coined at the Philadelphia Mint consisted of New York Assay Office bars manufactured from imported bullion and coin.

The number of pieces and the value of the total coinage were as follows:

	Pieces	Value.
Gold	10,111,113	$78,723,884 88
Silver	27,694,820	27,649,966 73
Minor	38,335,665	405,100 95
Total	76,143,600	106,788,940 70

The comparative values of the coinage of gold, silver, and minor coins executed during the fiscal year and the calendar year 1880 are as follows:

	Calendar year 1880.	Fiscal year 1881.
Gold	$72,308,279 00	$78,723,884 88
Silver	27,409,706 75	27,649,966 73
Total	89,717,985 75	106,303,830 78
Minor	391,395 95	405,100 95
Total coinage	90,109,381 70	106,788,940 70

The gold coinage of the mints prior to the year 1873 has been grouped and tabulated into three divisions. The first embracing the forty years from the commencement of coinage at the Philadelphia Mint in 1834 to the time of the change in the ratio of gold and silver and the reduced valuation of the gold dollar to correspond therewith, during which period $11,915,890 of gold were coined.

The second from 1834 to 1849, when gold from California first began to arrive at the mints, adding $64,425,550 to the gold coinage.

The third from 1849 to 1873, during which time $740,564,438.50 were coined.

The coinage of silver before 1873 is separated into two periods: The first containing the coinage prior to 1853, during which time all the silver coins, amounting in value to $79,213,371.90, were full weight and unlimited legal tender.

The second from 1853 to 1873, when fractional silver of reduced weight and limited tender to the amount of $60,389,564.70 was coined on government account; but, although the mints were open to individuals for the coinage of full weight silver dollars, only $5,538,948 of the latter were coined.

BARS.

Fine, standard, sterling, and unparted bars were manufactured during the year to the value of $100,750,649.94 in gold and $6,542,232.35 in silver.

At the New York Assay Office $89,643,135.29 of gold deposits were made into bars for conversion into coin at the mint at Philadelphia.

The value of fine gold bars manufactured at the mints and assay offices was $10,041,482.78 and of the unparted bars $1,066,031.87. Of the silver bars $5,857,276.98 were fine, $77,611.39 were standard and sterling, $88,296.45 unparted, and $519,047.53 were made at the New York Assay Office and transmitted to Philadelphia for coinage.

PARTING AND REFINING.

During the year, 11,449,704.19 gross ounces of bullion, containing both gold and silver or base metals, were sent to the acid refineries of the coinage mints and assay office at New York for parting or refining, from which were separated or refined 1,295,443.259 ounces of standard gold and 9,774,730.86 ounces of standard silver.

The following table exhibits in detail the gross ounces of bullion sent to the respective refineries and the ounces of standard gold and silver received therefrom:

OUNCES.

Mint or assay office.	Gross.	Standard gold.	Standard silver.
Philadelphia	535,770.27	125,700.460	389,617.83
San Francisco	6,507,762.50	612,429.779	5,591,629.12
Carson	525,785.05	27,819.475	507,723.00
New Orleans	13,886.37	2,793.545	11,860.91
New York	3,866,500.00	526,700.000	3,273,300.00
Total	11,449,704.19	1,295,443.259	9,774,730.86

VALUE.

Mint or assay office.	Gold.	Silver.	Total.
Philadelphia	$2,338,612 21	$453,373 47	$2,791,986 68
San Francisco	11,394,042 40	6,506,622 98	17,900,665 38
Carson	517,571 62	590,804 94	1,108,376 56
New Orleans	51,972 93	13,801 78	65,774 71
New York	9,799,069 76	3,809,629 09	13,608,698 85
Total	24,101,269 92	11,374,232 26	35,475,502 18

DIES AND MEDALS.

During the year the engraver of the mint at Philadelphia prepared 1,229 dies for coinage, and 13 for medals and experimental pieces, a total of 1,242.

The mints at San Francisco, Carson, and New Orleans are supplied with coinage dies by the Philadelphia Mint, the latter being the only one provided with an engraving department.

The number of medals made was 1,682, of which 112 were struck in fine gold, 1,196 in fine silver, and 374 in bronze copper.

SILVER PURCHASES.

At the commencement of the last fiscal year there were on hand in the coinage mints and New York Assay Office 5,403,980 ounces of standard silver bullion, worth, at its coining value, $6,283,613. This bullion in part consisted of 1,750,000 standard ounces procured prior to the passage of the resumption act, under the provisions of section 3545 of the Revised Statutes, and held as part of the bullion fund for the immediate payment of silver deposits in silver bars. A further portion, amounting to 2,500,000 standard ounces, had been purchased subsequent to January 14, 1875, the date of the resumption act, for the coinage of subsidiary silver, under the provisions of that act, or had been parted from gold or received in payment of charges on silver bullion, under sections 3520 and 3506. The remainder, about 1,400,000 standard ounces, was obtained by direct purchase for the coinage of the standard dollar, or in settlement for silver parted from gold, and in payment of charges on silver deposits.

Notwithstanding the regular monthly coinage of 2,300,000 and upwards of silver dollars, the purchases and deposits had increased the silver bullion on hand January 1, 1881, to 6,553,350 standard ounces, the cost of which was $7,145,487, and its coinage value $7,625,717. Of this amount, 2,928,752.49 standard ounces were at the Philadelphia Mint.

The limit of subsidiary coinage having been reached, no necessity existed for keeping on hand any silver for such coinage. It was, therefore, considered advisable by the Secretary of the Treasury to use in the silver-dollar coinage the balance of silver that had been procured for the subsidiary coinage, and to reduce the amount of monthly purchases, especially at the Philadelphia Mint, where, in view of the heavy amount of gold coinage required, it was thought that sufficient silver bullion had already been accumulated for the probable silver coinage of that mint during the remainder of the fiscal year.

By including the 2,250,000 ounces of standard silver as belonging to the account of purchased silver, to be used in the coinage of the standard dollar, it became necessary to reduce the amount on hand, so that not more than $5,000,000 above the resulting coinage should be invested in such purchases. The weekly purchases of the department were, therefore, much lighter during February and the succeeding months of the year.

In the month of May, owing to the higher prices asked and the small amounts offered for delivery at the Pacific coast mints, the weekly purchases of silver bullion were reduced for San Francisco and resumed at the Philadelphia Mint.

To enable the Philadelphia Mint to employ as much of its force as possible in the coinage of gold, the monthly allotment of silver coinage for the New Orleans Mint was increased and that for the Philadelphia Mint lessened, and to procure sufficient bullion to execute the required coinage at the New Orleans Mint, the owners of silver bullion were solicited to bid and send their bullion for delivery at that mint.

The prices for delivery in lots of less than ten thousand ounces at the New Orleans Mint were also fixed from time to time by the Director of the Mint, slightly below the equivalent of the London price, and notices of the rates and changes were given to the smelting and refining works in the Western States nearest to the mint, with the hope of inducing them to deliver their silver bullion at New Orleans. Two of these refineries have availed themselves of the advantages of direct shipment, saving the previous expense of double transportation to and from the Atlantic sea-board and benefiting the Government as well as themselves.

The purchases during the year, of silver bullion, were 21,904,351.54 standard ounces, at a cost of $22,339,728.67. The silver received for charges and parted from gold and paid for as provided by sections 3520 and 3506 of the Revised Statutes, costing $239,183.05, was 232,568.85 standard ounces, making the total amount purchased 22,136,920.39 standard ounces, at the cost of $22,578,911.72.

From the silver purchases of the year and the 2,250,000 standard ounces, directed to be used and carried into the silver purchase account, 23,751,368 standard ounces, exclusive of silver bullion wasted and sold in sweeps, were consumed in the coinage of 27,633,955 standard dollars, being an average monthly coinage of $2,303,166.

The London price of silver, during the year, averaged 51$\frac{11}{16}$ pence, which with exchange at par ($4.8665) equals $1.13852 per ounce, and at the New York average monthly price of sight exchange on London ($4.847) equals $1.13508 per ounce fine. The New York average price of silver during the year was $1.12957 per ounce fine.

The following statement shows the purchases at the coining mints and the New York Assay Office.

SILVER PURCHASES, 1881.

Mint or assay office at which delivered.	Purchases.		Partings and received for charges.		Total purchased.	
	Standard ounces.	Cost.	Standard ounces.	Cost.	Standard ounces.	Cost.
Philadelphia	6, 322, 103. 90	$6, 458, 604 34	21, 726. 01	$21, 726 01	6, 343, 829. 91	$6, 480, 330 35
San Francisco	10, 236, 585. 17	10, 412, 523 54	73, 373. 57	73, 629 04	10, 309, 958. 74	10, 486, 152 58
New Orleans........	4, 839, 852. 28	4, 954, 753 78	957. 11	957 47	4, 840, 809. 39	4, 955, 711 25
Carson City..........	505, 810. 19	513, 847 01	1, 912. 89	1, 912 89	507, 723. 08	515, 759 90
New York			134, 599. 27	140, 957 64	134, 599. 27	140, 957 64
Total	21, 904, 351. 54	22, 339, 728 67	232, 568. 85	239, 183 05	22, 136, 920. 39	22, 578, 911 72

DISTRIBUTION OF SILVER.

Including the amounts paid out at the mints and exchanged for gold as provided by law, $17,706,924 of the $27,637,955 silver dollar coinage of the year, have been transmitted and distributed under the regulations mentioned in my last report.

The amount of standard dollars in the mints at the close of the fiscal year, including $2,000,000 received at the New Orleans Mint, and $1,000,000 at the Philadelphia Mint from assistant treasurers, was $23,341,000.60, of which nearly $16,000,000 was in the San Francisco Mint.

The coinage and distribution at each mint, as shown by their statements to this bureau, appear in the following table:

AMOUNT of SILVER DOLLARS REPORTED by the COINAGE MINTS on HAND June 30, 1880, COINED during and on HAND at CLOSE of the FISCAL YEAR ended June 30, 1881.

	Philadelphia.	San Francisco.	Carson.	New Orleans.	Total.
On hand June 30, 1880.................	$875, 942	$5, 469, 769	$1, 119, 700	$2, 944, 618	$10, 410, 029
Coinage of year	9, 113, 955	11, 460, 000	539, 000	6, 525, 000	27, 637, 955
Total.............................	9, 989, 897	16, 929, 769	1, 658, 700	9, 469, 618	38, 047, 984
In mints June 30, 1881.................	*1, 250, 802	15, 941, 135	1, 060, 991	†5, 088, 132	23, 341, 060
Distributed	9, 739, 095	988, 634	597, 709	6, 381, 486	17, 706, 924

* Includes $1,000,000 transferred from the Treasury.
† Includes $2,000,000 transferred from the Treasury.

Besides the standard dollars remaining in the mints at the close of the year, considerable amounts had been deposited in the Treasury for the payment of outstanding silver certificates.

The following table, compiled from the Treasurer's monthly statements of assets and liabilities, shows in six months' periods from the commencement until the close of the last fiscal year and up to November 1, 1881, the amount (including that in the mints) in the Treasury, held for the payment of silver certificates and for other purposes and the amount in general circulation:

COMPARATIVE STATEMENT of the COINAGE MOVEMENT and CIRCULATION of STANDARD SILVER DOLLARS at the end of each six months from July 1, 1880, to July 1, 1881, and for the four months ending November 1, 1881.

Period.	Total coin-age.	In the Treasury.				In circulation.
		Held for payment of certificates outstanding.	For distribution.	Total.		
July 1, 1880	$63,734,750	$5,789,560	$38,635,746	$44,425,315		$19,309,435
January 1, 1881	77,458,005	36,127,711	12,062,807	48,190,518		29,262,487
July 1, 1881	91,272,705	39,110,729	24,423,993	63,544,722		26,827,983
November 1, 1881	100,672,705	58,838,770	7,737,608	66,576,378		34,066,327

APPROPRIATIONS, EARNINGS, AND EXPENDITURES.

The total appropriations for the support of the mints and assay offices during the fiscal year ended June 30, 1881, amounted to $1,178,250, out of which the sum of $1,100,347.71 was expended. In addition $97,311.60 was expended on account of the mints and $7,440.14 at the Treasury Department, a total of $104,751.74 from the appropriation contained in the act of February 28, 1878, authorizing the coinage of the standard silver dollar.

The appropriations for and expenditures at the several mints and assay offices are shown in the following table:

APPROPRIATIONS, 1881.

Institution.	Salaries.	Wages.	Contingent.	Coinage of the standard silver dollar, act of February 28, 1878—(indefinite).	Total.
Philadelphia Mint	$34,850 00	$295,000 00	$82,500 00		$412,350 00
San Francisco Mint	24,900 00	265,000 00	80,000 00		369,900 00
Carson Mint	24,570 00	72,000 00	30,000 00		125,570 00
New Orleans Mint	21,400 00	80,000 00	35,000 00		136,400 00
Denver Mint	10,970 00	10,000 00	6,000 00		26,970 00
New York Assay Office	32,900 00	22,500 00	9,000 00		64,400 00
Helena Assay Office	5,950 00	12,000 00	12,000 00		29,950 00
Boise City Assay Office	3,000 00		6,000 00		9,000 00
Charlotte Assay Office	2,750 00		1,000 00		3,750 00
	160,250 00	756,500 00	261,500 00		1,178,250 00

EXPENDITURES 1881.

Institution.	Salaries.	Wages.	Contingent.	Coinage of the standard silver dollar.	Total.
Philadelphia Mint	$34,850 00	$294,999 86	$82,497 57	$78,712 48	$491,059 91
San Francisco Mint	24,900 00	264,302 47	80,000 00	7,749 42	376,951 89
Carson Mint	23,345 61	71,686 30	22,619 86		117,651 77
New Orleans Mint	21,236 88	79,721 01	34,998 27	10,849 70	147,007 86
Denver Mint	10,835 80	9,996 75	4,111 82		24,945 37
New York Assay Office	32,900 00	21,776 00	8,554 90		63,230 90
Helena Assay Office	5,946 73	10,958 66	8,257 92		25,163 31
Boise City Assay Office	3,000 00		4,916 30		7,916 30
Charlotte Assay Office	2,750 00		1,000 00		3,750 00
	159,765 02	751,765 05	247,017 64	97,311 60	1,257,659 31

* Includes $3,000 for repairs and machinery.
† Includes $4,999 56 for repairs and machinery.

REFINERY EARNINGS AND EXPENDITURES.

During the year $255,939.78 was collected from depositors, and $274,784.64 paid on account of parting and refining bullion.

The following statement shows the amount collected for parting and refining, and the payments for expenditures in those operations, including that portion of the operative officers' wastages and the loss on sale of sweeps properly chargeable to that fund.

A much larger amount, consisting of undeposited refinery earnings of previous years, was deposited in the Treasury to the credit of the appropriation.

Included in the payments are expenses for railroad freight incurred in prior years, the bills for which were not rendered until the last fiscal year.

Institution.	Charges collected.	Expenditures.
Philadelphia Mint	$5,399 89	$9,753 05
San Francisco Mint	161,441 22	170,276 94
Carson Mint	9,008 33	10,397 79
New York Assay Office	80,090 34	84,356 86
Total	255,939 78	274,784 64

The net excess of the earnings of the refineries over the expenses, from the 1st of July, 1876, to June 30, 1881, as shown by the books of the Treasury Department, amounted to $121,238.90.

ANNUAL ASSAY.

The commission appointed by the President to test the weight and fineness of the coins reserved for the annual assay, performed the duty at the time designated by law, and the records of their proceedings show that all the coins tested by them were found to be within the limits of exactness required by law, as to weight, and that very few varied from the standard by one-half the tolerance.

As to fineness, the record states that in all cases, both in mass and single pieces, the coins from Philadelphia, San Francisco, and New Orleans were found to be correct, and safely within the limits of tolerance. But the committee on assaying reported that, in the case of the Carson Mint, they found the assay of mass melt of silver to be very low, but within tolerance, and that one single piece showed a fineness below the limits of tolerance. This fact was reported to the President, as required by law.

The assayer of the Mint Bureau, in October, 1880, in his assay of the coins required monthly to be forwarded to the Director for test, had discovered that a silver coin of the Carson Mint, from the coiner's July delivery of that year, was below the legal limit of tolerance. The superintendent of that mint was immediately directed not to pay out, but to retain in his possession all of the coins of that delivery, and to seal up, until further orders, all packages which might contain any of such coins, after selecting and forwarding to the Director sample coins from each package for further test. Ninety-six packages, each containing one thousand dollars, were thus sealed up and reserved for further assays at the bureau, and a special examination made by Andrew Mason, melter and refiner of the New York Assay Office, in conformity with the order of the President to investigate the matter, confirmed the previous assays, and demonstrated that the fineness of a certain bar of bullion, about to be melted for coinage, had been incorrectly stated to the melter and refiner of the Carson Mint, and that ingots of defective fineness made therefrom had afterward passed the assay department of that mint without detection. It did not appear that the error had occurred through the neglect of the assayer's subordinates, and as the assayer himself had died shortly after the first discovery of the defective coinage, it became unnecessary to take any further action, except to order all the coins contained in the 96 packages to be remelted for coinage, which was done.

ESTIMATION OF THE VALUES OF FOREIGN COINS.

The values of foreign coins were estimated by the Director of the Mint, and proclaimed by the Secretary of the Treasury on the first of January of the current year, as required by law. The computation of their values was made in the same manner as that of the previous year. No change in the value of the gold coins will be found, excepting that resulting from more accurate information or recent modificationsof the law prescribing their weight and fineness.

The commercial value of silver bullion for the time the estimation was made having fallen about 1.56 per cent. from its value for a like period of the preceding year, the value of silver coins based on the market rate of silver were correspondingly reduced.

By reason of this decline in the value of silver, and the more recent and reliable information, the values of foreign gold and silver coins were modified from those proclaimed in 1880, as follows:

The florin of Austria was reduced from 41.3 cents to 40.7; the boliviano of Bolivia from 83.6 to 82.3; the milreis of Brazil increased from 54.5 to 54.6; the peso of Ecuador reduced from 83.6 to 82.3; the rupee of India from 39.7 to 39. Japan having adopted the free-coinage system for silver, the yen, which was formerly given as 99.7 in gold, is now 88.8 in silver. The Mexican dollar from 90.9 to 89.4; the sol of Peru from 83.6 to 82.3; the rouble of Russia from 66.9 to 65.8; the mahbub of Tripoli from 74.8 to 74.3; the peso of Colombia from 83.6 to 82.3; the peso of Cuba was given at 93.2, and the bolivar of Venezuela at 19.3. The monetary unit of Egypt, which formerly was stated as the pound at $4.974, is now fixed as the piaster, .049.

EXAMINATIONS AND ANNUAL SETTLEMENTS.

The usual examinations and settlements were made at the close of the fiscal year at all the mints and at the New York Assay Office. The director personally superintended the closing of the settlements at Philadelphia and New York, and representatives of the bureau were detailed to take charge of the settlements at New Orleans, Carson, and San Francisco.

The magnitude and importance of these settlements are evident when it is known that they covered for the last year transactions and actual transfers·between the superintendent and operative officers of gold and silver bullion to the value of $603,230,121, and that bullion and funds amounting at the time of settlement to $128,318,274 were examined, counted, or weighed, and their value ascertained.

At each institution the superintendent, after the delivery to him of the bullion in the hands of the operative officers, was, upon taking account of the coin, bullion, and other moneys in his possession, found to ' the amount required by his accounts with the Treasury.

The wastage of each of the operative officers was found to be within the legal limit, and the total wastage during the year was, considering the amount received and worked, much less than that of the preceding year.

The total amount operated upon in the melter and refiner's department of the mints and the New York Assay Office was, of gold bullion, 16,319,460 standard ounces, on which the legal limit of wastage was 16,319 standard ounces and the actual wastage 1,608 standard ounces, and, of silver bullion, 54,798,707 standard ounces, on which the legal limit of wastage was 82,198, and the actual wastage only 4,453 standard ounces.

The amount operated upon in the coining department of the mints was, of gold bullion, 10,514,159 standard ounces, upon which the legal limit of wastage was 5,257 standard ounces, and the actual wastage 367 standard ounces; and of silver bullion, 48,182,982, upon which the legal limit of wastage was 48,183 standard ounces, while the actual wastage was only 4,021 standard ounces, being heavier in gold and less in silver than that of last year.

The total wastage during the year was $36,767.14 gold and $8,576.83 silver, a total of $45,343.97, which was no greater than that of the previous year, although three times as much gold was melted. Bullion, however, of the value of $8,406.12 was recovered during the year, from the deposit melting-rooms, and the melter and refiner of the New York Assay Office returned, on settlement, surplus bullion of the value of $24,733.24, making a total of $33,139.36 bullion gained. The net actual loss to the government on the immense amount received, redeposited, and reworked, during the year, was only $12,204.16.

Loss and wastage in the handling, melting, separating, refining, and coinage of the precious metals is unavoidable. It is contemplated and provided for by law, which limits and authorizes an allowance to be made in favor of the melter and refiner's accounts, to the extent of one thousandth of gold and one and a half thousandths of the silver, and, of the coiner's accounts, one-half thousandth of the gold and one thousandth of the silver delivered to them, respectively, during the year, if the superintendent is satisfied there has been *bona fide* waste of the precious metals.

At the last, as well as the preceding settlement, the melter and refiner's gold wastages at the Philadelphia and San Francisco Mints, although far within the legal limits, were heavier than the usual loss of those officers.

During the last two years large amounts, aggregating $90,000,000 of foreign coin and bullion, received and melted at the New York Assay Office, were transmitted to the Philadelphia Mint in the form of gold mint-bars alloyed with copper. The melter and refiner of that mint attributed his wastage, in part, to insufficient deductions on these bars for oxide of copper and other adhering impurities, the weight of which would occasion a loss in his accounts, but increase, to a corresponding extent, the surplus at the New York Assay Office, and, therefore, cause no real loss to the government.

The melter and refiner's wastage at the San Francisco Mint can, in part, be accounted for by greater deposits during the year of brittle, fine gold bars and unrefined gold bullion, containing refractory and volatile base metals, in the elimination of which loss of gold is a frequent, if not a necessary, consequence. How far this cause has operated to produce the wastage of that mint is under consideration; but, as yet, sufficient examination and analysis have not been made of the records and transcripts obtained for a comparison of the character of the deposits and the methods of weighing, assaying, and reporting the fineness of gold bullion, with those of previous years and of other mints and assay offices.

REVIEW OF THE MINT SERVICE.

During the year the regulations governing the mints and assay offices have been carefully revised so as to bring their directions in harmony with later provisions of the statutes, and the charges collected of depositors have been reviewed and modified in order that the rates at each institution may equal, but not exceed, the expenses of the operations for which they are imposed.

The mints and New York Assay Office have been required to make, as far as practicable, their purchases of supplies after public advertisement for bids and submission of the awards to this office, and to forward for examination original records of deposits and monthly statements showing the silver bullion purchased and the character and amount of the various classes of gold and silver bullion sent to and received from the refineries, and the charges collected and expenditures paid for parting and refining.

The data in regard to the annual production of precious metals in the United States, too imperfect at the time of submitting my last annual report for a reliable estimate of the production by States, after subsequent careful examination and comparison, were presented in both a summary form and detail as to localities, and the report has been published by order of Congress.

The collection and compilation of these monetary statistics, the more thorough inspection of the operations, reports, and accounts of the mints and assay offices, and a closer supervision of their expenditures, have largely increased the work, and, as is believed, the usefulness of this bureau.

PHILADELPHIA MINT.

On account of the continued heavy import of foreign gold coin and the payment of its value immediately upon assay in American coin it became necessary to increase the monthly gold coinage at the Philadelphia Mint to supply the Treasury with coin thus paid out. Its gold coinage had averaged previous to the heavy gold import of 1880 less than $10,000,000, but in 1881, besides coining $9,125,966.75 silver and $405,109.95 minor coins, its gold coinage amounted to $49,809,274, and at the close of the fiscal year the mint held $23,023,206.62 of uncoined gold bullion.

This increased coinage necessitated the employment of a larger working force and extra hours of labor, and also much heavier purchases of copper and other supplies.

By reason of these greater expenditures and in order to execute the monthly silver coinage required by law, it became necessary to make advances to the mint and use during the year $78,712.48 from the appropriation contained in the act authorizing the coinage of the standard silver dollar.

The following presents a comparison of the operations of the last and the preceding fiscal year:

	1880.	1881.
Deposits ....value..	$53,309,250 60	$70,651,442 91
Gold coinage ....pieces..	3,789,820	7,275,926
Silver coinage ....do...	15,223,400	9,174,820
Minor coinage ....do...	26,831,850	38,335,665
Total coinage....:..................................do...	45,845,070	54,786,411
Gold coinage ....value..	$27,639,445 00	$49,302,274 00
Silver coinage ....do...	15,194,437 50	9,125,966 75
Minor coinage ....de..	269,971 50	405,109 95
Total coinage ....do...	43,103,854 00	59,340,350 70
Gold bars ....value..	$145,200 85	$236,141 78
Silver bars ....do...	83,688 67	60,123 09
Total bars ....do...	228,889 52	296,264 87
Gold operated upon by melter and refiner ....standard ounces..	3,951,316	7,669,189
Silver operated upon by melter and refiner.........do...	26,640,003	16,551,054
Gold operated upon by coiner.......................do...	3,894,227	7,283,415
Silver operated upon by coiner.....................do...	26,326,668	16,259,728
Gold wastage of melter and refiner................do...	577	352
Silver wastage of melter and refiner ....do...		1,050
Gold wastage of coiner.............................do...		197
Silver wastage of coiner ....do...	3,047	1,869

On the large amount operated upon during the last year the wastage of the melter and refiner was, on gold, 4.5 per cent. of the legal limit of his allowance and 4.2 per cent. on silver, and of the coiner on gold 5.4 per cent. and on silver 11.4 per cent.

SAN FRANCISCO MINT.

A much larger amount of work was executed at this mint, both in coinage and in the refinery, during the past fiscal year than in 1880, the number of pieces of gold coined being nearly half a million more, and of silver about three and a half millions more.

The comparative values of the deposits, number of pieces coined, and bullion operated on in the refinery during the last and preceding years, are:

	1880.	1881.
Deposits...value..	$39,387,949	$41,959,062 71
Gold coinage ....pieces..	2,284,950	2,774,000
Silver coinage ....do...	7,910,000	11,460,000
Total coinage.....................................do...	10,194,950	14,234,000
Gold coinage ....value..	$28,143,000	$28,500,000
Silver coinage ....do...	7,910,000	11,460,000
Total coinage.....................................do...	36,053,000	39,960,000
Gold bars ....value..		$8,700 55
Silver bars ....do...	$2,355,252 07	1,110,045 74
Total bars ....do...	2,355,252 07	1,118,746 29
Gold received from the refinery .:................standard ounces	524,229	612,429
Silver received from the refinery ....do .	4,887,291	5,591,629
Gold operated upon by the melter and refiner.......do...	2,902,878	3,236,755
Silver operated upon by the melter and refiner ....do...	15,733,815	22,471,852
Gold operated upon by the coiner ....do	2,918,714	3,230,718
Silver operated upon by the coiner................do...	13,497,415	20,960,005
Gold wastage of the melter and refiner............do...	283	1,229
Silver wastage of the melter and refiner..........do ..	18,654	2,488
Gold wastage of the coiner ....do ..	118	118
Silver wastage of the coiner ....do ..	102	942

At the annual settlement, the melter and refiner's wastage in gold was 40 per cent. of the legal limit of allowance, and his silver wastage 7 per cent. His silver wastage was much less, but the gold wastage heavier than that of the preceding year. The coiner's gold wastage was 13¾ per cent. and his silver wastage 4½ per cent. of the amount allowed by law.

Improvements have been made at this mint in refining bullion by the use of the sulphuric-acid process. The charges for parting and refining the higher grades of bullion were, near the beginning of the year, reduced, yet, as a greater amount of bullion requiring to be parted or refined was deposited during the year, the charges collected for these operations exceeded those of the preceding year. The expenses of the refinery, however, owing to the larger amount of work performed, were slightly increased. Besides this heavier expenditure, the sum of $6,000 was expended in procuring apparatus and fixtures and making the necessary arrangements for operating the sulphuric-acid refinery, and nearly $4,000 was paid on account of freight bills of the previous year.

These necessary, but unusual expenditures made the payments during the year for expenses on account of partin and refining some $8,000 more than the charges collected.

CARSON MINT.

Coinage at the Carson Mint, which had been suspended in May, 1880, was resumed July 1, 1880, and was continued from that date until April 1, 1881, during which period $883,590 were coined, when, for lack of sufficient bullion, it was again discontinued, and so remained until the close of the year. The mint, however, was kept open for the reception and purchase of bullion, and payment was made, as usual, on deposits and purchases as soon as the value could be ascertained. No inconvenience or delay was therefore occasioned to depositors or to the mining interests of that portion of the country.

The work at this mint during the year compares with that of the previous year as follows:

		1880.	1881.
Deposits ....value..		$990,466 39	$1,108,376 6
Gold coinage...pieces..		39,567	52,189
Silver coinage...do...		408,000	539,000
Total coinage...do...		447,567	592,189
Gold coinage ....value..		$246,790 00	$344,590 00
Silver coinage...do...		408,000 00	539,000 00
Total coinage...do...		654,790 00	883,590 00
Gold operated upon by melter and refiner.............. standard ounces..		35,421	49,133
Silver operated upon by melter and refiner ....do...		869,478	1,129,355
Gold operated upon by coiner ....do...		25,735	40,467
Silver operated upon by coiner ....do...		704,486	1,010,408
Gold wastage of melter and refiner ....do...		7	24
Silver wastage of melter and refiner ....do...		135	249
Gold wastage of coiner...do...		2	3
Silver wastage of coiner..o...		138	148

At the annual settlement the wastages of the operative officers were as follows: of the melter and refiner, on gold 49.3 per cent. of the legal limit, and on silver 14.7 per cent.; of the coiner, 15.7 per cent. on gold and 14.7 per cent. on silver. The assayer of the mint, William P. Prescott, died December 5, 1880, and Josiah M. Hetrich was appointed to the position December 21, 1880, and entered upon duty January 4, 1881.

NEW ORLEANS MINT.

The work of this mint has been principally confined to the manufacture of standard silver dollars, for which the demand through the South continued heavy during the year and nearly equaled the coinage. The monthly allotment of silver coinage was raised to 500,000, and occasionally to 600,000 standard dollars, and executed with dispatch and little additional expense under the efficient management of the officers of the mint.

The following table exhibits the deposits and purchases of bullion and the coinage of the year compared with the fiscal year 1880:

	1880.	1881.
Deposits ....value..	$4, 599, 895 64	$6, 439, 652 39
Gold coinage ....pieces..	10, 525	8, 000
Silver coinage ....do..	4, 430, 000	6, 525, 000
Total coinage......................................do...	4, 440, 525	6, 533, 000
Gold coinage...value..	$128, 500	$80, 000
Silver coinage ....do...	4, 430, 000	6, 525, 000
Total coinage......................................do...	4, 558, 500	6, 605, 000
Gold operated upon by melter and refiner ....standard ounces..	16, 325	11, 850
Silver operated upon by melter and refiner ....do..	7, 925, 875	9, 976, 250
Gold operated upon by coiner.......................................do..	15, 316	9, 564
Silver operated upon by coiner.....................................do..	7, 773, 352	9, 952, 845
Gold wastage of melter and refiner ....do..		4
Silver wastage of melter and refiner ....do..		656
Gold wastage of coiner ....do..		
Silver wastage of coiner ....do..	807	1, 062

The wastage during the year of the melter and refiner was, on gold, 31.5 per cent. of the legal limit, and on silver 4.3; and of the coiner, nothing on gold, and on silver 10.6 of the legal limit.

Notwithstanding the amount of work performed at this mint during the year many necessary repairs were made in the rolling and coining rooms, and to the machinery; and it is expected that other repairs will be completed during the present fiscal year.

The deficiency of 1,000 silver dollars, to which reference was made in my report of last year, has been made good.

NEW YORK ASSAY OFFICE.

The business of the New York Assay Office assumed immense proportions during the year, owing to the continued and increased importation of foreign gold. The gold deposits were the largest in the history of the institution, $91,497,168.61 of the amount being foreign coin and bullion. The following table exhibits the value of deposits and of bars manufactured at the New York Assay Office during the fiscal years ended June 30, 1880, and June 30, 1881:

Deposits and bars..	1880.	1881.
Gold deposits..	$68, 273, 628	$99, 635, 544 46
Silver deposits	4, 491, 416	5, 285, 715 57
Total deposits	72, 765, 044	104, 921, 360 03
Gold, fine bars, manufactured	11, 378, 980	9, 805, 028 07
Gold, mint bars, manufactured......................................	57, 368, 701	89, 643, 135 29
Silver, fine bars, manufactured	4, 372, 705	4, 763, 180 08
Silver, sterling bars, manufactured.................................	24, 347	1, 418 03
Silver, mint bars, manufactured		519, 047 53
Total bars manufactured	73, 144, 795	104, 731, 818 00

There were paid during the year to depositors $99,603,605.42 in gold coin and bars and $4,976,641.10 in silver coin and bars, making the aggregate payments $104,580,246.52, and gold bullion of the value of $61,560,816.10 was transferred to the mint at Philadelphia for conversion into coin.

I was present at the close of the annual settlement, when the bullion and coin on hand, which had been carefully weighed and counted by representatives of this bureau, were found to agree with the balance, $65,194,122.56, as shown by the books to be on hand June 30, 1881.

On the annual settlement of his accounts the melter and refiner returned 1,329.100 standard ounces of gold bullion of the value of $24,727.44, and 4.98 standard ounces of silver bullion, valued at $5.80, in excess of the amounts with which he was charged, having recovered the same in his operations.

The aggregate of these sums, $24,733.24, has been deposited in the Treasury of the United States.

But, although the amount appears as an earning of the assay office, it is not available for payment of expenses, and was not credited to the appropriation for parting and refining, as, by law, only the charges collected from depositors for parting and refining bullion are authorized to be used for defraying the expenses of those operations.

DENVER MINT, AND ASSAY OFFICES AT CHARLOTTE, HELENA, BOISE CITY, AND SAINT LOUIS.

The assay offices were established for the local convenience and development of the mining interests in their vicinity and to afford miners and those owning, operating, and prospecting for mines facilities for ascertaining the value of ores and bullion, and for the exchange of their gold bullion for coin.

The work done by each during the year, including the Denver Mint (which, by law, can only be operated as an assay office), was—

	Denver.	Charlotte.	Helena.	Boise.	Total.
Gold deposits	$235,137 15	$86,919 59	$568,525 13	$163,469 86	$1,054,051 72
Silver deposits	3,805 77	626 80	84,314 97	2,828 50	91,576 04
Unparted bars manufactured	238,942 92	87,546 39	652,840 10	166,298 36	1,145,527 77
Charges collected:					
On deposits	239 17	133 94	666 05	185 10	1,224 36
On ore assays	921 00	260 35	1,718 00	186 00	3,085 35
Total earnings	1,843 31	995 37	2,551 71	441 69	5,631 96
Total expenses	24,968 37	3,750 00	25,163 31	7,940 15	61,821 83

Besides the work enumerated, the assayers in charge of the offices have rendered valuable assistance in collecting statistics of production in their respective States and Territories.

I have heretofore called attention to the necessity of the Denver Mint being put in better repair, and an appropriation should be made for that purpose.

The Saint Louis Assay Office was established so near the close of the fiscal year that nothing could be done except to have suitable rooms set apart in the United States building at Saint Louis, and to commence fitting them up and procuring the necessary fixtures and apparatus for the use of the office. Mr. E. C. Jewett was appointed assayer July 1, 1881, and has been placed in charge. The appointment of melter was delayed until his services should be required, and the office ready for the reception of bullion.

INTERNATIONAL MONETARY CONFERENCE.

The monetary conference called by France and the United States to consider propositions for an international agreement to coin gold and silver at a common fixed ratio, met at the city of Paris in April of the present year.

Although much instructive discussion occurred, and valuable facts were presented, no practical conclusions were reached, and, finally, on the 8th of July the conference was adjourned to meet in April, 1882, at the same place.

Delegates from several European countries gave little encouragement for the expectation of any effective aid from their governments in the effort to restore silver to its former place in the monetary circulation. The hope, however, seems to have been entertained that further deliberation, and a consideration of the inevitable complications and disturbances to commercial exchanges between Asiatic countries and the western world to be feared from the exclusion of silver from coinage, will enlist the co-operation of those nations in this, possibly the final, effort to retain silver conjointly with gold as a measure of values. In view, however, of the failure of the Conference to agree upon any practical measure, and while awaiting its future action, it is a question for our serious and early consideration, whether it is not desirable to suspend the further coinage of silver until, by international agreement and effective legislation, the unlimited coinage of silver and gold at a common fixed ratio shall have been authorized by the principal commercial nations of Europe and America.

The silver circulation of this country, before the close of this fiscal year, will amount to $200,000,000, and will suffice for the needs of our people, for coins of the denomination of one dollar and less.

The United States has done its part toward retaining silver as a monetary agent for measuring and exchanging values. For three years it has appropriated to coinage purposes one-third of the world's production of silver, and maintained its average bullion price nearly to the average of 1878. As was said in my first report, "should the $650,-000,000 of silver coin now full legal tender in Europe be demonetized, the United States could not, single-handed among commercial nations, with no European co-operation or allies, sustain the value of silver from the inevitable fall."

With that danger menacing us, we cannot, without serious embarrassment, continue such coinage, unless other commercial nations will agree upon the general use of silver as well as gold.

But should such international agreement be secured, neither our ratio of comparative valuation nor even one based upon the present exchangeable value of gold and silver will probably be adopted. The ratio of fifteen and a half to one, already approved and in use among the nations composing the Latin Union, would doubtless be chosen. This would, if the coinage of silver as well as gold at all the mints of the world were made free, as bimetallism implies, cause the voluntary withdrawal from circulation of the standard dollars, and their recoinage. In such case the further coinage of silver dollars of the present weight, unless needed for circulation, is a useless expenditure.

MONETARY STATISTICS OF THE UNITED STATES.

The statistics of the production, consumption, and circulation of the precious metals in the United States during the fiscal year ended June

30, 1881, have been sought, and inquiries prosecuted, in the manner and through the agencies employed in the previous year.

The results have been very satisfactory, both as to the extent and character of the information obtained.

It will suffice to present here in a summary form the conclusions deduced from the detailed statements and reports received at the bureau.

PRODUCTION OF THE PRECIOUS METALS IN THE UNITED STATES IN 1881.

For the calendar year 1880, embracing the first half of the last fiscal year, a special report on the annual production of the United States was submitted to the Secretary of the Treasury, in March last, and ordered to be published by Congress.

Further investigation has not materially changed the estimate I then made of the total production of the United States, and of each State and Territory, during the preceding fiscal year and the calendar year 1880.

From the data received at the Mint Bureau, I estimate the production for the fiscal year ended June 30, 1881, to have been, of gold $36,500,000, and of silver, at its coining value, $42,100,000, or, at its commercial bullion value, about $37,000,000.

The estimated production of each State and Territory for the fiscal years 1880 and 1881 are as follows:

State or Territory.	Fiscal year 1880.			Fiscal year 1881.		
	Gold.	Silver.	Total.	Gold.	Silver.	Total.
Alaska	$6,000		$6,000	$7,000		$7,000
Arizona	400,000	$2,000,000	2,400,000	770,000	$7,800,000	8,570,000
California	17,500,000	1,100,000	18,600,000	19,000,000	870,000	19,870,000
Colorado	3,200,000	17,000,000	20,200,000	3,400,000	15,000,000	18,400,000
Dakota	3,600,000	70,000	3,670,000	4,500,000	60,000	4,560,000
Georgia	120,000		120,000	150,000		150,000
Idaho	1,980,000	450,000	2,430,000	1,930,000	1,100,000	3,030,000
Montana	2,400,000	2,500,000	4,900,000	2,500,000	2,300,000	4,800,000
Nevada	4,800,000	10,900,000	15,700,000	2,700,000	8,860,000	11,560,000
New Mexico	130,000	425,000	555,000	120,000	270,000	390,000
North Carolina	95,000		95,000	75,000		75,000
Oregon	1,090,000	15,000	1,105,000	1,000,000	80,000	1,080,000
South Carolina	15,000		15,000	18,000		18,000
Tennessee				2,000		2,000
Utah	210,000	4,740,000	4,950,000	200,000	5,710,000	5,910,000
Virginia	10,000		10,000	11,000		11,000
Washington	410,000		410,000	100,000		100,000
Wyoming	20,000		20,000	7,000		7,030
Other	14,000		14,000	10,000	50,000	60,000
Total	36,000,000	39,200,000	75,200,000	36,500,000	42,100,000	78,600,000

CONSUMPTION OF THE PRECIOUS METALS.

It is a pleasure to report that the continuance of the inquiries heretofore instituted in regard to the annual consumption of gold and silver in the United States has resulted in the accumulation of very complete and satisfactory information.

Circular letters were again addressed, to the number of 6,417, to persons and firms reported to be using and consuming gold and silver in manufactures and the arts. At the date of this report, of the persons replying, 1,300 used no gold or silver in their business. It is believed that nearly all the principal manufacturers have responded to the request of this bureau.

The character of the gold and silver used was reported at—

Material used.	Gold.	Silver.	Total.
United States coins	$3, 315, 882	$72, 190	$3, 388, 072
Fine bars used	6, 171, 317	3, 127, 432	9, 296, 749
Foreign coin, jewelry, plate, &c.	599, 524	188, 799	788, 323
Total	10, 086, 723	3, 388, 421	13, 475, 144

From the information obtained it appears that 1,143 persons or firms use in the manufacture or repair of instruments, chemicals, leaf and foil, pens, plates, spectacles, watch cases, watches and jewelry, over ten millions of dollars gold and over three millions of dollars silver, a total of thirteen millions of dollars, of which three and a quarter millions is gold coin and seventy thousand dollars silver coin of the United States. The usual report was obtained from the New York Assay Office, which gives a full statement of the amount and character of the gold and silver supplied to manufacturers by that office:

Bars furnished to manufacturers.	Gold.	Silver.	Total.
Of foreign coin	$167, 368 00	$120, 791 00	$288, 159 00
Of foreign bullion	1, 380, 416 00	250, 207 00	1, 630, 623 00
Of domestic bullion	3, 653, 186 00	4, 579, 994 00	8, 233, 130 00
Of plate, &c.	522, 918 00	177, 940 00	700, 858 00
Total	5, 723, 838 00	5, 128, 932 00	10, 852, 770 00

A discrepancy similar to that of the preceding year appears between the amounts returned by manufacturers and those reported by the New York Assay Office. Taken together they indicate that last year's estimate of the consumption of silver in the United States should be increased to $6,000,000, and of gold to $11,000,000.

The estimate of last year, that, of the bullion produced in the United States, $4,000,000 of silver and $5,500,000 of gold were appropriated for use in manufactures and the arts, is not changed as to gold by the information thus far received, but must be increased $1,000,000 as to silver, and the consumption, therefore, of domestic bullion in the United States for the fiscal year may be estimated to be, of gold, $5,500,000, silver, $5,000,000.

COIN CIRCULATION OF THE UNITED STATES.

In the last annual report the circulation of United States coin was estimated from the amount previously on hand, and the annual coinage and import of United States coin to have been on the 30th of June, 1880, $358,958,691 of gold and $142,597,020 of silver. The net gain during last year from coinage and import was, in gold coin, $84,118,062, and in silver coin, $28,937,746. This would make the total circulation of United States coin on the 30th of June, 1881, $443,077,023 gold, and $171,534,766 silver.

Heretofore no deduction has been made for coin used in manufactures and the arts, as it was believed that it should be offset by the excess of United States coin brought by immigrants upon their persons above the sums if like manner taken out of the country by travelers; but the circulation of United States gold coin, and its consequent abrasion and use in the arts, have largely increased, while the amount held abroad has, as shown by its diminished import, become depleted, so that much less American coin than heretofore is obtained and brought into the country by immigrants.

13 Ab

It seems proper, therefore, that allowance should be made for use in the arts to the extent of the sum reported to this bureau to have been used by manufacturers, which was, for the last fiscal year, in round numbers, $3,300,000 gold, and $75,000 silver. This would reduce the circulation of United States gold coin at the close of the fiscal year to about $440,000,000, and of silver coin to $171,500,000.

During the first four months of the current fiscal year there has been a further coinage of $26,544,000 and a net import of $2,172,474 gold, and a coinage of $9,300,000 and net import of $310,858 United States silver coin, making a total gain to the first of November, 1881, in the circulation, of $28,609,000 gold and $9,600,000 silver. This, added to the amount estimated to be in circulation June 30, 1881, makes the coin circulation of the country, November 1, about $460,000,000 gold and $181,000,000 silver. At the latter date the mints and assay office at New York held of bullion $94,075,744 gold and $4,966,741 silver, swelling the stock of coin and bullion available for coinage to $563,000,000 gold and $186,000,000 silver, a total of $749,000,000, being a *per capita* of $14.93.

The following table shows the gain in the coin circulation of the United States from June 30, 1880, to June 30, 1881, and to October 31, 1881:

United States coin.	Gold.	Silver.	Total.
Circulation June 30, 1880	[$358,958,601	$142,597,020	$501,555,711
Coinage, less deposits for recoinage	78,203,087	27,642,660	105,923,747
Net import	5,824,975	1,295,086	7,130,061
Total..	443,076,753	171,534,766	614,611,519
Less amount used in the arts	3,300,000	75,000	3,375,000
Circulation July 1, 1881	439,776,753	171,459,766	611,236,519
Coinage to November 1, 1881	26,544,000	9,300,000	35,844,000
Net imports to November 1, 1881	*2,172,474	310,858	2,483,332
Circulation November 1, 1881..........................	468,493,227	181,070,624	649,563,851

* Imports for October at the port of New York only.

The coin circulation of the country, according to the reports of the Treasurer for the amount of coin in the Treasury on the 1st of November, and of the Comptroller of the Currency for the amount held by National banks on the 1st of October, 1881, estimated for other banks, appears to have been held by the banks, Treasury, and private parties as follows:

Held in—	Gold.	Silver.		Total.
		Legal tender.	Subsidiary.	
Treasury	$76,036,377	*$7,737,608	$25,984,647	$109,758,672
National banks	102,000,389	3,000,000	2,450,387	107,450,756
Other banks	20,000,000	} $89,862,392	51,964,936	433,790,572
Private hands	270,963,234			
Total	460,000,000	100,600,000	80,400,000	650,000,000

* Excess above amount held for payment of outstanding silver certificates.
† Including amount for which silver certificates are outstanding
‡ Includes $7,000,000 trade dollars.

MONETARY STATISTICS OF FOREIGN COUNTRIES.

The comprehensive reports obtained from our national representatives in foreign countries, and presented in my last annual report, contain so much valuable and recent monetary information that it will hardly be expected that additional statistics of equal importance can be gathered in the same fields during the year immediately succeeding. Through the agencies heretofore successfully employed, reliable information has been obtained for later periods, enabling me to continue the statistical summaries of previous years. To the replies received from foreign countries have been added, under the heading of the appropriate country, extracts from other official publications or reliable authorities, which form a part of the data upon which are based the conclusions submitted in the text and tables of this report. Again I desire to express my acknowledgements to the United States ministers, consuls, and official representatives of foreign countries, who have so courteously responded and heartily seconded these efforts to obtain the latest and fullest monetary statistics from all the countries of the world.

While the appended tabulated statements * conveniently group these statistics for comparison and use, a condensed statement of the facts communicated in the dispatches and accompanying papers may be found useful and convenient.

Great Britain.—The papers forwarded by Minister Lowell contain the following information:

The coinage of gold during the calendar year 1880 was £4,150,052, and of silver £761,508, which was largely in excess of that of the previous year. The exportation of gold coin and bullion exceeded the amount imported by about £3,500,000. The silver exported exceeded the amount imported by about £750,000. The specie circulation at the close of 1880 is estimated to be as follows:

Gold coin, £123,771,000.. $602,331,571
Silver coin, £18,959,000.. 92,263,973

These amounts include the bank reserves. The amount of gold in circulation is about £1,500,000 larger, and of silver a trifle less, than at the close of 1879. The paper circulation is stated at £42,536,000, of which £26,006,000 were notes of the Bank of England.

Australia.—The dispatches of J. H. Williams, United States consul at Sydney, furnish very complete financial statistics of New South Wales. The production of gold from the mines of the colony from 1851 to 1879, inclusive, is estimated at £33,042,362, and for 1879 the production was valued at £264,018. The value of the silver produced in this colony up to the close of 1879 is estimated to be between £300,000 and £400,000. The importation and exportation of gold and silver were as follows:

Gold imported, £1,262,371; exported, £718,617.
Silver imported, £136,433; exported, £106,615.

Canada.—The imports and exports of gold and silver, as given in the statement of the finance department of Canada, were for the calendar year 1880:

Imports.. $966,804
Exports.. 872,248

Small quantities of gold and silver are produced from the mines, valued for the year at about $900,000, being principally gold. The circulation is reported on the 31st day of December, 1880, to have been as follows:

Gold... $9,026,000
Silver... 1,020,000
Paper.. 41,562,711

Nearly all the gold was held by the banks and treasury, together with about one-half of the silver.

Germany.—The production of gold and silver in Germany during the year 1880 was about as follows:

* The documents here referred to are omitted for want of space, but they may be found in the volumes of the Director's report.

Gold, $280,693; silver, $4,893,061, a considerable portion of which was from ores mined in other countries, sent to Germany to be smelted. The imports and exports of silver coin and bullion were as follows: Imports, $4,987,200 silver; exports, $5,685,408 silver, showing a loss of silver of only about $700,000.

About $100,000,000 of old thaler pieces, partly of German and partly of Austrian coinage, are estimated to remain in circulation.

France.—A very interesting paper will be found in the Appendix, from Benjamin F. Peixotto, United States consul at Lyons, in which he treats upon the influences affecting the variation in the relative value of gold and silver.

Austria.—Minister Kasson transmits, under date of March 18, 1881, a copy of the new law of Austria in relation to the deviation allowed in the fineness of the minting of Austrian gold coin.

The Netherlands.—The papers transmitted by Hon. James Birney, United States minister at the Hague, furnish the following information: There was coined at the mint during the year 1880, 501,000 florins in ten-guilder pieces, and 25,372 golden ducats, and in silver 100,000 florins in ten-cent. pieces.

The imports and exports of gold and silver coin and bullion were as follows:

	Florins.
Imports, gold	7,301,193
Exports, gold	3,236,450
Imports, silver	4,432,458
Exports, silver	1,753,240

It is estimated that there was in circulation on the 31st of December, 1880, in standard gold coins, 72,897,320 florins, of which over 40,000,000 florins was in the Bank of the Netherlands, and of silver coin 140,518,785 florins, of which about 84,000,000 florins were held by the same bank. The paper currency issued for the State amounted to 10,000,000 florins, and by the Bank of Netherlands 198,549,505 florins.

Switzerland.—The reply of Minister Fish, transmitting from the Swiss Government the desired information in regard to the financial condition of Switzerland, contains statistics as to the imports and exports of gold and silver into and from the confederation and the amount in the treasury; also copies of two recent enactments of the Swiss Government, one concerning the emission of bank-notes, the other concerning the new coinage of 20-centime pieces. The paper money circulation amounts to about 86,000,000 of francs.

Greece.—The dispatch of B. O. Duncan, United States consul at Smyrna, shows that the entire debt of Greece amounted, December 31, 1880, to 317,276,572 dr.=$61,234,378, the annual interest of which amounts to $2,895,000, and that in addition to this the Chambers have voted a further loan of $23,160,000 (120,000,000 dr.) to cover the deficit of 1881 and to support the army on a war-footing.

Peru.—Minister Christiancy reports, under date of November last, that an attempt was made to introduce a forced paper currency in Peru called the "inca"; and, under date February of this year, that the attempt had failed, and that the paper soles are the only circulating medium of the country, gold and silver being commodities not circulating as money.

The value of a paper sole just prior to the taking of Lima by the Chilians was about five cents (twenty-one paper soles being about equal to one dollar United States coin); since the conquest of Peru by Chili the minister states that they have appreciated to seventeen paper soles *-* one dollar United States gold coin. The mountains of Peru, rich in the precious metals, owing to the unsettled condition, are not mined to any considerable extent.

Venezuela.—Mr. John Baker, United States minister, furnishes very satisfactory information respecting the monetary condition of Venezuela. He transmits a resolution adopted by the government of that country fixing a tariff of prices for various foreign silver coins. The importation of all foreign silver money, except those coined by the States of the Latin Union, is strictly prohibited. The principal foreign moneys in circulation are United States gold coins and Spanish-American doubloons. The paper money in circulation consists of notes issued by the Bank of Caracas, amounting to about $250,000 (1,300,000 bolivars), which circulate freely at their face value. The coinage of 5,000,000 bolivars, nearly $1,000,000, executed in Belgium, has been recently imported into Venezuela. With this exception, the importation of gold and silver has been insignificant. During the fiscal year 1880 there was exported in bullion nearly $1,500,000.

Hayti.—Minister Langston reports that the importation of American and Spanish gold during the year amounted to about $40,000, and of silver to $500,000; the export of the latter amounting to about $250,000 more. He estimates the money in circulation to be about $5,000,000, principally American and Mexican silver. He states that a law has been passed providing for the establishment of a national bank.

African States.—There was imported into Algeria during the year, in gold coin and bullion, 3,089,577 francs, and of silver 6,052,699 francs. No exports of gold or silver are reported. The coin in circulation amounts to about 50,000,000 francs, of which 30,000,000 are gold. The paper circulation is about 50,000,000 francs, in notes of the Bank of Algeria. Owing to the secrecy with which the affairs of the government are conducted, and the lack of official accounts, very little information in regard to the finances of Morocco can be obtained, but such as has been possible to secure has been furnished by Mr. Matthews, the consul.

Liberia.—The United States minister to Liberia furnishes the following information in regard to the finances of that country: Mining operations do not exist, nor is any coinage executed. The principal circulating medium is United States gold and silver coin, and those of Great Britain. It has a paper circulation amounting to $150,000.

Bulgaria.—Hon. Eugene Schuyler, consul-general at Bucharest, reports that the Russian silver ruble has been demonetized, and its place is to be supplied by 5-franc pieces, of which 7,000,000 francs are now ready for issue.

THE WORLD'S PRODUCTION.

My last report contained tables giving by countries the total productions of gold and silver for the years 1877, 1878, and 1879, based principally upon official statements or estimates communicated to this bureau.

The table is continued to embrace the year 1880, with such modifications of the former years as official intelligence since received required to be made. Troy ounces are reduced to or from kilograms at the valuation given by the United States statute: one gram = 15.432 grains, one kilogram therefore equals 15,432 grains.

In the reports for the years 1877, 1878, and 1879, the production as estimated for the rest of South America was correctly stated in kilograms, but an unnoticed clerical error misplaced one column to the right, the figures for the equivalent dollar valuation of 250,000 kilograms of silver. The amounts are correctly stated in this report.

The total product for the calendar year 1880 was, of gold, $107,037,697, and of silver, $87,543,072. The production of the United States is given for the fiscal year, which does not materially vary from the production of the calendar year.

THE WORLD'S CONSUMPTION OF THE PRECIOUS METALS.

The estimates and discussions contained in previous reports regarding the annual appropriation of the precious metals for manufactures, in the arts, &c., seem to have awakened the interest and attracted the attention of European statisticians, and a better appreciation is had of the propriety and necessity of subtracting largely from the world's apparent accumulated stock, for annual waste and consumption.

The total production since the discovery of America, and even since the discovery of gold in California, has, of late years, been frequently presented as an evidence of the mass of metal money in use or in stock for coinage. But few writers or statisticians have presented, in the same connection, estimates or statistics of the consumption.

From a review of the information published in this and preceding reports and other authorities, I estimate that, including the annual consumption in the United States of $11,000,000 gold and $6,000,000 silver, the annual consumption of the world in ornamentation manufactures and the arts is at least $75,000,000 of gold and $35,000,000 of silver.

COINAGE OF FOREIGN COUNTRIES.

The continued import of gold into the United States, with the retention of the domestic production, increased, as in the preceding year, the coinage of gold in the United States, and as largely diminished that of other countries.

In the year 1880, two-thirds of the gold and one-third of the silver coinage reported for nine of the principal countries of the world was executed by the mints of the United States.

A tabulated statement is appended giving the value in United States money of the coinage executed by a number of countries, for the years 1878, 1879, and 1880. It shows that, for the years and by the number of countries stated, the following amounts of gold and silver were coined:

Years.	Countries.	Gold.	Silver.	Total.
1878	18	$188,386,611	$161,191,913	$349,578,524
1879	18	90,714,493	104,888,813	195,603,306
1880	9	114,837,811	81,951,354	196,789,165

CIRCULATION OF THE PRINCIPAL COUNTRIES OF THE WORLD.

The tables presented in the last annual report showing the paper and specie circulation of thirty-one of the leading countries of the world, and the amounts of coin and bullion held by banks and national treasuries, have been corrected to the latest date possible.

Further replies to the circular of the Secretary of the Treasury from our ministers and consuls will, it is believed, contain additional information, which will be published in subsequent reports.

The estimated amount of gold circulation is $3,221,000,000; silver, full legal tender, $2,115,000,000; limited tender, $423,000,000; total specie,

$5,759,000,000; of paper, $3,644,000,000; and the total circulation, including the amounts held in government treasuries, banks, and in active circulation, is $9,403,000,000.

COURSE OF PRICES.

The table of the prices of exports, ascertained by dividing declared values by quantity, has been continued for the fiscal year 1881. It shows an advance of 5 per cent. on the previous year's export prices, but a decline on the gold prices of the same articles compared with other prices in 1870.

Tables have been prepared, under my direction, with great care and labor, by the computer of the bureau, Mr. Frederick Eckfeldt, which exhibit the average annual prices in the New York market from 1825 to 1880, inclusive, of leading staple commodities, the leading prices of each of the articles for 1856, and the percentage of each annual price compared with the mean price.

The prices quoted were obtained for the years 1825 to 1874, inclusive, from the tables of their average prices in New York, found in the Finance Reports of 1863, 1873, and 1874. For the succeeding six years, they were compiled in this office from the published semi-weekly quotations in the New York Shipping and Commercial List, from which paper it is understood the quotations were taken in compiling the tables found in the Finance Reports.

The comparative percentages for each year on all the articles taken will measure, as far as the varying prices of those commodities can do so, the varying purchasing power of money for the year.

The prices during the suspension of specie payments in the years 1837 and 1838 and from 1862 to 1878, during which there was a premium on gold, have been reduced to a gold basis.

The table of final averages, therefore, presents, for the years named, the purchasing power of gold in the United States, as shown by the prices of leading commodities in the New York market.

For instructive comparison, the circulation, paper and metallic, for the same years, as far as ascertainable, is given in additional columns, as well as the per capita circulation and estimated wealth. They show (as similar tables published in my last annual report showed as to France) that prices are less affected by circulation, paper or metallic, than by other potent agencies. They are worthy of special consideration at this time, and should tend to allay the prevalent fear of impending commercial disaster as a consequence of abundant and increasing monetary circulation, expanding with the growth of business and accompanied by enlarged production and substantial prosperity.

In closing this report it is a pleasure to again commend the zealous co-operation of the clerks in the Mint Bureau, and to acknowledge their efficient aid in preparing, tabulating, and verifying the statistics relating to those branches of the mint service assigned to them, as well as in the performance of their official duties.

I am, very respectfully,

HORATIO C. BURCHARD,
Director.

Hon. WILLIAM WINDOM,
Secretary of the Treasury.

REPORT OF FIRST COMPTROLLER OF THE TREASURY.

TREASURY DEPARTMENT,
FIRST COMPTROLLER'S OFFICE,
Washington, October 22, 1881.

SIR: In compliance with the request made in your letter of September 30, 1881, I have the honor to submit the following report of the transactions of this office during the fiscal year which ended June 30, 1881. The following-described Warrants were received, examined, countersigned, entered into blotters, and posted into ledgers under their proper heads of appropriations:

Kind.	Number of warrants.	Amounts covered thereby.
APPROPRIATION.		
Treasury proper	44	$ 54,032,021 96
Public debt	1	248,722,325 61
Diplomatic and consular	5	1,193,835 00
Customs	14	15,327,045 97
Internal revenue	5	5,034,488 74
Interior civil	12	9,832,632 90
Indians and pensions	51	32,765,740 19
War	26	45,492,539 84
Navy	15	16,137,139 06
	173	428,537,738 58
ACCOUNTABLE AND SETTLEMENT.		
Treasury proper	3,465	$ 28,630,103 14
Public debt	103	248,284,956 02
Quarterly salaries	1,248	531,237 28
Diplomatic and consular	2,532	1,176,057 64
Customs	4,765	19,451,322 96
Internal revenue	4,336	5,025,138 27
Judiciary	4,154	4,168,951 43
Interior civil	2,101	8,694,319 16
Indians and pensions	3,101	58,561,463 22
War	7,328	41,762,550 07
Navy	2,117	21,385,664 49
	35,250	437,671,763 79
COVERING.		
Customs	1,507	$ 198,150,676 02
Internal revenue	1,744	135,264,385 51
Public lands	1,091	2,201,863 17
Miscellaneous revenue	8,537	138,908,901 87
Indians and pensions repay	573	1,988,022 51
War repay	1,747	1,296,144 59
Navy repay	270	4,694,065 83
Miscellaneous repay	2,541	3,433,446 29
	18,010	485,884,505 72
Total	53,433	$1,352,094,028 09

Accounts have been received from the auditing offices, revised, recorded, and the balances thereon certified to the Register of the Treasury, as follow:

Kind.	No. of accounts.	No. of vouchers.	Amount involved.
FROM THE FIRST AUDITOR.			
1. *Judiciary:*			
Accounts of United States marshals, for their fees, and expenses of United States courts, and accounts of United States district attorneys, United States commissioners, and clerks of the United States courts, and rents of court rooms..'.........	3,874	145,483	$ 4,682,572 24
Judgments by Court of Claims examined and ordered paid.....	199	199	303,286 42
Total......	4,073	145,682	4,985,858 66
2. *Public debt.*			
Accounts of the Treasurer of the United States:			
For coupons payable in coin.............................·......	149	5,111,910	$ 37,174,068 21
For coupons of Treasury notes, Louisville and Portland Canal stock, and old funded debt of the District of Columbia.......	36	144,178	1,617,882 58
For registered stock of the District of Columbia redeemed.....	3	92	71,715 92
For District of Columbia 3.65 bonds purchased for sinking fund.	1	29	125,000 00
For United States called bonds redeemed......................	18	11,867	13,417,512 44
For United States bonds purchased for sinking fund............	10	63,467	91,606,298 16
For Louisville and Portland Canal stock redeemed.............	4	391	391,000 00
For sinking fund Union and Central Pacific Railroad Companies .	1	3	306,651 00
For interest on United States registered bonds (paid on schedules)...	37	16,917	12,086,159 80
For interest on Pacific Railroad stock (reimbursable).........	6	43	46,989,376 70
For checks for interest on funded loans of 1881, 1891, and consols of 1907	7	138,888	24,247,298 20
For gold certificates and refunding certificates................	26	86,299	3,822,550 76
For certificates of deposit (act June 8, 1872)................	12	2,462	21,585,000 00
For legal-tender notes, old demand notes, and fractional currency	25	976	30,562,317 59
For compound-interest, seven-thirty, and other old Treasury notes.......................................	24	404	14,189,32
For interest on Navy pension fund	1	1	420,000 00
Total	360	5,577,927	284,487,115 74
3. *Public buildings.*			
Accounts for the construction of public buildings throughout the United States, and the buildings for the Bureau of Engraving and Printing and the National Museum, Washington, D. C.; for the United States Fish Commission; for the construction of the building for the State, War and Navy Departments; the completion of the Washington Monument, and the care of the public buildings and grounds under the Chief Engineer, U. S. A.; for annual repairs of the Capitol and improving the Capitol grounds; for Coast and Geodetic Surveys; and for beneficiary and charitable institutions in the District of Columbia.	429	46,104	$ 4,391,312 12
4. *Steamboats.*			
Accounts for salaries and incidental expenses of inspectors of hulls and boilers...............................	868	10,199	250,000 00
5. *Territorial.*			
Accounts for salaries of Territorial officers and for the legislative and contingent expenses incidental to the government of the Territories...............................	121	1,009	230,181 00
6. *Mint and Assay.*			
Accounts for gold, silver, and nickel coinage; for bullion; for salaries of the officers and employés of the several mints, and for the general expenses of the same..................	859	84,037	1,575,171 76
Bullion deposits, purchases, and transfers..................	....	....	151,873,318 56
7. *Transportation.*			
Accounts for the transportation of gold and silver coin and bullion, minor and base coin, United States currency, national-bank notes, complete and incomplete coin certificates, registered and coupon bonds, mutilated currency, canceled and incomplete securities, national-bank notes for redemption, stamp-paper, stationery, boxes, parcels, &c................	211	33,292	111,478 54

Kind.	No. of accounts.	No. of vouchers.	Amount involved.
8. Congressional.			
Accounts for salaries of the officers and employés, and for contingent and other expenses of the United States Senate and House of Representatives..............................	154	5, 672	$ 873, 462 35
9. Outstanding Liabilities.			
Accounts arising from demands for payment of drafts and disbursing-officers' checks which have remained outstanding for three years, the funds from which they were payable having been covered into the Treasury	98	125	8, 615 87
10 District of Columbia.			
Accounts of the Commissioners of the District of Columbia and general accounts between the United States and said District.	20	10, 996	8, 542, 219 29
11. Public Printing.			
Accounts of the Public Printer for the salaries and wages of the employés of the Government Printing Office, for the purchase of materials for printing, and for contingent expenses of the Government Printing Office.	150	60, 761.	4, 651, 267 12
12. Treasurer's General Accounts.			
Quarterly accounts of the Treasurer of the United States for receipts and expenditures, including receipts from all sources covered into the Treasury, and all payments made from the Treasury	4	49, 422	2, 233, 010, 973 45
13. Assistant Treasurers' Accounts.			
Accounts of the several assistant treasurers of the United States for the salaries of their employés and the incidental expenses of their offices	81	1, 061	345, 686 22
14 Miscellaneous.			
Such as accounts with the disbursing officers of the executive departments for salaries of officers and employés, and contingent expenses of the same, accounts for salaries of Senators and Representatives in Congress, with the salaries of the judges of the United States Supreme Court, United States circuit and district judges, district attorneys, and marshals; for salaries and contingent expenses of the National Board of Health; and for the expenses of the tenth census	2, 378	79, 464	11, 504, 227 94
Total from First Auditor	9, 306	6, 105, 751	$2, 707, 339, 299 09
FROM THE FIFTH AUDITOR.			
15. Internal Revenue.			
Accounts of collectors of internal revenue	534	44, 851	$ 287, 748, 241 86
Accounts of same acting as disbursing agents..................	910	35, 838	5, 168, 996 42
Accounts of internal-revenue stamp agents	216	3, 683	3, 486, 738 75
Miscellaneous internal-revenue accounts, such as direct tax accounts with commissioners and with the States; six different monthly accounts with the Commissioner of Internal Revenue for revenue stamps, accounts with the disbursing clerk of the Treasury Department for salaries of officers and employés in the office of the Commissioner of Internal Revenue, and for the payment of internal-revenue gaugers; with the Secretary of the Treasury for fines, penalties, and forfeitures; with the Treasury Department for stationery, with revenue agents and distillery surveyors, drawback accounts; accounts for refunding taxes illegally collected, for the redemption of internal-revenue stamps, for the collection of legacy and succession taxes, for expenses of detecting and suppressing violations of internal-revenue laws, including rewards therefor, &c	2, 352	47, 836	457, 004, 547 38
	4, 012	132, 158	753, 430, 444 23
16. Diplomatic and Consular.			
Accounts for the salaries of ministers, chargés d'affaires, consuls, commercial agents, interpreters, secretaries to legations, and marshals of consular courts, accounts for the relief and protection of American seamen, for expenses of prisons in China and Japan, for contingent expenses of legations and consulates, for salaries and expenses of legations and consulates, for salaries and expenses of mixed commissions, accounts of United States bankers in London, accounts of the disbursing clerk Department of State, for miscellaneous diplomatic expenses, &c......................	2, 406	24, 819	5, 247, 772 00

Kind.	No of accounts.	No of vouchers	Amount involved.
17. *Transportation.*			
Accounts for transportation of internal-revenue moneys to the sub-treasuries and designated depositaries, and for the transportation of stationery, &c , to internal-revenue officers	44	7, 570	5, 470 61
Total from Fifth Auditor	6, 464	164, 547	$ 758, 673, 686 82
FROM THE COMMISSIONER OF THE GENERAL LAND OFFICE.			
18. *Public lands.*			
Accounts of surveyors-general and the employés in their offices	218	2, 534	$ 294, 263 68
Accounts of deputy surveyors	432	952	896, 253 83
Accounts of receivers of public moneys	474	7, 133	3, 752, 176 18
Accounts of same acting as disbursing agents	594	2, 689	848, 491 65
Accounts for the refunding of purchase money paid for lands erroneously sold...	370	2, 654	39, 569 34
Miscellaneous accounts, such as accounts with the several States for indemnity for swamp and overflowed lands erroneously sold, and for 2 per cent , 3 per cent., and 5 per cent., upon the proceeds of sales of public lands, accounts of surveyors-general for the contingent expenses of their offices; accounts for the salaries and commissions of registers of local land offices not paid by the receivers; accounts with the Kansas, Denver, Central, Northern and Union Pacific Railroads, for the transportation of special agents of the General Land Office; accounts for printing and stationery furnished the several surveyors-general, registers and receivers, accounts of special agents of the Interior Department, accounts for the transportation of public moneys from the local land offices to designated depositaries; accounts for salaries and incidental expenses of agents employed to examine and verify public surveys; for the return of deposits in excess of the amount required for the survey of private land claims, for the transportation of stationery to the several district land offices, &c	265	1, 640	312, 035 99
Total from Commissioner of General Land Office	2, 351	17, 602	$ 5, 942, 790 67

RECAPITULATION.

From—	Number.	Vouchers.	Amount involved.
First Auditor	9, 306	6, 105, 751	$2, 707, 329, 299 69
Fifth Auditor	6, 464	164, 547	758, 673, 686 82
Commissioner of the General Land Office..................	2, 351	17, 602	5, 942, 790 67
Total................................	18, 121	6, 287, 900	$3, 471, 955, 777 18

Requisitions for the advance of money from the Treasury, in the number following, have been examined and advances thereon recommended:

Internal revenue 1,523
Diplomatic and consular... 1,181
Judiciary 531
Public buildings... 139
Mint and assay... 201
District of Columbia... 74
Territorial 49
Public printing... 120
Miscellaneous 191

Total 4, 009

Suits, to the number following, have been instituted against defaulting officers:

Collectors of internal revenue... 4
Receivers of public moneys... 31

Total 35

Official letters written	12,559
Letters received, briefed, and registered	5,222
Powers of attorney recorded	2,027
Official bonds registered and filed	379
Miscellaneous contracts and bonds received and registered	583
Internal-revenue collectors' tax-list receipts recorded, scheduled, and referred	1,535
Orders of special allowances to collecters of internal revenue recorded, scheduled, and referred	258
Internal-revenue special-tax stamp books counted and certified	5,043
Internal-revenue tobacco-stamp books counted and certified	10,656
Internal-revenue spirit-stamp books counted and certified	8,612
Pages copied	8,652

Copies of accounts made, compared, and transmitted :

Internal revenue	1,665
Public lands	1,784
	3,449

The foregoing statement omits mention of a large amount of official work which does not admit of systematic classification and detailed report, and yet has occupied much time and care; such as, *e. g.*, examination of, and decision upon, applications for the issuing of duplicate bonds and other securities in place of securities lost and destroyed; examination of powers of attorney for collection of money due to creditors of the United States; decisions upon the rights of persons claiming to be executors, administrators, or heirs of deceased claimants, to receive money due from the United States; examination, registry, and filing of official bonds; copying of letters forwarded; answering calls for information made by Congress, the departments, and private persons; receiving and examining emolument returns of officers of courts; investigation of legal points arising in the adjustment of accounts; and other work of a miscellaneous character.

LAW CLERK AND STENOGRAPHER.

In addition to the regular daily work, which is onerous and steadily increasing, the Comptroller is frequently required to decide upon the validity of claims for large amounts of public money. Many of these claims involve difficult questions of law, and the claimants have, in most cases, the best legal assistance they can procure.

As to claims coming before the Comptroller, this office is not only in some sense a court of claims, but also a court from whose decisions there is no appeal as such—though subject to revision by Congress, and in certain cases by the judiciary. The head of the office discharges not only the duties of sole presiding judge, but also those of a solicitor for the government in the investigation of the claims; and he must be prepared to answer arguments of counsel for claimants. For these and other reasons stated in my last annual report, it is essential to the interests of the government that authority should be given to the Secretary of the Treasury to appoint a competent law clerk, and also a stenographer, for this office. It is physically impossible for any one man, in the position of Comptroller, to give to the multitude of important questions constantly arising before him such investigation and sustained attention, unaided by law clerk or stenographer, as they should receive before determination. There is no office under the government in which so many important decisions on questions involving immense demands against the National Treasury are made as in that of the First Comptroller. The officer who is daily called upon to make such decisions should, in justice alike to the government, to those preferring the demands, and to himself be furnished with all the assistance and facilities which are reasonably necessary in order to the prompt and efficient discharge of so momentous a duty; and it is respectfully urged that for these reasons the services of an able law clerk, and also of an experienced stenographer, are absolutely requisite. The salary of the law clerk should be such as not merely to secure for a brief interval, but to retain permanently, the services of an industrious, painstaking, well-trained, and trustworthy lawyer. I would suggest that the salary of the law clerk be not less than three thousand five hundred dollars; and of the stenographer, not less than eighteen hundred dollars.

DIVISION OF CLAIMS.

Claims involving difficult questions of law, which require not only much time, but special legal ability, for their proper investigation are constantly coming before this office for adjudication. If Congress were to establish in this office a Division of Claims, and authorize the appointment as its chief of a person possessing the requisite legal qualifications, and also of two additional clerks of class four, the work of the office would be more speedily and efficiently performed, and the public service be greatly benefited.

It is indispensable to the prompt adjustment of claims against the United States, and the settlement of the accounts of disbursing officers and of the Commissioners of the District of Columbia, that additional clerical assistance be furnished to this office. The accounts of the Commissioners of the District for the fiscal year 1879 are not yet all settled, and most of those for 1880 and 1881, as well as for the current year, remain unexamined. The accounts of the collector of taxes for the District have been subject to the revision of this office since July 1, 1878; but for want of sufficient clerical force they remain untouched. The Division of Internal Revenue Accounts has been so pressed with current business that the work of preparing statements for suits against delinquent collectors has been unavoidably delayed. The work of the Miscellaneous Division was largely increased last year by the accounts relating to the Tenth Census, all of which remain to be examined. The business of the office in most of its divisions increases relatively with the ordinary growth of the population and business of the country; and this increase necessitates an addition to its clerical force.

I respectfully invite and urge your attention to this subject as one which is of great importance as well to the interests of the government as to those of claimants having valid demands upon the United States Treasury.

ACCOUNTS IN ARREARS.

The First Comptroller is required by section 272 of the Revised Statutes to "make an annual report to Congress of such officers as shall have failed to make settlement of their accounts for the preceding fiscal year, within the year, or within such further time for settlement as may have been prescribed by the Secretary of the Treasury." This requirement is taken from section 13 of the act of ·March 3, 1817, providing for the prompt settlement of public accounts. I cannot find that it has ever been complied with, and I presume that the non-compliance has been caused by the impracticable nature of the requirement. No disbursing officer can, within the year, make settlement of his accounts for such fiscal year, and no time for settlement is prescribed by the Secretary of the Treasury. Besides the consideration that a strict compliance with the act of 1817 was impracticable, it was probably thought that the reports made in conformity to section 3 of the act approved March 3, 1809 (2 Stats., 536), contained substantially the information called for by the act of 1817. Said reports showed the accounts which had remained more than three years unsettled. They were discontinued in the year 1860; for what reason I am not advised. The law which required them is not contained in the Revised Statutes.

There must have been some doubt as to the meaning of section 13 of the act of March 3, 1817. (3 Stats., 366.) At the time of its passage the annual appropriations were made in and for the current *calendar* year, *e. g.*, the "Act making appropriations for the support of the government for the year one thousand eight hundred and seventeen" (3 Stats., 352), was passed March 3, 1817. The reports of the Comptroller required by section 13 of the "Act providing for the prompt settlement of public accounts" (3 Stats., 368), were to be laid "before Congress annually, during the first week of their session." From this it is clear that the reports could not have been intended to cover the calendar year in which they were made; and it might be inferred from the terms of section 6 of this act, that the reports required were intended to cover accountability accruing in the preceding calendar year, which was not settled during the year in which the report was to be made. Section 13 did not limit absolutely the settlement of accounts within each calendar year to which they pertained. The Secretary of the Treasury might extend the time; and if settlements were made within the following year, and before the time of reporting to Congress, such settlements would not have been considered cases of delinquency.

On the 9th of February, 1876, the Senate, by resolution, called for a special report of all delinquent public officers. This shows that the attention of Congress has been directed to the fact that the Comptroller had ceased to make the annual reports above mentioned.

It is my wish, no less than my duty, to observe strictly all the requirements of law relating to this office; and I should endeavor to make the reports mentioned in section 272, Revised Statutes, if it could be done satisfactorily; but this seems to be impracticable; and the facts that they were not made by my predecessors, and that those which were made under the act of 1809 were discontinued twenty years ago without objection from Congress or any member thereof, lead me to believe that they are not wanted.

FORMER RECOMMENDATIONS.

Your attention is again invited to the suggestions made in my last annual report (Ex. Doc. No. 46, Forty-sixth Congress, Third Session) on the following points:

1. That the heads of the other executive departments of the government be authorized by law to direct, pursuant to the request of the Secretary of the Treasury, any officer or agent of their respective departments to investigate any of the official transactions or accounts of officers or agents of the Treasury Department which, in the opinion of the Secretary of the Treasury, it may be of advantage to the government to have so investigated, and to make report of such investigation to the Treasury Department; and that the necessary expenses incurred in such investigation be made payable out of the appropriation which would be available if the investigation were made by an officer or agent of the Treasury Department.

2. That in cases of application for duplicates or for payment of lost or destroyed interest-bearing bonds of the United States, the Secretary of the Treasury be empowered to require an examination by the proper officers, with evidence under oath, into the financial status of parties

thorized by law or regulation to sell public property for cash, to be deposited by such officer in the Treasury and reported to the Secretary, or to the accounting officers for statement of an account. It is respectfully suggested that it would contribute to secure more reliable accountability if these officers were required to make reports substantially as in the Quartermaster's Department of the Army. (Rev. Stats., 1221.) It would seem proper that, before making the final adjustment of the accounts of a disbursing officer having the custody of public property, he should be required to show its delivery to his successor in office or other custodian. The Public Printer, for example, who is a disbursing officer of the class referred to, receives money from at least five sources: by warrant on the Treasury; from various officers and departments for work done; from sales of extra copies of documents, paper-shavings, and imperfections; from sales of waste-paper; and from sales of old material. For each transaction he is required by law to settle his account of receipts. (Rev. Stats., 3817.)

Moneys are paid out of the Treasury to the Public Printer, from the several appropriations to which the same are chargeable, for work done for various offices and departments, and the money so paid is by that officer deposited to the credit of the appropriation for " the public printing and binding." The statement made by the Public Printer of moneys received from offices or departments can only be verified by the First Auditor or Comptroller by a personal examination of the books of such offices or departments, or by an extensive correspondence; and, if omissions should be inadvertently made in the reports, the difficulty of correcting the errors would be very great. This difficulty would be lessened if the accounts rendered by the Public Printer for work done for offices or departments, properly authenticated by them, were transmitted to the Secretary of the Treasury and referred to the proper accounting officer, for statement of an account in favor of the Public Printer, the balance thereof to be charged to the proper appropriation, and, when paid, to be carried by counter-warrant to the credit of the appropriation for " the public printing and binding." Under the system suggested the records would show proper charges against the several appropriations for payment for doing such work, and corresponding credits to the appropriation for " the public printing and binding." This would, to a large extent at least, avoid the necessity of a verification of the amounts to be transferred, as each account would be verified by the head of the office, bureau, or department for which the work was done. It is respectfully suggested that this matter is worthy of consideration with a view to proper regulations, or legislation if necessary, on the subject.

Difficulties are frequently occurring in connection with the accounts rendered for the sale of movable public property. If the custody and disposal of such property in the hands of civil officers were subject to regulations similar to those applicable to the like property in the custody of officers in the military or naval service, and the property itself were subject to frequent inspection by properly designated officers, a stricter accountability for, and a more satisfactory disposition of, such property would be secured.

In connection with this subject your attention is respectfully directed to the fact that no provision is made by law for the payment of expenses incurred by public officers in the sale of old material and other property, in cases where the proceeds of the sales are required to be deposited and covered into the Treasury. Such expenses are usually paid out of the proceeds, but there is doubt whether this usage is in accordance with the requirement that *all* proceeds shall be deposited. (Rev. Stats., 3617, 3618.) The question should be settled by legislation.

PER CENTUM OF PROCEEDS OF SALES OF PUBLIC LANDS DUE TO, AND DIRECT TAX DUE FROM, KANSAS AND OTHER STATES.

The deficiency appropriation act of March 3, 1881, appropriates for the State of Kansas for amount due of the five, three, and two per centum fund to States, $190,268.27. The State of Kansas having been previously charged by the proper officer of the Treasury Department with $71,743.33 on account of direct taxes stated to be due to the United States from the State of Kansas, under the direct-tax act of Congress of August 5, 1861, and only a portion of this having been paid, the residue, $62,382.51, was retained by the Treasury Department out of the appropriation made by the act of March 3, 1881, and credited to the State on account of the charge for direct taxes. The State of Kansas, by its attorneys, insisted that the whole sum appropriated should be paid to the State without applying any part as a credit on account of the charge for direct taxes.

Some, if not all, of the questions which arose in relation to this claim are liable to arise as to charges against other States for direct taxes. A copy of the decision of the First Comptroller in relation to the subject is therefore herewith transmitted for information, in case Congress should deem it advisable to legislate on the subject.

ACTING SECRETARIES OF TERRITORIES.

By section 1843 of the Revised Statutes it is provided as to each Territory that "in case of the death, removal, resignation, or absence of the governor from the Territory, the secretary shall execute all the powers and perform all the duties of governor during such vacancy or absence or until another governor is appointed and qualified."

It is respectfully suggested that provision should be made authorizing some one to act as a deputy or substitute of the Territorial secretary, as to his office, under similar circumstances. Experience has shown the necessity for some provision on this subject.

LIMITATION OF CLAIMS.

There are statutes limiting the time within which some claims may be presented against the government, while as to others there is no limit prescribed by statute, and hence only such as may arise on common law principles from presumption of payment.* The existence of many old claims against the government, some of them often rejected but frequently renewed, would seem to suggest the propriety of considering the justice and necessity of providing a limitation generally applicable to claims.

I deem it due to those with whom I have been officially connected in this office, and to the employés therein, to express my appreciation of the intelligence, ability, and fidelity with which they have performed their respective duties.

I have the honor to be, very respectfully,

WILLIAM LAWRENCE,
First Comptroller.

Hon. WILLIAM WINDOM,
Secretary of the Treasury.

---

* I have had occasion, whilst a member of the House of Representatives, to consider the justice and necessity of prescribing a limitation applicable to claims generally House Rep. No. 134, second session Forty-third Congress, pp. 18, 242).

14 AB

REPORT OF SECOND COMPTROLLER OF THE TREASURY.

TREASURY DEPARTMENT,
SECOND COMPTROLLER'S OFFICE,
Washington, October 17, 1881.

SIR: In compliance with your direction, by letter of the 30th ultimo, I submit a report, in two tabular statements, of the transactions of this office during the fiscal year which ended on the 30th day of June, 1881. The first tabular statement shows the total number of accounts, claims, and cases of every kind settled and adjusted, and the amounts allowed thereon. The second table furnishes a more detailed statement of the same accounts, claims, and cases, showing the character of the accounts, the source from which received, the number of each kind, and the amounts allowed. A still more detailed statement is prepared and filed for preservation in this office, but it is deemed too voluminous for publication.

From—	Number revised.	Amounts.
Second Auditor	8,396	$22,905,529
Third Auditor	4,740	73,380,709
Fourth Auditor	1,804	16,203,818
	14,940	112,400,028
Various sources not involving present expenditure	2,995	2,076,516
Total number accounts and claims and amounts settled	17,935	114,476,554

ACCOUNTS REVISED DURING THE YEAR.

Character of accounts.	Number revised.	Amounts.
FROM SECOND AUDITOR.		
1. Of Army paymasters, for pay of the Army	521	$16,337,658
2. Of disbursing officers of the Ordnance Department, for ordnance, ordnance stores, supplies, armories, and arsenals	265	1,434,618
3. Of disbursing officers of the Medical Department, for medical and hospital supplies and services	52	204,798
4. Of recruiting officers, for regular recruiting service	427	131,151
5. Accounts of the Managers of the Soldiers' Home	13	87,813
6. Accounts of the National Home for Disabled Volunteer Soldiers	30	1,818,770
7. Miscellaneous accounts, including disbursements for contingent expenses (Army and Adjutant-General's Office), expenses of Commanding-General's Office, Artillery School, &c	164	90,216
8. Freedman's Branch, Adjutant-General's Office	1	1,680
9. Of Indian Agents' current and contingent expenses, annuities, and installments	2,197	7,665,885
Total	3,630	22,380,684
FROM THIRD AUDITOR.		
1. Of disbursing officers of the Quartermaster's Department, for regular and incidental expenses	915	11,921,147
2. Of disbursing officers of the Subsistence Department	572	2,918,037
3. Of disbursing officers of the Engineer Department, for military surveys, fortifications, river and harbor surveys and improvements	93	8,058,974
4. Of pension agents, for payment of Army pensions	140	49,143,605
Total	1,720	72,042,763
FROM FOURTH AUDITOR.		
1. Of disbursing agents of the Marine Corps	7	472,141
2. Of paymasters of the Navy proper (see pay)	114	4,176,888
3. Of paymasters of navy-yards	82	7,060,779
4. Of paymasters of the Navy as navy agents and disbursing officers	18	3,231,961
5. Of Navy pension agents, for payment of pensions of Navy and Marine Corps	93	954,402
6. Of miscellaneous naval accounts	76	97,775
7. Of financial agents' expenditures	4	23,315
Total	394	16,027,261

CLAIMS ALLOWED DURING THE YEAR.

Character of claims.	Number	Amounts.
FROM SECOND AUDITOR.		
1 Soldiers' pay and bounty	4,367	$395,183
2. Miscellaneous claims of pay division	349	49,653
FROM THIRD AUDITOR.		
1 For lost property paid under the act of March 3, 1849	398	48,521
2 Quartermasters' stores and commissary supplies under act of July 4, 1864, Army transportation, and miscellaneous..........................	2,597	1,199,082
3 Oregon and Washington war claims	28	4,290
4 State war claims..t...............	4	96,044
FROM FOURTH AUDITOR.		
1 Officers and sailors' pay and bounty	· 1,264	171,390
2. Prize money..	146	5,167
Total...	9,146	1,969,330

CASES NOT INVOLVING PRESENT EXPENDITURE.

	Number.	Amounts.
1. Duplicate checks approved...............................	458	$30,805
2. Financial agents' accounts...................................	4	2,039,456
3. Referred cases adjusted	2,061	
4. Special account, Second Auditor	472	6,255
Total..	2,995	2,076,516

	Number.
Bonds filed during the year..	92
Contracts filed during the year	2,115
Official letters written...	1,526
Requisitions recorded	14,800
Settlements recorded	8,172
Differences recorded, pages..	4,570
Clerks employed, average	62.5

All the public business intrusted to my charge is, I believe, promptly and properly attended to by the officers and clerks of the office, and has progressed with reasonable dispatch.

Very respectfully,   W. W. UPTON,
                                                           Comptroller.

Hon. WILLIAM WINDOM,
    Secretary of the Treasury.

REPORT OF THE COMMISSIONER OF CUSTOMS.

TREASURY DEPARTMENT,
OFFICE OF COMMISSIONER OF CUSTOMS,
Washington, D. C., October 29, 1881.

SIR: I have the honor to submit herewith for your information a statement of the work performed in this office during the fiscal year ending June 30, 1881:

Number of accounts on hand July 1, 1880	140	
Number of accounts received from the First Auditor during the year	6,703	
		6,843
Number of accounts adjusted during the year...........................	6,645	
Number of accounts returned to the First Auditor	14	
		6,659
Number of accounts on hand June 30, 1881		184

There was paid into the Treasury from sources the accounts relating to which are settled in this office:

On account of customs	$198,159,676 02
On account of marine-hospital tax	380,518 28
On account of steamboat fees	307,554 21
On account of fines, penalties, and forfeitures	150,433 49
On account of storage, fees, &c	860,144 21
On account of deceased passengers	370 00
On account of emolument fees	213,738 76
On account of mileage of examiners	1,197 90
On account of interest on debts due	1,236 00
On account of rent of public buildings	5,454 93
On account of relief of sick and disabled seamen	5,541 52
On account of proceeds of government property	24,058 76
On account of miscellaneous items	12 30
Aggregate	200,109,936 38

And there was paid out of the Treasury on the following accounts, viz:

Expenses of collection	$6,383,288 10
Excess of deposits	3,663,254 24
Debentures	1,722,184 35
Public buildings	2,284,053 13
Construction and maintenance of lights	2,642,668 99
Construction and maintenance of revenue cutters	839,914 77
Marine-hospital service	400,404 47
Life-saving stations	469,018 60
Compensation in lieu of moieties	32,509 73
Seal fisheries in Alaska	4,248 09
Metric standard weights and measures	5,388 27
Debentures and other charges	8 51
Detection and prevention of frauds upon the customs revenue	36,057 10
Unclaimed merchandise	129 77
Refunding moneys erroneously received and covered into the Treasury.	365 00
Protection of sea-otter hunting-grounds and seal fisheries in Alaska	619 12
Extra pay to officers and men in Mexican war—revenue marine	1,362 00
Relief of N. & G. Taylor	11,017 05
Relief of E. S. Sherman	1,130 79
Relief of keepers of Timbalier light station	100 00
Relief of E. E. Sanders	40 00
Relief of widows and children of surfmen who perished at Point Aux Barques, Lake Huron	1,000 00
Burial of surfmen who perished in rendering assistance to distressed vessels	150 00
Removal of remains of R. H. Carter, late inspector of customs, from Panama to Virginia	500 00
Aggregate	18,499,412 09

The number of estimates received and examined	3,103
The number of requisitions issued	3,103
The amount involved in requisitions	$15,196,725 36
The number of letters received	10,842
The number of letters written	10,844
The number of letters recorded	9,056
The number of stubs of receipts for duties and fees returned by collectors	206,145
The number of stubs examined	236,025
The number of stubs of certificates of payment of tonnage dues received and entered	10,020
The number of returns received and examined	82,882
The number of oaths examined and registered	2,568
The number of appointments registered	4,529
The average number of clerks employed	30

I inclose herewith a statement of the transactions in bonded goods during the year ending June 30, 1881, as shown by the adjusted accounts.

I am, very respectfully, your obedient servant,

H. C. JOHNSON,
Commissioner of Customs.

The SECRETARY OF THE TREASURY.

STATEMENT of WAREHOUSE TRANSACTIONS at the several DISTRICTS and PORTS of the UNITED STATES for the year ending JUNE 30, 1881.

Districts.	Balance on bonds to secure duties in warehouse July 1, 1880.	Warehoused and bonded.	Rewarehoused and bonded.	Constructively warehoused.	Increase of duties ascertained on liquidation.	Withdrawal, duty paid.	Withdrawal, for transportation.	Withdrawal, for exportation.	Allowances and deficiencies.	Balance on bonds to secure duties on goods remaining in warehouse June 30, 1881.
Albany	$520,615 08	$741,343 82	$13,779 63	$187,264 48	$9,649 54	$187,264 48	$55,839 08	$85,902 87	$12,863 61	$151,238 13
Baltimore	981 53	2,077 80	70,175 48	127,309 06	17 77	909,247 96	109 13	10,772 25		782 00
Bangor	42,156 75	20,866 71	167 30	191 87		2,339 77		281 38	11,355 28	579 40
Barnstable			620 15	439 40		46 48				43,068 77
Bath				1,453 80		80,845 76	572 39			1,020 15
Beaufort, S. C.				1,451 90		1,656 25				3,738,929 17
Boston and Charlestown	5,094,343 14	10,226,212 11	111,737 98	1,741,359 63	253,877 57	10,876,596 25	360,225 69	2,088,780 49	463,511 08	383 85
Brazos de Santiago	10,963 80	631,880 29	145,440 27	14,359 00	4 90	415,066 09	12,465 78	788,240 95	382 89	364 85
Buffalo Creek	1,543 77	28,983 64	3,602 15	480,438 81	13 27	74,383 06	68,502 13	387,639 70		214 78
Belfast	746 46			95 84				10 00		
Castine	38 12			42 43	3 81	120 04	82 43	1,254 87		67 28
Cape Vincent					108 50	4,158 00		10 00	60 37	9,785 80
Champlain	5,769 74	7,965 90	1,465 76	293,294 57	25 18	2,916 29	263,884 97	8,481 41	7,260 89	2,831 54
Charleston	278 08	153 70	2,596 38	2,284 57	9,697 56	1,364,105 19	15,486 06	8,439 53	14 15	173,647 74
Chicago	344,003 78	782,117 42	83,599 49	199,660 15	186 88	103,810 00	783 30			25,909 28
Cincinnati	25,988 50	63,148 26	10,263 92	30,438 21		1,870 00	1,094 65	8,481 41		4,676 58
Corpus Christi		18,812 46	9,843 50		146 80	49,077 84	1,708 56	20,574 72		2,696 89
Cuyahoga	7,763 56	8,123 96	21,840 15	15,602 22		13,709 11				1,363 46
Delaware			5,072 67		78 15	70,277 85	8,318 58	811,025 49	1,724 68	33,946 08
Detroit	422,729 03	85,746 09	55,960 99	809,088 14	08	1,045 52	1,742 70	907,787 86		
Duluth	432 86	20 69	20 69	909,077 89		10,887 37			996 72	
Dubuque	859 89	185 80	185 80			2,853 75	4,596 45	1,619 20	966 75	7,113 12
Erie				12 80	123 74	3,886 59		47,060 75		440 54
Fall River				2,853 75	2 70	70 20	11,124 11	77 00	701 23	13,672 03
Fernandina	9,816 45	10,824 47	7,881 58	4,296 43	284 89	97,543 19	1,715 69	46,585 03		4,780 85
Frenchman's Bay	265 98	570 52	7,823 64		198 98	23,765 07			8 50	11,631 20
Galveston	68,691 28	37,872 81	2,231 88	57,058 69	596 89	811 44		1,663,932 48		1,496 25
Genesee	9,608 64	2,387 25	4,766 80	15,722 38	29 53	2,962 04	101,910 58	456 16		
Gloucester	9,590 90	46,741 85	1,714 28					496 85		2,233 34
Georgetown, D. C.		957 85		2,178 12		138,615 84	20,627 70	127 66		27,586 03
Huron	71,099 96	100,065 85	3,223 34	1,784,943 06	8,874 70	24,801 64	211 50			7,507 77
Kennebunk	18,152 22	11,179 08	11,283 31	456 18	90 78	11,265 18				
Key West			8,940 81			14,433 13				1,183 61
Louisville	635 00		127 68	5,056 62	100 85	62,614 85	251 14			
Memphis			1,198 41	10,489 73	23 02					
Middletown	32,176 21		29,731 65	14,433 13						5,915 08

STATEMENT of WAREHOUSE TRANSACTIONS at the several DISTRICTS and PORTS of the UNITED STATES, &c.—Continued.

Districts.	Balance on bonds to secure duties remaining in warehouse July 1, 1880.	Warehoused and bonded.	Rewarehoused and bonded.	Constructively warehoused.	Increase of duties on ascertained on liquidation.	Withdrawal, duty paid.	Withdrawal, for transportation.	Withdrawn, for exportation.	Allowances and deficiencies.	Balance on bonds to secure duties on goods remaining in warehouse July 30, 1881.
Milwaukee	$14,871 19	$10,693 97	$968 89	$32,114 91	$35 83	$54,982 02	$208 45	$32,087 09	$896 16	$1,368 19
Minnesota	1,435 52	3,118 25	4,458 52	46,715 27	70 64	9,360 62	11,850 07	156 78	15,257 70	2,370 82
Mobile	27,580 60	6,686 34		997 15		14,606 05		154 57	39 90	5,400 34
Montana and Idaho				156 78						748 04
Nashville	16,680 32		1,398 04	1,391 25		185,125 46		3,521 30		2,370 54
Newburyport	8,247 50	240,262 52	2,370 54	154 57	3 33	15,787 92	41,949 19	130,621 23	1,226 88	21,751 40
New Haven	209,530 57	5,002 08	1,874 21	13,176 54	10,816 72	471,773 76	7,411 74	130,883,655 48	39,371 20	2,217 80
New Bedford		689,783 57	8,736 19	723,035 85	1,212,702 60	50,826,747 77	725,812 05	10,883,684 73	2,149,288 22	231,804 51
New Orleans	22,940,334 01	48,703,616 77	14,296 94	8,755,690 82			919,112 63	1,230,684 73		17,331,032 75
New York			497,512 63	8,416,404 39			185,719 08			
Niagara	201 91	15,860 85	1,971 46	91 92	12 32	5,963 06	420 88	1,463 63		107 04
Newark, N. J.	315 73	7,465 43		1,491 76		16,122 82				280 65
New London	1,792 15	696,314 95	3,178 82	38,283 22		1,566 88	21,761 58	18,066 63		5,586 96
Omaha	14,133 45	3,388 97	35,221 49	63,336 57	62 50	340,065 96	368,115 43	5,803 96		6,133 65
Oswegatchie	1,872 27	12,208 00	26,002 24	13,621 62	70 43	2,771 74	12,782 61		48 00	2,154 75
Oswego		3,584,699 19	92,231 52	81,867 01	200,314 44	1,317 98		61,746 26	123,417 25	44,732 25
Passamaquoddy	1,270,076 68	36,437 69	3,197 15	72,382 01		3,959,337 19	62,171 28			1,016,197 87
Perth Amboy	31,961 73	397,065 26	56,290 20	3,043,045 63	92 51	184,367 76	463 30	373 39	8,994 58	44,232 42
Philadelphia	38,387 17	1,557 64	1,845 43	3,950 08	130 56	36,068 82	52,580 37	3,036,398 92		5,510 39
Pittsburgh	16,567 63	22,299 53	14,240 56	10,102 96		280,332 79		1,965 39		170,825 71
Plymouth, Mass.				176 28		24,631 23				1,276 92
Portland and Falmouth				129 62		32,191 05				11,148 90
Portsmouth					16 10	3,446 44	698 82	176 20		
Providence					50 66	66		113 52		
Puget Sound	4,773 46		890 97					880 97	122,981 95	237 00
Saco		33,830 65		654,277 42	5 42	2,654,247 82	253,637 31	561,629 57		
Salem and Beverly	955,184 80	104,810 61	769 43	3,759 02	37,138 25	2,161,707 19	3,449 00			1,065,621 70
Sandusky	89,420 85			6 75	2 45	75				522 33
San Francisco		46,097 67	100,700 76	377,728 42		575,397 23		835,430 13	101 81	31,738 32
Savannah	28,995 49			694 00	111 21		229,748 01	1,220 11	1,674 88	
Saint John's		28,031 47	5,176 80	627,259 80		75,700 83	684 00			727 08
Saint Louis	1,569 48	75 04	3,782 70	129 27	336 37	174 47	694 00	27 04		2,200 07
Vermont				1,718 72	51	1,748 73				
Waldoborough	7,002 02	28,812 73	4,410 12	11,223 43	48 95	42,260 89				8,845 73
Wheeling										
Willamette										

* Not included in report for fiscal year ending June 30, 1880.

RECAPITULATION.

Balance July 1, 1880	$31,625,787 77
Warehoused and bonded	70,367,530 16
Rewarehoused and bonded	1,583,033 80
Constructively warehoused	22,684,855 00
Increase of duties ascertained on liquidation	1,798,783 19
Total	128,178,989 92

Withdrawal, duty paid	$73,944,007 35
Withdrawal, for transportation	3,697,044 70
Withdrawal, for exportation	23,258,453 75
Allowances and deficiencies	2,962,570 17
Balance June 30, 1881	24,321,304 96
Total	128,178,989 92

Arising from—

Increase in balance in New York from March 1 to June 30, 1880	11,584,901 05
Increase in balance in Boston from June 1 to June 30, 1880	184,707 85
Increase in balance in Mobile from December 1, 1879, to June 30, 1880	27,580 00

Balance taken up on this statement	$31,625,787 77
Balance reported by last statement	20,039,597 87
Difference	11,787,189 90

| | 11,787,189 90 |

H. C. JOHNSON,
Commissioner of Customs.

TREASURY DEPARTMENT, OFFICE COMMISSIONER OF CUSTOMS,
October 29, 1881.

REPORT OF THE FIRST AUDITOR OF THE TREASURY.

TREASURY DEPARTMENT,
FIRST AUDITOR'S OFFICE,
Washington, November 1, 1881.

SIR: I have the honor to submit the following exhibit of the business transacted in this office during the fiscal year ending June 30, 1881:

Accounts adjusted.	Number of accounts.	Amount.
RECEIPTS.		
Duties on merchandise and tonnage...............................	1,311	$199,909,976 53
Steamboat fees...	1,090	270,921 90
Fines, penalties, and forfeitures	698	120,589 57
Marine-hospital money collected.................................	1,446	374,921 37
Official emoluments of collectors, naval officers, and surveyors........	1,266	881,500 01
Moneys received on account of deceased passengers	52	980 00
Moneys received from sales of old materials, &c	281	314,156 89
Miscellaneous receipts..	612	713,271 98
Moneys retained from Pacific railroad companies for accrued interest on bonds.	18	3,734,909 75
Treasurer of the United States, for moneys received...............	3	541,426,739 43
Mints and Assay Offices	21	111,080,057 14
Water rents, Hot Springs, Arkansas	12	2,849 40
Accounts of collector of taxes for the District of Columbia, for taxes and water rents collected and deposited with the treasurer of said District......	2	1,610,214 98
Accounts of the treasurer of the District of Columbia for moneys received and deposited with the Treasurer of the United States	2	1,654,923 09
Total	6,814	862,006,061 94
DISBURSEMENTS.		
Expenses of collecting the revenue from customs..................	1,587	5,305,718 20
Detection and prevention of frauds on customs revenue	7	31,631 25
Debentures, drawbacks, &c..	196	1,429,063 53
Excess of deposits refunded	382	3,212,160 43
Revenue-cutter service	568	730,942 44
Duties refunded, fines remitted, judgments satisfied, &c...........	1,743	853,940 77
Marine-Hospital Service	1,118	399,749 76
Official emoluments of collectors, naval officers, and surveyors	1,257	778,257 46
Awards of compensation	167	42,648 73
Light-House Establishment, miscellaneous	44	46,180 00
Salaries of light-house keepers	340	437,549 86
Supplies of light-houses	83	267,581 62
Repairs of light-houses	72	209,416 91
Expenses of light-vessels...	79	211,669 49
Expenses of buoyage	73	228,375 80
Expenses of fog-signals	51	65,925 65
Expenses of lighting and buoyage of the Mississippi, Missouri, and Ohio rivers...	30	127,647 12
Expenses of inspection of lights....................................	6	1,842 18
Steam-tenders for the Light-House Service..........................	6	43,266 37
Commissions to superintendents of lights...........................	185	29,211 01
Salaries and mileage of Senators...................................	4	672,998 35
Salaries, officers and employés, Senate............................	11	233,999 63
Salaries and mileage, members and delegates, House of Representatives.......	1	3,239,557 44
Salaries, officers and employés, House of Representatives	11	265,889 34
Salaries of employés, Executive Mansion	6	39,319 73
Salaries paid by disbursing clerks of the Departments.............	294	5,744,654 34
Salaries, officers and employés, Independent Treasury..............	43	534,578 49
Salaries of the civil list, paid directly from the Treasury	1,315	551,451 01
Salaries, office of the Public Printer	4	13,000 00
Salaries, Bureau of Engraving and Printing	12	25,384 37
Salaries, Congressional Library	5	39,085 77
Salaries, standard weights and measures	5	10,554 25
Salaries, Steamboat-Inspection Service	3	120,014 96
Salaries, special agents, Independent Treasury.....................	6	3,646 28
Salaries, custodians and janitors	4	80,859 52
Salaries, Agricultural Department..................................	6	69,406 28
Salaries, Botanic Garden	6	12,787 54
Salaries and expenses, Southern Claims Commission	2	622 84
Salaries and expenses, National Board of Health	4	195,030 67
Salaries of employés, public buildings and grounds	5	38,042 39
Contingent expenses, Executive Mansion...........................	5	7,822 71
Contingent expenses, United States Senate	48	186,799 42
Contingent expenses, House of Representatives	58	209,999 23
Contingent expenses, Departments, Washington	407	381,980 17

Accounts adjusted.	Number of accounts.	Amount.
DISBURSEMENTS—Continued.		
Contingent expenses, Independent Treasury	213	$72, 517 78
Contingent expenses, Steamboat-Inspection Service	842	32, 082 74
Contingent expenses, public buildings and grounds	4	636 95
Contingent expenses, office of Public Printer	12	2, 171 95
Contingent expenses, National Currency, reimbursable	37	30, 617 34
Contingent expenses, Court of Claims	6	2, 825 83
Contingent expenses, Library of Congress	7	1, 021 81
Contingent expenses of the Executive offices, Territories	7	2, 609 88
Contingent expenses, Department of Agriculture	4	7, 879 06
Contingent expenses, Mints and Assay Offices	114	4, 969 00
Stationery, Interior Department	7	78, 510 57
Treasurer of the United States, for general expenditures	3	596, 760, 348 32
Treasurer of the United States, for sinking fund, Pacific railroads	3	1, 313, 254 21
Gold and silver bullion account	20	110, 403, 361 52
Ordinary expenses, Mints and Assay Offices	98	921, 688 52
Parting and refining bullion	17	151, 550 79
Coinage of standard silver dollars	39	76, 454 84
Freight on bullion and coin	10	36, 153 21
Transportation of coin and bullion	4	9, 847 05
Storage of silver dollars	4	8, 334 67
Manufacture of medals	1	7, 239 35
Legislative expenses, Territories of the United States	19	24, 606 90
Reapportionment of members of Territorial legislatures	4	346 80
Defending suits in claims against the United States	3	8, 223 76
Examination of rebel archives	3	4, 176 10
Collecting mining statistics	18	1, 111 96
Geodetic and Coast Survey of the United States	53	776, 210 47
Geological survey of the Territories and salary of director	25	176, 907 54
Illustrations for report on geological survey of the Territories	5	43, 748 85
Lands and other property of the United States	14	5, 448 71
Protection and improvement of Hot Springs, Arkansas	1	3, 034 86
Expenses of collecting rents, Hot Springs	13	355 60
Reproducing plats of surveys, General Land Office	5	22, 254 00
Adjusting claims for indemnity for swamp lands	6	9, 187 10
Protection and improvement of Yellowstone Park	3	13, 313 00
Commission to classify land and codify land laws	4	24, 447 69
Depredations on public timber	5	8, 480 36
Reclamation of arid and waste lands	3	9, 880 11
North American Ethnology, Smithsonian Institution	3	18, 733 73
Polaris report, Smithsonian Institution	6	2, 756 55
Judicial expenses, embracing accounts of United States marshals, district attorneys, clerks and commissioners, rent of court-houses, support of prisoners, &c	4, 967	4, 392, 268 59
Prosecution of crimes	5	17, 538 86
Suppressing counterfeiting and crime	28	33, 510 74
Investigation of frauds, Office of Commissioner of Pensions	3	15, 529 05
INTEREST ACCOUNT.		
Registered stock	45	44, 714, 719 37
Coupons	169	38, 962, 676 73
District of Columbia, Washington, Georgetown, and corporation bonds	25	1, 602, 022 57
Navy pension fund	1	420, 000 00
Louisville and Portland Canal Company's bonds	8	48, 330 00
REDEMPTION ACCOUNT.		
United States bonds, called:		
Principal	15	5, 049, 150 00
Interest		116, 657 99
United States bonds, purchased for sinking fund:		
Principal	13	89, 316, 050 00
Interest		1, 169, 060 57
Premium		2, 019, 029 85
Refunding certificates:		
Principal	12	718, 250 00
Interest		44, 669 74
Texas indemnity stock:		
Principal	1	1, 000 00
Interest		100 00
Certificates of deposit	35	27, 184, 360 00
District of Columbia stock:		
Principal	6	275, 476 74
Interest		892 83
Premium		12, 879 39
Louisville and Portland Canal Company's bonds		391, 000 00
Notes, one and two years, compound interest and 7-30s:		
Principal	41	17, 910 00
Interest		2, 928 76
Legal-tender notes destroyed	} 29	{ 44, 436, 549 00
Fractional currency destroyed		84, 239 06
Old demand notes destroyed		395 00

Accounts adjusted.	Number of accounts.	Amount.
DISBURSEMENTS—Continued.		
Refunding the national debt	9	$20,528 89
Expenses of national currency	19	25,491 11
Examination of national banks and bank-plates	6	832 30
Transportation of United States securities	15	5,612 17
Judgments of the Court of Claims	177	281,721 05
Reporting decisions of the Court of Claims	1	1,000 00
Outstanding drafts and checks	90	8,586 42
Post Office Department requisitions	8	971,735 86
Postage	24	196,000 15
Life-saving Service	49	294,785 79
Life-saving Service, contingent expenses	94	62,400 12
Establishing life-saving stations	18	19,106 95
Public printing and binding	151	3,480,073 48
Fire-extinguishers, Government Printing Office	1	1,000 00
Fire-escape ladders, Government Printing Office	1	385 55
Telephonic connection between the Capitol and Government Printing Office	17	424 09
Telegraph between the Capitol, departments, and Government Printing Office	4	906 86
Labor and expenses of engraving and printing	10	528,600 96
Removal of Bureau of Engraving and Printing	1	12,527 59
Propagation of food-fishes	25	106,845 86
Illustrations for report on food-fishes	2	942 88
Inquiry respecting food-fishes	3	3,500 00
Steam vessels (food-fishes)	10	57,450 85
Construction of fish pond on Monument lot	5	4,227 06
Increase of Library of Congress	6	11,750 85
Works of art for the Capitol	5	10,125 00
Library, Treasury Department	6	730 86
Statue of General Daniel Morgan	1	20,000 00
Construction of custom-houses	250	1,100,121 22
Construction of court-houses and post-offices	338	1,601,181 83
Construction of appraisers' stores	30	58,628 39
Construction of sub-treasury building, New York	8	984 74
Construction of National Museum	12	102,050 42
Construction of building for State, War, and Navy Departments	9	297,309 66
Construction of barge office, New York	21	75,276 73
Construction of light-houses	137	529,397 74
Construction of building for Bureau of Engraving and Printing	15	94,306 24
Construction of extension of Government Printing Office	9	5,894 52
Construction of marine hospitals	8	1,211 29
Plans for public buildings	6	2,986 07
Completion of Washington Monument	12	163,748 34
Reconstruction of Interior Department building	4	129,015 70
Repairs of the Interior Department building	5	13,553 45
Repairs, fuel, &c., Executive Mansion	6	30,419 27
Annual repairs of the Capitol	3	21,788 18
Annual repairs of the Treasury building	6	35,847 76
Repairs and preservation of public buildings	29	99,249 66
Fire-proof roof, building corner of Seventeenth and F streets	2	10,372 29
Rent of buildings in Washington	24	53,725 00
Completion of records, Southern Claims Commission	11	1,100 00
Summary reports of the Commissioners of Claims	1	2,000 00
Joint Select Committee to provide additional accommodations for Library of Congress	3	4,586 88
Lighting, &c., Executive Mansion	5	15,457 63
Lighting the Capitol grounds	4	29,191 61
Fuel, lights, and water for public buildings	60	465,192 54
Fuel, lights, &c., Department of the Interior	6	8,821 38
Furniture and repairs of same, public buildings	34	161,301 99
Furniture for new War Department building	2	7,500 49
Furniture for new Navy Department building	2	373 56
Vaults, safes, and locks for public buildings	13	87,580 79
Heating apparatus for public buildings	21	69,683 94
Heating apparatus for Senate	3	8,131 95
Heating apparatus for House of Representatives	2	999 40
Fire-extinguishers, Capitol	2	1,500 00
Improvement and care of public grounds	4	46,704 20
Improving Capitol grounds	6	54,309 43
Improving Botanic Garden and buildings	8	14,883 10
Improving grounds, Agricultural Department	5	5,530 68
Washington Aqueduct	5	19,383 14
Repairs of water-pipes and fire-plugs	5	2,639 41
Constructing, repairing, and maintaining bridges, District of Columbia	5	7,995 66
Preparation of receipts, expenditures, and appropriations of the government	4	1,481 27
Distributing documents, Bureau of Education	4	989 14
Experimental garden, Agricultural Department	4	7,446 14
Library, Agricultural Department	5	1,651 26
Museum, Agricultural Department	4	1,012 23
Laboratory, Agricultural Department	5	4,144 66
Furniture, cases, &c., Agricultural Department	3	4,981 27
Collecting agricultural statistics	6	10,466 27

Accounts adjusted.	Number of accounts.	Amount.
DISBURSEMENTS—Continued.		
Purchase and distribution of valuable seeds	6	$94,867 10
Commission to report on the cotton worm and Rocky Mountain locust	6	21,980 08
Investigating diseases of swine and other domestic animals	5	14,271 31
Investigating the history of insects injurious to agriculture	4	4,501 28
Machinery, apparatus, and experiments in the manufacture of sugar	4	17,149 41
Examination of wools and animal fibers	3	2,712 79
Report on forestry	3	2,611 55
Reform School, District of Columbia	3	35,605 38
Freedmen's Hospital and Asylum	5	40,993 60
Government Hospital for the Insane, buildings, &c	2	1,714 53
Government Hospital for the Insane, current expenses	4	140,217 36
Columbia Institution for the Deaf and Dumb, buildings, &c	2	6,372 58
Columbia Institution for the Deaf and Dumb, current expenses	4	52,949 48
Columbia Hospital for Women	5	9,509 13
Howard University	4	10,050 34
Saint Ann's Infant Asylum	4	5,001 02
Children's Hospital	4	5,186 29
National Association for the Relief of Colored Women and Children	4	6,362 27
Women's Christian Association	4	4,704 90
Industrial Home School	6	5,311 79
Maryland Institution for the Instruction of the Blind	4	5,275 00
Building for the Little Sisters of the Poor	1	5,000 00
Miscellaneous	358	529,456 16
Transfers by warrant and counter-warrant	220	297,504 15
DISTRICT OF COLUMBIA ACCOUNTS.		
Refunding taxes	12	23,063 34
Washington redemption fund	12	295 01
Redemption of tax-lien certificates	12	2,047 62
Redemption of Pennsylvania avenue paving scrip	12	816 88
Redemption of Pennsylvania avenue paving certificates	16	34,619 80
Relief of the poor	13	11,300 00
Salaries and contingent expenses	25	183,014 40
Improvement and repairs	19	467,750 35
Washington Asylum	19	47,876 45
Georgetown Almshouse	16	1,667 40
Government Hospital for the Insane	6	4,982 23
Transportation of paupers and prisoners	17	2,527 79
Reform School	16	19,567 40
Public schools	19	472,645 34
Metropolitan police	17	371,518 22
Fire department	19	128,837 62
Courts	15	16,853 24
Streets	16	284,250 84
Health department	19	30,509 43
Miscellaneous and contingent expenses	16	27,178 59
Washington Asylum, building and grounds	6	9,964 46
Contingent expenses	3	3,805 00
Markets	3	754 65
Penny-lunch house	15	1,500 00
Accounts of disbursements made by the Commissioners of the District of Columbia before the creation of the "permanent form of government":		
Payment of indebtedness of District of Columbia, 1875	1	1,062,807 28
General expenses, District of Columbia, 1875	1	77,765 86
General expenses, District of Columbia, 1875 and 1876	1	1,060,000 00
Removal of jail	1	14,000 00
Completing sewerage and filling Tiber valley	1	20,000 00
Fire department, District of Columbia, 1878	1	25,000 00
Total	20,308	1,016,464,134 81

Number of certificates recorded 15,396
Number of letters recorded 3,857
Judiciary emolument accounts registered and referred 572
Number of powers of attorney for collection of interest on the public debt examined, registered, and filed 3,539
Requisitions answered 924

SUMMARY STATEMENT of the WORK of the OFFICE, as shown by the REPORTS of the various DIVISIONS and MISCELLANEOUS DESKS.

CUSTOMS DIVISION.

Comprising the Accounts of Collectors of Customs for Receipts of Customs Revenue and Disbursements for the Expenses of Collecting the same, and also including Accounts of Collectors for Receipts and Disburse-ments in connection with the Revenue-Cutter, Steamboat, Fines, Light-House, and Marine-Hospital Serv-ices, with Accounts for Official Emoluments, Debentures, Refunds of Duties, Sales of Old Materials, and Miscellaneous Disbursements.

	Number of accounts.	Amount.
Receipts	6,684	$202,322,695 44
Disbursements	7,146	12,869,162 80
Total	13,830	215,191,858 24

JUDICIARY DIVISION.

Comprising the Accounts of District Attorneys, Marshals, Clerks, and Commissioners, Rents, and Miscel-laneous Court Accounts.

	Number of accounts.	Amount.
Disbursements	4,967	$4,392,268 50

PUBLIC DEBT DIVISION.

Public Debt Division, comprising all Accounts for Payment of Interest on the Public Debt, both Registered Stock and Coupon Bonds, Interest on District of Columbia Bonds, Pacific Railroad Bonds, Louisville and Portland Canal Bonds, Navy Pension Fund, Redemption of United States and District of Colum-bia Bonds, Redemption of Coin and Currency Certificates, Old Notes and Bounty Scrip, and Accounts for Notes and Fractional Currency Destroyed.

	Number of accounts.	Amount.
Interest accounts	248	$85,747,748 67
Redemption accounts	152	170,840,598 95
Total	400	256,588,347 62

WAREHOUSE AND BOND DIVISION.

STATEMENT of TRANSACTIONS in BONDED MERCHANDISE, as shown by ACCOUNTS ADJUSTED during the fiscal year ending June 30, 1881.

Number of accounts adjusted 1,106
Number of reports of "No transactions" received, examined, and referred .... 432.
Balance of duties on merchandise in warehouse per last report $15,735,130 57
Duties on merchandise warehoused 97,903,965 78
Duties on merchandise rewarehoused 1,944,292 42
Duties on merchandise constructively warehoused 30,818,641 05
Increased and additional duties, &c. 2,304,606 26

      Total 148,725,936 08

Contra:
Duties on merchandise withdrawn for consumption $96,450,296 91
Duties on merchandise withdrawn for transportation 4,340,148 51

Duties on merchandise withdrawn for exportation................... $31,419,814 41
Allowances for deficiencies, damage, &c........................... 3,714,304 16
Duties on withdrawals for construction and repair of vessels......... 155,078 12
Duties on bonds delivered to district attorneys for prosecution....... 11,044 53
Balance of duties on merchandise in warehouse..................... 22,635,319 44

     Total 148,725,936 08

MISCELLANEOUS DESKS.

No. 1.—Comprising Accounts of Disbursing Clerks of the Departments for Salaries, Salary Accounts of the various Assistant Treasurers, and of the Congressional Library, Public Printer, and Executive Office, Accounts for Salaries of the Officers and Employés, House of Representatives, and the Accounts relating to the Coast Survey.

	Number of accounts.	Amount.
Disbursements...	425	$7,285,096 92

No. 2.—Comprising the Accounts of the Disbursing Clerks of the Departments for Contingent Expenses, Contingent Expenses of the House of Representatives and Assistant Treasurers, Accounts of the Bureau of Engraving and Printing, Geological Survey, National Board of Health, Reform School, New Building for State, War, and Navy Departments, and a very great Number of Miscellaneous Accounts. The accounts on this desk during the last fiscal year covered one hundred and eighty different appropriations.

	Number of accounts.	Amount.
Receipts...	12	$2,849 40
Disbursements...	965	3,860,088 48
Total	977	3,862,937 88

No. 3.—Comprising Accounts for Construction of Custom-Houses, Post-Offices, Court-Houses, and other Public Buildings; Accounts of Light-House Engineers and Inspectors; Accounts of the Public Printer; Steamboat Inspection and Life-Saving Service; the Accounts of the Government Hospital for the Insane, Columbia Hospital for Deaf and Dumb, and many Charitable Institutions.

	Number of accounts.	Amount.
Receipts...	31	$3,931,994 54
Disbursements...	2,732	11,281,314 65
Total	2,763	15,213,309 19

No. 4.—Comprising the Account of the Treasurer of the United States for General Expenditures; the Salary and Mileage Accounts for the Senate and House of Representatives, and the Accounts for Contingent Expenses of the United States Senate.

	Number of accounts.	Amount.
Receipts...	3	$541,426,739 43
Disbursements...	67	601,095,658 16
Total	70	1,142,522,397 59

No 5 —*Comprising the Accounts of Mints and Assay Offices; Salaries of the Civil List paid directly from the Treasury on First Auditor's Certificates, Captured and Abandoned Property Accounts, and Accounts for the Legislative and Contingent Expenses of the United States Territories.*

	Number of accounts.	Amount.
Receipts	80	$111, 116, 665 06
Disbursements	1, 779	112, 282, 410 82
Total	1, 859	223, 399, 075 88

No. 6.—*Comprising the Accounts of the District of Columbia.*

	Number of accounts.	Amount.
Receipts	4	$3, 265, 138 07
Disbursements	348	4, 416, 959 30
Statement of account showing amounts appropriated for and revenue collected by the District of Columbia during the fiscal year 1879	1	3, 115, 277 94
Similar statement for the fiscal year 1880	1	3, 306, 722 94
Total	354	14, 104, 098 25

No 7 —*Under the Chief of the Warehouse and Bond Division, and Comprising Judgments of the Court of Claims, Outstanding Liabilities, Postal Requisitions, Transportation of United States Securities, Transfer of Appropriations, &c.*

	Number of accounts.	Amount.
Disbursements	1, 477	$2, 391, 027 47

The foregoing exhibits and enumeration of accounts examined and balances stated in this office, during the year just closed, show an increase of labor performed by the clerical force; and the accumulation of accounts presented for examination and settlement admonishes me that an additional number of clerks will be required to perform the official work of this bureau.

The changes made by statute in payment of interest upon the public debt, requiring quarterly instead of semi-annual settlements, have greatly increased the work of the Public Debt Division; and this division is in arrears from necessity, growing out of the additional requirements pressed upon it.

The changes made in the appropriations for expenses of the judiciary have largely increased the work of that division of the office. The growth of population and extended territory, as indicated by legislation relating to the Department of Justice, together with the change from general to specific appropriations, will compel an increase in the clerical force of the Judiciary Division.

The large amount of work, imposed by statute upon this bureau, by the transfer of all accounts relating to the receipts and disbursements of public moneys made by the honorable Commissioners of the District of Columbia, cannot be performed by the additional clerk granted by Congress; and one moment's examination of the work required in the examination and settlement of these accounts will satisfy the most exacting legislator that at least an additional clerk will be found absolutely necessary to dispatch work required. A temporary assignment of a clerk has been made to aid in this work, yet this has proved unsatisfactory, from the fact that he could remain only for a short time; while the work requires the most careful examination, by a clerk of good ability, after a patient and critical examination of statutes relating to the receipts and disbursements of the public moneys by the District of Columbia, as per accounts rendered.

While, in my judgment, an additional clerk beyond the necessities of a bureau, or office, is an injury to such office and a detriment to the public service, as well as a needless expenditure of the public money, I am constrained to make application for necessary clerical force, growing out of the increased work, which demands prompt attention, as well as careful investigation, before settlement of accounts can be properly made by this bureau.

The recommendation made in my last report relating to the organization of a new division in this office, is restated for consideration:

Attention is called to the number of accounts and the amounts involved in the settlement of what are known as "miscellaneous accounts," under the designation of "miscellaneous desks," from No. 1 to 7 inclusive. These embrace the largest part of the disbursements from the United States Treasury during the year, yet their examination is not under the supervision of a chief of division, as they do not belong to any class pertaining to divisions of the First Auditor's Office as now organized.

I would respectfully recommend that a new division be organized, to be known as the Division of Miscellaneous Accounts, to which should be referred all accounts not now assignable to existing divisions in this office.

While the accounts settled upon these desks are now carefully and critically examined by clerks in charge who would be a credit and honor to any office, for I except none, as to diligence, efficiency, and integrity, this will secure a supervision of the accounts stated by them, which will be an additional guarantee of their correct adjustment. In cases of enforced absence of clerks from duty on account of sickness or otherwise, the work of the new division will proceed with less embarrassment if under the charge of an efficient chief.

After a careful examination of the condition of the work required of this office, it was found entirely impracticable to make a temporary assignment of an "acting chief of division" to have charge of the miscellaneous desks, from the fact that the services of a competent clerk could not be spared from the pressing work specially assigned to him for his examination and report.

I am clearly of opinion that, after the examination of accounts, all reports, made in the first instance by clerks in an accounting office, should be carefully supervised before receiving the signature of the chief of the bureau.

It is a physical impossibility for any head of a bureau to carefully examine, or revise, all reports presented to him for approval and signature, and, of necessity, he must rely upon the clerical examination made and supervision had by some competent chief of division, who must share the responsibility of official action taken by the office, in any case.

Where a doubt arises in examination of accounts, or claims, as to the proper construction of the statute, the classification under existing appropriations, or the sufficiency of proof, &c., &c., the chief of bureau alone should make decision and direct official action; while the routine business of the office, when no doubt exists, is necessarily performed by the clerical force prescribed by law.

The deputy auditor and chiefs of division are specially commended for untiring diligence and kindly aid in the dispatch of the public business.

I desire to renew to them, and to the clerks and employés of the office, sincere expression of esteem and confidence.

I am, sir, respectfully, &c., your obedient servant,

R. M. REYNOLDS,
First Auditor.

The Hon. SECRETARY OF THE TREASURY.

REPORT OF THE SECOND AUDITOR OF THE TREASURY.

TREASURY DEPARTMENT,
SECOND AUDITOR'S OFFICE,
Washington, October 26, 1881.

SIR: In compliance with section 283 of the Revised Statutes, and your request of the 30th ultimo, I have the honor to submit my report of the business assigned to this office for the fiscal year ending June 30, 1881.

BOOKKEEPERS' DIVISION.

The application of money appropriated for those bureaus of the War Department whose accounts are adjusted in this office, and for the Indian service, cannot be shown in detail within reasonable limits, but its disposition is sufficiently indicated by the following condensed balance sheet of appropriations:

	War.	Indian.
CREDITS.		
Balance remaining to the credit of all appropriations on the books of this office July 1, 1880	61, 784, 389 54	85, 455, 718 63
Amount of repayments during the year	564, 393 96	306, 760 27
Amount repaid through the Third Auditor's office to the appropriation for "clothing, camp and garrison equipage"	1, 278 20	
Amount credited by warrants issued to adjust appropriations under section 5, act March 3, 1875, and by other counter-warrants	7, 940 03	18, 175 44
Amount of annual, permanent, specific, and indefinite appropriations made by law	16, 884, 306 52	11, 211, 104 83
Total credits	19, 242, 389 27	16, 994, 739 17
DEBITS.		
Amount paid out on requisitions issued by the Secretary of War and charged as follows:		
To Pay Department appropriations	12, 436, 090 55	
To Ordnance Department appropriations	1, 627, 717 36	
To Medical Department appropriations	713, 851 76	
To Adjutant-General's Department appropriations	80, 631 97	
To Quartermaster's Department appropriations, under section 5, act March 3, 1875	33 10	
To appropriations under the immediate control of the Secretary of War	127, 118 89	
To appropriations for the Commanding General's office	2, 500 00	
To the Soldiers' Home	87, 814 02	
To the National Home for Disabled Volunteer Soldiers	1, 088, 560 53	
To special acts of relief	7, 850 93	
Amount drawn through the Third Auditor's office from the appropriation for "clothing, camp and garrison equipage"	42 59	
Amount paid out on requisitions issued by the Secretary of the Interior		6, 822, 316 83
Amount charged by warrants issued to adjust appropriations under section 5, act March 3, 1875, and by other transfer warrants	6, 592 47	9, 842 79
Amount carried to the surplus fund under section 3691, Revised Statutes	963, 189 65	453, 685 79
Total debits	18, 086, 994 08	7, 286, 845 41
Balance remaining to the credit of all appropriations on the books of this office June 30, 1881	1, 155, 395 24	9, 707, 898 76

* Of the amounts drawn and repaid through the Third Auditor's office under "clothing, camp and garrison equipage," only so much is taken up in the above balance sheet as will close that appropriation on the books of this office, and hereafter the Third Auditor's drafts and repayments will not enter into the Second Auditor's statement of balances.

The aggregate amount appropriated for the Indian service, as reported in the foregoing balance sheet, $11,211,104.83, includes all sums that have been passed to the credit of Indian appropriations, by warrant, during the fiscal year, and is composed of the following items:

Amount appropriated for the service of the fiscal year 1881, per act of May 11, 1880	$4,657,262 72
Expenses of Board of Indian Commissioners, act June 16, 1880	10,000 00
Expenses of Ute Commission, act June 15, 1880	15,000 00
Removal, subsistence, &c., of Ute Indians, act June 15, 1880	401,000 00
Ute four per cent. fund, act June 15, 1880	1,250,000 00
Payment to the Miamies of Indiana, act March 3, 1881	221,257 86
Indemnity to the Ponca Indians, act March 3, 1881	165,000 00
Amount credited to the Osage Indians under the act of June 16, 1880	1,084,449 64
Amount received from sales of Indian lands	1,593,632 41
Interest on investments and on net proceeds of lands	553,437 85
Indian trust funds deposited in the Treasury in lieu of investment, act April 1, 1880	1,081,784 89
Special acts of relief	61,912 60
Amount appropriated to supply deficiencies, act March 3, 1881	107,379 23
Amount expended in connection with the purchase of Indian supplies in May and June, 1881, being part of the appropriation for 1882, which, being immediately available, was used during the fiscal year 1881	8,987 54
Total	11,211,104 83

The balance of $9,707,893.76, remaining to the credit of Indian appropriations June 30, 1881, includes items not subject to draft, as well as all moneys applicable to the current requirements of the Indian service, and may be divided as follows:

Balances subject to draft:		
Annuities, interest on investments and proceeds of lands, appropriations for beneficial objects, removal, subsistence, education and civilization of Indians, pay of officers and employés, incidental and contingent expenses, &c.		$2,518,385 59
Balances not subject to draft:		
Trust funds	$3,022,906 53	
Proceeds of lands	4,166,601 64	
		7,189,508 17
Total		9,707,893 76

The number of requisitions registered, journalized, posted, and indexed was 4,914, namely: War, 1,333 debit and 577 credit; Interior, 2,705 debit and 299 credit. One hundred and eighty-two miscellaneous settlements were made, involving $849,612.88; 1,289 certificates of deposit were listed; 621 repay or deposit requisitions were prepared for the War and Interior Departments; 55 appropriation warrants were recorded and posted; 61 official bonds of disbursing officers were registered and 342 certificates of non-indebtedness were issued, chiefly to officers having claims against the United States. The following settlements, confirmed by the Second Comptroller, were registered, journalized, and posted:

Disbursing accounts: War, 224; Indian, 333	557
Claims: War, 320; Indian, 1,934	2,254
Miscellaneous settlements, connected with overpayments, refundments, final adjustment of balances, &c	564
Total	3,375

PAYMASTERS' DIVISION.

Paymasters' accounts on hand unexamined July 1, 1880	130
Received from the Pay Department during the year	601
Total	731
Audited and reported to the Second Comptroller	419
On hand, unexamined, June 30, 1881	312

15 AB

The amount involved in 419 audited disbursing accounts and in 846 miscellaneous settlements was $9,593,555.39, as follows:

Disbursements by paymasters	$9,390,233 51
Fines, forfeitures, &c., paid to the Soldiers' Home	81,257 96
Transfers to the Third Auditor's books on account of—	
Tobacco sold to soldiers	87,238 77
Stoppages for quartermaster's and subsistence stores	7,842 40
Charges on account of overpayments, double payments, &c	9,111 36
Amount of overpayments refunded	4,427 84
Sundry charges and credits	13,443 53
Total	9,593,555 39

The accounts of five paymasters, of whom two were volunteers (additional paymasters), have been finally adjusted and the balance found due the United States, $10,271.20, collected and covered into the Treasury. The record of deposits by enlisted men (act May 15, 1872), shows that 9,521 deposits, amounting to $559,841.90, were made with paymasters whose accounts were audited during the year, and that there were 5,611 withdrawals, amounting to $314,598.14.

The longevity records of 103 officers have been revised in order to determine and fix their pay status under the acts of June 13, 1878, and February 24, 1881. The adjustment of this class of cases would be much simplified by the passage of an act declaratory of the intent and meaning of existing laws. Doubtful construction of these laws has already caused litigation, which is still pending.

MISCELLANEOUS DIVISION.

Unsettled accounts on hand July 1, 1880	446
Received during the year	1,732
Total	2,178
Accounts settled during the year	1,664
Remaining on hand June 30, 1881	514

The amount of disbursements allowed in the settlement of accounts was $3,883,560.04, chargeable to the following appropriations:

Ordnance, ordnance stores and supplies, ordnance service, armament of fortifications, arming and equipping the militia, repairs of arsenals, &c	$1,450,372 25
Medical and hospital department, artificial limbs, Medical and Surgical History and statistics, Army Medical Museum and library, &c	528,814 50
Recruiting service (regular and volunteer)	178,557 20
Contingencies of the Army, expenses of military convicts, secret service, publication of Official Records of the War of the Rebellion, contingencies of the Adjutant-General's Department, special acts of relief, Artillery school at Fort Monroe, expenses of the Commanding General's office, &c	102,228 84
Support of National Home for Disabled Volunteer Soldiers	1,623 587 21
Total	3,883,560 04

The compilation of a complete record of payments to officers, both regular and volunteer, is progressing as rapidly as circumstances will allow. The work is of sufficient importance to demand an early completion, but as it is not current work, strictly speaking, it has been made to give way whenever the services of the clerks engaged upon it were required for more pressing business. The record, when finished, will give the amounts paid to every commissioned officer who has served in the armies of the United States at any time since January 1, 1841, the periods for which payments were made, and references by numbers to the vouchers and settlements in which the evidence of payment can be found; so that the actual document upon which payment was made to any officer, for any given period within the last forty years, can be produced at a few minutes notice. The record commences in 1812, but prior to 1841 the mere fact of payment was entered. The payments to volunteer officers of the late war will fill forty-five large volumes of 450 pages each, thirty-five of which are completed, or nearly so. The entire record from 1812 to 1881 will fill one hundred and fifty volumes of various sizes. A comprehensive index to the volunteer record is in course of preparation. Last year 100,759 vouchers were examined for dates, &c., of payments, twenty cases of double payments being brought to light and reported.

INDIAN DIVISION.

The work of this division has been pushed forward so diligently that there were fewer disbursing accounts unsettled on June 30 than at any time during the last twenty-five years. It is very important that the property accounts of Indian agents, which constitute nearly eighty per cent. of the four hundred and fifteen accounts on hand, be brought up to date with as little delay as possible, in order that agents may be held to a prompt accountability for Indian goods and supplies, as well as public property, intrusted to them for issue or use; but with the small number of clerks available only slow progress can be made. The labor of examining property accounts has at least quadrupled within the last few years, in consequence of the additional evidence, in the shape of vouchers and returns, that agents are now required to furnish in support of their accounts. Although there are so many property accounts unsettled, it is gratifying to be able to report a continuous reduction in the number on hand, as evidenced by the following figures:

On hand June 30, 1876, 1,004; June 30, 1877, 822; June 30, 1878, 482; June 30, 1879, 352; June 30, 1880, 349; June 30, 1881, 331.

The general business of the division is briefly shown by the following tabular statement:

	Cash accounts.	Property accounts.	Claims.
On hand July 1, 1880..	343	349	143
Received during the year	847	354	2,062
Total	1,190	703	3,200
Settled during the year	1,166	372	2,970
Returned to the Indian Office since June 1, 1879.................			170
On hand June 30, 1881	24	331	60

The disbursements were as follows:

Expended by Indian agents and allowed on settlement of their accounts. $2,775,166 80
Paid by the Treasury Department in liquidation of 2,970 claims of contractors and others.. 4,087,805 51

    Total. 6,862,972 31

Fifty-nine transcripts of accounts have been forwarded to the Second Comptroller in order that suits may be entered against agents and their sureties to recover balances declared to be due the United States, amounting to $580,726.08; but it is only just to say that in none of the cases thus reported for suit is there any actual default, in the ordinary acceptation of the term. The balances consist mainly of sums that the accounting officers have been compelled to disallow under existing laws and regulations, although the moneys may have been expended in good faith for the benefit of the Indians or of the United States.

The claims returned to the Indian Office, as above reported, were forwarded to this office in the early part of 1879, indorsed by the Commissioner of Indian Affairs "Not approved." In some instances the lack of authority on the part of agents to incur the expense was assigned as the reason for non-approval. In others, no reason was given, nor was any apparent. All the claims were chargeable to appropriations that had been exhausted. Although the approval of the Commissioner is not a legal prerequisite to the auditing of claims, it was deemed proper to return those that bore the stamp of his disapproval, inasmuch as he, being the administrative officer to whose bureau the claims pertained, should have better facilities than the accounting officers for determining whether or not the services were rendered as stated, and whether the claims were correct and just.

In this connection I would invite special attention to a class of claims in regard to which inquiries and complaints are constantly made. The claims in question are for services rendered and supplies furnished for the Indian service during the fiscal year 1873, and subsequent years, and will probably amount to $500,000. The liabilities were contracted in disregard of the act of 1870, which prohibits any department of the government from exceeding its appropriations (section 3679 Revised Statutes.) The Second Auditor, as the records of the office show, persistently declined to entertain any claim of the class referred to until 1878, in which year Congress made it the duty of the accounting officers of the Treasury Department to continue to receive, examine, and consider the justice and validity of all claims under appropriations the balances of which have been exhausted or carried to the surplus fund, that may be brought before them within a period of five years. (Sec. 4, act June 14, 1878.)

The act of 1878, above alluded to, does not suspend or repeal the prohibitory law of 1870, and it may be questioned whether it confers upon the accounting officers any authority that they did not already possess; but, in the belief that Congress intended to open the way to a settlement of outstanding deficiency claims, the Auditor decided to examine and report to the Second Comptroller, for certification, all such claims as accrued while there was any balance in the Treasury to the credit of the appropriation from which they were payable, no matter whether the appropriation had been subsequently exhausted or not.

Accordingly 168 deficiency claims have been reported to the Second Comptroller, who has certified 25, retained 100, and returned 23 not certified on the ground that there are no funds applicable to their payment. In view of these facts it is suggested that section 4 of the act of June 14, 1878, should be so amended as to require the Commissioner of Indian Affairs to transmit all accounts and vouchers connected with the outstanding indebtedness of the Indian service to the proper accounting officers of the Treasury Department, who shall be authorized and directed to examine and adjust said accounts, and report the same to Congress in the manner prescribed by law.

PAY AND BOUNTY DIVISION.

The subjoined tabular statements show the work performed in the two branches of this division:

Examining branch.

Class of claims.	Claims pending July 1, 1880.	Received during the year.	Claims revived or not previously reported.	Claims disposed of.			Claims pending June 30, 1881.
				Sent to settling branch.	Disallowed.	Referred to other divisions and to Third and Fourth Auditors.	
White soldiers.							
Arrears of pay, original bounty, and bounty under act of April 22, 1872	16,040	6,619	....	1,489	4,294	22	16,854
Additional bounty, act July 28, 1866	2,317	....	507	158	31	4	2,631
Claims for pay prior to April, 1861	281	324	....	107	321	....	177
Claims of laundresses, sutlers, tailors, &c.	57	52	....	51	5	....	53
Colored soldiers.							
Arrears of pay and all bounties	8,098	1,180	....	693	1,860	572	6,153
Total	26,793	8,175	507	2,498	6,511	598	25,868

Settling branch.

Class of claims.	Claims pending July 1, 1880.	Received from examining branch.	Claims disposed of.			Amount involved.
			Allowed.	Disallowed.	Pending June 30, 1881.	
White soldiers.						
Arrears of pay, original bounty, and bounty under act of April 22, 1872	1,124	1,489	1,741	20	852	$186,627 29
Additional bounty, act July 28, 1866	308	158	313	55	98	85,549 08
Claims for pay prior to April, 1861	....	107	107	....	....	4,336 24
Claims of laundresses, sutlers, tailors, &c.	....	51	51	....	....	803 37
Colored soldiers.						
Arrears of pay and all bounties	1,425	693	1,988	13	117	184,509 75
Total	2,857	2,498	4,200	88	1,067	461,925 73

The number of claims on hand June 30, 1880, was stated in last year's report to be 29,470. The actual number was 29,650, namely, 26,793 in the examining branch and 2,857 in the settling branch. The discrepancy arose from the omission to count 180 old claims which are now classed under the heads of "claims prior to April, 1861," and "claims of laundresses," &c.

With regard to the receipt of 570 claims for additional bounty, although the time for filing such claims expired on June 30, 1880, it should be explained that some of these are old claims revived and reopened, the claimants being justly entitled to bounty that was withheld on the settlement of their claims by the Pay Department; others were filed within the limit allowed by law, but being included in applications for arrears of pay, with which they were classed and reported, it required a formal examination to develop the fact that the same claim embraced both arrears of pay and additional bounty.

In addition to the 26,935 classified claims on hand June 30, 1881, there are 5,812 cases in which settlements have already been made, but the claimants, in the hope that something additional may be due them, have presented new applications. These drag-net claims have to be received, recorded, and examined at an expenditure of time and clerical labor that should be devoted to more important matters. I am of opinion that in all cases where claims against the United States have been settled by the accounting officers, and the claimants, by accepting the amount awarded without demur, have tacitly acquiesced in the settlement, all further demands upon the government should be absolutely barred.

During the past year the sum of $2,145.58 was paid to the Soldiers' Home under section 4818 Revised Statutes, which provides that all moneys due the estates of deceased soldiers, remaining unclaimed for three years subsequent to the death of the soldiers, shall be appropriated for the support of said Home. If this law could have been strictly complied with, the Home would now be in possession of the unclaimed pay due all soldiers who died prior to June 30, 1878, but payments on this account are largely in arrear. They were entirely suspended for several years in consequence of the pressure of other business, and only two settlements have been made since July 1, 1879, the clerks engaged on that work being required to aid in the examination of claims of soldiers who served in the Mexican War for three months' extra pay under the act of February 17, 1879.

DIVISION FOR THE INVESTIGATION OF FRAUD.

This division is charged with the examination and investigation of such claims on account of military services as involve apparent, alleged, or suspected fraud; criminal personation of soldiers or their heirs; difficult identification; unlawful withholding of moneys from claimants by their agents or attorneys; contested heirship, &c.; also such cases of overpayments and double payments as it is deemed advisable to present to the Department of Justice for suit, after failure to collect the money by other means.

On July 1, 1880, 8,390 cases remained on hand; 608 new cases were received during the year, making a total of 8,998 before the division. Of these, 5,903 were examined and partially investigated; 1,175 were finally disposed of, and 7,823 remain for further consideration, namely:

Unsettled claims: white soldiers, 929; colored soldiers, 1,795	2,724
Settled claims: white soldiers, 1,068; colored soldiers, 3,648	4,716
Overpayments and double payments	383
Total	7,823

The sum of $24,014.28 has been recovered by suit and otherwise, as follows:

Recovered by suit, &c., and deposited in the Treasury	$5,318 91
Judgments recovered, but not yet satisfied	2,022 10
Pay and bounty due colored soldiers who have died since the settlement of their claims, or who have failed to demand their money for seven years after settlement, returned to the Treasury by the paymaster charged with the duty of making payments to colored soldiers and their heirs	15,904 21
Secured to claimants from persons unlawfully withholding moneys belonging to soldiers	769 06
Total	24,014 28

By reference to the Second Auditor's reports for 1875, 1877, 1878, 1879, and 1880, it will be seen that special attention has been repeatedly invited to the cases of colored soldiers who claim to have been defrauded of their arrears of pay and bounty by the agents of the late Freedmen's Bureau. Those people who have not received their money are still clamorous for a resettlement of their claims, but under the joint resolution of Congress approved March 29, 1867, (15 Statutes, 26), directing payment to be made to the Commissioner of said bureau, and charging him with the faithful disbursement of the funds, the accounting officers of the Treasury Department hold that they are *functus officio*, and that no claim can be resettled and paid without specific authority from Congress, accompanied by the requisite appropriation. The necessity of some action on the part of Congress, looking to an adjustment of these claims, is still urgent, and I respectfully suggest that a bill be prepared authorizing the proper accounting officers to reopen and resettle the claims of such colored soldiers as may present conclusive evidence that they have not received, in whole or in part, the pay and bounty to which they are entitled by law, the amounts found due such soldiers to be paid from any money in the Treasury not otherwise appropriated.

In this connection, and in simple justice to the late Commissioner of the Freedmen's Bureau, it is proper to recall the fact that certain charges against him, growing out of the irregularities above referred to, have been investigated by a military court and tried before a civil court. The special court of inquiry, convened by authority of a resolution of Congress approved February 13, 1874, not only exonerated General Oliver O. Howard from all blame, but also found that he did his whole duty, and expressed the belief that he deserved well of his country. The Supreme Court of the District of Columbia, before which suits were brought at the instance of this office to recover $153,173.57, rendered judgments in his favor on March 11 and 12, 1878.

PROPERTY DIVISION.

Property returns (clothing, camp and garrison equipage) on hand July 1, 1880.	7,561
Received during the year	3,649
Total	11,210
Settled during the year	4,969
On hand unexamined July 1, 1881	6,241

The sum of $12,657.35 has been charged to officers for property lost and otherwise not accounted for; $1,948.75 has been collected, and 328 certificates of non-indebtedness have been issued to officers out of service.

DIVISION OF INQUIRIES AND REPLIES.

The greater portion of the demands upon this division originated in the Pension Office and were received either directly from the Commissioner of Pensions or indirectly through the Adjutant-General of the Army in cases where the records of the War Department did not furnish the desired information.

On July 1, 1880, there were 4,772 inquiries unanswered, namely: From the Adjutant-General, 4,106; Quartermaster-General, 23; Commissary-General, 231; Chief of Ordnance, 1; Commissioner of Pensions, 278; Third Auditor, 70; Fourth Auditor, 3. Since that date 8,640 inquiries have been received and 9,442 replied to. leaving 3,970 to be answered—802 less than on June 30, 1880. In addition and incidental to the answering of inquiries 5,200 letters have been written asking for information; 2,419 signatures have been compared, and 3,146 pages of foolscap have been used in copying 3,385 documents, to wit: 466 rolls and vouchers for the Adjutant-General; 146 letters; 1,510 affidavits; 957 final statements; 70 certificates of disability; 51 general and special orders; 16 furloughs, and 169 miscellaneous papers.

Overpayments and double payments amounting to $11,428.17 have been discovered, and the sum of $3,137.37 has been collected, of which $2,338 was deducted by the Third Auditor from amounts certified to be due the payees for horses lost in the military service, and for commutation of rations while prisoners of war.

DIVISION OF CORRESPONDENCE AND RECORDS.

Letters received, 26,452; written, 25,277; referred to other offices, having been addressed to the Second Auditor in error, 1,408; recorded and indexed, 1,802; dead letters received and registered, 792; claims received, briefed, and registered, 18,175; miscellaneous vouchers received, stamped, and distributed, 60,934; letters containing additional evidence to perfect suspended claims briefed and registered, 16,786; pay and bounty certificates examined, registered, and mailed, 4,937; pay and bounty certificates examined, registered, and sent to the Pay Department, 5,317; reports calling for requisitions sent to the Secretary of War, 371; miscellaneous cases disposed of, 3,157.

ARCHIVES DIVISION.

Paymasters' accounts received from the Pay Department to be audited	574
Confirmed settlements received from the Second Comptroller, entered, indexed, and placed in permanent files: Paymasters'; 129; Indian, 2,313; miscellaneous, 1,027	3,469
Miscellaneous accounts withdrawn for reference and returned to files	1,372
Vouchers withdrawn from files for reference in the settlement of accounts and claims	13,548
Vouchers withdrawn for repairs	26,557
Vouchers returned to files	22,051
Vouchers briefed	94,901
Mutilated and worn vouchers repaired and returned to files	26,557
Number of pages copied	2,253

A fire-proof roof, for which an appropriation of $25,178.14 was made by the act of June 16, 1880, on the earnest recommendation of this office, has been placed on Winder's Building under the direction of the War Department. In preparing the building for the new roof, considerable space, which can be utilized whenever necessary, was added to the rooms of the upper story by increasing their height.

The building on the corner of New York avenue and Seventeenth street, known as the McKean building and occupied by the Property Division of this office since 1864, has been relinquished, and in lieu thereof the fourth and fifth stories of the new fire-proof building on Seventeenth street adjoining this office have been secured and fitted up with shelving and file-holders. Twenty thousand bundles of accounts, containing several million vouchers, have already been placed in the new rooms; 14,000 of the bundles, consisting of settled property returns (clothing, camp and garrison equipage), were removed from the McKean building, which is not fire-proof, and the remaining 6,000 bundles, consisting of old paymasters', Indian, and miscellaneous settlements, were taken from the corridors of Winder's Building which they had encumbered for many years.

Experience having demonstrated that bundles of muster rolls and vouchers, unprotected by file-cases of some kind, cannot be handled without wear and tear, no matter how much care is exercised, an appropriation of $10,000 was obtained last year for the purchase of shelving and file-holders, and those accounts to which reference is most frequently made are being properly protected. All the unbound records of the office should be placed in durable file-holders at as early a date as practicable, not only to preserve them from dust and injury, but to render them easier of access by dispensing with the cord and leather straps with which they are now imperfectly secured.

RECAPITULATION.

Number of accounts and claims of all kinds on hand July 1, 1880, as per last report 38,447
To which add old claims not heretofore reported 180
Number of accounts and claims received during the year........................ 18,917

Total 57,544
Number disposed of, including rejected cases 23,127

Number of accounts and claims on hand June 30, 1881 34,417

Amount drawn out of the Treasury in payment of claims and in advances to disbursing officers.. $23,940,486 15
Less repayments of unexpended balances, &c................................... 874,133 25

Net amount paid out 23,066,352 90

Total number of letters written 136,319
Average number of clerks employed.. 143

The detailed report of the Paymasters' and Miscellaneous Divisions show that the number of accounts settled last year was 322 less than in 1880, and that there are 250 unsettled accounts on hand in excess of last year's balance. This is accounted for by the fact that several clerks belonging to these divisions have been detached for temporary duty in other bureaus of the department, sixteen clerks being at one time absent from the office. It should also be stated, in regard to the Paymasters' Division, that the examination of accounts is much more rigid and exhaustive than at any former period. The liberality and latitude that were permissible in the adjustment of Army paymasters' accounts rendered during the haste and turmoil of a great war is no longer allowed, but those officers are now held to a strict observance of law and regulation.

CLAIMS FOR ARREARS OF PAY AND BOUNTY.

On referring to the reports of this office for the last eleven years, it will be found that the number of claims for arrears of pay and bounty rejected and disallowed is more than double the number allowed and paid. The figures are as follows:

Claims allowed and paid, 1871 to 1881, inclusive 80,476
Claims disallowed and rejected during same period.. 163,432

The amount paid out was $10,287,989.05. The amount of the rejected claims is not given, but, in the absence of evidence to the contrary, it is fair to assume that claims disallowed averaged about the same as those allowed, namely: $127.83, or $20,891,512.56 in the aggregate. A large proportion of the discarded claims are cases in which the claimants had been paid in full, but, after the lapse of a few years, had filed new claims, with affidavits that they had never been paid and had never made any previous application. The investigation of some of these cases has developed very remarkable instances of forgetfulness. These facts and figures would seem to indicate with sufficient significance that the time has now arrived when all claims for pay and bounty on account of service during the war of the rebellion, and prior thereto, may, without injustice, be barred by a statute of limitation. A precedent for this course will be found in the act of February 12, 1793, which required that all claims upon the United States for services, &c., prior to March 4, 1789, should be presented before May 1, 1794, or be forever barred and precluded from settlement or allowance. (1 Statutes, 301.) The necessity of a statute of limitation was so forcibly and clearly presented by Hon. E. W. Keightley, Third Auditor, in his annual report for 1879, that I cannot refrain from quoting and indorsing his remarks, which are as follows:

I respectfully renew the suggestion often made by my predecessors as to the necessity of some limitation to the time within which claims against the United States may be presented to the executive departments. In the absence of such a check the danger of frauds upon the government increases with every passing year. * * * As the danger of detection grows less, through the lapse of time, the temptation to present and the facilities for establishing fraudulent claims increase. Statutes of limitation are no longer looked upon with disfavor by courts or legislative bodies, and provisions of this kind respecting suits between individuals are, I believe, nearly universal. That which is everywhere conceded to be wise and just as between citizens of a State can but be considered fair and just as between the citizens and the State. Few claims that are fair and honest fail of presentation within six years from their origin, and the claimant who waits longer, if laboring under no legal disability, should be barred, in my opinion. One thing is certain, no one can be familiar with the business of this office for any period, however brief, without being thoroughly convinced that such a limitation would be of great value as a protection to the public Treasury, would remove a great temptation from the viciously inclined, and would give much needed relief to the executive departments.

OVERPAYMENTS.

During the last fifteen years a very large number of officers and men of the late volunteer forces have been charged with overpayments and double payments, ranging from forty cents to several hundred dollars. In the comparatively few instances where the payees have been found, attempts have been made to collect the amounts due the United States, recourse to law being had through the Department of Justice, when deemed advisable; but only a small proportion of the overpayments has been or ever will be recovered. The law of 1828 which prohibits payments to persons in arrears to the United States not being applicable to pensioners (sections 1766 and 4733, Revised Statutes), many persons are now in the receipt of liberal pensions who are indebted to the United States on the books of this office. There does not seem to be any valid reason for this discrimination.

In view of all the circumstances connected with overpayments, it has become a question whether the government would not really lose less by ignoring overpayments made during the war of the rebellion than by attempting to collect them; but, in the absence of legal authority to ignore them, it is the custom of this office to take action on all cases brought to its knowledge in which the Treasury has suffered by erroneous payments. I would suggest, however, that as, in my opinion, the time has arrived when all claims against the United States, growing out of the late war, should be barred by a statute of limitation, so, also, should claims by the United States against individuals be barred, with the exception, perhaps, of cases of double payment. It would doubtless be a measure of economy if Congress were to authorize the Second Auditor and Second Comptroller to make no further charges on account of overpayments prior to March 16, 1868, in cases where it is evident that payees did not knowingly and willfully obtain more than their just dues. This would cover all ordinary cases of overpayments, but, on the principle that no man should be permitted to take advantage of his own wrong, would except those cases in which officers drew their pay twice, or oftener, for the same period, or were otherwise overpaid on their own certificates. It should be mentioned that the paymasters who made the erroneous payments which have since been charged to the payees have been relieved of all responsibility by the act of March 16, 1868.

BONDS OF DISBURSING OFFICERS.

Numerous applications are made to this office for the surrender of the official bonds of disbursing officers whose accounts have been balanced and closed. These bonds are filed in the office of the Second-Comptroller, who has no authority to relinquish them. "No provision having been made by law for canceling or discharging official bonds to the government, the uniform practice has been for the government to retain the custody of the bonds, although the office of the principal may have expired and his accounts may have been satisfactorily settled." (Section 138, Comptroller's Digest, 1869.) Practically, therefore, the sureties of a public disbursing officer are never released, and a law seems to be needed making it obligatory upon the accounting officers to prepare and transmit to the Department of Justice, within a reasonable time, transcripts of the accounts of delinquent disbursing officers and all other persons who are in arrears to the United States; suit to be entered within ten years after the officer or other person became in arrears; otherwise, the United States to be estopped as regards the sureties—the principals, however, to be held.

CLERICAL FORCE.

The clerks of this office are entitled to commendation for diligence and efficiency. A change in the classification of the higher grade clerkships is desirable, in order that faithful and competent men may be more adequately remunerated, and has been made the subject of a special communication accompanying the annual estimates, to which your favorable attention is respectfully invited.

Very respectfully,

O. FERRISS,
Auditor.

The Hon. SECRETARY OF THE TREASURY.

REPORT OF THE THIRD AUDITOR OF THE TREASURY.

TREASURY DEPARTMENT,
THIRD AUDITOR'S OFFICE,
Washington, D. C., October 13, 1881.

SIR: I have the honor to transmit herewith report of the operations of this office, for the fiscal year ended June 30, 1881. The following statement shows, in tabular form, the number and amount of accounts and claims remaining on hand unsettled at the close of the last fiscal year, the number received and audited, and the number and amount of accounts and claims remaining unsettled June 30, 1881, viz:

Description of accounts.	Number of accounts remaining on hand June 30, 1880.	Number of accounts received in fiscal year ended June 30, 1881.	Number of accounts settled in fiscal year ended June 30, 1881.		Number of accounts unsettled June 30, 1881.	
	Monthly and quarterly.	Monthly and quarterly.	Monthly and quarterly.	Amount involved.	Monthly and quarterly.	Amount involved.
Quartermasters' money.....	836	2,739	3,153	$11,002,685 93	422	$2,554,626 96
Quartermasters' property...	552	3,617	3,090	....	1,079	....
Commissaries' money.......	440	1,657	1,565	2,234,257 00	532	1,221,500 58
Pension agents' money	359	449	555	54,973,659 39	253	37,806,670 52
Engineers' money...........	36	240	218	6,955,088 25	58	3,354,209 90
Signal officers' money	116	104	152	906,463 15	68	182,969 93
Signal officers' property	122	755	686	....	191	....
Claims for horses lost in military service	4,902	286	397	56,769 92	4,791	875,341 17
Claims for steamboats destroyed in military service	73	1	3	6,650 00	71	722,728 87
Oregon war claims..........	707	56	75	13,194 19	688	5,396 52
Miscellaneous claims	13,013	2,790	2,504	1,700,205 20	13,299	8,889,432 05
State war claims............	8	6	1	96,046 05	13	4,932,507 50
Total	21,164	12,700	12,399	77,945,019 09	21,465	60,548,476 00

BOOKKEEPERS' DIVISION.

The duty devolving upon this division is to keep the appropriation and money accounts of disbursing officers, which are settled in this office.

The annexed statement shows the amount drawn out of certain of its appropriation accounts, and also the repayments made through this office into the Treasury, and is a full exhibit of its financial operations during the fiscal year:

STATEMENT showing the FINANCIAL OPERATIONS of the THIRD AUDITOR'S OFFICE during the fiscal year ended June 30, 1881.

	Advances to officers and agents during the fiscal year.	Claims paid during the fiscal year.	Transfers not involving an expenditure from the Treasury.	Special relief acts.	Total.
Number of requisitions drawn by the Secretaries of War and Interior on the Secretary of the Treasury in favor of sundry persons, 6,286, amounting to $75,221,167.43, paid in the manner herein set forth and out of the following appropriations, viz:					
Regular supplies, Quartermaster's Department	$3,401,292 39	$33,194 15	$4,038 93	....	$3,438,525 47
Incidental expenses, Quartermaster's Department	962,312 03	59,962 57	38,131 85	....	1,060,406 45
Barracks and quarters, Quartermaster's Department	900,354 17	30,366 39	1,428 00	....	932,148 56
Army transportation	3,987,688 88	199,800 93	1,384 20	....	4,188,874 01
Army transportation (Pacific railroads)	....	138,950 08	273 65	....	139,223 68
Cavalry and artillery horses	198,671 75	8,950 40	23 60	....	207,645 75
Clothing, camp, and garrison equipage	1,071,441 39	72 91	....	....	1,071,514 30
National cemeteries	100,392 42	6 75	77 54	....	100,476 71
Pay of superintendents of national cemeteries	57,924 65	....	....	....	57,924 65
Observation and report of storms	375,051 70	....	....	....	375,051 70
Construction and repair of hospitals	78,401 22	3 00	....	....	78,404 22
Officers' transportation	....	230 58	51 00	....	281 58
Fifty per centum of arrears of Army transportation due certain land-grant railroads	....	66,513 40	....	....	66,513 40
Refunding to States expenses incurred in raising volunteers	....	129,583 40	26,604 05	....	156,187 45
Refunding to California expenses incurred in suppressing Indian hostilities	....	1,288 36	....	....	1,288 36
Reimbursing State of Kentucky for expenses in suppressing the rebellion	....	15,000 00	....	....	15,000 00
Awards for quartermasters' stores and commissary supplies taken by the Army in Tennessee, act March 3, 1881	....	8,759 25	....	....	8,759 20
Headstones for graves of soldiers in private cemeteries	25,000 00	....	....	....	25,000 00
Signal Service	10,507 38	....	....	....	10,507 38
Construction, maintenance, and repair of military telegraph lines	75,124 75	....	....	....	75,124 75
Buildings for headquarters at San Antonio, Tex	61,000 00	....	....	....	61,000 00
Buildings for military headquarters at Fort Snelling, Minn	130,000 00	....	....	....	130,000 00
Repair of government quarters at Fortress Monroe, Va	20,000 00	....	....	....	20,000 00
Military post near the northern boundary of Montana	80,000 00	....	....	....	80,000 00
Military post near Musselshell River, Montana	40,000 00	....	....	....	40,000 00
Macadamized road from Vicksburg to the national cemetery, Mississippi	8,000 00	....	....	....	8,000 00
Military road between Fort Missoula, Mont., and Coeur d'Alene, Idaho	20,000 00	....	....	....	20,000 00
Road from Fort Scott to national cemetery, Kansas	5,500 00	....	....	....	5,500 00
Construction of quarters at Fort Omaha, Nebr	25,000 00	....	....	....	25,000 00
Ringgold barracks, Tex	20,500 00	....	....	....	20,500 00
Payment to commissioners to appraise damages to lands in Fond du Lac County, Wis	5,010 00	....	....	....	5,010 00
Pay, transportation, services, and supplies of Oregon and Washington volunteers, 1855 and 1856	....	15,234 09	....	....	15,234 09
Miscellaneous claims audited by Third Auditor	....	15 00	....	....	15 00
Constructing jetties, &c., at South Pass, Mississippi River	....	125,000 00	....	....	125,000 00
Claims of loyal citizens for supplies furnished during the rebellion	....	344,359 36	....	....	344,359 36
Claims for quartermasters' stores and commissary supplies	....	359,780 11	....	....	359,780 11
Capture of Jefferson Davis	....	293 00	....	....	293 00
Sundry engineer appropriations	8,755,561 46	48 75	....	....	8,755,610 21
Subsistence of the Army	2,377,862 83	25,925 29	310 34	....	2,404,098 46

FINANCIAL OPERATIONS OF THE THIRD AUDITOR'S OFFICE—Continued.

	Advances to officers and agents during the fiscal year.	Claims paid during the fiscal year.	Transfers not involving an expenditure from the Treasury.	Special relief acts.	Total.
Support of Bureau of Refugees, Freedmen, and Abandoned Lands......	....	$1 00	....	....	$1 00
Support of military prison at Fort Leavenworth, Kansas	$55,910 80	....	....	....	55,910 80
Lost horses, &c., act March 3, 1849	....	105,797 24	$1,993 89	....	107,791 13
Commutation of rations to prisoners of war in rebel States..................	....	17,957 87	569 38	....	18,527 25
Army pensions	50,535,970 00	2,791 02	75	....	50,538,761 77
Relief of Judith Brown, act May 31, 1880.	....	....	....	$66 09	66 09
Relief of Samuel I. Gustin, act January 12, 1881	....	....	....	1,129 00	1,129 00
Relief of legal representatives of Henry M. Shreve, act January 13, 1881	....	....	....	50,000 00	50,000 00
Relief of estate of W. F. Nelson, act June 9, 1880	....	....	....	500 26	500 26
Relief of estate of N. Boyden, act June 8, 1880	....	....	....	75 00	75 00
Relief of Joseph Clymer, act March 2, 1881.	....	....	....	18,325 00	18,325 00
Relief of Henry F. Linea, act March 1, 1881.	....	....	....	360 00	360 00
Relief of W. A Reid, act March 1, 1881 ..	....	....	....	194 50	194 50
Relief of estate of J. M. Micou, act March 1, 1881	....	....	....	685 67	685 67
Relief of M. F Clark, act March 1, 1881 .	....	....	....	510 00	510 00
Relief of Martha Bridges, act March 2, 1881	....	....	....	72 06	72 06
Total	73,384,477 82	1,689,884 85	74,887 18	71,917 58	75,221,167 43

The number of credit and counter requisitions drawn by the Secretaries of War and Interior on sundry persons in favor of the Treasurer of the United States is 1,426, on which repayments into the Treasury have been made through the Third Auditor's Office during the fiscal year ended June 30, 1881, as follows:

Deposits...$1, 858, 131 41
Transfers...155, 171 75

Total...2, 013, 302 16

THE QUARTERMASTERS' DIVISION.

The accounts of quartermasters cover a wide range of money and property responsibility. The former embraces disbursements for barracks and quarters, hospitals, storehouses, offices, stables, and transportation of Army supplies, the purchase of Army clothing, camp and garrison equipage, cavalry and artillery horses, fuel, forage, straw, material for bedding, and stationery; payments of hired men and of "per diem" to extra duty men; expenses incurred in the pursuit and apprehension of deserters; for the burial of officers and soldiers, for hired escorts, expresses, interpreters, spies, and guides; for veterinary surgeons and medicines for horses, for supplying posts with water, and for all other proper and authorized outlays connected with the movements and operations of the Army not expressly assigned to any other department. Property purchased with the funds of the Quartermaster's Department is accounted for upon "returns" transmitted through the Quartermaster-General to this office (with the exception of "returns of clothing, camp and garrison equipage," which come under the supervision of the Second Auditor), showing that the disposition made of it is in accordance with law and Army regulations.

REPORT of the QUARTERMASTER'S DIVISION, THIRD AUDITOR'S OFFICE, for the fiscal year ended June 30, 1881.

	Money accounts.		Property returns.	Supplemental settlements	
	Number.	Amount.		Number.	Amount.
On hand per last report.....................	836	$2,144,673 26	552	....	....
Received during the fiscal year.............	2,739	11,412,639 64	3,617	236	$129,330 90
Total.................................	3,575	13,557,312 90	4,169	236	129,330 90
Reported during the fiscal year.............	3,153	11,002,685 94	3,090	236	129,330 90
Remaining unsettled	422	2,554,626 96	1,079	....	....
Total.................................	3,575	13,557,312 90	4,169	236	129,330 90

	Signal accounts.			Total.	
	Property.	Money.	Amount.	Number.	Amount.
On hand per last report	122	116	$571,655 78	1,626	$2,716,329 04
Received during the fiscal year............	755	104	517,777 30	7,451	12,059,747 84
Total.................................	877	220	1,089,433 08	9,077	14,776,076 88
Reported during the fiscal year.............	686	152	906,463 15	7,317	12,038,479 99
Remaining unsettled	191	68	182,969 93	1,760	2,737,596 89
Total.................................	877	220	1,089,433 08	9,077	14,776,076 88

Number of letters written, 4,792; number of clerks employed, 19; number of vouchers examined, 222,226; number of pages manuscripts written, 8,714.

SUBSISTENCE DIVISION.

The subsistence division examines the accounts of all commissaries and acting commissaries in the Army, whose duties are to purchase the provisions and stores necessary for its subsistence, and see to their proper distribution. These commissaries render monthly money accounts, with proper vouchers for disbursements of the funds intrusted to them, together with a provision-return, showing the disposition of provisions and stores purchased or derived from other sources. These accounts are received through the Commissary-General of Subsistence, and are examined and audited in this division. The money accounts and vouchers, together with a certified statement of the result of said examinations, are then referred to the Second Comptroller of the Treasury for revision. Upon their return from the Comptroller, with the settlement approved, the officers are notified of the result, and called upon to adjust or explain any omissions or errors that may have been discovered. The money and provision accounts, together with the papers belonging thereto, are then placed in the settled files for future reference, and remain permanently in the custody of this office. The engineer branch is engaged in the examination of the accounts of officers and agents of the Engineer Department, who, under the direction of the Chief of Engineers of the Army (except the Superintendent of the Military Academy at West Point, whose disbursements are directed by the Inspector-General), disburse moneys out of the various appropriations, now 248 in number, made from time to time by Congress for works of a public nature, which may be classed under the following heads, viz: The purchase of sites and materials for, and construction and repairs of the various fortifications throughout the United States; construction and repairs of roads, bridges, bridge-trains, &c., for armies in the field; surveys on the Atlantic and Pacific coasts; examination and surveys of the northern and western lakes and rivers; construction and repairs of breakwaters; repairs and improvement of harbors, both on sea and lake coasts; improvement of rivers and purchase of snag and dredge boats for the same; and the expenses of the Military Academy at West Point.

The transactions of the subsistence and engineer branches for the fiscal year are shown by the following statement, viz:

	Subsistence accounts.		Engineer accounts.	
	Number.	Amount.	Number.	Amount.
On hand per last report, June 30, 1880	440	$543,774 26	36	$2,470,226 88
Received during the fiscal year	1,657	2,911,983 32	240	7,839,071 27
Total..	2,097	3,455,757 58	276	10,309,298 15
Reported during the fiscal year	1,565	2,234,257 00	218	6,955,088 25
Remaining on hand June 30, 1881...................	532	1,221,500 58	58	3,354,209 90

Number of vouchers examined, 162,895; number of letters written, 1,852; number of differences written, 1,290; number of calls answered, 620; number of clerks employed, 9.

THE CLAIMS DIVISION.

This division has the settlement of claims of a miscellaneous character arising in the various branches of service in the War Department, and growing out of the purchase or appropriation of supplies and stores for the Army; the purchase, hire, or appropriation of water craft, railroad stock, horses, wagons, and other means of transportation; the transportation contracts of the Army; the occupation of real estate for camps, barracks, hospitals, fortifications, &c.; the hire of employés, mileage, courts-martial fees, traveling expenses, commutations, &c.; claims for compensation for vessels, railroad cars, engines, &c., lost in the military service; claims growing out of the Oregon and Washington war of 1855 and 1856, and other Indian wars; claims of various descriptions under special acts of Congress, and claims not otherwise assigned for adjudication.

MISCELLANEOUS CLAIMS for fiscal year 1880-'81.

	Miscellaneous claims.		
	Number.	Amount claimed.	Amount allowed.
On hand June 30, 1880	13,013	$8,175,232 09	....
Received during the year	2,790	52,414,405 16	....
Total..	15,803	10,589,637 25	....
Disposed of during the year...................	2,504	1,700,205 20	$1,303,252 63
On hand June 30, 1881..........................	13,299	8,889,432 05	....

MISCELLANEOUS CLAIMS for fiscal year 1880-'81—Continued.

	Oregon and Washington Indian war claims, 1855-'56.			Lost vessels, &c., under act of March 3, 1849.		
	Number.	Amount claimed.	Amount allowed.	Number.	Amount claimed.	Amount allowed.
On hand June 30, 1880......................	707	a$10,882 44	....	73	$727,378 87	....
Received during the year..................	56	f8,710 27	....	1	2,000 00	....
Total	763	19,592 71	....	74	729,378 87	....
Disposed of during the year	75	g13,194 19	$5,168 19	3	6,650 00	$4,500 00
On hand June 30, 1881......................	688	h6,398 52	....	71	722,728 87	....

a This is the amount claimed in 11,410 cases, the amount claimed in the other 1,603 cases not being stated.
b This is the amount claimed in 2,575 cases, the amount claimed in the other 215 cases not being stated.
c This is the amount claimed in 2,341 cases, the amount claimed in the other 163 cases not being stated.
d This is the amount claimed in 11,544 cases, the amount claimed in the other 1,655 cases not being stated.
e This is the amount claimed in 338 cases, the amount claimed in the other 369 cases not being stated.
f This is the amount claimed in 36 cases, the amount claimed in the other 20 cases not being stated.
g This is the amount claimed in 52 cases, the amount claimed in the other 23 cases not being stated.
h This is the amount claimed in 322 cases, the amount claimed in the other 366 cases not being stated.

The number of letters received during the year was 142; number written during the year, 2,334.

STATE AND HORSE CLAIMS DIVISION.

The duties of this division embrace the settlement, under the various acts and resolutions of Congress relating thereto, of all claims of the several States and Territories for the costs, charges, and expenses properly incurred by them for enrolling, subsisting, clothing, supplying, arming, equipping, paying, and transporting their troops employed in aiding to suppress the recent insurrection against the United States, and all claims arising out of Indian and other border invasions. Also the settlement of claims for compensation for loss of horses and equipage sustained by officers or enlisted men while in the military service of the United States, and for the loss of horses, mules, oxen, wagons, sleighs, and harness, while in said service, by impressment or contract.

State claims.	Original account.		Suspended account.	
	Number.	Amount.	Number.	Amount.
On hand June 30, 1880...............................	8	$4,096,750 33	31	$5,028,643 55
Received during the fiscal year	5	672,608 54	......	....
Total	13	4,769,358 87	31	5,028,643 55
Reported during the fiscal year	......	....	......	96,046 05
On hand June 30, 1881...............................	13	4,769,358 87	31	4,932,597 50

Horse claims.	Original account.			
	Number.	Amount.	Number.	Amount
On hand June 30, 1880................................	....	....	4,902	$891,715 12
Received during the fiscal year	....	....	224	31,897 47
Reconsidered during the fiscal year..................	....	....	62	8,498 50
Total..	....	....	5,188	932,111 09
Allowed during the fiscal year.......................	357	$44,826 60		
Disallowed during the fiscal year....................		6,293 05		
Rejected during the fiscal year......................	40	5,650 27		
Total..	397	56,769 92		
Deduct as disposed of during the year	....	....	397	56,769 92
On hand June 30, 1881...............................	....	....	4,791	875,341 17

Number of briefs, 522; number of claims examined and suspended, 2,089; number of letters received, 4,986; number of letters written, 5,590; number of clerks employed, 6.

COLLECTION DIVISION.

STATEMENT of BUSINESS TRANSACTED by the COLLECTION DIVISION during the year ended June 30, 1881.

	Entries on registers.	Number of special cases.	Accounts referred to.	Bounty-land and pension cases examined.	Letters written.	Names of soldiers of the war of 1812 abstracted.	Days comparing.	Cases prepared for suit.
July, 1880	833	313	3,204	114	255	13,585	10	5
August, 1880	689	307	5,908	155	184	9,579	.....	.....
September, 1880	250	195	2,991	390	176	10,251	10	.....
October, 1880	457	247	1,681	86	100	10,815	40	.....
November, 1880	509	435	3,398	370	193	13,463	80	.....
December, 1880	806	317	2,781	167	194	13,897	25	.....
January, 1881	722	371	3,806	218	236	11,234	.....	.....
February, 1881	774	257	3,529	186	222	14,900	24	2
March, 1881	714	261	4,175	282	252	9,929	48	3
April, 1881	1,008	351	5,478	216	342	15,234	26	4
May, 1881	975	200	3,213	175	249	19,608	45	1
June, 1881	.....	255	3,706	144	268	20,737	27	.....
Total	7,737	3,569	43,962	2,503	2,671	163,232	335	15

The current work of this division has steadily increased during the fiscal year and additional clerical force is required to keep it up. Work has been continued in abstracting the names of soldiers of the war of 1812, for the purpose of arrangement in alphabetical registers, with all the clerical force available. During the year, one hundred and sixty-three thousand two hundred and thirty-two payments have been abstracted, making a total, up to the end of the present fiscal year, of five hundred and nine thousand six hundred and sixty-four payments. In order to complete these registers within a period of time that will be available to the old soldiers and their widows, whose applications for pension are now pending in the office of the Commissioner of Pensions, but whose service cannot be traced for lack of data to base a search upon, and for historical purposes, an increase in the clerical force in this division is necessary.

In many cases (of widows especially, who know the fact by tradition that their former husbands served in the war of 1812) the claimants do not know the names of the officers under whom they (or their husbands) served. Until these alphabetical registers are completed, this office is unable to trace the service of any soldier without the name of the captain or colonel under whom the soldier served. When these registers shall be completed, a knowledge of the name of the soldier will be a sufficient clue to trace his military service. After the abstract slips shall have been entered upon registers, they may be sent to the respective States from which the soldiers enlisted, to become a part of the records of the State, and I recommend proper action looking to a distribution of these slips among the several States to which the service pertains.

ARMY PENSION DIVISION.

The duties of this division embrace the settlement of all accounts which pertain to the payment of army pensions throughout the United States. An account is kept with each pension agent, charging him with all moneys advanced for payment to pensioners, under the proper bond and fiscal year. At the end of each month the agent forwards his vouchers, abstracts, and money statement direct to this office, where a preliminary examination is made to see if the money advanced is properly accounted for. The receipt of the account is then acknowledged, and the account filed for audit. Each voucher is subsequently examined, and the payment entered on the roll-book opposite the pensioner's name. The agent's account, when audited, is reported to the Second Comptroller for his revision, and a copy of the statement of errors, if any, sent to the agent for his information and explanation. The account when revised, is returned by the Second Comptroller to this office and placed in the settled files, where it permanently remains. The following tables show the operations of this division during the fiscal year:

Army pensions 1878 and prior years:
    Amount refunded and deposited during the year ended June 30, 1881. $6, 152 17
Army pensions 1879:
    Balance to credit of appropriation June 30, 1880 .... 1, 242, 976 65
    Amount deposited during the year 2, 191 79

    Total 1, 245, 168 44
    Amount paid out on settlements 278 00

    Balance to credit of appropriation June 30, 1881 .... 1, 244, 890 44

Army pensions, 1880.	Army pensions	Pay, &c.	Surgeons.	Total.
Balance on hand June 30, 1880	$357 53	$6, 587 64	$111, 340 00	$118, 285 17
Amount deposited during the year	616, 556 73	18, 378 30	16, 874 00	651, 809 03
Total	616, 914 26	24, 965 94	128, 214 00	770, 094 20
Amount paid out on settlements........	1, 088 05	....	....	1, 088 05
Balance to credit of appropriation June 30, 1881	615, 826 21	24, 965 94	128, 214 00	769, 006 15

Army pensions, 1881.	Army pensions	Pay, &c.	Surgeons.	Total.
Amount appropriated, act Jan. 13, 1880..	$31, 475, 000 00	$250, 000 00	$100, 000 00	$31, 825, 000 00
Amount appropriated, act Feb 26, 1881..	17, 692, 031 69	....	28, 000 00	17, 720, 031 69
Total	49, 167, 031 69	250, 000 00	128, 000 00	49, 545, 031 09
Amount to credit of appropriation undrawn	3, 472 53	4, 918 42	1, 665 00	10, 055 95
Amount drawn to be accounted for	49, 163, 559 16	245, 081 58	126, 335 00	49, 534, 975 74
Amount disbursed by pension agents....	48, 751, 926 30	221, 848 30	113, 392 00	49, 087, 166 60
Unexpended balance in agents' hands to be deposited	411, 289 86	23, 233 28	12, 943 00	447, 466 14
Amount paid on miscellaneous settlements	343 00	....	....	343 00
Total	49, 163, 559 16	245, 081 58	126, 335 00	49, 534, 975 74

Arrears of Army and Navy pensions.	Army pensions.	Fees on vouchers.	Total.
Amount appropriated, acts January 29 and March 3, 1879 ..	$25, 000, 000 00	$15, 000 00	$25, 015, 000 00
Amount appropriated, act May 31, 1880	500, 000 00	....	500, 000 00
Total	25, 500, 000 00	15, 000 00	25, 515, 000 00
Amount disbursed by pension agents, 1879, "Army".......	4, 019, 527 33	1, 884 00	4, 021, 411 33
Amount disbursed by pension agents, 1880, "Army".......	19, 600, 843 78	10, 535 10	19, 620, 390 88
Amount disbursed by pension agents, 1881, "Army".......	667, 079 05	446 70	668, 425 75
Total...	24, 297, 362 16	12, 865 80	24, 310, 227 96
	1, 202, 637 84	2, 134 20	1, 204, 772 04

The following tabular statement shows the number of accounts received and audited during the fiscal year:

	Army pensions.		Arrears of pensions.		Total.	
	Number.	Amount.	Number.	Amount.	Number.	Amount.
Accounts on hand June 30, 1880.....	140	$20, 126, 051 03	219	$21, 989, 437 34	359	$42, 115, 488 37
Accounts received during the year..	244	49, 886, 933 18	205	779, 908 36	449	50, 666, 841 54
Total..........................	384	70, 012, 984 21	424	22, 769, 345 70	808	92, 782, 329 91
Accounts reported to the Second Comptroller......................	211	32, 396, 287 10	344	22, 577, 372 29	555	54, 973, 659 39
Accounts remaining unsettled June 30, 1881..........................	173	37, 616, 697 11	80	191, 973 41	253	37, 808, 670 52
Total..........................	384	70, 012, 984 21	424	22, 769, 345 70	808	92, 782, 329 91

Pensioners recorded	34, 515
Pensioners transferred..	929
Pensioners increased..	12, 665
Pensioners restored...	1, 674
Certificates reissued	2, 094
Changes noted	405
Corrections made...	7, 570
Arrears notifications recorded..	28, 394
Pension vouchers examined...	759, 773
Payments entered	734, 810
Pages of abstract added	25, 680
Pages of miscellaneous copied..	2, 252
Payments corrected	242
Copies of surgeons' certificates sent to Commissioner....................	308
Vouchers withdrawn from the files......................................	5, 380
Letters received and registered	3, 292
Letters written...	4, 154
Letters copied..	3, 288
Letters indexed	3, 286
Pension checks verified before payment, 92, amounting to	$6, 380 93
Settlements for lost checks made, 29, amounting to	1, 594 05
Settlements for forged checks made, 3, amounting to....................	78 00
Settlements for repayments, 3, amounting to	68 64
Amount paid Judith Brown, "special act" May 31, 1880	66 09
Amount paid for printing pension checks, being unexpended balance of 1880.	664 00
Checks unpaid covered to outstanding liabilities, 519, in amount	12, 069 89

The following tabular statement exhibits the number and amount of accounts on hand and unsettled July 1, 1869, together with those received and audited each fiscal year since:

	Received.		Audited.	
	Number.	Amount.	Number.	Amount.
On hand July 1, 1869............................	637	$34,811,593 83	....	$25,596,876 39
Received and audited fiscal year 1870.............	714	27,743,819 29	631	$25,596,876 39
Received and audited fiscal year 1871.............	930	28,513,262 44	789	32,312,384 28
Received and audited fiscal year 1872.............	684	28,661,597 26	900	40,000,205 68
Received and audited fiscal year 1873.............	711	28,756,702 92	795	33,926,556 19
Received and audited fiscal year 1874.............	864	29,708,332 26	786	96,431,956 71
Received and audited fiscal year 1875.............	798	20,572,855 54	619	19,888,428 52
Received and audited fiscal year 1876.............	741	28,348,161 99	1,150	48,432,036 92
Received and audited fiscal year 1877.............	834	27,809,350 30	952	34,067,985 43
Received and audited fiscal year 1878.............	538	33,194,149 18	715	24,133,591 52
Received and audited fiscal year 1879.............	256	26,123,111 64	281	25,765,870 58
Received and audited fiscal year 1880.............	547	61,010,132 95	277	31,169,748 01
Received and audited fiscal year 1881.............	449	50,066,841 54	555	54,973,659 39
Total......................................	8,703	435,009,920 14	8,450	397,201,249 62
Deduct amount audited...........................	8,450	397,201,249 62		
Balance on hand June 30, 1881	253	37,808,670 52		

The consolidation of agencies and the passage of various acts granting increase of pension, including arrears, have caused the accumulation of work now on hand, and if the work increases in future as it has in the past, the present force will be insufficient. A large amount of matter, such as verification of records before payment, requires immediate attention. Thirty-seven clerks and two copyists have been employed during the past year.

AMOUNT DISBURSED by PENSION AGENTS during the fiscal year ended June 30, 1881, as shown by their ACCOUNTS-CURRENT.

State	Agency	Agent	Invalids	Widows	Minors	Dependent relatives	War of 1812 Survivors	War of 1812 Widows	Surgeons	Salary	Voucher fees	Contingent	Total
California	San Francisco	W. H Payne	$271,497 57	$28,569 78	$10,484 35	$13,752 93	$4,498 13	$10,770 96	$564 00	$4,000 00	$254 85	$696 29	$343,068 86
Dist. Columbia	Washington	J. S Witcher	575,653 08	94,583 96	13,949 86	51,639 92	7,169 32	30,535 53	1,976 00	1,043 00	2,224 35	543 68	779,318 72
Do	do	Theop'e Gaines	2,266,978 67	332,151 95	46,198 36	184,862 71	21,665 62	90,338 70	5,176 00	2,957 00	7,320 80	1,948 84	2,964,608 65
Indiana	Indianapolis	Fred Kinelier	2,277,816 38	366,421 49	101,339 29	155,562 40	21,142 98	90,153 88	3,232 00	4,000 00	8,468 40	81 24	3,032,417 92
Illinois	Chicago	Ada C. Sweet	3,314,451 96	616,057 87	160,277 58	376,248 88	29,453 35	98,882 87	3,568 00	2,000 00	10,816 50	813 57	4,616,184 08
Iowa	Des Moines	B. F. Vine	1,489,531 16	145,815 36	35,144 43	116,725 06	7,664 28	32,590 84	2,700 00	4,000 00	3,112 80	903 30	1,837,270 33
Do	do	Jacob Birch	1,156,441 70	106,981 82	14,849 00	85,956 26	7,124 84	22,554 17	2,490 00	2,500 00	3,289 20	383 96	1,402,660 75
Kentucky	Louisville	R. M. Kelly	496,987 55	229,324 14	39,520 11	120,534 40	19,307 75	82,219 18	2,332 00	4,000 00	2,821 40	302 80	1,007,593 03
Massachusetts	Boston	D. W Gooch	173,714 29	566,129 73	39,190 66	337,082 35	46,438 27	176,606 66	6,990 00	4,000 00	10,177 85	89 46	1,387,081 41
Missouri	Saint Louis	Rufus Campion	2,198,508 08	296,148 97	105,448 53	134,092 42	20,327 21	83,563 36	4,457 00	4,000 00	5,630 80	742 05	2,848,621 41
Michigan	Detroit	Samuel Post	1,563,936 14	190,774 67	32,229 21	139,858 05	24,850 05	65,720 31	7,019 00	4,000 00	5,626 80	856 01	2,032,308 24
New Hampshire	Concord	E. L. Whitford	2,056,714 56	334,940 56	45,612 82	559,261 23	88,794 88	286,963 79	6,800 00	4,000 00	10,993 35	1,727 62	3,377,629 31
New York	Syracuse	T. L. Poole	2,274,651 37	397,018 20	38,139 05	393,389 08	71,490 97	210,271 63	5,050 00	4,000 00	10,128 75	1,283 18	3,387,172 23
Do	New York City	C. R Coster	1,536,855 35	423,781 74	46,068 00	278,131 59	38,384 30	124,708 48	13,008 00	4,000 00	13,082 10	942 12	2,468,992 57
Ohio	Columbus	A. T. Wikoff	2,970,579 96	642,706 86	99,683 18	362,850 40	50,320 55	187,516 58	8,640 00	4,000 00	6,073 05	1,587 13	4,344,695 75
Pennsylvania	Pittsburgh	W. A. Herron	2,011,917 63	280,025 07	44,659 41	272,873 99	16,951 17	76,039 38	10,443 00	4,000 00	8,956 95	734 75	2,725,665 54
Do	Philadelphia	H. G Sickel	2,187,992 46	444,039 60	40,482 64	282,353 99	15,769 08	84,416 13	4,494 00	4,000 00	8,277 00	45 42	3,080,369 34
Tennessee	Knoxville	D T Boynton	1,038,490 04	579,637 57	143,143 88	153,670 39	118,015 53	501,657 34	5,770 00	4,000 00	5,760 73		2,643,020 50
Wisconsin	Milwaukee	Ed. Ferguson	2,192,643 25	230,464 82	58,346 82	256,886 30	16,328 54	40,124 64					2,810,570 54
Total			34,033,340 90	6,305,453 68	1,114,986 70	4,295,757 70	621,636 80	2,381,944 35	113,392 00	68,000 00	132,645 73	21,210 80	49,088,368 84
Deduct credits on account of overpayments			433 34	198 12	125 86	6 00	48 00	382 67			8 25		1,202 24
Total			34,032,907 56	6,305,255 76	1,114,860 84	4,295,751 66	621,588 80	2,381,561 68	113,392 00	68,000 00	132,637 50	21,210 80	49,087,166 60

AMOUNT of "ARREARS OF PENSION" DISBURSED by PENSION AGENTS during the fiscal year ended June 30, 1881.

State	Agency	Agent	Invalids.	Widows.	Voucher fees.	Total.
California	San Francisco	W. H. Payne	$4,130 03	$1,142 93	$4 80	$5,277 76
District of Columbia	Washington	J. S. Witcher	15,731 16	14,815 28	17 70	30,564 14
Do.	do	Theophilus Gaines	18,892 62	6,902 78	18 00	25,813 40
Indiana	Indianapolis	Fred. Kneder	43,499 29	10,943 49	38 10	54,480 88
Illinois	Chicago	Ada C. Sweet	44,567 78	17,035 13	39 90	61,642 78
Iowa	Des Moines	B. F. Gue	26,085 89	1,474 14	17 10	27,577 13
Do.	do	Jacob Rich	5,889 82	....	4 80	5,894 32
Kentucky	Louisville	R. M. Kelly	13,250 75	10,880 47	14 40	24,145 62
Massachusetts	Boston	D. W. Gooch	20,063 41	7,513 96	22 30	27,599 57
Missouri	Saint Louis	Rufus Campion	32,943 27	12,275 83	29 10	45,248 20
Michigan	Detroit	Samuel Post	22,776 17	7,128 19	19 20	29,923 56
New Hampshire	Concord	R. L. Whitford	25,976 67	14,073 37	27 90	40,077 94
New York	Syracuse	T. L. Poole	31,211 25	12,727 35	28 20	43,966 80
Do.	New York City	C. R. Coster	43,886 65	19,494 57	42 80	63,424 12
Ohio	Columbus	A. T. Wikoff	16,719 68	12,514 54	21 80	29,255 22
Pennsylvania	Pittsburgh	W. A. Herron	29,426 15	4,977 99	30 30	34,434 44
Do.	Philadelphia	H. G. Sickel	19,586 83	29,363 11	23 10	48,973 04
Tennessee	Knoxville	D. T. Boynton	20,948 69	4,709 79	20 10	25,678 58
Wisconsin	Milwaukee	Ed Ferguson				
Total			470,032 44	196,614 92	446 70	669,094 06
Deduct credits on account of overpayments			644 31	24 00		668 31
Total			469,388 13	196,590 92	446 70	668,425 75

AMOUNT of UNEXPENDED BALANCES in HANDS of PENSION AGENTS, June 30, 1881.

State	Agency	Agent	Army pensions				Arrears of pensions		
			Army.	Surgeons.	Pay, &c.	Total.	Arrears.	Fees.	Total.
California	San Francisco	W. H. Payne	62,429 81	486 00	148 86	63,014 67	9,591 04	90 00	9,597 04
District of Columbia	Washington	Theophilus Gaines	9,401 64	8,520 00	3,764 40	16,575 04	29,135 81	7 80	29,144 61
Indiana	Indianapolis	Fred. Knefler	37,647 32	288 00	3,458 61	41,393 93	15,799 29	5 60	15,804 89
Illinois	Chicago	Ada C. Sweet	10,962 96	288 00	889 93	12,090 93	33,863 28	102 70	33,965 98
Iowa	Des Moines	B. F. Gue	516 10			516 10			
Do	do	Jacob Rich	6,202 41	4 00	1,816 84	8,019 25	4,110 48	5 20	4,115 68
Kentucky	Louisville	R. M. Kelly	27,127 17	1,866 00	1,275 80	28,406 97	5,888 33	11 40	5,899 72
Massachusetts	Boston	D. W. Gooch	5,638 04	540 00	1,232 89	8,638 93	75,108 25	109 70	75,217 95
Missouri	Saint Louis	Rufus Campion	61 49	43 00	427 10	1,028 59	15,689 61	4 80	15,694 41
Michigan	Detroit	Samuel Post	57,681 57	516 00	517 19	58,191 76	542 89	12 00	554 89
New Hampshire	Concord	E. L. Whitford	72,077 07	700 00	1,112 36	73,705 43	122,275 17	29 20	122,302 47
New York	Syracuse	T. L. Poole	35,070 43	357 00	688 07	36,858 07	33,726 72	7 80	33,734 52
Do	New York City	C. R. Coster	54,197 33	2,450 00	2,476 89	59,124 22	6,931 34	21 80	6,933 14
Ohio	Columbus	A. T. Wikoff	1,968 98	980 00	1,811 96	4,137 85	16,526 89	10 40	16,537 88
Pennsylvania	Pittsburgh	W. A. Herron	534 64	557 00	439 82	1,684 46	14,126 89	88 10	14,136 99
Do	Philadelphia	H. G. Sickel	2 41	6 00	2,126 58	2,685 99	11,919 01	215 10	12,134 11
Tennessee	Knoxville	D. T. Boynton	89,583 33	730 00	468 25	90,027 57	6,386 16	130 80	6,386 46
Wisconsin	Milwaukee	Ed. Ferguson	7 56		1,193 83	1,981 29	61,972 25	43 80	92,015 05
Total			411,289 86	12,943 00	23,749 38	447,982 24	443,422 46	755 40	444,177 86
Deduct amount due B. F. Gue, Des Moines, Iowa					516 10	516 10			
Total			411,289 86	12,943 00	23,233 28	447,466 14			

The records of this office have been augmented during the year by the addition of new settlements as follows: Money accounts of disbursing officers of the Army, 1,603; accounts of pension agents, 140; miscellaneous claims, 3,457, and property returns of Army officers, 3,648; making a total for the year of 8,848. The papers are in a good state of preservation, with the exception of some of the abstracts of pension accounts, which, being unbound, have been injured by long use. Within the last few months the new apartment assigned to this office has been occupied, and in it all the money settlements made since February, 1878, are filed. Meanwhile, in the other rooms several thousand old settlements have been rearranged and placed as far as possible in consecutive order. These file-rooms are now entirely filled.

There were nine lady copyists employed in this office during the year. The number of pages copied and compared was as follows: Miscellaneous papers, 18,995 pages; difference sheets, 1,443 pages; letters, 5,575 pages; total, 26,013. The papers received for copying and registered were: Miscellaneous, 2,220; difference sheets, 539; total, 2,759.

The necessity for a statute of limitations fixing the time within which claims against the United States may be presented to the Executive Departments, becomes more and more apparent every year. In many cases it is now practically impossible to determine the merits of claims growing out of the operations of the Army during the late rebellion, or in other wars of still earlier date. Most of the old claims pressed upon this office are of this class. Through the lapse of time the ascertainment of the truth grows difficult, but the temptation to present fraudulent claims is increased. The fair and honest claims that up to this date have failed of presentation must be so few in number as to be unworthy of consideration against the adoption of so wise a check upon the prosecution of fraudulent claims. By section 297 of the Revised Statutes the several auditors "are empowered to administer oaths to witnesses in any case in which they may deem it necessary;" but, without the power to compel the attendance of witnesses or the production of papers, and without any funds for the special investigation of claims, this section is practically a dead letter. At present the only provision of that character is in section 3488 of the Revised Statutes. It is limited to a class of claims now almost, if not quite, extinct. In the examination of all other claims, if the accounting officers desire to look beyond the case the claimant chooses to present, they are entirely dependent upon voluntary assistance from the officers and agents of other departments. Every special investigation must be limited to such as can be made *without expense* by aid of the files, records, and accounts. Hampered by these conditions, it is self-evident that such investigations must often be attended with great delay, and more often be found unsatisfactory in results. The accounting officers are required to act as judges between the government and its creditors, without those powers which have been always found most necessary for the safe, speedy, and efficient administration of justice. Dishonest claimants can look upon this situation with satisfaction and content; but the best interests of the government and of its honest creditors alike demand that these defects should be remedied by appropriate legislation.

Very respectfully submitted,

E. W. KEIGHTLEY,
Third Auditor.

Hon. WILLIAM WINDOM,
Secretary of the Treasury.

REPORT OF THE FOURTH AUDITOR OF THE TREASURY.

TREASURY DEPARTMENT,
FOURTH AUDITOR'S OFFICE,
Washington, November 5, 1881.

SIR: I have the honor to submit the following detailed report of the operations of this bureau for the fiscal year ending June 30, 1881, and of the expenditures of moneys appropriated for the support of the Navy for the same period:

APPROPRIATIONS AND EXPENDITURES.

Title of appropriation.	Year.	Amount appropriated.	Amount expended by warrants.
Pay of the Navy		$6, 965, 075 62	$6, 614, 820 00
Pay, miscellaneous	1881	475, 000 00	275, 578 52
Contingent, Navy	1881	111, 664 00	111, 061 11
Pay of Marine Corps		741, 025 89	586, 610 64
Provisions, Marine Corps	1881	67, 780 50	47, 047 91
Clothing, Marine Corps	1881	69, 579 50	65, 000 00
Fuel, Marine Corps	1881	18, 496 50	12, 597 50
Military stores, Marine Corps	1881	11, 286 50	11, 286 50
Transportation and recruiting, Marine Corps	1881	7, 000 00	7, 000 00
Repairs of barracks, Marine Corps	1881	10, 000 00	10, 000 00
Forage for horses, Marine Corps	1881	500 00	500 00
Marine barracks at Washington, Norfolk, and Annapolis		22, 336 69	21, 197 99
Contingent, Marine Corps	1881	20, 000 00	20, 000 00
Destruction of clothing and bedding for sanitary reasons		2, 919 41	958 68
Pay professors and others, Naval Academy	1881	54, 376 00	54, 160 00
Pay watchmen and others, Naval Academy	1881	24, 455 00	24, 455 08
Pay mechanics and others, Naval Academy	1881	16, 835 95	16, 835 95
Pay steam employés, Naval Academy	1881	8, 577 50	8, 577 50
Repairs, Naval Academy	1881	21, 000 00	21, 000 00
Heating and lighting, Naval Academy	1881	17, 000 00	17, 000 00
Library, Naval Academy	1881	2, 000 00	2, 000 00
Stationery, Naval Academy	1881	2, 000 00	2, 000 00
Chemistry, Naval Academy	1881	2, 500 00	2, 500 00
Miscellaneous, Naval Academy	1881	34, 690 00	34, 690 00
Stores, Naval Academy	1881	800 00	800 00
Materials, Naval Academy	1881	1, 000 00	1, 000 00
Board of Visitors to the Naval Academy	1881	2, 600 00	2, 600 00
Site for new Naval Observatory		70, 000 00	65, 000 00
Navigation and navigators' supplies	1881	104, 560 00	95, 183 31
Contingent, navigation	1881	2, 000 00	1, 981 86
Civil establishment, navigation	1881	10, 417 25	10, 417 25
Hydrographic work	1881	44, 000 00	36, 627 28
Naval Observatory	1881	24, 536 25	23, 234 05
Charts of Amazon and Madeira rivers		11, 000 00	3, 249 26
Charts of Pacific coast of Mexico		12, 000 00	5, 805 40
Nautical Almanac	1881	22, 500 00	18, 516 20
Ordnance and ordnance stores	1881	225, 000 00	206, 647 50
Contingent, ordnance	1881	3, 000 00	2, 779 91
Civil establishment, ordnance	1881	11, 886 23	11, 884 08
Torpedo Corps	1881	95, 000 00	58, 577 22
Equipment of vessels	1881	800, 000 00	733, 444 17
Contingent, equipment and recruiting	1881	55, 000 00	54, 707 95
Civil establishment, equipment and recruiting	1881	18, 251 75	18, 251 75
Maintenance, yards and docks	1881	440, 000 00	427, 295 16
Contingent, yards and docks	1881	20, 000 00	14, 631 98
Civil establishment, yards and docks	1881	37, 906 25	37, 901 79
Navy-yard, Mare Island, Cal	1881	112, 500 00	112, 500 00
Navy-yard, Pensacola, Fla	1881	150, 000 00	101, 275 62
Navy-yard, New London, Conn	1881	20, 000 00	14, 173 00
Navy-yard, Norfolk, Va	1881	125, 000 00	94, 446 90
Repairs and preservation at navy-yards	1881	300, 000 00	286, 562 87
Naval wharf, Key West, Fla	1881	30, 000 00	....
Navy-yard, Boston, repairs of rope-walk	1881–'82	20, 000 00	18, 792 75
Medical department, medicine and surgery	1881	45, 000 00	42, 889 81
Naval hospital fund	1881	50, 000 00	49, 796 64
Repairs, medicine and surgery	1881	30, 000 00	19, 814 52
Contingent, medicine and surgery	1881	15, 000 00	14, 102 47
Civil establishment, medicine and surgery	1881	40, 000 00	38, 565 11
Provisions, Navy	1881	1, 200, 000 00	966, 116 63
Contingent, provisions and clothing	1881	60, 000 00	29, 933 39
Civil establishment, provisions and clothing	1881	12, 411 50	12, 411 50

APPROPRIATIONS AND EXPENDITURES—Continued.

Title of appropriation.	Year.	Amount appropriated.	Amount expended by warrants.
Construction and repair................................	1881	$1,725,000 00	$1,614,538 73
Civil establishment, construction and repair..................	1881	40,105 75	40,066 22
Steam machinery..	1881	950,000 00	885,031 85
Contingent, steam engineering	1881	1,000 00	1,000 00
Civil establishment, steam engineering	1881	20,038 00	20,038 00
Total......:......		15,663,462 06	14,055,450 55

TABLE OF PERMANENT AND MISCELLANEOUS APPROPRIATIONS AND RELIEF ACTS.

Title of appropriation.	Amount appropriated.	Amount expended by warrants.
Completing torpedo-boat experiments United States steamer Alarm	$20,000 00	$15,000 00
Statue of Admiral Farragut	15,000 00	....
Payment to T. C. Basshor & Co., for ship-knees	22,692 00	12,957 29
Relief of widows and orphans of officers, &c., of the Levant, act June 16, 1880.	240 00	240 00
Naval stations and coaling depots Isthmus of Panama	200,000 00	....
Relief of widows, &c., United States steamers Cumberland and Congress.....	216 00	216 00
Relief of John H. W. Riley...................................	300 00	....
Medals of honor		6 00
Search for steamer Jeannette of the Arctic exploring expedition	175,000 00	166,536 92
New propeller for United States steamer Alarm	8,383 03	2,600 00
Relief of Absalom Kirby...................................	2,269 53	2,269 53
Relief of John Scott Cunningham	1,284 19	1,284 19
Relief Pay Director C. W. Abbot and Passed Ass't Paymaster W. W. Barry.	2,605 54	2,605 54
Payment to Jenkins & Lee for marine governor	825 00	825 00
Payment to Dr. Emil Bessels................................	10,233 70	10,233 70
Transporting contributions for the relief of the suffering poor of Ireland....	1,596 47	1,596 47
Prize-money................................		9,916 48
Indemnity for lost clothing............................	42 75	42 75
Gratuity to machinists in lieu of re-enlistment	30,000 00	30,000 00
Extra pay to officers and men who served in the Mexican war	9,964 00	9,964 00
Relief of persons impressed into the United States naval service.............	16,309 80	16,309 80
Relief of sufferers by wreck of United States steamer Huron	318 00	318 00
Observation of solar eclipse................................	1,206 68	941 92
Ordnance materials, proceeds of sales		21,801 21
Sales of small-arms......................................		19,968 83
Naval asylum, Philadelphia, 1881	59,309 00	47,427 78
Construction and repair, act June 14, 1878..................		72,293 40
Clothing, Navy		138,617 76
Small stores		64,554 50
Naval Observatory, 1880	236 25	236 25

The amount appropriated for officers of the active list was $3,913,600; for the retired list, $661,400; total, $4,575,000. The amount due and unpaid June 30, 1881, was $116,636.22. Net amount paid to officers, $4,458,363.78.

The amount appropriated for petty officers and men was $2,390,000. The amount due and unpaid June 30, 1881, was $615,643.80. Net amount paid petty officers and men, $1,774,356.20. The whole amount due and unpaid to officers and men at the close of the fiscal year was $732,280.02.

This balance in hand at the close of the fiscal year, in amount $732,280.02, represents the sum earned during the year, and subject to draft, when officers are finally settled with, when men are paid off upon discharge, and when claims are presented for payment to this office by the heirs of deceased officers and men who died in the naval service.

The balances in hand under the remaining appropriations, as shown in the foregoing table, may be applied still to the payment of reservations on public bills and the liquidation of other unpaid liabilities which were incurred during the fiscal year 1881.

The exigencies incident to the naval service require that disbursing officers doing duty upon vessels in distant waters and at stations in foreign lands shall anticipate their wants and draw money in advance to meet expenses which must inevitably be incurred.

It is impossible to foresee what the precise nature of the future expenses may be, or under what heads of appropriation the various expenditures may be required. In order to overcome difficulties arising from this condition of things, Congress passed an act in 1878 authorizing the issue of requisitions for advances in any amount not exceeding the total appropriation for the Navy, under a "general account of advances." Under this head all moneys for disbursement upon shipboard or at foreign stations are drawn. Summary statements are rendered monthly, showing the bills paid, the sums expended, and the appropriations to which these sums should be charged, respectively. The appropriations are adjusted in this office upon the officers' returns.

This explanation will account for any differences which may be observed between the expenditures as shown in the table given above and as they appear in the following statement made up from the books of this office:

STATEMENT of APPLICATION of MONEY as SHOWN by RETURNS RECEIVED from DISBURSING OFFICERS.

Title of appropriation.	Years.	Amount expended.
Pay of the Navy		96, 903, 581 35
Pay, miscellaneous	1881	330, 506 34
Contingent, Navy	1881	114, 847 96
Pay of the Marine Corps		550, 274 06
Provisions, Marine Corps	1881	47, 417 83
Clothing, Marine Corps	1881	67, 409 09
Fuel, Marine Corps	1881	12, 062 49
Military stores, Marine Corps	1881	11, 296 33
Transportation and recruiting, Marine Corps	1881	7, 123 09
Repairs of barracks, Marine Corps	1881	9, 362 30
Forage for horses, Marine Corps	1881	461 71
Marine barracks at Washington, Norfolk, and Annapolis		22, 246 26
Contingent, Marine Corps	1881	19, 596 14
Destruction of clothing and bedding for sanitary reasons		885 88
Pay, professors and others, Naval Academy	1881	3, 809 93
Pay, watchmen and others, Naval Academy	1881	24, 455 00
Pay, mechanics and others, Naval Academy	1881	16, 835 95
Pay, steam employés, Naval Academy	1881	8, 573 58
Repairs, Naval Academy	1881	18, 917 28
Heating and lighting, Naval Academy	1881	16, 656 08
Library, Naval Academy	1881	1, 720 05
Stationery, Naval Academy	1881	2, 000 00
Chemistry, Naval Academy	1881	2, 270 33
Miscellaneous, Naval Academy	1881	34, 504 57
Stores, Naval Academy	1881	800 08
Materials, Naval Academy	1881	1, 000 00
Board of Visitors to the Naval Academy	1881	2, 529 76
Site for new Naval Observatory		65, 000 00
Navigation and navigation supplies	1881	103, 012 77
Contingent, navigation	1881	3, 127 56
Civil establishment, navigation	1881	10, 417 25
Hydrographic work	1881	39, 944 94
Naval Observatory	1881	22, 737 25
Charts of Amazon and Madeira Rivers		3, 245 09
Charts of Pacific Coast of Mexico		4, 804 11
Nautical Almanac	1881	18, 366 87
Ordnance and ordnance stores	1881	206, 865 93
Contingent, ordnance	1881	3, 796 88
Civil establishment, ordnance	1881	11, 719 19
Torpedo Corps	1881	61, 438 47
Equipment of vessels	1881	812, 887 60
Contingent, equipment and recruiting	1881	66, 720 85
Civil establishment, equipment and recruiting	1881	18, 022 44
Maintenance, yards and docks	1881	435, 275 07
Contingent, yards and docks	1881	31, 550 55
Civil establishment, yards and docks	1881	37, 634 52
Navy-yard, Mare Island, Cal	1881	113, 466 84
Navy-yard, Pensacola, Fla	1881	96, 339 43
Navy-yard, New London, Conn	1881	11, 577 39
Navy-yard, Norfolk, Va	1881	92, 712 64
Repairs and preservations at navy-yards	1881	228, 796 68

STATEMENT of APPLICATION of MONEY as SHOWN by RETURNS RECEIVED from DISBURSING OFFICERS—Continued.

Title of appropriation.	Years.	Amount expended.
Naval wharf, Key West, Fla	1881	
Navy-yard, Boston, repairs of rope-walk	1881–'82	$18,614 75
Medical Department, medicine and surgery	1881	46,118 40
Naval hospital fund	1881	48,787 14
Repairs, medicine and surgery	1881	19,672 79
Contingent, medicine and surgery	1881	14,218 94
Civil establishment, medicine and surgery	1881	37,062 92
Provisions, Navy	1881	1,054,006 98
Contingent, provisions and clothing	1881	29,662 54
Civil establishment, provisions and clothing	1881	12,241 96
Construction and repair	1881	1,544,677 91
Civil establishment, construction and repair	1881	39,893 70
Construction and repair	1881–'82	103,476 63
Steam-machinery	1881	835,479 40
Contingent, steam-engineering	1881	1,000 00
Civil establishment, steam-engineering	1881	20,038 00
Steam machinery	1881–'82	64,507 75
Completing torpedo-boat experiments, United States steamer Alarm		
Statue of Admiral Farragut		15,000 00
Contingent, Marine Corps		207 31
Payment to T. C. Basshor & Co. for ship knees		12,957 29
Pay of Navy, prior to July 1, 1877		1,922 09
Pay, Marine Corps, prior to July 1, 1877		109 98
Relief of widows and orphans of officers, &c., of the Levant, act of June 16, 1880		240 00
Indemnity for lost clothing, prior to July 1, 1877		1,018 87
Enlistment bounty to seamen prior to July 1, 1877		2,907 48
Bounty for destruction of enemies' vessels, prior to July 1, 1877		954 31
Contingent, Marine Corps, 1879 and prior years		862 75
Ordnance, 1877 and prior years		37 53
Steam machinery, 1877 and prior years		45 81
Contingent, equipment and recruiting, 1877 and prior years		204 90
Contingent, provisions and clothing, 1878 and prior years		5,233 23
Contingent, medicine and surgery, 1877 and prior years		22 82
Contingent, navigation, 1877 and prior years		22 82
Naval Observatory, 1877 and prior years		416 88
Maintenance, yards and docks, 1877 and prior years		37 37
Relief of administrator of John D. McGill		102 00
Relief of Peter Meagher		170 00
Medals of honor		6 00
Search for steamer Jeannette of the Arctic exploring expedition		134,108 45
New propellor for United States steamer Alarm		2,304 26
Relief, Absalom Kirby		2,280 53
Relief, John Scott Cunningham		1,284 19
Relief of Pay Director C. W. Abbot and Passed Assistant Paymaster W. W. Barry		2,605 54
Payments to Jenkins & Lee for marine governor		825 00
Payment to Dr. Emil Bessels		10,233 70
Transporting contributions for the relief of the suffering poor of Ireland		1,596 47
Prize money		6,815 34
Indemnity for lost clothing		42 75
Gratuity to machinists in lieu of re-enlistment		28,458 00
Extra pay to officers and men who served in the Mexican War		8,008 00
Relief of persons impressed into the United States naval service		15,309 80
Relief of sufferers by wreck of United States steamer Huron		318 00
Observation of solar eclipse		941 92
Ordnance materials, proceeds of sales		21,799 88
Sale of small arms		19,967 80
Naval Asylum, Philadelphia	1881	47,130 20
Construction and repair, act of June 14, 1878		72,263 40
Clothing, Navy		140,800 93
Small stores		63,095 40
Pay, Marine Corps		2,000 00
Naval Observatory	1880	236 25
Illustrations for report on solar eclipse		1,500 00

EXCHANGE.

In the Auditor's last annual report some space was given to the subject of foreign exchange, and it was shown that quite heavy losses had been sustained by the government from this source. Efforts have been made during the past year to prevent as far as possible these losses; notwithstanding which, discount on bills sold amounts to $27,799.38, while the premium amounts to only $994.47, leaving a net loss to the department of $26,804.91.

The following statement will show in detail the gains and losses upon bills sold at the different ports in which it became necessary to procure money for disbursement:

	Amount.	Amount.	Amount received.	Loss.	Gain.
	£ s. d.				
Acapulco, Mexico		$5,100 00	$4,986 12	$113 88	....
Antwerp, Belgium	4,750 0 0	23,115 88	23,193 78	....	$77 90
Barbadoes, West Indies	1,400 0 0	6,813 10	6,804 00	9 10	....
Buenos Ayres, Argentine Republic...	5,000 0 0	24,332 50	23,762 49	570 01	....
Cadiz, Spain	1,000 0 0	4,866 50	4,806 35	60 15	....
Callao, Peru..........................	7,711 15 0	50,579 24	48,098 73	2,480 51	....
Chimbote, Peru.......................	2,293 18 0	12,963 26	12,849 25	147 96	33 95
Constantinople, Turkey	4,000 0 0	19,466 00	19,338 60	127 40	....
Copenhagen, Denmark	2,000 0 0	9,733 00	9,650 00	83 00	....
Coquimbo, Chili	1,000 0 0	4,866 50	4,714 43	152 07	....
Funchal Madeira	651 9 10	3,170 48	3,127 07	43 41	....
Genoa, Italy	3,000 0 0	14,599 50	14,561 85	37 65	....
Gibraltar, Spain	4,000 0 0	19,466 00	19,466 00	Par.......	....
Gravesend, England	4,000 0 0	19,466 00	19,466 00	Par.......	....
Havre, France.........................	2,000 0 0	9,733 00	9,746 50		13 50
Hong-Kong, China	14,100 0 0	68,617 65	68,610 93	275 83	209 10
Honolulu, Hawaiian Islands	....	7,250 00	7,352 50		102 50
Kobe, Japan..........................	1,500 0 0	7,299 73	7,231 82	67 93	
Leghorn, Italy........................	3,000 0 0	14,599 50	14,608 17		8 67
London, England	2,500 0 0	12,166 25	12,166 25	Par.......	....
Lima, Peru...........................	14,025 0 0	72,252 07	67,830 97	4,421 70	....
Marseilles, France....................	19,000 0 0	92,463 50	92,601 41	14 50	132 41
Mazatlan, Mexico		5,000 00	4,980 60	19 40	
Montevideo, Uruguay	45,000 0 0	218,992 50	216,835 28	2,271 75	114 53
Nagasaki, Japan	4,500 0 0	21,899 25	20,973 70	925 55	....
Naples, Italy	9,000 0 0	34,065 50	33,832 90	232 60	....
Nice, France..........................	55,784 6 0	271,474 30	271,190 21	467 22	183 13
Panama, United States of Columbia ..	5,000 0 0	50,136 80	48,814 30	1,332 50	....
Payta, Peru		5,940 00	5,940 00	Par.......	....
Rio de Janeiro, Brazil	6,150 0 0	29,928 08	29,673 00	277 59	21 61
San Diego, Cal		5,000 00	4,970 00	30 00	....
San Francisco, Cal		2,500 00	2,496 90	3 10	....
Santa Anna, Curaçao, West Indies ...		4,400 00	4,400 00	Par.......	....
Shanghai, China	61,400 0 0	298,803 10	292,162 54	6,640 56	....
Smyrna, Turkey..	7,000 0 0	34,065 50	34,058 00	7 50	....
Southampton, England	2,500 0 0	12,166 25	12,151 65	14 60	....
St George, Bermuda	145 0 0	705 63	705 65	Par...	....
Trieste, Austria....	2,000 0 0	9,733 00	9,698 25	34 75	....
Valparaiso, Chili	6,081 15 0	29,596 83	28,413 18	1,183 65	....
Yokohama, Japan	63,300 0 0	308,049 45	302,303 10	5,763 52	17 17
Total..........................	364,793 3 10	1,845,377 39	1,818,572 48	27,799 38	904 47

Of the above-mentioned settled claims, 224 were for the three months' extra pay authorized by the act of February 19, 1879, for service in the war with Mexico, and amount to $8,701.35, and 51 for the gratuity to machinists, granted by the act of June 16, 1880, amounting to $27,540 in the aggregate.

This division is also charged with the duty of furnishing the Commissioner of Pensions a complete naval history of all persons who file in his office claims for pensions, or for bounty land on account of service performed by themselves or by certain relatives in the United States Navy. As a rule, the service extends over a period of from one to three years, and in some instances much longer. It requires therefore a considerable length of time to properly examine the records in each case, and it often occurs that a clerk is obliged to consume in the examination an entire day in order to obtain the information required in a single claim. The result of this was, that at the commencement of the last fiscal year the letters from the Commissioner had accumulated to such an extent that it would have required between four and five months to dispose of the number then on hand. The settlement of the claims in the Pension Office was therefore necessarily delayed, and with the view of affording every facility in the adjustment of this meritorious class of claims, an additional force was employed in the examination of the records during a portion of the year, and it is very gratifying to be able to say that the work has been brought up to date, and that the inquiries from the Commissioner are now answered within a day or two after they reach the office.

NAVY PENSION ACCOUNTS.

STATEMENT of the WORK PERFORMED by the NAVY PENSION DIVISION for the fiscal year ending June 30, 1881.

Date.	Accounts received.	Accounts settled.	Letters received.	Letters written.	Amount involved.
1880.					
July	29	4	84	32	$7,197 82
August	24	25	74	52	96,190 14
September	10	3	61	33	64,286 42
October	13	12	84	32	79,534 51
November	19	18	85	32	116,119 42
December	13	19	100	45	157,668 42
1881.					
January	12	4	60	43	17,066 23
February	10	16	97	43	118,290 53
March	11	19	213	45	105,938 52
April	3	1	112	44	9,400 09
May	22	6	127	46	107,823 72
June	15	25	78	31	111,840 80
Total	181	152	1,115	478	991,376 62

ARREARS of PENSION PAID under acts of January 25 and March 4, 1879.

Date.	Accounts received.	Accounts settled.	Amount involved.
1880.			
July	1	7	$7,547 79
August	3	3	755 13
September	9	9	8,572 70
1881.			
January	5	5	2,034 15
February	3	3	3,323 90
April	4	4	1,096 86
Total	25	31	23,330 53

AMOUNT PAID NAVAL PENSIONERS.

Pension agencies.	Number of Navy invalid pensioners.	Number of widow pensioners and dependent relatives.	Total number of Navy pensioners.	Disbursements at each agency for the year ending June 30, 1881.
Boston, Mass	496	509	1,005	$240,559 18
Columbus, Ohio	66	112	178	38,580 36
Chicago, Ill	91	59	150	45,265 36
Concord, N. H	155	151	306	52,833 77
Detroit, Mich	23	26	49	7,330 83
Knoxville, Tenn	69	127	196	42,548 74
Louisville, Ky	11	24	35	10,053 09
Milwaukee, Wis	30	22	52	11,791 10
New York City	510	452	962	164,733 06
Pittsburg, Pa	46	74	120	26,974 97
Philadelphia, Pa	325	391	716	118,412 02
San Francisco, Cal	81	31	112	9,345 25
Saint Louis, Mo	31	27	58	19,050 76
Washington, D. C	345	503	848	176,780 93
Total	2,279	2,508	4,787	965,226 89

Number of accounts on hand June 30, 1881, 32; vouchers examined, 15,326.

The business of the bureau has been transacted with promptness and accuracy, and the chiefs of divisions, clerks, and other employés are deserving of high commendation for the faithfulness manifested in the discharge of their respective duties.

I have the honor to be, very respectfully, your obedient servant

BENJ. P. DAVIS,
Acting Auditor.

Hon. WILLIAM WINDOM,
Secretary of the Treasury.

REPORT OF THE FIFTH AUDITOR OF THE TREASURY.

TREASURY DEPARTMENT,
FIFTH AUDITOR'S OFFICE,
Washington, D. C., October 28, 1881.

SIR: I have the honor to submit herewith an exhibit of the business transacted in this office during the fiscal year ending June 30, 1881.

The accounts audited include the expenses and receipts of the foreign service, the internal revenue, disbursements by the disbursing officers of the Department of State, the Post-Office Department, and the Interior Department, besides numerous accounts under miscellaneous appropriations. These adjustments have required the examination of 192,098 vouchers, aggregating $837,891,644.94; and the fact that less than thirty clerks have been employed attests their fidelity and industry.

THE DIPLOMATIC SERVICE.

The accounts of ministers, set forth in the table marked Exhibit A, show that $324,550.74 were paid for salaries, $53,196.59 for contingent expenses, and $1,574.98 for loss by exchange, making a total of $379,322.31. Official and passport fees were received to the amount of

$5,132.14, which deducted from the total expense shows the actual cost of this branch of the foreign service to have been $374,190.17. It should be noted in this connection, however, as the table shows, that this does not include the accounts of the minister to Paraguay and Uruguay, nor have any accounts been received from the secretary of legation at Mexico.

THE CONSULAR SERVICE.

The tabular statement of consular salaries, fees, and expenditures is not complete, as a glance at the accompanying table, marked Exhibit B, will show. But all vouchers received by this office through the Department of State or otherwise have been adjusted and are included. The accounts audited may be recapitulated as follows:

Fees received for official services		$843,066 36
Received on account of extra wages		30,163 31
		$873,229 67
Paid consular salaries	$386,079 50	
Loss by exchange on same	2,275 52	
Fee emoluments	213,361 28	
		601,716 30
Relief of seamen	33,301 34	
Loss by exchange on same	337 33	
Passage of seamen	8,872 00	
		42,510 67
Contingent expenses of consulates		104,866 79
Allowance for clerks at consulates		54,261 15
Rescuing shipwrecked American seamen		3,355 46
Shipping and discharging seamen		4,384 42
Bringing home criminals		1,035 64
Rent of prison, American convicts in China		1,488 88
Rent of prison, American convicts in Japan		600 00
Wages of keepers, &c., American convicts in China		7,825 97
Wages of keepers, &c., American convicts in Japan		3,055 67
Rent of prison, wages of keepers, &c., American convicts in Siam and Turkey		1,409 81
Salaries of interpreters to consulates in China, Japan, and Siam		11,534 36
Salaries of marshals for consular courts		6,940 90
Expenses for interpreters, guards, &c., in Turkish dominions		3,000 00
		$847,966 02
Excess of receipts over expenditures		25,243 65

It will be observed from the above that the consular service is not only self-sustaining, but contributes in a measure to the support of the diplomatic service.

Several other accounts pertaining to the foreign service have also been adjusted as follows, specific appropriations being made therefor:

Salaries of the United States and Spanish claims commission, 1881	$4,200 00
Contingent expenses of the United States and Spanish claims commission, 1881	749 98
Contingent expenses of the United States and Spanish claims commission, 1879	58 67
Salaries of joint commission for settlement of claims between the United States and the French Republic, 1881	8,017 83
Contingent expenses of joint commission for settlement of claims between the United States and the French Republic, 1881	4,038 93
E. C. Wines, United States commissioner to international penitentiary congress at Stockholm, for expenses, 1879	4,000 00
S. Dana Horton, secretary to international bimetallic commission, for compensation and expenses, 1879	11,570 39
J. H. Ashton, agent United States and Mexican commission, for salary	170 56
Publication of consular and other commercial reports, Department of State, 1881	4,579 78
Allowance to Louis P. Di Cesnola, late consul at Cyprus, "for the official expenses of his consulate," act of March 2, 1881	5,500 00
Compensation to owners of lands ceded by the United States to Great Britain by treaty of Washington, dated July 9, 1842, act of March 3, 1877	1,561 27

17 Ab

The disbursements by Morton, Rose & Co., bankers of the United States at London, England, aggregate $311,393.37, and the receipts of fees from consular officers $205,909.65, and of extra wages and other money of seamen $12,176.30. The disbursements were as follows:

Salaries of ministers for fiscal year 1880	$40,338 19
Salaries of ministers for fiscal year 1881	165,094 34
Contingent expenses of foreign missions for fiscal year 1880	3,692 46
Contingent expenses of foreign missions for fiscal year 1881	28,007 07
Salaries of secretaries of legation for fiscal year 1880	7,095 42
Salaries of secretaries of legation for fiscal year 1881	26,562 33
Salaries of consular service for fiscal year 1880	2,456 18
Salaries of consular service for fiscal year 1881	9,697 45
Contingent expenses of consular service for fiscal year 1880	650 00
Contingent expenses of consular service for fiscal year 1881	1,980 37
International bureau of weights and measures for fiscal year 1880	982 58
International bureau of weights and measures for fiscal year 1881	1,900 00
International exhibition at Sydney and Melbourne for 1879 and 1880	10,046 71
International bimetallic commission	12,250 27
Expenses interpreters, guards, &c., in Turkish dominions, 1881	375 00
Expenses of Cape Spartel light for fiscal year 1881	285 00
Total	311,393 37

The following amounts were paid out of estates of decedents' trust fund, having been previously covered into the Treasury of the United States:

C. Barston, seaman, estate	$64 22
John Symons, citizen, estate	5,496 89
Alice Windsor, alias Evans, citizen, estate	139 87
Henry Willis, seaman, estate	80 00
John Adams, seaman	28 40
Edward A. Crocker, seaman	27 00
Charles L. Godfrey, seaman, estate	27 65
R. Hoeffgen, citizen, estate	134 68
Christopher Schmidt, citizen, estate	417 13
F. W. Clark, seaman, estate	9 00
Total	6,424 84

INTERNAL REVENUE.

The table marked Exhibit C shows the amount collected and deposited in each internal-revenue district, and the salary and expenses of each collector, together with the amount paid storekeepers in each district. The total amount of cash deposited was $127,866,755.16, exclusive of a deposit of $7,397,468.21 derived from sales of adhesive stamps, and collected by stamp agents.

The following sums constituting the expenses of collecting were disbursed, viz:

For salaries of collectors	$432,668 25
For salaries of deputy collectors, clerks, rent, fuel, and lights	1,467,836 97
For stationery, postage, expressage, and advertising	16,596 73
For compensation of storekeepers	1,423,786 00
For fees and expenses of gaugers	758,345 75
Aggregate cost of collecting	4,099,223 70

To arrive at the actual expenses of collecting the internal revenue, the following expenditures must be considered as incident to the system, although not included in the collectors' accounts, viz:

Cost of stamps, paper, and dies	$443,234 34
Salaries and expenses of internal-revenue agents	126,426 81
Salaries and expenses of surveyors of distilleries	5,651 56
Salaries of the office of the Commissioner of Internal Revenue	253,258 00
Incidental expenses of the Office of Internal Revenue, including counsel fees and rewards	210,089 10
Total	1,038,659 81

These expenses added to the collectors' accounts amount to $5,137,883 51, the whole cost of collecting the internal revenue, or 4 per cent. on the amount collected.   For the year ending June 30, 1880, $116,877,753.77 were collected at a cost of $4,463,558.95.

During the year there were paid for the manufacture of paper, printing, and imprinting of stamps, &c., the following sums:

To Bureau of Engraving and Printing	$348,636 62
S. D. Warren & Co	70,053 91
American Bank Note Company	20,762 12
John J. Crooke	3,731 69
The Graphic Company	50 00
Total	443,234 34

The accounts of the Commissioner of Internal Revenue for stamps, as set forth in the table marked Exhibit D, may be recapitulated as follows:

Distilled spirit stamps	$92,953,661 00
Special tax stamps	12,665,110 00
Beer stamps	14,978,051 42
Documentary and proprietary stamps	9,150,636 57
Stamps for tobacco, snuff, and cigars	51,321,612 92
Stamped foil wrappers	268,680 40
Stamped paper labels for tobacco	4,760 00
	181,342,512 31

The table marked Exhibit E gives a list of forty-two revenue agents, to whom were paid for salaries $82,880.65, for expenses, $41,619.08; to which should be added $229.20 for stationey, and $1,757.88 for transportation over Pacific railroads, making a total of $126,486.81.   To gaugers for fees, $711,231.86; expenses, $47,113.89; total $758,345.75.   To surveyors for salaries, $1,020; expenses, $4,631.56; total, $5,651.56.   For salaries in the office of Commissioner of Internal Revenue, $253,258.

In the adjustment of accounts of three hundred and thirty-one stamp agents, the amount involved was $4,905,524.19, and of 602 claims for the redemption of stamps, amounting to $24,957.93, there was discounted $183.82, leaving an amount actually paid of $24,774.11.

Accounts were adjusted for expenses incurred in the detection of fraud, for counting and issuing stamps, and for other purposes incident to the internal-revenue service, as follows:

Salary	$124,076 39
Traveling expenses	9,470 04
Expenses	24,319 98
Telegrams	1,317 84
Rent	5,416 67
Stationery	14,192 60
Expressage	7,053 96
Counsel fees and expenses	10,320 25
Rewards	13,861 67
Total	210,129 10

By the last report the Secretary of the Treasury had on deposit to his credit, on account of "fines, penalties, and forfeitures," a balance of $219,261.66.   During the year deposits have been made to the amount of $151,894.63, and disbursements made to the amount of $308,247.74, leaving a balance to his credit January 1, 1881, of $62,908.55.   An account has also been rendered by him on account of "offers in compromise," from December 1, 1879, to December 31, 1880, showing an amount deposited to his credit of $184,975.74, and disbursements amounting to

$146,102.07, leaving a balance on deposit to his credit January 1, 1881, of $38,873.67.

The following sums were refunded : Taxes erroneously assessed and collected, $34,559.07; drawbacks on merchandise exported, $39,511.93 ; and moneys refunded under private acts of Congress, $21,324.12.

The disbursements by George Waterhouse, chairman of the South Carolina Free School Fund Commissioners, amounted to $3,937.50.

DISBURSING CLERKS' ACCOUNTS.

Accounts rendered by Col. R. C. Morgan, disbursing clerk of the State Department, have been adjusted as follows :

Contingent expenses of United States consulates, 1881	$28,497 10
Contingent expenses of United States consulates, 1880	12,514 41
Contingent expenses of United States consulates, 1879	168 35
Contingent expenses of United States consulates, 1878	197 21
Contingent expenses of foreign missions, 1881	8,355 48
Contingent expenses of foreign missions, 1880	1,560 61
Contingent expenses of foreign missions, 1879	1,740 50
Rescuing shipwrecked American seamen, 1881	2,752 46
Rescuing shipwrecked American seamen, 1880	387 00
Rescuing shipwrecked American seamen, 1879	54 00
Return of criminals, 1880	547 91
Relief and protection of American seamen, 1881	84 00
Relief and protection of American seamen, 1880	139 00
International exhibitions at Sidney and Melbourne, Australia (1879 and 1880)	114 71
International exposition at Paris (1878)	4,207 74
International remonetization of silver, 1880	268 93
Berlin fishery exhibition (1880)	1,280 51
Publication of consular and other commercial reports, 1881	5,333 26
Monument marking the birthplace of George Washington	75 00
Stationery and furniture, 1881	3,463 61
Proof-reading and packing laws, 1881	1,710 80
Lithographing, 1881	1,200 00
Lithographing, 1880	108 70
Books and maps, 1881	2,893 04
Books and maps, 1880	99 13
Editing, publishing, and distributing Revised and Annual Statutes, 1881.	3,153 84

In order that the above exhibit might be complete in itself, it was necessary to include the following accounts, which have already been given in aggregating the expenses of the consular service:

Contingent expenses of consulates, 1881	$28,497 10
Contingent expenses of missions, 1881	8,355 48
Rescuing shipwrecked American seamen, 1881	2,752 46
Relief and protection of American seamen, 1881	84 00

Other amounts above appertaining to the foreign service have not appeared in any former statement.

Accounts rendered by Mr. Richard Joseph, disbursing clerk of the Department of the Interior, were adjusted as follows :

Contingent expenses, office of Commissioner of Patents, 1881	$15,518 75
Contingent expenses, office of Commissioner of Patents, 1880	384 85
Photolithographing, office of Commissioner of Patents, 1881	32,088 85
Photolithographing, office of Commissioner of Patents, 1880	1,215 13
Copies of drawings, office of Commissioner of Patents, 1881	16,871 48
Copies of drawings, office of Commissioner of Patents, 1880	5,636 47
Plates for Patent Office Official Gazette, 1881	14,768 71
Plates for Patent Office Official Gazette, 1880	3,910 90
Expenses for packing and distributing official documents, 1881	3,484 50
Expenses for packing and distributing official documents, 1880	252 60
Scientific Library, office of Commissioner of Patents, 1881	1,077 37
Scientific Library, office of Commissioner of Patents, 1880	1,114 66

Preservation of collections, Smithsonian Institute, 1881	$34,426	38
Preservation of collections, Smithsonian Institute, 1880	94	59
Preservation of collections, Smithsonian Institute (Armory Building), 1881	1,885	85
Preservation of collections, Smithsonian Institute (Armory Building), 1880	24	39
Furniture and fixtures National Museum, 1881	21,272	67
Expenses of the Tenth Census	122,940	54

Other accounts rendered by several disbursing agents of the Census Office were adjusted as follows:

Expenses of the Tenth Census	$101,739	10
Expenses of the Tenth Census for transportation over subsidized railroads, settled on approval of superintendent of the Census	4,003	79

Accounts rendered by Col. J. O. P. Burnside, disbursing clerk of the Post-Office Department, have been adjusted as follows:

Publication of Official Postal Guide	$16,037	69
Stationery	7,225	13
Carpets	4,996	90
Gas	5,774	80
Furniture	4,998	73
Telegraphing	1,664	08
Hardware	731	96
Rent of house No. 915 E street	1,500	00
Keeping horses and repair of wagons and harness	1,200	00
Plumbing and gas fixtures	3,975	89
Painting	3,999	95
Fuel	3,325	51
Miscellaneous items	9,452	28
Directories	200	00

Aside from the examination of 192,098 vouchers already noticed, there were 2,916 letters written, 9,220 reports recorded and copied, 22,361 coupon-books counted, and 23,576 books scheduled. An examination of the accompanying tables, which are too extensive to be incorporated in the body of this report, will further convey some idea of the extent of the work performed and clearly demonstrate the necessity for the additional clerical force recommended for this Bureau. In the Consular Division alone, accounts are received from 286 consulates, and 283 consular agencies. These accounts, as well as those growing out of the collection of internal revenue, are especially complicated, requiring much time and great care in their adjustment. It is true that the accounts adjusted are now carefully and critically handled by clerks in charge, whose industry, efficiency, and integrity cannot be successfully challenged, but it is also true that the clerical force has been gradually reduced until only with the greatest difficulty can the work be kept up as it is now required to be done.

I have the honor to be, very respectfully, your obedient servant,

D. S. ALEXANDER,
Auditor.

Hon. WILLIAM WINDOM,
Secretary of the Treasury.

REPORT OF THE SIXTH AUDITOR OF THE TREASURY.

OFFICE OF THE AUDITOR OF THE TREASURY
FOR THE POST-OFFICE DEPARTMENT,
November 8, 1881.

SIR: I have the honor to submit the report of the business operations of this office for the fiscal year ended June 30, 1881.

My annual report to the Postmaster-General exhibits in detail the financial transactions of the Post-Office Department during the last fiscal year.

REQUIRED INCREASE IN THE CLERICAL FORCE.

The failure of Congress to authorize the employment of the number of clerks asked for by my predecessor—which did not exceed the requirements of the office—together with the increase of business during the past year, will, in my opinion, more than justify my estimate for nineteen clerks, four female assorters of money-orders, and two assistant messengers.

The rapid growth of the money-order system, the large increase in the number of accounts for mail transportation and miscellaneous payments, the great number and variety of orders of the Postmaster-General affecting the accounts of contractors, subcontractors, for special and temporary service, and of postmasters, the close scrutiny, thorough examination and dispatch required in the settlement of all accounts rendered to this office, make an increase in the number of clerks necessary for the protection of the interests of the government.

Heretofore it has been impracticable, with the force employed, to make quarterly reports to the Secretary of the Treasury, of the money-order transactions. Annual reports of these transactions have been made to the Postmaster-General. It is my opinion that quarterly reports of the money-order business should be made to the Secretary of the Treasury, and for this purpose increased force is required.

From the date of the establishment of the money-order system, in 1864, to the present time, a large number of money-orders remain outstanding and unpaid, estimated to amount to about $1,250,000. The only existing record of these orders is that afforded by the weekly money-order statements of the postmasters who issued such orders, which statements cover nearly the whole period of the operation of the money-order system, and are difficult of access and inconvenient for reference. It is necessary that a complete, condensed record should be made of all these unpaid orders, for use in facilitating the payment of such as are from time to time presented, and of ascertaining at once the number, amount, and particulars of those still outstanding. To make such a record would require the services of about ten temporary clerks for one year, and I recommend that provision be made for the employment of the necessary force, as the importance and value of the record will warrant the expenditure.

The present diligent, faithful, and capable clerks find it impossible in many instances to perform the duties required of them within business hours, and it is the constant practice of a large number of them to work at night and on holidays in order to keep the work of their desks up to the requirements of the office.

The following is a comparative statement of the business of the office, as shown by the annual reports for the years ended June 30, 1878, and June 30, 1881, exhibiting the increase in some of the branches:

Number of postmaster's accounts settled during the year ended June 30, 1881	174,450
Number of same during the year ended June 30, 1878	152,211
Increase	22,239
Per cent. of increase	14.6
Number of accounts for the transportation of the mails and miscellaneous payments audited during the year ended June 30, 1881	119,148
Number of same during the year ended June 30, 1878	84,865
Increase	34,283
Per cent. of increase	40.4
Number of orders of the Postmaster-General, affecting accounts for the transportation of the mails, during the year ended June 30, 1881	15,274
Number of same during the year ended June 30, 1878	8,943
Increase	6,331
Per cent. of increase	70.8
Number of warrants and drafts passed and registered during the year ended June 30, 1881	45,924
Number of same during the year ended June 30, 1878	29,453
Increase	16,471
Per cent. of increase	56
Number of accounts of depositories audited during the year ended June 30, 1881	5,092
Number of same during the year ended June 30, 1878	850
Increase	4,242
Per cent. of increase	500
Number of certificates of deposit audited and registered during the year ended June 30, 1881	161,367
Number of same during the year ended June 30, 1878	12,094
Increase	149,273
Per cent. of increase	1,234
Number of foreign mail statements examined and registered during the year ended June 30, 1881	7,833
Number of same during the year ended June 30, 1878	6,388
Increase	1,445
Per cent. of increase	22.6

Number of drafts issued on late and present postmasters and contractors during the year ended June 30, 1881	3,705
Number of same during the year ended June 30, 1878................	2,394
Increase	1,311
Per cent. of increase	54
Number of money-order offices in operation June 30, 1881............	5,167
Number of money-order offices in operation June 30, 1878............	4,143
Increase	1,024
Per cent. of increase	24.7
Number of money-orders issued during the year ended June 30, 1881.	7,954,330
Number of money-orders issued during the year ended June 30, 1878.	5,733,905
Increase	2,220,425
Per cent. of increase	38.7
Amount involved in money-order settlements during the year ended June 30, 1881..	$205,244,434 97
Amount involved in money-order settlements during the year ended June 30, 1878..	152,821,986 72
Increase	52,422,448 25
Per cent. of increase	34.3
Number of communications sent out by mail during the year ended June 30, 1881..	198,709
Number of same during the year ended June 30, 1878................	180,436
Increase	18,273
Per cent. of increase	10.1

OBSOLETE FILES.

There are now stored in the archives of this office vast numbers of quarterly postal accounts and weekly money-order statements of postmasters, together with all the paid money orders. These accounts have, in part, accumulated since the fire which destroyed the Post-Office Department building, in 1836, and a portion antedate that occurrence. They have long since been audited and settled, and the items therein contained transferred to the registers and ledgers of the office; their further preservation is not material to the interests of the government or of individuals.

The greater part of the very large number of weekly money-order statements, dating back to 1864, may, with propriety, be dispensed with, after the record of unpaid money-orders therein contained has been transferred to permanent books.

I recommend that authority be requested from Congress for the sale or destruction of all unnecessary files over ten years old. Such action will relieve the office from the embarrassment now experienced for want of storage room, and afford space for the current accumulating files.

ADDITIONAL OFFICE ACCOMMODATIONS REQUIRED.

Attention is invited to the present overcrowded condition of the rooms occupied by this office. Many of the rooms, but poorly lighted and illy ᵈ, originally intended for the use of but two or three persons, are now occupied by five or six, and the available space diminished by file cases.

I recommend that suitable provision be made, at the earliest practicable date, for additional accommodations for this office.

I have the honor to be, very respectfully,

J. H. ELA,
Auditor.

The Hon. SECRETARY OF THE TREASURY,
Washington, D. C.

REPORT OF THE TREASURER OF THE UNITED STATES.

TREASURY OF THE UNITED STATES,
Washington, October 1, 1881.

SIR: I have the honor to submit the following report showing the operations of the Treasury of the United States for the fiscal year 1881.

SUMMARY OF TRANSACTIONS.

The receipts of the government show an increase over those for 1880 from nearly every source. The increase in the receipts from customs is $11,637,611.42; from internal revenue, $11,255,011.59; from sales of public lands, $1,185,356.57, and from miscellaneous sources, $3,177,702.01. The total increase is $27,255,681.59, which, added to a net reduction of $6,930,070.19 in expenditures, makes an increase in the surplus revenue of $34,185,751.78. The net revenues were $360,782,292.57, and the net expenditures $260,712,887.59. The excess of receipts over payments was $100,069,404.98, of which $85,432,381.05 was expended in the redemption of the public debt. The balance in the Treasury increased $48,667,603.93, from $203,791,321.88, at the beginning, to $252,458,925.81 at the end of the fiscal year. The amount expended on account of interest and premium on the public debt ran down from $98,552,895.53 in the fiscal year 1880 to $83,569,989.96, a reduction of $14,982,905.57.

The balance standing to the credit of disbursing officers and agents of the United States with the various offices of the Treasury, June 30, 1881, was $24,936,307.88.

The receipts for the fiscal year on account of the Post-Office Department were $39,757,664.72, and the expenditures $38,544,935.11, of which amounts $24,702,703.44 was received and expended directly by postmasters.

The unavailable funds of the Treasury stand at $29,521,632.72, having been increased $9,425.87 since the last report, by reason of taking up on this account certain items previously carried in the cash. The unavailable funds of the Post-Office Department account remain unchanged at $40,078.06.

During the year fifty-four national banks were organized and twenty went into voluntary liquidation, leaving 2,136 doing business at the close of the year. No national bank failed during the year.

The semi-annual duty accruing from national banks during the year was $8,493,552.55, all of which has been collected and paid into the Treasury, making the total amount collected by the Treasurer since the establishment of the national banking system in 1863, $108,855,021.90.

At the close of the year there was held by the Treasurer in United States bonds $360,505,900 as security for the circulation of national banks, and $15,295,500 as security for public deposits in national bank depositaries. During the year $276,899,700 in bonds was deposited for these purposes, and $277,527,350 withdrawn, exceeding by far the transactions of any former year. These changes were chiefly due to the continuance of the five and six per cent. bonds at three and one-half per cent., but were caused in considerable part by the substitution of the continued bonds for four and four and one-half per cents.

The United States currency outstanding at the close of the year was $362,539,437.65. There was redeemed during the year $71,069,974.95, making the total redemptions since the first issue of currency $2,300,141,073.36.

United States bonds amounting to $85,304,050 were retired during the year. The aggregate amount retired by purchase, redemption, conversion, and exchange, from March 11, 1869, to the close of the fiscal year, is $1,983,344,800.

Coupons from United States bonds, of the value of $22,797,667.52, were paid during the year, and quarterly interest on registered stock of the funded loans, amounting to $44,455,790.17, was paid by means of 305,101 checks drawn payable to the order of the respective stockholders and sent to them by mail.

The amount of national-bank notes received for redemption during the year was $59,650,259. The aggregate redemptions under the act of June 20, 1874, have been $1,099,634,772.

THE STATE OF THE TREASURY.

The liabilities and assets of the Treasury, at the close of September, for the last four years, are shown by the following statement:

	September 30, 1878.	September 30, 1879.	September 30, 1880.	September 30, 1881.
LIABILITIES.				
Post-Office Department Account.....	$2,151,698 76	$2,167,901 50	$2,600,489 16	$2,817,702 79
Disbursing Officers' Balances........	17,042,010 89	26,007,876 95	23,180,286 49	21,916,119 81
Fund for redemption of Notes of National Banks "failed," "in liquidation," and "reducing circulation"..	8,182,400 90	12,939,889 75	19,746,955 25	31,152,713 60
Undistributed Assets of failed National Banks	775,814 12	642,814 83	616,560 21	398,835 68
Five-per-cent. Fund for redemption of National-Bank Notes..	12,974,232 75	15,082,482 99	15,428,010 82	15,768,682 73
Fund for redemption of National Bank Gold-Notes ....*....	1,720 00	219,940 00	475,965 00	394,847 00
Currency and Minor-Coin Redemption Account	5,987 00	4,213 15	3,075 60	7,176 11
Fractional Silver-Coin Redemption Account......................		152,664 10	74,661 75	75,320 70
Interest Account	670,593 00	101,514 75	99,585 00	....
Interest Account, Pacific Railroads and Louisville and Portland Canal Company	15,650 40	6,270 00	8,400 00	4,930 06
Treasurer United States, Agent for paying interest on District of Columbia Bonds...................	40,811 27	298,435 54	366,532 59	253,795 34
Treasurer's Transfer Checks and Drafts outstanding	3,728,594 96	7,632,333 98	4,716,845 94	5,475,492 11
Treasurer's General Account: Interest due and unpaid...........	9,345,289 13	4,189,523 27	2,401,809 98	2,151,139 93
Matured Bonds and Interest........				3,004,205 94
Called Bonds and Interest..........	12,015,616 78	31,033,519 65	5,958,436 48	17,832,841 34
Old Debt..........................	877,864 26	840,608 41	816,585 07	798,488 28
Gold Certificates	$2,826,600 00	14,910,900 00	7,511,700 00	5,248,620 00
Silver Certificates	2,028,070 00	4,571,850 00	18,581,960 00	64,149,910 00
Certificates of Deposit (Act June 8, 1872)	40,890,000 00	31,335,000 00	9,975,000 00	8,395,000 00
Special Fund for redemption of Fractional Currency............	10,000,000 00			
Balance, including Bullion Fund..	182,845,615 52	151,848,666 70	156,664,083 17	151,336,178 73
Total .,.....................	327,424,964 74	303,485,995 07	267,676,912 40	331,961,210 11

	September 30, 1878.	September 30, 1879.	September 30, 1880.	September 30, 1881.
ASSETS.				
Gold Coin...............................	$126,987,235 10	$123,536,760 39	$68,868,091 10	$77,338,088 71
Gold Bullion...........................	9,049,067 10	96,290,810 90	66,772,094 67	97,458,477 70
Standard Silver Dollars...............	12,155,205 00	31,806,774 00	47,784,744 00	65,949,279 00
Fractional Silver Coin................	6,143,903 02	16,873,898 47	24,723,892 68	26,343,477 17
Silver Bullion........................	9,684,034 48	4,299,124 25	6,154,392 93	2,622,676 18
Gold Certificates....................	9,392,920 00	70,700 00	31,600 00	10,100 00
Silver Certificates..................	1,316,470 00	3,181,130 00	6,092,579 00	11,309,470 00
United States Notes..................	63,049,339 67	48,763,728 01	27,901,594 07	26,423,169 89
United States Notes, Special Fund for redemption of Fractional Currency...............................	10,000,000 00			
National-Bank Notes..................	9,256,043 81	4,279,958 76	3,268,404 57	4,457,713 59
National Bank Gold-Notes............	1,720 00	183,640 00	230,125 00	96,545 00
Fractional Currency.................	161,081 86	90,978 15	60,712 08	22,973 03
Deposits held by National Bank Depositaries.........................	75,661,403 15	17,836,816 48	11,212,315 94	12,677,454 48
Minor Coin...........................	1,410,898 50	1,524,700 57	1,063,665 22	552,585 06
New York and San Francisco Exchange.........................	367,000 00	1,799,334 51	1,443,000 00	1,483,000 00
One and Two Year Notes, &c	8,916 51	400 40	325 50	10 50
Redeemed Certificates of Deposit (Act June 8, 1872)...................	1,345,000 00	2,025,000 00	90,000 00	210,000 00
Quarterly Interest Checks and Coin Coupons paid.......................	256,900 48	189,579 78	141,517 91	193,452 68
Registered and Unclaimed Interest paid	370,482 80	22,355 00	19,303 50	900 00
United States Bonds and Interest....		507 64	997,343 91	2,016,876 70
Interest on District of Columbia Bonds	1,345 64	516 97	3,047 12	1,770 25
Refunding Certificates and Interest.		24,119 74		
Pacific Railroads, Sinking Fund.....		45,312 75		
Speaker's Certificates	123,802 00		126,215 00	118,916 00
Deficits, unavailable Funds..........	729,195 65	690,848 30	690,848 30	700,274 17
Total..............................	337,424,964 74	303,485,995 97	267,676,912 40	331,981,210 11

Comparing the condition of the Treasury September 30, 1881, with its condition on the same day last year, the most striking changes are the increase in the gold coin and bullion and standard silver dollars on hand and in the silver certificates outstanding. Deducting the gold certificates actually outstanding, the gold belonging to the government on September 30 of the last four years was $112,602,622.20 in 1878; $154,987,371.29 in 1879; $128,160,085.77 in 1880; and $169,552,746.41 in 1881. In 1880 the gold ran down nearly $27,000,000, but this decrease was much more than overcome in 1881, when it increased more than $41,000,000, reaching the highest point ever attained. This increase was largely due to the sale for gold coin in New York under the circular of September 18, 1880, of exchange on the West and South, payable in silver certificates. More than $23,500,000 in gold has been deposited with the assistant treasurer in New York on this account during the last fifteen months, exclusive of the amount deposited on account of standard silver dollars. The effect of these operations, so far as the Treasury is concerned, is to convert its silver dollars into gold, for the issue of the silver certificates transfers the ownership of the silver dollars which they represent from the Treasury to the public.

The gross amount of gold and silver coin and bullion held by the Treasury, without regard to the obligations outstanding against it, has ranged from $163,969,444.70, in 1878, to $222,807,368.01 in 1879, $214,303,215.38 in 1880, and $269,706,998.76 in 1881. The increase within the last year has been $55,400,000, of which $39,150,000 is in the gold and $16,250,000 in the silver. The increase in the gold has been greater, and in the silver less, in the last year than in any year since the coinage of the standard silver dollar began.

The amount of United States notes on hand, which largely decreased during the two preceding years, has slightly increased during the last year, notwithstanding the urgent public demand for notes for circulation. The amount on hand above the amount required for the payment of clearing-house certificates is $20,000,000, against $18,000,000 a year ago. The amount now held is not more than sufficient for the reasonable requirements of the various offices of the Treasury. The Treasurer, while freely furnishing new United States notes in redemption of old United States notes, and of national-bank notes, has endeavored to husband the supply by the use of gold, standard silver dollars, and silver certificates, in payment of demands on the Treasury. The practice during the past year has been to make ten per cent. of all payments in silver dollars or certificates, forty per cent. in gold coin, and fifty per cent. in notes. To this rule there is one important exception. Under the arrangement between the Treasury and the New York Clearing House all of the payments by the Treasury to this institution, aggregating two hundred and seventy-five million dollars a year, must be made in gold coin or United States notes; standard silver dollars are not receivable under its rules, although silver certificates are now being paid to it by the Treasury to some extent in large denominations, in lieu of gold coin for use in the payment of customs dues. Aside from any personal views as to the expediency of reviving the silver dollar, it would seem unwise for any branch of the government to encourage an arrangement by which a coin which the law has made a full legal tender is discredited.

The gross assets of the government, including the funds held for the redemption of gold, silver, and currency certificates, are $331,981,210.11, having increased more than $64,000,000 during the last year, and being larger than on the corresponding date in any year since 1878. This increase is due in chief part to deposits on account of silver certificates, which amounted during the year to $45,600,000. A large share of these certificates was issued for deposits of gold, which directly increased the assets, while so far as they were issued in payment of demands on the Treasury they protected the assets to a like extent.

THE RESERVE.

There is no provision of law requiring a specie reserve for the redemption of United States notes. In preparation for resumption of specie payments, a fund was created in the Treasury under section 3 of the resumption act of 1875, by the sale of $95,500,000 of bonds and the accumulation of surplus revenue, to protect the outstanding notes. The amount of this fund has never been definitely fixed, but it has been maintained at about forty per cent. of the United States notes outstanding.

The present fund is estimated by deducting from the cash in the Treasury the aggregate of current liabilities other than United States notes, and this excess of cash has been maintained and called the reserve. These current liabilities include coin and currency certificates, balances subject to checks of disbursing officers, the funds for the redemption of national-bank notes, interest due and unpaid, outstanding checks, matured bonds and interest, the balance due the Post-Office Department, old debts, undistributed assets of failed national banks, and various smaller items.

Aside from the coin and currency certificates there has been but little fluctuation in the aggregate amount of these items since the close of the refunding operations. The obligations which are the evidences of these liabilities are innumerable and widely scattered—comprising bonds and interest notes, the remnants of old loans and calls long matured; ˙ ˙ ˙ coupons, and many small amounts of unclaimed registered interest;

remnants of the circulation of failed, liquidating, and reducing national banks, all of which now find their way to the Treasury slowly, and could not be presented in any large amount without simultaneous action by many persons, which experience shows is impossible; and were it possible the various funds are always being replenished from the ample public revenues or by other deposits made in pursuance of law.

It has usually been assumed that a reserve of forty per cent. is sufficient for the protection of the United States notes, but it is plain that under this method of computation the reserve is not merely forty per cent. of the liability represented by United States notes, but also one hundred per cent. of all the other liabilities. So far as the gold, silver, and clearing-house certificates are concerned, it is necessary, under the laws authorizing their issue, that their full amount should be set aside in gold, silver, and United States notes, respectively, as funds for their redemption; but as to the other liabilities no such obligation exists, and it is submitted that no higher reserve is required for their protection than is required for the protection of the United States notes. In the changed condition of trade and commerce, unless some calamity shall overtake the nation, there seems to be no probability of a run upon the reserve of the Treasury. The total demand for coin in redemption of United States notes has aggregated since resumption but $12,029,086, and no notes whatever have been presented for redemption since February, 1881.

Should there ever be a run on the specie reserves of the Treasury, the United States notes will be made the basis of the demand, and not the other matured obligations, which compose the very varied current liabilities of the government mentioned above; the amount and nature of which may be seen in the following statement showing the excess of assets over the demand liabilities of the government, other than United States notes:

ASSETS.

Gold Coin in Treasury and Mints		$77,436,633 71
Gold Bullion,		97,453,477 70
Silver Bullion		2,622,676 18
Standard Silver Dollars		65,949,279 00
Fractional Silver Coin		26,343,477 17
Deposits with National Banks	$12,677,454 48	
United States Notes	32,879,883 48	
		45,557,337 96
		$315,362,881 72

LIABILITIES.

Old Debt	$796,488 28	
Less amount on hand.,	10 50	
		$796,477 78
Called Bonds matured		17,832,841 34
Bonds matured—Sixes of 1880 and 1881 and Oregon War Debt		3,004,205 94
Interest Due	2,151,139 93	
Less amount on hand	194,352 68	
		1,956,787 25
Gold Certificates	5,248,920 00	
Less amount on hand	10,100 00	
		5,238,820 00
Silver Certificates	64,149,910 00	
Less amount on hand	11,309,470 00	
		52,840,440 00
Clearing-House Certificates	8,395,000 00	
Less amount on hand	210,000 00	
		8,185,000 00

Disbursing Officers' Balances and other
   small accounts $22, 655, 398 39
Outstanding Drafts and Checks................... 5, 475, 492 11
Five per cent. Redemption Fund.................. 15, 768, 662 75
Fund for Redemption of Notes of Na-
   tional Banks, failed, liquidating, and
   reducing circulation........................... 31, 547, 560 60
Post-Office Department Account 3, 617, 703 79
                                                       $168, 919, 399 95

Reserve—Excess of Assets....................................... 146, 443, 491 77

Considering these liabilities as a whole it is clear that whatever percentage of reserve will protect the United States notes will protect the other liabilities. The Treasurer does not attempt to say what this percentage should be, but he is of the opinion that a uniform percentage should be fixed for all the current liabilities other than the three classes of certificates and that the excess of cash in the Treasury should be expended, from time to time, in the purchase or redemption of the public debt according to some definite and publicly announced plan. Should this be done, the policy of the Department would cease to be a subject of speculation and the influence of the Treasury on the money-market would be reduced to a minimum.

The following statement shows that while the present nominal reserve of the Treasury held exclusively for the protection of United States notes has since January 1, 1879, ranged from 36.2 per cent. to 44.5 per cent., and has averaged for that period 41.1 per cent. of the outstanding United States notes, there has really been for the same period a reserve of cash against all demand liabilities, including United States notes and excluding the amount of outstanding coin and currency certificates from both sides, of from 40.5 per cent. to 55.7 per cent., which has averaged 51.6 per cent.; in other words, the reserve, as it has been maintained exclusively against United States notes, has been kept some $46,000,000 in excess of what it would have been, had the same percentage been applied in computing the reserve to be held against all demand liabilities excluding coin and currency certificates.

Month.	Current liabilities excluding United States notes and coin and currency certificates.	Current liabilities excluding certificates and including United States notes, viz. $346,681,016.	Cash less amount of coin and currency certificates.	Percentage of cash, less coin and currency certificates, to demand liabilities including United States notes and excluding certificates.	Present reserve—percentage of excess of assets over liabilities to United States notes outstanding.
1879.					
January...............	$90, 653, 879 78	$427, 334, 895 78	$202, 026, 723 77	47. 2	36. 8
February..............	65, 103, 476 11	411, 784, 492 11	200, 434, 409 47	48. 6	37. 4
March.................	70, 167, 095 46	416, 848, 111 46	214, 008, 787 82	51. 3	38. 3
April	77, 716, 888 96	424, 397, 904 96	216, 399, 128 00	50. 9	38. 6
May	153, 804, 995 09	500, 486, 011 09	213, 838, 390 09	42. 7	39. 5
June	121, 645, 499 72	468, 326, 515 72	239, 493, 840 92	51. 1	42. 3
July	122, 888, 899 50	469, 569, 915 50	227, 188, 405 11	48. 3	38. 6
August	158, 395, 766 66	505, 076, 782 66	204, 811, 068 97	40. 5	38. 7
September	109, 865, 053 60	456, 546, 069 60	224, 625, 313 77	49. 2	40. 6
October	106, 938, 362 21	453, 619, 378 21	240, 161, 089 38	52. 9	40. 6
November.............	87, 643, 560 22	434, 324, 576 22	217, 241, 096 29	54. 6	43. 5
December	82, 793, 382 83	429, 474, 398 83	228, 679, 191 87	53. 2	42. 0
1880.					
January...............	83, 118, 494 71	429, 799, 510 71	222, 426, 811 33	51. 7	40. 1
February	77, 652, 037 12	424, 333, 053 12	225, 309, 798 63	53. 1	42. 5
March	78, 930, 514 42	425, 611, 530 42	221, 353, 928 60	52. 0	41. 0

Month.	Current liabilities excluding United States notes and coin and currency certificates.	Current liabilities excluding certificates and including United States notes, viz. $346,681,016.	Cash less amount of coin and currency certificates.	Percentage of cash, less coin and currency certificates, to demand liabilities including United States notes and excluding certificates.	Present reserve-percentage of excess of assets over liabilities to United States notes outstanding.
1880—Continued.					
April	$72,484,853 42	$419,165,869 42	$220,692,691 28	52.6	42.7
May	75,291,011 29	421,972,027 29	222,253,528 40	52.9	42.3
June	67,415,060 72	414,096,076 72	221,776,758 11	53.5	44.5
July	82,448,848 07	429,129,864 07	219,846,528 41	51.2	39.6
August	75,948,897 65	422,629,913 65	218,187,958 86	51.6	41.0
September	76,323,911 14	423,004,927 14	224,278,140 01	52.1	42.6
October	77,684,229 97	424,365,245 97	222,791,151 75	52.5	41.8
November	76,199,999 72	422,881,015 72	217,797,013 33	51.5	40.8
December	72,120,662 50	418,801,678 50	218,829,753 07	52.2	42.3
1881.					
January	83,057,655 48	429,738,671 48	215,040,205 57	50.0	38.0
February	76,264,634 27	422,945,650 27	217,988,929 14	51.5	40.8
March	89,349,715 30	436,080,731 30	240,877,135 86	55.2	43.7
April	90,565,183 74	437,246,199 74	240,911,186 11	55.1	43.2
May	89,987,758 03	436,668,774 03	243,030,705 60	55.6	44.1
June	94,425,753 84	441,106,769 84	245,880,409 05	55.7	43.6
July	110,955,327 33	457,636,343 33	245,505,531 91	53.6	38.8
August	89,025,825 41	435,706,841 41	237,543,416 36	45.5	42.8
September	120,603,239 63	467,284,255 63	246,189,312 79	52.7	36.2
October	105,643,243 65	452,324,259 65	244,730,999 94	54.1	40.1
Average for thirty-four months	91,268,050 52	437,949,066 69	225,948,559 97	51.6	41.1

At the present time the percentage of the surplus cash to the United States notes is only 40.1 per cent., while the percentage of the total cash to total liabilities (excluding certificates from both sides) is 54.1. Should 40 per cent. be fixed upon as a sufficient reserve for all the liabilities, the cash required to be held would be less than $181,000,000 instead of the $244,731,000 now held. Nearly $64,000,000 or, excluding $26,000,000 fractional silver coin not a full legal tender, $38,000,000 might gradually be applied to the extinguishment of the public debt.

UNITED STATES NOTES.

The following statement shows the changes which have taken place in the denominations of United States notes outstanding at the close of each of the last four fiscal years:

Denomination.	1878.	1879.	1880.	1881.
One dollar	$20,929,874 30	$18,209,980 80	$20,332,322 00	$22,645,761 68
Two dollars	20,910,948 20	18,092,653 20	20,352,813 00	22,244,122 10
Five dollars	54,669,556 50	54,107,118 00	65,432,548 00	69,569,078 04
Ten dollars	65,551,644 00	64,628,562 00	74,916,751 00	76,990,387 00
Twenty dollars	62,720,643 00	60,470,887 00	72,143,207 00	72,271,507 00
Fifty dollars	27,182,680 00	25,523,340 00	24,808,995 00	23,702,910 00
One hundred dollars	31,624,670 00	32,038,480 00	32,797,870 00	32,047,660 00
Five hundred dollars	30,878,500 00	32,569,500 00	19,224,000 00	14,570,000 00
One thousand dollars	33,212,500 00	35,070,500 00	16,532,500 00	12,024,500 00
Five thousand dollars		4,000,000 00	640,000 00	455,000 00
Ten thousand dollars		2,960,000 00	400,000 00	260,000 00
Total	347,681,016 00	347,681,016 00	347,641,016 00	347,681,016 00
Less unknown denominations destroyed in sub treasury in Chicago fire	1,000,000 00	1,000,000 00	1,000,000 00	1,000,000 00
Outstanding	346,681,016 00	346,681,016 00	346,681,016 00	346,681,016 00

During the last two years there has been a steady increase in the outstanding notes of the denominations of twenty dollars and under, and a proportionate decrease in the notes of higher denominations, the hundreds alone excepted. Of the five-thousand-dollar notes but ninety-one and of the ten-thousand-dollar notes but twenty-six remain in circulation. At the close of the fiscal year 1879 there were outstanding 48,497,283 notes; at the close of 1880, 55,573,301, and June 30, 1881, 59,839,069, an increase of nearly twenty-five per cent. in two years. During the last year there was an increase of $2,313,429 in one-dollar notes; $1,891,309 in two-dollar notes; $4,136,530 in five-dollar notes; $2,073,636 in ten-dollar notes; $128,390 in twenty-dollar notes, and $149,790 in one-hundred-dollar notes. The amount of ones and twos outstanding has increased $8,587,250 within the last two years. This increase is in part due to the discontinuance of the issue of notes of those denominations by the national banks upon the resumption of specie payments, though the chief cause is doubtless the revival of business and the demand for small notes for the payment of operatives and for use in small transactions.

The issues and redemptions during the last three fiscal years have been as follows:

Denomination.	1879.		1880.		1881.	
	Issued.	Redeemed.	Issued.	Redeemed.	Issued.	Redeemed.
One dollar	$6, 503, 133	$9, 223, 026 50	$9, 057, 863	$6, 935, 511 80	$9, 889, 034	$7, 575, 604 40
Two dollars.............	5, 892, 000	8, 710, 295 00	8, 232, 000	5, 971, 840 20	8, 752, 000	6, 860, 690 80
Five dollars............	11, 060, 000	11, 622, 443 50	19, 680, 000	8, 354, 565 00	14, 760, 000	10, 623, 470 00
Ten dollars	9, 280, 000	10, 193, 082 00	16, 520, 000	6, 241, 811 00	9, 160, 000	7, 086, 364 00
Twenty dollars	7, 400, 000	9, 649, 756 00	17, 360, 000	5, 687, 680 00	6, 240, 000	6, 111, 610 00
Fifty dollars	2, 400, 000	4, 059, 340 00	1, 400, 000	2, 114, 345 00	1, 200, 000	2, 306, 085 00
One hundred dollars ..	5, 007, 700	4, 593, 890 00	3, 052, 700	2, 293, 310 90	2, 944, 300	2, 794, 510 00
Five hundred dollars..	5, 650, 000	3, 959, 000 00	2, 300, 000	15, 645, 500 00	700, 000	5, 354, 000 00
One thousand dollars..	3, 900, 000	2, 042, 000 00	700, 000	19, 238, 000 00	900, 000	5, 406, 000 00
Five thousand dollars.	4, 005, 000	5, 000 00	1, 000, 000	4, 320, 000 00	....	225, 000 00
Ten thousand dollars .	3, 010, 000	50, 000 00	2, 000, 000	4, 500, 000 00	....	300, 000 00
Total............	64, 107, 833	64, 107, 833 00	81, 302, 563	81, 302, 563 00	54, 545, 334	54, 545, 334 00

Although the amount redeemed in 1881 is $26,757,229 less than in 1880, the number of notes constituting the amount is 1,617,045 greater. By virtue of a provision in the legislative, executive, and judicial appropriation bill for the current fiscal year making an appropriation of $50,000 "for the preparation and issue of new United States notes in place of worn and mutilated United States notes, and transportation of each to and from the Treasury," the express charges on worn and mutilated United States notes received for redemption in multiples of $500 since July 1, 1881, and on new United States notes returned, have been paid by the government. This appropriation was highly necessary, as no provision for the renewal of United States notes, without charge, had existed since 1875, and the condition of the circulation had much deteriorated in consequence. It has led to a considerable increase in redemptions, which will doubtless continue during the year. It is suggested that a similar appropriation for the next fiscal year be recommended by the Secretary.

The amount of United States notes presented for payment in coin during each month since the resumption of specie payments is shown by the following table:

Month.	1879.	1880.	1881.
January	$1,571,725	$71,500	$15,000
February	909,249	72,080	13,750
March	952,766	43,020	
April	690,773	16,000	
May	1,339,883	51,000	
June	2,503,302	47,200	
July	954,800	25,000	
August	981,400	22,000	
September	603,485	150,000	
October	740,295	9,000	
November	77,499	12,000	
December	122,359	25,000	

Redemptions have for the present entirely ceased, no notes having been presented for payment in coin since March 1, 1881. The entire amount redeemed in coin since January 1, 1879, a period of two years and nine months, is only $12,029,086, an average of less than $365,000 a month. The total redemptions thus far are less than 3½ per cent. of the United States notes outstanding, or a little more than one-tenth of one per cent. a month.

The amount of United States notes received in payment of duties on imports during each month since January 1, 1879, is as follows:

Month.	1879.	1880.	1881.
January	$6,864,839	$4,126,450	$1,689,728
February	9,340,452	4,477,161	2,049,856
March	11,919,876	3,702,737	1,890,813
April	10,562,006	3,231,897	1,310,292
May	9,703,566	2,888,133	1,402,118
June	9,236,778	3,951,588	1,479,506
July	10,588,145	4,029,892	1,641,006
August	11,261,307	2,844,858	1,872,788
September	12,506,018	2,241,305	1,476,118
October	9,281,243	1,802,288	
November	4,612,198	1,567,184	
December	3,051,219	1,405,964	

The aggregate amount so received is $160,050,101. The amount received during the year just ended is $19,528,788, which is $28,909,488 less than the amount received in the preceding year.

CLEARING-HOUSE TRANSACTIONS.

The transactions of the Treasury with the Clearing-House in New York during the last fifteen months are shown by the following statement:

Month.	Checks taken to clearing-house.	Checks received from clearing-house.	Balances paid clearing-house.	Balances received from clearing-house.
1880.				
July	$7,331,258 36	$25,917,765 27	$18,596,506 97	
August	7,446,734 73	28,782,183 30	21,382,304 60	$46,906 03
September	8,022,420 29	40,727,834 66	32,800,872 47	105,468 06
October	7,452,416 85	39,981,819 06	32,529,402 23	
November	7,249,489 67	21,201,962 43	14,098,675 26	146,212 50
December	6,381,584 70	32,258,363 82	26,024,473 16	47,694 04

18 Ab

Month.	Checks taken to clearing-house.	Checks received from clearing-house.	Balances paid clearing-house.	Balances received from clearing-house.
1881.				
January	$6,314,294 17	$26,861,820 38	$20,547,526 31	
February	11,901,271 88	20,385,496 47	12,392,579 44	$3,908,254 85
March	7,339,707 92	30,849,241 90	23,509,533 98	
April	4,162,802 18	39,433,300 07	35,270,556 79	
May	5,598,979 73	28,026,511 15	22,427,531 42	
June	4,030,937 00	19,642,352 81	15,611,615 81	
July	7,713,418 18	33,224,135 81	25,511,717 63	
August	12,066,887 20	22,850,716 21	11,838,531 12	1,354,792 11
September	9,571,313 04	42,436,882 28	32,929,946 85	64,377 61
Total	112,482,515 84	452,280,576 56	345,471,775 94	5,673,715 22

This statement may be thus summarized:

Cash paid to the Clearing-House in settlement of
  balances against the Treasury $345,471,775 94
Less cash received from the Clearing-House in settlement of balances in favor of the Treasury 5,673,715 22
                                             $339,798,060 72
Checks on banks sent to the Clearing-House....................... 112,482,515 84

Net amount of cash and checks sent to the Clearing-House.......... 452,280,576 56

Checks on the Assistant Treasurer U. S., New York, received from the
  Clearing-House... 452,280,576 56

The Treasury is almost invariably a debtor to the Clearing-House,
the aggregate balances against it during the fifteen months having
been $345,471,775.94 against balances of only $5,673,715.22 in its favor.
The Treasury membership of the Clearing-House has been of great advantage to both the Treasury and the banks in saving the useless handling of money, and in enabling the Treasury to conform to commercial
usage by accepting and collecting, without risk, drafts of banks and
bankers tendered in payment of public dues and for other purposes.

STANDARD SILVER DOLLARS.

The total amount of standard silver dollars coined to September 30,
1881, under the act of February 28, 1878, is $98,322,705, of which
$32,373,426, or nearly 33 per cent., is in circulation, and $65,949,279
remains in the Treasury. The amount coined during the last year was
$27,753,955, of which $9,589,420, or a little more than 34½ per cent., went
into circulation, and $18,164,535 remains in the Treasury. The amount
put into circulation in the preceding year was $11,956,680, or $2,367,260
more than in the year just closed, indicating a considerable falling off in
the demand. During the six months ending with June, 1881, the amount
in circulation ran down $445,775, but increased $4,250,091 in the next
three months. The amount going into circulation is invariably larger in
the last half of the calendar year than in the first half. This is largely
owing to the autumnal demand for Southern and Western exchange,
which is met to a considerable extent by shipments of silver dollars.
The dollars, being forwarded from the mints to all accessible points at
the expense of the government, for deposits of gold coin or currency with
any assistant treasurer, furnish a means by which exchange on any point
in the West or South can be obtained in New York without expense.
Silver certificates are paid out at the counters of the various sub-treasuries for deposits of gold coin with the assistant treasurer in New
York, but when required at any point at which there is no assistant
treasurer they are forwarded from the nearest sub-treasury at the ex-

pense of the person receiving them. For the purpose of placing funds at such points the silver dollars are therefore usually preferred. The dollars so placed are more likely to go into permanent circulation than those paid out in cities where there are assistant treasurers with whom they may at once be deposited for silver certificates. Any effort to put the dollars into actual circulation in such cities is frustrated by the return of the coins for certificates, which the holder is by law entitled to demand for them. As such attempts involve an unnecessary double handling of the coin by the Treasury, they have been generally abandoned, and when payments are to be made in silver the certificates are paid out in the first instance. Of the $98,322,705 in standard silver dollars coined, $72,001,777, or more than 73 per cent., has been paid out by the Treasury and mints. Of this latter amount $39,628,351 has been returned to the Treasury in payment of public dues or in exchange for silver certificates.

The following table gives the amount of silver dollars coined, on hand, distributed, and outstanding at the close of each month since the coinage was resumed in March, 1878:

Month.	Monthly coinage.	Coined to the end of the month.	Balance on hand at the close of the month.	Net distribution during the month.	Outstanding at the close of the month.
1878.					
March	$1,001,500	$1,001,500	$810,561	$190,939	$190,939
April	2,470,000	3,471,500	3,169,681	110,830	301,819
May	3,015,000	6,486,500	5,950,451	234,230	536,049
June	2,087,000	8,573,500	7,718,357	319,094	855,143
July	1,847,000	10,420,500	9,550,236	15,121	870,264
August	3,028,000	13,448,500	11,292,849	1,285,387	2,155,651
September	2,764,000	16,212,500	12,155,205	1,901,844	4,057,205
October	2,070,000	18,282,500	13,359,877	865,328	4,922,569
November	2,156,050	20,438,550	14,843,219	672,708	5,595,261
December	2,067,000	22,495,550	16,704,830	193,390	5,788,731
1879.					
January	2,066,200	24,555,750	18,025,228	139,806	5,982,837
February	2,132,000	26,687,750	20,049,181	703,042	6,632,549
March	2,087,200	28,774,950	21,799,206	337,175	6,975,744
April	2,381,000	31,155,950	23,909,047	181,159	7,156,963
May	2,330,000	33,485,950	26,386,154	....	7,099,795
June	2,315,050	35,801,000	26,353,589	285,506	7,443,411
July	1,650,000	37,451,000	29,347,203	661,383	8,105,799
August	2,787,050	40,238,050	30,962,254	1,171,997	9,275,796
September	2,396,050	42,634,100	31,806,774	1,551,530	10,827,328
October	2,572,100	45,206,200	32,203,358	2,175,516	13,002,842
November	2,499,000	47,705,200	33,503,888	1,198,470	14,201,312
December	2,350,450	50,055,650	33,827,552	2,526,786	16,728,098
1880.					
January	2,450,000	52,505,650	35,548,868	228,684	16,956,782
February	2,300,400	54,806,050	37,513,420	335,848	17,292,630
March	2,350,200	57,156,250	39,057,858	805,762	18,098,392
April	2,300,000	59,456,250	41,053,639	305,219	18,403,611
May	2,267,000	61,723,254	43,356,807	....	18,366,443
June	2,011,540	63,734,750	45,108,296	222,843	18,626,454
July	2,280,000	66,014,750	47,073,470	314,836	18,941,280
August	2,253,000	68,267,750	48,230,477	1,095,993	20,037,273
September	2,301,000	70,568,750	47,784,744	2,746,733	22,784,006
October	2,279,000	72,847,750	47,588,106	2,475,638	25,259,644
November	2,300,000	75,147,750	48,157,297	1,730,809	26,990,453
December	2,305,255	77,453,005	48,363,825	1,578,727	28,569,180
1881.					
January	2,300,000	79,753,005	51,445,339	....	28,307,666
February	2,307,000	82,060,005	53,771,356	....	28,288,649
March	2,299,500	84,359,505	55,905,617	165,239	28,453,888
April	2,300,000	86,659,505	58,341,491	....	28,318,014
May	2,300,000	88,959,505	60,968,897	....	27,960,068
June	2,413,200	91,372,705	63,249,300	192,797	28,123,405
July	3,250,000	93,622,705	65,130,646	368,654	28,492,059
August	2,300,000	95,922,705	66,300,847	1,129,799	29,621,858
September	2,400,000	98,322,705	65,949,279	2,751,568	32,373,426

The average monthly coinage has been $2,287,000, and the average net monthly issue $753,000.

The distribution of the standard silver dollars in the Treasury September 30 is shown by the statement below. Of the sixty-six million dollars on hand more than thirty millions are held by the mint and sub-treasury in San Francisco, and more than sixteen millions by the assistant treasurer in New York.

Treasury United States, Washington, D. C	$1,440,606
Sub-treasury United States, Baltimore, Md	443,311
Sub-treasury United States, Boston, Mass	1,053,939
Sub-treasury United States, Chicago, Ill	1,214,900
Sub-treasury United States, Cincinnati, Ohio	385,167
Sub-treasury United States, New Orleans, La	1,482,894
Sub-treasury United States, New York, N. Y	16,032,000
Sub-treasury United States, Philadelphia, Pa	5,870,190
Sub-treasury United States, San Francisco, Cal	12,315,000
Sub-treasury United States, Saint Louis, Mo	1,074,385
Depository United States, Tucson, Ariz	5,400
United States Assay-office, Helena, Mont	22,802
United States Assay-office, New York, N. Y	5,964
Mint United States, Carson, Nev	893,007
Mint United States, New Orleans, La	4,896,894
Mint United States, Philadelphia, Pa	1,005,250
Mint United States, San Francisco, Cal	18,097,040
Total	66,148,679

The difference of $199,400 between this and the preceding statement is the amount *in transitu.*

Of the 28,825,242 standard silver dollars put into circulation during the last year 12,600,314 were paid out at the counters of the various offices of the Treasury; 5,067,000 were forwarded by the mints in New Orleans, Philadelphia, and San Francisco for deposits with the assistant treasurers in the same cities; 10,102,428 were forwarded from the mints to banks and other private parties on orders from the Treasurer, for deposits with assistant treasurers, or remittances of money or checks to his office, and 1,055,500 were transferred from the mints under the Treasurer's direction to national bank depositaries and charged to them in their accounts with the government. During the same period $19,235,822 in silver dollars was returned to the Treasury in payment of dues or for silver certificates, making the net increase during the year in the amount outstanding $9,589,420.

SILVER CERTIFICATES.

There was a large increase during the fiscal year in the amount of silver certificates in circulation, the amount outstanding at the close of the year being $51,166,530 as compared with $12,374,270 outstanding June 30, 1880. This increase is due in part to the demand for notes for circulation, but chiefly to the operation of the departmental circular of September 18, 1880, under which exchange on the sub-treasuries in the West and South payable in silver certificates is furnished by the Department for deposits of gold coin with the assistant treasurer in New York. Under this circular large amounts of silver certificates, chiefly of the denominations of ten and twenty dollars, have been paid out at the sub-treasuries in New Orleans, Saint Louis, Chicago, and Cincinnati, for the purpose of moving the cotton and other crops. Since the close of the fiscal year the circulation of the certificates has still further increased; the amount now outstanding being $64,149,910, of which $11,309,470 is held by the Treasury. The amount of silver dollars in the Treasury at this date is $65,949,279, less than two million dollars in excess of the outstanding certificates. As the certificates cannot be issued in excess of the dollars held by the Treasury, the limit of their issue is likely soon to be reached, although, of course, the certificate s held by the Treasury in its cash can be paid out. Aside from this limitation, the issue of the silver certificates has little relation to the standard silver dollar. The Treasury pays them out because it finds it necessary to utilize in some way the enormous stock of silver which it is carrying, and they are taken by the public, without regard to the silver dollars behind them, because they constitute a convenient form of paper currency. To the extent of nearly two-thirds of the amount coined, the coinage and attempted circulation of the standard silver dollar have resulted simply in an addition to the paper circulation of the country. Whatever the ultimate result may be, the immediate effect has not been without positive advantages. The volume of the United States notes is limited by law, while the national banks do not find a sufficient profit in issuing circulation on United States bonds at present prices to induce them to supply the demand for additional paper circulation, caused by the increase of business. The issue of silver certificates, by meeting this demand, has averted what might have proved to be a serious public inconvenience.

The issues and redemptions of these certificates during the last fiscal year are shown by the following table:

Denomination.	Outstanding June 30, 1880.	Issued.		Redeemed.		Outstanding June 30, 1881.
		During fiscal year.	To June 30, 1881.	During fiscal year.	To June 30, 1881.	
Ten dollars	$2,147,340	$18,700,000	$20,874,000	$480,310	$506,970	$20,367,030
Twenty dollars	1,974,880	16,560,000	18,546,000	372,780	388,900	18,162,100
Fifty dollars	1,828,950	2,310,000	3,650,000	157,850	168,400	3,481,600
One hundred dollars	1,904,600	2,410,000	4,340,000	285,300	310,700	4,029,300
Five hundred dollars	1,229,500	632,000	3,650,000	215,000	2,003,500	1,646,500
One thousand dollars	3,789,000	300,000	10,870,000	609,000	7,390,000	3,480,000
Total	12,874,270	40,912,000	61,980,000	2,119,740	10,763,470	51,166,530

GOLD CERTIFICATES.

The amount of gold certificates issued and redeemed during each fiscal year from 1866 to 1881, the total amount issued and redeemed, and the amount outstanding at the close of each year, are exhibited in the following statement. None of these certificates have been issued since December 1, 1878, although the law authorizing their issue is unrepealed and may at any time be put in force. Only $5,782,920 was outstanding June 30, 1881, $2,221,680 having been redeemed during the year.

Period.	Issued during the fiscal year.	Total issued.	Redeemed during fiscal year.	Total redeemed.	Outstanding at the close of the fiscal year.
From Nov. 13, 1865, to June 30, 1866....	$98,493,660 00	$98,493,660 00	$87,545,800 00	$87,545,800 00	$10,947,860 00
Fiscal year 1867	109,121,620 00	207,615,280 00	101,295,900 00	188,841,700 00	18,773,580 00
Fiscal year 1868	77,960,400 00	285,575,680 00	79,055,340 00	267,897,040 00	17,678,640 00
Fiscal year 1869	80,663,160 00	366,238,840 00	65,256,620 00	333,153,660 00	33,086,180 00
Fiscal year 1870	76,731,060 00	442,969,900 00	75,370,120 00	408,422,730 00	34,547,120 00
Fiscal year 1871	56,577,000 00	499,546,900 00	71,237,820 00	479,660,500 00	19,825,300 00
Fiscal year 1872	63,229,500 00	562,776,400 00	51,029,500 00	530,690,100 00	32,086,300 00
Fiscal year 1873	55,570,500 00	618,346,900 00	48,196,800 00	578,886,900 00	39,460,000 00
Fiscal year 1874	81,117,780 46	699,464,680 46	97,752,680 46	676,639,580 46	22,825,100 00
Fiscal year 1875	70,250,100 00	769,714,780 46	71,278,900 00	747,918,480 46	21,796,300 00
Fiscal year 1876	90,619,100 00	860,333,880 46	83,734,000 00	831,652,480 46	28,681,400 00
Fiscal year 1877	58,141,200 00	918,475,080 46	45,250,000 00	876,902,480 46	41,572,600 00
Fiscal year 1878	50,342,400 00	968,817,480 46	47,548,000 00	924,450,480 46	44,367,000 00
Fiscal year 1879	12,317,400 00	981,134,880 46	41,370,700 00	965,721,180 46	15,413,700 00
Fiscal year 1880	....	981,134,880 46	7,409,100 00	973,130,280 46	8,004,600 00
Fiscal year 1881	....	981,134,880 46	2,221,680 00	975,351,960 46	5,782,920 00

CLEARING-HOUSE CERTIFICATES.

The clearing-house certificates outstanding at the close of the fiscal year amounted to only $11,615,000, the smallest amount outstanding at the close of any fiscal year since their issue began in 1873.

These certificates are issued under section 5193 of the Revised Statutes (act of June 8, 1872), for deposits of United States notes with the Treasurer and assistant treasurers, and are held by national banks as a part of their lawful money reserves. The falling off in their use since the resumption of specie payments is due to the extensive conversion of the bank reserves into specie and the increased demand for notes for circulation. Since the close of the fiscal year the amount actually outstanding has still further decreased, being only $8,185,000 on the thirtieth of September.

The following table shows the total amount issued and redeemed, and the amount outstanding at the close of each fiscal year from 1873 to 1881:

Fiscal year.	Total amount issued.	Total amount redeemed.	Outstanding as shown by the Treasurer's books.
1873	$57,240,000	$25,430,000	$31,810,000
1874	137,905,000	78,915,000	58,990,000
1875	219,000,000	159,955,000	59,045,000
1876	301,400,000	268,260,000	33,140,000
1877	378,285,000	324,305,000	53,980,000
1878	464,065,000	418,720,000	46,245,000
1879	554,730,000	525,400,000	29,330,000
1880	601,785,000	588,660,000	17,125,000
1881	612,850,000	601,235,000	11,615,000

FRACTIONAL SILVER COIN.

The amount of fractional silver coin in the Treasury, which on September 30, 1880, was $24,723,892.68, steadily ran up until August 1, 1881, when it reached $27,295,486.63. Within the last two months it has decreased, in consequence of the heavy shipments from this office, and now stands at $26,343,477.17, an increase of $1,619,584.49 in the last year but a decrease of $952,009.46 since August 1. Prior to March last no provision existed for the free distribution of fractional silver coins, and persons desiring them had to pay the charges for their transportation from the Treasury, although the minor coins of five cents and under could be obtained from the mints without expense. Under the operation of these causes and of the act of June 9, 1879, providing for the exchange of fractional silver coin for lawful money, the amount in the Treasury has increased more than $20,000,000 in the last three years, while the minor coin has run down nearly a million dollars within two years, although neither was coined to any extent, the bronze cents alone excepted. The coinage of fractional silver virtually ceased in 1878. The sundry civil appropriation act of March 3, 1881, however, contained an appropriation of $20,000, which was made immediately available, for the payment of the charges for the transportation of fractional silver to those applying for it. The regulations issued to carry the law into effect provided for the free shipment of the coins only from this office. Under this provision the shipments of fractional silver have largely increased, though its full effect was not felt until after the close of the fiscal year.

During the fiscal year there were shipped 1,339 packages, containing $1,106,467.85. During the next three months 1,524 packages, containing $1,256,445.93, were forwarded, of which $607,689.40 was shipped during the month of September. Of the $2,362,913.78 sent out during the last fifteen months, $1,717,395.18 or nearly three-fourths, was forwarded in the six and one-half months succeeding the date of the circular providing for the transportation of the coins at the expense of the government. The free distribution of the coins contributes greatly to the public convenience and it would be well to continue the appropriation for the purpose. At the present rate of shipment the appropriation already made will not last through the fiscal year. The large profit made by the government on the coinage of fractional silver warrants the pursuance of a liberal policy in its distribution and redemption.

MINOR COIN.

The amount of minor coin in the Treasury, which steadily increased from $157,000 in 1876 to $1,524,000 in 1879, has greatly decreased in the last two years. The amount now on hand is $552,585.06, as compared with $1,063,665.22 on September 30, 1880, and $1,524,700.57 on the corresponding date in 1879. The decrease within the last year has been entirely in the five-cent nickel coins, the amount of one-cent copper-nickel, two and three cent pieces on hand having slightly increased, as they are uncurrent, and are retained unissued. The amount of five-cent coins now held is $183,871.75, against $728,442.15 in 1880, and $1,184,232.95 in 1879. More than a million dollars in these coins has gone into circulation within the last two years. If the demand continues at this rate the supply will be exhausted in less than four months, and it will be necessary to resume their coinage, which virtually ceased in 1877. Until within the last six months these coins were forwarded to those ordering them, at the expense of the Mint for transportation, as authorized by section 3529 of the Revised Statutes. March 28, 1881, this practice was discontinued, and the public was notified by a departmental circular that the coins could be obtained only at the counters of the Treasurer and the assistant treasurers. Under this arrangement persons outside of cities in which there are offices of the Treasury are compelled to order the coins through their correspondents in those cities, and to bear the expense of their transportation.

The tendency of this change in a long-established practice has been to lessen the orders for the five-cent coins, of which there were plenty on hand, and to increase the orders for the bronze one-cent pieces, which, though often less desirable, can still be obtained directly from the Mint without expense for express charges, and which the government is compelled to coin to supply the demand, at a considerable expense for the metal and labor of coinage. It is recommended that the former practice be restored, and that the five-cent coins be again furnished by the Mint, and at its expense, to be paid from the minor coinage profit fund, the Mint to be kept supplied as heretofore by transfers of the coin from the Treasury.

The bronze two-cent pieces, whose coinage was discontinued by the coinage act of 1873, are used for recoinage into cents, and the supply in the Philadelphia Mint is intended for that purpose. The total amount coined was only $912,020, of which $695,030, or more than three fourths, was coined within three years from their authorization in 1864.

The amount of each denomination of minor coin held by each of the several offices of the Treasury September 30, 1881, is as follows:

Office by which held.	Five-cent nickel.	Three-cent nickel.	Two-cent bronze.	One-cent bronze, copper-nickel, and copper.	Mixed.	Total.
Treasury U. S., Washington.	$1,148 00	$2,652 00	$400 00	$345 00	$992 23	$5,537 23
Sub-treasury U. S., Baltimore	5,650 00	120 00	819 00	825 29	....	7,405 29
Sub-treasury U. S., New York	85,745 00	9,360 00	2,820 00	7,270 00	....	105,195 00
Sub-treasury U. S., Philadelphia	67,644 00	95,968 00	....	56,851 25	....	220,463 25
Sub-treasury U. S., Boston..	8,801 00	14,772 00	31 00	5,804 00	590 19	29,998 19
Sub-treasury U. S., Cincinnati	3,630 00	6,500 00	550 00	430 00	348 00	11,458 00
Sub-treasury U. S., Chicago.	1,050 00	9,510 00	....	155 00	2 32	10,717 32
Sub-treasury U. S., Saint Louis	....	5,812 31	113 90	2,274 44	....	8,200 65
Sub-treasury U. S., New Orleans	3,188 90	874 80	303 30	871 05	....	5,223 05
Sub-treasury U. S., San Francisco	5,650 00	2,100 00	200 00	1,050 00	....	9,000 00
Depository U. S., Tucson	....	....	....	....	136 13	136 13
Mint U. S., Philadelphia	1,389 85	1,960 80	10,620 98	122,997 26	....	136,948 89
Mint U. S., Denver	....	....	....	....	67 95	67 95
Assay-office U.S., New York.	....	....	....	....	06	06
Assay-office U. S., Helena...	....	....	....	....	2,224 05	2,224 05
Total	188,871 75	149,629 91	15,849 18	198,873 29	4,380 93	552,595 06

FRACTIONAL CURRENCY.

The redemptions of fractional currency have declined to a very low point, the amount redeemed during the year ending September 30 being but $83,434.35 out of $15,557,878.70 nominally outstanding a year ago, or a little more than one-half of 1 per cent., as compared with $189,628.89 for the preceding year. Of the $41,508,737.48 outstanding April 17, 1876, the date of the act authorizing the issue of fractional silver coin in exchange for fractional paper currency, $26,034,293.13 has been redeemed and $15,474,444.35 remains outstanding. Of this latter amount more than $14,000,000 has been lost or destroyed, and will constitute a profit to the Treasury. The steady decline in redemptions since the date of the cessation of the issue of fractional currency is shown by the following statement giving the redemptions for each year ending September 30, since 1876:

1877	$11,071,773 35
1878	2,489,212 69
1879	549,921 99
1880	189,628 89
1881	83,434 35

The total amount of each issue, the date of its discontinuance, and the amount and percentage outstanding September 30, 1881, are shown by the following statement:

Issue.	Total issued.	Issue ceased.	Outstanding September 30, 1881.	Percentage outstanding.
First	$20,215,635 00	May 27, 1863	$4,283,207 25	21.18
Second	23,164,483 65	Feb. 23, 1867	3,108,163 05	13.41
Third	86,115,028 80	Apr. 16, 1869	2,991,247 70	3.43
Fourth	176,567,032 00	Feb. 16, 1875	3,726,318 25	2.11
Fifth	62,661,900 00	Feb. 15, 1876	1,362,508 10	2.17
Total	368,724,079 45	....	15,474,444 35	4.19

Contrary to the usual rule, the percentage outstanding is in direct proportion to the age of the issues, varying from 21 per cent. for the first issue of postal currency, which ceased in 1863, to a little more than 2 per cent. for the last two issues, which ceased in 1875 and 1876. The percentage outstanding of the aggregate amount issued is nearly four and one fifth and cannot in all likelihood ever be reduced below 4 per cent.

MUTILATED, STOLEN, AND COUNTERFEIT CURRENCY.

There were detected by the counters of this office in remittances of currency received for redemption during the fiscal year, $7,434 in counterfeit United States notes; $449.45 in counterfeit fractional currency, and $3,721 in counterfeit national-bank notes, all of which were branded and returned to the persons from whom they were received. The counterfeit national-bank notes were from fifty-seven different plates. The amount of each denomination was as follows: $76 in twos; $1,275 in fives; $560 in tens; $560 in twenties; $150 in fifties; $1,100 in hundreds. There was also detected and rejected $450 in national-bank notes which had been stolen when unsigned and put in circulation with forged signatures. There was deducted, on account of mutilations, from the face value of United States notes redeemed during the year $9,125; from fractional currency $202.12, and from notes of failed, liquidating, and reducing national banks, $86.10, making the total deductions on this account $306,776.98 on notes of the face value of $2,300,447,850.34 redeemed.

The rule subjecting mutilated United States currency on its redemption to a discount proportioned to the part lacking is based on a false analogy to coined money, is unjust to the public and expensive to the Treasury, and should be modified. Almost the entire amount deducted is on account of mutilations which are plainly caused by ordinary wear and tear. The application of the rule requires a critical examination of each note and adds largely to the expense of redemption. A rule that fragments equal to three-fifths of whole notes would be redeemed in full, that half notes would be redeemed at half of the face value, and that fragments less than half would not be redeemed at all unless accompanied by proof of the absolute destruction of the missing parts, would be perfectly safe and fair. More than a thousand million dollars of national-bank notes have been redeemed under a similar rule, without loss to the banks or complaint from the public.

Of the stolen national-bank notes in circulation a part was stolen from the Treasury and a part from the banks of issue. For the redemption of the former an appropriation of $5,000 was made by the act of June 20, 1878, but it was not sufficient for the purpose and has been exhausted. A further appropriation sufficient for the redemption of the remainder of these notes should be made. There would seem to be no question that the loss should be borne by the government, through the dishonesty of one of whose employees the notes were stolen, rather than by innocent holders, who have no sufficient means of determining the character of the notes, which are genuine in all respects save the signatures. The notes stolen from the banks of issue are rejected under a decision of a State court that a State bank was not responsible for notes signed by but one of its officers, and put in circulation with forged signatures. It is doubtful whether this decision properly applies to national-bank notes, which have had the seal of the United States and the signatures of the Treasurer of the United States and of the Register of the Treasury imprinted on them before being forwarded to the bank and which have been charged to the bank on the books of the department and receipted for by it. As a matter of equity the loss ought to be borne by the banks through whose negligence, either actual or con-structive, the notes were stolen, rather than by the public.

SALES OF EXCHANGE.

During the fifteen months ending September 30, 1881, there was furnished to the commercial public through the various offices of the Treasury, exchange between different cities of the Union amounting to $52,266,714, exclusive of the standard silver dollars forwarded from the mints for deposits with assistant treasurers. Under the circular of September 18, 1880, $23,500,000 in gold coin was deposited with the assistant treasurer in New York, for which telegraphic orders, payable in silver certificates, were drawn by the Treasurer on assistant treasurers as follows: on New Orleans, $10,300,000; on Saint Louis, $7,110,000; on Cincinnati, $4,345,000; and on Chicago, $1,805,000. The orders for standard silver dollars under the same circular amounted to but $50,000, as the circular provides only for the payment of the coins at the counters of the sub-treasuries, while they are forwarded from the mints to any point under other regulations at the expense of the government. Under the circular of September 19, 1879, $7,026,500 in gold coin was paid or forwarded by the mint in Philadelphia on orders from the Treasurer for deposits of legal-tender notes with the assistant treasurer in New York. There was deposited with the same officer $12,140,000, for which tele-graphic orders, payable in gold coin, were issued by the Treasurer on the assistant treasurers in the following cities: Philadelphia, $6,540,000; New Orleans, $3,350,000, which was sold for a premium of $2,067.89; and San Francisco, $2,250,000. Currency exchange to the amount of $190,214 was drawn in the same manner. For the purpose of supplying their offices with funds the assistant treasurer in San Francisco was furnished with $9,000,000 in New York exchange, and the depositary at Tucson with $100,000 in New York exchange, and $200,000 in San Francisco exchange, to be disposed of for currency. The actual sales of exchange at these points during the fifteen months were $9,653,000, a balance of unsold exchange having been carried over from the preceding year.

The extent of these transactions, averaging more than $800,000 a week, and involving the transfer of funds between the various commer-cial centers of the country, illustrates the close connection between the necessary operations of the Treasury and the business of the country.

DRAFTS AND CHECKS.

During the fiscal year there were drawn and forwarded to the persons entitled to receive them 36,345 drafts on warrants of the Secretary of the Treasury, 14,713 drafts on warrants of the Postmaster-General, 305,101 checks in payment of quarterly interest on registered stock of the funded loans, and 42,992 transfer checks on assistant treasurers, making, in all, 399,151.

DEPOSITARY BANKS.

The receipts of public money by depositary banks during the fiscal year were $131,820,002.20, and the total amount received by them since 1863, $3,669,461,046.61. The average weekly balance held by them dur-ing the year to the credit of the Treasurer was a little less than eight million dollars, which, with other balances to the credit of disbursing officers, is secured by the deposit with the Treasurer of United States bonds to the amount of $15,295,500, and of $350,000 in personal bonds. There were 130 national banks acting as depositaries of public moneys at the close of the fiscal year, a decrease of one during the year.

The receipts and disbursements of public funds by bank depositaries during the last eighteen fiscal years have been as follows:

Fiscal year.	Receipts.	Funds transferred to depositary banks.	Funds transferred to the Treasury by depositary banks.	Drafts drawn on depositary banks.	Balance at close of the year.
1864	$153,393,108 71	$816,000 00	$85,507,674 98	$28,726,805 88	$39,976,738 75
1865	987,564,619 14	8,110,294 70	582,697,912 72	415,897,767 91	36,045,862 06
1866	497,566,676 42	13,523,972 62	363,085,565 65	149,772,756 11	34,296,319 34
1867	351,737,083 83	8,405,903 83	331,689,872 57	37,218,612 76	20,182,821 47
1868	225,244,144 75	9,404,392 00	215,311,460 69	22,218,187 92	22,301,709 61
1869	105,160,573 67	10,052,199 44	114,748,877 24	14,890,463 75	8,875,141 73
1870	136,084,041 79	2,466,531 06	111,123,926 18	11,818,228 61	8,483,549 79
1871	99,299,840 85	2,638,129 45	80,428,544 04	13,790,901 01	7,197,015 04
1872	106,104,855 16	3,058,444 65	94,938,603 76	13,635,887 49	7,777,873 66
1873	160,692,743 98	9,064,842 49	108,680,786 76	16,110,519 07	62,185,153 64
1874	91,108,846 70	2,729,958 81	134,869,112 57	13,364,554 52	7,790,292 08
1875	98,228,249 53	1,787,445 80	82,184,304 05	13,657,678 25	11,914,094 80
1876	97,402,227 57	2,445,451 49	89,981,146 99	13,909,616 83	7,670,920 13
1877	106,470,261 22	2,353,196 29	94,276,400 35	14,862,200 88	7,555,776 41
1878	90,781,053 48	2,385,920 88	90,177,963 35	12,606,870 60	6,937,916 32
1879	109,397,525 67	6,890,480 06	100,408,469 29	16,544,058 34	7,183,403 42
1880	119,483,171 94	6,489,634 17	109,641,232 84	15,625,023 03	7,996,952 96
1882	131,820,002 30	5,646,092 46	118,143,794 91	18,568,772 82	8,082,589 79
Total	3,089,461,046 61	98,145,887 70	2,816,744,577 84	841,928,805 68	

RETIREMENT OF BONDS.

During the year ending September 30, 1881, there were redeemed and paid for by this office called United States bonds, on which interest had ceased, of the face value of $75,223,200. The proceeds, including interest, amounted to $76,556,772.36. United States bonds to the amount of $28,327,650 were purchased during the year for the sinking fund, at a cost, including accrued interest and premiums, of $29,083,821.36.

PACIFIC RAILROAD SINKING FUNDS.

There are held at the date of this report on account of the Pacific Railroad sinking funds, established by the act approved May 7, 1878 (20 Statutes, 56), bonds as follows:

For the Union Pacific Railroad Company.

Pacific railway bonds, currency sixes	$361,000
Funded loan of 1891, 3½ per cents	256,450
Funded loan of 1907, 4 per cents	32,650
	$650,100

For the Central Pacific Railroad Company.

Pacific railway bonds, currency sixes	$444,000
Funded loan of 1891, 3½ per cents	194,900
Funded loan of 1907, 4 per cents	199,100
	$838,000

Bonds of the funded loan of 1881, to the amount of $256,450 held for the Union Pacific Railroad Company, and $194,900 for the Central Pacific Railroad Company, bearing five per cent. interest, were continued at 3½ per cent.

TRUST FUNDS.

The Indian Trust Fund.

The bonds and stocks of the Indian Trust Fund, at the close of the fiscal year, in the custody of this office, in conformity with the act of Congress of June 10, 1876 (19 Statutes, 58), amounted to $4,186,366.83½. Of this amount $2,466,550 was in United States bonds, as follows:

Loan of July and August, 1861	$500
Pacific railway bonds, currency sixes	280,000
Funded loan of 1891, 3½ per cents	2,186,050
	$2,466,550

In pursuance of a letter from the Secretary of the Interior, dated March 21, 1881, bonds of the funded loan of 1881, then held for the fund, amounting to $2,850, were withdrawn and sold, and the amount deposited in the Treasury to the credit of the Secretary of the Interior, trustee of the Shawnee Indians, for the purpose of reimbursing certain purchasers of lands from the Shawnee Indians, for which the government could give no valid title.

In pursuance of authority from the Secretary of the Interior, the remaining bonds of the funded loan of 1881, amounting to $2,186,050, were continued at 3½ per cent., and on the 11th day of July, 1881, under directions from the same officer, were forwarded to the assistant treasurer in New York, and sold at a premium of $44,971, and the proceeds, $2,231,021, deposited in the Treasury, as provided for in the act of Congress of April 1, 1880, in reference to such deposits in lieu of investments.

On the 1st day of July, 1881, the $500 bond of the loan of July and August, 1861, was, by request of the Secretary of the Interior, delivered to the Secretary of the Treasury for redemption, and the proceeds deposited in the Treasury to the credit of the former officer as trustee of various Indian tribes.

The only United States bonds belonging to the Indian Trust Fund at the date of this report are Pacific Railway bonds, known as currency sixes.

The amount of bonds of the Nashville and Chattanooga Railroad Company held for the Indian Trust Fund at the close of the fiscal year 1880 was $512,000. Of this amount, bonds amounting to $391,000 were due and payable July 1, 1881, and were transmitted to the assistant treasurer in New York, for collection, together with coupons attached and detached amounting to $15,360. The amount of the principal was deposited in the Treasury in accordance with the act of April 1, 1880; the interest was deposited to the credit of the Secretary of the Interior, trustee. The remaining bonds, $121,000 in amount, are due July 1, 1882. Current interest is paid on presentation of the coupons.

Non-interest paying bonds are held, belonging to the Indian Trust Fund, as follows: Arkansas funded debt, $168,000; Florida State stocks, $132,000; Louisiana State stocks, $37,000; South Carolina State stocks, $125,000; Tennessee State stocks, $335,666.66⅔; Virginia State stocks, $581,800; Virginia, Ohio and Chesapeake Canal bonds, $13,000.

North Carolina State stocks are held amounting to $192,000, on a portion of which interest is paid at irregular intervals by the receiver of the North Carolina Railroad Company.

There are also held $6,000 in Wabash and Erie Canal bonds, on which interest is paid semi-annually, and $8,350.17 in Maryland State stocks, on which interest is paid quarterly.

American Printing-House for the Blind.

Under the act of March 3, 1879 (20 Statutes, 467), $250,000 United States four per cent. bonds are held in the name of the Secretary of the Treasury, trustee, "to promote the education of the blind," the interest on which is paid to the trustees of the American Printing-House for the Blind, in Louisville, Ky., in conformity with that act.

Pennsylvania Company.

Under the provisions of department circular No. 146, dated November 29, 1876, $200,000, in registered bonds of the funded loan of 1891, are held in trust for the Pennsylvania Company for the security of un-appraised dutiable merchandise and dutiable merchandise in bond.

Manhattan Savings Institution.

United States bonds issued to replace those alleged to have been stolen from the vaults of the Manhattan Savings Institution, New York, are held in this office to the amount of $250,000 to protect the United States from loss, as provided by the act of December 19, 1878 (20 Statutes, 589).

Cincinnati Chamber of Commerce.

Forty thousand dollars in United States four per cent. bonds, in the name of the Treasurer of the United States, in trust for the Cincinnati Chamber of Commerce and Merchants' Exchange, are held in this office in pursuance of a contract between the Secretary of the Treasury and the Cincinnati Chamber of Commerce and Merchants' Exchange, made under the authority of a joint resolution of Congress approved February 27, 1879 (20 Statutes, 488), being the investment of a partial pay-ment for the site of the old post-office and custom-house in the city of Cincinnati. The bonds are to be sold, and the proceeds applied in pay-ment of the property named when a deed of conveyance is executed.

UNITED STATES BONDS HELD FOR NATIONAL BANKS.

At the close of the fiscal year 1880, the United States bonds held in trust for national banks amounted to $376,429,050. Of this amount $361,652,050 was held to secure circulation, and $14,777,000 to secure public moneys.

The bonds held to secure circulation were of the following classes:

Loan of February, 1861	$2,092,000
Loan of July and August, 1861	34,249,050
Loan of 1863 (8ls)	17,329,100
Consols of 1867	3,000
Consols of 1868	15,000
Ten-forties of 1864	1,379,900
Funded loan of 1881	138,378,750
Funded loan of 1891	37,760,950
Funded loan of 1907	126,076,300
Pacific Railway bonds	4,368,000
Total	361,652,050

During the fiscal year all of the bonds known as the sixes of 1880 and 1881, held to secure circulation, included in the first three classes above given, aggregating $53,670,150, having been called for payment or con-tinuance, were withdrawn, excepting $298,500. Of the $138,378,750 United States bonds of the funded loan of 1881, held for the same pur-pose, all were withdrawn excepting $43,814,950. A large proportion of all these bonds was continued at the rate of three and one-half per cen-tum per annum, and redeposited, as shown in the table in the appendix.

In addition to the large amounts withdrawn and deposited in these transactions, bonds of the funded loan of 1891, four and one-half per cents., and of the funded loan of 1907, four per cents., have been depos-ited and withdrawn to an aggregate of $75,548,200.

The amount of bonds deposited during the fiscal year was $276,899,700; of bonds withdrawn, $277,527,350, so that the total movement of United States bonds held in trust for national banks was $554,427,050.

SEMI-ANNUAL DUTY.

The semi-annual duty assessed upon and collected from the national banks by the Treasurer of the United States for the fiscal year is as follows:

On circulation	$3,121,374 33
On deposits	4,940,945 12
On capital	431,233 10
Total	8,493,552 55

This is the largest amount of semi-annual duty assessed and collected in one year since the establishment of the national banking system. It exceeds the amount for the fiscal year 1880 by $901,782.12, and for the fiscal year 1879 by $1,772,315.88.

The total amount of semi-annual duty collected by this office from the national banks for the fiscal years 1864 to 1881, as fully shown in the appendix, is:

On circulation	$49,062,536 26
On deposits	52,644,349 23
On capital	7,148,136 41
Total	108,855,021 90

THE DEPOSIT AND DISBURSEMENT OF THE POSTAL REVENUES.

The first section of the act of March 3, 1849, as incorporated into section 3617 of the Revised Statutes, requires that "the gross amount of all moneys received from whatever source for the use of the United States * * * shall be paid by the officer or agent receiving the same into the Treasury, at as early a day as practicable, without any abatement or deduction on account of salary, fees, costs, charges, expenses, or claim of any description whatever." From this requirement the revenues of the Post Office are, however, excepted. By virtue of this exception the greater part of the postal revenues is received and disbursed by postmasters without actually going into the Treasury at all, being carried into and out of the Treasurer's accounts by warrants for the gross amounts involved issued at the end of each quarter. During the last fiscal year, of aggregate revenues amounting to nearly $40,000,000, only $15,000,000, or about two-fifths, was deposited in the Treasury, and of this amount more than three million dollars was appropriated by the government to make good the deficiency in the postal revenues.

Since the close of the fiscal year the system of making payments by drafts of the Postmaster-General on postmasters, which had grown up without any specific warrant of law, has been abolished; but even after this change nearly half of the revenues will continue to be disbursed outside of the Treasury. This consists of funds expended by postmasters, without draft or warrant, for the expenses of their offices and for salaries of postal employees, on vouchers which are charged in their accounts with the department. It is evident that disbursements so made from funds already in the postmaster's possession, cannot be so efficiently controlled as disbursements which can be made only upon a warrant previously issued by the head of the department. The Treasurer regards the requirement of the act of 1849, that the public moneys shall be deposited in the Treasury without diminution in any way as most salutary and important, and he believes that there is no sufficient reason for excepting from it the public moneys collected by the Post-Office Department. To correct this, it would be necessary to repeal the clause in section 3617 of the Revised Statutes making the exception, and, if practicable, section 3861, permitting postmasters to pay their expenses directly out of their receipts, as well as section 4056, authorizing the transfer to contractors by means of "collection orders" of debts due to the Post-Office Department.

One other change is required to bring the Post Office under the system of accountability which applies to every other department. The revenues of the Post Office, unlike those of any other department, are not deposited to the credit of the Treasurer in his general account, but are carried to his credit in a special fund, over which the Treasury has no control. They are drawn out, not as the other funds of the government are, by the warrant of the Secretary of the Treasury countersigned by the First Comptroller, but by the warrant of the Postmaster-General countersigned by the Auditor of the Treasury for the Post-Office Department. To secure efficient control and uniform accountability they should, in the Treasurer's opinion, be deposited like all other revenues, without abatement, to the credit of the Treasurer's regular account, and be drawn out only on the warrant of the Secretary of the Treasury, based upon the requisition of the Postmaster-General.

THE REDEMPTION OF NATIONAL-BANK NOTES.

The amount of national-bank notes redeemed during the fiscal year shows a still further decrease as compared with previous years. The amount received for redemption was $59,650,259.43, the smallest amount received in any year since the establishment of the present system of redemption, and two million dollars less than the amount received during the preceding fiscal year. In accordance with the recommendation made in the Treasurer's last annual report, the order requiring the charges for the transportation of national-bank notes for redemption to be paid by the senders, which had already been modified so as to permit the charges on notes clearly unfit for circulation to be paid from the 5 per cent. redemption fund, was revoked January 13, 1881, and since that date the transportation charges on all bank notes, whether fit or unfit for circulation, received by the Treasurer in multiples of $1,000, have been defrayed out of the 5 per cent. fund. The effect of this order was shown in an increase of more than 60 per cent. in the redemptions of the last half of the fiscal year as compared with the preceding six months. This increase was entirely in worn, defaced, and mutilated notes, the notes fit for circulation assorted having fallen off $647,000 in the same time.

Of the $46,844,300 in notes assorted and charged to the banks of issue, $6,763,600 were fit and $40,080,700 unfit for circulation. The proportion of notes fit for circulation is much smaller than in any preceding year. In the fiscal year 1878, out of $204,022,700 assorted, $152,437,300, or nearly three-fourths, consisted of notes fit for circulation, while during the last year they constituted but a little more than one-seventh of the amount redeemed. This falling off is undoubtedly due to the increased activity of business.

The proportion of notes of failed, liquidating, and reducing banks was greater than during any preceding year, the amount redeemed, which consisted principally of notes of reducing banks, being $12,219,750, or more than one-fourth as great as the amount assorted and charged to the banks of issue. In no preceding year did this proportion reach one-seventh. This increase was due to the extensive reduction of bank circulation last spring during the pendency of the funding bill, when 140 banks within fifteen days surrendered nearly $19,000,000 of their circu-*lation by depositing lawful money for its retirement under the fourth section of the act of June 20, 1874. The redemptions of this class of notes were increased by the fact that, as soon as practicable after the veto of the funding bill, the banks that had just reduced their circulation began to increase it again—at the expense of the government for preparing the notes—many of them upon the self-same bonds which they had just withdrawn. A large share of the newly issued notes immediately came in for redemption and was charged to the lawful money deposits previously made. In all cases where these notes were received in separate packages or in blocks the senders were required to pay the express charges on them, but in most instances they were so mixed with other notes that they could not be separated, and the charges for transporting and assorting them were defrayed out of the 5 per cent. fund. By this means the banks which thus reduced and increased their circulation were enabled to escape the expense of redeeming their notes, and to throw it upon the banks which maintained their full circulation. The amount of notes of reducing banks redeemed ran up from $4,590,600 during the eight months preceding the large reduction of circulation to $7,629,150 during the remaining four months of the fiscal year, and they still constitute about two-ninths of the national-bank notes redeemed.

Aside from the mere difficulty of properly apportioning the expenses of redemption, the Treasurer is more firmly than ever of the conviction that the power now possessed by the national banks of throwing up their circulation at will is wrong in principle, unnecessary, and dangerous. Under a sound system of currency the circulation can be reduced only by the act of the holders in presenting it for redemption. Under the present system the issuers can suddenly and arbitrarily contract it to any extent; and it may be for their interest to do this when there is a legitimate demand for all the currency in circulation or even more. There may be—in fact often is—a profit to the banks in withdrawing and selling their bonds when the circulation is already deficient. A bank, having issued circulating notes, should be held responsible for them until they are redeemed or it goes out of business. There is no sound reason why, while continuing to do business, it should be permitted to throw the burden of the redemption of its promissory notes upon the United States, and there is no obligation resting upon the United States to assume that burden. The privilege of surrendering circulation by depositing lawful money for its redemption is not necessary to correct redundancy in the circulation, since any real redundancy will be naturally corrected by the return of the notes by the holders. If a bank finds that its issues are being redeemed so rapidly as to destroy the profit, the obvious remedy is to refrain from reissuing the redeemed notes and to retire them as permitted by section 5167 of the Revised Statutes, which provides for their surrender in sums of $1,000. Nor would the withdrawal of the privilege prevent banks from winding up their business and going into liquidation, inasmuch as the surrender of circulation by liquidating banks is made under prior and distinct provisions of law (sections 5220, 5221, and 5222, Revised Statutes).

Notwithstanding the decrease in redemptions and the increase in the proportion of notes of failed, liquidating, and reducing banks, on which no assessment can be levied, there was a slight decrease in the rate for the expenses of assorting as compared with the previous year. The number of notes assorted was 6,591,178, of which 539,245 were fit, and 6,051,933 unfit for circulation. The "costs for assorting," including salaries of bookkeepers, clerks, counters, and assorters, in the offices of the Treasurer and of the Comptroller of the Currency, printing and binding, stationery, and incidental expenses, were $92,368.26, making the average rate for each thousand notes $14.01½, against $14.38½ for the fiscal year 1880.   The "charges for transportation" were $33,843.86, which, when assessed upon $46,844,300, redeemed and assorted, makes an average rate of 72¼ cents for each $1,000, as against 63 $\frac{195}{1000}$ cents for the preceding year.   The increase is due to the payment out of the 5 per cent. fund of the charges for transportation on all the notes received during the last half of the fiscal year.   The following statement shows, in a summary form, the amount of notes of each class assorted and the expenses of redemption during each of the seven years which have elapsed since the passage of the act of June 20, 1874:

Fiscal year.	Notes fit for circulation.	Notes unfit for circulation.	Notes of failed, liquidating, and reducing banks.	Total redeemed and assorted.	Total expenses of redemption.
1875	$15, 213, 500	$115, 109, 445	$6, 579, 217	$136, 902, 162	$290, 965 37
1876	97, 478, 700	78, 643, 155	24, 927, 900	201, 049, 755	365, 193 81
1877	151, 842, 700	62, 518, 600	24, 439, 700	238, 801, 000	357, 066 10
1878	151, 786, 600	51, 629, 800	11, 852, 100	215, 268, 500	317, 942 48
1879	112, 293, 000	40, 162, 000	8, 281, 550	160, 736, 550	240, 940 95
1880	24, 977, 600	29, 860, 000	6, 500, 800	61, 338, 400	143, 728 39
1881	6, 763, 600	46, 080, 700	12, 219, 750	59, 064, 050	126, 212 12
Total......	560, 355, 700	418, 003, 700	94, 801, 017	1, 073, 160, 417	1, 842, 057 72

The third section of the act of June 20, 1874, although requiring each national bank to "keep and have on deposit in the Treasury of the United States, in lawful money of the United States, a sum equal to five per centum of its circulation, to be held and used for the redemption of such circulation," declares further on that the bank notes on presentation to the Treasurer in multiples of $1,000 " shall be redeemed in United States notes," and that each bank, on being notified of the redemption of its notes, shall deposit with the Treasurer "a sum in United States notes equal to the amount of its circulating notes so redeemed." Since the passage of the act it has always been considered by the Treasurer and acquiesced in by the banks that the intent of these provisions was to establish a system of redemption of national-bank notes in United States notes, and that the requirement that the 5 per cent. deposit should be maintained in lawful money was governed by the subsequent provisions in the same section specifying the particular kind of lawful money, to wit: United States notes, in which the bank notes should be redeemed and deposits for the credit of the 5 per cent. fund made. He accordingly required all deposits for this purpose to be made in United States notes, declining all tenders of gold or silver coin, and at the same time recognized the right of holders of national-bank notes to demand and receive from him United States notes in redemption of their bank notes.   The legality of this requirement having been questioned, the matter was referred to the Attorney-General, who held that both the redemption of bank notes and deposits for the 5 per cent. fund might be made in coin, declaring that "the government notes are promises to pay dollars; for such promises the thing promised may properly be substituted by the promisor."

A similar question arose concerning the deposits for the retirement of bank circulation under the fourth section of the act, which was decided in the same manner, so that a bank desiring to reduce its circulation may accomplish its object by depositing in the Treasury gold coin, or silver dollars, or United States notes.   The original theory of this provision was that whenever the paper circulation of the country became

19 Ab

excessive, the redundancy would be cured by the deposit by the banks of United States notes for the retirement of their circulation. Now, however, that the banks may reduce their circulation by the deposit of coin, it is evident that the original theory of the act is destroyed. In fact, the question was raised by banks desiring to reduce their circulation, who averred that it was difficult, if not impossible, to obtain United States notes for the purpose, plainly showing that banks may desire to reduce their circulation when the currency is already deficient.

RESTORATION OF SALARIES.

The Treasurer earnestly urges the restoration to their former amounts of the salaries of this office, which were reduced by the act of August 15, 1876.

The following is a list of the officers affected, their present salaries, the salaries proposed to be restored, and the amount required to effect the restoration in each case:

Title.	Present salary.	Former salary.	Amount asked to be restored to each.	Total.
Treasurer of the United States	$6,000	$6,500	$500	$500
Assistant treasurer of the United States	3,600	3,800	200	200
Cashier	3,600	3,800	200	200
Assistant cashier	3,200	3,500	300	300
Five chiefs of division	2,500	2,700	200	1,000
Chief clerk	2,500	2,700	200	200
Teller	2,500	2,700	200	200
Two tellers	2,500	2,600	100	200
Two assistant tellers	2,250	2,350	100	200
Assistant teller	2,000	2,200	200	200
Two principal bookkeepers	2,500	2,600	100	200
Principal bookkeeper reduced to asst. bookkeeper	2,400	2,500	100	100
Assistant bookkeeper	2,400	2,500	100	100
Total increase				3,600

The number of persons affected by the reduction was 22, while the entire saving made was only $3,900. Two of the positions have since been abolished, so that the number whose salaries it is proposed to restore is now 20, and the amount required but $3,600. This amount, which represents only the salaries of three clerks of the lowest grade, and is insignificant when compared with the aggregate amount appropriated for salaries for this office, has nevertheless inflicted hardship upon 20 officers upon whom are devolved duties of great importance and pecuniary responsibility. How grave their responsibilities are may be inferred from the following statement of the duties of this office.

All moneys deposited in the Treasury of the United States at all of the various sub-treasuries and depositories are placed to the credit of the Treasurer of the United States and can be drawn out only by his draft; all of the various classes of paper currency of the United States are issued and redeemed through his office; he has custody of the bonds deposited by national banks for the security of their circulation and public deposits, and assesses and collects the semi-annual duty on their capital, circulation, and deposits; he redeems and assorts the notes of all the national banks, redeems all bonds of the United States maturing or called in for redemption, pays by his check all dividends of interest on registered stock of the $3\frac{1}{2}$, 4, and $4\frac{1}{2}$ per cent. funded loans, receives, counts, and examines all coupons from United States bonds paid by the several assistant treasurers, has custody of the Indian and other trust funds, pays the salaries and mileage of the members of the House of Representatives, and performs numerous other duties connected with the receipt, custody, and disbursement of the funds of the United States. In addition to these general duties, he has direct charge of the Treasury Office at Washington, which performs substantially the same duties as those performed by a sub-treasury, including the receipt and payment of money, the keeping of accounts with disbursing officers, the payment of interest on the public debt, and the like. He also performs the duties formerly intrusted to the commissioners of the sinking fund of the District of Columbia, and, in this capacity, has entire charge and control of the management of the funded debt of the District.

During the last seven years the average annual amount in round numbers of United States currency issued by him has been $94,000,000; of United States currency redeemed, $111,000,000; of national-bank notes redeemed and assorted, $157,000,000; of United States bonds redeemed, $183,617,626; of coin coupons paid, $44,000,000; of quarterly interest checks issued, $24,000,000 (the number issued during the last year being more than 305,000); of semi-annual duty collected, $7,300,000; of bonds on deposit for security of national banks, $371,000,000; of drafts drawn on warrants, $673,000,000; and of moneys transferred from one office to another, under his direction, $752,000,000. The aggregate amount involved in the above transactions was $16,910,000,000. The average number of persons employed in his office during this period was 395.

In consideration of the growing importance and responsibility of his office, the salary of the Treasurer was increased from time to time until 1866, when it was fixed at $6,500. The duties of the office were afterwards greatly increased by devolving upon the Treasurer the entire charge of the redemption and assortment of national-bank notes, under the act of June 20, 1874; the payment of dividends to the creditors of the Freedman's Savings Bank; the issuing of the checks for registered interest on the funded loans; the custody and payment of the funds of the District of Columbia; the management of the funded debt of the District, and the custody of the sinking fund for its extinguishment; the custody of the Indian trust fund and of the Pacific Railroad sinking funds; the issue and redemption of silver certificates; and the distribution of the standard silver dollars and fractional silver coin. This immense addition to the labors and responsibilities of his office did not, however, prevent the reduction of his salary, which was cut down, along with the others mentioned.

Since the appointment of the present Treasurer on July 1, 1877, the force of his office, notwithstanding the increase in its duties and responsibilities, has been reduced from 405 to 286 persons, and the amount annually expended for salaries, from $473,927.86 to $346,331.92, a reduction of nearly 30 per cent. in number, and of nearly 27 per cent. in amount. Since 1875 the number of employees has been reduced 262, or not far from one-half, and the annual appropriation has been reduced $234,244. The amount asked for, to restore the salaries of the officers of this office, is but little more than one and one-half per cent. of this amount, and would still leave a net reduction in the appropriation as compared with 1875 of more than $230,000. As these salaries were fixed by sections 2 and 3 of the act of March 3, 1875 (18 Statutes, 397, 399), the only action necessary to effect the restoration seems to be to insert in the appropriation bill the amount required to pay them at the rates fixed by law.

Very respectfully,

JAS. GILFILLAN,
Treasurer of the United States.

Hon. WILLIAM WINDOM,
  Secretary of the Treasury.

REPORT OF THE REGISTER OF THE TREASURY.

TREASURY DEPARTMENT,
REGISTER'S OFFICE,
November 10, 1881.

SIR: I have the honor to transmit herewith a report in detail of the business transacted in the several divisions of this office during the fiscal year ended on the 30th of June last.

The report of the loan division shows a great increase in the work of that division caused by the continuance of the 6 per cent. and 5 per cent. bonds at the reduced rate of 3½ per centum, which necessitated the issue of a new bond in every case showing the change in the rate of interest.

The aggregate issues amounted to nearly $800,000,000, the number of bonds issued being over 140,000, while the number of bonds redeemed and canceled was 730,000.

The clerical force of the office was entirely inadequate to the performance of the work imposed upon it, and about forty clerks were detailed from other bureaus of the department during nearly the entire summer, and a great deal of extra labor was performed outside of the prescribed hours, for which, in my judgment, extra compensation should be paid.

Great credit is due for the prompt and satisfactory performance of this work to the clerks of this bureau engaged thereon, and also to those detailed from other offices.

A superior class of clerks was required to perform the important and responsible duties devolved upon them, and such were generally furnished by the offices called on by the honorable Secretary for details, the Bureau of Internal Revenue especially cheerfully sending a large number of its most efficient and faithful clerks.

I take pleasure in reporting the devotion to duty and general good conduct of the employés of the bureau.

LOAN DIVISION.

Total number of coupon and registered bonds issued..............	140,842
Total number of coupon and registered bonds canceled............	730,106

Amount issued:

Original issue, coupon and registered............................	$1,365,350 00
Direct issue of bonds continued at 3½ per cent....................	458,212,750 00
Coupon bonds issued on transfer (Oregon war debt)................	1,200 00
Registered bonds issued on transfer (including Spanish indemnity).	249,757,214 57
Registered bonds issued in exchange for coupon...................	72,972,500 00
Total..	782,309,014 57

Amount canceled:

Coupon bonds converted into registered..........................	72,972,500 00
Coupon bonds transferred (Oregon war debt)......................	1,200 00
Registered bonds transferred (including Spanish indemnity)......	249,757,214 57
Coupon and registered bonds redeemed...........................	224,712,600 00
Coupon bonds (5 and 6 per cent.) converted into 3½ per cent.......	85,134,400 00
Registered bonds (5 and 6 per cent.) converted into 3½ per cent....	373,078,350 00
Total..	1,005,656,264 57

A synopsis of the vault account shows that the amount of bonds on hand July 1, 1880, was—

Coupon bonds	$38,118,950 00
Registered bonds	642,699,650 00
District of Columbia bonds	3,258,700 00

Amount received during the year was—

Coupon bonds	18,400,000 00
Registered bonds	1,419,780,500 00
District of Columbia bonds	4,291,750 00
Total	2,126,549,550 00

Accounted for as follows:

Coupon bonds issued	$180,350 00
Registered bonds issued (exclusive of Spanish indemnity)	778,004,600 00
District of Columbia bonds issued (coupon and registered)	4,020,050 00
Delivered to destruction committee:	
Coupon bonds	10,000,000 00
Registered bonds	9,310,000 00
Canceled for specimen book	2,000 00
In hands of European agent June 30, 1881:	
Registered 3½ per cent. bonds	37,367,600 00
On hand June 30, 1881:	
Coupon bonds	46,337,600 00
Registered bonds	1,237,796,950 00
District of Columbia bonds	3,530,400,00
Total	2,126,549,550 00

STATEMENT showing the NUMBER and AMOUNT of COUPON and REGISTERED BONDS ISSUED during the fiscal year ended June 30, 1881.

Loans.	Bonds issued.				
	Direct issues, amount.	Exchanges, amount.	Transfers, amount.	Total amount issued.	Total number bonds issued.
Oregon war debt..............C.			$1,200 00	$1,200 00	4
February 8, 1861 (81s)........R.		$8,000	591,000 00	594,000 00	131
July and August, 1861 (81s)...R.		4,400,750	13,356,800 00	17,757,550 00	3,055
March 3, 1865 (81s)..........R.		1,012,250	3,963,700 00	4,945,950 00	1,176
5 per cent. funded (1881).....R.		46,691,500	43,604,400 00	90,296,900 00	8,500
4½ per cent. funded (1891)....R.		7,452,150	27,814,400 00	35,266,550 00	9,498
4 per cent. consols (1907)...{ C.	$179,150			179,150 00	1,070
	R.	498,150	12,121,850	127,641,550 00	140,261,550 00	43,860
Pacific Railroads............R.			6,045,000 00	6,045,000 00	1,217
1861, continued at 3½ per cent....R.	125,639,850		12,956,200 00	138,596,550 00	29,878
1863, continued at 3½ per cent.....R.	49,647,250		6,213,700 00	55,860,950 00	12,519
5 per cent. funded, continued at 3½ per cent.....R.	282,926,150		5,455,450 00	288,381,600 00	27,127
5 per cent. District of Columbia funded............R.		10,000	6,000 00	16,000 00	18
3.65 per cent. District of Co-{ C.	371,050			371,050 00	1,292
lumbia, funded ....{ R.	317,000	1,281,000	2,035,000 00	3,633,000 00	1,101
Spanish indemnity ....R.			104,014 57	104,014 57	8
Total...................	459,578,100	72,972,500	249,758,414 57	782,309,014 57	140,842

STATEMENT *showing the* NUMBER *and* AMOUNT *of* COUPON *and* REGISTERED
BONDS CANCELED *during the fiscal year ended June 30, 1881.*

Loans.		Bonds canceled.				Total number bonds canceled.
		Redemptions, amount.	Exchanges, amount.	Transfers, amount.	Total amount canceled.	
Oregon war debt	C..	$77,050	....	$1,200 00	$78,250 00	198
February 8, 1861 (81s)	{ C.. R..	3,008,000 5,071,000	$3,000	.... 591,000 00	3,011,000 00 3,662,000 00	3,011 1,454
July and August, 1861 (81s)	{ C.. R..	11,486,150 10,154,450	4,400,750	.... 13,356,800 00	15,886,900 00 23,511,250 00	22,785 6,465
March 3, 1863 (81s)	{ C.. R..	4,459,000 3,980,150	1,012,250	.... 3,933,700 00	5,471,250 00 7,913,850 00	7,728 2,627
5 per cent. funded (1881)	{ C.. R..	30,072,600 16,841,100	46,691,500	43,604,400 00	76,764,100 00 60,445,500 00	104,014 13,063
4½ per cent. funded (1891)	{ C.. R..	....	7,452,150	27,814,400 00	7,452,150 00 27,814,400 00	8,521 8,142
4 per cent. consols (1907)	{ C.. R..	950,000 550,000	12,121,850	127,641,550 00	13,071,850 00 123,191,550 00	44,650 44,672
Pacific Railroads	R..	....	....	6,045,000 00	6,045,000 00	1,383
1861, continued at 3½ per cent.	{ C.. R..	....	*23,289,900 *102,349,450	} 12,956,200 00	23,289,900 00 115,305,650 00	32,405 26,363
1863, continued at 3½ per cent.	{ C.. R..	....	*7,137,050 *42,510,200	} 6,213,700 00	7,137,050 00 48,723,900 00	9,178 11,562
5 per cent. funded, continued at 3½ per cent.	{ C.. R..	....	*54,707,450 *228,218,700	} 5,455,450 00	54,707,450 00 233,674,150 00	70,269 90,290
5 per cent. District of Columbia, funded	{ C.. R..	 3,000	10,000	6,000 00	10,000 00 9,000 00	10 9
3.65 per cent. District of Columbia, funded	{ C.. R..	1,900 125,000	1,281,000	2,035,000 00	1,282,900 00 2,160,000 00	2,888 692
Spanish indemnity	R..	....	....	104,014 57	104,014 57	15
1862—February 25	{ C.. R..	19,050 300	....	....	19,050 00 300 00	50 3
1864—March 3, 10-40s	{ C.. R..	20,458,250 2,157,800	....	....	20,458,250 00 2,157,800 00	30,332 530
1864—June 30	{ C.. R..	1,600 2,500	....	....	1,600 00 2,500 00	15 3
1865—March 3	{ C.. R..	5,000 35,000	....	....	5,000 00 35,000 00	15 4
1865—Consols	{ C.. R..	17,463,900 30,250	....	....	17,463,900 00 30,250 00	32,035 12
1867—Consols	{ C.. R..	93,326,400 244,700	....	....	93,326,400 00 244,700 00	204,327 189
1868—Consols	{ C.. R..	4,020,450 168,000	....	....	4,020,450 00 168,000 00	10,943 67
Total		224,712,600	531,185,250	249,758,414 57	1,005,656,264 57	730,106

* Five and six per cent. coupon and registered bonds surrendered for continuance at 3½ per cent.

NOTE AND COUPON DIVISION.

REDEEMED, EXCHANGED, *and* TRANSFERRED UNITED STATES BONDS, *with*
COUPONS ATTACHED, EXAMINED, REGISTERED, *and* SCHEDULED.

Loan.	Number of bonds.	Amount of bonds.	Number coupons attached.
March 3, 1865 (consols, '65)	18,686	$7,796,450	398,204
March 3, 1865 (consols, '67)	106,775	$7,092,500	2,725,360
March 3, 1865 (consols, '68)	5,081	1,794,000	185,151
Funded loan, 1881, 5 per cent.	24,899	19,505,050	77,654
District of Columbia funded debt, 1924	2,752	1,331,000	244,400
Total	218,193	117,582,000	3,432,668

INTEREST COIN-CHECKS.

Loan.	Number of checks.	Amount.
Funded loan, 1881, 5 per cent	36, 482	$13, 644, 370 09
Funded loan, 1891, 4½ per cent	32, 476	5, 499, 317 95
Consols, 1907, 4 per cent	115, 216	9, 535, 461 70
District of Columbia funded debt, 1924	1, 968	1, 685, 200 88
Total	186, 142	30, 364, 350 62

REDEEMED COUPONS DETACHED from BONDS and NOTES.

Arranged numerically 3, 069, 664
Registered 2, 749, 445
Examined 2, 978, 637

THREE YEARS' 7 3-10 PER CENT. TREASURY NOTES.

Authorizing acts.	Number of notes.	Amount.
June 30, 1864, and March 3, 1865	21	$2, 650

CURRENCY CERTIFICATES of DEPOSIT.

Authorizing act.	Number of certificates.	Amount.
June 8, 1872	2, 409	$21, 270, 000

GOLD CERTIFICATES.

Authorizing act.	Number of certificates.	Amount.
March 3, 1863	2, 950	$2, 693, 700

ONE and TWO YEARS' 5 PER CENT. NOTES.

Authorizing act.	Number of notes.	Amount.
March 3, 1863	120	$2, 100

THREE YEARS' 6 PER CENT. COMPOUND-INTEREST NOTES.

Authorizing acts.	Number of notes.	Amount.
March 3, 1863, and June 30, 1864	258	$8, 030

NOTE AND FRACTIONAL-CURRENCY DIVISION.

STATEMENT SHOWING the NUMBER of NOTES and AMOUNT of UNITED STATES NOTES, 4 PER CENT. REFUNDING CERTIFICATES, and FRACTIONAL CURRENCY EXAMINED, COUNTED, CANCELED, and DESTROYED for the fiscal year ending June 30, 1881.

United States notes.	Number of notes.	Amount.
New issue	124,181	$1,152,550
Series 1869	1,198,796	18,881,780
Series 1874	495,941	3,808,050
Series 1875	5,469,556	17,609,270
Series 1878	5,507,713	15,927,850
Series 1880	998,100	1,541,350
Demand notes	48	385
4 per cent. refunding certificates	63,391	633,910
Fractional currency, first issue	5,300	945
Fractional currency, second issue	6,000	890
Fractional currency, third issue	14,160	3,992
Fractional currency, fourth issue	97,055	16,520
Fractional currency, second series	11,500	5,750
Fractional currency, third series	18,300	9,150
Fractional currency, fifth issue	348,300	79,535
Total	14,357,243	54,757,477

4 PER CENT. REGISTERED REFUNDING CERTIFICATES.

Amount issued	$58,500
Amount funded	56,340

TONNAGE DIVISION.

The total tonnage of the country exhibits a decrease of 10,299.53 tons, the enrolled tonnage having increased 7,848.07 tons, while the registered tonnage has decreased 17,224.13 tons, and the licensed, under 20 tons, 924.03 tons.

The barge tonnage has decreased 58,264.26 tons under the operation of the act of Congress approved June 30, 1879, leaving 47,964.73 tons as the estimated increase in the tonnage during the past year.

Below are given the totals for the last two years:

	1880.		1881.	
	Vessels.	Tons.	Vessels.	Tons.
Registered	2,378	1,352,810	2,326	1,335,586.18
Enrolled and licensed	22,334	2,715,224	21,739	2,722,148.29
Total	24,712	4,068,034	24,065	4,057,734.47

The comparison of the different classes of vessels is as follows:

	1880.		1881.	
	Vessels.	Tons.	Vessels.	Tons.
Sailing vessels	16,830	2,366,258	16,760	2,350,393.14
Steam vessels	4,717	1,211,558	4,860	1,264,998.25
Canal-boats	1,235	106,590	1,327	116,978.73
Barges	1,930	383,628	1,118	325,364.35
Total	24,712	4,068,034	24,065	4,057,734.47

It may be seen from the foregoing that the steam tonnage has increased 53,440.25 tons, the canal-boat tonnage 10,388.73 tons, while the sailing tonnage has decreased 15,864.86 tons, and the barge tonnage 58,263.65 tons.

The proportion of the sailing tonnage registered is 50 per centum, and the steam tonnage registered 12 per centum.

SHIP-BUILDING.

The following table exhibits the class, number, and tonnage of the vessels built during the last two years:

Class.	1880.		1881.	
	Vessels.	Tons.	Vessels.	Tons.
Sailing vessels	460	59,057	493	81,209.57
Steam vessels..	348	78,854	444	118,079.55
Canal-boats	17	1,887	57	10,189.94
Barges	77	17,612	114	70,988.58
Total	902	157,410	1,108	280,458.64

From the foregoing it appears that the amount built during the past year was greater by 123,048.64 tons than that of the preceding year.

The tonnage built during the last two years in the several grand divisions of the country is shown below:

Division.	1880.		1881.	
	Vessels.	Tons.	Vessels.	Tons.
Atlantic and Gulf coasts................................	589	92,777	653	114,348.60
Pacific coast	41	8,943	58	11,417.49
Northern lakes	137	22,899	215	73,503.61
Western rivers	135	32,791	182	81,188.88
Total	902	157,410	1,108	280,458.64

The following table exhibits the iron tonnage built in the country since 1867:

Class.	1868.	1869.	1870.	1871.	1872.	1873.	1874.
Sailing vessels	....	1,039	679	2,067	....	....	....
Steam vessels	2,901	3,545	7,602	13,412	12,766	26,548	33,097
Total.............................	2,901	4,584	8,281	15,479	12,766	26,548	33,097

	1875.	1876.	1877.	1878.	1879.	1880.	1881.
Sailing vessels	....	....	....	....	....	44	36.04
Steam vessels	21,632	21,346	5,927	26,960	22,008	25,538	28,319.84
Total.............................	21,632	21,346	5,927	26,960	22,008	25,582	28,355.88

Tables showing the amount of iron tonnage outstanding may be found in the Report on Commerce and Navigation.

THE FISHERIES.

The tonnage engaged in the fisheries during the last two years is as follows:

Fisheries.	1880.		1881.	
	Vessels.	Tons.	Vessels.	Tons.
Cod and mackerel fisheries	2,822	77,539	2,120	76,137.16
Whale fisheries	174	38,408	173	38,551.53

Below is shown the amount of tonnage employed in the cod and mackerel fisheries, with the per centum of each State:

States.	Tonnage.	Per cent.
Maine	19,662.50	25.5
New Hampshire	1,068.78	1.4
Massachusetts	39,129.77	51.3
Rhode Island	2,081.34	2.7
Connecticut	4,349.44	5.7
New York	7,657.72	10.5
New Jersey	24.59	.03
California	2,162.93	2.87
Total	76,137.16	100

This shows a decrease of about 2 per cent. during the year.
The tonnage employed in the whale fisheries is given below:

Customs districts.	1880.		1881.	
	Vessels.	Tons.	Vessels.	Tons.
Boston, Mass	5	531	5	794.57
Barnstable, Mass	19	1,817	18	1,036.97
Edgartown, Mass	6	1,124	7	1,271.19
New Bedford, Mass	134	33,337	132	33,908.88
New London, Conn	10	1,599	11	1,749.61
Total	174	38,408	173	38,551.53

Of the above, nearly 86 per cent. belongs to New Bedford.

Fuller tables, showing the various classes of tonnage, may be found in the appendix to this report.

DIVISION OF RECEIPTS AND EXPENDITURES.

The following statement exhibits the work of this division for the year ending June 30, 1881:

The number of warrants registered during the year for civil, diplomatic, miscellaneous, internal revenue, and public debt expenditures and repayments was 25,254
In the preceding year 20,839

Increase 4,415

The number of warrants registered for receipts from customs, lands, internal revenue, direct tax, and miscellaneous sources was 12,881
In the preceding year 6,183 should have been 11,634

Increase 1,247

The number of warrants registered for payments and repayments in the War,
  Navy, and Interior (pension and Indian) Departments was................. 15,036
In the preceding year 11,833
                                                                         ─────────
  Increase 3,203
                                                                         ═════════

The number of drafts registered was..................................... 39,056
In the preceding year 32,179
                                                                         ─────────
  Increase 6,877
                                                                         ═════════

The number of journal pages required for the entry of accounts relating to the
  civil, diplomatic, internal revenue, miscellaneous, and public debt receipts
  and expenditures was 5,963
In the preceding year 5,437
                                                                         ─────────
  Increase 526
                                                                         ═════════

The number of certificates furnished for settlement of accounts was..... 13,341
In the preceding year 13,489
                                                                         ─────────
  Decrease 148
                                                                         ═════════

The number of accounts received from the First and Fifth Auditors and Com-
  missioner of the General Land Office was.............................. 23,646
In the preceding year 22,290
                                                                         ─────────
  Increase 1,356
                                                                         ═════════

In the appendix will be found a statement of the receipts and expenditures of the government, as required by the standing order of the
House of Representatives of December 30, 1791, and section 237 of the
Revised Statutes; also, statements of the money expended and the
number of persons employed, and the occupation and salary of each
person at each custom-house, as required by section 258 of the Revised
Statutes.

  Very·respectfully, your obedient servant,

                                       B. K. BRUCE, *Register.*

Hon. WILLIAM WINDOM,
       Secretary of the Treasury.

REPORT

OF THE

SECRETARY OF WAR.

WAR DEPARTMENT,
November 10, 1881.

To the PRESIDENT:

I have the honor to submit the following annual report of the administration of this department:

EXPENDITURES, APPROPRIATIONS, AND ESTIMATES.

The actual expenditures under this department for the fiscal year ending June 30, 1881, were $42,122,201.39.

The appropriations for 1882 were $44,889,725.42.

The estimates for 1883 are $44,541,276.91.

The estimates presented to me for revision included—

For armament of fortifications	$720, 000
Fortifications and other works of defense	4, 186, 500
Improving rivers and harbors	29, 101, 300
Improving Mississippi River, by commission	4, 323, 000
Public buildings and grounds in and near Washington	749, 000
Surveys of lakes	20, 000
	39, 099, 800

This amount has been reduced, on my revision, to aggregate $10,689,000, which sum, if judiciously allotted by Congress, will be, in my judgment, a reasonable allowance for this class of expenses during the next fiscal year.

The remainder of the estimates includes salaries and expenses of the departmental civil establishment and amounts for the support of the Army, for armories and arsenals, and for miscellaneous objects. For these purposes the estimates for 1883 are $33,852,276.91, being $296,321.37 in excess of the estimates for 1882, and $2,082,851.49 more than the appropriations for the current fiscal year. This increase grows out of apparent necessities in the public service, which are fully set forth by items in detail, accompanied with notes, in the book of estimates. While the estimates of expenses for this class show an increase, there is in the estimates of expenses for improvements, including rivers and harbors, a decrease which overbalances the difference, and makes the estimates for 1883 $348,443.51 less than the appropriations for 1882.

300

THE ARMY.

The report of the General of the Army contains recommendations of the highest importance. He again calls attention to the public necessity of legislation authorizing the Army to be recruited to a strength of thirty thousand enlisted men, as provided by section 1115 of the Revised Statutes. As is remarked by the General, our companies are too small for efficient discipline and for economical service. There are in the Army four hundred and thirty companies, which are necessarily widely scattered over our vast domain, to guard property and to prevent, as far as foresight can, complications and troubles of every variety and kind, at one time protecting the settlers against Indians, and again Indians against the settlers. When these occur, re-enforcements have to be hurried forward from great distances, and always at heavy cost for transportation of men, horses, wagons, and supplies. This cost in the aggregate is probably more than sufficient to supply an increase of twenty per cent. of *private soldiers*, which will add little, if any, to the annual cost of the Army, and yet give great relief to our overtaxed soldiers. In the last ten years our frontiers have so extended, under the protection of our small Army, as to add at least a thousand millions of dollars to the taxable wealth of the nation. This protection has enabled emigrants to settle up remote parts of the country, and is a principal cause of the great prosperity which is felt throughout all parts of our vast domain.

It should be remembered that of the enlisted force of any army a large part, not far from fifteen per cent., is, for many causes, not available at any one time as a fighting force; so that the legislation recommended would, after proper allowances, give an actual combatant force of about twenty-five thousand men.

I concur most earnestly in his recommendation.

Whilst the troops have been kept very busy during the past year, no serious Indian or other war has occurred, but great progress has been made in collecting and locating Indians, hitherto hostile, on their proper reservations. Sitting Bull and his adherents, who had fled into British territory, are now held at Fort Randall, Dakota, as prisoners of war, and the Utes have been moved to a new reservation in Utah. A sudden outbreak of a part of the Apaches occurred in Arizona, and it was found necessary to re-enforce for a short time the usual garrisons in Arizona by a strong detachment from New Mexico. Some of the guilty Apaches are now held as prisoners for trial; some have escaped into Mexico, while the greater part of the tribe remain on their reservation at San Carlos, under their proper civil agent.

The General recommends that section 1232 Revised Statutes be amended so as to read:

SEC. 1232. No officer shall use an enlisted man as a servant, in any case whatever, without proper compensation, or without his own consent and that of his commanding officer.

It appears that in many remote places no servants can possibly be obtained, and officers must not only cook their own meals, but groom their horses, or violate the law as it now stands. It would seem clear that no officer can habitually do such work and properly supervise his company and command.

In addition to the means for extended practical instruction for officers now given at the Artillery School at Fortress Monroe, and the Engineer Establishment at Willets Point, New York, arrangements are so far made for a School of Application for the cavalry and infantry at Fort Leavenworth that it will probably be in operation before January next. There will be, habitually, a garrison of one company of artillery, four companies of infantry and four of cavalry, to which will be attached, for instruction, one officer of each regiment of infantry and of cavalry for a detail of two years. These will receive instruction in the military art, and then rejoin their proper regiments, to be succeeded by a similar detail every two years, so that in time the whole Army will thus be enabled to keep up with the rapid progress in the science and practice of war.

The Signal School at Fort Myer provides for the instruction of eight subalterns each year in that branch of knowledge; but as it takes five years thus to instruct one officer of each of the forty regiments, practical instruction in all the signaling which is essential to the Army is also taught at West Point, at Fortress Monroe, and will be at Fort Leavenworth, thus embracing the whole Army.

The earnest attention of Congress is called to the need of legislation to prevent intrusion upon Indian lands, especially from Kansas into the Indian Territory. A large military force, at great expense, now patrols the boundary line; the only penalty which can be inflicted upon the intruder being removal by force and a pecuniary fine, the magnitude of which is not of the smallest importance to him, its collection being impossible. Section 2148 of the Revised Statutes should be amended by providing for imprisonment as well as fine in such cases.

ADJUTANT-GENERAL'S DEPARTMENT.

The Adjutant-General urgently recommends that legislative authority be given for the employment of civilian clerks at division and departmental headquarters, to do the work now performed by persons enlisted in the general service, as it is called, who are in name soldiers, but in fact clerks. Such a measure would restore 147 men to active duty as soldiers, and they could be replaced, it is estimated, by 113 clerks employed at salaries the aggregate of which would be nearly $20,000 less than now paid. This recommendation is approved, and I would also recommend a like enactment in respect to General Service clerks now employed in the War Department. The system grew out of the necessities of the war, and creates a certain amount of confusion, as "General Service" clerks, being nominally enlisted men of the Army, are not borne on the clerical rolls. This clerical work must be had, but it ought to be performed by regular clerks.

The Adjutant-General also calls attention to a discrimination, in the matter of compensation, against the clerks under him, which would be corrected by the abolition of the class of "General Service" clerks, and a new arrangement such as is shown in his report, which I recommend.

The Codified Army Regulations, prepared under the direction of my predecessor, are now being issued.

The Adjutant-General recommends that the Secretary of War be authorized to make a proper allowance to officers on court-martial or military board duties, to enable them to meet the exceptional expenses caused by such duties.

The rapidly increasing number of calls from the Pension Office for information from the rolls of the Army, in connection with claims for pension, led to the formation by the Adjutant-General of a new branch in his office last April, designated as the "Enlisted Volunteer Pension Branch." By the act of March 3, 1881, twenty-five additional clerks of the lowest class, viz, at an annual salary of $1,000, were authorized to be employed in this office, but their want of acquaintance with the minutiæ of Army rolls and records, and the consequent necessity devolving on the older clerks to devote much time to their instruction, has necessarily prevented the attainment of the highest results. The following table, however, is a gratifying exhibit of the labors of this branch and of other divisions of the office engaged in business relating to claims for pension, bounty, homestead grants, &c.:

Number of calls (from all sources):

On hand October 1, 1880	31,907
Received during the year	150,449
	182,446
Finished during the year	154,342
Remaining on hand October 1, 1881	28,104

INSPECTOR-GENERAL'S DEPARTMENT.

The report of the Inspector-General shows that the accounts of all officers of the Army who have disbursed public moneys during the past year have been carefully examined, and the reports of balances verified.

Nearly all the military posts have been inspected during the year. The discipline of the troops is reported as very good. They are well armed and well fed and clothed.

Great attention has been paid to target practice, and marked improvement is noted. A regular competition is now established throughout the Army, prizes being given annually in military departments and divisions, and biennially after a contest between the best marksmen of the three military divisions.

The Inspector-General's corps of officers, now limited to five, is too small a number for the important duties which devolve on them. The Inspector-General must necessarily be stationed in Washington, and should have at least one competent assistant with him. There are three military divisions and nine departments, each of which ought to have an inspector-general. This would necessitate fourteen officers in all— an increase in this corps of nine officers, each of whom should have the right to employ one clerk, with the same compensation which is now allowed to paymasters' clerks.

BUREAU OF MILITARY JUSTICE.

The number of general court-martial records received in the Bureau of Military Justice during the year ending October 1, 1881, was 1,792, an increase of 249 over the receipts of the previous year. The record of cases brought before inferior courts, reviewed and filed in the offices of the judge-advocates of the different military departments during the same period, was 8,500, an increase over the previous year of 267 cases.

The Judge-Advocate-General refers briefly to the various military tribunals, and to the usual course of procedure by which their proceedings reach the Bureau of Military Justice for consideration, and in this connection invites attention to the fact that, while the Judge-Advocate-General is empowered by statute to receive and revise the proceedings of courts-martial, yet the Secretary of War, whose subordinate he is, has no statutory authority to give effect to reports of revisions in such cases, even though he should concur therein, and remarks that to this extent the law is defective.

In connection with the nature, quality, and quantity of the work to be performed, attention is invited to the fact that, in view of the interests involved, an adequate force of clerks, possessing in the highest degree both capacity and fidelity, is imperatively necessary, and that the present inadequate clerical force has necessitated the transfer of officers of the corps of judge-advocates to duty in the Bureau of Military Justice, while their services are much needed at the headquarters of the various military departments.

The necessity for suitable furniture to replace that now in use, which is worn out and rickety, and the great need for an appropriation sufficient to furnish the library, at present incomplete and antiquated, with text-books and reports of recent date, is fully set forth.

The duties of the Judge-Advocate-General and of the corps of judge-advocates are enumerated, and in view of the advisability of having an officer of the corps at each of the ten geographical military departments, and at the Military Academy as professor of law, the repeal of the law limiting the number of judge-advocates to four, and the organization of the corps on the same basis as the other staff corps of the Army, are recommended, this being the only corps in which there is no promotion, to serve as an incentive to duty. In all other branches of the service officers can look forward to reaching the rank of colonel, while in the corps of judge-advocates all are of one rank—that of major—which has been held by its members for periods ranging from eight to nineteen years. It is not perceived why such a discrimination should exist against an expert corps, requiring in the exercise of its functions professional attainments of a high order, and I recommend appropriate legislation to remove it. With a properly organized corps, of sufficient strength to furnish each military department with one of its officers, it is believed that many trials by courts-martial could be avoided by thorough preliminary examination, and much expense to the government saved thereby.

Attention is invited to defects and omissions in the Articles of War (65–71 inclusive) relating to the arrest and confinement of officers and soldiers accused of crime, duration of confinement, copy of charges, and time of trial, being the only provisions of the Articles of War relating to this important portion of the criminal procedure before courts-martial, on account of the unjust discriminations involved and the inadequate provision for the subjects mentioned.

It is also recommended that the scope of the 91st Article be so enlarged as to provide for the taking of depositions in certain instances, to be used at the trial as secondary evidence, where, for any sufficient reason, primary evidence of the facts cannot be procured consistently with the public interests, the extended jurisdiction of courts-martial rendering it difficult, if not impossible, at times, to obtain the *viva voce* testimony of material witnesses at the time of trial.

Recommendations are also made for authority, under proper regulation, for the revision of charges before arraignment and plea; for compelling the attendance of witnesses in certain cases; for preventing the abuse of authority by non-commissioned officers; for amendment of the 72d Article of War, by expressly authorizing colonels commanding separate departments to appoint general courts-martial when necessary; for a penal sanction of the authority conferred upon a judge-advocate of a court-martial, by section 1202 of the Revised Statutes, "to issue process and compel witnesses to appear," &c.; for authority for a judge-advocate, or other officer of a court-martial, to administer oaths to witnesses or other persons in trials by courts-martial; and for amendment of that portion of the 90th Article of War which requires the judge-advocate to prosecute, as well as to a certain extent to consider himself as counsel for the prisoner, in order to prevent confusion and misunderstanding.

Accompanying the report are extracts from the reports of judge-advocates of departments (or officers acting and performing the duties of those officers), embodying recommendations on various matters pertaining to their respective departments.

MILITARY PRISON.

The administration of the affairs of the military prison at Fort Leavenworth, Kans., during the past year has been in a marked degree successful.

20 Ab.

During the fiscal year ending June 30, 1881, there were 373 men received into the prison and 273 discharged. But 1 death occurred during the year, and only 6 prisoners escaped during the same period. The actual number of men confined on June 30, 1881, was 447.

The board of commissioners have made the inspections required by law; have, at each visit, afforded the prisoners the fullest opportunity to make such representations or complaints as they desired to present for consideration; have carefully noted the character of the punishments imposed by the prison authorities for violations of the established rules and regulations, the methods and kinds of labor, the quality of food provided; and they have been fully satisfied, in all respects, with the condition and government of the prison. The governor, while on duty under his brevet rank of colonel, actually receives only the pay and allowances of his actual rank, viz, that of captain. Considering that his position demands the possession, in the incumbent, of administrative ability of the highest degree, combined with the rare mechanical powers required for the successful management of an institution embracing many and varied branches of industry, I most earnestly recommend that the local rank of colonel, with the pay and allowances of that grade, be attached to the office of the governor of the prison. This officer has a greater amount of labor and responsibility than any regimental commander. He governs and controls between 500 and 600 persons. Practically, he is at one and the same time the superintendent of a large manufacturing establishment, embracing diversified branches of industry, and the military director of all affairs within the prison.

I beg to renew the recommendation of last year that legislative authority be obtained to apply the earnings of the prison to its maintenance. A bill with this end in view was pending in the Senate last winter, and I sincerely hope it may become a law during the next session of Congress.

There were manufactured at the prison during the year 34,163 pairs of boots, 25,944 pairs of shoes, 4,356 corn brooms, 1,656 barrack-chairs, 110 arm-chairs, 100 chair-rungs, 220 chair-bolts, 1,263 packing boxes, 80 crates, 100 sets of four-mule ambulance harness, 75 sets of six-mule wagon harness, and, in addition to the above, all the doors, sashes, &c., for new buildings, and the work incident to the necessary repairs to buildings already erected. The prison farm produced a large quantity of vegetables, all from the labor of the convicts.

QUARTERMASTER'S DEPARTMENT.

The moneys appropriated for the service of the Quartermaster's Department during the fiscal year were $13,857,187.57; the balances of former appropriations, remaining in Treasury at beginning of fiscal year, were $1,027,815.68. These were applicable only to expenses incurred in prior years but not settled.

There were remitted to disbursing officers during the year, $11,203,-536.03; paid through the Treasury, $718,205.13; carried to surplus fund, $230,123.62; and there remained in Treasury, undrawn on June 30, 1881, $1,705,296.04.

The propriety of allowing to the officers of the line who are placed on duty as acting assistant quartermasters some compensation for the great pecuniary responsibility, to say nothing of the labor, imposed by these duties, is again mentioned by the Quartermaster-General. Such an allowance as is by law granted to acting commissaries of subsistence under the same circumstances is recommended.

The difficulty arising in the exhaustion of the depot stock of clothing and equipage, mentioned last year, has continued to be felt, though in a somewhat less degree because, the appropriation being made earlier, at the last or short session, it was possible to make contracts earlier, and thus the deficiency of supply in the earlier months of the year was less felt. The need of a special appropriation, however, to provide a working stock to be placed in depot to meet emergencies and to provide for the spring and summer distribution to the Army, remains, and unless an appropriation for this purpose is granted this winter, the old difficulties will be severely felt again next season.

Under several joint resolutions of Congress, tents and camp equipage were loaned to various organizations during the year, at a cost, in expenses, damages to material, and losses, of $2,038.31.

Helmets have been introduced both for officers and soldiers. For troops in severe climates buffalo coats, fur caps and gloves, and arctic overshoes are supplied by the United States. Their use has made campaigns possible without loss by frost in the severe climate of the Upper Missouri and the Canadian boundary.

The construction of 132 new military buildings by the Quartermaster's Department has been authorized during the year, at an estimated cost of $240,000. They are at military posts in twenty-one different States and Territories.

Repair of existing buildings has been authorized to the extent of $417,902; $13,428 of the above sum have been devoted to new buildings for schools and chapels at military posts, under the law of July 28, 1866; and $6,517 have been devoted to repair of wharves at military posts.

Of the $75,000 appropriated for hospital construction, $74,588 have been expended.

Seventy-six old buildings, no longer needed for the military service, have been sold, and their proceeds turned into the general Treasury balances.

With so many buildings under its charge, scattered throughout the country, there has been some loss by fire. Fourteen such fires have been reported, but, considering that the department is estimated to be in charge of 5,000 buildings, the losses have been comparatively small.

The new headquarters at Fort Snelling have been completed, excepting some of the minor buildings. The Quartermaster-General has lately inspected them, and reports them excellent buildings, of economical construction.

The Quartermaster-General renews his recommendation for the erection of a building for the safe-keeping of records of the executive departments not in frequent use. Such a building need not be costly; it should be fire-proof and safe, and so arranged that the records of the different departments could be stored in separate fire-proof rooms. There can be no doubt as to the value and economy of such a building, and the Quartermaster-General has submitted a design for such an one. An appropriation therefor has passed the Senate unanimously, but in the last hours of the late Congress it failed in conference.

Congress, at the last session, passed a law providing for the erection of a new building for the Pension Office. As the law imposed upon the Quartermaster-General of the Army the duty of selecting a site, subject to the approval of the Secretaries of War and of the Interior, he reports the progress made thereunder. It seems to have been the intention of the authors of this measure to provide, by the appropriation of $250,000 which was made, for the purchase of a site AND for the erection of the building, but the omission, apparently an accident, of the word *and* in the law has prevented any attempt to construct a building, and the whole matter has therefore remained undetermined, and needs further legislative action. The Quartermaster-General has, under the law, performed his duty of selecting and submitting for approval a site; he has also submitted plans for such a building as he believes, on information, to have been intended by the authors of this law; but in consequence of the omission of the important word noted above, preventing the construction of such a building as was believed by the Secretary of the Interior and myself to have been actually intended by Congress, it was not thought advisable by us to select a site until further legislation is had.

There are eighty national military cemeteries declared and established under the law, in which there have been 318,859 interments. These are independent of the cemeteries at military posts, which generally cannot be considered permanent, being vacated on the abandonment of posts as the frontier passes beyond them.

It is expected that the public road from Vicksburg to the military cemetery will be completed this fall. Further appropriations are asked to complete the roadways to the Fort Scott and to the Chattanooga military cemeteries, as the sums granted by Congress were not sufficient for the completion of either.

An appropriation for repairing the road from the capital to the Arlington Cemetery is recommended. The Quartermaster-General renews his recommendation that this cemetery, containing 208 acres, in which few more military interments are probable in the future, be constituted and established by law a national official cemetery for interment of officers of the government, members of Congress, and others in the public service, dying at Washington or elsewhere, whose friends may desire their interment in a cemetery maintained by the nation. There is space for this purpose. The cemetery is sufficiently remote from the city to be unobjectionable on the score of health, and yet near enough for easy communication. Being separated from the city by a great river, it is not liable to be encroached upon and ultimately destroyed by the growth of population.

Under the law of July, 1864, 3,813 claims for quartermaster's stores were investigated during the year by the agents of the Quartermaster's Department. Their amount as presented was $2,287,729.22. The cost of this work was $139,604.63. The total number of these claims on file for examination was 22,935, calling for $12,034,750.29. Of these the Quartermaster-General reported to the Third Auditor 1,149 with recommendation for settlement at $227,680.39, which is $344,898.93 less than claimed. During the year 1,995 claims, calling for $1,885,173.32, were rejected. The Quartermaster-General has not during the year been able to take up 2,018 other claims which had been prepared for such action. Thus, 5,162 cases were prepared during the year for adjudication.

The Quartermaster's Department moved, during the year, 46,658 persons, 10,355 beasts, and 136,632 tons of material.

Some of the railroads which purchased on credit, under executive orders, railroad material at the close of the war, continue in default.

Attention is called to the fact that, while appropriation has been made to pay land-grant railroads for service rendered in the years ending June 30, 1880 and 1882, no provision has been made in appropriations for paying for such service rendered in the year ending June 30, 1881. This inflicts loss upon those companies which have faithfully done their duty to the government during that and other years.

About 10,500 horses and the same number of mules are kept in the military service. The loss of animals during the year was 2,056 horses and 1,281 mules. The proceeds of sales thereof, deposited in the Treasury in the year, and not available under existing laws to replace those died, lost, or sold, was $80,207.97. The average cost of 1,438 cavalry and artillery horses purchased during the year was $125.12—total $179,926.71. The cost of 1,006 mules and 29 draft-horses purchased for the trains was $117,074.80; the average being for mules $111.07 each, and for draft-horses $183.79. Thus the sales of animals, worn out, produced about one-fourth of the cost of replacing them.

The duty of supplying lights to the Army, heretofore performed by the Subsistence Department, having been transferred to the Quartermaster's Department, contracts for mineral oil and for lamps have been made, and the first distribution thereof to the military posts is in progress. So far as can be at present estimated, the new method of lighting will cost about $2,500 per annum more than the old. As the Argand burner used gives the light of sixteen candles, the comfort of the troops will be very much increased by substitution of mineral oil for candles. The *morale* of the troops is reported to have improved at posts where the new lights have been introduced. The men, being able to read without injury to their eyes, spend more time in rational amusements and less time at the sutler store, at the grog-shops, and in the guard-house.

The law which abolished issue of fuel to officers causes great hardship to those who are stationed at military posts in inclement climates and on the prairies, where fuel is scarce and costly. It is much to be desired that this allowance be restored. It is considered by officers of the Army even more unjust to those in the wilderness than the abolition of the forage-ration was to those living east of the Mississippi. That complaint has been put an end to by the law of February 24, 1881, but the question of fuel has failed to meet Congressional remedy.

SUBSISTENCE DEPARTMENT.

Attention is invited to the clause in the appropriation acts requiring ten per centum to be charged officers and enlisted men in excess of original cost price to the United States on all subsistence stores sold them, and, as this addition is considered by officers and enlisted men to be onerous and unjust to them, legislation is recommended by the Commissary-General by which sales will hereafter be made to officers and enlisted men at cost prices, as was formerly the case.

The existing system of furnishing tobacco to enlisted men, by causing the small money values of the quantities drawn by each man to be charged on the pay-rolls and collected by the paymasters, to be subsequently transferred to the credit of the appropriations of the Subsistence Department upon the books of the Treasury on settlements made in the offices of the accounting officers, entails a very considerable expense to the government for clerical services in the Pay and Subsistence Departments which might, to a great extent, be saved by so modifying existing laws as to cause tobacco to be placed on sale in the Subsistence Department in the same manner as other articles are held for sale to officers and enlisted men under section 1144, Revised Statutes. This can be easily effected by repealing sections 1149 and 1301, Revised Statutes, and inserting the words "including tobacco" in section 1144.

The issues of subsistence for the Subsistence Department of the Army to Indians during the fiscal year 1881 are tabulated by the Commissary-General of Subsistence. It is a matter of annual recurrence that if, from any cause, an appropriation of the Indian Bureau for the support and care of an Indian tribe becomes at any time exhausted, requests are immediately made upon the War Department to furnish subsistence with which to feed the band or tribe unprovided for until an appropriation can be obtained from Congress; and, although section

3678, Revised Statutes, prescribes that "all sums appropriated for the various branches of expenditure in the public service shall be applied solely to the objects for which they are respectively made, *and for no others*," the overruling dictates of reason and sound policy toward these savages, who are capable of inflicting such untold misery upon individuals and expense upon the government, force executive officers to the adoption of expedients which are of doubtful legality. Such an instance occurred in May and June last in respect to certain Indians in the Indian Territory, who, for want of necessary funds on the part of the Indian Bureau, had to be subsisted from the appropriation for the subsistence of the Army until the appropriation for the fiscal year 1882 became available. This was done upon the express promise of the Interior Department to "present the subject to Congress upon the earliest opportunity, and urge upon that body the necessity for an appropriation to reimburse the War Department for such expenditures as shall be incurred in providing for these Indians." It would appear that the War Department should not be left, by inadequate provision for the Indian Bureau, to be made subject to contribution for the maintenance of the Indians whenever the appropriations for the Indian Bureau become, for any reason, exhausted.

The introduction of enlisted cooks into the Army, to prepare the rations of the companies, troops, and batteries, under such regulations as may be prescribed under section 1174, Revised Statutes, is recommended.

The question of the sufficiency or insufficiency of the Army ration for satisfying the requirements of the soldier for food is ably discussed, by officers who have given great attention to the subject, in reports appended to the annual report of the Commissary-General. The outcome of the whole discussion would seem to indicate the sufficiency of the present ration as a whole, if issued to and consumed by the men, or if the product of such of it as may be sold is applied exclusively to the purchase of food for the men.

MEDICAL DEPARTMENT.

The number of deaths of soldiers was 130 from disease, and 67 from wounds and injuries, being 9 per 1,000 of mean strength, the fatal results in cases treated being as 1 to 190.

The number of new official demands upon the Record and Pension Division during the fiscal year, for information as to the cause of death in the case of deceased soldiers and the hospital record of invalids, was 55,040. The average number of such demands, during the previous ten years, had been 22,245 annually, and the number during the fiscal year terminating June 30, 1880, was 39,241; the number received during the fiscal year ending June 30, 1881, being an increase of 40 per cent. over the previous fiscal year, and of 147 per cent. over the annual average of the previous ten years.

At the commencement of the fiscal year 6,964 cases remained unanswered, making 62,004 cases to be disposed of during the year.

Search was made and replies furnished to the proper authorities in 40,596 of these cases, leaving 21,408 unanswered cases on hand on the 1st of July, 1881.

This work becomes more difficult as the period elapsed since the close of the war increases, for the reason that claimants are in many cases unable to furnish accurate or definite data as to time and place of treatment; also, the volumes of hospital records on file in this office are becoming so very dilapidated, from constant handling, that the utmost care must be exercised in order that the entries contained therein may not be irretrievably lost, the clerical force not having been sufficient during the past fiscal year, or at any previous time, to permit of the copying of these original records.

The clerical force of the office was increased by forty clerks last March, under the provisions of the act of Congress approved March 3, 1881, but as, on account of the peculiar nature of the work, newly appointed clerks experience considerable difficulty in learning it, some time must necessarily elapse before they can be expected to perform it with the facility and accuracy exhibited by those who, from long experience, are more familiar with the records.

The Surgeon-General again invites attention to the necessity for a new fire-proof building for the Army Medical Museum and Library, and refers to the following extract from the message of the President to Congress at the commencement of its last session, and requests that the subject be again brought to the attention of that body:

The collections of books, specimens, and records constituting the Army Medical Museum and Library are of national importance. The Library now contains about 51,500 volumes and 57,000 pamphlets relating to medicine, surgery, and allied topics. The contents of the Army Medical Museum consists of 22,000 specimens, and are unique in the completeness with which both military surgery and the diseases of armies are illustrated. Their destruction would be an irreparable loss, not only to the United States, but to the world. There are filed in the Record and Pension Division over 16,000 bound volumes of hospital records, together with a great quantity of papers, embracing the original records of the hospitals of our armies during the civil war. Aside from their historical value, these records are daily searched for evidence needed in the settlement of large numbers of pension and other claims, for the protection of the government against attempted frauds, as well as for the benefit of honest claimants. These valuable collections are now in a building which is peculiarly exposed to the danger of destruction by fire. It is therefore earnestly recommended that an appropriation be made for a new fire-proof building, adequate for the present needs and reasonable future expansion of these valuable collections. Such a building should be absolutely fire-proof; no expenditure for mere architectural display is required. It is believed that a suitable structure can be erected at a cost not to exceed $250,000.

PAY DEPARTMENT.

The Paymaster-General reports the receipt by the Pay Department, during the last fiscal year, of $15,630,967.80; all of which is accounted for without loss.

He calls attention to the hardship upon officers at remote stations, caused by the deduction of one-half their pay during that part of a leave which is in excess of thirty days in any one year, remarking that most of them desire to come to the Eastern States, and that the great loss of time and the expenses of travel place them at a disadvantage; and recommends a repeal of the laws on the subject, the first of which was passed in 1863.

He asks for two additional clerks, and recommends that paymasters' clerks shall be classed and paid as other clerks.

He again urges the necessity of consolidating the appropriations for pay of the Army, mileage, and general expenses under one title.

The amounts to be disbursed under the above titles are, with two or three exceptions, limited by statute law. If the appropriation is in excess of these demands, the excess cannot be disbursed, but will be carried by operation of law to the surplus fund; but if the appropriation is not sufficient to meet the demands, the excess becomes a valid claim against the United States, and the subject of a deficiency estimate, thus forcing a very worthy class of claimants to a delay that is oftentimes very embarrassing. Many of the items are estimated upon expenditures of prior years, the best data obtainable. This estimate may be in some cases excessive and in others not sufficient, but in the aggregate the amount appropriated will be sufficient to meet all demands if the excess in one of them can be used to supply the deficiency in another. Again, the division of the appropriations into three heads, for each year, makes it necessary to keep in the hands of each disbursing officer a balance of funds much larger than if there were but one appropriation for each year, as he is obliged to carry a working balance under each appropriation. This, in case of a limited appropriation, makes it very difficult to properly distribute the funds over so scattered a field as that occupied by paymasters.

ENGINEER BUREAU.

I invite especial attention to that part of the report of the Chief of Engineers which refers to our sea-coast defenses. For many years, during which no work whatever has been done upon these defenses except for their preservation and repair, under small appropriations confined to these purposes by law, the Chief of Engineers has called attention in his annual reports to the very great danger which results from leaving our fortifications in their present condition.

The casemated works, which necessarily form a large part of our sea-coast defenses, were built before the invention of modern armor, and before the introduction of rifled guns into maritime warfare. They are built of masonry, unprotected by armor, and although in their day they were equal to any in the world, they are utterly unfitted to withstand the assaults of modern ships of war.

The Chief of Engineers shows that a defense by fortifications and torpedoes is the only one which is at all practicable for coasts as extended as ours, comprising so many rich maritime cities, extensive navy-yards, and depots of supply; that any attempt at any other mode of defense would be enormously expensive both for first cost and cost of maintenance, and that it is the only mode adopted by maritime nations.

Experience shows that modern wars come on suddenly; that serious international disputes occur between nations the relations of which are apparently the most unlikely to be other than friendly, and that a condition of readiness for defense and an attitude of belligerency are sometimes the best preventives of actual war. We know that the necessary new works and the proper modifications of our old works will require many years for their completion, and it seems simply a matter of common prudence that we commence without delay, and under liberal appropriations, to put our coasts in an efficient condition of defense.

I also commend attention to that part of the report of the Chief of Engineers which speaks of the needs of our torpedo system, and the importance of increasing the strength of the Engineer Battalion to 520 men, the minimum number consistent with reasonable efficiency. The work of engineer troops is more technical than is required in any other part of the Army, and while this is so, they are regular soldiers, thoroughly instructed in infantry tactics, and are as available in an emergency as any other troops of the line for any duty that may be required of soldiers. On our torpedo service much will depend in future wars, and 520 men in training for that service, for all our coasts and all our harbors, seems but a small number, and the desire of the Chief of Engineers for an increase of 320 men above the 200 to which the battalion is limited by orders, under the reduction of the Army to 25,000 men, is a reasonable one, and should be granted. No increase of officers is necessary, simply a provision of law authorizing the recruitment of the Engineer Battalion by the number necessary to raise its strength to 520 enlisted men, this number to be in addition to the 25,000 men who now constitute the entire Army, if my recommendation for a repeal of recent restrictions as to the enlisted force of the Army is not concurred in. The maximum strength of the battalion, as authorized by existing law, is 752, or 232 more than the strength recommended.

The funds applied to the improvement of rivers and harbors during the past fiscal year were derived from the appropriation of June 14, 1880, and balances remaining unexpended of previous appropriations, the total amount available for expenditure on July 1, 1880, being $13,549,455.41. To the above should be added certain small amounts from the appropriation of March 3, 1881, which were made available before the commencement of the present fiscal year. Operations have been carried on under approved projects for the improvements to which they relate, with results which have been generally satisfactory.

Detailed information in regard to the various works in progress during the year will be found in the report of the Chief of Engineers.

The preliminary arrangements which were in progress at the date of last annual report for making a practical test of the flume invented by Mr. M. J. Adams for increasing the depth of water in the Mississippi River, for which the sum of $20,000 was provided by act of March 3, 1879, have been continued during the fiscal year, under the direction and supervision of the inventor. .

The surveys and examinations of rivers and harbors, called for by the act of March 3, 1881, are in process of execution, and it is expected that the reports and maps will be ready for transmission to Congress in the early part of the session.

The Mississippi River Commission has been engaged in the further prosecution of surveys of the river and its tributaries, and in considering plans for the improvement of the main river, and in making the necessary arrangements for the application of the appropriation of $1,000,000 in the river and harbor act of March 3, 1881, for the improvement of the river below Cairo. Reports from the commission will be found appended to the report of the Chief of Engineers.

On the survey of the northern and northwestern lakes, a new chart of the west end of Lake Erie has been completed and published. The final report of this survey is now in course of preparation.

In the survey of the territory of the United States west of the one hundredth meridian work has been confined to the reduction of notes and the construction of maps. Six atlas sheets have been completed.

Volume VII, the last of the quarto reports of the fortieth parallel survey, has been published.

Eight officers of the Corps of Engineers have been on duty at the headquarters of the military divisions and departments, and have been engaged in making such surveys and preparing such maps as are required for the use of the Army. The maps prepared by these officers are of great value in the movement of troops, and the establishment of posts for controlling the Indians and protecting settlers. There is a great demand for the maps from citizens for use in the location of railroads, mines, and valuable lands. The small appropriation asked for the next fiscal year for continuing these surveys and for publication of maps required for military purposes is earnestly recommended.

ORDNANCE DEPARTMENT.

The report of the Chief of Ordnance shows that on July 1 we had in store only 37,526 small-arms. This is but little more than the annual consumption, and I concur in his opinion that increased appropriations for accumulating a large reserve are of great necessity.

The Chief of Ordnance recommends that the standing annual appropriation of $300,000, made in 1808, for arming the militia, should be largely increased. My opinion, derived from an examination of the debits and credits of the States, as they now stand under that law, is that it would be at least advisable to give legislative authority to the Secretary of War to give, after a specified time in each year, the allotments of States not called for to such States as make requisition therefor to arm their militia. Under the practical working of the present system, advances of arms strictly unlawful are made to those States which have a large force of organized militia, and a credit is left standing on the record to States which take no such steps for the public protection.

The "act making appropriations for fortifications and other works of defense, and for the armament thereof for the fiscal year ending June 30, 1882, and for other purposes," approved March 3, 1881, provides:

And the President is authorized to select a board, to consist of one engineer officer, two ordnance officers, and two officers of artillery, whose duty it shall be to make examinations of all inventions of heavy ordnance and improvements of heavy ordnance and projectiles that may be presented to them, including guns now being constructed or converted under direction of the Ordnance Bureau; and said board shall make detailed report to the Secretary of War, for transmission to Congress, of such examination, with recommendation as to what inventions are worthy of actual test, and the estimated cost of such test; and the sum of twenty-five thousand dollars, or so much thereof as may be necessary, is hereby appropriated for such purpose.

In conformity with the foregoing act, a board of officers has been appointed and is now in session for the purpose of making examinations of all inventions referred to in the law, and making a detailed report of such examinations, with recommendation as to what inventions are worthy of actual test, and the estimated cost of such test. Its report will undoubtedly be made and transmitted to Congress early the next session.

A special report from the Chief of Ordnance shows that under the act of March 3, 1881, there was sold, prior to July 1, 1881, 29,500 pounds of unserviceable and unsuitable powder, at 8 cents per pound, and that on June 24, 1881, a contract was made for the procurement of 500,000 pounds of hexagonal powder, at 25.4 cents per pound.

- Congress at its last session provided for convening a board of officers to examine magazine guns, with a view to the selection of some of the best for trial in service. The board is now in session.

REPORT OF THE CHIEF SIGNAL OFFICER.

Eight officers are, under present regulations, annually detailed for instruction in military signaling at Fort Myer, and, during the past year, an average number of seventy-nine enlisted men have been present subject to instruction in signaling and in the duties of observers at weather stations.

Six hundred and ten miles of sea-coast telegraph lines are operated by the Chief Signal Officer for the use of the Weather Bureau.

Five thousand and seventy-seven miles of frontier telegraph lines are also operated by him, and are of indispensable value to the military service.

A very brief summary of the work of the Chief Signal Officer includes the preparation of new instructions for observers; the preparation of new and improved forms for the recording and preservation of meteorological data; the preparation of special bulletins for the press, containing weather information of public interest; the forecasts of weather, of hot or cold waves for periods exceeding twenty-four hours; the forecasts of "northers" for the interior plateau; the adoption of a new storm signal (the Cautionary Northwest) for the interior lakes; the arrangement for increase of river service, and wider publication of warnings of floods or ice gorges; the changes and improvements in the publication of the International Bulletin, and the Monthly Weather Review, with their accompanying charts; the increased information added to the Farmers' and to the Railway Bulletins; the organization of a service for the special benefit of the cotton interests of the South; the extension of the special frost warning to the fruit interests of the country; the investigations into thermometric standards, and into barometric standards; the preparation of new hygrometric tables containing correction for altitude; the revised determinations of the altitudes of Signal Service stations; the computation of monthly constants for the reduction of observed barometric pressues to sea-level; the arrangements for original investigation in atmospheric electricity, in anemometry and in actinometry, and, in the last subject, especially with reference to the importance of solar radiation in agriculture and the absorption of the sun's heat by the atmosphere; the co-operation in an expedition to the summit of Mount Whitney, California, for the determination of problems in solar physics; in meteorology, the preparation of conversion tables for the English and metric systems; the co-operation in the dropping of time balls at Signal Service stations; the publication in quarto form of special professional papers; the offering of prizes for essays of great merit on meteorological subjects; the organization of State weather services; the new investigation of danger lines on western rivers; the organization and equipment of two expeditions for meteorological observation and research in the Arctic regions of America, one to be stationed at Lady Franklin Bay, the other at Point Barrow, Alaska, both co-operating in this work with a system of stations established in the Polar region by international conference; the establishment of a system of stations of observation in Alaska; the arrangements for organizing a Pacific Coast Weather Service; the display at the Paris Electrical Exposition; the experiments for improving newspaper weather charts; the increase since June 1 of telegraphic weather service, exceeding in value $34,000 per annum, without additional expenses to the United States, and the extension and construction of military telegraph lines.

Full details of these operations will be found in the report.

The total number of stations of observation was, on June 30, two hundred and ninety-six, in the management of which the enlisted force of five hundred men (excepting those under instruction) is constantly employed.

The plan of exhibiting as widely as possible in the agricultural districts throughout the United States, the results of the daily office studies, in the form of printed forecasts, for the benefit of the agricultural populations, frequently described in former reports, has been continued in operation.

The railway bulletin service has been increased during the year, and continues to give satisfaction as a rapid means of disseminating the Indications issued from the office. Ninety-three companies, with a total of two thousand nine hundred and thirty-seven stations, are now cooperating in this service.

Storm signals are displayed, when necessary, at 116 ports.

During the past year stations of observation on the habits and ravages of the Rocky Mountain locusts or grasshoppers were established by the Chief Signal Officer in those sections which the experience of past years has shown to be most exposed to the ravages of these pests. It is gratifying to state that not a single report of the ravages of locusts was received.

Attention is earnestly invited to the remarks of the Chief Signal Officer upon the subject of a permanent organization, to obviate the necessity of calling for details of officers from regiments. The work done by him undoubtedly requires the assistance of a number of officers in addition to the scientific staff of civilians. Officers of the Engineer and Ordnance Corps cannot properly be detailed on such duty, not only for the reason that their actual services in their own departments are constantly required, but because it would be an act of injustice to take them away from duties and studies of a very technical character, proficiency in which is a condition precedent to promotion. The taking of officers from the line of the Army is now the only course left, but this is objectionable, as the officer is nearly always detailed in opposition to the wishes of his commanding officers; the detail removes him from his proper military duties, imposes an undue share of company and regimental duty upon his brother officers remaining with the troops, and, at last, if the officer's services are valuable, results in conflicting claims for his return and his retention, always annoying, and sometimes difficult to decide.

It will be seen from the elaborate and interesting report of the Chief Signal Officer that the work of the Weather Bureau is highly scientific and wholly unmilitary, and that it depends for its value upon constant observations made at many stations, and continuous records of those observations. Any interruption, however short, at any station, makes a gap in the complete records, upon whose perfection rests the accuracy of calculated results. This work occupies all the time of the force under the Chief Signal Officer, detailed officers, civilian employés, and enlisted men, and would require an equal force under a permanent organization; and the detachment of any of them for signal duty in the field in time of war would cause a great and lasting injury, if not

educating the number authorized by law, even if some of them never enter the Regular Army, is well repaid by their availability in time of need as officers of Volunteers, or of an increased regular force.

If the full number authorized by law is educated at the Academy, no additional annual expense is incurred by keeping the cadets through a five years' course, and it is not unlikely that the decrease in the average number of annual graduates (one-fifth of the whole number being graduated each year, instead of one-fourth) would be so much affected by a decrease in the percentage of rejections and of dismissals for deficiency, that the graduates from the Academy would more nearly equal the annual casualties in the Army than is now the case. During the decade ending June, 1880, of nearly 750 appointments to the grade of second lieutenant in the Army, only about two-thirds were graduates of the Military Academy, so that under the present system less than two-thirds of the number of cadets possible, and provided for under the law, are graduated. From such consideration as I have been able to give the subject, I believe that this large deficiency is mainly owing to the compression of an undue amount of work into a term of four years, causing not only many failures by the way, but necessitating an exceedingly rigid preliminary examination. In a course of five years, not only would more time be given for the necessary studies, but a part of the first year could be considered as a period of probation, avoiding the necessity of a very severe preliminary examination, and better enabling the academic board to form a just idea of the general fitness of the young cadet to grapple with the higher studies.

EDUCATION IN THE ARMY.

Chaplain Mullins, the officer now in charge of this work, reports that at the various schools at military posts now in operation there is an average attendance of 912 enlisted men and 1,390 children of officers, enlisted men, and civilians. He calls attention to the difficulty of finding competent teachers among the enlisted men, and the interruptions caused by their military duties, none of which are omitted. I approve his recommendation for statutory authority for the enlistment of 150 competent men to be rated as schoolmasters, with the rank and pay of commissary-sergeant.

The reading-rooms established at most of the posts are very popular with enlisted men as well as officers. The average daily attendance upon them is about 4,800.

THE SOLDIERS' HOME.

The report of the Board of Commissioners of the Soldiers' Home shows that 550 members were receiving the benefits of the Home on September 30, 1880. During the year 318 permanent and temporary members were admitted; 46 members died; 197 were dropped, voluntarily and otherwise; leaving 588 members on September 30, 1881.

The board call attention to the evil effect of the unrestrained use of money by some members who are also in receipt of pensions.

GOVERNMENT HOSPITAL FOR THE INSANE.

The following is the number of persons admitted into the above-named institution, under orders of the Secretary of War, from October 1, 1880, to October 1, 1881:

Regular Army—
Commissioned officers	3
Commissioned officers (retired)	1
Enlisted men	35
Enlisted men (late of the Army)	4

Late volunteer service—
Commissioned officers	1
Enlisted men..	2
Hospital matrons attached to the Army	1
Inmates of the United States Soldiers' Home	5
Military prisoners..	3
Employés of the Quartermaster's Department, U. S. Army	1
Employés of the Subsistence Department, U. S. Army	1
Total	57

RECORDS OF THE WAR OF THE REBELLION.

The publication of these records is proceeding as rapidly as is consistent with accurate preparation. Two volumes have been published, and ten volumes have been made ready for the printer, seven being in his hands in various stages of preparation. Many contributions by gift or loan have been added during the year to the files of Confederate documents.

BUILDING FOR STATE, WAR, AND NAVY DEPARTMENTS.

The construction of this building, for the accommodation of the State, War, and Navy Departments, was confined, during the year, to the north wing, exclusively, and the walls of this wing were completed to the roof, of which the greater part of the iron-work is in place.

This wing forms one of the portions of the building to be used by the War Department, at present crowded, with some of its records, into a part of the wing allotted to the Navy Department. An appropriation of $100,000 for the completion of the north wing is recommended.

I also ask the favorable consideration of Congress upon the application for $450,000, included in the annual estimates of this department, to begin the erection of the west wing and the center wing of the building. The present isolation of some of the most important bureaus is not only inconvenient, but many of the outside buildings in use do

21 Ab

not afford adequate security to the public records. It is of the greatest importance that these records should be placed beyond the danger of destruction by fire at the earliest possible moment, and their safety cannot be assured until the new building is completed.

IMPROVEMENT OF THE SOUTH PASS OF THE MISSISSIPPI RIVER.

The last annual report from this department brought the history of this work to August 9, 1880, when there had been from July 8, 1879, a full year's maintenance of the channel required by law, after excluding days of non-maintenance, all of which occurred in the first two quarters. Uninterrupted maintenance was continued for the two quarters ending February 9, 1881. The engineer's certificate for the succeeding quarter showed that there was full maintenance, excepting through the pass itself, in which, as measured from the plane of the established gauge-mark, there was a slight failure for a distance of 240 feet; but during the time in question the stage of the river was such as to make its actual level, at low tide, 1.2 feet higher than the established low-water mark, so that the required channel was in fact maintained during the quarter. The facts being submitted by me to the Attorney-General for his opinion as to whether Mr. Eads was entitled to payment for maintenance during the quarter ending May 9, 1881, he answered in the affirmative, and payment was made accordingly. The next quarter extended to include August 13, 1881, four days being excluded in computation on account of the channel being in that time reduced to 110 feet in width at one point and given the required width by dredging. Four quarterly payments of $25,000 each for maintenance, and two semi-annual payments of $25,000 each for interest on the $1,000,000 retained, have accordingly been made to Mr. Eads.

The total expenditures of the government up to this time, on account of this improvement, are $4,550,000. It will be seen that there has been a substantial maintenance of the prescribed channel during the eighteen months last past, with a loss of only four days, and that the remarks in my predecessor's report concerning the permanency of this work are confirmed, to a large extent, by the results obtained during the second year of successful operation of this remarkable improvement.

THE FREE BRIDGE AT GEORGETOWN.

The difficulties met in attempting to carry out the provisions of the act of February 23, 1881, providing for a free bridge on the Potomac River, at or near Georgetown, have prevented much progress. The act forbids the incurring of any expense whatever for an entirely new bridge until a contract for its erection, at a cost not exceeding the prescribed limit of $140,000, shall have been made. There are, therefore, no funds to pay for preliminary surveys or for specifications on which to base a proper call for bids, and legally no funds out of which to pay for the advertisements for proposals.

I have no doubt that the wisest course is to use the piers of the present Aqueduct Bridge, for which an alternate provision is made in the act. It is, however, owned by one corporation and leased to another for a long term of years. The lessee offers to sell for the price named in the act, but the lessor refuses to sell. The United States acquired some interest in the old bridge, whose effect and extent must be determined judicially, if ever settled, by an advance of $300,000 to the corporation of Alexandria in 1837, which sum was expended in completing the canal and bridge. Bids for the construction of an entirely new bridge have been called for, but the result is not yet reported to me. If no bid is accepted, it is my opinion that such additional legislation should be had as to authorize a judicial condemnation of the present Aqueduct Bridge, the claims to the amount of compensation awarded to be settled as may be provided, and the old piers to be used for the construction of the free bridge. In this way the equitable rights of the government and of all parties in interest can be protected, and the actually needless construction of new piers for a free bridge be avoided. The subject, however, requires a more extended consideration than can be given at this time, and the attention of Congress will probably be invited to it in a special communication.

COWPENS MONUMENT.

By the joint resolution of Congress approved May 26, 1880, the duty devolved upon the Secretary of War to cause to be made a bronze statue of General Daniel Morgan, the commander of the American forces at the battle of Cowpens, South Carolina, and to cause the same to be delivered, through the governor of that State, to the Cowpens Centennial Committee, in time to be placed in position upon the memorial column before the 17th day of January, 1881, the centennial anniversary of the battle. With the approval of the President, my predecessor selected Mr. J. Q. A. Ward, of New York City, as the artist to execute the statue, and a contract was entered into with him for the sum named in the law, $20,000.

October 26, 1880, Mr. William A. Courtenay, the chairman of the Centennial Committee, advised Mr. Ward of the inability of the committee to complete the arrangements for unveiling the statue on January 17, 1881. To give the artist ample time to review his work carefully, the time for completion and delivery of the statue was extended until March 8, 1881. The statue was finished in bronze February 17, 1881, and, after inspection and acceptance, was shipped to Spartanburg, South Carolina. The chairman of the Cowpens Centennial Committee and the governor of South Carolina have certified that the statue was received in perfect order, and that the terms of the contract were fully complied with.

MONUMENT AT YORKTOWN.

The final report of the commission of artists selected by my predecessor to recommend a suitable design for the monument directed by the act approved June 7, 1880, to be erected at Yorktown, was received by me March 14, 1881, and at once submitted to the select committee of senators and members of the House of Representatives. The model was not received from the artists until May 26, and information of its arrival was on the same day given the committee.

The select committee, on June 30, 1881, notified me of their approval and adoption of the design submitted, and immediate directions were given to proceed with its construction, so far as could be done within the short time remaining before the 19th day of October, 1881, the time fixed for the national celebration at Yorktown. The site was selected by the joint committee of Congress July 7, 1881. It was not possible to proceed further by October 19, 1881, than the laying of the corner-stone, and this had to be done without awaiting the approval of the title to the site selected. The corner-stone having been laid, as a part of the celebration, further work of construction has been suspended, awaiting the approval of the title to the land occupied and its cession by the State of Virginia.

ROBERT T. LINCOLN,
Secretary of War.

PAPERS

ACCOMPANYING

THE REPORT OF THE SECRETARY OF WAR.

REPORT OF THE GENERAL OF THE ARMY.

HEADQUARTERS OF THE ARMY,
Washington, November 3, 1881.

SIR: I now have the honor to submit to you the following annual reports:

1st. Of Adjutant-General Drum, including tables which exhibit in great detail the organization of the Army according to existing laws; of the actual strength of organizations and distribution of troops; and statements of enlistments, casualties, recruitment, number of trials, &c., with comments and recommendations of which I will treat in due order.

2d. Of Inspector-General Sacket, giving results of the actual inspections of the various posts; of money accounts, property returns, and everything which contributes to the efficiency of the military establishment, with certain recommendations which I shall likewise consider in the proper place.

The above are the only two heads of the staff bureaus who report to me; all others are construed as branches of the War Department, and report direct to the Secretary of War.

I also transmit herewith the very full and exhaustive reports of all the commanding generals of divisions and departments, which record the changes made since their last annual reports, with a narrative of events which are most useful to the parties in interest and to the future historian. These are as follows:

3.—Military Division of the Missouri, Lieutenant-General Sheridan.
3 A.—Department of Dakota, Brigadier-General Terry.
3 B.—Department of the Platte, Brigadier-General Crook.
3 C.—Department of the Missouri, Brigadier-General Pope.
3½ C.—Report of Colonel Hatch.
3 D.—Department of Texas, Brigadier-General Augur.
4.—Military Division of the Atlantic, Major-General Hancock.
4 A.—Department of the East, Major-General Hancock.
4 B.—Department of the South, Colonel and Brevet Brigadier-General Hunt.
5.—Military Division of the Pacific and Department of California, Major-General McDowell, followed by 5 *a, b,* and *c.*
5 A.—Department of the Columbia: 1, Colonel and Brevet Brigadier-General Wheaton; and 2, Brigadier-General Miles.
5 B.—Department of Arizona, Colonel and Brevet Brigadier-General Willcox.

I also submit herewith (6) the reports of Brig. Gen. O. O. Howard,

Department of West Point, and (7) of Colonel and Brevet Major-General Getty, commanding Artillery School at Fort Monroe, Virginia.

All these are so full and interesting that I am sure they will receive your careful perusal. For a short time, viz, from January 31, 1881, to May 9, 1881, a Military Division "of the Gulf" was constituted by President Hayes, embracing Louisiana, Texas, Arkansas, and the Indian Territory, with Major-General Schofield in command; but as this division was found to fulfill no useful military end, it was discontinued by President Garfield, leaving boundaries as they existed before. These boundaries generally conform to political lines, and are the result of long experience, clearly limiting and defining the authority and consequent responsibility of each commanding general.

Whilst the troops have been kept very busy during the past year, no serious Indian or other war has occurred, but great progress has been made in collecting and locating Indians, hitherto hostile, on their proper reservations. Sitting Bull and his adherents, who had fled into British territory, are now held at Fort Randall, Dak., as prisoners of war, and the Utes have been moved to a new reservation in Utah, as fully described in the reports of Generals Terry and Sheridan. The sudden outbreak of a part of the Apaches in Arizona is explained in the reports of Generals Willcox and McDowell. In the latter case it was found necessary to re-enforce for a short time the usual garrisons in Arizona by a strong detachment from New Mexico, under Colonel Mackenzie, of the Fourth Cavalry. The guilty Apaches are now held as prisoners for trial. Some have escaped into Mexico, whilst the greater part of the tribe remains on their reservation at San Carlos, under their proper civil agent. I will append to General McDowell's report copies of all papers necessary to illustrate this event.

All these annual reports, with justice, dwell on the fact that our companies are too small for efficient discipline and for economical service. There are in the Army 430 companies, which are necessarily widely scattered over our vast domain, to guard property and to prevent, as far as foresight can, complications and troubles of every variety and kind—at one time protecting the settlers against Indians, and again Indians against the settlers. When these occur it is always sudden, and re-enforcements have to be hurried forward from great distances, and always at heavy cost for transportation of men, horses, wagons, and supplies. This cost in the aggregate will, in my judgment, be more than sufficient to supply an increase of 20 per cent. of *private soldiers*— all that I would ask for at this time, because I believe this increase will add little, if any, to the annual cost of the Army, and yet give great relief to our overtaxed soldiers. In the last ten years our frontiers have so extended, under the protection of our small Army, as to add at least a thousand millions of dollars to the taxable wealth of the nation; has enabled emigrants to settle up remote parts of the country, and is a principal cause of the great prosperity which is felt throughout all parts of the country. When the national Treasury was poor and loaded with debt, the Army endeavored, gracefully, to submit to overwork, but they now appeal for relief, and I do most earnestly ask the honorable Secretary of War to apply to Congress to repeal that clause of existing law which limits the enlisted force of the Army to 25,000 men, and to enact that each and every company in the Army may be enlisted to at least 50 privates, making 62 enlisted men and 3 officers to each of the 430 companies, thus increasing the Army proper to 26,660 enlisted men, which number in practice will probably never exceed 25,000. This should form the combatant force; and, as experience and universal practice have demonstrated the necessity for another or non-combatant force, I further urge that special provision be made by law for each of the following separate and distinct purposes, viz:

Engineer Battalion	200
Permanent recruiting companies and parties	1,250
Enlisted men detailed on general service (clerks)	420
Ordnance Department (laborers and mechanics)	400
West Point detachments (Military Academy)	192
Prison guard at Fort Leavenworth (special)	90
Hospital stewards	175
Ordnance sergeants	112
Commissary sergeants	150
Indian scouts	300
Signal detachment	500
Total	**3,789**

Which number, added to the 26,660 before explained, will make a total enlisted force of every nature and kind of 30,449.

By section 1115, Revised Statutes, the number of enlisted men of all arms of service is limited to 30,000; but for some years, in appropriation bills, the number has been further restricted to 25,000, which, in my judgment, has resulted in no real economy, and has imposed on the private soldiers of the Army too much manual labor and an undue proportion of risk to life and health.

In this connection I submit a statement of the actual strength of enlisted men in the Regular Army, compiled from returns received at the Adjutant-General's Office up to October 15, 1881, as follows: .

First Cavalry	700	
Second Cavalry	774	
Third Cavalry	681	
Fourth Cavalry	621	
Fifth Cavalry	557	
Sixth Cavalry	732	
Seventh Cavalry	658	
Eighth Cavalry	707	
Ninth Cavalry	744	
Tenth Cavalry	708	
Total cavalry		**6,882**
First Artillery	494	
Second Artillery	499	
Third Artillery	499	
Fourth Artillery	472	
Fifth Artillery	439	
Total Artillery		**2,403**
First Infantry	398	
Second Infantry	432	
Third Infantry	424	
Fourth Infantry	323	
Fifth Infantry	410	
Sixth Infantry	440	
Seventh Infantry	454	
Eighth Infantry	418	
Ninth Infantry	337	
Tenth Infantry	333	
Eleventh Infantry	377	
Twelfth Infantry	425	
Thirteenth Infantry	426	
Fourteenth Infantry	448	
Fifteenth Infantry	420	
Sixteenth Infantry	424	
Seventeenth Infantry	451	
Eighteenth Infantry	464	
Nineteenth Infantry	435	

Twentieth Infantry	429
Twenty-first Infantry	435
Twenty-second Infantry	384
Twenty-third Infantry	422
Twenty-fourth Infantry	500
Twenty-fifth Infantry	521
Total infantry	**10,530**
Combatants	**19,815**
Engineer Battalion	196
Permanent and recruiting parties, music boys, and recruits in depots	1,251
Enlisted men detailed on general service	421
Ordnance Department	406
West Point detachments	192
Prison guard	89
Hospital stewards	171
Ordnance-sergeants	112
Commissary-sergeants	149
Indian scouts	300
Signal detachment	494
Non-combatants	**3,781**
Total enlisted force of the Army of the United States, October, 1881	**23,596**

There are 120 companies of cavalry, 60 of artillery, and 250 of infantry. By dividing the total force of each arm of service by the number of companies, we have the average strength of company—

For cavalry, 58 enlisted men.

For artillery, 40 enlisted men.

For infantry, 41 enlisted men.

These numbers embrace 12 non-commissioned officers and musicians, leaving only 46, 28, and 29 privates, respectively—numbers so small that the companies are almost ridiculous, compelling commanding officers to group two and even four companies together to perform the work of one.

I also invite attention to the absurdity of styling in orders the companies of foot artillery, armed with muskets and without guns, "batteries." They are not batteries in any intelligent sense. The same as to "troop" for cavalry. All should be styled what they are in fact, "companies."

Nearly every general officer commanding troops on the frontier asks in his annual report for a larger increase than I have herein indicated, but this may be better accomplished by giving to the President the right to increase, at his discretion, the companies most exposed to danger to any number of privates, not exceeding 100, limited always in practice by the actual appropriations of money rather than by a fixed number of men.

In the report of Inspector-General Sacket you will find two points worthy of notice. He represents that his corps of officers is now limited to five, which is too small a number for the important duties which devolve on them. The inspector-general must necessarily be stationed in Washington, and should have at least one competent assistant with him. Then there are now, and probably always will be, three geographical divisions and nine departments, each of which ought to have an inspector-general. This would necessitate 14 officers in all—an increase in this corps of nine majors, each of whom should have the right to employ one clerk, with the same compensation which is now allowed to paymasters' clerks. I cordially unite with General Sacket in this latter recommendation, and further, that the President be allowed to select any increase of officers in the Inspector-General's Department from the majors and captains of the line. This is the only increase of commissioned officers asked for in the whole Army, and would, in fact, only be an increase of the same number of lieutenants needed to fill the vacancies occasioned by the promotion of the nine majors.

The second recommendation is in regard to officers' servants. I, myself, have seen occasions when no officer could afford to hire a servant, because a servant's wages exceeded the officer's pay; and as a rule the government compels its officers to live in remote places where no servant will go, of his own free will, for any wages. It is simply impossible for an officer to hire a servant at a hundred places where troops must necessarily be; and on one occasion, two years ago, in Western Montana, I had an escort of a company of cavalry, where, as soon as we reached camp, the captain and lieutenants had to pull off their coats, gather wood and water, cook their own meals, and groom their own horses. I honor labor as much as any man, and never was ashamed to cook my own meal or saddle my own horse; but no officer can habitually do this work and properly supervise his company and command. No soldier should ever be *compelled* to do menial labor without compensation, or without his own consent; but if a soldier is willing to cook and wash for his captain, and to groom his horse, for *pay*, there is no reason why he should be forbidden to do it, and I recommend that the law be repealed, or modified so as to read:

SEC. 1232. No officer shall use an enlisted man as a servant, in any case whatever, without proper compensation, or without his own consent and that of his commanding officer.

With this modification no wrong is possible to any soldier, and the officer will not be compelled, as now, to do menial service or to violate the law.

There is a subject of great importance, needing Congressional action, which has hitherto been discussed and will bear repetition. In the early days of the republic nearly every city and harbor on the Atlantic and Gulf coasts, as well as on the lakes, wanted a fort for protection against public enemies. These were built and still remain the property of the United States, and the Army is charged, in one way or another, with their care and preservation. Very many of them are now absolutely of no use, present or prospective, and should be disposed of. I will not mention names, because of local feeling. Every such city or town, from Maine to Texas and from Duluth to Lake George, has a local pride in its fort and garrison, and if in times past such a fort was built by the United States, any attempt to withdraw the garrison or remove the flag is met by local opposition, often impossible to overcome. I recommend that you apply to Congress for authority to submit the whole question of coast defense to a board of high officers of all arms of service, to consider the whole question, with instructions to report to the Secretary of War what coast forts shall be maintained, what sites shall be retained for future use, and what may be absolutely sold; and further, that authority be granted the President to sell the same, subject to any conditions which Congress may impose.

In like manner, inland, a great number of military posts and stations have either been reserved from the public domain, or have been purchased, which, by the progress of settlement, have become obsolete; yet they need a military guard for protection. These are worse than useless, because they absorb a large fraction of the small Army, which ought to be free for action. For these I would recommend a similar, but distinct board, to make a thorough study of the whole problem of internal defense, with similar authority to sell and dispose of all posts, except such as are deemed necessary for permanent occupation and future use. If the funds arising from these sales could be appropriated for the permanent sites, I am sure great economy would result to the Treasury, and durable barracks and quarters could be built in place of the temporary shelters which, from wear and tear, have proven the worst possible for economy. This is nothing more than what is occurring all over the United States, where the old log-cabins are giving place to the more lasting brick houses of the farmer and mechanic.

I am further of opinion that section 1136 of the Revised Statutes, forbidding the erection of permanent buildings except by special authority of Congress, should be wholly repealed. The time for temporary shanties has passed away, and no building should henceforth be erected at any of the permanent forts and military establishments except of stone or brick. This would be true economy, whereas wooden buildings with timber foundations and shingle roofs are in the end the most costly. Surely discretion as to the character of such structures can safely be reposed in the Secretary of War.

Beyond question some of the old forts are worth retaining, because they are finished, and are so located as to have little value for sale to private parties. To preserve these the government may, with propriety, economy, and charity, utilize the present corps of retired officers, for whom now there is no employment whatever. There are also in the Army many old soldiers who have served this government in war and peace faithfully for twenty-five and more years, in the assurance that they would be provided for in their old age. I recommend that the President be authorized to transfer, out of this class of enlisted men who have thus served for twenty-five or more years a number not to exceed 500, including the ordnance-sergeants (now 112), and establish a "Veteran Corps," to be stationed at these old forts, with the rank and pay they held at the close of their active career of Army service, to be subject to the Rules and Articles of War, but only to be used for guarding public property. One or two officers of the retired class and half a dozen of these old soldiers would compose a good garrison for an abandoned post or fort. They could hoist the flag, fire the evening gun, protect and account for the public property, and do what now costs the labor of an organized company. By granting the retired officers thus detailed fuel and quarters, we would provide homes for worthy veterans which would be most honorable and charitable to them and advantageous to the government. At the close of our civil war we had a similar arrangement in what was known as the "Veteran Reserve Corps;" and in Europe all, or nearly all, the governments thus or in some similar way provide for their old and faithful military servants.

The Adjutant-General enumerates 190 distinct military posts, 16 arsenals, 3 recruiting depots, and 1 engineer depot. Of these, 84 are on the Lakes, Atlantic or Gulf coasts; 11 on the Pacific; and the remaining 115 are "inland." Besides these are many "military sites," held by purchase long ago, or reserved out of the public domain, which the Attorney-General holds cannot be sold or abandoned without specific authority of Congress.

In the annual reports of Generals Sheridan, Hancock, and McDowell I find all subjects of recent interest so fully discussed that I ought not to repeat, but there is one of universal interest which I must discuss, "military education." The whole theory and practice of the Government of the United States has been, and continues to be, that the Regular Army must be small, as small as possible, and that for great occasions we as a people must rely on the volunteer masses of soldiery. No class of men better recognize this fact than the Regular Army, and as the science of war is progressive, we must keep pace with it, so as to impart to the volunteer militia, on the shortest notice, all that is known of the art and practice of war up to the moment of execution. In this sense the whole regular army is a school; but the bulk of the Army of the United States is fully employed otherwise in the daily work imposed on it, so that Congress has wisely provided that the Army shall lend assistance to military instruction in thirty of the civil colleges of the land. Each of these is a separate institution, and the thirty officers thus detailed fall absolutely under the control and authority of the faculty of the college to which each is attached. My own belief is that, inasmuch as the government loans the services of an officer to each of these institutions, they should be subjected to an inspection by an officer of that branch of the military service, whose report to the Secretary of War would enable him to decide whether this provision of law has fulfilled its purpose or not. There is now a great contest among civil colleges for this privilege, and the benefit of superimposing the military drill on the cadets of each college should be inquired into, from time to time, and reports made, so that the largest results possible may come from this investment.

West Point, however, has been, and must continue to be, the fountain-source of military education in time of peace. In the past it has fulfilled its destiny well, but we can no more restore the condition of facts of General Thayer's time than we can turn the dial of time back fifty years. You now have the report of the last Board of Visitors. I herewith submit the report of General O. O. Howard, the present Superintendent, and I beg you to consider them both together. Shall West Point go back to 1812 and become an engineer school, or shall it be a military academy for all arms of service? The Board of Visitors substantially recommend that the Superintendent of the Military Academy should be a colonel of engineers. The law is, the superintendent, while serving as such, shall have the local rank of colonel of engineers. Prior to 1866, the selection of superintendent was confined to the Engineer Corps, but not necessarily a colonel. A lieutenant colonel, major, or captain, could have been selected by the President, and when acting as superintendent the law gave him the local rank and pay of colonel of engineers. Great difficulty then existed in making a proper selection from the few officers eligible, which difficulty is now forgotten, and President Grant—himself a graduate, and deeply interested in the success of this National Academy—enlarged the field of selection so as to embrace the Engineer Corps and all the Army. Under his administration, Colonels Pitcher and Ruger, both of the infantry, were appointed superintendent, and finally Major-General Schofield. The present superintendent, Brigadier General Howard, was appointed by President Hayes. The Engineer Corps is in no manner excluded from the field of selection; on the contrary, if the President so chooses, he can select an officer of that corps, but is not limited to it exclusively, as is argued by the Board of Visitors.

I will concede to the engineers all the superiority in book knowledge they rightfully claim, but when war comes suddenly, as it most always does, with us, in the beginning the engineers naturally resort to scientific methods; whereas the Infantry, Cavalry, and Artillery, with superior practical knowledge acquired in contact with troops, must go in and do the fighting without further time for preparation. It was so

in 1812, in 1846, and in 1861-'65. West Point is intended to make
"soldiers," not professional engineers, and the word "soldier" embraces
everything in war.   If the engineer be a better soldier than the infantry officer, then let him in war and peace have all the honors and
emoluments; but our recent experience does not fulfill the assertion.
The honors of the civil war were not confined to the engineers; therefore I trust you will use your influence to leave the selection of the
head of the Military Academy, as now, from all arms of service.   Then
comes the question of rank for the superintendent.   Shall he be a
colonel or a general?   In my judgment it is a question of pay.   In
1830, the pay of a colonel was sufficient; now it is insufficient.   No
colonel can to-day be the Superintendent of the Military Academy without absolute distress.   Even the pay of a brigadier is scanty, and that
of a major-general, without outside help, is barely enough.   In 1830
few visitors went to West Point; now hundreds go from all parts of the
earth, and the superintendent has forced on him expenses of hospitality
that very few are aware of.   In my opinion the superintendent should
have a salary of $10,000 to maintain himself and family in that expen-
sive place, and if Congress will decree that sum, we can find captains
who are qualified, but it would be a cruelty to *order* any officer to occupy
the post on a colonel's pay.   Again, a "general" is common to all services; he is neither engineer, ordnance, quartermaster, artillery, cavalry,
nor infantry, but he pertains to all—therefore, I think, the superintendent should be a general officer.

Whether West Point should be a department or not is a small concern.   I think it should be, because the commander, as such, has the
lawful right to order courts-martial and execute their sentences on the
spot, not only against cadets, but the soldiers and officers stationed
there—a right of great value in maintaining the discipline which forms
the model for the whole Army.   I am perfectly conscious that the
Board of Visitors generally look upon modern times as worse than in
their young days.   To restore the "good old times" has been the dream
of man from the beginning, but time will not stop, and we must accept
this truth, and do the best we can *to-day*, sure that in due time those
who come after us will deplore the sad falling off of modern progress,
and compare the degeneracy of the year 1900 with "the good old times"
of 1880.   In my judgment the Military Academy of West Point *to-day*,
as in 1840, fulfills its uses, and can safely be trusted to prepare boys to
become the soldiers of the future.

The Artillery School at Fort Monroe is a specialty peculiar to that arm
of the service.   In former years we were content with 6, 12, 18, 24, and
32 pounder smooth-bore brass or iron guns.   Now all this is changed:
modern use calls for breech-loading steel rifle guns for field service, and
monster rifle-cannon of 100 tons weight, with a projectile weighing a ton,
impelled by 350 pounds of powder.   To mount and serve these guns requires
new machinery, and were the most skillful officer of the Mexican war
to rise from his grave he would be an infant in the use of modern artillery.
The object of this school is to familiarize our young officers with the
manipulation and use of these modern monsters, as well as to keep up
with the general progress of military science.

The engineer establishment at Willet's Point, New York, is believed
to be an admirable school for engineers, and for any officers who may be
called on to use torpedoes in connection with harbor defenses, but it
does not fall under my supervision or administration, and consequently
I merely mention it as one of the schools of instruction in successful
operation.

In like manner, the Signal School at Fort Myer provides for the instruction of eight subalterns each year in that branch of knowledge; but, as it takes five years thus to instruct one officer of each of the forty regiments, practical instruction in all the signaling which is essential to the Army is also taught at West Point, at Fort Monroe, and will be at Fort Leavenworth, thus embracing the whole Army.

Heretofore the officers of cavalry and infantry have been doomed to everlasting service in the very remotest parts of what was known as the "West," always in advance of civilization. No sooner than the settlements reached their post, which they had built of sods, or stone, or wood, they had to pull up stakes, move two or three hundred miles ahead, till the same game was repeated, and so on, *ad infinitum ;* but now this also is changed. Railroads traverse the continent east and west in the interest of trade and commerce, and these troops are shoved to the right and left to guard the embryo settlements against the Indians, or the Indians against the intrusive settlers, and the time has come when these officers should receive some consideration and some attention. With your approval, on the 7th of May last, I ordered Fort Leavenworth—a post on the Missouri River, occupied since 1819—to be got ready for a school of application for the cavalry and infantry, similar to that at Fort Monroe for the artillery. Under the supervision of General Pope, the necessary arrangements are well advanced, and I feel confident that before the 1st of January, 1882, we will have the plan complete and in successful execution. There will be habitually a garrison of one company of artillery, four companies of infantry, and four of cavalry, to which will be attached, for instruction, one officer of each regiment of infantry and of cavalry for a detail of two years. These will receive instruction in the military art, and then rejoin their proper regiments, to be succeeded by a similar detail every two years, so that in time the whole Army will thus be enabled to keep up with the rapid progress in the science and practice of war. This will complete the system, and I am certain that no matter how sudden war may come on us, we will be prepared for it, and the Regular Army will thus be the better enabled to impart to the vast mass of volunteers all the knowledge of the art of war which is possessed by the most skillful nations of the earth.

In conclusion, I beg to assure you that the enlisted men and officers of the present Army of the United States, in physique, in intelligence, in patriotic devotion to the honor and flag of the country, will compare favorably with any similar establishment on earth, and with our own Army at any previous period of our history.

During the past year recruitment has been slow, by reason of the general prosperity of the country affording better employment to the class of men who generally enlist; but winter and hard times will soon enable us to fill our ranks with a good class of men, and re-enlistments will increase by reason of the advantages the Army now holds out in the schools, in the better condition of the frontier posts, more abundant food and clothing, and the vastly diminished labor of the past by the completion of railroads to regions hitherto inaccessible except by long marches across arid, desolate plains. Now almost every post in the Army has railroad communication near, with mails, and connection by telegraph to all parts of the world. In my judgment, the condition of the Army, officers, and men, is incomparably better and more comfortable than it was twenty years ago.

For details of last year's work, and for progress in drill and rifle practice, I again invite your perusal of the inclosed reports of the several generals, which are very full and most interesting, supplemented by those of their own subordinates and staff, too voluminous to print, but which, in manuscript, are on file, accessible to you at all times.

With great respect,

W. T. SHERMAN,
General.

Hon. ROBERT T. LINCOLN,
Secretary of War.

REPORT OF THE ADJUTANT-GENERAL.

HEADQUARTERS OF THE ARMY,
ADJUTANT-GENERAL'S OFFICE,
Washington, October 25, 1881.

GENERAL: Pursuant to your instructions, I have the honor to submit the annual returns of the Army:

A.—Organization of the Regular Army.

B.—Return showing actual strength of the Regular Army.

C.—Distribution of troops in the Departments of Missouri, Texas, Platte, and Dakota—Division of the Missouri.

D.—Distribution of troops in the Departments of the East and South—Division of the Atlantic.

E.—Distribution of troops in the Departments of California, the Columbia, and Arizona—Division of the Pacific.

F.—Department of West Point.

G.—Military geographical divisions, departments, and posts, with distribution of troops, post-offices, telegraph stations, and nearest railroad stations or boat landings.

H.—Statement of casualties during the fiscal year ending June 30, 1881.

I.—Statement of the number of trials of enlisted men by general courts-martial during the fiscal year ending June 30, 1881.

K.—Statement of assignments of recruits and re-enlistments during the fiscal year ending June 30, 1881.

The number of enlisted men, now in service, who are drawing increased pay under act of Congress of August 4, 1854, is as follows:

Five years' continuous service	3,890
Ten years' continuous service	1,934
Fifteen years' continuous service	310
Twenty years' continuous service	140
Twenty-five years' continuous service	100
Thirty years' continuous service	50
Total	**6,424**

The number of those who will become entitled to increased pay, under act of Congress of May 15, 1872, during fiscal year ending June 30, 1883, is—

Re-enlisted pay	600
One dollar per month for third year of service	3,820
Two dollars per month for fourth year of service	3,834
Three dollars per month for fifth year of service	3,674
Total	**11,928**

: enlisted men now in service whose terms will ex-
l year ending June 30, 1883, is 3,596.

, compared with those in my last report, show an
:harges, 13 deaths, and 318 desertions; and, while
eyond human power to regulate, I am convinced
the number of discharges is ascribable to the grow-
) country, and equally satisfied that the desertions
> mainly to the fact that men joining the Army at
us are, from the necessities of the service, forwarded
egiments before they have learned the duties and
soldier. The sudden transition from the compara-
life to the strict discipline of the Army discourages
ie impulse of a discontented mood, and perhaps,
n an irresponsible condition, are led to disregard
is which they had assumed in all good faith. The
inted out in my remarks under the head of "The
but it rests with Congress to give the necessary
g into successful operation the plan suggested and
l.

f the true cause of the increase of desertions is
fact that of the men in the ranks who have already
service 1,964 (or nearly 13 per cent. of the nominal
r) have re-enlisted during the past year—an increase
ber of re-enlistments during the year 1879–'80.
he Adjutant-General's Department are properly
lischarge of their appropriate duties.

ON TO THE RANK OF FIELD OFFICER.

ny Regulations of 1863, prescribes that "all vacan-
giments or corps shall be filled by promotion accord-
ept in case of disability or other incompetency."
) established usage and custom of the service, re-
y in any one regiment of either of the three arms
)e filled by the promotion of the senior officer of the
it the officer promoted be commissioned in the par-
aring the loss which created the vacancy. This sys-
though sanctioned by long years of practice, is open

It sometimes happens that, during the permanent
iel of a regiment, through sickness or other cause,
necessarily devolves on either of the other field offi-
, the latter lack the elements required for the suc-
the duties of a regimental commander, and, in such
)w zealous and efficient the company commanders
; necessarily suffers loss in discipline and high tone;
evil, so far-reaching in its consequences, I beg to
st interests of the Army imperatively demand a
d of promotion to the rank of field officer below the
l this end can only be attained by promotion in the
iission in a particular regiment. In other words, on
racancy, the officer entitled to promotion should be
ajor of infantry," "lieutenant-colonel of artillery," as
tead of, as at present, "major of the—regiment of
effect of the proposed change will be to enable the
) to assign field officers of the line to the particular
s arm in which their services may be of the greatest

benefit, with a view to the highest efficiency of the regiment. This, it is conceived, would obliterate an evil which at any time may, through disgust or despair, threaten the demoralization of a regiment otherwise possessed of material not only able, but willing, to sustain its hard-earned reputation.

ARMY OFFICERS ABROAD.

But few of the officers who have enjoyed the privilege of visiting foreign countries have submitted reports of the results of their observations as is now required by orders; but from the well-known professional abilities and acquirements of those now abroad, and such as may hereafter be afforded the opportunity of visiting foreign countries, it is hoped much valuable scientific and military information may be obtained.

RESTORATION BY CONGRESS OF OFFICERS OUT OF SERVICE.

This most important subject so vitally affects the welfare and reputation of the whole Army that I beg most earnestly to reiterate my remarks on the subject made in my last report:

It has become the custom for officers dismissed by sentence of court-martial and dropped from the rolls of the Army to importune Congress for restoration to the position they have forfeited by the verdict of a court of their peers, reviewed and approved by the department commander, and confirmed by the President of the United States. The bill for restoration is referred to the Committee on Military Affairs, and by it, in many cases, placed in the hands of a subcommittee, before whom the claimant appears either personally or by attorney. The pressure of other duties not unfrequently prevents the subcommittee from giving the voluminous papers called for from the files of the War Department that careful and searching scrutiny such a case demands, having in view the baneful influence on the Army of the restoration to its rolls of a man unfit to hold a commission.

As a check on such claims, it is suggested that applicants for restoration be required, by statutory enactment, to present their claims to a board of officers to be appointed by the President, whenever, in his opinion, the applicant has an equitable claim to a further hearing.

VETERINARY SURGEONS.

By section 37 of the act of March 3, 1863 (section 1102, Revised Statutes), the grade of veterinary surgeon was created with assimilated rank of sergeant-major, and pay at the rate of $75 per month. The law of July 28, 1866, section 3, added four regiments to the cavalry arm, with the same organization as provided by law for cavalry regiments, but "with the addition of one veterinary surgeon to each regiment, whose compensation shall be one hundred dollars per month."

Thus, with precisely the same organization, *four* of the regiments have two veterinary surgeons, and *six* have but one, and at the lower rate of pay. If a cavalry regiment absolutely requires the services of two surgeons of that class, then all the regiments of that arm of the service should be placed on the same footing. In the contrary case, if only one suffices, then four of the ten regiments have one veterinary surgeon too many.

INFANTRY AND CAVALRY SCHOOL.

The gratifying results flowing from an enlargement of the field of professional acquirements and greater mental activity which have followed the establishment of a school of practice at Fort Monroe for the artillery arm of the service have long pointed out the advantages of establishing a school of application for infantry and cavalry similar to that above referred to, and orders were issued last May looking to the organization of a school at Fort Leavenworth, by assembling at that point at least four companies of infantry, four troops of cavalry, one light battery of artillery, and detailing for instruction one lieutenant of each regiment of infantry and cavalry, to be selected by the commander of the regiment and announced in general orders on or before the 1st of July of each alternate year, beginning with July, 1881, for the term of two years; the officers so detailed to be attached to the companies composing the school and to perform all the duties of company officers, in addition to those of instruction. The duty of carrying the above plan into execution was intrusted to the Lieutenant-General of the Army, and there is every prospect, although delay necessarily occurred by reason of inadequacy of officers' quarters at Fort Leavenworth, that ere long the school will be in successful operation, with, it is confidently hoped, marked benefit to those two arms of the service.

SIGNAL SCHOOL.

Signaling having become a necessary part of the military instruction of officers, a school of instruction has been established at Fort Myer, Virginia, and an annual detail authorized of eight officers, selected preferably from the lieutenants of the line of the Army who have served more than four years with their regiments and are possessed of sound health and good moral character, consideration being had also for service in the field, industry, soldierly habits, and aptitude for study.

RIFLE PRACTICE.

No teams from the Army participated this year in the Creedmore contest for marksmanship, owing to the limited appropriations from which the expenses for such contests could be defrayed. To counteract, as much as possible, the absence of this powerful incentive to effectiveness and to encourage general excellence in marksmanship in the Army the following plan has been adopted:

Three grades have been established for competition and Army prizes—1st, the department; 2d, the division; and, 3d, the Army.

From the reports of the best firing at posts and camps and other available data the department commander will select the most suitable man from the class known as "marksmen" of each company, troop, or battery, and assemble them at some central post to contest for the honor of a place in the department team of twelve. In like manner the commander of each of the three military divisions will assemble at some convenient post in his division the several department teams to compete for a position in the division team of twelve, and for the following prizes: First prize, a gold medal of the value of one hundred dollars, with a suitable inscription; to the next three, a marksman's rifle, with inscription on the butt; and to the remaining eight of the winning team of twelve each a silver medal of the value of five dollars.

Finally, every alternate year, beginning in 1882, the General of the Army, from the reports of rifle practice of the entire Army, will select a team of twelve of the best shots to compete for the Army prizes. The first prize will be a gold medal, with suitable inscriptions, of the value of two hundred dollars; the three next, a marksman's rifle, with inscription; and the remaining eight, a silver medal of the value of ten dollars.

To the public spirited citizens of Nevada the Army is indebted for an additional prize to the company or battery excelling in target firing.

22 Ab

The badge sent by citizens of that State—a very handsome and valuable one—having been accepted by the General of the Army, is now in my custody pending award, and the following rules to govern the competitive contest have been established and announced to the Army:

The competition for the trophy shall be open to all companies and batteries of the 'Army; the firing to be with the service arm and ammunition, and in strict accordance with the rules laid down in Laidley's Rifle Firing, supplemented by such as may, from time to time, issue from the headquarters of the Army. The commanding officer of the champion company or battery will be the custodian of the trophy and its possession noted on the Army Register.

INTOXICATING LIQUORS.

Fully recognizing the baneful effects of intemperance on the *morale* and efficiency of the Army, resulting in individual cases in serious injuries to the mental and physical health, and leading inevitably to demoralization and disgrace, the sale of intoxicating liquors was, early this year, by order of the President, prohibited at all the military posts and stations.

CERTIFICATES OF MERIT. ·

Section 1216, Revised Statutes, provides that when any *private soldier* shall have distinguished himself in the service, the President may grant him a certificate of merit, on the recommendation of the colonel of his regiment.

To bring non-commissioned officers, as well as privates, within the purview of the above-quoted section, it is suggested that it be amended by substituting for "private soldier" the words "enlisted man."

RECRUITING SERVICE.

The superintendencies of the General and Mounted Recruiting Service are still maintained at New York City and Jefferson Barracks, Missouri, respectively, with depots at David's Island, New York Harbor, and Columbus Barracks, Ohio, for the former and a subdepot for the latter in the city of New York.

At the date of my last report rendezvous had been established at the following points: Four in New York City; two in each of the cities of Boston (Massachusetts), Buffalo (New York), Baltimore (Maryland), Chicago (Illinois), Cincinnati (Ohio), Saint Louis (Missouri), and one each at Cleveland (Ohio), Harrisburg (Pennsylvania), Indianapolis (Indiana), San Antonio (Texas), San Francisco (California), and Washington (District of Columbia).

There being a government building at Pittsburgh, Pa., available for the purpose, the rendezvous at Harrisburg, Pa., was transferred to the former city October 8, 1880, and on the 20th of the same month the rendezvous at Buffalo, N. Y., was removed to Louisville, Ky., where it remained until recently, when it was transferred to Milwaukee, Wis.

The rendezvous which had been opened in Richmond, Va., last November was removed in the following April to Charleston, S. C., and in September finally transferred to Providence, R. I.

In February of this year the rendezvous at San Antonio (Texas), San Francisco (California), and in this city were discontinued, and last May the low ebb of the recruiting appropriation necessitated the closing of those in Baltimore (Maryland) and Cincinnati (Ohio). Recruiting in the Department of Texas and the Division of the Pacific was continued during the entire year, as it entailed no expenditure from the recruiting fund, and the commanding generals of the Departments of Missouri, Platte, and Dakota were authorized to designate officers to recruit for the regiments serving in these departments, the points designated being Fort Leavenworth (Kansas), Fort Omaha (Nebraska), and Fort Snelling (Minnesota).

The only organizations having their full complement of men were the colored regiments, and therefore recruiting for them was suspended last September, exception being made only in cases of men who, having honorably served one term of enlistment, desired to re-enter the service.

To remedy the serious injury to the efficiency of the recruiting service, resulting from the relief biennially of all the officers connected with that service and replacing the officers relieved by others necessarily inexperienced in the duties of recruiting officer, it was determined to inaugurate a new system, viz, of relieving yearly only one-half of the officers engaged in this important duty; thus allowing the new detail the benefit, during the first year of their tour, of the acquired knowledge and experience of the unrelieved officers of the previous detail.

The superintendents of the General and Mounted Recruiting Service have been ordered to break up what were known as the "permanent companies" at the depots and replace them by the following organization of the recruits: four companies to be organized at each depot, to be known as "companies of instruction," and to consist, each, of not less than eighty men, with six sergeants (who shall be permanent); each company, as nearly as possible, to be composed of twenty four-months' men, twenty three-months' men, twenty two-months' men, and twenty one-month men, or, in other words, dividing the recruits into four classes, according to the length of time they have been in the service. Recruits arriving at the depots to be assigned to these companies. Men re-entering the service to be considered as recruits of the first class and assigned as such. The clerks, band, company cooks, extra-duty men, &c., at each depot to be organized under the command of the depot adjutant and be known as the "depot detachment." Each company of instruction to furnish at least three men for duty as assistant cooks, that they may be properly and fully instructed in this important duty, and the details to be so regulated as to have always four, three, and two months' men under instruction; only four months' men being assignable to regiments.

As an encouragement to faithful and deserving non-commissioned officers serving at distant stations, and the better to promote the efficiency of the recruiting service, a number of sergeants, not to exceed eight, will be annually detailed from the infantry and cavalry regiments for service at the general depots, in the proportion of three to each of the General Service depots and two to that of the Mounted Service.

To inaugurate this system a sergeant (actually with his regiment), to be selected by the regimental commanders of the first six regiments of infantry and from the First and Second Regiments of Cavalry, were ordered by them to report to the Superintendents of the General and Mounted Recruiting Service, respectively, on the 1st of July last. These details are, as a rule, to be for one year; at the expiration of which term the men will be relieved by sergeants selected from such other regiments of infantry and cavalry as may be indicated from general headquarters.

The recruiting service has, under the impulse of the new system, furnished the Army with excellent men, who are prepared at the depot to at once enter upon company duty as soon as they join the regiment to which assigned, instead of, as formerly, having to undergo the setting-up process at posts and, possibly, in the field, where it was necessarily done in a very unsatisfactory manner. An opportunity, moreover, is afforded under the present arrangement of culling out worthless men before sending them, at considerable expense, to distant stations.

The table (marked L) exhibits in detail the nativities and occupation of accepted recruits, and the divers causes leading to the rejection of a large number of the applicants for enlistment.

As stated in my last report, the percentage of accepted recruits was not quite 22 per cent. of the total number of men offering themselves for enlistment. An examination of the table shows that the percentage during the past year reached nearly 23 per cent., evidencing a perceptible increase in the moral and physical tone of applicants.

For the reasons given in my last report, to which I beg to call your attention, and to give the service the full benefit of the new system, I earnestly renew the recommendation that one thousand men, in excess of the present authorized strength of the Army, be allowed for thorough instruction at the depots.

Respectfully submitted.

R. C. DRUM,
Adjutant-General.

General W. T. SHERMAN,
<blockquote>United States Army.</blockquote>

✳   ✳   ✳

REPORT OF THE INSPECTOR-GENERAL.

HEADQUARTERS OF THE ARMY,
INSPECTOR-GENERAL'S OFFICE,
Washington, D. C., October 15, 1881.

SIR: I have the honor to report that during the past year the officers of the Inspector-General's Department have been stationed and employed as follows, namely:

The undersigned was on duty at the headquarters of the Military Division of the Missouri, under the orders of the lieutenant-general commanding, until January, 1881, when he was promoted to the rank of brigadier-general, assumed charge of the office at these headquarters, and has since performed the various duties pertaining thereto. Besides making several special investigations under the orders of the Secretary of War, he has examined the accounts of certain disbursing officers, and made the quarterly inspections of the Leavenworth Military Prison, as required by section 1348, Revised Statutes.

Inspector-General Nelson H. Davis continued on duty as inspector-general of the Military Division of the Atlantic until July 1, 1881, when, by Special Orders No. 98, Adjutant-General's Office, April 29, 1881, he was assigned to the Military Division of the Missouri as inspector-general of that division.

Assistant Inspector-General Roger Jones continued on duty as assistant in this office until July 1, 1881, when, by the above-named order, he was assigned as inspector-general of the Military Division of the Atlantic.

Assistant Inspector-General Absalom Baird continued on duty at the headquarters of the Military Division of the Missouri until July 1, 1881, when, by the same order, he was assigned to duty as assistant in this office.

Capt. Joseph C. Breckinridge, Second Artillery, was appointed assistant inspector-general, with the rank of major, to date from January 19, 1881, and reported for duty in this office, as directed by Special Orders No. 24, Adjutant-General's Office, January 31, 1881. He was subsequently assigned as inspector-general of the Military Division of the Pacific, by Special Orders No. 98, Adjutant-General's Office, April 29, 1881, and reported for duty at the headquarters of that division July 1, 1881.

Brigadier and Inspector General Randolph B. Marcy continued in charge of the office at these headquarters until January 2, 1881, when, having served over forty consecutive years as a commissioned officer, he was, at his own request, by direction of the President, retired from active service, in conformity with the provisions of section 1243, Revised Statutes. On the occasion of his retirement, the following order was issued by the Secretary of War, viz:

[General Orders No. 1.]

HEADQUARTERS OF THE ARMY,
ADJUTANT-GENERAL'S OFFICE,
Washington, January 3, 1881.

The following order is, by direction of the Secretary of War, published to the Army: At his own request, after an active service of over forty-eight years, Brig. Gen. R. B. Marcy, senior Inspector-General of the Army, has been placed on the retired list, under section 1243, Revised Statutes.

In the war with Mexico; especially in the Utah expedition and movements connected therewith; in the later war with the Seminole Indians in Florida; in the war of the rebellion; and, indeed, throughout his long period of nearly half a century of constant duty, the career of Brigadier-General *Marcy* has been marked by distinguished military service.

In retirement, he bears with him the record and the honors of a life-time devoted to the cause of the country.

By command of General Sherman:

R. C. DRUM,
Adjutant-General.

Inspector-General Edmund Schriver continued on duty at the headquarters of the Military Division of the Pacific until January 19, 1881, when, being over sixty-two years of age, he was, by direction of the President, retired from active service, in conformity with the provisions of section 1244, Revised Statutes.

The following-named officers have been performing the duties of acting assistant inspectors-general since the date of the last annual report:

In Department of the Platte: Lieut. Col. William B. Royall, Third Cavalry.

In Department of the Missouri: Maj. John J. Coppinger, Tenth Infantry.

In Department of the East: Maj. Richard Arnold, Fifth Artillery.

In Department of Texas: Lieut. Col. John S. Mason, Fourth Infantry, until January 31, 1881; Capt. George B. Russell, Ninth Infantry, aide-de-camp, until June 2, 1881; Maj. James P. Martin, assistant adjutant-general, until August 27, 1881; and Capt. George B. Russell, Ninth Infantry, aid-de-camp from that date.

In Department of Arizona: Maj. James Biddle, Sixth Cavalry, until November 26, 1880; Lieut. Frederick A. Smith, Twelfth Infantry, until December 21, 1880; and Maj. Abraham K. Arnold, Sixth Cavalry, from that date.

In Department of the Columbia: Maj. Edwin C. Mason, Twenty-first Infantry, until June 25, 1881; and Capt. John A. Kress, Ordnance Department, from that date.

In Department of Dakota: Capt. Robert P. Hughes, Third Infantry, aid-de-camp, until March 9, 1881; and Maj. William W. Sanders, Eighth Infantry, from that date.

In Department of the South: Capt. George B. Russell, Ninth Infantry, until January 4, 1881, since which date no officer has been assigned.

The above-named officers have been engaged in inspecting the garrisoned posts of their respective departments, and, under the orders of the department commanders, performing, in general, the duties pertaining to the inspection branch of the service.

In compliance with the requirements of the act of Congress approved April 20, 1874, careful examinations have been made of the accounts of all officers of the Army who have disbursed public money during the year. The funds received and expended, with the balances reported due to the United States, have been compared and verified by official statements from the Treasury Department and designated depositories. All the reports of these inspections are herewith submitted, ready for transmittal to Congress, as required by the law above mentioned.

Nearly all of the military garrisoned posts have been carefully inspected during the past year, and reports of the same properly forwarded to this office, where they have been examined, and extracts made, and submitted to the authorities interested, of matters requiring action.

Department inspectors report the discipline of the troops as very good and constantly improving. They are well armed, clothed, and equipped, and, as a general rule, have been paid regularly, soon after each muster.

The stores furnished by the Subsistence Department, with rare exceptions, are of most excellent quality. The supplies furnished by the Quartermaster's Department are sufficient, and, as a rule, are of very good quality. It is reported that the mules purchased during the past year are far better adapted to the service than those received previously, being larger, deeper chested, with more roomy barrel, rendering them more fitted for the work required; and that more attention is paid to the care of animals than has been heretofore given.

Great improvements have been made during the past year in building, repairing, and renovating the barracks and quarters at most of the military posts, particularly at those posts in the West and Southwest. However, there is yet a great deal to be done to the buildings to make the occupants comfortable. Porches or verandas should be added to all permanent barracks, quarters, and hospitals in Texas, New Mexico, Arizona, California, and Utah; these would add much to the comfort and health of the troops, in fact, are indispensable on account of the heat and glare prevalent in those portions of our country during the greater part of the year.

Most of the work of building and repairing has been done by the troops. It would be a great thing for the discipline of the Army if more of the labor now performed by the soldier could be done by citizen employés, such as building posts, quarters, driving teams, &c. There is not a doubt that this constant hard work—not military—causes much dissatisfaction and a great many desertions, aided in part

by the demand for laborers and the high wages paid all over the West
for railroad building and other improvements.

Maj. A. K. Arnold makes a recommendation in his annual report, in
relation to the apprehension of deserters, as follows:

I recommend that the reward paid for the apprehension of deserters be increased to
$150. Thirty dollars is no inducement to citizens to apprehend deserters. In some
cases it has cost them nearly that sum. Soldiers should have the reward also. I believe that this method would, in a little time, do more to lessen desertion than anything heretofore proposed. Citizens do not look upon desertion as a crime, and the
consequence is that they are indifferent as to whether a deserter is caught or not, in
fact, they harbor them and shield them from arrest.

The following extracts, the first from Lieut. Col. W. B. Royall's annual report, and the second from that of Major A. K. Arnold, I concur
in fully:

First. "It is the object of the Army to raise the standard of the enlisted man and to
make him proud of his position, and to induce him to feel—as the soldiers of other
countries do—that he is certainly equal to the ordinary citizen of the country in which
he lives, but, in the orders or regulations that govern, we find them, inconsistently,
in favor of the citizen. When a quartermaster's employé travels, his expenses are
computed at $4 per day; when a soldier travels on detached service, 75 cents is allowed him per day for commutation of rations. I know of an instance that came
directly under my own eye, of a sergeant who was ordered from Fort Cameron, Utah,
to San Francisco, to identify a deserter; knowing that the amount of his commutation
would not be sufficient, his captain loaned him $50 to defray the necessary expenses
of the journey. The first meal the sergeant gets after reaching the railroad costs him
$1. This discrepancy is too apparent and needs no further comment. I would recommend that the ration, in such cases, be commuted to at least $1.50 per day, this being
the amount, I am informed, allowed to the Creedmoor team of last year. While on
this subject, I might mention that the extra-duty pay of clerks in the performance of
clerical labor in the quartermaster's department at posts ought, at least, to be rated
at the highest grade, instead of receiving 20 cents a day as laborer. Oftentimes this
class of men have very responsible positions to fill. They are frequently employed as
clerks by young officers without experience, who are often dependent upon the soldier
for the intelligent performance of the duties required. It does seem that this class of
men ought to be allowed the highest rate of extra-duty pay."

Second. "I recommend that officers serving west of the Mississippi—where travel is
mostly over stage routes and railroads, the fare per mile being largely in excess of that
allowed by law, for officers traveling under orders—be allowed actual transportation
and, in lieu of mileage allowance of $3 while traveling. This would be no more than justice,
as the expenses incurred are much more than is covered by the mileage now fixed by
law."

The following is an extract from a report of an inspection of Fort Sill,
Indian Territory, made September 1, 1881, by Maj. J. K. Mizner, Fourth
Cavalry, commanding:

"The Kiowa and Comanche tribes are the most numerous of the bands of Indians in
this vicinity. They, with several small bands, numbering in all about 4,000 Indians,
constitute what is known as the Kiowa, Comanche, and Wichita Agency, which is
situated on the Washita River, 35 miles north of Fort Sill, and a majority of the
Indians are grouped in that direction and established their villages. The general
conduct of these Indians has been friendly, and no serious trouble has occurred
during the past year. On June 7 the agent called upon me for troops to protect the
agency from the Indians, stating that he had information that the Kiowas, Comanches, Wichita, and others, had decided to go upon the war-path, and
would strike at the agency, dealing with friendly Indians as with the
rest. At this time the post had very fortunately been re-enforced by the
arrival of two companies of the Tenth Cavalry, which had been ordered from Texas
to join the Department. With these and all other troops available, I
moved to the agency, and it is believed that this prompt appearance of a
force averted what might otherwise have resulted in a serious outbreak. Experience with Indians, and a knowledge of their natural feebleness, and
a conviction that they had to submit to the ever varying exactions of the Indian agent, aggravations they are subjected to, makes it very important
that troops be maintained in the Indian Territory near the agencies. The
garrison has never been too large, and should, in my opinion, never be

less than seven companies, four of which should be full companies of cavalry—six companies of cavalry would be better. The quarters and stables are ample for six companies of cavalry, and with that number present it would be possible, when necessary, to re-enforce the garrison at Fort Reno. The necessity of re-enforcements at that post is likely to arise at any time."

Recent events demonstrate very forcibly the importance of strong garrisons being maintained at or near all Indian agencies as well as at Fort Sill. The wild Indian has great respect for *force;* a weak garrison only invites trouble, mischief, and outbreak.

Schools have been established at most of the military posts, school-houses and chapels built, or buildings set apart for school purposes and chapel. The great difficulty now is the lack of competent school-teachers and chaplains.

Regular target practice has been carried on during the year at all military posts and in every company in the Army. While it has been frequently necessary to dispense with drills, the target practice has been strictly attended to, and, as a consequence, the troops have improved wonderfully in the art of shooting. This is true of each individual company throughout the Army. In almost every company is a number of men who have attained to nearly the greatest proficiency.

With this great improvement in marksmanship, I believe it is now the opinion of most cavalry officers that for general cavalry service the carbine is superior to the rifle, particularly so were the charge of powder in the carbine cartridge somewhat increased. If the rifle is to replace the carbine in the cavalry it would be well that a board of cavalry officers be convened to fix upon some uniform mode of carrying the rifle while mounted. At the present time no two companies carry it alike.

The military prison at Fort Leavenworth has been inspected quarterly by an officer of the Inspector-General's Department as required by law. The prisoners confined here are fully supplied with ample and clean clothing and bedding, and with wholesome, well cooked, and sufficient food. They are permitted the use of newspapers and books, and the privilege of writing to their friends. The principal trades at which the convicts are employed are the making of boots and shoes, wagon and ambulance harness, and barrack chairs for the Army. The boots, &c., made by the prisoners are of most excellent quality and fine finish.

Cleanliness and good order are apparent everywhere in the shops, barracks, kitchens, grounds, hospital, &c. The government of the convicts is humane and kind, but withal firm and uniform.

During the past year many improvements and additions have been made to the prison buildings, offices, quarters, shops, &c. The work on the prison wall has been rapidly pushed forward and is completed, which adds much to the safekeeping of the prisoners and diminishes the number of sentinels required.

There is a limit to the capacity of this prison, and I would suggest that the number of prisoners to be confined within its walls be fixed; the health of the convicts demands this, and in my judgment that number should at no time exceed 450.

The disbursements of the funds appropriated for the maintenance of the prison have been examined and found to be properly made and necessary.

I fully concur in the following recommendations of Col. N. H. Davis:

"It is respectfully suggested that a concentration of the troops at a less number of military posts and in larger garrisons than now exist would increase their efficiency for Indian operations, promote their general welfare, and result in greater economy to the government. Now that railroads have been constructed and are being extended through the country inhabited or frequented by the Indian tribes, the necessity that formerly existed for numerous small and detached posts has ceased.

Large posts established at important centers for operation are in my judgment advisable, and I think also that the proper buildings to accommodate the troops and public stores should be erected from Congressional appropriations, and not in a piece-meal manner by the labor of the troops; their services are needed for military instruction and field services.

Attention is respectfully called to the large numbers of absentees on detached service, and of enlisted men on extra, special, and daily duty. The consequence is that companies are frequently reduced to a skeleton strength for duty. Under the circumstances of the policy pursued and orders to enforce it, this condition of things becomes a necessity, and it tends to destroy that pride which officers and men should take in their profession and respective commands. It would, in my opinion, be far better for the public interests if many of the duties, including clerical, now performed by soldiers, were executed by hired civilian employés."

The assignment of cavalry recruits to regiments and companies, before they are properly instructed at depots, to fill requisitions, is an unfortunate necessity.

It would, I think, be highly advantageous to the Army and promote its efficiency if some provision was made by Congress to anticipate by some months the reduction of regiments by discharge, &c., and to authorize enlistments, so that *all* recruits should be thoroughly instructed in their respective arms of the service before being sent from the depots to regiments.

General Orders No. 24, Adjutant-General's Office, February 22, 1881, in regard to the sale of intoxicating liquor at military posts and stations, is not having the effect desired—that is, of inducing temperance in the Army. Lieut. Col. W. B. Royall reports as follows:

"All the posts in this department have certain defined limits, say, generally, a reservation of three square miles. Outside of these reservations there are an unlimited number of grog-shops, to which the soldier can steal out of garrison when not on duty, and visit to his heart's content. Being out of sight of his officers and away from control, he has full scope to carouse and get drunk. Before this order went into force there were no inducements for the soldier to go out of the garrison for his grog, and should he become under the influence of liquor at the post, there was a remedy and a way to take care of him, a guard-house to confine him until he became sober, and to restrain him. Now he is under no restraint at these whisky shops, and he gets into rows with the *habitués* of the place, and sometimes is murdered by the lawless men of these dens. The commanding officer at Fort Bridger informed me that he had a soldier killed not long since by being in a drunken brawl with some citizens at one of these whisky ranches just outside the limits of the post, whom he believes would have been still living if he had not been denied the privilege of buying his dram at the post-trader's. An officer of the post of Niobrara informed me that Lieutenant Cherry's death might be remotely attributed to this same order. It has long been an established fact that you cannot legislate to restrain men's appetites or their passions. It has been tried in all our large cities, and the best way found is to license an evil you cannot destroy."

The employment of soldiers as servants, by officers, is in most cases unavoidable, on account of the exorbitant sums demanded for service; besides, at many posts, servants cannot be obtained at any price. The law in relation to the use of enlisted men as servants should be so modified as to enable an officer *to employ a soldier as servant*, without compelling him to violate the law or disobey existing orders. When servants cannot be had at reasonable rates of wages, an officer should be permitted to employ an enlisted man to wait upon him. No soldier should be required to act as servant to an officer except by the soldier's voluntary assent; he should be thoroughly instructed in his military duties before being so detailed; he should be regularly detailed for the duty in post orders; he should be so reported on the morning and monthly reports and muster-roll of his company; he should be required to keep his arms, &c., in good condition, and to attend all musters and inspections of his company. Further, the amount of *the pay proper* of the soldier should be dropped from the officer's pay account and be taken up and accounted for by the paymaster; and, in addition, the officer should be required to pay a fixed sum per month to the soldier.

Section 1232 of the Revised Statutes provides that "no officer shall use an enlisted man as a servant in any case *whatever*," and I am confident that a modification of this law, as above recommended, would prove beneficial to the service, and be satisfactory to officer and enlisted man. No officer of the Army wishes to violate the law in this regard, but in many sections of our country it is absolutely unavoidable.

I would respectfully ask, as has been frequently done by my predecessor, General Marcy, in his annual reports, that the Inspector-General's Department be placed on an equal footing with the other staff departments as regards clerical assistance. All other branches of the staff are provided with clerks, but for the officers of this department, with the exception of the senior here at the War Department, no provision is made.

The officers of this department are gentlemen of rank and of many years' service, and their status should not be that of beggars. Now, if an officer has more work or writing than he can possibly master, he must go (no matter how humiliating) to some other department, and borrow a clerk, if he can. There is much work that an officer of long service should not be required to do himself. Copying reports of inspections, investigations, keeping up the records of an office, &c., is properly the work of a clerk, and in every inspector's office there is much of this kind of labor to be performed.

I respectfully recommend that in the next annual estimates for the Army an item of $4,800 be embraced therein for the payment of three third-class clerks, for service in the office of inspector-general at the headquarters of the military divisions of the Missouri, Pacific, and Atlantic. I respectfully request a favorable indorsement by the General of the Army to this recommendation.

Inclosed I forward herewith copies of the annual reports of the different inspecting officers, so far as they have been received.

Respectfully submitted.

D. B. SACKET,
Brigadier and Inspector General, U. S. A.

The ADJUTANT-GENERAL UNITED STATES ARMY.

REPORT OF LIEUTENANT-GENERAL SHERIDAN.

HEADQUARTERS MILITARY DIVISION OF THE MISSOURI,

Chicago, Ill., October 23, 1881.

GENERAL: I have the honor to submit herewith, for the information of the General of the Army, the following report, covering the operations within the limits of my command, accompanied by the reports of the department commanders:

Since my last annual report, dated October 22, 1880, no permanent change has been made in the organization of the division, which consists of the Department of Dakota, commanded by Brig. Gen. A. H. Terry, comprising the State of Minnesota and Territories of Dakota and

Montana, garrisoned by twenty permanent posts, one cantonment where the Northern Pacific Railroad crosses the Little Missouri River, a camp at Poplar River Agency, Montana, and one small summer camp; the Department of the Platte, commanded by Brig. Gen. George Crook, comprising the States of Iowa and Nebraska, the Territories of Wyoming and Utah, and a portion of Idaho, containing seventeen permanent posts, including the post of Fort Thornburgh (just located but not constructed), near the junction of the Duchesne and Green rivers in Utah; the Department of the Missouri, commanded by Brig. Gen. John Pope, comprising the States of Illinois, Missouri, Kansas, and Colorado, the Indian Territory, and the Territory of New Mexico, and two posts in Texas, garrisoned by twenty-two permanent posts, with camps at White River, and the Uncompahgre River in Colorado, and at Snake River in Wyoming, also a camp at old Fort Cummings, and a temporary camp at Ojo Caliente, New Mexico; the Department of Texas, commanded by Brig. Gen. C. C. Augur, comprising the State of Texas, garrisoned by ten permanent posts and twelve camps and subposts along the southwestern frontier.

The Department of Texas and the Indian Territory were taken from the division december 18, 1880, on the organization of the Division of the Gulf, and the post of Fort Elliott, Texas, on February 4, 1881; but were restored to the division on May 6, 1881, when the Division of the Gulf was abolished.

To garrison these posts and furnish troops for active operations in the field, there are in this division eight regiments of cavalry, twenty regiments of infantry, twelve companies of which are mounted, and one battery of artillery, aggregating 14,076 officers and men, distributed as follows:

Department of Dakota, two regiments of cavalry, 1,505; one regiment of infantry, mounted, 435; six regiments of infantry, 2,548; total, 4,488. Department of the Platte, two regiments of cavalry, 1,252; three regiments of infantry, 1,160; total, 2,412. Department of the Missouri, two regiments of cavalry, 1,430; six regiments of infantry, two companies of which are mounted, 2,543; total, 3,973. Department of Texas, two regiments of cavalry, 1,440; one battery of artillery, 38; four regiments of infantry, 1,725; total, 3,203.

Although the Department of Dakota has, by far, the largest number of Indians from whom hostile acts might be expected, these have been at peace during the past year, and seem to have made some advancement in labor and in the cultivation of the soil, at the different agencies. The exceedingly annoying condition of having a small body of our hostile Indians, with Sitting Bull, just across the boundary line, in British Columbia, has been removed by the surrender of this head man. Nearly all of the Indians who clustered around him have come over, either with him or in advance of him, and have submitted to the authority of the government. So long as this body of Indians remained across the line, they formed a nucleus with whom all dissatisfied or disaffected ones, at the agencies, could take refuge. For this reason I supported General Terry in his efforts to get Sitting Bull back, and I think the results will be satisfactory. Although Sitting Bull was not much of a warrior, and had no prestige among Indians on that account, still he was stubborn in his resistance to the government reservation system, and naturally had many adherents among the disaffected. His original offense was his refusal to go to the reservation of his tribe, the Uncapapas, at Standing Rock; he wanted to live wild. He was not a chief in that tribe, but was the leader of a small band of about sixty lodges, who held with him the same feelings of bitter opposition towards being civilized. He was in the outskirts of the fight with Custer, but not conspicuous, and shortly afterwards struck out, with his small band, for British Columbia, being subsequently followed, from necessity, by other bands of Sioux. I have seen in newspapers long accounts and narratives purporting to be descriptions of the Custer battle, as related by Sitting Bull, which had, in my opinion, but little truth in them, and historians are cautioned against receiving them as correct. The Northern Cheyennes and the Ogallala Sioux, the former under two or three of their principal chiefs, and the latter under Crazy Horse, as their leaders, did the fighting at the battle of the Little Horn when Custer fell.

With the exception of the incursions of Indians and half-breeds belonging to British Columbia, and their passing through the cattle herds of Montana to kill buffalo south of the Missouri River, the condition of Indian affairs in the Department of Dakota has been favorable during the past year. The eastern frontier settlements are rapidly passing westward, and a year or two will carry them forward until they meet the frontier of Montana, which is advancing in this direction. The Northern Pacific Railroad will be at Fort Keogh in November, and will open up fine grazing and agricultural lands lying on the Yellowstone and between it and the Big Horn Mountains, from which section the road will undoubtedly reap a rich reward. To General Terry, for his good management, and to the troops who so faithfully served in the field during the bitter weather of last winter in collecting and bringing in bands of hostile Sioux who had surrendered, I return my sincere thanks. In this connection, the services of Maj. Guido Ilges, Fifth Infantry, and his command, are especially deserving of commendation.

In the Department of the Platte no event of military importance has occurred. The posts of Sheridan and Hartsuff have been abandoned, having fulfilled the purposes for which they were established. The post of Fort Niobrara has been completed and a new post has been located upon the new Ute Reservation, at the junction of the Duchesne and Green Rivers, in Utah. Although they have had plenty of time, the Uncompahgre Utes, who were to move to this vicinity from the Department of the Missouri, have not yet arrived at the new agency appointed for them, on the east side of Green River, not far distant from the new post above mentioned; nor have the White River Utes yet reached the Uintah Reservation, the place the commissioners have selected for them as their future home. Hopes are, however, entertained that, before the first of the new year, both the Uncompahgre and the White River Utes will reach their respective destinations without serious trouble. Still, some fears are entertained that they may not go there, and this impression has so firmly settled itself in the mind of the commission, that, at the request of Commissioner Russell, the General of the Army has directed that the White River Utes be driven to the Uintah agency. I am afraid, however, that but little can be done towards carrying out this order before spring, and will hope that better results will have obtained before that time. No one can form any idea, excepting by personal examination, of the rough and broken country of the Gunnison and White Rivers—the old home of the White River Utes—and I shall hope for a peaceful solution and settlement of this complication without necessity for military operations.

The cattle, mining, and agricultural interests have greatly increased in this department, especially in the Territories of Utah and Wyoming, and in that part of Idaho belonging to it. Along the base of the Big Horn Mountains, especially west of Fort McKinney, beautiful farms have sprung up; fields of wheat, oats, and barley, and hundreds of thousands of cattle, are now to be found where only two or three years ago was the land of the Indians and the buffalo.

The department has been economically administrated and the condition of the service improved. At its ensuing session Congress will be requested to make an appropriation for the new post at the junction of the Duchesne and Green Rivers, in Utah, on the reservation selected for the future home of the Uncompahgre Utes.

In the Department of the Missouri small raiding parties of Apache Indians, the remnant of Victoria's band, joined by a few young men from the Mescalero Reservation, in all not to exceed sixty in number, caused widespread alarm and serious loss of human life in Southern New Mexico last winter. The band came in from Mexico, south of Fort Cummings, and after making a raid of extraordinary boldness, recrossed into Mexico near their point of entrance. They killed a number of people, and, I am sorry to say, received but little punishment in return. This same band re-entered Southern New Mexico in July, and raided the same region of country, killing Lieut. G. W. Smith, Ninth Cavalry, and several people, and again escaping into Mexico without serious loss, so far as I have been able to learn from any official data received at these headquarters. I would advise that, if possible, the consent of the Mexican Government be obtained for our troops to cross and catch this small band of freebooters, or at least to break down the confidence with which the boundary line inspires them in their ability to escape punishment.

As previously stated, the Uncompahgre Utes have moved from the Uncompahgre Valley, in this department, for their new reservation and agency, near the junction of the Green and White Rivers, Utah, in the Department of the Platte. They would not have moved at all but for the presence of General Mackenzie and his command in the Uncompahgre Valley. About the same time the White River Utes also started from the White River Valley, near the scene of the Thornburg fight, to go to their new place in the Department of the Platte—the Uintah Reservation in Utah—but, as already mentioned, neither these nor the Uncompahgres have as yet arrived at their newly selected agencies.

Little Chief's band of Northern Cheyennes, in the Indian Territory, which gave some anxiety for a year or two past, has at last been sent back to their friends in the north, the Sioux. Little Chief's band was sent to Indian Territory originally because Congress had made provision for the Northern Cheyennes, by appropriation, with their kinsfolk, the Southern Cheyennes. The bands of Little Wolf, Dull Knife, and other chiefs went to the Indian Territory, seemingly satisfied with this arrangement, and were subsequently followed there by Little Chief. Congress had made appropriations for their support with the Southern Cheyennes; their reservation or lands were there; this they seemed to comprehend, but the misfortune was that a large number of the tribe were permitted to stay in the Sioux country, in the north—their natural home—and those so left there included many of the relatives of the bands of Little Chief, Little Wolf, and Dull Knife. This separation of families and friends, and the homesickness which Indians feel far more keenly than any other people, produced discontentment, and the escape from the Indian Territory of Little Wolf and Dull Knife, with their bands, was the well-known result. Then, after the eventual capture and surrender in the north of what remained of these escaped bands, they were not sent back to the Indian Territory, but were permitted to live in the north. This made a still greater separation of relatives and friends, so there was nothing to be done except to recommend, as I repeatedly did, that either Little Chief's band should be sent to the north or that *all* of the Northern Cheyennes should be sent down to the Indian Territory and be placed with the Southern Cheyennes. Apparently no heed was paid to this until lately, when the Sioux finally offered the Northern Cheyennes a home upon their own spacious reservation, and I presume that Congress will hereafter make appropriation for the latter-named Indians with the Sioux, instead of as heretofore with the Southern Cheyennes. I am glad this question is settled; it is a mistake to say that the Northern Cheyennes were treated with injustice, but it is no mistake to say that they were treated in a bungling and impolitic manner.

I earnestly recommend Congressional action to keep out intruders from the Indian Territory. Had it not been for the military, the territory of Oklahoma would have now been covered with settlements. . The intruders have been kept out by companies of troops marching from east to west and back again, on the south side of the line between the Indian Territory and the State of Kansas, while the intruders marched to and fro in Kansas, on the north side of the same line. The question, as I understand it, is this : Congress bought certain lands from Indians belonging to the Indian Nation for the purpose of colonizing other bands of Indians upon these lands. After some hostile Indians had been settled on portions of these lands, some of the members of Congress and Senators of adjacent States, becoming alarmed at the assembling of these Indians in the Indian Territory, secured the passage of an act prohibiting the removal of certain outside Indians to the Indian Territory. Then the people styled the "intruders" set up the claim that what was left of this purchase, which is now named Oklahoma, was subject to the same conditions of settlement as any other public domain, and they still persist in their purpose of obtaining possession of it. I therefore earnestly recommend some Congressional action which will settle this question and release the military from the complications involved by this Oklahoma trouble.

The completion of several lines of railway within the Department of the Missouri, and their rapid extension into country lying beyond it, have done much to facilitate the movement and supply of troops. The Atchison, Topeka, and Santa Fé Railway has been completed to Deming, connecting with the Southern Pacific road from the west, and both of these lines are now running to El Paso, on the Rio Grande, while the Mexican Central is rapidly pushing from that point into Chihuahua. The Atlantic and Pacific Railway is running from Albuquerque, via Fort Wingate, to beyond the western boundary of New Mexico, and is being rapidly constructed on the 35th parallel route, far into Arizona.

The service of this department has been economically and efficiently administered by General Pope. The commendation which, in his accompanying report, he bestows upon General Mackenzie, for the able management by the latter of the delicate details of the removal of the Uncompahgre Utes, is fully deserved, whilst the praise also awarded a number of young officers of the Ninth Cavalry, for their energetic pursuit and gallant action during the Indian raids in New Mexico, was doubtless well earned.

Military field operations in Texas during the year have been confined to the pursuit of small raiding parties from Mexico. The one which did most damage was severely chastised by First Lieutenant John L. Bullis, Twenty-fourth Infantry.

I coincide with the department commander, General Augur, as to the desirability of establishing the six small posts in the sections of country named by him in his accompanying report, and as soon as the exact locations are decided upon, the work of building can go on, as the money for construction has already been appropriated by Congress and is now available.

The extensive construction of railways in Texas has greatly contributed to the economical administration of this department and to the effectiveness of military operations. The good feeling which exists between our Mexican neighbors and ourselves along the Rio Grande frontier has almost entirely relieved the embarrassments which for a long time existed in that direction, and I most cheerfully pay tribute to the lamented General Canales, of the Mexican army, for his kindly feelings and cordial co-operation in the attainment of this most desirable result.

The department has been ably and economically administered, and the thanks of the division commander are tendered to Lieutenant Bullis for his successful pursuit and merited chastisement of the Indians who murdered Mrs. Lawrence and robbed her home.

The troops in this division are efficient and their discipline is very good, considering the smallness of the companies and the amount of hard work to be performed in fighting Indians, building posts, making roads, guarding settlements and railroads, and escorting parties engaged in surveying projected railways, boundary lines, and public lands in the Territories. The rights and the lands of the Indians have also to be protected against encroachments, and I have to reiterate what I have said in former reports, that the Army is much too small to efficiently and economically perform the duties required of it. I would recommend greater activity in enlistments. This could be brought about by modification of the rigid standards of weight and height for recruits.

The school of instruction for cavalry and infantry, at Fort Leavenworth, Kansas, will be organized shortly after the 1st of November.

I have the honor to be, general, very respectfully, your obedient servant.

P. H. SHERIDAN,
Lieutenant-General, Commanding.

Brig. Gen. R. C. DRUM,
Adjutant-General, United States Army, Washington, D. C.

*   *   *   *   *   *   *

REPORT OF BRIGADIER-GENERAL POPE.

HEADQUARTERS DEPARTMENT OF THE MISSOURI,
Fort Leavenworth, Kans., September 22, 1881.

COLONEL: I have the honor to submit the following brief report of affairs in this department since the date of my last annual report, October 1, 1880.

At the date of that report there existed no trouble from Indians within the department, although both in the Ute country and Southern New Mexico relations with the Indians were in such a delicate position that outbreaks at any time were not unlikely.

INDIAN TERRITORY.

At the date of my last report it was uncertain whether Payne, who had been indicted and was under bonds of the United States district court for invading unlawfully the Indian Territory with a band of so-called settlers, would, in his own critical position before the United States courts, again attempt to invade and locate in that Territory; but he began soon after to assemble a considerable following, numbering several hundred persons, along the southern line of Kansas, between Caldwell and Arkansas City, with the openly declared purpose, as announced by circulars over his own signature and notices in the newspapers, to force his way into the Indian Territory and occupy the district known as Oklahoma. Although there was no concealment of any kind on his part, or that of any one else, that his organization and its purposes were in absolute violation of the laws of the United States, and the proclamation of the President based thereon, yet he was permitted, for want of laws to cover the case, to organize a force of large dimensions and lead them down to the line of the Indian Territory, which he would undoubtedly have entered in violation of law and in the face of a certain outbreak of the Indians, which would have probably devastated the Kansas frontier and cost the lives of hundreds of innocent people, but for the presence and assured resistance of the cavalry forces of the United States which I had assembled along that line to prevent such an outrage. So persistent was Payne and his following that I was obliged to re-enforce considerably the first detachment of troops sent there, and to threaten any one who crossed the line into the Indian Territory that the animals, ridden or driven, should be killed the moment they crossed the line, and the men arrested and turned over to the United States courts. They marched to and fro along the line, keeping carefully within the State of Kansas, and finally encamped near Caldwell, where they remained during an extremely cold spell for three weeks, in the hope that the troops would finally return to their posts. Finding that there was no prospect that the troops would abandon their position, they finally, about the 6th of January, dispersed and scattered themselves among the settlements of Kansas, being compelled to it by extreme cold and suffering. Whatever may be Payne's object in all this, I think it certain that his followers firmly believed, through his representations and reasonably plausible legal authority, that they had the right to settle on these lands in the Indian Territory, and that their right to do so was obstructed unlawfully by the United States forces. It seems strange that such organizations can be openly made and every where announced to violate the laws of the United States at such fearful risk to exposed settlements, and that there should be neither law nor public sentiment to check it or to punish the criminals. Payne was afterwards tried for his invasion by the United States courts and sentenced under the law to pay a large fine, but as he is utterly impecunious, of course it never has been and never will be paid.

He is now engaged—although a sentenced criminal for the same act—in getting up another organization for precisely the same unlawful purpose, and no doubt will be so successful that troops must be again taken from their posts and legitimate duties to oppose his invasion by force. It would seem that in the light of these experiences some law should be passed to cover his case and that of others engaged in the same business. At present there are troops enough in that region to deal with all such attempts likely to be made, but it may well happen that pressing dangers or emergencies elsewhere may at some time leave us in such condition that the force in the Indian Territory will be entirely insufficient to protect it. Even now a great sensation has been occasioned by the reported discovery of silver in the Wichita Mountains, in the southern part of the Indian Territory, and it has already been necessary to use a considerable military force to prevent invasion in that quarter also. Whether there be really valuable discoveries of silver in those mountains or whether these sensational reports are merely parts of a concerted plan for invading the Indian Territory from both sides, is not yet known, but the resolute purpose of thousands of persons in this part of the country to occupy and possess the lands in the Indian Territory is unquestionable and must soon be met, if it be intended to prevent it, by much more stringent laws and heavier personal penalties than exist now.

There has been no serious trouble of any kind with the Indians in the Territory since my last report. The Northern Cheyennes, under Little Chief, have always been dissatisfied and have been the only disturbing element among the Cheyennes near Reno. Little Chief himself has behaved with great forbearance and consideration under a sense of deep wrong and want of good faith toward him—a feeling which I think amply justified by the facts. His return north with all his band is an act of justice which, in my opinion, and as frequently represented by me, should have been done long ago.

It does not appear at all likely that we shall at present have any troubles with the Indians in the Territory except what arise from the chronic complaints about food, unless the Indians are driven to hostilities by extensive invasions of their lands by white intruders, with whom we can probably deal satisfactorily, unless the military force be diminished by the necessities of other parts of the country.

*   *   *   *   *   *

GENERAL REMARKS ON THE INDIAN SITUATION.

In reviewing the history of Indian affairs west of the Missouri River, it is very striking to observe to what an extent the Indian frontier has been moved westward within the past twelve years. When I first assumed the command of this department, in May, 1870, the Indian frontier in the department was the line of the Kansas Pacific Railroad and the lines of the Indian Territory, and thence westward the whole country was dangerous to the whites. The Cheyennes and Arapahoes ranged through Western Kansas and all over the plains as far west as the vicinity of Denver and as far north as the line of the Platte River. The Utes came out of the eastern range of the Rocky Mountains, west and south of Denver, as far down as the Republican River of Kansas on the east, and as far south as the Panhandle of Texas, whilst the Comanches and Kiowas ranged through Northern Texas and along the eastern line of the Staked Plains into Western Texas and across the Rio Grande into Mexico. At that time—1870—all that region of country between Fort Riley and Texas on the south, Fort Riley and the Rio Grande on the west, and Fort Riley and the Platte River on the north, was dangerous Indian country, and was raided again and again by the Indians, the line of the Arkansas River being in the very center of hostile Indian country. To-day that whole region is as safe to white emigration and travel as any part of the United States, except a small strip near the Mescalero Agency, in the southern part of New Mexico. In short, the Indian frontier has been pushed westward roughly at least five hundred miles within the last ten years. The powerful tribes of wild Indians in the

Indian Territory—the Cheyennes and Arapahoes, the Kiowas and Comanches—were subdued by active campaigns against them in 1874 and 1875, and have been so civilized by the Indian Bureau since that they are now content to lie idly around the places where beef and coffee and sugar are issued to them. They only show signs of discontent when rations are not plenty, and then never undertake any campaign, except against their agent, who is under the protection of the troops, but for which he would be changed by "casualty of service" every time the Indians were unusually hungry. There is very little danger of any trouble from them in the future, unless provisions are scarce or the whites overrun their country. With a few years more of the civilizing process I do not believe they will be capable of resenting anything.

The Utes have been forced back and back until at last they have been compelled to give up (very reluctantly) their reservations on the White and Uncompahgre Rivers beyond the Continental Divide, and remove far west into Utah, whence another removal westward is impossible. Almost the same history has attended the great bands of the Sioux, between the Platte River and the British line. After much severe fighting and great loss of life, they are at last settled on reservations where they are undergoing the same civilizing process which has proved so successful with the Indians south of them. The Indians left practically at large are now sandwiched between the emigration from the East and that from the West, which has already begun to meet along the main line of the Rocky Mountains. Beginning at the Mexican line, these Indians are, first, the Apaches, probably seven thousand, all told; next the Navajoes, about fifteen or twenty thousand; and next the Utes, who extend now as far north as the Union Pacific Railroad, and number about five thousand. The waves of emigration, enormously hastened by the railroads, are now beating from both sides along this thin line of Indians, and, in the nature of things, must soon break through. This result is inevitable, and it should seem that the government should address itself at the very earliest moment to the question of preparing for it in such manner as will bring about its unavoidable accomplishment with the least injury and the greatest benefit to the Indians and to the country. It is impossible that this thin barrier of Indians can long withstand the pressure from both sides. To avoid the desperate conflicts which will precede the final ending, attended, as they would be, by great loss of life—the greater part of which would be visited upon the innocent whites and the savage, powerless in the end against such odds—is really the practical question to which the government should address itself with all haste. The time is short, at the best, in which to prepare for it, and no one can tell how circumstances now in progress may shorten it. I do not undertake to say without being asked what is best to be done in a matter involving such serious results, but it is not improper to suggest, 1st, that the agencies of the Apaches should be removed to some place remote from the Mexican line; and 2d, that the three tribes, Apaches, Navajoes, and Utes, should be withdrawn from between the advancing emigration on both sides of them and be placed in the rear of one or the other, and not left to be destroyed between them.

MILITARY POSTS.

The military posts in this department are generally in fair condition, except the posts in Southern New Mexico. Even had it been desirable to keep those in thorough repair, it would have been well-nigh impossible to do so because of the constant and harrassing field service of their garrisons, which are never long enough at the posts to work steadily or for a sufficient time; but the purpose to build a large post in Southern New Mexico, near the junction of the Atchison, Topeka and Santa Fé, and the Southern Pacific Railroads, near Fort Cummings, capable of sheltering all the troops needed in that part of the country, rendered it unadvisable to expend any more money on the small posts now occupied than was absolutely necessary to give shelter to the garrisons for temporary purposes. It is hoped that the needed appropriation for the large post above referred to may be made at this session of Congress, as otherwise we shall be obliged to expend considerable sums to keep the posts, which it is intended to replace, in anything like habitable condition.

The allowance to this department from the appropriation for barracks and quarters for the repairs of buildings at the posts, although a fair allotment of the money is made at division headquarters from the amounts allotted to the division for the several departments constituting it, is always ridiculously small and wholly insufficient for the most ordinary repairs. Either the appropriation for such purposes should be much larger or the troops should get a much larger amount of what is appropriated.

The amounts allowed for building posts on the frontier are so small that, notwithstanding the labor of troops—a labor which should not be imposed on troops serving in the field, for very manifest reasons—the posts are necessarily of the frailest and least substantial character, and require constant repairs, made by the same labor of troops, until within a few years hardly a remnant of the original material remains in the buildings. At the end of that time they are quite as worthless as they were in the beginning. Perhaps in times past such shelter was all that could be afforded for the numerous small posts we were obliged to keep up on the frontier, when communication was unfrequent and difficult, and the concentration and transportation of troops over considerable distances well-nigh impracticable; but at this day, when the railroad and telegraph lines have made communication rapid and transportation of bodies of troops almost equally so all over the Indian frontier, it should seem that troops can well be assembled in large garrisons and sheltered decently. That such concentration would be of immense benefit to economy, efficiency of military forces, and spirit and feeling of the troops, there can be no doubt. Their effectiveness for the service they are called on to perform would be greatly enhanced, and every interest of the government and the Army be benefited. I have, however, dwelt on this subject so much in almost every annual report for a number of years past, that it is superfluous, if not unpleasantly persistent, to repeat the recommendations here.

The posts in New Mexico and Southern Colorado, which will be sufficient, and are likely to be in a sense permanent, are, first, Fort Bliss; second, the large post to be built near the intersection of the Atchison, Topeka and Santa Fé, and the Southern Pacific Railroads, which should hold the garrisons of Craig, Selden, Cummings, and Bayard; third, Fort Wingate, in the Navajo country, holding five infantry and two cavalry companies—a garrison sufficient for precautionary measures against the Navajoes; and, fourth, Fort Lewis, on the La Plata River, in Southwest Colorado. This post covers all Southern and Southwestern Colorado, and is in the section of country where the Navajoes and Southern Utes hold common possession, their reservations being practically contermiuous. It is admirably located for the military purposes required. It holds five infantry companies—one mounted—but it should be enlarged and finished at an early day, so as to hold at least eight companies, three of which should be cavalry. With these posts I believe that New Mexico and Southern Colorado would be perfectly secure, and as soon as they can be built all other posts in that section could be abandoned, except perhaps Fort Stanton, which we shall be obliged to occupy until the Mescaleros are removed. I shall submit estimates for building the large post and completing the others, for which I trust Congress will make necessary appropriation. No contracts could be made for building Forts Lewis and Bliss for the amounts allowed for them. Indeed, the smallest bids were more than double the amount authorized. It was necessary, therefore, to buy the material and build the posts by the labor of troops. In the case of Fort Lewis this was accomplished in reasonable time, and with reasonable, though not entire, success. The troops at Fort Bliss, and indeed everywhere in Southern New Mexico, have been so constantly in the field that by no means the same progress has been made there. All that could be done was done, and I hope that for some time to come the troops will not again be taken off for other duty.

THE TROOPS.

The troops serving in this department are the Thirteenth, Fourteenth, Fifteenth, Nineteenth, Twenty-Third, and Twenty-Fourth Infantry, the Fourth and Ninth Cavalry, and four companies of the Tenth Cavalry, and are all in good discipline and general condition of effectiveness except the Ninth Cavalry and Fifteenth Infantry. These two regiments have for several years been almost continuously in the field, the greater part of the time in harassing and wearisome pursuit of small bands of Indians who infest the mountains of Southern New Mexico and Mexico, and are, therefore, much run down in every way. They need rest and recuperation, and I trust it will be in my power this autumn to replace them at their stations by fresh troops, and bring them into posts where they can have the opportunity not only to rest, but to re-establish discipline and tactical knowledge, which have been considerably impaired by the service they have had to perform for a number of years past.

Target practice has been carried on with zeal and industry and with gratifying success, as, I think, will be plainly illustrated in the competitive shooting required by the General Orders from Army headquarters. There is a great deal of interest on the subject everywhere in the department, an interest which I have encouraged by every means at my command. More and more every day, even in well organized armies, personal skill in the use of small-arms becomes essential and commands attention and encouragement. In Indian wars, which are of necessity running skirmishes in almost every case, the skillful sharpshooter is invaluable, and ours, of all the armies in the world, should do most to secure as large a number of good marksmen as constant practice, stimulated in every proper way, can secure for us. There is no doubt that the General Order from Army headquarters on this subject will prove of the greatest value to the Army.

SCHOOL OF APPLICATION.

The duties of the Army on this frontier since 1865 have consisted mainly, if not wholly, of continuous and harassing campaigns against Indians, generally in small detachments, in building shelters for the troops by their own labor, and in driving wagons, so that practically the Army in this region has consisted mainly of scouts, teamsters, and laborers. In the nature of things such service is the very opposite of being conducive to the proper discharge of military duty or the acquirement, either in theory or practice, by officers or soldiers, of professional knowledge or even of the ordinary tactics of a battalion. Everything, however, now indicates a condition of Indian affairs in the near future which will enable us to concentrate the troops at a few large posts, where all the essential instruction for well-organized armies can be readily and successfully undertaken. I think it may be fairly assumed, from practical results within the last ten years, that in much less time than that in the future our Indian relations will be so far settled that nearly all the small posts and cantonments on the western frontier can be dispensed with. Certainly, if the same progress be made in the next ten years toward such disposition of the Indians as will assure their harmlessness, as has been made within the last ten years, we may safely count upon such a condition of things that the government shall be able to determine precisely what military force it is its purpose to keep on foot and to select the points at which it shall be posted.

Fort Leavenworth, in the very center of one of the richest agricultural districts in the country, with easy communication to all parts of the country by rail, and with its ample reservation of 6,000 acres of land beautifully diversified, will, beyond doubt, be one of the principal points of occupation by a considerable part of our permanent army of the future. It seems eminently proper, therefore, that, in anticipation of such results, preparations should be begun to provide here the theoretical and practical instruction needed constantly by all armies, and certainly by ours as much, if not more, than most others. The organization of the "School of application" here, to go into operation as soon as the necessary buildings can be prepared, is an immense advance toward that condition of knowledge and efficiency in the Army which has been so long wanting and so sincerely craved by every grade of officer and enlisted man. It has been a genuine satisfaction to me that this school was determined on, and it will be a great source of pleasure to me to do all I can to make it successful. It is a great boon to the Army, and that its results will amply repay the government there is no doubt.

Every effort is being made to complete the arrangements for the shelter of the garrison for the school and of the officers to be sent here for instruction. I cannot venture to say when everything will be ready to open the school, but it will certainly be as soon as willing labor and deep interest can make it.

The administrative duties of the department have been most efficiently and satisfactorily performed by the respective chiefs of the staff departments serving at these headquarters. The troops have been well supplied in every respect, and the service is in as good condition as could be expected or desired. I wish here to express my entire satisfaction with these chiefs of staff departments, and think it simple justice that attention should be invited to them by name, as follows, viz: Maj. R. R. Platt, assistant adjutant-general; Lieut. Col. J. D. Bingham, chief quartermaster; Maj. George Bell, chief commissary; Maj. D. L. Magruder, medical director; Maj. J. J. Coppinger, inspector; Lieut. T. N. Bailey, chief engineer; Capt. D. M. Taylor, A. D. C., and chief of ordnance; Capt. W. M. Dunn, jr., Second Artillery, A. D. C.; Lieut. S. W. Groesbeck, judge-advocate, and Maj. George H. Weeks, depot quartermaster. All these officers are entitled to the thanks of the department commander, who hereby tenders them.

A roster of the department and a field return of troops serving in it are herein transmitted.

I am, colonel, respectfully, your obedient servant,

JNO. POPE,
Brevet Major-General, U. S. A., Commanding.

Col. W. D. WHIPPLE,
Assistant Adjutant-General,
Military Division of the Missouri, Chicago, Ill.

ANNUAL REPORT OF GENERAL MILES.

HEADQUARTERS DEPARTMENT OF THE COLUMBIA,
Vancouver Barracks, W. T., September 29, 1881.

SIR: In accordance with your communication of the 7th instant, I have the honor to submit the following report:

The important events and movements of troops in this department during the year preceding the time of my assuming command have been mentioned in reports of my predecessors already forwarded.

*   .*   *   *   *   *   *

The troops, at available points, occupy a wide extent of country, the greater portion of which is inhabited by defenseless settlers and numerous tribes of Indians.

The different Indian tribes in this department are, in the main, in a peaceable condition; most of the semi-civilized are making some progress toward self-support; yet there are vast tracts of country still occupied by bands of nomadic Indians, and between the latter and the remote settlers conflicts of race may be expected. The evils arising from injudicious and illy-defined treaties made with these Indian tribes are becoming apparent, and the constant clashing of interests between the Indians and the miners, ranchmen, and farmers, is almost inevitable, and quite likely to result in open hostilities.

The germs of future Indian disturbances are already noticeable in some localities.

Measures are being taken which, when completed, will better facilitate communication with and concentration of the available force in this department, and at the same time increase the efficiency of the troops and lessen the cost of supplies, the chief aim being to make the limited force (of 1,570 soldiers) of the least expense to the general government, and at the same time give the greatest protection to a people occupying territory (not including Alaska) of 250,000 square miles in extent. When it is remembered that our troops have contended in the past, and doubtless in the future will have to meet, an enemy of superior numbers where the natural obstacles are dense forests, trackless mountains, and almost impassable rivers, the difficulties to be encountered will be easily understood and appreciated.

In this connection I desire to invite especial attention to the weak and defective condition of the companies and regiments of this command, an evil which prevails through the entire service.

It must be apparent to every one familiar with the subject, that our little Army is defective in organization, and, consequently, greatly over-worked.

This nation of 50,000,000 of people calls upon its Army for more than double the labor required of any other troops in the world, and the testimony of those who have had the best means of knowing, from the humble frontier settler to the late Chief Magistrate, James A. Garfield, and in the words of the latter, is that the Army has been crippled and reduced "below the limit of efficiency and safety," and the people "expect Congress and the Executive to make the Army worthy of a great nation."

By the present system we have a sufficient number of officers and non-commissioned officers, but there is a great necessity for an increase in the number of soldiers in the different companies.

The "skeleton theory" has been found unwise, most expensive, and least effective.

Our Army is required to be efficient in every kind of military duty, including skilled marksmanship. It must guard our coast defenses and boundary lines, public arsenals, stores, and depots; it must protect the lives and property of citizens, scattered over vast Territories; and in cases of necessity those living in the populous States.

At the same time the troops are required to perform almost every kind of laborious work, constructing military posts, building roads and telegraph lines, also performing mechanical, clerical, and difficult manual labor.

This has a demoralizing influence upon the spirit of the troops, and causes desertion and other evils of the service.

In cases of emergency the skeleton companies are suddenly gathered up from distant points at great expense, and thrown into engagements illy prepared for such serious business, and expected to perform the work of well-organized and strong commands.

With our present facilities for the government and accommodation of troops, companies of 100 men can be easily maintained, and in every sense better fitted for the service required of them. There would probably be ten per cent. added to the yearly appropriation required for pay, food, and clothing of the men; but the efficiency of the Army would, in my judgment, be increased more than one hundred per cent.

I am satisfied that, in my own department, the yearly expenditures now made necessary by the weak condition of the companies and regiments could be greatly lessened.

If the companies were made of proper strength, not only would there be a large saving of the extra military expenses, but there would be greater benefit and security given to the people whose lives and property depend to a greater or less degree upon the protection guaranteed by the physical force of the general government.

I would therefore recommend that the authorized maximum number of enlisted men in the different companies be 100 per company where they are so stationed and employed that the public interest would be benefited thereby.

I would also call attention to the fact of the number of officers who are permanently absent from their respective commands through no fault of theirs, men who have become infirm through long years of hard service, or crippled or permanently disabled in the various wars in which our army has been engaged; also to the number of officers who have grown gray in the service and yet are occupying the subordinate grades of captains, first and second lieutenants. These facts have a very discouraging influence upon a zealous and faithful body of public servants.

In every branch of business or profession in life advancement or progress is absolutely essential, and the rule is no less applicable to the military service, and some system that will either promote retirements by commutation of retired pay, limiting the retired list to such number as would be suitable for our kind of service, or universal retirement at a given age, would undoubtedly improve the efficiency of the Army, and it is believed to be very generally desired by the officers of our service

I inclose the reports of the department staff officers, and invite attention to them for matters of detail in the different branches of the service.

I am, sir, very respectfully, your obedient servant,
NELSON A. MILES,
Brigadier-General, U. S. A., Commanding Department.
The ASSISTANT ADJUTANT-GENERAL,
Military Division of the Pacific, Presidio of San Francisco, Cal.

REPORT OF MAJOR-GENERAL O. O. HOWARD.

HEADQUARTERS DEPARTMENT OF WEST POINT,
UNITED STATES MILITARY ACADEMY,
West Point, N. Y., October 12, 1881.

SIR: I have the honor to submit my first annual report of the Military Academy:

LAW AND ORDERS; HOW COMPLIED WITH.

General Orders No. 84, dated December 18, 1880, from your headquarters, paragraph I, read as follows: "Brig. Gen. O. O. Howard is assigned to the command of the Department of West Point, and to do duty as superintendent of the United States Military Academy, according to his brevet of major-general, and will relieve Maj. Gen. John M. Schofield."

In compliance with the above instructions, I turned over the command of the Department of the Columbia to the next officer in rank, and proceeded to West Point, arriving the 20th of January, 1881. The next day I assumed formal command of this department, and entered at once upon the duties of superintendent of the academy.

Having been stationed here before, as an instructor, I was already comparatively well acquainted with the systems of instruction, government, and discipline which have long prevailed at this post and institution. The law of Congress (see Revised Statutes, section 1314) which declares that the superintendent, as well as all other officers on duty at the academy, may be detailed from *any arm* of the service has caused scarcely any modifications in the rules and practices differing from those which prevailed before.

In General Orders No. 15, series of 1877, I find the following:

PAR. I. The Military Academy and the post of West Point shall constitute a separate military department, the commander of which shall report directly to the General-in-Chief of the Army. The General-in-Chief, under the War Department, shall have supervision and charge of the academy. He will watch over its administration and discipline and the instruction of the corps of cadets, and will make reports thereof to the Secretary of War.

The effect of the law was, first, to open the largest possible field of selection to the President, instead of confining it to any staff corps of the Army; and, by the orders last quoted, the effect has been virtually to advance a post to the importance of a military department. In this way the field of selection of superintendent embraces the general officers as well as those of lower grade. There has been necessarily some increase of reports to be made, and a slight increase of clerical labor. Again, a captain and regular quartermaster has replaced the former detailed lieutenant. Every change made, in fact, has rendered the general administration here more consonant with the usual administration of a department and of army posts.

Three good objects, under present arrangement, appear to be gained, with very little, if any, additional cost : First, the authority of the commanding officer to order general courts for the trial of all enlisted men as well as cadets; second, to enable all concerned, officers and cadets, to be constantly familiar with practical Army methods of administration and government; and, third, to keep up the interest of the General-in-Chief and of all other officers of the Army in the management and welfare of the academy.

ACTING ASSISTANT ADJUTANT-GENERAL'S OFFICE.

· Though the limits of the department and the post are identical, the business is now so arranged as to prevent a duplication of records and accounts. For the sake of economy I have, as did my predecessors, dispensed with the services of an adjutant-general, having my senior aid-de-camp do the duty. This officer supervises the correspondence of an official kind, which now comes to us from the outside, and in the last decade has, for some evident reasons, grown to very large proportions. The present average will give about 2,000 communications a year. He also makes the post returns, receives the reports from the police, the detachments, engineer company, and general guards, and issues such orders as may be required which pertain to officers, soldiers, citizens living in the department, with reference to furloughs, leaves of absence, means of transit, visitors, excursionists who come and go, and such like operations.

ADJUTANT'S OFFICE.

The adjutant of the academy is, ex officio, the secretary of the academic board, and is also recruiting officer, commanding officer of the band and field music and of the general service detachment. In addition, he is charged with carrying out in detail all the direct correspondence with the heads of the various departments of instruction and with the corps of cadets; he prepares the academic reports that require transmission to Washington, and sees that the punishment and demerit rolls are kept with accuracy, submitting them daily to the superintendent. He must also attend to the proper working of the academy printing office, the preparation of the staff records, the keeping up of the official correspondence with parents or guardians of cadets, and must also reply to the daily requests for information made by members of Congress, schools, and colleges, and would-be candidates for admission.

I have been thus particular with reference to these two offices so as to make a brief exhibit of the labor performed.

I have been asked by members of the board of visitors if there was any advantage in a department. My answer was that I thought the departmental functions were of advantage to the academy. I still think so. The same duties can be done by a post organization, or even by a simpler academy organization. In fact, the academy, like the staff of the Army, could be reorganized. Yet, in the end, I do not think it would be bettered.

DISCIPLINE AND MANAGEMENT.

The academic board consists of the nine professors, the commandant of cadets, the chief instructors of ordnance and gunnery and practical military engineering, and the superintendent, who is, ex officio, president of the board. This makes up a membership of thirteen. Every interest of the academy is carefully weighed by this body of able men. In my judgment, it is the most powerful agent at work here. It is my earnest desire while superintendent to work in harmony with the board as at present constituted. This will give unity and strength to all official action.

Since my arrival a few changes have been made in the regulations. For example:

Paragraph 30, Regulations for the United States Military Academy of 1877, is revoked and the following substituted therefor:

"PAR. 30. This course will comprise topography and plotting of surveys with lead-pencil, pen and ink, and colors; problems in descriptive geometry, shades and shadows, and perspective; practical surveying in the field; free-hand drawing and landscape in black and white; constructive and architectural drawing in ink and colors. Lectures by the head of the department will accompany instruction, covering the subjects of: General rules for rectilinear and map drawing, scales, lettering, &c.; topography, different systems and methods of terrene drawing, &c.; methods of projection of meridians and parallels; plotting from field-work; field-sketching; general principles of triangulation, plotting, and filling in; free-hand drawing, light and shade, methods and material; theory of color; quality and character of pigments; methods of coloring and tinting in water-color; the orders of architecture; fundamental architectural forms and general proportions; drawing of plans."

Paragraph 72, Regulations for the United States Military Academy of 1877, is revoked and the following substituted therefor:

"PAR. 72. If any cadet shall have a total number of demerits thus recorded exceeding one hundred and twenty-five (125) for the time between June first and December thirty-first, both dates inclusive, or exceeding ninety (90) for the time between January first and May thirty-first, both dates inclusive (no credits being allowed other than those belonging to the time considered), he shall be reported to the academic board by the superintendent deficient in discipline; and the board shall consider and act upon such a deficiency as in cases of deficiency in studies."—(G. O. No. 22, A. G. O., February 19, 1881.)

Paragraph 75, Regulations for the United States Military Academy of 1877, is revoked and the following substituted therefor:

"PAR. 75. Every cadet of the first class who shall have been found proficient in all the studies and exercises of the entire academic course prescribed, including discipline, and whose character as shown by his conduct as a cadet shall be deemed satisfactory, shall receive a diploma signed by the members of the academic board, and shall thereupon become a graduate of the Military Academy.

"The names of the graduates shall be presented to the War Department, with the recommendation of the academic board for commission in the several corps of the Army, according to the duties each may be judged competent to perform.

"If the academic board doubt the physical ability of a graduate for military service, his case shall be referred to a board composed of the superintendent, the commandant of cadets, and the medical officers provided in paragraph 19, as prescribed in the last paragraph of this article."—(G. O. No. 22, A. G. O., February 19, 1881.)

The recommendation of the academic board that paragraph 129, Regulations of the United States Military Academy of 1877, be expunged, and that the following be substituted for it: "The use of tobacco in any form by cadets is prohibited," has been approved by the Secretary of War.—(G. O. No. 6, June 11, 1881, Headquarters United States Military Academy.)

These changes were recommended by the academic board after careful consideration, and I believe will prove decidedly beneficial to the academy.

I have myself made some modifications of existing orders, such as abolishing the cadet "all-night guard" in the barracks, relieving academic officers from company duty with the cadets, the confining of sergeantcies to the second class and corporalcies to the third class, the cutting down of Sunday permits recently given cadets to go beyond the limits, and a few others of relatively small importance. In each instance my purpose has been not to make changes, but to recall some already made which our experience has proved beyond question to be injurious to the cadets. My earnest judgment is in favor of a thorough discipline, but not of a martinetism which overloads the young men with espionage and punishments too numerous and too heavy to be borne. Of course, the cheerful, hearty performance of duty in the main effected by doing right because it is right is the best. The tendency here, with a view of keeping abreast of other institutions of learning, is naturally in the course of time to multiply the text-books and lengthen the lessons. The tendency in discipline is ever to multiply the reports of delinquency and to enforce the reporting by an almost inflexible system of action. The relief to these things, so far as the studies are concerned, is found in the conservative wisdom of the academic board, and in the discipline the burdens are relieved by the watchful kindness of the tactical and other executive officers. Thus believing, I have endeavored to diminish the number of reports, all possible, consistent with good order and good training, and to use all the influence in my power in favor of a kindly and paternal execution of our rules and regulations. The results are good. I have thus far met only good will. There was no hazing during the last summer encampment. Cadets generally appear contented and are very industrious. In order to facilitate the official intercourse between the cadets and the superintendent without interfering with the essential order of business, one hour every day, except Sundays, is now given to the cadet, if he so desires, to visit the superintendent. Further, he can easily obtain permission from the officer in charge to do so at any other time if necessity appears to him to warrant it.

DETAILS OF INSTRUCTORS.

There is every year a strong pressure brought to bear upon the superintendent to induce him to lengthen the term of service of the officers detailed to the academy as assistant professors and instructors. The period usually adhered to, especially as pertaining to the line officers, is four years. In my judgment, it is of great advantage to the young officer to have a term of duty at the academy. Besides the necessary review of past studies, it has become the custom for each officer carefully to prepare an exhaustive paper upon some important military subject, and to read it before an organized society, where full and free criticism is always invited. Further, the officers have the advantage of the large library to fill out any spare time by advantageous reading and research. It is then desirable to extend these advantages to as many officers of the Army as possible consistent with the best interests of the academy and the service. It might be well to extend the time to five years instead of limiting it to four. I recommend this extension.

I think that there are at present a sufficient number of permanent professorships Permanency promotes the tendency to increase the cadet's curriculum of instruction. I would not, then, make permanent the professor of law, the instructors in practical military engineering, in ordnance and gunnery, and in artillery. Five years will surely be a sufficient time to detain these able officers from their professional duties in the Army at large. From present knowledge and experience I am of the opinion that the same rule as to length of term should apply to the commandant and the superintendent. A change of administration has not heretofore proved, to any extent, detrimental. The institution in fact has been improved by bringing in a variety of talent, and as so many things are fixed and rigid in any military system, an occasional change in the manner of executing laws and orders is, I think, desirable. Again, in this, as in all other matters, the academy is established and maintained for the interest of the Army, and not the Army for the Academy. Therefore, worthy and capable officers in all the branches should, I believe, continue to have the opportunity of detail, as the law of Congress contemplates.

BUILDINGS.

The enlargement of the cadet barracks is progressing as rapidly as the appropriations will permit. As soon as completed there will be sufficient barrack room and therefore less crowding than usually occurs on the accession of the new cadets each year. Meanwhile, I have been able to reduce the number of officers at the academy, have added one new set of quarters, and have had put in habitable condition that of the professor of law, which was injured and partially destroyed by fire. I can now remove nearly all the academic officers from the cadet barracks and still have them comfortably quartered. Our needs in this direction will be still further subserved as soon as the new hospital shall have been completed and rendered fit for occupancy. The old hospital, with a few changes and repairs, can be made to extend our quarters' accommodations. The dentist also will have a new room, with adequate light, in the new hospital. These changes will operate to have the cadet barracks occupied, as they should be, only by the cadets and instructors in tactics.

I notice in several reports of the board of visitors and of the superintendent a recommendation that large panes be put in the place of the diamond lights in the windows of the cadet barracks. For some reason the appropriation asked for this object has hitherto failed. Certainly the light at present is insufficient. I think the change suggested, and the trimming of the trees, now large and during part of the year thick with foliage, will be all that is required to give sufficient light to the rooms. There are several changes that will soon be required in the heating and ventilating of the cadet barracks and the academic building. I believe that the academic building may be so changed, possibly by raising it one story, to fit it better to meet present necessities than it now does. Either an enlargement of the gymnasium-room, now in the basement of that building, should be made or a new building adapted to this purpose constructed. In several reports, since the cutting off by the railway of the cadets' bathing place, the necessity of supplying a swimming bath has been urged. I again call attention to this matter.

I have had a "system of gymnastic exercises" prepared, and also formal instructions for the swimming baths. The former are already in use, and the latter will be as soon as the swimming baths shall be constructed. I may add here that these exercises and those of the fencing and sword exercise, which did not prove this year to be as creditable as other performances of the cadets, the commandant has now placed under the more direct and immediate control of one of his skillful tactical officers.

It may appear to you that the Academy continually calls for new constructions. The reasons are, first, that it was built and arranged long since, and before modern improvements in the way of heating, lighting, water supply, &c., were in vogue, so that many of our buildings do not compare favorably with corresponding buildings of many other leading institutions of learning. Again, the numbers to be accommodated, both cadets and officers, have greatly increased. It would, indeed, be wise to have a board of skillful officers, appointed by the Secretary of War, visit the Academy, examine all the structures, the water supply, and the sewerage, and make such recommendations and detailed estimates as should be found necessary to give system, order, and completeness to the whole. Should this be done, and the essential appropriation be granted, the yearly requisitions would thereafter be much diminished, and the board of visitors and other friends of the institution feel better satisfied with the building accommodations. My full estimates, which have been forwarded, cover other repairs and constructions besides the above. The necessity for them is apparent on their face, and I hope the appropriations for them may be obtained.

FINANCES.

As you will probably be obliged to answer some objections which have lately been raised against the financial system in vogue at the Academy, I have called upon the treasurer to make a full and explicit statement of the funds in use, how they accrue, and how they are expended. It should be remembered that the intent of the law and regulations is that the cadet's monthly allowance, or, as officially denominated, his pay, should be made to cover his actual expenses. Hence the charge against him cannot be, for example, in regard to his subsistence, merely the cost in the market of provisions, but must cover the cooking and serving. The cost of a coat cannot be simply the cost of the cloth, but must include each cadet's portion of the cutting, the making, the repairing, and the account-keeping. This could, of course, all be avoided by a system of contract, but the changing forms of the young men and the necessity for special fitting under the immediate charge of the authorities of the Academy is plain to every thoughtful man interested in the institution. It is surely impracticable to purchase for the cadets ready-made clothing by the wholesale. Instead of being neatly dressed as now, with well-fitting uniforms, we should soon see a battalion of shabby appearance. Again, it would be next to impossible to keep up the excellent character of the material now furnished, and difficult at the best to maintain the present economy in prices.

It has been suggested in recent reports "that here there should be an appropriation to purchase a stock of provisions for which the commissary should account to the Treasury Department, as is done in the army," with the added assertion that "this would result in no loss to the government, but in a more perfect responsibility in the disbursing officer." I hope that this will not be done. For it would establish an objectionable ration system, necessitating the purchase of provisions so long in advance that certain supplies would deteriorate, and a loss necessarily fall upon the government, and it would eventuate in a rigidly monotonous system of daily subsistence not adapted to the needs of growing young men. Again, now there is much less wastage and loss under the present system of buying and issuing supplies when needed than there would be under any other system.

The only possible objection to requiring the commissary of cadets to *account to the Treasury Department* directly for supplies purchased and issued by him to cadets is that it will require additional clerical assistance, and add just so much to the deprecated cost. The treasurer is subjected now, by the inspector of accounts and by the board of audit, to repeated and constant supervision, as the treasurer's report shows.

The reasons for the existence of several separate funds, as "the laundry," "boat," "printing," &c., are that the needs have, from time to time, suggested to the officers in charge these methods of supplying them.

It would be generous on the part of the government to assume these charges and make direct appropriations therefor, but it would at once change the manner of dealing with each cadet's accounts and really give him an increase of compensation. For such changes careful legislation will of course be requisite.

*   *   *   *   *   *

The published report of the Board of Visitors to the Academy last June, as it appears in the public journals, contains the following in referring to the various funds appertaining to the Academy, viz:

The surplus balances of these various funds and property on June 1, 1881, amounted to little less than $50,000, all of which is the result of the percentage system, and to secure justice to former cadets for the levying of this tax, the Board are of the opinion that the money should be devoted to some purpose in which former cadets may have an interest and their successors a benefit, and a memorial hall is suggested at West Point to commemorate the services of such cadets as may have distinguished themselves or died in public service.

The foregoing statement in regard to the "surplus balances" of the various funds is erroneous.

1st. The cadet equipment fund, which on June 1, 1881, amounted to $25,568, and which was reduced $9,776 on the final settlement of the last graduating class, because of amounts paid to the individual members thereof, and which fund at date of last settlement amounted to $16,672, must not be considered a "surplus balance," because *it is the sum total of moneys retained from the monthly pay solely of those cadets now at the Academy,* and which is held in trust for them until they graduate, when they will receive personally the sum so retained, that they may have means sufficient to purchase an outfit, such as is required of every officer on first entering the service. Should a cadet sever his connection with the Academy prior to graduation, the portion of the "fund" contributed by him is then paid to him. No graduate of the Academy has ever contributed directly or indirectly a cent to the *present* equipment fund, and to appropriate any portion of this fund for any purpose other than that for which it is accumulated would be to perpetrate an act of injustice which is certainly farthest from the intention of the board.

2d. The corps of cadets' fund in the hands of the treasurer, and which amounted at date of last settlement of the accounts of the cadets to $3,185, must not be considered a "surplus balance," because it is the sum total of moneys *due* cadets personally on settlement of personal accounts, and which is held in trust for them until required for expenditure for their personal needs. No cadet is allowed to have in his possession money or to handle any portion of his pay; hence, sums *due* him remain in the hands of the treasurer, as before stated, until such time as the expenditure thereof is needed for his authorized personal requirements.

These two funds, amounting together to $19,857, must be subtracted from the sum total of all funds in the hands of the treasurer, viz, $35,003.41, before we can begin to speak of "surplus balances." Make the subtraction and there remains in the hands of the treasurer a balance of $15,146.41, which is made up of all other funds enumerated in the treasurer's accompanying statement.

The laundry fund of $5,421.86 may be considered a "surplus balance," but this sum or a large portion thereof will sooner or later be expended for repairs of the building occupied as a laundry, and for new machinery and equipments to the same. As long as there is no appropriation by Congress for the laundry, this fund cannot be expended except on account of the laundry without inflicting injury, and this fund should not be considered a "surplus balance." Deducting the laundry fund, $5,421.86, from the sum total of funds other than personal before mentioned, viz, $15,146.41, and there remains to be considered the sum of $9,724.55, which embraces all funds other than the "equipment," "corps of cadets," and "laundry" funds. Of this last amount the only fund which has accrued under the percentage system, is the cadet quartermaster's department fund of $4,707.95. This may be considered properly a "surplus fund," but in the absence of Congressional appropriations for the purchasing of required supplies other than subsistence, this amount is absolutely needed to enable the quartermaster of cadets to take advantage of the wholesale cash market, in order that supplies may be obtained when needed at advantageous prices. This fund increases and diminishes as the stock of supplies on hand in the cadet quartermaster's department diminishes or increases. This fund and the stock on hand must be considered together. To devote any portion of this to any purpose other than that of procuring needed supplies, and in the absence of Congressional appropriations, would be clearly wrong and paralyzing in its effects. All other funds are indispensable (in the absence of Congressional appropriations) in continuing the existence of the objects to which they are devoted.

I have shown that there are no "surplus balances" in the hands of the treasurer in excess of $15,146.41, and I trust I have shown with sufficient clearness that there are no "surplus balances" at all which are available for the object recommended by the Board of Visitors.

Since I have taken charge of this military department there has been a marked fidelity in the service and conduct of the professors, instructors, and other officers on duty here. I commend them to the favorable consideration of the General-in-Chief and of the Secretary of War. I append to the report a copy of the present roster.

The clerks, including those of the general service, are particularly efficient.

And certainly when discipline is so carefully maintained, the few cases of punishment shows a good record for the enlisted men of the several detachments on duty at or near the academy.

I do not feel that I have made an adequate exhibit of the work accomplished, and I have much in mind that should properly be reported upon, as with reference to the qualifications for admission, the expediency of September cadets, &c., but prefer a longer observation and experience before recommending any further changes.

I am, General, very respectfully, your obedient servant,

O. O. HOWARD,
Brig. and Bvt. Major-General, U. S. A.,
Superintendent U. S. Mil'y Acad'y, Commanding Department.

The ADJUTANT-GENERAL, U. S. ARMY,
Washington, D. C.

Roster of officers and troops serving in the Department of West Point, commanded by Brigadier-General O. O. Howard, Brevet Major-General U. S. Army, October 1, 1881.

DEPARTMENT OF WEST POINT,

UNITED STATES MILITARY ACADEMY, WEST POINT, N. Y.

Brig. Gen. O. O. HOWARD, brevet major-general, United States army, commanding.

DEPARTMENT STAFF.

First Lieut. J. A. SLADEN, Fourteenth Infantry, aide-de-camp, acting assistant adjutant-general.
First Lieut. CHARLES E. S. WOOD, Twenty-first Infantry, aide-de-camp, acting judge-advocate.
Capt. CHARLES H. HOYT, assistant quartermaster, chief and post quartermaster, and disbursing officer military academy.
Second Lieut. GUY HOWARD, Twelfth Infantry, aide-de-camp, detached (at Artillery School, Fort Monroe, Va.)

MILITARY STAFF OF THE ACADEMY.

First Lieut. JAMES L. LUSK, Corps of Engineers, adjutant.
Capt. WILLIAM F. SPURGIN, Twenty-first Infantry, treasurer, quartermaster and commissary of cadets.
First Lieut. GEORGE E. BACON, Sixteenth Infantry, acting commissary of subsistence.
Maj. CHARLES T. ALEXANDER, surgeon.
Capt. ROBERT H. WHITE, assistant surgeon.

ACADEMIC STAFF.

DEPARTMENT OF THE SPANISH LANGUAGE.

PATRICE DE JANON, professor.
First Lieut. JAMES O'HARA, Third Artillery, assistant professor.

DEPARTMENT OF NATURAL AND EXPERIMENTAL PHILOSOPHY.

PETER S. MICHIE, Ph. D., professor.
Capt. CLINTON B. SEARS, A. B., Corps of Engineers, assistant professor.
First Lieut. EZRA B. FULLER, Seventh Cavalry, } Acting assistant professors.
First Lieut. ARTHUR MURRAY, First Artillery, }

DEPARTMENT OF THE FRENCH LANGUAGE AND ENGLISH STUDIES.

GEORGE L. ANDREWS, A. M., professor.
First Lieut. JOHN R. WILLIAMS, Third Artillery, assistant professor.
Second Lieut. JOHN T FRENCH, Jr., Fourth Artillery, }
Second Lieut. JOHN H. PHILBRICK, Eleventh Infantry, } acting assistant professors.
Second Lieut. JOHN BIGELOW, Jr., Tenth Cavalry, }
Second Lieut. GEORGE P. SCRIVEN, Third Artillery, }

DEPARTMENT OF HISTORY, GEOGRAPHY, AND ETHICS.

Rev. JOHN FORSYTH, D. D., LL. D., chaplain and professor.
First Lieut. ERIC BERGLAND, Corps of Engineers, assistant professor of ethics.

DEPARTMENT OF CIVIL AND MILITARY ENGINEERING.

JUNIUS B. WHEELER, professor.
First Lieut. WILLARD YOUNG, Corps of Engineers, assistant professor.
First Lieut. SOLOMON W. ROESSLER, Corps of Engineers, acting assistant professor.

DEPARTMENT OF DRAWING.

CHARLES W. LARNED, professor.
First Lieut. CHARLES A. WORDEN, Seventh Infantry, assistant professor.
Second Lieut. EDWARD E. GAYLE, Second Artillery, } acting assistant professors.
Second Lieut. JAMES S. PETTIT, First Infantry, }

DEPARTMENT OF MATHEMATICS.

EDGAR W. BASS, professor.
First Lieut. JOHN T. HONEYCUTT, First Artillery, assistant professor.
First Lieut. WILLIAM M. MEDCALFE, Ordnance Department, }
First Lieut. WILLIAM CROZIER, Ordnance Department, }
Second Lieut. HENRY H. LUDLOW, Third Artillery, } acting assistant profes-
Second Lieut. SOLON F. MASSEY, Fifth Artillery, } sors.
Second Lieut. DOUGLAS A. HOWARD, Third Artillery, }
Second Lieut. JAMES E. RUNCIE, First Artillery, }

DEPARTMENT OF LAW.

GUIDO N. LIEBER, major and judge-advocate, professor.
First Lieut. ERIC BERGLAND, Corps of Engineers, acting assistant professor.

DEPARTMENT OF TACTICS.

Lieut. Col. HENRY M. LAZELLE, major First Infantry, commandant of cadets and instructor of tactics.
Capt. MARCUS P. MILLER, Fourth Artillery, assistant instructor of artillery tactics.
Capt. EDWARD S. GODFREY, Seventh Cavalry, assistant instructor of cavalry tactics.
First Lieut. EDWARD J. McCLERNAND, Second Cavalry, assistant instructor of infantry and cavalry tactics.
First Lieut. EDWARD W. CASEY, Twenty-second Infantry, assistant instructor of infantry tactics.
Second Lieut. QUINCY O'M. GILLMORE, Eighth Cavalry, assistant instructor of cavalry tactics.
Second Lieut. EDWARD S. FARROW, Twenty-first Infantry, assistant instructor of infantry tactics.

DEPARTMENT OF CHEMISTRY, MINERALOGY, AND GEOLOGY.

SAMUEL E. TILLMAN, professor.
First Lieut. JOHN P. WISSER, First Artillery, assistant professor.
First Lieut. JOSEPH S. OYSTER, First Artillery, } acting assistant professors.
Second Lieut. LEONARD A. LOVERING, Fourth Infantry, }

DEPARTMENT OF ORDNANCE AND GUNNERY.

Maj. CLIFTON COMLY, Ordnance Department, instructor.
First Lieut. CHARLES H. CLARK, Ordnance Department, assistant instructor.

DEPARTMENT OF PRACTICAL MILITARY ENGINEERING, MILITARY SIGNALING, AND TELEGRAPHY.

Capt. WILLIAM S. STANTON, Corps of Engineers, instructor.
First Lieut. HENRY S. TABER, Corps of Engineers, assistant instructor of practical military engineering.
First Lieut. CHARLES A. WORDEN, Seventh Infantry, assistant instructor of military signaling and telegraphy.
ANTONÉ LORENTZ, master of the sword.

TROOPS.

BATTALION OF CADETS.

Lieut. Col. HENRY M. LAZELLE (major, First Infantry), commandant of cadets, commanding.
Company A, Capt. MARCUS P. MILLER, Fourth Artillery, commanding.
Company B, First Lieut. EDWARD W. CASEY, Twenty-second Infantry, commanding.
Company C, Second Lieut. EDWARD S. FARROW, Twenty-first Infantry, commanding.
Company D, First Lieut. EDWARD J. McCLERNAND, Second Cavalry, commanding.

24 Ab

COMPANY E, BATTALION OF ENGINEERS.

Capt. WILLIAM S. STANTON, Corps of Engineers, commanding.
First Lieut. HENRY S. TABER, Corps of Engineers, attached.

UNITED STATES MILITARY ACADEMY DETACHMENT OF ORDNANCE.

Maj. CLIFTON COMLY, Ordnance Department, commanding.

UNITED STATES MILITARY ACADEMY DETACHMENT OF CAVALRY.

Capt. EDWARD S. GODFREY, Seventh Cavalry, commanding.

UNITED STATES MILITARY ACADEMY DETACHMENT OF ARTILLERY.

First Lieut. GEORGE E. BACON, Sixteenth Infantry, commanding.

UNITED STATES MILITARY ACADEMY BAND AND DETACHMENT OF FIELD MUSIC.

First Lieut. JAMES L. LUSK, Corps of Engineers, commanding.

*　　*　　*　　*　　*　　*

REPORT OF COL. GEORGE W. GETTY.

HEADQUARTERS UNITED STATES ARTILLERY SCHOOL,
Fort Monroe, Va., October 26, 1881.

SIR: I have the honor to submit my annual report on the operation
of the artillery school for the past year.

In my report for 1880 I have given an account of the present organization of the school, and have also exhibited the code of regulations
under which its service is performed. I therefore deem it to be unnecessary to say more in that regard in this paper than to invite attention to
the fact that the time embraced herein is a continuation of the school
term of two years, which commenced in May, 1880, and expires in May,
1882.

Last year's report left my hands while the instruction pertaining to
the division of the school known as the department of engineering was
in progress; that is, part of the class of officers was engaged upon an
actual reconnaissance of the country in the vicinity of Gloucester Court-
House, Va., under Capt. Lorenzo Lorain, Third Artillery (at that time
in immediate charge of the department), and part under Capt. James
Chester, Third Artillery, assistant instructor, were prosecuting a regular topographical survey of Yorktown and vicinity, in compliance with
a request from the Congressional Committee on the Yorktown Centennial.

With reference to the former, I have the honor to report that the work
was most satisfactorily performed, but that I am unable to exhibit the
result at this moment, because the work of compiling the map has been
unfortunately delayed by unforeseen causes. It is in progress, however, and when finished I shall forward a proper copy for your inspection. With reference to the latter, I am happy to be able to report the
production of as correct and beautifully executed a map as has come to
my notice in many years, and I cannot say too much in testimony of
the zeal and painstaking accuracy with which the gentlemen who were
employed upon this survey have performed the task allotted to them,

especially as it was somewhat outside of what is contemplated in the present arrangement of the school.

For this survey I have received, for the gentlemen who made it, a resolution of thanks by the honorable committee who had requested it. Active steps are now being taken to produce at the school photo-lithographic copies of the map, which, when finished, I shall have pleasure in forwarding. The map has been already used by the honorable committee in locating various historical points and in purchasing the site of the Yorktown monument, while copies of certain sections have been supplied to those officers of the general staff who have been employed in completing the military dispositions for the centennial which is about to be celebrated.

I have said that the survey of Yorktown was somewhat outside of what is contemplated in the present arrangement of the school, because the delicately adjusted instruments which are necessary to success in regular planimetry are not at hand, and, if they were, the time demanded by a proper use of them cannot now well be spared. I wish it to be understood, however, that the importance of surveying is by no means lost sight of. In fact, it is my intention that this branch of study, in its military sense, and the practical application of it particularly, shall receive the fullest development possible, because the importance of the part in warfare played by ground, and the extreme utility to an officer of a good ready method of procuring intelligence, is too glaringly apparent to be in the least neglected in any military school of application.

The remainder of the time allotted to the department of engineering, that is, until 20th of December, 1880, was devoted to practical work in engineering (including practical photography), in conformity with the code of regulations, during which time each of the officers were required to prepare in addition an essay on the attack and defense of a sea-coast fort, the locality chosen being Fort Monroe, Va., and the class being equally divided on the offensive and defensive sides.

The examination in the department of engineering took place on the 20th and 21st of December, being both written and practical. The results were eminently satisfactory and will form the subject of a special report.

* ^ = e = • •

DEPARTMENT OF ARTILLERY.

The time allotted to this department of study extends from January 5 to September 1 of the second year of the term. It is under the supervision of Maj. Richard Lodor, Third Artillery, who has been assisted by Capt. M. P. Miller, Fourth Artillery, and First Lieut. L. A. Chamberlin, First Artillery, and in the chemical branch by First Lieut. H. L. Harris, First Artillery.

• • e = = • ^

DEPARTMENT OF MILITARY ART.

This department is under the supervision of Maj. L. L. Livingston, Fourth Artillery, and Capt. J. H. Calef, Second Artillery, instructor. The time allotted to it extends from September 1, second year, to January 15, and it embraces theoretical and practical instruction in military history, military geography, infantry, and grand tactics. As the course commenced only with the month of September last, but little can as yet be reported upon regarding it.

• • • r .

DEPARTMENT OF LAW AND MILITARY ADMINISTRATION.

This department is under the immediate charge of Capt. S. S. Elder, First Artillery, but the time for its work will not arrive until January 10.

It is essential for the rendition of a complete report to record here, that, as in previous years, drills at all classes of artillery take place daily, except Saturdays and Sundays and such times as are devoted to infantry instruction; also that practice in small-arms firing receives all the time and attention which can be given to it. The latter is, however, interrupted, though not seriously, at the times of artillery practice; the situation of the range and scarcity of men compelling it.

DIVISION FOR ENLISTED MEN.

During the past year this branch of the school has been successful in its work under Capt. W. F. Randolph, Fifth Artillery, and First Lieut. E. M. Cobb, Second Artillery, instructor.

I consider it essential, however, to repeat my remarks of last year, inviting attention to the necessity of keeping up a rotation of enlisted men for attendance upon this division by sending for a year's instruction at the school a number of recruits destined for the artillery, and then assigning them to the service batteries. I also recommend that the policy be adopted of transferring, from time to time, enlisted men already belonging to the instruction batteries to the service batteries, thus giving a beneficial change to the school in the matter of enlisted men. But in recommending this action I do not refer to a change of the instruction batteries as organizations which would entail a transfer of officers in order to retain proper instructors at the school.

*   *   *   *   *   *

The present class numbers 25, and is in temporary charge of First Lieut. H. L. Harris, First Artillery, who performs this in addition to his regular duties.

Having thus sketched the work at the school, the amount of which is really greater than the length of this report will warrant a full exhibition of, I deem it to be my duty to express regret that it has been found expedient to make so many changes in the *personnel* of officers as have occurred in the past year. The school has lost nine officers and gained two, four of the former being of the class under instruction. While I would in no way wish to be understood as assuming an attitude for the school which is not in the most cheerful conformity with the best interests of the service at large, or which is not calculated to assist individual officers in their professional advancement, I cannot but draw attention to what would appear to be conducive to great embarrassment and discouragement to the school if allowed to become a precedent for future practice. The officers who have been selected for instructors and assistant instructors are those who, all things considered, have possessed special fitness for the duties assigned them; but as such duties demand study and experience for their efficient performance at a school of application, I submit that it might be in the interest of progress if some definite policy in regard to their tour of duty were indicated, so as to insure their timely replacement should more important interests demand their removal.

I also wish to draw particular attention to the recommendation in Major Lodor's report concerning the service of torpedoes, and to renew my own, made in former reports, in reference to the same subject. As I view it, too much practical knowledge of torpedo warfare cannot exist among artillery officers, and I fail to apprehend why there can be objection to at least enlarging their facilities for gaining it.

In another communication I have made known the necessity for a suitable fire-proof building for the school library, which I have reason to think has met with favorable consideration. I cannot, therefore, do more than mention this need here.

Experience has shown the desirability of a certain rearrangement of the various courses of study in view of making the course of instruction still more practical than at present; but as it is a matter for careful deliberation, I must reserve the presentation of it until another hour.

I am, sir, very respectfully, your obedient servant,

GEO. W. GETTY,
Col. Third Artillery, Bvt. Maj. Gen. U. S. A.

The ADJUTANT GENERAL U. S. ARMY,
Washington, D. C.

REPORT OF THE ADJUTANT-GENERAL.

WAR DEPARTMENT,
ADJUTANT-GENERAL'S OFFICE,
Washington, October 25, 1881.

SIR: I have the honor to submit my annual report for the year ending September 30, 1881.

MILITIA.

Deeming it unnecessary to reiterate the expression of my deep sympathy with everything that affects the well-being and development of the militia, I beg to invite your attention to the necessity of legislative authority to extend to the militia of the several States such aid, by furnishing them, on requisitions of the respective adjutant-generals, the tactical works and blank forms and books prescribed for the regular Army, as will still further assimilate the management, drill, and internal government of the two forces, due regard being always had to the fundamental conditions of their respective existence.

The Fourth Brigade of the South Carolina Volunteer troops, contemplating holding, in April last, a competitive drill between the artillery and infantry companies of the command, requested the detail of Army officers to act as judges; and in compliance with the request an officer was selected by the commanding general of the Department of the South to act as judge on the occasion.

It is greatly regretted that the non-receipt of any report from the officer selected to act as judge deprives me of the opportunity of placing on record his judgment, as well as, I doubt not, his recognition of the increasing interest manifested in military matters by the several organizations of the State troops of South Carolina participating in this friendly contest of skill and tactical knowledge.

At the request of the authorities of the States of Massachusetts, Connecticut, and Rhode Island, officers of the regular force were detailed to inspect the camps and troops of those States. From causes incident to the perturbed state of the country consequent on the assassination of the late President, and the movements of troops connected, later, with the Yorktown centennial celebration, the reports of the officers detailed have not been received in time to be incorporated with this report, and

It only remains for me to express the confident hope that the bright expectations raised by the inspection reports of last year have not only
been realized, but indicate still the justification of greater hopes.

MILITARY COLLEGES.

The subjoined table exhibits the apportionment of details corrected
up to October 1, 1881. The reports of the several officers detailed as
professors of military science at the several universities and colleges
show that, out of upwards of 3,600 youths over the age of 15, an average attendance has been secured as follows: Artillery drill, 563; infantry drill, 1,853, or over one-fifth of the entire number of students for the
first and over one-half for the last, besides attendance at recitations and
lectures on military points of interest. The average aptitude of pupils
is reported very good, while the interest manifested by the respective
faculties is steadily increasing as they realize the fact that, while military instruction does not, in anywise, interfere with the ordinary curriculum of studies at the several institutions, it proves of marked benefit
in maintaining a high degree of discipline and materially affects the
bearing and tone of the students.

Table showing apportionment of details at colleges, universities, &c., under section 1225 Revised Statutes.

States and groups.	No. of officers to which entitled.	No. on duty in State or group.	Aggregate population of States and group.	Officers detailed.	Colleges, &c., at which detailed.	Expiration of detail.
Maine			648,945	First Lieut. M. Crawford, Jr., Second Artillery	Bowdoin College, Brunswick, Me.	July 1, 1882.
New Hampshire			346,984			
Vermont			332,286	First Lieut. H. E. Tutherly, First Cavalry	University of Vermont, Burlington	July 1, 1884.
Massachusetts			1,783,012	Second Lieut. V. H. Bridgman, Second Artillery	Massachusetts Agricultural College, Amherst	July 1, 1884.
Connecticut			622,683			
Rhode Island			276,528			
	3	3	4,010,438			
New York	3	3	5,082,810	First Lieut. J. W. MacMurray, First Artillery	Union College, Schenectady	July 1, 1883.
				First Lieut. J. B. Burbank, Third Artillery	Cornell University, Ithaca	July 1, 1883.
				Second Lieut. Wm. S. Patten, Eighteenth Infantry	Riverview Academy, Poughkeepsie	July 1, 1883.
Pennsylvania			4,282,786	First Lieut. W. P. Duvall, Fifth Artillery	Pennsylvania Military Academy, Chester	July 1, 1884.
New Jersey			1,130,983	First Lieut. Geo. O. Webster, Fourth Infantry	Alleghany College, Meadville, Pa.	July 1, 1883.
Delaware			146,654	First Lieut. S. N. Holmes, Thirteenth Infantry	Rutgers College, New Brunswick, N.J	July 1, 1883.
Maryland			934,632	Second Lieut. Bogardus Eldridge, Tenth Infantry	Maryland Agricultural College	July 1, 1884.
	4	4	6,495,055			
West Virginia			618,443	Second Lieut. Geo. Le R. Brown, Eleventh Infantry	Hampton Normal and Agricultural Institute, Hampton, Va.	July 1, 1884.
Virginia			1,512,806			
North Carolina			1,400,047	Capt. G. W. Evans, Twenty-first Infantry	Carolina Military Institute, Charlotte, N.C	July 1, 1883.
	2	2	3,531,296			
South Carolina			995,622			
Georgia			1,539,048	First Lieut. Geo. S. Hoyle, First Cavalry	N. Georgia Agricultural College, Dahlonega	July 1, 1882.
	1	1	2,534,670			
Florida			267,351			
Alabama			1,262,794			
	1		1,530,145			
Mississippi			1,131,592	Second Lieut. E. B. Bolton, Twenty-third Infantry	Agricultural and Mechanical College of Mississippi, Starkville.	July 1, 1883.

Table showing apportionment of details at colleges, universities, &c., under section 1925 Revised Statutes—Continued.

States and groups	Aggregate population of States and groups	No. of officers to which State entitled	No. on duty in State or group	Officers detailed	Colleges, &c., at which detailed	Expiration of detail
Louisiana	940,103					
Texas	2,071,695	1	1	First Lieut. R. M. Rogers, Second Artillery	University of the South, Sewanee	July 1, 1883.
Arkansas	1,502,574			Second Lieut. W. C. McFarland, Sixteenth Infantry	Agricultural and Mechanical College of Kentucky, Lexington.	July 1, 1884.
	802,564					
	2,395,138	1	1			
Tennessee	1,542,463	1	1	First Lieut. Geo. Ruhlen, Seventeenth Infantry	Ohio State University, Columbus	July 1, 1884.
Kentucky	1,648,708	1	1	Second Lieut. Geo. Andrews, Twenty-fifth Infantry	Brooks Military Academy, Cleveland	July 1, 1884.
Ohio	3,198,239	2	2	Second Lieut. W. R. Hamilton, Fifth Artillery	Indiana Asbury University, Greencastle	July 1, 1883.
Indiana	1,978,362	1	1	Second Lieut. George K. Cecil, Thirteenth Infantry	Michigan Military Academy, Orchard Lake	July 1, 1882.
Michigan	1,636,331	1	1	First Lieut. H. T. Reed, First Infantry	S. Illinois Normal University, Carbondale	July 1, 1883.
Illinois	3,078,769	2	2	Second Lieut. W. T. Wood, Eighteenth Infantry	Illinois Industrial University, Champaign	July 1, 1883.
Wisconsin	1,315,480	1	1	First Lieut. John L. Clem, Twenty-fourth Infantry	Galesville University, Galesville	July 1, 1882.
Missouri	2,168,804			Second Lieut. Jno. J. Haden, Eighth Infantry	University of Missouri, Columbia	July 1, 1884.
Kansas	995,966			Second Lieut. Albert Todd, First Artillery	State Agricultural College, Manhattan, Kans	July 1, 1884.
Colorado	194,649	2	2			
	3,359,419					
Iowa	1,624,620			First Lieut. Geo. A. Thurston, Third Artillery	Iowa State University, Iowa City	July 1, 1883.
Minnesota	780,806			First Lieut. Isaac T. Webster, First Artillery	University of Nebraska, Lincoln	July 1, 1882.
Nebraska	452,433	2	2			
	2,857,859		2			
California	864,694			First Lieut. M. C. Wilkinson, Third Infantry	Tualatin Academy and Pacific University, Forest Grove, Oregon.	July 1, 1883
Oregon	174,767					
Nevada	62,265					
	1,101,718	1	1			

MILITARY PRISON.

The administration of the affairs of the military prison at Fort Leaven-worth, Kans., during the past year has been in a marked degree successful. The views expressed by its originators and promoters, that such an institution would become an important factor in the discipline of the service, have been fully verified. The prisoners confined therein are only such as have been convicted of purely military offenses by general courts-martial, and who, under the wholesome restraint and discipline to which they are subjected, joined to the system of mechanical instruction adopted, are discharged at the expiration of their terms of confinement better fitted to re-enter the service or to become useful members of society.

During the fiscal year ending June 30, 1881, there were 373 men received into the prison and 273 discharged. But 1 death occurred during the year, and only 6 prisoners escaped during the same period. The actual number of men confined on June 30, 1881, was 447. The *résumé* of the diversified labor of these men, taken from the reports of the prison officials, hereinafter noted, demonstrates the wisdom of the measures adopted, from an economical point of view, to keep them employed for the direct benefit of the Army. There still remain other industries to be introduced with the same end in view, so that there may be not a single case of enforced idleness. Thus far in the history of the institution a large number of the prisoners have been engaged in the work of constructing a circumvallating wall and upon the build-ings within the prison yard.

The board of commissioners have made the inspections required by law; have, at each visit, afforded the prisoners the fullest opportunity to make such representations or complaints as they desired to present for consideration; have carefully noted the character of the punishments imposed by the prison authorities for violations of the established rules and regulations; the methods and kind of labor; the quality of food provided; and they have been fully satisfied, in all respects, with the condition and government of the prison. The governor, while on duty under his brevet rank of colonel, actually receives only the pay and allowances of his actual rank, viz, that of captain. Considering that his position demands the possession, in the incumbent, of administrative ability of the highest degree, combined with the rare mechanical powers required for the successful management of an institution embracing many and varied branches of industry, I most earnestly recommend that the local rank of colonel, with the pay and allowances of that grade, be attached to the office of the governor of the prison. This officer has a greater amount of labor and responsibility than any regimental com-mander. He governs and controls between 500 and 600 persons. Prac-tically, he is at one and the same time the superintendent of a large man-ufacturing establishment, embracing diversified branches of industry, and the military director of all affairs within the prison. The adoption of the measure, not only suggested, but earnestly pressed from a pure sense of justice, would be a grateful recognition of the eminent services of an officer to whose zeal and fidelity, united to high executive and administrative ability, the success of the institution is almost wholly due.

I beg to renew the recommendation of last year that legislative au-thority be obtained to apply the earnings of the prison to its mainten-ance. A bill with this end in view was pending in the Senate last win-ter, and I sincerely hope it may become a law during the next session of Congress.

The improvements made during the fiscal year 1880–'81 were 1 set of cottage quarters, one-story frame, 3 rooms, each 16 feet square; an extension to the prison-shop building, two-story, 24 by 46 feet, brick, with slate roof; a frame building, 16 by 36 feet, one and a half story; an addition of one room, 12 by 16 feet, to a set of quarters already occupied; 1,620 lineal feet of board fence around the cottage quarters, and nearly two miles of fencing around the prison farm. This farm fence was all swept away by high water and rebuilt with old material. One set of cottage quarters (4 rooms each, 16 feet square) was in process of erection but not quite completed at the end of the year. A new floor of hard pine was laid in prison building No. 2, 37 by 97 feet.

The prison wall (except the coping) was completed, 186 feet being built during the year, making a total of 2,022 feet; and 381 feet of coping has been laid thereon. The stone for the wall has been quarried by prison labor on the military reservation, but the coping has been purchased, there being no stone suitable for the purpose on the government land.

There were manufactured 34,163 pair of boots, 25,944 pair of shoes, 4,356 corn brooms, 1,656 barrack-chairs, 110 arm-chairs, 100 chair-rungs, 220 chair-bolts, 1,263 packing-boxes, 80 crates, 100 sets of four-mule ambulance harness, 75 sets of six-mule wagon harness, and, in addition to the above, all the doors, sashes, &c., for new buildings, and the work incident to the necessary repairs to buildings already erected. Two thousand nine hundred and seventy bushels of lime have been, during the past year, burned and used in the erection of the buildings and wall and for sanitary purposes.

The cost per pair of boots and shoes manufactured during the year is, for boots, $2.90; shoes, $1.85; which includes cost of material, wages of foreman, and per diem allowances for prison labor.

The produce of the farm (although the latter was entirely inundated after the planting in the spring of 1881, and had to be replanted) amounted to 2,600 bushels of potatoes, 400 bushels of turnips, 3,900 heads of cabbage, 700 bushels of corn, 170 bushels of onions, 600 bushels of tomatoes, besides other vegetables, all grown by prison labor. About 50 acres are now under cultivation.

The work performed by prisoners for the Quartermaster's Department amounted to 30,241 days of skilled labor and 19,024 days of purely mechanical or unskilled labor.

The appropriation of $55,910.80 has all been expended, the larger amount being on account of permanent improvements.

I beg to invite your attention to the very full details and statistics of the operations of the prison for the past year, contained in the several reports, already submitted, made by the officers of the prison.

GOVERNMENT HOSPITAL FOR THE INSANE.

The following is a list of persons admitted into the above-named institution, under orders of the Secretary of War, from October 1, 1880, to October 1, 1881:

Regular Army:

Commissioned officers	3
Commissioned officers (retired)	1
Enlisted men	35
Enlisted men (late of the Army)	4

Late Volunteer Service:

Commissioned officers	1
Enlisted men	2
Hospital matrons attached to the Army	1
Inmates of the United States Soldiers' Home	5
Military prisoners	3
Employés of the Quartermaster's Department, U. S. Army	1
Employés of the Subsistence Department, U. S. Army	1
Total	**57**

OFFICERS ON DUTY AT REMOTE POINTS.

The great inconvenience to officers at distant stations, resulting in the difficulty, and in some cases the impossibility, of procuring assistance in supplying their personal wants and the care of their property, seems to demand that section 1232 of the Revised Statutes should be somewhat modified, so that officers at remote posts where private help cannot be procured may be authorized, with, in every case, the consent of the soldier himself, to secure the services of an enlisted man for the performance of those duties. The entire time and attention of officers serving with troops is required in looking after the comfort and wants of their commands and the care of government property and interests. Even if the performance of these domestic duties were suited to their positions, they could only do so by neglecting some of the important and responsible public duties so absolutely essential to the well-being and efficiency of their respective commands and the best interests of the service and government.

Instances could be cited of officers who, rather than violate the section named, have conscientiously abstained from the employment of their men in preparing their food or caring for their animals, and have themselves performed these duties. It is not believed that Congress contemplated such a condition of affairs, and I sincerely hope an effort will be made looking to the repeal of that section, or, preferably, to its modification, so that, in such cases, and conditional on the consent of the soldier and the approval of the department commander, officers may be allowed the services of an enlisted man of their immediate command, the pay proper of the soldier being withheld by the government and paid by the officer benefitted.

ALLOWANCES TO OFFICERS ON COURTS-MARTIAL AND MILITARY BOARDS.

Many cases have come to my knowledge of the hardships resulting from the detail of officers for duty on important courts-martial or military boards convened at points away from the proper stations of such officers, and I beg to invite your earnest attention to this matter. Selected by reason of eminent fitness for the special duty to which assigned, they have no control over the length of the period of time during which the court-martial or board must remain in session to complete its labors, and, under section 1269 of the Revised Statutes, forbidding any allowance being made to an officer in addition to his pay, the increased expenses incident to their stay in cities fall so heavily upon them in the discharge of imposed duty that, it seems to me, the action of Congress reviving, in such cases, the old *per diem* allowance would be a simple act of justice. That, however, there may be proper restriction and avoidance of abuse, I beg to suggest the decision, in each case, be left absolutely to the discretion of the honorable the Secretary of War.

RETIRED LIST.

The large increase·in the number of officers eligible to retirement by reason of having reached the age of sixty-two renders, or should render, inoperative so much of section 1243 of the Revised Statutes as provides for retirement after thirty years' service, and I earnestly recommend that the provision of the section printed in *italics* be repealed.

SEC. 1243. When an officer has served forty consecutive years as a commissioned officer, he shall, if he makes application therefor to the President, be retired from active service and placed upon the retired list. *When an officer has been thirty years in service, he may, upon his· own application, in the discretion of the President, be so retired, and placed on the retired list.*

The very liberal provisions made for the support of those officers who, by reason of old age and its attendant decrepitude, or in consequence of injuries received in service, are incapacitated for further active duty, would seem to make it obligatory on every officer in the service to sedulously·guard the retired list from having placed upon it any unworthy person. Unfortunately, this has not always been the case, and I beg to recommend, as a further guard, that a law be enacted that no officer of the Army be placed on the list of retired officers against whom charges are pending, or who is ·awaiting the promulgation of the sentence of a court-martial convened for his trial, and providing against the admission on that list of officers who, disabled temporarily from active life in the field by physical ailments not resulting from long service or wounds received in action, have become permanent pensioners of the government, although in many instances they have sufficiently recovered to énable them to secure and fill positions in civil life demanding, possibly, as' much physical exertion as is required for the performance of ordinary Army duty.

CODIFIED ARMY REGULATIONS.

The last edition of the Army Regulations was issued in 1863, and has been out of print for several years. With slight modifications, and an appendix containing the laws enacted during the two preceding years, it is simply a republication of the Army Regulations of August 10, 1861. An imperative need was felt for a new code which would embrace the numerous orders, decisions, &c., promulgated since 1863, and on my distinguished predecessor was imposed the task of preparing and codifying the Regulations, in addition to the important duties of his position. On the completion of his labors the Codified Regulations were submitted to a board of officers of large and varied experience and high rank. Finally, the work was approved by the honorable the Secretary of War, February 17, 1881, after which it was placed in the hands of the Government Printer. It will make a volume of some 1,400 pages, embracing not only the Regulations, but also the numerous blank forms in use in the several bureaus of the War Department and by the Army at large. The bulky volume, however, is unsuited for ready reference by officers away from their proper stations, on leave or traveling under orders, and with the approval of your predecessor, I caused an abridged edition to be prepared with great care, from which the blank forms are excluded, together with such paragraphs of the Code of Regulations as refer exclusively to the routine internal administration of permanent posts, care of national cemeteries, post schools, post gardens, clerks, and messengers at department headquarters, &c. This abridged edition will, I trust, be found to be a complete *vade mecum* of professional information, which officers can conveniently carry with them, at home and abroad, for the purpose of information and reference.

It is confidently expected that the Codified Regulations, in both forms, will soon issue from the government press and satisfy a need severely felt for many years past.

ILLUSTRATED ARMY REGISTER.

Some time ago it was thought desirable to attempt, in connection with and as supplementary to the publication of the official reports of the late war, the collection of approved photographs of all the general officers commissioned by the President of the United States during the eventful period of 1861-'65, including all officers who, although never commissioned as general officers, had actually commanded a brigade or division in the field; and a circular, setting forth the end in view, was addressed to every officer of that class whose address could be ascertained.

Responses, accompanied by a photograph of cabinet size, have been received from many of the men who, in the dark days of the Republic, responded to the call of duty and whose rank entitled them to those commands. Up to the present time some five hundred photographs have been received and preserved in temporary albums pending final arrangement. A full but concise "*etat de service*" has been prepared in many cases, and adds interest to the collection of the leaders in the great contest for the supremacy of the Union. I beg to call attention to this most interesting collection, and earnestly request authority may be obtained for the reproduction of the portraits obtained, either through the highly artistic ability of the Government Bureau of Engraving and Printing, or in any other manner that may be selected by Congress.

MILITARY RESERVATIONS.

A very important work (inaugurated a few years since, and steadily continued without interfering with the duties of the office) has been the collecting of *data* upon which to base complete histories of the military posts (whether abandoned or still garrisoned), giving location, date of establishment and occupation, plat of the site, from whom title to the land was obtained (either by purchase or reservation of public land), date of cession of State jurisdiction, &c. The prosecution of this work demands much intelligent labor and research, necessitating the consultation of the records of other bureaus of the government, and the attainment of the end in view is necessarily a slow process.

The work when completed will be a valuable one, not only to the executive departments of the government, but also to the historical societies of the country, and, in order that it may be properly conducted to completion at as early a day as practicable, I recommend that Congress be asked for authority to employ a competent clerk, at a salary of of $1,600 per annum.

* * * * * * *

The accompanying table gives a general exhibit of the work performed during the past year, omitting, of necessity, the higher class of duties, which it is simply impossible to reduce to a tabular form.

Respectfully submitted.

R. C. DRUM,
Adjutant-General.

Hon. ROBERT T. LINCOLN,
Secretary of War.

REPORT OF THE JUDGE-ADVOCATE-GENERAL.

WAR DEPARTMENT,
BUREAU OF MILITARY JUSTICE,
October 1, 1881.

SIR: In compliance with Circular of September 16, 1881, I have the honor to furnish the following report of the business of this bureau for the year between October 1, 1880, and October 1, 1881:

Number of general court-martial records received, reviewed, and registered .. 1, 792

Number of reports made and opinions furnished upon court-martial proceedings, applications for remission of sentence, &c., and upon miscellaneous questions of law referred to the Judge-Advocate-General for opinion by the Secretary of War 802

Number of official applications from the War and Treasury Departments and Pension Office for abstracts of proceedings of trials, &c., answered 336

Copies of Records furnished under the 114th Article of War, &c., pages...... 11, 452

The number of records of trials of enlisted men by inferior courts-martial received and filed at the different military departments during the past year, as appears from reports of Judge-Advocates received, is as follows:

Department of Arkansas	86
Department of California	819
Department of the Columbia	1, 002
Department of Dakota	1, 195
Department of the East	1, 268
Department of the Missouri	1, 370
Department of the Platte	1, 435
Department of the South	246
Department of Texas	1, 089
Total	8, 500

No report has been received from the Department of Arizona, and the number tried by inferior courts-martial in that Department is not embraced in the foregoing figures.

By Section 1199 of the Revised Statutes of the United States (as amended by the Act of June 23, 1874, Sec. 2, 18 Stat., 244) it is made the duty of the Judge-Advocate-General "to receive, revise, and cause to be recorded the proceedings of all courts-martial, courts of inquiry, and military commissions, and to perform such other duties as have been performed by the Judge-Advocate-General of the Army.

By the subsequent Act of March 3, 1877 (19 Stat., 310), the proceedings of garrison, regimental, and field officer's courts-martial are retained and filed in the office of the Judge-Advocate of the geographical department in which they are held, and do not reach this Bureau unless there is some alleged irregularity in the proceedings, or some question of law, practice, or procedure arises in the case on which the opinion of this Bureau is required. These courts are known as inferior courts-martial; they have no power to try capital cases or commissioned officers, or to inflict a fine exceeding one month's pay, or to imprison for a longer period than one month. The principal court-martial work of this Bureau, then, is confined to general courts-martial, being courts of superior and general jurisdiction over military crimes and offenses. In time of peace these courts are generally appointed by the commanders of separate departments, who are empowered to confirm and execute all sentences adjudged by such courts, except sentence of death, or of dismissal of an officer, or any sentence respecting a general officer, which are not to be carried into execution until confirmed by the President.

The proceedings of all general courts-martial convened by commanders of separate departments thus to be submitted for the action of the President, as well as the proceedings of all such courts as may be convened by the General of the Army, or by the President of the United States (when the general officer authorized to convene the court in the first instance is the accuser or prosecutor), are transmitted to this Bureau (by the Department Commander who appointed the court, or by the Judge-Advocate of the court appointed by the General of the Army or by the President), when the case is fully reported upon both as to the law and the facts, which report, with the proceedings of the court in the case, is then submitted to the Secretary of War for the consideration and action of the President as required by law.

The proceedings of all other general courts-martial where the sentences have been acted on by the officer ordering the court, and which have been transmitted to this Bureau for record, are, when necessary, revised, reported upon, and submitted to the Secretary of War.

It is to be remarked in this connection that while the Judge-Advocate-General is empowered by the statute above quoted to receive and revise the proceedings of courts-martial of the class last referred to, in the performance of which duty, as an official of the War Department, he is necessarily subordinate to the Secretary of War, yet the Secretary has no statutory authority to give effect to reports of revisions in such cases, even if he concurs therein, and to this extent the law is defective.

A Court of Inquiry is a tribunal called into being to examine into and report upon the facts of a transaction, accusation, or imputation against an officer or soldier. Under the provisions of the one hundred and fifteenth Article of War, it may be ordered by the President, or by any Commanding Officer, "upon a demand by the officer or soldier whose conduct is to be inquired of." Its object is to gather information with a view to ulterior proceedings by court-martial, or such action as the Commander who convened the court may deem proper.

A military commission is a tribunal called into being in time of war. It is mentioned in Section 1343 of the Revision as a tribunal for the trial of spies, but its organization and the pleadings, practice, and procedure before it are not prescribed by any statute.

I have thus briefly adverted to the military tribunals as well as the course of procedure by which their proceedings reach this Office for consideration. Upon this Bureau also devolves the duty of furnishing copies of the records of courts-martial to parties entitled to them, as provided by the one hundred and fourteenth Article of War. The extent of this work can be appreciated when it is considered that the records of some cases contain from 6,000 to 8,000 legal cap pages of manuscript, or over a million and a half of words, and of the 1,792 records received during the year each will average, say, 100 pages of legal cap, or 179,200 pages in all. These require to be read, revised, and reported upon, and very many of them to be copied, compared, and furnished, as stated.

It is evident, therefore, that in the quantity as well as in the nature and quality of the work to be performed by this Bureau, not only is an adequate force of clerks required, but in view of the interests involved in court-martial proceedings and other subjects confided to this Bureau, a force of clerks possessing in the highest degree both capacity and fidelity is imperatively necessary.

The insufficient clerical force allowed this Bureau has seriously crippled its efficiency, and has necessitated the transfer of officers of the corps of Judge-Advocates to duty in this office, thus depriving the geographical Military Departments of their much needed services. The large volume of business transacted and pressing upon this Bureau requires its employés to perform unusually severe and unremitting labor in order to keep up the current business.

This is neither wise nor just. An adequate and efficient clerical force is, for the reasons stated, of the utmost importance. With the view, therefore, of increasing its efficiency and rendering it adequate to the necessities of the public service, and in the interests of economy, there should be allowed:

One chief clerk, at a salary of $2,000 a year, as provided by section 215 of the Revised Statutes.

Two clerks of class 4.

Two clerks of class 3.

One clerk of class 2.

There should also be allowed one messenger and one laborer to convey the official messages and mails, to keep the office in order, and to handle and attend to its property and labor.

I have also to report that the office furniture generally is worn-out and rickety, and is unfitted for any public office. The law library is insufficient, incomplete, and antiquated. The reports of Wallace and Otto of the Supreme Court of the United States, the Opinions of the Attorneys-General of the United States, and a small number of text books, with a few scattering disconnected volumes of reports, constitute the library of the office.

To supply necessary furniture and books an adequate fund is required and has been estimated for; the sums allowed for several years past being barely sufficient to purchase necessary stationery for the office.

The other duties of the Judge-Advocate-General, referred to in the statutes, consist in rendering reports upon applications for clemency addressed to the President or Secretary of War by persons serving sentences of military courts, formulating and revising charges and specifications, advising courts-martial upon questions of law, practice, procedure and evidence arising before them, examining questions of law, and submitting opinions upon the same in matters arising in the course of the administration of the War Department, when called upon to do so by the Secretary of War, and, in short, when so required, it is the duty of the Judge-Advocate-General, as the law officer of the War Department, to advise in all questions touching the rights, duties, obligations, and limitations of authority of officers and others employed under the War Department, as fixed, defined, and limited by the Constitution and laws.

THE CORPS OF JUDGE-ADVOCATES.

The officers comprising this corps perform their duties under the direction of the Judge-Advocate-General (Sec. 1201, Revised Statutes), as amended by Act approved June 23, 1874 (18 Stat., 244).

These officers are stationed at the headquarters of the several geographical military departments, and their duties consist in preparing and revising charges, examining and reporting upon the proceedings of all military courts received at the Headquarters of the military departments at which they are stationed, assisting and advising the Department Commander (when required to do so,) in the examination of questions of law arising in the administration of his department, and officiating as Judge-Advocates of general courts-martial in the trial of important cases; appearing as counsel in behalf of the United States in civil courts, when the Department Commander may deem the same proper and for the best interests of the service.

This corps now consists of seven (7) officers, but is limited, however, by the act of Congress last cited to four (4), by gradual reduction (by the casualties of the service). I recommend the repeal of the clause in the statute making this reduction, and the organization of the corps of Judge-Advocates upon the same basis as other staff corps of the Army, this being the only corps in which the hope of promotion does not serve as an incentive to duty. The addition of four captains to the corps would render it able to meet all the requirements of the service, and I earnestly recommend that legislation in this behalf be urged by the Honorable Secretary of War. There are now ten geographical Departments, each of which should have a Judge-Advocate to advise in matters of law, but with the present strength of the corps of Judge-Advocates, four of these Departments—assuming all the members of the corps to be assigned to such Departments—must necessarily be deprived of the services of Judge-Advocates. In view of this fact, and as the addition of four captains would place the corps on a fair numerical basis, the importance of this slight increase becomes manifest, and I earnestly recommend it.

The seven members of the corps of Judge-Advocates are on duty as follows: Three are on duty in this Bureau, one in the Office of the Secretary of War, one as Professor of Law at the United States Military Academy, and two are on duty as Judge-Advocates of Departments. The importance of having a competent instructor of law at the Military Academy cannot be overestimated. It certainly requires no argument to make it clear to all that it is indispensable to a proper and intelligent discharge of the varied duties which devolve upon the Army officer that he should be as fully instructed in the general principles of law as possible. In the exercise of military command under this government, which is peculiarly one of laws, and where the increasing population surrounds military stations and military commanders, and where, as a consequence, questions of jurisdiction and of personal and property rights are necessarily constantly arising, it would seem proper that increased facilities should be furnished the young officer for acquiring such knowledge as an essential part of his military education.

I desire here to invite attention to some defects and omissions in our Articles of War.

The sixty-fifth, sixty-sixth, sixty-seventh, sixty-eighth, sixty-ninth, seventieth, and seventy-first Articles, relating to the arrest and confinement of officers and soldiers accused of crimes, duration of confinement, copy of charges and time of trial, being the only provisions of the Articles of War relating to this important portion of the criminal procedure before courts-martial, are unjustly discriminating and do not adequately provide for the subjects mentioned. By Article 66 a soldier may be held in confinement, and generally is so held, until his trial, no matter how long that period of time may be. By Article 71 an exact limit of time is fixed in which an officer may be kept in arrest, and if not brought to trial within the time fixed (48 days), the Article declares, "the arrest shall cease." I cannot understand why such a distinction should be made among any classes of persons amenable to military law. According to the practice now obtaining, any officer may prefer charges against another officer or enlisted man. No preliminary examination is required by law to be made into the grounds of accusation (although in some instances Department Commanders require this to be done to a limited extent), which in view of the length of time that elapses in many cases before a court-martial can be conveniently appointed for the trial, would seem to demand better regulation.

25 Ab

I desire also to invite attention to the sixty-first and sixty-second Articles of War, the Articles under which most military prosecutions are conducted. The sixty-first Article provides that "Any officer who is convicted of conduct unbecoming an officer and a gentleman shall be dismissed the service." This offense being undefined by any statute, or by the common law, in most prosecutions under it the facts alleged in the specification to the charge have never before passed into a precedent, being entirely novel in character and statement. The court-martial therefore in every such case, contrary to the fundamental maxim that "a court declares the law but may not make it" (*jus dicere*, but not *jus dare*), legislates as to what shall or shall not be deemed criminal under this Article. It rarely happens that the conviction and dismissal of an officer actually guilty of a crime or offence justifying dismissal, is founded alone on this charge, but is usually associated with other charges, which upon conviction justify dismissal, where sentence of dismissal is proper. For this reason, therefore, I would recommend the repeal of the sixty-first Article and the enactment of such legislation as may be deemed necessary to properly and definitely comprehend all offences which the said Article is intended to embrace.

The sixty-second Article reads:

All crimes not capital, and all disorders and neglects which officers and soldiers may be guilty of, to the prejudice of good order and military discipline, though not mentioned in the foregoing articles of war, are to be taken cognizance of by a general or regimental, garrison or field officers' court-martial, according to the nature and degree of the offence, and punished at the discretion of such court.

This sweeping provision has formed a part of our Articles of War since September 20, 1776, shortly after the Declaration of Independence, when it was adopted by the Continental Congress for the government of the Army, and has been continued through all the subsequent revisions of our Articles of War to the present time.

Like the preceding Article it was taken from the articles of war made by the Crown of England under a clause contained in the Mutiny Act (annually included in that Act since 3 Geo. I), empowering the Crown to make Articles of War; but whether the making of an Article in this form was a proper exercise of the power conferred, has not, so far as I am informed, received judicial consideration in England, nor has the Article been so considered in this country. While this Article is praised by some military men, it is also condemned by others. An eminent general and statesman termed it "The Devil's Article." Like the preceding one it neither mentions nor specifies any known crime or offence. In many of the prosecutions under it, the facts alleged are without precedent, and do not come within the terms of any statute, or of the common law, giving a court-martial jurisdiction to try and punish. The Article, therefore, is construed to deal out unknown punishments for unknown and undefined crimes and offences, *misera est servitus, ubi jus est vagum aut incertum.* As a consequence of this uncertainty with respect to this and the preceding Article, one court-martial may (and often does) consider actions as "conduct unbecoming an officer and a gentleman," or as "conduct to the prejudice of good order and military discipline," while another court-martial on substantially the same state of facts, and from equally conscientious motives, would consider them proper or excusable. The generality of these Articles induces the manufacture of new offences, and the frequency of trials by courts-martial, and the operation of the last-mentioned Article in connection with other Articles, result in the annual court-martialing of a large per cent. of the enlisted men of the Army (nearly 50 per cent. the present year), whereby large sums of the pay of the soldiers are regularly lost to them in the shape of fines, forfeitures, and penalties, aggregating about $150,000 annually, causing great dissatisfaction, discontent, and frequent desertions, and entailing great loss to the service in the matter of property, generally taken at the time of desertion.

The frequency of trials by court-martial should be prevented, and the specific crimes and offences contemplated by the Articles of War should be defined and limited, and the jurisdiction of courts-martial should be limited accordingly. The practice of imposing forfeitures of comparatively large sums of money by sentence of courts-martial, against the pay of enlisted men, is demoralizing in the extreme to the Army. For trifling neglects or disorders, or for what might be considered no more than bad manners, brief absences without leave, &c., fines are often imposed of ten dollars or perhaps the entire month's pay. This effect might be greatly ameliorated if the proceeds of such forfeitures, &c., could be appropriated to such uses as would inure to the direct benefit of those who faithfully performed their duties, by the establishing of post libraries, gymnasiums, bath-rooms, &c., &c.

So charges are preferred against enlisted men, and until tried by court-martial they must remain in confinement without bail or mainprise, until ordered released by the officer having authority to confirm the proceedings of the court. It sometimes happens that men are held in confinement for a year awaiting trial, the exigencies of the service not permitting trial sooner, and the trial results in an acquittal, or demonstrates that the offence was alleged to be more serious than the evidence would justify, and that an inferior court-martial would have been fully competent to act in the case at once, thus avoiding this long delay and confinement, all of which is the result of there being no preliminary examination into the merits of the case when the charges were preferred, thus bringing the essential facts to the notice of the officer who is authorized to appoint a court for the trial. Of course I here speak of cases deemed to be proper for the consideration of a general court-martial. These long delays not unfrequently cause failures of justice, where the witnesses for the prosecution cannot be found, or are induced by the accused to flee the country beyond the reach of process of the court at the time of trial.

The ninety-first Article of War provides in certain contingencies for the reading in evidence of the depositions of witnesses before courts-martial in cases not capital. If these depositions were taken at or near the time when the offence was committed, when practicable to do so, directly in the presence of the prisoner, so that he might cross-examine the witnesses if he would, and to be used in the trial, in the contingency that the case is not capital, or where it is shown to the satisfaction of the court that the witness is dead, or is so ill as not to be able to travel, or if he is kept out of the way by the accused, or is insane, or is residing beyond the limits of the State, Territory, or District in which the court may be ordered to sit, the administration of military justice would be greatly promoted by amending the law accordingly. The importance of this amendment of the law will be seen when it is considered that the territorial jurisdiction of a court-martial is so extended that a military offence committed in Maine may be brought to trial before a court-martial sitting in Oregon, rendering it difficult if not impossible at times to obtain the *viva voce* testimony of material witnesses.

So in case of arrest or confinement upon charges not felonious or aggravated, if the trial be not ordered within ten days, or other brief period, the commanding officer should be authorized to return the accused to duty until such time as trial may be ordered.

Regulations should be provided on the subject of framing the charges, and presenting them to the court for trial. No uniform practice now obtains on this important subject, and great incongruity of procedure and jarring of authority at times result as a consequence. The course now pursued may be briefly stated as follows: Charges are forwarded to the Department Commander recommending their trial. They are then referred to the Department Judge-Advocate for opinion. In very many cases this officer finds the specification of facts so defectively stated, or an omission of the *facts*, and statements of the evidence only, in support of the charge, that amendment or revision becomes essentially necessary. In many cases the officer preferring the charges objects to any revision by the Judge-Advocate, and declines to recognize his charges as thus revised, when it is proper in some cases that he should do so.

This matter ought to be set at rest by some authoritative provision empowering the officer authorized to appoint the court to cause the charges in all cases deemed necessary to be amended or revised (before arraignment and plea) by the Judge-Advocate of the Department, and the charges so revised and amended to be authenticated by the Judge-Advocate of the court appointed to try them, and empowering him to further amend them, with the consent of the convening officer, at any time before arraignment and plea, if the facts appear to warrant it.

Where charges are preferred against an officer or enlisted man, deemed proper for trial by general court-martial, it should be made the duty of the Commanding Officer, his Adjutant, or some disinterested officer, as soon as practicable, having regard to the circumstances attending the commission of the alleged crime or offence, to proceed to examine into the nature of such charges, and for this purpose he should have power to compel the attendance of witnesses residing within the limits of the command of the officer authorized to appoint the court. The witnesses should be sworn and examined by such officer, with a right on the part of the prisoner to cross-examine; the testimony should be written in the form of a deposition and subscribed by the witness, the accused to be a competent witness in his own behalf in the same manner as before a court-martial, and to be permitted to make and subscribe such statement as he may desire. The charges and depositions should then be forwarded to the officer authorized to appoint a court for the trial, who should be required to determine as soon as practicable whether it is proper to bring the case before a general court-martial. If he should not deem the case proper for trial by general court-martial, or if he should deem the case of an enlisted man to be a proper one for the cognizance of an inferior court-martial, his decision to that effect should be communicated to the commanding officer of the accused. An appeal from such decision, within a reasonable time, should be authorized to the Secretary of War, whose decision should be final.

An able writer on military law says:

No person should be put upon his trial before a general court-martial unless in consequence of a previous report by an inquest, on evidence laid before them that there appears sufficient grounds for calling upon the party to defend himself judicially against the matters of accusation. A preliminary form of this nature would be of infinite service in the repression of calumnious and frivolous prosecutions, and would tend more than any other measure to the checking of that extreme frequency of trials by court-martial, which has the worst effect upon the public mind, reflecting dishonor on the military character in general, spreading disunion and party divisions among the members of a corps, and frequently laying the foundation of permanent and even fatal animosities. (Tyler's Essay on Military Law, pp. 342–3.)

In reviewing court-martial proceedings, especially in cases of desertion, the prisoner very often is found to complain of ill-treatment at the hands of his superior officers, but more frequently at the hands of non-commissioned officers, and to attribute his desertion to that cause.

This complaint of ill-treatment is found repeated and reiterated in hundreds of trials for desertion, and sometimes for other offenses.

Whether the complaint be true or false, the opportunity which is afforded a superior to oppress an inferior is very great, and tends to give credence to the complaint. In the interests of the officer or non-commissioned officer, therefore, if the complaint be false, or in the interests of the soldier and the service if true, some remedy, either by legislation or regulation, should be adopted that would effectually prevent the possibility of an abuse of authority.

It is believed that the possibility of such abuse of power on the part of non-commissioned officers would be remedied if the men of the company were permitted at all proper times to lay all matters of complaint in person before the company commanders, and not as is now the general practice of requiring all complaints to be made through the first sergeant of the company.

The seventy-second Article of War should be amended by expressly authorizing the President of the United States and Colonels commanding separate Departments to appoint general courts-martial whenever necessary.

By Article 38 of the rules and articles for the government of the Navy, the President may appoint general courts-martial for the Navy whenever necessary.

So in maintaining the discipline of the Army like power should be conferred upon him by the Articles of War. Colonels are sometimes placed in command of separate Departments according to brevet rank of Brigadier or Major General. In view of the fact that there are now a great many colonels who have not the brevet rank of Brigadier or Major General, and that the number having such brevet rank is constantly diminishing, and that colonels may necessarily be called upon now and in the future to command Departments, the seventy-second Article should be amended as indicated, otherwise Colonels in command of Departments not having brevet rank will be unable to properly enforce the discipline of their Departments in view of the restrictions contained in that Article.

The authority conferred upon the Judge-Advocate of a court-martial by Section 1202 of the Revised Statutes, "to issue the like process to compel witnesses to appear and testify which courts of criminal jurisdiction within the State, Territory, or District where such military courts shall be ordered to sit may lawfully issue," should be penally sanctioned. While the Judge-Advocate may issue the process, there is no statutory authority to punish disobedience thereof. Witnesses not in the military service are now induced to attend solely by reason of a liberal compensation much exceeding that paid by any criminal court, whether State or National. As a matter of economy, then, if not of justice, power to punish reluctant and disobedient witnesses should be conferred by statute upon courts-martial or upon the Judge-Advocates thereof.

Except as provided in the eighty-fourth and eighty-fifth Articles of War, concerning the administration of oaths to the members and judge-advocate of a court-martial, no authority whatever is given by any statute to administer an oath before a court-martial, nor is it certain that the common law would confer such power. If, therefore, the judge-advocate or some official before a court-martial were expressly authorized to administer oaths to witnesses or other persons in trials by court-martial, many doubts and uncertainties in regard to this matter would be settled.

The operation of that portion of the ninetieth Article of War, which requires the Judge-Advocate of a court-martial to prosecute, as well as to a certain extent to consider himself counsel for the prisoner, tends to mislead. This Article was framed at a time when the person preferring the charges appeared and prosecuted them before the court-martial, or if he failed to prosecute, another person other than the judge-advocate was so appointed. As questions were asked through the judge-advocate, he could object to and decline to entertain criminating questions to the accused and witnesses; the party originating the charges and the accused being thus the actual parties before the court, and the judge-advocate being the official or nominal prosecutor. In this country, however, the judge-advocate of a court-martial prosecutes before it in as ample a manner as a United States Attorney prosecutes a criminal case before a Circuit or District Court, and a private prosecutor is not to be heard before a court-martial except in testifying as a witness. The prisoner not being permitted to testify before a court-martial till the passage of the Act of March 16, 1878 (20 Stat., 30), making persons charged with crimes and offences competent witnesses, no criminating or other question touching his guilt or innocence could properly be put to him as a witness. If, however, the prisoner now offers himself as a witness under the Act referred to, the understanding is that he becomes a general witness in the case, and must answer relevant questions, even if the answers would tend to criminate him.

Ignorant enlisted men, however, are led to believe that the judge-advocate is required to act as their counsel, when he cannot nor does he do so. Yet, adhering to the belief that he must, the prisoner frequently confides his defence to the judge-advocate, who is thus greatly embarrassed in the trial of the cause by reason of such knowledge. Obtained under such circumstances, a proper sense of honor will prevent its use to the prejudice of the prisoner.

In cases of conviction and sentence, the next thing heard from the prisoner comes in the form of a petition praying for remission or disapproval of his sentence, on the ground that he was deceived or misled by the advice of the Judge-Advocate of the court at the trial. The Judge-Advocates of courts-martial, unfortunately, are usually selected by the officers appointing the court (see Article 74) from the youngest and least experienced of the subaltern officers, apparently that they may thus acquire information, rather than that the court should be well advised and every legal right thus be secured to the prisoner.

Extracts from the reports of Judge-Advocates of Departments (or officers acting and performing the duties of those officers), embodying recommendations on various matters, are hereto appended, and, with this report, are respectfully submitted.

D. G. SWAIM,
Judge-Advocate-General.

The Hon. the SECRETARY OF WAR.

Extract from report of Judge-Advocate, Department of the Platte.

The administration of justice in this Department has received the usual attention of this office during the past year.

Questions submitted have been examined, and expressions of opinion made, as the law and justice of the matters involved required.

This Military Department extends over a large territory, and includes within its borders great numbers of Indian tribes, who hold portions of it subject to agreements and laws from time to time made and enacted by the national government. To protect them from external causes of demoralization, prevent internecine wars and bloodshed, as well as secure pioneers in their rights, not unfrequently involves delicate and perplexed questions as to their relative rights and responsibilities.

To insure respect for the law of the land by such tribes and these early settlers requires continuing familiarity with legal enactments, as well as with the objects upon which they are to operate and the subjects to be affected by their administration. To this end laws and decisions should be provided for each Department Headquarters.

The sum heretofore appropriated for libraries at Department Headquarters has not become practically available, but it is supposed it soon will, and it is hoped more adequate amounts will be hereafter appropriated to supply a want so plainly required for the best interests of the public and Army service.

The correspondence of this office with officers and others in this Department and beyond its boundaries has continued, and, it is believed, has been instrumental in the settlement of differences and the avoidance of conflicts relating to questions between officials involving the jurisdiction of the courts of the general and State governments.

The attention of this office has been repeatedly called (by grave events occurring within this Department) to the deficiency of adequate authority (in military courts) to punish murder in time of peace. It is believed the security and welfare of individuals and the good of the service demand that this offence (occurring in the Army) should be tried by its courts. As at present provided it practically goes unpunished; and this most atrocious crime is in the military service beyond the reach of proper investigation, or trial.

The reasons which operate to render unavoidable military laws and courts for the punishment of other offences apply to this also, and demand such trials.

The passion and cruelty which induces a person in the Army to shed the blood of his comrade, or send to an untimely grave the officer who directs and leads in the battle of danger, is less restrained by the apprehension of punishment in such case than in the perpetrator of a minor or trivial offense.

In the one speedy and substantial justice is meted out, while in the other the accused is passed over to the local courts of the frontier, sent to a distant place of incarceration (where witnesses can scarcely attend or be procured), and when, at last, the matter will drag slowly on, and can only with extreme difficulty be fairly met, an officer to punish crime or vindicate justice. Legislation upon this subject is believed to be necessary, and respectfully recommended.

The anomalous condition of Judge-Advocates in the matter of promotion has long attracted the attention of officers of the Army; and it is believed that the time has arrived when suitable legislation should provide for them such advancement of rank as is conceded to other officers.

The bill reported in Congress last winter seemed to embody the principle applicable to the subject, and its provisions are commended. The present system of military jurisprudence, under benign progress, brought order out of chaos, substituted established principles and authoritative decisions for conflicting findings, and made law the basis of conviction instead of personal dictum.

The efficiency and permanency of the corps, and the efficacy of its humanizing influence, depend in some degree upon the legislative provision which should assure to them the rights conceded to all other officers of the Army.

Extract from report of Judge-Advocate, Department of the East and Military Division of the Atlantic.

Under the direction of the Honorable Secretary of War, an effort has been made to secure from the Legislature of the State of New York an act granting certain riparian rights to the land occupied recruiting depot at David's Island, New York Harbor, so as to include facilities for landing on the main shore in Westchester.

By direction of the same authority a writ of error was taken to the United States Supreme Court for the southern district of New York from the district court, in the case of a case involving the construction of the one hundred and third Article of War. The cause is appointed for argument in November.

The various sentences of the different general courts-martial in the Division, on the same state of facts, involving discharge and confinement in the military prison, have been sufficiently noticeable in the past year to invite attention to the propriety of a thorough revision of the Articles of War, so that penalties for many offences may be more definite and certain.

* * * * * *

During the time covered by this report there have been seventy-six communications (not including charges and specifications submitted for examination and revision) referred to this office for recommendation and report. These have embraced not only applications for remissions of sentences and ordinary legal questions as to the construction of Articles of War or Regulations, but also questions of exercise of jurisdiction by State authority, as, for example, whether post-traders can be taxed, also whether the Executive authority in an incorporated village can compel the discontinuance of authorized rifle practice at a military post within its limits, over which the United States has, however, exclusive jurisdiction.

Also, as to the construction of deeds of cession of a military post where the State has reserved certain rights as to the quarrying upon or occupying portions of the ground.

Also, questions as to the custody of the minor children and property of a deceased soldier at a military post under the exclusive jurisdiction of the United States.

The appropriation recently made by Congress for the purchase of law-books for this office, although very small, will, it is hoped, be continued annually and increased in amounts until a working library shall be secured.

The want of books of reference and reports of the superior courts of law has, on several occasions during the past year, prevented me from presenting to the court a cited authority, when requested, during an argument.

*   *   *   *   *   *   *

In conclusion, it is to be hoped that, in the approaching session of Congress, the recommendations found in the last message of President Hayes, relative to the corps of Judge-Advocates, may receive early and favorable attention.

Extract from report of acting Judge-Advocate, Department of the Columbia.

From the foregoing exhibit it is seen that 35 cases of desertion were tried in the year ending August 31, 1880, and only 18 in the year ending August 31, 1881. The inference from this showing alone would be very gratifying, but the matter assumes a very different aspect when it is known that 101 desertions were reported in the past year and 93 in the previous year. The conclusion is unavoidable that, while the number of desertions per year remains about the same, the facilities for successfully accomplishing this crime have rapidly multiplied, and a much larger number of this class of criminals escape justice now than formerly.

During the seven months that the undersigned has acted as Judge-Advocate of this Department he has been detailed as judge-advocate of two important general courts—one at Fort Walla Walla, W. T., and the other at Fort Townsend, W. T.

The former court was ordered for the trial of a lieutenant-colonel upon charges preferred by another officer, a captain in the same regiment, and was ordered only after the failure of all other attempts at a satisfactory settlement of the matter at issue. After the convening of the court, however, and before the arraignment of the accused, an amicable and happy adjustment of the subject matter of the charges was arrived at by mutual explanations and concessions on the part of the accused and the officer preferring the charges, which resulted in the withdrawal of the charges by the Department Commander. This matter is touched upon here, inasmuch as, the court not having proceeded to the arraignment of the accused, no record of its proceedings was forwarded to the Judge-Advocate-General.

In conclusion, I have the honor to state that the recommendations made and opinions furnished by the undersigned have, without exception, been approved and concurred in by the Department Commander, and, in the only instance in which it was deemed advisable to apply to the Secretary of War for a more authoritative decision, the opinion delivered by the Department Judge-Advocate was approved and confirmed by the Judge-Advocate-General and Secretary of War.

Extract from report of acting Judge-Advocate, Department of Texas.

It is respectfully submitted that the necessity of detailing a judge-advocate for regimental or garrison courts-martial causes frequent embarrassment. At numerous small posts the requisite number of officers is not available. In such cases punishment must, of necessity, be arbitrary or long-delayed and expensive. The garrison court was, at best, a formal and unwieldy tribunal for disposing of petty offences, and now, it is confidently believed, the interests of the service demand a more prompt, summary, and certain substitute. For example, if a change of law could be effected, so as to authorize in time of peace a court after the manner of a field-officer's court: if, for instance, the eighty-second Article of War could be so modified as to permit the detail of a garrison court of less than three, when that number is not available, it would be an improvement on the present system, which seems unnecessarily slow, formal, circumstantial, and too liable to be beyond the reach of those who need it most.

Attention is respectfully invited to the vast sums of money derived from the soldier and applied to the Soldiers' Home.

Take this Department. For the past three years the strength of the enlisted force has averaged 3,419; exclusive of forfeitures of deserters and loss of all pay and allowances by those dishonorably discharged, the fines imposed upon soldiers remaining in service have alone aggregated $15,087 a year, on an average, to which adding $5,128, deduction of 12½ cents a month, it will be seen that $20,215 has annually been taken from soldiers still in service in this Department to support an establishment to which an average of three a year has been admitted. If analogy may be applied to the whole Army, $147,813 is annually taken from soldiers remaining in service to support the home, to which few ever get.

If the purport of the law be the benefit of the soldier who serves the government faithfully, it would seem but just and wise to apply a part of this money to his present actual needs. Could a portion of fines be set apart for the use of the soldiers at the post where imposed, they might enjoy decent quarters, and a better condition generally, without expense to the government. The soldier would then be certain to receive benefit of part of the money taken from him, and the service would be bettered by the improvement in the condition of its soldiers. The good soldier who does the work of the delinquent would in return enjoy the benefits of the fines imposed on the latter.

As it now stands, enormous sums of money are deducted from the small pay of the enlisted man and applied to the maintenance of a magnificent establishment, which comparatively few indeed may ever hope to enjoy.

As has been previously reported, the necessity of suitable books of law in this office is felt, and it is hoped a successful effort will be made to secure an appropriation of the few dollars required.

Extract from report of acting Judge-Advocate, Military Division of the Pacific and Department of California.

No commissioned officers have been tried in this Department during said period. Charges against one were received, but on investigation dismissed.

There is an apparent improvement in discipline indicated by this report, when compared with that of September 24, 1880.

The number of charges for trial by general court-martial received during the past year is 41 less than during the previous year, and the number of cases tried by general, garrison, and regimental courts-martial is 125 less, while the number of troops has remained the same.

Extract from report of Lieutenant Groesbeck, Sixth Infantry, in charge of Judge-Advocate's office, Department of the Missouri.

The following table was compiled mainly from cases of enlisted men convicted of desertion and now undergoing sentence in the military prison at Fort Leavenworth:

DESERTIONS.

Before serving one year	203
After serving one year	99
After serving two years	31
After serving three years	10
After serving four years	3

A tabulated statement of all the desertions in the Army during the past year would doubtless show a result much like the above, and from which it can be conclusively inferred that, whatever corrective is sought to be applied to the tendency to desertion, must have special regard to the needs of the recruit and of the young soldier of twelve and eighteen months' service. Excepting a small class of vicious men who always have been, and probably always will be, "run out" by the companies, or organizations to which they are assigned, my impression is that nearly all the recruits now accepted could be induced to remain until they become seasoned to the hard actualities of the service, and the danger of desertion thus largely eliminated. Among the causes that are now most baneful, and which ought to be assailed vigorously until corrected, is the brutality of non-commissioned officers. The American recruit is sensitive to restraint, feels any indignity keenly, broods over his sense of wrong and spreads a general feeling of discontent that influences hurtfully the foreign element in the ranks of the Army, which, owing to early habits and usages, would more readily submit to the methods of discipline employed. The crying need, then, is a system of instruction for non-commissioned officers, which shall enjoin, not only unflinching firmness in the exercise of their very responsible duties, but absolute forbearance in the use of profane and often disgustingly abusive language now too often accompanying their authoritative acts and commands. This is an old abuse, and its correction will not only make better non-commissioned officers, but maintain a more wholesome discipline and lessen the number of crimes.

A second and perhaps greater cause of desertion is found in the lack of effort put forth to arrest the deserter, and especially in the insufficiency of the reward offered for his apprehension and delivery, which ought to include cost of transportation of the prisoner to the "nearest military post," reckoned by mileage at 8 or 10 cents per mile. Many a deserter now feels comparatively safe because the sheriff could not "make it pay" to apprehend and undertake his delivery.

A third cause rests in the fact of the punishment imposed not being sufficiently deterrent. It has become a common remark among discontented men that two years' confinement in the military prison is not so great a hardship as five years of taxing service in garrison and field, where fatigue labor is the principal occupation. I am satisfied that many men desert with a view to accepting the alternative of conviction and sentence to hard labor for two years, and then be set at liberty, rather than face the certainty of four of five years of service which has become distasteful to them. Courts should be encouraged to impose at least three years confinement for desertion, and the labor at the prison should be sufficiently severe to contrast unfavorably with the ordinary labor of garrison life.

Extract from report of acting Judge-Advocate, Department of Dakota.

Attention is invited to the lack of uniformity in the practice before general courts-martial in respect to obtaining testimony by deposition under the provisions of the Ninety-first Article of War. From the records of this office it would seem that a wide diversity exists in the opinions of officers as to the nature and form of the "deposition" and the formalities necessary to be observed, in order that it may be safely received as evidence by the court. In some instances, these depositions are offered in the form of an affidavit. In many they are unaccompanied by proof of "reasonable notice," while in other cases, copies of interrogatories and cross-interrogatories are exchanged between the parties, and occasionally application is made to the court to issue a "*dedimus potestatem.*"

It is also, apparently, an unsettled question in what manner the expenses of such an examination are to be paid. The disbursement has been made in this department by the Quartermaster's Department, but at times with hesitation.

It is respectfully recommended that some mode of procedure be authoritatively adopted and promulgated.

REPORT OF THE QUARTERMASTER-GENERAL.

WAR DEPARTMENT,
QUARTERMASTER-GENERAL'S OFFICE,
Washington, D. C., November 1, 1881.

SIR: I have the honor to transmit herewith, for the honorable the Secretary of War, the report of operations of the Quartermaster's Department during the fiscal year ending June 30, 1881.

A synopsis of the report was forwarded to the War Department on the 26th ultimo.

Very respectfully, your obedient servant,

M. C. MEIGS,
Quartermaster-General, Bvt. Major-General, U. S. A.

To the ADJUTANT-GENERAL OF THE ARMY.

[First indorsement.]

ADJUTANT-GENERAL'S OFFICE,
Washington, November 2, 1881.

Respectfully submitted to the Secretary of War.

R. C. DRUM,
Adjutant-General.

WAR DEPARTMENT,
QUARTERMASTER-GENERAL'S OFFICE,
Washington, October 24, 1881.

SIR: I have the honor to submit the annual report of operations of the Quartermaster's Department during the fiscal year ending June 30, 1881.

The balance at end of June 30, 1880, in Treasury to credit of the Quartermaster's Department was, as by last report	$1,027,815 68
The appropriations made for the service of the Quartermaster's Department during the fiscal year were, in gross	11,498,758 19
The appropriations for deficiency for 1880 and prior years	215,466 41
Appropriations for 50 per centum to land-grant railroads	575,000 00
Amounts deposited to credit of appropriations and received from sales to officers of public property	540,147 29
Total	13,857,187 57
Remittances to disbursing officers have amounted to... $11,203,536 03	
Requisitions to pay settlements made by the Treasury. 718,205 13	
Carried to surplus fund, act 30th June, 1874 230,123 62	
Error in credit to clothing appropriation, 1879, now dropped 26 75	
	12,151,891 53
Balance in Treasury undrawn at end of June 30, 1881	1,705,296 04

A table accompanying this report gives the amount of the various items of appropriations, remittances, &c., in detail.

The Quartermaster's Department is charged with the duty of providing the means of transportation by land and water for all troops and all material of war. It furnishes the horses of the artillery and cavalry, and horses and mules for the trains. It provides and distributes clothing, tents, camp and garrison equipage, forage, lumber, and all material for camps and for shelter of troops and stores. It now provides lights for all military posts and buildings. It builds barracks, storehouses, hospitals; provides wagons and ambulances and harness, except for cavalry and artillery horses; builds or charters ships, steamers, and boats, docks, and wharves; constructs and repairs roads, railways, and bridges; clears out obstructions in rivers and harbors when necessary for military purposes; provides, by hire or purchase, grounds for military encampments and buildings; pays generally all expenses of military operations not by law assigned to some other department; and, finally, it provides and maintains military cemeteries in which the dead of the Army are buried.

Food, arms, ammunition, medical and hospital stores are purchased and issued by other departments, but the Quartermaster's Department transports them to the place of issue, and provides storehouses for their preservation until consumed.

About three hundred officers of the line, in each fiscal year, are placed on duty as acting assistant quartermasters, and are charged with the responsibility for public property, and many of them with the disbursement of public funds. A list of those to whom money has been remitted, or who have acted as assistant quartermasters during the fiscal year, is with this report.

For the responsibility thus involved, and the labor attending these duties, it seems to be just that they should be allowed by the government the same moderate monthly compensation which is allowed to acting commissaries of subsistence for duties somewhat similar, viz, $10 per month.

The want of post quartermaster sergeants still continues to be felt, and I am requested by officers who have the good of the service at heart to again recommend that their appointment be provided for.

The acting assistant quatermaster who is in charge of the military property of the Quartermaster's Department at any military post, as a rule, leaves the post whenever the garrison is exchanged or removed, and the sudden transfer of property, often of great value, is attended with risk of loss to the officers.

A post quartermaster sergeant, who would remain at the post, would be able to save officers and the government loss which results from such sudden and frequent changes. This care of supplies would prevent useless transportation and wastage.

The value of the service of ordnance and commissary sergeants is well established by experience, but the Quartermaster's Department, whose property at military posts generally exceeds in value all others combined, is without these useful non-commissioned officers.

DUTIES OF OFFICERS.

Col. Stewart Van Vliet, assistant quartermaster-general, was on duty in this office in charge of the inspection branch and as inspector to January 22, 1881, when retired from active service.

Col. S. B. Holabird, assistant quartermaster-general, has had charge of the finance branch and of the examination of accounts and returns of officers preparatory to their being transmitted to the Treasury for settlement, and of the supply and distribution and manufacture of clothing and camp and garrison equipage. Also, from January 23, 1881, in charge of inspection branch.

Lieut. Col. J. G. Chandler, deputy quartermaster-general, has had charge of the transportation, regular supplies, and miscellaneous claims branches of the office since May 20, 1881. Prior to that date Lieut. Col. H. C. Hodges was in charge of them. Colonel Chandler previously served as chief quartermaster Department of the South, at Newport Barracks, Ky., to February 12, 1881, and as chief quartermaster Military Division of the Gulf, at New Orleans, La., to May 20, 1881.

Maj. James M. Moore, quartermaster, has had charge of the claims branch and of the barracks and quarters branch of the office.

Maj. B. C. Card, quartermaster, has had charge of the maintenance and improvement of national military cemeteries since April 1, 1881, and has also done the duty of depot quartermaster at this station. Prior to that date Capt. A. F. Rockwell, assistant quartermaster, was in charge. Major Card had previously been on duty as chief quartermaster, Department of Texas, at San Antonio, Tex. Other principal regular stations have been occupied as follows:

Col. D. H. Rucker, assistant quartermaster-general, has been in charge of the Philadelphia general depot of the Quartermaster's Department, Philadelphia, Pa., the principal depot for purchase and manufacture of clothing for the Army.

Col. Rufus Ingalls, assistant quartermaster-general, chief quartermaster Military Division of the Missouri, Chicago, Ill., to February 17, 1881; since then in charge of the general depot of the Quartermaster's Department at New York City.

Col. L. C. Easton, assistant quartermaster-general, had charge of the general depot of the Quartermaster's Department at New York City to January 27, 1881, when retired from active service.

Col. C. H. Tompkins, assistant quartermaster-general, chief quartermaster Department of Dakota, Saint Paul, Minn., to February 15, 1881;

since then chief quartermaster Military Division of the Missouri, Chicago, Ill.

Lieut. Col. James A. Ekin, deputy quartermaster-general, in charge of the general depot of the Quartermaster's Department at Jeffersonville, Ind., disbursing officer of the Quartermaster's Department at Louisville, Ky., and in charge of the National Military Cemeteries in Kentucky and Tennessee, and of investigation of claims in Kentucky, Ohio, and Indiana.

Lieut. Col. Rufus Saxton, deputy quartermaster-general, chief quartermaster Military Division of the Pacific and Department of California, Presidio of San Francisco, Cal.

Lieut. Col. J. D. Bingham, deputy quartermaster-general, chief quartermaster Department of the Missouri, Fort Leavenworth, Kans.

Lieut. Col. A. J. Perry, deputy quartermaster-general, chief quartermaster Military Division of the Atlantic and Department of the East, Governor's Island, New York Harbor.

Lieut. Col. Henry C. Hodges, deputy quartermaster-general, until May 20, 1881, on duty in the Quartermaster General's Office, and since August 6, 1881, chief quartermaster Department of Arizona, Whipple Barracks, Prescott, Ariz.

Lieut. Col. William Myers, deputy quartermaster-general, depot quartermaster, Chicago, Ill., to February 17, 1881; since then chief quartermaster Department of Dakota, Fort Snelling, Minn.

Lieut. Col. Charles G. Sawtelle, deputy quartermaster-general, chief quartermaster Department, of Columbia, Vancouver Barracks, Washington Territory, to April 12, 1881; since then chief quartermaster Department of the South, Newport Barracks, Ky.

Maj. James J. Dana, quartermaster, chief quartermaster District of New Mexico, Santa Fé, N. Mex., to August 7, 1880; since then in charge of investigation of war claims in Tennessee, Nashville, Tenn.

Maj. R. N. Batchelder, quartermaster, in charge of the general depot of the Quartermaster's Department at San Francisco, Cal.

Maj. M. I. Ludington, quartermaster, chief quartermaster Department of the Platte, Fort Omaha, Nebr.

Maj. C. A. Reynolds, quartermaster, disbursing quartermaster, Buffalo, N. Y.

Maj. George B. Dandy, quartermaster, purchasing and shipping quartermaster at Portland, Oreg., to June 1, 1881; since April 12, 1881, chief quartermaster Department of Columbia, Vancouver Barracks, Washington Territory.

Maj. George H. Weeks, quartermaster, depot quartermaster, Fort Leavenworth, Kans.

Maj. William B. Hughes, quartermaster, depot quartermaster, Saint Louis, Mo., to March 31, 1881; since then chief quartermaster Department of Texas, San Antonio, Tex.

Maj. A. G. Robinson, quartermaster, disbursing quartermaster District of Montana, Helena, Mont.

Maj. E. D. Baker, quartermaster, depot quartermaster, San Antonio, Tex., to April 3, 1881; since then depot quartermaster, Saint Louis, Mo.

Maj. J. G. C. Lee, quartermaster, in charge of construction of buildings at Fort Assinaboine, Mont., to September 24, 1880; from November 13, 1880, chief quartermaster District of New Mexico, Santa Fé, N. Mex.

Maj. James Gilliss, quartermaster, post quartermaster, and quartermaster of artillery school, Fort Monroe, Va.

Maj. T. J. Eckerson, quartermaster, chief quartermaster District of the Rio Grande, Fort Brown, Tex., to April 5, 1881; since then depot quartermaster, Boston, Mass.

INSPECTION BRANCH.

This branch of the office reports the stations and duties of the officers of the Quartermaster's Department, and those of the line officers and officers of other branches of the staff on duty in the Quartermaster's Department as acting assistant quartermasters.

Three hundred and six have been on such duty for longer or shorter periods during the year. A list of their names and stations accompanies this report.

It prepares the monthly returns of officers of the Quartermaster's Department for the Adjutant-General's Office. It files and examines the annual reports of officers; files and distributes general and special orders, rolls of honor, and other printed documents relating to the Quartermaster's Department. It attends to procuring and distributing to military posts the reading matter furnished to them in connection with the system of military schools and instruction of soldiers and of their children. This reading matter consists principally of the current periodical literature of the day, for which, however, when desired by the post, a supply of school books is occasionally substituted. The total expenditure to supply the schools with reading matter during the year has been about $9,000.

Eighty-five thousand seven hundred and forty-nine general orders and other printed papers have been received, and 63,712 sent out during the year.

TRANSPORTATION.

The movement during the year was of 46,658 persons, 10,355 beasts, and 136,632 tons of material, costing $1,802,931.37, of which $393,156.27 was paid for transportation of persons and $1,409,775.10 for freight.

The larger movements of troops were:

Third Cavalry, Companies C, G, and L, from Department of the Platte to Department of the Missouri, 291 miles.

Second Artillery, Companies E, G, and L, from Department of Texas to Department of the South, 1,080 miles.

Sixteenth Infantry, headquarters and ten companies, from Department of the Missouri to Department of Texas, 705 miles.

Twenty-fourth Infantry, headquarters and ten companies, from Department of Texas to Department of the Missouri, 608 miles.

RAILROAD TRANSPORTATION.

There were moved by rail 32,820 persons, 8,782 beasts, and 83,516 tons of material and supplies.

The cost to the appropriation for transportation of the Army has been $212,729.00 for passengers and $307,912.66 for stock and freight.

The bonded Pacific railroads have earned $836,638.05 for military transportation, which sum is withheld by the Secretary of the Treasury to be applied, under the law of 7th May, 1878, to the liquidation of their indebtedness to the United States.

The value at full tariff rates of transportation over the land-grant railroads during the year is estimated at $250,000.

There is no appropriation available for the payment of military transportation over land-grant railroads during the fiscal year.

Under the existing laws, as interpreted by the courts, the land-grant railroad companies are entitled to compensation for all military trans-

portation service performed by them, respectively, subject to a fair deduction for the use of their respective railroads. Assuming this deduction to be 50 per centum of the ordinary rates in accordance with the acts of 24th February and of 3d March, 1881, the estimated amount due these railroads for service during the year is $125,000.

Unsettled railroad accounts, aggregating $200,000, are outstanding and cannot be paid until means are provided by Congress.

The total value at tariff rates of service rendered to the War Department by railroads during the year is $1,807,280.61.

BONDED PACIFIC RAILROADS.

The following tables state the military transportation during the fiscal year on the several Pacific railroads named:

Names of companies.	Number of persons transported.	Number of animals transported.	Freight transported.
			Pounds.
Union Pacific	6,102	3,266	53,137,214
Central Pacific	677	419	17,697,401
Kansas Pacific*	1,698	1,131	9,968,295
Sioux City and Pacific	616	24	1,345,077
Total	9,093	3,840	82,147,987

*Merged into Union Pacific Railway Company, and now styled "Union Pacific Railway Company, Kansas Division."

The cost of this service is stated as follows:

Names of companies.	Amount of accounts referred to Treasury for settlement.	Amount of accounts rendered and under examination June 30, 1881.	Estimated amount of accounts not yet rendered.	Total.
Union Pacific	$37 00	$319,411 91	$192,067 35	$511,516 26
Central Pacific	58,213 10	115,144 87	113,000 00	286,357 97
Kansas Pacific		31,998 21		31,998 21
Sioux City and Pacific	258 00		4,507 61	4,765 61
Total	58,508 10	466,554 99	311 574 96	836,638 08

The following is a statement of unsettled accounts with these railroads on 30th June, 1881, either in this office or in the Treasury Department, under adjustment:

Names of companies.	In Treasury.	In Quartermaster-General's Office.	Total.
Union Pacific	$130,936 36	$919,760 95	$1,050,706 31
Central Pacific	391,691 36	115,038 10	506,729 66
Kansas Pacific	50,540 60	81,262 35	131,802 95
Total	572,168 52	1,116 070 40	1,689,238 92

The total earnings of these railroads on account of military transportation, from their first opening to 30th June, 1881, is stated as follows:

Names of companies.	Amount paid in cash.	Amount credited on bonds under act of July 2, 1864.	Amount withheld under act of March 3, 1873 (Rev. Stats, 5260).	Amount withheld under act of May 7, 1878.	Total.
Union Pacific	$1, 693, 360 69	$1, 693, 360 87	$3, 177, 387 57	$468, 518 89	$7, 032, 626 02
Central Pacific	261, 106 21	261, 106 29	659, 124 07	232, 840 21	1, 414, 176 78
Kansas Pacific	881, 152 71	881, 152 76	545, 408 23	....	2, 307, 713 70
Sioux City and Pacific ..	3, 594 28	3, 594 29	39, 491 82	....	46, 680 39
Total...............	2, 839, 213 89	2, 839, 214 21	4, 421, 411 69	701, 359 10	10, 801, 198 89

The acts approved March 3, 1873 (section 5260, Revised Statutes), May 7, 1878 (section 2, 20 Statutes, page 58), and March 3, 1879 (20 Statutes, page 420), are the laws which govern the adjustment of bonded Pacific railroad accounts for military transportation.

These laws are quoted in the report of Leiut. Col. J. G. Chandler, in charge of the transportation branch of this office, which accompanies this report.

LAND-GRANT RAILROADS.

In the act making appropriations for support of the Army for the fiscal year ending June 30, 1882, approved February 24, 1881, an appropriation was made in the following terms:

For the payment for Army transportation lawfully due such land-grant railroads as have not received aid in government bonds, to be adjusted by the proper accounting officers in accordance with the decisions of the Supreme Court in cases decided under such land-grant acts, but in no case shall more than fifty per cent. of the full amount of the service be paid until a final decision shall be had in respect of each case in dispute, one hundred and twenty-five thousand dollars: *Provided*, That such payment shall be accepted as in full of all demands for said services.

In the act approved March 3, 1881, making appropriations to supply deficiencies, &c., an appropriation was made in the following terms:

To pay land-grant railroads fifty per centum of what the Quartermaster's Department finds justly due them for transportation during the fiscal year ending June thirtieth, eighteen hundred and eighty, and prior years, to be accepted in full of all demands for said services, two hundred and seventy-five thousand dollars.

Thus the law of February 24, 1881, provides for settlement for services rendered during the year ending June 30, 1882, and the law of March 3, 1881, provides for settlement of accounts for services rendered during the year ending June 30, 1880, and prior years, but no provision has been made for payment for services rendered by the land-grant railroads during the fiscal year ending June 30, 1881, an estimate for which has been submitted to Congress (see House Ex. Doc. No. 44, Forty-sixth Congress, third session, page 15).

Up to the 30th June, 1881, 230 accounts in favor of land-grant railroads had been presented to this office, amounting as rendered, at full tariff rates, to $484,991.85; 213 accounts had been examined, adjusted, and referred to the Treasury for settlement, amounting to $443,688.37; 17 accounts remain in this office, awaiting examination, amounting to $41,303.48; 113 accounts have been settled by the accounting officers of the Treasury at 50 per centum of rates fixed by this office, amounting to

$124,007.11; and 100 accounts are awaiting settlement in the Treasury, amounting at full rates to $181,321.63.

The following-named land-grant railroad companies have filed acceptances of the provisions and restrictions of the law of March 3, 1881, in settlement of accounts for services rendered the War Department:

Atchison, Topeka and Santa Fé.
Atlantic, Gulf and West India Transit Company.
Chicago and Northwestern.
Chicago, Rock Island and Pacific.
Chicago, Burlington and Quincy.
Illinois Central.
Northern Pacific.
Louisville and Nashville, for the Pensacola Railroad Company.
Louisville and Nashville, for the South and North Alabama Railroad Company.
Chicago, Saint Paul, Minneapolis and Omaha Line, for the Saint Paul and Sioux City Railroad Company.
Saint Paul, Minneapolis and Manitoba.
Saint Louis and San Francisco.
Northern Pacific, for the Western Railroad of Minnesota.

General Orders No. 69, September 30, 1880, and No. 57, June 22, 1881, prepared in this office and issued by the War Department, gives the names and classes of the several land-grant railroads, the termini of the land-grant and bonded portions of each road, and publishes extracts from the laws showing conditions of grant to each so far as relates to use of the road by the United States, together with instructions regulating settlements for military transportation over such roads as authorized and provided by existing laws. Copies of these General Orders accompany this report.

WAGON AND STAGE TRANSPORTATION.

On wagon-wheels the department moved by contract or hire and by Army teams 34,428 tons of military supplies, at a cost, as reported, of $853,007.45.

Sixty-two contracts for wagon transportation have been made and received at this office during the fiscal year.

Five thousand and forty-seven passengers and 24,744 pounds of stores have been transported by stage, costing $91,872.44.

WATER TRANSPORTATION.

There have been moved by water during the year 8,642 persons, 1,573 beasts, and 18,681 tons of materials and supplies, at a cost of $453,743.72. The work was done by vessels belonging to established commercial lines of water transportation, by contract, and by vessels owned and chartered by the United States.

The following-named vessels are in service of the department: Side-wheel steamer Henry Smith, in New York Harbor; propeller Ordnance, in employ of Ordnance Department, in New York Harbor; steam-tug Atlantic, in New York Harbor; steam-tug Resolute, in Boston Harbor; propeller General McPherson, in San Francisco Harbor; steam launch Thayer, at Fort Adams, R. I.; steam launch Monroe, at Fort Monroe, Va.; steam launch General Greene, at Fort McHenry, Md.; steam launch Hamilton, at David's Island, New York Harbor; steam launch General Jesup, at Governor's Island and David's Island, New York Harbor;

26 Ab

steam launch Barrancas, at Fort Barrancas, Fla.; steamboat General Sherman, employed on the Upper Missouri and Yellowstone Rivers; schooner Matchless, at Key West, Fla.; steam launch Chelan, employed on Lake Chelan, Washington Territory; steam launch Amelia Wheaton, on Lake Cœur d'Alene, Indian Territory; and steam launch Lillie Lee, at Fort Totten, Devil's Lake, Dakota Territory. The cost of maintenance and of running these vessels during the year has been $94,600.16.

The steam launch Lillie Lee was completed in July, 1879, and put into service on Devil's Lake, Dakota Territory. She is 43 feet in length over all, 10 feet 4 inches beam, and 5 feet hold, and about 40 tons burden. Reported cost, $2,500.

The lumber for her construction was cut in the vicinity of Fort Totten, and all the labor in connection with the construction of her hull was performed by enlisted men.

The machinery first placed in her proved on trial to be of insufficient power, and in January last a set of machinery, in store at the Philadelphia depot of the Quartermaster's Department, was ordered to Fort Totten to be placed in the launch.

In August, 1879, authority was granted for supply of a steam launch at Fort Cœur d'Alene, Idaho, and of one at Camp Chelan, Wash.

The steam launch for Fort Cœur d'Alene was completed in August, 1880. Her hull was built at the post, mostly by labor of the troops. Her machinery is reported to have cost $2,750. She is 40 tons burden, and named the Amelia Wheaton.

The steam launch Chelan was purchased at Portland, Oreg. Her reported cost is $3,510. She was transported by rail over the portages at the Cascades and the Dalles, and proceeded up the Columbia River to Priest's Rapids, at which point she struck on the rocks, was capsized and swamped. She was subsequently raised and transported by wagons to a point on the river opposite Camp Chelan. Her tonnage is 15 tons.

The total expenditure for water transportation during the year is reported at $453,743.72.

TRANSPORTATION ACCOUNTS AND CLAIMS.

One thousand four hundred and forty accounts and claims for transportation have been adjusted in this office during the year, amounting to $1,399,645.20; 1,307, amounting to $1,257,497.61, were reported favorably for settlement; 84, amounting to $77,668.22, were unfavorably reported and rejection recommended, and 49, amounting to $64,479.37, were suspended for additional evidence; 488, amounting to $1,269,207.63, were in the office unsettled at the close of the fiscal year.

INDEBTED RAILROADS.

At the beginning of the fiscal year the debts of the railroad companies for railway material, purchased by them from the United States at the close of the war, under Executive orders, and not compromised or settled under special laws of Congress, and excluding two railroads declared insolvent, amounted to $1,068,911.72. During the year interest and charges against these railroads amounted to $42,611.49. Payments by military transportation and postal service were credited to them, amounting to $5,088.66. Their debts on June 30, 1881, amounted to $1,106,434.55.

In addition to the payments by transportation service, there was received on account of the indebtedness of the Nashville and Northwestern Railroad Company the sum of $2,475.83, being the balance due the Quartermaster's Department from the postal earnings of that road.

The amount due the Mobile and Ohio Railroad Company, being 50 per cent. of its earnings as a land-grant railroad, is still withheld by the accounting officers of the Treasury, pending settlement of the account of that company for material purchased.

A communication has been sent to the governor of Tennessee in relation to the indebtedness of that State for property purchased for the Edgefield and Kentucky and the Memphis, Clarksville and Louisville Railroads, for which the United States holds the bonds of the State in double the value of the property purchased, requesting that if arrangements cannot be made at an early day to pay these debts, that the matter be submitted to the legislature of the State. No reply has been received, and the debts are still unpaid.

REGULAR AND MISCELLANEOUS SUPPLIES.

Animals.—One thousand four hundred and thirty-eight cavalry and artillery horses were purchased during the year, costing $179,926.71, averaging per head $125.12. Of these there were received in Department of Dakota, 277; Department of the Missouri, 494; Department of the Platte, 100; Department of Texas, 192; Department of California, 33; Department of the Columbia, 61; Department of Arizona, 221; Department of West Point, 31; at New York depot, 25; at Saint Louis depot, 4.

For the Army trains 1,006 mules and 29 draught horses were purchased; the mules costing $111,744.80, an average of $111.07 per head, and the horses $5,330, an average of $183.79 per head.

One thousand four hundred and eighty-seven horses and 594 mules were sold during the year. The horses brought $56,677.37 and the mules $23,530.60; total, $80,207.97; which is deposited in the Treasury to credit of miscellaneous receipts, except the small sum realized from sales of horses to officers.

The following is a summary of the number of animals purchased, sold, died, &c., during the year and remaining on hand June 30, 1881:

	On hand July 1, 1880.	Purchased.	Taken up, &c.	Total.	Sold.	Died.	Lost and stolen.	Total sold, died, &c.	On hand June 30, 1881.
Horses	10,704	1,467	131	12,302	1,487	446	123	2,056	10,246
Mules	10,722	1,006	90	11,818	594	529	158	1,281	10,537
Oxen	20			20					20

FUEL, FORAGE, AND STRAW.

The issues of fuel during the year have been 120,288 cords of wood and 39,386 tons of coal.

The issues of forage were 654,012 bushels of corn, 832,918 bushels of oats, 224,047 bushels of barley, 67,891 bushels of bran, 55,293 tons of hay, 31 tons of fodder, and 2,723 tons of straw.

The law of February 24, 1881, provides that there shall be no discrimination in the issues of forage against officers serving east of the Mississippi River, and the estimate of appropriation for purchase of forage for the fiscal year ending June 30, 1883, submitted by this office, has been increased accordingly.

The law which abolished issue of fuel to officers causes great hardship to those who are stationed at military posts in inclement climates, and on the prairies, where fuel is scarce and costly.

It is much to be desired that this allowance be restored. It is even more unjust to those in the wilderness than the abolition of the forage ration was to those living east of the Mississippi. That injustice has been put an end to by the law of February 24, 1881, but the question of fuel failed to meet Congressional remedy.

CONTRACTS.

During the year 822 contracts were filed in this office; 564 were for 34,784,602 pounds of corn, 23,500,099 pounds of oats, 9,953,000 pounds of barley, 907,600 pounds of bran, 97,867,970 pounds of hay, 6,090,084 pounds of straw, 100,755 cords of wood, 96,216,062 pounds of coal, 49,600 pounds of charcoal; 22 contracts for indefinite quantities of fuel and forage; 2 for work upon national cemeteries; 65 for clothing, camp and garrison equipage; 8 for horses and mules; 4 for harness; 68 for transportation; 12 for buildings; 2 for army wagons and ambulances; 4 for stationery; 10 for building material; 5 for veterinary supplies; 1 for mineral oil; 3 for lamps; 25 for miscellaneous services; 26 leases, and 1 charter party.

WAGONS AND HARNESS.

There were purchased during the year 245 six-mule army wagons; 125 two-horse wagons; 42 spring wagons; 3 trucks, and 1 ambulance. Of these, 225 six-mule wagons, purchased under contract at Leavenworth, Kans., cost $114.75 each; and 20, purchased under contract at San Francisco, Cal., cost $200 each. The two-horse wagons cost $104.75 each, and 25 spring wagons, manufactured at Leavenworth, cost $173.50 each, and 6 manufactured at San Francisco, cost $208 each.

There were purchased under contract 75 sets six-mule harness; 25 sets four-mule ambulance harness, and 50 sets cart harness. Fifty sets six-mule harness, manufactured at Leavenworth, Kans., cost $65.50 per set; and 25 sets, manufactured at San Francisco, Cal., cost $87 per set. The ambulance harness was manufactured in San Francisco for $79.56 per set, and the cart harness was manufactured in Oregon Territory for $19 per set.

Seventy-five sets six-mule harness and 100 sets ambulance harness have been manufactured for the Army at the military prison at Fort Leavenworth, Kans., and received during the year. The six-mule harness cost $83.07 per set, and the ambulance harness $58.07 per set.

Under the orders of the Secretary of War, communicated to this office on 22d June, 1881, all harness for the Quartermaster's Department will be manufactured at the military prison, the necessary funds for purchase of material and for other expenses incident to the manufacture to be supplied by this department.

STOVES.

Two hundred and fifty-six Army cast-iron heating-stoves were delivered to the department during the year by the Ordnance Department, which manufactures them at the Rock Island Arsenal, Illinois. Their aggregate cost was $3,727.82. Request was made on the Ordnance Department for 275 more, which have not yet been delivered.

LIGHTS.

In obedience to orders of the Secretary of War, a board of officers was convened at Fort Columbus, New York Harbor, by special orders from Headquarters Military Division of the Atlantic, dated June 30, 1879, to examine and report upon the subject of lighting barracks with mineral oil. Upon the report of the board, and the recommendation of this office, the Secretary of War authorized the trial of mineral oil and lamps in the public buildings at certain military posts.

Three different patterns of lamps were selected for the trials, one of brass, manufactured by John F. Donnell, of New York City, costing $8; one of bronze, manufactured by R. Hollings & Co., of Boston, Mass.; and one of brass, manufactured by the Manhattan Brass Company, of New York City, in accordance with drawings prepared in this office, at a cost of $4.40; 133 lamps of each pattern, and 10,000 gallons of mineral oil having a flash point not lower than 135° Fahr., were purchased and distributed to the several military posts located in different sections of the country selected for the trials. These trials have resulted in the selection of the brass lamp manufactured by the Manhattan Brass Company, in accordance with specifications prepared by this office, as the most suitable for the use of the Army, and its adoption for that purpose has been approved. It is made in two styles—a two-light pendant and a single-light bracket lamp. Copies of the specifications and drawings of the lamps, reflectors, brackets, and other parts of the lamps accompany this report.

In the annual estimates of appropriation for service of the Quartermaster's Department for the fiscal year ending June 30, 1882, a sum was included under the head of "regular supplies" for the purchase of lamps and oil for use of the Army, and an appropriation made accordingly in the act of Congress approved February 24, 1881.

General Orders No. 50, Headquarters of the Army, Adjutant-General's Office, May 24, 1881, publishes regulations for the supply, by the Quartermaster's Department, of all lights for the Army heretofore supplied by the Subsistence Department, except to troops in the field, on detached service, &c., where lamps cannot be used. To these the Subsistence Department will continue the issue of the established ration of candles.

Lamps and mineral oil are now being supplied to the Army in accordance with these regulations. So far as can be at present estimated the new method of lighting will cost about $2,500 per annum more than the old.

EXPLORING EXPEDITIONS.

The Quartermaster's Department has furnished supplies for the exploring expedition under Lieut. A. W. Greely, Fifth Cavalry, acting signal officer.

HORSE BLANKETS, ETC.

Standards have been adopted for Army horse blankets, saddle blankets, pack-saddle blankets, and paulins, specifications for which accompany this report.

MISCELLANEOUS CLAIMS AND ACCOUNTS.

On July 1, 1880, there were on file 12,911 miscellaneous claims, amounting to $6,965,673 42
And 364 accounts for 68,702 58
820 claims and accounts were filed during the year, amounting to 184,472 04

Total 14,095, amounting to 7,218,848 04

Forty-four claims were passed for $2,121.63, being a deduction in the amount, as presented, of $2,208.76; 255 claims, amounting to $35,644.17, were referred to other departments to which they pertained; 155 claims were transmitted to the Third Auditor for action of the accounting officers of the Treasury, amounting to $25,087.72; and 148 claims, amounting to $42,321.60, were rejected.

One hundred and eighty-six accounts, amounting to $13,554.20, were approved, being $239.30 less than their face. Three hundred and forty-eight accounts, for $84,185.19, were referred to other departments to which they pertained. Twenty, amounting to $3,224.28, were rejected. Total miscellaneous claims disposed of, 1,156 claims and accounts, amounting, as presented, to $208,586.85. Twelve thousand seven hundred and seven miscellaneous claims and 232 accounts remain on file, amounting to $7,010,261.19.

CLAIMS FOR QUARTERMASTERS' STORES PRESENTED UNDER ACT OF JULY 4, 1864.

The act of March 3, 1879, barred all those war claims for quartermasters' stores not presented prior to January 1, 1880. Claims presented and filed after that date are filed away or returned to claimants or their attorneys.

Claims presented to military boards, commissions, &c., instituted during the war, are held as having been presented before the statute of limitation began to run. Forty-four of these claims previously presented to military boards were called up during the fiscal year, and that number has been added to the docket of cases under consideration.

There were investigated by agents during the fiscal year, 3,813 claims, amounting to $2,287,729.22.

The total cost to the appropriation for the support of the Army for the service, &c., of agents and employés engaged on these claims amounts to $139,604.63.

The discharge on the 31st of March, 1881, of the agents and clerks and the reduction of salaries of others engaged on these claims, by reason of the low state of the appropriations for support of the Army, from which alone these salaries and expenses are paid, interrupted the work to some extent during the fiscal year.

The total number of claims on hand for consideration during the year was 22,935, amounting to $12,034,750.29.

One thousand one hundred and forty-nine claims were reported to the Third Auditor during the year with recommendation for settlement at $227,680.39, which was $344,898.93 less than claimed.

Nineteen hundred and ninety-five claims, amounting to $1,885,173.82, were rejected during the year. Thus 3,144 claims, amounting to $2,457,753.14, were finally disposed of by this office during the year.

The docket shows that 2,018 claims not finally acted on had been investigated and prepared for the action of the Quartermaster-General at the end of the fiscal year, making a total of 5,162 cases prepared for adjudication during the year.

The summary of the work for the year is very satisfactory.

In the report of the claims branch of this office will be found a table showing the work done since the passage of the act of July 4, 1864.

HALL OF RECORDS.

I renew a recommendation, frequently made heretofore, that an appropriation be made to erect near the executive departments a building for the safe keeping of public records, rolls of the Army, pay-rolls,

&c., which accumulate yearly in the costly buildings now devoted to executive business, and which now occupy rooms which have cost millions, to the great embarrassment of the public service. If such of these papers as are not in frequent use were placed in a cheap, thoroughly fire-proof storehouse, they would be safer than where they now are, and many costly rooms could be devoted to the transaction of current official business. Such a building, I believe, could be constructed for about $200,000, and I again submit a plan which I caused to be prepared some time since. The site which I have thought most appropriate, I have, while looking for a site for a new Pension Office, ascertained to be much divided, and I believe it will be well to provide for acquiring title and paying through the action of the courts of the District of Columbia the value of those parts of it which belong to minors, or for which prices deemed excessive may be demanded. An appropriation for this building passed the Senate unanimously, but was lost in conference in the last days of the last Congress. In connection with this matter I submit the following table, &c.

The following table of cost of various public buildings has been communicated to the Quartermaster-General. He adds the cost of the new fire-proof National Museum building in Washington, and of the new barracks lately completed at Fortress Monroe, Va.

Buildings.	Cubic feet.	Total cost.	Cost per cubic foot.
			Cents.
Sub-treasury and post-office, Boston, Mass	2,617,338	$2,080,507	77.88
United States branch mint, San Francisco, Cal	1,680,795	1,500,000	89.24
Custom and court house and post-office, Cairo, Ill.	444,376	271,081	61
Custom and court house and post-office, Columbia, S. C.	587,916	381,900	64.95
United States building, Des Moines, Iowa	413,987	221,437	53.48
United States building, Knoxville, Tenn	542,362	398,847	73.53
United States building, Madison, Wis	541,483	329,389	60.83
United States building, Ogdensburg, N. Y	447,585	216,576	48.38
United States building, Omaha, Nebr	654,703	334,000	51.01
United States building, Portland, Me	524,886	392,215	74.72
German Bank, Fourteenth street, Newport, R. I	600,000	475,000	79½
Staats Zeitung, New York City	508,000	475,100	93.52
Western Union Telegraph, New York City	1,330,000	1,400,000	105.218
Masonic Temple, New York City	1,763,839	923,889	53.38
Centennial Building, Shepherd's, corner Twelfth street and Pennsylvania avenue, Washington, D. C	931,728	246,073	26.41
United States National Museum, brick and iron fire-proof building	3,843,611	250,000	06.504
Brick barracks, company quarters, Fortress Monroe, Va.	1,000,000	59,000	05.9

BARRACKS AND QUARTERS.

The construction of 132 new buildings, comprising barracks, officers' quarters, stables, storehouses, guard-houses, &c., has been authorized during the year, at an estimated cost of $239,445. They are at military posts in twenty-one different States and Territories.

Repairs to existing buildings have been authorized at an estimated cost of $417,902 00

The cost of new buildings in Department of the East, is stated at 43,751 00
Repairs 96,386 00
Department of the South, new buildings 1,396 00
Repairs 10,832 00

Total, Division of the Atlantic 152,365 00

Department of the Missouri, new buildings.	$47,780 00
Repairs	71,134 00
Department of Dakota, new buildings.................................	54,821 00
Repairs	64,299 00
Department of the Platte, new buildings............................	12,776 00
Repairs ...., ...	54,877 00
Department of Texas, new buildings ...., ...	8,872 00
Repairs .:..	7,138 00
Total, Division of the Missouri.......,..........................	321,697 00
Department of Arizona, new buildings	32,409 00
Repairs	25,906 00
Department of the Columbia, new buildings........................	21,605 00
Repairs	52,698 00
Department of California, new buildings	16,035 00
Repairs ...., ...	34,642 00
Total, Division of the Pacific..	183,295 00

Of the above-mentioned sums devoted to construction and repairs of public buildings, $13,428 has been allotted to the erection of new buildings or the fitting up of existing ones for schools and chapels at military posts.

Repairs of wharves have been authorized at—

Fort Barrancas, Fla ....:.......................................	$2,117 00
Alcatraz Island, Cal	1,945 00
Angel Island, Cal	1,955 00
West Point, N. Y	500 00
Total	6,517 00

The site for the new military post authorized by act of Congress approved May 8, 1880, to be established at or near the Musselshell River, in Montana Territory, at a cost not to exceed $50,000, has, by authority of the Secretary of War, been located twelve miles east of Black Butte, opposite Cone Butte Pass on Ford's Creek, a tributary of the Musselshell River. The post has been named Fort Maginnis.

The site and buildings of Fort Logan, Mont., have been sold at public auction, as authorized and directed by the act of Congress approved May 8, 1880, and the amount realized therefrom, $4,525, will be expended in the establishment of the new post near the Musselshell River, as provided in the act referred to.

HOSPITALS.

Of the amount appropriated for hospital construction, $75,000, the sum of $74,588 has been expended for construction, repair, and alterations, as follows:

In the Department of the East, 19 hospitals.............................	$25,420 00
In the Department of the South, 8 hospitals	2,998 00
Total, Division of the Atlantic......................................	28,418 00
In the Department of Arizona, 6 hospitals	2,464 00
In the Department of California, 7 hospitals...........................	1,781 00
In the Department of the Columbia, 10 hospitals ...., ...	10,452 00
Total, Division of the Pacific.......................................	14,697 00
In the Department of the Platte, 7 hospitals...........................	10,673 00
In the Department of Dakota, 16 hospitals	9,364 00
In the Department of the Missouri, 19 hospitals	8,031 00
In the Department of Texas, 10 hospitals...............................	3,405 00
Total, Division of the Tennessee	31,473 00

SCHOOL-HOUSES.

During the year authority has been given under the act of 28th July, 1866 (Revised Statutes, sec. 1231), for the erection or fitting up of 12 buildings for school or religious purposes at the following military posts:

Fort Hamilton, New York harbor, costing	$1,500
Fort Wayne, Mich., costing	250
Fort Huachuca, Ariz., costing	1,765
Fort Boise, Ariz., costing	1,355
Fort Cœur d'Alene, Idaho, costing	1,500
Fort Vancouver, Wash., costing	1,788
Fort Walla Walla, Wash., costing	721
Fort Halleck, Nev., costing	404
Fort Elliott, Texas, costing	1,090
Fort Custer, Mont., costing	1,180
Fort Sisseton, Dak., costing	375
Fort Brown, Texas, costing	1,500
Total cost	13,428

In the sundry civil bill of June 20, 1878, an appropriation of $25,000 was made for beginning the erection of barracks at Fortress Monroe, Va., and an additional appropriation of $34,000 was made in the sundry civil bill of March 3, 1879, to complete the work. A plan of the buildings as erected accompanies this report. They were completed for the sum appropriated by Congress.

A plan of the barracks to be erected at Fort Leavenworth, as adopted by the Secretary of War, also accompanies this report. The appropriation made in the sundry civil bill, approved March 3, 1881, $30,000 for the erection of buildings at this post, is not sufficient to do all the work, and only one wing of the building has been commenced. It is estimated that the appropriation will complete this wing, containing barracks for three companies of troops.

The new headquarters at Fort Snelling have been completed, excepting some of the minor edifices, as the quarters for clerks. The Quartermaster-General has lately inspected them and finds them excellent buildings, very comfortable, and very well and economically built. No further appropriation is asked.

PROPERTY TRANSFERRED.

By General Orders No. 46, headquarters of the Army, dated May 12, 1881, the arsenal at Washington, D. C., was abolished, and the grounds and buildings transferred from the Ordnance Department to the Quartermaster's Department. The post is designated Washington Barracks, and is just now garrisoned by five companies of artillery.

SALES OF BUILDINGS.

Seventy-six old buildings, located in Nebraska and in the Territories of Wyoming and Montana, some temporary shelters in Idaho, and a quantity of old building material in Texas have been sold during the year. The proceeds go to the credit of miscellaneous receipts in the Treasury and not to the use of the military service.

MILITARY SITES IN TEXAS.

The title to the land upon which Ringgold Barracks is located has been perfected, and has been approved by the Attorney-General of the

United States, and the purchase money, $20,000, appropriated by act of Congress approved March 3, 1875, together with the sum of $500, appropriated in the sundry civil bill of June 16, 1880, to complete the purchase, has been paid into the hands of the proper officer of the district court of Starr County, Texas, in which court the decree for purchase of the land was granted. This site is now the property of the United States.

The question of purchase of the sites of Forts Brown and Duncan, for which special appropriations were made in the sundry civil act of March 3, 1875, remains unchanged since my last annual report, the owner still declining to accept the sums appropriated for the purpose.

A suit instituted in the district court of Cameron County, Texas, against the heirs of Maria Josepha Cavazos, owners of the site of Fort Brown, for condemnation of the land, has been decided adversely to the United States.

A tender of the sum appropriated by Congress for the purchase of the site of Fort Brown, $25,000, was made on 21st February, 1880, by the Secretary of War to the attorney for the owners, to which no reply has been received, so far as this office is informed.

By an act of Congress approved April 16, 1880, $200,000 was appropriated for the purpose of acquiring sites and erecting thereon such military posts on or near the Rio Grande frontier as may be deemed necessary by the Secretary of War for the adequate protection thereof.

Since the passage of that act, the construction of railroads through the State of Texas has materially changed the lines of military operations for the protection on that frontier, and the location of the military posts has not yet been determined.

POST CEMETERIES.

Orders have been given during the year for removal of remains buried at Forts Ripley and Ridgley, Minn., to the post cemetery at Rock Island, and from Fort Dalles, Oreg., to the Vancouver cemetery; also for the erection of a fence around the cemetery at Monterey, Cal., and the erection of a few headstones therein.

FIRES.

The department has suffered loss by fourteen fires during the year. At Prescott, Ariz., the headquarters office building was destroyed; at Fort Randall, Dak., a kitchen and dining room; at Fort Apache, Ariz., the bakery; at West Point, N. Y., Fort Supply, I. T., Fort Adams, R. I., Fort Verde, Ariz., and Fort Lincoln, Dak. T., each a set of officers' quarters; at Ogden, Utah, a warehouse and office; at Fort Keogh, Mont., barracks; at Fort Washakie, W. T., a saw-mill; at Jefferson Barracks, Mo., a lime-house; at Fort Russell, W. T., a stable, and at Fort Snelling, Minn., a wood-shed.

MILITARY RESERVATIONS DECLARED.

The following military reservations have been declared by a proclamation of the President:

For posts:

Hot Springs, Ark., November 17, 1880.

Fort Maginnis, Mont., April 8, 1881.

White River, Colo., April 26, 1881.

Fort Assiniboine, Mont., June 16, 1881 (in lieu of that of March 4, 1880).

Fort Totten, Dak., August 20, 1881, extending the boundaries.

Fort Cummings, N. Mex., November 9, 1880, extending the boundaries. Wood and timber reserves:

Fort Niobrara, Neb., June 6, 1881.

Fort Laramie, Wyo., February 9, 1881.

Fort Fred Steele, Wyo., November 4, 1880.

Fort Meade, Dak., April 18, 1881.

CLOTHING, CAMP AND GARRISON EQUIPAGE.

During the year some inconvenience has been experienced from not having a sufficient stock of clothing, camp and garrison equipage on hand to meet sudden demands upon the department. Illustrations of this will be found in the report of Col. S. B. Holabird, which accompanies this. He has had charge of this branch of the department since my last report. Means should be provided by special appropriation to enable this department to lay in a stock of clothing and camp and garrison equipage sufficient to meet any emergency, say at least a year's supply ahead.

Last year the Quartermaster-General recommended that provision be made by special appropriation of $1,000,000 for this purpose, which had the approval of the Secretary of War; but the project failed in Congress.

The amount appropriated for the current fiscal year was $1,100,000. The last session of Congress was a short one, and the department was therefore able to advertise for proposals and make contracts immediately upon the passage of the act making appropriation, in time to secure some deliveries of materials by 1st July, and providing an earlier partial supply of the needs of the Army than in the alternate years, when the appropriation is made later.

The estimate for the ensuing fiscal year, $1,400,000, will all be required for the purchase and manufacture of clothing and equipage to which the troops are entitled under existing laws and regulations. The exact cost of the articles, based upon the last contract prices, is estimated at $1,444,635.59. With the rise in business prosperity throughout the land prices have increased.

The manufacture of the clothing and equipage at our principal depots has been satisfactorily and economically accomplished. Under orders from this office the sewing is principally distributed to female operatives, preference being given to the widows and orphans of deceased Union soldiers, who thus receive the whole actual cost of the work, without any deduction for middlemen or contractors' profits or failures.

The following new standards have been adopted and distributed to the purchasing and manufacturing depots during the last fiscal year, viz: knit undershirts, cork helmets, canvas-lined great-coats, and flannels for lining capes of overcoats.

Of specifications the following have been distributed in addition to those heretofore adopted by the Quartermaster-General, viz: canvas-lined great-coats, conical wall-tents, Sibley or conical wall-tent stoves and pipe, dark blue wool shirting flannel, undershirts, and helmets. Copies of these specifications accompany this report.

Old-pattern clothing to the value of $29,387.20 was issued during the last fiscal year to the board of managers of the National Home for Disabled Volunteers, under the act of January 23, 1873, as equivalents for

1,334 suits of clothing, for which requisition was made upon this office on the 12th of January last.

On the 3d March, 1881, Congress passed a law directing the transfer to the board of managers of the Home referred to of all the old-pattern clothing still on hand. Orders to concentrate all this clothing at the principal depots at Jeffersonville, Saint Louis, and San Francisco, and to transfer it to the board, have been issued. A list of the articles which will thus be transferred will accompany the next annual report.

Issues of clothing, old and new pattern, to the value of $5,807.46 were made by this department during the last fiscal year, under authority of the War Department, to destitute citizens, sufferers from the overflow of the Missouri River.

Issues to the value of $2,784.56 were also made to certain Indian prisoners. Of this last amount $1,752 have been reimbursed to the appropriations of the Quartermaster's Department by the Indian Bureau.

Under the several joint resolutions of Congress, tents and other articles of camp and garrison equipage were loaned to various organizations during the last fiscal year, at a cost to this department, in loss, damage, and general expenses, of $2,038.31. A statement thereof in detail accompanies the report of Col. S. B. Holabird, assistant quartermaster-general, in charge of the clothing branch of this office.

The military prison at Fort Leavenworth, Kans., was indebted to the Quartermaster's Department on June 30, 1880, for clothing and equipage issued to the prison in excess of labor performed for the Quartermaster's Department in the amount of $536 20
There was issued to the prison by this department during the last fiscal year
clothing and equipage to the value of 11,307 37
Quartermaster's stores to the value of 2,011 32

13,854 89

The value of labor performed for the Quartermaster's Department during the fiscal year was 12,887 50

Leaving the prison account indebted to the Quartermaster's Department in the sum of 967 39

There were manufactured during the year 34,163 pairs of boots, at an average cost of $2.90 per pair; 25,944 pairs of shoes, at an average cost of $1.85 per pair; 1,656 barrack chairs, at an average cost of $1.22 each; and 4,356 corn brooms, at 16 cents each, all as reported by the governor of the prison.

The materials from which the boots and shoes were made were purchased by officers of this department at the Philadelphia depot of the Quartermaster's Department under contract, and were of unexceptionable quality.

Since my last report, upon recommendation of the board of commissioners of the prison and by order of the War Department, the purchase of materials for use at the prison has been transferred to the governor of the prison. This resulted, it is understood, because of the failure of this department to furnish materials in time, causing a suspension of work at the prison, it is alleged, during a part of the previous fiscal year.

The delay in supplying the materials was in no way the result of any negligence on the part of the officers or employés of this department. There was not at the time money to the credit of the appropriation available for the purchases. Besides, there was no immediate need for additional boots and shoes at that time. As soon as money was provided and contracts were made everything possible was done to hasten supplies forward and keep the prisoners employed.

Complaints having reached this department that some of the boots and shoes manufactured at the prison were of inferior workmanship, and specimens in support of the claims having been furnished by direction of the Secretary of War, a rigid inspection by a sworn inspector of the Quartermaster's Department is now made at the prison before shipment.

At the request of many officers, helmets have been authorized for wear by officers when they are desired in lieu of dress caps, and a general order of the War Department prescribed the pattern and directed the issue of helmets, dark blue overshirts, and knit undershirts to the enlisted men of all arms of the service, and they are now being furnished, with the exception of the overshirts, for which gray flannel ones have been temporarily substituted until a stock of the blue ones can be procured.

Owing to the changes in the patterns of clothing, it was found necessary, to avoid any increase in cost, to modify the table of allowance, and the unlined blouse and extra-lined great-coat have been dispensed with. The changes made have been for the benefit of the soldier, who is now better clad than at any time heretofore.

The old-style helmets are being altered to conform to the new pattern, at a cost of $6.50 per dozen.

Six thousand cork helmets have been procured, and issued to troops in warm climates.

Buffalo coats and fur caps and gauntlets have been procured for the Army. The price paid, $14.20, for the coats is due principally to the scarcity of the buffalo, and some other material will soon have to be substituted therefor.

Steps have been taken to concentrate at the general depots all surplus clothing in the several military divisions and thus prevent the undue accumulation of clothing at military posts, at the same time replenishing the stock at the depots, now almost exhausted.

By direction of the Secretary of War, upon recommendation of this office, service chevrons are now issued to the enlisted men without charge. They being considered in the nature of a decoration for good service, it was thought proper that the soldier should not be required to pay for them. A slight change has been made in them to conform to a decision of the General of the Army.

The governor of Missouri having informed the Secretary of War that some of the hospital tents loaned to that State for the use of sufferers from tornadoes were ready to be returned, this office has recommended that they be sent to the egeneral depot at Saint Louis, Mo., and that the Quartermaster-General be notified for record.

NATIONAL MILITARY CEMETERIES.

There are eighty national cemeteries, and on June 30, 1881, there were seventy superintendents.

Six superintendents were appointed, two died, two resigned, and three were discharged or dismissed during the year.

There were 219 interments made during the year, making the total number of interments in the national cemeteries on June 30, 1881, 318,859. All soldiers' graves in these cemeteries have been marked with marble or granite headstones as provided by law, and neat marble slabs will be erected at the graves of others than soldiers yet remaining to be permanently marked as fast as means will permit.

Only a few of the headstones required for soldiers' graves in private and village cemeteries have been erected. One of the contractors has failed to properly carry out his agreement, and the sureties on his bond have finally undertaken to complete the work.

The cemetery road at Vicksburg, Miss., will, it is hoped, be completed this fall, and the road leading to the Fort Scott National Cemetery will be constructed so far as the means appropriated will permit. These not being sufficient to finish this work, an additional sum of $7,000 is asked for the Fort Scott road.

The work of constructing the Chattanooga Cemetery roadway, which was authorized by Congress at its last session, has not been begun, as the title to the necessary right of way has yet to be secured.

The amount granted was $5,000, which is not sufficient to complete a substantial road. The estimated cost of a macadamized road, well drained, is $15,000, and the difference has been asked for.

The subject of improving the road to the Arlington Cemetery, near this city, is again referred to in this connection. The desirability of providing a decent approach to this beautiful cemetery is obvious on account of its proximity to the capital and the consequent large number of visitors. At present the road in some places is frequently almost impassable.

I repeat a recommendation heretofore made, that the Arlington Cemetery, containing 208 acres of land, now laid out and improved at the cost of the United States, be declared and constituted by law the official national cemetery of the government, and that its space, not needed for the interment of soldiers, be used for the burial of officers of the United States, legislative, judicial, civil, and military, who may die at the seat of government or whose friends may desire their interment in a public national cemetery. It is safe from encroachment of the rapidly extending cities of the District of Columbia. It is a safe distance from the population of the cities, while the existing Congressional Cemetery is rapidly filling up, and the extension of the inhabited and populous part of Washington threatens before many years to make it necessary to abandon the practice of interment within its limits. Almost all great cities have forbidden the use of cemeteries within their corporate bounds.

It has become evident that additional space will be required for a military cemetery near New York Harbor, and at Baltimore, Md. At Cypress Hills the United States owns a number of lots nearly filled, and the purchase of additional lots has been recommended, but the Quartermaster-General, deeming the purchase and improvement of the lots offered too costly, has instituted inquiry looking to the purchase of a few acres of land suitable for the purpose.

The purchase of an additional piece of ground adjoining the Loudon Park Cemetery at Baltimore has been ordered.

Several of the burial lots owned by the United States in the city of Philadelphia it would seem are in danger of being disturbed by the opening of new streets through the cemeteries, and it may therefore become necessary to establish a new national cemetery in the vicinity of that city and to remove the bodies thereto.

SITE AND BUILDING FOR A NEW PENSION OFFICE.

On the 28th of February last, I had the honor to be consulted by members of the Senate Appropriation Committee as to the possibility of constructing for $250,000 to $300,000 a fire-proof building of brick and metal, sufficient for the Pension Office, upon principles of construction somewhat like those which governed the design and erection of the new fire-proof National Museum building, which cost $250,000, and which contains 3,843,000 cubic feet of space, and about 110,000 square feet of floor surface. The sundry civil bill, approved 3d March, 1881, contained the following proviso:

For the purchase of a suitable site in the city of Washington for the erection of a brick and metal fire-proof building to be used and occupied by the Pension Bureau, the building to be erected in accordance with plans approved by the Secretary of War and the Secretary of the Interior, under the supervision of the Quartermaster-General of the United States Army, the site for which shall be selected by him, subject to the approval of the Secretaries aforesaid, both as to location and price, and the title to the land to be approved by the Attorney-General of the United States, two hundred and fifty thousand dollars.

From the discussion in committee-room I knew that the intention of the authors of this law was that the appropriation of $250,000 should be applicable to the purchase of the site and also to the erection of the building. The omission of the word "and," after the word "Washington," in the printed law, however, prevented any application of the money to construction. The question was submitted to the Department of Justice, and the honorable the Attorney-General thus decided.

Upon submitting the matter to the Secretaries of War and of the Interior, they held that the evident intention of Congress was to limit the cost of site to a small portion only of the appropriation, and with their verbal authority I proceeded to invite, through the public press, offers of sites deemed by the owners suitable for a Pension Office. I received many such offers, all of which received prior to the 19th April, 1881, I submitted, on that date, to the Secretaries, then designating as the site which I considered it my duty to select and submit for their approval the eastern portion of square No. 171, which lies near the State Department building, fronting on Seventeenth street, New York avenue, and E street, northwest. Here a plat containing 59,919½ square feet of ground was offered at the price of $1 per square foot. A few others, received later, were also submitted, but made no change in this selection. I am not yet advised that any conclusion has been reached as to this site.

I also caused to be prepared plans and drawings of a building to be 200 feet square, to be three or four stories high, to contain 91,200 square feet of floor, and to cost, including the site, from $250,000 to $300,000, which from long experience in conducting the business of a branch of the executive departments in Washington I believe to be well suited for the transaction of such business.

I find that the Pension Office needs accommodation for about 600 clerks, double the number named to me when first consulted, but the building as designed will come within the sum named, $300,000. It will have no dark corridors, passages, or corners. Every foot of its floors will be well lighted and fit for the site of desks at which to examine and prepare papers. It will be thoroughly ventilated, every room having windows on two sides, one opening to the outer air, the other into a central court covered from the weather by a non-conducting fire-proof roof, with ample windows above for escape of warm and foul air, and for the free admission of light. The windows are to be double glazed to prevent loss of heat in winter.

The public buildings of the executive departments are almost all subject to the disadvantages of dark and gloomy central corridors, which, being provided with windows at the extreme ends only, are both ill-lighted and ill-ventilated, and the accumulation of documents and records and of business has, in most of them, caused the construction of screens at the ends which form additional rooms for clerks, messengers, and others, but which cut off a large portion of the little light provided in the original designs.

The idea of the plan of the building recommended for a Pension Office is not new. It is the general plan of the best buildings for habitation and for public business in Rome and in many other cities of Europe, in climates like that of Washington. Such are the Palazo Farnese, the Cancellaria, the Vatican, and many others in Rome.

The improvements in manufacture of iron beams and of glass, and the progress in the building arts since those buildings were erected, during the revival of architecture known as the renaissance, or the cinquecento period, in Italy, have made possible the addition of durable and safe roofs of large span, covering central court-yards and making their whole space available for office purposes as well as for ventilation of the building.

The walls are intended to be constructed of brick; the window-dressings of either cast iron or of terra-cotta, i. e., of molded and baked brick, and the roofs and floors of masonry, resting upon iron beams. These plans I submitted to the honorable the Secretaries of War and of the Interior on the 22d September, 1881.

A building upon this method of construction has the advantage of being cheaply warmed. The National Museum, containing 3,843,000 cubic feet of space and about 110,000 square feet of floor, used during the last very severe winter, during which much of the coal was used to dry out the walls of the new building, 270 tons of coal. Its steam-heating apparatus cost only $20,000.

The building for some years occupied by the Quartermaster-General's Office, having only 21,000 square feet of floor, 323,000 cubic feet of capacity, uses each season 120 tons of coal. It is one-twelfth as large, and uses one-half as much fuel as the Museum.

In the course of years, the economy of fuel in such buildings as the Museum and the proposed Pension Office becomes important to the Treasury.

Since the propositions to sell sites for the new Pension Office were received, the owner of a small part of the site selected by the Quartermaster-General has died, and, as I am informed, intestate, leaving minor heirs; therefore it will be well, if the present Congress determines to erect a Pension Office, to provide for procuring title through the courts to any part of the site which it may be difficult to acquire by simple purchase. Indeed, it is probable that no site suitable for such a building could be acquired in this city without some such powers. The owner of a single lot might hold out for an excessive compensation after all others had agreed to a reasonable valuation.

Under the verbal authority of the Secretary of War and of the Secretary of the Interior, I advertised for offers of sites for this building and incurred the following bills:

The Washington Post, for advertising... $1 50
The Evening Star Newspaper Company, for advertising 2 25
The National Republican Printing and Publishing Company, for advertising.. 2 44

Amounting in all to 6 19

The Comptroller of the Treasury declined to allow and pay them; and I have also incurred a liability of $300 for preparation of finished drawings of the proposed building. All of these items I submit, with request that Congress be requested to make provision for their settlement.

None of the appropriation of $250,000 has been withdrawn from the Treasury or expended at this date, 24th October, 1881.

I have the honor to remain, most respectfully, your obedient servant,

M. C. MEIGS,
Quartermaster-General, Brevet Major-General, U. S. A.

Hon. ROBERT T. LINCOLN,
Secretary of War.

List of papers accompanying the annual report of the Quartermaster-General, for the fiscal year ending June 30, 1881.

1. Report of Col. S. B. Holabird, assistant quartermaster-general, United States Army, of the inspection branch of the Quartermaster-General's Office during the fiscal year ending June 30, 1881.

A.—Report of officers of the Quartermaster's Department for the fiscal year.

B.—Report of stations and duties of officers of the Quartermaster's Department.

C.—List of officers on duty as acting assistant quartermasters, and of the stations at which they have served during the fiscal year.

2. Report of Col. S. B. Holabird, assistant quartermaster-general, United States Army, of the operations of the accounts branch of the Quartermaster-General's Office during the fiscal year ending June 30, 1881.

3. Report of Col. S. B. Holabird, assistant quartermaster-general, United States Army, of the operations of the clothing branch of the Quartermaster-General's Office during the fiscal year ending June 30, 1881.

A.—Statement of articles of clothing and equipage on hand June 30, 1880; the quantities purchased, manufactured, received from posts and depots, gained, sold, transferred to other depots and posts, expended, issued to the Army during the year, and the quantity on hand June 30, 1881.

B.—Statement of remittances on account of clothing, camp and garrison equipage during the fiscal year.

C.—Statement of amounts received and remitted by the Quartermaster's Department on account of clothing, camp and garrison equipage during the fiscal year.

D.—Specifications of clothing, camp and garrison equipage adopted and distributed to officers of the Quartermaster's Department during the fiscal year.

E.—Phototypes of standard helmets adopted by the General of the Army.

F.—Statement of clothing, camp and garrison equipage issued to the National Home for Disabled Volunteers, under the act of January 23, 1873, during the fiscal year.

G.—Statement of clothing, camp and garrison equipage issued to Indians during the fiscal year.

H.—Statement of clothing, camp and garrison equipage issued to the military prison at Fort Leavenworth, Kans., during the fiscal year, and its money value.

I.—Statement of quartermasters' stores issued to the military prison at Fort Leavenworth, Kans., during the fiscal year, and its money value.

K.—Statement of clothing, camp and garrison equipage manufactured at the military prison for the Quartermaster's Department during the fiscal year, and cost of materials and labor.

L.—Statement of value of labor performed for the Quartermaster's Department by the military prison at Fort Leavenworth, Kans., during the fiscal year

M.—Statement of clothing, camp and garrison equipage issued by the Quartermaster's Department to sufferers from the overflow of the Missouri River during the fiscal year.

N.—Statement of camp and garrison equipage loaned by the Quartermaster's Department, under act of Congress, during the fiscal year.

O.—Statement of clothing, camp and garrison equipage issued by the Quartermaster's Department to the Lady Franklin Bay and Point Barrow expeditions during the fiscal year.

P.—Statement of returns of clothing, camp and garrison equipage received and examined, and of letters received and written during the fiscal year.

Q.—Statement of the clerical force employed in the clothing and equipage branch of the Quartermaster-General's Office during the fiscal year.

4. Report of Lieut. Col. J. G. Chandler, deputy quartermaster-general, United States Army, of the operations of the Quartermaster-General's Office pertaining to transportation, indebted railroads, regular and miscellaneous supplies, and miscellaneous claims and accounts, during the fiscal year ending June 30, 1881.

A.—Statement of all troops and property transported during the fiscal year.

27 Ab

B.—Statement of principal movements of troops during the fiscal year, and average length of march or movement in each case.

C.—General Orders No. 69, Adjutant-General's Office, 1880, publishing table of land-grant railroads.

D.—General Orders No. 57, Adjutant-General's Office, 1881, publishing extracts of laws relating to land-grant railroads.

E.—Abstract of contracts made by officers of the Quartermaster's Department for wagon transportation during the fiscal year.

F.—Abstract of contracts made by officers of the Quartermaster's Department for water transportation during the fiscal year.

G.—Statement of vessels owned and purchased by the Quartermaster's Department during the fiscal year.

H.— Statement of vessels chartered, impressed, or employed by the Quartermaster's Department during the fiscal year.

I.—Statement of the indebtedness of Southern railroad companies for railway material for the fiscal year.

K.—General Orders Nos. 40, 62, 67, Adjutant-General's Office, 1880, and Nos. 33 and 63, Adjutant-General's Office, 1881, in relation to contracts.

L.—Specifications for ambulance wagon, Army pattern.

M.—Circular publishing amendment to specifications for Army cast-iron coal heater also specifications for furniture, &c., for cooking-ranges.

N.—General Orders No. 50, Adjutant-General's Office, 1881, in relation to the supply of lights to the Army.

O.—Specifications and drawings of lamps, reflectors, brackets, &c., for lamps for military posts.

P.—General Orders No. 35, Adjutant-General's Office, 1881, in relation to supplies for exploring expedition under Lieut. A. W. Greely, United States Army.

Q.—Specifications for horse-saddle and packsaddle blankets and paulins.

5. Report of Maj. J. M. Moore, quartermaster, United States Army, of the operations of the barracks and quarters branch of the Quartermaster-General's Office for the fiscal year ending June 30, 1881.

A.—Plan and report of merit of the new barracks at Fort Monroe, Va.

B.—Plan of the new barracks to be built at Fort Leavenworth, Kans.

6. Report of Maj. J. M. Moore, quartermaster, United States Army, of the operations of the claims branch of the Quartermaster-General's Office for the fiscal year ending June 30, 1881.

7. Report of Maj. B. C. Card, quartermaster, United States Army, of the affairs relating to the care and maintenance of national military cemeteries for the fiscal year ending June 30, 1881.

A.—Statement of disbursements of appropriations for national cemeteries during the fiscal year.

REPORT OF THE COMMISSARY-GENERAL OF SUBSISTENCE.

WAR DEPARTMENT,
OFFICE COMMISSARY-GENERAL OF SUBSISTENCE,
Washington, D. C., October 10, 1881.

SIR: I have the honor to submit the following report of the operations of the Subsistence Department for the fiscal year ending June 30, 1881, with such remarks and recommendations in connection therewith as are thought to be for the best interest of the government and the Army.

RESOURCES AND EXPENDITURES.

The following statement exhibits the aggregate fiscal resources and expenditures of the department for the year mentioned, and the balances remaining unexpended at the close of the fiscal year:

RESOURCES.

Amounts in the Treasury to the credit of appropriations of the Subsistence Department on June 30, 1880, as follows:

Subsistence of the Army, 1877 and prior years, act June 16, 1880	$3, 368 95	
Subsistence of the Army, 1879	28, 331 99	
Subsistence of the Army, 1880	1, 081 85	
Commutation of rations to prisoners of war in rebel States, per act June 16, 1880	8, 221 38	$41. 004 17

Amount to the credit of officers of the Subsistence Department and of officers doing duty in the Subsistence Department, with the Treasurer, assistant treasurers, and designated depositaries, and in their personal possession, on June 30, 1880, as follows:

   Subsistence of the Army, 1880 .... $391,043 19

Amounts deposited to the credit of the Treasurer of the United States and in process of cover into the appropriations on June 30, 1880, since covered in, as follows:

Subsistence of the Army, 1878 and prior years	$9 71
Subsistence of the Army, 1879	160 30
Subsistence of the Army, 1880	90 91

         260 92

Amount in hands of representatives of deceased officer to be collected:

   Subsistence of the Army, 1878 .... 109 84

Amounts appropriated for the Subsistence Department for the fiscal year ending June 30, 1881, as follows:

Subsistence of the Army, 1878, and prior years, act March 3, 1881	2,212 44
Subsistence of the Army, 1881, act May 4, 1880.....	2,250,000 00
Commutation of rations to prisoners of war in rebel States, per act March 3, 1881	10,305 87
Claims for quartermaster's stores and commissary supplies, act July 4, 1864, per act June 15, 1880	15,062 29
Claims for quartermaster's stores and commissary supplies, act July 4, 1864, per act March 1, 1881	3,268 51

         2,280,849 11

Amounts collected from various sources and refunded to the appropriations of the Subsistence Department on the books of the Treasury during the fiscal year 1881, as follows:

Subsistence of the Army, 1878 and prior year........	349 89
Subsistence of the Army, 1879........................	473 36
Subsistence of the Army, 1880........................	41,257 13
Subsistence of the Army, 1881........................	104,258 70

         146,339 08

Amounts received by officers of the Subsistence Department and by officers doing duty in the Subsistence Department, from sales of subsistence stores to the following purchasers during the fiscal year 1881, and taken up for immediate disbursement under the appropriation, Subsistence of the Army, 1881:

   Sales to officers of the army, $461,912.58; to enlisted men, $239,884.33; to companies, detachments, and hospitals, $144,424.54; to civil employés, $15,297.06; to Fort Leavenworth Military Prison, $17,334.72; to civil engineers, $2,847.66; to railroad engineers, $780.98; to civil employés of Agricultural Department, $384.77; to Mullan road employés, $284.53; to steamers, $156.14; to Indians, $153.02; Indian Commissioners, $122.06; to Quartermaster's Department, $103.80; to railroad employés, $73.17; of condemned stores at auction, $6,697.23; of boxes, barrels, &c., $746.30; of garden seeds and agricultural implements, $1,325.41; total..... 892,528 30

Amounts received from sales of public property to be deposited as "miscellaneous receipts"... 54 10

Amounts taken up by officers doing duty in the Subsistence Department, on account of stores lost, damaged, &c., and in correction of errors in their accounts, &c., during the fiscal year 1881:

   Subsistence of the Army, 1881 .... 2,115 44

Amounts arising from various sources and deposited to the credit of the Treasurer United States during the fiscal year 1881, under the following appropriations, viz:

Subsistence of the Army, 1879........................	2 25
Subsistence of the Army, 1880........................	60 00
Subsistence of the Army, 1881........................	37 50

         99 75

Amounts charged against officers (deceased and resigned) on account of funds alleged to have been lost by theft, &c., as follows:

   Subsistence of the Army, 1879 and prior years 3,000 89

Amounts charged against officers, still in service, on account of funds alleged to have been lost by theft, &c., and for which relief can only be obtained in the Court of Claims under sections 1059 and 1062, Revised Statutes, (including all sums of this character heretofore entered in this statement), as follows:

Subsistence of the Army, 1879 and prior years....................	$2,772 86
Total resources...	$3,760,177 65

EXPENDITURES.

Amounts expended on the books of the Treasury from the appropriations of the Subsistence Department during the fiscal year 1881, as follows:

Subsistence of the Army, 1877 and prior years, act June 16, 1880....................................	$3,368 95	
Subsistence of the Army, 1878 and prior years, deficiency act March 3, 1881...........................	2,212 44	
Commutation of rations to prisoners of war in rebel States, per act June 16, 1880.....................	8,221 38	
Commutation of rations to prisoners of war in rebel States, per act March 3, 1881....................	10,305 87	
Claims "for quartermaster stores and commissary supplies, act July 4, 1864," per act June 15, 1880, being portion for "commissary" supplies..........	15,062 29	
Claims "for quartermaster stores and commissary supplies, act July 4, 1864," per act March 1, 1881, being portion for "commissary" supplies..........	3,192 91	
Subsistence of the Army, 1879	147 25	
Subsistence of the Army, 1880	20,184 15	
Subsistence of the Army, 1881	93 85	
		62,789 09

Amounts disbursed by officers of the Subsistence Department and officers doing duty in the Subsistence Department during the fiscal year 1881, as follows:

Subsistence of the Army, 1880....................	390,150 14	
Subsistence of the Army, 1881	2,835,953 36	
		3,226,103 50

Amounts dropped by officers doing duty in the Subsistence Department in correction of errors in their accounts during the fiscal year 1881:

Subsistence of the Army, 1881............................	260 04

Amount deposited to the credit of the Treasurer of the United States and covered into the Treasury as "miscellaneous receipts on account of sale of public property".....................................

	54 10

Amounts carried to the surplus fund on June 30, 1881:

Subsistence of the Army, 1878 and prior years.......	359 60	
Subsistence of the Army, 1879	28,818 40	
		29,178 00

Total expenditures....................................	$3,318,384 73

BALANCES UNEXPENDED.

Amounts in the Treasury to the credit of appropriations of the Subsistence Department on June 30, 1881, as follows:

Subsistence of the Army, 1880	22,575 45	
Subsistence of the Army, 1881	2 02	
Claims for "quartermaster's stores and commissary supplies, act July 4, 1864," per act March 1, 1881, being a portion for "commissary" supplies.......	75 60	
		22,653 07

Amounts to the credit of officers of the Subsistence Department, and of officers doing duty in the Subsistence Department, with the Treasurer, assistant treasurers, and designated depositaries, and in their personal possession, on June 30, 1881, as follows:

Subsistence of the Army, 1880	169 38	
Subsistence of the Army, 1881	412,327 70	
		412,497 08

Amounts refunded to the Treasury near close of fiscal year 1881, but not carried to the credit of the appropriations by June 30, 1881:

Subsistence of the Army, 1879	$2 25
Subsistence of the Army, 1880	60 00
Subsistence of the Army, 1881	37 50
	$99 75

Amount in hands of representatives of deceased officer to be collected:

Subsistence of the Army, 1878	109 84

Amounts charged against officers (deceased and resigned) on account of funds alleged to have been lost by theft, &c., as follows:

Subsistence of the Army, 1879 and prior years	3,000 89

Amounts charged against officers, still in service, on account of funds alleged to have been lost by theft, &c., and for which relief can only be obtained in the Court of Claims under sections 1059 and 1062, Revised Statutes, (including all sums of this character heretofore entered in this statement), as follows:

Subsistence of the Army, 1879 and prior years	2,772 86
Subsistence of the Army, 1880	393 96
Subsistence of the Army, 1881	265 47
	3,432 29

Total balances unexpended.................................... . $441,798 92

SOURCES OF SUPPLY OF SUBSISTENCE STORES.

The settled rule of the department of making all purchases of subsistence stores as near the points of consumption as practicable—regard being had to quality and prices; as compared with those of stores procurable at remote places, including cost of transportation—has been adhered to during the fiscal year. Tabular statements of the stores required in bulk for the various military departments where troops are serving in large bodies are, under existing orders, transmitted to the Commissary-General, at proper intervals, who orders the articles from the different purchasing stations; and thus stores of the best quality for Army use obtainable in particular sections or markets of the country are procured. In future it is intended to authorize chief commissaries of departments, after their tabular statements have been acted upon by the Commissary-General, to draw, directly upon the purchasing depots selected by him, at such times and for such quantities named on the tabular statements as in their opinion may be necessary. The Commissary-General will thus select the localities from which the supplies are to be obtained, with a view of obtaining for the Army the best and cheapest articles the markets of the country afford, leaving to the chief commissaries of the departments the details as to quantities and times of the respective shipments, which are often dependent upon or influenced by local contingencies, best known to the chief commissaries themselves.

CONTRACTS AND PURCHASES.

During the fiscal year ended June 30, 1881, 154 newspaper advertisements and 191 circulars and posters, inviting proposals for subsistence stores, were reported to this office. The disbursements for advertising for the year, on accounts approved by the Secretary of War, amounted to $7,829.45. There were also received, during the same period, 219 contracts for fresh meats, 29 contracts for miscellaneous articles, 34 contracts for complete rations for recruiting parties and recruits, and 2,384 informal contracts made under written proposals and acceptances.

The average price each month of each of the principal components of the Army ration, purchased at the principal subsistence purchasing depots, is reported monthly to the Commissary-General of Subsistence, under the Army regulations. The following table, prepared after the manner pursued in the preparation of like tables heretofore published, exhibits the average for the twelve months of the fiscal year, 1881, of these monthly average prices, taken from the monthly reports referred to, viz:

Average (for the twelve months of the fiscal year ending June 30, 1881) of the monthly average prices paid for the component parts of the ration purchased for the United States Army at the principal purchasing depots.

Purchasing depot at	Pork, per pound.	Bacon, per pound.	Salt beef, per pound.	Fresh beef, per pound.	Flour, per pound.	Hard bread, per pound.	Corn meal, per pound.	Beans, per pound.	Pease, per pound.	Rice, per pound.	Hominy, per pound.	Coffee, green, per pound.	Coffee, roasted, per pound.	Tea, black, per pound.	Tea, green, per pound.	Sugar, per pound.	Vinegar, per gallon.	Candles, per pound.	Soap, per pound.	Salt, per pound.	Pepper, per pound.
	Cents.	Cents.	Cents.	Cents.	Cents.	Cents.	Cents.	Cents.	Cents.	Cents.	Cents.	Cents.	Cents.	Cents.	Cents.	Cents.	Cents.	Cents.	Cents.	Cents.	Cents.
Boston, Mass.	7.68	11.00	7.01		2.17	5.46	2.28	3.02		7.95	2.22	14.83	20.07	55.05	58.34	8.30	16.21	15.59	5.75	0.81	20.75
New York, N.Y.	7.26				3.02		1.89	3.11	2.45	6.51	2.87	13.98		53.35	59.93	8.26	15.00	14.47	6.09	0.60	22.00
Baltimore, Md.	7.67	6.72	5.00		2.05	3.85	1.50	2.69		6.96	1.78	13.62		61.07	56.50	8.01	14.31	14.00	5.56	0.74	
Cincinnati, Ohio	7.87	9.50	6.25		2.74		1.41	3.24	3.13	6.67	3.20	15.27		53.33	50.75	9.63	12.80	14.66	5.05	0.65	20.20
Saint Louis, Mo.	7.76	8.58			2.19		1.56	3.53	3.25	7.30	2.50	16.23		56.25	53.13	9.06	18.00	13.67	4.82	0.81	21.67
Saint Paul, Minn.	8.41	9.46			2.07		1.10	4.17		6.68				45.00	55.00	8.24	12.90	13.00	5.19	0.50	
Fort Leavenworth, Kans.	7.44	9.25	6.42		2.62	4.44	1.15	3.47	4.50	6.22	2.04	13.83	17.60	66.67	67.50	8.80		16.00	4.25	0.78	13.00
New Orleans, La.	8.02	12.91	5.00		3.00	4.88	1.67	3.31	3.98	6.93	1.97			69.34	56.02	8.85	15.48	18.81	4.97	0.80	
Chicago, Ill.	7.67	8.63	7.44		2.45		0.81	2.90		5.85	3.20	13.47		44.07	60.00	8.85	21.50	15.45	5.40	0.87	15.45
San Francisco, Cal.	9.47	9.00			2.36					6.17						10.43	25.50	16.98	5.81	0.82	25.00
Omaha, Nebr.	7.30	12.50			2.63	4.15	2.14				6.25					10.24				0.96	
Yankton, Dak.					2.06	5.00															
Vancouver Barracks, Wash.					2.34																
Cheyenne, Wyo.																					
Helena, Mont.																					

A statement of the average prices per pound (independent of quantities purchased), in each State and Territory, for fresh beef, supplied to the Army on contract, during the fiscal years 1880, 1881, and 1882, is as follows, viz:

State or Territory.	Average price per pound.			State or Territory.	Average price per pound.		
	1880.	1881.	1882.		1880.	1881.	1882.
	Cents.	Cents.	Cents.		Cents.	Cents.	Cents.
Maine	7.00	8.75	10.50	Michigan	11.41	10.38	10.95
Massachusetts	8.85	8.89	11.38	Missouri	5.98	5.50	6.99
Rhode Island	7.90	6.90	8.00	Minnesota	6.06	6.17	8.15
Connecticut	7.95	7.23	8.97	Nebraska	6.51	7.21	7.23
New York	7.81	7.77	9.54	Kansas	6.45	7.40	7.93
Pennsylvania	9.19	9.87	12.25	Indian Territory	5.49	5.86	5.73
Maryland	7.13	7.93	9.00	Wyoming Territory	6.29	7.19	7.34
District of Columbia	6.00	6.64	8.06	Dakota Territory	8.30	8.79	9.30
Virginia	5.99	6.24	7.00	New Mexico Territory	6.57	7.75	8.32
North Carolina	7.75	7.87	....	Colorado	7.21	7.83	7.87
Georgia	7.06	8.85	9.68	Utah Territory	5.49	5.21	6.60
Florida	7.87	8.62	12.00	Montana Territory	4.16	6.50	6.34
Alabama	10.00	9.00	....	California	5.87	6.92	7.17
Louisiana	6.75	7.75	7.25	Arizona Territory	11.34	10.46	10.72
Arkansas	6.25	6.75	6.97	Washington Territory	5.16	6.73	6.71
Texas	5.43	5.18	5.48	Idaho Territory	7.63	6.05	6.75
Kentucky	5.25	6.50	6.75	Nevada	6.25	7.75	9.50
Ohio	6.00	6.15	7.25	Oregon	6.97	6.12	5.94
Indiana	8.00	8.00	8.00				
Illinois	7.29	8.00	7.00	Average for each year	7.06	7.39	8.19

The amounts expended on account of the purchase of subsistence supplies at the principal purchasing stations during the fiscal year ended June 30, 1881, were as follows:

Purchasing depot at—	For stores.	For property.	Total.
Baltimore, Md	$35,989 97	$486 83	$36,476 80
Boston, Mass	161,661 94	227 17	161,889 11
Cheyenne, Wyo	25,908 72	198 82	26,107 54
Chicago, Ill	450,289 21	6,748 74	457,037 95
Cincinnati, Ohio	13,820 11	242 25	14,062 36
Fort Leavenworth, Kans	206,235 37	8,171 87	214,407 24
Helena, Mont	24,967 58	224 35	25,191 93
Little Rock, Ark	211 11	289 50	500 61
New Orleans, La	46,590 65	464 14	47,054 79
New York, N.Y	349,318 80	3,141 17	352,459 97
Omaha, Neb	42,591 52	3,356 28	45,947 80
Vancouver Barracks, Wash	46,432 62	794 55	47,227 17
Prescott, Ariz	41,744 27		41,744 27
San Antonio, Tex	27,383 61	816 05	28,149 86
Saint Louis, Mo	103,916 21	921 63	104,837 84
Saint Paul, Minn	171,202 49	4,481 72	175,684 21
Santa Fé, N. Mex	7,874 39	18 62	7,893 01
San Francisco, Cal	155,182 56	4,762 51	159,945 07
Washington, D.C	126,156 38	1,564 08	127,720 46
Yankton, Dak	2,071 80	91 00	2,162 80
Totals	2,039,499 31	37,001 28	2,076,500 59

SALES OF SUBSISTENCE STORES TO OFFICERS AND ENLISTED MEN.

The *proviso* which has been introduced in the acts making appropriation for the support of the Army for the past two fiscal years, directing that "to the cost of all stores and other articles [subsistence] sold to officers and enlisted men, except tobacco, as provided for in section 1149 of the Revised Statutes, ten per centum shall be added to cover wastage, transportation, and other incidental charges," is considered onerous and

unjust by officers and enlisted men of the Army, and I would respectfully recommend that the *proviso* referred to be recommended by the
Secretary of War to be omitted from the appropriation act for the fiscal
year 1883, and the following be substituted therefor, viz: "*Provided,*
That hereafter sales of articles of subsistence supplies to officers and
enlisted men of the Army shall be made at the invoice price of the last
lot of the respective articles received by the officers by whom the sales
are made."

TOBACCO.

There were supplied to the officers and enlisted men of the Army,
during the fiscal year 1881, as appears by the returns of subsistence
stores rendered to this office for that period, 216,719$\frac{1}{16}$ pounds of chew-
ing tobacco, and 75,262$\frac{2}{8}$ pounds of smoking tobacco.

The value of such of the above tobacco as was furnished enlisted men
during the year under section 1149, Revised Statutes, was $107,658.24.
There was collected by the Pay Department from enlisted men on this
account, and returned to the appropriations of the Subsistence Department during the same period, the sum of $68,767.45.

By act of March 3, 1865 (section 1149, Rev. Stat.), Congress directed
the Secretary of War to cause tobacco, in quantities not exceeding 16
ounces per man per month, to be furnished to the enlisted men of the
Army at cost prices, exclusive of the cost of transportation, the amount
due therefor to be deducted from their pay, in the same manner as then
provided for the settlement of clothing accounts.

At the succeeding session, by act of July 28, 1866 (section 1144, Rev.
Stat.), the office of sutler was abolished, and the Subsistence Department
was required to furnish for sales to officers and enlisted men such articles as should be designated for the purpose by the inspectors-general
of the Army, and if not paid for when purchased, the amount due to be
deducted by the paymaster at the next payment following the purchase.

Measures for carrying into effect the tobacco law (section 1149, Rev.
Stat.) were taken as soon as practicable after the passage of the act, and
as the statute prescribed that the money due by enlisted men for tobacco
should be deducted from their pay as then prescribed for the settlement
of clothing accounts, an elaborate system of settlement had to be adopted,
involving accountability in both the Subsistence and Pay Departments,
and necessitating the making out and handling of many papers in drawing and issuing the tobacco to the enlisted men, in accounting for such
issues to the Subsistence Department, in charging such issues against the
men on the pay-rolls, in summing up those charges by the Paymaster
General on the pay-rolls of the entire Army, and in the final transfer, on
the books of the Treasury, of the aggregates so found due to the appropriations of the Subsistence Department. The system then perfected has
continued in operation to the present time. It is not only cumbersome,
but, as may be seen, the clerical labor involved in the Pay and Subsistence
Departments renders the system very expensive.

Upon investigation it furthermore appears that since the tobacco law
first went into operation, up to the date of this report, about $23,000
worth of tobacco has been issued to the enlisted men of the Army, the
money value of which will never be transferred from the appropriations
of the Pay Department to those of the Subsistence Department, owing
to deaths, desertions, forfeitures, and other contingencies of service
occurring after the men had drawn their tobacco and before the next
pay day had arrived.

When the law of 1866 (section 1144, Rev. Stat.) came to be put in operation, the existing system of furnishing tobacco to enlisted men was allowed to remain undisturbed. It has been supposed that section 1149, Revised Statutes, supplemented by section 1301, has vested a *right* in the enlisted men to have the tobacco furnished them on credit if they so elect, while it has been held optional with the Secretary of War whether sales under section 1144 shall be for cash exclusively, or on credit. In my opinion, this distinction between tobacco and other articles is an unreasonable one, and has arisen out of the fact that the two laws were passed at different times and without reference to each other. I can perceive no valid reason why tobacco for smoking purposes, for instance, furnished to enlisted men under section 1149 ought not to be required to be paid for in cash the same as is now required of him for the pipe in which to use it, which is sold him under section 1144. Sales of articles under that section cannot under existing orders be made on credit, except, in certain cases, where men are serving in the field or have not been regularly paid. As the amount of tobacco to be sold each man per month will be limited to the small quantity he can individually consume, it can impose no great hardship upon him if he is required to pay cash for it at time of purchase, during periods when he is regularly paid by the Pay Department.

With the view, therefore, of simplifying the accounts, and consequently of reducing the expenses connected with the furnishing of tobacco to enlisted men, I earnestly recommend that sections 1149 and 1301, Revised Statutes, be repealed, and that section 1144 be amended by inserting after the word "articles," in the third line, the words "including tobacco," so that the latter section will read:

1144: The officers of the Subsistence Department shall procure, and keep for sale to officers and enlisted men at cost prices, for cash or on credit, such articles, including tobacco, as may from time to time be designated by the inspectors-general of the Army. An account of all sales on credit shall be kept, and the amounts due for the same shall be reported monthly to the Paymaster-General.

If the repeal of sections 1149 and 1301, and the amendment of section 1144, hereinabove recommended, be adopted by Congress, tobacco will then take its place among the other articles directed to be kept for sale to officers and enlisted men, and be controlled by the same rules as to quantities to be sold to each individual, &c., resulting in a great simplification of accounts and consequent reduction of the expenses now connected with supplying tobacco to the enlisted men of the Army. I earnestly bespeak the favorable recommendation of the Secretary of War in behalf of the measures here proposed.

SUPPLIES CONDEMNED, LOST, DESTROYED, ETC.

The value of supplies inspected and condemned during the fiscal year ending June 30, 1881, was	$21,102 69
From such of the above as were sold there was realized the sum of	7,255 32
Net loss on account of supplies condemned	13,847 37
The value of stores reported on such of the returns of the fiscal year ending June 30, 1881, as have been examined, as lost in transportation and no one found responsible therefor, and as extraordinary wastage, &c., was	22,321 59

The value of stores lost in transportation during the fiscal year ending June 30, 1881, where responsibility for the loss has been fixed, was		1,013 40
The amount collected and taken up on officers' accounts, or covered into the Treasury on above account was	$312 35	
Collected and not yet covered in	32 39	
		344 74
Leaving a balance to be collected and accounted for of		668 66

SUFFERERS BY OVERFLOW IN DAKOTA.

During the month of April, 1881, a great freshet in the Missouri River caused the overflow of considerable tracts of land in the vicinity of Yankton, Vermillion and Fort Randall, in the Territory of Dakota. Upon appeals made to the Secretary of War for assistance for the people of the submerged districts, orders were given for the gratuitous issue of Army subsistence supplies to the sufferers. The character and quantities of stores so issued, and the cost thereof to the United States, are indicated by the following table, viz:

Articles.	Yankton and Vermillion, Dak.	Fort Randall, Dak.	Total amounts issued.	Value.
	Pounds.	Pounds.	Pounds.	
Pork	9,900	3,572	13,472	$1,116 54
Bacon		3,339	3,339	300 51
Beef, fresh	13,475		13,475	1,010 62
Flour	27,636	11,734	39,370	1,043 29
Hard bread		1,247	1,247	73 57
Beans		508	508	12 70
Rice		38	38	2 47
Coffee, green	1,176½	482	1,658½	364 83
Tea	190½	1	191½	64 30
Sugar	1,100	576	1,676	137 23
Soap		14	14	77
Salt	900	14	914	12 67
Yeast-powder	568		568	228 12
Potatoes		2,431	2,431	12 58
Total cost				$4,290 57

The majority of the people to whom issues were made at Yankton and Vermillion were farmers, the suffering falling heaviest on that class. No extra expense attended the issues at these places for store rent or transportation, &c., as prominent citizens and corporations afforded gratuitously every facility in the work of distribution, several citizens giving the matter their entire time without compensation. Issues at these places began April 14, 1881, and ceased on April 30, 1881. Full rations of flour, green coffee, and tea, and part rations of pork, fresh beef, sugar, salt, and yeast-powder were issued. In issuing, three children below ten years of age were considered equal to two adults. The only extra expense occasioned to the Subsistence Department by the issues to these sufferers, besides the value of the stores themselves, was $204.44 clerk hire.

OBSERVATION AND EXPLORATION IN THE ARCTIC SEAS.

Subsistence supplies for the expeditionary force to Lady Franklin Bay were directed by the Secretary of War to be provided by the Subsistence Department, and, in pursuance of directions from the Commissary-General of Subsistence, the purchases were made by Maj. J. P. Hawkins, Commissary of Subsistence, New York City, after conferring with the commander of the expedition, First Lieut. A. W. Greely, Fifth Cavalry, acting signal officer. The subsistence stores thus provided were for 4 officers and 21 enlisted men for a period of 395 days, and are to be held for sales to the officers and men of the expedition. The enlisted men were granted $1 per day "commutation of rations," the same that is allowed enlisted men on duty in the War Department bureaus in Washington, D. C. The money value of the subsistence supplies so sent out, was $10,309.78; of stationery, weights, measures, &c., for use in connection with those supplies, $67.78.

POINT BARROW EXPEDITION.

Subsistence supplies for this expedition were also furnished, by direction of the Secretary of War, by the Subsistence Department. As in the case of the Lady Franklin' Bay expedition, the enlisted men were granted "commutation of rations" at $1 per day. The supplies sent out were for 2 officers and 3 enlisted men and 5 civil employés for a period of two years, and were turned over by Maj. Thomas C. Sullivan, Commissary of Subsistence, San Francisco, Cal., on July 13, 1881, to Lieut. P. H. Ray, Eighth Infantry, acting signal officer, commanding the expedition. The money value of the subsistence stores was $3,533.47; of the stationery, weights, measures, &c., for use in connection with those supplies, $56.43.

LOSSES OF STORES AND PROPERTY.

The following is a statement of the value of stores and property reported lost by theft, flood, fire, &c., during the fiscal year ending June 30, 1881:

Where lost.	How lost, per reports.	Date of loss.	Value.
Fort McDowell, Ariz.	By theft	Between June 30 and July 12, 1880	$24 25
Fort Brown, Tex.	By storm	August 12, 1880	250 04
Fort Bowie, Ariz.	By theft	In August, 1880	100 48
Fort Custer, Mont	By fire	September 10, 1880	75 21
Camp Thorington, Mont.	By fire	September 22, 1880	91 65
Fort Maginnis, Mont	By theft	In November, 1880	24 39
Bismarck, Dak.	By theft	In December, 1880	60 31
Chicago, Ill	By flood	December 30, 1880	1,900 30
Whipple Barracks, Ariz.	By fire	January 28, 1881	*500 00
Willett's Point, New York Harbor	By theft	April and May, 1881	384 68
Fort McDowell, Ariz.	By ravages of bugs	In November, 1880	206 94
Total			$3,618 20

*Approximated.

MISCELLANEOUS ISSUES AND EXPENDITURES.

In the month of September, 1880, 1,000 pounds of flour were issued at Fort Davis, Tex., to Mexican troops, under command of Colonel Valle, who were entirely out of provisions. The issue was approved by the Secretary of War, and the flour returned in November, 1880.

Subsistence stores were issued during the fall of 1880 to civilians employed in repair of Mullan road, between Fort Missoula, Montana, and Fort Cœur d'Alene, Idaho, to the value of $284.53, which amount was refunded to the appropriation Subsistence of the Army, 1881, from the amount appropriated for the repair of that road per act approved June 8, 1880.

The number of rations issued to citizen prisoners during the fiscal year ending June 30, 1881, was 902, and to destitute citizens was 3,531.

The value of the rations issued to Indians during the fiscal year ending June 30, 1881, and not included elsewhere, was as follows:

To Indian prisoners of war	$2,804 99
To Indians visiting military posts under paragraphs 1202 and 1203, Revised Regulations, 1863	1,148 73
To friendly Indians	236 72
To destitute Indians	962 92
Total	$5,153 36

The issues of oil for exterior illumination at the different posts under the provisions of General Order No. 17, Headquarters of the Army, Adjutant-General's Office, series of 1870, during the fiscal year ending June 30, 1881, amount to 7,804⅜ gallons. The amount expended at Columbus Barracks, Ohio, for gas for above purpose was $360.

Issues of oil and candles for lighting evening schools, post libraries, reading rooms, and chapels have been made under the provisions of paragraph 13, of General Orders No. 24, and paragraph 2, of General Orders No. 84, Headquarters of the Army, Adjutant-General's Office, 1878, during the fiscal year ending June 30, 1881, to the extent of 1,821¼ gallons of oil and 19,062 pounds of candles. An expenditure of $50 has also been made for gas for above-named purposes at Columbus Barracks, Ohio.

The amount paid to enlisted men as "commutation of rations" while traveling to and from posts in connection with target firing during fiscal year ending June 30, 1881, was $1,303.50.

Accounts for the fiscal year ending June 30, 1881, show a disbursement of $30,211.03, for the subsistence of recruiting parties and recruits, the number of rations paid for being 61,998½, and the average cost per ration 48.728 cents, an increase of .775 of a cent per ration over the cost for the previous year.

Statement of supplies issued to Indians and transferred to Indian Department, during fiscal year ending June 30, 1881.

When issued.	Where issued.	To whom issued.	At whose request issued.	Refundment requested.	Subsistence stores.	Transportation.	Total.	Remarks.
July to Dec., 1880	Fort Keogh, Mont	Sioux Indians surrendered as prisoners of war	Interior Department.	Sept. 28, 1880, to Jan. 27, 1881.	22,782 37	3,243 51	26,005 88	Stores paid for Apr. 30, 1881.
Jan., 1881	do	do	do	Feb. 19, 1881.	5,815 95	857 55	6,673 50	Stores paid for in part Apr. 30, 1881.
Feb. to June, 1881	do	do	do	Mar. 28, 1881, to July 23, 1881.	27,775 70	3,580 15	31,355 85	Stores not paid for.
Totals					56,354 02	7,681 21	64,005 23	
Aug., 1880	Fort Stanton, N. Mex.	Mescalero Apache Indian prisoners	do	Request not made.	176 51		176 51	Returned in kind.
Dec., 1880, to Apr., 1881	Hackberry, Ariz	Destitute Hualpai Indians	do	Jan. 28 to May 20, 1881.	9,497 30		9,497 30	Paid for.
Feb. to Apr., 1881	Fort Mojave, Ariz	Destitute Mojave Indians	do	July 27, 23, and 29, 1881.	7,584 05		7,584 05	Not paid for.
July, 1880	Fort Custer, Mont	Destitute Crow Indians	do	Sept. 13, 1880	149 00		149 00	Do.
Oct, 1880	Fort Omaha, Nebr	Apache Indian boy	Department commander.	Jan. 11, 1880.	3 02		3 02	Paid for June 20, 1881.
Jan. to June, 1881	Fort Buford, Dak	Sioux Indian prisoners of war.	Post commander.	Request not made.	22,581 90		22,581 90	Not paid for.
Jan., 1881	Camp Poplar River, Mont.	do	do	do	579 53		579 53	Do.
June, 1881	Fort Yates, Dak	do	Interior Department.	Aug. 18, 1881.	9,385 27	1,267 63	10,653 90	Do.
Apr., May, and June, 1881	Fort Sill, Ind. T.	P. B. Hunt, agent for the Kiowa, Comanche, and Wichita Indians	do	Aug. 3, 1881.	22,536 06		22,536 06	Do.
Apr., May, and June, 1881	Fort Reno, Ind T.	John D. Miller, agent for the Cheyenne and Arapahoe Indians	do	Aug. 3 and 4, 1881.	35,860 96	534 09	36,395 05	Do.
Totals					164,995 53	9,482 93	174,451 44	

RECAPITULATION.

Total money value of subsistence issued during the year $184,998 93

Total paid to the Subsistence Department by Indian Department, on account of above stores $64,499 23

Returned in kind 176 51

Total paid for and returned $4,675 83

Total not paid for by Indian Department 130,322 99

The support and care of the Indians of the country being committed to a bureau of the Interior Department specially organized for the purpose, and specific appropriations being annually made by Congress to be disbursed under the direction of that bureau, the diversion of funds appropriated for other branches of the government to the payment of the legitimate expenses of the Indian Bureau is, upon whatever grounds it may be urged, a matter of very questionable legality, in view of the various restrictive laws which are spread upon the statute books. Nevertheless, it is a matter of annual recurrence that the appropriations for the support of the Army are called upon to meet current wants and contingencies of the Indian establishment, and although these requests may be coupled with the promise on the part of the Interior Department of securing reimbursement to Army appropriations by Congress, the whole responsibility for such application of appropriations made for other and specific purposes must be assumed, for the time being, by those by whom the expenditure is directed. The constitutional provision that "no money shall be drawn from the Treasury but in consequence of appropriations made by law," and the restraints of section 3678, Revised Statutes, that "all sums appropriated for the various branches of expenditure in the public service shall be applied solely to the objects for which they are respectively made, and *for no others*," must be ignored in all such instances. A strong claim of justification for such exercise of executive authority, in behalf of the restless or starving savages of the frontiers, lies in its pressing necessity oftentimes to prevent an outbreak on the part of the Indians, and in the fact that it is ultimately cheaper for the government to feed the Indians who have a claim upon it for subsistence, than to allow them to engender a state of war. The resources for meeting the latter contingency would necessarily come from the appropriations for the support of the Army, but it appears radically wrong, in the light of the laws above quoted, to leave the War Department, by inadequate provision for the Indian establishment, to be made subject to contribution to that establishment whenever its appropriations shall for any reason become exhausted.

An occasion of this kind occurred in May and June last, when, the Indian appropriations being exhausted, the Subsistence Department, at the request of the Interior Department, and by direction of the Secretary of War, purchased subsistence and issued it, during those two months, to the Arapaho, Cheyenne, Kiowa, Comanche, and Wichita Indians, in the vicinity of Forts Sill and Reno, in the Indian Territory, numbering in all about 10,000 souls. The cost of the subsistence thus issued appears by the above table to have been $22,836.96, and $36,395.05, respectively, or a total of $59,232.01. These supplies were furnished upon the express promise of the Secretary of the Interior that "this department will present the subject to Congress upon the earliest opportunity, and urge upon that body the necessity for an appropriation to reimburse the War Department for such expenditures as shall be incurred in providing for these Indians."

The issues to the Sioux Indians, as prisoners of war at Fort Keogh, during the fiscal year, were made with the approval of the Secretary of War, upon the application of the Secretary of the Interior, in the spring of 1880, for permission for the Sioux from the British Possessions to surrender themselves to the military authorities, and be fed until such time as other arrangements could be made by the Interior Department for their maintenance. The authority of the Secretary of War for such issues did not look to the continued subsistence of these Indians by the Subsistence Department, and bills have been rendered to the Interior

Department for reimbursement, but no such reimbursement has been made since April 30, 1881, presumably because the appropriations of the Indian Bureau became exhausted at or about that time. Another detachment of surrendered Indians came in to Fort Buford in the winter of 1880–'81, and were subsisted at the expense of army appropriations.

The issues to the destitute Mojave Indians, between February and April, 1881, were made at the request of the Interior Department, to preserve peace and prevent suffering, with the understanding that reimbursement would be made from such funds as may have been appropriated by Congress for the Hualpai and other destitute Indians in Arizona. No reimbursement, however, has yet been made on this account.

"ACTING COMMISSARIES OF SUBSISTENCE" AND "ACTING ASSISTANT COMMISSARIES OF SUBSISTENCE."

Section 1261, Revised Statutes authorizes the payment to an "acting assistant commissary" of "$100 per year in addition to the pay of *his rank*." It is observed that in the printed annual estimates submitted to Congress since 1876 the item for the pay of the Army has included an entry for "acting assistant commissaries of subsistence, in addition to pay *in the line*," and this same phraseology occurs in recent appropriation acts.

In my opinion, this allowance should only be made to *line* officers, and should be confined to subalterns, as was the case at the date of the revision of the statutes in 1874, and had been the case previous to that time for more than fifty years. Under the recent rulings of the accounting officers, however, the extra pay of $100 per year named in above section has been allowed, as "acting assistant commissaries of subsistence," to staff officers and to officers as high in rank as lieutenant-colonels. The following on the subject is quoted from my report of last year, and I now renew the recommendations then made:

The organization of the Subsistence Department was fixed by the sixteenth section of the act entitled "An act to increase and fix the military peace establishment of the United States," approved July 28, 1866, and all laws and parts of laws in conflict with the provisions of the act were repealed by the thirty-eighth section.

Among the laws so repealed was that portion of the act of March 2, 1821 (section 8), which authorized as many assistant commissaries of subsistence, not exceeding 50, as the service might require, to be taken from the lieutenants of the line.

The appointment of officers as "assistant commissaries of subsistence" was not provided for by the act of July 28, 1866, and no law has since been passed authorizing such appointments.

The Commissary-General of Subsistence, in his annual report of October 19, 1867, expressed the opinion that "it is very desirable that this grade of subsistence officers (viz, assistant commissaries of subsistence) be restored to the service." In this opinion I concur, and would respectfully recommend that Congress be requested to authorize the Secretary of War to appoint from the grade of lieutenant, on the recommendation of the Commissary-General of Subsistence, as many "assistant commissaries of subsistence" as the service may require, not exceeding 50; such officers, while performing duty as assistant commissaries of subsistence, to be paid $10 per month, in addition to the pay of their rank, and to hold their appointments until canceled by order of the Secretary of War, or by their promotion to the grade of captain. I would also recommend that it be provided by law that where there is no assistant commissary at any garrisoned post, or with any command, the commanding officer thereof may detail an officer to act as assistant commissary for the post or command, who, if a lieutenant, shall be entitled, while performing said duty, to the pay of an assistant commissary of subsistence; and that officers making such details shall forthwith report them to the Commissary-General of Subsistence.

Compensation for performance of the duty of assistant commissaries is thus limited to lieutenants by my recommendation, because if allowed to mounted officers of the rank of captain, or to higher grades, the aggregate pay of such individual officers would exceed that of the individual officers of the Subsistence Department of corresponding grades, which, I think, should not be allowed.

COMMUTATION OF RATIONS IN LIEU OF RATIONS IN KIND.

Payment of money to enlisted men as "commutation of rations" has constituted in late years a very considerable item in the expense of the military establishment.

The Army regulations from 1843 to 1857 fixed the rate of commutation to be paid enlisted men permanently detached, and having no facilities for messing, at 20 cents per ration. The regulations of 1857 changed this rate to "the cost or value of the ration at the post," but allowed 40 cents per day to soldiers "stationed in a city with no opportunity of messing." The latter allowance was increased to 75 cents per day by regulations of 1861, but by the regulations of 1863, commutation to soldiers on furlough, female nurses in hospitals, and to "persons entitled to rations when stationed where the government has not provided subsistence for them" was fixed at "the cost of the ration at the station where it is due." By regulations from 1835 to 1863, the rate of commutation to enlisted men "detached on command," where it was impracticable to carry rations with them, was 75 cents per day. The regulations of 1863 limited this allowance to the period "when a soldier is *traveling* on detached command and it is impracticable to carry rations with him." But I am unable to find any general law (with the exception of sections 1290 and 1294 Revised Statutes), which authorizes the allowance of any money as "commutation" to enlisted men in place of the articles of the ration to be furnished them under sections 1293 and 1146 Revised Statutes. To meet, as far as practicable, this apparent omission in the laws fixing the allowances of enlisted men, this bureau has in recent years included items in its annual estimates looking to provision for the increased cost of subsisting enlisted men detailed to duty in cases where "commutation" has heretofore been allowed them, and the words "for difference between the cost of rations and commutation thereof for detailed men," have been embodied by Congress in the acts for the support of the Army for the fiscal years 1880, 1881 and 1882. Should these words be omitted hereafter from the appropriation acts, the legality of such allowances in excess of the actual cost of the ration might, in my opinion, be properly open to serious objection under section 1765 Revised Statutes, which prescribes that no "additional pay, *extra* allowance, or compensation in *any form whatever*," shall be received by any person whose "salary, pay, or emoluments are fixed by law or regulations," unless the same is, 1st, "authorized by law," and 2d, "the appropriation therefor explicitly state that it is for such additional pay, *extra* allowance, or compensation."

In May, 1862, at a period of inflated prices consequent upon a state of war, the Secretary of War authorized the allowance of commutation of rations at the rate of 75 cents per day to the soldiers employed as clerks and messengers in the departments in Washington City, and on October 1, 1863, this rate was increased to $1 per day, the monthly commutation of quarters in that city being increased 100 per cent. by the same order, on account of "the great advance of rents." This last order allowing commutation of rations at $1 per day in Washington remains unchanged to the present day.

In 1868, by orders from the War Department, a "General Service" detachment of enlisted men, intended for duty as clerks, was authorized for each of the military division, department, and district headquarters throughout the country, with power to commanding generals to augment these detachments by details from regiments when necessary, and large rates of commutation were allowed for these services. The number of men authorized by this order was subsequently changed by other orders until in February, 1880, the entire subject of clerical duty in the Army was referred to a board consisting of the Quartermaster-General, Brigadier-General A. H. Terry, and the Commissary-General of Subsistence. The following is an extract from the report of the board:

The board has been able to find no law authorizing payment to general service and detailed men on extra duty at various headquarters except the annual appropriation bills. These, it learns, provide funds in accordance with estimates of the Quartermaster-General and the Commissary-General of Subsistence, which estimates are submitted by the Secretary of War to Congress. The details of items of the expenditure have not been always set forth in the consolidated estimates laid before Congress, but those original estimates in detail are on file in the office of the Quartermaster-General and of the Commissary-General. No express law authorizes the payment to a soldier of more money as commutation of fuel than his share of the allowance of fuel to his company costs the United States. So of commutation of rations. Rations are not an emolument, but an allowance of food. * * *

The board, therefore, recommends that the number of enlisted men on such duty, general service and detailed, be limited to the number set forth in the following table, that being the number for which appropriation was granted by Congress; that their allowance and commutation of quarters, fuel, and subsistence shall remain as it was fixed when the estimates for the appropriations made by Congress to pay their allowances were made up, and for payment of which rates the appropriation for 1879-'80 has provided funds. These rates are set forth in the accompanying tables. [Both tables omitted here.]

The board recommends that the War-Department do not attempt to fix in detail the number of enlisted men, general service or detailed, to be allowed at each separate headquarters in the Army. It recommends that the whole number available under laws and appropriations of Congress for this service be set forth in a general order, and that the General of the Army be authorized by letter of instruction or advice to division commanders to determine the distribution, from time to time, of these men among the divisions and departments according to the exigencies of the service.

A general order was thereupon issued by the War Department adopting the recommendations of the board. As in the case of enlisted men employed as clerks in the War Department and bureaus and offices, the rates of allowance of commutation of rations to these men on duty as clerks at military headquarters, was fixed by order at $1 and 75 cents per day, and the rate to men detailed as messengers at 50 cents per day.

The prevailing prices of table board paid by various grades of civil employés of the government in the city of Washington at the present time are from $15 to $20 per month. The estimated cost of the ration throughout the country is 20 cents. Enlisted men on duty in the War Department and bureaus and offices, however, are given $30 or $31 per month as commutation of rations. This excess—of $10 to $16 per month—over current prices of board paid to these men can hardly be considered other than an emolument intended to make up from "subsistence" what may be wanting under some other heading of income, which, in their present sphere of employment, is either partially provided for only, or is wholly unprovided for. This deficient heading is most probably "pay," since these men can only draw the *pay* of the enlisted men of the Army, which is fixed by Congress at from $13 to $17 per month, while the rates of "commutation" are not prescribed by that body. The same remarks are in the main applicable to the men on duty as clerks and messengers at the various military headquarters throughout the country. Speaking of this class of men on duty in the Adjutant-General's Office, the Adjutant-General, on December 18, 1880, in answer to Senate resolution of June 15, 1880, said: "Most of these men are excellent clerks, and, although having seen service in the regular or volunteer forces of the country during the late war, are in no sense *soldiers* now, but clerks, and the continuance of the system bur-

28 Ab

Character of duty.	Total number of men.	Number of days.	Rate of commutation per day.	Amount.
Signal Service enlisted men on duty in office of Chief Signal Officer	125	365	$1 00	$45,625 00
Signal Service enlisted men on signal duty at various signal stations	13	365	1 00	4,745 00
Signal Service enlisted men on signal duty at Lady Franklin Bay and Point Barrow, Alaska	20	365	1 00	7,300 00
On detached duty at Lady Franklin Bay and Point Barrow, Alaska	24	365	1 00	8,760 00
Enlisted clerks (general service) at headquarters military divisions, departments, and districts	148	365	75	40,515 00
Enlisted clerks (general service) at headquarters general recruiting service	7	365	75	1,916 25
On detached duty in various capacities at military posts	14	365	75	3,832 50
Signal Service enlisted men on signal duty at various signal stations	272	365	75	74,460 00
On detached duty as repairmen of United States telegraph lines	80	365	75	21,900 00
Traveling on detached duty	75	365	1 50	41,062 50
Detailed as messengers at headquarters military divisions, departments, and districts	60	365	50	10,950 00
Detailed as messengers at headquarters general recruiting service	2	365	50	365 00
Ordnance sergeant at Sandy Hook, N. J	1	365	50	182 50
Ordnance sergeants on duty at ungarrisoned posts	40	365	40	5,840 00
On furlough	432	365	25	39,420 00
Total	1,583	....	....	405,423 75

The enlisted men of the Signal Corps on duty at the various signal stations throughout the United States, with few exceptions, are allowed by the Secretary of War to draw commutation of rations at the rate of 75 cents per day. In the cases of 13 signal men outside of Washington and 125 in Washington, $1 per day is at present allowed. Rations in kind for 70 men only of the signal service are estimated for the fiscal year 1883. I find nothing in the statutes to exempt the enlisted men of the Signal Corps from the operation of sections 1293 and 1146 of the Revised Statutes, but as nearly all these men now draw "commutation," I would recommend that the number of men of that corps to whom commutation of rations shall be paid and the respective rates of commutation of rations to be allowed them may be fixed by law. This recommendation I make upon the same grounds as in the case of "general service" men above.

I have estimated in the estimate for subsistence of the Army for the fiscal year 1883, for commutation of rations for enlisted men *traveling* on detached duty at the rate of $1.50 per day. My opinion is that this sum is not at this time in excess of the average cost per diem of meals at points along lines of transportation throughout the country, and I think enlisted men traveling on detached duty, when it is impracticable to cook rations or to carry cooked rations, should be enabled to procure subsistence in the mode in which ordinary travelers usually procure their meals. I would recommend that even this amount may be authorized to be increased by the Secretary of War, in special cases of travel in the Territories and elsewhere where the cost of subsistence is known to be much in excess of the prices to be paid in more densely populated localities.

ARMY COOKING.

I invite the attention of the honorable Secretary of War to the following extract from my annual report for 1879, and urgently recommend that the attention of Congress may be invited to the subject, as one of the utmost importance, both in an economical and sanitary point of view:

ARMY COOKS AND BAKERS.

On the 8th of November, 1876, I stated, in a communication to the honorable Secretary of War:

"I am of the opinion that the efficiency of the Army would be materially increased, and desertions lessened, were a cook enlisted for each company with extra pay, say $4 in excess of the pay of a private, and schools for the instructions of cooks established at the recruiting depots at Fort Columbus, N. Y., and Columbus Barracks, Ohio."

In my annual report for the year 1876, I stated:

"I also think that bakers should be specially enlisted, paid extra-duty pay, say $4 per month, and assigned to posts as commissary-sergeants. I recommend that should schools for cooks be established at recruiting depots, bakers should also be instructed at the same schools."

I again invite the attention of the honorable Secretary of War to this subject in connection with the following extract from the report of the board on Army cooking, convened by General Orders No. 117, Headquarters of the Army, Adjutant-General's Office, series of 1877:

"The Army needs the enlistment of men who have an aptitude for cooking, and the establishment of a school for their education in the economy of the kitchen. * * *

"Extra compensation is allowed to enlisted men when on duty as mechanics, artisans, and laborers when performing such work, but none to the company cook, whose duty, if conscientiously done, is the most onerous performed by the enlisted men. Eight hours is the time fixed for the labor of the extra-duty men, who are rated and paid as such. The duties of the competent and conscientious company cook commence two hours before reveille, and frequently are not concluded before tattoo. The wear and tear of the clothes of a company cook is double that of any enlisted man in the same company, yet the cook receives no extra compensation therefor, whilst the carpenter, blacksmith, or laborer detailed from the same company does.

"An important aid to good soldiering is good cooking. This cannot be obtained without good cooks, and good cooks cannot be obtained without education and adequate compensation. If one company cook, while actually performing duty as such, was allowed 50 per cent. advance on his clothing allowance, and a monetary compensation of 30 per cent. per day, to be paid either from the Subsistence Department or the Quartermaster's Department, a class of men would be secured to the Army who would economically use the ration, cook it acceptably, and be anxious to retain his position for the extra compensation it brings, whilst at present he is only glad to be relieved from kitchen duty for lighter work."

I respectfully urge the Secretary of War to invite the attention of Congress to this subject, believing the subject one of the utmost importance in connection with the health, comfort, and efficiency of the enlisted men of the Army.

I would respectfully recommend the adoption of the following draft of a law intended to accomplish the object desired, viz:

There shall hereafter be enlisted, for each battery of artillery, troop of cavalry, and company of infantry in the service, under such regulations as the Secretary of War shall prescribe, a competent person as cook, whose clothing allowance shall be those of a private soldier, but whose pay proper shall be at the rate of twenty-two dollars per month, whose duty it shall be to cook the rations of the battery, troop, or company, under such regulations as may be prescribed under section 1174, Revised Statutes; *provided*, that cooks so enlisted shall not be entitled under any circumstances to extra-duty pay; and *provided further*, that the introduction of the grade into the Army shall not have the effect of increasing the strength of the Army beyond the number of men now authorized by law.

FIELD OVENS.

A board of officers consisting of Maj. George Bell, commissary o subsistence, Capt. Thomas B. Robinson, Nineteenth Infantry, First Lieut. O. B. Hall, Nineteenth Infantry, and Second Lieut. O. H. Hunter, Nineteenth Infantry, recorder, was convened by Special Order No. 262, Headquarters Department of the Missouri, Fort Leavenworth, Kans., series of 1880, to make a thorough and complete test of such field ovens as might be submitted to it. The report of the board has been received, and the revision of the pamphlets heretofore issued by the Subsistence Department on the subject of ovens has been made by Maj. George Bell, commissary of subsistence. It is the intention to publish to the Army the results of these experiments with ovens for field service, as well as notes upon the construction of permanent ovens for military posts.

THE SOLDIER'S RATION AND THE POST AND COMPANY FUNDS.

In the spring of 1880, a discussion sprang up in the department of Texas concerning the sufficiency, or insufficiency, of the present army ration. Under the direction of the commanding general of that department, and at the request of Surgeon J. R. Smith, medical director of the department, statistics of the company funds of the 78 companies in the department, for the average period of 17 months, and of savings of the post bakeries in the department during the same period, were collected. The *data* thus derived were subsequently subjected to a thorough and masterly reduction and analysis by Surgeon Smith, a copy of whose report, with the indorsements of the chief commissary of subsistence and the commanding general of the department of Texas, and of the Commissary-General of Subsistence thereon, is appended to this report and marked Appendix A. A review of this report was subsequently made by Col. John Gibbon, Seventh Infantry, at Fort Snelling, Minn., in connection with statistics gathered from the companies of the Seventh Infantry; and this review and the original report of Surgeon Smith were in turn reviewed by the chief commissary of subsistence and the medical director of the department of Dakota. These papers are also hereto appended, marked Appendix B.

The army ration, exclusive of the soap and candle components, was originally furnished by the government to the soldier solely for the purposes of alimentation; but ever since the Army Regulations of 1835 (see page 99 of those regulations) the flour component has been made tributary to the "post fund," to the extent of about one-third of the flour issued, wherever troops bake their own bread, and by the regulations issued after the passage of the law of July 5, 1838 (5 Stat. at Large 256)—which directed the issue of sugar and coffee in place of the former spirit or whisky component, and prescribed that "when not so issued, to be paid in money"—all the articles composing the ration, excepting flour, have been made tributary to another fund called the "company fund" (see Army Regulations, 1841, page 32). This fund accrues not only from the sale of sugar and coffee under the law, but from all other ration-articles, excepting flour, which are saved or not consumed by the men. In place of articles so saved, the company commanders receive from sales thereof the money value, and the fund thus accumulated (and added to from other minor sources) becomes the "company fund."

These laws and regulations are substantially in operation at the present time, and the obligation of the government to furnish subsistence to the soldier is practically fulfilled by the following system of issues and diminutions, viz:

1. The greater portion of each of the components of the full ration, drawn in kind, is consumed by the soldier.

2. A portion of some or of each of the components, excepting flour, not wanted by him, or not supposed to be needed by him under the varying contingencies of garrison or field duty, is not consumed by him, but its money-value, arising from the sale thereof by his company commander, is applied to the formation of the "company fund."

3. One-third of the flour to which he is entitled is, in garrison or where

a post bakery can be erected, diverted from him to pay the cost of baking the remaining two-thirds; this diversion, aided by the tax on the post-trader, if one be present, constituting the "post-fund."

If the post fund and the company fund are not, as such, to be considered longer available for procuring subsistence for the soldier when once accumulated, and he becomes hungry upon the quantity of food that is actually prepared for him, it is obvious that the rights of the enlisted man, under sections 1293 and 1146, Revised Statutes, are in a measure defeated, since the legal effect of those sections is to vest in him a right to an allowance of provisions sufficient for his daily subsistence, and this right ought not to be any more subject to unnecessary diminution than are his rights to his pay and other allowances under Title XIV, chapter 3, of the Revised Statutes.

For what purposes, then, are the post and company funds made available by the orders creating them?

The following are the objects (see General Orders No. 24, Headquarters of the Army, Adjutant-General's Office, 1878, as amended by General Orders No. 19, Headquarters of the Army, Adjutant-General's Office, 1881), to which the post fund (a portion of which is disbursed as a "regimental" fund), are applied, viz. As post fund: 1st. Expenses of bakehouse; 2d. Garden seeds and utensils (for all troops serving at the post); 3d. Post schools; 4th. Post library and reading rooms; 5th. Gymnasium; 6th. Chapel; 7th. Fruit and shade trees; 8th. Fruit-bearing vines and bushes; 9th. Printing press. As regimental fund: 1st. The maintenance of a band; 2d. When not needed for the band it may be transferred to the companies of the regiment as company fund.

The following are the objects (see General Orders Nos. 24 and 19, above cited) to which the company fund, "the savings arising from an economical use of the rations of the company, excepting the saving of flour," are to be applied for the exclusive benefit of the enlisted men of the company, viz: 1st. For enlisted men's mess; 2d. For garden seeds and utensils; 3d. For such exercise and amusements as may be, in the judgment of the company commander, for the benefit or comfort of the majority of the enlisted men of the company.

All these institutional comforts of the soldier are, then, to be provided for and maintained, not from direct congressional appropriations for the purpose, but indirectly at the expense of his allowance of food. What, then, is the remedy when soldiers "show symptoms of need of more food"?

Surgeon Smith submits:

That the soldier receive the whole of his ration, or the product of its barter in the shape of food.

The commanding general Department of Texas says:

The appropriation of money derived from the sale of any part of the soldier's rations to other purposes than providing food in greater variety is, in my opinion, contrary to law.

The chief commissary of subsistence of the Department of Texas says:

It should, however, be a principle established by regulations, that whatever the government allows as a ration, must, if sold, be replaced by its equivalent in *food* to the soldier.

Colonel Gibbon recommends:

That all expenditures of company funds be prohibited except for the purchase of food for the men.

The chief commissary of subsistence of the Department of Dakota says:

There should be nothing purchased with the proceeds of "savings" of the ration but food.

The medical director of the same department says:

The initial step in all efforts to improve the diet of the soldier should be to prohibit the expenditure of the proceeds arising from the sale of saved portions of the ration for anything but food.

Surgeon T. A. McParlin, U. S. A., in his report upon the nutritive value of the Army ration in 1875, recommended that it be ordered:

That no savings from the food portion of the ration shall be expendable for anything but food.

To increase the ration, as has been proposed by some officers, while the post and company funds and the institutions which they support are retained, will be to increase *pro tanto* the cost of subsisting the Army. Holding the views I do, as expressed in my indorsement of June 1, 1881, on Surgeon Smith's report, I cannot concur in the proposition of an increase until it shall be shown in actual service that the *full ration* now prescribed for the soldier is, when wholly consumed by him, either in kind or in nutritive equivalents obtained by barter, insufficient to completely satisfy his daily desires for food. As touching the subject of the sufficiency of the present ration, I append hereto, marked Appendix C, extracts from a letter of the late Commissary-General Eaton to the General of the Army in 1873, in the spirit of which I fully concur.

ACCOUNTS AND RETURNS.

There were received during the fiscal year ending June 30, 1881, from 516 officers performing duty in the Subsistence Department, the following accounts and returns, viz:

Accounts current	2,746
Returns of provisions	2,500
Returns of commissary property	936
Total received	6,182

During the same period there were examined in this office, and forwarded to the Third Auditor for settlement, the following:

Accounts current	2,666, accompanied by 38,153 vouchers.
Returns of provisions	2,281, accompanied by 32,168 vouchers.
Returns of commissary property	822, accompanied by 2,099 vouchers.
Total	5,769, accompanied by 72,420 vouchers.

In connection with the above there were 3,935 letters written, and 1,025 referred by indorsements, and 289 papers copied.

In addition to the above, returns of official postage-stamps to the number of 786, accompanied by 2,234 vouchers, have been examined and filed.

CLAIMS.

Act of July 4, 1864 (*Section* 300 B, *Revised Statutes*).—At the commencement of the fiscal year ending June 30, 1881, there were on file in this office, awaiting examination, 2,079 claims, under the third section of the act of July 4, 1864, and the acts and joint resolutions supplementary to said act, and during the year 32 more were received, making, in all, 2,111 to be acted upon. Formal decisions were rendered, during this period, in 249 cases of this class of claims. Of these, 33, amounting to $4,054, were allowed, and recommended to the Third Auditor of the Treasury for payment; and 216, amounting to $160,644.90, were rejected. The number decided embraced 21 cases, re-examined upon additional evidence, of which 1 was allowed, and 20 again rejected.

There remained on hand on July 1, 1881, awaiting examination and decision under this act, 1,862 claims.

Joint resolution of July 25, 1866, and third section of act of March 2, 1867.—At the commencement of the fiscal year there were on file in this office 2,644 claims for commutation of rations to Union soldiers while held as prisoners of war, and during the year 997 claims were received, making a total of 3,641 claims of this class for examination, &c. Of these, 17 were not reached for examination; 2,329 were partially examined; 1,295 examined and decided, of which 842 were rejected, and 453, amounting to $13,057.50, were allowed and recommended to the Third Auditor of the Treasury for payment. Besides this, 6 rejected (old) claims were re-examined upon additional evidence, 1 of which, amounting to $3, was allowed, and 5 again rejected.

Miscellaneous claims.—In addition to claims under the above-mentioned special acts of Congress, there were at the commencement of the fiscal year 532 miscellaneous claims on hand, and during the year 207 claims were received. Of these 739 claims, 122 were recommended for payment in the aggregate sum of $15,067.17; 126 were rejected; 420 have been partially examined; and 71 were not reached for examination. Besides this, 10 rejected (old claims) were re-examined upon additional evidence, 7 of which, amounting to $96.90, were allowed, and 3 again rejected.

Letters and indorsements.—In connection with the three classes of claims above mentioned, 11,127 communications were sent out during the year, and many briefs of evidence and extended examinations of records and reports were made.

CLERICAL AND OTHER FORCE IN THE OFFICE OF THE COMMISSARY-GENERAL OF SUBSISTENCE.

I have the honor to renew my recommendation of last year that Congress be urgently requested to allow to this office the following number and grades of employés, in lieu of the number and grades now authorized and employed, viz: One chief clerk; 2 clerks, class 4; 4 clerks, class 3; 5 clerks, class 2; 12 clerks, class 1; 5 clerks, class $1,000 (temporary); 1 messenger; 1 assistant messenger; 2 watchmen; 2 laborers. This force is absolutely required to perform the ordinary duties of the office, the 5 temporary clerks at $1,000 being required in connection with the examination of claims (now greatly in arrears), and to be retained only until such time as those claims are so far reduced in number as to be within the capacity of the regular force.

This reorganization of office *personnel* contemplates the discontinuance of the use of enlisted men as now resorted to. I believe that the necessary force should all be civilians, and that no part of the appropriations for the support of the army should be devoted to the payment of enlisted men for the performance of duties that are wholly of a civil nature.

DUTIES AND STATIONS OF OFFICERS OF THE SUBSISTENCE DEPARTMENT.

The duties and stations of officers of the Subsistence Department on the 10th of October, 1881, will appear from the roster hereto appended.

During the year the officers of the department have been actively and efficiently employed.

Very respectfully, your obedient servant,

R. MACFEELY,
Commissary-General of Subsistence.

Hon. the SECRETARY OF WAR.

REPORT OF THE SURGEON-GENERAL.

WAR DEPARTMENT,
SURGEON-GENERAL'S OFFICE,
Washington, October 1, 1881.

Sir: I have the honor to submit the following statement of finances and general transactions of the Medical Department of the Army for the fiscal year ending June 30, 1881:

FINANCIAL STATEMENT.

Appropriation for the Medical and Hospital Department, 1877:
Balance from previous fiscal year.................................... $1,029 46
Disbursed during the year.. 1,029 46

Medical and Hospital Department, 1878, and prior years:
Balance from previous fiscal year.................................... 1,421 59
Appropriated by act of March 3, 1881................................. 1,072 30
Refunded during the year... 56 00

2,549 89

Disbursed during the year.............................. $1,072 30
Carried to the surplus fund............................ 1,477 59

2,549 89

Medical and Hospital Department, 1879:
Balance from previous year... 95 22
Disbursed during the year.............................. $80 75
Carried to surplus fund................................ 14 47

95 22

Medical and Hospital Department, 1880:
Balance from previous fiscal year.................................... 47,251 62
Refunded during the year... 2,413 52

49,665 14
Disbursed during the year.. 46,373 08

Balance June 30, 1881.. 3,292 06

Medical and Hospital Department, 1881:
Appropriated by act of May 4, 1880...................................200,000 00
Disbursed during the year..142,894 57

* Balance June 30, 1881.. 57,105 43

Artificial limbs, 1877:
Balance from previous fiscal year.................................... 3,476 90
Appropriated by act of March 3, 1881................................. 138 40
Transfer warrant... 157 84

3,773 14

Disbursed during the year.............................. $296 24
Balance June 30,1881................................... 3,476 90

3,773 14

Artificial limbs, 1878:
Balance from previous fiscal year.................................... 1,927 77
Disbursed during the year.. 26 00

Balance June 30, 1881.. 1,901 77

---

* This entire amount will be required to meet obligations for which contracts were made prior to July 1, 1881; $53,929.28 of which has been disbursed since June 30, 1881, in fulfillment of said contracts.

Artificial limbs, 1879:
Balance from previous fiscal year..$30, 921 27
Disbursed during the year..   51 46

Balance June 30, 1881........,....................................... 30, 869 81

Artificial limbs, 1880:
Balance from previous fiscal year.................................... 62, 790 44
Disbursed during the year..   2, 975 28

Balance June 30, 1881... 59, 815 16

Artificial limbs, 1881:
Appropriated by act of June 16, 1880................................250, 000 00
Appropriated by act of March 3, 1881..............................200, 000 00

                                                                    450, 000 00
Disbursed during the year..420, 041 29

Balance June 30, 1881... 29, 958 71

Appliances for disabled soldiers, 1879:
Balance from previous fiscal year....................................   2, 887 00
Balance June 30, 1881..   2, 887 00

Appliances for disabled soldiers, 1880:
Balance from previous fiscal year....................................   790 00
Disbursed during the year..   80 00

Balance June 30, 1881...   710 00

Appliances for disabled soldiers, 1881:
Appropriated by act of June 16, 1880................................   3, 000 00
Disbursed during the year..   524 00

Balance June 30, 1881...   2, 476 00

Medical and Surgical History:
Balance from previous fiscal year.................................... 16, 353 05
Disbursed during the year..   2, 964 90

Balance June 30, 1881... 13, 388 15

Museum and Library, 1880:
Balance from previous fiscal year....................................   825 80
Disbursed during the year..   825 80

Museum and Library, 1881:
Appropriated by act of May 4, 1880................................. 10, 000 00
Disbursed during the year..   9, 380 14

Balance June 30, 1881..............................:...............   619 86

Expended in providing trusses for ruptured soldiers, seamen, and marines, under act approved May 28, 1872, extended by act of March 3,
1879...   5, 333 30

ARTIFICIAL LIMBS.

There were furnished during the fiscal year, in kind, trusses, 574; artificial legs, 652; arms, 14; foot, 1; apparatus for legs, 2; apparatus for
arm, 1. By commutation, legs, 2,546; arms, 2,754; feet, 55; apparatus
for legs, 343; apparatus for arms, 608.

The number of persons allowed artificial limbs or commutation up
to June 30, 1881, is 14,501. Of these 7,680 applied prior to June 17,
1870. From that time to June 17, 1875, 4,857 made their first applications; 1,716 to 1880, thence to June 30, 1881, 248.

As nearly as can be ascertained the dates of injuries for which applications for limbs have been made are: From 1813 to 1860, inclusive, 132; from 1861 to 1865, inclusive, 14,094; from 1866 to 1880, inclusive, 275.

The first issue, ending June 16, 1870, included 7,680 names; the second, ending June 16, 1875, 11,719; the third, 11,706; and that part of the fourth issue extending to June 30, 1881, 6,695.

Of the beneficiaries of the first period, 713 have not been heard from since 1870. With very few exceptions these are no doubt dead, indicating an annual death rate for that period of 11.6 per 1,000. Of the names occurring in the second issue, 1,831 have not appeared since, which incates a death rate of 31.25 per 1,000. If the same ratio were to continue till June 30, 1881, there would be a further loss of 2,195, making 4,740 in all. Hence it is probable that of the entire number there are little more than 10,000 now remaining.

MEDICAL AND HOSPITAL SUPPLIES.

The cost of the medical and hospital supplies actually issued during the last fiscal year was $183,253.42; and referring to my last annual report I deem it my duty to again call attention to the necessity for an increased appropriation to meet the actual expenses of the Medical Department, and to provide for emergencies which may arise for the fiscal year ending June 30, 1883.

The stock of supplies of durable nature left on hand at the close of the late war has become so nearly exhausted that, with few exceptions, they cannot be depended upon as heretofore to fill requisitions. I am of the opinion that the sum of $250,000 will be required for the use of the Medical Department for the next fiscal year for the purchase of medical and hospital supplies, for expenses of purveying depots, for pay of employés, for pay of private physicians and nurses employed in emergencies at posts or stations for which no other provision is made, and for other miscellaneous expenses of the Medical Department. Another important reason for recommending an increased appropriation is the fact that the Medical Department is obliged to furnish medical and hospital supplies for the use of several thousand Indians as prisoners of war.

HEALTH OF THE ARMY DURING THE FISCAL YEAR ENDING JUNE 30, 1881.

The monthly reports of sick and wounded received at this office up to September 5 represent an average mean strength of 21,160 white, 2,344 colored troops, and 300 Indian scouts.

Among the *white troops* the total number of cases of all kinds reported as taken on the sick list was 37,408, being at the rate of 1,768 per 1,000 of mean strength.

Of this number, 32,013, or 1,513 per 1,000 of strength, were taken on sick report for disease, and 5,395, or 255 per 1,000 of strength, for wounds, accidents, and injuries of all kinds.

The average number constantly on sick report during the year was 932, or 44 per 1,000 of mean strength. Of these, 739, or 35 per 1,000 of strength, were constantly under treatment for disease, and 193, or 9 per 1,000 of strength, for wounds, accidents, and injuries.

The total number of deaths from all causes reported among the white troops was 197, or 9 per 1,000 of mean strength. Of these 130, or 6 per 1,000 of strength, died of disease, and 67, or 3 per 1,000 of strength, of wounds, accidents, and injuries.

The proportion of deaths from all causes to cases treated was 1 to 190.

The total number of white soldiers reported to have been discharged the service on "surgeon's certificate of disability" was 723, or 34 per 1,000 of mean strength.

Among the *colored troops* the total number of cases of all kinds reported was 4,650, or 1,984 per 1,000 of mean strength. Of these, 4,090, or 1,745 per 1,000 of strength, were cases of disease, and 560, or 239 per 1,000 of strength, were wounds, accidents, and injuries.

The average number constantly on sick report was 106, or 45 per 1,000 of strength, of whom 81, or 34 per 1,000 of strength, were under treatment for disease, and 25, or 11 per 1,000 of strength, for wounds, accidents, and injuries.

The total number of deaths of colored soldiers reported from all causes was 48, or 20 per 1,000 of mean strength. Of these, 26, or 11 per 1,000 of strength, died of disease, and 22, or 9 per 1,000 of strength, of wounds, accidents, and injuries.

The proportion of deaths from all causes to cases treated was 1 to 97.

The total number of colored soldiers reported to have been discharged on "surgeon's certificate of disability" was 98, or 42 per 1,000 of mean strength.

The total number of deaths reported among the Indian scouts was 3, 1 from disease and 2 of wounds.

WORK PERFORMED IN THE RECORD AND PENSION DIVISION.

The number of new official demands upon this division during the fiscal year for information as to the cause of death in the case of deceased soldiers and the hospital record of invalids was 55,040. The average number of such demands during the previous ten years had been 22,245 annually, and the number during the fiscal year terminating June 30, 1880, was 39,241; the number received during the fiscal year ending June 30, 1881, being an increase of 40 per cent. over the previous fiscal year, and of 147 per cent. over the annual average of the previous ten years.

Six thousand nine hundred and sixty-four cases remained unanswered at the commencement of the fiscal year, making 62,004 cases to be disposed of during the year.

Of the new cases 53,438 were from the Commissioner of Pensions, 1,463 from the Adjutant-General of the Army, and 139 from miscellaneous sources.

Search was made and replies furnished to the proper authorities in 40,596 of these cases, viz, 39,388 to the Commissioner of Pensions, 1,081 to the Adjutant-General of the Army, and 127 to miscellaneous applicants, leaving 21,408 unanswered cases on hand on the 1st of July, 1881.

This work becomes more difficult as the period elapsed since the close of the war increases, for the reason that claimants are in many cases unable to furnish accurate or definite data as to time and place of treatment; also, the volumes of hospital records on file in this office are becoming so very dilapidated from constant handling, that the utmost care must be exercised in order that the entries contained therein may not be irretrievably lost, the clerical force not having been sufficient during the past fiscal year, or at any previous time, to permit of the copying of these original records.

The clerical force of the office was increased by forty clerks last March, under the provisions of the act of Congress approved March 3,

1881, but, as on account of the peculiar nature of the work newly appointed clerks experience considerable difficulty in learning the same, some time must necessarily elapse before they can be expected to perform it with the facility and accuracy exhibited by those who, from long experience, are more familiar with the records.

Because of the overcrowded condition of the building Nos. 509–511, Tenth street, northwest, in which the hospital records are filed, forty-two clerks were transferred to the building on the northeast corner of F and Tenth streets, northwest, the second and third floors of which were secured for their accommodation from the 1st of July, 1881, by authority of the Secretary of War.

During the past fiscal year 2,655 monthly reports of sick and wounded have been received from the medical officers in charge of the various posts and stations. These have been examined, consolidated on statistical sheets for use, and the deaths and discharges entered in the appropriate alphabetical registers. Eight hundred and sixty-six monthly meteorological reports were received from medical officers, which have been transmitted to the Chief Signal Officer of the Army for his use, and 992 reports of the medical examination of recruits were received and filed. Seven hundred and twenty-three volumes of hospital records were received from discontinued posts and commands, making the total number of such volumes on file 18,083.

DIVISION OF SURGICAL RECORDS.

The work pertaining to this division of the Surgeon-General's Office has embraced the reception, acknowledgement, and examination of the surgical reports of the medical officers of the Army, the correspondence referring to the reception and classification of specimens received for the Army Medical Museum, and the continuance of the publication of the Surgical History of the War.

Five thousand nine hundred and sixty-two cases of wounds, accidents, and injuries were recorded in Class V of the monthly reports of sick and wounded during the fiscal year ending June 30, 1881, in a mean strength of the Army of 23,804 men. The deaths from wounds received in action or from other violent causes numbered 91, being a proportion of 3.8 per 1,000 of mean strength.

From medical officers in charge of post hospitals, or with detachments of troops in the field, 2,436 official reports were received. Of these, 1,710 were regular quarterly reports, 54 were special, 661 miscellaneous and 11 reports of casualties.

The losses in actions with hostile Indians were 12 killed and 13 wounded; sustained in the following engagements: 1. At Rocky Ridge, Texas, July 30, 1880, in a fight between Companies C and G, Tenth Cavalry, and a number of Apache Indians, Acting Assist. Surg. C. K. Gregg reported 1 lieutenant and 1 private wounded, and 1 private killed by a shot through the chest. 2. Near Eagle Spring, Texas, August 3, 1880, a party of Indians, 15 in number, attacked a detachment of 5 men of the Tenth Cavalry. Acting Assist. Surg. C. K. Gregg reported 1 private killed and 1 wounded. 3. On August 4, 1880, at Taylor's Cañon, Guadalupe Mountains, Texas, 1 private of the Tenth Cavalry was killed, and 1 wounded; the report was sent by Acting Assist. Surg. M. F. Price. 4. A detachment of Company G, Ninth Cavalry, was attacked on September 1, 1880, by a party of hostile Mescalero Indians, at Agua Chiquito, sixty-six miles from the Mescalero Apache Agency, South Fork, N. Mex. Acting Assist. Surg. F. H. Atkins reported 2 privates wounded, death ensuing on the second and third days after; both were shot in the abdomen. 5. On the morning of September 7, 1880, Company A of the Fourth Cavalry and 20 Indian scouts, attacked Victoria's band of Indians in the Mogollon Mountains, about twenty miles from Fort Cummings, N. Mex.; 1 private and 2 scouts were killed, and 3 privates were wounded. No medical officer was present at the fight; an account of the engagement was sent by Assist. Surg. W. R. Hall. 6. At Ojo Caliente, October 28, 1880, from 20 to 30 Mexican Indians, supposed to belong to Victoria's band, attacked the pickets of the Tenth Cavalry; 1 corporal and 4 privates were reported as killed, by Acting Assist. Surg. W. Church Henderson. 7. One musician and 1 private of the Ninth Cavalry, were wounded in a fight at the Mescalero Indian Agency, N. Mex., December 2, 1880. Reported by Assist. Surg. R. C. Newton. 8. On January 24, 1881, an escort to a wagon train was attacked by Indians at Cruz Cañon, N. Mex. Acting Assist. Surg. F. S. Dewey reported 1 private of Company D, Ninth Cavalry, severely wounded; the man died on January 25, 1881. 9. On April 30, 1881, Acting Assist. Surg. W. Whitney reported a private of Company B, Ninth Cavalry, killed by Apache Indians in the Boca Grande Mountains.

At the close of the fiscal year ending June 30, 1879, 8,862 cases of injuries and operations reported in the Army since the publication of Circular No. 3, in 1871, had been collected; to these have been added, during the last fiscal year, 1,306 cases, viz, 215 injuries of the face, 4 of the neck, 37 of the trunk, 100 of the upper extremities, 100 of the lower extremities, 539 simple fractures, luxations, and sprains, and 221 miscellaneous injuries, making a total of 10,168 cases, namely, 2,489 injuries of the head, 356 of the face, 69 of the neck, 683 of the trunk, 1,766 of the upper extremities, 1,150 of the lower extremities, 2,553 simple fractures, luxations, and sprains, and 1,122 miscellaneous injuries.

Surgical statistics of the war.—From reports of pension examiners and through correspondence with medical officers who served during the war, additional information has been received in 102 cases of injuries received during the War of the Rebellion and from searches in the Pension Office the remote results were ascertained in 886 cases.

PROPERTY DIVISION.

The following is a summary statement of the work performed in the property division of this office during the fiscal year ending June 30, 1881, viz:

Letters received and recorded	3,571
Letters sent and recorded	1,946
Indorsements sent, charged	1,500
Indorsements sent, recorded	64
Accounts current examined, recorded and forwarded to Treasury	90
Vouchers pertaining to accounts current examined, recorded in *detail*, approved and forwarded	1,789
Accounts of sales with vouchers settled	64
Miscellaneous notifications	1,376
Statements of funds received, recorded, and forwarded to Treasury	22
Property returns examined and settled	463
Property returns examined and suspended	14
Certificates of non-indebtedness sent	49
Certificates of corrections sent	57
Property returns recorded	463
Property returns prepared in Surgeon-General's Office	6
Letters and indorsements sent, pertaining to property returns	68
Aggregate	**13,466**

ARMY MEDICAL MUSEUM.

Surgical section.

Specimens in the Museum, July 1, 1880	7,023
Specimens in the Museum, July 1, 1881	7,075
Increase during the year	52

Medical section.

Specimens in the Museum, July 1, 1880	1,534
Specimens in the Museum, July 1, 1881	1,570
Increase during the year	36

Microscopical section.

Specimens in the Museum, July 1, 1880	8,386
Specimens in the Museum, July 1, 1881	8,471
Increase during the year	85

Anatomical section.

Specimens in the Museum, July 1, 1880	2,070
Specimens in the Museum, July 1, 1881	2,121
Increase during the year	51

Section of comparative anatomy.

Specimens in the Museum, July 1, 1880	2,411
Specimens in the Museum, July 1, 1881	2,448
Increase during the year	37

Miscellaneous section.

Specimens in the Museum, July 1, 1880	672
Specimens in the Museum, July 1, 1881	707
Increase during the year	35
Specimens received	154
Specimens transferred	119

The contributors to the Army Medical Museum were 9 surgeons, 28 assistant surgeons, 15 acting assistant surgeons, 3 hospital stewards, 1 private, and 32 civilians.

The names of 34,479 visitors were registered at the Army Medical Museum during the fiscal year ending June 30, 1881.

Sixty-five negatives and 1,802 photographic prints of surgical objects were made, and 1,026 of them were distributed among correspondents and contributors.

Surgical History of the War of the Rebellion.—One hundred and ten drawings on wood, 96 engravings, and 4 lithographic plates were prepared for Volume II of Part III of the Medical and Surgical History of the War, and 152 pages of this volume were completed, advancing the work from page 382 to page 534, inclusive.

LIBRARY.

Nearly two thousand five hundred volumes, and 3,200 pamphlets have been added to the library during the past year, making the total number about 54,000 volumes, and 60,200 pamphlets.

The publication of Volume II of the Index-Catalogue has been completed, and the edition of 1,500 copies is being distributed. The manuscript of Volume III is now going to press.

An estimate has been forwarded for printing Volume IV of the Catalogue, and it is hoped that the appropriation asked for will be granted, in order that the progress of this important work may not be retarded.

A NEW FIRE-PROOF BUILDING A NECESSITY FOR THE ARMY MEDI-CAL MUSEUM AND LIBRARY.

I would again invite attention to the necessity for a new fire-proof building for the Army Medical Museum and Library, set forth in my last report, and would refer to the following extract from the message of the President to Congress at the commencement of its last session, and request that the subject be again brought to the attention of that body:

The collections of books, specimens, and records constituting the Army Medical Museum and Library are of national importance. The library now contains about 51,500 volumes and 57,000 pamphlets relating to medicine, surgery, and allied topics. The contents of the Army Medical Museum consists of 22,000 specimens, and are unique in the completeness with which both military surgery and the diseases of armies are illustrated. Their destruction would be an irreparable loss, not only to the United States, but to the world. There are filed in the record and pension division, over 16,000 bound volumes of hospital records, together with a great quantity of papers, embracing the original records of the hospitals of our armies during the civil war. Aside from their historical value, these records are daily searched for evidence needed in the settlement of large numbers of pension and other claims, for the protection of the Government against attempted frauds, as well as for the benefit of honest claimants. These valuable collections are now in a building which is peculiarly exposed to the danger of destruction by fire. It is therefore earnestly recommended that an appropriation be made for a new fire-proof building, adequate for the present needs and reasonable future expansion of these valuable collections. Such a building should be absolutely fire-proof; no expenditure for mere architectural display is required. It is believed that a suitable structure can be erected at a cost not to exceed $250,000.

MISCELLANEOUS.

The requirements of the Army as regards medical officers during the past year have been as follows:

Number of permanent posts	152
Number of temporary posts and substations	24
Total	176
Number of military expeditions in the field during the year	17

The services of 34 medical officers were required with these expeditions, and there were also 84 medical officers reported to this office as having been on duty with scouting parties during the year.

The Army Medical Examining Board, convened in New York City on the 7th of November, 1877, for the examination of assistant surgeons for promotion, and of candidates for appointment in the medical corps of the Army, has been continued in session throughout the past year, and since my last report 8 candidates have been found qualified and approved by the board; of whom 4 were appointed and commissioned assistant surgeons, on the 18th of February last, and the names of the remaining 4 have been submitted to the Secretary of War for appointment, and in due time will be presented to the Senate for confirmation.

The following is a recapitulation of the work thus far performed by the Army Medical Examining Board:

Number of assistant surgeons examined for promotion		44
Number of candidates for appointment in the medical corps invited to appear for examination		221
Number of candidates found qualified	29	
Number of candidates rejected	47	
Number of candidates who withdrew after partial examination	107	
Total number examined		183
Number of candidates who failed to appear for examination	17	
Number of candidates who declined to appear for examination	20	
Number of candidates remaining to be examined	1	
Total number invited but not examined		38

At the date of my last report there were 9 vacancies in the medical corps, all of which were in the grade of assistant surgeon. During the past year 1 assistant medical purveyor, with the rank of lieutenant-colonel, 1 surgeon, with the rank of major, 1 assistant surgeon, with the rank of captain, and 1 lieutenant-colonel, retired, have died, and 1 assistant surgeon, with the rank of captain, has resigned; 1 surgeon, with the rank of major, has been promoted to assistant medical purveyor, with the rank of lieutenant-colonel, and 2 assistant surgeons have been promoted to surgeon, with the rank of major; 4 appointments in the grade of assistant surgeons have also been made; leaving 9 vacancies in the medical corps at the present time in the grade of assistant surgeon.

There are at present 13 medical officers on sick leave of absence, 5 of whom have been found incapacitated for active service and recommended for retirement by army retiring boards, and 1 has been recommended to be brought before a retiring board with a view to his retirement from active service; 3 medical officers are on ordinary leave of absence after a tour of duty on the remote frontier; leaving 162 medical officers for duty.

The medical officers who have died during the year are as follows:

Lieut. Col. Richard S. Satterlee (retired), at New York City, November 10, 1880.

Lieut. Col. Geo. E. Cooper, assistant medical purveyor, at San Francisco, Cal., April 13, 1881.

Maj. George A. Otis, surgeon, at Washington, D. C., February 23, 1881.

Capt. John W. Brewer, assistant surgeon, at the Government Hospital for the Insane, November 15, 1880.

Lieut. Col. Richard S. Satterlee, chief medical purveyor (retired), entered the service as an assistant surgeon, February 25, 1822; was promoted to surgeon (with the rank of major), July 13, 1832; appointed lieutenant-colonel and chief medical purveyor, July 28, 1866, and retired from active service, as lieutenant-colonel, February 22, 1869. He was appointed lieutenant-colonel, colonel, and brigadier-general, by brevet, September 2, 1864, for diligent care and attention in procuring proper army supplies as medical purveyor, and for economy and fidelity in the disbursement of large sums of money. He served at Fort Niagara, N. Y., to March, 1823; at Detroit, Mich., to September, 1823; at Fort Howard, Wis., to June, 1825; at Fort Mackinac, Mich., to November, 1831; at Fort Winnebago, Wis., to September, 1833; at Fort Howard, Wis., to October, 1837; in Florida, to May, 1838; with troops removing the Cherokee Indians, to September, 1838; at Plattsburg, N. Y., to November, 1840; in Florida, to August, 1842; at Fort Adams, R. I., to October, 1846; with the Army in Mexico, to June, 1848; at Fort Adams, R. I., to October, 1853; accompanied Third United States Artillery to California, in December, 1853, and was wrecked on board the steamship San Francisco; attending surgeon and medical purveyor at New York City from March, 1854, to July, 1866; chief medical purveyor of the Army and stationed at New York City from July, 1866, to February 21, 1870; having been directed by the President to remain on duty as chief medical purveyor after his retirement from active service.

Dr. Satterlee was born at Fairfield, Herkimer County, New York, December 6, 1799, and entered the service from Michigan. He was on duty for many years among the Indians of the Northwest, where he became a great favorite and rendered important services. During the Seminole

29 Ab

war he was medical director on the staff of General Taylor. During the advance of the Army upon the city of Mexico he served as surgeon-in-chief of General Worth's division, and was mentioned for distinguished services at the battles of Cerro Gordo, Contreras, Churubusco, and especially at the battle of El Molino del Rey. After the occupation of the city of Mexico he became the medical director of the Army, and held that position until peace was declared and the country evacuated. During the War of the Rebellion he was on duty at New York City as the chief medical purveyor of the Army, where his services were of the greatest value. He was a most efficient, faithful, and conscientious officer, as well as a man of the most exemplary character, never losing an opportunity of doing good, and always laboring to promote the welfare of the medical corps of the Army, in which he took the greatest pride and deepest interest.

Lieut. Col. George E. Cooper entered the service as an assistant surgeon August 28, 1847, was promoted to surgeon, with the rank of major, May 21, 1861, and was made assistant medical purveyor, with the rank of lieutenant-colonel, December 2, 1876. He was appointed lieutenant-colonel, by brevet, September 1, 1864, and colonel, by brevet, March 13, 1865, for faithful and meritorious services during the war. He served with the "Army of Invasion" in Mexico from time of appointment to June, 1848; at Jefferson Barracks, Mo., to November, 1848; at Fort Wood, N. Y., to February, 1849; at Eagle Pass (Fort Duncan), Texas, to March, 1853; at Fort Monroe, Va., to May, 1854; with troops en route to New Mexico and at Fort Fillmore, N. Mex., to October, 1859; at Fort Mackinac, Mich., to May, 1861; medical director of the Department of Pennsylvania, to August, 1861; medical purveyor of General T. W. Sherman's expedition, to April, 1862; medical director of the Department of the South, to May, 1862; medical purveyor at Philadelphia, and acting under special instructions of the Secretary of War, to October, 1863; superintendent and inspector of hospitals at Louisville, Ky., to April, 1864; medical director of the Department of the Cumberland, to December, 1865; post surgeon, Fort Monroe, Va., to October, 1870; medical director of the Department of the Columbia, to May, 1874; post surgeon, Benicia Barracks, Cal., to December, 1874; post surgeon, Point San José, Cal., to March, 1877; was assigned to duty at San Francisco under his appointment as assistant medical purveyor, March 13, 1877, on which duty he remained until March 31, 1880, when relieved on account of sickness. Major-General McDowell, commanding the Military Division of the Pacific, in official orders announcing the death of Lieutenant-Colonel Cooper, made the following remarks as to the services of this officer:

Lieutenant-Colonel Cooper served faithfully in the Medical Corps, of which he was a gifted member, for nearly forty years, distinguishing himself in the war with Mexico, and also in the late war for the suppression of the rebellion. His devotion to duty and honesty of purpose commended him to all who knew him, and his loss will be deeply felt, not only by the members of his corps, but by all those who were his military associates.

Maj. George Alexander Otis entered the service as surgeon, Twenty-seventh Massachusetts Volunteers, in September, 1861; was appointed surgeon United States Volunteers, August 30, 1864; assistant surgeon United States Army, February 28, 1866, and was promoted to surgeon, with the rank of major, March 17, 1880; he received the four brevets of lieutenant-colonel of Volunteers, and captain, major, and lieutenant-colonel, United States Army, for meritorious services during the war of the rebellion. While surgeon of the Twenty-seventh Massachusetts Volunteers he served in Virginia, North and South Carolina, on special duty, in charge of the hospital steamer Cosmopolitan, in the Department of the South. He was assigned to duty in this office July 22, 1864, and was curator of the Army Medical Museum and in charge of the division of surgical records until his death. Dr. Otis was born at Boston, Mass., November 12, 1830. He graduated with the degree of A. B. and A. M. from Princeton College, and received his degree of M. D. from the University of Pennsylvania in 1850. He visited Europe, prosecuted his professional studies in London and Paris, and returning thence established himself in Springfield, Mass. He was a member of the leading medical societies of America, and corresponding member of similar societies in Europe. With personal observations of the surgical collections abroad, Surgeon Otis brought indefatigable industry and untiring energy to the development of the surgical and anatomical collections of the Army Medical Museum. The compilation of the Surgical Volume of the Medical and Surgical History of the War of the Rebellion has placed him among the most prominent contributors to surgical history, and his death will be deeply deplored, not only by the Medical Corps of the Army, but by the whole medical profession at home and abroad, and which has been evinced, in a measure, by the eulogistic remarks concerning him made during the recent meeting of the International Medical Congress in London.

Capt. John W. Brewer was appointed assistant surgeon November 22, 1862. During the war he was on duty as assistant medical purveyor at Memphis and with the Army operating in the Southwest; since the war he has been stationed at various posts in the Indian Territory and on the Western frontiers. He was appointed major, by brevet, March 13, 1865, for faithful and meritorious services during the war.

JOS. K. BARNES,
Surgeon-General, U. S. A.

REPORT OF THE PAYMASTER-GENERAL.

WAR DEPARTMENT, PAYMASTER-GENERAL'S OFFICE,
Washington, October 10, 1881.

SIR: In compliance with circular letter from your office of September 16, 1881, I have the honor to inclose my annual report to the Secretary of War, with a synopsis of the same.

Very respectfully, your obedient servant,

N. W. BROWN,
Paymaster-General, U. S. A.

The ADJUTANT-GENERAL *of the Army.*

[First indorsement.]

ADJUTANT-GENERAL'S OFFICE,
Washington, October 11, 1881.

Respectfully submitted to the Secretary of War.

C. McKEEVER,
Acting Adjutant-General.

WAR DEPARTMENT, PAYMASTER-GENERAL'S OFFICE,
Washington, October 10, 1881.

SIR: I have the honor to submit my annual report of the transactions of the Pay Department of the Army, for the fiscal year ending June 30, 1881.

Tabular statements herewith inclosed show in detail the fiscal operations of the department for that year, summarily stated as follows, viz:

RECEIPTS AND DISBURSEMENTS DURING THE FISCAL YEAR ENDING JUNE 30, 1881.

Balance in hands of paymasters July 1, 1880	$1,379,338 15
Amount received from Treasury	13,292,306 52
Amount received from soldiers' deposits	524,112 72
Amount received from paymasters' collections	435,210 41
Total to be accounted for	15,630,967 80

Accounted for as follows:

Disbursements:

To Regular Army	$12,966,200 09	
To Military Academy	190,259 07	
To volunteers, claims of freedmen, &c., on Treasury certificates	570,000 99	
	13,726,460 15	
Surplus funds deposited in Treasury	121,178 82	
Paymasters' collections deposited in Treasury	434,403 43	
Balance in hands of paymasters June 30, 1881	1,348,925 40	
Total accounted for	$15,630,967 80	

All the requirements of law have, I believe, been faithfully executed, and the Army has been regularly and promptly paid to the close of the year.

The amount received during the year from soldiers' deposits will be seen to be $524,112.72. The amount received for the previous year was $477,174.44, an increase of $46,938.28.

I again respectfully invite attention to the subject of pay to officers of the Army while on leave of absence.

The laws in reference to leaves of absence were passed, severally, on March 3, 1863; June 20, 1864; May 8, 1874; and July 29, 1876. The two latter acts are modifications of the former. Under these laws an officer can receive a leave of absence of thirty days each year—not to be cumulated more than four years—on full pay, and for any time in excess of that he is reduced to *half pay.*

It is considered that the first two laws above cited were enacted as *war measures,* and their effect was no doubt salutary among the large number of new and undisciplined officers gathered from the various walks of life; but the time has fully come, in my judgment, when they should be done away with. Their operation is harsh and very unequal. Very many of the officers are stationed at remote posts in the West, and when a leave is obtained the whole, or a large portion, of the thirty days is often necessarily consumed in travel to any of the Atlantic cities—where most of the officers desire to go—and in returning to their posts.

For any excess of thirty days they are reduced to *half pay,* and this, with the expense attending the journey, is very onerous to them. I therefore respectfully recommend that Congress be asked at the approaching regular session to repeal the laws in question. The extent to which leaves should be granted may safely be left to the recommendation of the department and division commanders and the General of the Army, and the decision of the Secretary of War.

The appropriation act now limits the number of paymasters' clerks to fifty-four. It often happens that the services of additional clerks are much needed in order to prevent delay and injury to public creditors.

I would therefore recommend that the number be increased to fifty-six, the two additional ones to be employed by the Paymaster-General, subject to the approbation of the Secretary of War, as in the case of other paymasters' clerks.

In this connection, I beg again to call attention to the inadequate compensation now allowed these clerks, whose duties are important and responsible, requiring an intimate knowledge of figures and considerable business capacity, and often necessitating long and toilsome journeys and exposure to danger. I therefore recommend that Congress be requested to repeal so much of section 1190, Revised Statutes of the United States, as fixes the compensation of paymasters' clerks, and provide that hereafter said clerks shall be classified and compensation regulated in the same manner as "civilian employés" in the other staff departments of the Army.

I would again urge the necessity of consolidating the appropriations for the pay of the Army, mileage, and general expenses under one title. The amounts to be disbursed under the above titles are, with two or three exceptions, limited by statute law. If the appropriation is in excess of these demands the excess cannot be disbursed, but will be carried by operation of law to the surplus fund, but if the appropriation is not sufficient to meet the demands the excess becomes a valid claim against the United States, and the subject of a deficiency estimate, thus forcing a very worthy class of claimants to a delay that is oftentimes very embarrassing. The interests of the service or economy in expenditures do not therefore demand the separation, while on the other hand there are good reasons for consolidation. Many of the items are estimated upon expenditures of prior years—the best data obtainable. This estimate may be in some cases excessive and in others not sufficient, but in the aggregate the amount appropriated will be sufficient to meet all demands, if the excess in one of them can be used to supply the deficiency in another; and thus a matron in a hospital will not be obliged to go without her pay until Congress meets and makes an appropriation for that purpose, while there is more than sufficient funds to pay the soldier whom she nurses. Again, the division of the appropriations into three heads, for each year, makes it necessary to keep in the hands of each disbursing officer a balance of funds much larger than if there were but one appropriation for each year, as he is obliged to carry a working balance under each appropriation. This, in the case of a limited appropriation, makes it very difficult to properly distribute the funds over so scattered a field as that occupied by paymasters.

Attention is invited to the report of Maj. A. B. Carey, paymaster, U. S. A., hereto appended, under whose immediate charge the payment of claims for bounty, arrears of pay, prize-money, &c., due soldiers, both white and colored, has been made, from which it will be seen that the payments devolved upon this bureau by the act of March 3, 1879, have been prompt, satisfactory, and economical.

The system of identification of claimants and placing the money in their hands seems as perfect as it can be made, and I have no change to recommend.

I am, sir, very respectfully, your obedient servant,

N. W. BROWN,
Paymaster-General, U. S. Army.

The Hon. the SECRETARY OF WAR.

WAR DEPARTMENT, PAYMASTER-GENERAL'S OFFICE,
BOUNTY DIVISION,
Washington, D. C., September 30, 1881.

SIR: In compliance with your instructions, I have the honor to submit the following report for the fiscal year ending June 30, 1881, relative to the payment of claims for bounty, arrears of pay, prize-money, &c., due colored soldiers, sailors, and marines, or their heirs, under joint resolution of Congress of March 29, 1867, and section 2 of an "act making appropriations for sundry civil expenses of the government for the fiscal year ending June 30, 1880, and for other purposes, approved March 3, 1879."

July 1, 1880, there remained in my hands 328 claims received from the Freedman's branch of the Adjutant-General's Office, aggregating $33,773.78; of these, 23 were paid, aggregating $2,430.46, leaving on hand June 30, 1881, 305 of these *old claims*, and 31,343.32 for their payment.

There also remained in my hands at that date, 79 Treasury certificates adjusted under the act of March 3, 1879, aggregating $7,928.94.

During the fiscal year, 2,209 Treasury certificates were received from the Second Auditor, making a total of 2,288, aggregating $203,945.58. Of these, 1,936, aggregating $159,621.93, were paid, leaving on hand June 30, 1881, 352 certificates and $44,323.65 for their payment.

All claims were prepared for payment in this office, and payments made as follows:

Maj. W. B. Rochester	12 claims, aggregating	$1,354 97
Maj. N. Vedder	66 claims, aggregating	7,774 14
Maj. G. W. Candee	493 claims, aggregating	72,548 85
Maj. A. B. Carey	1,388 claims, aggregating	80,374 43
Total	1,959 claims, aggregating	$162,052 59

One hundred and forty-nine claims, aggregating $15,503.80 were paid through the Post-Office Department by post-office money orders since March 3, 1881, the date on which the appropriation for the expense of these payments became available.

The total expense of all these payments during the year was $3,275.56, of which $1,950.05 was from the appropriation for the support of the Army for the fiscal year ending June 30, 1881, and $1,325.51 from the $5,595.02 appropriated by the act of March 3, 1881, which left a balance of $4,270.51 available for the fiscal year ending June 30, 1882.

The cost to the government in paying these claims for the last fiscal year was a trifle over 2 per cent. of the amount disbursed, or $1.67 for each claim paid.

In addition to the claims of colored soldiers paid as above, there has been paid from this office, by check, to white claimants, 3,925 Treasury certificates; aggregating $432,506.05.

Very respectfully, your obedient servant,

A. B. CAREY,
Paymaster, U. S. A.

Brig. Gen. N. W. BROWN,
Paymaster-General, U. S. Army.

REPORT OF PUBLICATION OF WAR RECORDS.

WAR DEPARTMENT, WAR RECORDS OFFICE,
Washington, D. C., October 12, 1881.

To the SECRETARY OF WAR:

SIR: I have the honor to report progress in the publication of the military records of the War of the Rebellion.

The examination of the files for 1861, 1862, and 1863, both Union and Confederate, and of the files of the Union Armies for 1864 and 1865, has been completed, and the necessary copying from them is nearly finished. Many of the Confederate files for 1864 and 1865 have also been examined. A few of the book records for 1863 and most of those for later years, of both armies, are yet to be searched.

The War Department agent for the collection (by gift or loan) of Confederate documents continues to be successful in obtaining valuable records from Confederate officers or their heirs. The more extensive contributions of that nature received since my last report have been from the collections of Generals E. P. Alexander, S. G. French, Johnson Hagood, Bradley T. Johnson, James H. Lane, T. T. Munford, J. C. Tappan, E. C. Walthall, and W. H. C. Whiting, and Colonels I. W. Avery and Charles Marshall.

The "Polk Papers" have been donated to the Government by Dr. William M. Polk, now of New York City.

By the act of June 16, 1880, Congress authorized the publication of 10,000 copies of each volume of the records that might be ready during the fiscal year ending June 30, 1881. Under that act seven volumes— five of Series 1 and one each of Series III and IV—were sent to the Public Printer. Of Series I, Vols. I and II have been given to the public. Vol. III, so far as this office is concerned, has been completed, and it will doubtless be delivered by the Public Printer before Congress assembles. The text of Vols. IV and V has been stereotyped and they are being indexed. The text of Vols. I, Series III and IV, has also been stereotyped.

Under the current appropriation Vols. VI and VII of Series I have been sent to the Public Printer; Vols. VIII, IX, and X are ready for him, and Vols. XI to XVI will be arranged during the current fiscal year. With proper regard for accuracy the volumes cannot be published more rapidly until the examination of the records is completed.

The contents of Vols. I to XI, Series I, are as follows:

VOLUME I.

Chapter I. Operations in Charleston Harbor, South Carolina. December 20, 1860–April 14, 1861.

Chapter II. The secession of Georgia. January 3–26, 1861.

Chapter III. The secession of Alabama and Mississippi. January 4–20, 1861.

Chapter IV. Operations in Florida. January 6–August 31, 1861.

Chapter V. The secession of North Carolina. January 9–May 20, 1861.

Chapter VI. The secession of Louisiana. January 10–February 19, 1861.

Chapter VII. Operations in Texas and New Mexico. February 1–June 11, 1861.

Chapter. VIII. Operations in Arkansas, the Indian Territory, and Missouri. February 7–May 9, 1861.

VOLUME II.

Chapter IX. Operations in Maryland, Pennsylvania, Virginia, and West Virginia. April 16–July 31, 1861.

VOLUME III.

Chapter X. Operations in Missouri, Arkansas, Kansas, and Indian Territory. May 10–November 19, 1861.

VOLUME IV.

Chapter XI. Operations in Texas, New Mexico, and Arizona. June 11, 1861–February 1, 1862.

Chapter XII. Operations in Kentucky and Tennessee. July 1–November 19, 1861.

Chapter XIII. Operations in North Carolina and Southeastern Virginia. August 1, 1861–January 11, 1862.

Messrs. Kirkley, of the Adjutant-General's Office, and Tasker, of the War Department, continue to render zealous and most valuable assistance to the work under my charge. In so doing they perform much extra labor, for which, in my judgment, they should receive extra compensation.

Very respectfully, your obedient servant,

ROBERT N. SCOTT,
Brevet Lieutenant-Colonel, U. S. A.

REPORT ON MILITARY PRISON, FORT LEAVENWORTH, KANSAS.

GOVERNOR'S OFFICE,
UNITED STATES MILITARY PRISON,
Fort Leavenworth, Kans., July 21, 1881.

To the ADJUTANT-GENERAL, UNITED STATES ARMY,
Washington, D. C.:

(Through headquarters Department of the Missouri, Fort Leavenworth, Kans.)

SIR: I have the honor to transmit herewith annual reports of the quartermaster, surgeon, and chaplain connected with the prison for the fiscal year ending June 30, 1881. I also inclose a tabular statement of labor performed, prisoners received, discharged, &c.

During the past year improvements have been made in and near the prison as exhibited by the following details:

Cottage quarters No. 6, three rooms, each 16 by 16 feet, one story, frame. South extension of shop building, first and second story, 24 by 46 feet, brick, and slate roof. A stable connected with the quarters for quartermaster's clerks, 16 by 36 feet, one and one-half story, frame.

An addition of one room, 12 by 16 feet, to quarters occupied by the prison farmer. There was also built 1,620 lineal feet of board fence around cottage quarters; and nearly two miles of fencing inclosing the prison farm, and which was destroyed by high water, was rebuilt of old material.

An additional set of cottage quarters, No. 7, of four rooms, each 16 by 16 feet, was erected, and is nearly completed.

A new floor of hard pine was laid on the first floor of prison building No. 2, dimensions 37 by 97 feet.

There has been built 186 feet of prison wall, completing the girth of the prison, making a total of 2,022 feet; 381$\frac{7}{12}$ feet of coping has been laid thereon.

Work in the shops has progressed very favorably, the only difficulty experienced being in the first quarter, owing to the failure of the Quartermaster's Department to furnish stock in time for the manufacture of boots and shoes, which caused a loss of 23$\frac{1}{2}$ days' labor in that department.

During the year there have been manufactured 34,163 pairs of boots, b. s.; 25,944 pairs of shoes, b. s.; 4,356 corn brooms; 1,656 barrack chairs; 110 chair arms; 110 chair rungs; 220 chair bolts; 1,623 packing boxes for boots, shoes, and harness; and 80 crates for packing chairs. Also 100 complete sets of 4-mule ambulance harness, and 75 complete sets of 6-mule Army-wagon harness.

Besides the above-enumerated articles, all doors, sash, &c., as well as the necessary repairs to buildings, &c., were made by prison labor. During the year there has been 2,970 bushels of lime burned and used in the building of wall, prison-building extension, sanitary purposes, &c.

In the shoe-shop care has been taken to save all scrap leather, and during the year there has been sold 48,713 pounds, realizing the sum of $2,150.77, which amount has been turned into the United States Treasury on account of miscellaneous receipts.

During the past year the prison farm has yielded 2,600 bushels of potatoes, 400 bushels of turnips, 3,900 heads of cabbage, 700 bushels of corn, 176 bushels of onions, 650 bushels of tomatoes, and a quantity of other vegetables for immediate consumption.

This year we have under cultivation about 50 acres, planted as follows: 29 acres in potatoes, 12 acres in corn, 3 acres in tomatoes, and 6 acres with a variety of vegetables, such as onions, beets, carrots, parsnips, &c.

Owing to the backwardness of the season, and the overflow of the Missouri River (which inundated the entire farm), the crops will not be as large as last year, and will be late on account of having to be replanted.

The fund of prison earnings has not been increased during the fiscal year, and the sum of $6,730.42 still remains deposited in the First National Bank, Leavenworth, Kans.

The work performed for the Quartermaster's Department during the past year has been as follows: 30,241 days' skilled labor, 19,524 days' unskilled labor.

The following will show the disbursements of funds appropriated for the support of the prison for the fiscal year:

Appropriated		$35,910 80
Expended:		
For subsistence of prisoners	$15,616 50	
For mess savings	2,913 22	
For lard oil and wicking	1,174 37	
For fuel	8,182 79	
For clothing for prisoners in shops	317 17	
For advertising for proposals	32 00	
For hay for bedding	216 58	
For stationery	224 67	
For stores, and miscellaneous stores, drainage, disinfectants, &c.	612 39	
For hats for prisoners at discharge	171 00	
For clothing for prisoners at discharge	738 72	
For donations at discharge	1,275 00	
For apprehension of escaped prisoners	240 00	
For straw hats for prisoners during summer	31 90	
For hose, tools, materials, &c., for use in shops, repair of transportation, cleaning and repair of machinery	3,857 46	
For tobacco for prisoners	399 77	
For pay of foremen, mechanics, and watchmen	7,867 50	
For pay of teamsters	1,800 00	
For pay of clerks	3,199 92	
For extra-duty pay of guard	486 00	
For paving-brick and stone for coping of wall	1,280 44	
For extension and repair of building	4,226 15	
For medical supplies	1,047 25	
		55,910 80

I wish to call attention to the fact that a considerable portion of the appropriation has been expended in permanent improvements, extension of buildings, &c.

The conduct of the prisoners has, on the whole, been very good, but few refractory cases, necessitating severe disciplinary measures, occurring.

Sixteen prisoners escaped; ten were recaptured, making a loss of six. The last three prisoners escaping from here did so while being guarded by a detachment of the Nineteenth Infantry.

The health of the institution, as shown by the inclosed report of the surgeon, has also been very good, considering the crowded condition of the dormitories, but three deaths occurring during the year, one of which was a prisoner, and two enlisted men—Hospital Steward Hartford T. Clarke, U. S. A., and Private Henry Rottmayer, provost guard, general service, U. S. A.; cause, pulmonary consumption and acute dysentery.

I desire to take this opportunity to acknowledge my sincere thanks to the department commander for his kind encouragement and substantial support which he has extended to me during the past year, and I am sure that whatever success has attended my labors here has been largely due to the aid he has given me in the performance of my duties.

It is also gratifying to me to acknowledge my obligations to the different officers on duty at the prison for the manifest interest they have taken in the performance of their arduous duties, their hearty co-operation, and exemplary conduct.

I am, sir, very respectfully, your obedient servant,

A. P. BLUNT,
Brevet Colonel, U. S. Army, Governor.

REPORT OF THE BOARD OF COMMISSIONERS OF THE SOLDIERS' HOME.

WASHINGTON, D. C., *November* 3, 1881.

To the Hon. SECRETARY OF WAR:

SIR: In obedience to a requirement of the regulations for the Soldiers' Home, I have the honor to submit the following report for the year ending September 30, 1881:

The commissioners have visited the Home and audited the accounts of the treasurer regularly, as required by law.

No additions have been made to the property by purchase or building during the year, and no expenses have been incurred except such as were necessary for the support of the inmates and the improvement or preservation of the buildings and grounds.

The management has been satisfactory and the duties devolving upon the officers have been properly performed. These duties have been during the past year probably more regular and routine in character, because of the absence of any of the special work in building and other new improvements which has demanded attention in previous years, but they have been nevertheless none the less important and responsible. The admissions of inmates have increased in number and the attention and care required have increased in proportion. This is particularly manifest in the matter of maintaining proper discipline. In the last annual report the fact was stated that pensioners who have contributed to the funds of the Home by the payment of twelve and one-half cents a month during their service in the Army now receive their pensions, instead of relinquishing them to the Home while they receive its benefits. In addition to the current payments on this account to pensioners, a great majority have had refunded to them by the United States a sum equal to their accrued pensions for a period of about four years. This money has been the means of bringing much damage to its possessors and much discredit upon the institution in which they have been kept. Many of them have either voluntarily forfeited their rights or have lost them as subjects of discipline, and have become burdens upon communities, in which the "Soldiers' Home" is judged according to the apparent evidences of neglect they witness in their midst. While inmates receive money in any considerable sums there will be no remedy for this state of things, and the strong measures adopted to restrain those who waste their means for intoxicating liquor will continue to be a hardship to those who are peaceable and well disposed.

In procuring the supplies for daily consumption the regulations governing purchases for the Army are observed as far as practicable. An abundance of good food well prepared and a sufficient supply of comfortable clothing are furnished. Each inmate has a single bed and is provided with a locker for his personal property and apparel. The rooms are kept perfectly clean and well ventilated, and the conveniences for all natural wants are as complete as circumstances will permit. All have access to a good library, and the current periodicals are regularly received. One of the inmates is employed to read for those who cannot read for themselves. The sick and infirm are cared for in a well-appointed hospital under the charge of an experienced medical officer.

Farming operations have been confined mainly to the production of fruits and vegetables, of which a good supply is raised, though not sufficient in quantity of the latter, and the deficiency is made up by purchase.

The officers of the Home who were relieved by the present detail at the close of the last fiscal year completed a most satisfactory tour of duty in their respective positions, and it is with gratification that this record of commendation is made.

The officers now on duty are:

Col. Samuel D. Sturgis, Seventh Cavalry (brevet major-general), governor.

Lieut. Col. John S. Mason, Twentieth Infantry (brevet brigadier-general) deputy governor.

Capt. Jonathan D. Stevenson, Eighth Cavalry, secretary and treasurer.

Assist. Surg. Calvin DeWitt, attending surgeon.

The officers relieved are:

Col. Joseph H. Potter, Twenty-fourth Infantry (brevet brigadier-general), as governor.

Maj. Milton Cogswell (brevet colonel, retired), as deputy governor.

Maj. Joseph H. Whittlesey (retired), as secretary and treasurer.

Surgeon David L. Huntington, as attending surgeon.

The register of inmates shows that during the year there were:

Receiving the benefits of the Home September 30, 1880	550
Admitted between October 1, 1880, and September 30, 1881:	
Regular	153
Temporary	68
Readmitted	77
	848
Dropped by voluntary withdrawal, for absence without leave, &c.:	
Regular	120
Temporary	66
Dismissed, regular	10
Died, temporary	1
Died:	
Regular	43
Temporary	3
Suspended	17
	260
Receiving the benefits September 30, 1881	588

Included in the 68 men temporarily admitted are 37 who were received as soldiers entitled to become inmates, and who were regularly admitted on receiving their discharges from the Army.

I have the honor to be, sir, very respectfully, your obedient servant,

J. K. BARNES,
Surgeon-General, U. S. Army,
President of the Board of Commissioners.

REPORT ON CONSTRUCTION OF THE STATE, WAR, AND
NAVY DEPARTMENT BUILDING, 1881.

OFFICE OF BUILDING FOR STATE, WAR,
AND NAVY DEPARTMENTS, OLD BUILDING,
NAVY DEPARTMENT, SEVENTEENTH STREET,
Washington, D. C., July 1, 1881.

SIR: I have the honor to submit the following report of operations
pertaining to the construction of the building for State, War, and Navy
Departments, in my charge, for the fiscal year ending June 30, 1881:

The east wing of the building having been entirely completed during
the last fiscal year, operations were confined exclusively to the north
wing. At the close of the year ending June 30, 1880, as shown by the
last annual report, the work, which had been proceeding slowly for some
weeks for want of funds, was nearly suspended, and the supply of materials practically exhausted.

An appropriation of $450,000 for the north wing was made by act of
Congress approved June 16, 1880, but owing to the facts that much of
the material required, consisting of manufactured iron and cut granite,
could not be contracted for until funds were available; that considerable
time was necessarily consumed in the preparation of those materials,
and that the iron-work was the first needed before the work could go on,
operations on the building could not be resumed with any vigor until
September 23, 1880. Even then, but few parts of the work could be
carried on simultaneously, as it was necessary to complete some floors
and interior walls to enable the derricks to be raised into advanced
positions for the handling of the stone.

After two or three weeks, however, the work moved along with system, and good progress was made up to November 22 with both the stone
and brick masonry, including the combined iron-work. At this time
freezing weather set in, which suspended the masonry for some days,
and, with the exception of one or two weeks of mild weather suitable
for laying masonry, was succeeded by one of the severest winters of this
latitude, effectually closing, on the 20th of December, all operations upon
the building.

The object of pushing the masonry work so late in the season was to
fit the building for the iron-work of the roof, for which the contractors
had prepared much of the material, expecting, according to the terms of
their contract, to erect it during the winter. The weather, however,
rendered all such out-door work impracticable, and it was necessarily
deferred until spring.

On February 23, 1881, the last of the stone for the court-yard walls of
this wing arrived at the building.

On March 28, 1881, the weather having become well settled, operations were resumed; but some loss of time was still suffered in the early
part of April from unfavorable weather.

On May 4, the erection of the iron-work of the roof was commenced,
and has progressed rapidly ever since. Being necessarily a complicated
structure, due to the architectural form of this wing of the building, considerable time, some three months, will be consumed in its construction.

On June 11, 1881, the last cut stones for this wing, being the last
stones wanted for the wing, exclusive of the approaches, were delivered
at the building, and the work of setting the granite masonry was completed on the 25th of that month.

At the close of the fiscal year the condition of the work is as follows:

The approaches have not been commenced, but, exclusive of this work, all the stone masonry is finished, and the same is practically true of the brick-work, only a piece of wall and floor in the attic and the backing of the mansards now remaining to be done.

The iron-work of all the roof excepting the part covering the center pavilion, which is in process of erection, is finished and ready to receive its covering of concrete, cement, and copper, and the slating of the mansards. The latter work was commenced on the 27th of June last, and is now in progress.

Throughout the interior of the building, all the walls, openings, brick-arched floors, and stairway wells are complete and ready for the cast-iron finish for doors and windows, and also for the granite stairways and heating apparatus to be put in place. Contracts for the prepared materials for all of these classes of work have been made, and the materials are to be delivered after July 1, 1881, when the new appropriation becomes available.

The following contracts were entered into and in force during the year:

Date of contract.	Subject of contract.	Contractor.	Amount.	Present condition.
1880.				
Mar. 19	Cement	J. G. & J. M. Waters	83 cents per barrel.	Completed.
Apl. 10	Sand	John B. Lord	75 cents per cubic yd	Do.
June 18	Cut granite for third story front.	Albert Ordway	$130,000	Do.
18	Cut granite to complete court-yard wall.	Bodwell Granite Company.	$17,000	Do.
July 2	Bricks	Washington Brick Machine Company.	$6.43 per M.	Do.
7	Cut granite to complete fourth and attic stories.	Albert Ordway	$70,000	Do.
8	Cast-iron columns and pilasters.	J. B. & J. M. Cornell	$7,344	Do.
9	Plate-iron girders	J. B. & J. M. Cornell	3.95 cents per pound	Do.
10	Small iron castings	Geo. White & Co	$712	Do.
10	Cement	J. G. & J. M. Waters	85 cents per barrel	In force.
10	Sand	John B. Lord	70 cents per cubic yd	Do.
15	Rolled-iron beams	J. F Bailey & Co	2.65 cents per pound	Do.
Nov. 5	Iron-work of roof, &c	J. B. & J. M. Cornell	$71,380	Do.
1881.				
May 5	Cut granite for stairways	Concord Granite Company.	$15,984	Do.
9	Boilers, tanks, &c., for heating apparatus.	Bartlett, Hayward & Co.	$7,108	Do.
9	Cast-iron flange pipe, &c., for heating apparatus.	do	$12,448	Do.
9	Fittings, valves, &c., for heating apparatus.	do	$6,698	Do.
10	Cast-iron door and window finish and wash-boards.	Joseph Hall & Co	$47,711 for doors and windows. 65 cents, 90 cents, $1 and $1.50 per ft. of wash-boards.	Do.
June 3	Iron furring, lathing, and partitions	Dwight & Hoyt	$11,567.45 (est.)	Do.
6	Wrought-iron pipe	National Tube Works.	$2,033	In force.
6	Sheet-copper and iron	C. G. Hussy & Co	20 cents, 35⅗ cents, 38⅗ cents, and $1 cents for copper, rivets, and burrs, and 7 cents per pound for iron	Do.
27	Lumber for floors	E. E. Jackson & Co	$45 and $35 per M	Do.

PROBABLE OPERATIONS FOR FISCAL YEAR 1881–'82.

During the months of July, August, and September, 1881, it is expected to introduce and complete the heating and steam apparatus, and to entirely finish the roof of the building.

The placing of the cast-iron frames, casings, and finish for the windows and doors, and the cast-iron wash-boards, will be commenced in July, and completed on January 1, 1882.

The two granite stairways will be built during the autumn of 1881, and at the same time all the fire-proof lathing, light iron partitions, and gas-piping will be put in place.

It is expected that the plastering and stucco work, requiring several months' time in execution, will be commenced on December 1, 1881, and that the plumbing work will be done during the early part of the winter.

During the spring and summer of 1882 it is expected that the floors and tiling and much of the painting will be finished, so that by the fall of 1882 but a comparatively small amount of work, pertaining partially to the painting, decoration, gas-fixtures, elevator, mantels, doors, clearing out, and cleaning down the exterior walls of the building, occupying perhaps two or three months' time, will be required to make the building entirely ready for occupancy.

At that time, however, it is believed that the approaches, if commenced at all, cannot be more than partially finished, owing to want of funds at the present time with which to make the necessary preparations, and the improbability that another appropriation will be made before the middle of the summer of 1882.

STATEMENT OF FUNDS.

Total amount expended to date on north wing	$1,363,786 49
Balance on hand, including new appropriation of $450,000, available this date	514,194 11
New appropriation desired to complete the north wing and approaches.	100,000 00

WEST AND CENTER WINGS.

As no appropriations have been made for those parts of the building, no work has been done looking to the preparation of the materials—a labor requiring much time.

At least a year should be devoted to the collection of the granite for the exterior walls before commencing the foundations. An estimate of $450,000 for these parts of the building is submitted, to be used in the preparation of materials, which sum, if granted, will enable ground to be broken for the foundation in the spring of 1883.

THOS. LINCOLN CASEY,
Lieutenant-Colonel, Corps of Engineers, U. S. A., in charge.
Hon. ROBT. T. LINCOLN,
Secretary of War.

REPORT ON EDUCATION IN THE ARMY.

OFFICE CORNER FOURTH AND ELM,
Saint Louis, Mo., November 1, 1881.
ADJUTANT-GENERAL UNITED STATES ARMY,
Washington, D. C.:

GENERAL: I have the honor to transmit herewith to the honorable Secretary of War my annual report on the subject of education in the Army; also an exhibit of grants obtained, of which I gratefully desire to make honorable mention.

Very respectfully, your obedient servant,
GEO. G. MULLINS,
Chaplain, Twenty-fifth Infantry, in Charge of Education in the Army.

SAINT LOUIS, MO., *November* 1, 1881.

The honorable the SECRETARY OF WAR,

Washington, D. C.:

(Through the Adjutant-General of U. S. Army.)

SIR: I have the honor to render my annual report on the subject of education in the Army.

'Since assuming charge of this work most of my time has been devoted to gathering data and information from reports and by informal correspondence with officers throughout the Army, so that I might understand the actual condition and need of the Army. The work is as yet in chaos, and no great progress has been made; but we have made a beginning which promises, through intelligent method and persistent toil, to lead to a noble success in the future.

A large number of officers have evinced a lively interest in the subject, and have been very kind and helpful in giving valuable information and suggestions.

The opinion is entertained that through this educational enterprise the enlisted man may at last be given that incentive and diversion so long and generally felt to be a pleading necessity in time of peace.

As to the number of buildings constructed during the current year for school and religious purposes I have not been advised; and am unable to state how many posts are still without suitable buildings for such purposes.

Thirty-eight posts report "no facilities for school."

The reading-rooms established in most of the posts, and supplied with reading matter by the Quartermaster-General's Department and by generous contributions from various benevolent societies, have already become a very pronounced success, and are popular both with officers and enlisted men. The approximate average daily attendance of enlisted men upon the reading-rooms has been 4,800.

The following is an exhibit of the average number of pupils who attended the schools in operation at the military posts during the year:

Enlisted men	912
Children of—	
Enlisted men	850
Officers	224
Civilians	316
Total average number	2,302

I find that there is a great want of libraries in the Army. Very few posts have good libraries; many have none at all; some not even an unabridged dictionary.

Inasmuch as the recognized libraries now are post libraries, and are fixtures at the posts, it is respectfully recommended that some arrangement be made whereby the few existing regimental libraries may be purchased for the posts.

I have the honor to call the attention of the Hon. Secretary of War to the difficulties met with in the effort to supply competent teachers for the post schools from the enlisted men of the Army. A soldier detailed for teacher in the post school now receives only thirty-five cents per diem extra pay, and is subject to all military duty (garrison or field), or such duties as may be prescribed by his post commander; and we have numerous instances where the teachers have been taken out of the schools and sent to the field with their companies, in which case the schools were broken up. This necessarily causes much inconvenience, loss of time, and almost destroys the interest which should characterize the subject of education in the Army.

While we have law for the establishment of schools, we have not adequate means provided to fulfill the evident intention of the law. There should be a distinct class of enlisted men for teachers, and an annual appropriation for the purchase by wholesale of books and school supplies.

It is respectfully and earnestly recommended that a law be passed by Congress authorizing the enlistment into the Army of the United States of one hundred and fifty young men to be rated as schoolmasters, with the rank and pay of commissary sergeant.

A mighty forward impulse would be given to the schools could the standard of attainments necessary for the non-commissioned officer be elevated; and it is respectfully recommended that a standard of education for non-commissioned officers be adopted, and then that all corporals and sergeants be compelled to attend school until educated up to that standard, or be required to show certificates witnessing that they have passed a satisfactory examination upon the prescribed standard.

I have been surprised to find that there are some sergeants who can neither read nor write; many non-commissioned officers who can do but little more.

The advanced science and art of modern warfare surely demands a higher standard, since the requisite quick intelligence and sound judgment cannot be expected, as a rule, of the ignorant.

My observation and study incline me to think that the companies and troops in which men are discontented, which have largest number of cases before general and garrison courts-martial, and from which there are most frequent desertions, will be found to be companies and troops which are afflicted with the most ignorant non-commissioned officers.

I am well advised that the majority of the superior officers of the Army would favor the adoption of some standard which would insure a higher order of non-commissioned officers, and the latter would be well pleased with the consequent increased dignity and honor of their very honorable and important position.

I am sir, very respectfully, your obedient servant,

GEO. G. MULLINS,
Chaplain, Twenty-fifth Infantry, in Charge of Education in the Army.

B.—*Grants of books and reading matter obtained and distributed to the Army by Chaplain G. G. Mullins since January 1, 1881.*

From American Bible Society, New York, through Dr. Alex. McLean, 5,100 Bibles and Testaments.

From American Tract Society, New York, 1,000 hymn and tune books; 150 copies Volksfreund; 50 copies Illustrated Christian Weekly; 100 copies American Messenger; 100 copies Morning Light; 100 copies Botschafter; 250 copies Child's Paper; 250 copies Apples of Gold; 2,000 copies tracts.

From leading publishers in United States, 300 volumes miscellaneous works.

From National Temperance Society, 2,000 tracts, 200 song-books.

From American Baptist Publishing Society, 100 Sunday-school books.

From Methodist Book Concern, New York, 300 Sunday-school books.

From Young Men's Christian Association of New York City, 600 papers and magazines each week, on which they pay $350 annual postage.

From Harlem Branch Young Men's Christian Association, 100 papers a week.

From unknown friend to cause of Christ and humanity, $500; expended in books, papers, and charts for Sunday schools in the Army.

GEO. G. MULLINS,
Chaplain, in Charge of Education in the Army.

30 Ab

RRPORT OF THE CHIEF OF ORDNANCE.

WAR DEPARTMENT, ORDNANCE OFFICE,
Washington, October 1, 1881.

SIR : I have the honor to submit the following report of the principal operations of the Ordnance Department during the fiscal year ended June 30, 1881, with such remarks and recommendations as the interests of this branch of the military service seem to require.

The fiscal resources and expenditures of the department during the year were as follows, viz:

Amount in the Treasury to the credit of appropriations on June 30, 1880.	$154,544 10
Amount in the Treasury not reported to the credit of appropriations on June 30, 1880......	7,155 44
Amount in government depositories to the credit of disbursing officers and others on June 30, 1880	135,996 13
Amount of appropriations for the service of the fiscal year ended June 30, 1881......	1,840,696 94
Amount refunded to ordnance appropriations in settling accounts during the fiscal year ended June 30, 1881......	6,769 09
Gross amount received during the fiscal year ended June 30, 1881, from sales to officers; from rents; from collections from troops on account of losses of, or damages to, ordnance stores; from Chicago, Rock Island and Pacific Railroad Company; from exchange of powder; from sales of condemned stores; and from all other sources not before mentioned.	138,286 83
Total	2,283,447 76

Amount of expenditures during the fiscal year ended June 30, 1881, including expenses attending sales of condemned stores, exchange of powder, &c.	$1,637,593 79
Amount deposited in Treasury during the fiscal year ended June 30, 1881, as proceeds of sales of government property	64,306 55
Amount lapsed into the Treasury from the appropriation "Ordnance material," under act of March 3, 1875, during the fiscal year ended June 30, 1881......	2 80
Amount turned into the "surplus fund" on June 30, 1881	3,042 75
Amount in government depositories to the credit of disbursing officers and others on June 30, 1881......	175,278 54
Amounts transferred from ordnance appropriations in settling accounts during the fiscal year ended June 30, 1881......	376 37
Amount in the Treasury not reported to the credit of appropriations on June 30, 1881......	2,658 85
Amount in the Treasury to the credit of appropriations on June 30, 1881.	400,186 11
Total	2,283,447 76

STATIONS AND DUTIES.

The stations and duties of the officers remain about the same as reported last year, viz: two at the Ordnance Office, twenty-nine at the arsenals, armory, and powder depots; nine at the ordnance agency, on the Ordnance Board, and at the foundries; seven at the different military headquarters and ordnance depots; four at the Military Academy; two under the orders of the Honorable Secretary of the Interior; and two on leave of absence (sick). Captains Dutton and Pitman have, on application of the Secretary of the Interior, been detailed for duty in that department, and Lieutenant Lyle still continues on duty in the Life-Saving Service, under the Secretary of the Treasury. Under the operations of existing laws, two officers have been transferred to the department from the line of the Army, after passing satisfactory examinations preliminary thereto.

The recent death of Col. J. G. Benton, commanding the National

Armory, has cast a gloom over the entire department. He was an officer of marked distinction, of the greatest professional attainments, with a public record without blemish, and a private life pure and noble. His death is a national loss. He gave to his country forty years of laborious and most valuable service, and has left a name and a memory that will be cherished by all lovers of the good and the true.

In the Revised Statutes are found the laws that fix the duties and responsibilities of the Ordnance Department. It provides armament for our extended sea-coast defenses, and arms and ordnance stores for the Army in all its branches, for the militia of the States and Territories, the Marine Corps of the Navy, all other governmental departments, when necessary to protect public money and property, and the thirty colleges authorized to receive arms for instruction. This is the mere supplying of the finished product. Its gravest responsibilities lie in the determination of the best war material, after long and close study and experiment, and its production of the best quality and workmanship. That the department has been fairly successful in its labors and operations, I cheerfully leave to the Army to decide.

Rock Island Arsenal.—The report of the commanding officer is herewith submitted. The erection of the workshops has been prosecuted with all expedition and economy.

Benicia Arsenal.—The appropriation made last session not being sufficient for the construction of the necessary workshops, work upon them has been postponed until Congress takes action on the estimate submitted. The necessity for the additional appropriation is most urgent, in view of the fact that Benicia is the only manufacturing arsenal on the Pacific coast, and should possess all the facilities and appliances to make it independent of our government workshops east of the Mississippi River.

Piccatinny Powder Depot.—The interesting report of the officer in command is herewith submitted, with the hope that Congress will make liberal appropriations for this important establishment. Railroad facilities are absolutely essential to the economical and successful carrying out of the plans adopted, and to connect with the railroad system for prompt and rapid transportation of gunpowder.

San Antonio Arsenal.—Estimates have been submitted for the necessary buildings at this arsenal. It supplies the entire Texas frontier, and its capacity for storage and repairs should be greatly enlarged. Most of the buildings are old and worthless, and should be at once replaced.

Frankford Arsenal.—The report of its operations is submitted. As it is the government cartridge factory, the arsenal should be kept in the best condition. The wall on the creek and river needs renovating, and an appropriation should be made.

Testing Machine at Watertown Arsenal.—The report of the commanding officer will be submitted for transmission to Congress.

SMALL-ARMS.

During the fiscal year ending June 30, 1881, there were manufactured at the National Armory 26,528 rifles and carbines. Much miscellaneous work in repairs of arms, spare parts, &c., was done.

On the 1st of July there were in store as a reserve supply, including those manufactured during the year, only 37,526 arms. This is but little more than the annual consumption, and increased appropriations for accumulating a larger reserve are indispensable to the safety of the country.

On my recommendation Congress at its last session provided for convening a board of officers to examine magazine guns, with a view to the selection of some of the best for trial in service. The board is now in session.

In this connection the question of ammunition becomes an important one. The capabilities of any arm can only be utilized by those experienced in its use, and target practice in its fullest development has become a necessity in all armies. The expenditure of ammunition for this purpose in considerable quantities, or in quantities sufficient to make our soldiers expert marksmen, is not waste or a useless expenditure. On the contrary, it is of vital importance. In an Indian fight the best marksman is the strongest man. Victory is not for the man of muscle, but the result of the quick eye and cool nerve of the fine shot. If our soldiers can pick off an Indian at one thousand yards, or even at five hundred yards, with unerring certainty, the Indian's occupation is gone. But we can make marksmen of our soldiers only by continued practice, and by a constant expenditure of ammunition. This costs money, but our Army is very small, and lack of numbers must be compensated by the greatest efficiency possible.

A close calculation shows that to supply each soldier with the ammunition required for target and gallery practice will cost $8.50 annually per man, or a total of $212,500.

Besides this, we require money for the ammunition for actual service and for a reserve supply. In my opinion the least amount that should be appropriated for ammunition is $300,000.

MILITIA.

In my last annual report I had the honor to refer at length to a very exhaustive report from the House Committee on the Militia on the powers of Congress and the rights of the States, accompanied by a bill.

Under the Constitution, Congress has the power:

To provide for calling forth the militia to execute the laws of the Union, suppress insurrections, and repel invasions.

To provide for organizing, arming, and disciplining the militia, and for governing such part of them as may be employed in the service of the United States, reserving to the States, respectively, the appointment of the officers and the authority of training the militia according to the discipline prescribed by Congress.

To make all laws which shall be necessary and proper for carrying into execution the foregoing powers, and all other powers vested by this Constitution in the Government of the United States, or in any department or officer thereof.

No State shall, without the consent of Congress, * * * keep troops, or ships of war, in time of peace, * * * or engage in war, unless actually invaded, or in such imminent danger as will not admit of delay.

For the purpose of more completely arming and equipping the whole body of militia, the permanent appropriation of $200,000 made in 1808 should be largely increased, and I so earnestly recommend. In war the country must depend upon its citizens for soldiers. Its militia, well armed, well organized, and thoroughly disciplined, must constitute its armed force. The absence of a large standing army must be compensated by the number of its citizen soldiers, and a large increase to the appropriation, as herein suggested, is the most economical way of solving this important question of a large armed force with a small standing army.

RETIRED LIST.

There are now ten ordnance storekeepers allowed by law. Of these, three are on permanent sick leave, being totally incapacitated for duty.

Several others are over sixty-two years of age. Both the old and the sick should be retired. The law of June 23, 1874, provides for the extinction of the grade of storekeeper by casualties. The retirement of these old and sick officers has been recommended, but the crowded condition of the retired list and the stronger claims of others have prevented any action. The interest of the public service, substantial economy, and the spirit of the laws call for favorable consideration.

In this connection I venture the expression of the opinion that the well-being and efficiency of the Army require the peremptory retirement of officers at the age of sixty-two years. The Army law governing retirements should be made to conform to that of the Navy, fixing by statute the age when the officer is retired. Such a law would shield the officer from apparent invidious selections to his disadvantage, and give, what is so much needed, a healthy flow of promotion to the advantage of the young and vigorous.

ARMAMENT OF FORTIFICATIONS.

The "Act making appropriations for fortifications and other works of defense, and for the armament thereof, for the fiscal year ending June 30, 1882, and for other purposes," approved March 3, 1881, provides:

And the President is authorized to select a board, to consist of one engineer officer, two ordnance officers, and two officers of artillery, whose duty it shall be to make examinations of all inventions of heavy ordnance and improvements of heavy ordnance and projectiles that may be presented to them, including guns now being constructed or converted under direction of the Ordnance Bureau; and said board shall make detailed report to the Secretary of War, for transmission to Congress, of such examination, with recommendation as to what inventions are worthy of actual test, and the estimated cost of such test; and the sum of twenty-five thousand dollars, or so much thereof as may be necessary, is hereby appropriated for such purpose.

In conformity with the foregoing act, a board of officers has been appointed and is now in session for the purpose of making examinations of all inventions referred to in the law, and making a detailed report of such examinations, with recommendation as to what inventions are worthy of actual test, and the estimated cost of such test.

As its report will undoubtedly be made and transmitted to Congress early the next session, I will at this time merely submit reports from the Constructor of Ordnance and the Ordnance Board on the progress made and the results obtained during the past year.

PAPERS ON ORDNANCE SUBJECTS, ETC.

I have also to transmit several very valuable and interesting papers on ordnance and other subjects, by officers of the department.

CLERICAL FORCE.

The clerical force, including the twenty enlisted men allowed by law, is found ample to perform the labors of this bureau. But I have again the honor to recommend that *three* clerks of class four may be provided, to take charge of the three important divisions of this office. I have also to recommend that the pay of the chief clerk may be increased. If the compensation should be commensurate to the capacity, experience, and to the duty performed, his present salary is entirely inadequate. I know of no more valuable and indispensable public servants than the chief clerks of our bureaus, and equal talents and services would in private business exact much larger compensation than is allowed by Con-

gress. This matter is respectfully submitted to your favorable consideration.

I have the honor to submit the following papers, heretofore referred to:

Appendix 1.—Statement of principal articles procured by fabrication
at the arsenals during the year ended June 30, 1881.

Appendix 2.—Statement of principal articles procured by purchase at
the arsenals during the year ended June 30, 1881.

Appendix 3.—Statement of ordnance, ordnance stores, &c., issued to
the military establishment, exclusive of the militia, during the year
ended June 30, 1881.

Appendix 4.—Apportionment for the fiscal year ended June 30, 1881,
of the annual appropriation of $200,000 for arming and equipping the
militia, under sections 1661 and 1667, Revised Statutes.

Appendix 5.—Statement of ordnance, ordnance stores, &c., distributed
to the militia from July 1, 1880, to June 30, 1881, under section 1667,
Revised Statutes.

Appendix 6.—Statement of ordnance, ordnance stores, &c., distributed
to colleges from July 1, 1880, to June 30, 1881, under section 1225, Revised Statutes.

Appendix 7.—Statement of arms and ammunition issued to the executive departments during the year ended June 30, 1881, under the provisions of the act of March 3, 1879.

Appendix 8.—Report of action taken during the year ended June 30,
1881, under the provisions of the act approved March 3, 1881.

Appendix 9.—Report of the principal operations at the Rock Island
Arsenal, Illinois, during the fiscal year ended June 30, 1881, Major D. W.
Flagler, Ordnance Department, commanding.

Appendix 10.—Report of the principal operations at the Benicia
Arsenal, California, during the fiscal year ended June 30, 1881, Col. J.
McAllister, Ordnance Department, commanding.

Appendix 11.—Report of the principal operations at the Piccatinny
Powder Depot, New Jersey, during the fiscal year ended June 30, 1881,
Major F. H. Parker, Ordnance Department, commanding.

Appendix 12.—Report of the principal operations at the Frankford
Arsenal, Pennsylvania, during the fiscal year ended June 30, 1881,
Major S. C. Lyford, Ordnance Department, commanding.

Appendix 13.—Experiments with small-arms having varying length
and weight of barrels and charges of powder and bullets, by Capt. John
E. Greer, Ordnance Department.

Appendix 14.—Report on fabrication of centers for paper targets at
Rock Island Arsenal, Illinois, by Major D. W. Flagler, Ordnance Department.

Appendix 15.—Description of harness manufactured at Rock Island
Arsenal, Illinois, for the Laidley cavalry forge, by Major D. W. Flagler,
Ordnance Department.

Appendix 16.—Physical properties of Ulster tube-iron, by Lieut. C. W.
Whipple, Ordnance Department.

Appendix 17.—Long-range firing, being a continuation of Appendix
25, Report of 1880.

Appendix 18.—Report on a telemeter sight invented by Capt. Luigi
Folta, Italian artillery, by Capt. John E. Greer, Ordnance Department.

Appendix 19.—Report on the inspection of contract small-arm ammunition, by Capt. Henry Metcalfe, Ordnance Department.

Appendix 20.—Report on the geology of the high plateaus of Utah,
by Capt. C. E. Dutton, Ordnance Department.

REPORTS OF THE ORDNANCE BOARD.

Appendix 38.—Proper mode of packing gunpowder.
Appendix 38ª.—Continued test of 8-inch breech-loading rifle, No. 1.
Appendix 38ᵇ.—3.20-inch breech-loading chambered rifles.
Appendix 38ᶜ.—11-inch muzzle-loading chambered rifle, No. 2.
Appendix 38ᵈ.—Hotchkiss single and triple wall shells.
Appendix 38ᵉ.—Hotchkiss mountain gun.

I have the honor to be, very respectfully, your obedient servant,
S. V. BENÉT,
Brigadier-General, Chief of Ordnance.
To the HON. SECRETARY OF WAR.

REPORT OF THE CHIEF OF ENGINEERS.

OFFICE OF THE CHIEF OF ENGINEERS,
UNITED STATES ARMY,
Washington, D. C., October 22, 1881.

SIR: I have the honor to present for your information the following report upon the duties and operations of the Engineer Department for the fiscal year ending June 30, 1881.

OFFICERS OF THE CORPS OF ENGINEERS.

The number of officers holding commissions in the Corps of Engineers, United States Army, at the end of the fiscal year was 106 on the active list and 7 on the retired list; the latter, however, under the law of January 21, 1870, not being available for duty. In the duties devolving upon the Corps by law and by its organizations, the employment of a number of scientists and assistant engineers has been necessary.

Since the last annual report the Corps has lost by death, resignation, and retirement, three of its officers: Capt. Charles B. Phillips, who died at Norfolk, Va., June 14, 1881; Lieut. Samuel E. Tillman, who resigned, to date December 31, 1880; and Col. John G. Barnard, who was retired January 2, 1881, in conformity with provisions of section 1244, Revised Statutes, being over sixty-two years of age, and having served over forty-five years as a commissioned officer.

There have been added to the Corps, by promotion of graduates of the Military Academy, two second lieutenants and three additional second lieutenants, whose commissions date from June 11, 1881, but who did not become available for duty till after the close of the year, and are, therefore, not included in the strength of the Corps.

On the 30th June, 1881, the officers were distributed as follows:

On duty, Office Chief of Engineers, including the Chief............................. 4
On duty, fortifications... 1
On duty, fortifications and light-house duty.. 1
On duty, fortifications and river and harbor works................................... 13
On duty, fortifications, river and harbor works, and light-house duty................ 1
On duty, fortifications, river and harbor works, and "The Mississippi River Commission".. 1
On duty, Board of Engineers.. 1
On duty, Board of Engineers and river and harbor works............................... 1
On duty, Board of Engineers, fortifications, and river and harbor works.............. 3
On duty, Board of Engineers, Battalion of Engineers and fortifications............... 1
On duty, Board of Engineers, and light-house duty.................................... 1

The officers detached were on duty as follows:

SEA-COAST AND LAKE-FRONTIER DEFENSES.

During the past fiscal year work upon our sea-coast defenses has been
limited, in accordance with the terms of the act of March 3, 1881, to
their protection, preservation, and repair.

It is again my duty to invite attention to the importance of early and
reasonable expenditures on our sea-coast defenses, but I can make no
better exposition of the necessity of a *commencement*, if nothing more,
in the modification of, and additions to, our works of fortifications on
which the safety of our maritime cities, our navy-yards, and depots of
supply must sooner or later depend, than by repeating the views which
were presented in my last annual report.

For many years no appropriations whatever have been made for the
construction of new works, or for the modifications of the old works which

were built before the introduction of modern ordnance and armored ships, and which latter, although there were none better in their day, are now most of them utterly unfit to cope with modern ships of war. The earthen batteries more recently built in the positions which are available for such batteries in our harbors are generally in effective condition, though by reason of the late increase in the power of ordnance some of them should be strengthened by thickening the parapets and coverings of magazines.

The casemated works of which our sea-coast defenses are necessarily largely composed were built when wooden walls were the only protection of guns afloat. Now, ships of war are clad in armor up to two feet in thickness, and the old smooth-bores have been replaced by rifled guns, the largest of which throw shot of nearly a ton's weight and which burn at each discharge nearly a quarter of a ton of powder.

While other maritime nations are adding to their already powerful navies heavily armored ships of war, which are armed with 81 and 100-ton guns and which cost, exclusive of armament, more than two and a half millions of dollars, they are building armored defenses for the protection of their own coasts. Great Britain has already more than 500 guns in position behind armored defenses.

We have not one such gun, nor have we any armored defenses whatever.

I think it is plainly demonstrated in the remarks which follow, taken from my last annual report, not only that reliance can be placed on no other mode of defense of our sea-coast, but that fortifications and torpedoes furnish the most efficient, most enduring, and least expensive mode of such defense; and I earnestly hope that Congress may be induced to grant for the next fiscal year a reasonable amount for the resumption of work on our sea-coast defenses.

*   *   *   *   *   *   *

The estimates submitted, based on the several estimates of the officers in charge, exhibit the amounts which are deemed necessary by this department for the commencement, the continuance, or the completion, as the case may be, of the several works of defense during the next fiscal year.

Special attention is invited to the estimate of $100,000 for providing torpedoes to be stored in our fortifications, and planted, on the advent of war, in the channels and fairways of our harbors, and for providing the electric apparatus by which the torpedo lines are to be fired.

The Board of Engineers for Fortifications, referring to this subject, in its annual report for the last fiscal year, says:

The annual appropriation made for the fiscal year 1880-'81 for providing materials to defend our coasts with submarine mines, &c. ($50,000), has been expended, upon the recommendation of this Board, chiefly in the purchase of torpedo cases and junction boxes to be stored for use in the channels leading to the harbor of Boston. A much larger sum could have been judiciously expended in providing for other important harbors, now quite neglected; and an increase in this appropriation for the coming year is urgently to be recommended. The material is not liable to deteriorate in store, and in the present condition of our sea-coast defenses and of their armaments an ample supply of torpedoes is a necessity which cannot be ignored without risk of disaster. Not less than $100,000 should be annually applied to this purpose for several years to come.

It is for procuring and storing torpedoes and such portions of the apparatus as cannot readily be obtained in the event of sudden hostilities that the appropriation is asked.

Special attention is also invited to the item of $200,000 for preparing our most important fortifications for operating torpedo lines, by providing bomb-proof chambers for the electrical apparatus, and the bomb-proof subterranean galleries through which the electric wires are to be carried to deep water; both of these being essential to the operation of the torpedo system of defense in connection with the fortifications themselves. The Board of Engineers for Fortifications remarks on this subject as follows:

Another matter in this connection demands immediate action. In its last annual report this board pointed out in some detail the necessity for a special appropriation to prepare our forts to serve as operating stations for submarine mines. Without such preparation only a very imperfect use could be made of the materials in store. Unless the electric cables connecting the mines with the casemate containing the batteries, &c., are so introduced as to be secure against bombardment, a single fortunate shot may open the whole channel to the enemy. This would be the condition of Boston to-day, and indeed of most of our great seaports. It is useless to provide mines without also constructing the shafts, galleries, and bomb-proofs necessary for their efficient service. An appropriation of $200,000 would go far towards supplying all our chief forts with these most necessary additions, and the appropriation of that sum is again recommended. The works require time for their construction, and at the outbreak of hostilities this would certainly be lacking.

I beg leave to quote the following extract from the report of the Board of Engineers for Fortifications for the fiscal year 1879–'80, respecting the necessity for increasing the number of enlisted men in the Battalion of Engineers:

For several years the board has urged in its annual reports the importance of increasing the number of enlisted men of engineers under training to fit them for submarine mining. The legal organization of the battalion provides for 752 enlisted men; but, in consequence of the reduction of the Army, and the necessity for troops on the plains, the force authorized to be enlisted is only 300 men, and of these 50 are stationed at West Point on special duty, which prevents their receiving drill or instruction in this new and important duty assigned by Congress to the engineer troops. We have, therefore, only 150 men, even on paper, who possess any knowledge of the planting or serving of the submarine defenses designed to cover our whole extensive sea-coast. The work is technical, requiring special qualifications and special training not to be found in the soldiers of the other arms of service, nor among the volunteers.

This statement is a sufficient reason for increasing our present force; but if additional argument be needed, it is found in the fact that now, in time of peace, Great Britain maintains at Bermuda or Halifax, almost in our own waters, six companies, or probably from three to four times as many engineer soldiers, instructed in torpedo warfare, as we have to depend upon to cover our whole coast from Maine to Alaska.

In this connection the board would invite attention to the last annual report of the General of the Army, which suggests providing troops for special needs not connected with service against the Indians, by a law authorizing their recruiting, in addition to the 25,000 men that now constitute the entire Army (except the Signal Service, which is already provided for upon a plan similar to that now suggested). If the importance of this increase were thoroughly understood, it might result in authorizing the minimum number of engineer soldiers (520) needed to be kept under training in submarine mining. No increase in officers nor change in the legal organization of the battalion would be required, and being regular soldiers, thoroughly instructed in infantry tactics, the men would be as available in any sudden emergency as any other troops in the service.

Upon this subject Lieutenant-Colonel Abbot, commanding the Engineer Battalion and Torpedo School, remarks:

The torpedo service is not like that of troops in line of battle, where any blunder by a private is quickly seen and corrected by his officers. There are many small details which must be intrusted to the individual soldiers; errors might be covered up in the progress of the work, and it is only when the mine is planted that they can be detected; and then hours of precious time must be lost in taking the group from the water to correct some little mistakes, which with trained men would never occur. Experience with newly-enlisted men at the torpedo school constantly confirms these views. Thoroughly impressed, therefore, with the absolute necessity for trained soldiers in torpedo operations, I feel it incumbent upon me to invite attention to the need of provision for a proper organization.

The following considerations have a bearing upon the subject: Torpedoes are planted by grand groups of 21 mines. To do this properly, requires 3 non-commissioned officers and 23 instructed privates of engineers, and about 40 boatmen, laborers, &c.,

which it is assumed could be hired in any of our seaports to do the parts of the work requiring no particular knowledge or skill. In important harbors and in times of haste, several grand groups could and should be planted simultaneously; but to arrive at the lowest judicious organization, 26 enlisted men of engineers will be assumed for each seperate channel to be defended. There are 30 such channels in the United States which would call for immediate defense. The minimum force then would be 26×30=780 effective soldiers. The legal war organization of the Engineer Battalion consists of five companies of 150 men each, or 752 men, including 2 staff sergeants. Evidently, therefore, for reasonable efficiency, the full strength should be maintained. Allowing, however, one-third as the maximum safe reduction below this estimate for a peace organization, and we have 520 men who must be kept thoroughly instructed and always available. Considering that in war time these men would be scattered along the whole sea-coast, these engineer troops, besides their duties with torpedoes, must be ready at any time to act as sappers and miners and pontoniers, and to make reconnaissances, and photograph maps with troops in the field; and, finally, that they are equally as available as other soldiers in any sudden emergency occurring in a time of peace calling for a military force, and it would appear that a minimum peace organization of 520 men should be maintained. This number is but little more than one-quarter of the police force of New York City, and is certainly very small compared with the enormous interest intrusted to it—the torpedo defense of the harbors along the whole coast of the United States.

The Board of Engineers for Fortifications in its annual report for the last fiscal year, which will be found further on in this report, again urges the importance of the torpedo service, and the increase of the Battalion of Engineers desired, and I heartily concur in its recommendations, which are thus stated:

It is the duty of the board to again urge the importance of increasing the number of enlisted men of engineers sufficiently to properly prepare for the service of our submarine mines in war. At present, owing to the reduction of the Army and to the need of troops on the plains, only about 100 men would be available in an emergency, hardly enough to defend the port of New York City. The service is technical, requiring qualifications and training not to be found in details from other arms of the service, or among the volunteers. No change in the organic law creating the Battalion of Engineers is required, but simply a provision authorizing it to be recruited to its full strength (752 enlisted men), in addition to the 25,000 men to which the Army is now limited. The Signal Service is already provided for upon this plan, which has also received the favorable indorsement of the General of the Army in his annual report for 1879. No increase of commissioned officers nor change in legal organization would be needful, and the men being thoroughly disciplined and well drilled as infantry, would be as serviceable in ordinary emergencies as those of any other arm of service.

* * * * * * *

WASHINGTON AQUEDUCT.

Officer in charge, Lieut. Col. Thomas Lincoln Casey, Corps of Engineers.

The funds appropriated for the Washington Aqueduct for the past year, were for maintenance and general repairs of existing works. These have been kept in good order, and have furnished to the city as great a supply of water as they are capable of giving with the present appliances.

Among the larger repairs made during the past year, were the plastering, with Portland cement mortar, of the exterior walls of the influent and effluent gate-houses of the distributing reservoir; the construction of a new timber bridge, 143 feet in length, with a 16-foot roadway, supported on trestles from 15 to 21 feet in height, over the waste channel of the receiving reservoir; the raising of the masonry of the chamber of the connecting conduit at the receiving reservoir, so as to bring up the water in the distributing reservoir to the level of 146 feet; and the plastering, with Portland cement mortar, of the exterior of the high service reservoir in Georgetown, in imitation of a rustic ashlar covering for this structure.

The necessity for the extension of the dam at the Great Falls, across the river, is again urged, and attention is invited to the remarks of the officer in charge upon this matter. The appropriation required for this purpose is recommended to favorable consideration; for unless this dam is built, the annoyance and embarrassment which many of the people of this city experience in consequence of a weak and limited supply of water, will in a short time be seriously increased, while the areas of limited supply will correspondingly enlarge.

The estimates of the officer in charge for the fiscal year ending June 30, 1883, are as follows:

For engineering, maintenance, repairs, and construction................ $255,000 00

IMPROVEMENT AND CARE OF PUBLIC BUILDINGS AND GROUNDS IN THE DISTRICT OF COLUMBIA.

Officer in charge, Lieut. Col. Thomas Lincoln Casey, Corps of Engineers, from July 1, 1880, to April 1, 1881; since that date Col. A. F. Rockwell, U. S. A.

The labor performed during the year upon the public grounds in the District of Columbia was confined principally to their care and preservation, the available appropriations permitting but little advance in the way of new work. Satisfactory progress was, however, made in the improvement of the grounds south of the Executive Mansion, while a marked improvement was made in Farragut Square, by the removal of the concrete roadway therefrom. Eleven of the smaller reservations at the intersections of streets and avenues were also improved by regrading and planting, and inclosing with park post and chain fence, and the introduction of water-pipe for irrigating purposes.

Attention is invited to the detailed report of the officer in charge, and his estimates for the coming fiscal year are recommended as follows:

For improvement and care of public buildings and grounds............. $193,500 00
For compensation of persons employed on and around public buildings
and grounds 48,400 00
For contingent and incidental expenses 1,000 00

242,900 00

MISSISSIPPI RIVER COMMISSION.

This commission, organized under the provisions of the act of June 28, 1879, reports to and receives instructions from the Secretary of War through this office. In addition to the continuation of the surveys of this river and its tributaries, and the consideration of plans for improving and giving safety and ease to the navigation of the main stream, the commission has been engaged in making arrangements for the application of the appropriation of $1,000,000, made by the river and harbor act of March 3, 1881, to the improvement of the extensive reaches of the Mississippi River in the vicinity of Plum Point and Lake Providence, where some of the worst of the obstacles to the navigation of the lower river are met with.

Much detailed information regarding the progress of the commission in its duties will be found in its reports, Appendix S S, which are attached at the suggestion of the president of the commission.

SURVEYS OF THE NORTHERN AND NORTHWESTERN LAKES.

Officer in charge, Maj. C. B. Comstock, Corps of Engineers, who had under his immediate orders First Lieut. P. M. Price, Corps of Engineers (relieved from duty on Lake Survey December 7, 1880), and the following named principal assistant engineers: E. S. Wheeler, A. R. Flint, O. B. Wheeler, R. S. Woodward, C. H. Kummell, Thomas Russell, J. H. Darling, T. W. Wright, and L. L. Wheeler.

Progress of the work during the year.—Longitudes have been determined between Detroit and the following named stations: Cambridge, Mass.; Toledo, Ohio; Fort McDermit, Nev.; and San Antonio, Tex.

The comparison of standards has been continued. The conduct of the zinc bar of Tube I., of the Repsold base apparatus, has been investigated.

The final reduction of the work of the lake survey and the preparation of the final report have been continued.

*   *   *   .   *   *   *   *

MILITARY, GEOGRAPHICAL, AND LAKE SURVEY MAPS.

In the Office of the Chief of Engineers.

Progress in the compilation of the new outline map of the Territory of the United States, west of the Mississippi River, scale $\frac{1}{1000000}$, has been made during the past year, and the northwestern sheet has been placed in the hands of the engraver.

The following maps have been photolithographed and an edition printed for distribution to the army:

Map of the Yellowstone National Park, Big Horn Mountains and adjacent territory, on a scale of 12 miles to 1 inch, by Capt. James F. Gregory, Corps of Engineers, 1881.

Map of Mexico, by Captain Noix, 1873, scale $\frac{1}{1000000}$.

Map of the United States, showing the locations of works and surveys for river and harbor improvement, on a scale of 52¼ miles to 1 inch, by Maj. H. M. Robert, Corps of Engineers, 1879.

Map of the Yellowstone River, in thirty-three sheets, from Fort Keogh to Fort Buford, scale $\frac{1}{5000}$, by Lieut. Edward Maguire, Corps of Engineers, 1879.

The following maps are now in the hands of the photolithographer:

Map of Nebraska, scale $\frac{1}{335000}$, by Capt. W. S. Stanton, Corps of Engineers, 1881.

Map of the Department of the Columbia, scale 16 miles to 1 inch, by Lieut. T. W. Symons, Corps of Engineers, 1881.

Map of the Ohio River, in forty-one sheets, scale 3 miles to 1 inch, by Maj. W. E. Merrill, Corps of Engineers, 1881.

The following lake survey charts have been engraved on copper:

Lake Erie.
Lake Erie coast chart, No. 1.
Lake Erie coast chart, No. 5.
Lake Erie coast chart, No. 6.
Niagara Falls.

Lake Erie coast chart No. 7 has been photolithographed and an edition printed in advance of the engraved edition. This chart is now in the hands of the engraver.

Plates 14 to 22, to illustrate the final report of the Survey of the Northern and Northwestern Lakes have been photolithographed and printed.

The following engraved plates of charts of the Northern and Northwestern Lakes have been electrotyped:

Lake Ontario.
Lake Michigan coast chart, No. 1.
Lake Michigan coast chart, No. 2.
Lake Michigan coast chart, No. 3,

Lake Michigan coast chart, No. 8.
Lake Michigan coast chart, No. 9.
Lake Superior charts, Nos. 1, 2, and 3.
Isle Royale.
Lake Saint Clair.
Lake Erie coast chart, No. 2.
Lake Erie.
Lake Erie coast chart, No. 3.
Lake Erie coast chart, No. 4.
Lake Erie coast chart, No. 6.
Lake Ontario coast chart, No. 1.
Lake Ontario coast chart, No. 5.

GEOLOGICAL EXPLORATIONS OF THE FORTIETH PAR-ALLEL.

The last of the quarto reports of this exploration, Vol. VII., Odontornithes, by Prof. O. C. Marsh, has been published.

GEOGRAPHICAL SURVEYS OF THE TERRITORY OF THE UNITED STATES WEST OF THE ONE HUNDREDTH MERIDIAN.

Officer in charge, First Lieut. M. M. Macomb, Fourth U. S. Artillery.

During portions of the year, in addition to the regular office force, the following gentlemen have been temporarily engaged upon special subjects: Prof. J. J. Stevenson, geologist, in completing the proof-reading of his report; Dr. C. A. White, paleontologist, in preparing an appendix to the above report, and reading proof of same; Mr. Miles Rock, computing geographical positions of main and secondary triangulation points in California and Nevada; Mr. Frank Carpenter, in completing the plotting of topographical data in Atlas sheet 73 in Southern California.

First Lieut. Willard Young, Corps of Engineers, U. S. A., was engaged at the office between June 7, 1881, and June 13, 1881, in supervising the plotting of notes taken by him in 1878 at Great Salt Lake.

No field-work was done during the year, there being no funds available for that purpose.

The duties of the regular office force have been confined to the reductions needed to place data already gathered in shape for publication.

Twenty longitudes and latitudes of primary and secondary triangulation stations have been computed, together with 126 distances and 39 azimuths.

Plotting has been done upon 5 regular and special sheets, not yet ready for publication, and new material has been reduced for revised edition of atlas sheets out of print.

Six regular atlas sheets in hachures, one large topographical map of the Lake Tahoe region, and one outline map have been completed during the year and placed in the hands of the lithographer.

Five other atlas sheets are now in the hands of the final draughtsmen and will be completed during the next fiscal year, together with two others not yet taken up.

Four new land classification sheets and three new geological sheets are now in the hands of the lithographer.

No maps will accompany extra copies of appendix, there not being sufficient funds available for the publication of large editions.

Vol. VII., Archæology, of the quarto reports authorized by act of Congress, has been in stereotype for some time, and will appear during the present year.

Vol. III., Supplement, Geology, by Prof. J. J. Stevenson, is now passing through the press, and the manuscript of an octavo report containing tables of geographical positions, altitudes, &c., is in preparation.

A new edition of the list of maps and reports issued by the office of this survey has just passed through the press.

The maps now in preparation will be issued as rapidly as they can be completed by the present small force.

There are a number of atlas sheets, aggregating in area about 57,000 square miles and lying in Oregon, California, and Arizona, in which much field-work has already been done, but in which further field-work must be done before publication in regular form would be possible.

Lieutenant Macomb estimates that $40,000 could be used to advantage in permitting the filling of gaps in the triangulation and topography by additional field-work, thus enabling full benefit to be got from material already at hand.

RECONNAISSANCES AND EXPLORATIONS.

The following-named officers have been on duty at the headquarters of the Army and at headquarters of the military divisions and departments, and have been engaged during the year in preparing such maps and making such surveys and reconnaissances as were required by their respective commanding officers:

Maj. O. M. Poe (colonel and aid-de-camp to the General of the Army) at headquarters of the Army.

Capt. James F. Gregory at headquarters Division of the Missouri.

Capt. W. R. Livermore at headquarters Department of Texas.

Capt. W. S. Stanton at headquarters Department of the Platte.

Capt. E. H. Ruffner at headquarters Department of the Missouri till February 5, 1881.

Lieut. T. N. Bailey at headquarters District of New Mexico, from September 15, 1880, to February 23, 1881, and at headquarters Department of the Missouri since March 28, 1881.

Capt. Edward Maguire at headquarters Department of Dakota.

Capt. W. A. Jones at headquarters Division of the Pacific.

Lieut. Carl F. Palfrey at headquarters Department of Arizona.

Lieut. T. W. Symons at headquarters Department of the Columbia.

The maps prepared by these Engineer officers are of great value to the War Department and to the Army in the movement of troops, the establishment of posts for controlling the Indians and for protecting settlers. There is also a great demand for the maps from citizens for use in the location of railroads, mines, and valuable lands. It is especially desired that funds be supplied to enable the Engineer Department to continue the mapping of the areas which are likely to be traversed by troops or by hostile Indians in future campaigns. The small appropriation asked for the next fiscal year will provide for the collection, plotting, and publication of a large amount of data required for the use of the War Department.

The attention of the honorable Secretary of War is earnestly invited to this subject.

Maj. O. M. Poe, Corps of Engineers, U. S. A., Colonel and aid-de-camp, has been on duty as aid-de-camp to the General of the Army and as a member of the Light-House Board.

He has completed the compilation of a map illustrating the capture of Savannah, December 21, 1864, and has made progress on other maps illustrating the operations of the armies commanded by General Sherman in 1864 and 1865.

He also made a tour of examination in Texas and part of New Mexico with reference to probable railroad, especially towards the Mexican frontier, and the changes in the military situation which would arise therefrom. The letter of instructions under which he acted and his report submitted to the General of the Army are given in Appendix V V.

Capt. James F. Gregory, on duty at headquarters Military Division of the Missouri, reports that the work of his office during the past fiscal year has consisted in correcting, mounting, and issuing maps for the use of officers in the division; in making copies, tracings, reductions, and enlargements of maps of military reservations, scouts, reconnaissances, &c., for file and for forwarding.

A map of the Yellowstone National Park, Big Horn Mountains, and adjacent territory has been compiled and drawn to a scale of 1 inch to 12 miles. This map, 26 by 16 inches, has been published in this office, and is ready for issue.

Sixteen autograph plates of military reservations and posts in the Department of Dakota have also been prepared for issue.

Captain Gregory states that owing to the lack of funds for employment of a draughtsman and the reduction of his force of topographical assistants from two to one by General Orders No. 7, A. G. O., headquarters of the Army, January 13, 1881, the work of his office cannot be conducted in such a manner as to make it of the value it should be in the administration of the affairs of the division.

Capt. W. S. Stanton, on duty with the general commanding the Department of the Platte, reports that a map of Nebraska has been made on a scale of 1: 500,000, embodying the fullest and latest information attainable from all reliable sources, embracing all surveys in the State, both under the Interior and War Departments, as well as a large mass of information secured from county officers, postmasters, and persons most familiar with the geography of the State.

Plans of all the posts in the department, with plots of their reservations, have been made in duplicate, comprising 50 sheets of drawings, with long inscriptions, embodying full information regarding both posts and reservations.

Five military reservations have been surveyed, and reconnaissances have been made of about 500 miles of routes.

One hundred and forty copies of large War Department maps have been mounted and issued, and the usual routine work of the office performed during the year.

Lieut. T. N. Bailey, engineer officer at headquarters, Department of the Missouri, has made complete surveys of the military reservations at Fort Lewis, Rio de la Plata, Colo.; Fort Cummings, N. Mex.; and Fort Bliss, Tex., and a reconnaissance covering 2,500 square miles north and west of the latter fort.

From astronomical observations and direct measurements he reports the geographical positions of Fort Bliss, Tex., and Fort Leavenworth, Kans.

Office work has consisted in reduction of his field notes, compilation of scout reports, and duplication and issuing of various maps required for file, and the use of troops in the field.

Capt. Edward Maguire, at headquarters, Department of Dakota, reports that the reservation of Fort Assinaboine, Mont., 869.82 square miles, was surveyed, and the boundary lines established. The latitude

31 Ab

and longitude were determined by sextant observations at the post, and by transit observations in Saint Paul. The latitude and longitude of Fort Meade, Dak., were determined by an accurate connection with the site of the old post-office in Deadwood, the position of which had been determined by Capt. W. S. Stanton, Corps of Engineers.

The longitude of Carleton College Observatory, Northfield, Minn., and the latitude and longitude of Fort Randall were also determined. In addition, a portion of the engineer force was called upon for a great deal of work in laying out parade grounds, carriage roads, &c., at Fort Snelling, under the direction of the Quartermaster's Department.

The office work consisted in computing and plotting field notes, revising and correcting the maps of Montana and Dakota, in making tracings and photographic copies for forwarding and for file, and in supplying such information and data as were called for by the department commander and other officers.

Capt. William A. Jones, engineer officer, headquarters Military Division of the Pacific and Department of California, reports that operations have been directed to the following purposes:

The survey of military posts and reservations.

Surveys for public buildings and works for water supply.

The collection of geographical information.

The cartographic work connected with the foregoing.

The distribution of maps and geographical information.

* * * * * * *

ESTIMATE FOR AMOUNT REQUIRED FOR MILITARY SURVEYS AND RECONNAISSANCES IN MILITARY DIVISIONS AND DEPARTMENTS.

For military surveys, reconnaissances, and surveys of military reservations by the engineer officers attached to the various headquarters of military divisions and departments, being an average of $5,000 for each of the nine military divisions and departments west of the Mississippi River, and $5,000 for publication of maps; total, $50,000.

OFFICE OF THE CHIEF OF ENGINEERS.

In the labors of the office the Chief of Engineers was assisted, on the 30th June, by the following officers in charge of the several divisions:

FIRST AND SECOND DIVISIONS.—*Fortifications, Battalion and Engineer depot, Lands, Armaments, Personnel, &c.,* Maj. George H. Elliot.

THIRD DIVISION.—*River and Harbor Improvements, &c.,* Lieut. Col. John G. Parke.

FOURTH AND FIFTH DIVISIONS.—*Property, Accounts, Estimates, Funds, Survey of the Lakes, Explorations, Maps, Instruments, &c.,* Capt. Henry M. Adams.

Very respectfully, your obedient servant,

H. G. WEIGHT,
Chief of Engineers,
Brig. and Bvt. Major-General.

Hon. ROBERT T. LINCOLN,
Secretary of War.

REPORT

OF THE

SECRETARY OF THE NAVY.

NAVY DEPARTMENT,
Washington, November 28, 1881.

SIR: The condition of the Navy imperatively demands the prompt and earnest attention of Congress. Unless some action be had in its behalf it must soon dwindle into insignificance. From such a state it would be difficult to revive it into efficiency without dangerous delay and enormous expense. Emergencies may at any moment arise which would render its aid indispensable to the protection of the lives and property of our citizens abroad and at home, and even to our existence as a nation.

We have been unable to make such an appropriate display of our naval power abroad as will cause us to be respected. The exhibition of our weakness in this important arm of defense is calculated to detract from our occupying in the eyes of foreign nations that rank to which we know ourselves to be justly entitled. It is a source of mortification to our officers and fellow-countrymen generally, that our vessels of war should stand in such mean contrast alongside of those of other and inferior powers.

The mercantile interests of our country have extended themselves over all quarters of the globe. Our citizens engaged in commerce with foreign nations look to the Navy for the supervisory protection of their persons and property. Calls are made upon the department to send vessels into different parts of the world, in order to prevent threatened aggression upon the rights of American citizens, and to shield them in time of civil commotion in foreign lands from insult or personal indignity. It is to be deplored that in many such instances it has proved impossible to respond to these calls from the want of a sufficient number of vessels.

These things ought not to be. While the Navy should not be large, it should at all times afford a nucleus for its enlargement upon an emergency. Its power of prompt and extended expansion should be established. It should be sufficiently powerful "to assure the navigator that in whatsoever sea he shall sail his ship he is protected by the stars and stripes of his country."

But the claims of the Navy to consideration and for its maintenance in a state of becoming usefulness and dignity rest not merely upon its power to protect the commerce and citizens of the nation in time of peace, or when they may become imperiled amidst the sudden ebullitions of hostility which occasionally burst forth in countries with which we are on terms of amity. Its claims rest upon the most sacred traditions of the Republic. It should be borne in mind that all the triumphs which illustrate the history of the Navy are connected with the glory of the nation.

From the day of the assertion of our independence down to the present time our Navy has borne a conspicuous part in the trials and vicissitudes of the wars through which we have passed. In the Revolution it was feeble and defective in organization; but by means of private cruisers and vessels contributed by the colonies it seriously crippled the commerce of Great Britain on the high seas, and, together with the naval forces of France, aided in achieving our independence. A few years after this, while yet in its infancy, at Tripoli and in the Mediterranean, it abolished the unjust tributes levied on commerce, and conferred new glory upon our national arms. In the last war with Great Britain, on the seas and on the lakes, its deeds of heroism and its brilliant victories fairly dazzled the eyes of the world, while they bore a most important part in the establishment of peace. In 1846 it was under the thunder of the guns of the Navy that we were enabled to land a large army at the port of Vera Cruz with a success almost unparalleled in warfare, and with but a trivial loss, while our ships patrolled the Gulf, and held the enemy's ports with a tight grasp. In our late rebellion it girdled our extensive coasts with a chain of vessels which sealed effectually all the southern ports from Virginia to the Rio Grande. It is believed that never in the history of the world has there been so extensive and effective a blockade. Besides this, in contests with the cruisers of the enemy upon the high seas and in our rivers, it accomplished a series of most wonderful and signal successes.

Achievements such as these constitute a strong claim upon the affections of a patriotic and grateful people. Their story becomes interwoven in the lessons of heroism that are taught at every fireside throughout the land. They inculcate that spirit of pride of country which imparts a chivalric charm to patriotism and is a stimulant to honorable ambition and the love of glory. Without such a history, a country has not that incentive to deeds of valor and self-sacrifice which fires the hearts and strengthens the arms of a people at their country's call, and adds especially to the power and perpetuity of a republic like ours.

Nor do the claims of the Navy rest solely upon its exploits on the seas and in times of war. It has made advances in meteorology and astronomy which have largely extended the limits of scientific knowledge. It has explored new seas, effected surveys of harbors and coasts at home and elsewhere and even of the waters under the earth, which have proved of the greatest practical advantage. Its strides in the domain of science have proved great in importance and extent.

It would be invidious to compare the officers of our Navy with those of other branches of the public service. It is but just, however, to say that they are alive to the importance of keeping up the high reputation of their predecessors in the Navy who have passed away, but left behind them the memory of an imperishable fame; that they have fully and faithfully profited by the example of their predecessors, and have availed themselves of the ample advantages which the government has extended to them for their thorough training in all the scientific, practical, and theoretical branches of their profession.

Upon the whole, whether it be as a means of self-protection to the long line of cities and harbors upon our coasts, or to guard our commerce on the high seas; or to insure our citizens sojourning in foreign lands and their property and persons against outrage; or to take and keep our proper place among nations; or to maintain the sentiment of patriotism connected with our Navy, and with the memories of its departed heroes; or to reap the advantages of the researches, and labors of its officers in the further progress of advanced science; it becomes the duty of Congress to see to it that the Navy of the United States should not be left to perish through inanition, but should be restored to a condition of usefulness in which it may upon occasion be so expanded as to become the ready means of protection at home or of active and aggressive warfare in the ports and waters of an enemy.

Considerations like these induced the department at an early period to adopt some means by which Congress should be induced to enlarge and restore to usefulness our languishing and neglected Navy. Warned by the history of such attempts, often resulting heretofore in failure, it was thought wise, so far as practicable, to present to Congress a scheme which would meet with the general approval of the different branches of the officers of the Navy.

The danger arising from the advocacy of different and conflicting views and theories, it was thought might be defeated by the creation of an advisory board. Such a board was accordingly ordered, and entered upon the discharge of its duties on the 11th day of July last. The members of the board were officers of recognized ability, experience, and attainments. Many of them had not yet reached the highest ranks in the service. It was deemed wise that those who were to command the new ships, to navigate and perhaps to fight them, should have a potential voice in directing their size, models, equipment, and armament.

The department has been gratified to observe with what alacrity the board entered upon its important and arduous duties. It has labored faithfully and well. It brought to the discharge of its duties, judgments enlightened by high scientific attainments, large practical experience, and a knowledge of the most advanced improvements in naval matters. Its recommendations avoid the perils and expenditures of experimental construction. It recommends proper and effective vessels, combining sufficient speed, facility of maneuver, and a power of resistance deemed sufficiently effective for practical purposes. They are adapted to the depth of water in our ports and harbors; and whilst requiring no fine work, extravagant and useless, it is believed they will adequately supply the pressing wants of this arm of our power. In reaching a result where there must necessarily have been divergent opinions, it is fortunate that there has been in the end so slight a difference in the views of the members of the board.

The department recommends as entitled to the entire approbation of Congress, the adoption of the views of the majority of the board. There is so slight a difference by a few members to it in its entirety, as to justify its being regarded as the unanimous judgment of the board. Indeed the minority of the board themselves declare that the points of difference between them and the majority "do not in any way militate against the objects of the department in calling an advisory board, but in their opinion further them by presenting additional arguments, and exhibiting the subject in a different light."

The report of the majority of the advisory board is appended to, and intended to form a part of, this report.

ARCTIC EXPEDITIONS—THE JEANNETTE, THE RODGERS, AND THE ALLIANCE.

The act making appropriations for sundry civil expenses of the government approved March 3, 1881, contained the following clause:

To enable the Secretary of the Navy to immediately charter or purchase, equip and supply a vessel for the prosecution of a search for the steamer Jeannette, of the Arctic exploring expedition (which the Secretary of the Navy is hereby authorized to undertake), and such other vessels as may be found to need assistance during said cruise, one hundred and seventy-five thousand dollars: *Provided*, That said vessel shall be wholly manned by volunteers from the Navy.

In the execution of this duty, which had devolved on me, the first step was to obtain a suitable vessel for the service to be undertaken. But little time remained in which to procure, prepare, equip, and man her, and to dispatch her to the Arctic regions in season to prosecute a search before severe winter should set in.

A course through Behrings Strait being manifestly the proper direction for the expedition, there was no time left to charter or purchase a vessel on the Atlantic coast and to send her round to the Pacific. A vessel had, therefore, necessarily to be provided on the Pacific coast. The department was able to find at San Francisco a steam whaler well adapted, with some alterations and additions, to the emergency.

The Mary and Helen, a comparatively new and strong vessel of proper size, was offered for sale to the government. A board of experienced officers thoroughly inspected her, and upon their recommendation and such knowledge of the vessel as could otherwise be obtained, the department decided to purchase her.   This step was considered more advantageous than to charter the vessel, as her qualities would render her a desirable vessel for use in the naval service upon her return from the expedition.   The sum of $100,000 was the least at which she could be purchased.   Under all the circumstances, that sum was not considered exorbitant, and she was accordingly purchased.

On the 14th of March I convened at the Navy Department a board of officers, to whom the duty was intrusted of suggesting the best plan for carrying out the act of Congress above mentioned.   The main subjects for the consideration of this board were: 1st, the direction of the search; 2d, the means best adapted to it; 3d, the details of the search expedition.

The board was composed of Rear Admiral John Rodgers, Capt. Jas. A. Greer, Lieut. Comdr. Henry C. White, Lieut. Wm. P. Randall, Lieut. R. M. Berry (recorder), Paymaster Albert S. Kenny, Surgeon Jerome S. Kidder.   They were officers of great experience, and most of them had been identified with earlier Arctic expeditions and explorations in that region.   They made a thorough investigation of the whole subject, in the course of which they examined many gentlemen who had been engaged in the whaling service, and some of whom were the last who had seen the Jeannette.   This board, on the 26th of March, submitted a full, interesting, and valuable report of the results of their deliberations.

The direction of the search, the means best adapted for it, and the details for it were minutely and admirably defined.   There was nothing remaining to be done but to carry out as far as practicable the suggestions of the board.

The name of the Mary and Helen was subsequently changed by me to the Rodgers, in compliment to the distinguished naval officer who was the president of the search expedition board.   The vessel was at once strengthened at the navy-yard, Mare Island, and officered and manned and provisioned not only with supplies for the officers and crew of the Rodgers, but also with ample provision for the relief of any of the people of the Jeannette or the missing whaling vessels that might be fallen in with.

The command of the Rodgers was given to Lieut. Robert M. Berry, an officer in whom the department has the greatest confidence, and who volunteered for this service.   The other officers were also volunteers. As on all previous occasions, where bold and hazardous services were to be required, the difficulty of the department lay in making a selection out of the number of gallant officers of the Navy who volunteered for this adventurous expedition.

The Rodgers sailed from San Francisco June 16, and arrived at Petropautooski, Kamtschatka, July 19, and at Saint Lawrence Bay August 18.   From the Russian authorities and the officers of the Russian vessels stationed or cruising in the arctic regions, Lieutenant Berry has received every facility and all the information which they were able to afford in furtherance of the object he has in view. The Rodgers left Saint Lawrence Bay August 19, and the next morning entered the Arctic Ocean in company with the Russian corvette, Strelock. After touching at Serdze Kamen for information, a partial examination was made of Herald Island by a boat sent in for the purpose, and on the 25th of August the Rodgers anchored in a harbor on the southern coast of Wrangel Land, to the westward of Cape Hawaii. She remained there until September 13, during which period Wrangel Land, or rather Wrangel Island, as Lieutenant Berry found it to be, was examined by three exploring parties organized for the purpose; but no tidings of the Jeannette nor of the missing whaling vessels could be obtained. Interesting reports from Lieutenant Berry, with charts and sketches of Wrangel Island, will be found in the appendix to this report. The whole coast of the island, with the exception of a few miles of outlying sand spits, was examined, and Lieutenant Berry believes it impossible that any of the missing parties ever landed there. The country is indebted to Lieutenant Berry and the party under his command for their energetic labors while at Wrangel Island, the results of which have satisfactorily established the character of that formation, and the probability that the Jeannette never touched there. On September 14 the Rodgers again visited Herald Island, and a boat was sent in for further examination. The eastern end of the island was pulled around, but no landing could be effected. On the 16th the Rodgers left Herald Island and proceeded to the northeastward as far as latitude 73° 44' north, longitude 171° 48' west, which was as far as the ice pack would permit; returned to the northeast point of Wrangel Island, and took a course in a northerly and westerly direction in the hope of finding the high land north of Wrangel Island, reported as "situated in 178° west longitude, and extending as far north as 73° north latitude, as the eye could reach," by Captain Smith, of the whale bark New Bedford. She crossed the 178th meridian and reached a position in latitude 73° 28' north, and longitude 179° 52' east, and then recrossed the same meridian in 73° north without sighting land, the horizon and sky being at the time clear to the northward.

The Rodgers returned to Herald Island and finished its examination, which was fruitless so far as finding any traces of the missing parties. Proceeding thence to the coast of Siberia, Lieutenant Berry examined the coast from the ship to the eastward to a point as far as Cape Serdze, and there put up a house and left a party of six, under command of Master C. F. Putnam, to remain for the winter. They were bountifully supplied with clothing, provisions for one year, dogs, sledges, &c., and will explore the coast in search of the Jeannette's crew and the survivors of the Mount Wollaston and Vigilant.

The Rodgers left on the 8th October, and arrived at Saint Lawrence Bay on the 15th, where the ship was to be put in winter quarters. When the ice opens next summer she will proceed first to Plover Bay, till up with coal, then to Saint Michaels for mails, and afterwards return to the arctic, take up the party at Cape Serdze, and continue the search.

In order to avail itself of every possible means of relieving the Jeannette, or her officers and crew in the event of her loss, the department determined, last spring, to send a naval vessel to search for the missing ship between Greenland, Iceland, and the coast of Norway and Spitzbergen, at least as far north as 77° latitude, and as far as 77° 45' if it should be possible to get there without danger from the ice. This determination was upon the suggestion of the liberal and public-spirited citizen through whose munificence and disinterested efforts to contribute to the cause of science the Jeannette was sent upon her voyage of exploration. The United States steamer Alliance was selected for this service, and Commander George H. Wadleigh was assigned to her command.

The vessel was ordered to proceed to the Norfolk navy-yard, where special preparations were immediately commenced for her cruise. The bow of the ship was sheathed with live oak of the proper thickness, with a strong iron guard on the stem to form a protection against drift ice. Every other precaution was taken to fit her, in all respects, for her voyage. On the completion of these preparations, full instructions having been given and all necessary charts and sailing directions having been furnished, the Alliance left Hampton Roads the 16th of June on her mission. While she was not fitted for arctic exploration, but only as a relief ship, her commanding officer was instructed to make such observations as opportunity permitted for the benefit of navigators and in aid of science. She carried an extra supply of provisions and clothing in case she should fall in with the Jeannette or any of her party. She reached St. John's, Newfoundland, after a passage of eight days, and, on the 9th of July, made the port of Reikjavik, Iceland. On the 24th of that month she arrived at the port of Hammerfest, Norway, having anchored *en route* off Seidis Fiord. While at Reikjavik, Commander Wadleigh distributed papers containing a description of the Jeannette, printed in Icelandic, and offered a reward for any reliable information in regard to that vessel. He was kindly aided in his efforts in this direction by Governor Finssen at Iceland, and Governor Blackstat at Hammerfest. On the 29th of July the Alliance proceeded to Bel Sound and Green Harbor, Spitzbergen. After cruising as far as latitude 80° 00' 36" north, and longitude 8° 14' 30" east, she was stopped by the pack ice. She sailed along the edge of this pack and succeeded, on the 20th of August, in reaching latitude 80° 10' north, longitude 11° 22' east, and as far east as longitude 13° 15' east and latitude 79° 58' north, about 10 miles northwest of Welcome Point, beyond which the ice was impenetrable. In latitude 79° 49' north, longitude 11° 15' east, on a bowlder in the middle of a small bight west of Hukluyts Headland, Amsterdam Island, a copper plate, marked with the ship's name, was spiked. A spike was also driven in a natural tablet on the cliff bearing northeast and north from the plate, and the cliff was also marked with the name of the ship. On the 27th of August the Alliance left Spitzbergen, and cruised under sail until September 11 when she returned to Hammerfest. She left that port on the 16th and again proceeded to Spitzbergen, and reached as far north as 79° 3′ 36″. While in port, Commander Wadleigh obtained specimens of the bottom; the beaches were searched for drift-wood; floral and geological collections were made, and specimens of birds and animals were collected. At sea, near the land or ice, a careful watch was kept for anything promising to throw light on the object of the cruise. Fishing vessels were communicated with, and furnished with a description of the Jeannette. The position of the Alliance, in a sealed bottle, was thrown overboard every day, and all observations were made as carefully as possible with the means at command. On the 25th of September the ship left Spitzbergen on her return to the United States; arrived at Reikjavik the 10th of October; at Halifax, Nova Scotia, the 1st of November; and on the 11th at New York. I regret to say that the Alliance proved unsuccessful in the main object of her cruise.

•

THE SQUADRONS, ETC.

The force on the NORTH ATLANTIC STATION is commanded by Rear-Admiral Robert H. Wyman, and consists of the Tennessee (flagship). Vandalia, Kearsarge, Alliance, and Yantic, regular cruisers; the five monitors in semi-commission on the James River, and the Wyoming and Pawnee at Port Royal, S. C.

The force on the SOUTH ATLANTIC STATION consists of the Shenandoah (flagship) and the Marion, and is under the command of Rear-Admiral James H. Spotts, who relieved Rear-Admiral Andrew Bryson on the station on the 25th of July last. The Brooklyn is preparing for sea at New York, and will relieve the Shenandoah.

The force on the EUROPEAN STATION is commanded by Rear-Admiral J. W. A. Nicholson, who left New York on the Lancaster, his flagship, on the 10th of October, and is now in the Mediterranean. Rear-Admiral John C. Howell, late in command of this station, hauled down his flag from the Trenton, at New York, on the 9th of November. The vessels on this station, at present, are the Lancaster, Quinnebaug, Galena, and Nipsic.

The force on the PACIFIC STATION is commanded by Rear-Admiral George C. Balch, who hoisted his flag on the Pensacola, at San Francisco, on the 18th of July last, succeeding Rear-Admiral Thomas H. Stevens, who was retired on the 27th of May. The Pensacola, Lackawanna, Alaska, Adams, Wachusett, and Ranger, with the Onward (store-ship), at Callao, comprise the force on this station. The Ranger is at present on detached special service, and the Wachusett is stationed in the waters of Alaska. The Essex, recently commissioned at League Island, will join the force in the Pacific.

The force on the ASIATIC STATION, commanded by Rear-Admiral J. M. B. Clitz, consists of the Richmond (flagship), Swatara, Monocacy, Ashuelot, Alert, and Palos.

The TRAINING PRACTICE SQUADRON is commanded by Capt. Stephen B. Luce, and consists of the New Hampshire, Minnesota, Constitution, Saratoga, and Portsmouth, only the three last-named of which are cruising vessels. The Constitution is to be put out of commission at New York, and the Jamestown, now at Mare Island, California, is fitting out and will be brought around to the Atlantic coast to take her place.

Engaged on SPECIAL SERVICE are the Powhatan, Despatch, Tallapoosa, Alarm, and Intrepid, on the Atlantic coast; the Michigan on the Lakes; and the Rodgers in the Arctic Ocean. The St. Mary's continues to be used by the State of New York as a marine school-ship.

The vessels above-mentioned, together with three monitors at Washington in partial commission, five receiving ships, one or two tugs at each of the yards and stations, and a monitor and old frigate at Annapolis make up the number of vessels at present in practical use.

There are one hundred and forty vessels on the Navy list, twenty-five of which are mere tugs, with a very large number of others entirely useless, and which could not, without a great expenditure of money, be made fit for service.

In the appendix to this report will be found a detailed statement of the movements and general service of all vessels which have been in commission for sea during the past year. It exhibits a commendable degree of activity and usefulness.

The reports of the Chiefs of the Bureaus of Steam Engineering and Construction and Repair represent the condition, in their respective departments, of the vessels of the Navy generally.

BUREAU OF NAVIGATION.

The Chief of this Bureau reports that the revised edition of the American Practical Navigator will be available for issue within the next year the type-work being already well advanced. This book will contain improved tables and formulæ used in navigation, nautical astronomy, and surveying, while its character as a popular hand-book for masters of sea-going vessels is still retained.

The longitudes of Yokohama, Nagasaki, Vladivastok, Shanghai, Amoy, and Hong-Kong have been established during the past summer by means of the electric telegraph. This work of determining in an accurate manner the meridians of principal sea-ports of the globe, as carried on by officers of the United States Navy for some years, is fully appreciated by foreign governments, and it is gratifying to note that thus far the owners of telegraph lines have rendered all the aid asked for by this department with a most commendable willingness.

Some new instruments for finding the position at sea and for determining the deviation of the compass, as well as improved implements for sounding depths of water, have been tested with interesting results.

It is proposed to experiment with the electric light for illuminating purposes in place of oil lamps and candles. It is expected that the electric light will eventually prove to be not only a better, but a safer and more economical means of lighting ships and for preventing collisions, while its use in time of war will be invaluable for detecting approaching torpedo-boats and for other purposes.

Systematic surveys of parts of the West Indies, the Spanish Main, the coasts of Mexico and Central America, the Marshall and Caroline groups of islands, as well as the examination of reported shoals and rocks in the Atlantic and Pacific Oceans, are recommended. These surveys are necessary for the construction of reliable charts of these localities, which are as yet imperfectly known, and for the safer navigation of the high-seas. It would seem to be the duty of the United States Navy, possessing the *personnel* educated for the purpose, to clear up the uncertainties in the tracks of ocean-going vessels, and to survey coasts not reliably laid down on charts or imperfectly known, especially in localities where our own commerce is most interested. No more useful work can be projected for available naval officers in time of peace. The department has encouraged all recommendations in that direction on the part of the Chief of the Bureau of Navigation as far as in its power; and some surveys have been successfully accomplished by our cruisers, aside from their regular duties. But for the want of suitable vessels and pecuniary means, much desired work of this kind has been left undone. The department has asked for additional funds for this purpose, and it is earnestly recommended that Congress may, in the interest of our own commerce and navigation in general, appropriate the means applied for.

In furtherance of this object, the United States steamer Despatch has been detailed for the purpose of surveying, during the coming winter months, the waters and shoals of the Gulf of Samana, in the island of San Domingo, which, from its geographical position and extent, seems destined to become of great importance commercially; and as soon as the United States steamer Pinta is ready for sea, she will be employed on similar service on the Spanish main.

The Hydrographic Office is reported as being in admirable working order. A number of junior naval officers find there much useful and instructive employment in collating and preparing for publication sailing directions and hydrographic notices to mariners, and in computing tables and translating foreign books and pamphlets. Although this office has only been in operation since 1866, it has already, through the energy and circumspection of its management, achieved a reputable station among the much older hydrographic institutions of other maritime nations.

This office is now the only source from which the merchants and navigators of this country can obtain authoritative charts and books for navigating the waters and harbors of the world, except those of the United States, which are published by the United States Coast and Geodetic Survey Office. Its importance becomes at once apparent, and its value as a national institution would be further enhanced if this country should become involved in a foreign war. It would seem good policy, therefore, to foster the objects of its creation by granting liberal appropriations in order to enable it to increase the number of its charts and other publications as fast as practicable, and in this way make this country eventually independent of others for its supply of charts, which to some extent have now to be purchased from abroad.

It is much regretted that during the past four years the appropriations for the Hydrographic Office have been less in amount than before, thus retarding the accomplishment of these objects.

Although this department has no control or supervision of anything pertaining to the merchant marine of this country, attention is called to the omission on the part of Congress during its last two sessions to pass an act adopting the revised international regulations for preventing collisions on the water, which originated from the Government of Great Britain, and have already been adopted by all other maritime nations except the United States. Thus the anomalous condition prevails that in the waters of the United States the regulations prescribed by section 4233 of the Revised Statutes must be observed, while in all other parts of the world a somewhat different law is to be obeyed. The Navy Department has issued the proper instructions in regard to this matter for the guidance of its vessels when in foreign waters, but merchant-vessels may be led into difficulty and disaster through the non-observance of the revised regulations obtaining in foreign waters.

The superintendent of the Naval Observatory reports the astronomical work performed during the past year, consisting of observations of stars, satellites, and comets; their reduction and partial publication; the discussion and publication of the results of the transit of Venus expeditions of 1874; the reduction of the photographic observations of the transit of Mercury of 1878, and the prosecution of experiments on astronomical photography. The report states also the number of navy chronometers and their treatment, and the manner of furnishing correct Washington and New York noon time.

In a separate report, hereto appended, the superintendent details the labors of the commission appointed under the authority of the act of February 4, 1880, to select a site for a new Naval Observatory, which resulted in the selection and purchase of the place belonging to Mrs. M. C. Barber, on Georgetown Heights, for the sum of $63,000. The height of the land is 280 feet above mean tide in the Potomac River. The place is salubrious, with a fine horizon, and contains a fraction over 70 acres of land. The character of the soil is gravel, sand, and clay, with a small portion of the latter, however, rendering the foundation of any building exceedingly firm.

Drawings, plans, and estimates for the new observatory have been prepared, and it is believed that for the sum of $586,138 the work can be completed without any subsequent appropriation.

In the preparation of the American Ephemeris and Nautical Almanac in advance, the volume for 1885 is nearly completed, that for 1884 having already been issued. Besides this current work, there have been prepared at the Nautical Almanac Office during the past year improved tables for the Ephemeris; and various researches, having for their object a more accurate determination of the constants of astronomy, are in progress.

The superintendent reports also the experiments made for determining the velocity of light, their progress, and the results thus far obtained

BUREAU OF ORDNANCE.

Besides the usual work of fitting the batteries of ships for sea, making the necessary repairs to ordnance material, and keeping up the stock of manufactured articles for current service, the Bureau of Ordnance has been engaged in improving the ballistic power of certain of the Parrott muzzle-loading rifles by converting them to breech-loaders with enlarged powder chambers.

A quantity of steel breech-loading howitzers for boat and field service have also been manufactured and fitted with field carriages, while a long 6-inch steel breech-loading rifle in process of manufacture at the South Boston Iron Works (from designs furnished by the bureau) approaches completion.

A number of 8-inch muzzle-loading converted rifles have been placed on board of ships fitted for sea, and carriages of improved design have been furnished on trial to some of them. A considerable number of machine guns (both heavy and light) of the most approved patterns have also recently been placed afloat.

The all-important subject of the suitable armament of the Navy with modern rifled breech-loading cannon presses for attention, and is dwelt upon at length in the report of the Ordnance Bureau. Our total lack of a really efficient armament is well known to Congress, and has been represented in the successive reports of this department for several years.

Our vessels of war are obliged to appear to great disadvantage beside those of ostensibly equal force belonging to other nations, and our battery power is so low as to justify the gravest apprehension in case we should be called upon to meet foreign ships of equal size in battle.

In view of these facts it would seem that the very moderate number of ten guns now estimated for by the Bureau of Ordnance should meet with favorable consideration, particularly as it is desired is to build them in our own country, except perhaps two or three which it may be thought advisable to procure abroad as models or exponents of the results of the practical experience of other countries.

It is time now that we should call upon our steel-makers for a serious effort to furnish material of proper quality for the manufacture of naval cannon, and the guns now asked for may perhaps constitute an inducement for some of our firms to study the subject more closely than they have heretofore done. A new armament should be procured without delay, and if it cannot be produced in this country we will be forced to go abroad for it.

During the year the torpedo station has done very useful work and has turned out a class of officers well instructed in the elements of torpedo attack and defense.

A new Lay torpedo, lately purchased by the department, shows a very considerable excess of speed above those previously furnished, and another movable torpedo has been experimented with, the results being encouraging. In addition, extensive researches have been made into the details of systems for defense of vessels against torpedoes, both by means of obstructions and by the electric light; and this work is still going on under the zealous and efficient supervision of the officer in charge of the station.

Experiments are also being made with a view to the introduction of a higher explosive than gunpowder into the torpedo service.

The impression prevails in some quarters that torpedoes alone would suffice for the defense of our coast against a hostile fleet. This view is not sustained by any of the military powers, and indeed hardly seems tenable. Torpedoes either for defense or attack must be covered and defended by the fire of powerful rifled guns, both afloat and ashore.

There are various methods in vogue for the destruction and removal of hostile torpedoes, and these appliances are being constantly perfected. In view of this state of affairs, it would be rash, indeed, to place our reliance upon torpedoes alone. The two destructive agents (artillery and torpedoes) supplement each other; and, as a rule, must be employed together.

I deem it proper to direct the attention of Congress to the invention by Capt. John Ericsson of a system of torpedoes for attack, as developed in the Ericsson torpedo boat, the Destroyer. Experiments of an interesting nature have been made of this invention, in the presence of the department and of scientific persons whose judgment is entitled to respect in such matters. The department deems the invention of sufficient importance to warrant the appointment of a board, to be charged with a full and thorough investigation of the methods employed, in order to accomplish the contemplated purpose. The board will be instructed to report the result of its investigation, and that report will be submitted hereafter to Congress for such action as, in its judgment, may be deemed proper.

BUREAU OF YARDS AND DOCKS.

Special attention is called to those parts of the report of the Chief of the Bureau of Yards and Docks which relate to the navy-yards at Boston, New York, New London, Norfolk, Pensacola, and Mare Island.

During the fiscal year ending June 30, 1881, the funds appropriated for the works coming under the cognizance of this bureau seem to have been economically and judiciously expended. They are deemed to have been inadequate to the requirements of the wants of the bureau. Due care has been bestowed upon the many and various objects embraced in its charge. Some idea of the magnitude of the work of this bureau may be conceived when it is known that the sole care of the vast property embraced within the limits of its various navy-yards devolves upon it; and much of this property, such as valuable buildings, wharves, docks, &c., has suffered serious deterioration from lack of funds to properly care for it. The repairs now absolutely necessary amount, in many instances, to reconstruction. On this account, the amount asked for at this time is in excess of that appropriated for many years past. From a personal inspection of some of the navy-yards, I am satisfied that the condition of things as set forth in the report of the chief of the bureau is not exaggerated.

Prompt action is required to save what has already been done on the stone dry-dock at Mare Island, California. This important and expensive structure has reached that stage where continued work seems absolutely necessary if it is to be prosecuted to a successful termination.

Wooden buildings, of which there are many in our navy-yards, are highly objectionable. They are unsubstantial and unsightly, affording inadequate protection to the property contained in them, and endangering its safety by fire. It is recommended that no more of this class of buildings be erected.

The recent accident at the Washington yard, from the explosion of a torpedo or rocket while being prepared for service, by which one man lost his life, two others were seriously injured, and a building was destroyed, again brings forward very prominently the question of the propriety of such work being carried on in a navy-yard, to the great risk of life, and of the vast and valuable property involved in the danger. In the opinion of the chief of the bureau, such works should be removed from the yard.

BUREAU OF EQUIPMENT AND RECRUITING.

During the past fiscal year 69 vessels have been wholly or partially equipped.

At home and abroad 38,244 tons of coal have been purchased.

Of hemp there have been purchased 168,210 pounds Manila, 112,205 pounds of American, and 108,580 pounds of Russian.

At the rolling-mill at the navy-yard, Washington, D.C., there have been rolled 797,643 pounds of iron, and 2,790 pounds of steel, all of superior quality, for the various purposes of the Navy.

The experiments of welding chain links by compression have been continued. During the year a quantity of specimens of the best English admiralty-made chains have been purchased, for the purpose of testing them with the chains made of the iron rolled in the rolling-mill.

The anchor and galley shops at the Washington navy-yard have been in constant employment, the former in making anchors as well as shafts for machinery, and the latter in making new as well as improving and repairing old galleys.

During the past fiscal year there were enlisted 4,519 men and 751 apprentices, and on the 30th June, 1881, there were 7,974 men and boys in the service.

Special legislation is asked for the employment of enlisted men who may be detailed to the Naval Academy and on vessels engaged in the Coast Survey and Fish Commission. They are at present taken from the quota of men allowed by law, and thus reduce the effective force of the Navy.

The chief of this bureau has submitted an increase of funds under appropriations "equipment of vessels" and "contingent."

BUREAU OF STEAM ENGINEERING.

The departments under cognizance of this bureau at the several navy-yards, under their present organization and equipment, are in good working condition, but, to render them more efficient, new and improved machine tools should from time to time be added.

THE ENGINEER CORPS.

I desire to call attention to the somewhat anomalous condition in which the grade of passed assistant engineer stands with regard to pay.

The officers of this grade holding, in a majority of cases, the relative rank of lieutenant, receive at present one increase of pay after a period of five years' service in that grade, and then the pay remains the same no matter how long promotion may be delayed.

It was evidently assumed that none would remain in that grade longer than ten years, whereas the term of service approaches twenty years.

The next higher grade receives four increases of service pay, and it would seem but justice, in view of the slow promotion of the passed assistant engineers, and of the fact that most of them will retire before being benefited by the longevity pay in the higher grade, that their pay should be graduated on the basis of length of service.

I earnestly commend their case to favorable consideration.

DOUBLE TURRETED MONITORS.

There are four double turreted monitors belonging to the government and remaining unfinished. They are the Terror at Philadelphia, Amphitrite at Wilmington, Del., the Puritan at Chester, Pa., and the Monadnock at Mare Island, California. To continue these vessels on the original plans, it is said would be to introduce a worthless class of vessels into the Navy at great cost to the government. To keep them in their present position without any work being done upon them involves a

32 Ab

heavy expense, and is besides a hardship to the builders, who, no doubt, require the room occupied by three of the vessels for their own purposes, and may properly charge the government for ground rent, inasmuch as it has been through no fault of theirs that the work does not progress.

In April, 1880, boards were appointed to report on the advisability of finishing these vessels on a somewhat modified plan, but it was thought the time spent in examining the vessels was not sufficient to enable the examiners to come to a correct conclusion, either as to the cost of finishing them, or the plan on which they should be completed.

The department is informed that there is nothing to prevent the launching of these vessels, although it has been stated that this cannot be done until the wood backing of the armor is in place, as the bolt holes necessary to receive it would be under water. If the hull proper was completed, in all respects, except only the wood backing and the side armor, the armor shelf on which the wood backing rests would be over three feet above the water.

When these vessels are once removed to a navy-yard, a careful examination of them can be made, and deliberate plans prepared for their completion. New contracts could be entered into, and the vessels be finished in a manner to confer some benefit to the government in spite of their irregularly designed plans.

The monitors are at present simply bad copies of old models built in an emergency, worthless for the defense of our coasts and entailing a considerable expense for their preservation.

The government cannot afford to throw away these vessels after spending so much money on them without first finding out whether they may be converted into useful ships.

BUREAU OF CONSTRUCTION AND REPAIR.

A reference to the report of the chief of the Bureau of Construction and Repair will show the condition of the ships composing our Navy at present. From this it will be seen that of 115 vessels of all kinds, exclusive of tugs, 27 are unfit for any service whatever.

The appropriation asked for that bureau, viz, $2,500,000, will keep in repair the vessels now in commission or awaiting repairs, and complete three other vessels, viz, the New York, Mohican, and Miantonomah.

BUREAU OF MEDICINE AND SURGERY.

A detailed report of the sanitary condition of the Navy, by the Surgeon-General, is hereto appended.

The returns show a most gratifying improvement in the health of the Navy over the previous year. There were admitted during the year, from the entire force, including the cases remaining over from the preceding year (amounting to 464), 13,387 cases, of which 11,485 were discharged recovered, 111 died, 990 invalided to hospital, 321 invalided from service, and 480 continued to the succeeding year.

The total loss of time to the service by disease and injury amounted to 179,435 days, giving a daily average sick-list of 491.6. The average duration of treatment was 13.4 days. In comparison with the previous year, these figures show a marked decrease in the admissions and invaliding rate, but a slight increase in the death rate, due principally to epidemic yellow fever on board the United States ship Marion.

The effective force of the Navy employed afloat during the year 1880 was 10,235, and corrected for time, 9,003, an increase of 134 men over the preceding year. The total number of admissions reached 9,752, of which 8,711 were discharged recovered, 758, or 84.19 per M, invalided to hospital, and 40, or 5.44 per M, discharged from the service; 28, or 3.11 per M, died, and 206 were continued to the succeeding year. The ratio of admissions was 1,083.44 per M of strength. These figures show a decrease of 99.10 per M in the admissions, 20.19 per M in the invaliding rate, and .95 per M in the death rate. The health has not only been better than for the previous year, but is also superior to that of several foreign navies. The English, Austrian, and Prussian reports show, respectively, 1,116.9–1,141.78 and 1,530.2 per M of admissions; 32.96–9.85 and 16.03 per M in the invaliding rate; and 6.23–5.1 and 8.8 per M in the date rate.

The number of sick days amounted to 82,623, giving a daily average sick-rate of 225.74, or 25.07 per M, a decrease of 2.52 per M from the previous year. The average duration of treatment was 8.88 days.

This is due to the vigilant attention paid by the Navy Department to all matters appertaining to the sanitary surroundings of the sailor. One of the most important of these is the ventilation of ships, which has been carried to the highest state of perfection in the Lancaster, Brooklyn, Hartford, and Richmond, and it is recommended that in future all ships undergoing repairs, or being built, be furnished with the same apparatus. It is also suggested that the system of cooking and rationing be made the subject of special investigation by a board of officers with a view of improving it, both as regards quality and preparation, by which it is believed that much sickness now prevalent can be avoided.

An allied and equally important subject for investigation is that of clothing, changes in which might be advantageously made in the interests of both comfort and a higher standard of health.

In the matter of recruiting, difficulties have been encountered in making physical examinations on ship-board on account of the disturbing influences of noise and other circumstances of ship routine. This important duty could be more efficiently performed in a room on shore specially arranged for the purpose at each station and by officers specially selected.

At the naval laboratory at Washington important work has been performed, with the assistance of a small appropriation made by the last Congress, in the causative relation of atmospheric impurities to disease, and it is hoped that the scope of these investigations may be enlarged so as to include other sanitary subjects bearing upon naval and general hygiene.

The amount of appropriations available for the present fiscal year ending June 30, 1882, is $14,874,269.55; also transferred from Navy pension fund to the Naval Asylum $59,813, making a total of $14,934,082.55. The amount drawn by warrant from the Treasury from July 1, 1881, to November 1, 1881, is $5,084,580.41; which, compared with the same period of last year, shows an increase of $43,009.96.

The estimates for the fiscal year ending June 30, 1883, are as follows, viz:

ESTIMATES FOR THE FISCAL YEAR ENDING JUNE 30, 1883.

Pay of the Navy	$7,609,025 00
Pay of civil establishment, navy-yards	201,303 50
Ordnance and Torpedo Corps	509,793 00
Coal, hemp and equipment	896,000 00
Navigation and navigation supplies	135,500 00
Hydrographic work	114,000 00
Naval Observatory, Nautical Almanac	52,336 25
Repairs and preservation of vessels	2,225,000 00
Building turrets, &c., for Miantonomah	275,000 00
Steam machinery, tools, &c	1,947,000 00
Provisions for the navy	1,200,000 00
Repairs of hospitals and laboratories	31,500 00
Medical department	45,000 00
Naval hospital fund	50,000 00
Contingent expenses of department and bureaus	300,500 00
Naval Academy	185,626 95
Support of Marine Corps	891,366 76
Naval Asylum, Philadelphia	90,197 00
Maintenance of yards and docks	490,000 00
Repairs and improvements of navy-yards	2,763,938 00
Contingent, Navy, 1881	630 00
	20,013,716 46
Add amount estimated for new building at Naval Academy	66,000 00
	20,079,716 46

The following statement shows the number and yearly amount of pensions on the rolls June 30, 1881, and the amount paid during the fiscal year:

	On roll June 30,1881.	Yearly value.	Amount paid for pensions.
Navy invalids	2,187	$427,227 06	$484,243 86
Navy widows and others	2,008	333,754 68	480,894 38
Total	4,195	760,981 74	965,138 24

THE NAVAL ACADEMY.

The Board of Visitors who witnessed the examination of the cadets at the Naval Academy in June last, and inspected the several professional departments of that institution, the sanitary condition of the buildings and grounds, &c., expressed themselves much gratified at the results. An additional wing to the new cadet quarters is recommended by the board in order that the entire body of cadets may be domiciled under the same roof, and the enactment of a law is suggested by which the library of the Academy can be furnished with all government publications free of cost. Legislation is also suggested which will provide against an increase in the number of cadet-midshipmen and cadet-engineers, so as to prevent them from growing old in these inferior grades, to the manifest detriment of the efficiency and usefulness of the service. Some other suggestions of an important nature are made by the board. These the department has authority to carry out, and they will be followed as far as the appropriations and circumstances will permit. The present condition of the Academy is efficient and entirely satisfactory.

On the 10th of June, Rear-Admiral Balch withdrew from the superintendency of the institution, and Rear-Admiral C. R. P. Rodgers succeeded him. It is due to this latter distinguished and enlightened officer to say that, in great part through his efforts, the present exemplary discipline of the school, and proficiency of the cadets in their studies and conduct, have been attained. The institution is a source of pride to the department and of usefulness to the country. It is believed that the Academy is, in all respects, at this time superior to any other naval school in the world. This excellence arises from the system of instruction originally introduced at the first formation of the school, and since then perfected by such reforms and improvements in its curriculum and general management and discipline as have become necessary in the course of time. The interest and zeal which have been exhibited by the corps of officers and instructors in charge of the Academy are entitled to commendation.

Particular attention is drawn to the report of the superintendent, Rear-Admiral C. R. P. Rodgers.

It is deemed proper that the salary of the professor of chemistry should be increased as recommended, and that the sum of $2,500, instead of $2,200, be hereafter paid as the salary of that chair.

TRAINING SQUADRON.

The training ships for the purpose of training boys to become seamen on men of war have recently been inspected by a board appointed for that purpose. They speak in the highest terms of the performances of the apprentice boys, and for the first time in our history the naval apprentice system seems to be established on a sure foundation, from which the Navy will soon reap material advantages. Heretofore the system has been conducted in a very irregular manner. The Admiral of the Navy has, however, devoted himself, with his accustomed zeal and ability, to the supervision of the squadron, relieving the department in a great measure from the responsibility connected with its operations. The squadron is under the command of Capt. S. B. Luce, who reported to the department on the 15th instant that he had ready for general service two hundred and fifty boys thoroughly trained as seamen. The younger boys have been transferred to the New Hampshire for the winter. The Saratoga and Portsmouth belonging to the squadron have been ordered to be repaired before going to sea again; and the Constitution has been taken to the navy-yard at New York for the same purpose, and to go out of commission.

It is believed by the department that this training squadron will maintain its present efficiency and may be relied on in future to furnish a nucleus for seamen for the Navy.

MARINE CORPS.

The commandant of the Marine Corps exhibits in his report the present condition of that branch of the service, which is very satisfactory.

The strength of the Corps on the 30th September last was 1,885 enlisted men, the majority of whom are doing duty on board ships in commission. An immediate increase of officers and enlisted men, to meet the requirements of the service, is represented as an absolute necessity, and the colonel commandant calls attention to his report of last year on this subject and urgently renews his recommendations then made.

The post of Pensacola, which has not been garrisoned for several years, is to be re-established next month, but the officers and men to be sent thither will be without suitable quarters or barracks. I recommend that provision be made to meet this want, and that an appropriation be also made for a similar purpose at the Norfolk navy-yard. New barracks have been constructed at Annapolis and Washington, which add greatly to the comfort and health of the garrisons at those places.

Somewhat more success has followed the measures for recruiting this year than in the prior one, especially at Philadelphia. The colonel commandant renews his recommendation for appropriate legislation as to the manner of appointments and promotions in the Corps and for the restoration of the grade of brigadier-general, both of which recommendations meet with my approval.

The urgent need of a prison, to which men serving out sentences of courts-martial can be sent instead of to State prisons, is well presented by the colonel commandant, and his suggestion that an appropriation be made for this purpose is well worthy of the attention of Congress.

WORKMEN IN NAVY-YARDS AND STATIONS.

The department deems it proper to invite Congress to consider some mode of relief for a class of public servants who are not adequately provided for under existing laws. Mechanics and laborers at the navy-yards and stations are often exposed, in the discharge of their duty, to unusual perils. In the preparation of ammunition, torpedoes, and ord-

nance stores, and in many other tasks to which they are assigned, it
seems impossible to guard at all times against accidents. There is no
provision for those who incur physical disabilities in this service. Recent instances have occurred in the naval service where injuries have
been sustained by meritorious persons while performing their duty
which appeal strongly to the sympathy and sense of justice of the government. The department is unable, under existing laws, to respond
favorably to such appeals.

This matter is put with simplicity and force in a report of the present
Chief of the Bureau of Steam Engineering, under date October 30, 1878:

> It matters not how long or how faithfully they may have served the government,
> nor how hazardous their duty or calling; an arm or leg is broken, an eye is lost, a
> hand is crushed, or, perhaps, instant death overtakes the laborer, and he is borne to
> his home by his fellow-workmen. He fails to answer at the next roll-call; his name
> is first checked, and then stricken from it altogether. * * * That is the last of
> him and his family, so far as the government is concerned!

Some legislation should be had with reference to cases of this nature,
by which persons should be relieved by the government from the cruel
hardship of such indifference.

COALING STATIONS ON THE ISTHMUS OF PANAMA.

In the act of Congress making appropriations for sundry civil expenses
of the government for the fiscal year ending June 30, 1882, and approved
March 3, 1881, the sum of $200,000 was appropriated "to enable the
Secretary of the Navy to establish at the Isthmus of Panama naval
stations and depots for coal, for the supply of steamships of war, to be
available for expenditure as soon as suitable arrangements can be made
to the proposed end."

Constantly, since the passage of this act, the department has been
importuned to expend the sum here appropriated in acquiring title to
certain rights upon the isthmus, claimed to belong to Ambrose W.
Thompson, as the representative of a corporation styling itself the
Chiriqui Improvement Company. The appropriation seems to have
been granted in pursuance of the recommendation of the Hon. N. Goff.
jr., Secretary of the Navy, in a report made by him to President Hayes,
under date of January 19, 1881. This report was submitted by President Hayes, in a message to the House of Representatives, dated February 2, 1881. It is evident that the report of the Secretary of the
Navy, and the message of the President contemplated the establishment of the naval stations and depots claimed to belong to the Chiriqui
Improvement Company, and Ambrose W. Thompson. Indeed, the Hon.
R. W. Thompson, Secretary of the Navy, in his report under date November 30, 1880, states that he had "caused coal to be deposited in
small quantities on these lands for use by our vessels whenever it may
be needed." This step was taken with a view to acquiring title to these
lands by our government. The appropriation, however, seems to have

carefully avoided all mention of the selection of these lands, or of any other specific lands for the contemplated coal stations. Under the general instructions of this authorization I have been unable to satisfy myself that the interests of the government will be advanced by the payment of this sum, or any portion of it, for the grant represented by Mr. Thompson. From reports made to the department from reliable sources, since the passage of the appropriation and before, I am not satisfied that the lands and harbors known as the Chiriqui grant are the best adapted for coal stations. Several parties claim to be owners of the grant which Mr. Thompson asserts belongs entirely to him and his company. It is also urged that the title of Mr. Thompson and the company is not valid; that it rested originally upon a grant conferred by the United States of Colombia under certain conditions, which have not been complied with by the grantees; that such coaling stations would result in a useless expenditure of money, involving large expense to the government in the maintenance of the stations, and probably resulting in their abandonment as being in an expensive, isolated, inconvenient, and unhealthy position. The sovereignty over these lands has undergone changes since the date of the original contract; and it is by no means certain that the obligations said to be conferred under that contract will be ratified and held valid by the government now in power there. It is further reported that land in this lagoon is almost valueless, and that any one settling there and cultivating it acquires title by mere possession. For these and other reasons, I have declined to treat for the lands offered by Mr. Ambrose W. Thompson and the corporation in whose name he acts.

DECAYED HULLS AND USELESS MATERIAL.

There are in our navy-yards large accumulations of property, consisting of the ancient hulls of vessels of war, launches, and other ships boats, old machinery and condemned stores and materials and other effects which have become unfitted for use in the Navy. This property is subject to a gradual process of deterioration and decay. It encumbers the wharves and grounds of our navy-yards, and presents an unsightly appearance sometimes ghastly and discouraging to those whose labors are to be performed near it, and to strangers and others who visit the yards. This property was originally paid for out of funds appropriated by Congress to the Navy Department. Under existing laws, if it be surveyed and sold at auction, the proceeds of such sales are turned into the general funds of the Treasury and cannot enure to the benefit of the Navy. It is expedient that this property, before becoming entirely worthless, should be surveyed and sold, and it is just that the proceeds of the sales should go to the credit of the construction and other funds of the Department. In order to bring about this desirable result a bill was introduced and passed in the Senate at the last session of Congress. It failed, for want of time, in the House of Representatives.

Day by day, the process of deterioration and decay goes on, and will continue, until the relief contemplated takes the form of a law of Congress, and the property is authorized to be sold in accordance with the plan approved by the Senate. As a measure of economy, it should be promptly adopted. The department incurs a heavy outlay daily, in guarding this property, and in endeavoring to preserve it. It is to be hoped that this matter will receive prompt attention from Congress.

THE CASE OF COMMODORE WHITING.

I deem it an act of justice to call attention to the case of Capt. W. D. Whiting, of the Navy. He has for some years served as Chief of the Bureau of Navigation, the arduous and responsible duties of which position he has discharged with ability and impartiality, and to the satisfaction of the department and of the officers of the Navy. As chief of that bureau, the law conferred upon him the relative rank of commodore. On coming to be examined for promotion to that full rank, he was reported as disqualified to obtain it, by reason of physical disabilities incurred in the performance of his duties in the service. This report involved his being placed upon the retired list. The Attorney-General was consulted by the department as to whether he might be retired in his relative rank of commodore. That officer gave an opinion that he could be retired only as a captain. In view of his long and meritorious service in the Navy, and of the fact that he has lost his eyesight whilst thus engaged, it seems to be eminently proper that an act should be passed by Congress, directing him to be retired as a commodore, and that his name be placed on the list of officers holding that rank from the date of his retirement, instead of on the list of captains.

WILLIAM H. HUNT,
Secretary of the Navy.

To the PRESIDENT.

PAPERS

ACCOMPANYING

THE REPORT OF THE SECRETARY OF THE NAVY.

ORDERS OF THE SECRETARY OF THE NAVY CONVENING THE NAVAL ADVISORY BOARD.

NAVY DEPARTMENT,
Washington, June 29, 1881.

I. In order to meet the exigencies of the Navy, it is highly important, in the opinion of the department, to present in the report of the Secretary at the next session of Congress a practical and plain statement of the pressing need of appropriate vessels in the service at the present time.

Such a statement can best be furnished by an Advisory Board who may consult together and be able to reconcile conflicting opinions and theories with reference to the number and class of such vessels as should be constructed, and to unite in recommending such as Congress would be most likely to approve.

II. Accordingly, the following officers in the service are detailed to constitute such a Board.

Rear-Admiral John Rodgers.
Commodore William G. Temple.
Capt. P. C. Johnson.
Capt. K. R. Breeze.
Commander H. L. Howison.
Commander R. D. Evans.
Commander A. S. Crowninshield.
Lieut. M. R. S. MacKenzie.
Lieut. Ed. W. Very.
Chief Engineer B. F. Isherwood.
Chief Engineer C. A. Loring.
Passed Assistant C. H. Manning.
Naval Constructor John Lenthall.
Naval Constructor Theo. D. Wilson.
Naval Constructor Philip Hichborn.

III. The Board will consider and advise the department upon the following subjects:

1st. The number of vessels that should now be built.

2d. Their class, size, and displacement.

3d. The material and form of their construction.

4th. The nature and size of the engines and machinery required for each.

5th. The ordnance and armament necessary for each.

6th. The appropriate equipments and rigging of each.

7th. The internal arrangements of each, and upon such other details as may seem to be necessary and proper, and, lastly, the probable cost of the whole of each vessel when complete and ready for service.

IV. The members of the Board will assemble in Washington City on the 11th day of July next, at 12 meridian, and will report to the department the result of their labors not later than the 10th day of November next.

WILLIAM H. HUNT,
Secretary of the Navy.

NAVY DEPARTMENT,
Washington, July 8, 1881.

SIR: You are informed that in consequence of the ill health of Capt. K. R. Breeze, his orders as a member of the Advisory Board of which you are president, have been revoked, and that Lieut. Frederick Collins has been ordered to supply the vacancy.

Respectfully,

WILLIAM H. HUNT,
Secretary of the Navy.

Rear-Admiral JOHN RODGERS,
Superintendent Naval Observatory, Washington, D. C.

REPORT OF THE BOARD.

UNITED STATES NAVY DEPARTMENT,
Washington, D. C., November 7, 1881.

Hon. WILLIAM H. HUNT,
Secretary of the Navy:

SIR: The Naval Advisory Board, convened by your order for the purpose of recommending the immediate construction of such number and classes of vessels as Congress would be most likely to approve, in order to satisfy the pressing need of appropriate vessels in the service at the present time, has been in session since the 11th of July last, and, having completed its labors, has the honor to submit the following report:

By the prescriptions of the order of the department, the Board was required to determine—

1st. The number of vessels that should now be built.

2d. Their class, size, and displacement.

3d. The material and form of the construction.

4th. The nature and size of the engines and machinery required for each.

5th. The ordnance and armament necessary for each.

6th. The appropriate equipment and rigging for each.

7th. The internal arrangements of each, and such other details as might seem to be necessary and, proper; and—

Lastly, the probable cost of the whole of each vessel when complete and ready for service.

After a thorough examination of the intentions and the scope of the order, it was decided by the Board to first determine the number, class, size, speed, armament, &c., of the unarmored cruisers necessary to fulfill the immediate necessities of the service. This decision was based upon the considerations, that—

The order explicitly stated that the necessities of *the present time* were to be provided for.

At present the unarmored vessels of the service are the only ones required to carry on the work of the Navy.

The unarmored vessels now in service are altogether inadequate in number and efficiency for the work that they are constantly called upon to perform.

In taking such vessels first under consideration, not only are the pressing needs of the service greatly relieved, but the basis of an efficient defensive and offensive force in time of war is established.

THE NUMBER OF UNARMORED VESSELS NOW TO BE BUILT.

The first step taken by the Board, in its determination of the number of vessels that should now be built, was to thoroughly investigate the present condition of the fleet; the number of vessels in service in the squadrons; the number of vessels in reserve available for relief; the estimated life-time of the vessels; the cost of putting them in condition for active service, and their comparative efficiency as measured by their speed, armament, size, &c. (See evidence given by the Chiefs of the Bureaus of Construction and of Steam Engineering, appended, pp. 91 to 105.)

In this manner a knowledge of the number of vessels now available was obtained, and it was found that of 61 unarmored cruising vessels now on the Navy-list (torpedo vessels, dispatch vessels, tugs, and sailing vessels excluded) but 32 either are available, or can be made so at a cost low enough to warrant the expenditure. Of these 32 vessels, 24 are at present in commission in the squadrons, leaving a reserve of 8 for the relief of ships requiring repair, &c., or 25 per centum of the whole number, while throughout the world it is recognized that, in order to keep up the strength of a wooden fleet, a reserve of 50 per centum is necessary.

It is the opinion of the Board that, taking into proper consideration the various requirements of the different squadrons for surveying, deep-sea sounding, the protection and advancement of American commerce, exploration, the protection of American life and property endangered by wars between foreign countries, and service in support of American policy in matters where foreign governments are concerned, 43 unarmored cruising vessels are required constantly in commission, or 12 more than are possibly available now in case of the most urgent necessity both in commission and in reserve. Increasing this number by 50 per centum, in order to obtain a reserve of sufficient strength to maintain the effectiveness of the fleet, a total of 65 vessels is obtained, which would be sufficient, were it not for the fact that the present condition and limited life-time of some of the vessels included will soon weaken the number very materially. To allow for this loss, it is the opinion of the Board that 5 more vessels should be added, giving a total number necessary to perform efficiently the work of the Navy at present of 70 vessels.

Taking from this the 32 vessels now available, the Board is of the opinion that 38 unarmored cruising vessels should now be built.

THE CLASS, SIZE, AND DISPLACEMENT.

In determining the class, size, and displacement of the unarmored vessels to be recommended, the Board is of the opinion that the first quality necessary to be developed, in order that a vessel shall be thoroughly efficient, is the capability of maintaining a high rate of speed at sea for a protracted period.

The Board decided that, in estimating the proper speed allowance for vessels, what is commonly known as maximum speed, or speed in smooth water on the measured mile, should not be considered, as such a basis is a deceptive one; but that the speed recommended should be the *average speed at sea* that the vessel would be capable of making under full power.

In order that a high rate of speed may be maintained at sea, a great weight of machinery is necessary, and also a great amount of space in the holds of the vessel. These demands alone place a limit upon the minimum displacement of the ship; while, on the other hand, the necessity of keeping within bounds in the draught of water of the ship, and of restricting the length and other measurements to limits that will permit a proper amount of handiness in maneuvering power, places a limit upon the maximum displacement, and consequently upon the speed.

It is the opinion of the Board that the maximum sea-speed that can be recommended as the measure of the size of the largest class of vessels is fifteen knots per hour.

Since the necessities of the service demand a class of vessels that should not draw over nine and one-half feet of water, and since a sea-speed of ten knots per hour is the greatest that can be depended upon with this draught (other qualities being given due weight), it is the opinion of the Board that ten knots should be recommended as the minimum sea-speed in measuring the sizes of vessels.

The Board is of the opinion that classes of vessels represented by sea-speeds of thirteen and fourteen knots are very useful in time of peace and of the greatest possible value in time of war, and that such vessels should now be built.

The sizes of the wooden vessels now in service and available correspond to sea-speeds of eleven and twelve knots. These speeds are not considered by the Board as efficient ones for war service; nor are these vessels capable of maintaining it as a rule. Still, the classes which they represent are excellent for ordinary service-work, and are more fully represented in foreign navies than the higher ones. (See tabulated statement of foreign unarmored vessels appended, p. 108.)

It is the opinion of the Board that the classes should be perpetuated by replacing these vessels as they wear out with modern vessels that shall be fully equal to the speed requirements. There is now, however, a sufficient number of vessels of these classes available for the duty required of them, and the Board does not recommend the building of any more at present.

The Board is of the opinion that the interests of efficiency and economy will best be satisfied in recommending that, of the 38 unarmored cruisers to be built, 2 should be 15-knot vessels of about 5,873 tons displacement; 6 should be 14-knot vessels of about 4,560 tons displacement; 10 should be 13-knot vessels of about 3,043 tons displacement; 20 should be 10-knot vessels of about 793 tons displacement.

MATERIAL OF CONSTRUCTION.

It is the opinion of the Board that owing to the large supply of suitable timber at present on hand in the navy-yards, which the interests of economy demand should be utilized, the familiarity of our eastern workmen with wooden ship-building, and their dependence upon it for a livelihood, the resources of the country with respect to this material, and the possibility of building wooden vessels of a limited size that shall be staunch, efficient, and economical, the 10-knot class of vessels should be built with live-oak frames, planked and ceiled with yellow pine.

The most difficult question brought before the Board for its decision has been that of the proper material of construction for the hulls of the vessels of the larger classes. It was at first decided that, since iron ship-building is now well developed in the United States, since the excellence and economy of this material for the hulls of vessels has long been indisputably established, and since iron vessels could be built with an absolute certainty that they would fully meet all requirements of efficiency, the Board should recommend iron as the material of construction.

Upon further investigation, however, the Board is of the opinion that, notwithstanding the greater cost of steel as a ship-building material, the lack of experience in the manufacture of steel frames in this country, and the experimental stage that steel ship-building is still passing through in Europe, it should be recommended as the material of construction for the hulls of the 15, 14, and 13 knot vessels, for the following reasons:

1st. The great saving realized in weight of hull, which, by making possible the acquirement of equal advantages on reduced dimensions, compensates in a great measure, if not entirely, for the difference in cost between steel and iron. (See evidence, p. 118, *et seq.*)

2d. The increased strength of hull and increased immunity from damage in grounding or in light collisions. (See evidence, p. 118, *et seq.*)

3d. The rapidly increasing success that attends the construction of steel hulls in Europe.

4th. The certainty that steel is in the very near future to almost entirely supplant iron in the construction of vessels. (See statement of the progress in steel ship-building in Europe, appended.)

5th. The impetus that such a step, taken by the government, would give to the general development of steel manufacture in this country.

6th. The necessity that, when the ships recommended are completed, they shall in all respects be equal to, if not better, than any of their class in foreign navies.

Finally, that for the reputation and the material advantage of the United States it is of prime necessity that in this country, where every other industry is developing with gigantic strides, a bold and decided step should be taken to win back from Europe our former prestige as the best ship-builders of the world.

It is therefore the opinion of the Board that the fifteen, fourteen, and thirteen knot classes of vessels should be built throughout of steel.

FORM OF CONSTRUCTION.

It is the opinion of the Board that the form of construction of the vessels should be such as to give a powerful fore-and-aft fire from the battery; and, in order to fully attain it, it is recommended that the fifteen, fourteen, and thirteen knot classes of vessels be provided with projecting half-turrets forward and aft; that they be provided with recessed bow-ports, capable of permitting both head and beam fire; that the necessary arrangements be made for permitting the installation of a stern pivot-gun that shall command stern, quarter, and beam fire; that channels shall be done away with, and the old style of standing cat-head be replaced by a swinging davit.

The Board is of the opinion that solid metal rams should not be applied to the stems of vessels, but that their bows should be strengthened for ramming.

The Board is of the opinion that all vessels should have as many water-tight compartments as can be consistently put in, and that double bottoms are desirable where practicable.

The Board is of the opinion that topgallant-forecastles should be fitted to all ships; for the protection of the bow-guns, to give increased berth-ing space to the crew, and to favor the strength and dryness of the forward part of the ship.

The Board is of the opinion that poop-cabins would be a disadvantage on the fifteen, fourteen, and ten knot vessels, but that such structures should be provided for the thirteen-knot class.

The Board is of the opinion that the fifteen and fourteen knot classes should have a covered gun-deck, while the thirteen and ten knot classes should have single decks. With regard to the fourteen-knot class it was found that the desired speed could be realized on a displacement of 4,200 tons, but that this tonnage would necessitate a single deck, which in turn would entail a sacrifice of armament of nearly one-half the battery that a vessel of that class should carry; this reduced battery would also be much exposed in action, yet again the berthing space would be quite insufficient for the number of men to be carried. It was decided that the displacement should be increased to 4,560 tons in order that an upper deck could be carried, realizing as far as possible all the advantages to be expected from a vessel of that class.

NATURE AND SIZE OF ENGINES AND MACHINERY.

The Board is of the opinion that the engines of the unarmored vessels recommended should be of the horizontal, back-action, compound type, with steam-jacketed cylinders, surface-condensers, and independent expansion-valves on each cylinder; that the boilers should be of the ordinary cylindrical type, with return tubes above the furnaces, and of a strength capable of carrying a working pressure of ninety pounds to the square inch.

That the screws should in all cases be fixed, four-bladed, and of a uniform pitch, one screw for each vessel. That all the machinery should be below the water-line, and should be further protected from shot by the coal in bunkers arranged for that purpose. That the smoke-pipes of the fifteen, fourteen, and thirteen knot classes of vessels should be telescopic, while for the ten-knot class it should be standing with such a hinged arrangement that in case of necessity it can be lowered fore and aft on deck and secured. That the smoke-pipe of the ten-knot class be made also a ventilator by means of an inner concentric pipe.

That in all classes of vessels the ashes be dumped into an iron tube, the upper end of which is within the fire-room hatch, the lower end leading through the bottom of the ship, so as to avoid carrying them to the side to be dumped overboard.

That all classes, except the ten-knot one, be provided with the most approved system of steam or hydraulic steering-apparatus; that the capstans be fitted to work with either steam or hand-power, and that all vessels be provided with a complete and thorough system of ventilation. (Reasons for adopting single instead of twin screws. Appended, pp. 126.)

THE ORDNANCE AND ARMAMENT.

It is the opinion of the Board, that, in order that the vessels of our service may be able to oppose to foreign men-of-war an armament of a power sufficient to place them on an equality in fighting strength, it is imperatively necessary that a reliable type of high-powered, rifled, breech-loading guns should be introduced into the service; that these guns should have a length of bore of at least twenty-six calibers, in order that their power may be fully developed; and that steel should be the metal used in their construction, in order that the greatest strength and safety may be combined with the least necessary weight.

That calibers of eight and six inches furnish the most satisfactory combination of total weight, individual power, and number of guns for the armament of unarmored vessels.

It is the opinion of the Board that while every gun should be given as great an arc of train as possible, the arrangement of the battery should be such as to do away as far as possible with the necessity for shifting pivot or transporting the gun from one port to another; and that, where possible, the heaviest calibers of a battery should be given the greatest command.

It is the opinion of the Board that the fifteen-knot class of vessels should carry 359 tons of armament, the fourteen-knot class 280 tons, the thirteen-knot class 161 tons, and the ten-knot class 32 tons. (For arrangement of batteries see report of Committee on Ordnance. Appended, pp. 130 et seq.)

It is the opinion of the Board that, owing to the rapid and complete development of a new and powerful gun-system known as the Hotchkiss Revolving Cannon, by which steel shell of from one and a half to two and three-quarters inches in caliber can be fired at the rate of from twenty to fifty shots a minute, the gun being aimed from the shoulder, and the shells being capable of piercing the sides of any unarmored vessel afloat at three hundred yards, the guns and crews of unarmored vessels should not only be protected wherever possible by bulwarks and decks, but wherever possible steel shields or mantlets of medium thickness should be provided in addition as a protection from bursting shells and flying splinters.

It is the opinion of the Board that at least four guns of this type should be provided for every vessel in the service, to give protection against torpedo attacks, to use in general action, and on land service.

That light machine guns should be provided for all vessels for use in torpedo attacks, in ship's tops during general action and on land service.

That a thoroughly approved type of magazine-rifle should be adopted for use in the service.

That hereafter in vessels provided with poop-cabins, such arrangements should be made as will permit the installation of a stern-gun equal in caliber to those of the broadside battery, and capable of commanding a complete stern, quarter, and beam fire.

EQUIPMENT AND RIGGING.

The Board is of the opinion, that all classes of vessels should have full sail power; the amount of sail surface not to be less than twenty-five times the area of the immersed midship-section.

The fifteen, fourteen, and thirteen knot classes of vessels should be ship-rigged, and the ten-knot class barquentine rigged.

The lower rigging in all cases should be set up at the side without channels.

33 Ab

THE INTERNAL ARRANGEMENTS.

The Board is of the opinion, that the fifteen and fourteen knot cruisers should have a bridge forward of the forward smoke-stack, and another one forward of and near the mizzen mast.

That there should be a pilot-house connected with the forward bridge, and a covering should be provided for the protection of the after helmsman, such as can be properly made consistent with his clear view of the sails.

That the head, for the use of the crew, should be under the topgallant forecastle, forward of and between the recessed bow-ports.

That the galleys should be on the gun deck.

That the after state-rooms of the ward-room should be so arranged as to have as nearly as possible the same cubical contents as the forward ones.

That the after compartment of the ward-room should be provided with bath-rooms.

That wash-rooms should be provided for the steerage officers.

That the thirteen-knot class of vessels should have a bridge forward of the smoke-stacks, having a pilot-house connected with it.

That the other internal arrangements of this class should conform as far as possible to those of the higher classes.

That the ward-room and steerages of the ten-knot class should form a single apartment.

It is the opinion of the Board that after its adjournment *sine die* the naval constructors, members, should be ordered to prepare the proper building plans of the vessels recommended by it, in conformity with the modifications adopted, together with the specifications embracing the size of the material, so that should these vessels be at any time ordered to be constructed there will be no delay in procuring the material and commencing the work. The plans and specifications, so prepared, to be deposited in the Navy Department.

In like manner and for like reasons the Board is of the opinion that drawings of the machinery of these vessels should be prepared under the supervision of the engineer members of this Board, or of such of them as may be directed.

THE COST OF EACH VESSEL READY FOR SERVICE.

The Board is of the opinion that the cost of a single vessel of each class, built in conformity with the foregoing recommendations, complete and ready for service, will be as follows:

Details.	15-knot class.	14-knot class.	13-knot class.	10-knot class.
Construction of hull	$1,040,0C0	$806,000	$512,000	$80,000
Engines and machinery	403,000	360,000	247,000	72,000
Ordnance outfit	237,000	180,000	113,000	3,000
Equipment	100,000	76,000	58,000	24,000
Total	1,780,000	1,422,000	930,000	214,000

IRON-CLADS.

After a thorough examination and discussion of the scope of the Department orders, it was decided by the Board that the determination of the number, class, size, &c., of iron-clads necessary to make the Navy thoroughly efficient should not be considered, for the following reasons:

1st. In times of peace iron-clads are not necessary to carry on the work required of the United States Navy. This type of vessels is therefore outside of the category of vessels that the Board is ordered to recommend.

2d. There must be a limit to the amount of money that Congress would be willing to appropriate for the construction of the Navy and this limit is without doubt a very restricted one. Efficient iron-clads could not be constructed at a cost of less than from three and a half to four millions of dollars apiece, and should an attempt be made to determine a number in any degree adequate to the necessities of defense in case of war, the result would certainly be that neither a satisfactory unarmored fleet for positive present needs nor an efficient armored defensive fleet for war purposes could be provided.

3d. Although our iron-clads do not compare favorably with those of foreign nations in size, speed, armor, or armament, it is considered that they are still capable of strengthening our harbor defense, and this strength may be greatly increased by the adoption of auxiliary means of defense that shall not call for the expenditure of such large sums of money as would prevent the full development of the unarmored fleet.

4th. It is the experience of foreign navies up to the present time that any type of iron-clad vessels introduced becomes so inferior as to be almost obsolete for general purposes in a period of about ten years. In order to, as far as possible, counteract this evil, it would be necessary for the Board to enter into the closest possible study of the present condition and course of development of iron-clad construction, so as to forestall the advances made in maritime warfare, if such a thing be possible. Not only must foreign designs be studied, but independent ones must be made, modified, and corrected; calculations must be made, and radical changes must be thoroughly examined. The limit of time given to the Board within which to prepare its entire report is altogether inadequate for the study of this branch of the subject alone, so that no thoroughly satisfactory result could be obtained.

Finally, no type of iron-clad vessel could be developed intelligently without knowing what weight and caliber of ordnance was to form her armament. A most serious obstacle to the establishment of this element, and one that is not generally known in this country, is the positive uncertainty that at present an efficient iron-clad armament could be procured otherwise than by purchase in a foreign market, which it is considered that the country would not permit. Within the past four years the development of artillery power has been immense. The first 16 and 17 inch guns provided for the British and Italian navies were rendered obsolete almost before they had left the foundries, through this development. It may be said, with equal truth, that almost all rifled guns constructed prior to 1878 are now so inferior in power as to be considered unworthy of future construction. It would be decidedly inadvisable to arm any iron-clad that might be built with other than what is known as high-powered, breech-loading ordnance, nor would caliber of less than 10 inches be at all satisfactory for iron-clad armament.

It is a matter of great uncertainty whether the construction of an efficient, high-powered, steel, breech-loading gun of 10 inches caliber could be successfully completed in this country. This is not due to any lack of skill in doing the work, but in the great hesitation of founders to accept the risk of attempting to furnish such large masses of steel of the necessary qualities, with no previous experience in the work to serve as a guide; also in the total absence of the proper appointments or plant in this country to produce the masses required. Such plants can readily be constructed, but only at such a great cost as to deter manufacturers from establishing them, since they could only be made remunerative by building heavy guns for *this* government.

It is not considered that this weakness of the country should give rise to unnecessary alarm. Preliminary steps have already been taken to overcome the obstacle, and although the results are now, and for some time to come will be, too uncertain to warrant any recommendation by the Board, it is of the opinion that satisfactory ordnance can be built in this country in the near future. It is considered, however, that this defensive weakness of the country should be made known to Congress and the people in order that obstacles may not be inadvertently thrown in the way of overcoming it.

By not recommending the immediate construction of iron-clads, the Board by no means pronounces against their necessity in the future. *Such vessels are absolutely needed for the defense of the country in time of war;* and if Congress be willing to at once appropriate the large sum necessary for their construction, thoroughly efficient vessels can be designed and built in this country.

The board is of the opinion that in any case this subject should receive the careful attention of naval officers. As developments are made abroad they should be carefully followed and noted by the Navy Department, and skilled officers should be permitted to familiarize themselves with the latest improvements, and especially with such developments as are not understood in the workshops of the United States, so that in case of sudden necessity it would be prepared to enter at once upon the construction of suitable vessels.

RAMS.

It is the opinion of the Board that one of the pressing necessities of the present time is to provide as far as possible for an efficient naval defense for the coasts and harbors of the country in case of a sudden emergency. Since it was decided that iron-clads must be left out of consideration, it became necessary to determine upon auxiliary means of defense, which, although not so far-reaching in their protection, should still hold foreign armored fleets in check until armored defense could be provided.

It is the opinion of the Board that a type of fast and handy marine rams would be especially valuable for such auxiliary defense. In determining the details of such a type, however, the Board was obliged to act entirely upon its judgment with regard to the possibilities, since experience with this type of vessels is entirely lacking throughout the world. But two actual types of such vessels are available on which to base a judgment. The first, a type designed by Rear-Admiral Ammen. U. S. N., whose correctness of details has never as yet been tested by actual construction; and the second, designs of the British Ram Polyphemus, now afloat, and whose main principles correspond with those of the American ram.

After mature consideration, the Board is of the opinion that five rams of the general design proposed by Rear-Admiral Ammen should now be built; that these rams should be of about two thousand tons displacement, and that they should be constructed of steel.

It is the opinion of the Board that the cost of any single vessel of this description would be, when complete and ready for service, $500,000.

TORPEDO VESSELS.

It is the opinion of the Board that a torpedo service completely organized as regards both *personnel* and *matériel* furnishes the most economical and efficient auxiliary coast defense attainable. Such a service, to be complete, must embrace not only means of protecting channels and harbors, but must extend its scope to the open sea in the immediate vicinity of the coast, so as to effectually prevent the establishment of blockades, the formation or free operation of hostile squadrons at any given point, or sudden attacks by single armored vessels.

It is the opinion of the Board that this open-sea work is best performed by a type of torpedo gunboats capable of carrying a powerful bow-gun in addition to the torpedo outfit; to be thoroughly sea-going; to have a length between perpendiculars of about 125 feet; a displacement of about 450 tons, and a maximum speed of not less than 13 knots per hour. The cost of such a vessel complete and ready for service would be $145,000.

It is the opinion of the Board that five such vessels should now be built.

For the strict harbor and channel service, the Board is of the opinion that ten steel vessels of the type known as the Herreshoff harbor torpedo boat should now be built; to be about 70 feet long, and to have a maximum speed of not less than 17 knots per hour. The cost of a single one of this type of vessels, complete and ready for service, would be $25,000.

The Board is of the opinion that these two types of torpedo vessels should be supplemented by ten steel cruising torpedo boats, that may be used as a re-enforcement, either to the rams and torpedo gunboats or to the harbor boats. These vessels to be about 100 feet long, and to have a maximum speed of not less than 21 knots per hour. The cost of a single vessel of this type, complete and ready for service, would be $38,000.

SUMMARY OF THE NUMBER, CLASS, TYPE, AND COST OF THE VESSELS THAT THE BOARD RECOMMEND NOW BE BUILT.

Two first-rate steel, double-decked, unarmored cruisers, having a displacement of about 5,873 tons, an average sea speed of 15 knots, and a battery of 4 VIII-inch and 21 VI-inch guns. Cost, $3,560,000.

Six first-rate steel, double-decked, unarmored cruisers, having a displacement of about 4,560 tons, an average sea speed of 14 knots, and a battery of 4 VIII-inch and 15 VI-inch guns. Cost, $8,532,000.

Ten second-rate steel, single-decked, unarmored cruisers, having a displacement of about 3,043 tons, an average sea speed of 13 knots, and a battery of 12 VI-inch guns. Cost, $9,300,000.

Twenty fourth-rate wooden cruisers, having a displacement of about 793 tons, an average sea speed of 10 knots, and a battery of 1 VI-inch and 2 60-pounders. Cost, $4,360,000.

Five steel rams of about 2,000 tons displacement, and an average sea speed of 13 knots. Cost, $2,500,000.

Five torpedo gunboats of about 450 tons displacement, a maximum sea speed of not less than 13 knots, and 1 heavy-powered rifled gun. Cost, $725,000.

Ten cruising torpedo-boats, about 100 feet long, and having a maximum speed of not less than 21 knots per hour. Cost, $380,000.

Ten harbor torpedo-boats, about 70 feet long, and having a maximum speed of not less than 17 knots per hour. Cost, $250,000.

Total cost of vessels recommended now to be built, $29,607,000.

NUMBER AND TYPES OF VESSELS THAT WILL BE AVAILABLE FOR SERVICE IN THE NAVY AT THE EXPIRATION OF EIGHT YEARS, ACCORDING TO THE PROGRAMME DEVISED BY THE ADVISORY BOARD.

Twenty-one iron-clads.
Seventy unarmored cruisers.
Five rams.
Five torpedo-gunboats.
Twenty torpedo-boats.

It is the opinion of the Board that this force will be thoroughly efficient for the work required of the Navy in time of peace, and that, due consideration being given to the geographical position of the country with regard to the great naval powers; to the great rapidity with which torpedo defense can be perfected both by laying mines and building torpedo vessels, and to the availability of our commercial steamers for conversion into fast commerce-destroying vessels, it will form an effective defense for our coasts in the sudden emergency of the outbreak of a war: permit of offensive measures of possible vital importance, and hold a naval enemy in check until armored vessels can be supplied to perfect the defense and undertake offensive operations,

Very respectfully, your obedient servants,

JOHN RODGERS,
Rear Admiral, President.
WM. G. TEMPLE.
Commodore, Member.
P. C. JOHNSON,
Captain, Member.
CHAS. H. LORING,
Chief Engineer, Member.
H. L. HOWISON,
Commander, Member.
R. D. EVANS,
Commander, Member.
A. S. CROWNINSHIELD,
Commander, Member.
CHAS. H. MANNING,
Passed Assistant Engineer, Member.
M. R. S. MACKENZIE,
Lieutenant, Member.
EDWARD W. VERY,
Lieutenant, Member.

The undersigned members of the Advisory Board being unable in several important particulars to coincide with the opinions and views of the members composing the majority, and our differences being on professional points, we are compelled to state these points of dissent, and to give our reasons therefor, as follows:

1st. We dissent from the weight of armament assigned to the different classes of vessels by the majority, and to the principles on which that weight was determined, as appeared from the statement on that subject read to the Board by the ordnance committee. The weights in question are in excess, caused by the assumption that they should be a certain percentage of the displacement of the vessel, a percentage obtained from foreign vessels, in which the coal carried was less than sufficient for three days maximum steaming, while in the vessels of the Board of quite different forms and proportions more than double this quantity was to be carried. No comparison of the weight of armament carried by the Board's vessels is possible with that carried by foreign vessels of equal displacement but much less machinery and coal. The propriety of such a method from any point of view is very questionable, but, if made, the weight of armaments can only be compared for what remains of the displacement of each vessel after deducting its weight of machinery and coal; consequently any comparison in this respect of the Board's vessels with those of foreign navies of quite different design and capabilities has no application. With the fallacious comparison of weight of armament to displacement, there would follow the irrational conclusion that the greater the speed and endurance of the vessel, due to a larger hull, more powerful machinery, and greater quantity of coal, the more should be the armament. In consideration that the highest practicable speed, and the means of sustaining it for the longest practicable time, are the governing ideas in the design of the Board's vessels, and that on these two depends essentially their value, it is judicious, in order to increase these qualities, to decrease the weight of armament carried, as well as of spars and all other weights not necessary to speed; for, to obtain this excessive speed, not only large vessels of the classes are required, but extremely sharp ones, and this sharpness in addition to the great space occupied by the powerful engines and boilers needed, and by the enormous quantity of coal to be carried, necessarily reduces the internal capacity of the vessel remaining for other purposes in a greater degree than in the case of vessels of less speed and endurance. Hence, it is unavoidable that armament, sail power, and crew must be proportionally less than in such vessels.

2d. We dissent from placing a poop cabin on the 13-knots single-decked sloop of war, as recommended by the majority. A poop cabin would increase the comforts of the commanding officer, but at the expense of that of all the other officers, whose quarters would consequently be removed farther aft where the space is less. It would prevent the use of a pivot-gun at the stern; and with boarding of a sea would be dangerous. Its weight is very injurious to the nautical qualities of the vessel, and it will impede her speed, a very slight reduction of which, when the speed is high, involving a large expenditure of coal to regain.

3d. We dissent from, and decidedly object to, the second rate 14-knots spar-deck vessel recommended by the majority. For, taking into consideration that our Navy will always be small in comparison with those of the great European powers, the few vessels we shall have ought to be first-rate of their type and possess the highest qualities, which can only be given by large dimensions and powerful machinery. Our hitherto naval superiority was thus produced; that is to say, by constructing larger and more efficient vessels of corresponding types to those in foreign navies, as was evident in 1812, and again in our late war. The size and correspondingly great qualities of the vessels we then built forced other maritime nations to follow our lead, which they admitted, and are doing, notwithstanding the excessive cost involved; and if our superiority is to be maintained it must be by progressing further in the same direction.

In modern war vessels the tendency is to increase the power of the guns and to reduce their number. If foreign nations have perfected artillery beyond our powers of improvement, and we can only copy what they have devised, then our superiority must be regained by the designs of our ships, for we know that subject is not exhausted, and we must compensate the want of superiority in artillery by greater speed and more endurance at sea. This will entail larger and faster vessels at necessarily greater cost, but the desired supremacy will be maintained. Hence, our vessels to be built of the different classes must be an advance on any existing ones of the same classes in any navy, and have greater speed. The complaint now made of our vessels is their want of speed, which is the fault constantly found with those sent abroad, exposing the Navy to the mortification of inferiority in this most important particular, and to certain disadvantage on all real service.

The second-rate 14-knots spar-deck ship recommended by the majority is, in every way, inferior to the first-rate 15-knots spar-deck, ship adopted by the Board. From the general principles of naval architecture, the smaller vessel must have relatively more beam and much greater resistance than the larger vessel of the same type, and be its inferior in speed, endurance, nautical qualities, and in accommodation for an admiral and his staff, the additional personnel to be provided for being thirty-four in number. The same cost, materials, and displacement in the form of a single-deck vessel would have a speed and endurance very nearly equal to that of the large 15-knots spar-deck vessel, and of course be greatly superior in these qualities to the second-rate 14-knots spar-deck ships recommended by the majority. The addition of the spar-deck to the second-rate ship of that type increases the weight of the machinery and lessens the quantity of coal carried. Foreign navies have numbers of such second-rate spar-deck ships, and the construction of similar ones for our Navy would only place us on a line with them—a position inferior certainly to that which we ought to occupy.

The difference to our naval prestige in the event of a maritime war would be immense, whether the actions between ships of the same type were fought on our side by first-rates of that type or by second rates, as in such combats the vessels are compared by types or classes; for instance, in former wars, of frigates against frigates, sloops of war against sloops of war, &c.

In place of the second-rate 14-knots vessels of the spar-deck type recommended by the majority, we propose to substitute ship-rigged first-rates of the single-deck type, with top-gallant forecastle decks extending to the foremast, without poop cabins, with speed of 14 knots, and with much superior coal-carrying capacity.

The speed of 14 knots, referred to, is the average speed of the vessel at sea for the maximum power the machinery can develop. In smooth water the speed will be 15 knots.

These single-deck vessels will have the following dimensions:

Total complement of officers and crew..........................persons..	322
Time for which provisions and stores are carried ....days..	150
Surface of sail..square feet..	20,000
Length on mean load line from the fore side of the rabbet of the stem of the iron hull to the aft side of the body stern post................feet..	315
Extreme breadth ....do..	45
Mean draught of water, exclusive of the keel.........................do..	19
Mean depth of keel and false keel.....................................do..	1.25
Depth of hold from the inside of double bottom to the lower side of the berth-deck beams...feet..	15.25
Height on berth-deck to under side of gun-deck beams...............do..	6.75
Height of lowest portsill on gun-deck above the mean load water line.do..	10.04
Lowest port sill awash at angle of ....degrees..	26
Area of the greatest immersed transverse section ....square feet..	738.6
Ratio of same to its circumscribing rectangle	0.654
Area of the mean load water line ....square feet..	11,096
Ratio of same to its circumscribing rectangle	0.783

Displacement per inch at mean load water section................tons..   26.4
Displacement of the body of the vessel........................cubic feet.. 151,758
Ratio of displacement to cylinder circumscribing the greatest immersed
    transverse section...   0.65
Center of bouyancy below the mean load water line..............feet..   7.873
Latitudinal meta center above the center of buoyancy............do..   9.581
Total displacement...tons..   4,354
Weight of hull, equipments, personnel, provisions, water; stores, &c.do..   2,576
Weight of ordnance...do..   182
Weight of steam machinery ....do..   780
Weight of coal in bunkers......................................do..   790
Excess of displacement...do..   26
Number of steam cylinders   3
Diameter of cylinders..inches..   65
Stroke of piston ....feet..   5
Number of boilers..   12
Diameter of boilers..feet..   12
Length of boilers ....do..   9
Number of furnaces in each boiler   3
Diameter of furnaces...feet..   3
Length of grate bars...do..   6
Total area of grate surface ....square feet..   648
Diameter of screw ....feet..   20
Pitch of screw ....do..   32.50
Length of screw ....do..   2.67

Of this type of vessel we consider our unarmored fleet should be mainly composed.

The machinery will consist of a horizontal back action compound engine, composed of three steam-jacketed cylinders of equal dimensions with an independent cut-off valve on each cylinder, surface condensation, and independent rotary circulating pump; and of two groups of cylindrical boilers, each group containing six boilers with an independent telescopic chimney, making two chimneys in all. The boilers will have cylindrical furnaces, above which the tubes are arranged, and will have strength for a working steam pressure of 90 pounds per square inch above the atmosphere. The screw will be four-bladed and fixed; that is to say, cannot be lifted out of the water when the vessel is under sail alone.

The armament will be two guns of 8 inches, and twelve of 6 inches. This battery of our proposed 14 knots single-deck vessel is three-fourths of that of the 14 knots spar-deck ship recommended by the majority; and, as regards space for berthing the crew, the reduction in the number of men required by the present system of determining the crew, owing to the reduction of sail surface due to the sharpness of the vessel, and to the adoption of breech-loading guns, steam capstans, and other mechanical appliances in connection with the long top-gallant forecastle deck provided, allows ample berthing accommodation for as large a crew as is needed.

4th. We dissent from the recommendation of the majority that five rams be immediately constructed. In the complete absence of experience with this kind of vessel, not more than one should be built, and that for experimental purposes.

5th. We dissent from the statement in the report of the majority that "It is the experience of foreign navies, up to the present time, that any type of iron-clad vessels introduced becomes so inferior as to be almost obsolete for general purposes in a period of about ten years." We know of no facts presented to the Board, or otherwise derived, to justify such an opinion, and consider it erroneous and misleading. The European iron-clads ten years old and older are exceedingly efficient, and compose the real strength of their navies. The types vary within very narrow limits, the differences being mainly in thickness of armor carried, every increase of which, involving larger vessels, causes the maximum to be quickly reached, owing to the difficulty and cost of construction. We wish to express decidedly the opinion that a modern navy must consist essentially of powerful iron-clads, and the constant tendency in their design has been to approximate them more and more to machines, and to depart farther and farther from ships of the unarmored type. Unarmored vessels cannot be properly considered as fighting machines, although they carry a respectable armament; but as the great maritime powers have, and always will have, many unarmored cruisers in their navies, ours could successfully encounter them in war; their war capability, however, would be limited to such encounters, and they would be compelled to fly the presence of all foreign iron-clads, even those of the least dimensions and thinnest armor.

6th. We dissent from the opinion of the majority that the material for the hulls of the vessels proposed, except those of the 10-knots gun-boats, should be of steel. We recommend iron instead of steel, and we do this after a careful comparison of the merits of the two. The term "steel," as applied to the material used under that name for shipbuilding, is a misnomer, as it has none of the physical qualities of steel; it will not temper, is deficient in elasticity, and is simply a high quality of iron made at greatly increased cost from cast ingots instead of by the puddling process. It originated in Great Britain, owing to the low quality of shipbuilding iron manufactured there, which has about one-fourth less tensile strength than the iron manufactured in the United States. Owing to the great difference in the quality of the British and United States iron, the comparison between the respective merits of British iron and this so-called steel, has no application to United States iron. In recognition that the shipbuilding material called steel is not properly so named, the term "mild steel" has been applied to it merely for the sake of distinction.

This mild steel, as now manufactured in Great Britain for shipbuilding, has a tensile strength of 28 tons per square inch of section when unannealed, but if annealing be necessary, which is frequently the case, this strength falls to 25 tons. It can be made of much higher tensile strength, but in that case its lessened malleability, ductility, and toughness, and its increased brittleness, renders it unfit for the purpose in question. Although the tensile strength of this material is as above stated, its shearing strength is only from 23 to 24 tons per square inch of section, offering a marked contrast in that respect to wrought iron whose shearing strength is about equal to its tensile strength.

In Great Britain the best merchantable iron for shipbuilding has a tensile strength of about 20 tons per square inch, and its inferiority to mild steel in strength is so marked that the inducement there to use the latter is very great; nevertheless, owing to the uncertainty both in the supply and in the quality of the mild steel, and to its enormous excess of cost, only a small percentage of the vessels constructed in Great Britain have been or are being made of it. In fact, the last and greatest transatlantic steamship built there is of iron. In that country, where the manufacture of this kind of material has been perfected to the highest degree, and competition has reduced its cost to the lowest limit, mild steel of the various dimensions employed in shipbuilding costs about 50 per centum per pound more than iron. The workmanship is also greatly more difficult and costly. The rivet holes in mild steel must be drilled—not punched, as in iron—because the injury to the steel is much greater by punching than to the iron. If the steel be punched the joint of the plates is largely weakened. Notwithstanding, therefore, the difference in strength between mild steel and British shipbuilding iron, and the consequently somewhat lighter steel hull, it is still a moot question in Great Britain whether the advantages of steel over iron are sufficiently great to warrant its substitution for the latter; especially when the far greater corrodibility of steel is taken into consideration, and the necessity for a certain thickness for stiffness irrespective of tensile strength. If this be the case in that country, where the tensile strength of the best shipbuilding iron is only 20 tons per square inch, and the cost of mild steel a minimum, how much stronger is the presumption in favor of iron in this country, which produces the finest merchantable iron in the world, with a tensile strength of 25 tons per square inch, and in which the manufacture of the proper mild steel for shipbuilding being unknown, its cost would be a maximum.

We assume that the great national vessels proposed are to be constructed of materials manufactured in the United States, and not imported from Great Britain. Before these vessels could be constructed of this mild steel, the manufacture of that material would have to be created in this country; enormous plant at correspondingly great cost, requiring much time to make and put in successful operation, would have to be obtained, and workmen would have to be educated to its use; also, as there is now no demand for this kind of steel for shipbuilding in the United States, the cost of educating the workmen and creating the plant to produce it would have to be entirely borne by the few naval vessels that might be constructed of it. Should mild steel be insisted on for the hulls of these vessels, the contracts for it would probably fall into the hands of a few middlemen or speculators, who, instead of having it manufactured here, would import it, while receiving for it an excessive price, based on what would be the great cost of its manufacture here. Under these circumstances no reasonable approximation can be made of the increased cost of our vessels if built of mild steel instead of iron, but evidently the increase would be very great.

It may be supposed by those who are practically unacquainted with the subject, that the weights of the same hull made of our iron and of mild steel would be in the ratio of the 25 and the 28 tons of tensile strength, respectively, and that this difference in the weights would correspondingly tend to equalize the costs, besides furnishing the advantage of a *pro rata* lighter hull. But the weights of iron and steel in the hull are by no means in the above ratio. The weakest parts of the structure are the joints, and the strength of the whole is measured by the strength of the weakest part. The strength of the joint is largely influenced by the shearing strength per square inch of the rivets uniting the plates, and, if steel rivets be used, that strength is only from 23 to 24 tons per square inch or less than that of first quality iron, so that rivets of the latter material are nearly always used. Hence, a very serious reduction of the ratio of 25 to 28 must be made, probably reducing the weights of iron and steel employed in the hull to the proportion of 26½ to 28, were both metals of the same specific gravity. In confirmation of this important fact that the strength of the joints of mild steel plates and of the joints of our first quality iron plates are very nearly the same, may be mentioned that the regular engineering practice is to give for cylindrical boilers of equal strength about the same thickness to the plates of both materials. A still further reduction of the above ratio of 26½ to 28 must now be made for the steel's greater specific gravity of not less than 2½ per centum over that of iron, so that the ratio becomes 26.5 to 27.3, leaving the steel portions of the hull only 3 per centum lighter than if made of iron. As the mild steel is much more corrodible than the iron, an additional thickness must be given to it in order that it may have equal durability in the hull. When a proper allowance for this is made there results that, practically, for hulls of equal value and durability, the weights must be substantially the same, whether constructed of British mild steel or of first-class American iron.

At the utmost, the substitution of steel for iron can apply to not more than three-fourths of the *metallic* portion of the hull. In the remaining metallic portion, the thickness of the material is determined by the rigidity rather than by the strength, and would thus be the same for both iron and steel. A large portion of the weight of the hulls of the proposed vessels is of wood, such as the decks, the linings, the external sheathing, &c., so that any difference of weight between iron and steel applies to only a portion of the hull, and not to the entire hull.

These important national vessels which, if properly designed and constructed, will, with insignificant repair, last for over half a century, must have not only strength enough, but rigidity enough, and thickness of material enough, to allow of considerable deterioration without impairing their efficiency below the limit requisite for service.

7th. We dissent from the report of the majority in its omission to state what we consider is very important to be known by the department in connection with the design of these vessels. It is that, owing to the greatly less depth of water at the entrance of our harbors and rivers than at the entrance of the great European harbors, and to the inferior steam-producing qualities of the anthracite used as fuel in our vessels, to those of the semi-bituminous coal used in the vessels of European navies, no comparisons of our vessels either in form or dimensions, or of our machinery either in relation to power produced relatively to quantity of boiler or to weight of fuel consumed per hour, can be made with the vessels and machinery of European navies. Our vessels must be adapted solely to our peculiar conditions, and servile imitation can have no part in their design. Owing to our want of protected coaling facilities abroad, our cruisers must necessarily carry more coal than the vessels of other navies which have military coaling stations; for, during war, they will have to remain longer out of port, cruise more in the open sea, and be farther from their base of supplies. Nor have we the colonies to protect, nor the difficult commercial relations to maintain, with barbarous and half-civilized nations that the great maritime powers of Europe have, and which make certain classes of vessels in their navies useful for such purposes, perhaps, but which have no analogues in ours.

In the matter of weight of machinery for equal power, our vessels are at a great disadvantage comparably with those of European navies. owing to the fact that our fuel is slow-burning anthracite, while theirs is rapidly-burning semi-bituminous coal. The rate of combustion in the two cases compares about as 1 to $1\frac{2}{3}$; consequently, to obtain an equal weight of steam in equal time, we have practically to give at least 50 per centum more boiler; the quantity of steam produced being in a less ratio than the rapidity of the combustion, because the economic vaporization is less at the higher than at the lower rate. Besides this, the anthracite contains about one and two-thirds times the refuse of the semi-bituminous coal. The greater labor, consequently, of cleaning anthracite fires per ton of coal consumed, requires more firemen than in the case of semi-bituminous coal; and less power is produced per ton. Thus, for equal powers developed, the fuel burnt in our vessels requires more boiler, more coal, and more firemen than the fuel burnt in European navies.

The advantages of anthracite over semi-bituminous coal are freedom from dust and smoke; both important in a war vessel, but particularly the latter. They have, however, to be paid ·for in the enormous excess of boiler required. So strongly marked is the inferiority of anthracite in this respect, that none of the transatlantic steamers voyaging to our ports use it for their return trips, although its cost per ton is fully one-third less. They prefer to pay this greater price rather than submit to the disadvantage of either loss of speed or larger boiler. A resolute attempt was made a few years since to burn anthracite in the British navy, but, although supported by the whole power of the admiralty, which appeared deeply interested in a favorable result, the failure was complete. The vessels, with their insufficient boilers for that fuel, could not make even mediocre speed, and the attempt had to be abandoned, though most unwillingly.

The small draught of water of our naval vessels, comparably with those of European navies having similar dimensions, places our machinery at a marked disadvantage in the less height available for it below the water-line, thereby requiring a greater length of vessel for its accommodation, and the same cause compels a greater length of vessel to be taken for stowing an equal quantity of coal. Thus no proper parallel is possible between our vessels and those of foreign navies having so much greater draught of water.

The more disadvantageous conditions to be encountered, and the greater difficulties to be overcome, as above described, in designing the vessels and machinery of our Navy, if not recognized by others, are of the deepest consequence to naval constructors and engineers, by whom that designing has to be done, and should be understood by all.

8th. In consequence of our substitution of iron for steel as the material of the hulls of the 15-knots, 14-knots, and 13-knots vessels; of our substitution of a different weight of armament for them; and of our substitution of a 14-knots single-deck sloop of war for the 14-knots spar-deck ship recommended by the majority, we have to submit the following estimate of the cost of a single ship of each class, dividing the amount among the appropriate bureaus of the department:

Fifteen-knots unarmored spar-deck ship, of iron sheathed with wood, having a displacement of about 5,873 tons, and a battery of four 8-inch and twenty 6-inch guns:

Bureau of Construction	$728,000
Bureau of Equipment	100,000
Bureau of Ordnance	195,000
Bureau of Steam Engineering	403,000
Total	1,426,000

Fourteen-knots unarmored single-deck sloop of war, of iron sheathed with wood, having a displacement of about 4,354 tons, and a battery of two 8-inch and twelve 6-inch guns:

Bureau of Construction	$514,000
Bureau of Equipment	76,000
Bureau of Ordnance	109,000
Bureau of Steam Engineering	341,000
Total	1,040,000

Thirteen-knots unarmored single-deck sloop of war, of iron sheathed with wood, having a displacement of about 3,043 tons, and a battery of twelve 6-inch guns:

Bureau of Construction	$358,000
Bureau of Equipment	58,000
Bureau of Ordnance	87,000
Bureau of Steam Engineering	247,000
Total	750,000

The foregoing "dissents" from the report of the majority are purely technical and in our special professions, and in no way militate against the necessity for increasing the number of vessels in the Navy. The need for additional vessels is pressing, and appropriations for them should be made at once; for without such addition we shall soon cease to have even the semblance of a Navy.

Respectfully submitted by your obedient servants,

JOHN LENTHALL,
Naval Constructor, U. S. N.
B. F. ISHERWOOD,
Chief Engineer, U. S. N.
T. D. WILSON,
Naval Constructor, U. S. N.
PHILIP HICHBORN,
Naval Constructor, U. S. N.

WASHINGTON, D. C., *November 26, 1881.*

────────

WASHINGTON, D. C., *November 26, 1881.*

SIR: We have the honor to acknowledge the receipt of the department's letter of the 18th instant, returning our minority report as members of the Advisory Board, with instructions to restrict our communication to simply stating dissents from the report of the majority, with our reasons therefor, and calling our attention to a naval regulation that "reports shall be signed by all the concurring members, and to have appended over their signatures the reasons of dissenting members."

We knew of this regulation as regards surveys in navy-yards and ships, on small objects of little value, but had not supposed it of application to so important a subject as an increase of the vessels of the Navy, involving an expenditure of over $30,000,000, and were under the impression we were furthering the wishes of the department in giving our opinions and the supporting facts *in extenso.* We have now, however, endeavored to comply with the directions of the department's letter, and herewith present our "dissents" in strict conformity with the orders received.

The difference between the majority and minority reports was wholly on technical matters, but the points from which we dissented and still dissent are such that we could not, as professional men, sanction by either acquiescence or silence. They do not in any way militate against the objects of the department in calling an Advisory Board, but, in our opinion, further them by presenting additional arguments, and exhibiting the subject in a different light.

The department, in its letter, seems to be under the impression that we objected to a vessel *not* recommended by the majority. This is a misapprehension; we made no objection to any such vessel, but we did and do object to the second-rate 14-knots spar-deck ship recommended by the majority, and for that objection we gave our reasons, which we still, after careful reconsideration, believe to be sound and proper. The majority of the Board directed the constructors and engineers to prepare the programme of a vessel according to certain conditions imposed. which was done, and in a manner that fulfilled the object desired by the majority; we, however, not only did not approve any such vessel, but objected to it throughout. We had already adopted, in conjunction with the majority, the best vessel of the type referred to, and we were opposed to any second best.

Another point referred to in the department's letter, namely, that of poop-cabins, seems also to have arisen from misapprehension. The question of poop-cabins could only apply to single-deck vessels, and we are not aware that any one proposed them for spar-deck vessels.

With regard to the nomenclature of the vessels recommended in our minority report, to which exception is taken, we would explain that we used only the regular professional terms, as they have the advantage of being descriptive of the kind of vessels to which they were applied; but we have now changed them in compliance with the department's order, and refer to the vessels by their intended speed.

Respectfully, your obedient servants,

JOHN LENTHALL,
Naval Constructor.
B. F. ISHERWOOD,
Chief Engineer.
T. D. WILSON,
Naval Constructor.
PHILIP HICHBORN,
Naval Constructor.

Hon. WM. H. HUNT,
   Secretary of the Navy.

MEMORANDA ACCOMPANYING THE REPORT, AND NECESSARY FOR REFERENCE.

Estimate of present condition, probable cost in construction and repair alone for placing in thorough condition for active service, and probable lifetime after such expenditure is made (minor repairs not considered), of each vessel at present represented on the Navy list.

[Evidence of Chief Naval Constructor J. W. Easby, U. S. N.]

Name of vessel.	Present condition and value to the service.	Cost of construction of outfit for active service.	Future lifetime.
	FIRST RATES.		*Yrs.*
Niagara	Cannot be put in a fit condition for active service at an expenditure small enough to warrant the outlay; worthless.	No estimate.	.....
Franklin	Belongs to an obsolete type; can be put in fit condition for active service, but only at a considerable cost.	$75,000	4
Colorado	Similar to the Franklin, but not in as good condition	150,000	4
Minnesota	Similar to the Colorado, but not in as good condition	150,000	4
Wabash	Similar to the Minnesota, and in no better condition	150,000	4
Tennessee	In active service and good condition; expensive and unsatisfactory type.	....	10
Connecticut	Good for nothing; unfinished and rotten..............	No estimate.	......
Florida	Not worth repairing	....do	......
New York	In frame; a good ship and worth finishing....................	400,000	20
Iowa	Good for nothing; rotten	No estimate.	......
Java	Not worth finishing; rotten	....do........	......
Antietam	Good for nothing, rotten	....do........	......
Pennsylvania	Good for nothing, rotten...	....do........	......
	SECOND RATES.		
Susquehanna	Not worth repairing	No estimate.	......
Powhatan	Excluded from consideration by the Board, being a ship only fit for special transport and towing service.	....	

Estimate of present condition, &c., of each vessel on the Navy list—Continued.

Name of vessel.	Present condition and value to the service.	Cost of construction of outfit for active service.	Future lifetime.
	SECOND RATES—Continued.		
Trenton	In good order and active service		20
Lancaster	In good order for active service		20
Congress	Not worth repairing; rotten	No estimate.	
Worcester	Not worth repairing; rotten	do	
Brooklyn	In good order for active service		20
Pensacola	Repairing for a service of one or two years; afterwards will require a large expenditure to give her a new lifetime.	100,000	10
Hartford	Under repairs for active service		20
Richmond	In good order for active service		20
Alaska	In good order and in active service		15
Benicia	No work of repair at present being done; could and should be repaired.	100,000	15
Omaha	No work of repair at present being done; could and should be repaired.	249,000	15
Plymouth	No work of repair at present being done, could and should be repaired.	250,000	15
Lackawanna	At present in active service and good order; will need extensive repairs after a time.	150,000	15
Ticonderoga	In good order and in active service; will need extensive repairs for a new life.	No estimate.	15
Vandalia	New; in order and in active service	20,000	20
Canandaigua	Should be condemned as worthless	No estimate	
Monongahela	Waiting repairs to put her in efficient order for active service.	50,000	15
Shenandoah	In good order and in active service		10
	THIRD RATES.		
Juniata	In good order for active service		20
Ossipee	Under repairs for active service	No estimate.	20
Quinnebaug	New; in good order and in active service		15
Swatara	do		15
Galena	do		15
Marion	do		15
Mohican	Under repairs for active service		25
Iroquois	Under repairs and nearly finished		15
Wachusett	In good order and in active service		12
Wyoming	In active service, should be condemned for further active use.	No estimate	
Tuscarora	Under repairs for active service	do	15
Kearsarge	In good order and in active service		15
Adams	New, in good order and in active service		15
Alliance	do		15
Essex	New, in good order for active service		15
Enterprise	New, in good order, but needing moderate repairs	No estimate	15
Nipsic	New, in good order and in active service		25
Ashuelot	In good order and in active service		20
Monocacy	do		20
Narragansett	Unfit for repairs		
Alert	In good order and in active service		20
Ranger	do		20
Kansas	Unfit for repairs	No estimate	
Saco	do		
Nyack	do	do	
Shawmut	do	do	
Yantic	New, in good order and in active service		20

Question by the Board.—Suppose 100 vessels to be kept in active service, how many would be required in reserve, or what percentage allowance must be made for ships growing old, requiring repairs, &c.?

Answer.—As vessels are now built in foreign navies, the allowance must be about 25 per cent. With such ships as we have, the allowance must be certainly 50 per cent.

SUMMARY OF CHIEF CONSTRUCTOR EASBY'S APPROXIMATE ESTIMATE OF IMMEDIATE EXPENSE FOR CONSTRUCTION ALONE.

At an expense of about $525,000 the Franklin, Colorado, Minnesota, and Wabash could be made serviceable for about 4 years' work. The Tennessee with ordinary repairs will last for some ten years, and for $400,000 the New York could be completed with a lifetime of fully twenty years. All the other first-rates are not worth repairing.

At an expense of $100,000 the Pensacola would be good for ten years to come, and for a further expense of $1,200,000 the Benicia, Omaha, Plymouth, Lackawanna, and Monongahela can be made serviceable for fifteen years. The Trenton, Lancaster, Brooklyn, Hartford, Richmond, and Vandalia, with ordinary repairs, may be reckoned upon for twenty years, and the Alaska and Ticonderoga for fifteen years, while the Shenandoah will last about ten years. The Powhatan is not considered as a cruiser. All other second rates are unworthy of repairs.

Of all the third-rates the Juniata, Ossipee, Mohican, Nipsic, Ashuelot, Monocacy, Alert, Ranger, and Yantic may be considered, with ordinary repairs, to have a lifetime of twenty years; the Quinnebaug, Swatara, Galena, Marion, Iroquois, Tuscarora, Kearsarge, Adams, Alliance, Essex, and Enterprise a lifetime of fifteen years, and the Wachusett of ten years. The others are worthless.

RECAPITULATION.

With ordinary expenditure there would be serviceable one first-rate, nine second-rates, and twenty-one third-rates; total, 31.

With extraordinary expenditure there would be serviceable five first rates and six second rates; total, 11.

Statement showing approximate estimates of cost of putting in repair for efficient service the engines, boilers, &c., of United States Navy vessels.

FIRST RATES.

Franklin.—Requires new boilers (on hand) to be put in; machinery thoroughly overhauled and repaired, $65,000.

Tennessee.—In good condition.

Colorado.—New boilers (on hand) and crank shaft (on hand) put in; machinery overhauled and repaired, $45,000.

Minnesota.—In fair condition.

Wabash.—Machinery overhauled and repaired; new boilers (on hand) put in, &c., $45,000.

New York.—Adapt present engines, construct and put in new boilers, $150,000.

SECOND RATES.

Powhatan.—Machinery in good condition; boilers fair.

Trenton.—In good condition.

Lancaster.—Work on machinery, &c., well advanced toward completion, $10,000.

Brooklyn.—Nearly ready for service, with new boilers.

Pensacola.—In good condition.

34 Ab

Hartford.—Work on machinery, &c., well advanced toward completion.

Richmond.—In good condition.

Alaska.—In fair condition.

Benicia.—Machinery repairs to be completed; new boilers to be constructed and put in, $75,000.

Omaha.—Machinery overhauled and repaired; new boilers (on hand) to be put in, $50,000.

Plymouth.—Machinery, &c., overhauled, $5,000.

Lackawanna.—In fair condition.

Ticonderoga.—Machinery, &c., overhauled and repaired; new boilers to be constructed and put in, $65,000.

Vandalia.—In good condition.

Monongahela.—Machinery, &c., overhauled and repaired; new boilers to be erected and put in, $85,000.

Shenandoah.—In good condition.

THIRD RATES.

Juniata.—Machinery, &c., overhauled and repaired; new boilers (on hand) put in, $40,000.

Ossipee.—Machinery, &c., requires extensive repairs; new boilers to be constructed and put in, $110,000

Quinnebaug.—In good condition.

Swatara.—In good condition.

Galena.—In good condition.

Marion.—In fair condition.

Mohican.—New compound machinery; boilers, &c., completed and erected, $50,000.

Iroquois.—Machinery, &c., repairs to be completed; new boilers to be completed and put in, $25,000.

Wachusett.—In good condition.

Wyoming.—Machinery, &c., generally overhauled and repaired; new boilers to be constructed and put in, $65,000.

Tuscarora.—Machinery, &c., to be overhauled and repaired; new boilers completed and put in, $65,000.

Kearsarge.—In good condition.

Adams.—In good condition.

Alliance.—In good condition.

Essex.—New boilers constructed and put in, $40,000.

Enterprise.—Machinery to be repaired; new boilers completed and put in, $40,000.

Nipsic.—In good condition.

Ashuelot.—In good condition.

Monocacy.—In good condition.

Alert.—Boilers should be replaced by new ones of improved design, $40,000.

Kansas.—Machinery, &c.; boilers fair; no estimate.

Yantic.—In good condition.

FOURTH RATES.

Tallapoosa.—In good condition.

Palos.—In good condition.

Despatch.—In good condition.

TORPEDO RAMS.

Intrepid.—In good condition.

Alarm.—In good condition.

Summary of the cruising efficiency of the unarmored vessels now in the service.

[NOTATION FOR COMPUTATION.—S = maximum speed; S = ⅔ maximum speed; C = coal per day at maximum speed; C′ = coal per day at ⅔ maximum speed; 3 log. S′ + log. C − 3 log. S = log. C′, or C × S′³ = C′.]

Name of vessel.	Maximum speed realized under steam alone, in knots.	Indicated horse-power at maximum speed.	Coal supply (bunker capacity.)	Tons coal consumed per day at maximum speed.	Days steaming at maximum speed on coal supply.	Two-thirds maximum speed in knots.	Tons coal consumed per day at two-thirds maximum speed.	Days steaming at two-thirds maximum speed on coal supply.
Franklin	7.75	1,076	580	46	12.7	5.12	14	6.4
Tennessee	11.00	850	381	36	10.6	7.26	11	34.6
Colorado	8.32	997	500	43	11.6	5.83	13	38.8
Minnesota	8.95	973	650	43	15.5	5.91	13	50.0
Wabash	8.11	1,088	560	44	12.7	6.00	13	43.0
New York								
Powhatan	11.5	1,246	680	58	11.8	7.60	16	39.3
Trenton	12.08	2,812	816	90	4.0	8.84	24	13.2
Lancaster					1.0			
Brooklyn	9.19	706	339	30	11.3	6.00	9	37.7
Pensacola	8.3	1,047	300	45	6.6	5.30	14	21.4
Hartford	7.06	785	225	34	6.6	5.00	10	22.5
Richmond	11.7	961	330	41	8.0	7.72	12	27.5
Alaska	9.3	784	151	34	5.3	6.13	8	18.1
Benicia	8.5	715	215	30	7.3	5.61	9	28.0
Omaha	7.8	457	200	20	16.0	5.15	6	23.9
Plymouth	10.00	864	175	37	4.7	6.60	11	15.9
Lackawanna	9.26	818	215	36	9.0	6.11	11	28.6
Ticonderoga	9.00	585	382	28	14.4	6.00	7	47.0
Vandalia	9.5	558	151	17	10.7	6.27	5	47.3
Monongahela	9.7	582	296	22	13.0	6.50	7	42.6
Shenandoah	8.4	755	365	34	10.7	5.84	10	36.5
Juniata	8.4	592	295	22	10.7	5.54	7	33.6
Ossipee	9.6	783	235	34	7.0	6.33	10	23.5
Quinnebaug	12.9	1,108	175	35	5.6	8.51	11	15.9
Swatara	10.5	776	186	25	7.4	6.98	8	23.3
Galena	10.96	826	195	24	4.8	7.26	8	15.6
Marion	12.4	897	160	30	5.5	8.16	9	17.7
Mohican								
Iroquois								
Wachusett	8.4	256	180	11	16.3	5.54	3	60.0
Wyoming	10.5	735	185	30	6.5	6.98	9	20.5
Tuscarora	7.6	500	185	21	9.0	5.00	6	30.8
Kearsarge	10.4	828	198	17	11.7	6.92	5	39.6
Adams	11.28	828	140	30	6.0	7.48	9	15.5
Alliance	11.26	508	130	16	8.1	7.43	5	26.0
Essex	10.2	582	158	17	8.0	6.78	5	30.6
Enterprise	10.66	500	140	16	8.7	7.04	5	28.0
Nipsic	10.78	840	139	26	4.3	7.08	8	17.4
Ashuelot	11.3	491	285	21	11.3	7.46	6	39.1
Monocacy	10.4	918	240	30	6.2	6.88	12	20.0
Alert	9.4	330	128	10	12.8	6.30	3	46.0
Kansas	9.9	327	115	14	6.3	6.58	4	29.5
Yantic	8.17	265	128	11	11.2	5.39	3	41.0
Tallapoosa	10.64	665	210	20	7.3	7.02	8	22.3
Palos	10.5	258	102	11	8.2	6.88	3	37.3
Despatch	14.00	500	130	16	4.0	9.34	5	24.6
Intrepid	10.51	642	180	21	8.6	8.94	6	26.0
Alarm								

Number of unarmored cruisers at present in commission on squadron service; individual estimates of the number of such vessels required for present necessary duties; number of vessels decided upon by joint action of the Advisory Board as necessary.

Squadrons.	Number of vessels at present in commission	Individual estimates.										Number adopted by the Board
		Rear-Admiral Rodgers.	Commodore Temple.	Captain Johnson.	Chief Engineer Loring.	Commander Howison.	Commander Evans.	Commander Crowninshield.	Passed Assistant Engineer Manning. Lieutenant Mask.	Lieutenant Very.	Naval Constructor Hichborn.	
North Atlantic	6	8	10	8	7	9	10	10	10	10	10	9
South Atlantic	2	4	5	4	4	5	6	6	6	4	4	5
European	5	8	10	10	8	7	6	2	10	2	10	7
Pacific	5	10	12	8	7	12	15	15	14	15	10	12
Asiatic	6	8	10	8	7	8	15	10	13	13	8	10
Special service					4							
Total	24	38	47	40	30	42	52	43	53	43	42	48

Tabulated statement of the unarmored sea-going vessels built by the six most prominent naval powers of Europe since 1867, and coming properly under the title of new cruisers.

[Yachts, tenders, and river gunboats excluded.]

(Compiled by Lieut. EDWARD W. VERY.)

Name of nation.	Over 6,000 tons.	6,000 to 5,000 tons.	5,000 to 4,000 tons.	4,000 to 3,000 tons.	3,000 to 2,000 tons.	2,000 to 1,000 tons.	1,000 to 500 tons.	Und'r 500 tons.	Total.
Austria		2		2	2	3	4		11
England	1		1	10	11	20	20	57	141
France		2		4	8	22	11		42
Germany				3	10	3	4		19
Holland				5	1	2	16		24
Italy				1	1	4			6
Total	1	4	1	24	34	64	65	57	250

Tabulated statement of British vessels in commission on squadron service January 1, 1881.

[Yachts, tenders, and river gunboats excluded.]

Squadron station.	Iron-clads.	Unarmored vessels.								Total.
		Over 6,000 tons.	6,000 to 5,000 tons.	5,000 to 4,000 tons.	4,000 to 3,000 tons.	3,000 to 2,000 tons.	2,000 to 1,000 tons.	1,000 to 500 tons.	Und'r 500 tons.	
China	2					2	4	8	6	22
Home	{ *4 †10						2	2	19	37
Pacific	2				1	7	1		11
Mediterranean	5					3	4	7		19
Detached service			2		1	3				6
East Indies					1		5	3	3	12
North America	{ ‡2 ‖1 ¶1						4	3	1	10
African				1			1	1	7	10
Australian	‖1					1	4	1		6
Brazilian							1	1	2	4
Total	28		2	1	3	7	30	23	45	138

*Channel. †First reserve. ‡Colonial. §Harbor. ‖Cruiser.

Abstract of approximate dimensions of unarmored cruisers.

[Submitted by Naval Constructor LENTHALL.]

General type of vessel.	Maximum speed.	Length on W. L.	Extreme breadth.	Mean draught.	Displacement.	Register tonnage.
	Knots.	*Feet.*	*Feet.*	*Feet.*	*Tons.*	*Tons.*
Flush-decked gunboat	10	170	26	9½	769	800
Single-decked third-class corvette	11	220	32	13½	1,558	710
Single-decked second-class corvette	12	250	36	15½	2,176	1,039
Single-decked second-class corvette	13	270	40	17½	2,967	1,416
Single-decked first-class corvette	14	315	45	20	4,269	2,035
Flush-decked frigate	15	358	50	21½	5,766	2,600

General type of vessel.	Wetted surface.	Sail area.	Complement.	Days' provisions.	Weight of armament.	Weight of machinery.	Weight of coal.
	Sq. feet.	*Sq. feet.*			*Tons.*	*Tons.*	*Tons.*
Flush-decked gunboat	4,673	6,000	95	65	24	150	165
Single-decked third-class corvette		12,000	150	100	63	250	280
Single-decked second-class corvette	10,054	16,000	190	100	81	475	496
Single-decked second-class corvette	13,086	19,000	217	125	125	550	563
Single-decked first-class corvette	17,347	23,000	345	150	220	760	770
Flush-decked frigate	21,680	26,000	530	150	352	900	908

General type of vessel.	Coal supply at maximum speed.			Coal supply at reduced speed.			Approximate cost.
	Knots.	Days' steaming.	Distance.	Knots.	Days' steaming.	Distance.	
Flush-decked gunboat	10	10¼	2,474	8	......	3,866	$168,000
Single-decked third-class corvette	11	10	2,540	10	......	3,520	320,000
Single-decked second-class corvette	12	10	2,857	10	......	4,114	458,000
Single-decked second-class corvette	13	8½	2,652	10	......	4,481	512,000
Single-decked first-class corvette	14	7½	2,584	10	......	5,064	896,000
Flush-decked frigate	15	5½	2,045	10	17	4,600	1,210,000

REPORT OF THE NAVAL CONSTRUCTORS TO THE BOARD WITH REGARD TO WEIGHT AND DISPOSITION OF THE ARMAMENT OF THE TEN-KNOT GUNBOAT.

GENTLEMEN: In answer to the following resolutions—

1st. That the constructors be requested to consider the armament of 40 tons, recommended by the ordnance committee, and to report as soon as possible whether it can be safely carried, giving, as far as possible, the reasons for their conclusions.

2d. That the constructors consider the practicability of giving half-turrets to the wooden gunboat, and give their conclusions to the board—

we have to submit the following report:

1st. We are of the opinion that there is not sufficient space or displacement in the design of the gunboat to admit of increasing the armament from 18 tons to 40 tons.

2d. We are of opinion that it is impracticable to put half-turrets on the wooden gunboat.

Very respectfully,

THEODORE D. WILSON,
PHILIP HICHBORN,
Naval Constructors.

REPORT OF THE COMMITTEE APPOINTED TO EXAMINE THE DESIGN OF THE TEN-KNOT GUNBOAT.

GENTLEMEN: The committee, after having carefully examined the designs of the ten-knot gunboat, with a view to reconciling the differences of opinion with regard to the modifications considered necessary, find that by reducing the weight of coal carried in these vessels 34 tons, there may be given to them a barkentine rig with not less than 5,600 square feet of sail, and a long topgallant forecastle extending to or beyond the foremast.

It is not considered judicious to apply the half-turrets to these vessels, and good fore-and-aft fire can be obtained from heavy Hotchkiss guns, mounted on the rail. It is not considered advisable to give these vessels poop-cabins and poop-wardrooms. They may carry 32 tons of armament.

NAVAL CONSTRUCTOR LENTHALL.
CHIEF ENGINEER ISHERWOOD.
CAPTAIN JOHNSON.
COMMANDER HOWISON.
COMMANDER CROWNINSHIELD.

REPORT OF THE COMMITTEE ON THE THIRTEEN-KNOT UNARMORED CRUISER.

GENTLEMEN: After examining carefully the designs of the thirteen-knot cruiser, with a view to reconciling differences of opinion with regard to the modifications necessary, we find as follows:

	Tons.
Weight of hull and equipments, including topgallant forecastle	1,759
Weight of machinery	550
Weight of coal	575
Total	2,884
Estimated displacement	3,043
Available weight	159

This available weight may be given to the armament, whilst the vessel can have 17,600 square feet of sails, 217 men, and her other weights, as shown. If a poop-cabin be applied to her it seems to be a question with some of the committee whether the additional weight, carried so far aft, would not affect here qualities as a sailer or steamer. This matter is left to the decision of the full Board.

Respectfully,

JOHN LENTHALL.
B. F. ISHERWOOD.
P. C. JOHNSON.
H. L. HOWISON.
A. S. CROWNINSHIELD.

REPORT OF THE NAVAL CONSTRUCTORS ON THE PROJECT OF PROVIDING THE 14-KNOT VESSEL WITH A SPAR-DECK.

GENTLEMEN: In compliance with the resolution of the Board, that the naval constructors prepare the programme of a spar-deck vessel having the same displacement as the single-deck vessel of the first class, retaining the latter's weight of hull, equipments, ordnance, steam-machinery, and coal; we report that such a spar-deck vessel on substantially the basis of the single-deck vessel of the first class, and designed as a substitute for it, will have a length of 268 feet and an extreme breadth of 46 feet; the draught of water remaining the same.

The area of the greatest immersed transverse section will be about 17 square feet greater and the form will be almost 9 per centum fuller. The total length, below the lower deck, occupied by the machinery and coal of the first-class single-deck vessel above referred to is 129 feet, and there thus remains, in the substituted spar-deck vessel, a length at each end of only 69½ feet for all other purposes.

Should the machinery and coal of the first-class single-deck vessel be retained in the substituted spar-deck vessel, the speed of the spar-deck vessel will not exceed 12¾ knots per hour in place of the 14 knots of the single-deck vessel.

Respectfully,

JOHN LENTHALL,
Naval Constructor.
THEODORE D. WILSON,
Naval Constructor.
PHILIP HICHBORN,
Naval Constructor.

REPORT OF THE NAVAL CONSTRUCTORS ON DOUBLE-DECKED 14-KNOT CRUISER.

GENTLEMEN: In compliance with the resolution of the Board requiring the naval constructors and the engineers to prepare a programme of a spar-decked vessel which should have a maximum speed of 14 knots per hour at sea, and carry sufficient coal to steam 4,000 miles at a speed of 10 knots per hour; also to carry 250 tons of ordnance, and to have 21,000 square feet of sail-surface; the vessel's draught of water being 20 feet inclusive of the keel; we have to submit the following:

There is no difficulty whatever in designing a vessel of any given displacement. The real problem and the one difficult of solution is to design her so that she shall have certain qualities for a special purpose; the aggregate weights for accomplishing which, whatever they may be, are called the displacement. Consequently, in designing the vessel in question the vessel could only be limited by the dimensions consistent with the qualities she was to possess. We find that the following dimensions &c., will embody the conditions imposed by the Board:

Length between perpendiculars	296′ 0″
Breadth, extreme	47′ 0″
Draught of water (exclusive of keel)	19′ 0″
Height of lowest port-sill above low-water line	9′ 0″
Area of greatest immersed transverse section, square feet	772
Displacement, tons	4,547
Coefficient of displacement	0.602

In consequence of the greater fullness of form and the larger immersed transverse section of the above vessel over the single-decked vessel designed by us, for which it is proposed by a majority of the

Board to be substituted, the steam-machinery had necessarily to be increased; and, for the same reason, the consumption of coal per day at the 14-knot speed had to be correspondingly increased; so that the endurance of the vessel at maximum speed or her coal-carrying capacity had to be reduced, and is now only six days.

REPORT OF THE NAVAL CONSTRUCTORS ON THE ESTIMATE OF COST OF CONSTRUCTION MATERIAL.

GENTLEMEN: The constructors desire to have it entered on the record that the estimates submitted by them of the cost of the hulls of the three classes of vessels were based on iron as the material, and not on steel.

If these hulls are built of steel, as the majority of the Board decided, that cost must be increased about 43 per cent., making the cost of the hulls alone as follows:

Fifteen-knot class.. $1, 040, 000
Fourteen-knot class 806, 000
Thirteen-knot class 512, 000
Ten-knot class 90, 000

The development of steel war-ship construction in Europe.

FIRST STAGE OF DEVELOPMENT.

[Vessels built with steel frames and iron plating.]

Nation.	Name of vessel.	Displacement.	Date of launch.
English	Corvettes:		
	Canada	2,380	1880.
	Carysfort	2,345	1878.
	Champion	2,348	1879.
	Cleopatra	2,348	1878.
	Comus	2,348	1878.
	Conquest	2,353	1880.
	Constance	2,380	1880.
	Cordelia	2,380	1880.
	Curacoa	2,353	1878.
	Calliope	2,548	1881.
	Calypso	2,363	1881.
Dutch.................	Corvettes:		
	Atjeh	3,106	1876.
	Tromp	3,106	1877.
	Koningen Emma	3,106	1878.
	De Ruyter	3,106	1879.
	Kortenaer..........	3,106	1880.
French...............	Iron-clads:		
	Duperré	10,515	1880.
	Devastation	9,680	1879.
	Foudroyant........	8,680	1881.
	Redoutable.........	9,064	1876.
	Dugueselin.........	5,705	1881.
	Vauban............	5,705	Building.
	Tonnerre	5,486	1877.
	Caiman............	5,486	Building.
	Fulminant..........	5,486	Do.
	Indomptable........	5,486	Do.
	Furieux	5,486	Do.
	Requin	5,486	Do.
	Tempête	4,452	1881.
	Tonnant	4,452	1880.
	Vengeur	4,452	Building.
Italian...............	Iron-clads:		
	Duilio	10,650	1876.
	Dandolo	10,650	Building.
Austrian..............	Iron-clad:		
	Tegethoff	7,390	1878.

The development of steel war-ship construction in Europe.—Continued.

SECOND STAGE OF DEVELOPMENT.

[Vessels built entirely of steel.]

Nation.	Name of vessels.	Displace-ment.	Date of launch.
English................	Iron-clads :		
	Collingwood	9,150	Building.
	Colossus	9,150	Do.
	Majestio	9,146	Do.
	Conqueror	6,200	Do.
	Dispatch-vessels :		
	Iris	3,730	1877.
	Mercury	3,735	1878.
	Leander	3,748	Building.
	Phæton	3,748	Do.
	Arethusa	3,748	Do.
	Ram :		
	Polyphemus	2,640	Do.
	Gunboats :		
	Bouncer	253	1881.
	Insolent	253	1881.
	Seahorse	70	1881.
Italian................	Iron-clads :		
	Italia	12,800	1880.
	Lepanto	12,800	Building.
	Dispatch-vessels :		
	Barbarigo	658	1879.
	Colonna	658	1880.
Argentine	Iron-clads :		
	Almirante Brown	4,200	1880.
	Almirante Martin	4,200	Building.
Chinese................	2 gunboats	1,350	1881.

Hoche, Marceau, Neptune, and Magenta, French iron-clads just laid down, probably will be finished all in steel. This point is awaiting the result of experiment on the action of salt-water on steel plates.

FOREIGN EXPERT OPINIONS ON STEEL FOR SHIP-BUILDING.

WILLIAM DENNY, Esq., member of council, Institute of Naval Architects (see Transactions of Institute of Naval Architects, vol. XXI, p. 185). This firm uses mild steel exclusively. Has worked steel since 1865. Built side-wheel steamer Rotomahana, which ran on a rock January 1, 1880; was docked for repairs; found bottom-plates and frames bent for a distance of 20 feet; seven frames badly bent at a sharp angle tending inwards and aft; no cracks; plates removed, heated, and replaced; frames heated and brought to proper curve without cracking. Opinion of dock-yard authorities that under the same circumstances an iron vessel would have filled and been lost.

"I believe that this reliability will, in the future, when it becomes sufficiently appreciated, enable a steel ship to be insured at a less cost than an iron ship, as the risk she runs, either in collision or in grounding or running on a rock, is very much less. Regarding steel there is but one doubt, and that is as to its corrosion. I will simply state my belief that as steel has conquered the doubt that beset the outset of its progress, it will with equal certainty overcome this last doubt, *which, for all practical purposes, is as groundless as those which preceded it.*"

HENRY H. WEST, chief surveyor to the underwriters' registry for iron vessels, gives official tests of British admiralty, Lloyds' and underwriters (see Trans. I. N. A., vol. XXI, p. 214). Advocates the exclusive use of steel for ships. Exhaustive discussion of the subject by the leading ship-builders of England. Verdict in favor of steel.

B. MARTELL, Esq., chief surveyor of Lloyds' Registry : "The time has come when it is said by many others besides the manufacturers that steel can be used with as much confidence as iron; and it is held that, whilst the properties of mild steel are in every respect superior to iron, the cost, having regard to the reduced weight required, will warrant the ship-owner in adopting the lighter and stronger material." * * * "In steamer construction the saving is 18 per cent. in weight of hull; in sailing vessels, 19 per cent."

Mr. J. D. SAMUDA, vice-president Institute of Naval Architects, president Thames Ship-Building Works, advocates an entire substitution of steel for iron in ship-building.

"If the Almirante Brown had been built of iron instead of steel, it would have involved 1,000 tons additional displacement, and 500 additional horse-power to give an equal result.

"I know that some doubts have been expressed as to the equal reliability of steel structures to those of iron; but I must here say that my experience does not agree in sustaining any such doubt. I have found steel, especially the Siemens-Martin steel used here, in all respects a superior metal to iron. It possesses one-third more tensile strength, is much more ductile, both hot and cold; can be efficiently worked cold in most cases when iron must be worked hot, and where properly prepared, and annealed where necessary, and, properly coated with paint, has in no instance given any symptoms of premature decay."

E. J. REED, late chief constructor R. N., advocates and builds steel ships. (See Trans. I. N. A., vol. XIX, p. 27; also, treatise on iron-ship building.)

Sir SPENCER ROBINSON, late chief constructor R. N., advocates steel for ship building. (See Trans. I. N. A.)

Mr. N. BARNABY, chief constructor R. N., advocates, and builds steel ships for the English navy.

Mr. WHITE, instructor in naval architecture, Royal Naval College, advocates steel for ship building. (See Trans. I. N. A., and treatise on naval architecture.)

Mr. P. DISLERE, naval constructor, French navy, advocates steel for naval ship building. (Seer "Guerre d'Escadre" and other treatises of which he is author.)

Mr. BERRIER FONTAINE, French naval constructor. The substitution of steel for iron in French hulls corresponds to an economy of 25 per cent. in the weight of hull of given dimensions. At the present time the hull of a French war-vessel comes out at a lower price when built of steel than of iron. In six years of developement the price of steelplates has fallen 56.2 per cent. and steel angles 46.2 per cent.

For a French fighting-ship, where all parts except the hull-plating are of steel, a saving of 17.1 per cent. in weight, and 7.7 per cent. in cost, is effected. If all steel, there is a saving of 20 per cent. in weight and 12.4 per cent. in cost.

If the Foudroyant's hull had been built of iron instead of steel it would have necessitated an increase of not less than 1,600 tons in the displacement.

Of all the reasons that have existed against the use of steel but one remains, and that is the behavior of steel in salt water. Steel plates rust much quicker than iron. The cause of this anomaly will without doubt soon be found and remedied, but until it is the French will continue to use iron plating on the wetted surface.

The ironmasters have so completely mastered the quality of their steel that they can obtain with certainty qualities satisfying all the conditions for acceptance imposed. To so great a degree is this result attained that the steel produced by different manufacturers cannot be distinguished by test.

Admiral DE ST. BON, Italian Minister of Marine, and BRIN, chief constructor Italian navy, advocate and build steel war-ships.

ROMAKO, chief constructor, Austrian navy, advocates steel for naval ship building.

Sir WILLIAM ARMSTRONG, president Elswick Works, advocates and builds steel war-vessels.

Evidence of Lloyd's Registry.—During the past year 25 per cent. of the vessels built in England and Scotland are entirely of steel.

The developement of steel merchant-ship building is as follows:

In 1878 there were classed at Lloyds' 4,500 tons of steel vessels.

In 1879 there were classed at Lloyds' 16,000 tons of steel vessels.

In 1880 there were classed at Lloyds' 35,400 tons of steel vessels.

On the 1st of January, 1881, Lloyds' had building, to class, 83,000 tons, and the entire steel-building in Great Britain at that date was 114,000 tons. This amount would have been larger were it not that the steel factories reached their limit of manufacture, although working night and day, Sundays included. The City of Rome was built of iron, for the Inman Company, solely because it was impossible to furnish the steel fast enough to enable her to be in the water this fall.

MEMORANDUM OF THE BOARD WITH REGARD TO SCREW-PROPULSION.

The following are the reasons why the Board has adopted single instead of twin screws for the vessels recommended:

Twin screws, for a given power require more weight of machinery and more space for it than single screws.

In vessels designed for the highest practicable speed, like those recommended by the Board, and to obtain which the greatest possible sacrifices of other requirements are made, it was of the first importance that within the space and with the weight which could be allotted for the machinery the maximum power should be placed. This condition rendered the use of single screws imperative.

With twin screws, the cylinders, twice as numerous as with single screws, would have been smaller, and as small cylinders are less economical of fuel than larger ones, that is, require a greater weight of fuel for a given power, the endurance of the vessel, or the length of time for which it could steam at a given speed, would be less with twin screws than with the single screw, the weight of coal carried being the same in both cases. Also, for equal power, more boiler would be required with twin screws than with single ones.

The outside brackets for the support of twin screws, and the outside pipes containing their shafts, lessen the speed of the vessel by the direct cross-section of the first, and by the surface resistance of both.

The propelling efficiency of twin screws is less for theoretically equivalent surface than that of the single screw, owing to their position beneath the counter of the vessel. The farther forward the screws, relatively to the hull, the less efficient becomes their propelling action. The twin screws consequently require more surface practically than the single screw for equal slip; and this additional surface, involving more resistance, absorbs additional power to overcome it.

In the rolling of the vessel, or when she is heeled by the sail, more of the surface of the screw is thrown out of the water with twin screws than with single ones and the propelling efficiency correspondingly reduced.

The steering power obtained from twin screws is but feeble for the long, sharp, and narrow vessels recommended by the Board. To turn a vessel with twin screws, less space is required, but the time is the same as with single ones.

The speed and endurance in these vessels are considered of such importance that no lessening of them could be compensated by any steering advantage which might be obtained from the use of twin screws.

Twin screws are not used in any merchant vessels on account of the greater space required for the machinery and the greater weight of machinery and coal involved for a given speed. In some exceptional naval vessels, mostly armored, in foreign navies, twin screws are in use, but in those cases they are employed of necessity and not from choice, because of continuous fore-and-aft bulkheads extending from stem to stern and dividing the wide vessel into two narrow ones. These narrow spaces not being sufficient for the accommodation of the proper horizontal engines, vertical ones have been resorted to extending high above the water-line. This can be done in armored vessels without exposing the machinery; but it is inadmissible in our unarmored vessels.

REPORT OF THE SUBCOMMITTEE OF THE UNITED STATES NAVAL ADVISORY BOARD ON THE DESIGN, ARRANGEMENT, AND COST OF ORDNANCE FOR VESSELS OF THE NAVY.

Mr. PRESIDENT AND GENTLEMEN OF THE BOARD: After having carefully studied the subjects with whose special investigation we have been charged, keeping in view the resolutions and limitations adopted by the full Board with regard to them, we have the honor to report as follows:

DESIGN OF GUNS.

At the present time there are no guns in the service, larger than boat howitzers, that will compare in power or efficiency with corresponding calibers of foreign new artillery. Our ordnance consists mainly of smooth-bores, supplemented by a limited number of rifles converted from the old guns. Of these, the smooth-bores are entirely obsolete; and the converted guns, although strong enough to be perfectly safe under all the ordinary circumstances of use, will not admit of high charges, and are therefore greatly deficient in power.

The development of ordnance in Europe has reached such a point that no gun can be considered thoroughly efficient that cannot give to its projectile an initial velocity of at least 1,600 feet per second without exceeding what are considered medium powder-pressures. In order to keep these pressures within safe limits of gun-strains, slow-burning powders must be used; and in order that these powders may develop the high velocities necessary, the charges must be very large, weighing from one-third to one-half as much as the projectile. The great amount of powder to be burned, and the necessity for completely burning it within the bore of the gun, require a certain length of bore, considerably greater than that found in smooth-bores or rifles of early manufacture. After examining the results of the latest experiments carried on in Europe, we are of the opinion that this length of bore must be at least 26 calibers, in order that our guns may be equal in power to the best foreign ones of similar calibers. The greatest initial velocity possible of attainment with guns possessing the limited strength and length of bore of our converted rifles is less than 1,500 feet per second. Foreign steel and composite guns having a length of bore varying from 25 to 30 calibers and using the same kinds of powder that we now use, give to their projectiles velocities of over 1,700 feet, reaching in some cases as high as 2,100 feet, per second. In other words, the actual power of the gun is from 20 to 60 per cent. more than that of our own.

We therefore recommend the construction of a new type of rifled guns, having a length of bore of at least 26 calibers, and having strength sufficient to withstand the pressures from charges of from one-third to one-half the weight of the projectile.

However much the character of slow-burning powders may be improved, the strains to which the gun must be subjected will always be very great, and the structure must be proportioned to them. The weight of ordnance allowed to a vessel of war is at best but a small percentage of the total displacement, so that every pound saved in the construction of the gun, beyond the weight that is absolutely necessary for controlling the powder-pressures, becomes a matter of importance as furnishing opportunity to increase the total power of the armament. For this reason *we recommend the adoption of steel as the metal for the new guns,* as this metal gives the greatest strength combined with the least weight.

The space allowed for maneuvering guns aboard ship is necessarily limited, and to such a degree that the increased length of gun which is necessary makes it difficult, if not impossible, to use muzzle-loaders for broadside batteries. Furthermore, the adoption of a good system of breech-loading permits the application of simple and secure means for centering projectiles in the bore, thus increasing the accuracy of the gun and preventing windage, so that the power of the gunpowder is fully utilized on the projectile. *We therefore recommend that the new guns be breech-loaders.*

In deciding upon the most efficient calibers of guns for *unarmored vessels,* it is considered that the first object to be attained is to so grade the calibers that the battery shall be at least equal in efficiency to those of similar foreign vessels. Since the penetrative power of rifled projectiles is so much superior to the resisting powers of unarmored ships, it is considered that, in the distribution of the battery, a greater weight should be given to number of guns for effectiveness than to caliber of individual guns. At the same time, since provision must be made for attacks on shore-defenses, for action at long range, and for possible conflict with armored vessels, batteries must possess an element of strength in individual guns greater than necessity might call for in a duel with a ship of a similar class. After examining the composition of the batteries carried by foreign unarmored vessels, making up batteries of different calibers and comparing them, and studying the powers and effectiveness of the different calibers, *we recommend that for the armament of our unarmored vessels the new guns be of calibers of 8 and 6 inches.*

Owing to the thoroughly established excellence of the Hotchkiss revolving cannon for defense against torpedo attacks, boat service, and general fighting service both afloat and ashore, *we recommend that these, or guns of a similar type, form a part of the armament of all unarmored vessels.* For the same reasons *we recommend that good types of machine-guns, magazine-rifles, and revolvers also form a part of the armament of all unarmored vessels.*

Summary of designs of guns recommended.

1st. Steel, breech-loading, rifled guns of not less than 26 calibers length of bore, and of calibers of 8 and 6 inches.
2d. Revolving cannon.
3d. Machine-guns.
4th. Magazine-rifles.
5th. Revolvers.

ARRANGEMENT OF ORDNANCE.

Of late years, one of the favorite subjects for argument amongst naval officers has been that of the advantages and disadvantages of end-on fighting, and, as a corollary, the development or neglect of fore-and-aft-fire. In our opinion, whatever superiority certain methods of attack may possess, the aim, in the distribution of the battery of a ship should be to give it the greatest possible command *all around.* No commander can, with certainty, choose his method of going into actoin; nor has he entire control when once engaged. His battery then should be so arranged as to give him good strength on all bearings, thus leaving him unhampered in his choice of maneuvers, and avoiding the most disastrous of all evils in case the ship is disabled in action, that of having a dead angle where an enemy may lie, and force a surrender with impunity.

By means of a simple graphic projection it is possible to compare different batteries and different arrangements and ascertain the true value that is represented by weight of metal and number of guns. This method we have used in arranging the batteries recommended. A horizontal line is divided into sixteen equal parts, the divisions representing bearings taken from the center of the ship and from right-ahead to right-astern. From one end of this line a vertical is let fall, divided into equal parts, which represent, as desired, either number of guns or pounds of metal thrown. A certain arrangement of battery having been made, its power on different bearings may be represented within these lines or axes, and may be directly compared with some different arrangement.

The allowance for armament given us by the Board for the 15 knot class of vessels is 352 tons. If all the guns of the battery be of one caliber, the number available for arrangement under the tonnage limit can be readily calculated. Thus, as a start in the comparison, two batteries are chosen; each made up of a single caliber, a 6-inch one as being the lowest caliber admissible, and an 8-inch one as being the highest caliber consistent with the fighting necessities of unarmored vessels. These two batteries having been laid down, a third or mixed one of 6 and 8 inch calibers is made up, in such a manner as to combine the excellencies of both the others and give to the ship the greatest possible command.

Battery No. 1, thirty-one 6-inch guns. Complete weight, 355 tons.

Gun-deck.—Eighteen guns in broadside.
Spar-deck.—Two guns in recessed bow-ports, two guns in forward half-turrets, two guns in after half-turrets, six guns in broadside, one stern shifting-gun.

Battery No. 2, twelve 8-inch guns.   Complete weight, 347 tons.

Gun-deck.—Eight guns in broadside.
Spar-deck.—Two guns in forward half-turrets, two guns in after half-turrets.

Battery No. 3, twenty-one 6-inch guns, four 8-inch guns.   Complete weight, 358 tons.

Gun-deck.—Eighteen 6-inch guns in broadside.
Spar-deck.—Two 6-inch guns in recessed bow-ports, two 8-inch guns in forward half-turrets, two 8-inch guns in after half-turrets, one 6-inch stern shifting-gun.

FIGHTING BEARINGS.

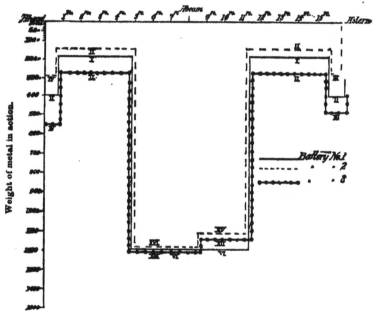

The Roman numerals denote the number of guns bearing.

An examination of the diagram shows that by judiciously combining the 8 and the 6 inch calibers, the weight of metal thrown, on any bearing, is greater than it would be with either of the single-caliber batteries, whilst the number of guns for head, bow, quarter, and stern fires is as great as it would be with the light caliber. The beam-fire gives an excellent combination of weight of metal and number of guns. With regard to the exposure of the spar-deck guns to musketry and machine-gun fire it is considered that the two bow-guns may and should be under the cover of a topgallant forecastle. It is easily possible to give thorough protection to the guns in the half-turrets by means of light steel shields that would not weigh over three-quarters of a ton per gun, or giving a total additional weight for armament of three tons. The stern-gun alone of all the battery would be unprotected.

We therefore recommend battery No. 3 as the most effective one for the allowance given. In order that a true idea may be obtained of its value when compared with corresponding armaments of foreign vessels, we respectfully submit diagrams showing the relative strength of the batteries of the British frigate Shah, the French frigate Tourville, and battery No. 3.

Shah, displacement 6,040 tons.

Gun-deck.—Eighteen 6-inch in broadside.
Spar-deck.—One 8-inch bow-gun, one 8-inch stern-gun, six 6-inch broadside.
Total weight of guns, carriages, and one hundred rounds of ammunition, 354 tons, or 5.9 per cent. of displacement.

Tourville, displacement 5,345 tons.

Gun-deck.—Fourteen 5½-inch in broadside.
Spar-deck.—One 7½-inch bow-gun, two 7½-inch forward half-turrets, two 7½-inch middle half-turrets, two 7½-inch after half-turrets.
Total weight of guns, carriages, and one hundred rounds of ammunition, 233 tons, or 4.4 per cent. of displacement.

American, displacement 5,768 tons.

Gun-deck.—Eighteen 6-inch in broadside.
Spar-deck.—Two 6-inch bow-guns, two 8-inch forward half-turrets, two 8-inch after half-turrets, one 6-inch stern shifting-gun.
Total weight of guns, carriages, and one hundred rounds of ammunition, 313 tons, or 5.4 per cent. of displacement.

After this arrangement of battery had been decided upon, a consultation was had with the subcommittee on construction, in order to ascertain if any obstacles existed to its establishment on the decks of the vessel that they had designed. It was found that whilst an increase of 52 tons in the displacement had been considered necessary, the committee had made no provision for a topgallant forecastle; the clear space on the gun-deck would not admit 18 guns in broadside, and they had felt constrained to recommend a reduction of 60 tons in the allowance for armament. These changes seriously affect the power of the battery, and whilst we urge the retention of No. 3, if it be possible, we have worked out a modified battery (called No. 4) and an alternate one (called No. 5), which we submit for the examination of the board.

Battery No. 4.

Gun deck.—Sixteen 6-inch guns in broadside.
Spar deck.—One 6-inch bow-pivot; one 6-inch stern-pivot; two 8-inch forward half-turrets; two 6-inch after half-turrets; two 6-inch in broadside.

Battery No. 5.

Gun-deck.—Sixteen 6-inch guns in broadside.
Spar-deck.—One 6-inch bow-pivot; one 6-inch stern-pivot; two 8-inch forward half-turrets; two 8-inch after half-turrets; two 6-inch in broadside.

The most objectionable feature in No. 4 is the reduction of the power, due to losing two of the 8-inch guns. Whilst in No. 3 two 8-inch guns are in action on almost every bearing, No. 4 allows only one, except right ahead where there are two, and on the quarter and stern bearings where there are none. An attempt is made in No. 5 to remedy this most serious disadvantage, but it is done at the expense of coal-supply. It is proposed to take from the weight of coal an amount equal to the extra tonnage required for carrying 8-inch guns in the after-turrets. In doing this a reduction is made in the steaming power of the ship from five and one-half days at full speed to five days; and from 4,600 miles at 10 knots to 4,300 miles.

FIGHTING BEARINGS.

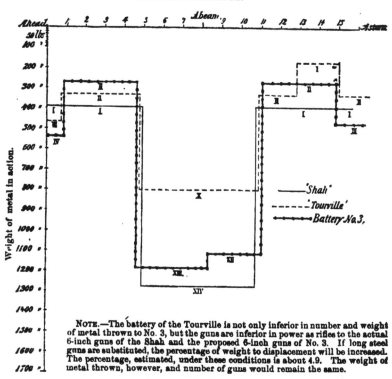

NOTE.—The battery of the Tourville is not only inferior in number and weight of metal thrown to No. 3, but the guns are inferior in power as rifles to the actual 6-inch guns of the Shah and the proposed 6-inch guns of No. 3. If long steel guns are substituted, the percentage of weight to displacement will be increased. The percentage, estimated, under these conditions is about 4.9. The weight of metal thrown, however, and number of guns would remain the same.

Fighting bearings.	Battery No. 3.		Battery No. 4.		Battery No. 5.	
	Number of guns.	Weight of metal.	Number of guns.	Weight of metal.	Number of guns.	Weight of metal.
		Pounds.		*Pounds.*		*Pounds.*
From ahead to one-half point on the bow	4	548	3	474	3	474
From one-half a point to 5 points	2	274	2	274	2	274
From 5 points to 8½ points	13	1,214	13	1,088	13	1,214
From 8½ points to 11 points	13	1,140	13	1,088	13	1,214
From 11 points to 15½ points	2	274	2	148	2	274
From 15½ points to astern	3	474	3	223	3	474

35 Ab

The allowance for the armament of the 14-knot class of vessels given us by the board is 220 tons. Three batteries were chosen for comparison as before. The first was the battery actually represented on the Trenton, substitutimg the new steel guns for the converted ones. The other two batteries were mixed ones of 8 and 6 inch.

Trenton's battery, nine 8-inch guns.

Gun-deck.—Six 8-inch in broadside.
Spar-deck.—Two 8-inch forecastle-pivots; one 8-inch stern-pivot.
The present battery of the Trenton is eleven 8-inch guns. The substitution of long steel guns calls for a reduction of two guns to keep the same weight.

Battery No. 2, two 8-inch guns, sixteen 6-inch guns.

Gun-deck.—Twelve 6-inch in broadside.
Spar-deck.—One 8-inch forecastle-pivot; two 6-inch forward half-turrets; two 6-inch after half-turrets; one 8-inch stern-pivot.

Battery No. 3, two 8-inch guns, seventeen 6-inch guns.

Gun-deck.—Twelve 6-inch in broadside.
Spar-deck.—Two 6-inch bow-guns; two 8-inch forward half-turrets; two 6-inch after half-turrets; one 6-inch stern-pivot.

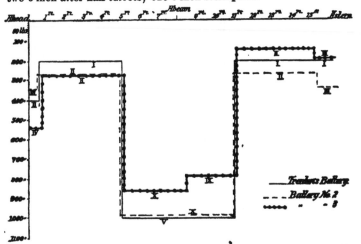

The graphic representation shows at a glance the inferiority of the Trenton's battery as compared with the others, which are of no greater tonnage. Battery No. 2 possesses the advantage of two 8-inch guns for broadside work, but in battery No. 3 the two 8-inch guns are available for bow-fighting, where it is thought heavy blows and long ranges are more necessary. The guns are mounted over water-borne sections of the ship, and the two 6-inch guns forward are of considerably less weight than a single 8-inch would be. Thus, this division of the battery is better distributed with regard to the strains on the non-water-borne sections.   The pivot-guns of No. 2 cannot be protected from small-arm fire, while the bow-guns of No. 3 are intended to go under a topgallant-forecastle.

We therefore recommend battery No. 3 as the most effective one for the tonnage allowance given.

As in the case of the 15-knot class, we have prepared a diagram showing the relative strength of the batteries of the British frigate Boadicea, the German frigate Leipsic, and the American 14-knot frigate:

Boadicea, *displacement* 4,140 *tons.*

Gun-deck.—Fourteen 7-inch broadside.
Spar-deck.—One 7-inch bow-pivot; one 7-inch stern-pivot.
Total weight of guns, carriages, and one hundred rounds of ammunition, 263 tons, 6.3 per cent. of displacement.

Leipsic, *displacement* 3,925 *tons.*

Gun-deck.—Ten 6.8-inch broadside.
Spar-deck.—One 6.8-inch bow-pivot; one 6.8-inch stern-pivot.
Total weight of guns, carriages, and one hundred rounds of ammunition, 181 tons, 4.9 per cent. of displacement.

American, *displacement* 4,269 *tons.*

Gun-deck.—Twelve 6-inch broadside.
Spar-deck.—Two 6-inch bow-guns; two 8-inch forward half-turrets; two 6-inch after half-turrets; one 6-inch stern-pivot.
Total weight of guns, carriages, and one hundred rounds of ammunition, 229 tons, 5.4 per cent. of displacement.

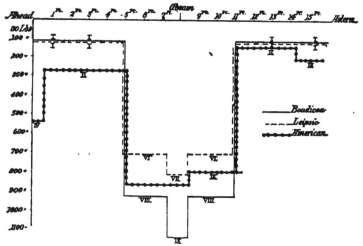

This battery was designed for a ship having a covered gun-deck, as we were under the impression that it was the intention of the Board that the class should be similar in type to foreign ships of a corresponding class and to the Trenton. We found, however, that in the design prepared by the construction committee, whilst an increase of displacement of 23 tons had been allowed, the ship was a single-decked one, with no topgallant-forecastle, and that the allowance for armament had been reduced 37 tons, thus necessitating a complete remodeling of our battery. As with the other class, we have prepared a modified No. 4 battery, and an alternate No. 5 one, for the examination of the Board.

Battery No. 4.—One 6-inch bow-pivot; one 6-inch stern-pivot; two 8-inch forward half-turrets; two 6-inch after half turrets; six 6-inch broadside.

Battery No. 5—One 6-inch bow-pivot; one 6-inch stern-pivot; two 8-inch forward half-turrets; two 8-inch after half-turrets; six 6-inch broadside.

It will be noticed that No. 4 battery is much injured in effectiveness by the loss of two 8-inch guns for beam, quarter, and stern fire. To save this bad weakening, which, in this case, is of more vital importance than in the case of the larger ships, on account of the loss in number of broadside guns, weight is transferred from the coal supply to the armament, reducing the steaming power of the ship from 7¾ days at full speed, to 7¼ days, and from 5,064 miles at ten knots to 4,800.

Fighting bearings.	Battery No. 3.		Battery No. 4.		Battery No. 5.	
	Number of guns.	Weight of metal.	Number of guns.	Weight of metal.	Number of guns.	Weight of metal.
From ahead to one half a point on the bow..........	4	548	3	474	3	474
From one-half a point to 5 points	2	274	2	274	2	274
From 5 points to 8½ points	10	866	6	570	6	696
From 8½ points to 11 points	9	794	6	570	6	696
From 11 points to 15¼ points	2	148	2	148	2	274
From 15¼ points to astern.............................	3	222	3	222	3	474

The allowance for the armament of the 13-knot class of vessels given us by the board is 125 tons. Two batteries were chosen for comparison, both entirely composed of 6-inch guns.

Battery No. 1.—Two 6-inch bow-guns, two 6-inch forward half-turrets, two 6-inch after half-turrets, six 6-inch broadside.

Battery No. 2.—One 6-inch bow-pivot, two 6-inch forward half-turrets, two 6-inch after half-turrets, one 6-inch stern-pivot, six 6-inch broadside.

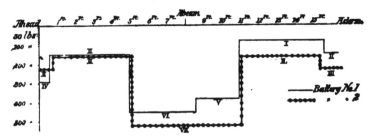

The graphic representation shows the advantage that battery No. 2 has in the greater weight and number of guns for beam and after fire, which more than counterbalances the increased straight-ahead fire of battery No. 1. In order, however, to gain this superiority it will be noticed the one 6-inch gun is mounted in the cabin. Although this style of mounting has been almost universally adopted abroad it has never found favor with us, although it must be acknowledged that its neglect has made our corvettes and gun-boats completely wanting in quarter and stern fire.

We recommend battery No. 2 as the most effective one for the tonnage allowance given, and in thus recommending a departure from established custom, we respectfully call the attention of the board to the fact that the surrender of the United States steamer Hatteras to the Alabama was directly due to the complete lack of stern and quarter fire of our ship. The Alabama took position under her stern in a dead-angle, and left the Hatteras not only disabled but totally unable to return a shot.

We have prepared a diagram showing the relative strength of the batteries of the British corvette Volage, the French corvette Duguay-Trouin, the Dutch corvette Atjeh, and the American 13-knot corvette.

Volage, displacement 3,078 tons.

One 64-pounder bow-gun, one 64-pounder stern-gun, sixteen 64-pounder broadside.

Total weight of guns, carriages, and 100 rounds of ammunition, 150 tons, 4.9 per cent. of displacement.

Duguay-Trouin, displacement 3,070 tons.

One 5½-inch bow gun, two 7½-inch forward half-turrets, two 7½-inch after half-turrets, one 5½-inch stern-gun, four 5½-inch broadside.

Total weight of guns, carriages, and 100 rounds of ammunition, 120 tons, 3.9 per cent. of displacement.

Atjeh, displacement 3,108 tons.

One 6.8-inch forward-pivot, one 6.8-inch after-pivot, four 6.8-inch broadside.

Total weight of guns, carriages, and 100 rounds of ammunition, 91 tons, 2.8 per cent. of displacement.

American, displacement 2,967 tons.

One 6-inch bow-gun, two 6-inch forward half-turrets, two 6-inch after half-turrets, one 6-inch stern-gun, six 6-inch broadside.

Total weight of guns, carriages, and 100 rounds of ammunition, 124 tons, 4.2 per cent. of displacement.

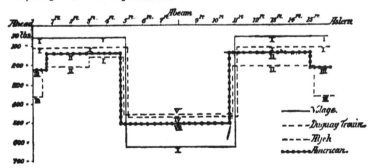

As with the other batteries, it was found on consultation that this one would have to be modified, as, although the displacement had been increased 19 tons, no topgallant-forecastle had been fitted and the allowance for armament had been reduced 22 tons. The modified battery No. 3 and the alternate No. 4 that we have prepared are as follows:

Battery No. 3.—One 6-inch bow-pivot, one 6-inch cabin-pivot, two 6-inch forward half-turrets, two 6-inch after half-turrets, two 6-inch broadside.

Battery No. 4.—One 6-inch bow-pivot, one 6-inch cabin-pivot, two 6-inch forward half-turrets, two 6-inch after half-turrets, four 6 inch broadside.

The additional pair of broadside guns gained in the alternate battery get their weight from the coal supply, which reduces the steaming capacity of the ship from eight and one-half days, at full speed, to eight days, and from 4,481 miles, at 10 knots, to 4,240.

Fighting bearings.	Battery No. 2.		Battery No. 3.		Battery No. 4.	
	Number of guns.	Weight of metal.	Number of guns.	Weight of metal.	Number of guns.	Weight of metal.
From ahead to one-half point on the bow	3	222	3	222	3	222
From one-half point to 5 points	2	148	2	148	2	148
From 5 points to 8½ points	7	516	5	370	6	444
From 8½ points to 11 points	7	516	5	370	6	444
From 11 points to 15½ points	2	148	2	148	2	148
From 15½ points to astern	3	222	3	222	3	222

The allowance for the armament of the 10 knot class of vessels given us by the board is 24 tons. Owing to the small allowance of space, there is but little opportunity to arrange batteries so as to develop their extreme effectiveness. The one that we chose contained but a single steel rifle of our proposed pattern—a 6-inch gun used as a midship-pivot. The relative strength of this battery, as compared with the Argentine gun-boat Parana and the British gun-boat Arab, is as follows:

Parana, displacement 800 tons.—One 10-pounder forecastle-pivot; one 6½-inch forward-pivot; one 6½-inch after-pivot; two 20-inch broadside.

Weight of guns and ammunition, 41.5 tons; 5.2 per cent. of displacement.

Arab, displacement 774 tons.—One 64-pounder forward-pivot; one 7-inch after-pivot; one 64-pounder stern-pivot.

Weight of guns and ammunition, 33 tons; 4.2 per cent. of displacement.

American, displacement 769 tons.—One 30-pounder forecastle-pivot; one 6-inch midship-pivot; four 30-pounder broadside; two 7-pounder poop-guns.

Weight of guns and ammunition, 29 tons; 3.7 per cent. of displacement.

The subcommittee on construction having designed a gun-boat with a flush-deck, and reduced the ordnance allowance from 24 to 18 tons, a reduced battery has been designed; although we recommend the other as being not only more effective, but better adapted to this class of vessels. The modified battery consists of one 30-pounder bow-pivot, one 6-inch midship-pivot, one 30-pounder stern-pivot.

The relative strength of the two batteries is as follows:

Fighting bearings.	Recommended battery.		Reduced battery.	
	Number of guns.	Weight of metal.	Number of guns.	Weight of metal.
From ahead to one-half point on the bow	1	30	1	30
From one-half point to 3 points	1	30	1	30
From 3 points to 5 points	2	104	2	104
From 5 points to 11 points	5	171	3	134
From 11 points to 15½ points	1	7	1	30
From 15½ points to astern........................	1	7	1	30

The attention of the board is respectfully called to the fact that while the modified battery is much weaker than the one recommended, and also quite inferior to foreign batteries, its weight amounts to 24 tons, which is the original allowance.

RECAPITULATION.

Batteries for the 15-knot class of cruisers.

Battery recommended; total weight of ordnance outfit, 359 tons ; adopted by the board.—Four 8-inch in half-turrets; two 6-inch in bow recessed ports; two 6-inch in spar-deck broadside; one 6-inch stern shifting gun; sixteen 6-inch gun-deck broadside; two 20-pounder saluting guns; one 3-inch, of 500 pounds, boat-gun; one 3-inch, of 350 pounds, boat-gun; six Hotchkiss revolving guns; one Gatling machine gun; 300 magazine rifles; 330 pistols and revolvers.

Modified battery ; total weight of ordnance outfit, 309 tons.—Two 8-inch in forward half-turrets; two 6-inch in after half-turrets; one 6-inch bow-gun; two 6-inch spar-deck broadside; one 6-inch stern-gun; sixteen 6-inch gun-deck broadside; two 20-pounder saluting guns; one 3-inch, of 500 pounds, boat-gun; one 3-inch, of 350 pounds, boat-gun; six Hotchkiss revolving guns; one Gatling machine gun; 300 magazine rifles; 330 pistols and revolvers.

Alternate battery ; total weight of ordnance outfit, 348 tons.—Four 8-inch in half-turrets; one 6-inch bow-gun; one 6-inch stern-gun; two 6-inch spar-deck broadside; sixteen 6-inch gun-deck broadside; two 20-pounder saluting guns; one 3-inch, of 500 pounds, boat-gun; one 3-inch, of 350 pounds, boat-gun; six Hotchkiss revolving guns; one Gatling machine gun; 300 magazine rifles; 330 pistols and revolvers.

Batteries for the 14-knot class of cruisers.

Battery recommended ; total weight of ordnance outfit, 252 tons ; adopted by the board, substituting two 8-inch for two 6-inch in after half-turrets.—Two 8-inch in forward half-turrets; two 6-inch in after half-turrets; two 6-inch in recessed bow-ports; one 6-inch stern-pivot; twelve 6-inch gun-deck broadside; two 20-pounder saluting guns; one 3-inch, of 500 pounds, boat-gun; one 3-inch, of 350 pounds, boat-gun; four Hotchkiss revolving guns; one Gatling machine gun; 250 magazine rifles; 275 pistols and revolvers.

Modified battery; total weight of ordnance outfit, 188 tons.—Two 6-inch in forward half-turrets; two 6-inch in after half-turrets; one 6-inch bow-pivot; one 6-inch stern-pivot; two 6-inch broadside; two 20-pounder saluting guns; one 3-inch, of 500 pounds, boat-gun; one 3-inch, of 350 pounds, boat-gun; four Hotchkiss revolving guns; one Gatling machine gun; 250 magazine rifles; 275 pistols and revolvers.

Alternate battery; total weight of ordnance outfit, 223 tons.—Two 6-inch in forward half-turrets; two 6-inch in after half-turrets; one 6-inch bow-pivot; one 6-inch stern-pivot; four 6-inch broadside; two 20-pounder saluting guns; one 3-inch, of 500 pounds, boat-gun; one 3-inch, of 350 pounds, boat-gun; four Hotchkiss revolving guns; one Gatling machine gun; 250 magazine rifles; 275 revolvers and pistols.

Batteries for the 13-knot class of cruisers.

Battery recommended; total weight of ordnance outfit, 161 tons; adopted by the board.—Two 6-inch in forward half-turrets; two 6-inch in after half-turrets; one 6-inch bow-pivot; one 6-inch stern-pivot; six 6-inch broadside; two 20-pounder saluting guns; two 3-inch, of 350 pounds, boat-guns; four Hotchkiss revolving guns; one Gatling machine gun; 200 magazine rifles; 220 pistols and revolvers.

Modified battery; total weight of ordnance outfit, 103 tons.—Two 6-inch in forward half-turrets; two 6-inch in after half-turrets; one 6-inch bow-pivot; one 6-inch stern-pivot; two 6-inch broadside; two 20-pounder saluting guns; two 3-inch, of 350 pounds, boat-guns; four Hotchkiss revolving guns; one Gatling machine gun; 200 magazine rifles; 220 pistols and revolvers.

Alternate battery; total weight of ordnance outfit, 132 tons.—Two 6-inch in forward half-turrets; two 6-inch in after half-turrets; one 6-inch bow-pivot; one 6-inch stern-pivot; four 6-inch broadside; two 20-pounder saluting guns; two 3-inch, of 350 pounds, boat-guns; four Hotchkiss revolving guns; one Gatling machine gun; 200 magazine rifles; 220 pistols and revolvers.

Batteries for the 10-knot class of gunboats.

Battery recommended; weight of ordnance outfit, 41 tons.—One 30-pounder forecastle-pivot; one 6-inch midship-pivot; four 30-pounder broadside; two 3-inch, of 500 pounds, poop-guns; one 3-inch, of 350 pounds, boat-gun; two Hotchkiss revolving guns; 60 magazine rifles; 65 pistols and revolvers.

Modified battery; weight of ordnance outfit, 24 tons—One 30-pounder forecastle-pivot; one 6-inch midship-pivot; one 30-pounder stern-pivot; one 3-inch, of 350 pounds, boat-gun; two Hotchkiss revolving guns; 60 magazine rifles; 65 pistols and revolvers.

Battery of 32 tons, adopted by the board.—One 60-pounder forecastle-pivot; one 6-inch midship-pivot; one 60-pounder stern-pivot; one 3-inch, of 350 pounds, boat-gun; two Hotchkiss revolving cannon; 60 magazine rifles; 65 pistols and revolvers.

COST AND WEIGHT OF ORDNANCE OUTFIT.

In computing the cost and weight of the ordnance outfit transcripts have been made from the regulation ordnance invoices as issued to ships, account being taken of the cost and weight of each detail, so that the total estimate is accurate within a very slight margin.

Cost and weight of ordnance for 15-knot class.

Items.	Recommended.		Modified.		Alternate.	
	Cost.	Weight.	Cost.	Weight.	Cost.	Weight.
		Pounds.		Pounds.		Pounds.
Guns, carriages, and projectiles...	$165,149 96	628,828	$150,497 68	528,929	$160,265 88	694,849
Light guns and equipments	16,420 23	11,777	16,420 23	11,777	16,420 23	11,777
Small-arms and equipments	14,702 24	7,734	14,702 24	7,734	14,702 24	7,724
Powder-charges, tanks, and magazine stores	37,222 75	148,618	32,508 12	131,167	35,117 80	142,039
Miscellaneous attachments	2,118 75	6,541	2,627 68	8,297	2,521 48	7,946
Books and papers..................	14 20	127	14 20	127	14 20	127
Torpedoes and torpedo stores.....	958 17	5,058	958 17	5,058	958 17	5,058
Total	236,586 32	803,673 or 359	217,813 26	693,079 or 309	230,000 00	779,520 or 348
Tons................						

Cost and weight of ordnance for 14-knot class.

Items.	Recommended.		Modified.		Alternate.	
	Cost.	Weight.	Cost.	Weight.	Cost.	Weight.
		Pounds.		Pounds.		Pounds.
Guns, carriages, and projectiles...	$121,544 39	436,990	$82,206 85	314,471	$111,710 01	375,730
Light guns and equipments.......	12,320 23	9,461	12,320 23	9,461	12,320 23	9,461
Small-arms and equipments	12,320 21	6,492	12,320 21	6,492	12,320 21	6,492
Powder-charges, tanks, and magazine stores....................	26,111 92	101,409	20,850 16	77,296	22,174 70	95,721
Miscellaneous attachments	1,935 44	5,951	2,526 16	7,911	2,378 48	6,931
Books and papers..................	14 20	127	14 20	127	14 20	127
Torpedoes and torpedo stores.....	958 17	5,058	958 17	5,058	958 17	5,058
Total	175,204 56	565,488 or 252	131,195 98	420,816 or 188	161,876 00	499,520 or 223
Tons.						

Cost and weight of ordnance for 13-knot class.

Items.	Recommended.		Modified.		Alternate.	
	Cost.	Weight.	Cost.	Weight.	Cost.	Weight.
		Pounds.		Pounds.		Pounds.
Guns, carriages, and projectiles ..	$72,517 83	274,881	$49,931 43	163,194	$61,224 63	210,038
Light guns and equipments.......	12,135 13	9,241	12,135 13	9,241	12,135 13	9,241
Small-arms and equipments	9,781 61	5,247	9,781 61	5,247	9,781 61	5,247
Powder-charges, tanks, and magazine stores.....................	15,828 42	61,169	12,067 81	44,823	13,945 61	52,394
Miscellaneous attachments	1,886 21	6,802	1,886 21	6,802	1,886 21	6,802
Books and papers..................	14 20	127	14 20	127	14 20	127
Torpedoes and torpedo stores....	692 83	2,831	692 83	2,831	692 83	2,831
Total	112,851 23	360,296 or 161½	86,509 22	232,265 or 104	99,680 22	295,680 or 132
Tons..................						

Cost and weight of ordnance for 10-knot class.

Items.	Recommended.		Modified.	
	Cost.	Weight.	Cost.	Weight.
		Pounds.		*Pounds.*
Guns, carriages, and projectiles............................	$19,289 44	61,460	$11,799 34	49,808
Light guns and equipments.................................	9,108 01	8,163	5,864 02	5,630
Small-arms and equipments...............................	3,170 74	2,086	3,170 74	2,086
Powder-charges, tanks, and magazine stores.............	3,945 05	13,287	3,192 06	11,182
Miscellaneous attachments	1,106 90	3,740	1,106 90	3,740
Books and paper	14 20	127	14 20	127
Torpedoes and torpedo stores.............................	692 83	2,831	692 83	2,831
Total	37,327 17	91,634	25,820 09	75,404
		or		or
Tons...		41		34

Cost and weight of ordnance of 32-ton battery adopted by the Board.

Items.	Cost.	Weight.
		Pounds.
Guns, carriages, and projectiles	$12,732 67	45,252
Howitzers and equipments	5,864 02	6,630
Small-arms and equipments	3,170 74	2,086
Magazine stores	3,434 06	12,151
Miscellaneous	1,106 90	37,740
Books, &c	14 20	127
Torpedoes, &c	692 83	2,831
Total	27,016 02	*72,817

* 32 tons.

In conclusion, we respectfully call the attention of the Board to a few points of great importance that have been developed by late improvements in ordnance.

Whilst the decks of vessels cannot be made wider, nor the hatchways narrower, the space occupied by these new guns and their carriages has been sensibly increased. It is, then, no longer proper to build a vessel and afterwards fit a battery to her. A vessel of a certain size must possess a certain amount of fighting strength, and this strength must neither be wasted nor curtailed. In the arrangement of decks, then, the constructor and the ordnance officer must work together; neither one is competent to attend to the subject alone. A bulkhead misplaced by a distance of 6 inches may cost the ship a pair of guns. A pump-box coming up through the deck an inch too far forward or aft can cost her a pivot. A single shroud or backstay having a few inches surplus spread may completely ruin the fore-and-aft fire; whilst, on the other side, a lack of knowledge in the ordnance officer of all the obstacles with which he has to contend prevents him from so arranging the details of slides and carriages as to make the most of the space allowed to him. Again, these new guns, in developing their enormous power, call most seriously upon the local strength of port and deck fittings. The recoil, which must be checked in a space of 3 feet or less, is altered into deck strains, and it becomes necessary for the constructor to provide extra strengthening where the local strains occur. In the solution of this problem the constructor knows where his limit is reached in the provision of strength; the ordnance officer knows how to arrange the attachments so that these strains shall be fairly distributed.

Another feature of still greater importance must be considered. The development of ordnance has given birth to a species of cannon firing from fifty to sixty shots a minute. This gun is fired from the shoulder, with all the ease and accuracy of a rifled musket. It throws steel shells weighing from 1 to 6 pounds that do actually pierce the sides of any unarmored ship afloat at a distance of 1,000 yards, the shell exploding inboard. These guns can effectually silence a gun in an open port at a distance of 1,000 yards by keeping an easy, steady fire on it.

From all this it follows that all guns must be protected. The old pivot-gun with its long sweep of dropped rail, must be condemned unqualifiedly. Were there no other reason, in the economy of shipboard, for putting topgallant-forecastles on our ships, the protection of the guns imperatively demands them. Let it be remembered that a fore-castle, like the traverse of an earthwork, protects the whole battery, fore and aft, in an end-on approach.

Wherever the displacement of a ship will permit, the protection of the battery absolutely requires a covered gun-deck. On single-decked vessels other means of protection are designed, and it must be remembered that the defensive power calls for a weight that must be taken from the guns and ammunition. The allowance is at best but a small percentage of the displacement. If a ship is built for fighting, it is certainly bad policy to deprive her of the means of offense. We therefore consider it necessary to strongly protest against the reduction of the fighting power below that carried in foreign navies. In the batteries that we have recommended for adoption we have kept the total weight below the average allowed in European vessels. This weight averages 5.9, and in no case passes 6.2 per cent. But in the modified batteries these weights have been cut down over 1 per cent. We respectfully submit to the Board that no fighting vessel, whatever be her speed, steaming qualities, strength, or safety, is in a position to realize the benefits of her excellences if her ordnance falls below a weight of 5.8 per cent. of her displacement tonnage, except in the single case of utilizing her speed to *escape* from vessels which she should overmatch.

Very respectfully, your obedient servants,

H. L. HOWISON,
Commander,
EDWARD W. VERY,
Lieutenant, U. S. N.

REPORT OF THE SUBCOMMITTEE ON DESIGN AND CONSTRUCTION OF HULL.

WASHINGTON, D. C., *October 5, 1881.*

SIR: The accompanying drawings of a spar-deck flag-ship, a single-deck ship of war of the first class, a ship of war of the second class, and a gunboat, have been prepared in conformity with the instructions of the Board.

The dimensions of the vessels as originally proposed have not been varied from, but a small increase in the estimated displacement was found necessary, and in order to obtain the high speed required it was absolutely necessary to allow a deeper keel aft to admit a propeller of the proper diameter; a temporary transfer of guns and men on the deck we find can readily bring the vessels on an even keel when occasion requires.

Allowing the vessels to have a topgallant-forecastle deck, not extending abaft the foremast, but which was not originally contemplated, has added somewhat to the weight.

The ordnance officers of the Board not having originally proposed any armament, nor given any estimate of its weight, the constructors had to assume the number of guns which in their opinion the vessels could carry. This was necessary, because the number of guns determines the number of the crew and the consequent weight of provisions, water, &c.

The estimated weight of the armament provisionally adopted by the constructor, corrected from the Ordnance Instructions of 1880, page 430, is, for the 24 guns assumed by the constructor for the spar-deck flag-ship, 292 tons; for the 14 guns similarly assumed for the first-class ship of war, 183 tons; for the 8 guns of the second-class ship of war, 103 tons, and for gunboat, 18 tons.

The weight of the equipments of all kinds, namely, masts, rigging, sails, boats, anchor and cables, crew, provisions, water, tanks, casks, fuel for cooking, galley, cooking utensils, furniture, books, clothing, small-stores, hospital stores, officers' stores and baggage, and stores in the various departments was estimated by us in the usual manner, which experience has shown to be nearly correct.

Estimating the weight of the hull, masts, boats, tanks, casks, and stores in construction department, and assuming the weight of the steam-machinery and coal to be as determined by the engineers of the Board, there will remain in the spar-deck flag-ship the weight of 919 tons for the armament and other equipments, consisting of rigging, sails, awnings, anchor and cables, crew, provisions, water, fuel for cooking, galley, cooking utensils, furniture, books, clothing, small-stores, hospital stores, officers' stores and baggage, and stores in the various departments. In the first-class ship of war there will similarly remain 642 tons for the same purposes; in the second-class ship of war, 398 tons; and in the gunboat, 93 tons.

The weight of the armament above estimated can only be increased by means of an equal reduction in the equipment or in the quantity of provisions and stores to be carried, for to reduce the steam-machinery and the coal will be a vital injury to the vessels in regard to their speed and ability to keep the sea under steam.

Should the surface of the sails be reduced by one-third, there would be a gain of 76 tons in the spar-deck ship, 62 tons in the first-class ship of war, and 48 tons in the second-class ship of war; with this reduction of spars there could be a small reduction in the anchors and cables.

If the vessels be more deeply immersed in the water to enable greater weights to be carried, their speed will be proportionally decreased and their general usefulness impaired.

The cost of the hull of the spar-deck ship, with masts, boats,
    tank and casks and stores, we estimate at..... .... $728,000 00
Same, first-class ship of war...... .... 514,000 00
Same, second-class ship of war 358,000 00
Same, gunboat................ .... 90,000 00 .

We are of opinion these vessels, as now submitted, will fulfill all the conditions originally required by the Board as sea-boats and fast steamers. They are sufficiently large, and it would be injudicious to increase their size and cost.

Respectfully,

                         JOHN LENTHALL,
                              Naval Constructor (retired).
                         THEODORE D. WILSON,
                              Naval Constructor, U. S. N.
                         PHILIP HICHBORN,
                              Naval Constructor, U. S. N.
Rear Admiral RODGERS,
        President of Board.

REPORT OF THE SUBCOMMITTEE ON DESIGNS OF ENGINES AND MACHINERY.

NAVY DEPARTMENT, *October* 5, 1881.

SIR: In accordance with the instructions of the Board, its committee on machinery has designed the machinery required to give the respective four classes of vessels ordered by the Board the speeds required.

In making these designs, the committee adopted horizontal back-action compound engines, with steam-jacketed cylinders, surface condensers, and independent expansion valves on each cylinder.

The boilers adopted are the ordinary cylindrical boilers, with return tubes above the furnaces, and having a strength capable of carrying a pressure of 90 pounds per square inch.

The screws are all fixed, four-bladed, and have uniform pitches; one screw for each vessel.

All the machinery is below the water-line, and is otherwise protected from shot by the coal, which has been placed in bunkers arranged for the purpose, and for convenient delivery upon the fire-room floor.

For the spar-deck ship the engine consists of three cylinders, each of 75 inches diameter and 5 feet stroke of piston. The boilers are sixteen in number, arranged in two groups of eight each; each group having a separate chimney, making two chimneys in all. The fire-room, which is in the fore-and-aft direction of the vessel, is 9 feet wide for the after group of boilers, and 8 feet wide for the forward group. The two groups of boilers are separated on each side of the vessel by a coal bunker 6 feet wide. Each boiler is 12 feet in diameter and 9 feet in length; it contains three cylindrical furnaces 3 feet in diameter, with grates 6 feet in length. The aggregate grate surface is 864 square feet. The screw is 22 feet in diameter, 34 feet pitch, and 34 inches length. The coal is carried in bunkers arranged on the starboard (but not on the port) side of the engine; between the boilers and the engine; between the two groups of boilers; in a hold forward of the boilers and below the lower deck; between the boilers and the sides of the ship; and along the sides of the lower deck for the entire distance occupied by the engine and boilers. The weight of the machinery will be 900 tons, and its estimated cost is $403,200. The weight of coal carried is 960 tons.

For the first-class sloop of war, the engine consists of three cylinders of 65 inches diameter and 5 feet stroke of piston. The boilers are twelve in number, arranged in two groups of six each, each group having a separate chimney, making two chimneys in all. The fire-room, which is in the fore-and-aft direction of the vessel, is 9 feet wide for the after group of boilers, and 8 feet wide for the forward group. The two groups of boilers are separated on each side of the vessel by a coal-bunker 4 feet wide. Each boiler is 12 feet in diameter and 9 feet in length; it contains three cylindrical furnaces 3 feet in diameter, with grates 6 feet in length. The aggregate grate surface is 648 square feet. The screw is 20 feet in diameter, 2⅜ feet in length, and 32½ feet pitch. The coal is carried in bunkers on the starboard (but not on the port) side of the engine; between the boilers and the engine; between the two groups of boilers; in a hold forward of the boilers and below the lower deck; between the boilers and the sides of the ship, and along the sides of the lower deck for the entire distance occupied by the engine and boilers. The weight of the machinery will be 760 tons, and its estimated cost is $340,480.

For the second-class sloop of war, the engine consists of a high-pressure and a low-pressure cylinder; the former having a diameter of 48 inches, with a 3-foot stroke of piston; and the latter having a diameter of 65 inches with a 4-foot stroke of piston. The boilers are ten in number and form a single group; all deliver their gases of combustion into the same chimney. The fire-room is 9 feet wide and extends in the fore-and-aft-direction of the vessel. The boilers are arranged in pairs, on opposite sides of the fire-room, and facing each other. Each boiler is 9¼ feet in diameter and 9 feet in length, and contains two cylindrical furnaces 3 feet in diameter, with a 6-foot length of grates. The total grate surface is 360 square feet. The screw is 16 feet in diameter, 2 feet in length, and 25 feet uniform pitch. The coal is carried in bunkers arranged on the starboard (but not on the port) side of the engine; between the engine and boilers; in a hold forward of the boilers and below the lower deck; between the boilers and the sides of the vessel, and along the sides of the vessel, on the lower deck, for the entire distance occupied by the engine and boilers. The weight of coal carried is 575 tons. The weight of the machinery is 550 tons, and its estimated cost $246,400.

For the gunboat, the engine consists of a high-pressure cylinder of 24 inches diameter, and a low-pressure cylinder of 40 inches diameter; stroke of piston for both, 30 inches. The boilers are four in number, 9 feet 4 inches in diameter, and 8 feet 6 inches in length. Each boiler contains two cylindrical furnaces, 3 feet in diameter, with grates 6 feet in length. Total grate surface, 144 square feet. The boilers are placed in pairs, each pair facing the other, with an athwartship fire-room between them, 9 feet wide. The four boilers have one chimney in common. Between the boilers, on each side of the fire-room, is a fore-and-aft passage 4½ feet wide, and over each of these passages is a hatch 6 feet long by 4 feet wide, for ventilation. The screw is 10 feet in diameter, 15 inches in length, and has a uniform pitch of 16¼ feet. The coal is carried partly forward and partly abaft the boilers, and weighs 160 tons. The weight of the machinery is 160 tons, and its estimated cost is $71,680.

The four accompanying general plans, drawn to scale, show, for each vessel, the arrangement of the entire machinery, and coal-bunkers, hatches, ladders, &c., together with the dimensions of the spaces occupied.

We are of opinion that the machinery submitted for the four classes of vessels will give the required speeds; that it is well adapted to the vessels, can be properly placed in them, and will prove satisfactory in its working when constructed.

Very respectfully, your obedient servants,

B. F. ISHERWOOD,
Chief Engineer, U. S. N.
CHAS. H. LORING,
Chief Engineer, U. S. N.
CHAS. H. MANNING,
Passed Assistant Engineer, U. S. N.

Rear-Admiral JOHN RODGERS, U. S. N.,
President of the Advisory Board.

REPORT OF THE SUBCOMMITTEE ON EQUIPMENT OF VESSELS.

WASHINGTON, D. C., *October* 4, 1881.

SIR: The committee to whom was referred the subject of equipment of vessels submit the annexed table of weights and costs of outfits, stores, &c.; also, weights of provisions and clothing for 100 men for three months.

Very respectfully,

P. C. JOHNSON,
Captain, U. S. N.
R. D. EVANS,
Commander, U. S. N.
M. R. S. MACKENZIE,
Lieutenant, U. S. N.

Rear-Admiral JOHN RODGERS, U. S. N.,
President of Advisory Board.

Weights and costs of outfits and equipment of proposed vessels.

Outfits, stores, &c.	Displacement 5768.		Displacement 4269.	
	Weight.	Cost.	Weight.	Cost.
Anchors and chains	203, 946	$15, 018 70	158, 050	$11, 911 68
Grapnels and buoys	420	110 00	360	100 00
Hawsers and towlines	20, 049	4, 410 78	14, 000	8, 080 00
Rigging	118, 627	41, 636 75	69, 865	27, 108 25
Sails	14, 856	38, 800 00	12, 142	29, 900 00
Furniture	2, 500	2, 200 00	2, 000	2, 000 00
Galley and utensils	14, 577	2, 327 84	11, 809	1, 575 72
Stores	31, 589	9, 034 61	22, 691	6, 776 96
Weights and costs, including stores	399, 564	108, 648 68	293, 908	82, 452 61
Weights and costs, exclusive of stores	367, 975	99, 614 07	270, 217	75, 675 65

Outfits, stores, &c.	Displacement 2967.		Displacement 769.	
	Weight.	Cost.	Weight.	Cost.
Anchors and chains	127, 527	$10, 401 60	48, 641	$3, 116 41
Grapnels and buoys	360	100 00	264	80 00
Hawsers and towlines	12, 000	2, 640 00	8, 000	1, 760 00
Rigging	40, 752	16, 830 00	15, 000	8, 250 00
Sails	10, 856	24, 700 00	2, 428	7, 800 00
Furniture	2, 741	1, 802 00	2, 241	1, 602 99
Galley and utensils	6, 602	1, 063 24	5, 504	986 38
Stores	21, 049	5, 993 08	15, 795	4, 517 31
Weights and costs, including stores	221, 887	63, 529 92	93, 873	28, 113 09
Weights and costs, exclusive of stores	200, 838	57, 536 84	78, 978	23, 595 78

Weight of provisions and clothing for 100 men for three months.

	Pounds.
Provisions	26, 625
Clothing	5, 063
Small stores	200
Total weight	31, 888

REPORT OF THE SUBCOMMITTEE ON INTERNAL ARRANGE-
MENTS OF VESSELS.

NAVY DEPARTMENT,
Washington, D. C., October 3, 1881.

SIR: On the part of the committee on internal arrangements, I have
the honor to make the following report:

The deck plans of the 15-knot cruiser, herewith presented, show the
proposed internal arrangement.

The large amount of coal which must of necessity be carried on the
berth deck of this vessel reduces very materially the space that would
otherwise be available for quarters, &c.

The idea of placing the wardroom on the gun-deck of this ship was
favorably considered, but it was found impossible to carry out such a
plan, owing to the fact of there not being sufficient room for it abaft the
after guns; and, as the ship is designed without a poop, the space referred to was required for captain's and admiral's cabins. The ward-
room was therefore left in its old position, the fore-and-aft bulkheads
being drawn together as they approach the stern, in order to give
greater deck room in the after rooms.

Wash rooms have been provided for the midshipmen and steerage
engineers, which will add much to the health and comfort of their quarters.

A drying room for the wet clothing of the men has been proposed by
inclosing a space one foot wide around the bulkheads of the fire-room
hatches on the berth deck. In ordinary weather this space could be
used for hanging up the men's pea-jackets. This committee are of the
opinion that it is very desirable that this or some similar arrangement
for drying clothing in continued bad weather be provided.

The *head* we think should not be placed on the gun deck, where it
must necessarily be in close proximity to the galley and the living quarters of many of the ship's company. We think it should by all means
be placed on the spar deck, where it alone can receive proper ventilation, and therefore we have so located it.

We also recommend a thorough system of ventilation by mechanical
means for the entire ship, and space for the necessary blowers and engines for this purpose has been provided for on the berth decks.

We would propose that this ship be provided with two bridges, one
forward of the smoke-pipes, and the other over the quarter deck, connected by a fore-and-aft bridge. These bridges, if made detachable and
given additional buoyancy, would, we think, be very useful in saving
life in case of a fatal accident to the ship. We have located a pilot-
house and chart-room on the forward bridge.

The sick-bay has been placed on one side of the berth deck, and bag
racks provided on the forward part of the same deck.

The general arrangement of the quarters, &c., of this vessel we would
propose for the 14 and 13 knot cruisers as far as practicable, though a decided reduction must be made in the space devoted to living and messing purposes in these two classes of vessels (13 and 14 knot cruisers),
owing to the fact that, as they are designed without a gun deck or top-
gallant forecastle, all arrangements for living, cooking, and messing
must be on the berth deck.

A drawing of the berth deck of the 10-knot gunboat, showing the interior arrangements of quarters, &c., is also submitted.

This committee is of the opinion that in small vessels of this design it would be very desirable to combine the wardroom and steerage into one apartment—at best, the amount of space that can be given to officers' quarters in this class of vessels is very limited—and that, instead of dividing it into two very restricted spaces, it would be better to make of it one fair-sized apartment, and to have but *one* officers' mess.

We would also recommend that all quarters, as far as possible, be finished in hard wood, which we believe to be more economical and more sightly than the ordinary method of covering wood-work with paint.

The science of lighting by electricity is now so far advanced that we believe it desirable to introduce that method of lighting our vessels of war.

In conclusion, we desire to say that we have carefully examined the plans of an unarmored cruiser, submitted to the department by Master Samuel Seabury; also those of Lieut. J. C. Soley for a similar vessel. Though they both contain several features that are novel, and which we would like to see incorporated in new cruisers, we found it impossible to do so, for the reason that the vessels designed, together with the location of their batteries and coal, did not permit it to be done.

Very respectfully,

A. S. CROWNINSHIELD,
Commander, U. S. N.

Rear-Admiral JOHN RODGERS, *U. S. N.*
President of the Advisory Board.

NAVAL ACADEMY.

REPORT OF THE BOARD OF VISITORS, 1881.

UNITED STATES NAVAL ACADEMY,
Annapolis, Md., June 10, 1881.

SIR: The Board of Visitors appointed to attend the annual examination at the United States Naval Academy met on the 1st instant and organized as follows: Rear-Admiral C. R. P. Rodgers, president; Hon. John F. Miller, vice-president; Lieut. C. Belknap reported for duty as secretary.

The board resolved itself into the usual committees for the purpose of more thoroughly examining into the workings of the institution, holding meetings as occasion required, and now, having completed its labors, it has the honor to submit the following report:

SEAMANSHIP, GUNNERY, AND NAVIGATION.

We have been at much pains to inquire into the character of the examination papers of all the classes in these departments and the general methods of instruction therein. Here are the three pre-eminently professional departments and the standard set cannot be too high; and it affords us pleasure to say that those in charge of them seem fully impressed with the importance of their duties; that they are all satisfactorily conducted, and that the proficiency of the cadets is of a high order.

In this connection we desire to suggest, in consideration of the great importance of these professional departments, the greatest possible weight be given to seamanship, gunnery, and navigation in determining the final standing of members of the several classes.

36 Ab

The increasing importance of iron-ship building renders it highly desirable that some additional models, in iron or steel, of the longitudinal system of framing, stern framing of iron-clads, and the different keels showing methods of uniting them to stem and stern posts, should be furnished to the department of seamanship.

In the department of gunnery we find that only the old and almost obsolete smooth-bore muzzle-loading guns are provided for instruction of the cadets in this most important branch of professional studies.

We feel that the eminently sensible recommendation of the head of this department, that a battery of breech-loading rifle guns of proper caliber with the most improved carriages, to replace a portion of the VIII-inch smooth-bore guns, should at once be carried into effect. It seems to us absurd that the naval cadets of this great country should continue to be instructed by methods and means which the experience of the rest of the naval world has laid aside as things of the past.

The board recommends that a suitable steam vessel of war, to be armed with rifled and smooth-bore guns, be provided, in order that gunnery may be taught the cadets from vessels under way, either under steam or sail, or both, and that instruction in seamanship, in combination with steam, may be practically taught.

STEAM ENGINEERING.

This department shows improving thoroughness and efficiency. By the recent introduction of what is known as the Russian system of instruction in practical mechanics, a notable advance has been made. Through its excellent methods, the student obtains intimate knowledge of the material with which he has to deal, acquires judgment regarding its qualities, and skill in its manipulation. To carry out this system in its entirety, a small cupola for melting iron, and a coppersmith's shop are needed. Space for these objects can be had within the building of the department by providing elsewhere shelter for the steam fire-engine now awkwardly placed. With the facilities thus provided, all the smaller repairs to the machinery of the vessels on the station can be made. It is estimated that about nineteen hundred dollars will be required for these alterations and additions.

PHYSICS.

The department of physics in all its branches evidently keeps pace with the progress of modern science. Its apparatus, selected with excellent judgment, includes pieces for the demonstration of the most recent discoveries in the science to which the department is devoted.

The chemical laboratory is well adapted for analytical work, and fairly supplied with apparatus. We believe it would be to the advantage of the Academy and of the Navy to utilize its resources in making any chemical examination of such stores and material of uncertain character as may be referred to it by the Navy Department and its bureaus for which no other provision exists.

MATHEMATICS.

We have no recommendations to offer with regard to the course of instruction pursued in this branch of study.

We have examined the rooms used by the professor of mathematics for descriptive geometry, right-line drawing, &c., and find that, situated as it is, directly under the roof, with inadequate ventilation and insufficient space, it is entirely unsuited for the use to which it is put. The room in question is in the eastern end of the building; in the opposite or western end is the space devoted to the purposes of the professor of drawing, equally unsuitable and uncomfortable. It is recommended that a proper place be provided to accommodate the working rooms of both of these branches of instruction.

MECHANICS.

The board has no recommendations to make regarding this department. The course appears to be ample and the instruction thorough; its incidental importance in the education of those who are to practice the art of war, and provide the instruments with which it is to be carried on, can scarcely be overestimated.

ENGLISH STUDIES AND MODERN LANGUAGES.

The work of instruction in these departments is well performed, and the results, considering the amount of preparation required for admission into the Academy, are not only equal to any just expectation, but are in a very high degree creditable to the heads of the departments and to all the instructors whose work has come under our notice.

Considering how limited is the time which can be given to English studies, and how great the difficulties which instructors encounter in the defective earlier education of many of the cadets, it would seem difficult to enlarge the comprehension of English studies, but it would be a most desirable addition to this course to bring into it more of study of the government whose servants they are, and of the people whose rights and honor they are appointed to defend; and we would emphasize our conviction that elementary studies in mental and moral science cannot be excluded from the education of the youth here assembled, without damage to the proper harmony of their education, and to its completeness for the purposes of command for which they are in training.

The effects of inadequate preparation for admission to the Academy are apparent, not only in the fourth class, but in the higher classes. Cadets best prepared have an advantage over their fellows, which, other things being equal, continues to the end.

The apparatus of education here possessed and at work is of the very best character; it has the wealth of the government for its support, and it cannot but be in the utmost sense desirable that the youth who come to these great opportunities should come fully prepared to avail themselves of their benefits.

We would therefore respectfully submit as worthy of inquiry whether the standard remaining as it is, it could not be interpreted in a higher sense—whether the standard could not be supported in a higher interpretation by making fifteen years the lowest age at which a cadet could be received, or whether the standard might not actually be raised, even if in order to this end it should be found necessary to provide for a temporary sub-cadetship, to insure that those who enter the prescribed course shall in no case be deficient at the beginning.

To raise the standard of admission would be only to put the Naval Academy in harmony in this respect with the colleges and other advanced schools of the country, whose terms of admission are steadily rising with the general advance of education.

PUBLIC GROUNDS, BUILDINGS, AND SANITARY CONDITION.

All the matters which have been submitted to us for consideration under this head seem to have been under the careful consideration of the officers connected with the Academy for several years, and the recommendations have been uniformly in the same direction.

Medical Inspector A. C. Gorgas, head of the medical department, states the health of the cadets, officers and families, sailors and marines, to be excellent. For the treatment of the cadets the sick quarters are adequate. For the accommodation of the sick among the sailors and marines no proper provision exists. To meet the requirement, we recommend the erection of a pavilion ward, to contain twelve beds, in the rear of the sick quarters, preferably to an extension of the present building.

The presence of malaria in limited extent is operative. To lessen its influence, the recommendation of Medical Inspector Gorgas to ditch, employ oyster shells, and sow pine cones in the two swamps on the " Farm" belonging to the Naval Academy is indorsed.

The old quarters are inadequate for their purpose, being without proper ventilation, subject to draughts, destitute of baths, and possessed of defective water-closets in the rear of the buildings. For these reasons, in addition to those made in the reports of former Boards of Visitors, the recommendation for the addition of a wing to the rear of the new quarters, in order that the entire corps of cadets may be domiciled under one roof, is fully concurred in.

The location selected for the erection of a new barracks is, in our opinion, not well taken, being upon low, newly-made ground, and in close proximity to the outlets of sewers, one of which is used to convey the sewerage matter from a portion of the city of Annapolis. We have to recommend the selection of another site, which will comply with the sanitary requirements.

The system of sewerage is defective. Grave faults are found in the water-closets, soil-pipes, waste-pipes, and traps. The urinals within, and the water-closets without the new quarters of the cadets, are offensive to sight and smell, and pernicious in their pollution of the air. These should be removed and the clean and effective water-closets of modern invention should be substituted. The other defects to be corrected require that the drainage system be as free as possible from foul matter; that every part of the system be separated from the atmosphere of the house by suitable traps and tightness of the conduit; that as far as may be, the system opened to the admission and circulation of fresh air; that a positive separation be secured between the water supply of the house and the drainage system; that the connection between the works occasions no communication between different rooms or floors, or with the spaces between the floors and ceilings and in partitions. The suggestion made by Medical Inspector Gorgas for the extension of the sewerage-pipes out into the stream, so as to keep their outlets covered at low-water is indorsed. We believe that the proposed improvement of the sewerage system should apply-to the entire collection of buildings, and that it may be carried out in a manner advocated by the highest authorities, we recommend the employment of a sanitary engineer, who can make intelligent estimates of the cost, upon which a request for an appropriation may be based. The suggestion to employ the services of a sanitary engineer is also made by Medical Inspector Gorgas.

We are clearly of the opinion that the inhibition of tobacco among the cadets should be enforced. The reasons set forth by Medical Director Gihon for the prohibition are sufficiently conclusive, and the conclusion has obtained in several preceding Boards of Visitors, who have recommended it as a wise sanitary provision. Contrasting the condition of the cadets during the enforcement of the prohibition with that stated in the report of Medical Inspector Gorgas, during the period of practice, the physiological and hygienic benefits resulting from the inhibition are too pronounced to warrant a hesitancy of opinion as to the expediency of prevention of the use of tobacco.

ADMINISTRATION, DISCIPLINE, AND POLICE.

The board gives its unqualified approval of the general conduct and management of the Academy, and of the admirable system under which the effective discipline of the cadets is maintained. After a very critical examination, the board is unable to find any fault, either of system or management, and deems it proper to express the highest commendation of the officers charged with the difficult and delicate duties of this department of the institution. These duties would be more easily performed should the requisite addition to the quarters of the cadets be constructed, as recommended in another part of this report. All cadets would then be quartered under the same roof, giving the officer in charge more perfect control over their conduct, with less labor and expense.

The system of demerits practiced is regarded as admirable, and it is believed it is carried out in perfect fairness and impartiality. The reliance placed upon the honor of the cadet in the matter of excuses cannot fail to develop those characteristics which denote the gentleman, and to stimulate the practice of a high morality.

FINANCE AND LIBRARY.

We would report as the result of our investigation into the financial affairs of the Academy that the annual appropriations for the support of the Academy are strictly applied to the objects contemplated by the laws making them, and are honestly, intelligently, and prudently disbursed.

The books and accounts of the various officers, through whom these disbursements are made, are kept in an orderly manner, easily understood, and show such a system of checks and balances as renders practically impossible an improper disbursement of the funds.

We were much interested in the library and its orderly management; both are highly creditable. There are now upon the shelves of the library about 23,000 volumes, and these are being gradually added to, to the extent of the annual appropriation for that purpose, in such manner as to best meet the actual needs of the school.

The appropriation for the present fiscal year, annually renewed, is deemed sufficient for this purpose. In this connection we would suggest that many of the government publications are of value to the Academy; but there is no law obliging the officers who have charge of these publications to furnish them to the Academy. We would therefore recommend the enactment of a law covering the case, which will regularly secure to the library, free of charge, all government publications as they are issued.

MISCELLANEOUS.

In the opinion of the board it is necessary that only enough cadets shall graduate from the Naval Academy to make good the annual waste of the Navy, and that Congress should, by careful legislation, provide against the accumulation of midshipmen and cadet engineers to grow old in those inferior grades to the manifest injury of the Naval service, its discipline and its usefulness.

In this connection the board desires to refer to the report of the Superintendent of the Naval Academy, dated November 13, 1877, and published with the report of the Secretary of the Navy for that year. The present system seems to the board very fruitful of evil.

We suggest, in order to supplement the instruction in natural history given at the academy, that officers who show an aptitude for these pursuits should be given an opportunity between their cruises to study the vast and valuable collection at the National Museum, so that the Navy may possess a class of officers trained in the habits of study and observation which obtain in natural history, and which would especially fit them to serve upon the expeditions for exploration and scientific research which the Navy is so frequently called upon to undertake.

C. R. P. ROGERS,
Rear-Admiral, President.
JNO. F. MILLER, U. S. S.,
Vice-President.
JNO. T. MORGAN, U. S. S.
OLIN WELLBORN, M. C.
THOMAS M. BROWNE,
House of Representatives.
JNO. SCOVILLE, M. C.
S. P. CARTER,
Commodore, U. S. N.
J. M. BROWNE,
Medical Director, U. S. N.
CHAS. H. LORING,
Chief Engineer, U. S. N.
D. B. McCREARY,
Pennsylvania.
W. O. BIBB,
Alabama.
S. S. CUTTING,
New York.
WM. M. CALDWELL,
Newport, R. I.
JAMES PARKER,
Perth Amboy, N. J.
FRANCIS W. LAWRENCE,
Brookline, Mass.
BEVERLY TUCKER,
Berkley Springs, W. Va.

REPORT OF THE SUPERINTENDENT.

UNITED STATES NAVAL ACADEMY,
Annapolis, Md., November 10, 1881.

SIR: After an absence of three years on foreign service, I resumed command at the Naval Academy on the 13th June, and now have the honor to submit its annual report.

During the summer the cadets were embarked on board the practice-ships Constellation and Dale, and the steamers Standish and Mayflower, and their cruise along the coast of the United States was directed with zeal and success by their commanding officers, whose reports I herewith transmit.

The change that has been made in sending all the cadets to sea every year, and in giving them at the end of the summer cruise a month's leave, is an improvement upon the old system, except in two particulars: the cost of fitting out and manning so many vessels; and, secondly, in the inability of many of the cadets to incur the expense of going on leave, paying for civilian's clothes, and traveling expenses, an expense that those who have not private resources are little prepared to encounter, and by which they are tempted to incur debts.

Before and at the beginning of the academic year, an effort was made to continue the unmanly and unseamanlike habit of hazing the new cadets, in violation not only of law but of those principles of hospitality and kindness to strangers for which all sea-faring people have been noted.

The effort, as soon as discovered, was summarily dealt with; the third class, to which the attempt to haze is chiefly confined, was informed that evil consequences could only be averted by the most prompt assurance offered the Superintendent that the practice should instantly cease.

The cadet engineers of the third class gave the assurance; the cadet midshipmen were not ready to do so, and they were at once separated from the new-comers and transferred to the Constellation and Santee, where they were messed, lodged, and instructed under careful supervision, and only permittted to land to be marched in military formation to the prescribed drills. A court of inquiry was convened, and efficient steps were taken to discover who had violated the law approved June 23, 1874, "to prevent hazing at the Naval Academy."

So effective were these steps that before any testimony was taken by the court all the cadets of the second, third, and fourth classes hastened to pledge their word of honor that, while at the Naval Academy, they would never haze, maltreat, harass, render ridiculous, subject to indignities, or in any way molest the cadets of the fourth class. Such pledges are always kept, and may be implicitly relied upon. The first class never joins in hazing.

When the new cadets arrive next year they will find every cadet at the Naval Academy thus pledged, and the succession of hazing is therefore broken.

During the summer a large and much-needed armory and drill room has been erected, two hundred and fifty feet long and eighty feet wide; a handsome brick structure, that will be very valuable. It would have now been under roof had not one of the contractors failed to fulfill his agreement, but it will doubtless be under cover during the present month.

Large and convenient marine barracks have been built and are now being finished. They will afford the marine garrison handsome and comfortable quarters in the place of the unsuitable sheds in which the marines have been hitherto lodged.

The professors and officers at the Naval Academy are able and zealous, and are very successful in their methods and instruction. I cannot speak too highly of their ability and devotion. The country, always anxious to foster the education of its people, has good reason to be satisfied with its Naval Academy, to which Congress has been most liberal and considerate. As an old officer I am very proud when I have the opportunity to show it to officers from other countries.

I beg to renew the recommendation so often made, that Congress be moved to vote the necessary appropriation to build an additional wing to the new cadet quarters so that the cadets may be quartered under one roof, to the great benefit of their discipline, their health, and the economy of the administration of the school. At present, in addition to the cadet midshipmen, we have one hundred cadet engineers at this institution.

In my opinion the number both of cadet midshipmen and cadet engineers might be advantageously decreased.

We have now in the Navy nearly two hundred young gentlemen who have passed successfully through the academic course of four years, have completed their studies at this school, and are awaiting their promotion to the grade of ensign, the lowest commissioned grade, a grade attained by the cadets at West Point in four years, but for which some of the naval aspirants who finished their course at Annapolis last June must wait for at least eight years longer, twelve years after their admission to this establishment. The average age of the ten lowest of these young officers who will be the last promoted is at this moment twenty-two years.

Under our present system this number of midshipmen will increase every year; a sorry sight of an ever-increasing number of graduates, waiting, with hope long deferred, for promotion to the lowest grade of commissioned officers. We shall, also, under the present system, graduate, every year, many more cadet engineers than will supply the annual waste of their corps.

I therefore respectfully renew the suggestions I made four years ago, and I venture to make them in the same words I used at that time, in my annual report dated November 13, 1877.

I would respectfully recommend that either the number of cadet appointments be largely decreased, or that a new system be adopted which would produce far better results than the one now in force. I would suggest that some able actuary be found to calculate the annual waste of the Navy, both of the line and of the engineer corps; and, further, that he should compute how many cadets should each year enter the second class to supply that waste and keep the number of officers in the lower commissioned grades of the Navy always full. This table could be made more easily than the tables of the life-insurance companies, and might be rearranged every five or ten years. The number of cadets for the second class being thus decided, admission to it should be the prize for which all entering the Naval Academy should compete during the first two years of their novitiate. Those who failed to win the prize might graduate at the end of their first two years, and return to their homes with an honorable diploma; and would well repay the country for the cost of their training by carrying to every congressional district in the land the habit of discipline, the traditions of military life, and a practical knowledge of the use of arms which would make them invaluable in the organization of volunteer regiments whenever the country found occasion to call its citizens to arms.

There is a subtle power in military discipline which cannot be readily defined, but which gives to those who have learned to obey a great capacity to command with ease and with ready acceptance. Under this system no cadet need be found deficient, except for grave misconduct, or for contumacious and inexcusable neglect of study.

All countries are following the example of the United States in raising their standard of naval education; for all the world begins to recognize that a scientific training is highly desirable in those who are to command the ships of war of to-day (and of the future), with their new engines of destruction, their complicated machinery, and their novelties of structure. When I entered the Navy the wooden line-of-battle ship, a short ship, easily handled under canvas, was the highest type of a fighting vessel. Its guns were weak and of small caliber, having upon them no sights worthy of the name; the powder was poor; flint-locks were used; the whole ordnance equipment was very bad; there were no torpedoes, no rifled cannon, no steam engines, no armor, nor any of those extraordinary provisions of strength, such as foreign iron-clads now exhibit, to enable them to endure the shock of battle and the terrible strain to which their own machinery subjects them when they are driven by it at their greatest speed.

The education given at the Naval Academy lays the foundation upon which the graduates of this school may build the highest professional education. It gives them keys by which they may unlock the mysteries of ship-building, and ordnance and gunnery, and all the intricacies involved in the torpedo system, and at the same time it trains them to the use of all arms; it exercises their muscles so as to develop the manliest habit, and during four years practical work as "topmen," it teaches them the duty of a private seaman, a training that was not given to the naval youth of my day, and which, to my mind, gives to our graduates a great advantage by enabling them to sympathize with those whom they are to command, from having themselves performed a private seaman's duty both aloft and at the guns.

There is naturally great complaint now from the disappointed friends of cadets who have been too idle to profit by the opportunities given them here, or, in some rare cases, perhaps, too dull. It is my carefully considered belief that any lad of even a little less than average ability can complete successfully the course of studies here if he will study faithfully and diligently. Those of more brilliant capacity can attain the same result with a very moderate amount of study. To take honors at the school requires both capacity and hard work.

The government offers to its young men at the Naval Academy an honorable career and an excellent education at the country's cost, and it demands from them only that they shall not be dull, idle, unfaithful, or vicious.

The professors and officers are uniformly desirous to graduate as large a class as possible; they are ready to give all the assistance in their power, and it is, of course, a matter of anxiety to the academic board to avoid the great concern its members feel when witnessing the disappointment of parents and friends, caused by the failure of those whom they had hoped had secured an honorable calling.

It is sometimes claimed that the course of instruction here is too severe, and I venture to give it as my opinion that such is not the case, and I think that if the demands of the course were largely decreased we should have no more graduates. As the demand decreased the effort of the student would diminish; for it is now not the love of learning, but the fear of failure to enter the Navy, which prompts the majority to exertion; and with the larger number the effort is to do as little, instead of as much, as possible.

It is sometimes objected that we lay too much stress upon the study of mathematics; that the cadets are not needed as mathematicians, but as sea-officers. I know of no study that will so carefully train the mind to quick, clear thought, and to the ready application of principles, as the study of pure and applied mathematics.

The course of mathematics here leads directly to those principles of physics and to the scientific knowledge which has now become essential to the sea-officer who would fully understand the engines of war committed to his care. He must still be a seaman, but a scientific seaman, and his science and mental training will in no degree detract from his nautical skill.

The instruction in seamanship at this school seems to me excellent, for it is very practical, enabling the cadets to do the duty of a seaman aloft, and to do it well; to steer; to heave the lead; to bend and unbend the sails; to send up and down the different spars, and, as officers of the watch, to handle the ship under canvas. During three months of every year the cadet midshipmen make a practice cruise in the Constellation and Dale, the lower classes doing the duty of topmen, while the first-class men are officers of the deck.

I was brought up in the old Navy, so called; I am familiar with the new system, and I know perfectly well that no midshipman of my day ever acquired in four years as much of purely naval training as is given to their successors of this generation, at this school, in the same length of time.

In my later commands I have been much associated afloat with graduates of the Naval Academy serving as watch officers, and I desire to assert that, as seamen, they are in no respect inferior to the sea-officers with whom I served forty years ago, and in the other branches of professional knowledge they are greatly superior.

I have the honor to be, very respectfully, your obedient servant,
C. R. P. RODGERS,
Rear-Admiral, Superintendent.

Hon. WILLIAM H. HUNT,
Secretary of the Navy, Washington, D. C.

REPORT OF THE CHIEF OF THE BUREAU OF ORDNANCE.

BUREAU OF ORDNANCE, NAVY DEPARTMENT,
October 1, 1881.

SIR: I have the honor to submit the annual report of this bureau, and also to transmit estimates for the fiscal year ending June 30, 1883, viz:

1. Labor, tools, material, and fuel used in fitting ships for service, and in the production and preservation of ordnance and ordnance stores; repairs to buildings, magazines, gun parks, wharves, tugs, lighters, and boats $244,793 00
2. Torpedo service 45,000 00
3. Miscellaneous items, freight, telegrams, postage, advertising, &c..... 5,500 00
4. Civil establishment at navy-yards..................................... 11,886 25
5. Supplementary estimate for 10 steel rifled breech-loading cannon and equipments 220,000 00

527,179 25

These estimates are moderate in amount, and are divided into two classes.

1st. (Items 1, 2, 3, and 4.) Those embracing funds to be devoted to the current uses of the bureau.

2d. (Item 5.) Supplementary estimates, the principal items of which are the material and labor necessary for commencing (in a very small way) the armament of the Navy with modern guns.

The operations of the bureau for many preceding years, and for nearly the whole of the year now closing, were directed by Commodore William N. Jeffers, whose ability and experience are so well known to the department and to the Navy generally. He introduced improvements of vital importance, and the adoption of almost all the modern ordnance appliances now in use in the Navy is due to his direction and efforts.

During this year the Ordnance Department has been largely employed in the preparation of outfits for such ships as were needed for service.

The batteries of these vessels consist mainly of smooth-bore guns, on account of the want of funds and facilities for the introduction of a suitable rifled armament. In all cases, however, at least one converted 8-inch rifled muzzle-loading gun and a converted 60-pounder breech-loading rifle were placed on board each ship.

One vessel, the Lancaster, is provided with an entire battery of 8-inch converted muzzle-loading rifles, mounted upon carriages worked by mechanical gearing, and so pivoted as to give an unusual horizontal arc of fire, together with greatly increased facilty of training.

The improved rapid firing Gatling gun has been placed on all the ships lately commissioned; and, in addition, one of these guns has been sent to each vessel on the Asiatic station.

The Hotchkiss magazine rifle has also been issued as occasion offered, and is now in use on most of the ships in commission.

The 300 Lee breech-loading rifles, caliber .45, ordered for the Navy, are in course of manufacture at the Remington Armory, Ilion, N. Y. When the guns are received they will be issued to service on trial.

Twenty-one Hotchkiss revolving cannon of 1.45-inch caliber, and throwing a projectile weighing about a pound, were purchased by my predecessor. Seventeen of these have been delivered by the manufacturer and have been issued to service.

Two heavier guns of this class are in course of manufacture for the bureau by Mr. Hotchkiss. These throw projectiles of 2.42 pounds, and 4 pounds respectively, and it is understood that larger calibers are being designed.

The chief province of heavy machine guns has heretofore been defense against torpedo boats. But their caliber and power having been greatly increased of late, these pieces can now play an important part in naval engagements, as their projectiles are capable of piercing the sides of unarmored ships of war. They also penetrate about one and a half inches of steel plate at moderate ranges, and their introduction will doubtless soon render necessary the shielding of all great guns not already covered by armor. It is highly probable that still heavier calibers of machine guns will be found very effective and useful in the future.

The most important question of armament now pressing for attention is the manufacture of suitable high power rifled cannon for the navy; and that steel is the proper material to be employed in the construction of such guns is admitted by most naval men.

It is very desirable to reduce the weight of naval guns as much as practicable, as thereby a relatively greater number, or heavier calibers, can be mounted on any given ship, her battery power being correspondingly increased.

Owing to its great strength, steel can bear high powder pressures with a less thickness of wall than would be necessary if any other metal were used, and hence its peculiar fitness for use on shipboard.

To be suitable for such a purpose, however, the steel, besides being perfectly sound, must possess a particular combination of strength, elasticity, and ductility. Rigid tests are in use to ascertain the existence and proper combination of these qualities; and if the metal fails to meet the requirements, it must be rejected, and is consequently thrown upon the hands of the producer.

As the combination of qualities referred to is difficult to obtain with certainty, especially in large masses, such as gun tubes and jackets, and as the demand for ordinary merchant steel is constantly increasing, steel makers are reluctant to attempt the production of gun ingots, besides which only a very few works in the country have steam hammers heavy enough to properly forge such masses.

The machine work required for converting the rough forgings into finished guns also calls for time and care, so it will be seen that the manufacture of heavy ordnance (even in time of peace) is a slow operation, and previous experience is absolutely necessary in order to turn out guns with speed and success in case of emergency.

It is also apparent that a comparatively small gun is more easily manufactured than one of larger size, and that in the endeavor to effect the production of cannon it would be best to attempt the smaller calibers first.

Owing to want of funds, the Navy has not been able to keep pace with the immense development in the power of artillery that has taken place abroad of late years. Some of our smooth-bore guns have been converted to rifles, and are thereby much increased in power. An excellent form of breech closure has also been introduced. But beyond this our great guns are of necessity in the same state as they were twenty years ago, and the batteries of our ships are still mainly composed of smooth bores.

The contest between guns and armor having been to all appearances settled in favor of the gun, the material and general form of the latter may be considered as established for the present, and since steel has been almost universally decided upon as the only metal that has the strength necessary for building a light and powerful naval gun, it becomes my duty to strongly recommend that Congress be urged to grant funds for manufacturing the ten guns and equipments which I have inserted in the estimates for 1882–'83. It is probable that two or three of these guns should be purchased abroad as examples of a branch of manufacture in which our people have but little experience.

The number asked for is of course wholly inadequate to the needs of the Navy, and is, indeed, intended only as a commencement, for the purpose of settling upon types, and also for testing the ability of our steel makers to produce what is required. In fact, the bureau has not heretofore had sufficient funds at its disposal to justify it in giving orders large enough to induce steel makers to enter upon this comparatively new and difficult branch of their business.

It is now time that producers should be encouraged to turn their attention into this important channel, and if they fail to come up to requirements, then we must necessarily look abroad for an armament.

The previous experience of the bureau shows that delay will probably be encountered in obtaining the proper metal, and therefore a beginning should be made as soon as practicable.

I beg that the necessity for immediate commencement upon the work of re-arming the Navy may be particularly pressed upon the attention of Congress, as it is certainly by far the most serious and important matter the bureau has to present at this time.

TORPEDO STATION.

Since the date of the last annual report of the bureau, Capt. F. M. Ramsay has been relieved of the charge of the Torpedo Station at Newport by Capt. Thomas O. Selfridge.

The usual class of officers has been under instruction during the summer months, and their examination was in all respects satisfactory to the board of officers assembled to witness it.

Practical exercises were had in the management of batteries and connections, in the fabrication of explosives and torpedo fuses, in the manufacture of torpedoes, both offensive and defensive, and opportunities were afforded to witness the manipulation of movable torpedoes. (See report appended, marked E.)

During that part of the year when instruction is not going on the attention of the officers at the station has been turned towards general researches bearing upon torpedo work.

Among other things a movable torpedo has been experimented with. It promises well, and trials with it will be continued.

An improved form of the Lay torpedo (called the Lay-Haight) has been received and tried, with favorable results, showing very considerable reduction of weight, and a gratifying increase of speed over those formerly purchased by the bureau.

Captain Selfridge has been engaged in perfecting a system of electric lighting for the use of ships of war, and an exhibition of it given before the board of examiners was considered highly satisfactory by them. (A description of this light will be found in the appendix, marked E.) He has also been engaged upon a method of defense for ships against movable torpedoes. This plan is ingenious, and promises very well.

Experiments are also being made with a view to improvement in the method of firing great guns by electricity.

An addition to the explosive laboratory has been lately made. Its need has been much felt, and when completed the officers on duty at the station will be enabled to familiarize themselves more fully than they heretofore could do with the nature, manufacture and characteristics of the high explosives.

It is necessary to commence the introduction of a higher explosive than gunpowder into the service torpedo, and efforts in that direction will be prosecuted as rapidly as prudence will permit.

Extracts from some of the reports of Captain Selfridge are appended. Besides being very interesting, they are progressive in their character, and afford a good indication of the kind of work that the torpedo station is engaged in when not occupied with the instruction of classes of officers. It is of vital importance to the country and to the Navy that we should keep fully abreast with foreign powers in this most important branch of attack and defense.

The dangerous business of handling explosives cannot be prosecuted without risk, and it is conceded that as a rule the work at the torpedo station has been reasonably exempt from accident. We have, however, this year to lament a most painful occurrence whereby two officers of the greatest promise, Lieutenant Commander Benjamin Long Edes and Lieutenant Lyman G. Spalding, lost their lives.

A very important exhibition, which embodies the progress made in electric research of late years, is now being held at Paris. It is hoped that great benefit to practical electricity will result therefrom; and the bureau will receive reports of all matters that come within its province.

I am, sir, with high respect, your obedient servant,

MONTGOMERY SICARD,
Chief of Bureau.

Hon. WILLIAM H. HUNT,
Secretary of the Navy.

REPORT OF THE CHIEF OF THE BUREAU OF NAVIGATION.

BUREAU OF NAVIGATION, NAVY DEPARTMENT,
Washington, November 5, 1881.

SIR: I have the honor to submit the following report of the Bureau of Navigation for the past year, together with the estimates for its support, and for the expenditures that will probably be required in that division of the naval service committed to its immediate charge, for the fiscal year ending June 30, 1883.

Included in this report, and transmitted herewith, are the reports and estimates of the several offices under its cognizance, and an abstract of offers for supplies received.

Having but recently assumed charge of this Bureau, I confine myself to its records and to the appended reports.

NAVIGATION.

American Practical Navigator.—Since the last report, all the manuscript of the revised American Practical Navigator has been placed in the hands of the printer; the proof-sheets of the text have been read twice, also the proofs of the tables to table 28 inclusive, and it is expected that the work will be finished and ready for issue within one year.

Magnetism of ships.—The magnetic record of ships in commission is regularly kept up and coefficients calculated. This subject will demand increased attention when more iron vessels shall be added to the present naval force. A number of very valuable observations have been made by Commander W. T. Sampson, commanding the United States steamer Swatara, for local deviation, absolute declination, horizontal intensity and dip, with fine instruments specially provided for the purpose.

The necessary instruments for taking magnetic observations have also been supplied to the United States steamer Rodgers for her cruise in the Arctic Ocean via Behring Straits, and to the United States steamer Alliance for her cruise between Spitzbergen and Iceland, both in search of the Jeannette, and important results in this respect are anticipated.

Determinations of longitudes.—In the spring of this year Lieut. Commander F. M. Green and a party of officers started on their mission to measure differences of longitude between a number of the principal seaports on the coast of Asia, by the aid of the telegraph, and as far as reported the longitudes of Yokohama, Nagasaki, Vladivostok, Shanghai, Amoy, and Hong Kong have thus been successfully determined; also the latitudes of Yokohama, Nagasaki, and Shanghai. It is gratifying to note that foreign governments take the liveliest interest in this important scientific work, and that the owners of the respective telegraph lines render all necessary facilities for accomplishing the same with appreciative willingness. It may be remarked that this work, so essential for geography and navigation, is now performed at no additional outlay of funds beyond that for transportation of officers and instruments, as the same instruments are being used that served in previous longitude-expeditions in the West Indies, Brazil, Cape de Verdes, England, and Portugal.

Nautical instruments.—The attention of the Bureau having been drawn to a new instrument called the "Navisphere," invented by Captain

Magnac, French navy, two have been purchased and are being tested. This instrument promises to be a useful aid in navigation, and will receive due attention.

The Bureau has also ordered the purchase of another new instrument, the invention of Lieut. Josef Peichl, of the Austrian navy, for determining compass deviations.

Experiments have recently been made by Capt. George E. Belknap, commanding the United States steamer Alaska, with the "Navigational Sounding Machine," designed by Sir Wm. Thomson, and with the "Bassnett Atmospheric Sounder," which prove that these implements can be used with advantage for sounding in depths of about a hundred fathoms while the vessel is in motion. The "Bassnett Atmospheric Sounder" has also been successfully tested on board the United States steamers Kearsarge and Tallapoosa.

A new speed-indicator, designed and improved by Master B. A. Fiske, United States Navy, has been favorably reported upon after a trial on board the United States ship Tallapoosa.

Navigation supplies.—The revision of the allowances of the various navigation stores for ships of the Navy has been completed, and the list awaits printing. It will be an improved guide in the fitting of vessels, and an aid in administering the affairs of this Bureau.

As stated in previous reports, I find from the records that the navigation storerooms at the different navy-yards contain a large number of old implements unfit for service or repairs, and I concur in the request made by my predecessor that legislation be obtained for the disposal of those articles of obsolete form, being of no practical utility, and that the proceeds of the sale of such material be devoted to procuring articles of an improved kind.

The question of lighting ships by means of electricity demands attention. In some European ships of war this method has been in use for some time, and it is proposed to try it also on some of our naval vessels. Hitherto the electric-light machines have been held at such prices as to preclude their introduction on shipboard; but the more extensive use of the electric light for illuminating the streets of cities, hotels and other large buildings, has brought about competition and a consequent reduction in cost. The electric light would be extremely useful in preventing collisions at sea, and in detecting approaching torpedo-boats in time of war. An estimate for experimenting in lighting ships of war by means of the electric light, has therefore been submitted, which it is hoped will be granted.

I find that the appropriations made for this Bureau are inadequate to the demands of the branch of the service under its charge, and the increase asked for is needed for the maintenance of the present naval establishment. Higher prices than formerly are now invariably demanded for all supplies to be purchased; notably is this the case with illuminating oil.

Simultaneous international meteorological observations.—The system of taking meteorological observations on board of all naval vessels, at given moments three times each day, has been continued during the past year, and the results forwarded to the Army Signal Office for collation and publication.

HYDROGRAPHY.

I beg leave to invite your attention to the comprehensive report of the Hydrographer, hereto appended, detailing minutely the operations of the Hydrographic Office during the past year; enumerating the surveys accomplished and the hydrographic information furnished by commanding officers of vessels at home and abroad, and also the office work and foreign surveys still needing attention.

The work accomplished in this office during the past year, as detailed in the first part of the Hydrographer's report, shows that its affairs were systematically and economically managed, and the best possible use made of the comparatively small appropriation for this branch of the service. A number of new charts have been issued, by engraving and photo-lithography; sailing directions have been collated and published, and all changes in lighting and buoying the sea-coasts and harbors of the world, as well as all reported dangers to navigation, have been made public by means of printed notices to mariners and hydrographic notices.

The usefulness of the Hydrographic Office is acknowledged by all citizens of this country who are interested in commerce and navigation, and its publications are highly appreciated, both at home and abroad. The office is in admirable working order, and prepared to do much more useful work if the means are provided by Congress. I heartily indorse all the Hydrographer has to say in regard to the proposed extension of the usefulness of the office, and trust that the additional funds asked for its support and for engraving on copper a number of charts quickly produced by photo-lithography in order to supply the demand, may be granted.

The part of the report detailing the hydrographic and surveying work done by naval vessels during the past year is a fair exhibit of the readiness with which officers comply with the requests of the Bureau for occasional surveys and examinations of reported dangers; their labors are very useful, and the manner of execution highly creditable to them.

My predecessors have already urged the necessity of a systematic examination of many reported dangers in the Pacific and Atlantic Oceans, and also the thorough survey of the Marshall and Caroline Islands, the coast of Mexico, parts of the West Indies, and the Spanish main. Of these projected surveys, that of the west coast of Mexico has been undertaken and successfully carried on under Commander J. W. Philip, now commanding the United States steamer Ranger; all the other desired surveys have been left undone.

I earnestly recommend that the department give this important subject its serious consideration; that it may, so far as possible, detail the necessary vessels for service in the Atlantic and Pacific, and invoke the aid of Congress in furnishing the funds for carrying the projects into execution.

SIGNAL OFFICE.

Referring to the appended report of the Chief Signal Officer of the Navy, I desire to bring to your notice the omission on the part of our national legislature to make statutory the revised international regulations for preventing collisions at sea, which have been adopted by all other maritime nations of the world. The Navy Department, by its General Order No. 253, dated July 16, 1880, directed that its vessels be guided by these revised regulations, in so far as the navigation of naval vessels outside of United States territorial waters is concerned. Within the waters of the United States, the regulations as specified in section 4233 of the Revised Statutes must be observed.

As serious complications and losses to American ship-owners may occur from a non-observance of these revised regulations by American

navigators when in foreign waters, and as the fact of our having different regulations to guard against collisions from those of other maritime nations will sooner or later lead to difficulty, confusion, and disaster, Congress should be urged to remedy this evil by enacting as law the revised international regulations for preventing collisions adopted by all other countries.

NAVAL OBSERVATORY.

The appended report of the Superintendent of the Naval Observatory contains a statement of a large amount of astronomical work performed during the past year, consisting of observations of stars, satellites, and comets; their reduction and partial publication; the discussion and publication of the results of the Transit of Venus Expedition of 1874; the reduction of the photographic observations of the transit of Mercury in 1878, and the prosecution of experiments on astronomical photography.

The report treats also of the manner of furnishing New York and Washington mean time, the condition of the library of the institution, and gives the number and condition of navy chronometers now on hand, as well as those received and issued during the year.

Attention is respectfully called to the remarks regarding the vexatious delays in printing the annual volumes of observations and results. It is hoped that some method may be devised for completing the printing now in arrears, and that arrangements may be made for their prompt publication in the future.

NAUTICAL ALMANAC.

The superintendent of the Nautical Almanac reports that the volume for 1884 has been issued, and that for 1885 is nearly completed. During the fiscal year ending June 30, 1881, 479 copies of the large volume, and 2,997 of the small edition, were sold, and 909 copies were distributed for the public services and for educational purposes.

The work of preparing improved tables for the Ephemeris, and various researches, having for their object a more accurate determination of the constants of astronomy, are in progress.

The report of the experiments made for determining the velocity of light, and of the results obtained, is very interesting.

Respectfully submitted.

J. G. WALKER,
Chief of Bureau,

Hon. W. H. HUNT,
  Secretary of the Navy.

REPORT OF THE HYDROGRAPHER.

NAVY DEPARTMENT, BUREAU OF NAVIGATION,
            HYDROGRAPHIC OFFICE,
      Washington, D. C., October 29, 1881.

SIR: In accordance with the order of the Bureau of Navigation, I have the honor to submit the following report of the operations of the Hydrographic Office for the fiscal year ending June 30, 1881, with such

37 Ab

recommendations as the great importance of the work confided to this office demands.

I. WORK LEFT UNFINISHED IN THE PREVIOUS FISCAL YEAR, 1879–'80.

The increased activity of the hydrographic institutions of the various maritime powers, especially in the preceding year, is shown in the publication of an increased number of new surveys.

The necessity of keeping our issues corrected to the latest dates being paramount, this new matter has entailed so much labor of addition and correction of manuscript and plates, not only of charts on issue, but of new charts in process of engraving, that our small force of draughtsmen and engravers has been severely taxed, and the publication of important general charts by this office has been greatly retarded.

General Chart of the South Pacific Ocean, 8 half sheets.—Publication retarded as mentioned above. Further corrections are still to be made on the plates, before the new plates can be placed on issue.

General Chart of the Indian Ocean, 4 half sheets.—This chart is now on issue. There has been added to the northwestern sheet an outline chart of the world for laying down courses across the entire ocean, and for purposes of general reference.

General Chart of the North Atlantic Ocean, 4 half sheets.—The completion of the engraver's work has been delayed for the purpose of introducing new matter to be derived from the revised charts of the Spanish West India possessions now being published by the Spanish Hydrographic Office.

General Chart of the South Atlantic Ocean, 4 half sheets.—The engraving of this chart is still in progress.

Chart of the Mediterranean Sea, in 3 sheets.—The third (eastern) sheet has been completed, and the proof sheet is undergoing corrections from the new surveys recently published. The manuscript of the middle sheet is being corrected from the surveys by the French and Italian governments, the results of which have become available only in the past few months. The corrected portions of the western sheet are being engraved.

Chart of Guadeloupe, West Indies.—The work of engraving the extensive mountain topography of Guadeloupe has been completed, and the chart is now on issue.

Chart of the South Side of Oahu, Sandwich Islands.—The engraving has been completed, and the chart is now on issue.

Chart of the North Sea, 2 sheets.—The pressure of other work has caused the engraving of this chart to be temporarily discontinued.

Chart of the channels between the North and Baltic Seas.—Part of the work is in the hands of the engraver, while the manuscript of other parts is in preparation and nearly completed.

Chart of the Amazon River, 6 sheets, from the survey of Commander T. O. Selfridge.—The engraving is in progress, and will be completed before the close of the present year.

Chart of the Madeira River, 5 sheets, from the survey of Commander T O. Selfridge.—The completion of the engraver's work, which is now in rapid progress, will be effected before the close of the present year.

The following engraved charts of *Harbors and Anchorages on the West Coast of Mexico and Guatemala, from the surveys of Commander J. W. Philip,* have been completed and placed on issue:

No. 872. Acapulco Harbor.

No. 873. Anchorages off Champerico and San José.

No. 874. Anchorages off Morro Ayuca and Escondido.

No. 875. Anchorages off Angelos and Sacrificios.

No. 877. Harbors of Guatalco, Santa Cruz, and Tangola Tangola.

No. 878. Harbor of Istapa or Isla Grande.

No. 879. Harbors of Sihuatenejo, Petatlan, and Tequepa.

No. 876. Coast chart of Mexico, from Chiquepa Point to Ventosa Bay, from surveys by Commander J. W. Philip.—The survey of the *Coasts of Mexico and Guatemala* not yet being continuous, no chart of that coast has yet been prepared on the scale of the coast charts of Lower California; but No. 876, which embraces a number of good anchorages, has been prepared on a large scale, and is being engraved. The following-named books, which at the date of my last annual report were still in the hands of the Public Printer, have been published and placed on issue:

List of Reported Dangers in the North Pacific Ocean (Supplement), &c., by Commander William Gibson.—This supplement contains nearly 500 reported dangers, whose positions are uncertain, including in its scope the China and Japan seas and the East Indian Archipelago.

Sailing Directions for the West Coast of Mexico from the United States boundary line to Cape Corrientes, including the Gulf of California, compiled by Lieut. Samuel Belden, from data by Commander George Dewey, and other authorities.—The report on *Telegraphic Determinations of Longitude on the East Coast of South America, by Lieut. Commander F. M. Green,* which was in an advanced state at the date of my last annual report, has been published.

II. CURRENT WORK AND NEW WORK COMPLETED DURING THE YEAR.

In the Draughting and Engraving Division.—More or less extensive corrections and additions, from recent foreign surveys and other sources, have been made on 44 charts, and engraved on 38 plates; while the corrections on 6 plates yet remain to be engraved.

The corrections of sheet charts of the coast of Brazil have also been numerous and extensive, and the work of engraving on the plates will not be completed for several months.

Minor corrections, such as changes of the positions of isolated islands and dangers, the placing of new reported dangers, or the erasure of such as have been proved not to exist, have been made on 73 plates.

The following new charts by photolithography were published during the year:

No. 869. Portland Bay, in Patagonia, from a recent British survey.

No. 870. Ohama Harbor, Japan, from a Japanese survey.

No. 871. A-San Anchorage, West Coast of Korea, from a Japanese survey.

No. 880. Dangers on the South Coast of Oko-Siri, Japan, from a French survey.

No. 881. Examinations of the islands, &c., south of Fatsizio Sima, Japan, by the U. S. S. Alert.

No. 882. Anchorages and Passages in the Waters of the Southwest Coast of Alaska, by officers of the U. S. S. Jamestown.

No. 883. Reconnaissance in the same waters, by officers of the same vessel.

No. 884. St. Paul River, Liberia, surveyed by the officers of the U. S. S. Ticonderoga.

No. 898. Harbor of St. Thomas, West Indies, from a British survey.

No. 890. Ruk or Hogolu, an island of the Caroline group, North Pacific Ocean, from a sketch by the master of the missionary ship Morning Star.

Second editions of the following photolithograph charts were also published:

No. 353 *a* and *b*. Trinidad Island, West Indies, 2 sheets.
No. 360. Martinique, West Indies.
No. 350. Harbor of Jamaica.
No. 606. Harbors on the West Coast of Newfoundland.
No. 303. Barcelona, Spain.
No. 305. Alicante, Spain.
No. 328 *a*. Sea of Marmora.

Additions by photolithography were made on the following charts:
No. 347. Jamaica.
No. 718. Approaches to Port Royal and Kingston Harbor, Jamaica.
No. 608. Northeast coast of Newfoundland.—Important tracings or manuscript charts were made for the Archives Division of this office, for the Coast and Geodetic Survey and for other branches of the government.

In the Archives Division.—There have been published during the year 139 notices to mariners, containing 453 pages, and 99 hydrographic notices, containing 443 pages; also 4 quarterly statements, containing an index of charts published and canceled; and notices published by this office; index to notices for 1880; catalogue of documents contained in the Archives Division; besides which the following are in preparation for publication: United States Light List, Nos. 1, 1*a*, 2, 3, and 4.

A great amount of labor was involved in translating and reading proof, and in the correction of charts and Sailing Directions, most of which has been most creditably done by officers of the Navy, whose services in this work have been of great value.

In the Division of Library and Books.—All books of Sailing Directions for issue to naval vessels have been kept corrected to the latest dates, using chiefly the information given by the Notices to Mariners, and Hydrographic Notices published by this office.

During the year, 1,088 volumes of Sailing Directions have been sold to authorized agents, and in addition 2,841 volumes of various nautical publications have been issued to United States naval vessels, United States Coast and Geodetic Survey, United States Revenue Marine, libraries, and to foreign Hydrographic Offices.

In the number 2,841 are included reissues to naval vessels.

The following books have been compiled and published during the year: Arctic Azimuth Tables for Parallels of Latitude between 70° and 88°, by Lieut. Seaton Schroeder.

Kattegat Sound, and the Great and Little Belts to the Baltic Sea, by Commander William Gibson.

The operations of the Chart Division have been as follows:

Charts received.—Hydrographic Office charts from Hydrographic Office printing room, 7,656; from other sources, 4,575. Plans to be pasted on Hydrographic Office charts, 1,150. Charts from Coast and Geodetic Survey, 1,059; from British Admiralty (complimentary), 157; by purchase, 1,229. Total receipts of charts and plans, 15,826.

Charts issued.—To naval vessels, Hydrographic Office charts, 2,685; British Admiralty charts, 2,821; Coast and Geodetic Survey charts, 1,869; French charts, 33. Total issued to naval vessels, 7,408.

To Mare Island Depot, Hydrographic Office charts, 582; British Admiralty charts, 721; Coast and Geodetic Survey charts, 199; French charts, 17. Total to Mare Island Depot, 1,519.

To Executive Departments of United States Government, Hydrographic Office charts, 378; British Admiralty charts, 45. Total to Executive Departments, 423.

To Archives and other divisions of Hydrographic Office, Hydrographic Office charts, 1,750; British Admiralty charts, 57; Coast and Geodetic Survey charts, 15. Total to divisions of Hydrographic Office, 1,822.

To agents for sale of Hydrographic Office publications, Hydrographic Office charts, 4,636; Meteorological Portfolios, 5. Total to agents, 4,641.

To masters of merchant vessels, in consideration of keeping meteorological journals for the office, Hydrographic Office charts, 319.

To foreign correspondents and Hydrographic Offices (complimentary), 480.

To home correspondents and agents (complimentary), 270. Total of charts issued, 16,882. Grand.

In the same division the following work of plate printing was done: Hydrographic Office charts for issue, 7,656 copies; proofs from unfinished and corrected plates, 192; plates for American Practical Navigator, 14,710; penalty stamp on official envelopes, 3,800; letter heads, 1,190; Nebulæ in Orion (for Naval Observatory), 1,540; labels, 1,100; thermometric scales for meterological journals, 350; meteorological diagrams, 250; compass roses, 150 sheets; office seals, 50; publication notes, 50.

The manuscript of 102 hydrographic notices and 145 notices to mariners has been verified by careful comparison with the charts, and all printed charts have been kept corrected up to the latest dates.

In addition to the regular work of the Chart Division, much work has been done for the Meteorological Division of this office, and for various offices of the Navy Department.

In the Meteorological Division—The work of compiling and reducing meteorological data, obtained from the log-books of vessels, has been continued. That immediately in hand, pertaining to the North and South Atlantic Oceans, of which charts on a graphic plan are in hand, will be published, it is hoped, this year.

Since the operations of the Meteorological Division were inaugurated, September 1, 1876, 838 blank journals have been distributed; of these 178 have been returned as completed, of which 44 per cent. are "Good," 28 per cent. "Fair," and 28 per cent. "Bad."

During the past fiscal year, 86 journals have been returned, 43 per cent. of which are "Good," 26 per cent. "Fair," and 31 per cent. "Bad."

III. WORK ENTERED UPON AND STILL IN PROGRESS.

During the year, the following charts were prepared, and are now in process of engraving.

No. 307. Havana Harbor, from a recent Spanish survey.

No. 856. Jamaica, from recent British surveys.

No. 348. Port Royal and Kingston Harbors, Jamaica, from recent British surveys.

No. 349. Harbors of Jamaica, from recent British surveys.

No. 456. Gulf of Yedo, Southern Part, from a Japanese survey.

To complete the series of navigating charts of the West Coast of North America, it is necessary to publish charts extending from the northern boundary of Lower California to Dixon Entrance, Alaska. These will be on the same scale as the navigating charts of the series which will extend from Cape Horn to the Arctic Sea.

The following are now in the hands of the engraver:

No. 900. West Coast of North America, from San Diego to Piedras Blancas.

No. 901. West Coast of North America, from Piedras Blancas to Cape Orford.

Chart No. 225. West Coast of North America, from Dixon Entrance to Cross Sound, of which the office possesses a lithographic stone, has been extensively corrected from the reconnaissances of the officers of the U. S. S. Jamestown.

The sheet charts of the coast of Brazil, published by this office, extend only as far north as São Joao Island. Preparations are now being made to continue the series northward.

Since the Amazon has now been surveyed by a United States vessel, it becomes desirable that the sheet charts should be extended to include the mouth of the Amazon.

An appendix to the Sailing Directions of the Coast of Brazil has been prepared, and is now being bound with the latter, to form Sailing Directions of the Coast of South America, vol. I.

Coast of South America vol. II is in preparation; also Azimuth Tables of the World, from Latitude 61° North to Latitude 61° South.

In these publications, the work of compilation and revision has been performed by Lieut. Seaton Schroeder.

I. SURVEYS AND HYDROGRAPHIC EXAMINATIONS BY UNITED STATES NAVAL VESSELS DURING THE FISCAL YEAR 1880–'81.

Much valuable hydrographic information has been furnished by the officers of the following vessels, the character and extent of the work reflecting credit upon the zeal and industry of those interested in obtaining it:

U. S. S. Tuscarora and Ranger, Commander J. W. Philip, have sent in very satisfactory and extensive work on the west coast of Mexico; also lines of deep-sea soundings across the Gulf of California, which enhance the value of the charts already published of that locality. In the course of this work a very good anchorage was discovered and surveyed at Agua Verde Bay, on the western shore of the gulf.

U. S. S. Jamestown, under Commander L. A. Beardslee, and later under his successor, Commander H. A. Glass, has rendered good service, and sent in a mass of information pertaining to the coast and interior waters of Alaska, from which important changes and corrections have been made through the commendable zeal of the officers of that vessel; among them Lieut. F. M. Symonds and Master G. C. Hanus, deserve especial mention. These officers have explored a large sheet of water, penetrating many miles into the land to the northwest of Chatham Strait, and studded with numerous islands, heretofore not shown on any chart; also the headwaters of the Lynn Canal, leading to regions which are said to contain rich deposits of precious ore.

A number of harbors and anchorages, of which no charts existed, were surveyed. Positions of islands and dangers to navigation were corrected, and heretofore unknown dangers located.

A new and very complete survey was made in the previous year of the harbor of Sitka and portions of Sitka Sound.

All this valuable information, and all other information relating to the coasts and harbors of the United States, has been promptly submitted to the office of the Coast Survey for its use; and this office is much pleased with the gratification expressed by the Coast Survey in its letters of acknowledgment.

U. S. S. *Alert*, Commander C. L. Huntington, examined the islands and dangerous reefs to the southward of the Bay of Yedo, Japan, from Fatsizio down to the Marianne Group, and established the non-existence of several islands and a number of reefs shown heretofore on the charts as doubtful. From the fact that Commander Huntington was on the ground at the time that a submarine volcano was in action, and that he obtained soundings in from 5 to 20 fathoms, where deep water had previously existed, it is quite apparent that shoals and reefs are thrown up from time to time in these seas by volcanic action, and that their subsidence follows on the cessation of the expanding forces beneath the earth's surface.

U. S. S. *Swatara*, Commander W. T. Sampson, has furnished valuable data in regard to shoals in the harbor of Amoy, China, and Hakodadi, Japan, and has given directions for entering the harbor of Vladivostok (Russian Tartary); also a chart of a dangerous reef extending south of Okasima Island in the Sea of Japan, on which one of the English iron-clads had recently grounded.

U. S. S. *Lackawanna*, Capt. Ralph Chandler, established positions in the Samoan and other groups of islands in the South Pacific; also furnished directions for entering harbors of the Marquesas and Samoan Islands of the Gilbert Archipelago, and examined positions of reported dangers within those regions.

U. S. S. *Marion*, Commander F. M. Bunce, has supplied valuable information and tracings relating to anchorages in the straits of Magellan and the Skyring waters, with directions for entering them.

U. S. S. *Alaska*, Capt. George Brown, established positions of islands and reefs in the South Pacific. Capt. George E. Belknap, who succeeded Captain Brown in command of the Alaska, has made additions to valuable deep sea-soundings done by him previously in the Pacific Ocean.

U. S. S. *Palos*, Lieut. Commander F. M. Green, in addition to the important work of establishing secondary and tertiary meridional positions on the eastern shores of Asia and in the Indian Archipelago, is collecting hydrographic information and examining reported dangers on his route through the China Sea.

U. S. S. *Adams*, Commander J. A. Howell, has contributed a valuable survey of the harbor of Golfito, in the Gulf of Dulce, west coast of Costa Rica, and has examined its adaptability for a coaling station.

U. S. S. *Kearsarge*, Commander H. F. Picking, has furnished results of a similar examination of the Boca del Toro on the eastern or Atlantic coast of that State. The anchorage off Cumana, Venezuela, was also surveyed by the officers of the Kearsarge.

U. S. S. *Alliance*, Commander A. R. Yates, examined the eastern shoals lately discovered on the Newfoundland banks eastward of the Virgin Rocks, as well as other localities in that region where dangers were reported.

Information regarding the harbors of Tampico, Tuspan, and Vera Cruz, on the east coast of Mexico, has been furnished by the same officer; who also examined the entrance to the harbor of Pensacola, Fla., where important changes about the middle ground were discovered and reported to the Coast Survey.

U. S. S. *Yantic*, Commander E. T. Woodward, examined the approaches to the harbor of Celestun, on the west coast of Honduras, where dangers were reported.

U. S. S. Wyoming, Commander J. C. Watson, furnished information relating to harbors on the Mediterranean coasts of France and Spain.

U. S. S. Saratoga, Commander R. D. Evans, furnished deep-sea soundings in the North Atlantic Ocean.

U. S. S. Vandalia, Capt. R. W. Meade, has furnished copious remarks on the numerous ports in the West Indies and British Canadian possessions visited by that vessel.

II. RECOMMENDATIONS.

The appropriation for the survey of the west coast of Mexico, as originally projected and intended, to extend to the Gulf of Fonseca, is nearly exhausted; the amount remaining will be insufficient to complete the work. In the stretch of coast thus far surveyed, a greater number of good anchorages were found than was anticipated. Special charts of them were required, which have proved a heavy tax upon the originally small appropriation. A thorough knowledge of the entire west coast of Central America, from Panama to the Gulf of Fonseca, is of such importance to the California trade that it has been necessary to extend the Mexican survey so as to include the entire coast and harbors of the west coast of Nicaragua and Costa Rica as far south as the Gulf of Dulce.

Many imperfectly known harbors exist on these coasts, and the necessities of commerce require that they should be thoroughly surveyed. Foreign powers naturally leave the survey of the coasts of this continent to the American Government, which is expected to do a fair share towards obtaining and disseminating knowledge of such great value to the commerce of the world. This survey will probably not be complete before the winter season of 1882–'83, but much of the current work can be placed in the hands of engravers during the progress of the survey. An additional sum of $14,000 is therefore asked to complete unfinished work on the Mexican coast, and to extend the survey over the west coast of Nicaragua and Costa Rica to the Gulf of Dulce.

The number of charts published and issued by this office is not commensurate with the demands of the commerce of this country and the necessities of the naval service. The American Navy is dependent upon the British Admiralty for means of safely navigating remote seas and coasts, at a time when this office possesses all the data necessary for publishing the same charts, but is denied the means of meeting the expense of engraving. A wise and liberal policy would soon relieve us from such annoying dependence, by enabling us to increase year by year the number of engraved plates from which to print American charts.

During the past year, 1,229 British Admiralty charts have been purchased, and 2,821 issued by this office; and since January, 1878, nearly 9,000 British Admiralty charts have been purchased. In order to emphasize this point, I reluctantly present a comparison of the number of charts published by the Hydrographic Offices of Great Britain, France, and the United States, from engraved copper plates.

British Admiralty Catalogue, 1880, including 51 at branch office, Calcutta, 2,755 engraved plates.

French Hydrographic Office Catalogue, 1878, including 385 engraved plans, 3,157 engraved plates.

United States Hydrographic Office, 205 engraved plates.

Five hundred and thirty additional photolithograph charts are issued by this office, making total issues of all kinds 735.

This comparison is hardly flattering to American energy or independence. Five-sevenths of the small number of charts which the insufficient appropriations of Congress permit to be printed in this office are cheap, unsatisfactory photolithographs, disliked by navigators, and unworthy of issue as a government work, except in special emergencies.

In addition to the government hydrographic offices in Great Britain and France, there are private establishments which provide the merchant marine with charts compiled from the official publications in a shape specially desired by masters of merchant vessels.

In this country no establishment exists, except the United States Hydrographic Office, from which late and reliable hydrographic information can be obtained for the use of naval and merchant vessels of the United States.

The facilities now possessed by this office for greatly extending the supply of information are ample, and masses of data have accumulated in its archives which should be given to the world, as other progressive nations distribute the knowledge which they obtain.

Increased appropriations to accomplish this end and to relieve us from dependence upon foreign offices have been frequently asked in the interest of commerce, for the purpose of enabling this office to suitably return the attentions of foreign offices by sending the results of our work in return for theirs; but Congress has not seen fit to make the necessary appropriations.

The demand for United States charts has been increasing. To supply this demand of the American merchant marine, and for want of means to issue engraved charts, it has been found necessary from year to year, in order to supply such as were most in demand, to resort to the cheap process of photolithography. This policy has been pursued quite far enough, since 530 of the 735 charts issued are of the cheap kind.

It must be remembered that while these charts are relatively cheap for a single issue, they are in the end often more expensive than the engraved plate, since the latter can be corrected from time to time as may be found desirable, while the former, when important corrections are needed, must be destroyed and a new chart made from new tracings. These charts are less clear in figures and outlines than engraved charts, and have never been received with satisfaction by the navigator, who in many cases prefers to buy the far more expensive foreign originals when they can be obtained. Therefore, of late the publication of charts by this process has been restricted to preliminary plans and sketches, for which it answers very well, and to a few second editions of larger charts, which could not be dropped from the catalogue. Of the 500 and odd photolithographed charts now on issue a considerable number will either have to be dropped or second editions prepared, if means are not provided for replacing them by engraved charts. I therefore most urgently recommend a special appropriation of $15,000 annually for four years, until the photolithographs are replaced by durable and creditable copper-plates.

The last annual report from this office urged the importance of a survey of the Caroline and Marshall group of islands in the Pacific Ocean. The importance of a thorough survey of these very imperfectly known groups is so great that I will repeat the recommendation contained in that report, viz: "The Marshall and Caroline groups, located in the Western Pacific Ocean between the equator and 15° of north latitude, and covering roughly an extent of ocean about 900 miles in latitude by 1,200 in longitude, are very imperfectly known, and filled with dangers whose position and numbers are uncertain. Occasionally information and sketches are sent to this office by venturesome masters of trading or missionary vessels of apparently safe harbors and passages into the lagoons of the several atolls visited by them, which were previously unknown. This important information cannot be utililized for publication by this office in consequence of many evident faults and inaccuracies.

An examination of a chart of the North Pacific Ocean will immediately develop the vast importance to commerce of a thorough knowledge of these two groups.

Casting the eye eastward from the Caroline group, and examining that part of the ocean lying between the equator and 20° of north latitude as far as the American Isthmus, one sees at a glance that this belt, in which are found the ceaseless northeast trade winds, and currents setting to the westward, is the natural and necessary highway of the great trade which will be developed and stimulated by the completion of an interoceanic canal through Central America, at whatever point it may be located. Vessels bound to Japan, China, the Philippines, and to the East Indian Archipelago must necessarily take this broad way of the sea; and just near its western extremity lie the two groups above mentioned, with their thousand unknown dangers disputing and obstructing the passage of the world's commerce with the distant East. A careful survey of these two groups is a necessary supplement to the construction of the proposed canal or ship railway, and inseparable from the benefits which commerce and navigation are to experience from the completion of any means of Isthmian transit for ships. To accurately locate and make known these grave dangers will be the work of several years, and I cannot too urgently invite attention to the necessity for equipping at least two vessels, fully prepared for surveying and for deep-sea soundings, to develop the dangers as well as harbors and shelters which doubtless exist among these islands. A special appropriation of $20,000 is asked for this work.

The recommendation in regard to a survey of the Spanish Main made in the last annual report is renewed. It will be remembered that there are discrepancies of thirteen miles in the charts of these coasts. The charts of the Spanish Main now in use are, with very few exceptions, mostly from old Spanish charts and surveys, dating back to 1794 and 1826. Very few revisions have taken place.

Reliable charts of this coast, answering the demands of commerce, can only be obtained by a new continuous survey, which the governments bordering thereon are hardly prepared to inaugurate. The United States being specially interested in developing knowledge in regard to the coasts of the American continent, where the native governments are unable to do so, could with great profit detail a vessel, fitted expressly for surveying, to collect the data necessary in constructing reliable charts of that region.

The coasts of South America eastward of Trinidad, extending to the western border of British Guiana and from the eastern border of French Guiana to the mouth of the Amazon, are very imperfectly known, and are generally avoided. The extent of this coast, including the off-lying islands, is about 2,200 nautical miles. The detail of a vessel for this and other surveying work in and among the adjacent islands is specially urged. It is believed that to carefully collect all the data necessary to a thorough knowledge of this region, five winter seasons of steady work will be necessary.

While the work of the Hydrographic Office is steadily accumulating, and the amount of information which should be given to navigators without delay is continually being increased, the appropriations for maintaining this office have decreased from $100,800, in 1874, to $49,000, in 1881-'82.

An annual appropriation of not less than $100,000 is necessary to keep up the work required from this office, and to make American commerce independent of foreign sources of supply in matters of hydrographic information.

The refusal to make more liberal appropriations for American hydrographic publications amounts to a species of prohibition of copper-plate chart printing in this country, while it perpetuates our dependence upon foreign Hydrographic Offices, which in some cases are the first to publish to the world data sent them from this office.

Every foreign government, including Japan, is doing earnest work in contributing to the hydrographic development of the globe, and in speedily disseminating its discoveries; while the meager sums appropriated for the use of this office place us in the awkward situation of receiving contributions from the Hydrographic Offices of the world without the means of making suitable exchanges or returns.

Very respectfully, your obedient servant,

J. C. P. DE KRAFFT,
Commodore, United States Navy, Hydrographer.

Commodore JOHN G. WALKER, U. S. N.,
Chief of Bureau of Navigation.

REPORT OF THE CHIEF SIGNAL OFFICER.

NAVY DEPARTMENT,
OFFICE OF CHIEF SIGNAL OFFICER,
Washington, D. C., October 29, 1881.

SIR: In compliance with the order of the Bureau of Navigation, of the 27th instant, I have the honor to submit the following report of the operations of the Signal Office during the past year.

A new system arranged for use with Very's night signals has been perfected and introduced into the service, and reports received from cruising vessels where the system has been used speak of it as working with entire satisfaction, being superior to the old methods both in certainty and rapidity of communication.

During the year several letters from the Department of State and the British Government with regard to the operation of the new international road rules have been referred to this office for consideration. In so far as the Navy is concerned, compliance with these rules is rigidly enforced, but as yet there has been no legislation by Congress with regard to the matter, so that our merchant marine is as yet without positive instructions with regard to them.

The adoption of the rules by the United States being a matter of serious importance, it is respectfully recommended that, in the apparent absence of interest by other departments of the government, the Navy Department should bring the matter to the attention of Congress.

I take the liberty of renewing the recommendations made in former reports with regard to improvements in signal instruction aboard ship, namely, that instead of paying exclusive attention to instruction in Myer's code, all blue-jackets be instructed in the naval day and night codes, in the names and uses of flags and symbols, in national and foreign pilot and buoyage rules, in the rules of the road, and in lookout duties. The Signal Office has prepared a complete schedule of such instruction, which can be introduced into the service at a very slight cost, and it is believed will result in great benefit to the petty officers and seamen.

Very respectfully, your obedient servant,

C. H. WELLS,
Commodore and Chief Signal Officer.

Commodore J. G. WALKER, U. S. N.,
Chief of Bureau of Navigation.

REPORT OF THE SUPERINTENDENT OF THE NAVAL OBSERVATORY.

UNITED STATES NAVAL OBSERVATORY,
Washington, November 4, 1881.

SIR: I have the honor to submit herewith the report of the operations of the Naval Observatory for the past year, called for by the bureau's order of the 27th ultimo.

THE 26-INCH EQUATORIAL.

This instrument has been in charge of Prof. A. Hall, with Prof. E. Frisby as assistant. It is now in good working order, and has been used, as in previous years, for observations of satellites, double stars, and some of the periodical comets.

The repairs made lately have produced a decided improvement in the turning of the great dome, so that it has worked more easily. The timbers in the lower part of the dome having become decayed, it will be necessary to remove them.

The observations of double stars, made by Professor Hall from 1875 to 1880, have been collected, revised, and published. Professor Frisby has computed parabolic and elliptic elements of the comet discovered by Mr. Lewis Swift on October 10, 1880. This comet has a period of about five and a half years. He has also computed parabolic elements and an ephemeris of the great comet of 1881. The above elements have been published in the Astronomische Nachrichten.

A very careful series of observations of *a Lyræ* was begun here in 1862 with the prime vertical transit, and these were continued until 1867. The objects in view were the determination of the annual parallax of this star, and a new determination of the constants of aberration and nutation. Unfortunately, these observations did not give trustworthy results. Since it is probable that the Naval Observatory will be moved from its present site within a few years, it was thought best, while in our present position, to make some differential observations with the 26-inch equatorial for the annual parallax of *a Lyræ*. These observations were begun by Professor Hall on May 24, 1880, and were finished July 2, 1881. A series of similar observations was begun on 61 *Cygni* October 24, 1880; and these will be completed during the present month. At the same time a series of observations has been made to test the value of a revolution of the micrometer-screw, at the extreme temperatures at which the observations for parallax have been made. The observations for parallax have not been reduced further than to compute the probable error of a single comparison, but these errors show that we may expect a trustworthy result.

A great number of observations of the satellites of Mars, Saturn, Uranus, and Neptune have now been made with this instrument; and it is very desirable that these observations should be completely reduced and discussed, and that they should be used for correcting the orbits of the satellites, for determining the masses of the primary planets, and in the formation of the tables of the satellites.

THE TRANSIT CIRCLE.

This instrument has been employed under the direction of Prof. J. R. Eastman, who was assisted by Prof. E. S. Holden until January 1; and by assistant astronomers A. N. Skinner, Miles Rock, and W. C. Winlock during the year. Mr. Winslow Upton was employed as a computer until April 1, when he was succeeded by Mr. Albert S. Flint. Lieuts. E. Longnecker and A. H. Vail have been employed in reducing observations.

The observations have been confined to—

1. Stars of the American Ephemeris for clock and instrumental corrections.

2. Sun, moon, major and minor planets.

3. Stars whose occultations were observed in connection with observations of the Transit of Venus in 1874.

4. Standard stars for a catalogue of zone-observations.

5. Such stars of the British Association catalogue, between 120° 0′ and 131° 10′ N. P. D., as have not been observed here three times in both right ascension and declination.

6. Stars used in the observations of comets with the 26-inch and 9.6-inch equatorials.

The whole number of observations made with the Transit Circle since the last report is 4,480. Of these observations 79 were of the sun, 57 of the moon, 146 of the major planets, and 120 of the minor planets. Comet c, 1880, was observed six times, and comet b, 1881, 16 times.

THE 9.6-INCH EQUATORIAL.

This instrument was under the direction of Prof. J. R. Eastman, who had the same assistants as on the work with the Transit Circle. Mr. Upton made several observations of comets in 1880, with this instrument. The work has been confined to the observations of comets and of occultations of stars, and in determining the approximate corrections to the ephemerides of such minor planets as are not readily found with the Transit Circle.

The meteorological department is under the direction of Professor Eastman, and the usual observations at intervals of three hours, beginning at midnight, have been made throughout the year by the watchmen, Messrs. Hays, Horigan, and Cahill. Lieut. E. K. Moore rendered excellent service in reducing and compiling meteorological observations from January 6 to April 1.

The control of the system of wires within the Observatory with the central switch-board, and of the connections of the wires of the Western Union Telegraph Company, is under the direction of the officer in charge of the Transit Circle; while the immediate charge of all the batteries, wires and their connections, is confided to the instrument-maker, Mr. W. F. Gardner.

The connections for astronomical work within the building remain substantially the same as during the past year.

Outside of the Observatory, this department is responsible for the control, by means of the *motor* clock, of the several clocks in the State, War, Navy, and Treasury Departments.

PRINTING.

The annual volume for 1876 has been printed, bound in two parts, and distributed since the last report. The volume for 1877 is nearly ready for binding, and a portion of the volume for 1878 is now in press. The reductions of the work of 1879 and 1880 are well advanced.

The delay in issuing the annual volumes of observations and results is due chiefly to the fact that the printing fund of the Navy Department is generally exhausted before the end of the fiscal year, and our work is stopped. The font of type used in our volumes is nearly worn out, and the printing office claims to have no money to purchase new type. During the sessions of Congress it is difficult to keep the usual number of compositors employed on our work. These are the principal sources of delay; and unless some remedy be found, it will be impossible to bring up the work already in arrears.

TRANSIT OF VENUS.

The first part of the report of the observations upon the transit of Venus in 1874 was published in March last by the Senate. The resolution providing for the printing allowed the Observatory only 250 copies, scarcely enough for foreign distribution. It is therefore hoped that our colleges and scientific men at home will be supplied by their Senators or Representatives in Congress.

The printing of the second part, comprising the observations made at the several stations, has been delayed for want of assistance in finally preparing them for the press. This assistance has been secured through an appropriation made at the last session of Congress; and the first batch of the observations is now in the hands of the printer.

Part III, containing the final discussions of the longitudes of the several stations, is also nearly ready.

PHOTOGRAPHIC OBSERVATIONS OF THE TRANSIT OF MERCURY.

In the reduction of the photographic observations of the transit of Mercury of May, 1878, Professor Harkness has been assisted by Mr. Albert S. Flint, from May 25 to September 19. In addition to the 112 photographs measured by Lieut. T. D. Bolles, and the 101 measured by Lieut. Thomas Perry in 1878 and 1879, Mr. Flint has, during the present year, measured 17 photographs, and Professor Harkness 8, making 238 plates; but as each plate was measured twice, the actual number of separate photographs is 119. Of these, 25 were made at Cambridge, Mass., 30 at this Observatory, and 64 at Ann Harbor, Mich. The numerical reductions of the measurements of these plates are now completed, and the results may be summarized as follows:

Each plate having been measured in duplicate, if the positions of Mercury upon the sun's disk given by the first observer are subtracted from those given by the measures of the second observer, the mean of the two results thus obtained will be the constant error due to personal equation in measuring. Its amount for each station is:

	In altitude.	In azimuth.
	"	"
Cambridge	—0.10	—0.08
Washington	—0.09	+0.08
Ann Arbor	+0.15	—0.03

Thus it appears that for the mean of the three stations the constant error is practically zero.

If the mean of the readings by the two observers is accepted as the truth, the probable error of a position of Mercury upon the sun's disk, as determined from a single set of readings by one observer, is:

	In altitude.	In azimuth.
	"	"
Cambridge	±0.18	±0.20
Washington	±0.19	±0.18
Ann Arbor	±0.24	±0.28

The locus of the average probable error, therefore, lies within a circle whose radius is $0''.21$.

The corrections found at each station to Le Verrier's tables of mercury, as represented by the British Nautical Almanac for 1878, are:

	Right ascension.	North polar distance.
	s	"
Cambridge	+0.079	—0.23
Washington	+0.105	—0.12
Ann Arbor	+0.063	+0.47

The correction to the north polar distance given by the Ann Arbor plates seems to be affected by a constant error, and an effort will be made to discover its origin.

The probable error of a position of Mercury depending upon two sets of readings made upon a single photograph is:

	Right ascension.	North polar distance.
	"	"
Cambridge	±0.570	+0.562
Washington	±0.635	—0.579
Ann Arbor	±0.436	+0.514

The probable errors in right ascension have been reduced to arc of a great circle. We may infer from the mean of all the stations that on the average the locus of the probable error is a circle whose radius is $0''.553$.

These results are of great importance as showing what may be expected from the application of photography to the approaching transit of Venus; and it is desirable that the report of which they will form a part should be issued soon. With this view, sixteen sheets of drawings have been prepared for the necessary illustrations, and the writing of the text will be pushed forward as rapidly as possible.

In the prosecution of the experiments on astronomical photography, Professor Harkness has been assisted by Mr. Joseph A. Rogers, from October 1, 1880, to February 1, 1881, and from April 1, to September 13.

Forty-nine sets of positives on glass, amounting in the aggregate to 238 pictures, have been made from the negatives of the total solar eclipse of July 29, 1878; and last February they were distributed among the most prominent observatories and astronomers in this country and Europe. It was found exceedingly difficult to make satisfactory copies of the original negatives, but as scientfic men attach far more importance to photographs than to the most careful drawings, the large amount of time, and labor expended in reproducing these pictures is thought not to have been misapplied.

Twenty-four samples of pyroxyline have been prepared at temperatures of 150° and 165° Fahrenheit, and with various proportions and strengths of the acids. As there has always been great difficulty in producing pyroxyline possessing uniform properties for photographic purposes, the utmost care has been exercised in every step of the process by which the 24 samples in question were manufactured; and it is hoped that the exact repetition of these processes will furnish gun-cotton at least closely resembling the original samples. Meanwhile, these original samples are being made up into collodions which will be tested with respect to their fitness for astronomical photography.

With the aid of Professor Harkness' private apparatus, a series of experiments has been made in photographing the spectra of the sun and moon, the object aimed at being to determine the exposure coefficients for different parts of the spectra, and thus to obtain some data respecting the best form of apparatus for use in attempting to photograph the spectrum of the corona during total solar eclipses. In connection with this investigation, a six-inch equatorial camera has been mounted, and some photographs of the lunar eclipse of June 11, 1881, were obtained.

To clear up some points respecting the relative advantages of silvered and unsilvered heliostat mirrors in the photographic apparatus to be used for observing the coming transit of Venus, a twenty-foot horizontal photoheliograph has been mounted alongside of the 40-foot one, and the investigation will be proceeded with as soon as the weather is sufficiently cool. In this connection it may be well to mention that all our photographic operations are much impeded by the cramped and unsuitable character of our photographic house. It was erected in 1873 as a temporary structure in which to make certain experiments relating to the then approaching transit of Venus, and has been used almost without change ever since. During the past summer the temperature in it has generally been above the boiling-point of ether; and last winter it was sometimes below the freezing-point of water, in spite of a stove which was kept constantly burning.

From March 25 to November 4, 1879, pictures of the sun were taken with the 40-foot photoheliograph on every fine day, the whole series amounting to 108 pictures; but as it is scarcely worth while to attempt this work unless it can be kept up continuously, it has not been resumed during the present year.

Ensign S. J. Brown was detailed to assist Professor Harkness on July 19; and he has begun work upon the long-deferred catalogue of stars, which is to be made from the zones observed, under the direction of the late Capt. James M. Gilliss, by the Naval Astronomical Expedition to Chile in 1850-'51-'52.

CHRONOMETERS.

There are now in the chronometer-room 228 chronometers, of which 21 are ready for issue, 17 are on trial, 58 need repairs and will be repaired as wanted, and 132 are condemned to be used only as "hacks." Thirty-two have been received from vessels and other sources of service, and run down for repairs, having run their allotted time, four years, since cleaning. Fifty-two have been issued to vessels afloat, and for other service. Forty-four have been cleaned and repaired, and there are now 27 in the hands of T. S. & J. D. Negus, of New York, being put in order.

There were 6 new chronometers on trial at the beginning of the year, preparatory to purchase from Messrs. Negus, all of which passed the test, and were accepted March 1, 1881. On their trial they showed an excellent record, taken as a lot, better than that of any ever before purchased for the Navy.

The time continues to be sent out over the wires of the Western Union Telegraph Company to New York for three minutes and five seconds before New York noon, and the ball to be dropped on the building of the company at mean noon of that meridian (longitude 4 hours, 56 minutes, 01.6 seconds). The time is also sent over the same company's wires for three minutes and fifteen seconds before Washington mean noon, to wherever that company may choose to switch, in the limit of their wires, it being entirely under their control. The time-ball of this observatory is dropped at our mean noon for the use of the city.

The fire-alarm bells connected with the Observatory are struck from the chronometer-room at 7 a. m., 12 m., and 6 p. m. each day, Sundays excepted, which tests their connections as well as giving the time to the public.

There are several horological establishments in Washington, connected directly with the Observatory, which regulate their clocks each day at noon; and in New York City over a hundred different places are connected by special arrangement with the Western Union Telegraph Company, through which their clocks are corrected daily by direct comparison with the Naval Observatory signals.

The New York ball has occasionally failed to drop, owing to some unknown cause, apparently outside of the Observatory, as the Observatory ball has only failed twice during the year—once occasioned by everything being covered with ice, and once dropping three seconds too soon, by reason of a cross and leak of the wires. The latter caused a failure in New York the same day.

The greatest error that has occurred in telegraphing out the time was one second and thirty-four-hundredths. This was due to cloudy weather for eight days, when a transit observation could not be obtained; during which time a great change took place in the temperature, altering slightly the rate of the standard clock.

With very little additional expense and labor in the clock-room the local time could be furnished, and the time-balls dropped at other cities, as now done in New York, had we the use of a Western Union or other telegraph wire for two or three minutes before noon at each place. It is a question whether Congress will go to the expense of furnishing the cost of such wires to give Washington time to the country at large.

38 Ab

THE LIBRARY.

The library, in charge of Mr. E. F. Qualtrough, Master, U. S. N., has been increased during the year by the addition of nearly two thousand volumes and pamphlets, obtained by purchase, exchange, and donation.

Since the last report, thirty incomplete volumes of periodicals have been filled up by the purchase of the missing numbers, and about the same number of unfinished sets still remain.

In June last 250 volumes were sent to the bindery, of which number 240 still remain in the hands of the binder.

The volumes in the library are classified about as follows:

1. Works on astronomy, mathematics, physics, meteorology, geography, geodesy, and naval science, including transactions of learned societies; 7,900 volumes.

2. Pamphlets and papers on the same subjects, classified and placed in drawers; about 1,300 numbers.

3. Miscellaneous works of reference, &c.; about 650 volumes.

4. Publications of the United States Senate and House of Representatives; 600 volumes.

Total, 10,450 volumes and pamphlets.

A card catalogue of over 20,000 cards has been arranged, and is found to be very convenient for reference. It is not yet in condition for printing.

It seems advisable that the library should be provided with fire-proof quarters at the earliest possible date, since many of the rare and very valuable works which it now contains would be difficult to replace.

The list of correspondents to whom our publications are regularly distributed contains at present 886 names.

During the year, about 4,000 separate numbers of the publications of the Observatory have been distributed. These consisted mainly of the annual volume of Observations and Results, for the year 1876, Parts I and II; the reports on the Total Solar Eclipses of July 29, 1878, and January 11, 1880, of which 1,750 copies were received from the printer; Appendices I and II, Washington Observations for 1877, and Observations of Double Stars, by Prof. A. Hall.

In addition to the above, about 300 numbers of the back publications have been issued to fill sets which had been left incomplete in former distributions, and to supply new institutions.

There are at present remaining in reserve about 2,000 separate volumes of the Observatory publications.

It is desirable that some of our sets of valuable foreign publications be completed back to the date of their commencement, but this can hardly be done with the annual appropriation for books without interfering with the purchase of modern scientific works and periodicals. The required volumes can doubtless be procured at any time within a few years, and their purchase might perhaps be deferred until the library shall be in safe and more commodious quarters.

Very respectfully, your obedient servant,

JOHN RODGERS,
Rear-Admiral, Superintendent.

Commodore JOHN G. WALKER, U. S. N.,
Chief of Bureau of Navigation.

REPORT OF THE SUPERINTENDENT OF THE NAUTICAL ALMANAC.

NAUTICAL ALMANAC OFFICE,
BUREAU OF NAVIGATION,
Washington, D. C., October 31, 1881.

SIR: I have the honor to submit the following report of the operations of this office during the past year:

Since my last annual report, both the American Nautical Almanac and American Ephemeris for the year 1884 have been issued. The printing of the Nautical Almanac for 1885 is complete except the last three months of lunar distances. Of the entire Ephemeris for 1885, 305 pages are in type.

During the fiscal year ending June 30, 1881, 479 copies of the large Ephemeris were sold, and 909 were distributed for the public service and for scientific and educational purposes.

Of the Navigator's Almanac 2,997 copies were sold. The number sold at each agency is as follows:

Boston	608
New York	913
Philadelphia	636
Charleston	14
Savannah	1?
New Orleans	98
San Francisco	716
Total	2,997

The computations for future years are making their accustomed regular progress. The general policy is to issue the Ephemeris three years in advance in order to be available for ships starting upon long voyages of exploration. It is expected that hereafter the Navigator's Almanac will be issued about December of the fourth year preceding, and the large Ephemeris about the following June.

ASTRONOMICAL RESEARCHES.

Progress has been made in the following researches, having for their object a more accurate determination of the constants of astronomy and the construction of improved tables, for the use of the Ephemeris.

The catalogue of 1,098 standard stars, referred to in my last annual report, has been printed and distributed.

Mr. Hill's work on the perturbations of Jupiter and Saturn has been continued by him with great assiduity during most of the year, but is still unfinished. His work on Gauss's method of secular variations has been concluded and printed.

Le Verrier's tables of Mercury have been partially reconstructed in order to make them more convenient in use, and the work of comparing them with meridian observations since 1750 has been commenced. The discussion of all past transits of Mercury, mentioned in my last annual report, has been continued, but the final completion is delayed until the transit of November 7, 1881, has been observed.

The computation of places of the moon from Hansen's tables for the purpose of comparing observations since 1750 has been completed, and the work of reducing the occultations is now in progress. Recent observations of the moon concur in showing a constant increase in the errors of Hansen's tables,[and render it desirable to obtain definitive corrections to their elements. The provisional corrections now applied have, however, proved satisfactory up to 1880.

Preparations for the mathematical computation of the perturbations of all the planets produced by their mutual attraction are in progress. The work on the four inner planets will be first undertaken.

During the last four years a continuous record of the solar spots has been kept up, under the auspices of this office, by Mr. D. P. Todd, assistant, at the request of the Chief Signal Officer of the Army. This record has been regularly published in the Signal Service Bulletin. Mr. Todd has also assiduously observed occultations of stars by the moon, and eclipses of Jupiter's satellites. It is proper to add that these works have been without the range of official duty, and are to be regarded as a gratuitous contribution to the scientific work of the offices concerned.

VELOCITY OF LIGHT.

The measures of the velocity of light between Fort Meyer and the Observatory were completed last spring. The reflecting mirrors were then removed from the Observatory to a station at the base of the Washington Monument, in order to have a second set of determinations from a different station. The distance to the monument is 3,720 meters, or two miles and a quarter. Much trouble however, was experienced from the unstability of the made ground on which the piers supporting the reflectors rested, and when success was finally attained in this respect it was found that the revolving mirror, which, in the course of the experiments, had made several millions of revolutions at rates of speed between 200 and 250 turns per second, showed the effects of wear of its pivots. This has just been corrected by Messrs. Alvan Clark & Sons, but the advance of the season and the exhaustion of the appropriation will probably prevent further operations at present.

The following are the results in kilometers per second of the three series of measures thus far made, when reduced to a vacuum:

	K. M. per sec.
From Observatory, in 1880	299,680
From Observatory, in 1881	299,720
From Monument, in 1881	299,750

The following are the results of previous measures by other investigators:

	K. M. per. sec.
Foucault, 1862	298,000
Cornu, 1874	300,400
Michelson, 1879	299,940

The differences between the three results of the present series above exhibited far exceed the probable accidental errors of the separate determinations, and render further experiments necessary to the complete success of the work.

Very respectfully, your obedient servant,

SIMON NEWCOMB,
Professor, U. S. N.,
Superintendent Nautical Almanac.

Commodore J. G. WALKER, U. S. N.,
    Chief of Bureau of Navigation, Navy Department.

REPORT OF THE CHIEF OF THE BUREAU OF STEAM ENGINEERING.

NAVY DEPARTMENT,
BUREAU OF STEAM ENGINEERING,
Washington, November 2, 1881.

SIR: In obedience to your order, I have the honor to submit to the department the annual report of this bureau.

By act of Congress approved May 3, 1880, there was appropriated for the Bureau of Steam Engineering for fiscal year ending June 30, 1881, the sum of $800,000. The bureau also received one-half—$75,000—of $150,000 appropriated "for the Bureau of Construction and Repair and the Bureau of Steam Engineering," act approved March 3, 1881, making a total of $875,000, which amount has been expended as follows, viz:

Labor in navy-yards and stations in constructing new engines, boilers, and their dependencies; repairing old boilers, machinery, &c., and fitting vessels for sea service; preservation of tools, handling and preservation of materials and stores	$479,994 11
Purchase of materials, stores, machine tools, and patent rights; freights and incidental expenses	332,548 31
Payments made on foreign stations for repairs, materials, &c	53,673 76
Total	866,216 18
Less repayment by transfers in adjustment of appropriations	1,125 65
Total actual expenditure	865,090 53
Balance on hand November 1, 1881	9,909 47
Total amount appropriated for 1880–'81	875,000 00

The balance of $9,909.47, however, is covered by obligations of the bureau for purchases, &c., at home and abroad, the vouchers for which have not yet been received, or the accounts not yet settled.

Of the amount appropriated for fiscal year 1881–'82, act approved February 23, 1881, the sum of $75,000 was made "immediately available for the purpose of repairing and converting the ships Brooklyn and Lancaster into flag-ships." This sum has been expended for these vessels towards these objects, and both ships are now in commission.

There yet remains to be paid from the deficiency appropriation act, approved June 14, 1878, for work not yet completed, or accounts not yet settled, the following sums, viz:

To Harlan & Hollingsworth Company	$12,881 68
To William Cramp & Sons	22,850 00
Total to be paid	35,731 68

GENERAL OPERATIONS OF THE BUREAU.

The following will exhibit the extent and character of the work done under cognizance of this bureau since my last report, upon the machinery, boilers, &c., of naval steamers:

Alaska (2d rate).—Limited repairs made at Mare Island, to fit the vessel for temporary service. Ship in commission.

Brooklyn (2d rate).—Extensive repairs to machinery, including new crank-shaft, new boilers, new stern-bearing, and a new four-bladed screw-propeller of bureau design, completed at New York navy-yard.

This ship has been fitted with a new steam capstan, and is in commission as flag-ship.

Canandaigua (2d rate).—Machinery, boilers, &c., being removed from ship and stored at Norfolk navy-yard.

Enterprise (3d rate).—New boilers of bureau design constructed and put in; machinery, &c., thoroughly overhauled and repaired. Work very near completion at Washington navy-yard.

Essex (3d rate).—General overhauling and repair of machinery, &c., completed at League Island navy-yard.

Fortune (tug).—Engines overhauled and repaired; new boilers of bureau design constructed and put in. Work very nearly completed at Norfolk navy-yard.

Hartford (2d rate).—Work in completing new engines, placing new boilers in the vessel, and fitting new screw propeller, has advanced as rapidly at Boston navy-yard as the funds of the bureau would permit. A steam capstan has been fitted to this vessel.

Iroquois (3d rate).—Extensive repairs to machinery, with new boilers of bureau design, and a new screw propeller, are nearly completed at the Mare Island navy-yard.

Lancaster (2d rate).—The extensive work of putting in and connecting new machinery, placing and connecting new boilers, &c., has been completed at Portsmouth, N. H., navy-yard. This ship has been fitted with a new steam capstan and new steam steering apparatus, and is in commission as flag-ship.

Leyden (tug).—Sundry repairs to machinery, &c., completed at the Portsmouth, N. H., navy-yard. Tug is in service.

Monocacy (3d rate).—Machinery of this vessel has received very considerable repairs at Shanghai, China.

Pinta (tug).—New boilers, and thorough repair of machinery, &c., nearly completed at Washington navy-yard.

Omaha (2d rate).—Machinery, &c., being removed at Portsmouth, N. H., navy-yard, preparatory to extensive overhauling and repair.

Ranger (3d rate).—General overhauling and repair of machinery, with construction, placing and connecting new boilers on the vessel, and fitting new steam capstan, has been completed at Mare Island navy-yard. Vessel in commission.

Tallapoosa (4th rate).—New boilers of bureau design completed and connected on board the vessel. Machinery, &c., thoroughly overhauled and repaired, and new steam capstan fitted at Washington navy-yard. Ship is in commission.

NAVY-YARDS.

The departments under cognizance of this bureau at the several navy-yards, under their present organization and equipment, are in good working condition, but to render them more efficient, new and improved machine tools should from time to time be added.

I would also renew the recommendation made in my last report, that Congress be requested to pass an act permitting condemned material, stores, machinery, &c., to be sold from time to time at public auction, and the proceeds used in the purchase of new material, construction of new machinery, or repairs, as required and the best interests of the service shall seem to demand.

WORK REQUIRED.

The following will show the work required to be done to engines, &c.,

of United States naval steamers to fit them for efficient sea service (exclusive of what will probably be done under appropriation 1881–'82), viz:

Alaska (2d rate).—To be thoroughly overhauled and repaired.

Alert (3d rate).—Should have engines, &c., thoroughly overhauled and repaired, and new boilers of bureau design (for which material is on hand) substituted.

Benicia (2d rate).—Requires new boilers to be constructed and put in.

Colorado (1st rate).—In service as receiving-ship at New York navy-yard. Requires new boilers and crank-shaft (on hand) to be put in, and machinery thoroughly overhauled and repaired.

Dictator (iron-clad, 2d rate).—Engines should be put in condition for service and new boilers constructed and put in.

Essex (3d rate).—New boilers to be completed at New York navy-yard (the material on hand), and put in vessel.

Franklin (1st rate).—Is in service at the Norfolk navy-yard as receiving-ship. If required for sea service, should have new boilers (now on hand) put in, and machinery thoroughly overhauled and repaired.

Juniata (3d rate).—Should have thorough repairs to the machinery, new boilers (now on hand) placed in the ship, a new four-bladed screw-propeller of bureau design, and a new crank-shaft put in.

Lackawanna (2d rate).—Requires general overhauling, and repair of machinery, boilers, &c.

Mohican (3d rate).—Work should be continued on new compound engines, &c.

Marion (3d rate).—Requires general overhauling and repair of machinery, &c., and new boilers of bureau design substituted.

Monongahela (2d rate).—Requires new boilers, with thorough overhauling and repair of machinery.

Michigan (4th rate).—Needs new boilers.

New York (1st rate).—New machinery ready for erection on board ship; new boilers to be constructed; portion of material on hand.

Omaha (2d rate).—Machinery, &c., should be thoroughly overhauled and repaired, new boilers (now on hand) placed on board and connected.

Ossipee (3d rate).—Machinery, &c., requires to be thoroughly overhauled and repaired. New boilers (material on hand) should be constructed and placed on board.

Shenandoah (3d rate).—Machinery, &c., should be thoroughly overhauled and repaired.

Saugus (iron-clad, 4th rate).—If this vessel is required for sea-service, should have new boilers.

Ticonderoga (2d rate).—General overhauling and repair of machinery; new boilers (material on hand) to be constructed and put in.

Trenton (2d rate).—Requires thorough overhauling and repair.

Tuscarora (3d rate).—Thorough overhauling and repair of machinery required; new boilers (material on hand) completed and put in.

Wyoming (3d rate).—Thorough overhauling and repair of machinery required. New boilers should be constructed and put in.

DOUBLE-TURRETED MONITORS.

I would once more respectfully renew the recommendations made under date of February 13, 1879, and my reports, dated November 10, 1879, and November 15, 1880, with reference to the double-turreted monitors Puritan, Amphitrite, Terror, and Monadnock. These monitors, as well as the boilers intended for them, are now, and have been, occupying valuable space on the premises of the contractors, and it would seem that the best interests of the public service demand that some action should be taken to avoid the prospective damages to the government growing out of delay.

PERSONNEL OF THE ENGINEER CORPS.

The number of vacancies existing in the grade of assistant engineer is now twenty-seven, but in a few years, it is fair to assume, the grade will be filled by graduates from the Naval Academy.

The reports from ships where cadet engineers are now serving are very favorable, and show them as intelligent, zealous, and capable to a marked degree. Their duties as watch officers have been performed in the most satisfactory manner.

I desire to call the attention of the department to the somewhat anomalous condition in which the grade of passed assistant engineer stands, with regard to pay. The officers of this grade, holding in a majority of cases the relative rank of lieutenant, receive at present one increase of pay after a period of five years' service in that grade, and then the pay remains the same, no matter how long promotion may be delayed.

It was evidently assumed that none would remain in that grade longer than ten years, whereas the term of service approaches twenty years.

The next higher grade receives four increases of service pay, and it would seem but justice, in view of the slow promotion of the passed assistant engineers, and of the fact that most of them will retire before being benefited by the longevity pay in the higher grade, that their pay should be graduated on the basis of length of service. I earnestly commend their case to your favorable consideration.

PENSIONS FOR DISABLED MECHANICS.

I respectfully renew the suggestions made in this connection in my annual report for 1878.

VENTILATION OF THE EXECUTIVE MANSION.

During the illness of the late President, James A. Garfield, it became necessary, owing to the intense heat of the weather, to ventilate and cool his apartments by extraordinary methods.

To accomplish this, and in obedience to your order, the necessary machinery was erected under the cognizance of this bureau in the basement of the Executive Mansion, and when ready for operation the whole was placed in charge of three of our most skilled engineer officers, with instructions to take notes and data bearing upon ventilation and refrigeration, as developed with machinery and appliances under their care. Their report is annexed hereto as a matter of public interest.

ESTIMATES.

I have the honor to submit herewith the annual estimates of this bureau for the fiscal year ending June 30, 1883.

Very respectfully,

W. H. SHOCK,
Chief of Bureau.

Hon. WILLIAM H. HUNT,
Secretary of the Navy, Washington, D. C.

Estimates of appropriations required for the service of the fiscal year ending June 30, 1883, by the Bureau of Steam Engineering, Navy Department.

Detailed objects of expenditure, and explanations.	Estimated amount which will be required for each detailed object of expenditure.	Amount appropriated for the current fiscal year ending June 30, 1882.
CIVIL ESTABLISHMENT.		
Portsmouth, N. H., navy-yard:		
One clerk to chief engineer, appropriated February 23, 1881.	$1,400 00	$1,300 00
One store clerk, same act	1,300 00	1,017 25
Boston, Mass., navy-yard:	$2,700 00	
One clerk to chief engineer, same act	1,400 00	1,300 00
One store clerk, same act	1,300 00	1,017 25
Brooklyn, N. Y., navy-yard:	2,700 00	
One clerk to chief engineer, same act	1,400 00	1,400 00
One store clerk, same act	1,300 00	1,300 00
One clerk, same act	1,300 00	1,017 25
League Island, Pa., navy-yard:	4,000 00	
One clerk to chief engineer, same act	1,400 00	1,300 00
One store clerk, same act	1,300 00	1,017 25
Washington, D. C., navy-yard:	2,700 00	
One clerk to chief engineer, same act	1,400 00	1,300 00
One store clerk, same act	1,300 00	1,017 25
One writer, same act	1,017 25	1,017 25
Norfolk, Va., navy-yard:	3,717 25	
One clerk to chief engineer, same act	1,400 00	1,300 00
One store clerk, same act	1,300 00	1,017 25
Pensacola, Fla., navy-yard:	2,700 00	
One writer, same act	1,017 25	1,017 25
Mare Island, Cal., navy-yard:	1,017 25	
One clerk to chief engineer, same act	1,400 00	1,400 00
One store clerk, same act	1,300 00	1,300 00
	2,700 00	
	22,234 50	20,038 00

NOTE.—The small increase in estimates for clerk to chief engineer and store clerk in the several navy-yards, is to give them the same pay as now appropriated for clerks of same grade and similar services in the three other principal departments of these yards.

SALARIES.		
Chief clerk, March 3, 1881	1,800 00	1,800 00
Chief draughtsman, same act	2,250 00	2,250 00
Assistant draughtsman, same act	1,400 00	1,800 00
One clerk of class two, same act	1,400 00	1,400 00
One clerk of class two (submitted)	1,400 00	
One clerk of class one, March 3, 1881	1,200 00	1,200 00
One clerk, same act	1,000 00	1,000 00
One assistant messenger, same act	720 00	720 00
Two laborers, same act	1,320 00	1,320 00
Restoring messengers to rank and pay (submitted)	120 00	
Restoring two laborers to pay previously given (submitted)	120 00	
	12,730 00	11,290 00

NOTE.—Up to June 30, 1878, the messenger and laborer received $840 and $720, respectively, and these submissions in the estimate are to return them to their former salaries.

CONTINGENT.		
For stationery and miscellaneous items, March 3, 1881	1,500 00	1,500 00

STEAM MACHINERY.		
For preservation of machinery, boilers, &c., in vessels on the stocks and in ordinary; purchase and preservation of all materials and stores and patent-rights; purchase, fitting, and repair of machinery and tools in the navy-yards and stations; wear, tear, and repair of machinery, boilers, &c., of naval vessels; incidental expenses, such as freights, foreign postages, telegrams, advertising, photographing, books, instruments, &c.; and would recommend that at least $75,000 of this estimate be made immediately available upon passage of the act making the appropriation, appropriated February 23, 1881	1,947,000 00	875,000 00
CONTINGENT.		
For drawing materials, &c., for draughting room, appropriated February 23, 1881	1,000 00	1,000 00

VENTILATION, ETC., OF THE EXECUTIVE MANSION.

WASHINGTON, D. C., *October* 31, 1881.

SIR: We respectfully submit the following report as the result of our observation of the operation of the cooling apparatus used at the Executive Mansion during President Garfield's illness:

There were two systems of cooling apparatus employed, one delivering the cool air directly into the President's room, and the other delivering into the corridor outside of the room.

Mr. R. S. Jennings, of Baltimore, offered, and had accepted for the purpose of cooling the room occupied by the President, a machine used by him for manufacturing purposes, and which is represented in Plate A.

This machine consisted of a cast-iron box 2′ 3″ by 2′ 3″ on the end and 6′ 6″ long, which contained a number of screens made of terry-cotton, stretched over thin iron frames, and placed in the box longitudinally and vertically and $\frac{1}{4}$ of an inch apart; suspended inside and at the top of the box was a shallow pan made of galvanized iron, which was corrugated and perforated at the bottom. On the top of the box was placed a galvanized iron tank of about 134 gallons capacity, which was filled with granulated ice and salt, composed of 64 parts cracked ice, 3 parts salt, and 33 parts water; this brine was taken from the bottom of the tank through $\frac{5}{8}$-inch pipe and delivered into the shallow pan in the top of the box, through which it percolated, and was distributed over the screens, wetting them and reducing their temperature to that due to the composition of the brine. Attached to this apparatus was a 14-inch Sturtevant blower, which was used to draw the air into the box, and between the screens, reducing it to a corresponding temperature, and delivering it at any desired point. This apparatus of Mr. Jennings was connected with the heating flue leading to the President's chamber, and the air to the box was supplied from outside through an air duct which passes along the top, and the whole length of the corridor in the basement of the Executive Mansion.

This cooling machine was soon found to be of insufficient capacity to affect the temperature of the President's room with the windows open, but with the windows and doors closed it would have reduced the air in the room to the desired temperature. As, however, it was required that the windows and doors of the sick chamber be left open, the problem of how to cool the room under those conditions was presented, and the attention of certain scientific gentlemen was called to the subject. Mr. Jennings proposed to enlarge the capacity of his apparatus by adding two additional boxes, of wood, containing the same system of screens, to the circuit of air, and by this enlargement he claimed the desired result would be effected, but in view of the necessity of supplying the cool air as quickly as possible, Prof. Simon Newcomb and Major Powell, of the United States Geodetic Survey, suggested the addition of an ice-box to the Jennings machine, of sufficient capacity to hold the amount of ice necessary to meet the emergency, and by a change of pipe connections requiring the air to pass first through the Jennings machine, and then into the ice-box at the top, and after circulating over the ice to be taken by the blower and forced up into the President's room. These suggestions were carried out, and the effect was a rapid and continuous supply of air at about 55° Fahr. at the register in the President's room, giving the air in the room an agreeable temperature during the warm weather which prevailed at the time. This apparatus is represented in Plate A, the notes on the plate indicating its different features.

Subsequently it was ascertained that when a fresh breeze from the south was blowing directly into the President's room, through the open windows which faced in that direction, it was impossible to affect the temperature of the room by the small 14-inch blower then in use. It was therefore determined to substitute a 36-inch blower, and reverse the circuit so that the air would pass first through the ice-box, then through the Jennings machine to the blower, thence up to the President's room. By this arrangement the temperature was kept at the desired point during the extremely hot weather which prevailed on August 13 and 14, which may be regarded as a good test of the efficiency of the apparatus.

By the first arrangement, represented in Plate A, it was observed that all the air delivered into the President's room did not pass through the Jennings machine, but that a large portion was drawn through the leaks in the ice-box; arrangement in Plate B obviated this difficulty, and assured the passage of the air through the pipes leading from the air-duct and not from the corridor through the leaks, and by extending the induction pipe into the box a better distribution of the air over the ice was effected.

The data taken during the running of this cooling apparatus was incomplete, as those who had constant access to the President's room were too busily occupied to take a systematic series of observations in the room, and it was not until after President Garfield was removed to Elberon that we were able to take the temperatures in the room be occupied, and this was done September 7 and 8, during a run of the apparatus for twenty consecutive hours, under circumstances as nearly as possible like those which existed during the President's illness at the Executive Mansion, excepting the last hour of the run when the windows and doors were closed.

The outside temperature during the special trial averaged 84°.9 Fahr., and running the engine at an average of 102 revolutions per minute, and forcing 22,796 cubic feet of air into the room per hour, resulted in the reduction of the temperature of the room 5°.4 Fahr., and this with one window and door open, and a southerly breeze blowing. Although this was in a measure disappointing, so far as the reduction of temperature was concerned, yet the character of the air was so greatly changed by the reduction of the relative humidity of the air that it was agreeable, and could not have been reduced to a lower degree with impunity had the patient been present.

We were told by one of the President's attending physicians that the first effect observed when the cooling machine was started was the change in the character of the air, and, even before a sensible change of temperature occurred, a benefit from the machine was experienced in the dryness of the air in the room, which reduced the temperature of the skin by a more rapid evaporation of the moisture at its surface. This effect is not the least in importance; for, as commonly observed, a warm day is not necessarily an oppressive day, if the relative humidity of the atmosphere is not great. The reduction of the relative humidity of the air in the President's room was obtained by the operation of a well-known law in physics, by which the air is deprived of a percentage of its moisture, which it contains at high temperatures, when that same air is reduced to lower temperatures.

The capacity for holding moisture, or vapor, by the atmosphere is greater at high than at low temperatures, and is consequently deprived of a part of its moisture when passed over the surfaces of the cooling machine, and this moisture the air cannot regain until it escapes from the system of pipes through which it is conducted; at the point of its escape, however, as its temperature rises, it claims that percentage of moisture of which it has been deprived in the cooling machine from the surrounding atmosphere. An examination of the accompanying Table A will demonstrate the truth of this law. The data were taken during the twenty hours' trial after President Garfield was removed. The relative humidity of the air outside averaged 60, and that of the air in the President's room after passing through the cooling apparatus averaged 54.3. This shows conclusively that the air of the room gave up a part of its moisture to supply the loss of moisture to the air entering through the cooling apparatus. What the condition and dryness would have been had the cool air been delivered into a closed room we have no means of ascertaining; but from the result of this experiment, where the relative humidity of the air in the room was maintained at a lower percentage than that of the air outside, with which it was in communication through an open window, it is safe to assert that the relative humidity of the air in a closed room can be maintained at any desired point. Charles Hood, in his book on Warming and Ventilation, says: "The most healthy state of the atmosphere will be obtained when the dew-point of the air is not less than 10° nor more than 20° Fahr. lower than the temperature of the room. When these limits are exceeded the air will be either too dry or too damp for healthy respiration." Examination of Table A shows the dew-point to average 18°.5 lower than the temperature at the center of the room, which proves by Hood to have been the most desirable condition of the atmosphere to maintain.

In order that the President's room might by no accident be deprived of its supply of cold air, Major Powell devised a second machine, which was constructed by labor and material from the navy-yard, the difference between it and the other apparatus consisting in the arrangement of the compartments of the ice box, as shown in Plate C, and doing away with the box containing the terry-cotton screens. The ice-box was divided into three compartments, an upper, middle, and lower. The air was first taken through the induction pipe and passed over the ice in the upper compartment, from thence down through rectangular holes into the middle compartment, which it traversed, and was then drawn into the lower compartment, and at the opposite end the air was taken by a 36-inch blower and forced through a drying-box up through a system of pipes to the corridor outside of the President's chamber.

The peculiar feature of this apparatus was the drying-box, which was placed in the circuit for the purpose of drying the air. This purpose was supposed to be accomplished by cooling the bars of iron contained in the box, by causing a freezing mixture of ice and salt to fall on the ends of the bars, thereby cooling them, and by their low temperature causing the air to deposit on their surface another portion of its moisture, after having been deprived of a certain percentage in the ice-box. The purpose for which the drying-box was intended was not accomplished, as the bars could not, by the means employed, be reduced to a lower temperature than the air when it entered the box.

By examining Table B, the data for which were taken at various times as opportunity occurred during the time machine No. 2 was employed, we find that the temperatures taken just before entering the drying-box average 56° Fahr., and those temperatures taken just after the air left the box average 59° Fahr., or 3° higher, showing that no reduction of temperature was effected; the relative humidity of the air entering was 85°.8 and increased to 86°.2 on leaving the box, or 0°.4 greater on leaving than when it entered, and proving the box to be of no use as a dryer.

Comparing results at the two ice-boxes, we find the air on leaving ice-box No. 1 to be 40°.7 Fahr., and leaving ice-box No. 2 to be 53°.5 Fahr., by which we conclude that the arrangement of the box into compartments, did not produce the best results, and may be accounted for by the air passing over the top surface of the ice as it lay packed upon the floors of the compartments, and not coming in contact with the other surfaces, while in the other box, which was not divided but contained shelves upon which the ice was packed, a greater surface of the ice was exposed to contact with the circulating currents of air, which was consequently more effectually cooled. Deflecting diaphragms might have been used with advantage in box No. 2, so as to cause the air to deflect from the direct course and come in contact with the sides of the ice as well as the top, and thus forcing the cold air resting between the cakes of ice into the circuit.

The effect of the air delivered by this apparatus at the average rate of 39,217.9 cubic feet per hour, was to keep the air in the corridor at a pleasant temperature, although no observations were taken, excepting at the point the air issued from the pipe, where the average temperature was 63.5° Fahr. In the effort to complete this apparatus as quickly as possible, right-angle elbows were used in all the pipe connections; the effect was to produce eddying currents at all the bends, the nature of which was noticed at the point of delivery into the corridor. This elbow was 10 inches in diameter, and the passage of the air through it produced an eddy at the point of delivery, the outer circle of which was four inches in diameter, the vertical diameter extending one inch above, and three inches inside the elbow, the horizontal diameter touching the inner bend of the elbow. This eddy is represented in plate C at N.

The eddy was due to the shape of the elbow, allowing a dead space at M, into which the emerging cold air falls. By reason of its being of greater specific gravity than the outer atmosphere, it falls until it is again taken up by the main current of air which causes it to complete the circle. When the elbow was replaced by a curved elbow the eddy disappeared.

The conditions under which the President's room was cooled precluded all considerations of economy. The experiments, therefore, are without value for the purpose of determining the cost of ice sufficient to keep the President's room at an agreeable temperature under more favorable conditions. The problem as presented was the same as to ascertain the price of coal sufficient to keep the room warm on a cold day with the windows open.

During the twenty hours' run 8,734 pounds of ice were melted, or 436.7 pounds per hour. This at $5 per ton, or one-quarter of a cent per pound, would be $1.09 per hour; or this was the cost necessary to supply 32,799 cubic feet of air at 50° Fahr. at the register per hour.

Had time been offered for experiment or had experience suggested a more economical method of cooling the President's room much of the waste of cooling material might have been avoided, as for instance, the water of liquefaction which was allowed to run to waste might have been used as a first cooling medium for the air.

'The experiments were also conducted under circumstances unfavorable for determining the most accurate results, as the observations would be interrupted at any time the air became too cool for the comfort of the President, the experiments, being, of course, entirely secondary in consideration; yet a sufficient number of temperatures were observed to show the value of the cooling apparatus, not only as affecting the temperature of the room occupied by the President, but affecting the best hygrometric condition of the air in the room.

A more general system of experiments would be interesting, and would furnish most valuable information as regards the cost as well as the effects of cooling apparatus.

Our operations at the Executive Mansion have brought to our notice the great importance of a proper hygrometric condition of the atmosphere we breathe and in which we live. Great stress is laid upon the subject by various authorities upon ventilation and warming, and notwithstanding its importance appears · to be so fully realized, yet but crude attempts have been made to control the hygrometric condition of the air used in ventilating and warming our houses. In summer, with the windows open, the general condition of the atmosphere outside is maintained inside our houses, but in winter, with windows closed, and the ventilation mostly dependent upon the warm air which has passed through the heaters, the conditions are entirely changed. As, for example, the temperature of the air outside we will suppose to be 20° Fahr.; it is passed through the heaters and delivered into a room where the temperature is maintained at 70° Fahr.; supposing the windows to be closed and only leakage sufficient to permit ventilation, we will have in this room air at the temperature of 70°, the dew-point of which is not above 20°; for in the manner our heaters are usually constructed there are no means by which the air can receive moisture after it has left the outside of the house.

The most healthful condition of the air is found to exist when its relative humidity is from 50 to 70 per cent. In the hypothetical case cited, the relative humidity is as low as 15 per cent., an extreme that must be not only unpleasant but injurious. Of course crude attempts have been made to remedy this evil by urns of water placed over or near the heaters, but in most instances even this is wanting. It being necessary that the dew-point should not be less than 20° below the temperature of the room, it may be increased as it enters from the outside by passing it through water at a given temperature, say 55° before entering the furnace, saturating the air and establishing the dew-point at that temperature, the relative humidity being 58.

Our operations at the Executive Mansion have proved that it is possible to place the dew-points, or relative humidity of definite quantities of air, at any desired point, and there is no reason why this hygrometric condition may not be maintained with as much certainty as the amount and temperature of air supplied for proper ventilation and warming. This field of study presents great opportunities for effecting a better condition of the atmosphere of our rooms, and our personal comfort and health may be improved in proportion to our careful observation of the hygrometric condition of air in which we live. Hospitals and public buildings ought to be especially protected from the evil results attending a vitiated condition of the air, and we can see no reason why their atmosphere may not be made comfortable and healthful at all seasons and under all conditions of the outside air.

Hoping the few results obtained from our experiments may be useful in calling more general attention to this subject, and expressing our thanks to the United States Signal Officer for valuable information and the use of instruments,

We are, very respectfully, your obedient servants.

WM. L. BAILIE,
Passed Assistant Engineer, U. S. N.
RICHARD INCH,
Passed Assistant Engineer, U. S. N.
W. S. MOORE,
Passed Assistant Engineer, U. S. N.

Engineer in Chief W. H. SHOCK, U. S. N.,
Chief Bureau of Steam Engineering,
Navy Department, Washington, D. C.

REPORT OF CHIEF OF THE BUREAU OF CONSTRUCTION AND REPAIR.

NAVY DEPARTMENT,
BUREAU OF CONSTRUCTION AND REPAIR,
November 4, 1881.

SIR: I have the honor to submit herewith, in conformity with your instructions of the 1st instant, statements of the work performed during the past year, and estimates of the money required by this bureau for the year ending June 30, 1883.

Amount appropriated for the fiscal year 1880-'81, act May 3, 1880......	$1,500,000 00
Amount appropriated for the fiscal year 1880-'81, act March 3, 1881....	75,000 00
Amount appropriated for the fiscal year 1880-'81, act February 23, 1881.	150,000 00
Total	1,725,000 00

Expended:

For labor at navy-yards from July 1, 1880, to June 30, 1881.........	$1,300,730 00	
For materials, &c., at navy-yards from July 1, 1880, to June 30, 1881.........	313,689 73	
		1,614,419 73
Balance on hand July 1, 1881		110,580 27

	For timber.	For contractors.
Amount appropriated to meet a deficiency on account of the fiscal year 1876-'77...........	$416,819 32	$901,134 55
Expended from June 15, 1878, to June 30, 1880	390,153 78	826,805 78
Balance on hand July 1, 1880	26,165 54	104,528 77
Expended from July 1, 1880, to June 30, 1881...........	17,648 40	54,615 00
Balance on hand July 1, 1881...........	8,517 14	49,913 77

Vessels repaired at the different navy-yards during the fiscal year 1880-'81.

Adams.	Galena.	Monadnock.	Rodgers.
Alarm.	Hartford.	Monongahela.	Rescue.
Alaska.	Independence.	Montauk.	Rose.
Alliance.	Intrepid.	Monterey.	Saratoga.
Antietam.	Iroquois.	Nahant.	Snowdrop.
Benicia.	Jamestown.	New Hampshire.	Speedwell.
Brooklyn.	Jason.	Nina.	Standish.
Canandaigua.	Juniata.	Ossipee.	St. Louis.
Colorado.	Kearsarge.	Passaic.	Tallapoosa.
Constitution.	Lackawanna.	Pensacola.	Tennessee.
Constellation.	Lancaster.	Pilgrim.	Ticonderoga.
Dale.	Lehigh.	Pinta.	Tuscarora.
Despatch.	Mahopac. .	Powhatan.	Triana.
Dictator.	Manhattan.	Portsmouth.	Vandalia.
Enterprise.	Mayflower.	Puritan.	Wachusett.
Essex.	Miantonomoh.	Quinnebaug.	Wyoming.
Fortune.	Minnesota.	Ranger.	Yantic.
Franklin.	Mohican.		

We have on our register, exclusive of tugs, one hundred and fifteen vessels. These may be divided into four classes, as follows:

In commission and variously employed	39
In ordinary, repairing, or waiting completion or repairs.........	27
Employed either as receiving, practice, store, training, transport, dispatch, or stationary vessels	22
Unfit for repairs or completion.........	27
Total, exclusive of tugs	115

The 27 vessels last mentioned are worthless for naval service, but must, nevertheless, be protected from damage by fire or water, and also from loss by depredation; and for this purpose it is necessary to employ a large number of ship-keepers, at an annual expense of over $30,000. It would, therefore, be greatly to the interest of the government to sell or break up these vessels.

To keep in repair the vessels worth repairing, the appropriations for this bureau for the last four years have been devoted, and experience proves that the amount appropriated annually, viz, $1,500,000, is too small for the purpose. I have, therefore, asked for an appropriation of $2,500,000 for the year ending June 30, 1883. This will enable the bureau to keep the vessels now in the service in repair, and also to complete the New York, now on the stocks in the Brooklyn navy-yard, the Mohican at the Mare Island navy-yard, and to erect the turrets and pilot house required for the completion of the monitor "Miantonomoh," at the League Island navy-yard.

A large number of our ships now employed as cruisers, while answering all the purposes of a peace establishment, cannot be relied upon in actual warfare; but it is nevertheless necessary to keep them in repair during the time which must elapse while we are building ships better fitted for the wants of the service at the present day.

In the Kittery navy-yard we have just completed the extensive repairs required on the Lancaster. Many modern appliances have been introduced in this ship, and free circulation of air has been secured to an extent equal to any ship now afloat. The repairs of the Omaha have just been commenced at this yard.

In the Boston yard the Hartford is still under repair, and will be ready for service early in the coming year. At this yard we have been preserving, under a contract with the American Wood Preserving Company, a quantity of white-oak and yellow-pine timber. The report of the board of chemists appointed to examine the process used by this company has not yet been acted upon, and as the subject is one of much importance to the Navy, I respectfully recommend the appointment of another board, composed of officers of the Navy who are officially interested in this matter, to take up the whole subject of preserving timber, examine carefully the report of the board of chemists above referred to, examine all processes known in our own country and in Europe, and report their conclusions to the department.

The funds of the bureau will not admit of an extension of the contract with the American Wood Preserving Company, or of the employment of any other process, during the present fiscal year; therefore no time will be lost in this investigation.

In the Brooklyn navy-yard the repairs of the Brooklyn have been completed, and, with the many new appliances introduced, she is probably a better ship now than when first put in commission.

The repairs of the Juniata are advancing, and in a few months she will be ready for sea.

The New York is here on the stocks waiting completion, and, under orders of the department, will be taken in hand as soon as the funds of the bureau will admit of it.

At the League Island yard the Ossipee is undergoing extensive repairs.

For want of a dry-dock at this yard the bureau finds it impossible to complete the repairs of vessels commenced, and is subjected to the additional expense and delay of sending them to other yards for completion.

At the Washington yard the Tallapoosa has been very thoroughly repaired, and is now in good condition for service for many years.

The repairs on the Enterprise are nearly completed, and she will be ready for sea in a few months.

At the Norfolk yard we have been employed principally in making such light repairs to vessels belonging to the North Atlantic station as they may from time to time require.

The Vandalia has just been docked, and the Kearsarge is now in dock under repair.

At the Pensacola yard we shall be able in the course of next year to repair such vessels as can be taken on the floating dock now building for that place.

At present the small force at work is employed in preserving the public property, repairing the small vessels in use at the yard, and fitting up shops for future use.

At the Mare Island yard we are employed in repairing the Iroquois and the Tuscarora, and in completing the Mohican. The Benicia and Monongahela are waiting repairs. It is at this yard we have the greatest difficulty with our limited appropriation in doing all the work required. We could with great advantage and economy finish in a short time the various ships now waiting repairs at this yard, had we the means of doing so.

In China the work of repairing the Monocacy has been completed, and she is now in good condition for service.

The four double-turreted monitors, viz, Terror, Puritan, Amphitrite, and Monadnock, now on the stocks in private yards, and upon which large sums of money have been expended, are a continual expense to the bureau as they now are, and I respectfully recommend that an arrangement may be made with the builders of these vessels to secure their being launched and delivered to the nearest navy-yard as soon as the money can be appropriated to pay the necessary cost of the work.

I have the honor to be, very respectfully, your obedient servant,

J. W. EASBY,
Chief of Bureau.

Hon. WM. H. HUNT,
Secretary of the Navy.

39 Ab

REPORT

SECRETARY OF THE INTERIOR.

DEPARTMENT OF THE INTERIOR,
November 1, 1881.

SIR: I have the honor to transmit herewith the reports of the chiefs of bureaus of this department and of the superintendents of the institutions under its supervision, showing the operations of the department for the past year. I also submit such recommendations and suggestions touching the administration of the department as I deem necessary and appropriate.

INDIAN AFFAIRS.

The Indian question, as it is called, has lost nothing of its interest or importance, and the methods by which it shall be finally settled are not yet fully recognized. All who have studied the question unite in the opinion that the end to be attained is the civilization of the Indians and their final absorption into the mass of our citizens, clothed with all the rights and instructed in and performing all the duties of citizenship. The difficulty lies in devising and executing the means by which this end shall be accomplished.

The difficulties to be overcome are mainly these: The Indians do not speak and do not wish to learn to speak our language; hence all business with them by the government and by individuals has been and must be transacted through the medium of interpreters. Misunderstandings must continue to arise in the future, as they have arisen in the past, between the government and the Indians, under this condition of affairs, and so long as it shall continue, the Indians, unable to carry on in person ordinary business transactions with our citizens generally or even with their agents, are completely isolated, and are compelled to adhere to that tribal relation which so greatly stands in the way of their advancement. It is not probable that much can be done in the way of teaching our language to adult Indians, but much may be done and is being done in the direction of so teaching those of school age, and our efforts to maintain and extend Indian schools should be earnest and

610

constant. The civilization fund, which has been devoted largely to educational purposes, will be exhausted before the end of this fiscal year if the schools already established shall be continued. The schools at Carlisle and Forest Grove are supported wholly from this fund, and a number of Indian youth of both sexes are maintained at Hampton therefrom. These schools must be abandoned unless Congress shall make provision for their support. The schools at the agencies should be cherished and strengthened. It is idle to expect any material advancement by the Indians in civilization until they have learned to speak and write our language and to labor for their living, and these things to a great extent go hand in hand. Those of middle age and over are I fear beyond our reach. We must depend mainly upon the proper training of the youth. To do this we must teach them, and to teach them will cost money. If we really mean to civilize them we must incur the expense necessary to that end. Our whole Indian policy, in my judgment, has been characterized by a parsimony which has borne the more respectable but undeserved name of economy. We have acted very much as does the man, who, burdened with a heavy debt, contents himself with paying the interest without diminishing the principal. I am satisfied that in the management of our Indian affairs we have found, as many have found in the management of their private affairs, that the policy which, for the time being, seemed the cheapest, in the end has proved the most expensive. When the Indian shall have learned to speak and write our language, to earn his own living by his own labor, to obey the law and aid in making and administering it, the Indian problem will be solved, and not until then. Money wisely applied to these ends will be well spent; money withheld from these ends will be extravagance.

Again, all the traditions of our Indians teach them that the only proper occupation for a brave is war or the chase, and hence they regard labor, manual labor, as degrading. We should not be impatient with them on that account, for while it may be curious that it should be so, it is, I fear, true that this opinion of these people standing on the confines of savagery is held by many who believe themselves to have reached the very topmost heights of civilization and refinement. Be that as it may, the fact remains that the Indian does not willingly engage in manual labor. But if he is to make upward progress—to become civilized—he must labor. The game on which he lived is gone, or so nearly gone that he cannot longer rely on it for food, and yet he must have food. The government, recognizing this situation, has undertaken to and does furnish a large portion of our Indians food and clothing, and at the same time has been endeavoring to teach them to become self-supporting by assigning to them land for cultivation, furnishing them with farming tools, horses and harness, and encouraging them to work. But two difficulties have attended this system, although it has met with considerable success. The first is that adult Indians, thoroughly grounded in the faith that labor is degrading, prefer pauperism to independence; that is, prefer to live upon food furnished by the labor of others to earning their food by their own labor—a preference which is perhaps shared with them by some white men. This is not true, however, of all Indians. Many individuals of some of the tribes are willing to work, and are working, under difficulties, but it still remains true that many others are content to be and will remain mere paupers.

The other difficulty in the way of making the Indians self-supporting is that we have not given them a fair chance to become so. The titles of the Indians to most of their reservations, perhaps to all of them except those in the Indian Territory, are not such as the courts are bound to protect. They are compelled to rely largely, if not entirely, upon the executive and legislative departments of the government. The reservations set apart by treaty, or law, or executive order, have been usually many times larger than necessary (if cultivated) for the support of the tribes placed thereon. Our people, in their march westward, have surrounded these reservations, and seeing in them large tracts of fertile land withheld from the purpose for which they believe it was intended—cultivation—have called upon the executive and legislative departments to make new treaties, new laws, and new orders, and these calls have generally been heeded. Now, it is clear that no Indian will with good heart engage in making and improving a farm with the knowledge or the prospect that after he has so done he may at any time be required to leave it and "move on." In the case of the Indian, he may have the privilege of keeping his home if he will sever the ties of kinship and remain behind his tribe; but few do this. I wish to emphasize the point that we are asking too much of the Indian when we ask him to build up a farm in the timber or on the prairie, with the belief that at some future time he will be compelled to choose between abandoning the fruits of his labor, or his kindred and tribe. White men would not do so, and we should not ask Indians to do so.

I therefore earnestly recommend two things, in case the present number of reservations shall be maintained: First, that existing reservations, where entirely out of proportion to the number of Indians thereon, be, with the consent of the Indians, and upon just and fair terms, reduced to proper size; and, second, that the titles to these diminished reserves be placed by patent as fully under the protection of the courts as are the titles of all others of our people to their land. I would not, in reducing the reservations, so reduce them as to leave to the Indians only an area that would suffice for an equal number of whites. Their attachment to kin and tribe is stronger than among civilized men, and I would so arrange that the Indian father of to-day might have assurance that his children as well as himself could have a home. I would also provide in the patent for the reservations that so long as the title to any portion of the reservation remained in the tribe, adult Indians of the tribe who would locate upon and improve particular parcels of the reservation, should have an absolute title to the parcels so improved by them; and I would provide against alienation, either by the tribe of the tribal title, or by individuals of their personal title, for a limited time. As an additional inducement for heads of families to take land in severalty and engage in farming, provision should be made to aid such of them as do so in building houses thereon. The sum of $50, carefully expended by a judicious agent, will enable an Indian on many of the reservations, with his own labor, to build a house as comfortable as those occupied by many of our frontier settlers, and much more comfortable than the lodges in which they have been accustomed to live; and when so situated in his own house, on his own land, with a beginning made in the way of farming, a feeling of personal ownership and self-reliance will be developed and produce good results. And in building houses preference should be given to those who have selected land in severalty and made a certain amount of improvement thereon, and the offer of such aid should be held out as an inducement so to do. If a liberal sum was placed in the control of the Indian Office every year to be expended for this purpose exclusively, the effect would be excellent. A wise liberality in this direction would, in my judgment, be true economy.

There are now in the States and Territories west of the Mississippi River 102 reservations, great and small, on which are located, in round numbers, 224,000 Indians. The numbers on the different reservations vary from a few hundred to several thousand. There are attached to these reservations sixty-eight agencies, each with its staff of employés. There are also established near them, for the protection alike of the whites and Indians, thirty-seven military posts, with larger or smaller garrisons. The transportation of supplies to so many and so widely scattered agencies and military posts is very expensive, and our Army is so small that the garrisons at many of the posts are not sufficient either to prevent outbreaks or to suppress them promptly when they occur. It is my duty to say, and I say with great pleasure, that the military authorities have, when called upon by this Department, always responded with promptness and efficiency; but it must be apparent to all who have had occasion to note their operations, that they have been seriously embarrassed in their efforts to concentrate speedily at particular points sufficient force to meet emergencies. The peculiar conditions attending the transaction of public business for some months have prevented me from giving this subject the attention that in my opinion it deserves; but I am strongly inclined to believe that if all the Indians west of the Mississippi were gathered upon four or five reservations, our Indian affairs could be managed with greater economy to the government and greater benefit to the Indians.

In view of the facts stated as to existing reservations, I recommend that Congress be asked to create a commission of three or four eminent citizens to visit during the next year the reservations west of the Mississippi River, for the purpose of recommending to Congress, if they shall deem it wise to do so, the concentration of the Indians on four or five large reservations, to be selected in different parts of the West, on which the different tribes shall be located; and if this shall in the judgment of the commission not be wise, then to recommend the concentration of existing small agencies, where that can properly be done, and the reduction of the area of others to dimensions proportionate to the number of Indians now located thereon.

.I expected to transmit herewith a statement showing the acreage of each reservation, distinguishing between farming land, pasture land, timber and waste land, by comparing which with the number of Indians on each reservation, it would be easy to determine whether in justice to the Indians and in the public interest any of the reservations could be reduced in size. The necessary information for such statement has not as yet been received, but I hope it will be in the possession of the Department at an early day.

The tribal relation is a hinderance to individual progress. It means communism so far at least as land is concerned. It interferes with the administration of both civil and criminal law among the members of the tribe, and among members of the tribe and non-members. The Indians should learn both to know the law and to administer it. They will not become law-abiding citizens until they shall so learn. In my judgment it would be well to select some tribe or tribes among those most advanced in civilization, and establish therein a form of local government as nearly like, as may be, to the system of county government prevailing in the State or Territory in which the reservations are located, allowing the Indians to elect corresponding county officers having corresponding power and authority to enforce such laws of the State or Territory as Congress may deem proper to declare in force on each reservation for local purposes. Should the experiment prove successful it would, I think, be a long step forward in the path the Indian must travel if he shall ever reach full and intelligent citizenship. The ballot and trial by jury are tools to which Indian hands are not accustomed, and would doubtless be used by them awkwardly for a time, but if the Indian is to become in truth a citizen, he must learn to use them, and he cannot so learn until they are placed within his reach. It is better to move in the right direction, however slowly and awkwardly, than not to move at all.

DEFINITION OF CRIMES.

Further legislation is, in my judgment, necessary for the definition and punishment of crime committed on reservations, whether by Indians in their dealings with each other, by Indians on white men, or by white men on Indians. A good deal of uncertainty exists on these points, which should be removed. It is also important that the liability of Indians who engage in hostile acts against the government and our people should be declared more clearly and fully. During the present year the Apaches have committed many outrages in New Mexico and Arizona. A number of those thus engaged are now in confinement. Are they prisoners of war or criminals? Should not the liability of Indians thus engaged be clearly defined? Should not all crimes committed on reservations be clearly defined, the punishment thereof fixed, and the trial therefor provided in the United States courts? We know that polygamy prevails among most if not all the Indian tribes, and all history shows the degrading influence of that system wherever it prevails. We are endeavoring to civilize the Indians; should we not take measures to remove this obstacle to their civilization?

STOCK RAISING.

I am satisfied that some of the reservations now occupied by Indians are not well adapted to farming purposes, for the reason that the rainfall is not sufficient to make the raising of good crops reasonably certain. This is the case, in my opinion, in that portion of the Indian Territory occupied by the Cheyennes and Arapahoes near Fort Reno, and by the Kiowas and Comanches near Fort Sill. The soil is fertile but cannot be farmed profitably, as I am informed, without irrigation, the necessary works for which the Indians have neither the knowledge nor the means to establish.

It would, I think, be much better to teach the Indians on such reservations to become herdsmen, than to endeavor to teach them farming. If the government would, at each of the Agencies named, provide a herd of cattle to be cared for and managed by Indians, under the supervision of the agent, to be added to by annual purchases and natural increase, and not to be diminished for the use of the Indians until it should have attained such size as to be sufficient for all their wants, and then, under proper restrictions, turned over to them, with the distinct understanding that they must depend upon it and not upon the government, we would, in my judgment, make them self-sustaining much sooner than by attempting to make farmers of them on lands not adapted to that purpose.

THE INDIAN TRUST FUND.

This fund, amounting to $2,186,050, of which the Treasurer of the United States is custodian and the Secretary of the Interior is trustee, was invested in United States 5 per cent. bonds issued under acts of July 14, 1870, and January 20, 1871. On the 16th of May last, I was notified by the Treasury Department that interest would cease on these and other like bonds August 12, 1881, and the bonds be paid, but that if desired the bonds could be continued at three and a half per cent. Believing that such continuance would be to the profit of the fund, request to that end was duly made, and on the 28th of June, 1881, notice of such continuance was communicated to this department by the Treasurer. I then requested the Treasurer to sell the bonds thus continued, which he did, selling $500,000 July 15, 1881, at 2¼ per cent. premium, and the balance, $1,686,050, August 11, 1881, at 2 per cent. premium, realizing a gross premium of $44,971 to the profit of the fund. The principal sum of $2,186,050 has been, under the law, covered into the Treasury and draws five per cent. interest, and the premium above stated has been, under the decision of the First Comptroller, carried to the interest account of the fund.

RIGHT OF WAY TO RAILROADS THROUGH INDIAN RESERVATIONS.

During the last fifteen months, quite a number of railroad corporations have made application to the department for permission to construct their railroads through Indian reservations, urging the necessity of supplying the needs of the white people on our frontier, and the civilizing influence of railroads on the Indians, as reasons why their requests should be granted.

The Chicago, Milwaukee and Saint Paul Railway Company obtained permission, on May 24, 1880, to cross the Sisseton Reserve, in Dakota, occupied by the Sisseton and Wahpeton Sioux. The treaty with these Indians provides for the construction of railroads, under certain conditions, which I am advised have been carried out.

The Republican Valley Railroad Company, of Nebraska, in October and December of 1880, obtained permission from the Otoes and Missourias to cross their reservation in Nebraska. The treaty with these Indians provides for the building of railroads.

The Saint Paul and Sioux City Railroad Company, on April 19, 1880, obtained permission to cross the Omaha Reservation, under the provision of the treaty with the Omahas which provides for the building of railroads.

The Carson and Colorado Railroad Company, on April 13, 1880, made an agreement with the Pi-Utes to cross the Walker River Reservation, Nevada, which was established by executive order. This privilege has not yet been confirmed.

The Dakota Central Railroad Company, on June 12, December 23, and December 31, 1880, entered into an agreement with the mixed tribes of Sioux living on the Sioux Reservation in Dakota, to build a railroad east and west through their reservation, in accordance with treaty stipulations.

The Chicago, Milwaukee and Saint Paul Railroad Company, on November 2, 1880, made a similar agreement with the same Indians to cross the Territory east and west.

The Oregon Railway and Navigation Company, on June 10, 1881, in accordance with treaty stipulations, made an agreement with the Walla-Wallas Cayuses, and Umatillas to construct its line across the Umatilla Reserve in Oregon.

On July 18, 1881, by authority of the President, on the application of the Utah and Northern Railroad Company, an officer of the government obtained an agreement from the Shoshones and Bannocks living on the Fort Hall Reservation, Idaho, by which the right of way and the necessary lands for railroad purposes east and west across the reservation were granted on the payment of suitable compensation; the agreement, however, to be ratified by Congress. The treaty with these Indians makes no provisions for railroads.

On August 22, 1881, the Crow Indians, on the Crow Reserve, Montana, entered into an agreement permitting the Northern Pacific Railroad Company to construct its road through the reservation, subject to ratification by Congress, there being no treaty providing for the same.

On June 18, 1881, the Atchison and Nebraska Railroad Company obtained permission from the Iowa Indians on the Iowa Reserve, Nebraska, to construct a road north and south through their reservation, in accordance with treaty stipulations.

My purpose is to submit to Congress, with my recommendation, the above-mentioned agreements for such action as may be deemed appropriate.

In addition to the above negotiations, an agent of the department is now in the Choctaw country, with directions to submit to the constituted authorities of that Nation the application of several railroads which desire the privilege of constructing their lines through the Choctaw country north and south. If the Nation acts favorably on the applications, and the same meet my approval, I will also transmit them to Congress for its action.

In May, 1880, in accordance with the provisions of the treaty with the Ute Indians in Colorado, the President issued a proclamation giving permission to the Denver and Rio Grande Railroad Company to cross over and occupy so much of the Ute Reservation in Colorado as might be necessary for the right of way. Last spring, while the company was constructing its road under the proclamation, I received information that the Indians on the reservation had become alarmed at the presence of the working force of the railroad, and I immediately notified the president of the company that it must compensate the Indians for its occupation of their lands, or directions would be given to stop its construction. I have received no satisfactory answer to this and other similar communications, neither has any compensation been paid to the Indians for the occupation of their lands. I understand that the railroad has been constructed and is now in operation through that part of the Ute Reservation which is still occupied by Indians. I beg to recommend that suitable action be taken by Congress looking to an adjustment of the rights of the Denver and Rio Grande Railroad and the Indians in this transaction. It cannot be expected that the Indians will remain satisfied so long as the railroad company shall continue to make use of their lands without suitable compensation.

SAN CARLOS RESERVATION.

This reservation was established by Executive order on the 14th of December, 1872. Its boundary has not been surveyed. It is ascertained, however, that on the southern part of the reservation there are extensive deposits of coal. Fuel is scarce in the Territory of Arizona, in which this reservation lies, and hence the coal deposit is supposed to be very valuable. Parties have sought to contract with the Indians for the privilege of mining the coal, and during the last summer a contract of this kind was submitted to the department for approval. The contract was disapproved, as neither the Indians nor the department had lawful authority to make or approve such contract. I consider this matter of sufficient importance to call it to your special attention. The reservation is a large one, and might perhaps be so lessened without injury to the Indians as to exclude the deposits of coal, or, if this cannot be done, it may be enlarged to a corresponding extent elsewhere, and the coal bearing portion withdrawn from the reservation. The coal is and will be needed for the proper development of Arizona, but in providing for the sale of the land care should be taken that the coal is not monopolized by a single or a few parties to the injury of the Territory.

THE SIOUX AND THE PONCAS IN DAKOTA.

I refer with great pleasure to that portion of the report of the Commissioner of Indian Affairs in which is set forth a copy of an agreement signed by the principal chiefs of nearly all the different bands of Sioux, at a council held in this city in August last for the benefit of the Poncas in Dakota. The conduct of the Sioux chiefs who signed the agreement was manly and generous, and deserves, I think, high commendation. Should the agreement receive the necessary number of signatures of adult male Sioux, it will be submitted for the consideration of Congress.

DEFICIENCIES.

I consider it very important that the attention of Congress be specially called to the following extracts from the report of the Commissioner of Indian Affairs:

DEFICIENCY APPROPRIATIONS.

•As stated under the head of "Appropriation," owing to the large increase in the price of beef paid during the fiscal year 1882, the appropriations for the Indian service during 1882 will in many cases be insufficient. On the 20th of July last, the War Department turned over to this bureau 2,813 Sioux Indians, belonging to Sitting Bull's band, and for whose support no appropriation was made by Congress. Under your authority a deficiency of $195,000 was incurred for the purchase of the supplies and clothing for these Indians, and the amount will be included in the deficiency estimate to be submitted to Congress. Additional funds for the support of the following Indians for the present fiscal year, and for other purposes, will also be required, as follows: Support of Apaches in Arizona and New Mexico, $25,000; support of Arapahoes, Cheyennes, Apaches, Kiowas, Comanches, and Wichitas, $100,000; support of Blackfeet, Bloods, and Piegans, $15,000; support of Indians in central superintendency, $7,500; support of Modocs, $5,000; support of Navajoes, $5,000; support of Nez Percés of Joseph's band, $7,500; support of schools, $50,000; telegraphing and purchase of Indian supplies, $5,000; transportation of Indian supplies, $25,000. Large sums are also due different parties for goods and supplies furnished and for services rendered in 1873 and 1874, which have repeatedly been reported to Congress for appropriation, but none has so far been made. There is due the Western Union Telegraph Company, for messages transmitted during May and June, 1879, the sum of $361.65; contractors for transporting Indian goods and supplies during the fiscal year 1879, $9,556.63; during the fiscal year 1880, $44,882.14, and during the fiscal year 1881, about fifty thousand dollars. This indebtedness was incurred by this office under an absolute necessity, and early provision for its payment should be made by Congress.

Early in last spring it was found that the amount appropriated by Congress for the support of the Arapahoes, Cheyennes, Apaches, Kiowas, Comanches, and Wichitas, located at the Cheyenne and Arapahoe and Kiowa, and Comanche Agencies, Indian Territory, for the fiscal year 1881, was insufficient to furnish them with beef, coffee, and sugar until the end of the fiscal year. The agents in charge were notified of the insufficient appropriations and directed to reduce the issue of beef, but in reply thereto submitted statements which convinced the department that to reduce the rations of those Indians was to invite a war. Copies of these letters were transmitted to Congress with a request for an additional appropriation, but the same was not granted. After the adjournment of Congress the case was submitted by you to the President, and, upon consultation with the honorable Secretary of War, it was decided that the War Department would furnish the agents at Cheyenne and Arapahoe, and Kiowa and Comanche Agencies with beef and flour until the end of the last fiscal year, the cost of these supplies to be reimbursed from any appropriation which may hereafter be made by Congress for that purpose. Accounts amounting to $59,232.01 have been presented by the War Department for reimbursement, and it is hoped that Congress, at an early day, will furnish this office with the means to cancel this debt.

TRANSPORTATION OF INDIAN SUPPLIES.

Owing to the failure of Congress to appropriate during the fiscal years 1879, 1880, and 1881 sufficient funds to pay for the transportation of goods and supplies to the different agencies, this office has been greatly embarrassed this summer by not having its stores promptly delivered. Contractors to whom the government owes over $100,000 for transportation services performed under former contracts are not very anxious to render services and wait for their pay several years. Flour delivered to the contractors for different agencies in October, 1880, was not delivered until July or August, 1881, and when this office urged them to comply more strictly with their contracts, their reply, that this office had no funds to pay them after service was rendered, appeared a sufficient excuse for the delay. The failure of Congress to appropriate last winter sufficient funds to pay outstanding indebtedness for transportation costs the government in increased price of transportation for the present fiscal year more than the interest on the money due, and while there are such large sums lying idle in the United States Treasury, the policy of not paying debts lawfully due appears to me very short-sighted. It cannot be expected that contractors will wait years for money due and honestly earned without attempting to get even with the government by charging increased rates of transportation, and for this reason it is urged that sufficient means be furnished this office to liquidate these debts. This would certainly be true economy.

The right of this office to incur this indebtedness above the amount appropriated cannot be questioned. Congress appropriates a certain amount of money to be used in the purchase of clothing and supplies, mostly due the Indians under treaty stipulation. Of what avail are these goods and supplies to the Indians, if sufficient funds are not appropriated to pay for transporting them to the different agencies, where they are required ?

The attention of Congress has repeatedly been called to the insufficient amount appropriated yearly for transporting the goods and supplies, and it is earnestly hoped that the efforts of this office in obtaining means to pay the old indebtedness incurred, as well as in securing sufficient funds for the pesent and next fiscal year, will have better success than heretofore.

The Sioux, turned over by the War Department in July last, were prisoners of war, held as such until that time by the military authorities, and for whose support no estimates had been made by the Indian Office.

The administration of our Indian affairs is, at all times, and under all circumstances, embarrassing and difficult, but when to all other troubles is added that of insufficient appropriations, the embarrassment and difficulty are greatly increased.

SALARY OF COMMISSIONER AND APPOINTMENT OF ASSISTANT COMMISSIONER.

There is disbursed yearly, under the supervision of the Commissioner of Indian Affairs, in round numbers, the sum of about $6,000,000. Of this sum about $2,500,000 is paid for Indian supplies bought under contract, or in open market under his direction. The money and the supplies representing the whole amount are distributed at sixty-eight agencies scattered over our vast country between the Atlantic and the Pacific oceans. It is needless to say that to supervise this work requires a man of untiring industry, great business skill and training, and sterling integrity, because it is evident that upon the proper performance of this work depends not only the careful and economical expenditure of the public moneys, but to a great extent the preservation of peace among the Indian tribes. I submit that the government does not provide sufficient compensation for such service, when it is fortunate enough to have it, or to secure it at all times when it is needed. The salary now provided by law is $3,500 per annum. It is in my judgment wholly inadequate, and I earnestly recommend that it be increased to $4,500. I also recommend that provision be made for the appointment of an assistant commissioner, with a salary of $3,000 per annum. Such provision is in my judgment necessary for the prompt and proper discharge of the duties of the bureau, and I am convinced would prove of benefit to the public service.

PUBLIC LANDS.

During the year ending 30 June, 1881, public lands were disposed of as follows:

Acres.

Cash sales:

	Acres
Private entries	666,289.11
Public sales	2,279.40
Timber and stone lands	42,987.92

	Acres.
Pre-emption entries	721,146.26
Desert lands	108,560.02
Mineral lands	27,179.68
Coal lands	4,975.58
Excesses	12,339.06
Abandoned military reservations	1,910.21
Total cash sales	1,587,617.2
Homestead entries	5,028,100.69
Timber-culture entries	1,763,799.35
Military-warrant localities	55,662.36
Agricultural College scrip locations	360.00
Supreme Court scrip locations	28,253.74
Valentine scrip locations	392.15
Sioux half-breed scrip locations	2,519.27
Chippewa half-breed scrip locations	800.00
Porterfield scrip locations	16.86

Lands certified or patented for railroad purposes to States.

	Acres.
Alabama	383.23
Iowa	73,391.58
Minnesota	483,466.63
Kansas	281,277.28
To corporations:	
Pacific railroads	211,992.04
State selections approved for—	
School idemnity	15,880.00
Internal improvements	1,780.00
Agricultural colleges	1,370.45
Seminaries	3,964.14
Donation claims	18,237.06
Swamp	569,001.18
Grand total	10,128,175.25

The cash receipts from all sources, sales, fees, and commissions, for the last fiscal year amounted to $4,402,112.53.

The total area of the land States and Territories is 1,814,788,922 acres, of which 784,906,980 acres have been surveyed.

The area of lands surveyed the last fiscal year was greater by 6,058,759 acres than that of the previous year.

The area of public lands disposed of the last fiscal year was less by 3,898,974.60 acres than that of the previous year; the aggregate cash receipts were greater by $2,508,642.56.

Besides these public lands, there were disposed of during the last fiscal year by the General Land Office, Indian lands amounting to 765,221.80 acres, for which was received the sum of $1,006,691.63, deposited in the Treasury for the benefit of the Indians.

THE GENERAL LAND OFFICE.

I invite especial attention to that portion of the letter of the Commissioner of the General Land Office to me of date October 25, 1881, relating to the clerical force required for his office for the fiscal year ending June 30, 1883. The work of the office is much in arrears. It is very important to the many individuals whose interests are affected by its action that such action shall at all times be prompt and that delay in settling the questions before the office shall not occur. Such delay is not only unjust to the parties whose interests are involved, but tends to embarrass and hinder the work actually done by requiring a portion of the force now employed to answer the numerous letters of inquiry written by parties who are impatient at the (to them) unaccountable delay in having their business disposed of. If permitting the work to fall in arrears dispensed with doing it altogether, we might congratulate ourselves that we had saved the expense of doing it, although our failure to do it had worked great injury to those whose work the office was created to do and who share in the cost of maintaining it. But the work must and will be done sooner or later, and I submit that it is not only just and right, but it is in the long run cheaper to provide sufficient force to do it promptly.

I concur in the recommendation of the Commissioner that authority of law be given for the appointment of a deputy commissioner who shall assist him in the discharge of his duties and perform such other duties as may be prescribed.

I also concur in the recommendation of the Commissioner for the appointment of three inspectors of surveyor-general and district land offices. It is impossible for the Land Office with the means now provided to keep careful supervision over their offices, situated so far from the seat of government. The information received concerning them is usually ex parte and often contradictory, and in many cases is not received until it is too late to prevent much maladministration.

If surveyors-general and district land officers were aware that an agent of the government might at any time visit their respective offices, with authority to examine their books and papers, and by personal examination to ascertain their condition, it seems that great benefit would thereby result to the public service.

Said inspectors would also be of great assistance when new land districts are created and offices opened, and when a change of officers occurs.

SURVEYS UNDER DEPOSIT SYSTEM.

For the reasons named in the report of the Commissioner (pages 6, 7, and 8), I recommend the repeal of the act of March 3, 1879, entitled "An act to amend section twenty-four hundred and three of the Revised Statutes of the United States, in relation to deposits for surveys." Under the present law there seems good reason to believe that extensive surveys are made far in advance of any legitimate demand; it is impossible to test the accuracy of the field work, and it is probable that when, in the future, a survey shall be needed, the work will have to be done again.

PRIVATE LAND CLAIMS IN NEW MEXICO, ARIZONA, AND COLORADO.

I call special attention to that portion of the letter of the Commissioner of the General Land Office relating to private land claims in New Mexico, Arizona, and Colorado. The uncertainty existing as to the validity of these claims and their extent makes the title to them of merely speculative value and retards the sales and settlements, greatly to the injury of the sections in which these claims are situate. The present system for the settlement of these claims appears to be wholly inadequate, and some more efficient system should be speedily provided.

LAND-GRANT RAILROADS.

Fifty miles of the Atlantic and Pacific Railroad west of Albuquerque, New Mexico, were accepted by President Hayes on the 17th December last; and fifty miles by President Garfield on the 18th April last. One hundred additional miles of this road are now ready for examination, and commissioners have been appointed for that purpose.

Fifty miles of the Northern Pacific Railroad in Dakota Territory, west of the Missouri River, were accepted by President Hayes on the 20th December last, one hundred additional miles, partly in Dakota and partly in Montana, have recently been examined, but have not yet been accepted. Two hundred and twenty-five miles in Eastern Washington and Idaho are now under examination by commissioners.

One hundred and thirty miles of the New Orleans Pacific Railroad have recently been examined, but have not yet been accepted. One hundred and twenty-three additional miles are now ready for examination.

REPAYMENTS.

The price of reserved sections within the limits of railroad land grants is by law double the minimum price for similar lands outside such limits. It has happened in many instances that local land officers have supposed parcels of land to be within land grant limits when in fact they were not, and have sold them to purchasers at double minimum price, thus placing in the Treasury of the United States in each case a sum of money to which the government was not entitled, and which in all good conscience belonged to the party by whom it had been paid.

Accordingly Congress, by act of June 16, 1880, provided that "in all cases where parties have paid double minimum price for land which has afterwards been found not to be within the limits of a railroad land grant, the excess of one dollar and twenty five cents per acre shall in like manner be repaid to the purchaser thereof, or to his heirs or assigns." (Supplement to Revised Statutes, page 565.)

Under this provision the First Comptroller of the Treasury has held that where the purchaser has conveyed the land since June 16, 1880, his grantee, and not the purchaser, is entitled to the money, for the reason that the grantee is the assignee within the meaning of the act. Aside from the question whether the word "assignee" in the act shall be construed to mean the grantee of the land, which I do not admit, there is what seems to me to be involved a grave question. If it be admitted, as this act clearly admits, that the government honestly owes a particular person a sum of money, and therefore should pay it, can the government acquit itself of that obligation by paying the amount to another person?

I have not been able to reach the conclusion that Congress so intended to declare in the act of June 16, 1880, and have therefore declined to approve requisitions upon the Treasury for payment in this class of cases to the grantee of the land instead of the original purchaser until Congress shall declare its intention in more clear and precise terms than are contained in the act mentioned.

OFFICE OF COMMISSIONER OF RAILROADS.

The report of the Commissioner of Railroads, herewith presented, gives the operations of that office during the fiscal year ending June 30, 1881, under the law relating to indebted Pacific railroad companies and certain land-grant railroads.

Two inspection trips have been made during the year for the purpose of examining the properties and accounts of the several subsidized railroads—one by the then Commissioner, extending from April 20 to June 18, 1881, and the other by the bookkeeper temporarily in charge of the office, extending from August 18 to October 7, 1881.

About 6,900 miles of subsidized and land-grant railroads subject to the supervision of the bureau have been examined, and their books (especially those of the Union and Central Pacific roads) carefully compared with the reports as rendered by the companies.

Among the properties included in the inspections, aside from the Union and Central Pacific, were those of the Southern Pacific, Atlantic and Pacific, Central Branch Union Pacific, and the Sioux City and Pacific Companies, in all of which the United States is interested as creditor or otherwise.

Although the past severe and protracted winter was accompanied by unusual floods and storms, which destroyed much property and materially increased the expenditures for maintaining the same, it was noticeable that a substantial improvement in the property of the roads in which the government has a direct interest had been made, and in general the reports rendered indicate a marked increase in their business.

The Union Pacific Railway is building an extension from Granger—a station on their main line, 156 miles east of Ogden, to Baker City, Oreg., via Port Neuf, on the Utah Northern Railroad—which will connect at

Baker City with the Oregon system of railroads, and thus acquire an outlet to the Pacific coast, independent of the Central Pacific. It is represented that the work will be completed at an early date.

The Central Pacific Railroad Company has, by lease of the Southern Pacific of Arizona and New Mexico, which is now completed to Deming, N. Mex., and there connects with the Atchison, Topeka and Santa Fé Railroad, secured a through route from the Pacific coast, independent of the Union Pacific.

The Atlantic and Pacific Railroad is being rapidly constructed from the east and the west.

THE UNION PACIFIC RAILWAY COMPANY.

The property and business of this company is reported on in full, and has been found in good condition, with business increasing.

The company has furnished reports, from which the following statements are derived:

Length of line subsidized with bonds..........................Miles..	1,432.62
Length of line subsidized with lands............................do...	1,783.17
Leased to the Central Pacific....................................do...	5.00
Operated by the Union Pacific ....do...	1,818.80
Stock subscribed	$61,000,000 00
Stock issued	60,673,745 00
Par value...	100 00
United States subsidy bonds	33,539,512 00
Other funded debt	81,987,405 00
Total stock and debt.................................	176,200,662 00
Increase of stock during the year........................	9,911,445 00
Floating debt and interest account to June 30, 1881, on subsidy and other bonds..............................	28,430,686 60
Bonds and stocks of, and investments in, other companies...........	28,718,560 42
Material on hand...	$2,794,893 97
Cash on hand	2,333,343 45
Accounts receivable	2,870,998 81
	7,999,236 23
Cost of road and equipment, per company's books	155,708,861 58

The following statement shows the earnings for the fiscal year ending June 30, 1881, as per reports submitted by the company:

Passenger..	$4,970,646 85
Freight	15,957,560 64
Miscellaneous	1,837,544 59
	22,765,752 08
Operating expenses.....................................	11,474,910 08
Net earnings	11,290,842 00
Interest paid..	6,147,859 94
Dividends paid	3,607,448 13

40 Ab

Under the sinking-fund act of May 7, 1878, the "25 per cent. of net earnings" due the United States from that part of the road to which the act applies has not yet been determined for the year ending December 31, 1880, items amounting to the sum of $762,440.87 not being adjusted.

CENTRAL PACIFIC RAILROAD COMPANY.

The property and accounts of this company have been examined and the details of the same embodied in the Commissioner's report.

The condition of the property is improving and the business materially increasing. This company leases and operates the Southern Pacific Railroad in California, Arizona, and New Mexico.

The following statement is taken from reports furnished by the company:

Number of miles subsidized	860. 66
Number of miles owned	1,204. 50
Number of miles leased	1,513. 00
Average number of miles operated during fiscal year ending June 30, 1881	2,614. 00
Locomotives owned, 226; leased, 70	296
Passenger cars owned, 261; leased, 49	310
Baggage, mail, and express cars owned, 56; leased, 24	80
Freight and other cars owned, 5,616; leased, 2,351	7,967
Stock subscribed	$59,275,500 00
Stock issued	59,275,500 00
Par value	100 00
Subsidy bonds outstanding	27,855,680 00
Funded debt	55,301,000 00
Floating debt	7,028,442 44
Interest accrued on subsidy bonds	21,778,122 61
Interest due and accrued on funded debt	1,433,095 00
Total debt	113,396,340 05
Capital stock and debt	172,671,840 05
Cost of road	136,994,849 80
Equipment	8,047,103 42
Real estate	2,639,148 10
Total cost of road and equipment	147,681,101 32
Cash, materials, and sinking funds	8,455,566 81
Bonds and stocks	334,604 90
Miscellaneous investments	1,899,995 66
Total	10,600,167 37

The earnings for the fiscal year ending June 30, 1881, are reported as follows:

Passenger	$6,188,388 56
Freight	15,216,554 65
United States mail	463,861 27
Miscellaneous earnings	1,024,540 09
Total	22,893,344 57
Operating expenses and rentals	13,502,504 48
Ordinary net earnings	9,390,840 09
Interest paid	3,642,965 02
Dividends paid	3,557,530 00

Under the sinking-fund fund act of May 7, 1878, the "25 per cent. of net earnings" found due the United States by this company to December 31, 1880, amounted to $1,037,225.28, which has been covered into the Treasury as follows:

Credit of bond and interest account	$428,388 67
Credit of sinking-fund account	608,836 61
Total	1,037,225 28

The company rendered transportation services amounting to $892,788.54, and made a cash payment of $144,436.74.

CENTRAL BRANCH UNION PACIFIC RAILROAD.

This road, with the leased lines controlled by it, is operated as a division of the Missouri Pacific Railway Company.

From the meager reports submitted by the company the following is derived:

Miles owned and subsidized	100
Miles leased	262
Stock issued	$1,000,000 00
Subsidy bonds	1,600,000 00
Interest on subsidy bonds	1,357,808 25
Gross earnings for year ending June 30, 1881, whole line	$914,398 58
Operating expenses	566,562 85
Net earnings	347,835 73

SIOUX CITY AND PACIFIC RAILROAD COMPANY.

Until the year ending June 30, 1880, this road had not earned enough to pay operating expenses and interest on its first-mortgage bonds, consequently there was no "5 per cent. of net earnings" for the government, under the Supreme Court decision.

The length of road operated is 264.13 miles; road owned, 107.42; road subsidized, 101.77; number of locomotives, 12; passenger cars, 9; baggage, mail, and express cars, 6; freight and other cars, 232. The earnings for the year ending June 30, 1881, are reported as follows:

Passenger	$140,887 81
Freight	434,448 91
Miscellaneous	30,359 52
Total	605,196 24
Operating expenses	540,502 66
Net earnings	64,693 58

The liabilities and assets are follows:

Stock issued	$2,066,400 00
Subsidy bonds	1,628,390 00
Interest on subsidy bonds	1,268,899 09
First-mortgage bonds	1,628,000 00
Interest on same	52,485 00
Miscellaneous indebtedness	531,561 51
Total stock and debt	7,177,665 60
Cost of road and fixtures	5,397,226 15
Materials on hand	65,439 62
Cash and bonds	27,706 76
Miscellaneous investments	312,800 00
Accounts receivable	167,896 81
Total assets	5,971,001 34
Deficit	1,206,664 26

OREGON AND CALIFORNIA RAILROAD COMPANY.

The reports of this company show the length of road operated, 316.93 miles; number of locomotives, 20; number of passenger cars, 16; number of baggage, mail, and express, 6; number of freight and other cars, 441. Par value of shares, $100; stock issued, $19,000,000; funded debt, $15,940,000; floating debt, $6,112.513.39; total debt, $22,052,513.39; total stock and debt, $22,052,513.39. Cost of road, $12,019,154.90; cost of equipment, $813,784.08; cost of road and equipment, $12,832,938.98. Passenger earnings, $244,578.95; freight earnings, $350,239.82; miscellaneous earnings, $31,920.04; total earnings, $626,738.81. Operating expenses, including taxes, $528,589.18; net earnings, $98,149.63.

ATCHISON, TOPEKA, AND SANTA FÉ RAILROAD COMPANY.

This company reports operations for the year ending December 31, 1880, as follows:

Miles owned, 470.58; miles leased, 1,031.74; stock issued, $24,891,000; increase during year, $12,256,600; par value, $100; funded debt, $15,873,000; floating debt, $6,149,366.99; total debt, $22,022,366.99; stock and debt, $46,913,366.99; cost of road and equipment, $26,866,325.72;

investments in other companies, $18,604,126; materials and supplies on hand, $1,118,488.93. Passenger earnings, $1,786,947.10; freight earnings, $6,515,527.30; miscellaneous earnings, $270,093.74; total earnings, $8,572,568.14; operating expenses, including taxes, rentals, &c., $4,905,902.89; net earnings, $3,666,665.25. Interest and discount paid, $1,457,090.21; dividends paid, $1,727,195. The company owns and leases 157 locomotives, 76 passenger cars, 33 baggage, mail, and express cars, and 5,227 freight cars.

SOUTHERN PACIFIC RAILROAD COMPANY.

For the year ending June 30, 1881, the company reports as follows: Miles operated, 160.89; miles owned, 711.56; leased to Central Pacific, 550.67; number of locomotives, 48; passenger cars, 74; baggage, mail, and express, 15; freight and other cars, 1,158; stock issued, $36,763,900; funded debt, $28,774,000; floating debt, $699,279.43; interest due on first-mortgage bonds, $482,145; total debt, $29,955,424.43; stock and debt, $66,719,324.43; cash, material, and accounts due, $1,402,632.37; cost of road, $62,439,447.70; cost of equipment, $1,847,815.43; total cost of road and equipment, $64,287,263.13. Passenger earnings, $476,611.03; freight earnings, $602,434.40; miscellaneous earnings and rentals, $1,680,166.46; total earnings, $2,759,211.89; operating expenses, including taxes and insurance, $710,694.41; net earnings, $2,048,517.48; interest paid, $1,754,500.94.

TEXAS AND PACIFIC RAILWAY COMPANY.

Work upon this road is being pushed rapidly forward, and it is anticipated that the line will be completed and trains running through to El Paso not later than January 1, 1882. At present trains are running to Antelope, Tex., 640 miles west of Marshall, and 120 miles east of El Paso. The grading is completed to the latter point, and bridging and track are being pushed at a rapid rate.

The annual report of the operations of the road for the year ending June 30, 1881, has not been received at this department.

NORTHERN PACIFIC RAILROAD COMPANY.

For the year ending June 30, 1881, the company reports as follows: Miles operated, 754; number of locomotives, 104; passenger cars, 53; baggage, mail, and express, 15; freight and other cars, 3,021; capital stock, $100,000,000, less $8,687,411.05, canceled; funded debt, $21,586,800; floating debt, $1,472,090.65; total debt, $22,058,890.65; total stock and debt, $113,371,479.60; cost of road and equipment and lands, including lines under construction, $108,324,280.42; cash, $11,567,944.33; materials, $2,082,947.08; accounts receivable, $975,440.65. Passenger earnings, $668,420.92; freight earnings, $2,144,782.12; miscellaneous earnings, $118,599.44; total earnings, $2,931,802.48; operating expenses, $1,946,157.08; net earnings, $985.645.40.

The Commissioner's report is accompanied by an appendix and tables, containing compilations and statements of facts relating to the Pacific and land-grant railroad companies, the laws affecting them, statements of their affairs, their receipts, expenditures, and operations, and other matters of interest to railroad companies.

It is respectfully suggested that the act of May 7, 1878, amending the act entitled "An act to aid in the construction of a railroad and telegraph line from the Missouri River to the Pacific Ocean, and to secure to the government the use of the same for postal, military, and other purposes," be so amended as to embrace the subsidized portion of the Kansas division of the Union Pacific Railway, formerly the Kansas Pacific Railway, within the operations of said act requiring the establishment of sinking-funds and the payment of "25 per cent. of net earnings."

THE TENTH CENSUS.

The report of the Superintendent of the Tenth Census indicates the near completion of the important work under his charge. He estimates that five-sixths of the clerical work has been done, and the one-sixth remaining will be mostly in the line of tabulation. With the exception of obtaining the statistics of ship-building, production of petroleum, quarrying industry, and those relating to the population and resources of Alaska, the field work of the Tenth Census may be considered practically finished. Six agents are still employed on this work, and it is expected that within a few weeks their labors will be completed.

Rapid progress has been made during the year in the tabulation and compilation of the statistical material received, and early publication is assured.

The total population by States and Territories, as finally determined by the Tenth Census, is as follows:

Alabama	1,262,505
Arizona	40,440
Arkansas	802,525
California	864,694
Colorado	194,327
Connecticut	622,700
Dakota	135,177
Delaware	146,608
Dist. of Columbia	177,624
Florida	269,493
Georgia	1,542,180
Idaho	32,610
Illinois	3,077,871
Indiana	1,978,301
Iowa	1,624,615
Kansas	996,096
Kentucky	1,648,690

Louisiana	939,946
Maine	648,936
Maryland	934,943
Massachusetts	1,783,085
Michigan	1,636,937
Minnesota	780,773
Mississippi	1,131,597
Missouri	2,168,380
Montana	39,159
Nebraska	452,402
Nevada	62,266
New Hampshire	346,991
New Jersey	1,131,116
New Mexico	119,565
New York	5,082,871
North Carolina	1,399,750
Ohio	3,198,002
Oregon	174,768
Pennsylvania	4,282,891
Rhode Island	276,531
South Carolina	995,577
Tennessee	1,542,359
Texas	1,591,749
Utah	143,963
Vermont	332,286
Virginia	1,512,565
Washington	75,116
West Virginia	618,457
Wisconsin	1,315,497
Wyoming	20,789
Grand total	50,155,783

The increase of population since 1870 appears to have been about 30 per cent.

Tables accompany the report, exhibiting the distribution of Representatives in Congress, according to the Tenth Census, upon the plan heretofore pursued in determining the number to which each State has become entitled. The scheme proposed by Col. C. W. Seaton (the present Superintendent) for the distribution of Representatives is also illustrated by appropriate tables. This has the approval of Superintendent Walker as a more equitable plan than that heretofore employed.

The Superintendent devotes considerable space to a statement of the financial embarrassments which, at one time, threatened to suspend the active work of his office, and which would have made suspension an absolute necessity had not the services of a volunteer force been accepted. He assumes the responsibility for the inadequate appropriation allowed by Congress, and gives the reasons for the mistaken estimates submitted. When the $500,000 asked for the completion of the work was granted, it was thought that it would be sufficient to cover the required expenditures. Important field work was then in progress in the departments of mining, manufactures, and social statistics. The cost of its completion could not be definitely known, and proved to be heavier than was anticipated. In addition to this, the tabulations undertaken in the Central Office were upon a scale far exceeding that of any previous census, and entailed labor and expense which could not well be calculated in advance of the actual performance of the work. The investigations instituted demanded the utmost accuracy and completeness, so that all the statistical material brought into the office should challenge criticism, and be as near perfect as intelligent labor could make it. The defects and inaccuracies of the ninth census have been avoided. The act of March 3, 1879, widened the field of intelligent supervision and made possible through its better machinery a more complete and perfect census. It has led to a great improvement in the quality of the material gathered, and afforded the office opportunities for revision and verification, which were quite impossible under the defective law of 1850. The superintendent believes it wholly practicable to bring every class of facts presented in the census up to the standard of absolute or approximate accuracy. Facts are cited by the superintendent showing the necessity of expenditures in certain branches of his work, far in excess of his original estimates. These necessities could not be foretold, nor by close calculations in advance could they be provided for. They grew out of the work as it progressed, and were known only when met in the practical work of the office. When it became fully known that the appropriation was inadequate to complete the work to be done, the only alternative was to disband the office force and suspend all work until Congress should meet and provide the money to go on, or to accept the service of such of the old employés and officers as should volunteer to work without pay, without involving the United States in any legal obligation for their employment. To have closed the office and disbanded a force trained to the work in hand would have added largely to the expense when the resumption of labor was authorized by Congress. Valuable clerks would have found other employment. New material would have to be accepted and the slow process of training again undertaken, while a delay of six or eight months at a most critical period of the work, when the country was impatiently waiting for results already in hand, would have been disastrous in the extreme.

Under these circumstances the Superintendent felt justified in calling the attention of the Department to the practicability of obtaining a sufficient volunteer force to carry on the work of his office and to ask its sanction of the plan proposed.

After a careful consideration of the question, weighing all possible objections with the advantages presented, the suggestions of the Superintendent were concurred in and instructions given to permit those who desired to volunteer to do so, with the full understanding on their part that the government had no legal right to make any contract, express or implied, that should bind it in anticipation of appropriations. At the same time assurance was given that all of the facts necessary to a full understanding of the case would be laid before Congress at the earliest practicable moment.

The average force employed, under the conditions named, has been 700. It represents the best of the old force and in point of efficiency has steadily improved upon what, at an earlier period, was considered a high standard of clerical work. So rapid and satisfactory has been the labor performed that it is confidently expected that by the time Congress meets in December the compilation of the Tenth Census will be substantially completed. This accomplished, a comparatively small force will be required to reduce the statistical matter to tabular form and to prepare it for the printer.

While the peculiar condition of affairs which made necessary the acceptance of a volunteer force is to be regretted, no one will be inclined, in view of all the facts, to question the sincerity and good faith of the efficient Superintendent, General Francis A. Walker, nor to find fault, on mere technical grounds, with the expedient adopted, which happily made possible an early and prompt completion of the work which had commanded so much of his time and attention. The course pursued was the wisest possible under the circumstances, and any other which looked to the suspension of the work would have resulted in grave injury to the public interests. No stronger evidence of the Superintendent's unselfish devotion to the service could be afforded than the fact that out of his limited means he placed at the disposal of the Department sufficient funds to meet those pressing obligations which had been incurred, and the payment of which could not be postponed without serious inconvenience. The amount thus expended will amount to about five thousand dollars, for the repayment of which he could receive no guaranty or security from the government. In referring to this, in his report, the Superintendent says: "Should it please Congress to make an appropriation to cover the amounts so expended I shall be glad to be reimbursed for expenditures made in good faith and for the public interest. If not, I shall accept the decision of that body and regard the amount so expended as my personal contribution to the success of a great public work."

It is estimated that $540,000 will be required to complete the Tenth Census, and of this amount $330,000 will be applied to the payment of the volunteer force, provided Congress shall authorize the same to be done.

This subject will form the basis of a special communication to Congress when it meets, at which time all the facts necessary to a more perfect understanding of the situation will be laid before that body.

With the additional amount, $540,000, required, the total expenses of the Tenth Census will be proportionally less than those of the Ninth Census. For this $3,336,000 were appropriated. The present census shows an increase of thirty per cent. in population, and this percentage, added to the cost of the last census, would call for an expenditure at the present time of four and a third millions. Including the cost of printing and engraving, for which an appropriation has been made of $250,000, the proportional cost would still be less than that of the census of 1870. As the act of April 20, 1880, appropriating $210,000, imposed duties upon the enumerators altogether additional to those required in the previous census or provided for in the act of 1879, this amount should not be included in instituting a comparison between the expenditures of the Tenth and Ninth Censuses.

It can be safely asserted that better and far more reliable work, comprehending departments of public and private industry never before included in a census, distinguishes the Tenth Census from any that has preceded it. For the first time it has collected the statistics of railroads, the telegraph, fire, life, and marine insurance, while the bulk of material returned in the departments of agriculture and manufactures has been at least double that of any former census. In relation to taxation and public debts the investigations have been extended to embrace details which exist in regard to the indebtedness of no other country of the world. Special attention has been paid to mining and fishing industries, and the results obtained cannot be other than advantageous to the nation.

In commenting upon the work accomplished the Superintendent says: "There is not one direction in which the published results of the present census will not cover more ground, divided into greater detail, than any preceding, while the character of the results will testify to a more rigid examination and a more careful revision of the results of the enumeration."

A tabular statement accompanies the report, showing in detail the expenditures on account of the Tenth Census to October 31, 1881. The following reports have been prepared, and are now in the hands of the Public Printer: Population; Fisheries; Power and Machinery used in Manufactures; Interchangeable Mechanism; Water Supply of Cities; Milling and Flouring Industry; Water-power of the Southern Atlantic Coast; Water-power of the Northwest; Water-power of the Missouri River Basin; Pumps and Pumping Engines; Shop Tools and Production of Cereals in the United States; The Newspaper Press; Manufacture of Iron and Steel; Manufacture of Silk Goods; Debt and Taxation; Public Debts of the United States; Cattle and Sheep Industry; Social Statistics of Cities; Tobacco Culture; Production of the Precious Metals. It is expected that most, if not all, of the reports named will be ready some time in December of this year.

It was with regret that the resignation of Superintendent Walker was accepted, although tendered at a time when the work of the census was practically ended. Faithful and capable in the discharge of his duties, he labored early and late to make the Tenth Census a model for accuracy and comprehensive statistical information. It is confidently believed that the result of his labors will be in every way worthy of his ripened experience, and add to his well-earned reputation as an accomplished scientist. His successor, Charles W. Seaton, who was the efficient chief clerk of the Bureau, brings to the work of completion all the earnestness of his old chief. His long training and thorough knowledge of statistical matters eminently fit him for the duties of his important office.

PENSIONS.

On the 30th of June, 1881, there were 268,830 pensioners on the rolls, classified as follows: Army invalids, 153,025; Army widows, children, and dependent relatives, 76,683; Navy invalids, 2,187; Navy widows, children, and dependent relatives, 2,008; soldiers and sailors of the war of 1812, 8,898; widows of solders and sailors of that war, 26,029.

During the year, 28,740 names were placed on the pension-roll; and 10,712 were dropped, making the increase for the year in the number of pensioners, 18,028.

The whole amount paid on account of pensions, was $49,723,147.52, of which, $23,628,176.61 was paid to pensioners whose names were placed on the roll during the year ending June 30, 1881, whose pensions, generally, extended back over a period of many years.

The average annual pension of the pensioners on the roll on the 30th of June, 1881, was $107.01. It would require $28,769,967.66 to pay, for one year, the pensioners on the roll at the end of the last fiscal year, at the rate they were then receiving.

Since the year 1861, 431,439 claims of invalid officers and soldiers for pension have been filed in the Pension Office, of which 190,250 have been allowed, and 289,240 claims of widows, children, and dependent relatives have been filed, of which 197,414 have been allowed.

In addition to the above, since the 14th of February, 1871, 34,548 claims of officers and soldiers of the war of 1812 have been filed, of which 25,585 have been allowed; and 41,305 claims of widows of officers and soldiers of that war have been filed, of which 31,863 have been allowed.

Since 1861 the sum of $506,345,044.21 has been paid to pensioners.

There are on file 319,748 unadjudicated claims for pension (exclusive of those made on account of service in the war of 1812), of which 50 per cent. were filed between July 1, 1879, and June 30, 1881.

The proportion of the whole number of cases which will be further prosecuted cannot at present be determined.

The Commissioner states that with the present force of the office the expenses will exceed the appropriation for the present year by $30,000. The condition of the business is such that the force should be retained. The recommendation of the Commissioner that an appropriation be made for the deficiency, and to enable the office to promote those who deserve higher compensation, is therefore concurred in.

The Commissioner recommends legislation to provide for the identification of Indian pensioners and to authorize payment to them by a pension agent in person, at some convenient point in the Indian Territory, and that the payments be made in money in place of drafts.

He also recommends legislation more definitely defining the circumstances under which the pensions of persons who are held as inmates of the Soldiers' Home for Disabled Volunteer Soldiers shall be paid to the Home, in order to obviate the contests which arise between the Home and the pensioners for the possession of the pension money, and also renews the recommendation of his predecessor that authority of law be given for the payment of the pensions of insane and imprisoned pensioners to their families.

Section 4707 Revised Statutes provides that the pension of the children of a soldier shall commence at the date of the remarriage of the widow. It often occurs that, through ignorance or design, the widow continues to draw the pension after her remarriage. Under these circumstances it was decided by my predecessor that the pension of the children should commence at the date to which the widow was paid. In order to have this clearly expressed in the law itself, it is recommended that section 4702 of the Revised Statutes be amended so as to provide for the commencement of the pension in such cases at the date to which the widow was paid.

It is also recommended that the cohabitation of the widow of a soldier with a man as man and wife, when no valid marriage contract exists, should be made a bar to the receipt of pension by her. As this has been the practice of the office, based on departmental decision, it should be made part of the law.

The Commissioner renews the recommendation of his predecessor, that the law fixing the date of the commencement of increase of pension at the date of the surgical examination establishing the right to increase be repealed, and that authority be given for the readjustment in certain cases of rates of pension which were allowed.

The Commissioner gives the opinion that the change in the law relative to fees of attorneys in pension claims, made by the act of June 20, 1878, was disadvantageous alike to the interests of claimants and the government, and that the laws upon the subject in force prior to June 20, 1878, should be re-enacted. Under existing law it is found that fees are taken in advance by persons who render no service to applicants.

It is believed that it is better for the interests of the government and claimants to have the fee dependent upon the successful prosecution of the claim, and that the payment be secured to the attorney from the pension allowed. The successful prosecution of claims for pension, so long after the close of the war, requires more labor than is compensated by a fee of $10. I concur in the view of the Commissioner that a law allowing more liberal compensation to attorneys, to be paid from the pension when allowed, be enacted.

The secret investigation of pension claims by special agents operating at the residence of claimants has been abolished by the Commissioner and open investigation substituted, without, in his opinion, detriment to the interests of the government.

Under the authority of a law passed at the last session of Congress he has extended this method of investigation to a larger proportion of cases than heretofore.

He recommends that provision be made by Congress for the employment of a larger number of examiners upon this work, at a compensation of $1,400 per annum, and $4 per diem, and necessary traveling expenses, and that provision be made for the payment of the expenses of the applicant when required to accompany the special examiner, and also for the compelling of the attendance of witnesses and for the payment of their expenses.

It is recommended in the report that the fee of examining surgeons be increased to $2 for each examination, and that provision be made for their expenses and a per diem allowance when they are required to examine, at their homes, pensioners who are unable to travel.   ·

The Commissioner states that under existing laws the compensation of pension agents averages about $2,500, and that this amount is altogether disproportionate to their labors and responsibilities. He recommends that provision be made for an increase of their compensation, and that they be required to aid in the detection of fraudulent pension claims.

The Commissioner calls attention to the necessity for more-definite legislation for the following purposes: to define by what officer commutation for artificial limbs shall be paid; to define the jurisdiction of the accounting officer of the Treasury in the matter of allowance made by the Commissioner of Pensions; to give authority to grant pensions in certain cases to soldiers who left the service without a discharge; and to give authority to fix dates for the commencement of pensions, upon the presumption of a soldier's death, when proof of the fact and date cannot be obtained.

In the sundry civil bill, approved March 3, 1881, provision was made for the purchase of a suitable site, in the city of Washington, for the erection of a fire-proof building for the use of the Pension Office; and $250,000 was appropriated for the purpose. The purchase of the site and the approval of the plans for the building were placed under the supervision of the Secretary of War, Secretary of the Interior, and Quartermaster-General of the Army. While it is believed to have been the intention of Congress to provide in the sum named for the erection of the building, the wording of the act precluded such construction, and it was therefore deemed proper to defer action until the defect could be cured by additional legislation on the subject.

PATENT OFFICE.

The report of the Commissioner of Patents shows an increase of business for the year ending June 30, 1881. The number of applications for patents was 22,932, an increase of 1,942 over the previous year. Applications for designs, 585; reissues, 588; caveats 2,342; trade-mark, 464; appeals, 771; disclaimers, 18; labels, 337.

The number of patents granted, including re-issues and designs, was 15,175, an increase over the former year of 1,526.

Number of trade-marks registered was 462; labels registered, 181; patents withheld for non payment of final fee, 1,439; patents expired, 4,272.

The total receipts of the office was $789,895.52, an increase over the previous year of $59,348.40.

The aggregate of appropriations for the office, including a deficiency of $8,429.06, was $607,299.06. Amount expended for printing, binding, &c., out of the appropriation for printing and binding for Department of the Interior, $142,432.47. Total expenditure on account of Patent Office, $749,731.53. Total receipts in excess of all expenditures for the year ending June 30, 1881, $40,163.99.

On account of the increase in the business of his office the Commissioner asks for an increase in the appropriation for the next fiscal year. He submits for salaries of officers and employés $518,820, an increase of $37,950; for publication of the Official Gazette, $29,000, an increase of $6,000; for photolithographing, $45,000, an increase of $10,000; for reproducing burnt and exhausted copies of drawings, including pay of temporary draughtsmen, $45,000, an increase of $10,000.

Under the law providing for the abridgment of patents, $10,000 were allowed. Work has been commenced in accordance with the plan laid down. It includes a brief statement of the invention patented, together with the claims of the inventor, and illustration of the device. For the continuation of this work the Commissioner asks for $50,000. This will provide for the abridgment of 15,000 patents, and the publication of an edition of 10,000 copies. The Commissioner urges the necessity of this abridgment, and is of opinion that the sale of copies will cover the expense of making the same.

An appropriation is also asked of $6,000 for the completion of the illustrations for the Patent Office Report of 1870. With the publication of this work the reports of the office up to the present time will be completed.

A deficiency of $722.15 for the publication of the Official Gazette during the last fiscal year and $1,000 for the current year are also submitted; likewise an estimated deficiency for the present year of $9,000 for photolithographing or otherwise producing copies of the weekly issues of drawings of patents, designs, and trade-marks.

The necessity for additional room for the Patent Office is becoming more urgent every year. With the present limited space at the disposal of the office, rooms are overcrowded, and proper disposition cannot be made of the files and records which are yearly accumulating. It has been found absolutely necessary to occupy a portion of the newly constructed model hall in the west wing both for the clerical force and for the accommodation of the files. There can be no relief from this condition of affairs until additional room shall be provided elsewhere for some of the other bureaus whose necessities for more room are quite as urgent as those of the Patent Office.

The question, how far the Secretary of the Interior has controlling or appellate power over the Commissioner of Patents has been from time to time presented to the department by parties in interest, invoking the supervisory powers of the Secretary in cases decided by or pending before the Commissioner.

Secretary Chandler, under date of March 9, 1876, decided that no power was vested in him to review the decisions "honestly" made by the Commissioner of Patents in cases within his jurisdiction.

While claiming the right to exercise supervisory power over the administrative action of the Commissioner in the direction of executive duties, he expressly disclaimed all appellate jurisdiction over his judicial actions.

In this opinion he says:

I am unable to learn that any appellate jurisdiction has ever been exercised or claimed by any Secretary of State or of the Interior Department over the judicial action of the Commissioner of Patents since the creation of the office by act of July 4, 1836.

My immediate predecessor, Secretary Schurz, under dates of September 13, 1877, April 29, 1878, and June 25, 1879, concurred substantially in this opinion.

In the opinion rendered September 13, 1877, my predecessor, while holding that he had no right to examine into the merits of an application for a patent or to review the judicial action had thereon, used the following language:

I think it is quite clear that the supervision and direction with which the Secretary of the Interior is charged means something more than an approval of the act of the Commissioner of Patents. The responsibility of seeing that the work is properly done by the Commissioner of Patents is with the Secretary of the Interior. This includes negative as well as affirmative acts.

The Commissioner of Patents is to "superintend or perform all duties respecting the granting and issuing of patents," but these duties are to be performed under the direction of the Secretary of the Interior.

If the Commissioner neglects or refuses to perform any duty required by law to be performed by him under the direction of the Secretary of the Interior or performs a ministerial or administrative duty improperly, I am of the opinion that the Secretary of the Interior, by virtue of his supervisory power, may direct him in its performance. To be charged with the responsibility of the supervision and direction of any kind of work or business by law, and not be able to require that it shall be in accordance with the law would be anomalous indeed.

There being such a shadowy line of distinction between what might be properly adjudged as ministerial and judicial acts on the part of the Commissioner, the one being oftentimes essential to give expression and force to the other, I considered it my duty when the question was again brought before the department for its decision to refer the whole subject to the Attorney-General for his opinion thereon.

Under date of August 20, 1881, the Attorney-General rendered an opinion differing widely from the conclusions of my predecessors. He says:

I think the key to the whole question is found in sections 441 and 481 of the Revised Statutes. By the former "the Secretary of the Interior is charged with the supervision of the public business relating to (*inter alia*) patents for inventions"; and by the latter it is provided that "the Commissioner of Patents, under the direction of the Secretary of the Interior, shall superintend or perform *all* duties respecting the granting and issuing of patents directed by law." To my mind every section imposing a duty or conferring a power on the Commissioner of Patents should be read as if the words "under the direction of the Secretary of the Interior" were inserted.

It is not necessary to the validity of all acts of the Commissioner that the direction of the Secretary should be expressed. That will always be presumed except in the cases which require his express approval, to wit, the adoption of regulations (sec. 483 R. S.), the refusal to recognize a person as patent agent (sec. 487), and the actual granting of a patent (sec. 4883). The latter section requires the patent to be signed by the Secretary of the Interior, while the name of the Commissioner appears only by way of counter-signature. Lexicographers unite in defining countersign to mean " to sign what has already been signed by a superior, to authenticate by an additional signature."

This distinction between the two officers palpably means that the Secretary's signature is not for mere purpose of authentication. It would be absurd in face of sections 441, 481, and 4883 to say that the act of the Secretary in issuing the patent is purely ministerial, the act of a clerk of a court registering the decree delivered by some tribunal. I find no clause or section relieving the Commissioner from the directing powers of the Secretary, and I am irresistibly led to the conclusion that the final discretion in all matters relating to the granting of patents is lodged in the Secretary of the Interior.

While concurring in this decision it is proper to add that its adoption will necessitate some radical changes in the practice of the office. Sections 4909, 4910, and 4911 of the Revised Statutes provide for appeal in uncontested cases from the primary examiners to the examiners-in-chief; from the examiners-in-chief to the Commissioner; and from the Commissioner to the Supreme Court of the District of Columbia, and section 4934 provides for the fees to be paid on appeal to the examiners-in-chief, and to the Commissioner. There should be no right of appeal to the Secretary in uncontested cases so long as the Supreme Court of the District has appellate jurisdiction, and unless the present laws are wholly remodeled I respectfully recommend that this jurisdiction be made exclusive by distinct enactment. Unless Congress, by proper legislation, shall restrict the supervisory power of the Secretary to acts purely administrative on the part of the Commissioner, provision should be made in the law authorizing a fee for an appeal from the Commissioner to the Secretary; but, if so restricted, exclusive jurisdiction to hear appeals in interference cases as well as in uncontested cases should be conferred on the courts.

The labor entailed upon the Secretary's office consequent upon the decision of the Attorney-General will necessitate an increase of clerical force. This must also be provided, and will form the subject of a subsequent communication to Congress.

The Commissioner of Patents has called my attention to what appears to be an injustice upon the public, sanctioned by law. Innocent purchasers of patented articles and devices exposed for sale in open market occasionally find themselves prosecuted for infringement. It is sometimes determined, as construed by the courts, that two patents have been issued to different parties for the same invention. One of these must therefore be regarded as void, yet both may have placed their patented articles upon the market in good faith and found ready purchasers who never questioned their liability under the law. Yet the purchasers of the articles or devices manufactured and sold by the patentee of the patent declared void, after the decision of the court, are liable to a requirement to pay royalty to the successful patentee, although it may be shown that the purchase was made in ignorance of the decision and in perfect good faith.

This is wrong, and in many cases tends to grievous hardship. It should be remedied by proper legislation exempting innocent purchasers in open market from any liability for the use of such patented articles or devices.

EDUCATION.

The Commissioner of Education reports an increased amount of work done by his office. During the year the annual report, seven circulars of information, and seven bulletins have been issued. Other circulars are being prepared. Among the subjects that will be presented in them are normal schools, city systems, the care of the eye and ear, and the condition of education in France. The documents which have been distributed numbered about 131,000, or nearly twice as many as were issued last year. For the purpose of obtaining statistics for the annual reports 8.093 blank lists of questions have been sent out; and similar forms have been issued for the purpose of obtaining material for other publications. The letters written number 4,190. Many of them furnish statistics and facts to educational writers and school officials, the result of extensive research and patient labor. About 4,000 letters and 2,549 documents have been received. About 1,000 volumes and 1,200 pamphlets have been added to the library. The card catalogue, which has been in preparation, is now nearly completed, and is already of service in rendering available the contents of the library.

The Commissioner is of opinion that in order to meet the multiplying demands for educational information, an increase of clerical force is required. He states that the present employés are assigned duties which demand their full time and strength, and until additional clerks are provided the choice foreign works in the library cannot be catalogued, the progress of education abroad cannot be watched as closely as desirable, and other branches of educational work must of necessity receive less attention than their importance demands. He reports the progress of education during the year as substantial and satisfactory. New Kindergarten have been opened, and the principles of this system more largely introduced into primary schools. The importance of wisely directing the mind in its earlier efforts to acquire knowledge is being better understood. Proof of this is found in active measures taken for the improvement of rural and elementary schools and in efforts to provide normal training for all who intend to teach. Recently established chairs of pedagogy and normal classes in leading universities and colleges are giving correct ideas of the teachers' work to those who are being liberally educated; and the increase of normal schools and teachers' institutes has made the facilities for special training more accessible to the rank and file of the teaching force. Especially is this the case in the South. The income of the Peabody fund is now devoted to the education of teachers for that section. Through its aid Florida has the benefit of an efficient normal school; and the schools of Arkansas, North Carolina, and Texas have been enabled to offer greater advantages to the teachers of those States.

A disposition is manifest on the part of many colleges to make the standards of admission more uniform. Elective and optional studies are growing in favor, and scientific and special courses are more frequently selected. Schools for industrial training have been heartily supported. The colleges of agriculture and mechanic arts are fulfilling more faithfully the requirements of the law of July 2, 1862, by which grants of land were made to the several States for the establishment of such institutions. Professional schools are exercising more care in admitting students and conferring degrees.

The Commissioner recommends that the superintendents of public instruction in the Territories be appointed by the President; that the net proceeds of the sale of public lands be devoted to educational purposes and divided among the several States and Territories in proportion to their illiterate population, and that all facts necessary to the information of Congress upon the disposal of grants made by it for educational purposes, and upon the condition of education in the Territories and the District of Columbia, be presented through his office.

THE UNITED STATES GEOLOGICAL SURVEY.

The report of the Director of the United States Geological Survey gives an account of the work of the organization during the second year of its existence. The first director, Clarence King, resigned his office in

in the communication to the public of the initial work of the new organization, but regards it as in some sense unavoidable.

It is anticipated that the majority of the monographs announced in the last annual report as in preparation will be offered for publication during the approaching winter.

In the department of economic geology the alliance of the survey with the Tenth Census, which was described in the last annual report, has been continued, and the chief work of the corps consisted in the gathering and discussion of the statistics of the mineral resources of the country. Examinations in the field by experts of the Census under the direction of the geological survey were continued through the summer of 1880 and did not entirely cease before the close of the fiscal year. The complementary office work, which consisted partly of the combination and tabulation of the statistics, but chiefly of the analysis of the ore samples gathered, which has been conducted upon a large scale, was in an advanced stage at the close of the fiscal year, but no final report was ready for publication.

The survey has at the same time carried forward independently two economic investigations of importance; the first, that of the Comstock Lode, Nevada; the second, that of the mines of Leadville, Colo. The field examinations in each district were completed in the year 1880, and assistants who conducted them have since been engaged in accessory investigations in the laboratory and in the preparation of their reports. The report on the mines of Leadville will be comprised in a single volume; that upon the Comstock Lode will embody the work of a larger corps, and will fill three volumes. It will include a history of the Comstock Mines, a report on the geology of the lode, and a report on the mechanical appliances used in mining and milling.

I beg leave to call the especial attention of Congress to the remarks made by the Director in regard to the expansion and extension of the work of the survey. He announces that the organization is now complete, and that—

Work so presses upon it in all its departments that the restrictions imposed by the limited amount of its appropriations are felt to greatly impair its usefulness. As at present endowed, it is unable to carry on work simultaneously in the several districts where important mining industries are prosecuted, and at the same time maintain such a standard of excellence as shall give a true and permanent value to its results.

He urges also with cogency the extension of the domain of the survey so as to include the entire area of the United States, arguing that in that way only can the most valuable contributions be made to geological science, pure and applied.

It is not local work which demands the attention or should command the endowment of the nation. The study of the individual mine may safely be intrusted to the interest of the mine owner, and the study of the structure of a restricted locality may be left to the zeal and enterprise of the private geologist; but the higher walks of science and all the great economic interests of the country are replete with problems which can only be comprehended through the broad view, and which for the most part involve expenditures which are beyond the means of the private individual. The best means of combining the various minerals which go to the production of such a staple as iron, for example, cannot be ascertained by the examination of a single State, nor by the collation of such information as may fall within the purview of a single individual, but may be reached by the systematic collaboration which a great survey only can provide.

The report is accompanied by a series of scientific papers which are elaborately illustrated. Among them are abstracts or *résumés* giving a general account of the scientific results achieved by the survey—results which will receive a fuller presentation in its quarto publications; and there are also a number of essays on special topics associated with the general work.

ENTOMOLOGICAL COMMISSION.

The Commission has, during the year, published its second report, which is a fully illustrated volume of over 400 pages, and in great demand. It is also supplementary to the first report, which treated of the destruction of the young or unwinged locusts as they hatch out in the more fertile portions of the trans-Mississippi country. The second report deals with the problem of preventing the winged swarms from increasing and devastating the country.

With the assistance of a large map, in six sections, so arranged that they may be put together on canvas, or cloth, and hung up in school-rooms or other public buildings, the surface characteristics of plains, mountains, plateaus, and basins are considered, especially from the point of view of the relative areas in which the vegetation is susceptible of being burned over.

The Commissioner has also published Bulletin No. 6, by Professor Riley, being a general index to the Entomological Reports of Missouri, which are out of print and difficult to obtain, and which contain much original matter, in reference to the insects, of national importance, which the Commission has been charged with studying. Bulletin No. 7 on forest tree insects, by Dr. Packard, is going through the press; the third report is being prepared, and a final report on the cotton-worm is nearly ready for the printer.

The following record of field work will show how extended and important have been the operations during the year. Utah and Montana were visited by Dr. Packard and an assistant, Mr. Lawrence Bruner. The result of the summer's work in the Western Territories, showed that during the past season locusts were no more abundant and destructive than in Dakota, and portions of Minnesota and adjacent regions, including Nebraska and Kansas, the insect being few in numbers anywhere. Hence, it was predicted that during 1881 there would be no swarms anywhere in the Western Territories large enough to cause extensive damage.

During the summer of 1880, Mr. Thomas made an extensive visit through the Northwest for the purpose of making observations with regard to the locusts, gathering all additional facts possible in reference to their past history and depredations and all that could be ascertained as to the probability of their proving disastrous during that or the present season of 1881. On his return he communicated to Governor Pillsbury, of Minnesota, the result of his operations, which appears in the second report.

Prof. J. G. Lemmon, of Oakland, Cal., was engaged to visit various sections in Western Utah, Nevada, and California, where the locusts were present in injurious numbers during the past season. Prof. Samuel Aughey, of Nebraska, was also engaged to study the diseases of insects, especially those arising from fungus growths.

Professor Riley has had charge of the southern part of the work on insects affecting the cotton plant. With a corps of capable assistants he organized the investigation, and it is believed has gathered valuable information in that direction.

The results of this work, which are being embodied in a revised edition, ordered by Congress, of the work on the cotton-worm, are of the highest practical value, as not only have the principles been established which should guide the planter in his warfare with his worst enemies, but important mechanical discoveries have been made which cheapen and simplify the instruments and appliances of warfare.

By the action of the last Congress, the Entomological Commission has been transferred from this Department to the Department of Agriculture, where it more properly belongs. The Commissioners are entitled to credit for the valuable work produced, and for the faithful manner in which they performed their duties.

YELLOWSTONE NATIONAL PARK.

The Superintendent of the Yellowstone National Park reports successful prosecution of improvements during the past season. Roads damaged by the severe winter and spring floods were repaired, new roads were built, connecting leading points of interest, and the action of the geysers carefully watched and noted. His report will contain a record of the temperature, winds, rainfall, and a daily record of the geysers, showing the maximum and minimum of their eruptive elevation. The number of tourists visiting the park is reported as largely in excess of that of any previous year.

REDWOOD AND MAMMOTH TREES.

I renew the recommendation of my predecessor that Congress, by appropriate legislation, authorize the President to withdraw from sale or other disposition an area at least equal to two townships in the northern coast range and an equal area in the southern part of California, containing the best specimens of the Redwood (*Sequoia sempervirens*).

and the mammoth trees (*Sequoia gigantea*). These trees are without doubt the most magnificent specimens of a species now almost extinct. Towering to a height of from 350 to 400 feet, and with an estimated age of upwards of a thousand years, they may justly be ranked as among the greatest of natural curiosities. Men of science, in both Europe and America, have petitioned for the protection of these relics of the primeval forests. Unless the government, at an early day, intervenes for their protection and preservation, they will be entirely destroyed. I, therefore, earnestly commend the subject to the attention of Congress.

CAPITOL BUILDING AND GROUNDS.

The Architect of the Capitol reports the near completion of the elevator in the south end of the east corridor.

The gallery of the old hall of Representatives, the rooms connected with it, and the rooms in the loft of the northern part of the central building have been made substantially fire-proof. The body of the Senate chamber, together with rooms and corridors, has been painted and regilded. The iron panels have been taken from the ceiling of the Senate chamber and glass used instead, and additional sky-lights have been placed in the roof.

The apparatus for heating and ventilating the Hall of Representatives has worked in a satisfactory manner and been productive of good results.

The dynamo-electric machines continue to give satisfaction in lighting the gas of the Capitol. Experiments have been made with the electric light with a view of lighting the hall, but as yet no satisfactory result has been obtained. The incandescent system costs about double that of gas, while those cheaper than gas must be rejected because of their unsteady lights.

The architect reports progress made in the improvement of the grounds.

The intense severity of last winter injured a number of choice plants and trees, and caused some damage to the roads and pavements.

The 15 per cent. reserved for three years on paving contracts finished in 1877 has been paid, the pavements having been repaired as stipulated.

The work on the extension of the court-house has progressed in a satisfactory manner. The severe storm of June 27 unroofed a portion of the old building. It being necessary that the damage should at once be repaired, in order to protect valuable property and official records, a deficiency was incurred amounting to $1,830.70, which should be provided for at the next session of Congress.

The extension to the Government Printing Office has been pushed forward as rapidly as possible, and its completion is assured at an early day.

A brick stable, with accommodation for twenty horses, wagons, forage, &c., has been erected in a substantial manner.

Plans have been made, in accordance with the requirements of the law, for five school buildings. These have been approved by the trustees, and information received by the architect that they are in process of erection.

The appropriations for the fiscal year ending June 30, 1881, were as follows:

For Capitol extension	$57,000 00
For Senate heating apparatus	10,000 00
For House of Representatives heating apparatus	1,000 00
For lighting Capitol and grounds	32,000 00
For Capitol grounds	60,000 00
For retained percentages	6,246 72
For enlarging court-house	117,000 00

Accompanying the report is a table showing observations made by the chief engineer of the heating and ventilating department, House of Representatives, during the months of January and February, 1881. These observations relate specially to the movements of air, temperature of the same, relative humidity, velocity and direction of wind, amount of fresh air afforded each person per minute, and condition of the weather as indicated by barometrical observation.

HOSPITAL FOR THE INSANE.

The report of the board of visitors of this institution shows a satisfactory condition in its management during the year ending June 30, 1881.

The number of patients remaining in the hospital June 30, 1880, was 897, of which 691 were males and 206 females.

The number remaining June 30, 1881, was 925, made up of 700 males and 225 females.

During the year 223 were admitted, 161 being males and 62 females.

The number discharged, including deaths, was 195. Recovered, 72; improved, 36; unimproved, 6; died, 81.

Of the patients under treatment June 30, 1881, 448 were from the Army; 44 from the Navy; 10 from Marine Hospital Service, and 423 from civil life.

Of the 423 from civil life, 383 were indigent residents of the District of Columbia, 21 were indigent non-residents, and 2 were non-resident criminals.

Interesting tables accompanying the report show monthly changes of population, physical condition of those who died, duration of the mental disease of fatal cases, duration of disease on admission, nativity of patients, form of disease, complications, time of life when insanity developed, history of annual admissions, mean annual mortality and proportion of recoveries.

The general sanitary condition of the hospital has been good, exemption from disaster and epidemic diseases being specially noted.

The recently erected buildings for special classes have afforded needed relief and proven the wisdom of their erection. The money value of the farm and garden products was $21,389.49. In addition to this, there were consumed on the farm products estimated at $9,207.85.

The farm is reported as moderately remunerative, and is especially useful in affording the necessary exercise and employment for a large number of the inmates.

The estimates for next year are as follows:

For the support of the institution... $202,500
For general repairs and improvements 10,000
For special improvements 38,500
For erection of a distinct hospital building for the female insane............ 250,000

The appropriation asked for the support of the hospital includes clothing and treatment, and is based on an average support of 900 patients at $225 per year.

That for general repairs and improvements is regarded as necessary for the proper care of the buildings and grounds.

The special improvements for which an appropriation is asked include a supply of pure water, increased accommodation for hay, stock, and farm implements, a detached kitchen and cooking apparatus, with scullery, fire-walls between sections of building, and the erection of a mortuary building.

There is a vital necessity for the water-supply asked for. At present water is pumped from the Anacostia at a point where it ebbs and flows by the hospital grounds. As this supply is liable to be contaminated by the sewage of Washington, and is taken from a place in close proximity to the dumping-grounds of the dredging machines at work on our channel, it can readily be seen that it is unfit for the use of a great hospital, wherein pure water is as great a necessity as pure air. The water supply of Washington can be carried over the Anacostia through pipes and stored in reservoirs built for the purpose, and from thence pumped to the hospital. This should be done without delay, and to this end $25,000 is asked, to be made immediately available, out of the special improvement estimate.

The other items included in special improvement estimate are urgently required for the protection of public property and for the care and comfort of the insane, and should be provided for without delay.

The necessity for an additional building for the female insane has long been recognized, and I fully concur in the recommendation of my predecessor on this subject. The importance of making distinct provision for the female insane cannot be too strongly urged. The experience of some of the leading institutions of the country has proven that the separation of the sexes affords decided advantage and leads to more positive improvement in their care and treatment.

Aside from the benefits growing out of the separation of the sexes, the present overcrowded condition of the hospital demands additional room. The space now available is barely sufficient to afford comfortable accommodations for the male patients now under treatment. The proposed building should be of sufficient size to accommodate at least 400 females, should be built of brick, thoroughly fire-proof, and should embody the best ideas of modern science in regard to comfort and cure of the insane. In order that this improvement may be completed with as little delay as possible, I concur in the recommendation of the Board of Visitors, that $100,000 of the $250,000 required be appropriated for the year ending June 30, 1883, and that it be made immediately available.

To the efficient services and good management of the superintendent, Dr. W. W. Godding, the government is largely indebted for the present excellent condition of the hospital. In his report he submits an itemized account of the receipts and expenditures for the fiscal year ending June 30, 1881. The total expenditures reported were $226,146.76, made up as follows: Subsistence, $77,314.73; house-furnishing, fuel, lights, &c., $29,237.64; dry goods, clothing, books and stationery, &c., $15,567.26; medical supplies, &c., $4,040.23; farm, garden, and stable, $10,192.58; repairs and improvements, $18,676.31; salaries and wages, $71,118.01. Total receipts for board of patients, $53,311.65.

FREEDMEN'S HOSPITAL.

The report of the surgeon in charge shows that on the 30th of June, 1880, the number of patients remaining in hospital was 228. Of this number, 33 were white and 195 colored.

The number remaining June 30, 1881, was 225; 35 white and 190 colored. During the year 841 were admitted, 51 were born, and 40 were transients. Of this number, 297 were white and 595 colored.

During the same period 776 were discharged, 40 of whom were transients needing no treatment; 157 died; 2 still-born.

Of those discharged, 660 were reported cured and 76 relieved.

A dispensary has been supported during the year for the benefit of the poor; 2,134 names have been entered as out-patients, and over 3,000 prescriptions were put up for them.

The report is accompanied with tables showing the nativity of the patients admitted, the diseases treated, the number of cases of each disease resulting fatally, and the more important surgical operations performed.

The aggregate number of days of support afforded to patients during the year was 88,481. Exclusive of rent, the cost of each patient for subsistence, medicines, nursing, and partial clothing was less than 43 cents per day.

The report concludes with a suggestion that the name of the hospital be changed, the patients now admitted being radically different in character from those for whom it was originally established.

The estimates for the next fiscal year are for $50,500.

INSTITUTION FOR THE DEAF AND DUMB.

One hundred and fourteen pupils have received instruction during the year. Sixty-eight of them, representing twenty-one States and the Federal District, have been connected with the collegiate department, and forty-six with the primary department.

Four deaths have occurred among the students and pupils, two resulting from sickness and two from accident. The general health of the institution has, however, been good.

The governing board has lost three members by death, viz, Hon. William Stickney, secretary; George W. Riggs, esq., treasurer, and Henry D. Cook, a director.

The gymnasium has been completed and fitted up at a cost of about $14,600. The building contains a bowling alley, a swimming pool, and a hall for gymnastic exercises.

The apparatus was prepared and set up under the direction of Dr. D. A. Sargent, director of the Harvard University Gymnasium.

The total receipts of the institution for the year ending June 30, 1881, were $66,571.99. Of this amount $53,500 was received from the United States Treasury for support of institution, $7,500 from same source for buildings and grounds, and $5,571.99 from miscellaneous sources.

The total expenditures amounted to $65,425.35, leaving balance on hand July 1, 1881, of $1,146.64.

The estimates submitted for the year ending June 30, 1883, are: For support of the institution, $55,000; for farm barn, two dwelling-houses for professors, and inclosure and improvement of grounds, $15,000. Total for next year, $70,000.

LAWLESSNESS IN NEW MEXICO AND ARIZONA.

For some time past there have been complaints of lawlessness in the Territories of Arizona and New Mexico which the authorities of those Territories have been unable to repress.

Bands of robbers have operated there and in the adjoining parts of Mexico upon an extensive scale. Complaints of the depredations committed by them have been received from the Government of Mexico, through the Department of State. This department has information of one organized band of robbers numbering one hundred and twenty men in Arizona, who are robbing the citizens of Mexico and the United States of horses and cattle, and disposing of the same or converting them to their own use. Owing to the sparseness of the population, the local authorities are unable to cope with such combinations. The use of United States troops to assist in enforcing the laws is forbidden by the law relating to the use of any part of the army as a *posse comitatus.* The governors of those Territories have represented to this department that if the United States military authorities were free to assist in repressing the lawlessness which prevails there, and would so assist, the lives and property of the citizens would be more secure, the advancement of the interests of the people would be promoted, and causes which threaten to disturb the peace between the United States and Mexico would be removed. I have therefore to recommend that the law prohibiting the use of the army as a *posse comitatus* to assist in the execution of the laws be repealed so far as it applies to the Territories of Arizona and New Mexico.

RECONSTRUCTION OF THE DEPARTMENT BUILDING.

The reconstruction of the building made necessary by the great fire of 1877 is now fully completed. The new halls afford a third more room than the old ones and are a decided improvement in point of architectural beauty.

The north hall is being fitted up with iron model cases, some of which are already completed and occupied. The west hall being needed for clerical purposes, no cases will be, for the present, placed therein. For this reason about $45,000 of the $80,000 appropriated for the completion of the model cases will remain unexpended. I recommend that authority be granted to use this amount for the purpose of aiding in the construction of a fire-proof roof over the south and east wings, or, if it be deemed more advisable, in the reconstruction of the south hall upon the plan adopted in the north and west halls.

The roof in question is little better than a standing invitation for another fire. It is constructed of wood, covered with copper roofing, and in many places is already charred by close contact with the defective flues which it covers. There can be no question as the necessity of immediately replacing such a dangerous roof with one substantially fire-proof.

In referring to this subject my predecessor, in his last annual report, said:

It is little better than a tinder-box, and, covering imperfect and badly constructed flues, may at any time endanger the safety of the building. The changes necessary to construct a fire-proof roof and remedy the evils growing out of a faulty plan, would be so radical and expensive that I deem it in the interest of public economy to recommend the reconstruction of both wings on the plan adopted in the rebuilding of the north and west halls.

I commend this subject to the attention of Congress, and earnestly hope that ample provision may be made to protect this building against all possible danger from fire.

While not prepared to make any definite recommendation as to how far the reconstruction should go, whether it should be confined to a fire-proof roof, or extend to the body of the halls, I desire to emphasize my belief that the building is not safe and cannot be made so until the roof covering the south and west wings is replaced by one of fire-proof construction.

A careful inspection of the walls and arches and general arrangement of the flues should be authorized by a board of experts and the plan of reconstruction agreed upon by them should be adopted.

ADDITIONAL ROOM NEEDED.

The necessity for additional room to accommodate the growing wants of the Interior Department has from time to time been brought to the attention of Congress. Each year adds to the necessity. Several important offices connected with the department, namely, the Pension, Census, Bureau of Education, Office of the Geological Survey, cannot be accommodated in the present building, and to the detriment of the public interests and an expense of $45,960 a year are forced to find room elsewhere. The bureaus within the building are cramped for room, the hall-ways in many instances being used for cases to contain the files of the office. Rooms are overcrowded, endangering the health of employés and seriously inconveniencing the transaction of business. With the increase of work and the continued accumulation of the files of the department, the public business must soon be greatly embarrassed unless the necessary room is provided. So great has been the pressure for more room that the occupation of the west Model Hall, lately reconstructed, has been resorted to as a temporary expedient on the part of the Patent and Land offices. As this hall was intended for the exhibition of models, its conversion into rooms for a clerical force has been attended with some difficulties. While it answers the temporary purpose for which it is used, its occupation for office room should be tolerated only as a matter of absolute necessity, and until such time as proper quarters can be provided elsewhere.

A new building should be erected without delay for the use of the Interior Department. It should be large enough to accommodate, in connection with the present building, all of the bureaus of the department. The erection of a substantial brick structure, thoroughly fire-proof, situated in an eligible locality, should, in my opinion, be authorized without delay.

SAMUEL J. KIRKWOOD,
Secretary of the Interior.

The PRESIDENT.

PAPERS

REPORT OF THE SECRETARY OF THE INTERIOR.

REPORT OF THE COMMISSIONER OF THE GENERAL LAND OFFICE.

DEPARTMENT OF THE INTERIOR,
GENERAL LAND OFFICE,
October 25, 1881.

SIR: I have the honor to submit the following synopsis of the annual report of this office for the fiscal year ending with June 30, 1881, viz:

Abstract of operations under the laws relating to the survey and disposal of public and Indian lands during the fiscal year ending with June 30, 1881.

	Acres.
Cash sales:	
Private entries	666,229.11
Public sales	2,279.40
Timber and stone lands	42,987.92
Pre-emption entries	721,146.26
Desert lands	104,568.03
Mineral lands	27,189.68
Coal lands	4,975.56
Excesses	12,332.06
Abandoned military reservations	1,910.21
Total	1,587,617.24
Homestead entries	5,022,100.69
Timber culture entries	1,763,799.35
Locations with military bounty land warrants issued under acts of 1847, 1850, 1852, and 1855	55,682.36
Agricultural college scrip locations	360.00
Supreme court scrip locations	28,253.74
Valentine scrip locations	322.15
Sioux half-breed scrip locations	2,519.27
Chippewa half-breed scrip locations	866.60
Locations with Porterfield scrip	15.86
Lands certified or patented for railroad purposes to States:	
Alabama	363.23
Iowa	72,391.56
Minnesota	483,466.63
Kansas	281,277.26
To corporations:	
Pacific railroads	211,992.04
State selections, approved for—	
School indemnity	15,880.00
Internal improvements	1,780.00
Agricultural colleges	1,370.45
Seminaries	3,964.14
Donation claims	18,237.06
Approved to States as swamp	569,001.18
Total	10,126,176.25

654

Indian lands, sales of, during the fiscal year of 1881:	Acres.	Acres.
Osage ceded	4,629.21	
Osage trust and diminished reserve	613,951.05	
Kansas trust	25,736.53	
Kansas trust and diminished reserve	18,971.86	
Pawnee	15,219.55	
Sioux	50,299.64	
Sac and Fox	57.40	
Cherokee strip	20,086.12	
Otoe and Missouria	16,036.87	
Cherokee school	240.57	
		765,221.80

Which added to the sales of public lands makes a grand total of 10,893,397.05

Cash receipts:	
From sales of public lands	$3,534,550 98
*From sales of Indian lands	1,006,691 63
Homestead fees and commissions	555,766 16
Timber culture fees and commissions	154,739 35
Fees on military bounty land warrant locations	1,484 00
Fees on locations with different classes of scrip	17 00
Fees in pre-emption and other filings	59,366 00
Fees in mining applications and protests	28,310 00
Fees on timber land entries	3,330 00
Fees for reducing testimony to writing, by local officers	47,625 24
Fees on railroad selections	3,581 27
Fees on state selections	4,199 63
Fees on donation claims	1,415 00
Fees for transcripts, furnished by the General Land Office, during the fiscal year of 1881	6,727 90
Total	5,408,804.16

SURVEYS.

	Acres.
Total area of the land States and Territories	1,814,788,922
Surveyed up to June 30, 1880	752,557,194
Surveyed but not heretofore reported	10,561,775
Surveyed during the fiscal year ending with the 30th of June, 1881	21,788,011
	784,906,980
Leaving	1,029,881,942

acres of public and Indian lands yet to be surveyed, inclusive of private land claims surveyed at the close of the fiscal year ending with the 30th of June, 1881.

The surveys during the past fiscal year show an increase of 6,058,759 acres over those executed during previous year. This extraordinary showing is mainly attributable to the great demand for surveys under the deposit system, and to which reference is hereinafter made.

The sales of public lands as compared with those of the previous fiscal year, show a decrease of 3,898,974.60 acres, while the aggregate of cash receipts, under various heads, is greater by $2,508,642.56.

During the year there were received 83,864 letters, and 68,427 were written and recorded, covering 60,325 pages of record books, and during the same period there were issued and transmitted 56,979 patents. This amount embraces patents for private land claims, mining claims, lands granted for railroad purposes, swamp lands, Indian lands, and for lands sold under the pre-emption and homestead laws.

There were also audited, adjusted, and reported to the First Comptroller of the Treasury 2,800 accounts, embracing accounts of surveyors

* This money is deposited by the receivers of public moneys in the United States Treasury, to the credit of the Indian funds, for the benefit of the Indians, under treaty stipulations.

general, deputy surveyors, registers and receivers, special agents, &c., covering 13,350 pages of record.

In addition to the clerical work performed in the several divisions of the office, the following is a list of papers accompanying the annual report.

1. Statement showing the number of acres called for by military bounty land warrants located in the several land States and Territories.

2. Decision rendered by the Secretary of the Interior in regard to the question of jurisdiction over the assignments of warrants after their issue and delivery by the Commissioner of Pensions.

3. Condition of business relating to revolutionary bounty land scrip—Virginia military district in Ohio—warrants under act of July 27, 1842, and Porterfield warrants.

4. Tabular statement showing condition of bounty land business since the commencement of operations to the close of the fiscal year last past.

5. Decisions and rulings relating to desert lands.

6. Decisions and rulings under the timber culture acts.

7. Decisions and rulings under the homestead laws.

8. Withdrawal of lands in the States of Wisconsin and Minnesota for reservoir purposes.

9. Condition of military reservations—Fort Ripley, Dalles, Fort Kearney, and Fort Harker.

10. Indian lands; Osage trust and diminished reserve lands; absentee Shawnee lands.

11. Statement showing disposal of Indian lands in Kansas.

12. Indian reservations: Pawnee, in Nebraska; Sac and Fox and Otoe and Missouria Reservations.

13. Decisions relating to private land claims in California, New Mexico, and Missouri.

14. Construction of act of June 15, 1880, affecting heirs or legal representatives of Israel Dodge, deceased.

15. Table showing the apportionment to the several surveying districts of the sum of $300,000, appropriated for the survey of public lands by act of Congress approved June 16, 1880.

16. Abstract of surveying operations in the sixteen surveying districts under the supervision of the respective surveyors general.

17. Table exhibiting the comparative progress of surveys, number of surveying districts, land districts, cost of surveys, number of acres surveyed, and number of acres disposed of during the five years ending with June 30, 1881.

18. Surveys under the deposit system, authorized by sections 2401, 2402, and 2403, United States Revised Statutes.

19. Survey and subdivision of Red Cloud and Spotted Tail Indian Reservations in Dakota.

20. Military reservations declared reduced or enlarged during the fiscal year.

21. Lists of surveyors general and their residences.

22. Principal meridians and bases.

23. Tabular statement showing the areas of the land States and Territories; the extent of surveys of public and Indian lands; total area of land surveyed from the beginning of the surveying system, and the area remaining unsurveyed in each of the land States and Territories at the close of the fiscal year.

24. Estimates of appropriations required for surveying the public

lands and private land claims—for compensation of surveyors general and clerks in their offices, and for contingent expenses of surveyors general.

25. Decisions affecting railroad grants.

26. Status of the "Old Cherokee Indian Reservation" in Arkansas.

27. Statement exhibiting land concessions by acts of Congress to States and corporations for railroad and wagon road purposes from 1850 to June 30, 1881.

28. Statement showing what town sites have been patented since September 27, 1878.

29. Decisions affecting pre-emption rights.

30. Decisions relating to swamp lands and indemnity for swamp lands.

31. Tabular statements showing the quantity of land selected, approved, and patented to the several States as swamp.

32. Swamp land laws, regulations, and rulings.

33. Tabular statements showing operations under the laws governing the survey and·disposal of public lands and Indian lands, sales and receipts under various heads, with amount of fees and commissions derived therefrom, &c.

34: Estimates of appropriations required for the General Land Office and for local land offices.

35. List of mining claims patented during the fiscal year.

36. Recent decisions affecting rights under the mining laws of the United States.

37. Circular issued under act of January 22, 1880.

38. Construction of act of January 22, 1880.

39. Condition of business relating to depredations upon the public domain by the cutting and removing of timber therefrom.

40. List of local land offices.

41. Reports of United States surveyors general, numbered from A to P inclusive.

42. Historical and statistical table of the United States and Territories, showing the area of each in square miles and acres, the date of organization of Territories, date of admission of new States into the Union, number of acres surveyed and remaining unsurveyed, and the population of each State and Territory at the taking of the last census in 1880.

In all the land districts there is a large and legitimate demand for copies from the official records, and for copies or tracings of the maps and plats of survey, &c. As the country is settled and improved, values increase and interests multiply, the records of the local land offices are more frequently consulted, and such copies more largely required. Those who desire transcripts from the records are willing and desirous to pay for the same, but registers and receivers are precluded, under penalty of removal from office, from receiving fees or other rewards not authorized by law (see section 2242, Revised Statutes), and no authority of law exists for any fee for such copies except in consolidated land districts where, under section 2239, Revised Statutes, such fees are authorized to be charged by the land officers as are authorized by the tariff existing in the local courts of the district.

It has, until a comparatively recent date, undoubtedly been the general practice·of local officers to furnish such copies, receive pay for the same, and use the money in part at least to pay for the clerical labor made necessary by this work. The local officers justified themselves on the general ground that it was not by law made their duty to furnish such transcripts, &c., and hence it was no.infraction of law to perform.

42 Ah.

a legitimate act and receive pay for the same. This proceeding was clearly illegal, however, and led to abuses of considerable magnitude, upon discovery of which instructions were issued to all the local land officers definitively advising them what fees they were authorized to charge or receive, and forbidding the receipt of any other rewards under penalty of recommendation for dismissal from office.

The matter now is in this condition: there is a legitimate and public necessity for copies from the records and files of district land offices; there is no sufficient appropriation to pay for the clerical labor essential to prepare such copies, and the only way they can be had is by allowing outside parties to have access to the official records and make the copies themselves. This course is obviously unadvisable, and I have the honor to recommend that legislation be speedily had authorizing the preparation of copies by registers and receivers, and a fee for the same at the rate of 15 cents per 100 words and $2 for copies of township plats or diagrams, and that the receivers of the several land offices shall make returns of all moneys so received, and shall pay over the same in the manner now provided by law for other moneys received by them in their official capacity.

And, in view of the fact that the clerical labor necessary to be employed will be increased in proportion to the amount of said class of work, I further recommend as absolutely essential to the furnishing of such copies that all moneys received therefor be placed to the credit of the appropriation "for incidental expenses of the several land offices," and be available for clerk hire in said offices under authority of the Secretary of the Interior.

I would also recommend that the same provisions be extended to all consolidated land offices and substituted for those of section 2239, Revised Statutes.

In this connection I would call attention to sections 460 and 461, Revised Statutes, under which it is made my duty to furnish exemplifications of patents, or papers on file or of record in this office, to parties interested, upon payment of certain rates therein named. The labor thus involved is not expended upon the adjustment of entries—a work so much in arrears and so earnestly demanded by the public, who need their evidences of title at the earliest moment—but relates almost exclusively to patented claims, or to land which is in litigation in the courts; and the fees received for such copies are turned into the Treasury. It is thus apparent that a portion of the clerical labor which Congress provides is diverted from its contemplated channel, and engaged upon work which does not relate to the current disposition of any class of land claims.

For the year ending June 30, 1880, there were received and turned into the Treasury for such copies $7,043.05, and for the year ending June 30, 1881, $6,727.90.

I recommend legislation to the effect that the moneys so annually received be credited to the appropriation for clerical services in this office for the fiscal year in which they are received, and made available for the payment of the clerical labor necessary for the preparation of said copies. In this connection I would state that, owing to the difficult character of much of the copying done as aforesaid, and to the necessity of careful comparison with the original, the fees authorized to be charged are not estimated to be in excess of the actual cost of the clerical labor expended upon the preparation of exemplifications.

Section 2325, Revised Statutes, specifies the proceedings necessary to obtain a patent to mineral lands. It was held by this department that the application for such patent, which includes an allegation of compliance with law, must be sworn to by the owner of the claim. By act of January 22, 1880 (page 61, pamphlet edition, statutes of 1879–80), amendatory of sections 2304 and 2305, Revised Statutes, it was provided that the authorized agent of the claimant might make said affidavit when he was conversant with the facts sought to be established thereby and the claimant was not a resident of the land district wherein the claim was located. In view of the fact that a large proportion of the mining claims are managed by such agents, who are thereby better qualified to make the required affidavit than the owner, I would recommend that the duly authorized agent of the claimant, when conversant with the material facts, be allowed to make said affidavit in any case, and that legislation to that effect be had.

Under section 2401, 2402, and 2403, Revised Statutes, it is provided that when settlers in any township, not mineral or reserved, desire a survey of the same under authority of the surveyor general, they shall be entitled thereto, upon filing a written application therefor, and depositing a sum sufficient to pay for the survey and all expenses incident thereto; that said sums so deposited shall be placed to the credit of the proper appropriation for the surveying service, and that the amount so deposited by any such settlers may go in part payment for their lands situated in the township, the surveying of which is paid out of such deposits.

By act of March 3, 1879, amendatory of section 2403, Revised Statutes, the certificates issued for such deposits were made assignable by indorsement, and receivable in payment for pre-emption and homestead claims.

Since the passage of this act of 1879, the deposits for surveys have increased to an unprecedented extent, and numerous representations which are believed to be true have been made to this office, that lands of no present practical value and on which there are no settlers have been largely surveyed; that applications for surveys are fraudulently made by or through the instigation and management of deputy surveyors, who, for the purpose of securing the contract for making the survey, either themselves or through friends advance the money for deposit, thereafter sell and assign the certificates, and thus reimburse themselves and secure their profit from the surveying contracts.

The appropriation for surveys for the last fiscal year was $1,000,000. The amount of deposits for the same period, and which was placed to the credit of the said appropriation, was $1,804,166.47, and the amount of the certificates surrendered in payment of pre-emption and homestead claims for the same time was $1,346,109.26.

It is believed that the practical result of said act of March 3, 1879, has been to cause the survey of vast areas of lands of no present and perhaps of no prospective, value, and the surrender of tillable lands in payment for such surveys.

With the intent to secure as far as possible the following instructions under said law, I issued the following instructions to —

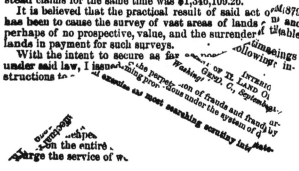

ments of applicants for survey, to satisfy themselves of the truth thereof, and unless found to be *bona fide* in every respect they shall not accept such applications nor furnish the estimates requested.

II. Believing that in a great many instances applications for survey, particularly in sections of country unfit for settlement, have been procured or invited at the instance of deputy surveyors seeking contracts, you are instructed that such proceedings on the part of deputy surveyors are unlawful, and that contracts thus unlawfully procured will not be recognized as valid. The surveyor general must minutely examine into all applications for surveys under the deposit system. If he is satisfied that the deputy has acted in the manner described, the commission of such deputy shall be forthwith revoked, and the surveyor general shall report all the facts, with his findings in the case, to this office. Upon approval thereof such deputy shall be deemed unfit to exercise the functions of a deputy surveyor, and the approval of a finding against a deputy will be communicated by this office to each surveyor general for his information and guidance; and any surveyor general who shall fail to report such deputy, or who shall employ any deputy so barred, will be open to charges to be preferred by the Commissioner of the General Land Office to the Secretary of the Interior.

III. Surveyors general are required to exercise the utmost care and vigilance to prevent frauds and irregularities of any kind regarding surveys under the system of deposits by individuals, as also of surveys made under any other appropriation of moneys by Congress, whether general or special, and they will report each and every fact that may come to their knowledge of any attempted fraud, by whomsoever made, with all obtainable particulars, to this office for consideration and action.

IV. The plats and field notes of surveys under the system of deposits by individuals, as returned to this office, do not usually show the settlements and improvements of the settler at whose instance the surveys are ostensibly made. In a majority of instances the location of the settler, whether *bona fide* or otherwise, is entirely omitted, while the improvements, if any, are never noted. In order, therefore, to still further check the uses and dishonest practices to which this system of surveys has become subject, the attention of surveyors general and deputy surveyors is specially directed to the requirements of pages 18 and 19 of the Manual of Surveys, and pages 43 and 44 of the instructions of the Commissioner of the General Land Office, dated May 3, 1881. The requirements therein contained must be strictly adhered to, and surveyors general are required and enjoined to see to it that their deputies comply therewith.

Surveyors general are directed to instruct their deputies that they must designate the field notes and plats of their surveys the location of each and every settle, within a township surveyed under the deposit system, whether it be permanent character or not, together with the names of such settlers and their improvements, if any. Cattle corrals are not considered as constituting improvements.

When no settlers are found within a township surveyed under the system of individual deposits, the field notes of survey must *distinctly and unequivocally state that* fact any omission so to describe and designate the settlements and their surface improvements, or the *absence* of one or both in the field notes and plat, will be held a sufficient cause to infer fraud, and the accounts of the deputy will be held until such omission shall have been supplied to both plat and field notes. Action of the commission of the deputy will in the meantime take place, and facts will be reported to this office for consideration and action.

Surveyors general are directed to make known to their several deputies the import and nature of this order, and will be held strictly accountable for its faithful execution. Ignorance of the terms of this order will not be held an excuse for failure to comply therewith by deputies.

This order will be observed by deputies now in the field, and surveyors general are directed to so inform them with the least practicable delay.

Surveyors general are reminded of the important trust confided to them, and are instructed to exercise their whole authority to secure correct and honest surveys as by their deputies.

This order will take effect from and after the receipt of the same, and its receipt immediately acknowledged by each surveyor general.

In every case in which a contract heretofore approved which the surveyor general has reason to believe was unlawfully procured, such contract and the accounts thereof be investigated, and the facts reported to this office.

         N. C. McFARLAND,
            Commissioner.

           A. BELL,
         Secretary of the Interior.

...ceedings new remedy by this department in...

act, in its purpose and intent, in my opinion, is well adapted to the wants of actual settlers who desire to obtain title to their settlements without being subject to the enforced postponement incident to surveys under the present system; but the temptation to irregularity and fraud are too great, and the means of evading the law too easy, to justify a reasonable expectation that the law can be administered in the public interest. The repeal of said act of March 3, 1879, would still leave prior provisions as found in Revised Statutes, sections 2401, 2402, and 2403, available for actual settlers; and these provisions are as liberal as, in my judgment, can safely be extended for their relief, for in addition to the irregularities hereinbefore named, it is to be considered that it is very difficult to examine and prove the proper execution of the surveys covering so large areas, and very probable that those who would fraudulently procure a surveying contract would fraudulently execute it. I therefore recommend the repeal of said act of March 3, 1879, and an increased appropriation for surveys.

The fact that the monuments now used to mark the boundary corners of the public surveys on our vast plains, devoid of suitable stone or timber, and very destructible and liable to be wholly obliterated by the rubbing of cattle and other causes, leads me to call attention to the advisability of some provision whereby some metallic monument of cheap but durable form and material could be substituted, at least for township corners.

EXAMINATIONS OF SURVEYS IN THE FIELD.

The very unsatisfactory manner in which examinations of surveys in the field are made by deputy surveyors, under the direction of the several surveyors general, and the general slighting of this very important work, needs, in the opinion of this office, a radical and wholesome change. It is an absurdity to suppose that truthful and honest returns of examinations in every particular will be made by deputy surveyors, upon whom surveyors general are more than ordinarily dependent for examiners, when it is considered that the examining deputy will at some time, if not already under obligations, have his own work examined by the very deputy whose work he has, if honest, condemned. The temptation of overlooking defects, either in the survey of lines or the marking of the same, has proven too great to be resisted by them. It is safe to say that not one per cent. of the number of examinations are satisfactory to this office in the results obtained.

It is therefore earnestly recommended that the amount set apart for examinations of surveys, either by appropriation or construction of the law by the Treasury Department as applicable to the same, be disbursed directly by this office, through agents appointed for the purpose, who shall be removable only for cause, and who shall make all examinations required, either at the suggestion of the surveyors general or at the instance of this office; to report directly to, and be responsible to this office alone, and be in every way independent of the surveyors general; to receive such fair compensation as may be determined upon by the Secretary of the Interior.

It is firmly believed that only by making them independent of the surveyors general, and responsible to this office alone, that honest and faithful returns of examinations can be secured; that it is the best as well as the cheapest method pecuniarily, and will have a most salutary effect upon the entire surveying service, and is the only means by which to purge the service of worthless and contaminating individuals.

SURVEY OF THE MODIFIED BOUNDARIES OF THE WHITE MOUNTAIN INDIAN RESERVATION.

Though properly belonging to the jurisdiction of the office of Indian Affairs, it has nevertheless been the subject of some correspondence between the Department of the Interior and this office, by reason of the probable extension of the public surveys in the vicinity of the reservation, and other causes.

Under date of August 30, 1878, the surveyor general of Arizona submitted certain recommendations relative to proposed modifications of all the boundaries of the reservation. At a later date, December 2, 1878, he addressed a letter on the subject to John P. Clum, esq., which, together with a petition of citizens requesting a change in the western boundary of the reservation, there being rich deposits of minerals along the immediate present boundary, was submitted to the Hon. Secretary of the Interior, under date of January 22, 1879. In response to a former communication to the Hon. Secretary, an estimate of $1,440 was submitted for the survey of the same. The correspondence on the subject developed the fact that the classification of the lands along said boundary did not come within the scope of classes for the survey of which the funds of this office were applicable under existing laws.

A modification in accordance with the petition of the citizens above referred to, as also in part of the recommendations of the surveyor general, it is believed would be of benefit to the status of the reservation, and also furnishing better lines upon which to close the lines of public surveys. An appropriation for this purpose should be made at an early day in order to avoid probable complications between settlers and those entitled to the reservation, particularly as the reservation is the most permanent in the Territory.

RESURVEY OF THE SIOUX INDIAN RESERVATION WEST OF BIG STONE LAKE, DAKOTA.

Serious complaints have been addressed to this office in time past by several parties as to the seriously erroneous or wholly fraudulent surveys of the Sioux Indian Reservation west of Big Stone Lake, in Dakota, which complaints upon examination have been proved to be only too well founded.

These surveys were made in 1865 by a deputy surveyor, and payment therefor was made from the proceeds of sales of these Indian lands. It is ascertained that no titles to lands anywhere within the limits of the reservation can be perfected until a correct survey and subdivision of the lands embraced therein has been made. This work may involve also the resurvey of the west boundary of the reservation.

There being no law authorizing the application of public funds for the prosecution of resurveys of public lands, the resurvey of these lands, if done at all at the expense of the government, must be provided for by act of Congress.

In order therefore to consummate an early adjustment of the difficulties that have grown out of these erroneous surveys, and to prevent further complications arising from the same cause, an estimate of $4,000 was submitted, under date of April 15, 1880, to the Hon. Secretary of the Interior, and by him submitted to the appropriation committees of Congress.

In view of these facts, and the complications which have arisen from pretended surveys upon which disposals have been made to settlers who are, however, unable to find or define the limits of their claims or purchases, it is earnestly recommended that the appropriation above estimated may be made available at an early day, as resubmitted in estimates for 1883.

At the instance of the Office of Indian Affairs, these lands were proclaimed for sale by the President of the United States during the last fiscal year, but owing to the complicated condition of affairs within the reservation, the proclamation was withdrawn during the present fiscal year in order to have correct survey made of the lands, so that the purchasers of the same can identify their premises and secure titles according to the proper metes and bounds.

Referring to the act approved September 27, 1850, entitled "An act to create the office of surveyor general of the public lands in Oregon, and to provide for the survey, and to make donations to settlers of the said public lands," and to legislation supplemental thereto, my predecessor caused an examination to be made of all claims initiated under said acts and filed in the district land offices in Oregon and Washington Territory. It was ascertained that a large number of said claims had been voluntarily abandoned prior to a compliance with the law, but that no formal relinquishments or notices of abandonment had been filed with the local land officers.

The said laws did not limit the number of claims that might be filed upon by any one person, nor limit the time within which final proof thereon would be necessary. It was therefore not within the power of this office to cite said claimants to complete their claims within any certain time, and no means could be legally resorted to for clearing the record. It was known meanwhile that the abandoned lands had in many instances been entered and disposed of under the general land laws.

I therefore deem it important that Congress should pass an act fixing a definite time after survey, and after the act, within which all such donation claimants shall file final proof on their several claims, and that in default thereof the claims shall be forfeited and canceled.

As section 2447, Revised Statutes, authorizes the issue of patents for those claims only which had been confirmed by law at the date of its adoption, I would further recommend that said section be so amended as to authorize the issue of patents for all claims which have since been, or may hereafter be, confirmed by law when no provision is made in the confirmatory statute for the issue of patents.

I deem it my duty to call special attention to the private land claims in Colorado, New Mexico, and Arizona. For convenience I quote from my predecessor's report of 1877:

PRIVATE LAND CLAIMS IN THE STATE OF COLORADO AND THE TERRITORIES OF NEW MEXICO AND ARIZONA.

The basis of the present mode of settling these claims is the eighth section of the act of July 22, 1854 (10 Stats., p. 308), which in substance makes it the duty of the surveyor general of New Mexico to examine, under instructions by the Secretary of the Interior, and report upon the validity or invalidity of Spanish and Mexican titles therein, which said report, the act further provides, shall be "laid before Congress for such action thereon as may be deemed just and proper, with a view to confirm bona fide grants." This legislation applied only to that part of New Mexico which was included within the lines defined by the treaty of Guadalupe Hidalgo until the act of August 4, 1854 (10 Stats., p. 575), which provided that, "until otherwise provided by law, the territory acquired under the late treaty with Mexico, commonly known as the Gadsden treaty, be, and the same is hereby, incorporated with the Territory of New Mexico, subject to all the laws of said last named Territory."

Under this act the honorable Secretary of the Interior, in his decision, dated February 17, 1872, addressed to this office, held that the laws therein referred to were

United States laws, including the above act of July 22, 1854, and hence that the juris-diction of the surveyor general of New Mexico for the settlement of these claims ex-tended over all the territory acquired by the Gadsden treaty, unless, in the words of the act of August 4, 1854, some other mode had been "provided by law." Since the date of this act the settlement of a part of these claims in the Gadsden purchase has been otherwise provided for by law.

By the act of February 24, 1863 (12 Stats., p. 664), a part of the Gadsden purchase was incorporated into the Territory of Arizona, and by the same act authority was given for the appointment of a surveyor general for that Territory. By the subse-quent act of July 15, 1870 (16 Stats., p. 304), the provisions of the eighth section of the act of July 22, 1854, were extended to Arizona, and the surveyor general thereof was thereby clothed with as ample jurisdiction over grants therein as was vested in the surveyor general of New Mexico over like claims in the Territory of New Mexico.

The provisions of the eighth section of the said act of July 22, 1854, were extended to Colorado by the seventeenth section of the act of February 28, 1861 (12 Stats., p. 176), so that, as the law stands, there are three Territories, New Mexico, Colorado [since become a State), and Arizona, in which there are provisions of law for the set-tlement of Spanish and Mexican titles, the protection of which is guaranteed by treaty stipulations.

On the 25th of August, 1854, the Secretary of the Interior issued instructions to the United States surveyor general for New Mexico, as required by the legislation afore-said, and that officer thereupon entered upon his duties, as prescribed by said instruc-tions and the acts of July and August, 1854, and he has since transmitted to Congress a number of reports on this class of claims, some of which have been approved by Congress, and some of which are now awaiting action before either the Senate or House.

On the 9th of January and 11th of April, 1877, this office issued instructions to the surveyors general of Arizona and Colorado, approved by the Secretary of the Interior, respectively, on the 11th of January and 1st of May, 1877, directing those officers to proceed, in compliance with the requirements of said act of July 22, 1854, and sup-plemental legislation, to report to Congress the origin, nature, and extent of all pri-vate land claims within their respective districts. The issue of these instructions has been delayed partly because it was hoped that Congress would, in view of the evident necessities for further legislation, make some provision for a more speedy adjustment of these claims, and partly for the reason that the *quasi* judicial duties conferred by the acts aforesaid could not be exercised without injury to that branch of the duties of the surveyor general more properly appertaining to his office.

During the past four years this office has, by reports and otherwise, repeatedly called the attention of Congress to the defects in the present system of settling these claims; and to these I add my opinion that the present method prescribed for the determina-tion of the validity of these grants is not sufficiently speedy to do justice either to the claimants or settlers or to the United States. Nor does it secure the requisite ability for a proper settlement of such grants; nor does it provide for the settlement of all such claims, the protection of which is guaranteed by treaty.

It is now more than twenty years since the surveyor general of New Mexico com-menced the examination of claims in that Territory, and he has since reported to Con-gress less than one hundred and fifty claims, though in 1856 he had more than one thousand upon his files, and of the number reported Congress has confirmed but seventy-one. From these data it will be seen that the probable date when the last of these thousand claims in New Mexico alone will be reported on and confirmed is in the far future.

In the mean time the claimants must wait without remedy, and their grants, which would be valuable if the title were completed by a United States confirmation or patent, must remain comparatively worthless, as is all property where the vendor offers for sale an incomplete title and prospective litigation.

The settler dares not settle and improve land lest it be subsequently found to be within the limits of some unconfirmed and unsurveyed grant; and the United States by such delay not only loses the sale of its land, but, judging from past experience with private land claims in other localities, the development of the resources of that country will create additional incentives for the manufacture of fraudulent title papers, with the view of securing public land therewith. Each year's delay, with the con-sequent death of living witnesses and loss or destruction of ancient records relating to land, adds to the probabilities that such forged and otherwise fraudulent title pa-pers will pass without detection the scrutiny of the officers whose duty it may become to determine their character.

This delay is neither the fault of the surveyor general nor of Congress. A proper attention by the surveyor general to his executive duties leaves him but little time to attend to the examination of complicated and confused evidences of title, most of which are in a foreign language. And when the claim, having been reported to Con-gress, has been assigned to its appropriate committee, no member of such committee can conscientiously recommend that the United States convey the large tract of land which most of these grants contain without giving to each case that careful, patient, and protracted examination which belongs to the judge rather than the legislator. In the multitude of business pressing upon Congress during its session, it cannot be expected that these claims will be attended to to the exclusion of business more important to the general welfare.

However able, competent, and valuable a surveyor general may be as an executive officer, or to conduct the usual business arising in a surveyor general's office, he may, and probably will, lack the technical legal knowledge which will enable him to cope successfully with voluminous title papers, complicated by the sophistry of skillful attorneys. Yet, under the present system, the surveyor general must surmount these difficulties, or they cannot be surmounted; for, however carefully Congress may re-examine his work, it must not be forgotten that Congress acts on a *copy* of the papers filed with the surveyor general, and hence cannot possibly know whether the grant be antedated or forged, or contains any of those defects which can be detected only by an inspection of the original record.

The practical result of this system appears in the confirmation of immense tracts of land, the location of which is now boldly asked by the claimants and their agents, not in accordance with the limits of their grant from Mexico, but within the limits of their grant as defined in the recommendation and report of the surveyor general, and as confirmed by Congress.

The present method of surveying these claims is also defective. At present, the whole weight of correctly locating a grant by survey rests with the United States deputy surveyor, who executes the survey in the field.

The greater part of these grants are bounded by adjoining grants or natural objects; such, for example, as on the north by the grant to A, on the south by the stream called B, on the east by the table lands of C, and on the west by the spring of D. Now, it is often a matter of the greatest difficulty, in a country such as the Southwest, abounding in springs and streams, and covered with table lands, to determine which of two springs, several miles apart, is the spring D, or which of two streams or table lands, likewise miles apart, is the stream B or the table land C. To aid him in reaching a correct conclusion, the deputy surveyor has no guide other than such information as he can glean from statements of persons in the vicinity, not under oath, and perhaps interested in extending or curtailing the limits of the grant about to be surveyed. When the deputy surveyor has performed his duty to the best of his ability, under these adverse circumstances, he returns the survey to the surveyor general, who, not being required to examine these natural objects in the field, transmits the survey to this office, and the claimants appear and ask for a patent in accordance therewith. Manifestly, if this office acts upon such a survey, by approving it, it acts blindly.

It is difficult to suggest a remedy that will be entirely satisfactory, but, as the result of a careful examination of the settlement of these claims elsewhere, I recommend that a law be passed authorizing the surveyor general to publish each survey for a period not exceeding six weeks in two newspapers, one publication being in the newspaper nearest the land and one at the principal business or political center of the Territory or State in which the claim is located; the said publication to call upon all parties interested to appear and show cause, if any there be, why the said survey should not be approved, and such objection as may then be made, or such evidence as may then be produced, to be transmitted, with the opinion of the surveyor general, to this office. Provision should also be made for a return of the papers, a further notice, and the taking of further testimony, where deemed necessary by the Commissioner of the General Land Office.

The success which has attended this method in a similar class of claims in California warrants me in predicting a favorable result, should it be adopted in the adjustment of the claims now under consideration.

In addition to the foregoing, I might add that, while these private land claims remain in their present unsettled condition, it will continue to retard emigration to and settlement in said Territories; for, until the titles thereto are ascertained, and the land segregrated from the public domain, it will be impossible to determine which is public land subject to appropriation and settlement under the public land laws and which is not; therefore, settlement made with a purpose of acquiring title under the public land system is necessarily at the risk of finding in the future the land settled upon included within the limits of a private land claim, and the improvements lost to the party who made them. There has already occurred many cases of severe hardship in this respect.

The experience of the past fully demonstrates that after these claims have been reported to Congress, as required by the aforesaid act of 1854, Congress is loath to take them up and confirm them without more definite knowledge regarding their genuineness, extent, and location, which it is impossible to have under the present defective system.

I feel disinclined at this time to recommend any specific plan for the adjustment of said claims. Whether a commission be appointed and the same provisions made as by act of March 3, 1851, for the settlement of like claims in California, or a law enacted requiring proceedings to be commenced directly in the courts within a certain time, is left to the discretion of Congress. My present duty will be performed when I shall have directed attention to the pressing necessity for some legislation which will be adequate to the speedy ascertainment of just what lands these claims embrace, and to their final disposition within such period as may be essential to judicial proceedings. Colorado is already a flourishing State, daily increasing its population, its industries, and its wealth. New Mexico and Arizona are becoming easily accessible by reason of the construction of railroads; and the mineral resources of both the State and Territories are drawing to them the wealth and enterprise of large numbers of our best citizens. It is manifest not only that they are entitled to such legislative relief as shall secure title to their lands at the earliest date compatible with due proceedings, but that it is a matter of interest to the whole country. The longer Congress defers action in the premises, the more complicated and the greater are the difficulties which must ultimately be met and overcome.

The investigation of trespasses upon the timber lands of the United States has resulted in the apprehension and prosecution of many depredators. Where the trespass was the result of mistake the party has been allowed to settle by the payment of a fair valuation of the timber taken, and many suits have been adjusted by payment for the timber, when the trespass was of a character to justify compromise. The government has thus realized a very considerable sum of money for timber so illegally taken, and depredators have been measurably deterred from their business, which was swiftly denuding the public lands of their best timber.

The present appropriation, however, is quite insufficient for the necessities of this branch of the service. With it I am unable to keep in the field more than fifteen agents. With this number it is impossible to even cursorily examine the vast timber districts, and extensive depredations undoubtedly are undetected. I earnestly recommend an increased appropriation for this service. Not only will the public interests be subserved by the protection of its timber, but the Treasury will profit by the payments made.

The existing provisions of law permitting citizens to fell and remove timber on the public lands for mining and domestic purposes, as found in act of June 3, 1878 (20 Statutes, 88), are, in my opinion, very defective. The only lands from which such cutting is authorized are the *mineral* lands.

1st. The mineral lands are to a great extent undefined, and necessarily must so remain.

2d. Large quantities of timber are absolutely necessary for the development of mines, while the said act authorizes the cutting thereon of the timber for other purposes. The purchaser of a mining claim has as much (if not a greater) need for the timber thereon as the agriculturist, and the transportation of timber to the mines from a distance is very expensive.

3. The law furnishes no relief to such as reside at a distance from such lands. The situation is practically this: The settlers on lands devoid of timber need timber for fuel, building, &c. Very frequently they cannot get it, except from the public lands. If they cannot get it legally, still they will take it, and when taken solely for said purposes it is under circumstances which largely mitigate the technical legal offense.

While parties who steal the public timber for speculation and profit deserve severe punishment, those who use it solely for home purposes under the imperative necessities above mentioned should have their privileges accurately and reasonably defined. I deem the enactment of some law which will accomplish this end to be very desirable and in the public interest.

I am unwillingly constrained to invite attention, so soon after taking charge of this office, to its necessities in the matter of its clerical force, but a close and careful study of its immense work and a knowledge derived from personal contact with, and participation in, the proceedings compel me to bear witness to the magnitude of the difficulties surrounding its proper administration. The views of my three immediate predecessors are set forth in the annual report from this office for 1880, and for the purpose of showing the uniformity of opinion entertained by them in relation to this matter, I quote from said report:

I deem it appropriate for me here to submit some remarks with reference to the disadvantages under which the General Land Office labors in performing the important duties with which it is charged, in consequence of existing conditions with regard to its clerical force, and in other respects—a matter which has heretofore been made the subject of remark alike by myself and some of my predecessors.

Hon. Willis Drummond was appointed Commissioner of this office February 11, 1871. In his first annual report (see General Land Office Report for 1871, page 8) he said:

"Upon assuming control of this office in the month of February last, I found nearly every branch of the business greatly in arrears. As almost, if not quite, the entire clerical force of the office is requisite and necessary to the prompt and proper execution of current work, the task of bringing up the business thus found in arrears has been a difficult one. Such progress has been made, however, as to justify the belief that this work may be accomplished in time with the force at present employed; but I am fully satisfied that it would be to the interest of both the government and parties having business with this office for Congress to provide for a temporary increase of the clerical force, as, with such increase, a large amount of business which has been in arrears for months and years could be brought up immediately, and a great saving of time to the government and of expense to parties affected thereby."

In Commissioner Drummond's annual report of 1872, page 5, he said:

"In my last annual report I referred to the fact that when I assumed control of the General Land Office in February, 1871, nearly every branch of the business was largely in arrears. The returns of local land offices remained unposted for periods ranging from several months to two years. The adjustment of registers' and receivers' accounts was in a similar condition. The field notes of township surveys, to which it is necessary to make frequent reference, had not been indexed for ten years. About 47,000 pieces of agricultural college scrip which had been located remained on the files of the office uncanceled, and, consequently, in such a condition as to involve the risk of its being abstracted and disposed of fraudulently. Notwithstanding the current business of the office has increased constantly and rapidly, all these arrears and many others have been brought up, and such progress made in the disposition of suspended and contested cases as to justify the belief that by the end of the present fiscal year they will be adjusted, and that thereafter parties who purchase lands of the government will not, as heretofore, be subjected to the suspense, anxiety, and loss consequent upon a delay of half a dozen years or more in the adjustment of their entries. These results are mainly attributable to the industry and faithfulness of the clerks employed in the office, many of whom not only performed what was required of them, but voluntarily contributed much of their time after office hours to the service of the government.

"I beg leave to repeat the suggestion made in my last annual report in relation to the reorganization of the clerical force and appointment of special agents. When the vast extent of the public domain is taken into consideration, and when it is remembered that the validity of title to each and every tract on which a home may be made depends upon the accuracy with which the first details of transfer from the government to its grantees are executed, the importance of exercising critical care in the adjustment of all matters pertaining to the disposal of public lands will be apparent.

"There is not an owner of a home in many of the States in the prosperous valley of the Mississippi, nor in the rapidly growing regions beyond that river, who does not depend upon the records of this bureau for evidence to complete the chain of title by which his home is held. Even from those regions of the West which have been peopled for the greatest length of time, this office is in constant receipt of applications for certified transcripts of records affecting the validity of title to lands which for ten, twenty, and even fifty years, have been under cultivation.

"Were every acre of land now owned by the government sold or otherwise disposed of, there would still be ample necessity for the perpetuation of this bureau, with a clerical force by no means small, to afford information and furnish papers respecting the original transfer of title from the government. In many instances the necessity for these transcripts of records arises from errors and inadvertencies, either in construing laws or in the execution of the details of transfer, both of which inevitably lead to expensive and protracted litigation.

"With a view to prevent, as far as may be possible, the further occurrence of such cases, I am impelled to call your attention, with the hope that proper legislation to meet the case may be invoked, to the great importance of placing within the reach of this bureau the means of securing such clerical aid as may be equal to a proper adjustment of the important questions constantly arising before it.

"The work of the bureau should not only be done, but it should be done well. When performed imperfectly it requires double labor to make corrections, and parties are subjected to vexatious delays and unnecessary expense in matters which it is the duty of the government to render as speedy, simple, and inexpensive as possible. A knowledge of the laws and rulings of the land system cannot be acquired in a day, but it takes as long and careful study as to acquire a knowledge of any of the professions, and also much experience before the necessary degree of proficiency is attained. When clerks have once gained this knowledge and experience their services are invaluable to the government; but it is difficult to retain them, for the reason that the utterly inadequate salaries now paid too often fail to induce the more competent clerks to remain in the bureau after becoming fully conversant with the laws and departmental rulings relating to our land system, there being always more advantageous opportunities to exercise that knowledge in legitimate pursuits outside of the office, at rates of compensation with which the government, under existing laws, cannot compete. The statutes relating to public lands are numerous and complicated. In construing them, and in the adjustment of adverse claims arising under them, the questions this office is required to decide are sufficiently intricate to demand the best legal ability. The interests at stake are almost invariably of great moment, in most cases involving the lawful and peaceable possession and enjoyment of the lands of men struggling through property to secure, by hard industry, for themselves and families a home. To dispose of these questions in a proper manner, competent clerks should be employed and retained. This cannot be done for the compensation now allowed by law.

"The heads of the various divisions of the bureau are charged with a responsibility second only to the head of the bureau, and should, in my opinion, receive a salary of not less than $2,400 per annum. The number of clerks of the higher grades should be increased; a proportionate number could be taken from the 'clerks of the first class. Under a reorganization like this the work will be done better, and there will be an actual saving of time and money by the avoidance of errors in its execution."

In Commissioner Drummond's report for 1873, page 5, he said:

"Notwithstanding this increase in the survey and sale of lands, which involves a corresponding increase in the work of this office, I have thus far been able to transact the current business and largely reduce the vast accumulation of unfinished work which I found on assuming control of the office, and to which I have alluded in previous reports, and the work of the office is now well advanced in most of its branches. The adjustment of ex parte homestead and pre-emption cases is now kept up to current dates. The number of contested cases awaiting adjustment has been much reduced, but, owing to the insufficiency of the clerical force, this class of work still remains somewhat in arrears.

"When I took charge of the office there was a large accumulation of California private land claims unadjusted. This accumulation has been removed, and at this time only four cases are awaiting examination.

"Notwithstanding the satisfactory progress thus far made in bringing up arrearages the business of the office is increasing so rapidly as to justify the conclusion that present arrearages cannot be brought up and the current business of the office transacted promptly without a thorough reorganization and increase of the clerical force of this bureau. I therefore respectfully, but earnestly, renew the recommendations made by me on this point in my last annual report."

In the annual report for 1874, page 7, Commissioner Burdett said:

"In the annual reports of my immediate predecessor for the years 1871 and 1872, the necessity for a thorough reorganization and increase of the clerical force of the General Land Office was adverted to and discussed at length. I do not deem it essential to reiterate in form the facts and reasons by him clearly set forth in support of that necessity. My own experience amply justifies the belief that the urgency of his statement was moderate in view of the facts. Though very much was done during the efficient

administration of the affairs of the office for the past three years to correct the evils flowing out of the accumulation of business theretofore existing, I am yet almost daily made painfully aware of the fact that both the public and private interests are suffering on account of a lack of adequate clerical force, and while I appreciate the purposes of economy which thus far prevailed against the urgent representations heretofore made to Congress on the subject, I must yet discharge my imperative duty in the premises by declaring that with the existing organization and force I am not able to execute the laws relating to the disposal of the public domain with that efficiency and economy demanded for the protection of both the public and individual interests."

In Commissioner Burdett's annual report for 1875, page 21, he said:

"In my last annual report, and in those of my immediate predecessor for the years 1871, 1872, and 1873, the necessity for a thorough reorganization and increase of the clerical force of the General Land Office was urged as indispensable to the proper transaction of its business.

"These representations resulted in provision being made by the last Congress for such increase in the number of clerks as has enabled me to put the business of the office in better condition than it has heretofore been for the past twenty years.

. "The current work is now dispatched with as great rapidity as is consistent with accuracy and safety to public and private interests. There remains, however, large accumulations of old suspended cases, which, from their nature, are difficult and slow of adjustment. They require the attention of the most competent and experienced of the office force. It is to be regretted that the final adjustment of these cases must be still longer delayed, owing to the want of a sufficient number of skilled men to take charge of their final disposition. I deem it my duty to again urge that steps be taken to bring to the notice of Congress the necessity of the reorganization of the clerical force heretofore referred to. I have no hesitation in declaring it to be my judgment that, considering the large body of laws to be administered, the manifold forms of proofs to be examined, the watchfulness against fraud constantly required, the immensity of the trust imposed, and the special skill and learning required in the settlement of the foundations, as is here done, of the titles of the whole estate of the people in lands derived from the government, places this bureau in a position of importance second to none other, and entitles it to an organization commensurate with the interests it is intended to subserve. It will be found, however, on comparison, that it is still restricted within the meager wants of its early organization, and that the salaries of its employés are among the lowest provided for the public service.

"OFFICE ROOM.

"The question of room for the use of this bureau has become an important one. There is now urgent need for larger space for the proper, safe, and economical transaction of its business and the preservation of its records. The space available for desks is now overcrowded; the file rooms are filled to their utmost capacity; the meager space now available for desks and files has been preserved by thrusting out into the public halls of the department building some of the most important records of this office; should they be returned to the proper rooms, where they are in hourly use, and where upon every consideration of their great value and importance the expenditure, to be, there would be left no working space whatever. The records going into insecurely placed are mainly the 'tract books.' They are the only indexes. These the General Land Office by which its varied transactions can be traced, and themselves, in a large sense, the original evidences of title to an estate of public lands last census to be valued at $4,749,409,940.

"The relief which this system of storage has heretofore given has reached to the office, limit; space in the halls available for the purpose is now exhausted upon important accumulation of letters, returns, and records must henceforward be answered at once, too-limited working room unless relief can be found by the assignment manner as the rooms within the department building.

"These records are of too great importance to be deposited in buildings, courtesy, as well of department, unless constructed specially for such purpose with matters of great fire, and even as now arranged in the department they are insecure lands, be speedily parties to take advantage of homes and improve-

In my first annual report, 1876, page 14, I said:

"Upon assuming the office of Commissioner I found a clerical and often doubly vexa-considered by my predecessors in office inadequate to the efficiency, and expense devoted to of the work pertaining to it. Since then Congress, by act other in arrears. The exami-reduced the force more than 25 per cent., making it less since the reorganization of the office by act of Congress, novices in official life, nor by the business of the office is constantly increasing as rapidly, without legal training, and ing laws governing the disposition of the public and judicial observation which enter our railroad land grants, the pre-emption and honest admission to departmental clerk-the timber culture act, and the various Congress all tending to complicate and increase the work of this bureau. I find, moreover, upon comparing the salaries allowed clerks in this bureau with those allowed to clerks in other bureaus under the control of the Secretary of the Interior that they are much lower, as the following table will show:

Tabular statement showing the number of clerks in each bureau of the Department of the Interior and salaries allowed by law.

Bureaus.	$3,000.	$2,500.	$2,250.	$2,000.	Class 4, $1,800.	Class 3, $1,600.	Class 2, $1,400.	Class 1, $1,200.	Copyists, $900.	Total number of clerks.
PATENT OFFICE.										
Assistant Commissioner	1									1
Examiner in chief	3									3
Principal examiners		23								23
Chief clerk			1							1
Examiner			1							1
Clerks				1	27	28	43	38	40	177
										206
PENSION OFFICE.										
Deputy Commissioner			1							1
Chief clerk				1						1
Medical referee			1							1
Clerks					26	52	84	123	25	310
										313
GENERAL LAND OFFICE.										
Chief clerk				1						1
Recorder				1						1
Law clerk				1						1
Principal clerks					3					3
Clerks					5	23	41	70		139
										145
INDIAN OFFICE.										
Chief clerk				1						1
Clerks					5	9	13	13	6	46
										47
BUREAU OF EDUCATION.										
Chief clerk					1					1
Clerks					3	2	1		4	9
										10

"This year the Land Office is authorized by law to employ 145 clerks, including a chief clerk, recorder, and law clerk, at a yearly salary of $2,000 each; 3 principal clerks at $1,800; 5 clerks of class 4; 23 of class 3; 41 of class 2; and 70 of class 1, thus making 8 clerks who receive a salary of $1,800 each, or about 1 in 20 of the whole force above the third class, and not one who receives a salary of over $2,000, while the Patent Office (which it will not be claimed is of more importance to the country than the General Land Office, upon whose records the title to almost every acre of land west and northwest of the Ohio to the Pacific is dependent) has a deputy commissioner and three examiners-in-chief, who receive a salary of $3,000 each; 23 examiners and clerks at $2,500 each; 1 chief clerk and an examiner at $2,500; me on 1 clerk at $2,000; 27 assistant examiners and clerks at $1,800; 28 at $1,600; $1,400; 38 clerks at $1,200; and 40 copyists at $900; making 57 clerks who receive salaries ranging from $1,800 to $3,000, or about one in three of the whole force with a salary above $1,600. By continuing the comparison with other necessary in the department, we find the Pension Office with 29 clerks receiving salaries above the third class, being about one in ten of its clerical force; the Indian Office with 47 clerks, 6 of whom receive salaries above the third class, being in the proportion of one to eight; and the Bureau of Education, with its whole clerical force of 10 clerks, has 3 who receive $1,800.

"It will readily be seen by this statement that the General Land Office, which, considering the character and amount of work it has to perform, and needing the best talent that can be procured, has in fact the poorest provision in the matter of salaries, and consequently the poorest organization.

"If it is assumed that the work of this bureau is of less importance than that of others, and requiring clerks of less ability, then that would be an apparent reason for the fact: but it is not true that the labor is less important or more easily performed. It differs only in character, but not in importance.

"The difficulty, however, which the office labors under at present is not so much the lack of numbers as inability to obtain the talent required for the salaries allowed. A knowledge of the laws and rulings of the public land system cannot be acquired in a day, but takes as long and as careful study almost as to acquire a knowledge of any of the professions, and much experience before the necessary degree of proficiency is attained. When clerks have once acquired this knowledge and experience their services become invaluable to the government; but it is difficult to retain them, owing to the inadequate salaries now paid by the government, and their services are eagerly sought for by railroad corporations, land companies, and legal firms having business before the office, at rates of compensation with which the government, under existing laws, cannot compete. Unless Congress provides more adequate compensation, there is nothing to induce a clerk having acquired a thorough knowledge of the laws and rulings relating to our land system to retain his position; and I must confess that, unless Congress provide by law for the reorganization of the clerical force now under my control, and for the payment of salaries adequate to the ability required, I feel myself unable to properly administer the laws relating to the public lands and do justice to the thousands of cases now pending, awaiting action for the want of clerks possessing the ability to adjudicate them.

"I would therefore respectfully request that the earnest attention of Congress be called to the subject, with a view that such legislation may be had as the exigencies of the case demand."

In my annual report for 1877 (see page 1) I said:

"By reference to the statements of the condition of the work in the several divisions of the bureau, it will not escape your observation that a very large arrearage is shown, much of it the accumulation of former years, while a considerable percentage has been added during the year in consequence of the insufficiency of the clerical force to keep up with the constant press of the current business. Year after year my predecessors in this office have urged upon Congress the necessities of the public service in this regard, and since my induction as Commissioner I have labored with renewed effort to the same end. Thus far, however, it does not appear to have reached the judgment of Congress that a paramount need of the country is daily sacrificed upon the altar of a false economy, and the most sacred interest of the hardy pioneers of civilization, that of speedy acquisition and security of their homes and hearthstones, is continually ignored and disregarded.

"By the regular appropriations for the current fiscal year provision is made for one Commissioner, one chief clerk, one recorder, one law clerk, three principal clerks, five clerks of class four, twenty-two clerks of class three, forty clerks of class two, seventy clerks of class one, one draughtsman, one assistant draughtsman, two messengers, three assistant messengers, eight laborers, and two packers, to which an additional allowance was made by a clause in the sundry civil act to the amount of the expenditure of ten thousand dollars, available from March 3, 1877, to enable me to bring into market the vacant lands in the Southern States, under act of June 22, 1876. These allowances and provisions were greatly reduced from the estimates submitted, and have not sufficed, as before stated, to keep up the current work of the bureau. As an illustration, I would mention the fact that the correspondence in the public lands division is six months behindhand, not only causing great inconvenience to the office, but absolute wrong to individuals, who, addressing the government upon important matters, are obliged to wait months for reply, instead of receiving answers at once, as would be the case were private individuals concerned in the same manner as the department.

"It would seem to be a matter of the merest and commonest courtesy, as well of individual right, that letters received by the office, often involving matters of great moment to the settlers and others interested in acquiring the public lands, be speedily and properly answered in such reasonable time as will enable parties to take advantage of the season in the preparation for crops and the making of homes and improvements, without risk of an adverse decision tardily rendered, and often doubly vexatious and burdensome on account of the added time, labor, and expense devoted to the improvement of the lands of which they are deprived.

"The contests relating to conflicting claims are still further in arrears. The examination of these conflicts cannot be undertaken by mere novices in official life, nor by men possessing even the highest order of clerical ability, without legal training, and the acquisition of those habits of care, research, and judicial observation which enter into the judgments of courts. No ordinary tests of admission to departmental clerk-

certified transcripts of records affecting the validity of title to lands which for ten, twenty, and even fifty years, have been under cultivation.

"Were every acre of land now owned by the government sold or otherwise disposed of, there would still be ample necessity for the perpetuation of this bureau, with a clerical force by no means small, to afford information and furnish papers respecting the original transfer of title from the government. In many instances the necessity for these transcripts of records arises from errors and inadvertencies, either in construing laws or in the execution of the details of transfer, both of which inevitably lead to expensive and protracted litigation.

"With a view to prevent, as far as may be possible, the further occurrence of such cases, I am impelled to call your attention, with the hope that proper legislation to meet the case may be invoked, to the great importance of placing within the reach of this bureau the means of securing such clerical aid as may be equal to a proper adjustment of the important questions constantly arising before it.

"The work of the bureau should not only be done, but it should be done well. When performed imperfectly it requires double labor to make corrections, and parties are subjected to vexatious delays and unnecessary expense in matters which it is the duty of the government to render as speedy, simple, and inexpensive as possible. A knowledge of the laws and rulings of the land system cannot be acquired in a day, but it takes as long and careful study as to acquire a knowledge of any of the professions, and also much experience before the necessary degree of proficiency is attained. When clerks have once gained this knowledge and experience their services are invaluable to the government; but it is difficult to retain them, for the reason that the utterly inadequate salaries now paid too often fail to induce the more competent clerks to remain in the bureau after becoming fully conversant with the laws and departmental rulings relating to our land system, there being always more advantageous opportunities to exercise that knowledge in legitimate pursuits outside of the office, at rates of compensation with which the government, under existing laws, cannot compete. The statutes relating to public lands are numerous and complicated. In construing them, and in the adjustment of adverse claims arising under them, the questions this office is required to decide are sufficiently intricate to demand the best legal ability. The interests at stake are almost invariably of great moment, in most cases involving the lawful and peaceable possession and enjoyment of the lands of men struggling through property to secure, by hard industry, for themselves and families a home. To dispose of these questions in a proper manner, competent clerks should be employed and retained. This cannot be done for the compensation now allowed by law.

"The heads of the various divisions of the bureau are charged with a responsibility second only to the head of the bureau, and should, in my opinion, receive a salary of not less than $2,400 per annum. The number of clerks of the higher grades should be increased; a proportionate number could be taken from the clerks of the first class. Under a reorganization like this the work will be done better, and there will be an actual saving of time and money by the avoidance of errors in its execution."

In Commissioner Drummond's report for 1873, page 5, he said:

"Notwithstanding this increase in the survey and sale of lands, which involves a corresponding increase in the work of this office, I have thus far been able to transact the current business and largely reduce the vast accumulation of unfinished work which I found on assuming control of the office, and to which I have alluded in previous reports, and the work of the office is now well advanced in most of its branches. The adjustment of ex parte homestead and pre-emption cases is now kept up to current dates. The number of contested cases awaiting adjustment has been much reduced, but, owing to the insufficiency of the clerical force, this class of work still remains somewhat in arrears.

"When I took charge of the office there was a large accumulation of California private land claims unadjusted. This accumulation has been removed, and at this time only four cases are awaiting examination.

"Notwithstanding the satisfactory progress thus far made in bringing up arrearages the business of the office is increasing so rapidly as to justify the conclusion that present arrearages cannot be brought up and the current business of the office transacted promptly without a thorough reorganization and increase of the clerical force of this bureau. I therefore respectfully, but earnestly, renew the recommendations made by me on this point in my last annual report."

In the annual report for 1874, page 7, Commissioner Burdett said:

"In the annual reports of my immediate predecessor for the years 1871 and 1872, the necessity for a thorough reorganization and increase of the clerical force of the General Land Office was adverted to and discussed at length. I do not deem it essential to reiterate in form the facts and reasons by him clearly set forth in support of that necessity. My own experience amply justifies the belief that the urgency of his was moderate in view of the facts. Though very much was done during th

administration of the affairs of the office for the past three years to correct the evils flowing out of the accumulation of business theretofore existing, I am yet almost daily made painfully aware of the fact that both the public and private interests are suffering on account of a lack of adequate clerical force, and while I appreciate the purposes of economy which thus far prevailed against the urgent representations heretofore made to Congress on the subject, I must yet discharge my imperative duty in the premises by declaring that with the existing organization and force I am not able to execute the laws relating to the disposal of the public domain with that efficiency and economy demanded for the protection of both the public and individual interests."

In Commissioner Burdett's annual report for 1875, page 21, he said:

"In my last annual report, and in those of my immediate predecessor for the years 1871, 1872, and 1873, the necessity for a thorough reorganization and increase of the clerical force of the General Land Office was urged as indispensable to the proper transaction of its business.

"These representations resulted in provision being made by the last Congress for such increase in the number of clerks as has enabled me to put the business of the office in better condition than it has heretofore been for the past twenty years.

"The current work is now dispatched with as great rapidity as is consistent with accuracy and safety to public and private interests. There remains, however, large accumulations of old suspended cases, which, from their nature, are difficult and slow of adjustment. They require the attention of the most competent and experienced of the office force. It is to be regretted that the final adjustment of these cases must be still longer delayed, owing to the want of a sufficient number of skilled men to take charge of their final disposition. I deem it my duty to again urge that steps be taken to bring to the notice of Congress the necessity of the reorganization of the clerical force heretofore referred to. I have no hesitation in declaring it to be my judgment that, considering the large body of laws to be administered, the manifold forms of proof to be examined, the watchfulness against fraud constantly required, the immensity of the trust imposed, and the special skill and learning required in the settlement of the foundations, as is here done, of the titles of the whole estate of the people in lands derived from the government, places this bureau in a position of importance second to none other, and entitles it to an organization commensurate with the interests it is intended to subserve. It will be found, however, on comparison, that it is still restricted within the meager wants of its early organization, and that the salaries of its employés are among the lowest provided for the public service.

"OFFICE ROOM.

"The question of room for the use of this bureau has become an important one. There is now urgent need for larger space for the proper, safe, and economical transaction of its business and the preservation of its records. The space available for desks is now overcrowded; the file rooms are filled to their utmost capacity; the meager space now available for desks and files has been preserved by thrusting out into the public halls of the department building some of the most important record of the office; should they be returned to the proper rooms, where they are in hourly demand, and where upon every consideration of their great value and importance the ought, for safety, to be, there would be left no working space whatever. The rec'ds thus insecurely placed are mainly the 'tract books.' They are the only indexes found in the General Land Office by which its varied transactions can be traced, and are in themselves, in a large sense, the original evidences of title to an estate felt by the last census to be valued at $4,749,409,940.

"The relief which this system of storage has heretofore given has reached utmost limit; space in the halls available for the purpose is now exhausted. The daily accumulation of letters, returns, and records must henceforward be now too-limited working room unless relief can be found by the assignment additional rooms within the department building.

"These records are of too great importance to be deposited in b̲ courtside the department, unless constructed specially for such purpose with a fire, and even as now arranged in the department they are insecure. the lands, parties to take of homes and improve-

In my first annual report, 1876, page 14, I said:

"Upon assuming the office of Commissioner I found a clerk and often doubly vexa- considered by my predecessors in office inadequate to the offic and expense devoted to of the work pertaining to it. Since then Congress, by act reduced the force more than 25 per cent., making it less other in arrears. The exami- along the reorganization of the office by act of Congress services in official life, nor by the business of the office is constantly increasing as only without legal training, and the laws governing the disposition of the public and judicial observation which enter on railroad land grants, the pre-emption and hone admission to departmental duties the timber culture act, and the various Congress all tending to complicate and increase the work of this bureau. I find, moreover, upon comparing the salaries allowed clerks in this bureau with those allowed to clerks in other bureaus under the control of the Secretary of the Interior that they are much lower, as the following table will show:

Tabular statement showing the number of clerks in each bureau of the Department of the Interior and salaries allowed by law.

Bureaus.	$3,000.	$2,500.	$2,250.	$2,000.	Class 4, $1,800.	Class 3, $1,600.	Class 2, $1,400.	Class 1, $1,200.	Copyists, $900.	Total number of clerks.
PATENT OFFICE.										
Assistant Commissioner	1									1
Examiner-in-chief	3									3
Principal examiners		22								22
Chief clerk			1							1
Examiner				1						1
Clerks					1	27	28	49	98	60	177
										300
PENSION OFFICE.										
Deputy Commissioner			1							1
Chief clerk				1						1
Medical referee			1							1
Clerks					26	52	84	129	25	310
										313
GENERAL LAND OFFICE.										
Chief clerk					1					1
Recorder					1					1
Law clerk					1					1
Principal clerks					3	5	23	61	70	130
Clerks										145
INDIAN OFFICE.										
Chief clerk					1					1
Clerks					5	9	13	13	6	46
										67
BUREAU OF EDUCATION.										
Chief clerk					1					1
Clerks					2	2	1		4	9
										10

"This .... Office is authorized by law to employ 145 clerks, including a chief cl......... clerk, at a yearly salary of $2,000 each; 3 principal clerks ...book.........4; 23 of class 3; 41 of class 2; and 70 of class 1, thus ma...ms........ ...ry of $1,800 each, or about 1 in 20 of the whole force a...es are.........ives a salary of over $2,000, while the Pa...standin......... more importance to the coun- try th... of the ....le to almost every acre of lan...ges cannot..........ent) has a deputy .... without a th......... $3,000 each; 23 bu...au. I therefore res.........miner at $2,500 me on this point in my .... $1,800; 23 at $1,600; .... ; making 57 clerks In the annual report for......... ....be in three of the "In the annual reports of :......... ....parison with other necessity for a thorough reorg.........ks receiving salaries Land Office was adverted to an......... ....se; the Indian Office iterate in form the facts and rea.........u, being in the pre- sity. My own experience amply.........ole clerical force of was moderate in view of the fact.........

.........which, con-

administration of the affairs of the office for the past three years to correct the evils flowing out of the accumulation of business theretofore existing, I am yet almost daily made painfully aware of the fact that both the public and private interests are suffering on account of a lack of adequate clerical force, and while I appreciate the purposes of economy which thus far prevailed against the urgent representations heretofore made to Congress on the subject, I must yet discharge my imperative duty in the premises by declaring that with the existing organization and force I am not able to execute the laws relating to the disposal of the public domain with that efficiency and economy demanded for the protection of both the public and individual interests."

In Commissioner Burdett's annual report for 1875, page 21, he said:

"In my last annual report, and in those of my immediate predecessor for the years 1871, 1872, and 1873, the necessity for a thorough reorganization and increase of the clerical force of the General Land Office was urged as indispensable to the proper transaction of its business.

"These representations resulted in provision being made by the last Congress for such increase in the number of clerks as has enabled me to put the business of the office in better condition than it has heretofore been for the past twenty years.

. "The current work is now dispatched with as great rapidity as is consistent with accuracy and safety to public and private interests. There remains, however, large accumulations of old suspended cases, which, from their nature, are difficult and slow of adjustment. They require the attention of the most competent and experienced of the office force. It is to be regretted that the final adjustment of these cases must be still longer delayed, owing to the want of a sufficient number of skilled men to take charge of their final disposition. I deem it my duty to again urge that steps be taken to bring to the notice of Congress the necessity of the reorganization of the clerical force heretofore referred to. I have no hesitation in declaring it to be my judgment that, considering the large body of laws to be administered, the manifold forms of proofs to be examined, the watchfulness against fraud constantly required, the immensity of the trust imposed, and the special skill and learning required in the settlement of the foundations, as is here done, of the titles of the whole estate of the people in lands derived from the government, places this bureau in a position of importance second to none other, and entitles it to an organization commensurate with the interests it is intended to subserve. It will be found, however, on comparison, that it is still restricted within the meager wants of its early organization, and that the salaries of its employés are among the lowest provided for the public service.

"OFFICE ROOM.

"The question of room for the use of this bureau has become an important one. There is now urgent need for larger space for the proper, safe, and economical transaction of its business and the preservation of its records. The space available for desks is now overcrowded; the file rooms are filled to their utmost capacity; the meager space now available for desks and files has been preserved by thrusting out into the public halls of the department building some of the most important records of the office; should they be returned to the proper rooms, where they are in hourly demand, and where upon every consideration of their great value and importance they ought, for safety, to be, there would be no working space whatever. The records thus insecurely placed are mainly the 'tract books.' They are the only indexes found in the General Land Office by which its varied transactions can be traced, and are in themselves, in a large sense, the original evidences of title to an estate found by the last census to be valued at $4,749,409,940.

"The relief which this system of storage has heretofore given has reached its utmost limit; space in the halls available for the purpose is now exhausted, and the daily accumulation of letters, returns, and records must henceforward trench on the now too-limited working room unless relief can be found by the assignment of additional rooms within the department building.

"These records are of too great importance to be deposited in buildings outside the department, unless constructed specially for such purpose with a view to safety readily fire, and even as now arranged in the department they are insecure from mutilation

In my first annual report, 1876, page 14, I said:

"Upon assuming the office of Commissioner I found a clerical force that had vexaconsidered by my predecessors in office inadequate to the efficient and prompt discharged to of the work pertaining to it. Since then Congress, by act approved August 15, 1874 reduced the force more than 25 per cent., making it less at this time than it has been since the reorganization of the office by act of Congress approved March 3, 1855, which by the business of the office is constantly increasing as new legislation is added to the land ing laws governing the disposition of the public lands, as evidenced by the multifarous railroad land grants, the pre-emption and homestead laws, with their amendments, the timber culture act, and the various Congressional grants

ships will properly fill these positions. It is in consequence of these facts that this office is at present so far from efficient organization.

"The compensation allowed to the classes of clerks necessarily assigned to the making up of official decisions in all branches of the bureau is too small to secure first class men acquainted with law, and especially with land statutes, and with the current and routine of departmental practice, and possessing the requisite tact, discretion, and power of discrimination to act upon these important questions covering the elements of title to the entire body of lands disposed of by the government. The number of clerks should be largely increased in all the higher grades. Into these classes should then be introduced men of first class talent and legal acquirements, ready versed in the law, and familiar, as far as possible, with the practice in land cases. The salaries of the heads of divisions appointed to superintend the work of these classes, including the recorder and law clerk, should be raised to $2,500 each, and the chief clerk, who is required by law to act as Commissioner in the sickness or absence of the head of the bureau, or in case of vacancy in that office, and who must, therefore, be fully qualified for its duties, should receive not less than $3,000 per annum.

"With ten heads of division, including the recorder, law clerk, and three principal clerks, at $2,500 each, ten clerks of class four as assistants, at $1,800 each, a principal draughtsman at $2,000, and an addition of ten to each of classes three and two above the number allowed by the last appropriation, I could so arrange the work as to double the efficiency of the office in a very short time. Without some additional assistance of this kind it must remain for an indefinite period in its present very unsatisfactory condition."

In my annual report for 1878, page 145, I said:

"In the foregoing report I have endeavored to present a brief statement of the business transacted by this office during the fiscal year ending with the 30th June, 1878, and to exhibit, at least approximately, the character and extent of the duties devolved upon it by existing laws. It will be seen therefrom that the work to be performed is far in excess of the clerical force provided, and that much of it is of a character calling for more than merely clerical ability for its proper performance. The result is to be seen in the extent to which the work of the office has fallen in arrears. Thousands of letters, which should be answered, remain unattended to on the files. Returns of transactions in the surveying and land districts, which should be posted into the books provided for the purpose, remain unposted. Hundreds of contested cases, which should be promptly examined and decided as fast as they arise, are untouched. This condition of things cannot be changed for the better, but on the contrary must grow worse from day to day as long as the inadequacy of the clerical force is permitted to continue. In the discharge of my duty in this respect, I can but refer to the representations made in my last annual report of the need of an increase of the number of clerks and a reorganization of the office. It rests with the legislative authority to supply this need by appropriate legislation."

The land commission appointed under act of Congress approved March 3, 1879, making appropriation for the sundry civil expenses of the government for the fiscal year ending June 30, 1880, after a laborious tour through the public land States and Territories, where the workings of the land system were carefully examined, the testimony of hundreds of witnesses taken, and the necessities of the service most cautiously estimated, in their report to Congress (see pages xi to xiv, inclusive) said:

The machinery of the land system lies at the threshold of the successful administration of the law. If defective and incomplete in its organization, it will not be operative from inherent weakness; and the law will, in the ratio of such weakness, remain a dead letter upon the statute book. If cumbersome and complicated it will, by cumulative delays and excessive cost, impair and retard the operation of the law it was intended to execute. The commission has sought to put the officers of the land system on such footing in point of numbers and powers as would, at a minimum expenditure, secure a maximum efficiency. The present organization was adopted many years since, and it has not been perfected to keep even step with the administrative growth of the system. In the last twenty years the surveying districts have increased from 10 to 16; the district land offices from 53 to 94; the acres annually surveyed from four millions to more than double that quantity; and the acres annually disposed of from three millions to over nine millions. During nearly the same period the system of land grants to aid the construction of railroads and wagon roads has been matured: the swamp land, agricultural college, and other grants to States have been made: the homestead laws and the timber culture laws have been enacted; the practice of selling the fee to the mineral lands has been engrafted upon our legislation; and by Indian treaties and the acquisition of Mexican lands the area of our public domain has been enlarged. The adjustment of each of these involves the settlement of difficult questions of the most important character both to the settler and to the government. The business imposed upon the land organization has been thereby largely augmented, and the executive labor arising therefrom has been proportionately increased. But Congress has heretofore met their increased demands only with teemporary expedients, and the permanent organization of the General Land Office is even smaller to-day, when the population of the country has swollen to 48,000,000, than it was when only 27,000,000 acknowledged one national authority. The prosperity of a nation is interwoven with the security of its land titles; and the titles to our public domain depend largely for their security upon the accuracy and promptness of the operations of the Land Bureau and its subordinate agencies. It is important that the officers of that organization should be of sufficient integrity and trained capacity to qualify them for the lawful adjustment of the intricate and delicate questions of fact and of law constantly arising in the administrative construction of the various statutes which constitute our land system. Duties of such responsibility require men of experience and ability, and for their employment and their retention an adequate compensation should be provided. The temporary expedients heretofore resorted to in Congressional enactments have been uniformly an increase of low-grade officers, with small compensation. But brains command a market price as well as merchandise; and while the increase of small salaries has augmented the hands and feet of the organization, it has not materially enlarged the volume of intellectual power to direct their movement. The organization has had an excess of physical force, and a deficiency of brain force. The commission has sought to increase the latter, and to diminish the former. Taking the entire land organization, the Commission has increased the compensation and the number of the higher grade officers, and has thus augmented the expenses by about $50,000; but it has also abolished useless officers, and reduced the number of low grade employés, so as to diminish in that direction the expenses about $90,000. An aggregate saving of about $40,000 would result to the annual appropriations for the land service if the whole of our recommendations should be adopted, which we do earnestly recommend in the interest of a wise and sound economy.

"GENERAL LAND OFFICE.

"The Commission respectfully ask a careful consideration by Congress of its statement regarding the officers and clerical force of the General Land Office, their salaries, and the duties they perform, and the recommendations for securing greater efficiency in that office.

"The General Land Office was organized as a separate bureau in the Treasury Department by an act of Congress approved April 25, 1812. The duties, though important, were simple, and without many complications at that time. The public lands were disposed of only by sales for cash. No grant of any kind had then been made; no mining laws were in existence; the population of the country was comparatively small, and settlement upon the public lands proportionately slow. The thirteen original States were sparsely populated, and immigrants and native-born citizens found homes mostly within their limits, while settlements were founded but slowly in the Northwest Territory. The Commissioner of the General Land Office, for the comparatively unimportant duties then to be performed, was allowed the same salary as was allowed the 'Auditor' of the Treasury; and it remained the same until the year 1836, when the office was reorganized, and the salary of the Commissioner was fixed at $3,000 per year, and has since been raised to $4,000, which amount is not adequate to the duties and responsibilities of the office. The salary should be equal to that of any other bureau officer of the government.

"At the date of the reorganization, in 1836, there was still comparatively little to do in the General Land Office. The method of disposal of the public lands was the same as in 1812, the amount disposed of being greater. The territory acquired by the treaty of Guadalupe Hidalgo and by the Gadsden purchases was very great in extent, and consisted largely of grants and private holdings which were not segregated from the mass of public domain acquired by said treaties. The work of ascertaining the nature, extent, and boundaries of the grants and private holdings, and segregating and patenting the same, which was devolved upon the General Land Office by laws made in pursuance of those treaties, has been for many years more difficult, requiring a higher order of ability than all the work of the office prior to the date of the treaties named. In addition to the private land claims, and since the date at which their settlement became a duty of the office, all, or nearly all, land grants by the government, such as grants to aid in the construction of railroads and telegraph lines, the grants of swamp and overflowed lands to the States, the grants for wagon roads, agricultural colleges, internal improvements, university grants, common-school grants, and grants for slackwater navigation have been made, and their adjustment added to the other duties of the Land Office. The homestead, timber-culture, mineral, and bounty-land acts have also to be added to the great volume of work that has in the last quarter of a century been laid upon the General Land Office under the various acts of Congress. The work of selling lands for cash and the adjustment of Virginia military scrip, which comprised nearly the whole duty of the office until about the year 1850, would not make any perceptible difference in the work of the office to-day if it were entirely withdrawn or added to it; and yet, strange to say, the clerical force

43 Ab

of the office was greater during some part of that time than it was in the years 1877 and 1878, and nearly equal to what it is in the year 1880.

"The conflicts arising between the government and grantees and between settlers and grantees require the best ability for their adjustment. Questions which thus arise are at all times pending before the office. Cases involving greater amounts come before the General Land Office than before any other branch of the executive department of the government. The difference between what the beneficiaries of a land grant may claim and what may be awarded often amounts to millions of dollars in value. The adjudication of many cases involving millions of dollars' worth of property is not infrequent. Prior to the acquisition of the territory in which private land claims are situated and the enactment of laws granting lands equal to the area of one and a half States the size of Pennsylvania to a single corporation, and the enactment of laws for the sale of mineral lands, cases involving more than a few hundred dollars could not often arise.

"Notwithstanding the great increase of labor in this office, and the change in the character of the work, requiring higher and better qualifications, the law officer of the bureau and its principal clerks are paid only the salaries fixed by law forty-four years ago, when the salaries of members of Congress were fixed at $8 per day for the time employed. Since then all grades of salaries, save those of low-grade officers who toil throughout the year without vacation have been greatly increased. Increase of numbers of clerks at low salaries has from most urgent necessity been allowed by law.

"The Commission, with a view to bettering the service, would respectfully recommend the reorganization of the General Land Office, shown in the following tables, which show the difference between the present and proposed organization:

"PRESENT ORGANIZATION.

1 Commissioner, at $4,000	$4,000
1 chief clerk, at $2,000	2,000
1 recorder, at $2,000	2,000
1 law clerk, at $2,000	2,000
1 principal clerk public lands, at $1,800	1,800
1 principal clerk private land claims, at $1,800	1,800
1 principal clerk surveys, at $1,800	1,800
6 clerks, class four, at $1,800 each	10,800
1 draughtsman, at $1,600	1,600
22 clerks class three, at $1,600 each	35,200
1 assistant draughtsman, at $1,400	1,400
40 clerks, class two, at $1,400 each	56,000
80 clerks, class one, at $1,200 each	96,000
30 clerks, class one, at $1,000 each	30,000
9 copyists, at $900 each	8,100
9 assistant messengers, at $720 each	6,480
6 packers, at $720 each	4,320
12 laborers, at $660 each	7,920
223	273,220

"PROPOSED ORGANIZATION.

1 Commissioner, at $6,000	$6,000
1 assistant commissioner, at $3,000	3,000
1 chief clerk, at $2,500	2,500
1 solicitor, at $2,700	2,700
1 recorder, at $2,400	2,400
1 clerk in charge of surveys	3,000
9 chiefs of division, at $2,400 each	21,600
1 chief draughtsman, at $2,200	2,200
10 assistant chiefs of division, at $2,000 each	20,000
15 clerks, class four, at $1,800 each	27,000
35 clerks, class three, at $1,600 each	56,000
40 clerks, class two, at $1,400 each	56,000
50 clerks, class one, at $1,200 each	60,000
10 draughtsmen, at $1,200 each	12,000
20 clerks, at $1,000 each	20,000
10 copyists, at $900 each	9,000
2 packers, at $840 each	1,680
1 chief messenger, at $840	840
9 assistant messengers, $720 each	6,480
12 laborers, at $720 each	8,640
229	321,040

"The Commission would recommend a much larger force for one or two years if there were room in which to advantageously place it. The room allotted to the General Land Office is not quite the worst that it could be, nor is it wholly inadequate, but it approximates both. The immense bulk of valuable records of the office is stored in cheap wooden cases in dark rooms, and darker halls, to which clerks must constantly go for examination of files of papers and volumes of records, which, when found, cannot, in dark or cloudy weather, be read without carrying them to a window, which may be a hundred feet away. It may be safely estimated that the want of more convenient and suitable room costs the government the one-fourth part annually of all money appropriated for clerical force in the General Land Office.

"If there were sufficient and suitable room for the purpose, it would be both wisdom and economy to add as largely to the clerical force as might be necessary to enable the Commissioner to thoroughly inspect the records of the office and ascertian errors, reproduce all mutilated and worn out records while it may be done; but the room is not sufficient, and the best thing that can be done, until room is provided, is to give the maximum force that can be employed, and pay salaries high enough to get good, if not the best, talent."

After the necessity for a reorganization of this office has been thus called to the attention of Congress for nine successive years by three different Commissioners and by a commission of eminent men appointed under an act of Congress for the specific purpose of ascertaining the condition of the public land system of laws and service, I am constrained to believe that further evidence to show that the public interests require a thorough reorganization of the clerical force of this office should be altogether unnecessary. The reasons, however, upon which said annual recommendations were based are continually assuming a more imperative character.

The following is a statement of the clerical force of this office, exclusive of messengers, laborers, and packers, annually provided, commencing with 1876:

For the year ending June 30, 1876 156
For the year ending June 30, 1877.. 145
For the year ending June 30, 1878.. 145
For the year ending June 30, 1879.. 151
For the year ending June 30, 1880.. 196
For the year ending June 30, 1881.. 195

The work of the office in 1876 was largely in arrears. The total disposals of lands in the year 1876 were 6,524,326.36 acres. The total disposals in 1880 were 14,792,371.65 acres, showing an increase of over 126 per cent. The increase in the clerical force in 1880 over 1876 was about 26 per cent.

The increase in sales of land for cash and under the homestead and timber-culture laws, commencing with the year ending June 30, 1876, is shown in the following table:

Number of acres sold for cash in the years ending June 30—

1876 640,691
1877 740,686
1878 877,555
1879 622,573
1880 850,741

And in the same period there were entered under the homestead laws—

1876 2,875,909
1877 2,178,098
1878 4,418,344
1879 5,280,111
1880 6,045,570

And under the timber-culture act—

1876 607,984
1877 520,673
1878 1,870,434
1879 2,766,573
1880 2,193,184

But the necessities of this branch of the public service, and in the interests represented in its transactions, cannot be understood from said figures alone.

Laws have multiplied; no session of Congress closes without new and varied legislation involving the public lands. Lands are of greater value than formerly, and as the country is settled and filled up, this increase in value will continue, and with it contests by conflicting claimants will be more numerous and more vigorously prosecuted. The existing cases, which have been pending and in controversy for years, are complicated and difficult, requiring for their correct disposition the *best legal talent.*

The mineral lands are inviting the capital and enterprise of the country for their development; and in these cases, not unfrequently involving millions of dollars in value, and in which the best legal talent of the country is employed as counsel, manifestly should be examined and decided by able lawyers; and the controversies growing out of conflicting claims of every character, all render it simply beyond reasonable question by any sensible person that a high standard of ability in those who decide these cases, involving the homes and fortunes of individuals no less than the public interests dependent upon peace of title and the sound administration of law, is imperatively demanded. Yet it will be seen, by a comparison of the clerical force provided in 1876 with that for the present year, that the increase is almost entirely represented by clerks at salaries of $1,200, $1,000, and $900. Now, while a limited number of copyists can be profitably used, yet, with a practical personal knowledge of this office and its work since the spring of 1876, I would be recreant to my trust should I fail to declare with the greatest emphasis that it is *absolutely absurd* to expect that the immense and varied interests adjusted by this office can be properly disposed of by clerks who can be hired at $1,000, $1,200, or $1,400 salaries.

The *necessity* of this office is able men of legal education and mature judgment, and without them the administration of its affairs must be measurably defective and discreditable.

With the force employed at the salaries now provided, it practically results that a very few of the ablest men in the entire office are overworked days, nights, and Sundays, in the effort to properly perform the grave duties imposed by law; and it is beyond question necessary that a higher grade of ability should be secured than can be had in the market at the low salaries above named.

The history of this office for the past ten years proves the almost invariable rule to be, that its ablest men resigned from the office, after acquiring proficiency in the business, for more lucrative positions. Whenever a man is employed who develops uncommon ability and value, it is confidently expected that he will remain for a limited time only. The work is difficult, and the pay is insignificant in comparison; hence the result cannot be doubtful.

The Patent Office has a deputy commissioner at a salary of $3,000. In my judgment there is an equal necessity for the deputy commissioner for the General Land Office at a salary at least as great, for no office in the executive branch of the government requires men of greater ability, or needs more diligent service, than the General Land Office.

Now the chief clerk performs the duties of the Commissioner during his absence from any cause, and receives a salary of $2,000.

The following provision should be made for this office in addition to the Commissioner:

1 deputy commissioner	$3,000
1 chief clerk	2,500
1 law officer	3,000
1 chief of division of surveys	3,000
1 chief of division of mineral lands	3,000
1 chief of division of private lands	3,000
1 chief of division of homesteads	2,400
1 chief of division of pre-emptions	2,400
1 chief of division of railroads	2,400
1 chief of division of swamp lands	2,400
1 chief of division of accounts	2,400
8 assistant chiefs of division, at $2,000	16,000
1 receiving clerk	2,000
1 recorder	2,000
20 clerks, class 4	36,000
60 clerks, class 3	96,000
50 clerks, class 2	70,000
40 clerks, class 1	48,000
15 copyists, at $900	13,500
9 assistant messengers, at $720	6,480
12 laborers, at $660	7,920
6 packers, at $720	4,320

The number of clerks above mentioned is all that can profitably be employed with the office room furnished.

The large and increasing accumulation of tract books, plats of surveys, field notes of surveys, records of patents, registers of official papers, records of correspondence, dockets of contested claims, returns of registers and receivers, records of testimony in contested cases, and the files of ex parte entries and proof, and correspondence, &c., occupy a very large space. The rooms are crowded with clerks' desks, books, files, &c., and large numbers of tract books, which contain the record of every entry, filing, selection, grant, or other disposition of every tract, and which have to be consulted continually in the daily work of the office, as well as records of patents, are stored in the corridors of the building to a degree rendering these invaluable records insecure, and involving a vast and unnecessary waste of labor, both by reason of their position remote from the clerks, and the fact that the light is so dim that the books have to be carried to some place where light can be secured and then returned again to their places.

The want of sufficient and conveniently arranged rooms unquestionably involves a large percentage of loss annually, and I feel well assured that were this fully remedied the saving to the government, in work accomplished, would in a few years actually reimburse it for the expenses necessary to construct the proper building to accommodate the office and preserve its records for all time. Much of the business of this office is far-removed from merely clerical work, and the embarrassments resulting from examination of large records of testimony, and writing important and difficult decisions, in rooms overcrowded with clerks engaged in various duties, can be readily understood. No well regulated private business would fail to receive improvement in the respect named.

The recommendations herein are substantially the same as have been made by my predecessors in office, and others, whose investigation of the subject entitles their conclusions to great respect. I differ only in respect to the prices which should be paid for competent services, and possibly, though not probably, in my estimate of the benefits to be derived from proper and commodious office room. I am not, however, necessarily at variance with my predecessors in any respect, inasmuch as I contemplate the condition of the office *as it is at the present time*, and speak with the advantage of additional experience, and a knowledge of existing difficulties. The necessity of the office, and the public and private interests involved is, to-day, a far more competent corps of men, and additional office room.

In conclusion, I frankly acknowledge my embarrassment in presenting again the pressing necessity for a thorough reorganization of this office. Every year for ten years last past the same subject has been called to the earnest attention of Congress. The leading men in the office have with almost superhuman efforts labored unceasingly to sustain the character of the bureau and carry forward its great work, the adjudication of the land titles of our vast territory, which has swiftly been organized into wealthy and populous States. The magnitude, the difficulty, and the national importance of the work can hardly be overstated, and it would seem self-evident that it cannot be done, and *well done;* except by able men, and, so far, no provision at all commensurate with the magnitude of the interests involved has been made.

I further suggest, in order that Congress may be fully advised of the necessities of this office, that a committee, composed of members from the Senate and House of Representatives, make a thorough examination of the office, and report their conclusions and recommendations to that body.

Very respectfully, your obedient servant,

J. A. WILLIAMSON,
Commissioner.

It seems unnecessary that I should add to what has been heretofore said, except to state that, in my opinion, the necessity for a higher grade of ability for the discharge of the official duties of this office is simply imperative.

One of the difficulties under which this office has heretofore labored has been the want of sufficient room to properly accommodate the requisite number of clerks. During the last summer about seventy clerks have been moved into the western hall of the model rooms of the Patent Office. This was done to obtain relief from the overcrowded rooms theretofore occupied, and also to enable the office to accommodate an additional number of clerks, made necessary by the accumulation of business, for the disposal of which pre-emptors, homesteaders, mineral land, and other claimants in all sections of the country are anxiously waiting. In this connection it may be stated that during the last fiscal year there were nearly twice the number of mineral entries than was made the year previous. These cases involve large values, and require ability and great care for their proper adjustment.

Their examination is now over one year in arrears, and with the current accumulations the period of delay must indefinitely increase. In these claims laborers and capitalists in every part of the country are interested.

In the single division of public lands there are now over 60,000 entries and legal notices of settlement claims unposted on the tract books, and unexamined, and about 1,300 contests unexamined, together with a large number of contests in the various stages of progress towards final adjudication. Other divisions are as much or more in arrears. There are 97 district land offices and 16 surveyor general's offices, under the supervision of this office. All their work and all their accounts come here for examination and adjustment.

This office contains the record of original sales of land, and of final adjustments of controversies relating to the public domain. It annually furnishes an immense amount of information to interested parties, at a great outlay of labor. I deem it quite impracticable to give in this communication any full detail of the vast work which has for several years seriously embarrassed this office, because of an insufficient clerical force of the requisite ability.

My estimate already submitted to you for the clerical force for the fiscal year ending June 30, 1883, is as follows:

Commissioner	$5,000 00
Deputy commissioner	3,000 00
3 inspectors of surveyor general and district land offices, at $3,000 each	9,000 00
Chief clerk	2,500 00
Law officer	2,500 00
Recorder	2,000 00
3 principal clerks, of public lands, private lands, and of surveys, at $2,000 each	6,000 00
6 chiefs of division, at $2,000 each	12,000 00
Receiving clerk	2,000 00
Chief draughtsman	2,000 00
35 clerks of class 4, at $1,800 each	63,000 00
50 clerks of class 3, at $1,600 each	80,000 00
60 clerks of class 2, at $1,400 each	84,000 00
55 clerks of class 1, at $1,200 each	66,000 00
35 copyists, at $900 each	31,500 00
Chief messenger	900 00
8 assistant messengers, at $720 each	5,760 00
6 packers, at $720 each	4,320 00
12 laborers, at $660 each	7,920 00
	389,400 00

It will be observed that the above estimate embraces more clerks at somewhat less salaries than were asked for last year by my predecessor. He did not ask for a greater number of clerks because at that time there was no room to accommodate them, and in the matter of my estimate for salaries I have sought to name the very lowest figures which, in my judgment, would possibly justify a reasonable expectation of retaining what good and competent men are now employed and thoroughly skilled in the business, and of obtaining from the outside a class of ability which the public have a right to expect will be employed to adjust the vast interests committed to this office.

I conceive it to be of great importance that a deputy commissioner be speedily authorized for this office.

The executive duties devolving upon the head of the bureau are so great and varied, as is well known, that it is impracticable and beyond physical possibilities for any Commissioner to personally discharge them in a proper manner. With a deputy commissioner a division of these duties can be made which will result largely to the benefit of the public business. I therefore recommend that this officer be authorized at as early a date after Congress convenes as may be practicable.

I have also estimated for an appropriation for three inspectors of surveyor general and district land offices, at a salary of $3,000 each. It has been the practice to detail clerks from this office, or employ special agents from the outside, to investigate irregularities and frauds, and to inspect the local offices. This proceeding is, however, open to serious objection. Not only is the agent comparatively unskilled in most instances, but the system of an occasional examination does not meet the demands of the service. The local land officers are subject to frequent change by death, resignation, or removal, and new and unskilled officers are appointed; errors in business methods are perpetuated, and by reason of defective proceedings in the local offices, claimants frequently suffer and additional work is imposed upon this office. The local offices should be under continued and intelligent supervision. A system of fraud not infrequently continues for a considerable time before this office is advised of its existence, and then it has but imperfect remedies at its command. In this, as in most other matters, prevention is better than cure.

The inspectors named should be tried, trusty, intelligent men, well versed in land laws and in the business of this office. Their duty should be, under direction from this office, to aid in the opening of all new land offices; to instruct new officers in their duties; see that the offices are legally and properly administered; detect and report fraud, irregularities, and inefficient officers, and, in short, to do and perform any duties in connection with the land service for which special agents have heretofore been appointed, or as the Secretary of the Interior or this office may direct.

Many of the same reasons which render the employment of inspectors in the Indian Department advisable apply with equal force to the land service. I am confident that the employment of such inspectors would cost less than the present system, would be far more effective, and would result in speedy improvement of the service.

Respectfully submitted.

N. C. McFARLAND,
Commissioner.

Hon. S. J. KIRKWOOD,
Secretary of the Interior.

REPORT OF THE COMMISSIONER OF INDIAN AFFAIRS.

DEPARTMENT OF THE INTERIOR,
OFFICE OF INDIAN AFFAIRS,
Washington, October 24, 1881.

SIR: I have the honor to submit herewith the annual report of the Indian Bureau for the year 1881.

In the outset, I desire to urge with earnestness the absolute necessity for a thorough and radical change of the Indian policy in some respects, and in so doing I shall touch upon points which will be referred to more at length hereafter under special headings.

It is claimed and admitted by all that the great object of the government is to civilize the Indians and render them such assistance in kind and degree as will make them self-supporting, and yet I think no one will deny that one part of our policy is calculated to produce the very opposite result. It must be apparent to the most casual observer that the system of gathering the Indians in bands or tribes on reservations and carrying to them victuals and clothes, thus relieving them of the necessity of labor, never will and never can civilize them. Labor is an essential element in producing civilization. If white men were treated as we treat the Indians the result would certainly be a race of worthless vagabonds. The greatest kindness the government can bestow upon the Indian is to teach him to labor for his own support, thus developing his true manhood, and, as a consequence, making him self-relying and self-supporting.

We are expending annually over one million dollars in feeding and clothing Indians where no treaty obligation exists for so doing. This is simply a gratuity, and it is presumed no one will question the expediency or the right of the government, if it bestows gratuities upon Indians, to make labor of some useful sort a condition precedent to such gift, especially when all of the products of such labor go to the Indian. To domesticate and civilize wild Indians is a noble work, the accomplishment of which should be a crown of glory to any nation. But to allow them to drag along year after year, and generation after generation, in their old superstitions, laziness, and filth, when we have the power to elevate them in the scale of humanity, would be a lasting disgrace to our government. The past experience of this government with its Indians has clearly established some points which ought to be useful as guides in the future.

There is no one who has been a close observer of Indian history and the effect of contact of Indians with civilization, who is not well satisfied that one of two things must eventually take place, to wit, either civilization or extermination of the Indian. Savage and civilized life cannot live and prosper on the same ground. One of the two must die. If the Indians are to be civilized and become a happy and prosperous people, which is certainly the object and intention of our government, they must learn our language and adopt our modes of life. We are fifty millions of people, and they are only one-fourth of one million. The few must yield to the many. We cannot reasonably expect them to abandon their habits of life and modes of living, and adopt ours, with any hope of speedy success as long as we feed and clothe them without any effort on their part.

In this connection I wish to call attention to the fact that in almost every case it is only the non-laboring tribes that go upon the war-path, and the stubborn facts of history compel me to say that the government is largely to blame for this.

The peaceable and industrious Indian has had less consideration than the turbulent and vicious. One instance in proof of this can be found at this moment in the case of the White River Utes (the murderers of Meeker) and the Utes on the Uintah Reservation. The White River Utes have just been moved to the Uintah Reservation alongside of the peaceable Uintah Utes. We feed the White River murderers and compel the peaceable Uintahs to largely care for themselves. This course induces the Indians to believe that if they are to get favors from the government they must refuse to work, refuse to be orderly and peaceable, and must commit some depredations or murder, and then a commission will be appointed to treat with them, and pay them in goods, provisions, and money to behave themselves. This looks to an Indian very much like rewarding enemies and punishing friends, and gives him a singular idea of our Christian civilization and our manner of administering justice, which has so much the appearance of rewarding vice and punishing virtue.

Another cause of the unsatisfactory condition of our Indian affairs is the failure of the government to give the Indian land in severalty, and to give it to him in such a way that he will know that it is his. He has learned by painful experience that a small piece of paper called scrip is not good for much as a title to land. He has again and again earnestly solicited the government to give him a title to a piece of land, that he might make for himself a home. These requests have, in a great many instances, been neglected or refused, and this is true even in cases where, by treaty stipulations, the government agreed to give the Indian a patent for his land. Under this state of facts, it is not to be wondered at that the Indian is slow to cultivate the soil. He says, when urged to do so, that he has no heart to do it, when in a month or a year he may be moved, and some white man be allowed to enjoy the fruit of his labor. That is the way the Indian talks, and that is the way a white man would talk under similar circumstances.

Another just cause of complaint which the Indians have is that in our treaties with them, in some instances, we agree to give them so many pounds of beef, flour, coffee, sugar, &c., and then a certain sum of money is appropriated for the purpose of fulfilling the promise, which sum so appropriated (as is the case the present year, because of the increased price of beef, &c.) will not buy the *pounds*; consequently, the Indians do not get what was promised them. This they construe as bad faith on the part of the government, and use it as an excuse for doing something wrong themselves; and thus troubles of a serious and extensive nature frequently arise. This would all be avoided if appropriations were sufficiently large to cover all contingencies, and such appropriations would not interfere with or violate the rules of strict economy; for any surplus (if there should be any) would be turned into the Treasury, as is always done, at the end of the fiscal year, when an unexpended balance remains of any particular appropriation. This would be keeping our contracts to the letter, and would inspire confidence and respect on the part of the Indian for our government, and give him no excuse for wrong-doing.

But I am very decidedly of opinion that ultimate and final success never can be reached without adding to all other means and appliances the location of each family, or adult Indian who has no family, on a certain number of acres of land, which they may call their own and hold by a title as good and strong as a United States patent can make it. Let it be inalienable for, say, twenty years; give the Indian teams, implements, and tools amply sufficient for farming purposes; give him seed, food, and clothes for at least one year; in short, give him every facility for making a comfortable living, and then *compel* him to depend upon his own exertions for a livelihood. Let the laws that govern a white man govern the Indian. The Indian must be made to understand that if he expects to live and prosper in this country he must learn the English language, and learn to *work*. The language will enable him to transact his business understandingly with his white neighbors, and his labor will enable him to provide the necessaries and comforts of life for himself and family. The policy thus indicated will in a few years rid the government of this vexed "Indian question," making the Indian a blessing instead of a curse to himself and country, which, judging the future by the past, will never be done by the present policy.

REMOVAL OF THE MESCALERO APACHES.

I wish to call attention to the fact that some Indians in Arizona and New Mexico have always been troublesome and difficult to manage.

Lawless Indians, belonging to no particular reservation, and desperate white men compose bands of marauders who commit depredations and when pursued fly to the mountains of Chihuahua and Sonora. My opinion is that the most effectual remedy for all this is to remove the Mescalero Apaches, and eventually all other Indians, north of the center line of New Mexico and Arizona, so as to keep them at a distance from Chihuahua and Sonora. The removal of the Mescaleros would not seem to be difficult of accomplishment, inasmuch as a special Indian agent, who was recently dispatched to their agency for the purpose of ascertaining their views upon the subject of removal, reports them as expressing a willingness to remove to the Jicarilla Reservation on the north line of New Mexico.

For the past five years the office has been importuned to take measures for the removal of the Mescaleros from their present reservation and settle them permanently on some other reserve, where they can be more easily guarded and will be far less liable to commit depredations. The citizens of New Mexico and Texas have urged this, and the military authorities have regarded such a movement as indispensable to the protection of the citizens and the welfare and good conduct of the Indians. The county of Lincoln, in which this reservation is situated, has for a population the very worst elements that can be found in the Territory or upon the borders of Mexico—Spanish and Mexican refugees from justice, outlaws from the States, &c. In brief, as stated by Inspector Watkins, who made a thorough investigation of affairs in that section and that reservation in 1878, "the whole county of Lincoln is under the control of cut-throats and thieves." He was also of the opinion, concurred in by many others who have been personally cognizant of affairs there, that a large share of the crimes committed by this class of settlers are charged to the Indians. · There is abundant evidence before the office to show that these outlaws have for years been in the habit of enticing the Indians to go out upon their raids, &c., and are the recipients of their plunder. Indians under such circumstances and with such surroundings will not progress very far in civilization. The result has been that over one-half of these Indians within the past five years have been scattered and exterminated; depredations have been committed by them, and large sums of money have been expended by the government in military operations against them.

Two inspectors and one special agent within the past six or eight months have visited this reserve, and all concur in the opinion that the Indians should be removed. The reservation is not adapted to agricultural purposes. It is overrun with prospectors for mining purposes. &c., and numerous claims have been taken, many of them antedating the establishment of the reservation, and it will be impossible to remove the claimants without much litigation and large expenditure of money for their improvements.

To guard these 400 Indians and prevent them from going into Southern New Mexico, Texas, and Old Mexico three companies of cavalry and one of infantry are stationed some 40 miles north of the agency, at Fort Stanton, where large expenditures have been made for barracks, buildings, &c. If the Indians are removed these troops will not be needed there, and thus a large amount of money would be saved to the government annually. Because of the contemplated removal no improvements have been made upon the reservation to any extent for some time; but if the Indians remain there for any considerable time longer, buildings will have to be erected at an expense of $3,000 to $4,000 (the agent estimates their cost at $6,000) which must ultimately be abandoned, for no one believes that this reservation can be a permanent home for these Indians. If removed to the Jicarilla Reservation, one agent can take charge of the two bands, Mescaleros and Jicarillas (the former affiliate well with most of the latter and have intermarried), and the cost of removal will be less than the proposed expenditure for buildings and for troops to guard the Indians where they are.

The agent of the Mescaleros and our special agent advised the office, when the removal to the Jicarilla Reservation was first contemplated, that the military at Fort Stanton and certain persons who have large contracts with that branch of the service would prevent such removal if possible; and, as predicted, these influences are now busily at work to prolong the disastrous state of affairs which for the past ten years have existed in Southern New Mexico, to continue the large expenditures resulting therefrom, and to prevent the government from settling the question now and permanently.

The Indian problem is at best difficult of solution; but by removing the Indians from unfavorable surroundings and bad men, as far as possible, a long step will have been taken in the direction of success.

INDIAN DISTURBANCES IN NEW MEXICO AND ARIZONA.

In this connection I wish to call attention briefly to recent Indian disturbances in New Mexico and Arizona, which are the only Indian disturbances of any magnitude that have occurred during the year and which have been greatly exaggerated in the accounts published in the newspapers.

For a few months after the destruction of Victoria and his band in Old Mexico, in October, 1880, Indian raids in New Mexico ceased; but last summer depredations and murders again began, chiefly in Socorro County, which were charged to the "remnant of Victoria's band." It was known that a portion of that band, by their temporary absence from the main body at the time of the fight with Victoria, saved themselves from destruction or capture. This "remnant," under Chief Nana, naturally became a nucleus for renegade Indians in that part of the country, and their number, which General Terrasas reported as 30, has been reported this last summer as about seventy. They have been again followed up by troops and chased toward Sonora.

The following extract from report of Agent Llewellyn, dated July 28, 1881, would show that the return of these Indians to a marauding life was not wholly without excuse :

As to who these Indians are, I can assure the Department that they are not from this agency, at least have not been here for over one year; it is certain, however, that they belong here, and had it not been for the San Carlos scouts and the soldiers, they would have come into the agency at least two weeks ago.

It seems that some few months since a Lieutenant of the United States Army, then stationed here, gave a written permit to three Indians at this agency to go to Old Mexico and bring back here a party of their friends whom they claimed had left at the time of the Victoria troubles. This party were due here three weeks ago, and at that time attempted to come in, but were chased and driven into the mountains thirty miles from the agency to the south. Since that time they have made, according to the statement of one of the packers for the scouts, who is now at this agency badly wounded, three ineffectual efforts to get into the agency, being prevented each time by the scouts and soldiers; finding that they could not return to the agency, as they had been led to believe they could, they commenced to go on the war-path. I learn on good authority that there are about seventy Indians in this party.

In June and July reports that these "hostiles" were being driven by General Hatch towards Arizona caused some anxiety on the part of the San Carlos agent and the military in the vicinity of that reservation, lest the hostiles might cause disaffection among a few of the Indians there who were related to the renegades, and various precautions were taken and preparations made to resist any attack. These fears, however, were not realized, and, reports to the contrary notwithstanding, the San Carlos Indians seem to have had no part whatever in the Indian raids in New Mexico; on the contrary, at different times they have had no small share in the scouting carried on against them.

In 1875 the Camp Apache Agency, located in the northern part of the San Carlos reserve, was abolished, and the White Mountain Apaches belonging thereto, about 1,800 in number, were turned over to the San Carlos agent. Most of them were removed to the southern part of the reserve and located on the Gila (where a sub-agency was established), and regularly rationed; but some, preferring to take the chance of self-support on their old hunting-grounds, remained behind, and were gradually rejoined by others until they numbered between 600 and 700, whose headquarters were on Cibicu Creek, in the northwestern part of the reserve, about 40 miles from the agency and 30 from Camp Apache. In June last, considerable excitement was occasioned among these Indians by the proposition of a medicine-man named Nock-a-de-klenny, at the expense of large gifts of horses, blankets, &c., to bring to life again some chiefs who had died a few months previous. The agent remonstrated with the Indians on the ground of the folly of the thing and the waste of their goods, but they decided to wait till the time specified, and in case the "resurrection" failed, to demand the restoration of their property. Whether he desired only to appease the Indians for his failure, or whether he intended to bring about a revolt, cannot be known; but when Nock a de klenny announced that the spirits had notified him that the dead warriors could not return to the country until the whites had left it, and fixed the date of their leaving at the time of the corn harvest, it was feared both by the agent and the military authorities at Camp Apache that the medicine man was working upon the superstitions of the Indians to bring about an outbreak, or would bring them into such a condition that they could easily be induced to join in any demonstration made by hostiles from New Mexico.

It was accordingly decided that the military should arrest the man at a "medicine-dance" which he proposed to hold at Camp Apache on August 20th. The dance having failed to come off, Colonel Carr, commanding post, sent a messenger to tell Nock a de klenny that he wanted to see him on the following Sunday. Only an evasive reply being received, he started on Monday, August 29th, with 6 officers, 79 soldiers, and 23 Indian scouts for the Indian village, reached there the following day, and arrested Nock a de klenny, who surrendered quietly, professing no desire or intention of attempting escape. But as the troops were making camp for the night, their own Indian scouts and many other Indians opened fire on them. A sharp fight ensued, the medicine-man was killed, the Indians repulsed, and the command reached the post the next day, to be again attacked by the Indians, who had already killed eight men on the road to Camp Thomas and run off some stock. The loss in the two fights was 11 killed and 3 wounded. The mutinous scouts were themselves White Mountain Apaches, and though a few of them are exonerated from complicity in the treachery, it is believed that most of them left the post with no intention of aiding in the arrest of the medicine-man.

Re-enforcements were sent to Camp Apache and troops were stationed at the agency, and preparations made for an attack at either point. The White Mountain Indians, however, were not long in discovering the folly of their action, and came into the agency and subagency in small parties, where they were required to surrender to military officers unconditionally, except that they asked and were promised a fair trial for their individual crimes. Six days' notice was given throughout the reserve that a "peace line" would be declared on the reserve September 21st, outside of whose limits all Indians found would be considered hostile, with the exception of Pedro's band near Camp Apache. On the 20th of September the five chiefs who had been leaders in the affair surrendered, and during the ensuing week 60 of their principal men followed their example. Several of the mutinous scouts had been arrested and brought in by the agency Indian police force and delivered up to the military, and by the close of the month nearly all were in or accounted for, and little remained to be done but to proceed with the trials.

It appears, however, that chiefs George and Bonito, who had come in to the subagency, and had gone with Issue Clerk Hoag to Camp Thomas, and there surrendered to Gen. Wilcox, September 25, had been paroled by that officer and allowed to return to the subagency. September 30, Colonel Biddle, with some troops, was sent to the subagency to take them and their bands back to Thomas. Unfortunately this was issue day, and a large number of Indians were assembled. They agreed to go as soon as the issue of beef (which was then in progress) had been made, but later in the afternoon sent word that the troops need not wait for them as they would follow soon with Issue Clerk Hoag. Colonel Biddle replied that they must go at once, and started his command towards George's camp, whereupon he and Bonito fled to the Chiricahuas and so alarmed them that during the night 74 Chiricahuas, including women and children, fled from the reserve, leaving much of their stock behind. The troops followed and are reported to have overtaken and attacked them. In their flight the Indians have captured 8 teams and killed 6 teamsters. Bonito went with them. These are some of the very Indians who under chief "Juh" were induced by Captain Haskell, to come in from Old Mexico in January last. The following, from Agent Tiffany, shows that these Indians were not concerned in the White Mountain troubles, and that their flight was occasioned by fear, not hostility:

These bands have been perfectly quiet during the whole White Mountain trouble. They have been reported out on the war-path in New Mexico and committing depredations all over the country, but every time inquiry has been made the chiefs and men have always been found in their camps, and on two occasions they were in the agency office talking to me when telegrams arrived as to their whereabouts; and on one of these occasions, R. S. Gardner, Indian inspector, was present. Ten days or thereabouts before the present outbreak they came to me to hear what was going on, and what so many troops meant about the agencies. I explained it to them and told them to have no fear, that none of the Indians who had been peaceable would be molested in any way. They said they had been out on the war-path and had come in in good faith and were contented, that they did not want war or to fight. The only place they would fight was if the White Mountains would come to the agency or subagency they would fight them there.

They inquired if the movements of troops had anything to do with what they had done in Mexico. I assured them it had not. They shook hands, much delighted and went back. Then the military move was made on the subagency to arrest Chiefs George and Bonito, of White Mountain Indians, and Issue Clerk Hoag at subagency, who has been very efficient and judicious in all this trouble, tells me that they were literally scared away by this movement of troops.

I desire to call attention to the loyalty shown by five-sixths of the Indians on the San Carlos reserve. They have rendered invaluable and hazardous service as police and scouts, in finding, arresting, and guarding the guilty ones, and as messengers for both agent and military when communication was interrupted by the cutting of the telegraph wires.

GENERAL STATISTICS.

The following tables show:

First. The distribution of population.

Second. The objects and purposes of the expenditures from appropriations for the fiscal year 1880 and the present year.

Third. The work accomplished and the gain made during the year by the Indians of the country in the way of farming, stock-raising, house-building, &c.

Population.—According to the last annual report, the number of Indians in the United States, exclusive of Alaska, was 255,938; the present number is 261,851, an increase of nearly six thousand, which is probably largely accounted for by the more accurate census taken during this year, and by the surrender and return to their agencies of the Sioux who, under Sitting Bull, have been living in Canada since 1877. These are distributed among 68 agencies established in the following States and Territories:

States and Territories.	Aggregate number of agencies.	Aggregate Indian population.
Arizona	4	18,600
California	4	4,741
Colorado	2	3,600
Dakota	10	30,660
Idaho	3	3,562
Indian Territory	5	18,205
Indian Territory (5 civilized tribes)	1	56,877
Kansas	1	732
Iowa	1	355
Michigan	1	9,795
Minnesota	1	6,136
Montana	5	20,519
Nebraska	4	4,228
Nevada	2	7,811
New Mexico (including Jicarilla subagency)	1	18,683
New York	1	5,235
Oregon	5	4,119
Utah	1	674
Washington Territory	7	13,167
Wisconsin	2	7,250
Wyoming	1	3,668
Total	68	246,417

Those Indians not under the control of the agents of the government, numbering 15,134, are principally in the Territories of Arizona, Idaho, and Utah, and in the States of California, Indiana, Kansas, North Carolina, Oregon, and Wisconsin.

Expenditures.

Objects and purposes for which the appropriations have been expended.	1880.	1881.
Amount appropriated..	$4,674,573 44	$4,418,390 76
Pay of Indian agents..	76,569 13	80,493 15
Pay of special agents.......................................	3,917 58	3,897 23
Pay of interpreters..	21,696 97	94,555 53
Buildings at agencies and repairs..........................	40,715 91	43,147 20
Vaccination of Indians	192 00	404 34
Medicines and medical supplies.............................	17,273 08	15,974 51
Annuity goods	477,370 39	584,825 47
Subsistence supplies	1,867,348 27	1,804,505 88
Agricultural and miscellaneous supplies....................	418,487 94	291,450 43
Expenses of transportation and storage	309,394 60	284,680 73
Purchase and inspection of annuity goods and supplies.....	17,941 97	21,668 80
Advertising expenses and telegraphing.....................	5,478 05	8,347 90
Payment of annuities in money.............................	281,336 57	306,987 64
Payment of regular employés at agencies..................	307,468 41	335,458 65
Payment of temporary employés at agencies................	16,786 16	17,302 37
Support of schools...	152,411 76	206,996 47
To promote civilization among Indians generally, including Indian labor..	73,647 89	117,574 44
Traveling expenses of Indian agents.......................	16,306 33	13,908 52
Traveling expenses of special agents......................	2,995 25	1,129 76
Incidental expenses of agencies	6,786 18	3,387 20
Pay of Indian police, scouts, and equipments	48,234 46	63,442 30
Presents to Indians	1,030 00	50 00
Survey of Indian reservations..............................		251 28
Pay and expenses of Indian inspectors.....................	10,744 56	19,779 43
Expenses of Indian commissioners..........................	13,963 98	6,300 00
Agricultural improvements..................................	4,696 10	11,935 46
Miscellaneous..	12,974 00	7,610 29
In hands of agents at date of this report..................	134,716 01	16,489 58
Total amount expended from all appropriations	4,204,271 73	4,297,322 74
Balance unexpended at date of this report.................	335,585 70	184,507 44

A comparison of the expenditures of the two years shows that during the current year particular effort has been made to push forward the educational interests of the service, and to advance the process of civilizing the Indian by inducing him to labor, paying him therefor. A large part of the items of "expenses of transportation, &c.," $284,680.73, and "to promote civilization, &c.," $117,574.44, has been paid to Indians for services which formerly were performed by white contractors. The willingness exhibited by the Indians to engage in industrial pursuits is constantly increasing, and is one of the most gratifying features connected with the service. Again, a comparison shows clearly that a more careful supervision of the funds appropriated is had from year to year, the amount of funds in the hands of agents at the date of this report being only $16,489.58, against $134,716.01 at a corresponding date last year; and a balance remaining on the books of this office of only $184,507.44 against $335,585.70 the previous year.

Results of Indian labor.

INDIANS EXCLUSIVE OF FIVE CIVILIZED TRIBES.	1879.	1880.	1881.
Number of acres broken by Indians........................	24,270	27,105	29,558
Number of acres cultivated...............................	157,056	168,340	205,367
Number of bushels of wheat raised	324,637	408,812	451,479
Number of bushels of corn raised	643,286	604,103	517,642
Number of bushels of oats and barley raised..............	189,054	294,899	343,444
Number of bushels of vegetables raised...................	390,698	375,843	488,799
Number of tons of hay cut.................................	48,333	75,745	76,763
Number of horses owned...................................	199,739	211,981	188,402
Number of cattle owned...................................	66,894	78,989	80,684

Results of Indian labor—Continued.

	1879.	1880.	1881.
INDIANS EXCLUSIVE OF FIVE CIVILIZED TRIBES—Continued.			
Number of swine owned	32, 537	40, 381	43, 913
Number of sheep owned	863, 585	864, 516	877, 017
Number of houses occupied	11, 634	12, 507	12, 883
Number of Indian houses built during the year	1, 211	1, 639	1, 409
Number of Indian apprentices who have been learning trades	185	388	456
FIVE CIVILIZED TRIBES.			
Number of acres cultivated	273, 000	314, 386	348, 000
Number of bushels of wheat raised	568, 400	336, 494	105, 000
Number of bushels of corn raised	2, 915, 000	2, 346, 042	618, 000
Number of bushels of oats and barley raised	900, 000	134, 569	74, 300
Number of bushels of vegetables raised	236, 700	595, 000	305, 000
Number of tons of hay cut	176, 500	125, 500	161, 500
Number of bales of cotton raised	10, 530	16, 800	(*)
Number of horses owned	45, 580	61, 453	64, 600
Number of mules owned	5, 500	5, 138	6, 150
Number of cattle owned	278, 000	297, 040	370, 000
Number of swine owned	120, 000	409, 382	455, 080
Number of sheep owned	32, 400	34, 034	23, 408

* Not reported.

The decrease in quantities raised by the civilized tribes in the Indian Territory is largely attributable to the long-continued season of drought.

APPROPRIATIONS.

The appropriations made by Congress for the fiscal year ending June 30, 1882, for the support of the Indians under treaty stipulations and otherwise, are entirely insufficient, and unless an additional amount is appropriated this winter, this office will be greatly embarrassed in the work of civilization, and want of funds may lead to serious difficulties. Owing to the severe weather of last winter the price paid for beef for the fiscal year 1882 is 30 per cent. higher than that paid last year, which, taking into consideration that this office purchases nearly 40,000,000 pounds gross, makes a difference of $400,000 for that article alone. In some instances the treaty with the Indians provides a specific amount of clothing or subsistence to be furnished them, yet Congress in almost every instance fails to provide sufficient funds to carry out these provisions. The agreement made with the Sioux, dated February 28, 1877, provides in article 5 as follows:

In consideration of the foregoing cession of territory and rights, and upon full compliance with each and every obligation assumed by the said Indians, the United States does agree to provide all necessary aid to assist the said Indians in the work of civilization, to furnish to them schools and instruction in mechanical and agricultural arts, as provided for by the treaty of 1868; also to provide the said Indians with subsistence consisting of a ration for each individual of a pound and a half of beef (or in lieu thereof one-half pound of bacon), one-half pound of flour, and one-half pound of corn ; and for every 100 rations four pounds of coffee, eight pounds of sugar, and three pounds of beans, or in lieu of said articles the equivalent thereof, in the discretion of the Commissioner of Indian Affairs.

On a basis of 25,000 Indians (the reports of the agents give a population of over 25,000, including 2,800 turned over recently by the War Department) these Indians are entitled, under the foregoing agreement. to 27,375,000 pounds gross beef, 4,562,000 pounds flour, 4,562,000 pounds corn, 365,000 pounds coffee, 730,000 pounds sugar, and 273,750 pounds beans, costing, at prices at which contracts were made for the fiscal year 1882, over $1,250,000; and this does not take into consideration the promise also made by Congress in the article above quoted "to provide all necessary aid to assist the said Indians in the work of civilization, to furnish them schools," &c. The amount appropriated by Congress for 1882, for both subsistence and civilization, under the above agreement, is only $1,000,000, leaving a deficiency of over $250,000 to be provided for, for subsistence alone, and an additional sum of at least $100,000 for aiding these Sioux in civilization and agricultural pursuits. There are other instances in which additional sums must be had for subsistence, and a deficiency estimate will be submitted to you at an early date for transmission to Congress.

The amount appropriated for schools ($85,000) is entirely inadequate. At almost every agency day-schools, as well as a boarding-school, must be supported from this fund, since in but few instances does the treaty or agreement provide sufficient means for that purpose. It is confidently expected that Congress will be more liberal in the future than in the past in appropriating money for the education of the Indians.

The amount appropriated for the support of the Blackfeet Indians in Montana ($35,000) is insufficient, and $50,000 at least should be granted by Congress for that purpose for the next fiscal year. In this connection I call your attention to the following letters from Col. Thomas H. Ruger, commanding district of Montana, in regard to the additional supplies required for the support of these Indians:

HEADQUARTERS DISTRICT OF MONTANA,
Helena, Mont., September 1, 1881.

SIR: I have the honor to request the attention of the department commander to the propriety of action with a view to procuring an increase of subsistence supplies for the Indians attached to the Blackfeet Agency.

By letter of the 26th of May last, I urged the agent, Mr. John Young, to present the case in full to the department. He passed through here on the 29th instant before my return from Maginnis, and stated, as I learn, that he should go to Washington and endeavor to get more supplies for the Indians under his charge. If anything can be done to further such object, I think, action to that end very desirable. The facts pertinent are, that the supplies provided for these Indians are entirely inadequate for their subsistence the coming winter; the game obtainable on their reservation is not sufficient, if added to the issues by the agent, to prevent great suffering and even starvation. Should the Indians be permitted to leave the reservation, the nearest region where game could be had is the Musselshell country, to reach which would require, by their usual route by the Judith Valley, a journey of about twenty-five days through a country now practically destitute of game, but occupied by settlers and for cattle-ranges. The Indians would not start provided with food for such journey. Whether they committed depredations or not, their presence in the settlement would be taken as conclusive evidence that they were killing cattle from necessity. Should they move in a body and under escort to the Musselshell their presence there, so near the cattle-ranges east of the Judith and Snowy Mountains and the lower ranges of the Musselshell, would be a source of trouble. Last winter these and other Indians in that country were the prey of illicit-whisky traders, and consequently derived very little benefit from the robes and peltries procured, and no doubt that experience would be repeated.

There has been for the past two years, as the settlements have spread and ranges for cattle have been occupied, embracing generally all the country to the south of the Marias River and the Missouri and west of the Musselshell, an increasing feeling of hostility on the part of cattle-owners and settlers concerned, to the presence of any Indians in the region mentioned, and recently several organizations of stock-owners have had meetings with apparent intent to prevent Indians from crossing the ranges; and some, no doubt, would not hesitate, if opportunity offered, to act with a purpose of bringing matters to a crisis in expectation of a final settlement resulting, by which the Indians would be confined to their reservations; and this applies as well to the settlers on the Yellowstone with respect to the Crows, Flatheads, &c.

The time has come when the Indians attached to the Blackfeet Agency at least should be supplied with sufficient food on their reservation. I have not the data from which to make an accurate estimate of the amount requisite for this winter in addition to the present appropriation, but not less than $15,000 is necessary, and which should be expended for food only.

Very respectfully, your obedient servant,

THOS. H. RUGER,
Colonel Eighteenth Infantry, Commanding District.

To the ADJUTANT GENERAL DEPARTMENT OF DAKOTA,
Fort Snelling, Minnesota.

44 Ab

DEFICIENCY APPROPRIATIONS.

As stated under the head of "Appropriations," owing to the large increase in the price of beef paid during the fiscal year 1882, the appropriations for the Indian service during 1882 will in many cases be insufficient. On the 20th of July last, the War Department turned over to this bureau 2,813 Sioux Indians, belonging to Sitting Bull's band, and for whose support no appropriation was made by Congress. Under your authority a deficiency of $195,000 was incurred for the purchase fo the supplies and clothing for these Indians and the amount will be included in the deficiency estimate to be submitted to Congress. Additional funds for the support of the following Indians for the present fiscal year. and for other purposes, will also be required, as follows: Support of Apaches in Arizona and New Mexico, $25,000; support of Arapahoes, Cheyennes, Apaches, Kiowas, Comanches, and Wichitas, $100,000; support of Blackfeet, Bloods, and Piegans, $15,000; support of Indians in central superintendency, $7,500; support of Modocs, $5,000; support of Navajoes, $5,000; support of Nez Percés of Joseph's band, $7,500; support of schools, $50,000; telegraphing and purchase of Indian supplies, $5,000; transportation of Indian supplies, $25,000.

Large sums are also due different parties for goods and supplies furnished and for services rendered in 1873 and 1874, which have repeatedly been reported to Congress for appropriation, but none has so far been made. There is due the Western Union Telegraph Company, for messages transmitted during May and June, 1879, the sum of $361.65; contractors for transporting Indian goods and supplies during the fiscal year 1879, $9,556.63; during the fiscal year 1880, $44,882.14, and during the fiscal year 1881, about $50,000. This indebtedness was incurred by this office under an absolute necessity, and early provision for its payment should be made by Congress.

Early in last spring it was found that the amount appropriated by Congress for the support of the Arapahoes, Cheyennes, Apaches, Kiowas, Comanches and Wichitas, located at the Cheyenne and Arapaho and Kiowa, and Comanche Agencies, Indian Territory, for the fiscal year 1881, was insufficient to furnish them with beef, coffee, and sugar until the end of the fiscal year. The agents in charge were notified of the insufficient appropriations and directed to reduce the issue of beef, but in reply thereto submitted statements which convinced the department that to reduce the rations of those Indians was to invite a war. Copies of these letters were transmitted to Congress with a request for an additional appropriation, but the same was not granted. After the adjournment of Congress the case was submitted by you to the President, and, upon consultation with the honorable Secretary of War, it was decided that the War Department would furnish the agents at Cheyenne and Arapaho, and Kiowa and Comanche Agencies with beef and flour until the end of the last fiscal year, the cost of these supplies to be reimbursed from any appropriation which may hereafter be made by Congress for that purpose. Accounts amounting to $59,232.01 have been presented by the War Department for reimbursement, and it is hoped that Congress at an early day will furnish this office with the means to cancel this debt.

Owing to the failure of Congress to appropriate during the fiscal years 1879, 1880, and 1881 sufficient funds to pay for the transportation of goods and supplies to the different agencies, this office has been greatly embarrassed this summer by not having its stores promptly delivered. Contractors to whom the government owes over $100,000 for transportation services performed under former contracts, are not very anxious to render services and wait for their pay several years. Flour delivered to the contractors for different agencies in October, 1880, was not delivered until July or August, 1881, and when this office urged them to comply more strictly with their contracts, their reply, that this office had no funds to pay them after service was rendered, appeared a sufficient excuse for the delay. The failure of Congress to appropriate last winter sufficient funds to pay outstanding indebtedness for transportation costs the government in increased price of transportation for the present fiscal year more than the interest on the money due, and while there are such large sums lying idle in the United States Treasury-the policy of not paying debts lawfully due appears to me very short, sighted. It cannot be expected that contractors will wait years for money due and honestly earned without attempting to get even with the government by charging increased rates of transportation; and for this reason it is urged that sufficient means be furnished this office to liquidate these debts. This would certainly be true economy.

The right of this office to incur this indebtedness above the amount appropriated cannot be questioned. Congress appropriates a certain amount of money to be used in the purchase of clothing and supplies, mostly due the Indians under treaty stipulation. Of what avail are these goods and supplies to the Indians, if sufficient funds are not appropriated to pay for transporting them to the different agencies, where they are required?

The attention of Congress has repeatedly been called to the insufficient amount appropriated yearly for transporting the goods and supplies, and it is earnestly hoped that the efforts of this office in obtaining means to pay the old indebtedness incurred, as well as in securing sufficient funds for the present and next fiscal year, will have better success than heretofore.

INDIAN POLICE.

The organization of a United States Indian police force is no longer an experiment. The system is now in operation at forty-nine agencies; the total force employed being eighty-four commissioned officers, and seven hundred and eighty-six non-commissioned officers and privates. In answer to circular letter from this office, dated August 19, 1881, special reports have been received from nearly all agencies as to the value, reliability, and efficiency of this service. These reports are uniformly gratifying in their testimony as to the zeal, courage, and fidelity of the members of the force, and their almost invaluable service to the agents. The Indian police are fully recognized as an important agency in the civilization of their brethren.

The immediate work of this force is to preserve order, prohibit illegal traffic in liquor, and arrest offenders. In the line of these duties, they act as guards at ration issues and annuity payments; take charge of and protect, at all times, government property; restore lost or stolen property to its rightful owners; drive out timber thieves and other trespassers; return truant pupils to school; make arrests for disorderly conduct and other offenses, and especially protect the reservations from the traffic in liquor, which, in the language of one of the agents, is "the root and cause of nine-tenths of all crimes committed." These varied and important duties are performed with a fidelity and thoroughness that is fully appreciated by this office, and its agents.

The indirect results and ultimate influence of this system are even more important than its direct advantages. Well trained and disciplined, the police force is a perpetual educator. It is a power entirely independent of the chiefs. It weakens, and will finally destroy, the power of tribes and bands. It fosters a spirit of personal responsibility. It makes the Indian himself the representative of the power and majesty of the Government of the United States. These latter features constitute its main strength for permanent good. It is true that the Indians need to be taught the supremacy of law, and the necessity for strict obedience thereto; it is also true that where the Indians themselves are the recognized agents for the enforcement of law, they will the more readily learn to be obedient to its requirements.

The force is, at present, limited by law to one hundred officers and eight hundred privates. This limit should be extended so as to allow the appointment of one hundred and twenty officers and twelve hundred privates. There are requests now on file for an increase of force, at points where such increase is absolutely necessary. The requests cannot be granted without violating the above law. There are also nineteen agencies without police, a majority of whom would be benefitted by its introduction.

A very important matter in connection with the police service is the amount of the annual appropriation therefor. The compensation of eight dollars per month for officers, and five dollars per month for privates, is properly characterized by some of the agents as simply ridiculous. In some cases, members of the force spend fully that sum for traveling expenses in the discharge of their duties; they also furnish their own ponies and feed them. The pay of commissioned officers should be not less than fifteen dollars per month, and privates should have at least ten dollars monthly. The best men of the tribes can be had, if the compensation is commensurate with the value and importance of the work. The appropriation should be such that rations can be furnished at non-ration agencies, and that uniforms, arms, and accouterments, may be of the best quality as a matter of mere economy. A large increase in the annual appropriation is necessary to secure the best men, and to promote the highest interests of the service.

Some selections from recent reports of agents will give intelligent information as to the value, reliability, and efficiency of this service.

Agent McGillycuddy, of Pine Ridge agency, Dakota, says:

The force, to a man, are prompt to obey orders in making an arrest. It is immaterial to them whether the offender be a white man or an Indian, a head chief or a young brave, the arrest is always made. The white men in this region recognize the fact that to resist an Indian policeman would be to resist a United States official in discharge of his duty. The Indians generally recognize the police authority, for from time immemorial there has existed among the Sioux and other tribes native soldier organizations, systematically governed by laws and regulations. Some of the strongest opposition encountered in endeavoring to organize the police force in the spring of 1879 was from these native soldier organizations, for they at once recognized something in it strongly antagonistic to their ancient customs, namely, a force at the command of the white man opposed to their own. The police were threatened in various ways, but as time passed on we secured the requisite number of members, and among them many of the *head soldiers*, so that to-day the United States Indian police have, to a great extent, supplanted the soldier bands and exercise their ancient powers.

Up to the present time nothing has occurred to cause doubt as to their trustworthiness and efficiency. The Indian freighters and employés at this agency are paid in standard silver dollars to avoid disputes and trouble in cashing their checks by traders. It is expressed through from the Philadelphia mint in quantities of $10,000 to Fort Robinson, Neb., our nearest express office, sixty-three miles away. It is my custom to proceed to that point with ten of the police as an escort, receipt for the money, and *turn it over to the police;* they then transport the same to the agency, camping out *en route.* The money remains in wooden boxes in their charge until wanted, and so far this trust has not been violated, and I feel assured will not be.

In former years this agency was the rendezvous and asylum for the hardest class of white men in the West, such as horse-thieves, road-agents, and escaped convicts. Safely concealed in the camps of the Indians, with whom they affiliated, they successfully defied all efforts to arrest them. Now, with a United States court commissioner and deputy United States marshal stationed at the agency, efficiently backed by the police, things have changed, and a man—white or Indian—is guaranteed better protection for his life and property on this portion of the Sioux reserve than in any of the bordering States or Territories, as the intervening country between the villages, which are located at various distances up to forty miles from the agency, is continually patrolled by the police, so that no depredation could be committed without soon coming to their knowledge.

In this connection the question might be pertinently asked, "Why is it that the Oga-lallas, a people numbering over 7,000, have just passed three of the quietest and to the government and themselves most gratifying years of their existence, and the first that they have passed without the presence of military at their agency?" For this condi-tion of affairs much is due to the police system. The majority of the Indians appre-ciate the fact that, sooner or later, a regularly organized armed force has to be introduced and play a part in agency affairs. Heretofore that force has been the Army, against which it is but natural there should be a feeling of antagonism among the Indians, and the very presence of which at an agency is a constant reminder that the white man cannot and will not trust the Indian. Recognizing this fact, these Indians have chosen the lesser of (to them) two evils, the Indian police in preference to the white soldier. Here the old adage that "confidence begets confidence" comes into play. Placing, as has been done at this agency, the entire control of the people, the care of their supplies, and the enforcing of the law in their own hands, has certainly given them confidence in themselves, and put them on their good behavior.

Agent Tufts, at Union Agency, Indian Territory, says:

The police system is good, and if well paid and properly managed would be valuable to the Indian service, and the means of saving much money to the government. It would be valuable to the service at this agency, because, while there are fifteen thou-sand persons in this agency not amenable to the laws of these nations, there is no offi-cer who can make an arrest without obtaining a warrant from the United States court at Fort Smith, Ark., except the Indian police. Crime in this Territory is almost always the result of whisky, and takes place at Indian gatherings. If a United States officer is present with authority to keep order, there will be little trouble. I am certainly of opinion that while it costs the Indian Department something to keep the police on duty, the government has saved much more than their cost to the Departments of War and Justice.

Agent Dyer, of Quapaw Agency, Indian Territory, says:

We now have a force of reliable and efficient men, and as proof of this I would sim-ply call attention to the fact that the eight men in garrison at Camp Quapaw perform the same duties as did the company of troops recently removed. Upon a large reserve, they are invaluable as messengers. As an escort in making annuity payments to the tribes distant from the agency, their worth cannot be estimated except by the amount of treasure in charge. Ready for duty at any time and in any emergency, I consider it the right arm of an agent in the successful conduct of his reservation. Ever alert to the detection of the introduction of liquor, they are a factor that cannot be dispensed with.

Agent Wilbur, of Yakama Agency, Washington Territory, says:

All the members are faithful, prompt, and efficient in the discharge of their duties, though of course there are degrees of merit. Their usefulness in the detection and pun-ishment of crime and preservation of order can hardly be overestimated. Their dis-cipline is good; their general appearance and demeanor among the people is such as to command the respect and confidence of all. They are prompt and obedient, never hesitating to obey an order though it may involve great personal danger to them-selves.

Agent Andrus, of Yankton Agency, Dakota, says:

The knowledge that there is a body of organized police upon a reservation serves as a powerful restraint upon both whites and Indians, and checks the inception as well as the commission of much crime. The police have proved prompt and efficient in the performance of the various duties assigned, steadily breaking down and overcoming the strong opposition at first manifested toward them. The chiefs have, I think, with-drawn all opposition because they perceived its futility.

These selections fairly represent the many reports received by this office from all parts of the Indian country. Originally introduced as an experiment, an organized police force has become a necessity. One of the principal duties of the Indian policemen, as specified in the law creating the force, is to prevent the introduction of liquor into these Indian communities. This duty is faithfully performed. At Navajo Agency, New Mexico, the Indians refuse to have a police force because of the small compensation offered, yet the necessity for such a force is well shown in a report from Captain Bennett, acting agent, under date of October 14, 1880. He says:

The evil that has the most damaging effect upon this people is whisky. There are several traders at many points ranging from forty to one hundred miles from the reservation where whisky of the vilest description is dealt out to these people in open violation of law, being an incentive to crime, and greatly impoverishing many of them. Decisive and prompt measures should be adopted by the government to put a stop to this nefarious traffic; otherwise results of the most deplorable character may be expected. At several councils, the sensible chiefs and headmen universally deprecated this liquor traffic, and said, "We have no rivers, streams, or lakes of whisky; why does not the Great Father at Washington, who can do anything he pleases, put a stop to this trade and keep white men from bringing or selling whisky to us?" I again urge that the most decisive measures should be adopted to stop this whisky trade.

The civilization, Christianization, and general well-being of the Indian tribes depends in great measure upon the arrest and punishment of these criminals, who not only destroy the happiness and lives of the Indians, but continually jeopardize the peace and quiet of our Western frontier life. The most powerful and efficient agency for the destruction of this traffic that has yet been proposed is a thoroughly organized and well-equipped United States Indian police force.

PENAL RESERVATIONS.

In 1879 one of my predecessors called attention to the necessity of providing a more effectual way to punish Indians who may engage in hostilities against the government, commit crimes against one another, or who may become dangerous to the peace on reservations; and he earnestly urged the establishment of penal settlements for this purpose. No action was taken by Congress on the subject, and I now again invite attention to the matter in the hope that provision to this end may be made.

At least two such reservations should be created: one on the Pacific coast, and one east of the Rocky Mountains; and they should be located in a good agricultural region. Fort Gibson military reservation, in Indian Territory, is suggested as a very suitable location for the reservation east of the Rocky Mounains. It embraces 5,541 acres, or a little more than 8 square miles, and is thus described in an "Outline description of United States military posts and stations," published by authority of the War Department:

The post is situated in the Cherokee Nation, upon the south bank of the Neosho, two and a half miles above its confluence with the Arkansas. * * * There is scarcely an acre of land, except upon the ranges of high hills along the Grand, Verdigris, and Illinois Rivers, that is not arable and susceptible of cultivation. Soil, loam and clay; and will grow well and abundantly all kinds of cereals, vegetables, fruit, cotton, and tobacco. The principal crops now raised are corn, wheat, potatoes, and oats; fruit (apples, pears, and peaches), of the finest quality, is very plentiful. The country is well watered, and abounds in springs. The prairies are small, being usually from three to four miles wide. Timber is scarce, and growing only in the bottoms along the rivers and bayous, and on the mountains, but there very densely; it consists chiefly of oak, walnut, hickory, pecan, and cotton-wood; grass, wild prairie. * * grows rank and heavy, and is cut for hay in the season in large quantities. * * Climate, mild; average temperature of the seasons for 1868, as follows: January, February, and March, 41° 13; April, May, and June, 61° 04; July, August, and September, 79° 41; October, November, and December, 61° 66. The country is generally healthy. Chills and fever are very common among the people living in the bottom lands; on the high lands but little sickness is known.

A similar suitable location west of the Rocky Mountains would not, it is believed, be difficult to find.

These penal reservations, or colonies, should be surrounded by a cordon of military posts, and be under the exclusive control of the military authorities. On them should be placed all predatory Indians who refuse to recognize treaty obligations or to go on reservations, and who, by their depredations, endanger the peace and safety of remote frontier settlements; also, Indians belonging to reservations who commit depredations upon white settlers or other Indians, or who may become turbulent or ungovernable, or who may commit crimes for the punishment of which there is at present no authority of law. Such are crimes committed by one Indian against another, for which, under the existing law, there is, for the most part, no punishment except such as may be meted out by the local law of the tribe, and this is usually the barbarous law of retaliation. Indians confined on such reservations should be compelled to cultivate the soil, the proceeds of their labor to be applied to their sustenance; and schools should be provided for the younger Indians, and attendance thereon made compulsory, and they should be instructed in the mechanic arts, so that when the term of their colonization shall have expired they may be fitted to support themselves.

Deprivation of personal liberty is the severest punishment that can be inflicted upon an Indian, and if the plan herein suggested were carried into practical operation it is believed that a want long felt in the Indian service would be met.

ALLOTMENT OF LAND IN SEVERALTY AND A PERMANENT LAND TITLE.

No question which enters into the present and future welfare and permanent advancement of the Indians is of so much importance as the question of allotment to them of lands in severalty, with a perfect and permanent title. On the 24th of January, 1879, a report was submitted to the department upon this subject, in which the views of this office were fully set out, accompanied by a draft of a bill the enactment of which it was believed would bring about the desired end. The subject was treated at length in the annual report of this office for the year 1878, and was touched upon in the reports of 1879 and 1880. A bill to carry out this beneficial object was introduced into the Forty-fifth Congress, and was favorably reported upon by the committees of both Houses, but failed to receive final action. A bill similar in its provisions was submitted to the extra session of the Forty-sixth Congress. (H. R. No. 354). At the second session of the Forty-sixth Congress. House bill No. 5038 was reported by the House committee as a substitute for House bill No. 354, but it also failed to become a law. A bill with the same objects in view was also introduced in the Senate at the third session of the Forty-sixth Congress (S. No. 1773), and was discussed at some length by the Senate, but no final action was reached.

Much has been said in Congress, in the public press of the country, in public meetings, and otherwise, and various plans suggested with reference to solving the "Indian question," but no definite and practical solution of the question has been reached. In my judgment, the first step to be taken in this direction is the enactment of a law providing for the allotment of land in severalty, similar in its provisions to the bills above referred to.

The system of allotment now in force under the various treaties and acts of Congress is crude and imperfect, with no provisions for a title which affords sufficient protection to the Indians. In some of the treaties which authorize the allotment of land in severalty, provision is made for the issuance of patents, with restricted power of alienation, (with the consent of the President or the Secretary of the Interior). In others allotments are authorized with no provision for the issuance of patent, but simply authorizing the issuance of a certificate of allotment, which caries with it no title at all. This system of allotment, so far as carried into effect, has been fraught with much success and encouraging improvement. The fact, however, that the Indians are not guaranteed a title affording them perfect security from molestation, and the fear that their lands may be taken from them, has created apprehension in the minds of many, and has been a bar to progress in this direction.

The allotment system tends to break up tribal relations. It has the effect of creating individuality, responsibility, and a desire to accumulate property. It teaches the Indians habits of industry and frugality, and stimulates them to look forward to a better and more useful life, and, in the end, it will relieve the government of large annual appropriations. As stated in the annual report of this office for the year 1880, the desire to take lands in severalty is almost universal among the Indians. They see that in the near future the settlement of the country by whites, and the consequent disappearance of game, the expiration of the annuity provisions of their treaties, and other causes will necessitate the adoption of some measures on their part providing for the future support and welfare of themselves and their children. As illustrating the desire on the part of the Indian to take land in severalty, to adopt the habits and pursuits of civilization, to provide a home for himself and family, and to guard against future want, I invite attention to the following extracts from a report made by C. A. Maxwell, United States special agent, dated September 23, 1881, upon a council held with the Crow Indians at their agency, in Montana, on the 22d of August last, viz:

It will be observed by reference to the minutes of the council that the main point of conversation on the part of the Indians was the subject of more cattle, houses to live in, farming, and a general desire to live like the white man and to adopt the habits and pursuits of civilized life. The Indians are very anxious in regard to the manner of payment for the right of way of the Northern Pacific Railroad through their reservation, an agreement for which they signed on the 22d of August last, and also the money which they believe is due them for the western portion of the reservation, an agreement for the cession of which they signed June 12, 1880. It appears to be almost the unanimous wish of the tribe that the money due or to become due them under both agreements should be invested in cattle for the heads of families and individual members of the tribe, the erection of houses, and the purchase of agricultural implements, which certainly shows a commendable spirit on the part of such wild and untutored savages, and tends to demonstrate the fact that, no matter how wild and nomadic Indians are, they can be taught to follow the pursuits of the white man and to enter upon a more useful life, and, in time, become self-supporting. It is but a question of short time when the rapid settlement of the country and the disappearance of the buffalo will necessitate the confinement of the Crows to their reservation, in which event they will, for the greater portion of each year, be in a destitute condition unless some measures are adopted to render them self-supporting.

From what I observed while at the agency, the Crows are very willing to be instructed in and learn of the white man the ways of civilization. It appears that as late as the spring of 1879 not one of the Crows was engaged, or had attempted to engage, in agriculture, while at the present time quite a number of the leading chiefs are occupying comfortable log cabins and cultivating small parcels of ground, some of them having their land inclosed. The Indians manifest great interest and considerable pride in this step toward civilization and the self-support of themselves and families, and the example has had a good effect upon the other chiefs of the tribe. Not a day passed while I was at the agency but what some of the leading chiefs asked Agent Keller for houses to live in, and for tracts of land to cultivate for themselves and their followers. In fact, this subject appears to be uppermost in their minds, and considerable jealousy appears to exist as to whom provision shall be first made for. About one hundred Indians have selected locations for farms, and the agent will erect houses at the points selected as rapidly as possible. While at the agency authority was received for the erection of twenty houses and the breaking of five hundred acres of land, by contract. The Indians received this information with many manifestations of joy and expressions of satisfaction. As stated by them, it made their hearts feel good.

The disposition manifested upon this subject by such a wild, untutored, and uncivilized tribe as the Crows is certainly very encouraging, and is one of the strongest recommendations in favor of the allotment system. As a further illustration of this desire on the part of the Indians, and of its practical and beneficial results, attention is also invited to the following extracts from some of the annual reports of agents. James McLaughlin, agent at the Devil's Lake Agency, Dakota, in speaking upon the subject of the advancement of the Indians at his agency, says:

Nearly all of them are located on individual claims, living in log cabins, some having shingle roofs and pine floors, cultivating farms in severalty, and none are now ashamed to labor in civilised pursuits. A majority of the heads of families have ox-teams, wagons, plows, harrows, &c., and a desire to accumulate property and excel each other is becoming more general. One thousand acres are under cultivation. Four hundred and five acres of new land were broken this year preparatory to sowing wheat next spring. This breaking was done entirely by Indians on 110 different claims adjoining their old fields.

Capt. W. E. Dougherty, acting agent at the Crow Creek Agency, Dakota, says:

Last summer one band of the tribe was located on land in severalty, each family taking 320 acres, upon which it began some kind of improvement. Last spring the demand of the Indians for the subdivision of the land and the allotment of it in severalty became general. A surveyor was accordingly employed for the purpose, and up to the present time the following-named persons have been allotted land, and are living on their allotments or are preparing to move upon them. [Here follows a list of 173 allotments, with the quantity of land allotted to each.] All the improvements made during the year have been made on these allotments, and consist of the erection of houses, stables, fences, corrals, &c., and the breaking of new land. The latter was done by the government, the other by the Indians. During the past year every family on the reservation has contributed more or less to the advancement of its condition and welfare, while some, with the assistance obtained from the agency, have made themselves very comfortable, and are the possessors of considerable personal property. Forty-five houses have been erected, and about twenty-five moved from the common lands and re-erected on land taken in severalty, by the Indians, unaided.

Isaiah Lightner, agent for the Santees, in Nebraska, says:

Just here I feel that I should speak again of the land title, as it is a subject I have been writing about for the last four years, and nothing special accomplished. I must confess I feel somewhat discouraged. But as I have told the Santee Indians, with my hands uplifted, that I would stand by them until they received a more lasting title to their homes, I must repeat here, to you and all who may read what I have formerly said, that the Santees should have this land given to them by a law that could not be changed, so that the white man could not take their homes from them. At present they have but little assurance that they can remain here, and I know it has been a drawback to them in the way of self-support, for they have repeatedly informed me that they do not wish to open up a farm for a white man to take from them when the whites may feel like doing so. They want a lasting title to their homes the same as a white man, and I think it wicked in the first degree for us, as a nation, to withhold any longer such a sacred right—that of liberty and a free home for these people, who eventually will be recognized as a part of our nation, exercising the rights of citizenship as we do. In the name of the power that rules, cannot we bring force to bear that will make right prevail, and produce such a law as will allow the Santee Indians, and those similarly situated, to select their land and hold it as a permanent home.

The reports of nearly all the agents show a similar state of facts existing among the Indians at their respective agencies. The Indian wants his land allotted to him. He wants a perfect and secure title that will protect him against the rapacity of the white man. He is not only willing but anxious to learn the ways of civilization. He is desirous of being taught to work and to accumulate property. His mind is imbued with these ideas, and some decisive steps should be taken by the law-making branch of the government to encourage him in his laudable and praiseworthy desires and efforts toward civilization, self-support, and a better and more useful life.

An approximate estimate shows that 5,972 allotments have been made on the various reservations in the United States, and that 2,793 of this number have been patented to the allottees; also that 1,355 allotments have been made for which certificates have been issued. An before stated these certificates carry no title with them. They are only evidence of the right of one Indian as against another to occupy the tract of land which they describe. It should be stated in explanation of the difference between the number of allotments and number of patents issued, that under the provision of some of the treaties the lands allotted to the several members of a family are embraced in one patent issued to the head of the family.

INDIAN HOMESTEAD ENTRIES.

On the 19th of May, 1880, my predecessor submitted to the department a draft of a bill to enable Indians to enter land under the provisions of the 15th and 16th sections of the act of Congress, approved March 3d, 1875, extending to Indians the benefits of the provisions of the homestead act of May 20th, 1862, and the acts amendatory thereof (now embodied in sections 2290, 2291, 2292, and 2295 to 2300, inclusive,) without the payment of the fees and commissions now prescribed by law in such cases. A great many Indians in different parts of the United States are desirous of availing themselves of the benefits conferred by the act of 1875, but owing to their poverty and improvidence few of them can command the amount necessary to pay the fees and commissions required by law. In many instances, more especially the Mission Indians in California and the Spokanes and others in Washington Territory, the Indians, and their fathers before them, have been residing upon, cultivating, and improving small tracts of land for generations. When these lands are surveyed and brought into market, the Indians, through ignorance of the law and the want of funds to pay the fees and commissions necessary to enter the land occupied by them, fail to take advantage of the benefits of the act of 1875 within the time prescribed by law after filing of the plats of survey in the district land-office, the result of which is that white men enter the Indian's land, drive him therefrom, and appropriate his improvements and the fruits of his industry and labor.

A condition precedent to an Indian taking advantage of the act of 1875 is that he must have abandoned his tribal relations. The policy of the government being to break up tribal relations among the different bands of Indians, and to encourage them to take land in severalty, and to adopt the habits and pursuits of civilized life, they should receive every encouragement in their efforts in that direction.

Until a change in the law as above recommended is made, it is of great importance that the department should have at its disposal a fund that can be used for the payment of entry fees and commissions, and with that end in view, an estimate for the sum of $5,000 has been submitted.

SURVEYS OF INDIAN RESERVATIONS.

The want of a proper and exact definition of the boundary lines of some of the reservations by plain and permanent marks is the cause of great and ever recurring embarrassment to the Indian service, and if not speedily supplied must inevitably result in serious conflicts between the Indians and white settlers. The Indians are naturally jealous in respect to their land rights, while the whites, covetous and hard to restrain, hover on their borders, and, in the absence of lines officially established and that are easily traceable, are not apt to be very punctilious, to say the least, in deciding whether or not they are encroaching upon the Indians. On the other hand, the Indians, by reason of this indefiniteness of boundary, do not hesitate to extend, pretentiously, the limits of their possessions whenever it suits their convenience to do so.

Hence disputes arise engendering the bitterest hostility, and the agent, left to decide between them, often finds himself incapable of doing so with fairness, and, to avoid actual conflict, is sometimes driven to arbitrary measures. I know of no one thing that is more fruitful of discord in the Indian country than the absence of proper marks and monuments to indicate the outboundaries of our Indian reservations.

The San Carlos division of the White Mountain Reservation in Arizona Territory is a case in point. Extensive and valuable coal deposits have been discovered along its southern line, and that these deposits are within the limits of the reserve there is but little doubt. But the boundary lines have never been marked upon the ground or otherwise by official survey, and consequently the miners and prospectors, flocking into the neighborhood from all directions, dispute the jurisdiction of the agent, who, by astronomical observations, has approximately determined the location of the boundary, and declares the discoveries to be within the reservation. In regard to this he says:

The great wrong in not surveying these reservation lines and monumenting them leaves all these border complaints for continuance, and it is along these the wrangles commence; the ranchmen and the prospectors claim they are off, the agent and Indians that they are on, the reservation: at any rate the whites crowd the line to the very greatest extent, and only on assurance of removal and loss of improvements do they hesitate to make them. It is a hard matter to take a crooked line 70 miles long, and ranging from peak to peak, and decide within a mile whether a ranch is off or on the reservation, and become responsible for the observation and action. If the government will not appropriate funds to survey the line, I do not think any agent will or can run the risk of deciding the exact location of it. I believe, had these lines been surveyed and determined belonging to this reservation, that thousands of dollars would already have been saved to the government, and if it does not do so soon it will cost thousands of dollars more, and many lives.

The agents at the Klamath Agency, in Oregon, and the military officers as well, have repeatedly warned the department of the imminent danger growing out of the disputed boundary question at that agency. Herds of cattle are driven and grazed upon what is no doubt a part of the Klamath Reservation, and the Indians claim that lands acquired by them under solemn treaty stipulations have been sold to white settlers who are now in full occupation and enjoyment of them. It is admitted by the General Land Office that the treaty lines of the east and south, and a portion of the west side of the reservation were not followed by the surveyor who made the survey of the reservation in 1871, but that certain lines of the public survey lying considerably inside of the reservation, as defined by the language of the treaty, were followed instead. Hence it would appear that the Indians have good grounds for complaint. Agent Nickerson has recently made this matter the subject of a special report to this bureau, in which he again warns the government of the danger of further delay in the settlement of this vexed question. He says:

While there is a patient waiting on the part of the Indians for the government to redress what they believe to be their wrongs, there is also a deep and growing conviction in their minds that nothing will be done unless some complication shall arise that will compel action.

Not to heed these repeated warnings is to assume a responsibility that this office is unwilling to take upon itself.

Tillable lands within the reservations should in all cases be subdivided, where it has not already been done, in order that allotments may be made to individual Indians, and that all such lands may be made available for that purpose, whether remote from the agency or adjacent thereto.

It is hoped that this matter may be pressed upon the attention of Congress at its coming session, in order that the necessary appropriations may be had to relieve the department of this most serious embarrassment.

RAILROADS THROUGH INDIAN RESERVATIONS.

Since the date of the last annual report negotiations have been perfected, under the sanction of the department, with the several tribes or bands of Sioux Indians, occupying the great Sioux Reserve in Dakota for a right of way across the reserve to the Dakota Central Railway Company and the Chicago, Milwaukee and Saint Paul Railway Company (extension to Black Hills), respectively; also, with the Indians occupying the Umatilla Reserve, in Oregon, for a right of way to the Oregon Railway and Navigation Company. These arrangements have been made in accordance with treaty stipulations with the Indians interested, relative to the construction of railroads upon their lands, and reasonable compensation to them by the railroad companies for the quantity of land required has been provided for in each case.

Successful negotiations have also been had, by special agents appointed by the department, with the Shoshone and Bannack Indians, for the extinguishment by the government, under the several acts of Congress in that behalf, of their title to so much of the lands of their reservation in Idaho as may be necessary for the purposes of the Utah and Northern Railroad Company in the construction of a road from east to west across said reservation; also, with the Crow Indians for the cession of so much of their reservation lands in Montana as are required by the Northern Pacific Railroad Company for the construction of its road westwardly through the same. Agreements embodying the terms of purchase by the government in each case have been prepared and executed by the Indians, and bills for the necessary ratification thereof by Congress will be submitted by this office in due course.

The incursions of the Missouri River have compelled the Atchison and Nebraska Railroad Company to set back its track upon the Iowa Reserve in Nebraska. The requisite quantity of land has been obtained from the Indians, and reasonable compensation has been stipulated to be paid them by the railroad company therefor.

In the Indian Territory an unauthorized attempt was made in April last by the Missouri, Kansas and Texas Railway Company to survey a branch line to Fort Smith, Ark. Upon complaint of the Cherokee authorities to the department, the local agent was directed to stop the survey and remove the intruders, which was successfully accomplished. The company, however, still claims the right, under statutory provisions, to construct the branch road, and the matter is now pending before the department for adjudication.

It is gratifying to remark that the Indians have offered no opposition to the passage of railroads over their reservations; on the contrary, they hail their construction with every evidence of satisfaction.

MILITARY OCCUPATION OF INDIAN RESERVATIONS AND DESTRUCTION OF TIMBER THEREBY.

Under this heading I desire to call your attention to a subject which occasions serious embarrassment to this office—the continued occupation of Indian reservations and destruction of timber thereon by the military, where the necessity for their presence in large numbers no longer exists.

The Standing Rock Agency in Dakota forms a striking illustration in point. The history of this case is, briefly, as follows: In December, 1874, United States Indian Agent Palmer, then in charge of the agency, when about to enroll his Indians, met with strong opposition, and called for a company of troops to make arrests of one or two insubordinate

Indians and preserve order. The department commander furnished him with a detachment of sixty men and three commissioned officers from Fort Lincoln, stating that this force was "amply sufficient to meet the wants of the situation." According to a report of Major-General Terry, commanding department of Dakota, dated the 7th September last, the garrison at Fort Yates at the present time consists of four companies of infantry and two of cavalry, and a sum of no less than $80,000 has been expended in the construction of the post, independent of the work accomplished by the labor of the troops.

It is not, however, so much the actual presence of troops upon an Indian reservation which embarrasses this office as the inordinate consumption of wood and timber cut upon the reservation and used under the direction and authority of the military, not only in the erection of barracks, &c., but also in the filling of contracts awarded by military officers to post traders, and other persons, for supplying steamers with wood—contracts made without consulting the agent or this office in the matter. Remonstrances have heretofore been made by this department upon the subject, and the War Department has been requested to cause the necessary orders to be issued restraining the officers at Fort Yates and other posts from cutting any timber except such as is absolutely necessary for the use of their respective posts. But so far as Standing Rock Agency is concerned, there has been but little change for the better, and there is every reason to believe that if the present military force is continued at the agency, and the wood disappears as it has for the past five years (at the rate of about 4,000 cords per annum) the Indians will in a short time be entirely destitute of fuel and timber for building purposes, there by entailing a heavy expense on the government for the necessary supplies, or, as the only alternative, the removal of the Indians to another reservation.

In the report of Major-General Terry, before referred to, and which was called forth by one from this office to the department of the 8th July last, setting forth the evils complained of, and renewing the recommendations previously and repeatedly made for the reduction of the garrison at Fort Yates to not more than one company,[*] as being amply sufficient for any emergency likely to arise, that officer admits that the strong force maintained at Fort Yates since the autumn of 1876 has not been kept there solely in the interests of the Indian service, but also for the protection of the property and persons of settlers in the surrounding country, within a radius of perhaps 300 miles, from Indian depredations; also for the protection of the interests of the Northern Pacific Railroad Company, now prosecuting its work of construction between the Missouri and the Yellowstone, which railroad company protests against the withdrawal of the troops from Fort Yates, as a measure calculated to deter settlements along the line of its road. In regard to the fuel and timber question, which is admitted to be an important one, General Terry contends that very little, if any more, wood will be needed for building purposes at the post, and that after this year "lignite" can be substituted for fuel, at an increased cost, however, to the government. But whatever difference in expense there may be, he frankly admits that the importance of the wood to the Indians is so great that the fuel necessary to the troops of the post should no longer be taken from the forests in the vicinity. I think this admission of itself, without further comment, sufficiently demonstrates the mischief which has already been done.

A similar state of things exists at Cheyenne River, from which, ow-

[*] It should be stated that since the transfer to the Standing Rock Agency, July 21st, of nearly 3,000 Sitting Bull Indians, the Indian Office has considered it advisable that no reduction should be made in the garrison at Fort Yates, at least at present.

ing to the extravagant use of timber by the military stationed at the neighboring posts, it will in all probability become necessary to remove the Indians at an early date.

I have no desire to provoke a controversy between co-ordinate branches of the government, least of all with the War Department, to which this office is under many and lasting obligations for the prompt and valuable assistance it has ever rendered in many and serious emergencies; but as an officer of the government, intrusted under your direction with the management of Indian affairs and the material welfare of the Indians, I do seriously protest against the reckless consumption of timber upon Indian reservations by the military, and request that measures may be taken to define and restrict their rights in this respect, and with that view I have deemed it my duty to call your attention to the matter.

I will add, in regard to the protection demanded by the Northern Pacific Railroad Company, that it appears to me that the troops at Fort Yates, sixty miles away, could afford but little protection; but that Fort A. Lincoln, and other military posts along the line of the road, could be more advantageously used, and are amply sufficient to keep any and all raiding parties in check, and to effectually prevent any obstruction in the settlement of the land or the construction and operation of the road.

LIQUOR IN THE INDIAN COUNTRY.

Existing statutes prohibit the introduction of ardent spirits into the Indian country under any pretense, unless introduced therein by the War Department [sections 2139 and 2140 U. S. Revised Statutes], the penalty being "imprisonment for *not more than* two years, and a fine of *not more than* three hundred dollars."

Numerous complaints have been received during the year of the insufficiency of the law to prevent Indians from obtaining liquor from white persons who reside in the vicinity of Indian reservations. And although the penalty for furnishing it *may* be severe, yet the difficulty of detecting offenders and the frequent leniency of courts in prescribing and enforcing punishment make the law to a great extent inoperative. A case in point is brought to attention by the agent at Warm Springs Agency, Oregon. He reports that while most of his Indians will not touch liquor some will drink every time they go where it is, and the parties furnishing it will make the Indians promise not to reveal the fact; and he cites a recent occurrence in which one Indian complained of another for severely beating him. Examination of the matter before the Indian council disclosed the fact that both the Indians had been drunk (having obtained three bottles of whisky at The Dalles, on the Columbia River), and while drunk the stronger and least intoxicated had committed the assault. The council fined him a good horse for his crime, and the Indian assaulted was fined an ordinary horse for being drunk. The white man who furnished the liquor was detected, brought before the United States court, plead guilty, was fined *ten dollars*, and liberated after confinement *one night!* In this case the witness fees. paid by the United States, amounted to nearly five times the amount of the fine imposed by court, and the other expenses were doubtless fully as much more. The agent aptly remarks :

Until such flagrant violations of the laws can be more severely punished, an agent need hardly waste time and money in hunting up offenders and having them punished.

The danger to be apprehended from drunken Indians certainly calls for such legislation as will not only totally prohibit the introduction of liquor into reservations but will also, as nearly as may be, make it impossible for Indians to obtain it; and experience has shown that where soldiers obtain liquor Indians do get it. I know of no good reason why authority should be conferred upon the War Department to introduce it into the Indian country. If it is bad for Indians it is no less so for soldiers, and, therefore, with a view more effectually to suppress the traffic among Indians I respectfully recommend that Congress be urged to amend sections 2139 and 2140 of the United States Revised Statutes by repealing the provisions therein which permit the introduction of ardent spirits into the Indian country by authority of the War Department, and that the penalty for furnishing liquor to Indians be a fine of *not less than* one hundred dollars for the first offense, and imprisonment for *not less than* one year.

As a more effectual remedy for the evil complained of, I also recommend that Congress be asked to enact a law absolutely prohibiting the manufacture or sale of ardent spirits in any of the Territories of the United States, or if this should not be practicable at present, that a law be passed prohibiting the manufacture, sale, or other disposal of intoxicating liquors within twenty miles of any Indian reservation.

INDIAN EDUCATION.

Schools for Indians are divided into three classes—day-schools and boarding-schools for Indians in the Indian country, and boarding-schools in civilized communities remote from Indian reservations. Although varying greatly in the extent and character of their results, each holds its own important place as a factor in Indian civilization.

In many tribes the less expensive and less aggressive day-school prepares the way for the boarding-school, and occupies the field while buildings for boarding pupils are being erected and furnished, or while Congress is discussing the desirability of appropriating funds necessary for their construction. It disarms native prejudice and opposition to education, and awakens a desire for the thorough fundamental teaching which the boarding-school gives. The sending of twenty Pueblo children to Carlisle is the direct result of the inroads made by day-schools on the superstition and prejudice of the most conservative tribe on the continent. In more civilized tribes like those in Michigan and California the government day-school supplies the place of the State common school.

Exclusive of those among the five civilized tribes, the day schools during the past year have numbered 106, and have been attended by 4,221 pupils. Two schools have been opened among the Mission Indians, the first ever given these hard-working, much-abused people by either government or State. Three others will open soon. At Pine Ridge day-schools in the various Indian settlements are having a very good influence, pending the erection of the new boarding-school building; and they will be needed after its completion in order to extend to the 1,400 children of the agency who cannot be accommodated therein some small degree of civilizing influence—an influence which will not be confined to the pupils, but will extend to the families in the vicinity of the schools, whose remoteness from the agency renders it specially important that some civilizing force should be exerted in their midst.

Of the 106 schools one is supported by the State of Pennsylvania, and 28 are located in and supported by the State of New York as part of its common-school system. As a result, of the 1,590 Indian children of school age in that State 1,164 have attended school some portion of the past year, and the average daily attendance has been 625.[*] This provision for Indian schools has been made by New York for twenty years, at an annual expense of about $7,000, and last year the New York Indian agent reported that nearly all the Indians in his agency could read and write. For the support of these schools New York does not depend on the uncertainties of a local tax, but gives to her Indians their *pro rata* share of the State school-tax and of the income of the permanent invested fund of the State. The State law on the subject is as follows, being an extract from the "general school law of the State of New York":

SECTION 5. The money raised by the State tax, or borrowed, as aforesaid, to supply a deficiency thereof, and such portion of the income of the United States deposit fund as shall be appropriated, and the income of the common-school fund when the same are appropriated to the support of common schools, constitute the State school moneys, and shall be divided and apportioned by the superintendent of public instruction.

*   *   *   *   *

SECTION 6. * * * He [the superintendent of public instruction] shall then set apart and apportion for and on account of the Indian schools under his supervision a sum which will be equitably equivalent to their proportion of the State school money upon the basis of distribution established by this act, such sum to be wholly payable out of the proceeds of the State tax for the support of common schools.

The amount expended last year in the support of these schools was $8,000, and the superintendent asks that on account of the establishment of three new schools another $1,000 be added. New York is also expending about $8,000 a year in the support of an Indian orphan asylum.

Were this example followed by other States—Michigan, Minnesota, Wisconsin, Nebraska, North Carolina, and California, for instance—States which have within their borders considerable numbers of Indians who are semi-civilized and practically self-supporting, the status attained by the next generation would attest both the wisdom of the course pursued and its economy. That it is cheaper for a State to educate her lower classes than to allow them to grow up in ignorance and superstition may be considered a truism, but, so far as it relates to Indians, the truth of it needs practical acknowledgment in many localities.

Sixty-eight boarding schools have been in operation during the year; an increase of eight over last year. They have been attended by 3,888 pupils. Of the new schools six have been opened at Colorado River, San Carlos, Pima, Pueblo, Siletz, and Uintah Agencies. They will accommodate 351 pupils, and are the first boarding schools ever provided for the 27,000 Indians of those agencies who represent a school population of not less than 5,000. A second boarding-school has been given the Omahas, who are waking up to the importance of education, and a boarding-school for boys has been established at Cheyenne River, where a mission school for girls has been in successful operation for several years. Delay in the erection of buildings has prevented the opening of the other five schools referred to in last report.

Three new school buildings have been completed, furnished, and occupied during the year, eight more are now ready for use, and five are in process of erection. These buildings will give accommodation for ten new schools and additional room, which has been sorely needed, for three old ones. Buildings are needed at nine other agencies for whose 16,000 Indians no boarding-schools have yet been furnished, and where there are now but six day-schools, with accommodations for 175 pupils. Another building must be erected for the Pueblo school, which is only temporarily provided for in a rented building not adapted for the purpose.

[*]From the Annual Report Superintendent Public Instruction of the State of New York, January 5, 1881.

The interest, aptness, docility, and progress of the pupils is remarked on by their teachers as being fully equal to that of white children. Their acquirements, of course, are much behind those of white children. The first two school years, at least, must be spent mainly in acquiring the English language and the white man's way of living, lessons which the child of civilized parents learns in the nursery, and in these two branches progress is impeded by the reluctance of Indians to use any but their native tongue, and is seriously interrupted by the annual vacation, which returns the children to the old ways of speech, thought, and life. The interest of parents in education continues to increase, and some schools have been overcrowded.

The agency boarding-school is the object lesson for the reservation. The new methods of thought and life there exemplified, while being wrought into the pupils, are watched by those outside. The parents visit the school, and the pupils take back into their homes new habits and ideas gained in the school-room, sewing-room, kitchen, and farm. Though more or less dissipated in the alien atmosphere of a heathen household, these habits and ideas still have an influence for good, real and valuable, though it cannot always be distinctly traced. The agency school takes the pupils as it finds them; the dull and frail have a chance with the quick-witted and robust; and since Indians are much less willing to send away their daughters than their sons, it furnishes the girls of the tribe almost their only opportunity for acquiring a knowledge of books and of home-making.

But so long as the American people now demand that Indians shall become white men within one generation, the Indian child must have other opportunities and come under other influences than reservations can offer. He must be compelled to adopt the English language, must be so placed that attendance at school shall be regular, and that vacations shall not be periods of retrogression, and must breathe the atmosphere of a civilized instead of a barbarous or semi-barbarous community. Therefore, youth chosen for their intelligence, force of character, and soundness of constitution are sent to Carlisle, Hampton, and Forest Grove to acquire the discipline and training which, on their return, shall serve as a leverage for the uplifting of their people.

The reports from these schools are in every respect encouraging. At Carlisle 295 pupils have been in attendance, of whom 29 per cent. were girls. They represent twenty-four tribes and fourteen agencies. Seventy are learning trades, and have been so faithful and successful in their labor that the articles manufactured and job work done by apprentices in the harness, shoe, tin, and blacksmith shops have netted the school $776.62 over the cost of materials, salaries of instructors, and wages of apprentices—the wages being 16¾ cents per day for the time actually employed. The carpenter and tailor shops have also more than paid expenses.

Stimulus to the industrial work of the school has been given by the clause in the Indian appropriation act of May 11, 1880, which provides that the Secretary of the Interior is "authorized, whenever it can be done advantageously, to purchase for use in the Indian service from Indian manual and training schools, in the manner customary among individuals, such articles as may be manufactured at such schools, and which are used in the Indian service." A market has thus been found for all articles manufactured, and this year the Carlisle school has shipped to forty-two Indian agencies 8,929 tin cups, coffee-boilers, funnels, pails, and pans; 183 sets double harness, 161 riding-bridles, 10 halters, 9 spring wagons, and 2 carriages, valued (according to the low contract rates paid by this office for such articles) at $6,333.46.

45 Ab

The parents are proud of the skill attained by their children, and the boys are interested to have specimens of their handiwork sent to their homes.

Among those "graduated" from the Cheyenne and Arapaho Agency boarding-school were found, last spring, sixteen young men who offered to pay their own traveling expenses from the Indian Territory to Carlisle, provided the government would there give them instruction in various trades. Their request was granted, but a similar request from one of the Sioux agencies has had to be refused for lack of funds with which to support the applicants after reaching Carlisle. Interesting details of the year's work at Carlisle will be found in Lieutenant Pratt's report, on page 242.

At the Hampton Institute, 81 Indian pupils have been in attendance, two-thirds of whose support is furnished by government, the remainder being obtained from charitable sources. The principal event of the year has been the return this month to their homes in Dakota of 30 of the 49 Sioux youths who went to Hampton three years ago, and with the returned Florida prisoners initiated the experiment out of which the Carlisle and Forest Grove schools have grown. Of the remaining 19 youths, 5 had died at Hampton; 12 had been previously returned to their homes, ten on account of ill health, one for bad conduct, and one at his own request; by consent of their guardians 2 will remain at Hampton for further training.

The ability of Indian youth to acquire civilized ideas and habits has been proved. Their ability to resolutely apply and continue them amid great disadvantages is now to be demonstrated. It cannot reasonably be expected that every one of a company of 30 boys and girls taken out of heathenism and barbarism will be transformed by a three-years' course of training into enlightened Christian men and women, with character and principles sturdy enough to successfully resist all the degenerating and demoralizing influences which they must encounter in their old homes. That white men with every inherited advantage fail under this test is too often exemplified upon Indian reservations. A longer stay at Hampton would undoubtedly have diminished the risk of relapse; but the promise made the parents that their children should be retained but three years could not be broken. Every endeavor, however, has been made by General Armstrong, with the co-operation of this office, to have suitable employment provided for these youth at the various agencies as interpreters, apprentices, assistant teachers, &c., and it is confidently hoped that the proportion who hold fast to the "new road," and induce others to adopt it, will more than compensate for the labor and money which have been expended in their education. It is just here that the government must look to missionaries on the various reservations for invaluable service—the continuance of the religious influence which was relied on as an indispensable part of their training at Hampton, and which is the foundation of American civilization.

All of the 22 Florida prisoners who remained North after their release from Saint Augustine have now returned to their homes. Three, educated by Mr. Wicks, of Syracuse, N. Y., in his own family, are devoting themselves to earnest missionary work among their people. The stand taken by most of the others, who spent two or three years at Carlisle and Hampton, is eminently satisfactory. Of those belonging to the Cheyenne and Arapaho Agency, Agent Miles says:

The last of the Florida prisoners returned to the agency during the year, and are, with the exception of one or two, standing firm on the side of right, and as a result from their careful training while prisoners in Florida and while at Hampton and Car-

Rule, they are the strongest lever we have at this agency in building up strength and hope for the future of their people. A majority of the Indian employé force of the agency is composed of these men, and a better class of laborers you could not find. Some are engaged in the shops at their trades, while one (Daniel Pendleton) is preaching the gospel to his people in their own tongue, and a better Christian man we do not find. Such results are indeed wonderful, and the example of these trained few, together with the red from Carlisle and Hampton, and the well-directed efforts in the agency schools, is going to kill much of the "Indian" in the Indians of this agency in due time.

The school at Forest Grove has been in operation 20 months and is now attended by 79 pupils. Unlike the Carlisle and Hampton schools it began with nothing and the school-boys under skilled supervision have themselves done most of the work of erecting necessary buildings and making the furniture. As in the other two schools, instruction is given in school-room, workshops, and kitchen, and the English language occupies the most important place in the school curriculum. At present its greatest need is sufficient land for farm and garden purposes. As Lieutenant Wilkinson's report on page 256 shows, the methods and results of the school are not only awakening an interest in its workings among neighboring white people, but are overcoming a wide-spread skepticism as to the practicability of Indian civilization. This disadvantage the school has had to contend with from the start. It has, however, the advantage of being near the Indian country while out of it, so that the expense of taking Indian children to and from Forest Grove is much less than that incurred by the two schools in the East. Moreover, the pupils are not required to undergo a change of climate in addition to an entire change in the conditions of life.

Sixty-four of the Forest Grove pupils represent bands in Washington Territory and Oregon, the other twelve are from Alaska—the first step taken by the government toward the reclamation of the Alaska Indians from the lower depth of ignorance and vice into which they have been descending since the purchase of that country from the Russian Government. Twice the number of pupils now at Forest Grove could be accommodated, and could easily be obtained from the reservations and from Alaska, if the funds at the disposal of the office would justify the expenditure.

It becomes more evident with each year that the obstacle to the education of the Indian children of this generation lies not in their inability to be taught, nor in the indifference or hostility of the parents to education, but in meager appropriations. For the education of its 49,000 children of school age, in day and evening schools alone, the State of Rhode Island expends annually $600,000. For the education of the same number of Indians (which is about the number to be provided for exclusive of the five civilized tribes in the Indian Territory) the United States Government last year appropriated, in fulfillment of specific treaty stipulations, $64,000, and "for schools not otherwise provided for," $75,000, making a total of $139,000 with which to maintain day-schools, furnish books to all pupils, erect and furnish school buildings, and support boarding-schools! From other funds appropriated for general civilization, but which can be applied to schools after other demands not more important but more immediately urgent have been met, the office has been able to expend about $85,000. - This, of course, has fallen so far short of meeting the needs of the service, that requests for increased school accommodations at various agencies have repeatedly been refused. For the current fiscal year an increase of $10,000 was made by the last Congress, but this will hardly cover the increase in the cost of beef and flour consumed in the schools, to say nothing of maintaining new boarding-schools opened this fall in the new buildings before referred.

to, of supporting throughout the year schools opened near the close of
the last fiscal year, and of erecting new buildings at hitherto neglected
agencies. Consequently requests for new boarding-school buildings at
seven agencies and for needed enlargement of school buildings at five
other agencies have already been refused; and unless a deficiency appropriation is made by Congress at its next regular session more Indian boarding-schools will have to be closed early next spring and
the children remanded to the debasing surroundings from which the
school was intended to redeem them.

It must not be supposed that by the appropriation of $864,000, above
referred to, treaty provisions with the various tribes have been fulfilled.
This covers only *specific sums* called for by treaty. In the treaties of
1868, made with the Sioux, Navajo, Ute, Kiowa, Comanche, Cheyenne,
Arapaho, Crow, Shoshone, and Pawnee tribes the educational provision is a general one, and is substantially as follows:

> In order to insure the civilization of the Indians entering into this treaty the
> necessity of education is admitted; especially of such of them as are or may be
> settled on said agricultural or other reservations, and they therefore pledge themselves
> to compel their children, male and female, between the ages of six and sixteen years
> to attend school, and the United States agrees that for every thirty children between
> said ages who can be induced or compelled to attend school, a house shall be provided
> and a teacher competent to teach the elementary branches of an English education
> furnished, who will reside among said Indians and faithfully discharge his or her
> duties as teacher. The provisions of this article to continue for not less than twenty
> years.

These tribes number in the aggregate 60,000, and have at least 12,000
youths of school age. For these children the tables herewith show that
after a lapse of thirteen years only twelve boarding and seven day
schools have been provided, which will accommodate respectively
and 565 pupils. To furnish day-schools only, according to the treaties
for the remaining 10,000 youth would require the erection and furnishing of 250 school-houses at an average cost of not less than $800 each
total, $200,000, besides an annual expenditure of $150,000 for salaries
of 250 teachers at $600 per annum, and $80,000 for books, school appliances, &c. (at an average of $8 per pupil), or more than the entire
amount expended during the past year at all agencies for both boarding and day schools. The shortsightedness and dishonesty of the
policy hitherto pursued in this connection is beyond question.
Lieutenant Pratt says, after making a similar estimate:

> The injury done by the United States Government to this large number of
> boys and girls who have grown up during this period by withholding this
> and valuable intelligence, and the actual injury and loss to the country hav-
> ing been an ignorant, pauper, peace-disturbing, life-destroying, impoverishing
> of an intelligent, producing element could not be stated in figures.

STOCK CATTLE.

Owing to the insufficient appropriations made by Congress for the
support of the Indian service during the present fiscal year, no more
cattle could be purchased for the benefit of those Indians who had not
been supplied in former years. Experience has shown that the Indian
is able and willing to take care of his cattle, and it is hoped that the
appropriations made for the coming fiscal year will be sufficient to supply at least a part of those who desire cattle. Since 1878 stock cattle
were furnished to different agencies as follows: Blackfeet A
Cheyenne and Arapaho, 500; Crow, 82; Crow Creek, 300;
700; Fort Hall, 200; Kiowa, 1,089; Klamath, 225; Lower Br
Osage and Kaw, 2,725; Pawnee, 400; Pine Ridge, 907; P
Rosebud, 1,000; Sac and Fox, 212; San Carlos, 1,125;

Bannack, 765; Sisseton, 437; Standing Rock, 500; White Earth, 52; Western Shoshone, 200; Yankton, 495; total, 13,264 head.

FREIGHTING DONE BY INDIANS.

During the year 1878 the 13,000 Sioux Indians under control of Spotted Tail and Red Cloud were induced to begin the work of civilization by hauling their annuity goods and supplies from the Missouri River to their new agencies, a distance of about 150 miles. Wagons and harness were furnished, and they successfully accomplished the undertaking. Since that time a large number of wagons have been furnished other Indians, and at present not only those above mentioned, but many others, especially those located in the Indian Territory, successfully transport their annuity goods and supplies from the nearest railroad station to their respective agencies. Their wages are paid, in cash, at the rate of $1 to $1.50 per 100 pounds per 100 miles, according to the condition of the roads over which the supplies are carried. Herewith is a statement of the number of wagons furnished each agency since July 1, 1877.:

Names of agencies.	1878.	1879.	1880.	1881.	1882.	Total.
Blackfeet, Mont.		32	15		15	68
Cheyenne and Arapaho, Ind. T.	40	56	15	42		153
Crow, Mont.	11	1	10	2	20	44
Crow Creek, Dak.	11	10	24		27	86
Cheyenne River, Dak.	51		66	1		118
Colorado River, Ariz.		1				1
Devil's Lake, Dak.		11	34		25	79
Fort Belknap, Mont.		1	3	11	6	21
Fort Berthold, Dak.		16	35	20		71
Fort Hall, Idaho.	10	24	10	15		59
Fort Peck, Mont.	31	20		10	4	65
Flathead, Mont.		12			20	32
Great Nemaha, Nebr.		4	2	17		31
Green Bay, Wis.			43			43
Pottawatomie, Kans.			10			10
Kiowa, Comanche, and Wichita, Ind. T.		56	12	15	10	93
Klamath, Oreg.		12	18		1	31
La Pointe, Wis.		4	52			56
Lemhi, Idaho.			4	15		19
Los Pinos, Colo		1	1	1	2	5
Lower Brulé, Dak.	13	20	24	20		77
Mackinac, Mich			25			25
Malheur, Oreg.				4		4
Mescalero, N. Mex			1	1		2
Moquis Pueblo, Ariz.		1	2			3
Navajo, N. Mex.		2	11			13
Nevada, Nev.		3		25		28
Omaha and Winnebago, Nebr.		2	60			62
Osage, Ind. T.	50	30	95		20	195
Kaw, Ind. T.	5	4				9
Pawnee, Ind. T.		20	68			88
Ponca, Ind. T.		41	42	40	2	125
Pima, Ariz.		1				1
Quapaw, Ind. T.	3	26	12	11		51
Pine Ridge, Dak.	56	251	51		50	408
Rosebud, Dak.	57	201	55		50	363
Sac and Fox, Ind. T.		22	4		5	31
San Carlos, Ariz.		2			2	4
Santee and Flandreau, Nebr.	9	10	134	2		155
Siletz, Oreg.			1		5	6
Sisseton, Dak.		1	135		25	161
Shoshone and Bannock, Wyo.	2	36	123			161
Southern Ute, Colo	1			1		2
Standing Rock, Dak.		36	51	1	50	150
Tule River, Cal.		1	22		1	94
Uintah, Utah			31	1	27	59
Umatilla, Oreg.			8	12	20	40
Union, Ind. T.			2			2
Western Shoshone, Nev.		5				5
White Earth, Minn. (consolidated)		10	53			63
White River, Colo		3	3			6
Warm Springs, Oreg				5	6	11
Yakama, Wash			7	10	16	33
Yankton, Dak.	50		7			57
Otoe, Nebr.				12	51	63
Total						3,556

PURCHASE OF ANNUITY GOODS AND SUPPLIES.

All goods and supplies for the Indian service are contracted for in the spring of each year, after due advertisement for bids in the principal newspapers in different parts of the country, the contracts being awarded to the lowest and best bidders. The schedule of goods required for the present fiscal year comprises over 1,800 different articles required to meet the wants of the Indians. There were received at the opening of bids in New York, May 2, 1881, 301 bids; at a subsequent letting in this city for beef 12 bids were received, and in San Francisco 24, making a total of 345 bids for furnishing goods required by the department for the present fiscal year; 161 contracts were executed, made out in quadruplicate, each one accompanied with a bond for the faithful performance of the same. The contracts were awarded by me, with the assistance of the Board of Indian Commissioners, after the samples offered with the bids had been properly examined by inspectors appointed for that purpose.

The delivery, inspection, and shipment of goods is mostly done in New York, in a warehouse rented for that purpose. There all goods are delivered, properly marked with a number which must correspond with the number on the invoice of the articles furnished; all invoices must be made out in quintuplicate, and must give the number, weight, and contents of each package charged for. After delivery of the goods they are inspected by a person appointed for that purpose, and each package stamped by the inspector with his name. A copy of each invoice is forwarded by first mail to the agent for whom the goods are intended, in order that he may compare the quantities received with the articles invoiced. A complete record of all packages received is kept, giving the name of the articles, date of inspection, of shipment, &c.; and when it is considered that from May 2, 1881, to October 15, 1881, there were shipped from the New York warehouse 25,893 packages, weighing 4,536,092 pounds, not one of which is unaccounted for, the magnitude of the business will be understood and appreciated.

No attempts have this year been made so far by contractors to deliver goods inferior to the sample upon which the contract was awarded, and I can say that all goods and supplies furnished during the present fiscal year were of good quality and entirely satisfactory to this office.

CASH ANNUITIES.

Winnebagoes.—At its last session Congress passed an act, which was approved on the 18th of January last, to aid that portion of the Winnebago tribe of Indians residing in Wisconsin "to obtain subsistence by agricultural pursuits, and to promote their civilization." It provides that an account shall be stated between the two branches of the tribe, so that those in Wisconsin may be paid their full share as found to be due from those in Nebraska, and it directs that future distribution of annuities shall be made *pro rata,* according to the number of the whole tribe. This act also provides that before any person shall be entitled to the benefits accruing thereunder, it shall be made to appear that he, or the head of the family of which he is a member, has taken up a homestead, with a *bona-fide* intention of complying with an act approved March 3, 1875.

In pursuance of this just and beneficial measure, Congress further directed that a census be taken which would show the entire number of Winnebagoes in Wisconsin and Nebraska, separately, and also all the facts necessary to justly decide in regard to the rights of those claiming to participate in the benefits of the act.

When the scattered condition of these Indians in Wisconsin, and the data and proof required in the case of each, is considered, the magnitude of the work will be understood. It was the purpose and is yet the hope of this office to have the money due these Indians under this act paid to them during the current year, but Congress having failed to provide any funds to pay the necessary expenses incident to the taking of this census, and no funds being available for the purpose, nothing could be done in the matter until after the beginning of the present fiscal year. Then, in consideration of the desirability of the measure, and in compliance with repeated requests from members of Congress and others, I consented to have the work done by a clerk from this office, and the expense paid from the contingency funds of the Indian Department for the fiscal year 1882. Consequently, on the 12th of August last, a clerk was detailed to proceed to Wisconsin, and he is now there engaged in this duty. In the mean time the regular agent at Winnebago Agency in Nebraska has been instructed in regard to taking the census of those at that place, and both lists will no doubt be completed at an early day.

Sac and Fox, Iowa.—Continued efforts are being made to induce the Sac and Fox Indians in Iowa to sign a pay-roll for annuities now four years over due. They still refuse, however, notwithstanding that the last season has been a very unfavorable one for farming and they are suffering in consequence. During January last I instructed the agent at Iowa Agency to take a census and make a list of these Indians, arranging them in families in the manner established by the department. This he succeeded in doing after great difficulty, and only by obtaining the necessary information from parties who were not members of the tribe, but who had lived with them long enough to become thoroughly acquainted. The chiefs in the mean time used all their influence to prevent the names of the women and children from being enrolled. This list shows a total number of 356, viz, 92 men, 104 women, and 160 children. Owing to the circumstances under which it was completed this may not be strictly correct, but may be useful in the division of annuities payable to the whole tribe under the various treaties.

These Indians are industrious and temperate, but are suspicious of whites, and stubbornly refuse to abandon their Indian traditions and customs. It is to be regretted that they will not consent to receipt properly for their annuities, as many of them are in want, and I am persuaded almost all would make a good use of the money. It might be wise and humane, now that they are permanently located in Iowa, with the approval of the State, and on land bought with their own money, to make. if possible, a satisfactory arrangement between them and that part of the tribe now in Indian Territory, so that the census just taken, or one more complete, if obtainable, may be agreed upon as a basis for a permanent division of their annuities, and a compliance with the law, which says, "They (the whole tribe) shall be paid *pro rata,* according to their numbers." *

Wyandottes.—By an act to supply deficiencies in appropriations, and for other purposes, approved March 3, 1881, the sum of $28,109.51 was appropriated to pay the Wyandottes their claim under treaty of February 23, 1860. Soon after the passage of this act the United States

---

*Since the above was written a delegation of these Indians has visited Washington and consented on behalf of their people to the signing of the new roll. The money due them will therefore soon be paid.

Indian agent at Quapaw Agency, Indian Territory, was instructed to take a census of the Wyandottes, distinguishing between those who are citizens and those who are not, that the payment might be made *per capita*, and as directed.

Since that time he has referred to this office, under different dates, the names of a number of claimants for enrollment, whose rights to share in this fund are disputed by members of the council of the tribe on various grounds, and many communications have been received from Wyandottes who became citizens under the treaty of January 31, 1855, asserting their right to participate in this fund, claiming that it was appropriated in pursuance of the findings of a commission appointed in accordance with an amendment to the treaty of 1867. In order to determine the rights of the various claimants in the premises, a thorough examination of the report of that commission became necessary, as well as a careful and impartial consideration of all evidence and proofs submitted by claimants, particularly by those whose claims are contested.

A claim has also been filed by Isaiah Walker to a ferry franchise purchased of the Wyandottes, under treaty of 1855, amounting to $17,900, which, in view of statements made by his attorneys, requires examination and final decision, before these funds can be paid to the Wyandottes. A conclusion has not as yet been reached in the matters above set forth, and therefore the payment has been withheld.

Poncas.—The same act contains a provision for the purpose of indemnifying the Ponca Indians for losses sustained in consequence of their removal to the Indian Territory, and directs that $20,000 of the money thereby appropriated be paid to them, in cash, the sum of $10,000 to those now in that Territory and a like sum to those in Dakota. No cash payments having been made to these Indians since 1878, a correct and reliable list of them was not on file, and one of the Indian inspectors was instructed to take a census of those in the Indian Territory. On the 27th of May last he reported that an enrollment had been completed by him, containing the names of 506 persons then living, and the names of 14 others now dead, but who were alive on the 3d of March last, the date on which the act was approved; in all, 520 names. In accordance with this enrollment payment was made by the agent on the 28th of June.

Those of the tribe in Dakota not being under the charge of any agent of this department, but nearly all living in the vicinity of Santee Agency, Nebraska, the agent there was instructed to prepare a complete and correct roll of them. This roll, containing 175 names, after examination, was approved on the 27th of the following July, and returned to the agent, with instructions to pay, *per capita*, to the parties therein named, the $10,000 which had already been placed to his credit; and the payment was accordingly made.

Miamies of Indiana.—This act also appropriates $221,257.86 to pay the Miami Indians residing in Indiana and elsewhere the principal sum that became due them on the 1st day of July, 1880, in accordance with the amended fourth article of the treaty concluded with them on the 5th day of June and ratified on the 4th day of August, 1854. To effect this payment the fourth section of the act provides for the appointment of a competent person to take a census and make a list of such of these Indians as were living on the 1st of July, 1880, and were embraced in a corrected list agreed upon by said Indians, in the presence of the Commissioner of Indian Affairs, in June, 1854, and the increase of their families. It also provided for the appointment of an agent to make the payment.

Accordingly, on the 2d day of the following April an agent was appointed to take the census and make the list, and was fully instructed in regard to his duties. As the tribal relations of these Indians is broken up and they are much scattered, notice of this appointment was given by publication, for three weeks prior to the 31st of May last, in a leading paper in each of the States of Indiana, Michigan, Kansas, and Missouri, calling upon all claimants to make their claims known on or before that day, or be forever barred. Much difficulty was experienced in tracing many claimants to their ancestors on the original roll, through the great liability to change the spelling of Indian names and their custom of often changing their names entirely. As the payment is large (nearly $685 to each man, woman, and child), the agent was instructed to use all possible care to guard against fraudulent enrollments. In the discharge of this duty he visited almost every family and claimant, and received much valuable assistance from various members of the tribe, nearly all of whom are civilized, and numbers even well educated.

Time was required to accomplish the enrollment according to law and in a manner satisfactory to the Indians, this office, and the department, so that the list was not finally submitted for your approval until the 29th of September last. This list, with its notes, references, &c., appears to be very full, complete, and satisfactory, and will be valuable for future reference as a true exhibit of this people at the time it was taken. The necessity for the delay incident to preparing it can be appreciated by those only who are familiar with the circumstances and the labor and research connected therewith.

The Hon. Calvin Cowgill, of Wabash, Ind., having been appointed and having duly qualified as agent to make this payment, it will be completed without unnecessary delay, probably during the current month.

In this connection I desire to call attention to the fact that, with the exception of that for the Sac and Fox Indians, the foregoing legislation may be termed special, and the extra work thereby entailed on this office must have been unforeseen when the clerical force allowed this bureau for the present year was under consideration. An addition of at least one-fifth was thereby unexpectedly added to the general work of this office, so that the several acts mentioned could not be carried out as promptly as they should have been, and the current work of the office has consequently been much retarded.

It may also be observed that the funds necessary to carry out these enactments were not always provided, and this office was obliged to use for the purpose the appropriation for "Contingencies, Indian Department," a fund that has always been insufficient for the regular requirements of the service.

SANITARY.

The sanitary condition of the Indians remains about the same as at last annual report. The aggregate number of cases of sickness treated, however, has materially increased, being 83,899 against 67,352 for last year, while the number of deaths reported is only 1,440 against 1,936. The number of births is 1,290, but these numbers are probably not strictly accurate, as the physician reports only those which come under his actual knowledge; and as the disposition of the Indians of some of the tribes is to keep these facts secret, perfectly reliable statistics are difficult to obtain. The increase in cases of sickness treated indicates the growth of confidence in the agency physicians and in the civilized mode of treatment of disease, and a tendency to abandon the barbarous practices of the native medicine-men. The number of cases vaccinated is 1,576.

The monthly sanitary reports from physicians have been for the most part satisfactory, and the ratio of mortality to the number of cases treated indicates a remarkable degree of success. The agency physicians at many of the agencies are not provided with the necessary hospital accommodations, and as the sick have to be treated in their quarters and camps, where no hygienic nor dietary measures can be enforced, the physician is embarrassed in the effort to better the condition of those for whom he feels great responsibility. The medical corps consists of 65 physicians, and it is fair to infer that their duties were faithfully performed. A tabulated statement will be found on page 367 showing the number of patients treated, diseases, &c. From this it appears that the greatest morbific agents have been malarial and pulmonary diseases, especially the former. This is particularly noticeable among the Indians in the Indian Territory.

HUALAPAIS.

For several years the Hualapais Indians roamed unmolested among the mountains of Northwestern Arizona, in the vicinity of Camp Beale Springs, and subsisted themselves in the Indian way. But in 1873, when it was represented that they were on one of the principal lines of travel, and that mining camps were springing up all around them, it was recommended, by both civil and military officers, that they be removed from that section and located upon some reservation. Accordingly, in the spring of 1874, 580 of them were removed to the Colorado River Reserve, and there regularly rationed. Partly on account of their dissatisfaction with the location, and partly owing to their unwillingness to submit to the requirement that they should labor for a portion of the ration, they left the reservation the following spring, and returned to their old haunts; and the agent reported that, on consultation with the commanding officer of the department, it had been decided to allow them to remain there during good behavior.

The projection of the Southern Arizona Railroad brought settlers into that country; their stock ranged over the grounds on which the Indians had depended for nuts and seeds; game grew scarce; and the Hualapais became so destitute that it was feared that their poverty would lead them to depredate on settlers, and that a collision would result. Such reports led Governor Frémont to visit them in person in December, 1878, and he found them impoverished but friendly, and exceedingly desirous of being allowed to remain there and hunt. Nothing further was done until the fall of 1879, when the Hualapais became so desperately poor that, as a measure of both humanity and policy, rations were issued to nearly 700 of them by the War Department, until spring opened. During the succeeding summer they subsisted themselves, but in the fall of 1880 their destitution again called for relief, and the War Department provided for another issue of rations, with the understanding that the funds expended therefor should be reimbursed the military by the Interior Department, whenever the necessary appropriation should be obtained. In the deficiency act of March 3, 1881, $15,000 was appropriated for the Hualapais, with which the War Department accounts were paid.

The needs of these Indians are this fall greater than ever. The office has no fund with which to provide for them, and the War Department has again agreed to issue rations on the same conditions as to reimbursement. An estimate of funds needed therefor will be submitted to Congress at its next session; but it is important that some permanent arrangement should be made, whereby the Hualapais may be put in the way of becoming civilized and self-supporting.

At their request, General Wilcox, under date of July 8, 1881, ordered that a tract about 30 miles wide and 100 miles long, lying along a bend in the Colorado River, be set apart as a "military reservation for the subsistence and better control of the Hualapais Indians." But the military officer who recommends the boundary lines of this tract reports that they include little or no arable land, and that "the water is in such small quantities, and the country is so rocky and devoid of grass, that it would not be available for stock-raising." Either a reserve suitable for agriculture or grazing should be set apart for them, or, which is far better, they should be settled under the care of an agent upon some reserve already established, and should be assisted in the way of house-building, farming, or herding, and schools. Their friendliness and willingness to render service as scouts entitle them to generous treatment by the government; but they should be so placed that support by their own efforts is possible, and then gradually be compelled to depend on it for support. This will require an ample appropriation on the start, but will be more economical in the end, and more creditable, than to allow them to continue to be idle consumers of rations in a barren country.

UTES.

The commissioners appointed under the act of June 15, 1880, ratifying the Ute agreement of March 6, 1880, have selected a reservation in the vicinity of the confluence of White River with Green River, Utah, adjacent to the Uintah Indian Reservation, for the Uncompahgre Utes, who were formerly located at Los Pinos Agency, Colorado. The Uncompahgre Utes have been removed thereto; the agency buildings at the former Los Pinos Agency have been sold, and new ones have been erected at the new agency, which is designated Ouray Agency, in recognition of the friendship and faithfulness to the whites of Ouray, former head chief of the Utes.

The White River Utes have been removed to Uintah Agency, where lands will be assigned to them in severalty, as provided in the Ute agreement, so soon as the requisite surveys shall have been made.

The Southern Utes still occupy their old reservation in the southern part of the Ute Reserve. Their agent reports that the lands on the Rio La Plata and vicinity, assigned for their location in severalty by the Ute agreement, are being surveyed with a view to the definite location of these Indians so far as practicable, but that there is not a sufficient amount of agricultural land on the reservation in that vicinity to furnish to each Indian the amount of land specified in the agreement. In this contingency the act of June 15, 1880, stipulates that the Southern Utes shall be located "upon such other unoccupied agricultural lands as may be found on the La Plata River or in its vicinity in New Mexico."

SITTING BULL INDIANS.

In July last the military authorities turned over to the Indian agent at Standing Rock Agency, Dakota, 2,858 Sioux Indians who had been with Sitting Bull in the British possessions, and who had, from time to time, surrendered to the military. Of this number 139 were permitted to join their relatives at Cheyenne River Agency, the balance remaining at Standing Rock Agency for the present, where arrangements have been made to subsist them. Sitting Bull himself and his more immediate followers, 137 in number, are still prisoners, under the surveillance of the military, at Fort Randall, Dakota Territory.

At all of the Sioux agencies quietness has prevailed and progress has been made during the year, and no event of importance has occurred except the death of Spotted Tail, hereditary head chief of the Sioux, who was killed by another Indian at Rosebud Agency. A full account of the affair will be found in Agent Cook's annual report herewith, page 112. The murderer is in the custody of the judicial authorities for trial, the United States Attorney-General having expressed the opinion that he is subject to trial by the United States courts.

PONCAS.

By mistake, the United States, in 1868, ceded to the Sioux the land in Dakota which had previously been ceded to the Poncas, and in 1873 the Poncas were removed to their present location in Indian Territory, where a reservation containing 101,894.31 acres of land was assigned to them in the Cherokee country, west of the 96th degree of longitude. where, upon payment to the Cherokees for the same, it was provided by the sixteenth article of the Cherokee treaty of July 19, 1866, that the United States might settle friendly Indians. The Poncas were at first dissatisfied at their removal, but, as stated in the last annual report of this office, in October of last year the Ponca chiefs then on the reservation in Indian Territory forwarded to this office a petition earnestly requesting to be permitted to come to Washington to formally part with their right to all lands in Dakota, and to obtain a title to their present reservation, and to settle all their matters with the government. Their request was granted, and while in Washington they entered into an agreement of the kind indicated in their request of 25th October, 1880.

By act of March 3, 1881, Congress appropriated the sum of $165,000 to enable the Secretary of the Interior "to indemnify the Ponca tribe of Indians for losses sustained by them in consequence of their removal to the Indian Territory, to secure their lands in severalty on either the old or new reservation, in accordance with their wishes, and to settle all matters of difference with these Indians;" the amount so appropriated to be expended under the direction of the Secretary of the Interior: (1) For the purchase of the aforesaid reservation in Indian Territory, $50,000; (2) for distribution *per capita* among the Ponca Indians in Indian Territory, $10,000; (3) to purchase stock cattle and draught animals for the Poncas in Indian Territory, $2,000; (4) to erect dwelling-houses, purchase agricultural implements, stock and seed, for school purposes, and to distribute *per capita* to the Poncas in Dakota, $25,000 Seventy thousand dollars were also appropriated "to be held as a permanent fund in the Treasury of the United States, at 5 per cent. interest, the interest to be distributed annually among all the Ponca Indians in cash." The amounts thus appropriated have been, so far as practicable, expended for the purposes for which they were appropriated. It has not been practicable as yet to devote the money appropriated for the erection of houses for the Poncas in Dakota to that us for the reason that they have as yet no settled title to any land in that Territory.

With a view to securing a permanent home for those Poncas who left the Ponca Reservation in Indian Territory under the chief Standing Bear—being the Indians referred to in the aforesaid appropriation bill as the "Poncas now in Dakota"—delegations from the Omaha and Winnebago Indians in Nebraska, and from the Sioux in Dakota, were brought to this city in August last, and under date of 20th of that month the delegations of Sioux from Rosebud, Pine Ridge, and Standing Rock Agencies signed an agreement to give to these Poncas land for homes where they formerly resided. The agreement is as follows:

Whereas by a mistake made in the treaty between the United States and the Sioux Indians on April 29, 1868, injustice was done to the Ponca Indians by taking away from them and giving to the Sioux lands which belonged to the Poncas; and

Whereas the Sioux Indians, in council assembled in the city of Washington, are desirous of correcting that mistake in order to do justice to the Poncas; and

Whereas the United States has given lands to a portion of the Poncas who removed to the Indian Territory, upon which they are now living and contented; and

Whereas it is desired to provide lands for such of the Poncas as are now in Dakota, as well as those in the Indian Territory:

Now, therefore, this agreement, made this 20th day of August, 1881, by the Sioux Indians resident upon the reservation in the Territory of Dakota, represented by their chiefs and headmen now present in Washington, and under the supervision and with the approval of the Secretary of the Interior of the United States, witnesseth:

The said tribes of Sioux Indians do hereby cede and relinquish to the United States so much of that portion of the present Sioux Reservation as was formerly occupied by the Ponca tribe of Indians, set forth and described by the supplemental treaty between the United States of America and the Ponca tribe of Indians concluded March 10, 1865 (14 Stats., 675), as may be necessary for the settlement of that portion of the Ponca tribe under Standing Bear now on or residing near the old Ponca Reservation, for their use and occupation, in the proportion and to the extent of as many tracts of 640 acres each as there are heads of families and male members now of the age of twenty-one years and upwards and unmarried.

If it should be found that there are of the adult Poncas, males or females, not connected with any family, but standing wholly alone, there shall be reserved from the lands thus ceded sufficient to allot to each of such Indians 80 acres, and the remainder shall be allotted to heads of families and to such male members over the age of twenty-one years as shall marry.

The selections and allotments shall be made by such person as the Secretary of the Interior shall designate for that purpose, and subject to his approval; and thereupon the United States shall give to each allottee, when he shall have settled on his land, title in fee-simple for the land. The title to be acquired by the Poncas shall not be subject to alienation, lease, or incumbrance, either by voluntary conveyance of the grantee or his heirs, or by the judgment, order, or decree of any court, nor subject to taxation of any character, but shall be and remain inalienable and not subject to taxation for the period of twenty years, and until such time thereafter as the President may see fit to remove the restrictions, which shall be incorporated in the patent.

This agreement shall not be binding until it shall have been executed and signed by at least three-fourths of all the adult male Indians occupying or interested in the present Sioux Reservation, and ratified by the Congress of the United States.

In witness whereof we have hereunto set our hands and seals on the day and date above written.

Ogalalla Sioux and Brulé Sioux:
    Mahpiyaluta, his + mark (Red Cloud).
    Wakinyanska, his + mark (White Thunder).
    TasunkeKokipapi, his + mark (Young Man Afraid of his Horses).
    Miwakanyuha (Captain George Sword).
    Asanpi, his + mark (Milk).
    Wobela, his + mark (Cook).
Standing Rock Sioux:
    Cetanwakinyan, his + mark (Thunder Hawk).
    Nasunatanka, his + mark (Big Head).
    Mato-cuwiyuksa, his + mark (Bear's Rib).
    Cantepeta, his + mark (Fire Heart).
    Tatankaluta, his + mark (Red Bull).
    Wakutemani, his + mark (Shooting Walker).
I certify that the foregoing agreement was read and explained by me and was fully

understood by the above-named Indians before signing, and that the same was executed by the above Ogalalla, Brulé, and Standing Rock Sioux, at the Department of the Interior, Washington, D. C., on the 20th day of August, 1881.

JOHN P. WILLIAMSON,
Interpreter.

Attest:
A. BELL,
E. P. HANNA.

INTERIOR DEPARTMENT,
August 20, 1881.

The foregoing agreement is approved by us.

S. J. KIRKWOOD,
Secretary of the Interior.
H. PRICE,
Commissioner of Indian Affairs.

An agent is now among the Sioux Indians parties to the treaty of April 29, 1868, to obtain the ratification by them of the foregoing agreements as indicated in the last clause, and as required by the twelfth article of the said treaty of 1868. It will, doubtless, be thus ratified, and if Congress shall then assent to it, the question as to the settlement of the Poncas under Standing Bear will have been settled.

TURTLE MOUNTAIN BAND OF CHIPPEWAS IN DAKOTA.

The unsettled condition of affairs with these Indians has long been a matter of deep concern, not only to the Indians themselves, but to this bureau as well. Prominent among their troubles is the uncertainty on their part as to the view held by the government relative to the status of the lands claimed by them, and the purposes of the department in the matter of their ultimate disposal.

The tract of country inhabited and claimed by them is north and northwest of Devil's Lake, in Dakota, and is estimated to contain 9,500,000 acres. These lands have never been ceded to the United States, and the claim of the Turtle Mountain Band to ownership is based upon continuous possession and occupation by them and their ancestors for many generations. That the Indian title to the country in question has never been extinguished or successfully disputed cannot be denied, and, according to the theory that has been adopted by the government, it would seem that these Indians have all the original rights in an unceded territory. Effort has been made from time to time to remove them to the White Earth Reservation, in Minnesota, but they have steadfastly resisted such removal, lest the abandonment of the country claimed by them might be looked upon as a willing relinquishment of their title thereto.

The condition of these people is deplorable in the extreme; they have no permanent abiding place, are very poor, and, owing to the scarcity of game, which indeed may be said to have almost entirely disappeared, they have only the most scanty means of subsistence. Last year the agent at Devil's Lake Agency reported that chief Little Bull and his people were in great danger of actual starvation. Emigration is fast flowing into the country, to the great discomfort of the Indians, and they desire and have repeatedly asked protection from the government. That their condition requires the attention of the government is manifest. Petitions have been presented from both sides, Indians and whites, asking for a settlement of their difficulties, and I propose to make the matter the subject of a special report, with a view to securing early Congressional action looking to their permanent relief.

I will add that the number of Indians roaming about over this vast area, homeless, destitute, and almost hopeless, is variously estimated at from 500 to 600 full-bloods and from 1,000 to 1,500 half-breeds.

LITTLE CHIEF'S BAND OF CHEYENNES.

Little Chief's band of Northern Cheyennes, taken from Sidney Barracks, Nebraska, reached the Cheyenne and Arapaho Agency, Indian Territory, December 9, 1878. It appears that before leaving Fort Keogh, Montana, a hope was held out to them, which they construed into a promise, that if they were not satisfied with the Indian Territory they would be permitted to return North. They have never been contented there, and have always urged to be taken back North. While some of the Cheyennes have been insubordinate and disposed to give trouble, Little Chief, whose influence has been great, has always counseled patience, refusing to sanction any movement looking to the return of the Cheyennes to the North without the consent of the government; and when, in the autumn of 1880, some of his young men armed themselves and prepared to go to the agency to unite with other Cheyennes in precipitating a disturbance, Little Chief armed himself and directed his folowers to remain in their camp, threatening to kill any who should attempt to leave.

Believing that the time had come when any promises which might have been made could be fulfilled with safety, and the condition of these Indians improved, Little Chief was called to Washington, in August last, to meet delegations of Sioux from several of the Sioux agencies in Dakota. As a result of the conference, arrangements have been made to locate Little Chief and his band at Pine Ridge Agency, Dakota, among the Sioux Indians comprised in the bands over which Red Cloud has been recognized as head chief. Red Cloud's people and these Cheyennes are extensively intermarried and speak the same language, and many of Red Cloud's relatives are still at the Cheyenne and Arapaho Agency, in Indian Territory. The desire was expressed in the council that all the Cheyennes who were taken to Indian Territory from the North—about four hundred—should go to Pine Ridge Agency; but, as before stated, it was finally determined that only those who went with Little Chief—about two hundred and thirty-five—should return with him; but promise was made that their request in behalf of those remaining in Indian Territory should be laid before Congress.

Little Chief and his band were transferred to Capt. W. A. Thompson, Fourth Cavalry, on the 6th instant, he having been selected by the military authorities to conduct them to Pine Ridge Agency. Before leaving the Cheyenne and Arapaho Agency they were furnished with their proportion of such annuity goods as had been received, and subsistence for sixty days was issued to them. In reporting their departure Agent Miles says:

Now that this band has gone it only remains to make a final and irrevocable decision in regard to the balance of the Northern Cheyennes now here, who are as eager to go as these people were. The promise of the Hon. Secretary of the Interior to bring the matter before Congress at its next session is viewed by them as a direct promise that they shall go North next summer; and if not allowed to go, the same disquietude which has visibly affected the Southern Cheyennes will exist, and it will be in the interest of peace and progress to let them go. The coming of these Northern Indians in two parties, leaving part of their numbers still North, has retarded the old Southern Indians and created difficulties in their management, and it is hoped that the further advancement of these people may not be retarded by the attempt to settle a discontented element permanently among them.

As these Northern Cheyennes have always lived in the North near
the Sioux, and will advance much more rapidly than if compelled to
remain in Indian Territory, I respectfully recommend that provision be
made to permit them to rejoin their relatives.

FREEDMEN IN CHOCTAW AND CHICKASAW NATIONS.

The third article of the Choctaw and Chickasaw treaty of April 28,
1866 (14 Stat., p. 769), provides that the sum of $300,000, which was
the consideration for the cession to the United States of their territory
west of 98°, known as the "leased district"—

Shall be invested and held by the United States, at an interest not less than 5 per
cent., in trust for the said nations, until the legislatures of the Choctaw and Chickasaw
Nations, respectively, shall have made such laws, rules, and regulations as may be necessary to give all persons of African descent resident in the said nations at the date of
the treaty of Fort Smith, and their descendants, heretofore held in slavery among said
nations, all the rights, privileges, and immunities, including the right of suffrage, of
citizens of said nations, except in the annuities, moneys, and public domain claimed
by, or belonging to, said nations, respectively, and also to give to such persons who
were residents as aforesaid, and their descendants, forty acres each of the land of said
nations on the same terms as the Choctaws and Chickasaws, to be selected on the survey of said land, after the Choctaws and Chickasaws and Kansas Indians have made
their selections, as herein provided. * * * On the enactment of such laws, rules,
and regulations, the said sum of three hundred thousand dollars shall be paid to the
Choctaw and Chickasaw Nations, * * * less such sum, at the rate of one hundred dollars per capita, as shall be sufficient to pay such persons of African descent
before referred to as, within ninety days after the passage of such laws, rules, and
regulations, shall elect to remove and actually remove from the nations, respectively.

The said article further provides that:

Should the said laws, rules, and regulations not be made by the legislatures of the
said nations, respectively, within two years from the ratification of this treaty, then
the said sum of three hundred thousand dollars shall cease to be held in trust for the
said Choctaw and Chickasaw Nations, and be held for the use and benefit of such of
said persons of African descent as the United States shall remove from the said Territory in such manner as the United States shall deem proper; the United States agreeing, within ninety days from the expiration of the said two years, to remove from said
nations all such persons of African descent as may be willing to remove; those remaining or returning after having been removed from said nations to have no benefit of
said sum of three hundred thousand dollars, or any part thereof, but shall be upon the
same footing as other citizens of the United States in the said nations.

The fourth article of this treaty defines the rights of freedmen in
said nations, and the forty-sixth article provides how the money due
the Indians under this treaty shall be paid.

In fulfillment of these treaty stipulations, Congress, by act of July 26,
1866, appropriated $200,000 of the $300,000 to be advanced to these
Indians, as provided in said forty-sixth article, and by the same act,
and by the act of April 10, 1869, $30,000 was appropriated as interest
on the aforesaid fund of $300,000, when two-thirds of the fund had
been advanced and paid over to the proper authorities of said nations,
and that, too, before a step had been taken by said Indians to comply
with their part of the agreement. In fact, the Choctaws and Chickasaws allowed the two years to elapse without granting the freedmen the
rights and privileges therein specified, and up to this date have failed to
take action thereon, and thereby have forfeited all claim to the interest
advanced therein. Neither did the government, within the ninety
days from the expiration of the said two years, remove, or attempt to
remove, said freedmen, willing or unwilling, from the said nations, nor
have any of said freedmen removed themselves; but all remain, as
provided in the fourth article of the treaty.

One of the embarrassments in the settlement of this question is that provision of the treaty which requires joint or concurrent action by the legislative councils of the two nations. The Chickasaws desiring the removal of all freedmen from their country, persistently refuse to concur in any legislation granting their freedmen the rights, privileges, and immunities of citizens of said nation, while the Choctaws show a disposition to adopt all the requirements of said third article of the treaty.

An act to extend to freedmen the privileges of citizenship was introduced in the Choctaw council in 1873, and was passed by the house, but failed in the senate. At a later period, in 1875, Hon. J. P. C. Shanks was appointed a commissioner to visit these nations and secure an adjustment of the status of persons of African descent residing in the Choctaw and Chickasaw Nations, reference being had to the provisions of the third and fourth articles of the aforesaid treaty; but, meeting the same difficulty, was unable to effect terms satisfactory to both nations. Not satisfied or disheartened by these failures, the Choctaw national council, at its legislative session of 1880, passed a memorial to the Government of the United States, which was approved November 2, 1880, by the principal chief, J. F. McCurtain, wherein it is proposed to adopt their freedmen as citizens upon the basis of the third article of the treaty of 1866, and they ask the government to enact the necessary legislation to authorize them to adopt said action without the co-operation of the Chickasaw Nation. The only objection to this legislation comes from the freedmen themselves, who ask to be granted all the privileges accruing to them under these treaty stipulations, but protest against being placed under the jurisdiction of the Choctaw laws.

These freedmen are upon the lands not from their own option, have had no voice in these treaty provisions, have made valuable improvements in the country of their enforced adoption, and do not now desire to leave that country, and should be protected in all their rights in the Choctaw and Chickasaw Nations by the adoption separately of such acts by each council as will, with the approval of Congress, give the freedmen living thereon forty acres of land each and all the rights and privileges which were contemplated to be given them by the treaty.

CREEK AND SEMINOLE BOUNDARY.

By the third article of the treaty of June 14, 1866 (14 Stat., p. 785), the Creek Indians ceded to the United States the west half of their entire domain, to be divided by a line running north and south, to be sold to and used as homes for such other civilized Indians as the United States might choose to settle thereon. By the eighth article of this treaty said divisional line was to be forthwith accurately surveyed by the Secretary of the Interior, under the direction of the Commissioner of Indian Affairs.. By the third article of the treaty of March 21, 1866 (14 Stat., p. 755), the United States granted to the Seminole Nation a portion of the above-ceded tract of Creek country bounded and described as follows:

Beginning on the Canadian River where the line divides the Creek lands according to the terms of their sale to the United States by their treaty of February 6, 1866 following said line due north to where said line crosses the north fork of the Canadian River; thence up said north fork of the Canadian River a distance sufficient to make two hundred thousand acres by running due south to the Canadian River; thence down said Canadian River to the place of beginning.

In explanation of the discrepancy in the dates of the Creek treaty above given, it should be stated that after the treaty of February 6, 1866, was made and forwarded to the President for ratification by the Senate, objections were made by the delegates representing the South-

46 Ab

ern Creeks to certain stipulations not therein contained; that two subsequent treaties, dated respectively May 9 and May 21, 1866, were prepared, covering the objectionable features of the former treaty; but not until the 14th of June, 1866, was a satisfactory treaty presented that all the delegates were willing to sign. In the mean time the Seminole treaty was made.

In order to carry out the provisions of the third and eighth articles of the Creek treaty of 1866, the superintendent of Indian affairs for the southern superintendency, under office instructions, made a contract December 28, 1867, with Mr. J. C. Rankin, for the above-named survey. By the sundry civil appropriation act of July 28, 1866 (14 Stat, p. 320), $4,000 were appropriated for this survey, which being insufficient, Congress, by the deficiency appropriation act of March 3, 1869, appropriated $5,000 to complete the survey of the divisional line and the out-boundaries of the Seminole Reservation (15 Stat., p. 315). Mr. Rankin, in the execution of his contract, located the divisional line, which is the western boundary of the Creek Reservation, two and a half miles east of the point where the agency buildings are now located. The Seminoles had in the mean time been located thereon by the United States, and had made considerable improvements in their new home before the execution and completion of the survey. The protests of the Creeks against the acceptance and approval of this survey were so urgent that this office deemed it advisable to withhold its approval for the time being, and to require a review of the survey made and to complete whatever evidences were required in the survey to determine the true western boundary of the Creek Reservation.

On the completion of the survey in 1871 (in which Frederic W. Bardwell, esq., was employed by the contractor to assist in the review of the survey and in the computations of the area of the country as well as in the definite location of the line of division), which was approved by the department February 5, 1872, it was found that nearly all the extensive improvements which the Seminoles had made since their settlement thereon, together with the agency buildings, were east of the true divisional line and, consequently, upon Creek lands. As soon as this was definitely determined, the Creeks claimed, and began to exercise, jurisdiction over the country occupied by the Seminoles; and the Seminoles, fearing the loss of their improvements and lands, appealed to the government for protection and relief, whence has arisen a question which, though it has been the subject of much correspondence and negotiation, still remains unsettled and as difficult of solution as ever.

Under an act of Congress, approved March 3, 1873, authorizing the Secretary of the Interior to negotiate with the Creek Indians for the cession of a portion of their reservation, occupied by friendly Indians (17 Stat., p. 626), a commission, consisting of Supt. Enoch Hoag, Judge Thomas C. Jones, and John M. Millikin, esq., was sent to that country to negotiate and arrange with said tribes for a final and permanent adjustment of the boundaries of their reservations, but with fruitless results. The Creeks were unwilling to part with any more of their lands, but were willing to incorporate the whole Seminole tribe into their nation, which proposition received no consideration whatever from the Seminoles who had been settled thereon by the United States. In 1875, Hon. J. P. C. Shanks was commissioned to visit and negotiate with the Creeks for the cession of these lands and authorized to offer the sum of one dollar per acre for all their lands in the possession of the Seminole Nation; but this offer was accepted only upon the condition of the settlement of all their outstanding claims against the government.

Subsequently, however, the Creek council appointed a committee to negotiate for the sale of the Seminole tract upon such terms as would " give the best satisfaction to the Muskogee people", with instructions to report their negotiations to the next annual session of the national council for its approval or rejection. The Creek delegation, in February last, signified through the department their willingness to sell to the United States, for the use of the Seminoles, 175,000 acres of their land, lying east of the divisional line and embracing the land occupied by the Seminoles, at the rate of one dollar per acre, in full settlement of all differences and demands on the United States growing out of the question of Seminole occupation of their lands.

The improvements of the Seminoles are not confined to any particular portion of the reservation as first defined by Mr. Rankin, but extend over the whole, from the eastern boundary located by him in his first survey to the eastern boundary as located by him in 1871, and reaching from the north fork of the Canadian River, on the north, to the main Canadian River, on the south. While it is not attempted to deprive the Creeks of these lands, yet the Seminoles certainly should not be subjected to the jurisdiction of the Creeks, nor should they be compelled to lose their improvements or abandon their lands.

Believing that the rights and equities of both Creeks and Seminoles can be best preserved by means of purchase, and the Creeks now showing a willingness to dispose of these lands at a reasonable price after being deprived of their use for fifteen years, it is respectfully recommended and urged, as the only means of relief, that Congress adopt the necessary legislation and provide the necessary means to purchase said land, and thereby relieve, as the opportunity now offers, not only these nations of a fruitful source of irritation, but this office of a subject of much embarrassment and anxiety.

KICKAPOO ALLOTTEES UNDER TREATY OF 1862.

Attention is called to the condition of affairs relative to the estates of deceased and minor allottees, under the provisions of the Kickapoo treaty of June 28, 1862 (13 Stat., 623), and to certain tracts of land reserved thereby for certain purposes. By the terms of said treaty it is provided that the lands of said tribe shall be allotted in severalty or held in common as the members thereof shall elect; that the President of the United States may cause patents in fee-simple to issue to the adult allottees " being males and heads of families," when satisfied of their ability to control their own affairs, and provided they had obtained certificates of naturalization from the United States district court for Kansas. No provision, however, is made by which female allottees can become citizens and obtain patents for their lands.

Many of the allottees deceased before having, by a compliance with the above provisions, obtained patents for their allotments, and frequent applications are made to this office by the heirs of such deceased allottees for the settlement of their estates, and by female allottees, that some action may be taken to enable them to acquire citizenship, and to obtain patents for their lands. Some legislation should be had by which female allottees under said treaty can obtain citizenship and patents for their land, and also for the settlement of the estates of deceased allottees who had not become citizens as provided by the treaty. The same difficulty having arisen as to the settlement of the estates of deceased Pottawatomie Indians, allottees under their treaty of 1862, the treaty of 1867 (Senate amendment) provided that where allottees had deceased, or should thereafter decease, such allottees should be regarded, for the purpose of a careful and just settlement of their estates, as citizens of the United States and of the State of Kansas.

By the terms of said Kickapoo treaty certain tracts of land were reserved as a site for a saw and grist mill, and for missionary purposes, respectively, which are to be disposed of when the objects for which they are reserved shall have been accomplished, in such a manner and for such a purpose "as may be provided by law." The said tracts have not for years been used, and probably never will be used, for the purposes for which they were reserved, and being several miles distant from the tribal reservation, it is not possible for the agent to exercise such care in their protection as will prevent trespasses upon them by white men. Congress should provide for the disposition of these tracts, and for the application of the fund derived therefrom to the benefit of the Kickapoo Indians.

AGENCIES IN THE INDIAN TERRITORY.

This year has been one of general quiet at all the agencies of the Indian Territory, and with the exception of some excitement over the action of "Captain Payne," who with a small party of whites claimed the right to homestead certain lands that the civilized Indians had ceded to the United States for the purpose of settling friendly Indians and freedmen thereon, and whose prompt arrest and conviction is a matter of publicity, nothing of special moment has occurred.

The great drought of this summer, which has so terribly scourged a goodly portion of our country, extending as it has in a wide belt from the Eastern through the Middle and Western States, has left its withering track at all the agencies in this Territory, and so thorough has been its work of devastation that at most of the agencies an almost total failure of crops is reported. The loss to a white farmer of his crop for one year is keenly felt, but the loss of a crop to an untutored Indian is a great calamity; and especially is it disheartening when it is remembered that this is the third successive year that, from the same cause, the crops there have been either a partial or general failure.

To induce the Indians to labor in some one of the civilized pursuits is the paramount aim of this office, but the great and perplexing question that constantly presents itself is, What shall they do? Since the year 1877, when Agent Miles so successfully inaugurated Indian freighting at the Cheyenne and Arapaho Agency, the Indians of this and other agencies in the Indian Territory have generally freighted not only their own agency goods and supplies, but also goods and supplies belonging to the military and traders. At the Cheyenne and Arapaho Agency the Indians have freighted this year over 400,000 pounds of freight for the military at Fort Reno. But this field of industry of course is not large, as it should be remembered that the Indians are shut in upon their reservation without the chance or opportunity of working for outside parties. If this Territory were well adapted to agriculture it would be the better policy of the department to gather there all of the Indians of the country, excepting only those in the most northerly portion, but the expression of agents upon this subject has uniformly been that, owing to frequent droughts, agriculture cannot with any certainty be depended upon. From reports of our agents for the last eight years it is found that farming in the Indian Territory for about one-half of the time has been a failure. Owing to the fact that there are no hill or mountain streams in this country, irrigation is impossible

cable. In connection with the above-named subject, and embodying in substance what is said in other reports, attention is called to the following extract of a report made to Agent Miles by Mr. J. A. Covington, farmer at the Cheyenne and Arapaho Agency, who has resided in the Territory for ten years:

As the spring opened early, with plenty of rain and warm weather, the Indian stock was in a condition to work much sooner than usual, and the result was a much larger area was prepared than usual for the seed, and having been enabled by an early requisition for seed to supply all who were ready, no delay was experienced, and the crops of corn and vegetables were planted in good condition early in the season, and plentiful crops of all kinds were almost assured. The ground plowed and planted embraced all of last year's tillage, and some few new farms were opened up; these new locations were mostly on the Canadian River, a few, however, were on the north fork of Canadian. Agency employés, under direction, planted 90 acres of corn and 39 acres of millet, and the entire agency farm and mission manual-labor tract were inclosed with a substantial post and board fence, the logs being cut and hauled to agency saw-mill, where they were converted into lumber, and the posts, which were of cedar, being hauled a distance of 15 miles on the Canadian River. However, "man proposes and God disposes." The extreme heat and drought from which this country has suffered so severely the present season set in early in June, and from that time until the middle of July we had absolutely no rain, and as a matter of course the crops are a total and complete failure, and early vegetables only about half matured. This is a heavy disappointment to our Indian farmers, who had much the best prospect for corn ever realized before. The agency field, although plowed late and thoroughly cultivated three different times, is almost a complete failure, there not being corn sufficient to pay for gathering, and the millet also, which was sowed in excellent condition, dried up immediately after sprouting, and is a complete failure.

If further evidence were wanting in regard to this country being a failure as an agricultural country this season would furnish it, but in the light of the experience gained during a residence of ten years in this country, we say *without hesitation* that owing to the uncertainty of the seasons that agriculture cannot be relied upon as a source of living, and the sooner the Indians turn their attention to pasturage and the raising of stock the more immediate will be the benefits and the less burdensome their disappointments.

If, then, instead of agriculture, the Indians could be induced to engage in stock-raising to any great extent it would be necessary, at least at some of the agencies, to issue full rations (instead of one-half and three-fourths rations as at present), so that there would be no deficiency to be made good by the killing of their stock to satisfy the cravings of hunger, and this should continue until such time as they could become, by the increase of their stock, self-supporting. With proper encouragement in this direction, added to the already acquired industries of many of the Indians of this Territory, including freighting, brick-making, lime and charcoal burning, stone-hauling, &c., it is believed that the time is not far distant when even the "wild tribes" will become as the five civilized tribes have already become, self-supporting and independent.

The five civilized tribes of Union Agency (Cherokees, Chickasaws, Choctaws, Creeks, and Seminoles) number about 60,000, and comprise more than one-fifth of our entire Indian population. They are not only self-supporting and self-governing, but are fully competent to regulate their own domestic and international affairs. Each tribe or nation has its executive, legislative, and judicial branches of government on the plan of the States, and their courts have exclusive jurisdiction when the parties are citizens of the nation. There is no court, however, where civil cases can be tried where one party only is an Indian, or where both parties are whites, and this renders it necessary in many cases that the agent act as arbitrator. A United States court should be established with criminal jurisdiction only (as the treaty provides), at some convenient point in the Territory.

During the year Tullehasse Mission and Asbury school buildings were burned. They were large brick buildings belonging to the Creeks. Immediate arrangements were made, however, for the erection of a much larger building, in place of Tullehasse Mission, at a cost of about $25,000. and the same will be completed during the present year. Asbury school will also be rebuilt at once. One of the most encouraging features connected with the civilized tribes is the increased and increasing interest which is taken in all educational matters. These Indians are not retrograding or going back into barbarism (as it is sometimes contended they will), but are marching forward steadily and sturdily under the banner of progress into all the avenues of civilization, until now they stand almost abreast of their white neighbors around them, never considering any outlay too great when required to aid the great cause of education. In addition to the enlargement of their schools, agricultural interests are extended and herds increased, and their condition is better and their prospects brighter than that of any other great number of our American Indians. All this is largely attributable to the fact that the Indians of the Five Nations own and control the land upon which they live—in fact, have a title vested in the nations tantamount to a fee-simple—and thus feel an interest in the cultivation of the soil, and the consequent advance of civilization, which other Indians not so favorably situated do not and, in the very nature of things, cannot feel.

Upon the subject of intruders, Inspector Pollock, in a recent report upon the condition of Union Agency, says:

The greater portion of the troubles that arise here are occasioned by white intruders, American citizens whom the United States by treaty are obligated to, and should promptly, remove from the Territory. These intruders do not come here because there are no other unoccupied lands. Millions of acres better than this are to be found in our Western States and Territories against the settlement of which there is no inhibition. They come here from an inherent disposition to transgress, to evade the payment of taxes, and to escape the restraints of law. To them Indian laws do not apply. By regularly-enacted laws of the Five Nations their members are prohibited from carrying deadly weapons, but these white intruders—pale-faced cut-throats, the terrors of the country—go armed to the teeth continually. The United States should keep their own transgressing citizens out of this Territory, and should sacredly keep and perform every other obligation entered into with these people. No excuse can be made current for a failure to do this.

The United States should establish a district court with limited criminal jurisdiction at Muscogee or Fort Gibson. The cutting or stealing of timber, hay, or stone, the grazing or raising of stock, and all other wanton, and willful trespassing by United States citizens upon lands held *in common* or *in severalty* by these people should be made a criminal offense, punishable not only by fine (which is usually not collectable), but also by imprisonment. And as the United States cannot extend civil jurisdiction over this country without violating treaty stipulations, the Indian agent here should be clothed with authority somewhat similar to that of a foreign consul or commercial agent, that adjudications in civil cases between United States citizens and Indian citizens might be adjusted before him. As simple as this plan is, it would, if inaugurated and carried out in good faith, solve the vexed question of Indian matters in this Territory—of one nation existing within another—and enable these people to maintain intact their own institutions. And if the American people were as honest, magnanimous, and just as they are wise, selfish, and shrewd, not another Congress would pass without inaugurating some such measure.

The buildings of the agency are situated at a point very inconvenient for its business, being about 3½ miles from the town of Muscogee, and it is necessary for the government to keep the road from Muscogee to the agency in repair, which is done at an annual cost of $600. The Creek Nation has made a proposition to erect suitable and necessary buildings at Muscogee for the use of the government and agency, and take in exchange the present agency building for a school for the freedmen of their nation. The proposition has been accepted by the department, and preliminary steps have been taken to obtain land sufficient to erect said buildings upon, which action has been taken subject to the ratification of the same by Congress.

The Indians of the Cheyenne and Arapaho Agency still show a steady improvement. The present year has been remarkable for health; and as a consequence the Cheyennes show an increase of 430, and the Arapahoes 126. One-half of the cost of subsistence of the Indians of this agency has been provided this year by their own labor, and the other half by the government. Owing, however, to the *entire* failure of their crops this season, it is probable that further provision will have to be made for their necessities. During the year 42 wagons were purchased by the Indians themselves and 40 were issued to and paid for by the Indians in labor, making at present 211 wagons at this agency owned by Indians. As the amount of freighting is limited, the agent is sorely taxed to find employment for these Indians and their teams. In addition to freighting, the agent furnishes as much employment as possible to his Indians in making brick, burning lime, hauling stone, &c. The removal of Little Chief and his band from this agency has been referred to on page L.

The nine different tribes of the Kiowa, Comanche, and Wichita Agency have made fair progress, have manifested a disposition to acquire the habits of civilized life, and, until the disheartening effect of the drought, took more than usual interest in their farm-work. Although it was feared that the consolidation of the Indians of the Kiowa and Comanche Agency with the Indians of the Wichita Agency, effected in the fall of 1879, might cause some clashing and trouble between the Indians of the different tribes, yet, on the contrary, the agent reports that no difficulty has been experienced, and that the members of the different tribes are in constant daily intercourse with each other, and as yet not one personal or tribal difficulty has occurred. The Wichita and affiliated bands are further advanced on the road towards civilization than the Kiowas or Comanches; yet the progress made by the latter tribes has been satisfactory. The number who wear citizen's dress in all the tribes is steadily increasing, and the prejudice against labor is steadily disappearing. The agent has more applications for positions on his force of Indian laborers than he can grant. In this connection Agent Hunt says:

I am becoming more and more convinced that the money expended for the hire of Indian labor is wisely appropriated, although they do not always labor faithfully, nor is the work always important, yet it is surely effecting much good by removing the prejudice against work. A young man tempted by the wages offered to lay aside his blanket and work for one month will never again be affected by his old-time prejudices or the ridicule of his associates.

The tribal system here is fast disappearing. The change from Fort Sill to the Washita is believed to be one of the causes, dispersing the members of the different tribes through the new settlements; and the issuing of rations to individual Indians, instead of to chiefs of bands, is another, and perhaps the principal, cause. The agent is of opinion that the Indians of his agency could engage profitably in stock-raising if their rations were sufficiently increased to preclude the necessity of their killing their stock-cattle to satisfy the pangs of hunger. The proceeds of freight hauled by the Kiowas during the year has amounted to $11,445.56; and other labor has been performed, such as burning of charcoal, cutting of logs, &c.

The Osage Indians, while reluctant to adopt the white man's way, so far as dress is concerned, yet continue greatly interested in house-building. During the year nearly 60 houses have been built. The Indians cut the logs, hauled the same to the agency mill (where it was cut by one or two white employés, assisted by Indians), and hauled the lumber to where they wanted their houses built. They have also carried and hauled their own rock for chimneys, and are generally abandoning their lodges, as soon as their houses are completed. The agent expects to complete about 25 more houses before winter sets in, and to have all the Osages comfortably housed before another winter. The Kaws are rapidly decreasing, owing, mainly to disease, and number now but about 250 full bloods and 50 mixed bloods. Some of them have raised good patches of corn this year, and good care is taken of their stock-cattle. The barbarous custom of selling their daughters for wives, even when they are not over eight or nine years of age, still continues. The Quapaws living among the Osages number between 150 to 200; most of them have built log huts, and earn something by working for the mixed-blood Osages.

At the Pawnee Agency but little progress is noted. Of all the Indians in the Territory the Pawnees have practically made the least advance. Under the very best auspices and under the best of agents their progress at no time in the past has been encouraging, and to-day they are far removed from civilization. Owing mainly to the drought farming operations have not been successful. Last season 400 head of young cattle were issued to these Indians to encourage them in stock raising, but very soon after the issue some of the hides of these young cattle were brought to the agency trader to be sold. The policy of giving annunity goods to Indians is often questioned on the ground that that which is not the product of labor of the individual, civilized or savage, is not appreciated or valued, and it would certainly seem that in the case of the Pawnees the giving of annuity goods is of doubtful utility. Yet out of the gloom that seems to surround the future of these unfortunate people is a gleam of hope, which is found in the rising generation. The pupils in the industrial boarding-school are reported to be working in a very creditable manner. The idea of it being discreditable *per se* to labor finds no place in the school, and the crops of corn, millet, and amber cane show gratifying evidence of work performed and progress made. The money received from the sale of products will be distributed among the pupils who do the work, a plan which it is believed will work well. Another school should be added to this agency according to the terms of the treaty.

The eight different tribes under Quapaw Agency are already well advanced in the arts of civilization, and this year encouraging progress is noted. The drought not having wrought so disastrously here as at other agencies in the Territory, fair crops are reported. There are 311 pupils in the different schools. The great obstacle here, as elsewhere, is the fact that the title to their homes, earned by their own industry and built by their own hands, is insecure; and Agent Dyer says:

The Indian is a man, and should be treated as such. Let us give him the same rights we enjoy; make him responsible to the law. To insure them justice in them, let us deed to each individual in severalty his share of the land they hold in severalty; let us protect them in its possession for 25 years; make them citizens, and they to responsibility of self-support upon them.

Decided action should be taken by Congress to settle the title of these lands in individual Indians, and thereby place them on a new basis, when improvements would steadily and rapidly progress. —

The Poncas have already been referred to on page XLVII.

CESSIONS OF PORTIONS OF CROW AND FORT HALL RESERVE

It is earnestly hoped that Congress will ratify the agreement entered into last year with the Crows and the Shoshones and Bannocks of Fort Hall for the cession to the United States of portions of their respective reservations, as detailed in the last annual report of this office. The Indians cannot understand the delay, and are impatient to have the agreements carried into effect. By this means a large quantity of valuable mineral land will be thrown open to settlement.

OTOES AND MISSOURIAS.

By act of Congress, approved March 3, last, provision was made, provided the consent of the Indians was obtained thereto, for the survey, appraisement, and sale of the remainder of the reservation of the Confederated Otoe and Missouria tribes of Indians in the States of Nebraska and Kansas, and for their removal to other reservation lands to be secured for their use by the Secretary of the Interior. Accordingly (the consent of a majority of the Indians having first been obtained), a reservation has been selected for them in the Indian Territory, south of and adjoining the Poncas and west of and adjoining the Pawnees, under the provisions of the 16th article of the Cherokee treaty of July 19, 1868 (14 Stat., 804). It contains 129,113.20 acres; is well watered and otherwise admirably adapted to agricultural pursuits. The location was selected by a delegation of the confederate tribes which visited the Territory for the purpose, in charge of Inspector McNeil, and has since been designated and assigned by the department for their use and occupation.

The work of removal, which began on the 5th of October, was completed on the 23d, and all the Indians recently in occupation of the old reservation are now in their new home in the Indian Territory, save only a very few, who, by reason of the valuable improvements made by them, prefer and will be permitted to remain on the old reservation.

The appraisement and sale of the lands embraced within the old reserve will be proceeded with at an early day. The full consent of the Indians has been obtained thereto, and they are anxious to see an early termination of the whole matter.

EASTERN BAND OF CHEROKEES IN NORTH CAROLINA.

These Indians are located in Cherokee, Graham, Jackson, Macon, and Swain Counties, in the extreme southwestern section of the State. Most of their lands lie in Jackson and Swain Counties, and are known as the "Qualla Boundary," comprising about 50,000 acres. Their other lands are in detached tracts lying in several counties, and aggregate some 15,000 acres. These lands, as originally contemplated, were purchased with Indian funds, at sundry times, by their late agent, William H. Thomas, who proposed when he had completed his purchases, to convey the same to the Indians. Before the execution of this purpose, however, the war came on, and, Mr. Thomas being involved in debt and having become insane, nothing was done until Congress, by the eleventh section of the act of July 15, 1870 (16 Stats., p. 302), authorized and empowered these Indians to institute suit in the circuit court of the United States for the western district of North Carolina against said Thomas for all claims, including lands, which they might have against him. Under the award of Rufus Barringer and others, dated October 23, 1874, which was confirmed by said court at its November term, 1874, and act of Congress approved August 14, 1876 (16 Stats., p. 139), these Indians became possessed of the lands in question.

Adverse claims of white men have been made upon some of these lands, and I am credibly informed that under the land laws of North Carolina "any citizen can obtain a State grant or patent for any land in the State regardless of the fact that the State may have parted with its title to the same to another party." Under this law any one may obtain a grant or patent from the State for a tract of land embracing the town of Asheville, or any other town or other body of land in the State, by paying 12½ cents per acre for it, though the same land may have been sold and patented fifty years ago; but his title to the tract must be determined in the courts. I am further informed that the State, since the date of said award and decree, has issued grants or patents for lands within the "Qualla Boundary" which were entered by Thomas and others many years ago, and the only proper proceeding in respect to white men settled upon Indian lands is to bring suit against them in the courts, which is the only power they will respect; and this, too, must be done within seven years from their entry.

To institute suits, however, involves the outlay of money. This band has funds under section 3859 of the Revised Statutes, and by the Indian appropriation act of March 3, 1875, this fund was authorized to be applied, under the direction of the Secretary of the Interior, to perfecting titles to lands, to payment of expenses of suits, to purchase and extinguish the titles of any whites within the "boundary," and for the education, improvement, and civilization of said Indians (18 Stats., p. 47). But by the Indian appropriation act of August 15, 1876 (19 Stats., p. 197), after the payment of certain amounts to certain claimants therein named—

The balance of the fund appropriated by the act of March 3, 1875, shall, upon the 1st of July, 1876, be placed to their credit upon the books of the Treasury Department, to bear interest at the rate of 5 per cent. per annum; and the Secretary of the Interior is authorized to use annually for agricultural implements and for educational purposes among said Indians so much of the principal of said fund as, with the interest annually accruing thereon, shall amount to $6,000.

By the Indian appropriation act of March 3, 1877, the sum of $1,500 was appropriated from this fund to complete the survey of their lands, $300 for attorney fees to examine titles, and the Secretary of the Interior was authorized to use a portion of the fund for the support of schools among the Eastern Band of Cherokee Indians in aid of schools among said Cherokees residing in Tennessee and Georgia (19 Stats., p. 291).

Thus it will be seen that these Indians are subject to continued encroachments upon their lands by white claimants, and that, while they have funds belonging to them, Congress has so legislated that their moneys now can be used only for the purchase of agricultural implements and educational purposes. This band is without a superintendent or agent, and, so far as this office has supervision, is in an anomalous and unsatisfactory condition. The bitter feuds that have existed so long between the several factions have added to the many difficulties which embarrass the band and retard its progress in civilization and wealth.

The Cherokee national authorities in Indian Territory last spring appointed a delegation to visit North Carolina and to invite and induce these Indians to remove to the Indian Territory. The principal chief of the nation, D. W. Bushyhead, offered every reasonable inducement to them to remove, and this office encouraged the effort, and it was hoped Congress would have furnished the necessary authority and means for removal. Notwithstanding this disappointment, quite a number of applications have been filed asking assistance to effect their removal, and one party, consisting of forty-one adults and thirty-two children, started on their own resources; but on reaching Tennessee their means were exhausted, and, on their urgent appeal, this department furnished the means whereby they reached their destination. Since then nineteen others have arrived in Indian Territory, and I have no doubt many more, if not all, might be induced to remove were the proper facilities furnished them. That is their home and there they should be settled.

INDIANS IN WASHINGTON TERRITORY AND OREGON.

The treaty provisions with the "confederated tribes and bands" and the Walla Walla, Cayuse, and Umatilla tribes in Oregon, and the D'Wamish and other allied tribes, Makahs, Quinaielts, Quillehutes, S'Kallams, and Yakamas in Washington Territory, expired with the fiscal year ending June 30, 1880. Congress, however, in compliance with the request of this department, made appropriations for their benefit, and their condition is still such that the aid and assistance heretofore extended should be continued.

An inspection made this year of all the agencies in the Territories above alluded to has added to the desire of this office that increased educational facilities be provided, and that the several reservations occupied by them be surveyed and titles in severalty given to the Indians. The principal agency by which these Indians can be elevated is believed to be the "industrial school." Several such schools are now in successful operation at their agencies and others are contemplated, and the requisite appropriations for this purpose and for other necessary objects are respectfully recommended.

MALHEUR RESERVATION.

The appraisement and sale of the Malheur Reservation in Southeastern Oregon, as recommended in the last annual report of this bureau, is required in carrying out the intentions of the department in respect to the Indians of that section. The reservation is no longer needed for Indian purposes, and, by the direction of the President, the agency has been finally abandoned, and a considerable portion of the public property and supplies appertaining thereto has already been removed. The remainder will be disposed of in such manner and at such time as may seem to be most advantageous.

A memorial from the legislative assembly of the State of Oregon praying for the restoration of the lands included in this reserve to the public domain, for pre-emption settlement and sale, was referred to this office in February last by the chairman of the Senate Committee on Indian Affairs. The proposition to dispose of the lands in the manner therein indicated did not receive the approval of the office, and it may be well to add that any plan looking to the disposal of the reservation that does not contemplate and provide substantial return to the Indians, for whose sole benefit it was established and set apart, should not receive the sanction of the department. These Indians will need assistance in the future in their efforts at self-support, and the proceeds of the sale of their reservation will, if properly invested, afford such assistance, and relieve the government of the burden. The reservation contains 1,778,000 acres. The Indians who formerly occupied it are either at the Yakama Agency, in Washington Territory, or in the vicinity of Camps McDermott and Bidwell and the town of Winnemucca, where they meagerly support themselves by labor among the whites or by cultivation of the soil.

UMATILLA RESERVATION—TOWN OF PENDLETON.

The town of Pendleton, Oregon, adjoins the Umatilla Indian Reservation on the north. Indeed, the northern line of the reservation runs through the town, so that a considerable portion of it is within the reservation limits. A tract about 30 acres in extent, forming a part of the land claim of M. E. Goodwin, the original proprietor of the town site, acquired under the pre-emption laws, and for which patent was issued by the government August 30, 1869 (the reservation was established by treaty in 1855; proclaimed April 11th, 1859), is within the reservation, and is occupied by substantial warehouses, stores, residences, &c. Other buildings, including "Odd Fellows Hall," a large school-house, tenement-houses, and residences, are within the reservation lines, where no shadow of title to the land exists. Land is much needed to meet the growing necessities of the town, and it appears that there is none to be had elsewhere than upon the reservation.

A petition numerously signed by citizens of Pendleton was referred to this office by your predecessor, and was made the subject of a report to the department in May last. The petitioners ask that the title to the Goodwin tract lying within the reservation be quieted, and that some plan be adopted by which they may secure, by purchase from the Indians a sufficient quantity of land to meet the absolute requirements of the town. The Indians have already signified their entire willingness to dispose of so much of their reservation as is required to meet the demand, at a price to be fixed upon by the government, and it is suggested that Congress be asked at the next session to grant authority for a proper adjustment of the whole matter.

LEGISLATION NEEDED.

Upon reference to previous annual reports from this office, I observe that repeated recommendations have been made for additional legislation in behalf of the Indians, and upon examination I find that Congress has hitherto failed to afford the desired relief.

Foremost among the subjects which call for attention by Congress is that of the law relating to—

Intruders upon Indian reservations.

Existing laws (intercourse act, June 30, 1834; act of August 18, 1856; sections 2147, 2148, R. S.) are, in the changed order of things, entirely insufficient for the purpose. Under these laws an intruder must first be removed from the reserve, and then if he returns he is liable to a penalty of $1,000. As a general rule, intruders are of a class having no property subject to execution, and as the penalty can only be collected by an action of debt, the result is invariably a barren judgment, and the delinquent goes scot-free, only to renew his attempts at settlement at a later date, and perhaps in some other direction.

A notable illustration of the inadequacy of the law is found in the case of the notorious Captain Payne, of Oklahoma fame, who, after repeated attempts at settlement in the Indian Territory, and removal therefrom by the military, was finally arrested July 15, 1880, and taken to Fort Smith, Ark., where he was released on bail to appear at the ensuing November term of court. At the subsequent May term of said court a civil suit in the nature of an action of debt, brought against Payne, in the name of the United States, to recover the statutory penalty of $1,000, was tried, and judgment rendered against him. It is altogether improbable that the judgment can ever be collected from Payne, and the result is that he is at large, organizing another scheme for invasion of the Territory.

I suggest an amendment of the law so that an intruder on Indian lands shall be liable to prosecution for the first and every subsequent offense, and, upon conviction, be punishable, not simply by fine, but by fine and imprisonment; and provision should also be made in the act for confiscation and sale by the government of the entire outfit of an intruder or party of intruders.

Another crying evil, and a never-ending cause of complaint to this office, is the ineffective character of existing laws to prevent—

Timber depredations upon Indian lands.

Especially in the Indian Territory, spoliation of valuable walnut timber has been and is still being constantly carried on, and unless some stringent and effective measures are devised to stop it, that whole section of country will be completely denuded of timber; and it is apprehended by those competent to judge, that disastrous climatic effects will follow. The whole subject was fully presented in the report of the Hon. Commissioner of Indian Affairs for 1879 (pp. XLVII–XLVIII), and the inefficacy of the law pointed out, with a recommendation for the enactment of such measures as would effectually prevent the wanton cutting or destruction of timber on Indian reservations.

At the second session of the Forty-sixth Congress, Senate bill No. 1812 was introduced, so extending the provisions of section 5388, Revised Statutes, and of other laws of the United States for the protection and preservation of timber belonging to the United States, and for the punishment of offenders who cut, destroy, or take the same, as to make them apply to the preservation of timber upon the following classes of Indian reservations, viz: Lands to which the original Indian title has never been extinguished, but which have not been specially reserved, by treaty, act of Congress, or otherwise, for the use of the Indians, or for other purposes, although the Indians' right of occupancy thereof has been tacitly recognized by the government; lands expressly reserved by treaty or act of Congress or set apart for the use of the Indians by executive order of the President; lands allotted or patented to individual Indians who are not under the laws of any State or Territory; lands patented to Indian tribes; and lands which have been purchased by or ceded to the United States for the purpose of settling Indians thereon, but which are as yet unoccupied. The punishment of offenders committing depredations upon such timber was also provided for by said bill. I cannot too strongly urge the absolute necessity for the early passage of some kindred measure in this behalf.

For the last four years urgent appeals have been made by this office for—

The enactment of laws for Indian reservations.

Various measures looking to this end have been introduced in Congress, among the latest being House bill No. 350, Forty-sixth Congress, second session, which, as amended, was favorably reported by the House Committee on Indian Affairs. This bill reads as follows:

Be it enacted by the Senate and House of Representatives of the United States of America in Congress assembled, That the provisions of the laws of the respective States and Territories in which are located Indian reservations, relating to the crimes of murder, manslaughter, arson, rape, burglary, larceny, and robbery, shall be deemed and taken to be the law and in force within such reservations; and the district courts of the United States within and for the respective districts in which such reservations may be located in any State, and the Territorial courts of the respective Territories in which such reservations may be located, shall have original jurisdiction over all such offenses which may be committed within such reservations.

In respect to all that portion of the Indian Territory not set apart and occupied by the Cherokee, Creek, Choctaw, Chickasaw, and Seminole Indian tribes, the provisions of the laws of the State of Kansas relating to the crimes of murder, manslaughter, arson rape, burglary, larceny, and robbery shall be deemed and taken to be the law and in force therein; and the United States district court held at Fort Scott, Kans., shall have exclusive original jurisdiction over all such offenses arising in said portion of the Indian Territory. The place of punishment of any and all of said offenses shall be the same as for other like offenses arising within the jurisdiction of said respective courts.

This bill, as well as others of a kindred nature, died a natural death at the close of the last Congress. In commenting upon this subject the Hon. Commissioner of Indian Affairs, in his annual report for 1879, said:

It is a matter of vital importance that action should be taken to secure the passage of the above bill, or of some measure of equal efficiency to provide law for Indians, to the end that order may be secured. A civilized community could not exist as such without law, and a semi-civilized and barbarous people are in a hopeless state of anarchy without its protection and sanction. It is true that the various tribes have regulations and customs of their own, which, however, are founded on superstition and ignorance of the usages of civilized communities, and generally tend to perpetuate feuds and keep alive animosities. To supply their place it is the bounden duty of the government to provide laws suited to the dependent condition of the Indians. The most intelligent amongst them ask for the laws of the white men to enable them to show that Indians can understand and respect law, and the wonder is that such a code was not enacted years ago.

I fully concur in the views above quoted, and earnestly hope that Congress will find time to bestow attention upon this important subject.

I also beg to draw attention to the necessity of legislation in regard to—

Indian marriages.

This subject has also been fully treated of in prior annual reports of this office. The importance of the enactment of a law to prevent polygamy and to provide for legal marriages among Indians is self-apparent. I respectfully reiterate the recommendation of my immediate predecessor that the necessity and propriety for such legislation be laid before Congress at its next session.

Other subjects calling for special legislation have already been referred to under appropriate headings, and may be summarized as follows:

Legislation is needed to provide for—

Removal of the Mescalero Apaches to the Jicarilla Reservation.

Deficiencies necessarily incurred in current and prior fiscal years.

Increase in number and pay of Indian police.

Establishment of penal reservations for refractory Indians.

Allotment of lands in severalty and issue of patents therefor, with restrictions as to alienation.

Remission of fees and commissions on homestead entries by Indians.

Survey of boundaries of Indian reservations and of arable lands rein.

Prohibition of introduction of liquor on Indian reserves by authority of War Department, and modification of penalty for sale of liquor to Indians.

Relief of Hualapais.

Relief of Turtle Mountain Band of Chippewas.

Removal of remainder of Northern Cheyennes from Indian Territory to Dakota.

Adjustment of status of freedmen in Choctaw and Chickasaw Nations.

Purchase of Creek lands occupied by Seminoles.

Settlement of estates of deceased Kickapoo allottees, issue of patents to female Kickapoo allottees, &c.

Ratification of cession of portions of Crow and Fort Hall Reserves.

Appraisement and sale of Malheur Reservation.

Sale of portion of Umatilla Reserve occupied by town of Pendleton.

I have the honor to be, sir, very respectfully, your obedient servant,

H. PRICE,
Commissioner.

The Hon. SECRETARY OF THE INTERIOR.

REPORT OF THE COMMISSIONER OF RAILROADS.

DEPARTMENT OF THE INTERIOR,
OFFICE OF COMMISSIONER OF RAILROADS,
Washington; D. C., November 1, 1881.

SIR: In compliance with the statutory requirements of the act creating this bureau (20 U. S. Statutes, 169, sec. 3), I have the honor to submit the following report in regard to the bureau and its operations, and of the condition of the property, business, and accounts of the several railroad companies who have complied with the requests of this office under the law in rendering proper reports, and to which, or their predecessors, the United States have granted, and which have directly or indirectly received, any subsidy in bonds or grant of public lands, and the geographical location of whose railroads is in the whole or in part west, north, or south of the Missouri River.

PROPERTY AND ACCOUNTS OF THE PACIFIC AND OTHER RAILROADS.

During the present year two inspection trips of the property and accounts of the subsidized and land-grant railroads have been made; one by the then Commissioner, Theophilus French, accompanied by the railroad engineer of this office, and extending from April 20, 1881, to June 18, 1881; the other trip by the bookkeeper, in company with the railroad engineer, and extending from August 18, 1881, to October 7, 1881, both trips covering about 6,900 miles of aided railroads.

The full and comprehensive report of Capt. Henry Blackstone, railroad engineer of this office, is made a part of this report, and immediately precedes the appendixes and tables.

Special attention is called to his suggestions regarding the great lack of uniformity in train signals of the different railroads of the United States. Serious accidents, entailing both loss of life and property, have frequently occurred from this cause alone, and will undoubtedly continue until all the railroads in the country are compelled to use one uniform set of signals, which shall have the same meaning upon all roads. There can be no serious objection raised to the adoption of such system by any of the railroad managers. Railroad train men are quite nomadic in their habits, and frequently, when employed upon a road, are compelled to adopt signals the meaning of which differs widely from that of the road which they have just left.

The railroad property inspected and reported on, is as follows:

Miles.

Union Pacific:
Council Bluffs to Ogden 1,036.00
Kansas Division.. 745.00

    Inspected 1,781.00

Central Pacific:
Visalia Division.. 146.08
Junction with Union Pacific to San Francisco 872.59
San José Branch to Tres Pinos 100.00

    Total miles owned... 1,118.67

Leased and operated:
Union Pacific Road.. 5.00
Southern Pacific... 550.20
Southern Pacific of Arizona...................................... 293.93
Los Angeles to Santa Monica...................................... 18.00

    Total leased and operated :................................... 867.13

    Owned and leased (inspected) 1,985.80

Central Branch Union Pacific, operated by Missouri Pacific:
(Owned) Atchison to Waterville, Kans............................. 100.
(Leased) Atchison, Colorado and Pacific.......................... 261.00

    Total miles 361.00

Saint Louis, Iron Mountain and Southern Railroad:
(Owned) Main Line, Saint Louis to Texarkana 488.50
Branch, Poplar Bluff to Birds Point.............................. 71.00
Bismarck to Columbus 121.00
Mineral Point to Potosi.. 4.00

    Total amount operated 684.50

Chicago, Rock Island and Pacific:
(Owned) Chicago to Council Bluffs................................ 498.00

    (No branch or division was passed over.)

Northern Pacific Railroad:
(Owned) Kalama to Takoma... 105.00
Puyallup Branch.. 31.00

    Total 136.00
From Ainsworth the new road has been extended eastward 124 miles, which was gone over.

Atchison, Topeka, and Santa Fe:
(Owned) Atchison to New Mexico State line........................ 470.58
Leased.. 843.42

    Total 1,314.00

Atlantic and Pacific Railroad:
(Owned) Inspected latter part of April, new road was then extended from Albuquerque to Navajo Springs.................................. 213.00

Oregon and California:
(Owned) Portland to Roseburg 200.00

Miles.

Saint Louis and San Francisco:
    (Owned) From Pacific, Missouri, to line of Indian Territory 293.00
    (Leased) Atlantic and Pacific, Indian Territory 34
    Saint Louis, Wichita and Western, Pierce City, Mo., to Oswego,
        Kans., and branch to Joplin, Mo................................. 83
    Missouri and Western, Oswego to Wichita 144
    Joplin, Mo., to Girard, Kans.................................... 38
    Joint use of track, Saint Louis to Pacific 37   336.00

        Total.. 629.00

Sioux City and Pacific Railroad:
    (Owned) Sioux City to Missouri Valley Junction, Iowa, and Fremont,
        Nebr.. 107.42
    Leased) Fremont, Elkhorn and Missouri Valley Road.............. 109.99

        Total leased and owned 217.41

ACCOUNTS EXAMINED FROM COMPANY'S BOOKS.

The general books and accounts of the Union Pacific Railway Company (which now operates the Kansas Pacific Railroad as a division of its own road), in Boston, have been carefully examined and compared with statements rendered by it. The operating books, which are kept in Omaha, Nebr., have also been examined; the general books of the Central Pacific Railroad Company, in San Francisco, Cal., have been examined and compared with statements sent to this office, likewise the books of the Sioux City and Pacific Railroad at Cedar Rapids, Iowa, and those of the Central Branch of the Union Pacific Railroad now being operated by the Missouri Pacific, at Saint Louis, Mo.

It is gratifying to state that free access has been granted by all these roads to their books and accounts, which are all kept in good business-like order, and in such form that an expert accountant would find no great difficulty in ascertaining the true condition of the financial affairs of the companies.

Although the past severe and protracted winter, followed by unusual floods and storms, destroyed much property and materially increased the expenditures of maintaining the same, it is noticeable that a substantial improvement in the general property of the roads has been made, and in general the reports rendered by the different roads specified indicate a marked increase in their business.

The construction of new and the extension of old railroads in the West, and notably the leasing and rapid building of new lines by the Central and Union Pacific Companies since the last report are marked features of railroad history.

The Union Pacific is building an extension from Granger, a station on their main line 156 miles east of Ogden, to Baker City, Oreg., via Port Neuf on the Utah Northern Railroad, which will connect at Baker City with the Oregon system of railroads, and thus acquire an outlet to the Pacific coast independent of the Central Pacific Railroad.

This extension when completed will be about 600 miles long, and steel rails to lay the entire length have been contracted for.

It is represented that the work will be completed at an early date.

The Central Pacific has this year, by leasing the Southern Pacific of Arizona and New Mexico, which is now completed to Deming, N. Mex., and there connecting with the Atchison, Topeka, and Santa Fé Railroad, secured a through route from the Pacific coast independent of the Union Pacific Railroad.

47 Ab

The Atlantic and Pacific Road is being extended towards the Pacific coast at a rapid rate, and is expected to reach there at an early date.

The Northern Pacific is being rapidly constructed from both the east and west.

The indications are that within a short time there will be five different routes to the Pacific coast, where less than a year ago there was but one.

The accompanying map will give a very good idea of the roads already built and those under course of construction, and those contemplated.

The dotted lines refer to roads whose construction is contemplated, the other lines to roads already built.

The railroads have been instrumental in developing the country at a rapid rate; capital has been invested in immense sums; and still the tendency is towards increased developments, principally in the West and Southwest.

It is believed that the operations in railroad construction this year will exceed those of any previous year, and in consequence large tracts of mineral and agricultural lands will be made accessible.

An interesting article in the Railway Age, of a recent date, treats of railroad building in 1881 as follows:

RAILWAY BUILDING IN 1881.

Railway construction has proceeded at such a rapid and unprecedented pace during the present year that it has been more difficult than ever before to keep an accurate record of it. Unfortunately there is no source for obtaining information in regard to the most important element in the financial situation, the investment of money in railway undertakings. The general government makes no pretense of obtaining statistics in regard to railway construction, and even the railroad commissioners in the different States, who could without much difficulty keep a record each month of the work done and in progress, seldom pay any attention to it. It is left to two or three railway and financial papers to compile statistics from their own sources of information, and it is evidently impossible for them to make the record complete until some time has elapsed. Nevertheless, even the approximate statistics which they can furnish during the year are of interest and value.

The season of active railway building is now nearly ended, at least in the North, as work is liable to be interrupted at any time by the coming of winter. Still, an open season would witness the addition of a very large mileage, as grading is finished for numerous extensions and great efforts will be made to complete the tracks before January. The track laid during the ten months of the year ended October 30, aggregates from the best estimate that we can make, fully 6,000 miles. This is at least 25 per cent. more than the mileage reported completed at this time last year. The total mileage laid during 1880 was about 7,400 miles, and at the increased rate the year 1881 will have witnessed the addition of at least 9,250 miles of new road. But the actual construction seems certain to exceed even these large figures. Last year winter set in very early, putting a stop to the completion of many hundreds of miles of road that were ready for the rails, and the long-continued severity of the winter and spring delayed the recommencement of operations, so that up to April 1 of this year only about 650 miles of new track had been reported laid. The greater part of the immense amount of new line ironed this year has been completed within the last four or five months, and if the weather permits the mileage to be added in the next two months will greatly exceed the proportion for the same period in any previous year.

There is another evident reason why a very great increase of track mileage this year is certain. Our columns have recorded the incorporation of and the inauguration of work upon an extraordinary number of new enterprises—much greater than any previous year. While the mileage which will be actually constructed by these various new companies is of course a very difficult matter to estimate in advance, some idea may be obtained by summarizing the list thus far given. The Financial Chronicle has undertaken to compile from the railway papers a list of the new enterprises inaugurated during the year on which definite engagements have been entered into for construction, and it makes the following estimate:

Between the Atlantic coast and the Upper Mississippi River, and north of the Ohio and Potomac Rivers, 4,791 miles.

Between the Atlantic coast and Mississippi, and south of the Ohio and Potomac Rivers, 2,352 miles,

Between the Rocky Mountains and Mississippi River, and south of the latitude of Saint Louis, 4,140 miles.

West of the Rocky Mountains, 540 miles.

Total miles expected to be laid between October 1, 1881, and December 31, 1882, 15,786.

While the Chronicle's list fails to include a considerable number of the enterprises which we have already noted, and some which now give promise of speedy construction, and while the mileage of track may be laid during the period named is of course only estimated and subject to events not yet known, at the same time it is apparently within reason to say that if a financial disaster occurs, the close of 1882 will probably see at least 15,000 miles of new railways more than the mileage reported in operation at the present date. As for 1881, we now venture the prediction that it will show nearly, if not quite, 10,000 miles of new railway, making the mileage in the United States on January 1, 1882, not far from 105,000 miles. This, it should be remembered, is in the United States alone, and does not include the large number of miles being added in Canada and in Mexico. In the Dominion alone over 1,200 miles are now in process of construction, with many other lines proposed, and in Mexico several thousand miles of new lines have either been commenced or give promise of being soon undertaken.

A prodigious amount of money evidently has been expended and pledged in the last year on these enterprises. Assuming an actual cost of $200,000,000 will have been expended on the roads completed in 1881, while the nominal capital invested is much greater, the Chronicle estimates the par value of stocks and bonds issued or subscribed to from January 1 to September 1, 1881, at $314,000,000, while it believes that the cost of the equipped roads undertaken and to be completed between October 1, 1881, and December 31, 1882, fifteen months, will be about $397,000,000. These vast figures naturally raise the question whether railway building is progressing too rapidly for safety. It is certain that many lines are being built which cannot be immediately profitable, and which will depend upon the development of new regions for their existence. But this development is going on and is bound to go on until all the vast habitable areas in the country shall be peopled, and this evidently affords an, as yet, unlimited field for the employment of enterprise and capital. Whether the speed of development is becoming too rapid for stability, however, affords a subject for reflection.

CONDITION OF THE BOND AND INTEREST ACCOUNTS.

The public debt statement, issued by the Treasury Department June 30, 1881, shows the condition of the accounts with the several Pacific railroad companies, so far as regards moneys which have been actually covered in to their credit, but takes no account of moneys in the sinking fund held by the Treasurer of the United States, or of the compensation for services performed by them for the government, not at that time settled by the accounting officers. The following extract from the statement is here given:

Name of railway.	Principal outstanding.	Interest accrued and not yet paid.	Interest paid by the United States.	Interest repaid by companies.		Balance of interest paid by the United States.
				By transportation service.	By cash payments 5 per cent. net earnings.	
Central Pacific	$25,885,120 00	$776,553 60	$19,560,787 27	$3,496,942 83	$648,271 96	$15,424,572 48
Kansas Pacific	6,966,000 00	182,090 00	5,162,883 09	2,565,443 44		2,618,439 65
Union Pacific	27,236,512 00	817,095 36	20,872,373 61	8,135,878 56		12,736,495 05
Central Branch Union Pacific	1,600,000 00	48,000 00	1,309,808 26	93,515 38	6,926 91	1,209,365 97
Western Pacific	1,970,560 00	59,116 80	1,872,664 94	9,367 00		1,363,297 94
Sioux City and Pacific	1,626,820 00	48,849 60	1,220,049 49	124,979 14		1,095,070 35
Totals	84,622,512 00	1,938,705 36	49,528,566 66	14,426,126 35	655,198 87	34,447,241 44

As regards the total indebtedness of all the subsidized Pacific railroads to the United States, Appendix 7 of this report shows the following:

Total debt, principal and interest, to June 30, 1881....................	$116,090,784 02
Total credits, transportation and money in the Treasury to June 30, 1881	17,000,275 48
Balance yet due to the United States	99,090,508 54

CONDITION OF TRANSPORTATION ACCOUNTS.

From Appendix 7 the following summary is made, showing the condition of the transportation accounts of the indebted Pacific roads with the government:

Transportation service performed for the United States to December 31, 1880, as per the companies' books............................		$23,095,907 50
Transportation service on roads not subsidized		1,951,888 39
Transportation service on subsidized roads.........................		21,144,019 11
One-half paid to companies prior to 1873	$4,295,187 98	
One-half retained and applied prior to 1873............	4,204,471 03	
Amount settled for prior to act of 1873		8,499,659 01
Remainder applicable to "repayment of interest," to the payment of "five per cent. of net earnings," and to the payment of "requirement for sinking fund"...		12,644,360 10

The cash payments which have been required from the companies, in addition to the retention of the entire compensation for services, are as follows:

Central Pacific..		$1,203,114 53
Central Branch Union Pacific................................		1,953 77
Union Pacific	$1,177,566 43	
Less balance due the Kansas Pacific Railway...........	865,920 71	
		311,645 72
Total..		1,516,714 02

The Central Pacific Company has deposited the above amount of $1,203,114.53 in the Treasury, and the balance of $311,645.72, due from the Union Pacific Railway Company (which owns and operates the Kansas Pacific Railway as its Kansas division), is in course of settlement.

CONDITION OF THE SINKING-FUND ACCOUNTS.

Appendix 8 of this report shows in detail the condition of the sinking funds of the Union and Central Pacific Companies, respectively, held by the Treasurer of the United States under the act of Congress approved May 7, 1878.

Reports furnished this office by the Treasury Department show that the amount in the sinking fund on the 30th of June, 1881, was $1,919,950.26 of which the Central Pacific Company had $1,069,904.62 and the Union Pacific Company $850,045.64.

The same statements show the investment of these sinking funds to have been as follows:

Character of bonds.	Union Pacific.	Central Pacific.	Total.
Funded loan of 1881, 5 per cent	$256,450 00	$194,900 00	$451,250 00
Funded loan of 1907, 4 per cent	32,650 00	199,100 00	231,750 00
Currency sixes, 6 per cent	361,000 00	444,000 00	805,000 00
Principal	650,100 00	838,000 00	1,488,100 00
Premium paid	124,085 43	168,727 73	292,798 16
Total cost	774,185 43	1,006,727 73	1,780,893 16

Leaving the amount uninvested on June 30, 1881, as follows:

Union Pacific $75,880 21
Central Pacific 63,176 89

Total 139,057 10

No investment has been made since April 6, 1881.

The companies have repeatedly protested against the heavy cost of these investments. As high as 135 has been paid, as, for instance, $198,000 was invested by the Treasurer on April 6, 1881, in currency sixes, premium 35; $76,000 on same date at premium of 34.95, and $220,000, same date, premium 33.9.

I quote from last year's report of this office:

The honorable the Secretary of the Treasury, in December, 1879, and again in June, 1880, informed Congress of the difficulties which lay in the way of a just and profitable investment of these moneys, the funded loan of 1881 five per cent. bonds having so short a time to run; but the session closed without any action being taken, and the investment was made in "currency sixes" at that large premium as a better investment than was offered by any other United States bond, to which the law limited the Secretary of the Treasury. The first-mortgage bonds of the company—first payable from the sinking fund—are undoubtedly the best investment for this fund; but better than any investment in bonds, which is always more or less liable to influence the market value of the securities sought, the amounts as covered in these sinking funds should be credited with interest at, say, six per cent. per annum, payable semi-annually. This plan would make the investment secure, would avoid all question of market influence, and would pay the companies a sum on the investment much nearer that which they could obtain by investing the moneys themselves. These sinking-fund moneys belong to the companies entirely, the United States bonds having no lien whatever upon the one-half of transportation compensation devoted to this purpose, *only on the other half*, which is, and has been, regularly applied to the payment of the bonds and interest under the act of July 2, 1864 (sec. 5, 13 U. S. Statutes, 359).

I renew this recommendation of my predecessor, and agree with him that it is due to the companies affected by the act of May 7, 1878, that the Secretary of the Treasury be given authority to credit the amounts covered into the sinking funds, with interest at 5 or 6 per cent. per annum, payable semi-annually; or, I will add, to invest the sinking funds in either the company's first-mortgage bonds or such bonds as have been issued to the companies by the United States.

LAWS OF THE UNITED STATES AFFECTING RAILROADS AND TELEGRAPHS.

A compilation of the laws relating to the railroad and telegraph companies has been embodied in previous reports made by this office, and has been found useful for reference.

For convenience, and for the information of all branches of the government service, it has been deemed advisable to republish some of these laws, adding those which have been passed since the last report.

THE UNION PACIFIO RAILWAY COMPANY.

This company is the successor, by consolidation January 26, 1880, to the Union Pacific Railroad Company, the Kansas Pacific Railway Company, and the Denver Pacific Railway and Telegraph Company.

The property and accounts of this company have been examined in full by duly authorized members of this bureau. From an examination of their books, and reports rendered, the following statements are derived:

Length of line subsidized with bonds	miles..	1,432.62
Length of line subsidized with lands	do...	1,783.17
Leased to the Central Pacific Railroad Company	do...	5.00
Miles owned and operated and upon which the capital stock and funded debt are based amount to	miles..	1,818.80
Leased and operated by the company	do...	1,597.50
Total miles operated		3,415.30
Stock subscribed		$61,000,000 00
Stock issued		60,673,745 00
Par value		100 00
Increase of stock during the year		9,911,445 00

The following statement shows the financial condition of the company on June 30, 1881:

LIABILITIES.

United States subsidy bonds	$33,539,512 00
Interest on United States bonds	27,062,442 06
Other bonded debt	81,987,405 00
Interest due and accrued	1,974,978 90
Pay-rolls and vouchers	2,147,588 34
Bills payable	1,846,500 00
Accounts payable	1,202,238 70
Dividends payable	1,089,852 76
Capital stock	60,673,745 00
Total	211,524,262 76
Balance, surplus, or credit to income account, including land sales, &c	3,155,797 10
	214,680,059 86

ASSETS.

Road and equipment	$155,708,861 58
Fuel, material, &c	2,794,883 97
Cash	2,333,343 47
Company's bonds and stocks	1,097,524 42
Other bonds and stocks and investments	28,735,568 33
Bills receivable	487,568 00
Accounts receivable	2,870,908 00
Due from the United States	7,090,321 00
Interest repaid to the United States	6,892,914 10
Premiums paid on United States sinking fund	64,835 40
United States sinking fund	554,004 00
Sinking fund with trustees	206,857 00
	208,837,702 4
Land contracts, land cash, &c	5,842,357 4
	214,680,059 5

The following statements for settlement of the account with the United States to December 31, 1880, have been prepared by the bookkeeper of this office from the general books and accounts of the company.

The tables are inserted with a view of showing the method of settlement, which has not yet been consummated, owing to items for the year ending December 31, 1880, aggregating $762,440.87 not being adjusted. The further sum of $209,181.68 for prior years will depend upon this adjustment.

A.

Statement showing the indebtedness of the United States to the Union Pacific Railroad Company up to June 30, 1878.

Balance due the Union Pacific Railroad Company after satisfying all demands for five per cent. and applying all amounts claimed for half-transportation up to June 30, 1878, as per their statement of May 10, 1879, which was assented to by the then Auditor of Railroad Accounts in his letter of August 9, 1879 .... $780,695 46

Included in which there is charged one-half of the amount claimed by the railroad company for transporting the United States mail, which charges since February 1, 1876, exceed the allowance by the Post-Office Department, the following amounts:

The railroad company charges monthly from February 1, 1876, to June 30, 1878, twenty-nine months, at $49,731.25.		$1,442,206 25
The Post-Office Department allows monthly from February 1, 1876, to March 31, 1878, twenty-six months, at $27,095.25	$704,476 50	
And monthly from April 1, 1878, to June 30, 1878, three months, at $31,405.38	94,216 14	
		798,692 64
Excess charged by the railroad company and not allowed by Post-Office Department to June 30, 1878		643,513 61
One-half of which is included in their claims for transportation		321,756 80
Deduct five per cent. on the total amount disallowed, i. e., $643,513.61		32,175 68

Leaving the amount to be deducted from the above admitted balance (by the Ex-Auditor of Railroad Accounts) due to the railroad company to June 30, 1878.. 289,581 12

Balance due the Union Pacific Railroad Company up to June 30, 1878. 491,244 34

B.

Statement showing earnings and expenses of the Union Pacific Railroad Company for the six months ending December 31, 1878.

EARNINGS.

United States:			
Passenger and freight		$296,217 82	
Mail	$298,389 50		
Less difference between amount charged by railroad company and that allowed by Post-Office Department....................	109,955 22		
		188,439 28	
			$483,650 10
Commercial:			
Passenger and freight		6,194,403 88	
Express		258,618 68	
Miscellaneous		77,180 76	
		6,530,203 30	
Total earnings			7,013,853 40

EXPENSES.

Conducting transportation	$490,749 14	
Motive power	907,219 64	
Maintenance of cars	190,696 75	
Maintenance of way......................................	691,837 57	
General expenses and taxes...............................	277,952 92	
		$2,567,456 02
Interest on first-mortgage bonds..........................		820,679 75
Total expenses under law of May 7, 1878......................		3,388,135 77

Net earnings, so ascertained $3,695,717 63

"Twenty-five per cent." 906,429 41
Deduct United States transportation above (six months) 483,650 10

    Remainder, cash or additional payment required by law 422,779 31

APPLICATION.

One-half transportation service $241,825 05
Cash payment, 5 per cent. net earnings 181,285 88

For credit on bond and interest account $423,110 93
One-half transportation service 241,825 05
  Cash payment, being that portion of the $850,000, named
  in section 4 of the act, which is required 241,493 43
          483,318 48

C.

Statement of the earnings and expenses of the Union Pacific Railroad Company for the year ending December 31, 1879.

EARNINGS.

United States:
  Passenger $150,965 23
  Freight 401,947 78
  Mail $596,775 00
Less difference between amount charged by
  railroad company and that allowed by the
  Post-Office Department 217,921 92
             378,853 08
                     $931,766 09

Commercial:
  Passenger 3,056,944 69
  Freight 7,424,516 52
  Express 360,840 90
           10,842,302 11
Company freight 865,949 94
Car service, balance 20 74
Rent of buildings 44,624 60
Miscellaneous 298,492 26
           1,209,087 54

    Total earnings 12,983,155 74

EXPENSES.

Conducting-transportation 1,004,507 89
Motive power 2,004,334 16
Maintenance of cars 447,012 81
Maintenance of way 1,397,696 78
General expenses and taxes 621,951 80
           5,475,504 94
Interest paid on first-mortgage bonds 1,636,530 00
Premium on gold 29 99
           1,636,559 99

Total expenses under law of May 7, 1878 .... 7,112,064 93

Net earnings so ascertained 5,871,092 31

  "Twenty-five per cent." 1,467,773 08
  Deduct United States transportation above 931,766 09
  And express and telegraph business for the United
    States, included in commercial, express, and miscel-
    laneous earnings 10,335 27
  And "other roads" for 1879 .... 1,633 34
           943,734 70

Remainder (cash or additional payment required by law) 594,038 38

APPLICATION.

Half-transportation service	$471,867 35	
Cash payment—five per cent. net earnings	293,554 62	
		$765,421 97
Half-transportation service	471,867 35	
Cash payment—being that portion of the $850,000 named in section 4 of the act which is required for the year 1879	230,483 76	
Payable in established sinking fund...............................		702,351 11

D.

1880.

Statement showing earnings and expenses of the Union Pacific Railway Company for the year ending December 31, 1880.

UNION DIVISION.

EARNINGS.

United States:			
Passenger..		$215,635 74	
Freight..		383,147 67	
Mail..	$596,775 00		
Less difference between amount charged by railroad company and amount allowed by Post-Office Department....................	179,479 18		
		417,295 89	
			$1,016,079 23
Commercial:			
Passenger..		3,502,547 52	
Freight..		9,358,109 61	
Express..		522,470 46	
			13,383,127 59
Company freight.......................................		976,130 91	
Car service		56,598 67	
Rent of buildings		27,799 70	
Miscellaneous...		295,790 26	
			1,356,319 54
Total earnings			15,755,596 36

EXPENSES.

Conducting transportation	1,315,784 65	
Motive power..	2,352,958 11	
Maintenance of cars	613,010 02	
Maintenance of way...................................	1,993,514 85	
General expenses and taxes............................	584,157 53	
		6,859,425 16
Interest on first-mortgage bonds, paid...................		1,626,570 00
Total expenses under law of May 7, 1878		8,485,995 16
Net earnings so ascertained............................		7,269,531 20
"Twenty-five per cent."	1,817,382 80	
Deduct transportation above, 1880	1,016,079 23	
Remainder, additional payment required by law		801,303 57
Add 5 per cent. of $65,408.47, being additional allowance for transportation of United State mails from February 14, 1876, to June 30, 1878..		3,270 42
Total payment required for 1880		804,573 99

Less :

Amount included in miscellaneous matters under heading of "other service"	$7,908,87	
And services for government transportation "branch-line service," ledger folio 219, transferred from Omaha to Boston books	3,863 79	
Balances on Omaha books:		
Troops and supplies, Colorado division, 1879	789 59	
Mail, Colorado division, 1879	1,003 90	
Services on non-aided lines as reported by the auditor at Omaha	37,943 87	
Credit them with one-half of the $65,408.47 which was an additional allowance for mail transportation by the Post-Office Department, but which has not been included in the earnings of this statement	32,704 23	
Total	84,214 25	
Deduct amount taken up in settlement of 1879..	1,633 34	$82,580 91

Amount now ascertained to be due to the United States according to law for 1880	721,993 02

APPLICATION.

One-half transportation services	508,039 61	
Cash payment, 5 per cent. of net earnings	366,746 98	
For credit on bond and interest account		$874,786 59
One-half transportation service	508,039 62	
Cash payment, being that portion of the $850,000 named in section 4, act May 7, 1878, which is required for the year 1880, payable into the sinking fund established in the Treasury of the United States	437,827 01	
		$945,866 63

E.

THE UNION PACIFIC RAILWAY COMPANY, TREASURER'S OFFICE,
Boston, Mass., July 1, 1881.

Statement of the amounts due from the Union Pacific Railway Company to the United States for 5 per cent. of the net earnings of that part of its Kansas division which was subsidized by the United States, for the year from November 2, 1879, to November 1, 1880, both inclusive, and the amounts due the company for transportation services to December 31, 1880.

EARNINGS, MAIN LINE.

November, 1879, $420,667.55—11	$406,645 29	
December, 1879	461,627 03	
January, 1880	387,013 50	
February, 1880	395,392 71	
March, 1880	539,247 96	
April, 1880	579,247 18	
May, 1880	554,201 10	
June, 1880	523,737 47	
July, 1880	462,819 47	
August, 1880	516,575 12	
September, 1880	536,897 83	
October, 1880	557,875 80	
November, 1880, $496,498.83—10	16,549 96	
		$5,937,830 4

EXPENSES AND TAXES, MAIN LINE.

November, 1879, $191,891.85, 8	$185,582 45
December, 1879	331,731 23
January, 1880	236,796 61
February, 1880	174,006 37

March, 1880	$217,482 62	
April, 1880	285,407 96	
May, 1880	298,037 59	
June, 1880	258,212 52	
July, 1880	273,153 11	
August, 1880	253,365 23	
September, 1880	304,069 83	
October, 1880	325,120 56	
November, 1880	11,624 47	
		$3,154,589 55
Surplus earnings, main line Kansas division		2,783,240 87
₁₁₄, subsidized road		1,716,114 09
Less:		
New construction *	66,288 00	
New equipment, † 350,984.94, ₂₁₄	216,413 25	
		282,701 25
Net earnings		1,433,412 84
Five per cent		71,670 64
Cash portion due the company for transportation service in 1880		170,455 05
Balance due the company on Kansas division, account for 1880		98,784 41
Balance due the company on Kansas division, account to December 31, 1879		767,136 30
Balance due December 31, 1880		865,920 71

MEMORANDA.

Particulars, new construction:

Right of way	494 47
Right of way, and side track, Kansas City	3,614 39
Right of way, November, 1880, all on 394 miles, ₁/₁₀ of $50 =	1 67
Graduation	255 74
Knowles pump, Armstrong	479 21
Fire apparatus	4 68
Telegraph line	3,098 73
Bismarck Grove	33,872 07
Freight-house at State line	296 60
Office at Armstrong shops	3,021 05
Lathes at Armstrong shops	6,581 10
Additions to Armstrong shops	12,680 09
Machines at Armstrong shops	1,958 29
Total	66,288 00

Particulars, new equipment:

Car equipment	229,002 09
Locomotive equipment	120,901 84
Fire engine and water car	1,281 01
	350,984 94
₂₁₄	216,413 25

The Union Pacific Railway Company to the United States, Dr.

For balance due for the six months ending December 31, 1878, as per statement B herewith	$422,779 31	
For balance due for the year 1879, as per statement C herewith	524,038 38	
For balance due for the year 1880, as per statement D herewith	721,993 08	
		$1,668,810 77

* Apportioned an actual location.
† Apportioned on basis of subsidized road, viz, ₂₁₄.

CONTRA.

By balance due them up to June 30, 1878, as per statement
  A herewith $491,244 34
By balance due the Kansas division (Kansas Pacific Rail-
  way) to December 31, 1880, as per statement E attached.   865,920 71
                                                                          $1,357,165 05

Balance due the United States...   311,645 72

The following comparative statement shows the earnings and expenses of the Union Pacific Railway Company for the fiscal years ending June 30, 1880 and 1881:

	June 30, 1881.	June 30, 1880.
Passenger earnings	$4,970,646 85	$5,173,289 83
Freight earnings	15,957,560 64	13,806,275 09
Miscellaneous earnings	1,837,544 59	1,536,241 39
Gross earnings	22,765,752 08	20,517,806 52
Operating expenses	11,474,910 08	9,322,041 38
Net earnings	11,290,842 00	11,195,765 44

Showing an increase of $2,149,285.55 in freight, of $301,302.69 in miscellaneous, and a decrease of $202,642.98 in passenger earnings; a total increase of $2,247,945.26 in earnings being nearly offset by an increase of $2,152,868.70 in operating expenses, leaving an increase of $95,076.56 in net earnings.

THE CENTRAL PACIFIC RAILROAD COMPANY.

This company was operating, on June 30, 1881, 2,722.05 miles of road, of which 1,204.5 miles are owned, and 1,517.55 miles are leased, as against 2,487.2 miles operated last June, 1,204.5 miles owned and 1,282.7, miles leased.

Of the 1,204.5 miles owned, 860.66 have been subsidized by the United States with bonds, and 1,012.47 with lands.

This company leases and operates the Southern Pacific Railroad in California, Arizona, and New Mexico, connecting with the Atchison, Topeka and Santa Fé Railroad at Deming, N. Mex.

The condition of the property is good and improving, and the business materially increasing.

The following statement is submitted as showing the financial condition of the company on June 30, 1881:

LIABILITIES.

United States subsidy bonds... $27,855,680 00
Interest on subsidy bonds 21,778,122 61
Other bonded debt 55,301,000 00
Interest due and accrued 1,433,095 00
Bills payable...   696,023 00
Accounts payable 5,741,006 26
Dividends...   5,403 00
Capital stock...   59,275,500 00
Sinking fund uninvested 349,009 17
                                                                      ──────────────
                                                                      172,334,839 04
Trustees land-grant mortgage..   337,001 01
                                                                      ──────────────
    Total 172,671,840 05

ASSETS.

Road and fixtures	$136,994,849 80
Equipment	8,047,103 42
Real estate	2,639,148 10
Cash	2,166,168 45
Material, &c	2,022,489 19
Company's bonds and stocks	334,604 90
Other bonds and stocks and investments	1,809,995 66
Bills receivable	1,710,063 36
Sinking fund with trustees	4,266,909 17
Accounts receivable	2,360,778 57
United States transportation account ⎱ United States sinking-fund account ⎰	5,884,891 60
	168,237,002 22
Balance, deficit	4,434,837 83
	172,671,840 05

The comparative earnings and expenses of the road for the fiscal years ending June 30, 1880 and 1881, are shown below.

	1881.	1880.
Passenger earnings	$6,188,388 56	$5,235,573 62
Freight earnings	15,216,554 65	11,169,085 87
Miscellaneous earnings	1,488,401 36	1,397,738 67
Gross earnings	22,893,344 57	17,802,448 16
Operating expenses	13,502,504 48	11,586,482 92
Net earnings	9,390,840 09	6,215,965 24

Showing an increase of $952,814.94 in passenger, $4,047,468.78 in freight, $90,612.69 in miscellaneous, and an aggregate total increase of $5,090,896.41 net earnings, or an increase of $3,174,874.85, or 51 per cent. during the year, which is considered highly flattering.

A settlement with this company for the year ending December 31, 1880, was effected by the then Commissioner French, whereby the company were shown to owe the United States for that year a balance of $144,436.74, which has been paid into the Treasury.

A copy of the settlement is herewith submitted.

Statement of earnings and expenses of the subsidized line of the Central Pacific Railroad for the calendar year 1880, ascertained in accordance with the act of Congress approved May 7, 1878.

Gross earnings from operation			$9,457,083 60
Dividends on and proceeds of Wells, Fargo & Co.'s stock ($432,468.18 × .709456)			306,817 14
Through business done on non-aided line but which might have been done on aided line		$435,625 77	
Less operating expenses at 41.66 per cent... $181,481.69 .35705 per cent. for additional mileage ..... .64,798 04		246,279 73	
			189,346 04
Total			9,953,246 78
Operating expenses		3,780,269 63	
Rental		40,303 55	
Taxes		143,300 74	
General expenses, legal expenses, and engineering, $356,736.29 × .461138		164,504 66	

Interest on first-mortgage bonds $1,668,390 00
Additional general expenses, &c., on allowance for di-
    verted business as above 7,577 08

    Total.. $5,804,345 08

Net earnings under the act 4,148,901 12

Twenty-five per cent 1,037,225 28

*Transportation service done for the United States by the Central Pacific Railroad Company
during the calendar year 1880.*

	On aided line.	On non-aided line.	Total.
Mails....................................	$343,057 28	$89,059 37	$432,116 65
Miscellaneous..........................	98,829 95	195,953 60	294,782 55
Total.......................	441,887 23	285,011 97	726,899 20

Other transportation not heretofore considered in annual settlement.

Southern Pacific, per auditor's books, 1877-'78-'79......	....	131,814 21	131,814 21
Branch lines, per auditor's books, 1879	....	2,655 59	2,655 59
Branch lines, Post-Office Department, 1880 and prior....	....	31,419 54	31,419 54
Total...........................	....	165,889 34	165,889 34
Total of all..............................	441,887 23	450,901 31	892,788 54

Application of "Net earnings" of the subsidized line of the Central Pacific Railroad Company for 1880.

Twenty-five per cent. of net earnings as ascertained.................... $1,037,225 28
Transportation services performed............................ ......   441,887 23

Cash requirement 595,338 05
Transportation on other lines—equivalent to cash......................   450,901 31

Net cash required:.....................................   144,436 74

DISPOSITION OF SAME.

One-half of transportation on subsidized line............................. $220,943 61
Five per cent. of net earnings as ascertained......................   207,445 06

Total for credit of bond and interest account............................   428,388 67

One-half transportation on subsidized line.............................   220,943 62
Additional payment under the law..   387,492 39

Total for sinking-fund account.......................................   608,436 01

THE SIOUX CITY AND PACIFIC RAILROAD COMPANY.

This road has been aided by the United States by the issue of
$1,628,320, in bonds and a grant of 41,318 acres of land.

Until the year ending June 30, 1880, the road had not earned enough
to pay operating expenses and interest on its first-mortgage bonds:
consequently there was no 5 per cent. of net earnings for the government, under the Supreme Court decision.

Length of road subsidized...................................Miles.. 107.48
Length of road owned ....do.... 107.48
Length of road leased.......................................do..... 156.71
Length of road operated.....................................do..... 264.19

Number of locomotives owned.. 12
Number of locomotives leased.. 9

 Total 21

Number of passenger cars owned... 14
Number of passenger cars leased.. 4

 Total 18

Number of freight cars owned... 164
Number of freight cars leased.. 410

 Total 574

Number of other cars owned.. 91

The following is a comparative statement of the earnings and expenses of the subsidized portion of, the road for the fiscal years ending June 30, 1880 and 1881:

	Year ending June 30, 1881.	Year ending June 30, 1880.
Passenger earnings............................	$102,884 60	$105,788 03
Freight earnings...............................	327,735 40	328,276 89
Miscellaneous earnings.......................	23,636 55	21,380 31
Gross earnings............................	454,236 55	455,440 23
Operating expenses............................	341,087 37	297,343 10
Net earnings.............................	113,149 38	158,097 13

Whilst the gross earnings are about the same for the two years, the expenses of 1881 were 15 per cent. greater than those of 1880.

The financial condition of this company on June 30, 1881, is shown by the following statement:

LIABILITIES.

United States subsidy bonds...... .... $1,628,320 00
Interest on subsidy bonds.. 1,968,809 09
First-mortgage bonds... 1,628,000 00
Interest on bonds... 52,485 00
Pay-rolls and vouchers... 58,837 17
Bills payable... 398,800 00
Accounts payable $53,223 77
Company's accounts, traffic................................ 2,097 95
Company's accounts, leases................................ 18,602 62

                  73,924 34

                  5,109,265 60
Capital stock.. 2,068,400 00

 Total 7,177,665 60

ASSETS.

Road and fixtures.. $5,392,236 15
Fuel, material, &c 65,439 02
Cash.. 27,204 76
Company's bonds.. 500 00
Miscellaneous investments... 312,800 00
Accounts, receivable $46,947 09
Accounts, traffic.. 26,496 62

                  72,373 71

                  5,875,548 24

Applied on interest accrued on United States bonds.................................   ███,███ ██
Due from United States...   ██,███ ██

                                                                                        █,███,███ ██
Deficit, or debit to income..▪.......   █,███,███ ██

    Total..▪....................   7, 177,███ ██

CENTRAL BRANCH UNION PACIFIC RAILROAD.

This road and its leased lines are operated by the Missouri Pacific Railway Company as one of its divisions. One million six hundred thousand dollars in bonds have been loaned and 187,608 acres of land granted by the United States, subsidizing 100 miles of road from Atchison to Waterville, Kans.

The earnings and expenses for the fiscal years ending June 30, 1880 and 1881, were as follows:

	June 30, 1881.	June 30, ████.
Gross earnings..	███14,███ ██	██,███,███ ██
Operating expenses..	███,███ ██	███,███ ██
Net earnings..	███,███ ██	███,███ ██

TEXAS AND PACIFIC RAILWAY COMPANY.

This company was operating, on the 30th of June, 1881, 820.86 miles of road, and work towards its completion was rapidly being pushed forward.

It is anticipated that the line will be completed and trains running through to El Paso not later than January 1, 1882.

From the annual report of this company for the year ending June 30, 1881, and which is published in full under the head of Appendix 13 of this report, the following statements are derived:

Financial condition of the Texas and Pacific Railway Company June 30, 1881.

Capital stock :
    Authorized -- $██,███,███ ██
    Issued ---   14,███,███ ██
    Full paid ------------------‡--------------------------------   14,███,███ ██

LIABILITIES.

First-mortgage 6 per cent. gold construction bonds, Eastern Division,
    $8,000 per mile, payable March 1, 1905 .... $4,050,███ ██
Consolidated mortgage 6 per cent. gold bonds, Eastern Division, $17,000
    per mile, payable June 1, 1905 ....   9,███,███ ██
Income and land-grant 7 per cent. currency bonds, limited to an issue
    of $8,908,000, dated May 15, 1875, payable June, 1905 ....   8,███,000 ██
First-mortgage construction 6 per cent. gold bonds, Rio Grande Division, $25,000 per mile, payable February 1, 1930 ....   █,███,███ ██
Land-grant bonds, old issue...   ███,███ ██
Coupons old land-grant bonds ....   ██,███ ██
Fractional bond scrip, income and land-grant bonds ....────   ██,███ ██
Land department fractional scrip ....   ██,███ ██
School-fund loan, State of Texas ....   ███,███ ██
Unpaid coupons construction bonds ....   ██,███ ██
Sinking-fund first-mortgage, Eastern Division, bonds, payable October
    1, 1881...   ██,███ ██
Current balances ....   ██,███ ██

    Total ....   28,███,174 ██

ASSETS.

Property accounts...	$335,764 62
Bills and accounts receivable	438,146 14
Cash in treasury	120,750 84
Material on hand	389,208 75
Land department	165,013 06
	1,448,883 41

Add 821 miles of constructed and equipped road and telegraph line, the value of which does not fully appear on our books because of unadjusted balances, but the construction accounts show an expenditure of 40,356,816 40

Also, 4,738,308 acres of land in Texas and about 4,000 acres in California, a portion only of which has been valued ; also, 5,052,160 acres of unlocated lands in Texas.

Receipts from all sources and how applied for the year ending June 30, 1881.

On hand June 30, 1880, balance from last report........................		$294,817 49
By receipts from:		
Passengers............................	$712,593 73	
Freight...............................	2,500,083 26	
Express................................	40,245 10	
Mail...................................	54,480 77	
Telegraph	17,690 30	
Miscellaneous.........................	6,075 00	
	$3,331,168 16	
To payment for :		
Conducting transportation.............	675,907 19	
Motive power..........................	615,110 00	
Maintenance of cars...................	198,951 64	
Maintenance of way...................	1,069,457 59	
General expense	208,950 31	
	2,768,376 73	
By net earnings from operating road......		562,791 43
By receipts from other sources:		
Texas land sales	29,680 16	
Less bonds and scrip received in payment for land	26,601 79	
	3,078 37	
From lot sales.........................	33,846 77	
Construction bonds....................	8,687,000 00	
Capital stock	6,287,000 00	
Interest on loans, &c..................	19,872 85	
Bills and accounts receivable	140,970 68	
Liabilities accounts, balance...........	60,347 78	
		15,232,116 45
Total..		16,089,725 37
Against which there is charged—		
For interest on bonds..................	788,295 00	
For construction and equipment........	14,156,873 05	
For sinking-fund first mortgage........	71,750 00	
For land department...................	48,439 46	
For loans, &c.........................	307,133 32	
For sundry accounts...................	52,534 81	
	15,425,025 58	
Balance on hand June 30, 1881—		
Cash	120,750 84	
Material..............................	389,208 75	
Due from agents, &c.................	154,740 20	
	664,699 79	
		16,089,725 37

48 Ab

NORTHERN PACIFIC RAILROAD COMPANY.

Half-yearly reports for the six months ending December 31, 1880, and June 30, 1881, not having been received at this office, the following items are gleaned from the company's annual report to its stockholders for the fiscal year ending June 30, 1881.

At the close of the year the road operated by the company was as follows:

	Miles.
Saint Paul to Brainerd	136
Duluth to Bismarck	450
Casselton to Blanchard	32
Miles operated on eastern division	618
Tacoma to Kalama	105
Tacoma to Wilkerson	31
Miles operated on Pacific side	136
Total operated	754

In addition to this, 311 miles were in operation principally for construction; the earnings derived from commercial business being credited to construction account until the divisions are completed and turned over to the operating department.

From returns made to this office on our form 8–003 the following comparative statement of earnings and expenses for the fiscal years ending June 30, 1880 and 1881, is made:

	June 30, 1881.	June 30, 1880.
Passenger earnings	$698,420 92	$549,473 97
Freight earnings	2,164,783 12	1,588,560 50
Miscellaneous earnings	118,500 44	92,080 54
Gross earnings	2,981,802 48	2,380,114 31
Operating expenses	1,946,187 08	1,416,144 84
Net earnings	985,645 40	812,969 47

Showing an increase in earnings of 31½ per cent.; in expenses of 38 per cent., and in net earnings of 20 per cent.

There remained outstanding on June 30, 1881, of—

Preferred stock	$42,312,588 90
Common stock	49,000,000 00
Total capital stock	91,312,588 90

The divisional mortgage bonds authorized are:

Missouri division	$2,500,000 00
Pend D'Oreille division	4,500,000 00
Total	7,000,000 00

The net proceeds of the sales of land pertaining to these divisions are pledged to the cancellation of these bonds. The amount outstanding on June 30, 1881, was:

Missouri division bonds	$2,484,300 00
Pend D'Oreille division bonds	3,915,000 00
Total	6,399,300 00

which will probably be absorbed in a short time by the sales of lands. There remains to be constructed to complete the main line—

	Miles.
Between Lake Superior and the Pacific Coast	816
Thomson Junction to Montreal River	122
Wallula Junction to Portland	238
Portland to Kalama	39
Cascade Mountain branch	219
Total	1,434

Eight million seven hundred and fifty-six thousand nine hundred and eighty-seven dollars and fourteen cents were expended in new construction of track, bridges, and buildings during the fiscal year ending June 30, 1881.

The equipments consists of 32 locomotives, 17 passenger and sleeping cars, 1,150 freight cars, and 54 hand, section, and miscellaneous cars, costing the sum of $1,084,416.51.

The financial condition of the company on June 30, 1881, as made up from its auditor's balance-sheet, was:

ASSETS.

Cost of road, equipment, &c	$106,324,290 42
Material on hand	2,082,947 08
Investments	3,846,856 96
Accounts receivable	975,440 65
Cash	11,774,275 16
Total	127,003,800 27

LIABILITIES.

Funded debt	$21,586,800 00
Interest accrued on same	562,149 32
Unpaid vouchers	883,889 33
Net proceeds of land sales in preferred stock, bonds, deferred payments, and cash	10,212,899 44
Profit and loss	2,445,473 23
Capital stock	91,312,588 95
Total	127,003,800 27

The report further says that as to future progress the purpose of the company is at once to put under contract the grading of the entire 816 miles of uncompleted line forming the gap between the eastern and western portions of the road, which, it is expected, will be completed some time in 1883.

ATCHISON, TOPEKA, AND SANTA FÉ RAILROAD COMPANY.

Inspection of this road was made in April, 1881. Since the last annual report the road has been extended to Deming, N. Mex., where it connects with the Southern Pacific Railroad, forming with it what is now termed the southern route to the Pacific coast.

The following statements are taken from their annual report for the year 1880:

	1880.	1879.	Increase.
Passenger earnings	$1,786,901 41	$1,353,230 62	$433,670 79
Freight earnings	6,499,980 79	4,883,434 95	1,616,545 84
Miscellaneous earnings	270,093 74	144,776 94	125,316 80
Total	8,556,975 94	6,381,442 51	2,175,533 48
Operating expenses and taxes	4,343,205 40	2,966,965 32	1,376,240 08
Net earnings	4,213,770 54	3,414,477 19	799,293 85

Being an increase in gross earnings of 34.09 per cent.; in operating expenses of 46.38 per cent.; in net earnings of 23.4 per cent. The percentage of operating expenses to gross earnings for the year 1880 was 50¾, and for 1879, 46¼.

	1880.	1879.
Gross earnings per average mile of road operated..........................	$6,237 27	$5,400 96
Operating expenses per average mile of road operated......................	3,165 81	2,976 04
Net earnings per average mile of road operated	3,071 46	3,434 92

There was charged to new construction and new rolling stock during 1880, the sum of $1,801,025.31.

Repairs and renewals were much more extensive than during the preceding year, and the operating expenses were proportionately increased.

One hundred and thirty-three and two-tenths miles of track were relaid with steel rails, and 25.6 miles with iron, using in these renewals 472,828 cross-ties. The company also built 40.2 miles of fence this year, a matter of considerable importance to a road running through a great live-stock country.

Four hundred and two-tenths miles of new road were constructed during 1880. The rolling-stock owned and leased by the company on December 31, 1880, was 107 passenger cars, 153 locomotives, 4,129 freight cars, 61 miscellaneous cars.

Contracts were made for the following additional rolling-stock, for delivery in the spring and summer of 1881: 50 locomotives; 29 passenger, baggage, and postal cars; 2,500 freight cars; 40 way cars.

The financial condition of the company on December 31, 1880, was as follows:

ASSETS.

Construction and equipment......................................	$26,866,325 72
Proprietorship in leased roads, represented by stocks and bonds......	18,604,126 10
Material and supplies on hand...................................	1,118,488 33
Sundry securities...	619,065 82
Accounts receivable...	3,847,578 97
Cash	885,071 58
	51,940,656 02

LIABILITIES.

Funded debt..	$15,873,000 00
Capital stock	24,891,000 00
Interest on funded debt	564,431 24
Dividends	503,358 08
Accounts payable	2,059,157 57
Profit and loss, and income accounts	8,049,609 71
	51,940,656 02

SOUTHERN PACIFIC RAILROAD COMPANY (NORTHERN DIVISION).

Inspection of this property was made in the latter part of June last. This company has leased all but 160.89 miles of its track to the Central Pacific Railroad Company. The capital stock authorized is $90,000,000, of which there has been issued and is now outstanding $36,763,900, all held by thirty-six stockholders.

The following statement shows the earnings (including rentals of leased lines,) and expenses of the line operated by the company, for the fiscal years ending June 30, 1880 and 1881:

	June 30, 1881.	June 30, 1880.
Passenger earnings	$451,782 32	$399,340 34
Freight earnings	602,434 40	455,382 51
Miscellaneous earnings	1,704,995 17	1,680,049 56
Gross earnings	2,759,211 89	2,534,781 41
Operating expenses	710,694 41	756,683 88
Net earnings	2,048,517 48	1,778,097 53

This company owns the following rolling-stock: 48 locomotives, 89 passenger cars, 915 freight cars, 243 miscellaneous cars; of which it has leased to the Central Pacific Company, 18 locomotives, 19 passenger cars, 345 freight cars and 156 miscellaneous cars.

The financial condition of this company on June 30, 1881, is shown by the following report:

ASSETS.

Cost of road equipment and real estate	$64,900,058 87
Material and supplies on hand	104,633 57
Cash	293,157 12
Stocks and bonds, other than company's	425,000 00
Accounts receivable	1,004,841 68
Total	66,727,691 24

LIABILITIES.

First-mortgage bonds	$28,774,000 00
Interest on first-mortgage bonds	482,145 00
Pay-rolls and vouchers	94,003 06
Accounts payable	605,276 37
Profit and loss	8,366 81
Capital stock	36,763,900 00
Total	66,727,691 24

OREGON AND CALIFORNIA RAILROAD COMPANY.

This company is formed by the consolidation of the Oregon Central Railroad Company, by purchase September 1, 1880; Western Oregon Railroad Company, by purchase October 9, 1880; and Albany and Lebanon Railroad Company, by lease December 15, 1880.

Inspection of this road was made in May last, the result of which is detailed in the civil engineer's report.

The authorized capital stock of the company is $19,000,000, of which all has been issued and is now outstanding, being held by five persons.

The Oregon and Trans-Continental Company, which was organized June 28, 1881, with a capital stock of $50,000,000, among other objects, contemplates the extension of the Oregon and California Railroad southward to a connection with the railroad system of California.

Below is a statement of the earnings and expenses of the Oregon and California Railroad for the fiscal years ending June 30, 1880 and 1881:

1880 and 1881.	June 30, 1881.	June 30, 1880.
Passenger earnings	$232,512 72	$192,183 75
Freight earnings	331,136 40	247,009 63
Miscellaneous earnings	51,134 70	66,439 06
Gross earnings	614,783 82	505,632 44
Operating expenses	491,279 83	383,579 16
Net earnings	123,508 99	122,053 28

The financial condition of the company on June 30, 1881, was:

ASSETS.

Cost of road and equipment	$12,832,988 98
Real estate	774,315 99
Material and supplies on hand	115,935 65
Cash	26,141 77
Sinking fund in hands of trustees	17,173 75
Bills and accounts receivable	21,393,024 02
Total	35,159,619 66
Deficit	5,892,893 73

LIABILITIES.

First-mortgage bonds	$12,950,000 00
Interest on same	5,087,930 35
Other funded debt	2,990,000 00
Interest on same	748,036 35
Bills and accounts payable	295,546 80
Capital stock	19,000,000 00
Total	41,052,513 39

The equipment of the company on June 30, 1881, was as follows: 30 locomotives, 22 passenger cars, 350 freight cars, 91 miscellaneous cars.

About three-fourths of the tonnage of this road consists of grain and flour.

ATLANTIC AND PACIFIC RAILROAD COMPANY.

This company was incorporated by act of Congress approved July 27, 1866, and after a long delay began construction from Albuquerque, N. Mex., westwardly.

One hundred miles of road has been completed and, through the recommendation of the commissioners appointed to inspect and report upon the same, accepted by the President of the United States.

At this writing, commissioners are examining a second one hundred miles of completed road.

The civil engineer of this office reports that the location of this line of road has been carefully and judiciously made; the grades light, making the construction of road-bed cheap and future maintenance thereof easy.

A tripartite agreement in 1880, between this company and the Saint Louis and San Francisco and the Atchison, Topeka and Santa Fé companies, providing that this company should construct that part of its line extending from the Rio Grande River to the Pacific Ocean, resulted in the issuance of an income mortgage of $10,000,000, which was promptly taken up by the Saint Louis and San Francisco and the Atchison, Topeka and Santa Fé companies.

The following statement shows the financial condition of the Atlantic and Pacific Railroad Company on December 31, 1880, as taken from their report to the stockholders for the year ending that date:

ASSETS.

Cost of road and equipment Central, Missouri and Western divisions.	$23,500,744 22
Income account, Missouri and Western divisions	715,828 16
Accounts receivable	836,510 35
Cash on hand	55,701 85
Total	25,108,784 58

LIABILITIES.

First-mortgage bonds $3,784,905 00
Capital stock 19,760,300 00
Notes and accounts payable 1,556,072 17
Interest.. 7,507 35

Total... 25,108,784 52

On December 31, 1880, the rolling-stock owned by the company was as follows: 17 locomotives, 9 passenger cars, 659 freight cars, 20 hand cars.

SAINT LOUIS AND SAN FRANCISCO RAILWAY.

A portion of the original road of the Atlantic and Pacific Company is now owned and operated by the Saint Louis and San Francisco Railway Company.

That portion of the road, 253 miles, extending from Pacific Station to Pierce City, and that from Pierce City to Wichita, 218 miles, were examined during the latter part of April, 1881.

The company own 293 miles, and lease 336 miles of road, making a total of 629 miles operated.

Valuable improvements have been made during the year, among which may be mentioned 95 miles of steel rails, and 150,000 new cross-ties placed in the track. 6½ miles of additional side tracks have been added during the same period.

The earnings and expenses of the road for the fiscal years ending June 30, 1880 and 1881, were as follows:

	June 30, 1881.	June 30, 1880.
Gross earnings..	$3,061,353 18	$2,259,594 57
Operating expenses..	1,500,076 89	1,006,709 88
Net earnings	1,561,776 29	1,252,888 69

From the report of the company to the directors, for the calendar year 1880, the following is ascertained:

This company holds 97,795½ shares of the capital stock of the Atlantic and Pacific Railroad Company (the Atchison, Topeka and Santa Fé Company holding an equal amount), and all future issue of the stock of the Atlantic and Pacific, the total authorized amount being one hundred millions of dollars, is to be delivered, one half to this company and the other to the Atchison Topeka and Santa Fé Company.

The two companies (the Saint Louis and San Francisco and the Atchison, Topeka and Santa Fé) have entered into an agreement with the Atlantic and Pacific Company, wherein they guarantee to supply, from the gross earnings derived from their inter-traffic, sufficient to meet any deficiency which may occur in the payment by the Atlantic and Pacific Railway Company of the interest on its first-mortgage bonds issued and to be issued to the extent of $25,000 per mile. This appropriation, whatever its amount, is to be in the nature of a loan and to be returned with interest.

The financial condition of the Saint Louis and San Francisco Company on December 31, 1880, was as follows:

ASSETS.

Cost of road and equipment	$38,015,381 86
Material and stock on hand	138,407 34
Cash	873,427 96
Company's stocks and bonds	1,138,619 74
Other stocks and bonds	1,485,349 46
Bills and accounts receivable	3,039,277 22
Total	44,690,463 58

LIABILITIES.

Funded debt	$17,900,000 00
Interest on same unpaid	364,648 50
Dividends unpaid	144,693 50
Accounts and bills payable	433,504 72
Income on profit and loss account	847,616 86
Capital stock	25,000,000 00
Total	44,690,463 58

At the close of the year the company had 59 locomotives, 39 passenger, mail, and baggage cars, and 2,145 freight cars.

The company has built 14 stock cars and 8 cabooses at its shops in Springfield, Mo., and has sufficient accommodations for the repairing of all rolling-stock.

SAINT LOUIS, IRON MOUNTAIN, AND SOUTHERN RAILWAY COMPANY.

This road has been aided through the States of Missouri and Arkansas by a grant of 1,386,384 acres of land.

The operations during the year 1880 developed greater progress than in any year of its existence.

Inspection of the property of this company was made by the civil engineer of this office in September, 1881, being the first one made by an officer of this bureau.

The present company was formed in 1874 by the consolidation of the Saint Louis and Iron Mountain; the Arkansas Branch; the Cairo and Fulton, and the Cairo, Arkansas and Texas Railroads.

The original gauge of the road was 5 feet, but was changed to the standard gauge of 4 feet 8½ inches on June 29, 1879.

The gross earnings of the road for 1880 were $6,265,597.30, being an increase over the previous year of $972,986.03. Operating expenses amounted to $4,075,226.37, or 65 per cent. of the gross earnings.

The company reports that this exceptionally large expenditure was the result of the policy adopted to put the road in first-class order as rapidly as possible.

The following statement shows the financial condition of the company on December 31, 1880:

ASSETS.

Road equipment and lands	$50,841,125 77
Supplies and material on hand	365,822
Sundry investments	611,351
Union Trust Company of New York	52,951
Cash	251,323
Bills and accounts receivable	493,407
Total	52,616,014
Deficit	1,706,141

LIABILITIES.

Bonded debt	$30,078,810 00
Interest on funded debt	1,056,319 46
Bills and accounts payable	1,727,205 29
Capital stock	21,459,821 00
Total	54,322,155 75

The equipment of the road on December 31, 1880, consisted of 137 locomotives, 90 passenger, baggage, mail, and express cars, 3,983 freight and caboose cars, and 8 miscellaneous cars.

The freight traffic of the road consists largely of iron-ore and cotton. A large and increasing Texas passenger business is also being done.

MISSOURI, KANSAS AND TEXAS RAILWAY.

The date of incorporation of this company was September 20, 1865. It has been consolidated with the Sabette and Sedalia Railway Company, the Tebo and Neosho Railroad Company, and the Neosho Valley and Holden Railway Company.

The entire road has lost its individuality and is now operated by the Missouri Pacific Railway Company as its "Kansas and Texas Division." One hundred and eighty-three and two-tenths miles have been aided, through the State of Kansas, by a grant of 397,643 acres of land.

The earnings and expenses of the road for the fiscal years ending June 30, 1880 and 1881, were as follows:

	June 30, 1881.	June 30, 1880.
Passenger earnings	$879,195 13	$779,984 82
Freight earnings	3,272,050 70	3,096,948 71
Miscellaneous earnings	245,317 41	203,389 89
Gross earnings	4,396,563 24	4,062,322 92
Operating expenses	2,239,214 02	1,904,096 83
Net earnings	2,157,349 22	2,178,226 09

DECISIONS OF UNITED STATES COURTS.

The Court of Claims has during its last term decided several cases in which the rights of the Pacific railroads, under the original acts and the act of May 7, 1878, were involved.

A case of interest is that of the Union Pacific Railway Company vs. the United States (No. 12,380), in which the company, among other things, claimed full compensation for carrying the mails over that portion of the Kansas Pacific Road west of the 394th mile-post, for which the company received no subsidy of bonds. Although this suit related especially to the unsubsidized portion of the Kansas Pacific Railroad, it had a direct bearing on the question of whether the leased lines of the Pacific railroads, which were unsubsidized, should receive full compensation in money for all services performed by them for the government. The company claimed, further, that the Secretary of the Treasury had no right to withhold more than one-half compensation for services performed by the Kansas Pacific Railroad, it being contended, however, by the government that under the act of March 3, 1873, and the act of May 7, 1878, the Secretary had authority to withhold all compensation due either the Central or Union Pacific Railroad Company, whether such compensation was earned over leased, unsubsidized or subsidized lines.

Chief-Justice Drake, in delivering the opinion of the court in this matter, said:

To this petition the defendants demur, and the demurrer raises the question whether, upon the facts set forth in the petition, the claimant has any right to recover.

This question arises, first, as to the 394 miles for which subsidy bonds were issued, and it is contended, on behalf of the defendants, that, notwithstanding the above-cited provision of the act of 1864, declaring that only one-half of the compensation for the services rendered to the government by the road should be required to be applied to the payment of those bonds, there is yet a right in the government to withhold payment of the other half.

In our opinion there is no just grounds for this position. The right of the government to withhold any of the money earned by the company for services rendered to the government, for the purpose of ultimately applying it to the payment of the bonds, rests not upon any general principle of law, but upon statute; and when the statute, after requiring all of that money to be applied, is changed so as to require "only one-half," it is a clear authority for the payment of the other half to the company. So far, then, as concerns the claim of the one-half of the compensation for carrying the mails over the 394 miles, the claimant appears entitled to recover.

As to the $19,180.25 earned for carrying the mails over the 344 miles, it is claimed on behalf of the defendants that the government having paid interest on the bonds which the company ought to have paid and was bound to reimburse, it should be fully be permitted to hold that amount for reimbursement, without regard for the question of how far the lien of the mortgage created by the issue of the bonds should extend.

It is claimed that because the Union Pacific, the Kansas Pacific, and the Denver Pacific Companies have been consolidated, and so the Kansas Pacific Company and its road have become a part of the consolidated company, therefore the compensation earned on the former road of the Kansas Pacific Company became after the consolidation subject to section 2 of the act of May 6, 1878 (20 Stat. L., 58, ch. 96), which is as follows:

"That the whole amount of compensation which may from time to time be due to said several companies respectively for services rendered for the government shall be retained by the United States, one-half thereof to be presently applied to the liquidation of the interest paid and to be paid by the United States upon the bonds as issued by it as aforesaid to each of said corporations severally, and the other half to be turned into the sinking fund hereinafter provided for the uses therein mentioned."

We are unable to perceive how this section can have any bearing on this case for the following reasons:

1. That act nowhere refers in any way to the Kansas Pacific Railway.

2. The "several companies" referred to in that section cannot be considered to be any other than the companies to which the act in its terms applies.

3. The only companies intended to be affected by the act were manifestly the Union Pacific and the Central Pacific.

4. The bonds referred to in that section are plainly those which had been issued to those two companies and no other.

It seems to us clear that the mere perusal of the act must lead to these conclusions, and they are re-enforced by the fact that the act was passed nearly two years before the consolidation of the roads took place. It is therefore not to be presumed to apply to any conditions produced by such consolidation.

This view is strengthened by the consideration that by the 16th section of the act of 1864, such a consolidation was expressly authorized, and Congress, with this act before it, made no provision in the act of 1878 looking to the not improbable formation of such consolidation.

If that body intended in that event to change the previously-defined relations towards the government of any road which might thereafter become consolidated with any other of the roads it would surely have enacted its will to that regard.

It did not enact anything on the subject, and we are therefore led to the conclusion that section 2 of the act of 1878 was intended to apply only to the Union Pacific and Central Pacific roads as they then stood, and to their respective liabilities to the government based on the bonds issued to them respectively by the government.

We are led to the further conclusion that when the Kansas Pacific became consolidated with the Union Pacific the pre-existing legal relations of the road of the first company to the government, as to compensation for services performed for the government, remained unchanged; and that whatever compensation was after the consolidation be earned on the road from Kansas City to Denver must be dealt with just as it would be if no consolidation had taken place.

The conclusion from the whole case presented by the petition is that the claimant is entitled to recover one-half of the compensation earned by the transportation of the mails over the 304 miles for which subsidy bonds were issued, and the whole of the compensation earned in that way ou the remaining 944 miles.

In Appendix 12 will be found the full text of the opinion.

In No. 12,515, Court of Claims, the Union Pacific Railroad Company brought suit for compensation in addition to that allowed by the Postmaster-General for carrying the mails, on the ground that by section 6 of the act of 1862, the railroad company was entitled to receive from the government compensation equal to the amount paid by private parties, for the same kind of service, alleging that the company's express business was the same kind of service performed as the mail service performed for the government. The court, Nott, J., delivering the opinion, says:

We do not understand the act of 1862 either to make a contract for all prospective services, or to bind the government to pay precisely the same rates which are paid by private parties for the same kind of service. Its language is:

"SEC. 6. * * * That the grants aforesaid are made upon condition that said company shall pay said bonds at maturity, and shall keep said railroad and telegraph line in repair and use, and shall all times transmit dispatches over said telegraph line, and transport mails, troops, and munitions of war, supplies and public stores upon said railroad for the government, whenever required to do so by any department thereof, and that the government shall at all times have the preference in the use of the same for all the purposes aforesaid (at fair and reasonable rates of compensation, not to exceed the amounts paid by private parties for the same kind of service); and all compensation for services rendered for the government shall be applied to the payment of said bonds and interest until the whole amount is fully paid"

Obviously and really, the section means, we think, that the company shall transport the government's mails, munitions, troops, &c., whenever required so to do, and that the government at all times shall have the preference over private parties; but that the transportation in all cases shall be done at fair and reasonable rates, which in no case (of preference or otherwise) shall exceed the rates paid by any private party for the same kind of service, while in all cases, even where the ordinary rates are fair and reasonable per se, the government shall have the benefit of those exceptional reductions of rate which railroads frequently make, sometimes as a matter of policy and sometimes as a matter of favor.

Another suit was brought by the Central Branch Union Pacific, which was similar to the first suit cited by me.

I also respectfully call your attention to the case of Thomas Wardell, appellant, vs. the Union Pacific Railroad Company et al., recently decided by the Supreme Court, Mr. Justice Field delivering the opinion, in which the legality of the contract made by the officers of the Union Pacific Railroad Company, by which certain parties were permitted to mine coal from land of the Union Pacific Railroad company, was passed upon. The court says that—

The scheme disclosed by this agreement has no feature which relieves it of its fraudulent character; it was a fraudulent proceeding on the part of the directors and contractors who devised and carried it into execution, not only against the company, but also against the government, which had largely contributed to its aid by the loan of bonds and by the grant of lands.

The court before this conclusion says—

Hence all arrangements by directors of a railroad company to secure an undue advantage to themselves at its expense, by the formation of a new company as an auxiliary to the original one, with an understanding that they, or some of them, shall take stock in it, and then that valuable contracts shall be given to it, in the profits of which they, as stockholders in the new company, are to share, are so many unlawful devices to enrich themselves to the detriment of the stockholders and creditors of the original company, and will be condemned whenever brought before the courts for consideration.

In Appendix 11 will be found the full text of the opinion.

LEGISLATIVE RECOMMENDATIONS.

It is respectfully suggested that section 4 of the act of May 7, 1878, amending the act entitled "An act to aid in the construction of a railroad and telegraph line from the Missouri River to the Pacific Ocean and to secure to the government the use of same for postal, military, and other purposes," be so amended as to embrace the subsidized portion of the Kansas division of the Union Pacific Railway, formerly the Kansas Pacific Railway, within the operations of said act requiring the establishment of sinking funds and the payment of "25 per cent. of net earnings," and that the annual requirement shall be a sum not less than $300,000.

I repeat, with approval, the recommendation of my predecessor in his report for 1880, that—

Sufficient appropriation be made to enable all land-grant companies which have covenanted to transport troops and supplies free of toll or other charge to be paid 50 per cent. of their ordinary charge for government transportation, on the condition that if this amount is accepted, it be in full of all demands and claims upon the government for such services.

In addition to this, I would recommend that Congress consider the question whether provision should not be made to establish permanently, or for a stated period, the rate of compensation to be paid by the government to the railroads mentioned.

After due consideration of the subject, I have reached the conclusion that 50 per cent. of the tariff, or ordinary rate of the companies, would be a compensation just to the railroads and the government, and proper for permanent application.

THE PERSONNEL AND EXPENSE OF THE BUREAU.

The following-named persons were employés of this office on June 30, 1881:

	Annual salary.
Theophilus French, auditor	$3,600
F. B. Pickerill, bookkeeper	2,400
W. M. Thompson, assistant bookkeeper	2,000
Henry Blackstone, engineer	2,000
Miss E. W. Rogers, clerk	1,600
Miss Kate Schmidt, copyist	900
A. S. Seely, messenger	720
Thomas Hassard, (temporary) draughtsman	1,200
E. J. Lockwood, (temporary) copyist	900
Miss M. L. Barnard, (temporary) copyist	720
Henry S. Leonard, (temporary) messenger	600

On this day, November 1, 1881, the *personnel* is as follows:

	Annual salary.
Joseph K. McCammon, commissioner	$4,500
F. B. Pickerill, bookkeeper	2,400
W. M. Thompson, assistant bookkeeper	2,000
Henry Blackstone, engineer	2,500
Luther W. Hickork, clerk	1,400
Miss Kate Schmidt, copyist	900
A. S. Seely, messenger	720
Thomas Hassard, (temporary) draughtsman	1,200
E. M. Hardin, (temporary) copyist	900
James S. Phillips, (temporary) copyist	900

Of the appropriations for this office for the fiscal year ending June 30, 1881, amounting to $15,700, the following sums have been expended, viz: Salaries, $12,897.21; traveling and incidental expenses, $2,199.07; in all, amounting to $15,096.28.

The appropriations for the current fiscal year ending June 30, 1882, are as follows: "Salaries, office of the commissioner of railroads," for commissioner, $4,500; bookkeeper, $2,400; assistant bookkeeper, $2,000; railroad engineer, $2,500; one clerk, $1,400; one copyist, $900; one messenger, $600=$14,300.   Traveling expenses, $2,500; contingent expenses, $300=$2,800; making in all, $17,100.

The estimates which have been submitted for the fiscal year ending June 30, 1883, are as follows: Commissioner, $5,000; bookkeeper, $2,500; assistant bookkeeper, $2,000; railroad engineer, $2,500; one clerk, $1,600; one clerk, $1,400; one copyist, $900; one messenger, 720= $16,620.   Traveling expenses, $3,000; contingent expenses, $500= $3,500; making in all, $20,120.

I take this opportunity to commend the general efficiency of the employés of the bureau.

I have the honor to be, sir, very respectfully, your obedient servant,

JOS. K. McCAMMON,
Commissioner.

Hon. SAMUEL J. KIRKWOOD,
Secretary of the Interior.

REPORT OF RAILROAD ENGINEER.

DEPARTMENT OF THE INTERIOR,
OFFICE OF. COMMISSIONER OF RAILROADS,
Washington, D. C., November 1, 1881.

SIR: The following is a report of the inspection of railroads named in the act of Congress approved June 19, 1878, establishing the office of Auditor of Railroad Accounts, made since my appointment as railroad engineer in February last.

Two inspection trips have been made within this period.   The first was made in the months of April, May, and June of the current year, and embraced the Missouri Pacific Railway, from Saint Louis to Pacific Station; the Saint Louis and San Francisco Railway, from Pacific to Wichita; the Atchison, Topeka and Santa Fé Railroad, from Wichita, via Newton, to Albuquerque and to Deming (the junction with the Southern Pacific Railroad of Arizona and New Mexico); the Atlantic and Pacific Railroad, from Albuquerque, running southwest a distance of about 160 miles, and terminating at a point west of Fort Wingate; the Visalia division of the Central Pacific Railroad; that portion of the Southern Pacific Railroad leased to the Central Pacific Railroad of Arizona and New Mexico; the Pacific and Pend D'Oreille divisions of the Northern Pacific Railroad; the Oregon and California Railroad and the Oregon Central Railroad; the Central Pacific Railroad; the Union Pacific Railway, including the Colorado division, running from Cheyenne to Denver; and the Chicago, Rock Island and Pacific Railway.

It is gratifying to find these roads in such general good condition, they having recently passed through a rather severe winter season, without sufficient time and opportunity for any general repair and surfacing of track, &c., showing that the improvements spoken of by my predecessor were of substantial character.   However, the favorable condition of these railroads, under all the circumstances, still leaves much to be done in order to bring them to that standard condition that true economy in their maintenance and operation suggests.

This last remark will apply particularly to the bridges.   Comparatively few of them are supplied with safety floors and iron guard-rails, to save trains that may be derailed from bunching the cross-ties or breaking the floor-beams and dashing through to the stream below, or from going through the side of the bridge.

766 PAPERS ACCOMPANYING THE

Ballast is in very limited supply at many points on the roads, and drainage is also much needed.

The second trip of inspection covered the period from August 18 to October 1, and the following-named roads were examined in detail: the Sioux City and Pacific Railway; the Saint Louis, Iron Mountain and Southern Railroad; the Kansas Division of the Union Pacific Railway; the Little Rock and Fort Smith Railroad; and the Central Branch Union Pacific Railroad.

There remains abundant opportunity for improvements in the bridges and trestles on many of these roads, as well as the widening of embankments and cuttings, in drainage, and in ballasting the road beds.

In the annual reports for 1879 and 1880, the railroad engineer has spoken very plainly of the defects in the floors of many of the bridges and trestles on the Western railroads; that especially are they wanting in the proper guard-rails to save derailed trains from going through bridges into the streams below; and cites one case where the coroner's jury report, among other defects, that the railroad company's "floor system in use at the time of the accident, while in accordance with approved practice at the time of its construction, was not altogether safe, and it lacked the necessary precaution against disaster resulting from derailed trains."

No satisfactory reason can be given for the failure to supply such guards as shall give to the traveling community satisfactory assurance of protection from destruction, in case of derailment of locomotive or cars in passing over bridges.

As iron or steel will probably be adopted in the place of wood in the construction of important bridges on all railroads built or to be built, there would seem to be a necessity for the provision of some satisfactory testing of the material to be used in their construction. It is equally desirable that a constructing engineer should either design the bridge or have the plans submitted to him for his approval.

In order to demonstrate the great disparity in the uniformity of train signals, your attention is invited to the table of "whistle signals in use on the railroads of the United States and Canada," compiled by W. F. Allen, and published in the Traveler's Official Guide for October, 1881. An examination of this table reveals the fact that among the two hundred roads embraced therein, with the exception of three short whistles for backing, there is no signal employed having the same meaning in all cases. I therefore earnestly recommend that the attention of Congress be invited to this subject, in order that the proper steps may be taken to establish a uniform system of signals throughout the United States.

In compiling this report, the several railroads have not been taken up in the order in which they were inspected, but have been considered, as far as practicable, in the same order as in former reports.

1st. Roads that have been aided with bonds, lands, right of way, &c., granted by the United States.

2d. Roads that have been aided with lands and right of way by the United States.

3d. Roads that have been aided with lands, right of way, &c., granted by the United States to sundry States for that purpose.

UNION PACIFIC RAILWAY.

This line is still operated in two grand divisions, viz, the Union Division, embracing the line from Council Bluffs to Ogden and controlled branches, and the Kansas Division, embracing the line from Kansas City to Cheyenne and controlled branches.

These grand divisions will each be considered separately.
The road owned is:

	Miles.
Council Bluffs to junction with Central Pacific	1,038.458
Kansas City (State line) to Denver	638.6
Leavenworth to Junction	31.9
Denver to Cheyenne	105.80
Total owned	1,814.848

Road controlled and operated June 30, 1881, was:

	Miles.
Omaha and Republican Valley	199.2
Omaha, Niobrara and Black Hills	162.9
Colorado Central	184
Saint Joseph and Western	252
Marysville and Blue Valley	50.6
Summit County	8
Utah and Northern	479.8
Carbondale Branch	32
Junction City and Fort Kearney	70
Solomon Railroad	57
Salina and Southwestern	51
Boulder Valley	27
Golden, Boulder and Caribou	6
Total	1,597.5

Five miles of the road owned, west from Ogden, is leased to the Central Pacific Company, leaving grand total owned and operated June 30, 1881, 3,412.348 miles.

UNION DIVISION, MAIN LINE, COUNCIL BLUFFS TO OGDEN.

Inspection was made in June, 1881.

Various improvements in alignment and grades, as well as in graduation and bridging, have been made. A very important change in grades, referred to in last year's report, at Elkhorn Hill, has been progressing. Up to June 1, 61,000 cubic yards of earth excavation had been removed and 52,502 cubic yards of embankment had been built, leaving at that date 78,248 cubic yards of excavation to be removed, and 65,000 cubic yards of embankment to be built, in order to finish that important improvement. The work is expected to be completed during the coming winter, when the maximum grade of 79.2 feet per mile will be reduced to 21 feet per mile. Many of the narrow embankments have been widened, and the line and surface of the track much improved; but there still remains considerable similar work to be done at various points on the road.

The floods and high-water of the spring of 1881 caused much damage to the road, overflowing and washing the embankments badly in the valley of Platte River, especially between Elkhorn and Columbus, a distance of 60 miles. Since that time much has been done in raising the grade of the road bed at the exposed points, in order to place it above similar high-water in the future. About one mile of track in the vicinity of Fremont has been raised 2 and 2½ feet; also at and near Elkhorn River bridge. Between Council Bluffs and Ogden there has been laid this year 17,559.5 tons of steel rails, weighing severally 56, 58, and 60 pounds per lineal yard. Taking 58 pounds as the average weight, the above amount of rails would be equivalent to 192.6 miles of track. Twenty-seven and one-quarter miles of new side track was laid this year.

There has been no change made in the frogs, switches, or targets within the present year. No considerable additions have been made in ballasting the track. Where it has been done it has been chiefly of gravel, which is accessible at a few points on the road.

The total number of cross-ties put into the track from January 1 to August 1, 1881, was 173,809 (covering about 66 miles of road, at 2,640 per mile). Of this number 32,777 were cedar, 122,293 common pine, and 18,739 oak, and cost, respectively, 55, 55, and 90 cents. This would hardly supply the natural decay and wear.

Ten iron truss bridges have been substituted for wooden bridges, generally in spans of 150 feet each, making a total of 1,535 feet of new iron bridging. Truss and pile bridges of the aggregate length of 5,345 feet have been rebuilt during the past year. The truss bridges have guard rails placed on them, to save derailed trains from passing off.

The specifications for the standard water station adopted consist of a circular frost-proof tank 24 feet in diameter and 16 feet in height, mounted on cast-iron columns, which are set on stone and concrete foundations; Halliday windmill, with wheels 25 feet in diameter.

The pump pits are lined with cast iron, and the wells 12 feet in diameter curbed with oak plank, iron bound. Water stations of the above description have been erected at the following-named stations between November 1, 1880, and October 1, 1881: At Gibbon, with well 26 feet deep; Brady Island, 15 feet deep; Kearney, 22 feet deep; Willow Island, 13 feet deep; at Echo the well was dug last year. At Clark's, water-works as described are in the course of construction and approaching completion. At North Bend and Columbus the tanks and wells have been replaced by new ones; at North Bend the well is 16 feet deep, and at Columbus 22 feet deep. New tanks are completed to replace the old ones at the following stations: Alkali, Ogalalla, Lodge Pole, and Potter.

A new water tank is being built at Laramie, to be supplied from a spring. At Rawlins the machinery for boring a well is being erected, but the boring not begun. At Fillmore and Table Rock, present depth of boring 750 feet each. At Salt Works, work is in same condition as at Rawlins.

Coal sheds on stone foundations are being erected at Columbus and at Medicine Bow; each shed contains 16 coal bins, with a capacity of 20 tons each, and 32 chutes, with a capacity of 4 tons each. For the convenient unloading of coal into the chutes, the cars are run into the building by locomotives.

Buildings for locomotives and car department have been added or are in contemplation at the following points, viz: At Omaha, car shops (wood) 200 by 300 feet, commenced; Grand Island, smith shop (stone) 75 by 150 feet, completed; car shop (stone) 100 by 150 feet, completed; North Platte (old engine-house destroyed by storm on the 25th June, 1881), new engine-house (brick), 25 stalls, completed; new boiler shops (brick), 50 by 125 feet, completed; oil house (brick), 40 by 60 feet, completed; and store room (brick), 40 by 60 feet, completed.

Cheyenne, smith shop (wood), 25 by 80 feet, completed; store room (wood), 25 by 40 feet, completed.

Rock Springs, engine-house (wood), 2 stalls, completed.

At Green River the following are contemplated: new machine and car shop (wood), 25 by 80; new pump and boiler house (wood), 26 by 34; and new smith shop (wood), 36 by 44.

New machinery has been placed in the shops at North Platte, Omaha, Laramie, Evanston, Rawlins, and Cheyenne.

The coal department has erected at the Carbon mines 14 tenement houses, engine-house, boiler-house, and dump-house, all of wood.

At Rock Spring mines, 12 tenements for white laborers, 18 tenements for Chinese laborers, engine and boiler house, and slack-house.

At Almy mines, 12 tenement houses for white laborers and 20 for Chinese laborers.

At Shelton, Denver Junction, and Echo, new passenger stations have been built, and at Denver Junction a freight depot and a dwelling-house for the agent.

Connecting roads, operated in the interest of the Union Pacific Railway, were extended during the year 1880 as follows:

	Miles.
Omaha and Republican Valley Railroad	67.2
Marysville and Blue Valley	12.6
Omaha, Niobrara and Black Hills	81.9
Echo and Park City	27.2
Utah and Northern	75.8
Selma and Southwestern	15
Making increased mileage	279.7

The Julesburg branch, extending from Denver Junction (on the main line) to Omaha Junction, on the Denver division, is located in the South Platte Valley, crossing the river 16 miles from Omaha Junction.

The length of the line is 151.16 miles, of which 131.4 miles are tangent. The maximum degree of curvature is one degree, and the total curvature of the line is but 769° 21'; the maximum grade, both east and west, is 15.84 feet per mile. The greater portion of this road is built on light embankments, with very few cuttings, thus securing cheap maintenance and immunity from snow blockades in winter.

Excellent water is readily obtained from wells and from the Platte River. The entire line is laid with steel rails; that portion of the track constructed in 1880 was of 56 pounds to the yard, and that of 1881 of 60 pounds to the yard.

The crossing of the South Platte is accomplished by an oak pile bridge, 2,800 feet in length, the work on which is rapidly approaching completion.

Another very important and extended branch, called the Oregon Short Line, leaves the main line at Granger, running northwest, crossing the Utah Northern Road at Port Neuf in Idaho, and extending to Baker City in Oregon, some 600 miles in length.

The company report 100 miles of road-bed graded, and 25 miles of track laid in September, and they are actively at work grading and preparing to extend the track to Baker City, there to connect with the Oregon Railway and Navigation Company's lines, thus reaching the Pacific coast by another and independent route, and opening a broad belt of country for occupancy.

The snow-sheds and fences have had no additions or extensions made to them, and have only received ordinary repair. Considerable further repair to both, to make them effective, should be made before the coming winter.

There are very valuable deposits of mineral on the line of the road, especially in iron and coal, and very large deposits of fine white sand, equal to the best in the country, and admirably adapted to manufacture of fine glass; also large deposits of soda. The extent and richness of some of these strata of iron ores (assaying from 60 to 70 per centum) in close proximity as they are to rich veins of bituminous coal, would invite capital to be employed in their manufacture for various uses and purposes, and especially for the manufacture of the "Bessemer" rail, for which there is, and will be for years to come, a large demand, in the maintenance of roads already constructed, as well as for those to be built in connection with the further development of this section of the country.

The strata of coal found at various points near the main line of the road are of various thicknesses, running from 4 and 5 feet to 9 feet, and

49 Ab

in some places to 27 feet in thickness. On the Oregon Short Line I am informed that the road is tunneled through a stratum of superior bituminous coal 80 feet in thickness, and of better quality than any other on the Union Pacific Railway.

The company report having contracted for 60,000 tons of steel rails for repairs of tracks and to lay extensions and branches now under construction.

KANSAS DIVISION, UNION PACIFIC.

This division was inspected in September, 1881.

There have been various and important improvements made in the past year. The permanent way has evidently received considerable attention, in order to place it in its present improved condition, more especially on the Smoky Hill division. At many points embankments have been widened, and the ditches received proper attention; but over a considerable portion of the road this class of work has been neglected.

Laborers are scarce and high prices demanded, but it would be poor economy to allow the road to run down because of increased expense in this particular.

The Kaw division has shared more largely in improvements than any other portion of the road. The short intervening sections of iron between the steel rail track have been removed, and the gaps filled with steel, thus making a continuous all steel rail track from the Kansas State line to the 174.6 mile, the remaining distance of 25.4 miles being laid with iron rails.

On the Smoky Hill division there are 50.8 miles of steel and 161.6 miles of iron-rail track, and on the Denver division 54.9 miles of steel and 161.6 miles of iron rails. There are no steel rails on the Cheyenne division. The total amount of steel track on the Kansas division is 280.3 miles, leaving 464.4 miles to be supplied. During the past year 662,678 new cross-ties have been used.

At Armstrong, Lawrence, Wamego, Salina, Brookville, Ellis, Cleveland, Wallace, Hugo, and Denver, new platforms have been erected; and coal chutes at Wamego, 28 pockets; Hugo, 24 pockets; Brookville, 24 pockets; Ellis, 24 pockets; Wallace, 28 pockets; and Denver, 28 pockets. A combination platform and chute of 4 pockets is also located at Cheyenne Wells.

Buildings, &c.

The company has made many additions in new buildings for shops, depots, &c., among which the following deserve mention: At Kansas City, frame freight house and office with extensive covered freight platform; at Armstrong, office, storehouse, and oil-house, with additions to locomotive, smith, and car-shops, dry-house, charcoal-house, and fire-department building; at Brookville and Collyer, station buildings; at Wallace, ice-house and tenement-house; at Box Elder, frame freight-house; at Denver, stone freight-house and office, stone oil and powder house, extensive open platforms, a stone engine-house with 28 stalls and very complete in all appointments, with office attached. Houses provided with tanks for storing oil have been erected at Brookville, Ellis, Wallace, and Denver.

Water supply.

Standard water-tanks with a capacity of 50,000 gallons each are located at the following points: Eureka Lake, Bismarck, Ellsworth, Black Wolf, Hays, Wakeeny, Collyer, Cleveland, Sheridan, Wallace, Cheyenne Wells,

Mirage, River Bend, Byer's Station, and Denver. Poage's standard water columns are located at Kansas City, Armstrong, Bismarck, and Wamego. New wells have been dug and windmills erected at Evans and Pierce.

Bridges.

Over all the principal streams where truss bridges are required, with the exception of Wolf Creek and Delaware River, wrought-iron structures have been erected.

CENTRAL PACIFIC RAILROAD.

Inspection of this road was made in June, 1881.

On June 30, 1881, the company was operating on the main line, branches, and leased lines 2,722.05 miles of railroad. Of this amount 1,204.50 miles are owned and 1,517.55 miles operated under lease. The line is in good order, the track being smooth, well ballasted and surfaced. Of the 1,204.50 miles owned by the company, it has received from the United States a grant of land for 1,012.47 miles of the road, and bonds to aid in the construction of 860.66 miles.

At Oakland the shops of the Western division are located, and consist of an engine-house with 24 stalls, machine, car, and blacksmith shops, and are well adapted for ordinary repairs.

The principal shops of the company are at Sacramento, and are extensive and complete in all their arrangements. The buildings are generally of brick, with galvanized-iron roofs, and comprise an engine-house with 25 stalls, machine, car, paint, boiler, and blacksmith shops, rolling-mill, furnaces for making locomotive and car springs, foundry for making car-wheels, castings, &c. The company also has shops and engine-houses at Rocklin, Truckee, Wadsworth, Winnemucca, Carlin, Wells, and Terrace. Between Blue Cañon and Truckee the company has established a very complete system of watchmen's signals, by telegraph and telephone, for use in the snow-sheds. The circuit is 41.3 miles in length, with 5 day and night telegraph stations and 34 boxes and 8 telephones as auxiliaries. There is also a dial having 12 numbers, which will give notice of any damage or accident that may occur.

A locomotive with water-cars is also stationed conveniently for the protection of the snow-sheds in case of fire.

The company report that during the past year no iron rails were laid in the main track; 96.73 miles were relaid with steel rails, nearly all of which weighed 60 pounds to the yard, and 205,608 new cross-ties were placed in the track. The length of the various sidings was increased 4.80 miles. The "Wharton" or the "Lorenz" safety switches have been adopted as the standard, 28 having been placed in the track during the past year.

No iron bridges or trestles were built during the year, nor any important renewals made in the wooden bridges or trestles other than necessary repairs required to keep them in safe condition.

The Humboldt bridge, near Oreana, was raised 23¾ inches, and new floor-beams, stringers, and cross-ties put on.

New standard frost-proof water-tanks have been constructed at the following points: Blue Creek, 50,000 gallons; Ogden, 50,400 gallons; and at Beowawe, Peko, and Stone-House 30,000 gallons each.

At Ogden Station new car repair shop, blacksmith shop, lumber-shed, section of new round-house, cattle-pens and platforms, oil and lamp house of brick, fuel-house, platforms, office, &c., were constructed.

Buildings for the accommodation of section gangs were erected at the following points : Deseret, Golconda, Humboldt, Mill City, Palisade, Quarry, Rose Creek, and Winnemucca. New transfer platforms have been built at Ogden, to replace those destroyed by fire in June last.

It is gratifying to note the progress of the work in improving the alignment and surface of the track and the removal of defective rails and decayed cross-ties ; but a liberal supply of broken stone or gravel ballast is much needed.

SOUTHERN PACIFIC RAILROAD.

Inspection was made in the latter part of April, 1881.

This road is leased by the Central Pacific Company, and extends from Huron, Cal., to the Colorado River at Fort Yuma, a distance of 530 miles. There is a land grant for the entire length of the road.

Near Pomona, about 215 miles west of Yuma, an extensive and valuable tin mine is now being worked

At Mojave there is an engine-house for 15 engines, which are chiefly employed on the 116-foot grades of the Tahatchapi Mountains. There is also a small repair shop at this point.

At Lancaster, Wilmington, and Santa Monica are frame engine-houses of one, two, and three stalls each.

At Tulare, the shops of the Visalia and Tulare divisions are located, and consist of an engine-house with 13 stalls, machine-shop, blacksmith-shop, and store-room and offices. These shops are supplied with tools for all ordinary work. There is an engine-house with 6 stalls, at Sumner.

At Los Angeles, the shops of the Yuma and Los Angeles divisions are located, and comprise an engine-house with 18 stalls, machine and car shop. A stationary engine building of brick, with iron roof, contains large store-rooms and offices of master mechanic and shop clerk of the division.

At Yuma, there is an engine-house of wood with 15 stalls, which is supplied with hand tools for doing light engine repairs, and a store and car tool-house.

The track and road bed are generally in very fair order, being smooth and well graded and the embankments in repair. The company report 340 miles of the entire distance of 550 miles, laid with 50-pound steel rails, and the balance with 56-pound iron rails. These are comparatively new. The road is ballasted with such material as was available, principally of sand, but occasionally gravel or broken stone is used.

The bridging is nearly all of pile and trestle, and conforms to the plans adopted on the Central Pacific Road.

There has been no material change in the station buildings during the past year.

The water supply over much of the road is deficient, both in quality and quantity, and water trains are run through much of the desert land for general supply, not only for locomotives, but for the employés along the road.

The tunnels are lined with wood, faced with galvanized sheet-iron as a protection against fire.

The Southern Pacific of Arizona and New Mexico, extends from Yuma, Cal., via El Paso, in Texas, to Deming, where it connects with the Atchison, Topeka and Santa Fé Railroad. This is not a subsidized road, but it forms an important link in the new southern route of the Central Pacific system.

The road and rolling stock are in very fair condition, and the shops and engine-houses at Yuma and Tucson are sufficient for the present business of the road.

The local traffic is almost entirely connected with the mining interest of the country, and in the rapid development of these mines the business of the road must necessarily be materially increased.

NORTHERN PACIFIC RAILROAD.

PACIFIC DIVISION.

Inspection of this division was made in May, 1881. No inspection was made of the Eastern division.

From Kalama the road extends a distance of 105 miles to Tacoma, on Puget's Sound, and is well graded and in good surface. The track is laid with 56-pound iron rails, with flat splice bars breaking joint on the same cross-ties, and is ballasted with gravel. The number of trestles on this line is a serious drawback, which can only be overcome at great expense by substituting embankments. The alignment is faulty, there being a number of places where sharp curves are reversed, with no tangents intervening, and at other places the tangents are too short.

All the bridges and trestles lack the necessary provisions for the protection of derailed trains.

The company have made some betterments during the year, among which may be mentioned the rebuilding of Youth River truss bridge, a span of 180 feet, and supplying stone masonry abutments; renewing the Olequa bridge of 120 feet span; renewing about 1,400 piles at the Tacoma wharf; laying 8 miles of steel rail track, &c.

The Puyallup branch extends from Tacoma to Carbondale, a distance of 34 miles, and is in a fair condition for a coal road. The track is laid with 56-pound iron rails, flat splice bars, with joints opposite and generally suspended between the cross-ties.

The company has shops at Tacoma for the repair of locomotives and cars; large warehouse; extensive coal wharves; and a large hotel, which is well kept.

The locomotives are fair, but the passenger cars are without air-brakes or safety platforms. The rolling stock is old style.

From Ainsworth, the company is extending its line eastward, and on May 20, 1881, had constructed 124 miles. Owing to the scarcity of timber, the cross-ties are laid 4 feet apart, but this defect will be remedied as soon as the track is extended into the timber region. About 8 miles is ballasted with gravel, the balance being unballasted.

The alignment is good, and the maximum grade 52.8 feet per mile, except in a few places, which will be reduced from 63.36 feet. The track is laid with 50-pound steel rails, with flat splice bars on tangents, and flat and angle bars on curves. The company has on hand and in transit steel rails to lay 80 miles of track. It has 8 water stations on this section of the road, and the water is generally of an excellent quality. There are also about 50 trestles, the longest of which is 90 spans of 16 feet each—1,440 feet. The telegraph line has been built for 57 miles, and a sufficient number of poles are on hand to finish the 124 miles.

No part of this line has been accepted by the President of the United States.

A tract to connect the road at Ainsworth with the Oregon Railway and Navigation Company's line at Wallula, a distance of 12 miles, has been completed, and the road used in common.

CENTRAL BRANCH UNION PACIFIC RAILROAD.

This company owns the subsidized line from Atchison to Waterville, Kans., a distance of 100 miles, and leases the lines of the Atchison, Colorado and Pacific Railway Company, 261 miles, making a total owned and leased of 361 miles; the whole being operated as a part of the Missouri-Pacific system.

Subsidized line.

Inspection was made in September, 1881.

The general characteristics of the road are very fair, the line quite direct, and the grades moderate. The line is undulating, the steeper grades being short, so that the momentum of the heavier trains aids materially in passing them over.

The whole length of the road was originally laid with iron rails 50 pounds per yard, and with the old style wrought-iron chair fastening. In the past year 19 miles of the track have been relaid with new rails of 54 and 56 pounds per yard, and 12 miles of the track have had the chairs removed and their places supplied with the double-angle splice bar. There are 1½ miles of steel rail track at Atchison, which is all the steel rail in the entire road.

A number of new sidings have been laid during the past year for the more convenient passing of trains and the loading and unloading of freight at stations; their total length being 11,000 feet.

During the year 60,000 white-oak cross-ties have been put into the track, at a cost of 55 cents each, and 11 miles of the road have been ballasted with stone, and 10 miles with good gravel. The company expect to continue this operation until the whole road shall be thoroughly ballasted.

There are eleven bridges in all on the road; ten are of the Howe truss pattern, one of three spans, and nine of one span each. The one over Clay Creek has been renewed with a double track steel plate bridge. One of the Howe truss bridges was renewed in the last year, and several of them in 1879 and 1880; and all are in good condition. There are 16 pieces of trestling of various lengths, from 20 to 130 feet each; the spans are from 16 to 20 feet each, resting on abutments and piers of masonry, and generally in good condition.

Several of the embankments, where they had settled, have been raised to grade and widened to proper dimensions. Many of the cuts have also been widened and proper ditches provided, but there still remains considerable similar work to be done.

A fair force is employed in the maintenance of way, there being from 8 to 10 men on each subdivision of 5 or 6 miles, two gravel trains with a force of 30 men on each, besides extra gangs of men employed in raising sunken embankments, surfacing of track, and laying new iron in the track. This force should, in a short time, make a decided improvement in the condition of the road bed and superstructure.

About 20 bridge carpenters are also employed in the work of repair and reconstruction of bridges and trestles.

A new passenger and freight depot has been built at Bigelow Station; one new water station with two frost-proof tanks 16 by 36 feet, and more; a new coal platform 16 by 130 feet, with five chutes for loading engines, at Atchison; and a new wood turn-table, 50 feet, at Greenleaf. With the exception of an addition to the machine-shops, a new foundry and stationary engine room, and a new shop for painting cars, the buildings of the company remain about the same as last year.

CHICAGO, ROCK ISLAND AND PACIFIC RAILROAD.

This company has received aid in lands granted the State of Iowa for 317.75 miles between Davenport and Council Bluffs.

Inspection was made on regular train; but as a considerable portion of the journey was traveled at night, there was no favorable opportunity for a satisfactory examination; but, so far as could be observed, the road generally was in fair condition. There are parts, however, where it is not in good order, the road bed being narrow, the ditches foul, and the ballasting deficient. These defects should be remedied promptly, and the road kept in first-class condition, so that express trains could make more than 22 miles per hour.

The track is being laid throughout with steel rails, generally ballasted with gravel, and the cross-ties are in good condition. There is a double track from Chicago to Morris, a distance of over 60 miles. The rolling stock is first-class and in good condition.

The wrought-iron bridges crossing the Mississippi and Missouri rivers appear to be sufficient to meet any demands that may be made upon their strength. The wooden bridges were not examined closely, but appear to be well constructed.

ATLANTIC AND PACIFIC RAILROAD.

Inspection was made in the latter part of April, 1881.

This company was incorporated by act of Congress, approved July 27, 1866.

After a long period of inactivity, this company finally began the construction of its road from Albuquerque, N. Mex., westward, and on December 17, 1880, 50 miles had been inspected and accepted by the President of the United States. On March 29, 1881, two other sections of 25 miles each had been accepted, making in all, 100 miles of completed road. Since the latter date, the road has been extended to Navajo Springs Station, and is now opened for public use a distance of 213 miles west of Albuquerque.

The location of this line has been carefully and judiciously made, being generally in light embankments, thus making a road-bed of cheap construction and easy maintenance. The maximum degree of curvature on the accepted portion of the road is 8°. The grades are also quite moderate, the maximum being 52.8 feet per mile.

The track is laid throughout with 56-pound American steel rails, and the joints secured with the Sampson fish-plate on each side. The cross-ties are principally of yellow pine, and are laid 2,816 to the mile. White-oak ties are used in the curves. There is but little broken stone or gravel ballast on the road, earth being used for filling between the cross-ties. The excavations and embankments are generally of full width, but the ditches require cleaning. The company has five sidings of 1,600 feet each, on the western section of fifty miles. A telegraph line has been constructed over the 100 miles, and is provided with suitable buildings for offices.

The rolling stock is all new and of superior build, and ample for all demands likely to be made upon it.

There are no Howe truss bridges on this part of the road. Pile bridges have been exclusively used except where there was solid rock in the stream bed, in which case, framed bents, with the sills securely bolted to the rocks, were used. The spans are uniformly 15 feet each, and from

4 to 24 feet in height. The timbers are of Michigan and native pine, the posts and caps being 12 by 12 inches, and the stringers of three pieces 7 by 16 inches each, securely bolted together. Wooden guard rails are used. All of the culverts are of wood, with the exception of four, which are of stone, 3 by 4 feet.

Standard frost-proof water-tanks with a capacity of about 35,000 gallons each, are located at the following points: Isleta, El Rita, McCarty's, Grant, Blue Water, Cranes, Gallup, Manulito, and Houcks.

Among the substantial improvements made by the company, the following are noticeable:

At Albuquerque: section of a stone engine-house with six stalls; wrought-iron turn-tables, machine, carpenter, and blacksmith shops; and the general offices, built of adobe, 50 by 70 feet, two stories, with stone foundations. At Cranes: stone engine-house with 6 stalls, and wrought-iron turn-tables. Materials are on hand for the construction of a depot building, smith shop, and a hotel.

ATCHISON, TOPEKA AND SANTA FÉ RAILROAD.

Inspection was made in the latter part of April, 1881.

Under an act of Congress approved March 3, 1863, granting lands to the State of Kansas to aid in the construction of certain railroad and telegraph lines, this road received aid for 470.58 miles, extending from Atchison to the western boundary of the State.

On June 30, 1880, the company owned 470.58 miles, and leased 843.42 miles, making a total of 1,314 miles owned and operated. Since that date it has extended its line as follows: The Marion and McPherson Branch, from McPherson to Lyons, 30.6 miles; the Cowley, Sumner and Fort Smith Branch, from Wellington to Caldwell, 23.3 miles; the Manhattan, Alma and Burlingame Railway, connecting with the Union Pacific, 56.6 miles, making a total of 110.5 miles of extension in Kansas. The Pueblo and Arkansas Valley Railroad has been extended from Pueblo to the salt works at Rockvale, a distance of 37 miles in Colorado.

The main line was completed April 15, 1880, to Albuquerque, N. Mex., a distance of 250.4 miles from the boundary line between Colorado and New Mexico, and on October 1, 1880, to San Marcial, 102½ miles further.

Connection was made with the Southern Pacific Railroad at Deming, in March, 1881.

During the year the company relaid 133.2 miles with steel rails, 25.6 miles with iron rails, and renewed 472,828 cross-ties; but heavy repairs are still needed to put the track in proper condition. With this object in view, the company has contracted for 25,000 tons of steel rails and 550,000 cross-ties, to be placed in the track during the coming year.

The company report large additions to its rolling stock, about $250,000 having been expended for that purpose during the year. It has also contracted for the delivery, during the coming year, of 50 locomotives, 15 passenger, 7 baggage, 7 postal, and 2,500 freight cars.

The general condition of the bridges on the road has been improved. One new span has been supplied in the bridge over the Kansas River at Topeka; one steel plate girder bridge at Atchison, and several of the wooden truss bridges have been rebuilt; and, west of Nickerson, a number of the pile bridges have been renewed.

The company has built 40.1 miles of fencing on the main line and branches in the past year, and expects to make large additions in the future, having paid $31,528.47 damages for live stock killed during the year.

The buildings of the company have been kept in good condition and many new structures have been added, among which are a large brick union depot and hotel, and a stone freight-house at Atchison; a brick passenger depot at Topeka, five station-houses and offices, and 12 section foremen's houses. A new stone machine-shop and two blocks of tenement houses are in course of construction at Eaton, and the dining hall has been removed from Larkin to Sargent, and considerably enlarged.

The company has ordered the erection of new passenger depots at Lawrence, Emporia, and other points, and round-houses at Kansas City, Topeka, Lawrence, Florence, Newton, Dodge City, Sargent, La Junta, and Trinidad.

Machine-shops, with the necessary tools, have also been built at these points, and coal-chutes, water-stations, and section-houses where needed.

SAINT LOUIS AND SAN FRANCISCO RAILWAY.

Inspection of the Eastern Division, from Pacific to Pierce City, 253 miles, and of the Kansas Division, from Pierce City to Wichita, 218 miles, was made in the latter part of April, 1881.

At the present time the company operates the same lines as in 1879, viz:

	Miles.
Road owned:	
From Pacific, Mo., to line of Indian Territory	293
Leased:	
Atlantic and Pacific, in Indian Territory	34
Saint Louis, Wichita and Western, Pierce City, Mo., to Oswego, Kans., and branch to Joplin, Mo	83
Missouri and Western, Oswego, Kans., to Wichita, Kans	144
Joplin Railroad; Joplin, Mo., to Girard, Kans	38
Joint use of track, Saint Louis to Pacific, Mo	37
Total leased	336
Total leased and operated	629

This road passes through a range of rich farming lands extending from Pierce to the neighborhood of Rolla, thence entering the Ozark Hills. This latter section abounds in scrub oaks, but as it is rapidly being cleared up, the lands improve in value.

The traffic of the road is derived principally from the Missouri, Kansas and Texas Railway, and the Joplin Railroad extending into the lead region. The transportation of iron ore to the Saint Louis market is an important item of its local business.

Valuable improvements have been added during the year. The bridge across Beaver Valley, near Rolla—800 feet in length—has been removed, the crossing filled with embankment, and a stone arched culvert of 24 feet span substituted. In order to complete this work it required 1,590 cubic yards of masonry and 160,000 cubic yards of embankment, at a cost of $48,000.

The wooden bridges on this line have, with one exception, been renewed within the last three years. The combination bridge across the Gasconade River at Arlington was built in 1874, but the timbers for its renewal are being delivered and will be put in place this season.

Between Pacific and Springfield three spans of wrought iron—two of 150 each and one of 162 feet—have been erected. Two spans of 100 feet each, two of 50 feet each, two of 40 feet each, and three of 30 feet each, have been contracted for. The masonry is generally in good order. All wrought-iron bridges are proportioned for the heaviest traffic and are provided with guard-rails.

The track has been improved by the supply of 95 miles of steel rails and 150,000 cross-ties, and 6½ miles of side track have been added during the year. Sixty per centum of the road is tangent. The maximum grade is 100 feet, and the maximum degree of curvature is 10°.

Springfield to Vinita—123 miles.

An iron bridge of 100 feet span was erected at Verona last year, and all bridges on this section have been renewed since 1878. Four of them were raised a sufficient height to place them above high water. New pile trestles were built near Pierce City, and the masonry generally repaired, and all are now in good condition.

A new station building has been erected at Plymouth, the junction of the Arkansas Branch, and extensive renewals of cross-ties have been made.

Sixty per centum of this section is tangent, the maximum degree of curvature is 4°, and the maximum grade 60 feet per mile.

The principal shops are located at Springfield, and comprise an engine-house with twelve stalls, machine, car, and paint shops, iron turn-table, water-station, &c. The machine-shop is supplied with machinery for turning driving-wheels, hydraulic press, quartering and facing machines, steam hammer, planer, 60 inches by 17 feet, &c., and is sufficient for the present needs of the company.

KANSAS DIVISION.

Pierce City, Mo., to Wichita, Kans.—218 miles.

About 145 miles of this division was built during the years 1879 and 1880. Portions of the road are ballasted with broken stone, but it is generally filled in with earth. The track is all laid with steel rails and is in good surface, but many of the ditches require cleaning. All important streams are crossed on wrought-iron bridges, resting on substantial masonry. Eighty-five per centum is tangent, the maximum degree of curvature is 4°, and the maximum grade 63 feet per mile.

ARKANSAS DIVISION.

From Plymouth to Fayetteville—68½ miles.

No inspection of this division was made; but it is reported that the track has been laid for a distance of 35 miles, and construction is progressing at the rate of three-fourths of a mile per day. The road is opened for business to Seligman, 30 miles.

The short branches from Oronogo to Joplin, and from Girard to Joplin, were not inspected.

The road from Pacific to Pierce City, and from Pierce City to Wichita, is being extensively laid with steel rails, secured with double fish plates and the Verona nut lock. More ballast of broken stone or gravel is required over much of the road, and the proper cleansing of the ditches suggested.

SAINT LOUIS, IRON MOUNTAIN AND SOUTHERN RAILWAY

Inspection was made in September, 1881.

The Saint Louis, Iron Mountain and Southern Railroad was incorporated January 12, 1867. The Saint Louis, Iron Mountain and Southern Railway was organized May 6, 1874, by consolidation with the

Arkansas Branch, the Cairo and Fulton, and the Cairo, Arkansas and Texas Railroad Companies. The through line was opened for traffic in 1874, and the gauge of the road (formerly 5 feet) changed to the standard June 29, 1879.

The total length of the main line is:

	Miles.
From Saint Louis, Mo., to Texarkana, Ark.................................	488.5
Branch, Poplar Bluff to Bird's Point.................................	71
Branch, Bismarck to Columbus...	121
Branch, Mineral Point to Potosi	4
	—— 196
Total length of road..	684.5

Of this distance, the line from Pilot Knob to Poplar Bluff, 80 miles, and from Bird's Point to Texarkana, 393.5 miles, making a total of 473.5 miles, has received aid in lands under the act of February 9, 1853, granting "land to the States of Missouri and Arkansas to aid in the construction of a railroad from a point on the Mississippi, opposite the mouth of the Ohio River, via Little Rock, to the Texas boundary near Fulton, with branches to Fort Smith and the Mississippi River."

The road passes through a country of varied soil, and is thickly interspersed with valuable timber, white oak and cypress being the prevailing growths.

The alignment of the road is very direct. Ninety-five per centum of the Arkansas and Texas divisions (394 miles) is tangent, and the sharpest curvature on the line is 8°. From Little Rock to Piedmont the road is practically level, with grades so short that the momentum of trains aids materially in passing them without difficulty. On Hogan Mountain, for a distance of 3½ miles, the grades are 98 to 103 feet per mile, and on the next 3 miles they are from 65 to 80 feet; but it is intended to reduce them all to 45 feet per mile.

The line was originally laid with iron rails of 56 pounds per yard, the joints breaking on the same cross-ties and fastened with the flat splice bar. At the present time 436 miles of the track have been relaid with steel rails of 60 pounds per yard, with double splice angle bars. The cross-ties are generally of oak, sound in appearance, and evenly distributed. The "Elliott" steel frog and the split-rail switch are used. The switch stands have targets, but no provision is made for lighting them at night.

The Arkansas Division had, on January 1 last, 64 miles of broken stone and gravel ballast. Since that date the Arkansas and Texas Division has been supplied with 6 miles of broken stone and 34 miles of gravel ballast. The company is pushing this class of work energetically, and it is contemplated that the remaining 220 miles will be properly ballasted within the next two years.

The company owns a valuable quarry at Ball Knob, 287 miles west of Saint Louis. It is of an excellent quality of sandstone, easily split into desirable sizes and shapes for bridge and other masonry, and is extensively used for ballast.

The principal shops are located at Saint Louis, De Soto, Belmont, Baring Cross, and Texarkana, and consist of machine, boiler, smith, car, and paint shops, engine-houses, &c., and are sufficient for the present needs of the road. Engine-houses are located at Saint Louis, De Soto, Belmont, Iron Mountain, Bismarck, Piedmont, Baring Cross, and Texarkana.

There are 16 turn-tables, 8 track scales, and 39 water-stations, with capacity of cisterns ranging from 16,000 to 48,500 gallons, distributed at suitable points along the line of road.

On the four divisions of the road there are 62 Howe truss bridges, of 100 to 150 feet; 5 Carter combination bridges, of 130 to 150 feet, and 9 truss-girder bridges, of 30 to 50 feet span each, all of wood, and in general good condition; but many of them will require renewal in the near future. In addition to these, there are three wooden bridges, which the company has made provision to replace by iron superstructures, viz, the Ouachita bridge will be three spans of 135 feet each, the Saline bridge two spans of 135 feet each, and the Little Red bridge, with one draw span of 263 feet, and one fixed span of 114½ feet.

There are 61 wooden and 46 stone culverts of various spans, and 384 pieces of trestling, ranging from 8 to 1,300 feet in length, all in general good order.

The road is well supplied with sidings; the Saint Louis Division having 71.08 miles; the Arkansas Division, 28.28 miles; the Texas Division. 18.43 miles; the Belmont Branch of the Missouri Division, 17.46 miles: and the Cairo Branch, 22.6 miles, making a total of 157.85 miles, or about 23 per cent. of the entire length of the main line.

A considerable portion of the road runs through a flat country where the water stands on the surface through much of the summer season. and it is difficult and expensive to do the ditching in the ordinary way. but the superintendent, Mr. Buchanan, has invented and put in operation a machine which does the work rapidly and economically.

THE MISSOURI DIVISION.

This division extends from Poplar Bluff, on the main line, to Bird's Point, on the Mississippi, opposite Cairo, with which it is connected by a steam ferry. The inconvenience of this connection with other roads is a serious drawback, and can only be obviated by the construction of a bridge across the Mississippi River.

The alignment of this branch is very direct. Not over 5 miles of its entire length is curved, the maximum being 3°. The grades are almost level, with the exception of a stretch of 2,000 feet, which is 52.8 feet. and three short grades of 40 feet per mile.

The track is laid throughout with iron rails of 50 pounds per yard. About 5 miles is of British and the remainder of Cambria iron. As these rails have been in the track for nine years, many of them are considerably worn and require renewal. The old chair fastening is used on 5 miles, and the flat splice bar on the balance of the road. No angle splice bars are in the track.

The cross-ties are of white oak and cypress, and are generally laid 3,000 to the mile, but in a few places they are 2 feet from center to center. The embankments are narrow and require widening, and the ditches for a large portion of the road should be cleaned.

Bridges and trestles are numerous on this division of the road, and there seems to be no available remedy of the difficulty, as the broad flat lands are flooded in the spring, and require large openings for the outflow of the waters. There are three Howe truss bridges, one of 70 feet and two of 140 feet span each, and 210 pieces of trestling, placed on pile foundations, ranging from 10 to 2,000 feet in length.

Two new passenger and freight stations have been erected during the year. There are four frost-proof water-tanks and eight foremen's houses on this division.

The road is fenced for a distance of 40 miles, 6 miles being of wire, miles of rail, and the balance of board.

LITTLE ROCK AND FORT SMITH RAILROAD.

Inspection was made in September, 1881.

This road extends from Argenta, opposite Little Rock, to Fort Smith, Arkansas, a distance of 165 miles. It passes up the Arkansas Valley on the north side of the river to Van Buren, thence south to Fort Smith.

The location of the road is not beyond criticism, and at many points improvements might have been made with profit to the company.

The crossing of the Arkansas River at Van Buren is made by means of a steam ferry-boat capable of carrying two passenger or four loaded freight cars, but the company proposes, at an early date, to erect a substantial iron bridge at this point.

The entire road is laid with iron rails of 56 pounds to the yard, but many of them are badly worn and require renewal. The cross-ties are 6 by 8 inches and 8½ feet in length, and are laid 2,640 to the mile. There is very little broken stone or gravel ballast, earth being generally used. The switches are of the square stub pattern, with the exception of a few of the French split pattern.

The cuts and embankments require widening, and the ditches should be cleaned.

There are two combination bridges on the road, each of 200 feet span, one being of the Pratt patent and one of the Post patent, and ten covered Howe truss bridges of 75 to 150 span each, resting on first class masonry, all being in good condition. A Pratt iron bridge will be substituted this fall for the Post combination bridge. There are also about 200 open culverts ranging from 4 to 30 feet span, and 30 pieces of trestling from 30 to 100 feet in length. They are also in good condition, having had about 300,000 feet of timber put in them in renewals during the year.

During the year the company has erected 5 new depot buildings, all conveniently arranged for passengers and freight. The company also contemplates building a new passenger station at Fort Smith, where it is much needed, and a passenger and freight depot at Russell Station.

There are ten water-stations on the road, none of them being frost-proof, as that is unnecessary in this climate. Three are supplied by horse-power pumps, one by hot-air engine, and six by steam-power. All of the water is of good quality with the exception of that pumped from the Arkansas River, which is foul and muddy and clogs the boilers very badly.

OREGON AND CALIFORNIA RAILROAD.

Inspection was made during the latter part of May, 1881.

This road is located in the valley between the Coast and Cascade ranges of mountains, and extends from Portland to Roseburg, a distance of 197.36 miles. It has a land grant of ten alternate sections from Portland to the south boundary of the state, the design being that it should connect with the Oregon Branch of the Central Pacific, formerly the California and Pacific Railroad. Both of these roads are unfinished, and have made no progress during the past year.

The track for the first three miles is laid with iron rails, then 15 miles with 56 pound steel rails, and thence on to Roseburg with iron rails. Flat splice bars are used on the iron rails and flat and angle bars on the steel rails. Stub switches with targets and steel rail frogs are used.

The road is generally ballasted with gravel, very little broken stone being supplied.

All of the bridges are of the Howe truss pattern, the one at Eugene City having been renewed within the year. They have no masonry under them, but are supported on cribbing or trestling. There are over 60,000 feet of trestling on the entire road, and one long piece was renewed last year. The bridge floors are provided with guard rails.

The rolling stock is in fair condition, but the passenger and baggage cars are not supplied with patent air-brakes nor with safety platforms.

The traffic of this road is largely dependent upon the transportation of wheat, and many thousands of tons are now stored awaiting an advance in the price of that article before being shipped.

The company has an engine-house with 10 stalls, a machine shop, car shop, and a blacksmith shop, all of limited extent and not in good condition. With the exception of one new building, no change has been made in passenger and freight stations.

The company still owns and operates the steam ferry across the Willamette River, at Portland, which is kept in good condition.

WEST SIDE DIVISION, FORMERLY THE OREGON CENTRAL RAILROAD.

Inspection was made the latter part of May, 1881.

This road extending from Corvallis to Saint Joseph, a distance of 50 miles, was built in 1879, under the name of the Western Oregon Railroad Company, and is laid throughout with steel rails of 50 pounds per yard.

The alignment and grades are very fair, but near the city of Portland there is a short grade of 198 feet per mile, and a curve of 12°. The track for three-fourths of its length is in good order and ballasted with gravel. The graduation has been well done, the road-bed is kept in fair condition, and the ditches well cleaned.

The character of the country through which the greater portion of the road passes is well adapted to the construction of a cheap line, but near Portland it becomes very uneven, crossing deep ravines and streams on high bridges and trestles, and, owing to the treacherous nature of the soil, makes it difficult to maintain a road-bed in permanent and good condition.

SIOUX CITY AND PACIFIC RAILROAD.

Inspection was made in September, 1881.

This company owns and operates railroads as follows, viz:

	M'···
Owned:	
Sioux City, Iowa, to Missouri Valley, Iowa, and Fremont, Nebr	1·7.4.
Leased:	
Fremont, Elkhorn and Missouri Valley	1(·)
Total owned and operated	217 -4

The alignment of the road is very direct. On the Iowa Division from Missouri Valley to Sioux City, a distance of 75.7 miles, 94.8 per cent is tangent. The sharpest curvature on the subsidized portion of the road is 4°.

The total length of the road in Iowa, from Sioux City to the middle of the Missouri transfer, is reported as 74.63 miles, and from the middle of the Missouri transfer to Fremont, the end of the subsidized portion of the road, 26.95 miles.

The road throughout its entire length is laid with American iron rails, 56 pounds per yard, breaking joint opposite on the same cross-tie, and are connected with the flat splice bar, except in case of renewal, when the angle splice bar is used. Much of the track is badly worn and requires large renewals. Many varieties of frogs were used in the track as originally laid, but all renewals are of the steel rail pattern. The stub or square switch, with painted vanes, is exclusively used, and on the Iowa Division all of the switch stands are revolving so that signal lights can be used upon them.

Connection between the lines at the Missouri River is still made by means of a steam ferry, and is a serious drawback to all their operations. Owing to the frequent shiftings of the channel of the river, the location of the inclined tracks is liable to constant change and an entirely new arrangement of them. These shiftings are so great and so continuous as to discourage the selection of any site for a bridge at this point.

There are three Pratt combination bridges on this road: one at Sioux City, over Perry Creek, 80 feet span; one across Floyd River, 180 feet span; and one across the Little Sioux River, 160 feet span. These have all been built since March, 1878, and are apparently in good order. There are 61 pieces of trestling of various lengths from 10 to 190 feet, but there is no masonry under any bridge or piece of trestle on the road, piles and timber abutments being used. There are no Howe truss bridges on the road.

The freight house at Missouri Junction, which was burned in October, 1880, has been rebuilt on about the same area, but with extended platforms. No new stations or foremen's houses, or water stations, have been built during the year, but extensive repairs have been made to a number of them.

The company has an engine-house with 8 stalls, and shops for the ordinary repair of locomotives and cars at Missouri Junction; an engine-house with 4 stalls at Sioux City; and an engine-house with 7 stalls at Blair. Turn-tables and "Y's" are located at Sioux City and Missouri Junction.

During the year the company has made the following additions to its rolling stock: two new passenger and three new freight locomotives of an average weight of 32 tons, 4 passenger, 150 box, 50 flat, and 50 stock cars, but they are all held by trustees. It has also added two caboose cars built in the company's shops.

The company report that it has extended its road from Missouri Valley to Atkinson, 210 miles, and intends to construct about 100 miles further to Fort Niobrara. It has also built a branch from Norfolk, extending 42 miles towards the town of Niobrara.

It is confidently looking forward to large additions in freights, especially in live stock, and has commenced the erection of extensive cattle yards, amply supplied with water, with a view to accommodate this class of business.

CONCLUSION.

It is gratifying to observe the large improvements already attained, but as the population and business interests of the country continue to increase, the railroads must conform to the additional demands to be made upon them in the transportation of passengers and of manufactured, agricultural, and mineral products. It is also very important that they should be thoroughly equipped with all the modern appliances for comfort and safety, and that special attention should be given to the approval of the plans and the inspection of all materials used in the construction of bridges and trestles, in order that danger of accidents may be reduced to the minimum.

It affords me pleasure to acknowledge the uniform courtesy extended by officers of all the roads it has been my duty to examine.

Very respectfully,

H. BLACKSTONE,
Railroad Engineer.

Hon. JOSEPH K. McCAMMON,
Commissioner of Railroads, Department of the Interior.

REPORT OF THE SUPERINTENDENT OF CENSUS.

DEPARTMENT OF THE INTERIOR,
CENSUS OFFICE,
Washington, D. C., November 1, 1881.

SIR: I have the honor to present the annual report of the operations of this bureau. The last annual report bore date the 1st of December. 1880. In the interval the field-work of the census has been completed in all the departments, except those relating to the statistics of ship-building, to the production of petroleum, the quarrying industry, and to the population, resources, etc., of Alaska. Owing to the difficulty of securing the proper agents, the field-work in these departments was not begun until long after the others were in full operation, and the completion of the work has consequently been delayed. Only a few weeks of field-work, however, now remain to be performed by the six agents still employed in these departments.

The year has also witnessed the rapid progress of the tabulations and compilations required to reduce the raw material of the enumeration into statistical form.

It is perhaps not generally understood that nearly as many days' labor are required to complete the tabulations and compilations at the central office as are needed to perform the entire work of enumeration in the field. An efficient enumerator can, in a city, or even in a well-settled rural district, take down, upon a page of his schedules, the names of fifty persons living in ten families, with all the particulars required by law to be collected, in a shorter time than the same man could distribute those fifty names according to the various classes of facts taken for compilation, viz, by age, by sex, by color, by place of birth, by occupation, by the places of birth of parents, by illiteracy, by conjugal condition, etc., and make all the various combinations thereof which go to form the tables usually published in the census reports.

The work of tabulation and compilation has been pressed forward with great rapidity, from the fact that the Superintendent felt that it was of the highest consequence to secure an early publication of the results of the census. In the last annual report of the bureau the number of persons employed on the 1st of December, 1880, was stated as 1,084. The maximum of clerical force was reached on the 15th of March, 1881, when the number of employés of all grades was 1,495.

The co-operation of so large a clerical force has allowed a very rapid progress in the compilation and tabulation of results. Five-sixths, at least, of the clerical labor of the census has already been accomplished. The results of the compilations are now being put into the form of tables for publication.

The following statement gives the population of the several States and Territories, as finally determined. The total differs by 2,917 from that contained in the report of this office under date of January 7, 1881. This, however, is but the net result of individual changes, amounting to many times that number, due to the exclusion of persons twice returned in the census (as, for instance, once at their homes, and again in asylums, prisons, almshouses, etc.), and to the supplying of the names, in even greater number, of persons ascertained to have been omitted from the enumeration.

Population of the United States, according to the Census of 1880.

Alabama	1,262,505
Arizona	40,440
Arkansas	802,525
California	864,694
Colorado	194,327
Connecticut	622,700
Dakota	135,177
Delaware	146,608
District of Columbia	177,624
Florida	269,493
Georgia	1,542,180
Idaho	32,610
Illinois	3,077,871
Indiana	1,978,301
Iowa	1,624,615
Kansas	996,096
Kentucky	1,648,690
Louisiana	939,946
Maine	648,936
Maryland	934,943
Massachusetts	1,783,085
Michigan	1,636,937
Minnesota	780,773
Mississippi	1,131,597
Missouri	2,168,380
Montana	39,159
Nebraska	452,402
Nevada	62,266
New Hampshire	346,991
New Jersey	1,131,116
New Mexico	119,565
New York	5,082,871
North Carolina	1,399,750
Ohio	3,198,062
Oregon	174,768
Pennsylvania	4,282,891
Rhode Island	276,531
South Carolina	995,577
Tennessee	1,542,359
Texas	1,591,749
Utah	143,963
Vermont	332,286
Virginia	1,512,565
Washington	75,116
West Virginia	618,457
Wisconsin	1,315,497
Wyoming	20,789
Grand total	**50,155,783**

In the appendix to this report will be found tables exhibiting the distribution of Representatives in Congress, according to the Tenth Census, upon the plan heretofore pursued in determining the number to which each State has become entitled.

A second series of tables exhibits the distribution of Representatives

50 Ab

according to the scheme proposed by Col. O. W. Seaton, the
of the bureau, who has been nominated to the Senate and
confirmed as my successor in office. Colonel Seaton
he has taken for determining the number of Represent
each State has become entitled more equitable than the
employed, and in that opinion I concur.

During the first half of 1881, the suspension of the work
tion in this office was threatened by a very serious obst
the failure of the appropriation for the service.

When, on the 5th of January last, this office recommend
tional appropriation of $500,000, to complete the work of th
was done in perfectly good faith, in the belief that the sum n
be adequate to that end. At that time, however, a very la
the field-work in the departments of mining, manufactures
statistics, still remained to be done. The cost of completing
has been found to be heavier than was at the time anticipa
over, the tabulations which had been undertaken in the ce
upon a scale far exceeding that of any preceding census
be more laborious and expensive than was expected. Ano
of expense beyond the estimates of the Superintendent, and
as important as either of the two just indicated, has been f
occasions, which have developed in the course of our investi
securing accuracy and completeness in the statistical mater
into the office by the enumeration, beyond the degree he
tempted in a census of the United States.

When I had the honor to submit the several reports of the
sus I felt compelled, in simple truthfulness, to say, in respe
few of the tables comprised in the three volumes, that th
contained were, to a great extent, incomplete and defective,
some cases the material gathered by the enumeration was
cient or inaccurate that it would be more creditable not to
tables at all, did the Superintendent feel at liberty to sup
Remarks of this character will be found scattered through
umes of the Ninth Census.

During the years that have intervened, the investigations
of the Superintendent have deepened his conviction of the
and inaccuracy of many classes of statistics as gathered
enumerations under the act of May 23, 1850.

It is doubtful, for instance, whether any of the three cen
under that law has obtained one-half of our mineral prod
compassed two-thirds of the total number of the defective,
and delinquent classes (the deaf and dumb, blind, insane, idiot
and criminals), who have by law been made the subjects
enumeration.

In regard to still other large classes of statistics, the pe
omission or error has not been equally great; but in all d
of investigation, concerning alike agriculture, manufactur
mining interests of the country, as well as education, p
ities, the wages of labor, and other departments of soci
the statistics of the United States census have failed to p
validity and authority which were to be desired, by reason
or suspected error. Much was done to improve the char
classes of statistics to be recorded in the census, through
of the enlightened law of March 3, 1879. Greatly wid
of the census was by that enactment, I venture to
provement in the quality of the statistical material ga
marked than the extension in amount; yet, notwith

value of the material brought into the central office through the new agencies provided by the act of 1879, opportunities for revision and correction have frequently presented themselves in the course of the examination and tabulation of that material. Of such opportunities the Superintendent has not been able to refrain from availing himself, whenever the cost was not disproportionate to the value of results. Instead of publishing table after table, as he was obliged to do in 1870, branded as fragmentary and incomplete, if not altogether inaccurate and misleading, the Superintendent has desired, and with great gratification he is able to announce that he believes it wholly practicable, to bring every class of facts which have been embraced in the publication of previous censuses up to the standard of absolute or approximate accuracy, so that no class of statistics shall be put forth at the Tenth Census which are not sound and reliable. This, however, has involved the expenditure of no little time and labor in many departments. For example, in the department relating to the defective, dependent, and delinquent classes, three times as much clerical labor has been expended upon the returns prior to taking them up for compilation as was expended in this department, in all, up to the point of publication in the census report of 1870. The Superintendent is confident that the results will fully justify the effort put forth.

From the causes indicated, viz: first, the unexpected cost of completing the field-work in the departments of mining, manufacture, and social statistics; second, the weight of the new compilations and tabulations undertaken, for the first time, at this office, greatly exceeding the Superintendent's estimate; and third, the labor involved in bringing the statistical material of the census up to a higher point of completeness and accuracy, the expenditures of this office were so enhanced that it became manifest, during the month of May, that the appropriation would not be sufficient to complete the service.

In this emergency two courses were open: first, to disband the office force, retaining only a small number of clerks to prepare for publication whatever statistical matter had already been compiled, and, for the rest, to await the action of Congress upon the recommendation of a new appropriation when it should meet in the December following; or, second, to accept the service of volunteers, upon the condition of their expressly disavowing any claim against the government being created by their services, and with their aid to carry forward the compilations of the census as rapidly as possible towards completion.

Respecting this alternative, the Superintendent conferred with the honorable the Secretary of the Interior and with the honorable the Attorney-General, who concurred in the opinion that it would be exceedingly unfortunate to disband the office force and discontinue, for eight or ten months, the work of tabulation and compilation; and that, if a sufficient number of the employés of the Census Office should be found disposed to volunteer their services, upon the condition indicated, no legal or political objection interposed. As the result of this conference the following letter was addressed to the honorable the Secretary of the Interior, viz:

DEPARTMENT OF THE INTERIOR,
CENSUS OFFICE,
Washington, D. C., May 27, 1881.

Hon. ALONZO BELL,
Acting Secretary of the Interior :

SIR : I have the honor to ask your attention to the following considerations and to a suggestion based thereon.

By an error of calculation, for which I am alone responsible, the estimate for the appropriations required for carrying on and completing the work of the Tenth Census were framed, as the result proves, too low. The vast extent and complexity of the investigations undertaken by this office have caused a more rapid exhaustion of the amount appropriated for this service than was contemplated, and I find myself now in a position of being obliged to suspend the work upon considerable portions of the field until the next session of Congress, unless some exceptional arrangement can be made which will allow the continuance of my present office force.

Such a suspension would be a matter of regret on two accounts: first, because the public interest in the results of the enumeration makes the earliest possible completion of the tabulations and compilations of the office a matter greatly to be desired; and secondly, because such a suspension would involve the disbanding of a clerical force which I sincerely believe is not surpassed in efficiency through all the departments of the government. To disband the force and to recruit another, at a later date, should Congress make appropriation of additional funds for carrying on the service, would of itself involve a certain loss of efficiency.

Fully appreciating the fact that no contract, express or implied, can lawfully be made with any person for services or supplies on behalf of the government in anticipation of an appropriation therefor, I venture to suggest whether it might yet not be consistent with the provisions of law, as well as decidedly for the interest of the public service, to accept as volunteers in completing the work of the census during the coming season such of the members of the present office force as are willing to continue in the office under a complete disclaimer of any claim thereby to be created against the government, and with a formal profession of their willingness to submit the question of their compensation to the decision of Congress, without any alleged obligation to make appropriations on such account.

I am satisfied that at least two-thirds of my present force would esteem it a privilege to be permitted to continue work upon these terms, while the result to the government would be that, at the meeting of Congress in December, it would find the tabulations of the census completely finished, and a considerable portion of the statistical tables in type, ready for distribution.

If this suggestion is deemed practicable, I should be greatly pleased to give effect thereto on being duly authorized, and I pledge myself to use my utmost energy to finish the work with the least possible expenditure of clerical labor.

I have the honor to be, very respectfully,

FRANCIS A. WALKER,
Superintendent of Census.

·To this communication the following reply was received, viz:

DEPARTMENT OF THE INTERIOR,
Washington, June 3, 1881.

General F. A. WALKER,
Superintendent Tenth Census:

SIR: I have fully considered your letter of May 27, in relation to the condition of the appropriation for the Tenth Census and the necessity of a suspension of important work unless some exceptional arrangement can be made which will allow the continuance of your present office force. Your suggestions in relation to the acceptance of a volunteer force (provided such can be secured, willing to disclaim all claims against the government on account of services rendered) are fully concurred in by me.

The postponement of the important work upon which you are engaged, on account of a lack of clerical force, would work serious inconvenience and loss to the public interests, and while it should be clearly understood that the government has no legal right to make any contract, express or implied, that shall bind it in anticipation of appropriations, you are authorized to say to all who desire to serve without pay, and with an express disclaimer in relation thereto, that all of the facts necessary to a full understanding of the case will be laid before Congress at the earliest practicable moment.

Very respectfully, &c.,

A. BELL,
Acting Secretary

Acting under the authority given in the above letter,* an average

* The following has been the form used in notifying clerks and other employés of the acceptance of their services as volunteers, viz:

DEPARTMENT OF THE INTERIOR,
Washington, D. C., June 22, 1881.

—— ——:

SIR: Your resignation as a clerk of class —— in the Census Office has been received, and is hereby accepted to take effect on the 15th instant.

In compliance with the request contained in your letter of resignation, you will be

force of seven hundred assistants has been retained from the 15th of June to the present time. Not only has no falling off in efficiency been manifested by the clerical force as a consequence of the peculiar and regretable condition of service, but the average amount of work done in every division of the office has steadily improved.

The work in every department has made rapid progress, and it is my confident expectation that by the time Congress meets the compilation of the Tenth Census will be substantially completed.

A comparatively small force will further be required to reduce the statistical matter to tabular form and to prepare it for the printer; but it is safe to say that at least eight months have been saved, in the publication of the final results of the census, by keeping the clerical force at work during the summer, as compared with what would have taken place had the office been disbanded, and subsequently organized a second time after the meeting of Congress.

While I have spoken thus in regard to the increase in the cost of the Tenth Census above my estimates and calculations, it should not be understood that the census so taken has been expensive, as compared with any preceding enumeration, reasonable allowance being made for the increase of population and other elements of expense.

The Ninth Census cost three millions and a third ($3,336,000). Our population has, in the interval, increased 30 per cent., and other elements of the cost of a census have increased at least proportionally.

An increase of 30 per cent. upon three millions and a third would amount to four millions and a third. By the twentieth section of the act of March 3, 1879, Congress provided only three millions for the expenses of the Tenth Census, *exclusive of printing and engraving*, being a million and a third below its proportional cost, as compared with the census preceding. By the act of March 3, 1881, $500,000 additional were appropriated, making the total appropriation for the purposes of the act of 1879 three millions and a half, or $836,000 below the proportional cost of the Ninth Census. This is all that has thus far been appropriated for this service, exclusive of the amount provided for printing and engraving ($250,000), and of the amount appropriated ($210,000) to meet the expenses involved in carrying out the provisions of the sixth section of the act of April 20, 1880, which act required of the enumerators services altogether additional to those prescribed by the act of 1879. Should, therefore, an additional $540,000 be appropriated for this service, according to the recommendation hereafter to be made, the expense of the Tenth Census, according to the scheme of the act of March 3, 1879, would still be considerably below that of the census of 1870. But such a comparison would not be fair without reference to the vastly wider range of the present census, the minuter and more extensive compilations undertaken, and the improvement in the quality of the results obtained.

The census has, for the first time, collected the statistics of railroads and telegraphs; of fire, marine, and life insurance; while, in the departments of agriculture and manufactures, the information obtained has been at least double, in mere matter of bulk, what has heretofore been obtained.

permitted to continue at work for such time as in the judgment of the Superintendent may seem proper, upon the conditions indicated in your said letter, viz: That the services to be rendered by you shall create no claim against the United States, either expressed or implied.

Very respectfully,

A. BELL,
Acting Secretary.

In the inquiries respecting taxation and public debts, the investigations of the census have been extended to embrace an amount of detail which exists in regard to the public indebtedness of no other country of the world. In the great field of our mining and fishing industries, the worse than worthless statistics of 1850, 1860, and 1870 will be found replaced by a body of economical, social, and technical information respecting these great and growing interests which will be of incalculable value to the country. There is not one direction in which the published results of the present census will not cover more ground, divided into greater detail, than any preceding, while the character of the results will testify to a more rigid examination and a more careful revision of the results of the enumeration.

Out of a total appropriation of $3,960,000 (inclusive of the appropriation of $250,000 for printing and engraving, and of $310,000 for the purposes of the act of April 20, 1880), $3,860,068 67 have been expended, leaving a balance of $2,120 50 on the general appropriation (all in the hands of the disbursing officers of the mining and fishery investigations), and of $97,810 83 on the appropriation for printing and engraving. The accompanying table shows the various objects of expenditure, classified under certain general heads.

It appears from this exhibit that $2,094,947 95* have been paid to enumerators and interpreters, $133,457 54 to supervisors of census, while certain re-enumerations, under the orders of the Secretary of the Interior, have cost $8,099 67.

The enumeration of the manufacturing statistics of cities, conducted by 345 special agents, cost $87,085 37. The collection of the statistics of mining industries, including both the precious and the non-precious metals, both east and west of the Mississippi river, have cost $149,897 23, while the collection of the statistics of the fisheries has cost $45,329 19, and other investigations by special agents, smaller sums. The expenses of the central office at Washington have aggregated $1,063,468 48, of which $817,359 40 has been expended as compensation for clerks and other employés.

---

* Tables F and G in the appendix of this report exhibit the rates of per diem payments to enumerators in the several supervisors' districts.

Statement of disbursements on account of the Tenth Census to October 31, 1881.

Ledger pages.	Branch of investigation.	Name of person in charge.	Compensation.	Travelling, ex-penses.	Stationery and printing.	Furniture and fittings.	Rents and fuel.	Miscellaneous.	Pay of inter-preters.	Total.
25	Enumerators' accounts		$2,003,423 67					$2,538 80	$1,524 28	$2,004,947 95
22	Supervisors' accounts		127,244 12	$2,294 85	$339 02	$316 75	$9970 00	51 10	10 50	183,457 60
27	Re-enumeration of Saint Louis.		3,532 57	485 60	225 83		70 00	13 50		4,373 60
28	Re-enumeration of South Carolina.		1,444 80	2,284 57						3,728 07
101/15	Superintendent's office	Francis A. Walker, superin- tendent.	817,359 40	947 14	138,346 79	32,745 75	26,770 62	27,298 76		1,063,468 46
31	Manufacturing statistics of cities.	345 special agents.	82,970 53	2,138 56	143 38		1,090 33	50 57	72 00	87,085 37
	Statistics of the mining industries east of the Mississippi river.	Prof. R. Pumpelly and 57 as- sistants.	49,232 22	19,522 72	824 96	581 62	1,925 46	11,706 24		84,743 22
39	Statistics of the mining industries west of the Mississippi river.	Clarence King and 54 assist- ants.	57,183 38	22,000 00	1,782 56	383 51	891 67	1,923 90		65,154 00
41	Statistics of the fisheries.	Prof. G. Brown Goode and 26 assistants.	30,970 58	13,323 49	197 10		147 75	690 27		45,329 19
56	Statistics of meat production	Clarence Gordon and 19 assist- ants.	15,970 49	12,213 77	507 88	193 58	7 00	447 12		29,389 84
70	Social statistics of cities.	Col. G. E. Waring and 23 assist- ants.	20,400 17	4,778 18	1,078 20	539 24	819 90	535 76		28,151 45
48	Statistics of Indians not taxed.	Maj. John W. Powell and 4 assistants.	19,981 09	5,368 53				151 94	877 75	25,779 91
104	Statistics of forestry and the lumbering in- dustry.	Prof. C. S. Sargent and 24 as- sistant.	13,749 01	7,106 00	10 00	75 00		1,484 05		22,349 06
71	Statistics of wealth, debt, and taxation.	Robert P. Porter and 2 assist- ants.	16,856 27	5,071 83	8 30	65 51		29 44		22,041 03
52	Statistics of power and machinery used in manufacture.	Prof. W. P. Trowbridge and 8 assistants.	8,455 39	9,730 77	98 00		130 00	735 54		19,285 21
59	Statistics of the defective, delinquent, and de- pendent classes.	Rev. F. H. Wines and 8 assist- ants.	14,484 27	2,910 28	558 60			63 98		18,097 98
44	Statistics of the cotton culture.	Prof. E. W. Hilgard and 14 as- sistants.	12,330 80	2,175 94	7 50			394 08		14,908 41
57/57	Statistics of fire and marine insurance. Statistics of schools, churches, and libraries.	Charles A. Jenney...... Dr. Henry R. Waite and 15 as- sistants.	12,040 64 / 9,472 41	1,424 21 / 1,875 59	161 53 / 181 06	81 50 / 15 00	25 00	158 71 / 74 79		13,896 59 / 11,618 87
59	Statistics of orchard-fruits, hops, and the manufacture of tobacco.	Jacob R. Dodge and 14 assist- ants.	7,086 00	936 78				7 00		8,009 78
52	Statistics of the manufactures of glass and coke, and wages in manufacturing industry.	Joseph D. Weeks and 4 assist- ants.	5,423 89	1,720 30	111 93	77 00	298 00	81 44		7,564 56
59	Statistics of the quarrying industry of the United States.	Dr. George W. Hawes and 19 assistants.	4,140 10	2,346 14				102 93		6,789 17

Statement of disbursements on account of the Tenth Census to October 31, 1881—Continued.

Ledger page.	Branch of investigation.	Name of person in charge.	Compensation.	Traveling expenses.	Stationery and printing.	Furniture and fittings.	Rents and fuel.	Miscellaneous.	Pay of interpreters.	Total.
63	Statistics of the tobacco culture	Prof. J. B. Killebrew and 5 assistants.	$5,230 68	$1,158 55		$36 00	$99 00	$22 63		$6,547 18
18	Vital and mortuary statistics	C. S. Mixer and W. A. g...	5,144 08	224 17						5,378 25
61	Statistics of the silk industry	W. C. Wyckoff and 1 a tant.	4,034 50	816 30	12 80			4 20		4,867 80
72	Statistics of the production of cereals	Prof. William H. Brew...	2,918 56	1,149 00						4,067 56
58	Statistics of railroad, transportation, express and telegraph companies.	J. H. Goodspeed, R. P. rter, and 2 assistants.	2,547 00	1,149 30						3,696 30
85	Statistics of Alaska, its population, industry, and resources.	Ivan Petroff and 1 ass nt	2,019 00	1,621 49	14 00			25 00		3,679 49
75	Statistics of newspapers and the publishing interests.	S. N. D. North	3,069 00	463 16	38 83		22 00	30 31		3,623 32
64	Statistics of the movement of population	Henry Gannett and 1 assistant.	2,313 00	644 30	50 83			23 17		2,957 30
96	Statistics of the production of petroleum	Prof. S F. Peckham	1,877 50	754 06	40 50			58 40		2,723 56
88	Statistics of the manufacture of iron and steel	James M. Swank	2,294 25	132 25		14 65	120 00			2,551 40
88	Statistics of the manufacture of wool	George Wm. Bond and 1 assistant.	2,275 48	40 20						2,450 33
80	Statistics of the chemical manufacturing industry.	Henry Bover and 2 assistants.	1,546 30	753 70				22 75		2,322 75
80	Statistics of the factory system of the United States.	Carroll D. Wright	1,536 00	689 50						2,225 50
74	Statistics of ship-building	Henry Hall	1,482 00	928 97						2,410 97
162	Miscellaneous investigations		490 50							490 50
			3,442,963 82	132,781 29	164,652 84	34,825 41	33,038 73	48,732 23	1,984 53	3,800,068 67

The volunteer service thus far (to November 1, 1881) rendered, under the arrangements hereinbefore detailed, would, if paid for according to the rates of compensation received prior to June 15, 1881, by the several individuals rendering such service, amount to $243,640 92. This statement includes both the clerical force at Washington, and the experts and special agents engaged upon field-work, or in the preparation of their reports outside of Washington.

I regret to have to add that, beyond the service thus rendered under an express disavowal of any claim being created against the United States thereby, a small body of liabilities have unavoidably been created in bringing the work of the census to a conclusion. As soon as I apprehended the danger of a deficiency I whistled down brakes, and tried to stop the train before it reached the draw; but a service so gigantic, moving so rapidly, has a momentum which it is not always possible to calculate with nice accuracy, and in spite of every effort to escape an actual deficiency (aside from the personal volunteer service heretofore referred to), the office found itself subject to certain calls for which no funds were provided. These were of three classes:

First. The rent of the Main Census Building since the 1st of July, 1881, being at the rate of $1,083 33⅓ per month. The lessors have expressed their entire willingness to await the action of Congress.

Second. Certain amounts from subsidized railroads for transportation of officers and agents of the census, amounting to $3,642 48. Even had sufficient funds been available for the payment, these accounts for transportation could not, up to this time, have been paid, inasmuch as the railroads concerned are delinquent in respect to the repayment of certain sums extorted as regular fare from the agents of the Census Office traveling under instructions, and presenting duly authenticated orders for transportation at government rates.

Third. Certain miscellaneous expenses for traveling, for supplies and for minor services, in respect to which no arrangement could properly be made for postponing payment. Being unwilling that the persons entitled to these sums, generally in small amounts, should be required to await the action of Congress, upon their just and proper claims, I addressed a letter to the honorable the Secretary of the Interior in the following terms, viz:

DEPARTMENT OF THE INTERIOR,
CENSUS OFFICE,
Washington, D. C., October 3, 1881.

Hon. S. J. KIRKWOOD,
Secretary of the Interior:

SIR: I have the honor to state that upon ascertaining, in May last, that the appropriation of the Tenth Census would necessarily prove inadequate to the needs of the service, I shut down as quickly and peremptorily as possible upon all sources of expense.

With a service so vast, however, and so widely spread, with between thirteen and fourteen-hundred employés in the Washington office, and with several hundred special agents scattered over the country, all the way from Arizona to Alaska, it was not possible to estimate closely the total of unadjusted accounts, while there were some points at which expenditure could not be abruptly terminated (for instance, as by recalling an agent from a distant field already nearly canvassed) without a great loss to the service, amounting to the practical abandonment of what had been done in that field.

I regret to say that, in consequence of the accounts for obligations incurred at the date mentioned proving larger than was anticipated, and of the seemingly imperative necessity of keeping up some small disbursements in several directions for the reason just indicated, there will be required to carry this office through to the meeting of Congress, several thousands of dollars; it may be three, it may be five thousand.

As no appropriation is available for this purpose, and as it would not be creditable to allow these accounts to remain unpaid, I respectfully propose to the department that it give its sanction to my depositing with the disbursing agent of the department a sum of money, out of my own private resources, sufficient to meet the charges related to, all accounts to be approved as usual by the Secretary of the Interior, and asked for payment in the accustomed form.

Should Congress consent to make appropriation for the uncompleted work of the census, I can be reimbursed; if not, the loss will be my own—a loss I would rather submit to than have those who have rendered service to the government, or incurred expenditures on its behalf, suffer for my error in calculating the probable needs of the service.

Very respectfully,

F. A. WALKER,
Superintendent of Census.

To this letter a reply was received from the department as follows, viz:

DEPARTMENT OF THE INTERIOR,
Washington, D. C., October 4, 1881.

General FRANCIS A. WALKER,
Superintendent of the Census:

SIR: I have the honor to acknowledge the receipt of your communication of the 3d instant, relative to the exhaustion of the appropriation for the expenses of the Tenth Census, and requesting my sanction to your depositing a certain amount of money, from your private means, in the hands of the disbursing clerk of this department to meet certain obligations already incurred, etc.

In consideration of the fact that it is difficult to estimate closely for the expenditures under this head, and that to abruptly terminate all disbursements would necessarily cause great loss to the service, I hereby sanction the proposition you make for meeting these obligations from your own private funds, to be done through the disbursing clerk or in any other way you may desire. In doing this, however, you will understand that I assume no responsibility in the matter, and that such vouchers as you may pay cannot be considered as constituting any claim against the government, and any risk that may be incurred as to your repayment must be assumed by you, pending the future action of Congress in the matter.

Should you do this, it should be officially communicated to Congress at its next session.

Very respectfully,

S. J. KIRKWOOD,
Secretary.

Under the foregoing arrangement $4,889 97 have been paid out of my own private funds in liquidation of these accounts, which are all adjusted to date. Seven or eight hundred dollars more will probably be required to be paid in the same manner, prior to the meeting of Congress, of which a full account will be rendered. Should it please Congress to make an appropriation to cover the amounts so expended, I shall be glad to be reimbursed for expenditures made in good faith, and for the public interest. If not, I shall accept the decision of that body, and regard the amount so expended as my personal contribution to the success of a great public work.

At the present date the following reports have been prepared, and are all, or nearly all, in the hands of the Public Printer:

First. The report on population, by the Superintendent, assisted by Mr. Henry Gannett, comprising the statistics of population by States, counties, and minor civil divisions, with distinction of white and colored, foreign and native, male and female. This volume will be illustrated by about seventy-five quarto pages of maps and charts, all of which are now in the hands of the engraver.

Second. From the department of fisheries (Prof. G. Browne Goode, chief special agent) reports on the oyster-industry, by Mr. Earnest Inger-soll; on the whale-fishery, by Messrs. James Temple Browne and A. Howard Clark; on the river fisheries of the United States, by Mr. C. W. Smiley; on the seal fisheries of Alaska, by Mr. H. W. Elliot. All the reports in this department, as in that next to be mentioned, will be fully illustrated by maps, charts, and diagrams already in the hands of the engraver.

Third. From the department of power and machinery used in manu-factures (Prof. W. P. Trowbridge, chief special agent) reports on the manufactures of interchangeable mechanism, by Mr. C. H. Fitch; on the water-supply of cities, by the chief special agent and Mr. Walter G. Elliott; on milling and the flouring industry, by Mr. Joseph W. K. Nef-tel; on the water-power of the Southern Atlantic coast, by Mr. Geo. F. Swain; on the water-power of the Northwest, by Mr. James L. Green-leaf; on the water-power of the Missouri River Basin, by Mr. Dwight Porter; on steam-pumps and pumping-engines, by Mr. F. R. Hutton; on shop-tools, also by Mr. Hutton.

Fourth. A report on the production of cereals in the United States, by Prof. W. H. Brewer.

Fifth. A report on the newspaper press, by Mr. S. N. D. North.

Sixth. A report on the manufacture of iron and steel, by Mr. James M. Swank.

Seventh. A report on the manufacture of silk goods, by Mr. Wm. C. Wyckoff.

Eighth. From the department of wealth, debt, and taxation a report on the public debts of the United States, comprising the statistics of State, county, city, town, village, and school-district indebtedness, to-gether with a history of the debts of the several States, by the chief special agent, Mr. Robert P. Porter, and a full statistical account of the debt of the United States, by Mr. Rafael A. Bayley.

Ninth. From the department of meat production reports on the cattle and sheep industry of California, Oregon, Texas, Nevada, Washington Territory, and Idaho, by Mr. Clarence Gordon, chief special agent. These reports are illustrated with maps showing the range of cattle and sheep occupation.

Tenth. From the department dealing with the social statistics of cities, reports on the cities of New Orleans and Austin.

Eleventh. A report on the tobacco culture of the United States, by Mr. J. B. Killebrew.

Twelfth. A report on the production of the precious metals during the census year 1879–'80, by the Hon. Clarence King, chief special agent.

The work of the printing-office and of the engraver is so far advanced as to justify the anticipation that all, or nearly all, of these reports will be printed and laid upon the desks of members when Congress shall as-semble in December, or within a few days thereafter.

In view of the exhaustion of the appropriation for this service, as re-cited, I respectfully recommend that the further sum of $540,000 be ap-propriated for the compensation of those who have rendered services as volunteers, as hereinbefore stated, and for the completion of the Tenth Census. Of this sum about $330,000 would be applied to the payment of the volunteer force of the office, down, say, to the 15th of December, and to the liquidation of the three classes of obligations referred to. The balance would be sufficient to complete all the compilations and tabulations remaining to be effected in order to secure the fullest statement and publication of the results of the enumeration.

I have the honor to be, very respectfully, your obedient servant,

FRANCIS A. WALKER,

Superintendent of Census.

Hon. S. J. KIRKWOOD,
Secretary of the Interior.

REPORT OF THE COMMISSIONER OF PENSIONS.

DEPARTMENT OF THE INTERIOR,
PENSION OFFICE,
Washington, D. C., October 15, 1881.

SIR: I have the honor to submit herewith the annual statement showing the operation of this bureau for the fiscal year ending June 30, 1881.

There were at the close of the year, June 30, 1881, 268,830 pensioners on the rolls, classified as follows: Army invalids, 153,025; Army widows, minor children, and dependent relatives, 76,683; Navy invalids, 2,187; Navy widows, minor children, and dependent relatives, 2,008; surviving soldiers and sailors of the war of 1812, 8,898; and widows of deceased soldiers and sailors of that war, 26,029.

There were added to the roll during the year the names of 27,396 new pensioners, and the names of 1,344, whose pension had previously been dropped, were restored to the rolls, making an aggregate increase to the roll of 28,740.

The names of 10,712 pensioners were dropped from the roll during the year for various causes, leaving a net increase to the roll of 18,028 pensioners.

At the close of the year the annual pension to each pensioner on the roll averaged $107.01, and the annual aggregate value of all pensions was $28,769,967.46.

The annual payments, however, exceed this sum by several millions of dollars; *i. e.*, the total amount paid for pensions during the year exclusive of the arrears due in pensions allowed prior to January 25, 1879. was $49,723,147.52, which is accounted for by what is known as arrears of pension, or accrued pension covering the period since discharge in the case of a soldier, and since the soldier's death in the case of a widow, &c.

The amounts paid during the year upon first payment to new pensioners is $23,628,176.61, and by examination it is shown that this sum was paid to 25,887 pensioners, averaging to each case as follows: Army invalids, $953.62; to Army widows, minor children, and dependent relatives, $1,021.51; to Navy invalids, $771.42; to Navy widows, minor children, and dependent relatives, $790.22; to the surviving soldiers and sailors of the war of 1812, $329.97; and to the widows of deceased soldiers and sailors of that war, $314.58.

The complete details of these statements will be found in Table 1. with the value of pension allowed, increased, and dropped; and Table 2 will show the various causes for which the names of the 10,712 pensioners were dropped; also an analysis of the widows' roll, showing the number of widows with and without minor children, guardians, dependent fathers, and dependent mothers, &c.

The amount appropriated to meet the payment of pensions was $50,302,306.68, exclusive of the amounts for the salaries and expenses of the pension agents and the fees of examining surgeons. A statement in detail of the same will be shown by Table 3, which also shows the payment of arrears of pension in the case of those provided for by the act of January 25, 1879, who were at that date in receipt of a pension.

The disbursements on account of this class during the year was $679,137.23.

Table 4 is a classified statement of the number of pensioners on the rolls of each agency, and compares the whole number of pensioners on the roll with that of the preceding year, and shows the total disbursements and cost of same at each agency during the year.

Table 5 is an interesting exhibit of the number of each class of original pension claims filed and allowed during each year since 1861, and the amounts paid for pension, with the cost of disbursement each year since 1860.

During this period it will be seen that 431,439 claims for original pension for invalid soldiers, and 289,240 claims for widows, minor children, and dependent relatives of the Army and Navy were filed.

There have been allowed of these two classes 190,250 claims of invalids, and 197,414 claims of widows, minor children, and dependent relatives.

Besides these are those provided for by acts of February 14, 1871, and March 9, 1878, for service in the war of 1812, there having been filed since February 14, 1871, 34,548 claims of surviving soldiers and sailors of the war of 1812 and 41,305 claims of widows of the soldiers and sailors of that war.

There have been allowed from the first class 25,585 claims, and from the second class 31,863, making in the aggregate since July 1, 1861, 796,422 pension claims filed, out of which number 445,112 have been allowed, and already a sum of $506,345,044.21 since 1860 has been paid on account of these pensions, an average of nearly $25,000,000 per annum.

In the 319,748 original pension claims, excluding those on account of service in the war of 1812, reported in Table 6 as on file, are included those which have been rejected and abandoned. But out of this number on file more than 50 per cent. have been filed in the office during the last two fiscal years, or, in other words, from July 1, 1879, to June 30, 1881.

The number which can be regarded as *dead* claims must be entirely conjectural, but I hope in a few weeks to present such an analysis of the files as will give definite data on this point, which I will refer to later on.

The results of the office have shown during each year, for several years past, an interesting exhibit of but slight varying percentage of allowances relating to the year in which the claims were filed, each year, since 1862, after the third or fourth year since filing; e. g., in 1871 8,837 original invalid Army claims were filed; during the same year 1,268 were allowed; in 1872 1,947 were allowed; and in 1873 1,094 were allowed.

In each year since, the following numbers have been allowed, to wit: 1874, 441; 1875, 298; 1876, 220; 1877, 192; 1878, 128; 1879, 97; 1880, 219.

The comparison by each year since 1861 is the more remarkable as covering a much larger period with the same features presented. In the year 1880, out of 9,723 original Army invalid claims allowed, 675 of them were filed prior to 1866, and 1,520 prior to July 1, 1870.

I have deemed it of sufficient importance to determine as far as practicable how many of the claims which are reported as on the files may be reasonably regarded as "dead" claims, and what proportion may be regarded as ultimately likely to be placed on the pension roll.

To have this information complete and substantial I have caused a thorough analysis of the files to be made, and a history of each case in regard to the date of filing, how many times, and the date rejected, and how long, if an apparently abandoned case, since the last action was had. It will be some few weeks before I will be able to submit the complete results of this analysis, but I hope to have it complete prior to the assembling of Congress.

Table 6 shows the number of claims of each class believed to be on the files at the beginning of the year, the number allowed and rejected during the year, also the number believed to be remaining on hand at the close of the year.

Table 7 shows the operations of the special service under the provisions of section 4744 of the Revised Statutes.

Previous to the completion of the fiscal year ending June 30, 1881, which this report is intended to cover, my predecessor had control of the Pension Office, and practically this is a report of the work accomplished under his supervision, which he would have reported himself had he remained in office until after June 30.

Great credit is due to him for the industry, ability, and watchful integrity with which the business of this office has been conducted under his management, and the increase of work accomplished and results reached during the past year call for warmest commendation.

Owing to his foresight and recommendation the laws were so amended and supplemented as to enable me to effect changes in organization and management of the clerical force of this office, which it is hoped will to some extent alleviate the difficulties surrounding an *ex parte* system which has been so long in vogue.

Since July 1 the force of this office has consisted of a Commissioner, two deputy commissioners, medical referee, chief clerk, and a clerical force averaging 675 in number, organized as follows:

DEPARTMENT OF THE INTERIOR,
PENSION OFFICE,
Washington, August 16, 1881.

[302.]

ORDERED:

The force in this office is reorganized, from this date, into the following-named divisions:

1. *Board of review.*—C. B. WALKER, deputy commissioner, in charge; J. H. HOBBS, assistant; to be composed of expert examiners to review all claims before final action is taken by the office. Details for the board will be made by the Commissioner.

2. *Medical division.*—Dr. T. B. HOOD, medical referee, in charge; Dr. N. F. GRAHAM assistant; to have charge of the work required of examining surgeons; to review their reports, and to determine the degree of pensionable disability found in invalid claims, and to perform such other duties touching medical and surgical questions as the interest of the service may demand.

3. *Division of special examinations.*—H. R. McCALMONT, chief; W. E. DULIN, assistant; to have charge of claims requiring special examination in vicinity of claimant; and witnesses; to direct the method of inquiry by responsible examiners; to have charge of all matters pertaining to attorneys practicing before the office; to keep a record of the official character of notaries and justices of the peace, and to aid in prosecuting offenders against the pension law.

4. *Old War and Navy division.*—W. H. WEBSTER, chief; T. W. DALTON, assistant; to have charge of the settlement of all claims on account of service in wars prior to March 4, 1861; claims on account of service in the Regular Army and the Navy, and in all other general organizations not belonging especially to any State or Territory.

5. *Eastern division.*—FRED. MACK, chief; J. M. CURTIS, assistant; to have charge of

the settlement of all claims arising out of military service during the late war in organizations from the several New England States, and also from the States of New York, New Jersey, and Delaware.

6. *Middle division.*—F. D. STEPHENSON, chief; A. F. KINGSLEY, assistant; to have charge of the settlement of late war claims on account of military service in organizations belonging to the States of Pennsylvania, Ohio, and Michigan.

7. *Western division.*—JOHN M. COMSTOCK, chief; D. A. MCKNIGHT, assistant; to have charge of settlement of late war claims on account of military service in organizations belonging to the States of Indiana, Illinois, Iowa, Wisconsin, Minnesota, Nebraska, Kansas, Nevada, Colorado, California, Oregon, and the several Territories.

8. *Southern division.*—L. E. DICKEY, chief; J. D. SMITH, assistant; to have charge of the settlement of claims arising out of military service during the late war in organizations belonging to the States of Maryland, Virginia, West Virginia, North Carolina, South Carolina, Florida, Georgia, Alabama, Mississippi, Louisiana, Texas, Kentucky, Tennessee, Missouri, Arkansas, and the District of Columbia, and the several organizations of colored troops.

9. *Record division.*—W. T. FORD, chief; E. E. FULLER, assistant; to have charge of the recording and numbering of the claims as they are received in the office, and to have custody of the records; and to brief the evidence filed to secure its transmission to appropriate claims.

10. *Certificate and account division.*—FRANK MOORE, chief; M. B. JOHNSON, assistant; to have charge of the issuing, numbering, and recording of certificates granting pensions, and designating the agency at which payable; also, to audit accounts, under section 4718, Revised Statutes, for expenses of last sickness and burial of pensioners.

11. *Agents' division.*—C. F. SAWYER, chief; to have charge of the disbursement of pension funds, and of all correspondence with the several pension agents, and accounting officers of the Treasury, in reference to official action of this office.

12. *Mail division.*—DAVID L. GITT, chief; JOHN RICHMOND, assistant; to have charge of the stamping, recording, and proper distribution of all mail coming to the office, and of the proper dispatch of the mail going out; also to have charge of jacketing and briefing the jackets of claims received.

13. Mr. J. W. HOWELL is designated as appointment and financial clerk, and will have supervision of all public property, keep the accounts between the office and the various appropriations for clerical and contingent expenses, and report through the chief clerk to the Commissioner, upon the first of each month, a balance sheet showing the exact condition of each fund at the close of the preceding month; and shall prepare such estimates and reports as may be called for by the Commissioner from time to time.

14. *The miscellaneous work* of the office and its necessary clerical force, now under Mr. A. VANGEUDER, the laborers and watchmen, under Mr. JOHN DICKERSON, the general messengers, under Mr. JOSEPH JACKSON, and all other clerks and employés not especially assigned to any division, as well as the general oversight of the clerical force of the office, will be under the immediate control of the chief clerk, to whom chiefs of divisions will make monthly reports of the condition of the work of their divisions, and of the clerical force under their charge, as to numbers, efficiency, and general attention to duty. The chief clerk will make a consolidated report to the Commissioner, at the end of each month, showing the condition of the business of the office and its clerical force.

Any order conflicting with the foregoing is hereby rescinded.

WM. W. DUDLEY,
Commissioner.

Upon July 1, 1881, the clerical force of this office consisted of 784 employés, requiring an annual payment for their service of $931,350.

The appropriations available for this purpose, for the fiscal year then beginning, aggregate $794,630.

This made necessary a very large reduction of the force, already too small to keep up with the increasing annual influx of cases, as will be seen by Table 5, and upon July 15, 1881, over one hundred discharges and a large number of reductions in salary were made.

It was necessary, in discharging so many, that many efficient men, whose services were greatly needed, should be dropped.

This, and the reductions in salary were soon and disastrously felt in the work of the office, and from the necessities of the case, a few reinstatements were made, so that now the pay roll of the force is still too large for the appropriation by about $35,000 per annum.

It is to be hoped, for the sake of the important character of the work intrusted to this office, as well as the necessities of those who are dependent upon our labors for the pensions, so long past due, and so nobly earned in defense of the country, that Congress will make early and liberal provision for this deficiency, and add enough, so that well earned promotions may be made; or else at once indicate their unwillingness to do so, to the end that such further reductions may at once be made as to bring the pay roll within the appropriation for the year.

In this connection I would respectfully call your attention to the fact that the clerical force of such an office as the Pension Office can be disposed and arranged upon a much more business-like basis, were Congress to vote its appropriation therefor in the aggregate, instead of limiting the number of each class of clerks to be employed. The Secretary could then arrange the classes of clerks so that merit might be rewarded by earned promotions, and the positions having higher pay be filled by those performing the higher grades of work.

Such is not the case as the appropriations are now divided, and as the force is now necessarily arranged.

INDIAN PENSIONS.

Much trouble and delay has arisen in the payment of Indian pensions. There are 98 of this class now upon the rolls, requiring the annual payment of $9,108. In his report for a former year, my predecessor has called attention to the particular defects and hindrances encountered in this matter, and exhibited to the last Congress the report of the commission sent out to investigate and report thereon.

The principal trouble seems to grow out of the inadequate means of identification, and the procuring of cash upon the checks necessarily given them in payment, under sections 4764, 4765, 4766, and 4767 of the Revised Statutes.

It is respectfully suggested that such modifications of these sections be made as to allow the payment of this class of pensioners upon a suitable voucher—the form and manner of identification to be prescribed by the Secretary of the Interior—by the pension agent in person, at some convenient point in the Indian Territory, such payment to be made in standard silver.

The necessity for some such provision of law is made apparent from a perusal of said report. (See pp. 9, 10, of Report of Commissioner of Pensions for the year ending June 30, 1880.)

SOLDIERS' HOME PENSIONS.

Much annoyance and unpleasant friction has been caused by the imperfect legislation upon the subject of the payment of pensions of inmates of the National Military Home by the pension agents, to the treasurer of said home.

The act of February 26, 1881, provides that such payments shall be made upon the execution by such treasurer of good and sufficient bonds to the satisfaction of the board of managers.

The statute, making such inmates amenable to the rules and regulations prescribed for the governing of the Army, is thought by many to be unconstitutional, and that such inmates cannot be considered in the light of enlisted men, else the right to pension ceases during such enlistment if the pay of an enlisted man is received, to which if enlisted they would be entitled, and consequently the practice of summarily and voluntarily leaving such home just previous to pension pay day, and declaring themselves no longer inmates has been frequently resorted to, greatly to the annoyance of the pension agent and to the detriment of the discipline of the home, and consequent damage to the welfare of the beneficiaries.

It is to be hoped that Congress will thoroughly inquire into this matter, and cure such defects of legislation as permit this unpleasant friction, to the end that there may be harmonious action between the Pension Office, its agents, and the Home, and so promote the well being of the defenders of the Nation intrusted to their care.

INSANE AND IMPRISONED INVALID PENSIONERS.

My predecessor very properly called attention in his report of 1880, page 12, to the imperfect legislation with regard to insane and imprisoned invalid pensioners.

The same necessity exists for amendment and new enactments upon that subject in order to make proper payment of the pension to this class as then existed, and I again urge your attention thereto.

He also recommended that the following clause be added to section 4702 of Revised Statutes, to wit: "That when the children have resided with and been supported by the widow of the soldier the pension shall commence at the date to which the widow was last paid."

This is a wise and just provision and will be conducive to good morals and be equitable to all. I again call your attention thereto, and would also recommend that it and the following be enacted as an amendment to said section 4702, "That marriage must be proven in pension cases to have been performed in accordance with the law of the place where the parties resided at the time of the alleged marriage, in proving the title of the widow to pension, and that adulterous cohabitation of a widow shall operate to terminate her pension from the date of the commencement and during the continuance of such cohabitation."

This is a necessary and just provision, and should, I think, become a law.

INCREASE, RERATING, AND REISSUE.

Under section 4698½ no increase can commence at an earlier date than the date of the medical examination made under an order therefor after the filing of the application for such increase.

In an office four to six years behindhand with its work, as this is, it is a manifest injustice to make an increase depend upon such an uncertain date as that of a medical examination that may not be ordered for six months or a year after filing application therefor, and my predecessor's recommendation upon that subject should be heeded.

I therefore recommend the passage of such a provision and quote his recommendation in his Report of 1880, as follows:

INCREASE OF INVALID PENSION, SECTION 4698½—REVIEW OF PREVIOUS RATINGS.

The statutes relating to the subject of increasing invalid pensions on the ground of an increased degree of disability and regulating reviews of former ratings alleged to have been unjust are meager and indefinite; indeed, touching the latter point there is no statute whatever, and the proceedings in such cases rest entirely upon precedent, and as almost every case presents circumstances differing from former cases the consequence is a great want of uniformity of action.

* * * * * *

I respectfully recommend, therefore, that section 4698½ be repealed and an act passed containing substantially the following provisions: That if any invalid pensioner shall think his pension is not commensurate with the degree of his disability, either because it has been improperly rated by the Commissioner of Pensions, or because the disability for which he was pensioned has increased, or because he has another disability incurred in the service, for which he is not pensioned, he may apply to the Commissioner of Pensions for an increase of his pension, and said application shall be considered and determined in the same manner as his original application, so far as such proceedings may be applicable to his case; and the Commissioner of Pensions shall cause any invalid pensioner to be examined by a surgeon as often as he shall deem it for the interest of the government or of the pensioner, and if, upon such examination, it shall appear that the pension enjoyed by the pensioner is not according to the degree of his disability, the same shall be readjusted and rerated according to right and justice, provided that in cases where the increase is granted for the reason that the disability has increased since the pension was last rated by the Commissioner of Pensions, such increase shall commence at the date of filing application therefor; and provided further, that all applications for increase on the ground that the pension has been improperly rated, made more than one year after such alleged improper rate was fixed by the Commissioner of Pensions, shall be treated and settled as in the case of increase claims on the ground of an increase of disability.

AGENTS AND ATTORNEYS.

Upon this subject much has been said, but in my opinion the actual results-of the enactments of June 20, 1878, have been deleterious to the interests of claimants and agents alike; to the claimants, in that the abolishment of the contingency of success, and removal of the security to the agents, has stimulated many irresponsible persons, who could be of no possible service to the claimants, to invite a general application of soldiers for pension, regardless of disabilities incurred, by which, after filing the claim, they may obtain in advance the legal fee of $10, and thenceforth abandon the claim, thus incumbering the files of this office, and hindering and delaying meritorious claimants; to the agents, by degrading the profession and bringing into disrepute an otherwise legitimate employment. Agents in good standing and well informed in pension law and practice, when their fee depended upon the successful prosecution of the claim, would, and I believe did, examine and scrutinize the merits before risking years of labor, and refused to file cases without merit.

Unpleasant friction between the principal and agent was avoided by the contingent fee and security of payment, because of the identity of interests.

I recommend that Congress re-enact the laws in force prior to June 20, 1878, upon this subject, and make such provision as will protect the department and claimant alike from ignorant and useless agents, and protect and assist well-informed and useful ones.

Owing to the large number of pending claims, out of the many thousands of applications filed during the past eighteen years, there are thousands of claimants justly clamorous for settlement of their long-delayed claims; and from each of them, through every avenue of approach, come letters of inquiry. An answer conveying any valuable information costs an examination of the case, which clerical labor, if spent in adjudication, would have settled a case. Hence, it follows that the vast correspondence of this office consumes in its consideration and answer nearly the labor of one-third of the clerical force of the office, which would otherwise be spent in the real work of the bureau.

The claimant cannot be blamed for wishing frequently to know why his claim, filed two, five, eight, ten years since, has not been settled, and Members of Congress and Senators feel this pressure, and are compelled to spend much valuable time and a vast amount of postage in replies and communications to satisfy the demand. So long as the work of this office is behind, as it now is, this tax upon Members and Senators must and will continue and increase. Senators and Members should be relieved of this improper burden by allowing an official postage stamp for their use, or extending to them the use of the penalty frank.

In order to relieve this great pressure, bring up the back business, and allow current work to be settled speedily, I shall submit a plan hereafter in a special report, which it is believed will be practicable, should it be desired by you.

SPECIAL INVESTIGATION AND EXAMINATION.

The results of the operations of this portion of the office force is shown by Table 7.

The system in vogue until July 15, 1881, was that used by each of my predecessors since 1862, and involved secrecy in obtaining and using evidence secured thereby.

The report of the special committee of the last Congress gives evidence that the system was defective, and, in many instances, arbitrary and unjust and prejudicial to the interest of both claimant and government, and deprecated its continuance.

By a happy wording of the appropriation act, and the generous appropriation given therefor, suggested, as I understand, by my immediate predecessor, I was able to extend special examination to a large number of cases hitherto precluded therefrom, and have since July 15, 1881, put into operation an entire change of system respecting this class of examinations.

The examiner now works up his case upon the ground, brings all witnesses face to face with the claimant or his attorney, and frequently establishes a meritorious claim when the claimant would have failed, either for want of means or for want of opportunity to procure testimony of important witnesses. In this class of cases the government comes in to help the poor but worthy claimant, and gives him the benefit of her strong arm and generous purse, and to this end authority of law should be given the Commissioner of Pensions to defray the expenses of the claimant in accompanying the special examiner when in his opinion the necessity for such expense exists.

This change does not appear thus far to be attended with any results detrimental to the interests of the government, and if after a fair and open investigation the claimant fails to establish his right to pension, he is satisfied and content with rejection. The principal obstruction is in the lack of power to compel the attendance of witnesses. The special examiner of this bureau should, and I hope will, be empowered and clothed with authority to take depositions in cases pending before this bureau, so that the provisions of sections 184, 185, and 186 shall be extended to examinations in pension claims. Section 186 should be amended, so that the United States marshals will be authorized to make payments of witnesses' fees thereunder.

Such special examiner should be authorized to employ stenographer, when deemed necessary by the Commissioner of Pensions, to take down testimony in important cases, inasmuch as the amount involved is often very large; who should be paid by said special examiner, and the same allowed in his accounts.

This service should be broadened and extended largely; but to do so, Congress, I think, should authorize the employment of large numbers of additional examiners, whose pay should be fixed for all who serve in this capacity, at $1,400 and $1,600 per annum, and the $4 per diem now provided by law, when employed, and necessary traveling expenses, at which compensation, it is believed, the services of fit and proper men may be had. And there should be authorized six special agents at same pay and allowances, whose duty it should be to visit and scrutinize the proceedings and value as such of medical examiners, located at different points for the examination of applicants for pension.

These medical officers are the most important, and, if trustworthy and competent, reliable adjuncts in disclosing the merits or demerits of claimants; but being so important should be well paid and carefully looked after.

In my opinion, examining surgeons should be paid $2 fee in each case, and should be required to make full and complete description of the physical condition of each claimant, after a personal and thorough examination.

The provisions for per diem and expenses should be extended to this class of officers, who are now often required to visit a sick or helpless pensioner for purpose of examination, at considerable expense and loss of valuable time, without pay.

PENSION AGENTS.

This class of officers have the hardest work and are most poorly paid therefor, considering their responsibilities, of any officers in the government service.

The law provides a salary to each agent of $4,000 per annum, and $15 for each 100 vouchers paid in excess of 4,000 vouchers per annum.

From this compensation the law provides that the agents shall pay for the postage upon vouchers and checks sent to pensioners, and all the expenses of their offices, so that, with the increased labor and responsibilities devolving upon these officers, they find in most instances an inability to save from their compensation more than $2,500 per annum, and this by paying small salaries for clerk-hire, which in most instances is inadequate compensation for the services required.

These reductions seem to have gradually grown by indirect, rather than by direct, provisions of law.

These officers are compelled to give bond in sums varying from $50,000 to $150,000, and for which sureties are compelled to justify in double the amount. Agents handle annually millions of dollars each, and are held to a strict accountability through the accounting officers of the Treasury for all errors of calculation or payment. Their accounts and other requirements of the Pension Office and Treasury require elaborate and extremely accurate and responsible accounting clerks, so that the necessary payments for clerical force come from the agents' compensation. I therefore respectfully recommend a thorough reconstruction of this section of the law bearing upon these officers, their duties and responsibilities, as well as their compensation, to the end that they may be properly paid and required to aid in the detection of fraud.

COMMUTATION FOR ARTIFICIAL LIMBS.

I would respectfully call attention to the defective legislation upon the subject of commutation for artificial limbs and surgical appliances, as construed by the Comptroller of the Treasury. In a recent decision he has held that such payment must be made by the Commissioner of Pensions.

There being no appropriation available to the Commissioner of Pensions, it is difficult to see how such payment can be made, unless Congress shall pass an appropriation for that purpose.

REIMBURSEMENT FOR FUNERAL EXPENSES, &C.

There are a large number of claims for reimbursement for funeral expenses, under section 4718 R. S., which have been examined and allowed, and for which certificates have been issued by this office and instruction given to agents to pay, but which the accounting officers of the Treasury find themselves unable, under their view of the law, to allow to the credit of agents, if paid by them.

Hence, a great hardship has accrued by compelling claimants to wait for their money past due.

It is manifestly improper to require agents to make payments which they are notified in advance will be disallowed from their accounts, and I trust you will recommend that Congress take early occasion to remedy this trouble by necessary enactment.

DISHONORABLE DISCHARGE AND DESERTION.

Until recently the War Department has been accustomed to grant to soldiers without a record of discharge, upon request and a proper showing, a discharge, either honorable or dishonorable, as the facts might warrant, by which the date of commencement of pension might be fixed.

That department now declines such action, and under the provision of the act of January 25, 1879, and your recent ruling, I am obliged to deny otherwise worthy pensions, because no date can be fixed for commencement. I would respectfully recommend that this defect be cured by an amendment to said section.

There should be some provision of law by which a presumption of the death of the soldier might be raised in certain cases.

Many widows and dependent relatives are denied pension because of the lack of some such reasonable provision of law.

CRIMINAL PROSECUTIONS.

I cannot close without calling attention to a matter which I deem essential to the proper protection of the rights of pensioners and claimants for pensions.

It often happens that irresponsible persons falsely and maliciously swear that the pension, or claim to pension, of soldiers or their widows or dependents has been obtained, or is sought to be obtained, by fraud. There seems to be no law by which such persons can be successfully prosecuted in the Federal courts, and certainly those swearing falsely and maliciously against a meritorious and worthy claimant's right to pension should be subject to indictment and prosecution in the Federal courts, in the same manner as those swearing falsely in support of a fraudulent claim.

The only law touching this subject (and the same is believed to be inadequate for the purpose which I have pointed out), is contained in sections 5292 and 5293 of the revised Statutes, and reads as follows, to wit:

SECTION 5392. Every person who, having taken an oath before a competent tribunal, officer, or person in any case in which a law of the United States authorizes an oath to be administered, that he will testify, declare, depose, or certify truly, or that any written testimony, declaration, deposition, or certificate by him subscribed is true, willfully and contrary to such oath states or subscribes any material matter which he does not believe to be true, is guilty of perjury, and shall be punished by a fine of not more than two thousand dollars, and by imprisonment, at hard labor, not more than five years; and shall, moreover, thereafter be incapable of giving testimony in any court of the United States until such time as the judgment against him is reversed.

SECTION 5393. Every person who procures another to commit any perjury is guilty of subornation of perjury, and punishable as in the preceding section prescribed.

I recommend that after the word "*deposition,*" in section ██ be added "*affidavit,*" and after the words "*which he does not be true,*" in the same section, there be added "*or which, in part not true, of the falsity of which the affiant had knowledge,*" and 5393, after the words "*to commit any perjury,*" there be added "*as described in section 5392.*"

Table 8 shows the name and residence of the surviving ██ those who served in the Revolutionary war, and were in ██ pension at the close of the year.

I am, sir, very respectfully,

WM. W. DUDLE██
Commi

Hon. SAMUEL J. KIRKWOOD,
    Secretary of the Interior.

REPORT OF THE SUPERINTENDENT OF THE YELLOW██ NATIONAL PARK.

OFFICE OF THE SUPERINTENDENT OF ·
THE YELLOWSTONE NATIONAL PAR██
Mammoth Hot Springs, December ██

SIR: I herewith submit my report of operations for the ██████ improvement of the Yellowstone National Park during the ██ with the request that, if approved, it may be printed.

Very respectfully,

P. W. NORRI██
Superintendent of the Yellowstone National

Hon. S. J. KIRKWOOD,
    ·*Secretary of the Interior, Washington, D. C.*

SIR: As you are doubtless aware, the winter of 1880–'81 com██ very early, with unusual severity, and with attendant heav; throughout the United States, and continued so in those porti of the Rocky Mountains. Such was not the case in the regio and beyond them, in which localities the latter part of the win very mild, followed by a continuously pleasant early spring. T dition of affairs resulted in a prematurely heavy rise in many rivers, notably the Bighorn, Yellowstone, and Missouri, whose waters, swept a resistless, devastating flood over a great agri valley, still robed in winter's mantle of snow. From these fl elevation of the National Park preserved it, and allowed the n continuous daily rays of an unclouded sun to render the deep-sl glens and valleys luxuriant with herbage and fragrant with l flowers, while the winter snows still rested low and chill, u; mountain slopes above and around them. Rarely has man wi scenes more strangely mingling the weird and repellent with the ingly beautiful, than these borders to fire-hole basins, or the shee; slanting sunbeams from ice-clad cliffs begirting geyser basins of ing hot water, or the sulphur-lined fumerole escape-vents of sun fires. These were among the scenes which greeted my return Park. In the East I had left the frugal farmer, with shelter, gr care, nursing his starveling animals, hoping for the scanty her a tardy spring; upon the Platte and the Great Plains I had a carcasses of thousands of animals claimed by the princely-impro fortune-trusting herdsman of the border, decaying where they s or frozen, fell; and, in the valleys of the Madison, the Gallatin, and the Upper Yellowstone, witnessed animals in only passable heart and flesh; while in the Park, at an elevation of 6,450 feet, in our little cliff-and-snow-girt valley, with its matchless hot springs, I found all our animals sleek, fat, and able, engaged in grading a road up the cañon of the east fork of the Gardiner River. In fact, the season in the valleys was as advanced by the middle of April, this year, as it was upon the 1st of July of last, and the roads in better condition; so that the limited amount of funds under my control available before the 1st of July alone prevented me from at once organizing my force and pushing improvements. Finding that, with the utmost prudence, I could keep only my assistant, O. M. Stephens, gamekeeper Harry Yount, and two additional men, I employed them in duties deemed most advantageous at this time. As Yount was no longer needed at the gamekeeper's cabin on the Soda Butte, and was a trusty person as well as an excellent hunter and scout, he was stationed at our headquarters (the gun-turret of which is a commanding lookout station) with instructions to daily scan, with a field-glass, our surroundings, visiting so much thereof as was convenient, paying attention to the repairing of roads and bridle-paths, and returning each night, with game when needed, to the proper care of our buildings and other property. With the remaining men, one wagon, team, necessary tents and other outfit, I moved to our grade in the cañon of the East Gardiner, about four miles distant. By this plan we daily saved an eight-mile trip; in addition to which, I, being weary of city life, books and writing, the men of a winter's confinement to the house, and all longing for the freedom of camp life and blanket, these longings were thus gratified.

This cañon of the East Fork of the Gardiner is 3 miles long, 2,000 feet deep, with no egress from its vertical basaltic-capped cliffs, save by our bridges over the East and the Middle Forks, near their confluence, towards our headquarters, or past the falls and cascades to the Blacktail plateau. At this point we made our camp, moving it to little sheltered grassy nooks or glades, as we pushed forward our grade between the roaring torrent and the craggy cliffs. Here, beneath cloudless skies, the stately bighorn, the ferocious grizzly, and the royal eagle watched us from the cliffs, while grouse, deer, and elk were ever in sight and often within pistol-shot of our camp-fire; there were countless speckled trout in the dashing snow-fed stream beside it, and our quiet animals were half-hidden in pasturage and flowers. These scenes, with nights of refreshing sleep and days of cheering progress upon our new route from the cañons of the Gardiner—in short, our sports, our labors, and surroundings, all combined to render these bright camp-fire days among the most pleasant of those which I have ever spent in the mountains.

Late in May, with Harry Yount, I visited the Fire Hole regions, and besides noting geyser eruptions and removing fallen timber from the roads, planned and marked out much of our season's work in that direction, and thence alone proceeded to our gamekeeper's cabin on the Soda Butte. Meeting Rowland there, we together explored and marked a bridle-path to where checked by snow-fields upon the slopes of the Hoodoo Mountain; and on the route of return made interesting discoveries of Indian fortifications and fossil forests. A succession of long hot days early in June were telling rapidly upon the elevated snow-fields of the Sierra Shoshone range; each little rill joining its fellow, that another, thus deeply furrowing and undermining the softening ice-field or tottering crag, until launched a resistless snow-slide or avalanche of ice, rock, and crushed and tangled timber, with roar of thunder, crashing into the streams, rendering them for a time as turbid as the Missouri of the plains, and from their velocity and floating timber therein, far more dangerous to cross. I apprehend that three days of such experience as mine in crossing these mountain torrents while returning from the Soda Butte, would convey a more adequate conception of the resistless power of the mountain floods and their all-eroding effect upon the contour of mountains during countless ages, than the perusal of any work which has ever been written upon the subject.

Leaving the men to complete the cañon grade, I followed, noted, and sketched traces of the Indians, and of some unknown earlier occupants of these regions, from the Sheepeater Cliffs and Sepulcher Mountain, above the Mammoth Hot Springs, to the borders of the Park in the Yellowstone Valley. Then, while en route to Bozeman, for the purpose of selecting and forwarding our season's supplies, I improved my first leisure from urgent duty since 1875, in tracing and sketching such remains through the second cañon and Gate of the Mountains, upon the Yellowstone, together with the first terrace below, and the Bottler Park between the first and second cañons, a distance of fully 60 miles; and thence proceeded along the Trail Pass to Bozeman. These explorations are a continuation of those reported in my communication of 1877, as may be found under the head of "Prehistoric Remains in Montana," pages 327 and 328 of the Smithsonian Report of 1879. As it is my purpose (should there be no official objection) to furnish a fully illustrated report of these, and other traces, tools, weapons, and utensils of a supposed prehistoric people, to the Bureau of Ethnology, Smithsonian Institution, under the charge of Maj. J. W. Powell, I will here only state that they are deemed of peculiar historic interest and value. For the purpose of economizing valuable time, the latter part of June was devoted to hiring men, and the selection and forwarding by government teams of our supplies of tools, provisions and other outfit, for use after the 1st of July, and to be paid for with funds then available. From experience, I considered it best to work simultaneously upon both the Yellowstone and the Fire Hole routes from the headquarters, keeping up our communication there by weekly couriers. The men, wagons, teams, tools, and provisions were divided, and in readiness for an early start upon the morning of the 1st day of July, when, as before stated, our season's funds for improvement of the Park first became available. At dawn of that day the members of each detail were in harmonious but spirited rivalry for the start, anterior to which I read the names and duties of the various members of each, as well as the following address and instructions, furnishing a copy to the foreman of each party:

OFFICE OF THE SUPERINTENDENT, MAMMOTH HOT SPRINGS,
Yellowstone National Park, July 1, 1881.

MOUNTAIN COMRADES: Organized as we are for the protection and improvement of the Park, every member is expected to faithfully obey all the recently published rules and regulations for its management, and to vigilantly assist in enforcing their observance by all persons visiting it.

While labor in the construction of roads and bridle-paths will be our main object still, with trifling care and effort, much valuable knowledge may be obtained of the regions visited, especially by the hunters and scouts, all of which, including the discovery of mountain passes, geysers, and other hot springs, falls, and fossil forests, are to be promptly reported to the leader of each party.

As all civilized nations are now actively pushing explorations and researches for evidences of prehistoric peoples, careful scrutiny is required of all material handled in excavations; and all arrow, spear, or lance heads, stone axes and knives, or other weapons, utensils or ornaments; in short, all such objects of interest are to be regularly retained and turned over daily to the officer in charge of each party, for transmittal to the National Museum in Washington.

P. W. NORRIS,
Superintendent of Yellowstone National Park.

FIRST PARTY, YELLOWSTONE ROUTE.

P. W. NORRIS, *in charge.*

Thomas Scott, foreman and wagon-master; George H. Phelps, hunter and scout; Julius Beltezar, packmaster; Clement Ward, cook; N. D. Johnson, Andy Johnson, Patrick Kennedy, R. E. Cutler, and Philip Lynch.

Supplied by one government wagon, four-mule team, and pack-train, the saddle animal of each man, and a good outfit of tents, tools, and provisions.

SECOND PARTY.—FIRE HOLE ROUTE.

C. M. STEPHENS, *Assistant, in charge.*

James E. Ingersoll, foreman and wagon-master; Harry Yount, game-keeper, hunter and scout; John W. Davis, packmaster; George W. Graham, blacksmith; Robert Clayton, cook; George Rowland, Frank Roy, Andrew Hanson, James Jessen, John Cunningham, Henry Klamer, Samuel S. Mather, Thomas H. Smith, George R. Dow, William Jump.

Supplied by one heavy wagon and a four-horse team, hired for the season. One medium-sized government wagon and two-horse team, with the blacksmith's forge, tools, and also pack-train, tents, and supplies; be-sides, as usual, each man with his own saddle animal, outfit, and weapons.

C. H. Wyman, my comrade of 1875, in the Soda Butte region, was left sole occupant of our headquarters save when George Arnhold, as for the past three years, made his weekly visits with the mails and supplies of articles as needed, and our couriers, who then received them for each party, and kept up a regular communication between them. As nearly all these men had shared the toils, privations, and dangers of the snowy pass, the weary watch, and the welcome camp-fire, and had been employed for their known worth and fidelity, either continuously, or during each season of labor, for from one to four or five, and one of them for eighteen years, they were truly comrades, treated and trusted as such, and are believed to be worthy of the above record of their names and respective duties. Although thus organized upon this occasion, such is now their knowledge of the routes which we have traversed, of each other, and of the various duties, that, aside from the assistant, blacksmith, and wagon-master, they could be reorganized in nearly any desired manner (and in fact were during the season with some addition to their numbers), without seriously impairing their efficiency; and I confidently challenge the mountain regions to furnish an equal number of men who, in the situation, circum-stances, and peculiar difficulties under which we have labored, ever have shown, or are capable of showing, a better record of caring for public property or of making public improvements than is theirs.

Our day of starting being upon Friday, that day and the next, July 1 and 2, were spent by Stephens and party in repairing the grades and bridges to and beyond Willow Park, where they camped, spending the Sabbath and the national anniversary of the fourth in welcome rest and successful hunting; and as there were no intoxicating stimulants in camp, there was neither wrangling then, nor head nor heart aches when, with an ardent spirit of emulation in the performance of duty, they commenced the labors of the next morning. Important repairs and improvements were rapidly made at Obsidian Cliffs and the Lake of the Woods, and again repaired after a terrific water-spout (here called cloud-bursts), as well as at the Norris Geyser Basin and Gibbon Meadows; and the beautiful cone of a pulsating geyser, and some scalloped borders to adjacent pools, was, with much labor and difficulty, got out of a secluded defile two miles above the Paint Pots, for conveyance to the National Museum in Washington. Improvements were also made at Cañon Creek and other localities to and throughout the Fire Hole Basin. Thence, Stephens with his pack train reopened the great bridle-path, via the Shoshone and Yellowstone Lakes, to the Natural Bridge and Great Falls of the Yellowstone, returning by way of Mary's Lake to his wagons, and commenced pushing a road up the East Fork of the Fire Hole River toward the Great Falls. Meanwhile, I had with my party built a bridge over the East Fork of the Gardiner, at the head of its middle falls, another at the forks of the Blacktail Creek, there camping, with no other stimulants than the excitement of the use of rod and gun in securing a good supply of trout and elk meat, during the Sabbath and Independence Day.

We had ascended fully 2,000 feet by the only route possible for a wagon-road from the cañon of the Gardiner to the open, beautiful plateau of the Blacktail, whence a greater and more abrupt descent was requisite to reach the Yellowstone River, where Baronette's Bridge spans it from its East Fork to Pleasant Valley, this being the only place of approach through its terrible cañons, from 2,000 to 3,000 feet deep, between the Great Falls and the confluence of the Gardiner River, a distance of more than 40 miles. Previous long and careful research having failed to reveal a satisfactory route for a road, the 3d and 4th days of July were spent by Baronette, builder of the first house within the Park and the first bridge upon the Yellowstone River, and myself in a terribly trying but fruitless and final effort for a roadway through the yawning fissure region. Adopting a route which I had previously explored through an open pass in the Blacktail divide, we constructed a road with only a moderate amount of grade and bridging in passing between the vertical basaltic walls of a very modern lava overflow, and an impassable fissure vent fully 1,000 feet deep, to Elk Creek, and through a geode basin to the famous "Devil's Cut," or Dry Cañon (as I more politely if less appropriately call it), to the stream skirting Pleasant Valley. While grading down the terribly broken banks of this stream we unfortunately broke our plow beyond repair by any person nearer than our blacksmith with Stephens, to whom our energetic wagonmaster, Scott, with a four-mule team and heavy wagon, took our broken plow and the fragments of another from our shop at headquarters to Stephens at Cañon Creek, exchanged it for the one with his party and returned, making the round trip of 100 miles within four days.

We were compelled to scale a sharp hill to escape an impassable cañon in reaching Pleasant Valley, and to traverse a boggy cañon to avoid a craggy cliff in leaving it, near the forks of the Yellowstone, and by steep grading and climbing reached the cliffs overlooking Tower Falls. Without sufficient time or means to construct a road into the yawning cañon of Tower Creek, we left our wagon and carried our plow into and across it above the falls; then attaching a span of mules, we plowed a furrow for a present bridle-path and one track of a proposed wagon-road over the lovely terraces, the grassy glades, and up the long foot-hill slopes of Mount Washburn to the snowy line within a mile of Rowland's Pass, which, in distance and elevation, is about midway between the foaming river, in the yawning cañon, and the storm-swept summit of the mountain crest. From this place Scott returned with the team, wagon, and two men to the Mammoth Hot Springs, where he quickly repaired the fences, filled our barn, besides securing a rick of excellent hay. They then hoed and irrigated our garden, and, with a supply of potatoes and other delicious vegetables therefrom, and supplies from Bozeman, proceeded to join Stephens in the Fire Hole regions. In the mean time, with the pack-train and the remainder of my party, I proceeded to greatly improve the bridle-path through Rowland's Pass, opened a new one two miles through timber, crags, and snowfields, to the summit of Mount Washburn, and, leaving the party to repair the bridle-path down the mountain and along the Grand Cañon to the Great Falls, I made a visit to Stephens and party, near the forks of the Fire Holes. Finding them energetically pushing the construction of a road towards Mary's Lake, I returned to my party, making ladders and various other improvements at and near the Great Falls, including a good bridle-path 5 miles below the falls to the roaring Yellowstone River in the Grand Cañon, where it is nearly 2,000 feet deep; and after planning and marking out a line of road, skirting Sulphur Mountain and the Mud Volcano, to the foot of Yellowstone Lake, united my party with that of Stephens.

After failing in a long-continued exploration for the discovery of a practicable pass through the Madison divide, towards the Yellowstone, we engineered a line of grade along its nearly vertical face, where little less than 1,000 feet high, and then through the cañon and along the route of General Howard in the Nez Percé campaign of 1877, to Mary's Lake. During the progress of this work, I embraced the first leisure of the season to visit the party of Justice Strong, Senators Sherman and Harrison, Governor Potts, the artist Bierstadt, and other gentlemen of prominence, accompanying them through the Fire Hole Basins, and with some of them—including Lieutenant Swigert, of Fort Ellis, in charge of their escort—to the Great Falls.

Prominent among the parties of visitors who were swarming to the Park early in August was that of Governor Hoyt and Col. J. W. Mason, the civil and military officers of regions embracing the Park, who were united in an expedition in search of a practicable pass for a wagon road from the inhabited portions of Wyoming to the National Park, of which they have a full appreciation and a pardonable pride. Having failed in a determined effort for the discovery of a pass at the head of the North Fork of the Wind River, after nearly a month of dauntless mountain climbing, they had just arrived at our camp, guided from the Two Ocean Pass by Harry Yount, whom I had sent to meet them.

Having been informed from Washington that want of funds would prevent the United States Geological Survey from making an exploration of these regions during this season, and deeming it very desirable to learn all possible regarding them in time for important legislation next winter concerning the Park and its boundaries, I accompanied Governor Hoyt, Colonel Mason, and party through the Sierra Shoshone Mountains to the head of the Great Cañon of the Stinkingwater, which they descended, while I completed the exploration, making important discoveries, and returned over the Soda Butte and Baronette's bridge from fearful snow-storms in the Goblin land, as will be shown under the head of explorations. While personally thus employed, and making but one brief visit to my men at the Mud Volcano, they, with highly commendable energy, completed a good road upon the line which I had laid out to the Yellowstone River, with a branch ascending it past the Mud Volcano to the foot of the lake, and another around the Sulphur Mountain to the mouth of Alum Creek, 4 miles above the Great Falls. They then returned through severe snow-storms, bringing in teams and outfit in good order to headquarters; and judging the employment of so large a force in autumn storms injudicious, most of the men were discharged, but provisionally engaged for next season if desired.

The remaining field operations with small parties were as follows:
One with Davis, securing a fine collection of natural objects of interest
and Indian relics from the fossil forests of the Soda Butte and Amethyst
Mountain regions. Another was made, through severe snow-storms, to
check vandalism and note geyser irruptions in the Fire Hole region,
which was completed by Wyman and Rowland; another, by Stephens
and Miller, in planning bridge sites and grades for next season upon
the East Fork of the Yellowstone. My faithful gamekeeper, Harry
Yount, having made his final tour and report, tendered his resignation;
records of all of which will be found in their proper order.

The final trip of the season was made with the teams in October, hauling out to Fort Ellis, Montana, a large and valuable collection of natural
and anthropological objects of interest for the National Museum in
Washington; and then to Bozeman, 4 miles distant, for the purpose of
closing the business affairs of the season, and the purchasing and forwarding of our winter's supplies.

Our buildings are well repaired, and wagons, tools, and other outfit
secured for winter; during which it is my purpose to retain only my
trusted assistant, Stephens, and Packmaster Davis, for the care and
protection of the building, animals, and other public property.

The season for profitable labor in the Park closed, as it had commenced, unusually early; but the practical knowledge which has been
acquired of the climate and peculiarities of these regions, the careful protection of teams, tools, and provisions, the excellent character and organization of my men, enabled me to make large and substantial improvements, and win the approbation of the candid, practical portion of the
numerous and prominent tourists to the wonder-land. Neither myself
nor others are as well satisfied with the season's protection of the forests
from fire, or the geyser cones or other objects of natural interest from
vandalism; all of which, with my suggestions as to a practical remedy,
will be found in appropriate sections of this report.

The unavoidable failure of all my aneroid barometers to register correctly is a source of deep regret and a serious loss; but the thermometer
readings, which have been regularly and carefully noted and preserved
at the Mammoth Hot Springs during the entire season, as well as during my explorations of the Rocky and Sierra Shoshone Mountains, and
those of Wyman in the Geyser basins, it is believed will be perused with
interest, as greatly increasing our meager knowledge of the peculiar
climate of those regions.

AREA OF THE PARK.

Two matters in connection with the Yellowstone National Park tend
to great and general misapprehension regarding it. These are, first, its
name, and second its area; or, as are perhaps best treated, inversely.

The large, beautiful, and (so far as then explored) correct map by
Henry Gannet, M. E., topographer of the United States Geological
Survey of the said Park during 1878, now in press, shows it to be an
oblong square, 62 miles in length from north to south and 54 miles in
width from east to west, containing 3,348 square miles. The extra
census bulletin, by Mr. Gannet, now geographer of the tenth census
of the United States, under date of September 30, 1881, page 4, shows
that the area of the State of Delaware is 1,960 square miles; State of
Rhode Island, 1,085 square miles; District of Columbia, 60 square miles;
and page 17 of said bulletin shows the aggregate area of the counties of
New York, King's, and Richmond, of the State of New York, is 150, equal

to 3,255 square miles. Thus the most recent and reliable authorities extant show that this great national land of wonders contains 93 square miles in excess of the aggregate area of two of the original thirteen States of the Union, the District of Columbia, containing the capital, and the three counties of the State of New York, which embrace the commercial emporium of the first and third cities of the nation, having an aggregate population of about 2,500,000. Nor is this a full statement of the case; as, if to this account were added the actual excess of surface measurements of this peculiarly broken region, over those relatively level eastern ones, it would (see bulletin, page 4) certainly exceed that of Connecticut, 4,845 miles, and, with the adjacent Goblin Land and other regions which I have explored during the past two seasons, fully equal that of New Jersey (bulletin, page 4)—7,455, or Massachusetts (same page)—8,040 square miles, or several other of the original States of the Union.

Prominent among the bordering points of observation of this vast region is Electric Peak, near the northwestern border, elevation 11,775 feet; Mount Norris in the northeast, 10,019; Mounts Chittenden, Hoyt, Langford, Stephenson, and others in the eastern Sierra Shoshone border, and Mounts Holmes and Bell's Peak upon the western, ranging between 10,000 and 11,000 feet high, and Mount Sheridan, near the southern border, 10,385 feet high, still backed by the Grand Teton, landmark of all those mountain regions, which is over 13,000 feet in height. But Mount Washburn, towering upon the brink of the yawning Grand Cañon waterway of the Yellowstone Falls and Lake, 10,340 feet high, is the most central, accessible, and commanding for a general view of the park and its surroundings. From its isolated summit can be plainly seen on a fair day, as upon an open map, not only this lake and cañon but many others also; countless flowery parks and valleys, misty sulphur and steaming geyser basins, dark pine and fir-clad slopes, broken foot-hills, craggy cliffs, and snowy summits of the sundering and surrounding mountains. No tourist should fail in securing this enchanting view, the best plan of obtaining which is, upon reaching the meandering rivulet-fed lawns of the Cascade, the Glade or the Antelope Creeks, to go into camp, and await the dawn of a cloudless summer's morning. Then, to the scientist, the artist, or the poet, and to the weary and worn pilgrims of health and pleasure, from our own and other lands, ardent to secure the acme of mountain-climbing enjoyment, or in viewing the lovely parks and yawning cañons, the crests of glistening ice and vales of blistering brimstone, the records of fire and flood, the evidences of marvelous eruptions and erosions of the present and the past, and day-dreams of the future in the commingling purgatory and paradise of the peerless Wonder Land of earth, I would say, leisurely ascend the terraced slopes of Mount Washburn, and from its oval summit, with throbbing heart but fearless eye and soul expanding, look around you. One day thus spent would more adequately impress the mind with the magnitude and marvels of the Park, and the vast amount of exploration and research necessary in finding routes, and the enormous amount of labor and hardship unavoidable in the construction of buildings, roads, bridle-paths, trails, and other improvements, even when unmolested by hostile Indians—as during the past two years only—than a perusal of all the reports and maps of the Park which have ever been published.

Owing to the lack of natural curiosities worth retaining, in the three-mile strip of the Crow reservation in Montana, upon the north, or the four-mile strip in Montana and Idaho upon the west, the desirability of having the entire Park under one jurisdiction, as well as for other and weighty reasons fully set forth in my report of 1880, I again earnestly

recommend re-ceding to the jurisdiction of those Territories all of the
Park not embraced by the now surveyed northern and western boundaries of Wyoming, leaving to future explorations and development the
fixing and surveying of the remaining borders. It is hoped this may be
done next season by the United States Geological Survey.

This necessarily lengthy explanation of the first question as to the magnitude of the Park so nearly disposes of the second, as to the name, that
I only add that although it is so vast and broken by mountains and
cañons into countless partially or wholly isolated parks and valleys, still
the whole of it is nearly encircled by snowy mountains with few passes,
being thus park-like in character, and the name correct, or at least difficult to substitute by one more appropriate.

THE TWO MAIN APPROACHES TO THE PARK.

The explorations of myself and others, previous to my assuming the
superintendency of the National Park, led to the correct conclusion that
there were only two natural valley routes of access for wagon or railroads thereto, viz: the one up the Yellowstone River to the initial point
on the northern boundaries of the Park, at the confluence of the Yellowstone and the Gardiner Rivers, some five miles below the Mammoth Hot
Springs ; and the other from the West via Henry's Lake and the Upper
Madison River to its head at the confluence of the Fire Hole Rivers.
The elevated passes over the Rocky and Sierra Shoshone ranges will
be noted in their proper connections.

EASTERN APPROACHES TO THE PARK—THE VALLEY OF THE UPPER
YELLOWSTONE AND THE TWO OCEAN PASS.

There are many and important indications that the towering lava cliffs
which border the Yellowstone Valley above the lake were once lashed
by the waves of its then extended little finger, fed by mountain torrents
in yawning gulches, and drained through Two Ocean Pass into Snake
River and to the Pacific Ocean, much as the ancient lake Bonneville (of
which Salt Lake is a dwindled remnant) once drained through the Porte
Neuf Cañon ; and that the present Yellowstone and Bridger's Lakes, as
well as the deep blue alpine-like appearing waters of the Upper River
between them, are only remnants of this matchless mountain lake, since
a less elevated outlet was elsewhere worn. Two Ocean Pass is either a
natural gap or a broadly and smoothly eroded pass directly through the
continental divide, trending from Bridger's Lake, near the head of the
ancient one, southwesterly towards Jackson's Lake, at the foot of the
Grand Tetons. Some 4 miles from the main valley this becomes a smooth
open marshy meadow, fully half a mile wide; for the first 6 miles of
which the waters creep sluggishly towards the Yellowstone, and then,
in like manner, towards the Snake River. From these circumstances, the
first slope is called the Atlantic, and the last the Pacific Creek ; and are
both fed along their courses by torrents from the snowy mountains upon
each side as usual, the only novel feature heretofore known of this, being
that one of these streams from the south enters the pass so near the summit that portions of its snow-fed waters discharge through these creeks
towards both the Atlantic and Pacific Oceans, and hence the names of those
creeks, the side creek, and the pass. Our camp of this year was made
upon the left-hand side of the Pacific Creek, where a comparatively modern overflow of lava has not only pushed encroaching basaltic walls far
into the pass from the north, but a narrow stream, of the same material 20
or 30 feet in thickness, entirely across, and for a time severing it and form-

ing the summit and divide of the pass. Through this, from erosion or other causes, two openings have been formed. I had never, from record or narrative, heard of a creek upon the north side, nor had I specially observed it until in crossing the mountain towards Barlow's Fork of Snake River I found that while the small but permanent and uniformly flowing Two Ocean Creek drained a snowy basin high above, but within a mile or two of the pass, a much larger one, in fact a fair-sized mill-stream, cuts a yawning gorge in descending over 2,000 feet within 4 miles from the snowy summit of the Rocky Mountains to the north of the pass. This enters directly opposite the other creek, a knowledge of which at once solves the whole mystery which has always shrouded this pass; for with but one feeder, no matter what its angle of entrance to the pass, it would have, as is commonly the case, cut and followed a channel to one ocean, not both, but, with both torrents cutting their gorges and depositing the débris directly opposite, a broad dam has slowly but steadily accumulated entirely across the pass (there less than a mile wide) from the convex or sloping ends and sides of which the streams, broken into smaller channels by the ever descending and changing masses of rock and timber, actually does divide the waters, and portions of each flow through thousands of miles of yawning cañons and mighty rivers to opposite oceans. Although, during this year, a somewhat larger portion of these waters drained into the Atlantic, there is a liability to fluctuation naturally, and little labor would be necessary each season to throw all of these waters, from off this sloping divide, into their former course to the Yellowstone, or through these two openings in the former lava divide, 200 yards upon the Pacific side of it.

In search, not of a better pass or approaches than that at the matchless "Two Ocean," but rather a shorter and better route than the one through dense, and, for the most part, fallen timber, through Trail Pass and by the fingers of the Yellowstone Lake, we scaled the main divide, and, shivering in the snow among the clouds, searched our maps and scanned the surroundings, especially those upon the desired route northwesterly. The scene was grand and inspiring, but the practical part of it was that we could distinctly trace the Grand Tetons, Mounts Sheridan, Hancock, and other familiar snowy peaks, with traces of the numerous fountain heads of the Snake River, and their valleys or cañons, and notably the main one, the Barlow Fork, apparently to our feet, and the desired pass in the main range to Pacific Creek, some miles below us. Buoyant with hope of a warmer region, we frightened scores of big-horn elk and grizzlies, in an impetuous descent of over 2,000 feet into a deep, narrow valley, connecting the Falls Fork of the Yellowstone with a stream which we were rapidly descending, hopeful of a nooning in the lovely Barlow Valley, when, with a sudden turn to the left, it cut directly through the mountain to the Pacific Creek, leaving us to follow the Barlow when we could find it. This we did by way of a pass and mountain spur, which certainly could not have been visited by Jones or Hayden, as neither these nor other portions of a region 6 or 8 miles in width are represented upon the maps of either of these gentlemen. But, as elsewhere stated, the pass to Fall Creek is evidently that traversed by Phelps in 1864, and hence given his name.

A thorough exploration of the region between the Barlow Valley, Mount Sheridan, and Heart Lake to Riddle Lake and the fingers and thumb of the Yellowstone, renders it evident that the route as proposed by Captain Jones and Professor Comstock, in 1873, and by Governor Hoyt and Colonel Mason this season, from Wind River over Tog-wa-tee Pass to the Buffalo Fork and Pacific Creek, waters of the Snake River, can utilize the old Two Ocean and Upper Yellowstone route, or a new one through the lower end of Phelps Pass, and a side one from it, through which we reached the magnificent timber and charming valleys of the Barlow and the Heart Rivers, and the low timbered plateau summit of the Continental divide where there is no mountain, past Lake Riddle, to connect with our bridle-path from the Fire Holes and Shoshone Lake at the western end of the Thumb of the Yellowstone.

I may here add as an objection to the adoption of a water-shed as a boundary of the park, that in this exploration between Phelps Pass and Heart Lake, I traversed the main continental divide, following a tolerably direct course, no less than eleven times in one day.

The interlocking fountain-heads of stream in the Sierra Shoshone range render its water-shed equally tortuous and objectional.

NEW PASS OF THE SIERRA SHOSHONE RANGE.

The narrow elevated pass discovered by Captain Jones in 1873, south of Mount Chittenden, several similar ones explored by myself at various times north of it, and Sylvan Lake, discovered, named, and sketched, together with its supposed drainage, as correctly as possible in a snow-storm, by members of the Hayden expedition of 1878, was all known of passes in the entire Sierra Shoshone range prior to this season. From mountains at a distance I had often observed a deep depression in the serried crest of this range which could not be seen when among its broken foot-hills. The length of time expended by Governor Hoyt and Colonel Mason in their outward route from Wind River would not allow of the search for a pass there, in our crossing to the Stinkingwater, or while following it to its great cañon, which they descended, leaving me to prosecute the exploration. This I did, ascending several creeks, and from lofty peaks viewing all the others, as well as passes of the range above the cañon, finding few trails and no practical passes until on the north bank of the second creek below Jones's I found an ancient but very heavy lodge-pole trail, which I traced eight miles to the forks of the creek, and camped in a grove of cottonwood and other timber—indicating a sheltered and warmer location than is common at that elevation—and some pine trees 150 feet in height. Phelps caught trout, Roy kept camp and cooked supper, while Yount ascended the south and I the north fork of the creek. He reported impassable, snowy barriers; myself, indications of a pass some 5 miles distant; and the evening with the glistening of a glorious sunset and the haloes of the harvest moon of other lands upon the Giants' Castle, towering athwart the glittering stars, was spent in plans, preparation, and hopes of a morrow's crossing of the divide.

Pressing ahead of the packs in the morning, I was blazing the trail along the steep acclivity, when it dwindled, and, in Shoshone guttural. kay wut; or, according to border provincialism, "played out," and a sharp turn to the right at once revealed the cause to be the branching of the trail for various elevations in ascending to a low, clear-cut, but very narrow pass directly through the range, unlike all others, which are elevated, with very steep, rocky climbing from one or both approaches to the sharp, narrow crest. We reached the summit in time for a romantic noon camp on a velvet lawn of grass and frost flowers, beside an Alpine lake supplied by a snow-fed rivulet, skipping in several fifty-feet leaps from the cliffs; and as meat was wanting, Yount killed a blacktail, myself an elk. the surplus of which, and want of other provisions, caused the return of Phelps and Roy, with the most of it and all the pack animals save one each for Yount and myself, to our main camp at the Mud Volcano, they not returning to us. This pass has more the appearance of a natural gap, not quite closed by two mountains of eruption, than by the erosion of a narrow pass; but whatever the cause, it is a very low, direct one, with good approaches for a trail or wagon road, the only drawback being several heavy mountain slides, some very ancient, and others of comparatively recent occurrence, the latter with immense masses of angular rocks filling it for at least a mile from fifty to two hundred feet deep, and the former causing a chain of three lakes, the most western of which is evidently the Sylvan Lake of Hayden's map of the explorations of 1878. This is shown correctly, but not its drainage, which I did not find; but, as the next lake in the pass drains toward this, its outlet cannot be to the Stinkingwater—as the one at the cascade probably is—but even this only by percolating through these modern rock-slides. As this pass is nearly abreast the eastern side of the Yellowstone Lake, affording a fine route *via* Clear Creek to and a route each way around it, and there appears to have been comparatively little recent rock-sliding in the pass, it seems to promise its old pre-eminence as such of the range, by the making of a rocky road, as I did at the Obsidian Cliffs in 1878, over that portion of the pass which doubtless caused its abandonment by the Indians for at least a generation. In reply to my pressing inquiry of We-saw regarding a pass in that direction, while upon the range going out, his only answer was a French-like shrugging of the shoulders and ejaculation, "*Me no go there; maybe Bannock Indian, long time 'go.*"

DIRECT CONNECTING ROAD.

One of the early and important plans of the park was the exploration and opening of a line of wagon road, upon the most direct practicable route, from the headquarters across the park to and through the other entrance thereto, thus connecting them for the convenience of our laborers, the public, and the military for their protection.

Important explorations were made in 1877 upon my route of 1875, and were completed and a rough road opened during the Bannock raid of 1878. This was somewhat changed and shortened through the earthquake region, in order to meet the new entrance over the Plateau of the Madison instead of through its cañon, in 1880, and with the improvements since made at Cañon Creek and elsewhere only requires important grades to save crossing the Gibbon in its cañon, and opening of the routes through the Middle Gardiner Cañon, to render it a direct and permanent route connecting the two main entrances.

CIRCUIT OF ROADS.

Another improvement contemplated in the first general plan of developing the park, and which, though often delayed, has never been abandoned nor forgotten, but persistently pushed at every opportunity each year, has been the construction of a bridle-path upon a route to be mainly followed by a wagon road connecting these two main entrances, from the Mammoth Hot Springs via the Forks, Great Falls, and Lake of the Yellowstone, to the Forks of the Fire Holes, so that tourists could ultimately enter the park by one of these main approaches, visit the principal points of interest with wagons; those of less importance by branching bridle-paths, leaving it by either. Bridle-paths were early opened, and important changes made, with exploration and opportunity, until the whole line was planned, and although the greater part of 1880 was unavoidably devoted to opening the new route over the Madison Plateau instead of its cañon, still, a good start was made in the cañon of the East Gardiner River, from the Mammoth Hot Springs at one end, and up the East Fire Hole River from their forks at the other, during 1880; and the main improvements of this season have been in the construction of this line of road from both ends. As elsewhere stated, the remarkably favorable spring of this season would have permitted the advantageous use of a much larger appropriation than was at my command, but what I had was promptly and prudently expended in the warm sheltered cañon of the East Gardiner.

After July 1, when this year's appropriation became available, until the untimely heavy snows of September rendered such field-work injudicious, the construction of this road was pushed with a vigor, skill, and success, resulting from thorough previous exploration, preparation, and experience, aided by a reliable and active assistant and force of veteran laborers, well understanding their duties and emulous in surmounting the attendant difficulties of climate and surroundings.

The proposition of responsible parties to introduce a portable steam saw-mill for the purpose of sawing lumber for a steamboat upon the Yellowstone Lake, hotels at its foot, and falls of the river, as well as for the government in the construction of bridges, added to the necessity of reaching the foot of the lake this season. After the construction of bridges, culverts, and grades in the open valley of the East Fire Hole, much of which was boggy, and the failure of long and laborious exploration to reveal a practicable pass through the precipitous Madison Divide, it was crossed by a long and uniformly excellent grade along its nearly vertical face to the narrow, dry cañon outlet of the ancient Mary's Lake, along the grove-girt border of its clear but brackish waters, uninhabited by any kind of fish, through the adjacent noisome sulphur basin to the deep valley and grassy lawns of Alum Creek. Thence, winding amid the bald, eroded, and still eroding hills of a short divide, down the open meadows of Sage Creek to the old trail near the Yellowstone River, midway between Sulphur Mountain and the Mud Volcano. From there, one branch was pushed up the river past the Mud Volcano, Nez Percé Ford, and a succession of enchanting groves and flowery lawns, beside the broad, placid, blue waters of the peerless Yellowstone, to Toppin's Point and miniature harbor at the foot of its lake. The other branch was constructed by winding ways, amid verdant hills, passing the stifling fumes of Sulphur Mountain, to the mouth of Alum Creek, four miles up the Yellowstone, above its Great Falls. The other end of this circling line of road was forced through the cliff-walled cañon of the East Gardiner, the grassy plateaus and lava beds of the Blacktail, beside the yawning, impassable fissure vents fronting Hellroaring Creek, through the Devil's Cut (which I am trying to rechristen Dry Cañon, and down the mountain slopes fully 2,000 feet to Pleasant Valley and the Forks of the Yellowstone, in this only practicable gap of the Grand Cañon for a distance of more than 40 miles. By careful research, we carried our road to the summit of the cliffs overlooking alike one of the finest views of the Grand Cañon, the Tower Falls, and the meeting of the foaming blue waters between them. This leaves a gap of less than 20 miles in distance between the Tower Falls and the terminus of the other end of our road at the mouth of Alum Creek, and hence the completion of our much-desired circuitous line of road to the main points of interest in the Park, situate west of the Yellowstone Lake and its Grand Cañon. As before shown, the two main routes of access, as well as the direct or Norris Geyser Basin route, being open, this little gap is all remaining to complete the plan of roads originally adopted and persistently adhered to through vexatious difficulties, and delays, and annoying public misapprehensions.

Although this gap is so short and some portions of it an excellent natural roadway, yet the yawning cañon of Tower Creek, with its vast amount of rock-work, culvert, and bridging above the Falls, the scaling of Mount Washburn through Rowland's Pass, extensive bridging, timber-cutting, and grading along the Grand Cañon and near the Triple Great Falls, together with the absolute necessity of several small bridges and extensive grading, or twice bridging the Yellowstone above the Falls, to connect with the other road at Alum Creek, renders it incomparably the most expensive of any equal portion of the route, and hence it was left until the last; and $10,000 is deemed necessary, and is specifically recommended to be appropriated, for these purposes during the coming fiscal year. This sum, in addition to the amount annually appropriated, might perhaps complete this road, were all others neglected. But this would appear injudicious, as, although the road over the Madison Plateau is deemed an excellent one, save the grades at each end, and they as good as are possible to have been made there, with the limited time and means at my command when this was done, still, they are very steep for hauling heavy boilers or mill or steamboat machinery, and need extensive change of grade, or else of the entire line, and returning to the circuitous Cañon route, with its unavoidably long and expensive grades, or bridging, or both, and which cannot properly be longer delayed. With nearly equal force, this necessity pertains to the extension of the road up the East Fork of the Yellowstone and Soda Butte, as the only route to the gamekeeper's cabin, the fossil forests, medicinal springs, and extension to the borders of the park, of a very important at least bridle-path route via the Clark's Fork mines to the Big Horn Valley and Fort Custer.

There is also a necessity for important bridle-paths up the East Fork Valley to the Goblin Land, and by a newly-discovered pass to Pelican Creek and Steamboat Point, on the Yellowstone Lake. This route also necessitates the purchase of the Baronette Bridge, recognition of it as a toll bridge, or building another, with better approaches, near it. The great desirability of constructing a road via the Middle Gardiner Cañon is believed to be rendered evident in the section devoted to that subject. Nor should the views of the governor, the military officers, and leading citizens of Wyoming Territory, in which the park is mainly situated, their explorations for a route to this Wonder Land, and their efforts to open it, as elsewhere explained, be ignored, but at least a substantial bridle-path route should be opened from some of ours to the borders of the park near the Two Ocean Pass, or via the new one which I explored during the past season through the Sierra Shoshone Range to the Great Cañon of the Passamaria, or both of them. . In this connection I may state that my former knowledge and this season's explorations alike sustain the views of Governor Hoyt and Colonel Mason as to the practicability and necessity of a wagon-road from the Wind River and Two Ocean or the Stinkingwater (Passamaria) route to the park; and, as such, I do most cordially indorse their report favoring the appropriation of a sum sufficient to open a good wagon-road from the Wind R ver Valley or from the Stinkingwater to the borders of the park.

CAÑON OF THE GARDINER RIVER.

In addition to long, yawning, and interesting cañons upon all of the forks of the Gardiner River, high in the snowy ranges not traversed by any of our roads or trails and hence not necessarily mentioned here, there are four of great interest and importance within five miles distance and in plain view of our headquarters at the Mammoth Hot Springs, viz: One upon each of the three forks, or branches, cut in their precipi tous descent of nearly 2,000 feet down the basaltic cliffs to our deep sheltered valley, by them eroded in some remote period, and another carved fully 1,000 feet deep by their united waters in escaping to the Yellowstone. Winding along the western terraces above the latter cañon, we have constructed our road to the main Yellowstone Valley, also one over the elevated Terrace Pass, around that portion of the cañon of the West Gardiner—which is utterly impassable for even a game trail—on our road towards the Fire Holes and through the beautiful cañon of the East Gardiner, ornamented by basaltic column-capped cliffs above and around the falls and cascades, on our road of this season to the Forks of the Yellowstone. The remaining cañon of the middle, and far the largest, fork is utterly impassable, but a bridle-path was made in 1879 along the precipitous face of Bunsen's Peak above it as preliminary to a road line. This bridle-path, as stated in some preceding report, has been in practical use and has demonstrated the feasibility of the route for a road to connect with that to the Fire Holes near Swan Lake. With no increase of distance this route will save several hundred feet in ele- vation, afford a picturesque view of the Mammoth Hot Springs, govern- ment buildings, and sheltered cliff-girt valley from one end of the pass, the upper valley with its rim of snow-capped mountains from the other, and within it the Sheepeater Glen, the vertical walls and uniquely inter- esting rotatory or fan-shaped basaltic columns, the roaring falls and splashing cascades of the Middle Gardiner, in wild, majestic beauty second only to those of the Grand Cañon of the Yellowstone, in the Wonder Land. Long and careful search and engineering resulted in the selection of a route along our timber road to a terrace overlooking the lower cascades of the West Fork of the Gardiner, which is to be crossed upon a short but very high timber bridge, and thence by a moderate and uniform grade along the pine-clad face of Bunsen's Peak to the sum- mit of the pass, amid the spray and thunder of a cataract nearly 200 feet high, in an eroded cañon more than 1,000 feet deep—a route com- bining so much of surpassing interest and practical value that only the want of means to divert from the pressing necessity of opening new routes to the Great Falls and other leading points of attraction has pre- vented its construction, and will insure it, with the first means at my command to properly thus expend.

MOUNT WASHBURN BRIDLE-PATH.

Successive seasons of exploration and research have resulted in the partial abandonment of the old route, with its several steep ascents upon the cold snowy side of Mount Washburn, the gulches of Dunraven's Peak, and the beautiful, but, in places, boggy valley of Cascade Creek, for the bridle-path route of a road ascending by long, easy grades from the pleasant meadows of Antelope Creek to the elevated but only sum- mit of the route, in Rowland's Pass, and thence in like manner down its warm sheltered face to the grassy glades and sulphur basin, between it and the Grand Cañon, and skirting the latter, with its matchless scenery, to the Great Falls. An easily accessible peak upon the very brink of the Grand Cañon, about half a mile east of Rowland's Pass, affords a commanding view of it in all its windings and yawning side cañons, from the Forks to the Great Falls of the Yellowstone, and the terribly eroded, gashed, and repellant-looking unexplored region beyond it. By a short moderate ascent west from the summit of the pass, an open spur is reached, which, in less than two miles of gradual ascent, scales the highest peak of Mount Washburn if desired, although it is but little more elevated and commanding than portions of the snowy crest before reaching it.

PAINTED CLIFFS—BRIDLE-PATH INTO THE GRAND CAÑON.

This path leaves the main one, from Mount Washburn, at the eastern end of an open marsh, about 5 miles below the Great Falls, and, passing fully a mile through an open pine forest, reaches the head of the cañon, and winds along the face of a mountain slide to the small, but beautiful and noisy, Safety Valve pulsating geyser, situated in the narrow valley between this slide and the mountain face. For a proper understanding of this location it is necessary to explain that, evidently at a comparatively recent period, the eroding river and the erupting fire-holes along it have undermined portions of the nearly vertical walls, some of which are fully a mile along it and nearly half as wide and high, precipitating them into and damming it until cut asunder by the resistless current of the foaming river, often leaving long portions of these enormous mountain-slides with the timber undisturbed upon them. It thus presents the appearance of a lower bank, or terrace, with a nearly vertical face of the peculiar ancient lake formations of this region, above and below it. Along the line of contact above this mountain slide, skirting the river below, and at the terribly ragged ends of it, is a line of noisy escape vents of smothered fire, of which one is the "Safety Valve," thus named at its discovery last year, from its powerful and distinct reverberations along the cliff, which were then much more audible than during this season. This is nearly a mile in distance, and 1,000 feet in descent, below the summit of the cliffs, or one half of the entire distance and descent in the cañon, the lower half of which was made through a line of mingled active and extinct and crumbling geyser and other hot-spring formations, along the ragged edge of the lower end of the mountain slide to the foaming river drainage of the mountain snows. This stream we found literally filled with delicious trout of rare size and beauty, and so gamy that all desired of them were caught at each of our visits of this year, during our brief nooning, using as bait some of the countless salmon flies which were crawling upon the rocks or on our clothing, upon hooks fastened to one end of a line, the other being merely held in the hand or attached to some chance fragment of drift-wood; but the sport seemed harder upon the hooks and lines than upon the trout, which were abundant, both in the river and out of it, after the loss of all our lines. Although this is strictly true in our experience, it is but just to state that some other persons who were there at a later hour of the day or period of the season, while seeing countless trout, found them less voracious.

The beautiful tinting of the cliffs in this locality, not unlike beauty elsewhere, seems only skin-deep; i. e., the material beneath is often nearly white, and the brilliant coloring only brought out by surface oxidation of the various mineral constituents; and, although not deeming our path dangerous, I would suggest that anglers who may visit this place should not become so engaged with the beautiful speckled trout as to forget that their charming lady companions may need their nerve and assistance in the horseback ascent of the cliffs. Here, only, between Tower Creek and the Great Falls of the Yellowstone, does a bridle-path reach the foaming, white surfaced, ultramarine blue vein of the "Mystic River," and the long, horizontal, cornice-like groove of its clearly banded and rainbow-tinted walls and tottering cliff; in short, the seclusion, the scenery, and the surroundings of this hidden glen of the Wonder Land render it one of the most uniquely attractive so that the few tourists who fail to visit it will never cease to regret their neglect.

THE TRIPLE OR GREAT FALLS OF THE YELLOWSTONE, AND THE BRIDLE-PATH AND TRAILS THERETO.

These, as is well known, are the Upper Falls, of 150 feet, or about the same height as those of Niagara: the Lower Falls, nearly one-half mile below, of about 350 feet; and, upon the west side of the river, midway between them, the Crystal Falls, or Cascades of Cascade Creek, near its mouth, in height about equaling the Upper Falls. Upon the very brink of the latter the main bridle-path to the lake passes, affording a fine view of them—the foaming rapids above and the rippling river below them—to the head of the Lower Falls, which is reached by the 500-feet descent of a good trail from the main one, or bridle-path, which crosses the creek upon a good bridge constructed last year from two projecting trachyte rocks, nearly 40 feet above the famous Grotto Pool, between the upper fall of 21 feet, and the lower, of more than 50 feet, beside a leaping cascade below it. This pool is caused by the sheet of water in the upper fall being at right angles with the stream, thus facing and undermining the eastern wall, and beneath it forming a broad, deep pool of placid water, nearly hidden under the narrow shelf of rocks between the two leaps of the cataract, and from its peculiarities named by me in 1875, Grotto Pool. From a pole railing to the cliff between the bridge and the brink of the cliff overlooking the lower leap I this year placed a substantial, well-supported ladder to a projection of the wall and thence there another to the foot of the Grotto Pool and thence the footless for the convenience of tourists, beneath an overhanging rock and the lofty bridge along the narrow way between the wall and the water's edge. See Fig. 1. A sudden but violent hail and thunder shower, ... and ... regret, compelled us to ... this newly ... while waiting it, and for a brief period the ... a low ... the bottoms of earth, with their ... and waters are ...

Near the ... Sulphur ... bridge, and danger ... in the Point Lake ... and Grotto ... a chief of ... while the lower ... back the great lake ... and the southern edge of the ... are evident ... park (Crater) of ... a great mass of ... the ...

... the ...

Such ... a ladder, lead the ... pages ...

of my report of 1880, I have so changed the route of the bridle-path as to invite an excellent view of the archway at several points of observation within the distance of a mile below or fronting it, and then, after crossing a warm creek near some beaver ponds, ascend by a winding way to and across it. Thence the trail, within a distance of two miles, descends through a beautiful pine forest, meanders along the shore of the nearly severed extension of Bridge Bay, and across some lovely grove-girt lawns to the old route upon the shore of the lake. The danger of a general conflagration alone deterred me from burning out several miles of nearly impassable fallen timber, thereby materially shortening the trail to the thumb of the lake. No other substantial natural bridges over a permanent water-course have been discovered, but several wind and storm worn tunnels, high amid the tottering crests of the Sierra Shoshone Range, were found and sketched; also one between the first and second peaks from the southwestern slopes of Mount Norris, nearly fronting the famous extinct geyser cone of Soda Butte, although high above and scarcely perceptible from it, but showing a clear cut outline of blue sky directly through the craggy crest, from the great terrace of Cache Creek. At that distance, and even nearer, this opening so closely resembles the adjacent snow-drifts that Rowland, who was with me at the time of its discovery, wagered me a new hat that it was one.

EXPLORATIONS.

Successive years of active exploration, hunting, and road or trail making in the park, have rendered the most of it, west of Yellowstone Lake and its Grand Cañon, so familiar that research is perhaps now more appropriate than exploration, for our observations therein. Still, there are new many localities of considerable area, as much of Mounts Stephens and Dunraven ranges, as little known as before Washburn scaled the peak which bears his name. Traversing such regions are truly explorations, prominent among which, of this season, is that of the Madison Divide, in search of a pass to avoid the cliffs near Mary's Lake. Those to the south were explored last year and found utterly impracticable, although a depression observed this year in the crest of the range to the north afforded a hope that a pass might be discovered there. The long, open, but unsafe valley of hot springs and sulphur vents on the head of Alum Creek was traced to its connection with a branch of the Rocky Fork of the East Fire Hole River, and one mountain feeder of this, through an elevated divide, to the seething brimstone basin of Violet Creek, and another to a similar repellent sulphur region overlooking the Norris Geyser Basin and Fork of the Gibbon, and thence down the Rocky Fork to our camp on the East Fire Hole, and the effort there abandoned. Although this exploration failed in its main object, it led to the discovery and opening of a fine bridle-path route from above the mouth of Rocky Fork, through the earthquake region to the Paint Pots on the main road, which proved a good 20 miles saving of distance for our couriers and pack-trains from the headquarters to our camp on the Mary's Lake route. It also greatly extended our knowledge of the fire holes in those regions, and afforded proof positive that a band of bison wintered there, at an elevation of nearly 9,000 feet. Much was also learned of the broad elevated timbered plateau of Elephant's Back, and its extension above the Natural Bridge; and exceedingly interesting knowledge was obtained of its apparently most recent shattering of the earth's crust, with still awning impassable vents and lava overflow in this region of the Park, upon the various branches of the Blacktail, skirting the Great Cañon

of the Yellowstone between the mouth of Crevice Gulch, via the head
of Pleasant Valley to Tower Creek. By far the most extensive, interesting, and valuable exploration of the season is that in connection with,
or continuation of, that of Governor Hoyt and Colonel Mason, in the
Sierra Shoshone and main Rocky Ranges, during twenty-six days of
continuous and arduous cliff and cañon climbing among the snowy lava-
capped crests of a region of as wild chaotic grandeur, and as little known
or understood as any other in the United States, if not indeed in North
America. A journal of the transactions of each day was regularly kept,
water-courses mapped, prominent mountain peaks sketched, passes noted,
and the weather and elevations recorded at least three times a day.
Only the size and purposes of this report preclude its publication entire herein, but the preceding descriptions of the Two Ocean and other
passes, the subjoined record of weather and elevations (the former accurate, and the latter, for want of reliability in the readings of the aneroid barometer, approximate only), the mountains and streams as
shown upon the map, will be found tolerably correct, and it is hoped will
prove of sufficient interest to encourage the attention of scientists better prepared and outfitted than myself to do this wonderful region justice.

HEADQUARTERS OF THE PARK.

One of my first and most important official duties in the Park was the
search for a location for its headquarters, which should combine, in the
fullest degree, nearness and accessibility throughout the year, through
one of the two main entrances to the park, to the nearest permanent
settlements of whites and a military post, remoteness from routes inviting Indian raids, and a proper site for defense therefrom, for ourselves,
saddle and other animals, good pasturage, water, and timber, as well
as accessibility to the other prominent points of interest in the Park.
The want of any public funds in 1877 prevented other than exploration
of routes to and throughout portions of the park (cut short by a severe
injury at Tower Falls, just in advance of Chief Joseph's Nez Percé Indian raid), and the publication of a report.
The Bannock Indian raid of 1878 rendered unsafe the construction of
public buildings or the retention of public property in the Park during
the following winter, but the road constructed that year, connecting the
two entrances from the Mammoth Hot Springs to the Forks of the Fire
Holes, together with its value to myself in making other improvements,
to the Hayden geological explorations, and to Generals Miles and Bris-
bin, in their military operations, confirmed my opinion, in which these
gentlemen concurred, that the Mammoth Hot Springs was then, beyond
question, the proper location for the headquarters of the Park. The
buildings of hewn timber were mainly constructed in 1879, upon a commanding site for outlook and safety, the main one being surmounted by
a loopholed gun-turret for defense from Indians. Subsequent explorations and improvements in the Park have justified the selection, alike of
the location and of the building site. These are well shown, with the
adjacent cliff fences to our large and valuable pasturage, in the frontispiece of the Park Reports of 1879 and of 1880; and the buildings as they
now are in the frontispiece of this report.
As explained in my report of 1879, there was found at the Mammoth
Hot Springs only one building site not overlooked by others, which one,
besides its position commanding every locality within rifle range, was
desirable from its gradual slopes and accessibility from the Upper Terraces, as well as direct connection with the matchless pastures and

meadows beside and below it. The elevation of this building site from actual measurements is found to be: Above the Cedar Grove toward the Great Terraces southwesterly, 84 feet; above the Liberty Cap northwesterly, 152 feet; above the Little Meadows southeasterly, 226 feet; while towards the northeast the descent by terraces is nearly continuous for over a mile in distance, and fully 1,000 feet in descent, to the Great Medicinal Springs in the cañon of the Gardiner. Although so elevated and commanding a site for observation or defense, a depression down its least elevated side affords an excellent roadway upon each side of it, and between them a convenient location for a reservoir of warm water, which has proved alike useful for ourselves, for our animals, and for the purpose of irrigating our garden, especially for its protection during frosty nights. This hill was originally a sage-brush dotted, grassy mound, having a few dwarf firs and cedars upon it, and with a regular supply of cold water in a natural depression for a reservoir near the house, which might, with little expense, soon be shaded and screened by an evergreen grove, and with a supply of the terrace building water, furnish bathing rooms and ornament any desired portion of the slopes with peerless bathing pools like the ancient ones fronting it. For convenience, for symmetry, as well as for safety from gales, the main building, 40 by 18 feet, was built upon a stone foundation embracing our cellar, with one lean-to wing, 22 by 13 feet, for office and small bedroom, another, 25 by 13, for family sitting-room and bedroom, and a rear kitchen, 18 by 13 (see cut of ground plan, Fig. 2).

All these, together with the main edifice, are built of well-hewn logs notched and spiked or pinned together log by log as laid up, the attic portion of the wings thus sustaining the upper story of the main building, which is surmounted by an octagon turret 9 feet in diameter and 10 feet high from a solid foundation of timbers upon the plates, the upper ends of the well hewn and fitted timbers of which, extending above the roof, are loop-holed for rifles. From the evident infrequency of injury by lightning in the park, I ventured upon an additional mode of sustaining the building during wind-storms, as well as for providing a substantial flag-staff. This was done by planting a fine liberty-pole firmly in the rocky foundation of the building around which it was constructed, and to which it was firmly attached by several heavy iron bands, which allowed for the natural settling of the building, and thence extended through the center of the shingle-roofed octagon turret, above which, 53 feet from the main floor of the building, are the globe and flag-pulley. Altogether it is a sightly, substantial, and commodious building for a headquarters, only needing ceilings in the lower and partitions and ceilings in the upper story—both of which are high and airy—for its completion. The other buildings are an earth-roofed timber, 32 by 18, one end of the lower story of which is for a stable, and the other is an open front room for our wagons, &c. From the adjoining large and substantial corral, one gateway leads to the lane in front, and the other to the pasture in the rear.

A large, warm, and convenient hennery in the hillside near the barn has proved less valuable than was anticipated from the ceaseless destruction of our domestic fowls by the ever pestiferous mountain skunks. In the cedar grove near the old corral and reservoir is our round-log, earth-roofed blacksmith shop, 20 by 14. Amid the cedars at the foot of the cliffs is our rude partitioned bath-house, and at a proper distance in the rear of our main building is a commodious out-house. A large wire-screened box in the cool, sheltered nook at the north angles of the build-

ing is found valuable as a protection from blow-flies upon the elk meat
and venison, which seldom taints at any season of the year.

All these buildings are detached and isolated beyond danger of ordinary fires, the constant fear of which induced the recent construction of
a fire, frost, and burglar-proof vault, 12 by 16 feet, in the face of the dug-

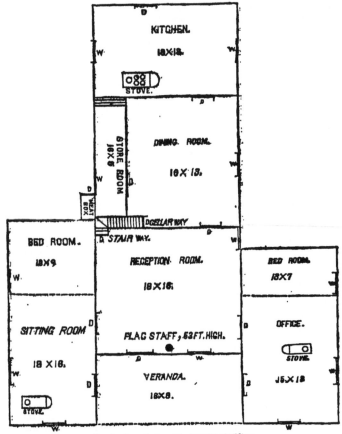

FIG. 2.—Ground plan of headquarters building.

way in rear of the main building, as a provision, tool, and outfit storehouse. These buildings have proved convenient, well adapted for the
public purposes, and, saving improvement in a supply of good cold water,
which is still more difficult to obtain in the Fire Hole regions, ample and
substantial enough for headquarters, until the rapidly-approaching railroads demonstrate the necessity of others, and the proper location for them.
This will admit of all the funds which may be appropriated for the park
being expended for its protection, and the construction of roads, bridges,
and other necessary improvements. Meanwhile some of the finest loca-

tions in the Fire Hole regions should be reserved from sale or leasehold to persons or railroad companies, from which to select a site for the headquarters of the superintendent or his assistant, as may then be deemed best; it being evident that after the completion of railroads to the Mammoth Hot Springs, and to the forks of the Fire Holes, a leading officer of the park, with adequate buildings, will be a necessity at each of these places.

MAMMOTH HOT SPRINGS.

The characteristic tendency of these springs to dwindle or fail in one place and burst forth in another not remote has been very marked during this season in both location and power. We have been compelled to culvert the outlet of a hot spring which burst forth in our road at the foot of the Devil's Thumb during the past winter, and which is still active, while the springs near McCartney's Hotel dwindled until it was necessary to remove his bath-houses, and then burst forth anew in full power. The water, which has heretofore been too hot for comfort at our bathhouse, was this year too cold for that purpose, or to properly protect our garden by irrigation during frosty nights, while a new pool, too far below it for use, is a veritable boiling caldron, and similar changes are observable on all of the terraces. Not only this, but the aggregate quantity of water upon these terraces is evidently diminishing, while that of the Hot Creek, which is fully 1,000 feet below, near the McGuirk Spring, on the Gardiner River, is surely increasing, but is not now of the terrace building, but of the medicinal class of springs.

LIBERTY CAP.

The suggestions contained in my report of 1880, in reference to recoating this famous extinct geyser cone by a jet of water from the terrace building, Mammoth Hot Springs, having been approved, I decided to practically test whether these waters deposit at the orifice of a tube by evaporation only, or by deposition its whole length. For this purpose the open-ended double-barrels of a shot-gun were placed where a current of the hot water in a boiling spring passed steadily through them to the muzzle end, which alone protruded from the scalloped border. Repeated trials, resulting in filling the barrels within a week, demonstrated that *these* springs do certainly fill a tube by deposition the whole length, and not by evaporation at its exposed extremity, as had been believed. Hence the negotiation for the purchase of gas-pipe was abandoned and water conveyed in troughs made for the purpose to the Devil's Thumb, and with perfect success, it having been covered and enlarged by a coating of beautiful white geyserite. The flow of water is now discontinued for the purpose of learning if this coating will endure the frosts of winter; and if so, it only requires about 300 feet of scaffolding from 25 to 45 feet high to conduct the water from the Devil's Thumb to the Liberty Cap, and by building around the base, filling the fractures, and recoating it to thus preserve and beautify one of the unique marvels of the Park.

LAWS RELATING TO THE PARK.

All the enactments by Congress in reference to the vast regions included in the Yellowstone National Park may be found, first, in two brief sections approved March 1, 1872, dedicating it as a national health and pleasure resort, and placing it absolutely under the appropriate control of the Department of the Interior; and, second, by virtue of the annual appropriations during the past four years, aggregating up to July 1, 1882, the sum of $50,000, to enable the honorable Secretary of the Interior to protect, preserve, and improve it. For a knowledge of the enactment, see appendix marked A and regarding the second, or a proper showing of the management of these funds, and the manner and results of the expenditure, reference is made to the annual reports of the honorable Secretary, containing those of the superintendent thereof. The park has been wholly managed without the aid of the civil or military authorities of those regions, save occasional assistance by the latter in repelling hostile Indians, under rules and regulations as prescribed by the honorable Secretary of the Interior, somewhat modified by experience. Those now in force will be found in appendix marked B. While under these rules and management, as fully shown in these reports, and included in maps, plates, &c., much has been peacefully accomplished (so far as the whites are concerned), in both protection and improvement of the park, it is believed that additional provisions by Congress, by the council of Wyoming Territory, or by both of them, are necessary, as well as the proposed organization of a county of Wyoming, with a seat of justice near enough to insure legal co-operation and assistance in the management of the park, as it is neither desirable nor in accordance with the spirit of our institutions, or of our people, to continue the control of so vast a region, teeming with people from nearly every land, by mere moral suasion, occasionally sustained by more potent appeals from the muzzles of Winchester rifles.

GUIDES OF THE PARK.

From the statements and letters of persons who visited or attempted to visit the park, I have no more doubt that many persons have been deceived, and have suffered from the greed, ignorance, or inefficiency of persons in the adjacent regions professing to be able to properly convey or guide tourists to and throughout the park, than of my utter inability or power to prevent such impositions. In addition to my present purpose of publishing a complete and accurate map and guide book of the park, for use during the coming season, I may add that I know of many good, honorable men, thoroughly acquainted with the park, its approaches, and its wonders, who will neither deface nor destroy guide-boards or represent that the park is destitute of roads, and that valiant guides and an arsenal of arms are indispensable to reach or safely visit its marvels or swindle or neglect those employing and confiding in them. If, in compliance with the earnest request of such persons now pending, I should adopt the policy of granting licenses operative during good behavior, each season, which should cost such persons only the expense of badges, license, and record, holding each in a degree interested and responsible for the prevention of fires and acts of vandalism, and observance of the other rules and regulations for the management of the park, by the parties in their charge, I cannot doubt the result would be far more beneficial to the park, and its visitors, than pleasant to the superintendent, from the machinations of those whom he might deem unworthy to receive or retain such a license.

SUGGESTIONS REGARDING A POLICE FORCE FOR THE PARK.

As will be found in the interesting report of the gamekeeper, his experience and observations, as such, leads to the conclusion that an officer especially for the protection of game is not necessary in the park, but rather that there should be a small force of men, hired by the superintendent for their known worth, and subject to discharge for cause, or some of them, at the close of each season, in which opinion, from years of experience, I heartily concur.   Selected as these men would be, from those hired as laborers, the hope of winning promotion to this more attractive and responsible duty would prove alike an incentive to win and faithfulness to retain it; and I am unaware of any other plan promising such efficient assistants in the indispensable protection of game, prevention of fire and vandalism, keeping regular records of the weather, and geyser eruptions, and in general asisting the worthy, and restraining the unworthy visitors of the various geyser basins, as well as for patrol for like purposes and for seeing to the roads and bridle-paths.   There has not occurred a serious fire in the park since the Bannock raid from the camp-fire of any of our laborers or of the mountaineers; but such is the inexcusable carelessness of many tourists, that without great watchfulness disastrous conflagrations, utterly impossible to check when once started, may yet destroy the matchless evergreen groves, and cover much of the park with impassable fallen timber.

Since writing the above, I am in receipt of a synopsis of Lieutenant-General Sheridan's report to the Adjutant-General of the Army, of his recent tour through the National Park, and his views and suggestions in reference thereto.   Owing to his entrance to the Park from Fort Custer and and Clarke's Fork pass, he crossed the Yellowstone River at its forks, while Governor Hoyt, Colonel Mason, and myself were crossing it at the foot of the lake, some 40 miles above, en route to the Stinkingwater, and hence I failed in a desired interview with him, but it is with great pleasure that I acknowledge, in behalf of the park, my obligations to him for authorizing the reconnaissance of Colonel Mason, Captain Stanton, and Lieutenant Steever, and also to the first of these gentlemen for the courtesy (and assistance when needed) which has ever characterized the military officers with whom I have met in the park, as well as for a manuscript synopsis of his past season's explorations; and to the last two officers for their tables of odometer measurements—the first ever made of any of our roads or bridle-paths within the park. From the route taken by General Sheridan, via Mount Washburn bridle-path, he was unable to visit our headquarters or main line of improvements then completed in the park, but the tone of his remarks upon the magnitude of the National Park, the difficulties of its protection and improvement, the inadequacy of the means heretofore provided therefor, and his views as to a remedy, evince alike his intuitive comprehension of a subject or a region, and his military stand-point of view in the management of them.

REGISTERING THE NAMES OF TOURISTS.

The register of the names of tourists at the headquarters, is so incomplete regarding those known to have been there as not to justify publication; that of Job's Hotel, at the Mammoth Hot Springs, has not been received, but that of the Marshall House at the Forks of the Fire Holes, the remaining residence within the Park, although very incomplete, is published, hoping that it may prompt more attention to the matter hereafter by all parties.   Various suggestions have been made as to the best mode of obtaining the names of all visitors to the park, one of which is the establishment of a gate and keeper at each of the two main entrances to the Park to compel registration of names, residence, and dates, which, besides the cost of the gates and keepers, would, I fear, prove unreliable to intercept or prevent false registration by those desirous of avoiding it, and which certainly would be incomplete, as the mountaineer tourists will hereafter enter the Park from nearly all quarters. Besides it may appear to many so like unjustifiable annoyance, that I incline to leave to time, the approaching railroads, increase of hotels, and wishes of the constantly multiplying number of tourists, for a solution of this matter.

REGISTER OF VISITORS.

Copy of the register of the Marshall Hotel at the forks of the Fire Hole rivers, Yellowstone National Park, from June 27 to August 25, 1881.

Date.	Name.	Residence.
1881.		
June 27	Charles R. Brodix	Bloomington, Ill.
July 14	Patrick Walsh	Virginia City, Mont.
26	James R. Johnson	Prickley Pear, Mont.
25	C. L. Dahler	Virginia City, Mont.
25	N. I. Davis	Do.
26	John McManus	Kirkville, Mont.
25	E. Panabacker	Do.
26	James R. Johnson	Prickley Pear, Mont.
26	Francis Collins	Pittsburgh, Pa.
26	R. K. Cooper	Silver City, Mont.
28	William Collins and wife	Glasgow, Scotland.
29	I. W. Thorne	Helena, Mont.
29	I. L. Mears	Wicks, Mont.
29	E. H. Metcalf	Do.
Aug. 3	George Huston and two men	Clarke's Fork, Mont.
3	E. Panabacker	Do.
3	R. Pearsall Smith	Philadelphia, Pa.
3	Hannah Whithall Smith	Do.
3	Mary W. Smith	Do.
3	Alys W. Smith	Do.
3	David Scull, jr	Do.
3	Edward L. Scull	Do.
3	William E. Scull	Do.
3	I. Tucker Burr	Boston, Mass.
3	Winthrop M. Burr	Do.
3	William S. Mills	Wilmington, Del.
3	Bond V. Thomas	Baltimore, Md.
3	Justice W. Strong	Washington, D. C.
6	Senator John Sherman	Ohio.
6	Senator Benjamin Harrison	Indiana.
6	Gov. B. T. Potts	Helena, Mont.
6	Albert Bierstadt, artist	New York.
6	P. W. Norris, superintendent	National Park.
6	Judge W. H. Miller	Indiana.
6	Gen. Thomas A. Sharpe	Do.
6	E. Sharpe	Do.
6	Alfred M. Hoyt	New York.
6	E. W. Knight	Helena, Mont.
8	Dr. D. S. Snively	U. S. Army.
8	Lieut. W. D. Huntington	Do.
8	Miss H. D. Huntington	Fort Ellis, Mont.
8	Miss A. J. McKay	New York.
8	Z. H. Daniels	Bozeman, Mont.
9	Judge William Gaslin	Kearney, Neb.
9	Com. T. T. Oakes	New York.
9	James Gamble	San Francisco, Cal.
9	I. H. Hammond	Evanston, Ind.
9	Edward Stone	Walla Walla, Wash. Ter.
9	Gen. L. S. Willson	Bozeman, Mont.
9	L. W. Langhorne	Do.
9	E. L. Fridley	Do.
9	George Ashe	Do.
9	R. McDonald	Do.
9	L. V. Bogart	Scutogambia.
9	Fred. de Gamga	Do.
9	Commodore Bell	Boston, Mass.
12	Wm. F. Bowers	Cheyenne, Wyo.
14	Gov. John Hoyt	Fort Washakie Wyo.
14	Col. J. W. Mason	Do.
14	Capt. John Cummings	National Park.
14	P. W. Norris, superintendent	Cheyenne, Wyo.
14	Keppler Hoyt	Fort Washakie, Wyo.
14	J. A. Mason	National Park.
14	Harry Yount, gamekeeper	Towanda, Pa.
14	G. W. Watkins	

Copy of the register of the Marshall Hotel, &c.—Continued.

Date.	Name.	Residence.
1881.		
Aug. 14	Frank Grounds	Bozeman, Mont.
14	W. H. Young, sr.	Butte, Mont.
14	W. H. Young, jr., and wife	Do.
14	H. Rumsbach	Do.
14	T. G. Corris	Do.
15	Miss Lizzie Astle	Do.
15	Francis Frances	England.
15	V. W. Bunting	New York.
15	Lieut. Edgar Z. Steever	U. S. Army.
20	John F. Forbes	Butte, Mont.
20	W. T. Hawley	Do.
	J. V. Long	Do.
	John Farwell	Do.
	Geo. N. Givin	Do.
	I. F. Rumsey	Chicago, Ill.
	Prof. W. I. Marshall	Fitchburg, Mass.
20	C. R. Hernon	Saint Louis, Mo.
20	W. R. Larcey	Bozeman, Mont.
24	Walter Cooper	Do.
24	Geo. W. Wakefield	Do.
24	R. Korh	Do.
24	Fred. La Shaw	Do.
25	Thomas Dennison	Cold Bluff, Pa.
25	W. C. Cody	New London, Ct.
25	P. W. Lytle	Oakdale, Pa.
25	A. J. Fisk	Helena, Mont.
25	Henry Cannon	Do.
25	G. R. Multas	Do.
25	W. E. Sanders	Do.
25	John Porter	Do.
25	C. A. Brown	Virginia City, Mont.

FISHES OF THE PARK.

Suckers, catfish, and the bony white mountain herring, abound in the Yellowstone River and some of the lakes, but far the larger portion of all the fishes found in the known waters of the Park are trout. These appear to me to be of many different varieties. Several of these are peculiar to a certain lake, as the red-gilled and red-finned trout of the famous Lake Abundance, at the head of Slough Creek, which has an area of less than a square mile. These trout are very beautiful as well as palatable when in flesh—then weighing nearly a pound each—but they often so overstock the lake as to become as voracious as sharks and too poor for food.

TROUT LAKE.

This noted lake or pond is situated about two miles above the famous Soda Butte, and is wholly supplied by a snow-fed rivulet less than a mile in length and only a good pace in width, and drained by another of similar dimensions, each having impassible cascades within one-fourth of that distance from it; and yet in this little isolated pond are found incredible numbers of one of the largest, most beautiful, and delicious trout of the entire mountain regions. In the spawning season of each year they literally fill the inlet, and can be caught in countless numbers. From my journal of June 3, 1861, I quote as follows:

Wishing a supply of trout for our men in the Gardiner Cañon, Rowland, Cutler, and myself rode to Trout Lake, and, after pacing around and sketching it, with brush and sods I slightly obstructed its inlet near the mouth. Within eight minutes thereafter the boys had driven down so many trout that we had upon the bank all that were desired, and the obstruction was removed, allowing the water to run off, and within three minutes thereafter we counted out 82 of them from 10 to 26 inches in length. Of these, 48 of the larger ones, aggregating over 100 pounds, were retained for use, 30 of the smaller ones returned to the lake unharmed, and the remaining 19 were together with a fine supply of spawn, distributed in Longfellow's and other adjacent ponds, which, although as large, and some of them apparently as favorable for fish as the Trout Lake, are wholly destitute of them.

Although the boys declared this was not a favorable morning for trout, and they do doubtless often make greater hauls, still this is as large a fish story as I dare publish, and qualify even this with the statement that the pond is unusually full of weeds and grass, and the food supply of insects so abundant that the fish are not reduced in numbers by the rod as in many other ponds, and hence the incredible number in its small inlet during the spawning season. Trout varying greatly in size and appearance are found in the snow-fed rivulet branches of Alum Creek and other streams, whose waters are too hot and too full of minerals to sustain ordinary life.

FISHES OF THE YELLOWSTONE LAKE.

The only variety of fishes known to inhabit this great lake is the yellowish speckled salmon trout, which are usually found of from 15 to 25 inches in length. These are proverbial alike for their taking the hook so near boiling pools at various localities along the shore line that they may with ease be cooked in them upon the line without the fisherman changing his position, and for the large number of them being infested with long slender white worms. The proportion of them thus diseased has increased from something over one half in 1870 until all are apparently infested, as I have neither seen nor heard of one of the countless numbers caught this season which was clear of these parasites; and so many were dying along the shores, and so great the quantity of weeds with adherent sacks of yellowish-green jelly, that they drift in lines—sometimes in small windrows—along the shore. Not only this, but it is the opinion of those the best acquainted with this lake that its waters are more discolored with these weeds and less pure than formerly. What degree of connection, if any, these various peculiarities hold to each other, is only conjectural, but to assist in an investigation I have sent the skin, a portion of the meat, entrails, and worms of one of these trout in a bottle of alcohol, and some of the sprigs of this weed and sacks, as well as porous yellowish stone tubes of some worm or insect which are found in abundance along the bank of the lake, to Prof. S. F. Baird, director of the Smithsonian and National Museum, and United States Commissioner of Fish and Fisheries. It has been suggested that some other more voracious fish might exterminate the trout and stock the lake, but whether the latter would prove any more exempt from the parasites, evidently depends upon whether the disease is peculiar to the trout, or to the lake; the evidence now known favoring the latter theory, as trout thus diseased are found only in this lake, or in waters so connected with it as to indicate that they frequent it. Thus, I have no knowledge of a worm-infested trout having been found in the Yellowstone River below the Great Falls; although many of the trout there are apparently of the same species with those of the lake, and presumably some of them may, at some period of their growth, have safely passed the falls; or, waiving this theory, trout of the same variety are never, as I am aware, found thus infested in the numerous mountain feeders of the Snake branch of the Columbia, which so interlock in the Two Ocean and other passes, that there is strong probability that the trout, like the waters, do actually intermingle, and would become diseased also did the cause pertain to the fish and not to the lake. These are the facts so far as now known, and the subject being one of both scientific and practical importance, in connection with a lake of about 200 miles shore line, and far the largest of its elevation upon the globe, I earnestly invite a thorough investigation and pledge all the assistance in my power to render it as complete as possible.

Sufficient time has not elapsed as yet to determine the results of my experiments in stocking various lakes this season with trout, but I propose to extend the effort in larger lakes, like Shoshone and Lewis, and shall report progress from time to time.

In view of the paucity of species of fishes in the Park, it is my earnest intention during my next season's explorations to endeavor to find suitable waters in which to attempt the culture of carp, a subject which is now engrossing quite a large share of the attention of those interested in cheap and nutritious food fishes.

HISTORY OF THE PARK.

Since embracing in this chapter of my report of 1880 my previous private and official publications regarding the aboriginal inhabitants and early white rovers of the park, the accumulation of material from exploration, research, and the narratives of trappers and miners in these regions, as well as the perusal of rare publications in the east, is deemed sufficient to justify a synopsis of them herein. This material, for brevity and clearness, is arranged as follows:

First. Traces of a people who inhabited these regions prior to their occupancy by the present race of Indians.

Second. Remains of Indians.

Third. Evidence of early white trappers.

Fourth. Narrations of prospecting white men before the Washburn exploring expedition of 1870.

Fifth. Explorations of this year.

TRACES OF A SUPPOSED PREHISTORIC PEOPLE.

These consist mainly of utensils, weapons, and implements not now or known to have ever been used by the present race of Indians in or adjacent to the park. Also, rude stone-heap drive-ways for game, which I have recently found therein, or adjacent thereto, some of which are here represented.

Notes regarding ollas, vessels of stone, &c., found in the Yellowstone National Park in 1881.

Fig. 3. Fragment of steatite vessel, size restored about as follows: Inches.
   Greatest diameter 11
   Height externally 10
   Depth of vessel inside 8
   Breadth of rim 1

Much thicker in the bottom, pecked into oval shape outside. No evidence of fire, but some pestle marks in the bottom of the cavity. Found upon the surface in the Upper Madison Cañon.

Fig. 4. Fragment of steatite vessel, size restored: Inches.
   Greatest diameter 8
   Height externally 10
   Depth of vessel inside 9
   Breadth of rim .... ⅓

Very uniform throughout and finely finished, but not polished or ornamented; showing very evident *fire marks.* Found outside up, nearly

covered with washings from the volcanic cliffs, together with various
rude stone lance-heads, knives, and scrapers, in the remains of ancient

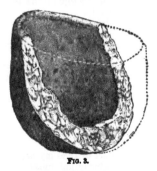

FIG. 3.

FIG. 4.

camp-fires disclosed by the recent burning of the forest border of the
upper end of Pleasant Valley, on the right of where our road enters it
from the cliffs.

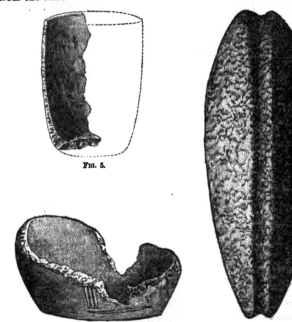

FIG. 5.

FIG. 6.   FIG. 7.

Fig. 5. Fragment of a steatite vessel, size restored: Inches.
    Greatest diameter.. .
    Height externally... 12
    Depth of vessel inside 10
    Breadth of rim 4

Very uniform, well finished outside, but showing much evidence of fine tool-marks inside. Found upon the surface of the mines at the head of Soda Butte.

Fig. 6. Soapstone or very soft steatite vessel, fragment:

	Inches.
Greatest diameter	5
Smallest diameter	3¼
Height externally	2¾
Depth of vessel inside	2
Breadth of rim	½

Well finished inside and out, with flat bottom. No evidence of fire; found with fragments of pottery and rude lance-heads at an ancient camp on the eroding bank of the Blacktail Creek.

It may be mentioned that these steatite vessels are the first found between the Atlantic and Pacific coasts, and are entirely different in form from those found in either direction.

Fig. 7. Sinker: natural size.

	Inches.
Length	3¼
Greatest thickness	1½
Narrowest at ends	1

Grooved entirely around it, endwise; made of rough, volcanic sandstone.

Fig. 8. Sinker: natural size.

	Inches.
Length	3¾
Greatest diameter	1⅛

Hole, ⅜ of an inch from one end; made of coarse, green-veined marble.

Fig. 8.

There is abundant evidence that the Sheepeater Indians habitually made brush and timber driveways and arrow coverts to secure game, and little to show that their progenitors or predecessors ever found timber so scarce in the park as to require driveways to be made of long lines of small stone-heaps such as are found; and this year I traced and sketched from the commencement of the open valley of the Yellowstone, upon the borders of the park below the mouth of Gardiner River, through the Bottler Park and the Gate of the Mountains, to the open plains, a distance of fully 60 miles. As this is mainly outside of the park, and the exploration exhausted none of the funds appropriated therefor, the report and numerous sketches of these stone-heaps, the cliffs over which at least the buffalo were driven, traces of bone-heaps, rude stone foundations of dwellings, together with their burial cairns, mining-shafts, and the tools, ornaments, and weapons obtained from them, will be published elsewhere in due time.

Fig. 9 is a representation of a line of rude stone heaps, probably intended as a driveway for game over the cliffs upon the banks of the Yellowstone. The stone circles shown are evidently the foundations of very ancient dwellings, as the stones like those of the driveway are about one-half covered with accumulated débris. This sketch may be considered as typical of others, many of which are much larger.

I will only here add that there is proof positive of the early and long occupancy of these mountain parks and valleys by a people whose tools, weapons, burial cairns, and habits were very unlike those of the red Indians, and who were the makers of the steatite vessels, &c., we discovered; but whether they were a branch of the cliff-dwellers of the cañons of the Colorado, progenitors of the Sheepeaters, or both or

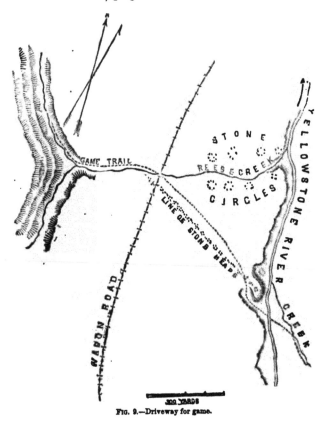

FIG. 9.—Driveway for game.

neither, are questions better understood with exploration and research in that direction, which I have commenced and hope may be continued.

INDIAN REMAINS.

These are, first, of the various kinds usually found in regions until recently only occasionally visited rather than inhabited by the nomadic hunter tribes, such as trails, lodge-poles, brush wick-e-ups, peeling of timber, and rude storm or timber wind-brakes upon commanding sites or narrow passes, for observation, ambush, or for protection from their enemies or the elements, as well as rude stone axes, or flint or obsidian knives, lance and arrow heads and scrapers; and, second, those pertaining to the timid Sheepeater occupants, such as remains of camp-fires in the secluded glens or cañons, and occasionally in caves or niches in the cliffs, for shelter from the storms, or seclusion or defense from their enemies; timber driveways for animals to some well-chosen place for arrow-covert ambush and slaughter, and notably an occasional circular breastwork of timber or stone, or, as is common, partly of each, as to the real builders of which, and the purposes for which constructed, opinions differ. Four of these were discovered during this season, viz, one beside our camp, in a grove north of the crossing of Willow Creek, some three miles below Mary's Lake, which was seen by Hon. John Sherman and party, including the artist Bierstadt, who sketched it. It is about thirty feet long by twenty wide, and constructed of fragments of logs, stumps, poles, and stones, with ingenuity and skill proverbial

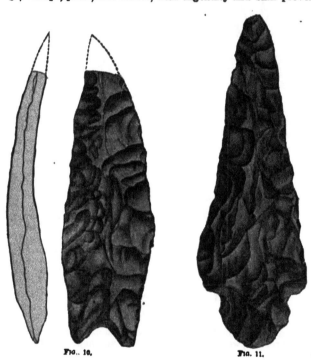

FIG. 10.   FIG. 11.

to the beaver; nearly weather, wind, and bullet proof; about breast high, which is certainly less than when built, and situated, as usual, in a wind-fall then screened by a thicket of small pines, which are now large enough for bridge or building timber. A similar one was found upon the Stinkingwater side of the pass, which I discovered this season, in the Sierra Shoshone range, east of the Yellowstone Lake; another near Bridger's Lake, and the newest one on a small branch of Barlow Fork of Snake River. Although these and some of those previously found do not appear older than some of the evidences of white men, others certainly do, but none of them in any part of their construction as yet known show an iron ax or hatchet hack upon them, and very few and faint marks of even stone tools or weapons. There is usually little

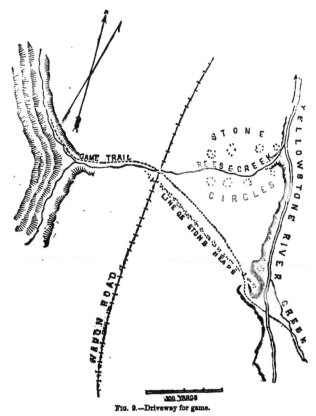

evidence of a door or gateway, and none of a roof, but abundant proof of a central fire, and usually of bones fractured lengthwise for the extraction of the marrow, as practiced by many barbaric peoples.

While these constructions much resemble a Blackfoot Indian fort, the infrequency of the visits of these Indians to a region of few horses, the

Fig. 13.   Fig. 14.   Fig. 15.

Fig. 12.

utter lack of marks of hatchets, which they have long possessed · and always use, dispels this theory, and, as Sheepeater wick-e-ups and pole coverts under low and heavily branched trees are common for summer use, and on cliffs for winter, the only remaining and most probable theory is that these are really winter lodges of the Sheepeaters in the thicket borders of warm, sheltered valleys, where the abundant timber of the decaying wind-falls, in which they are always found, could be liberally used in an inclosure so large as to not take fire, while it was a great protection against the cold, even if, without being wholly or in part covered with the skins of animals, and as necessary against the prowling wolf and wolverine in winter, the ferocious grizzly in spring, or human foes on occasions. Two Shoshone Indian scouts and guides accompanied the exploring expedition of Governor Hoyt and Colonel Mason during the past season, one of whom, We-saw, had accompanied Captain Jones in his explorations of 1873. As arranged with Governor Hoyt at Mary's Lake, I en route tried the Nez Percé ford, and deeming it then barely passible for those well acquainted with the channel both sides of the island, posted a notice so informing him at the Mud Volcano, and then ascended the river to its head, laid out some work for my laborers, constructed a raft, and crossed in time to intercept the governor and party, who, after visiting the Great Falls, had crossed at the Nez Percé ford under the skillful guidance of We-saw, although this was his first visit since the one with Captain Jones, eight years before, and the channel had meanwhile changed materially. While the rest of the party were camped at Concretion Cove, We-saw and myself went over to the Jones trail on the Pelican, and thence followed it as near as possible for large areas of timber fallen since his visit, to the entrance of his pass of the Sierra Shoshone range, and in order to avoid this timber selected a route via the Hot Springs feeder of Turbid

Fig. 17.

Fig. 16.

Fig. 18.   Lake. During this and other occasions I could not fail to admire the intuitive accuracy of his judgment as to Jones's and other routes, even where no trace was visible, and in various conversations as well as comparisons of our daily sketches, which each regularly kept in his own style, obtained much valuable information. I found him an old but remarkably intelligent Indian, and so accurate in his sketches that I could readily trace them, although they were destitute of the point of compass, date, or word of explanation; and yet in that, as in all else, he manifested the true Indian character, which, like their farms, *is all long and no wide, i. e.*, a keenness of perception rather than a broad or general comprehension of a subject, or even a region. Hence, although a person skilled in Indian sketching could by his map or sketch easily follow them through a long journey in all its turns and windings, neither one or both of them could therefrom make a general map of the region or of the relative positions of various mountains or other portions of the route, even approximately, and this is in fact the main difficulty with the maps and journals of white rovers also. We saw states that he had neither knowledge nor tradition of any permanent occupants of the Park save the timid Sheepeaters, his account of whom is embraced in the history of them. He said that his people (Shoshones), the Bannocks, and Crows occasionally visited the Yellowstone Lake and river portions of the Park, but very seldom the geyser regions, which he declared were "*heap heap bad*," and never wintered there, as white men sometimes did with horses; that he had made several trips before the one with Captain Jones, one of which was, as I understood him, to assist some friends who had intermarried with the Sheepeaters to leave the Park after the great small-pox visitation some twenty years ago. Among the most recent as well as the most interesting of Indian remains are those heretofore reported of the rudely fortified camp of Chief Joseph and his Nez Percés in 1877. Of these, the corral east of Mary's Lake, corral and small breastwork between the Mud Volcano and the river, and others upon Pelican and Cache Creeks, and their dugways in descending into the cañons of Crandall and Clarke's Forks, possess peculiar historic interest. Figs. 10 to 24, inclusive, represent natural size scrapers, knives, lance or spear heads, perforators, and arrow-heads chipped from black obsidian. These were found in various places, such as caverns, driveways, or at the foot of cliffs over which animals had been driven to slaughter, and are typical of a collection of over two hundred such specimens collected this season.

EARLY WHITE ROVERS IN THE PARK—JOHN COULTER.

Since the publication in my report of 1880 of a reference to the trip of the Indian gauntlet-running Coulter across the National Park, in 1808 or 1809, I have, through the kindness of General O. M. Poe, Corps of Engineers, U. S. A., obtained a trace of the prior wanderings of this famous mountaineer, of which, as well as of the map exhibiting them, I had no previous knowledge. This map is contained in the first of three rare volumes now in the military library of the War Department, Washington, and is an English reprint in 1815 of the journals of Lewis and Clarke to the head of the Missouri River, and across the continent to the Pacific and return, during the years 1804–'05 and '06. The portion of this map showing the routes of these explorers, is remarkably accurate and the rest of it a fair representation of what was then known of those regions; but, as that was a medley of fact and fiction, of truth and romance, gleaned from the narratives of three centuries of Spanish rovers from Mexico, two of French missionaries or traders from Canada, and the more recent and more accurate accounts, English or American, between them, far the most valuable fact shown was the existence of an elevated snowy fountain-head and point of divergence for nearly all of the mighty rivers of central North America, while the real or relative location of the upper portion of all save those visited by Lewis and Clarke, as there shown, are at best only approximate, and are now known to be mainly erroneous. A knowledge of these facts is alike uscessary to properly estimate the truth and the errors of this map, and especially those portions of the country shown to have been visited by Coulter in 1807. After his honorable discharge, as stated by Lewis and Clarke, in 1806, near the mouth of the Yellowstone, he ascended it to Prior's Creek, a southern branch of the Yellowstone, between the Clarke's Fork and the Bighorn, where he probably wintered, and, as shown by the map, the next year traversed the famous Prior Gap to the Clarke's Fork, which he ascended nearly to its head, and thence crossed the Amethyst Mountain to the main Yellowstone River, and that at the best ford upon it. This is the famous Nez Percé ford at the Mud Volcano, the location of which is accurately shown under the name of Hot Brimstone Spring. But, most strangely, neither the Great Falls of the Yellowstone, 10 miles below, nor the lake, 8 miles above, are represented; but the river is correctly shown as a very wide one, not only to where the foot of

Fig. 20.

the lake really is, but also incorrectly throughout its length, and the locating of one of the fingers to and as being the outlet of Eustus Lake, which he reached by crossing the main divide of the Rocky Mountains without knowing it. This is pardonable, as from the peculiar situation in the mountains of the lake he called Eustus (evidently Shoshone) Lake which was mistaken by Professor Hayden and others as Atlantic and not Pacific waters, only they thought it drained into the Madison, and Coulter supposed it drained into the Yellowstone, while it is in fact the head of one fork of the Snake River of the Columbia, although from its size (12 miles long) Coulter deemed it the large lake at the head of the Yellowstone, of which he must have heard.

From this lake his route seems to have been through or near Two Ocean and Tog-wo-tee Passes to lake Riddle, which, though far too large, is, from its location and drainage into the Upper Bighorn River, probably the Great Hot Spring at the present Fort Washakie, near the Wind River Shoshone Indian Agency. He thence traversed the mountains to Coulter's Fork of the Rio del Norte, as he naturally deemed it, discharging into the Gulf of Mexico, while it is in fact the Green River of the Colorado, of Major Powell's Grand Cañon to the Gulf of California. In traversing the South Pass he crossed the Continental Divide probably for the sixth time, without knowing it, to the Platte, which he calls the Rio de la Plata, and thence across the mountains and Bighorn River, through fossil regions, to the Salt (really South) Fork of the Stinkingwater, to the great Stinking Spring near the forks, and hence the name which, Indian-like, does not signify

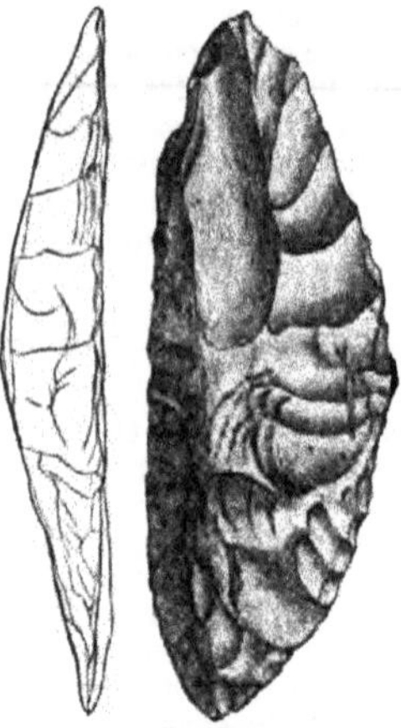

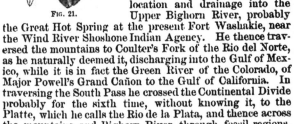

Fig. 21.

Fig. 22.

the river of stinking water, but the river which passes or is near the *stinking water*.

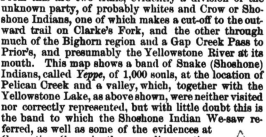

From this are two trails, evidently a division of the unknown party, of probably whites and Crow or Shoshone Indians, one of which makes a cut-off to the outward trail on Clarke's Fork, and the other through much of the Bighorn region and a Gap Creek Pass to Prior's, and presumably the Yellowstone River at its mouth. This map shows a band of Snake (Shoshone) Indians, called *Yeppe*, of 1,000 souls, at the location of Pelican Creek and a valley, which, together with the Yellowstone Lake, as above shown, were neither visited nor correctly represented, but with little doubt this is the band to which the Shoshone Indian We-saw referred, as well as some of the evidences at Concretion Cove, in the preceding section

Fio. 23.

upon Indian Remains. I have devoted unusual space to this matter, which I think is of great interest, as being the earliest known record of white men in any portion of the National Park, and is nearly as valuable for what is erroneously as well as for that which is correctly represented, from being a compilation by the highest authority of all that was at that period known of those vast mountain regions, and in no way conflicts with the account of the death of Potts, during Coulter's gauntlet-running expedition upon the Jefferson, or his return through the Park, as that was a subsequent expedition, and probably unknown to Lewis and Clarke at the time of their first publication of their journals, of which this English edition was mainly a reprint.

Fio. 24.

RECORDS OF THE EARLIEST WHITE MEN FOUND IN THE PARK.

The next earliest evidence of white men in the Park, of which I have any knowledge, was discovered by myself at our camp in the little glen, where our bridle-path from the lake makes its last approach to the rapids, one-fourth of a mile above the upper falls. About breast-high upon the west side of a smooth pine tree, about 20 inches in diameter, were found, legibly carved through the bark, and not materially obliterated by overgrowth or decay, in Roman capitals and Arabic numerals, the following record:

J. O. R.
AUG. 29. 1819

Fio. 25.

The camp was soon in excitement, the members of our party developing a marked diversity of opinion as to the real age of the record, the most experienced favoring the theory that it was really made at the

date as represented. Upon the other side of tl
small wooden pins, such as were formerly often u
verine and other skins while drying (of the actu
was no clew further than that they were very old), l
hatchet hacks near the record, which all agreed v
and that by cutting them out and counting the laye
the question should be decided. This was done, an
were unusually thin, they were mainly distinct, an
present, decisive; and as this was upon the 29tb
only one month short of sixty-two years since some
had there stood and recorded his visit to the roarin
tic River," before the birth of any of the band of
and grizzled mountaineers who were then groupe
all which was then or subsequently learned, or y
of the maker of the record, unless a search which
results in proving these initials to be those of some
regions. Prominent among these was a famous :
named Ross, whose grave I have often seen (the
the Bighole battlefield for the bones of Lieutens
where he was long since killed by the Blackfeet Inc
as parks were then called—at the head of the Ros
branch of the Hell Gate, in Montana, and which v
as was also, perhaps, the branch of Snake River
Shoshone Indian Agency is situated. The "R" ir
rather than proves, identity, which, if established,
as confirming the reality of the legendary visits of t
pers to the Park at that early day. Thorough s
which this tree is situated only proved that it was a l
ing ground. Our intelligent, observant mountain
upon this, as upon previous and subsequent occasio
date claimed by any one, of the traces of men, anc
be correct.

The narrowest place of the Yellowstone River
knowledge below the lake is between our camp
Upper Falls; and upon the eastern rock, just al
often seen a medium-sized stump, which Phelps
himself when returning with two or three comrades
fruitless Big Horn expedition of 1864, or sevento
time, and that if we would cross the river he would sho
camp-fire also. This we soon after did with a raft
too high to cross as I have frequently done later in
the measurements of the river for a future bridge, a
Phelps found the charred fire-brands of the camp
picket-pins for the lariats of the horses, intact, and
of the ground, but little decayed; in fact, the hate
the poles, including the ends of the pins, although c
were uniformly clear and distinct. In company
subsequently visited a scaffold for drying meat, at
which I had often at a glance in passing deemed
which he accurately described before reaching, an
as one of their camps of 1864, although he had n
time visited the vicinity. From the appearance
other camps which were subsequently visited with
his description at various places in the mountains (
that of Two Oce_____ which I thus particulai
save those of O_____ y hereafter mentionec

white men in the Park, of which we have positive data, I learned to judge of the relative age of certain marks, which, from signs hard to explain, were unmistakably recognized as the traces of unknown white men.   In addition to the old loop-holed log ruin near the brink of the Grand Cañon below Mount Washburn; the cache of old Hudson Bay marten traps, near Obsidian Cliffs; decaying stumps of foot-logs over Hellroaring and Crevice streams, and other evidences of early white men, heretofore mentioned in my reports, I saw many during this season's explorations, a few only of which will be here noticed.

In the grove-girt border to the small lake back of Concretion Cove of Yellowstone Lake are the traces of very old tree and brush shelters for horses, larger and differently formed from those of Indians, and the numerous decaying bones of horses, proving that they died probably by starvation during some severe winter, or, as is less likely, were killed by the Indians in an attack before carrying the camp, (as they were not at that day properly armed with guns), for they would certainly have saved and not slaughtered them thereafter.   Stumps of trees, remains of old camps, and the fragments of a rough dugout canoe, prove that white trappers long since frequented the famous willow swamps around the mouths of the Upper Yellowstone and the Beaver Dam Creek.   Our first noon camp in ascending the east side of the Yellowstone above the lake was purposely made where Harry Yount found a human cranium in 1878.   This skull we failed to find, but we utilized some of the wood cut and split, but not corded, by white men so long ago that, though the upper cross-sticks were apparently not decayed, they were dried into curvature from the heart and seams in the well-known manner of timber unearthed from peat bogs or beaver dams, and were easily broken over the knee by a sudden pressure of the hands upon the ends; also one end of a long pole for camp purposes, thrust through the fork of a pine, was there much overgrown.   This camp was made near the eastern edge of a then new wind-fall of timber, as shown by the fragments of logs chopped, extending from the river to a lovely lawn skirting the towering cliffs; a well-chosen place for defense, or for secretion, unless betrayed by the presence of horses.   A little distance above the camp are the stumps of trees cut and one of the logs not used in the construction of a raft.   This wind-fall is now overgrown by trees, certainly not less than fifty or sixty years old; and the skull, fire-wood, raft log, and other circumstances indicate that a party of white men were attacked, and, after loss of horses, at least some of them hastily left their camp and attempted to escape by descending the river.   Just south of the trail between the South Creek and the summit of the Two Ocean Pass is one standing and several fallen posts, and some poles of what may have been a very large oblong square tent, or more probably a conical lodge, as the appearance of the notches in the top of these posts, to sustain strong ridge and plate poles, seem to indicate that it was inclosed with skins and not canvas.   But as the notches in the top of the posts were unquestionably made by white men, it was probably constructed for some grand council between the early trappers and the Indians, of which we have no other record or tradition than these decaying remnants.

The deep broad, and often branched bridle-paths up the Pelican Creek have usually been attributed to the thousands of horses of the retreating hostile Nez Percés or Bannocks and their white pursuers in 1877 and 1878, but this year I followed heavy trails from Camp Lovely, near the open pass from the South Fork of Pelican Creek, down an unknown branch (which these Indians did not follow) to the East Fork of the Yellowstone, finding constant evidences of camps and other distinctly recognized traces of white men, made long years before the miles of burned and fallen timber—now much decayed—caused the abandonment of the route.

In closing this interesting subject it is only added that to tradition and slight published records I find abundant wide-spread, and, to my mind, conclusive evidence that white men frequented these regions nearly or quite from the visit of Coulter in 1807 until the waning of the fur trade after the discovery of gold in California, and in a lesser degree continuously thereafter. What portion of these rovers were trusty trappers and what hiding outlaws will never be known. Nor is it material to history, as the interest of each conduced to a successful concealment from the public of a knowledge of the cliff and snow girt parks and valleys of the National Park, fully two generations after the surrounding regions, some of which are fully as inaccessible, were well known, correctly mapped, and published to the world.

WHITE PROSPECTING MINERS.

The dwindling of placer mines in California, and their discovery elsewhere, greatly increased the numbers of the worthy prospecting successors of these roving trappers, and these were joined during the war of the rebellion by many deserters from the Union and Confederate armies, and by refugees from the devastated borders between them, and bold men from elsewhere, who preferred fighting Indians in the West to white men in the East, being mostly armed with long-range breech-loading rifles. Scarce since the days of the Pilgrims of the Cross, and the wild crusade of the mailed warriors of Europe for the sacred tomb in Palestine, has the world witnessed an onset more wide-spread, daring, or resistless than that of the grim gold-seeking pilgrims to Wyoming, Idaho, and Montana. Streaming from the East, organized, often broken up and reorganized upon the plains, under Bridger, Bozeman, or other daring leaders, they, with wagon trains, pack trains, on horseback or afoot, collectively or separately, fought their way through the Cheyenne, the Sioux, and other of the fiercest fighting Indian nations of the plains, with bull-boat, raft, or wagon, afoot or on horseback, forded, ferried, or swam the mighty rivers, and in bands, in squads, or alone, poured a resistless stream through nearly every mountain pass, yawning gulch, and dangerous cañon, to all the main parks and valleys from the Platte to the Columbia.

Of some of these parties and pilgrims we have knowledge, but doubtless many prospectors have traversed these regions, visited portions of the park prior to 1870, but as they were seeking mines, and not marvels, and better skilled in fighting Indians than in reporting discoveries, the little known of them is being learned from their own recent publications, or by interviews with those of them still living, the list embracing many of the wealthiest and worthiest citizens of these regions, the narratives of some of which are added.

On page 113 of the first volume of the History of Montana is found the commencement of a very interesting narrative by Capt. W. W. De Lacy, now and long a prominent and esteemed surveyor and engineer of Montana, of the wanderings of himself and party of prospecting friends during the latter part of 1863. Leaving Alder Gulch, now Virginia City, in Montana, August 3, they crossed the main divide at Red Rock Creek, and proceeded thence, via Camas, Market Lake, and the forks of Snake River, and through the broken regions of East Fork, so graphically described in Irving's Astoria and Bonneville, reaching Jackson's Lake, at the very foot of the towering Tetons. Here the party divided, one portion returning via Lewis Lake and the Fire Hole and Madison Rivers to Virginia City, while Captain De Lacy, with twenty-six men, missed Lewis Lake, but discovered and skirted a lake which was very properly called after their leader, De Lacy. This was named and published in maps for years before Professor Hayden or any of his men saw it; and some of them, for some unknown cause, gave it the name of Shoshone, which, though a fitting record of the name of the Indians who frequented it, is still in my view a gross injustice to its worthy discoverer, as, even if my interpretation of Coulter's visit in 1807 is correct, it was then unknown. From this lake De Lacy and party crossed the main divide of the Rocky Mountains to the East Fire Hole River, which they descended to the forks, and down the main Madison, through its upper cañon, then across the North Fork and through mountain defiles to the head of the west branch of the Gallatin Fork of the Missouri. The above narrative, the high character of its writer, his mainly correct description of the regions visited, and the traces which I have found of this party, proves alike its entire truthfulness, and the injustice of changing the name of De Lacy's Lake; and fearing it is now too late to restore the proper name to it, I have, as a small token of deserved justice, named the stream and park crossed by our trail above the Shoshone Lake after their discoverer.

The journey of G. H. Phelps and comrades connected with the armed expedition of James Stuart early in the spring of 1864, to the Bighorn regions, for the purpose of avenging the slaughter of some, and the terrible sufferings of the rest, of his party, in 1863; failing to find the Indians, they broke up into prospecting parties, that of Phelps wandering through the mountains to the Sweet Water, through the South Pass to Green River, then to the Buffalo Fork of Snake River, crossing the main divide in the pass near Two Ocean, which, as before stated, I recognized from his description, and attached his name. Thence they descended to Bridger's Lake, crossed the Upper Yellowstone, and continued upon the east side of it, as well as of the lake and lower river, past Pelican Creek and the falls, as before shown, to the trail of another party of white men, which they followed to Emigrant Gulch, near the Gate of the Mountains.

From a well-informed and truthful mountaineer, named Adam Miller, I learned the history of this party. In the spring of 1864, H. W. Wayant, now a leading citizen of Silver City, Idaho, William Hamilton, and other prospectors, to the number of forty men, with saddle horses, pack train, and outfit, ascended the east side of the Yellowstone from the Gate of the Mountains to Emigrant, Bear, and Crevice Gulches, forks of the Yellowstone, East Fork, and Soda Butte; thence over the western foothills of Mount Norris to the bluffs upon the south side of Cache Creek, where their horses were all stolen by some unknown Indians, but their only two donkeys would not stampede, and remained with them. Here the party broke up; Wayant, Harrison, and ten others, with one jack, and what he and the men could carry, ascended Cache Creek to Crandall Creek, Clarke's Fork, Heart Mountain, thence by way of Index Peak and the Soda Butte returned to the cache made by the other party of what they could not carry, aided by their donkey, from where set afoot, and hence called Cache Creek. They then crossed the East Fork, scaled the Amethyst Mountain, forded the main Yellowstone, at Tower Falls, and thence returned via the mouth of Gardiner River, Cinnabar, and Cañon Creek, where I saw traces of them in 1870, to Alder Gulch, now Virginia City, Montana. Meanwhile the other party had returned, and some of them assisted in planting the mining camps of Crevice, Bear, and Emigrant.

Later in the same season George Huston and party ascended the main Fire Hole River, and from the marvelous eruption of the Giantess and other geysers, and the suffocating fumes of brimstone, fearing they were nearing the infernal regions, hastily decamped. These, with the visit of Frederick Bottler, and H. Sprague, Barronette, and others mentioned in preceding reports, are the most important of those as yet known, until 1870.

Upon a pine tree, below the confluence of the North Fork of the Stinking Water and the creek which we ascended to the new pass, is plainly and recently carved as follows:

Fig. 36.

Evidently showing that some one, on the 5th day of some month, the name of which commences with A, failed in an effort to ascend the stream, and so informed some person or party, who would then have known the date and circumstances. This record may have been left by a member of A Company, Fifth Infantry, this company having been with General Miles in the Bannock campaign of 1878, or the famous mountaineer and guide, Yellowstone Kelley, may have carved it.

A square pen of logs, with a huge dead-fall at its only entrance, found on Orange Creek, is certainly a white man's bear-trap, and like many other traces is of uncertain date, and not of sufficient interest for further notice.

INDIAN TREATIES.

The first white visitors to the National Park found the timid, harmless Sheepeater Indians the only permanent occupants of it; their nearest neighbors, the Bannocks, Shoshones, and Mountain Crows, its most frequent visitors; and the occasional prowlers therein, the rapacious Blackfeet and Sioux, robbers of their race, and the early white trappers of these regions. Decimation by war and disease, with the occupancy of intervening regions by whites, guarantee future safety from the Blackfeet; a nearly impassable mountain range and a cordon of military posts and armed ranchmen, from the Sioux.

SHEEPEATERS, BANNOCKS, AND SHOSHONES.

The recent sale of the National Park and adjacent regions by these Indians insures future freedom from any save small horse-stealing bands of these tribes also. To prevent these forays, in council at their agency on Ross Fork of Snake River, in Idaho, and in Ruby Valley, in Montana, early in 1880, I obtained a solemn pledge from them to not thereafter go east of Henry's Lake, in Montana, or north of Hart Lake, in Wyoming, to which, as stated on page 3 of my report of 1880, they faithfully adhered. This pledge was renewed at Ross Fork when I was en route from Washington this year, and has again been sacredly observed. Unable to visit the Lemhi Agency of these tribes, by letter I represented the matter, and sent printed copies of the rules and regulations for the management of the Park to Maj. E. C. Stone, their agent, who, in reply under date of May 26, stated that, after mature deliberation in council, he felt justified in pledging that the Indians of his agency would not thereafter enter the Park. The only known disregard of this pledge was by a band of three lodges of hunters upon the North Branch of the Madison, which was promptly reported and checked, and is not likely to occur again.

MOUNTAIN CROWS.

These Indians, numbering about 3,000, have as a tribe never been hostile to the whites, but often their valuable allies in conflicts with others, and though beset with their proverbial craving for horses, without a special observance of brands or collar-marks, besides some minor failings too prevalent with other races also, they have by the sale of much of their lands, and granting the right of way for a railroad through the remainder, proven that, although in common with their race they may be the guilty possessors of a valuable region desired by the all-absorbing white man, still they are not intentional obstructors in the pathway of progress.

As shown in my preceding reports, sustained by memorials of the officers and other leading citizens of Montana, and proven by the records, the following facts are established:

First. No portion of the northern or western watershed of the Yellowstone Range, between the Gate of the Mountains and the borders of Wyoming, including a three-mile strip of the Yellowstone National Park in Montana, was ever occupied, owned, or even claimed by the Crows, save only as being embraced in the then unknown boundaries of their reservation as set off in 1868.

Second. In 1864, or four years prior to the cession of this land to the Crows, the Sheepeater Indians, owners of Emigrant, Bear, and Crevice Gulches, had been dispossessed by the white miners, who have since constantly occupied portions and controlled all of it, with the full knowledge and acquiescence of the Crows.

Third. Upon the discovery of mines upon the northeastern watershed of the said Yellowstone Range, below the Gate of the Mountains, which had always been owned and occupied by the Crows, they promptly sold the entire range, embracing alike that occupied by the miners and that by themselves, including the old agency, buildings and improvements, as well as valuable agricultural lands, and have for many months allowed white men to occupy it, although, by the delay of Congress to appropriate the funds, they are still without one dollar of pay therefor. Besides this, they have, as before stated, shown their peaceful and progressive tendencies by promptly granting for a mere nominal sum a very liberal right of way along the whole river front of the remainder of their reservation for a railroad artery of civilization. Meanwhile, mines, mills, ranches, and the site and buildings of at least one village (Emigrant, or Chico), with a United States post-office, are, in the absence of all lawful organization or protection, held only by actual possession, without legal right of transfer or even improvement, which are alike indispensable to attract capital for the development of a most promising mining and agricultural region. Hence, in justice and good faith alike to the white man and to the Indian—to the Crow who surrendered a region without remuneration, and to the miner who holds it without title; to the race dwindling away for want of civilization for the means which are their due of obtaining it; to the poor but dauntless path-finding prospector of boundless hidden wealth for the race of resistless destiny sure reward for its discovery and development, and for the peaceful adjustment and legal occupancy of a border of the Wonder Land of earth, and the safety of those who may visit, improve, or occupy it, do I urge, through the active influence of the department, the speedy appropriation by Congress of the means to cancel treaty obligations by paying this confiding people for a valuable region long since peacefully surrendered.

As the hostile incursion of Chief Joseph and his Nez Percés in 1877 was the armed migration of a people, anomalous in all its features, and impossible to ever again occur, with the peaceful adjustment of these Crow difficulties closes all claims or danger of Indians in any portion of the Park, and with it the necessity or semblance of an excuse for tourists to traverse it stalking arsenals of long-range rifles and other weapons, merely to slaughter or frighten away the dwindling remnant of our noblest animals, which it should be the pride as it is the duty of our American people to here preserve from threatened extinction.

HOODOO OR GOBLIN LAND.

A trail was opened this season upon a nearer route than that followed last year, and some new discoveries made around the base of Mount Norris, upon Cache Creek, and thence in nearly a direct line to and beyond the Hoodoo Mountain to Mason's Creek, at the head of the Great Stinkingwater Cañon, near the forks of which is a yawning cañon bordered by unearthly goblin forms as hideous as any conjured in wildest dreams.

C. M. Stephens accompanied me from the Mud Volcano to Clarke's Fork, with his transit for the purpose of taking daily and nightly observations; but although in early September we were terribly annoyed by fogs and storms, from the summit of Mount Chittenden we, protected by overcoats and gloves, through occasional rifts in the fog-clouds, got fair views of the Yellowstone Lake and Pelican Creek regions, but not of the Hoodoo, and upon the latter during the entire day of September 6 we remained, amid chilling fogs which were ascending from the melting snows in all the adjacent valleys, standing behind our monument of last year with compass and field-glass, ready to catch every glimpse of sunshine or opening in the shifting mists below or about us, and at various times obtained fair bearings of most of the leading points of interest, save Index Peak, which was not visible during the entire day. We proposed renewing our observations the next day, and then descend the Middle Fork of Crandall Creek to an open grassy plateau which we had plainly seen from the mountain, but a few miles distant upon Clarke's Fork, to the northeast. But the terrific snow-storm, which had kept us in a clump of fir trees at our camp of last year during much of the 4th and all of the 5th, recommenced with such fury that we had descended along our new trail about 30 miles to the gamekeeper's cabin on the Soda Butte, where the weather was warm and pleasant, with little snow. Determined to complete the exploration, leaving our pack animals and outfit, we ascended the Soda Butte 20 miles to Clarke's Fork Mines, and spent the rest of the day in viewing the pass to Clarke's Fork and a route to Crandall's Creek for the morrow's effort. With the dawn came a snow-storm so furious that we yielded to the inevitable, and pressing through the storm, which as we descended decreased to a snow and a bright sunset at the cabin that night. The next day I returned through mingled snow and sunshine, 35 miles, reaching our headquarters on the eve of September 10, which I had only visited once for a few moments since the morning of July 1.

METEOROLOGICAL RECORD.

Weather record, kept by P. W. Norris, during the exploration of the Sierra Shoshone and a portion of the Rocky ranges.

[*Indicates approximate elevation only.—P. W. N.]

Date.	Camp.	Location.	Time.	Elevation.	Ther.	Weather.	Wind.
1861.				Feet.	°		
Aug. 16	1	Two miles below Mary's Lake...	7 a. m...	7,500	51	Cloudy	SW.
16	N.	Mud Volcano................	Noon...	7,725	65	Rainy	SW.
16	2	West side of the foot of Yellowstone Lake.	6 p. m...	7,738	61	Clear	S.
17	2	......do...............	6 a. m...	7,738	41	...do	N.
17	2	......do...............	Noon...	7,738	70	...do	SW.
17	2	......do...............	6 p. m...	7,738	62	Fair	SW.
18	2	......do...............	6 a. m...	7,738	42	...do	NE.
18	3	Concretion Cove, on Yellowstone Lake.	Noon...	7,738	68	Cloudy	SW.
18	3	......do...............	Sunset..	7,738	51	Windy	S.
19	3	......do...............	Sunrise.	7,738	40	Cloudy ...	N.
19	N.	Jones' Pass of the Sierra Shoshone Range.	Noon ...	9,444	60	...do	SW.
19	4	Mouth of Jones' Creek, near Jones' Camp No. 38.	Sunset..	6,683	54	Fair	SW.
20	4	......do...............	Sunrise.	6,683	34	Clear	S.
20	5	Jones' Camp No. 35, at head of the Grand Stinkingwater Cañon.	1 p. m...	6,319	35	...do	N.
20	5	......do...............	Sunset..	6,319	65	...do	SW.
21	5	......do...............	Sunrise.	6,319	51	...do	SW.
21	N.	Snow field on Bald Mountain...	1 p. m...	*10,650	28	...do	SW.
21	5	Camp No. 5, on the Stinkingwater.	3 p. m...	6,319	65	...do	SW.
22	5	......do...............	Sunrise.	6,319	64	Slight shower	NW.
22	N.	Noon halt on the Norris Creek...	Noon ...	*7,500	73	Clear	NW.
22	6	Forks of Norris Creek............	Sunset..	*7,813	50	...do	W.
23	6	......do...............	Sunrise.	7,812	31	...do	W.
23	N.	At pond and cascade in pass.....	Noon ...	*8,476	43	...do	NW.
23	7	Forks of Clear Creek............	Sunset..	*7,950	70	...do	W.
24	7	......do...............	Sunrise.	*7,950	51	...do	W.
24	N.	Signal Point, Yellowstone Lake.	Noon ...	*7,500	70	...do	NW.
24	8	Terrace at the head of the left finger of the Yellowstone Lake.	Sunset..	7,800	65	...do	S.
25	8	......do...............	Sunrise.	7,800	50	Thunder-shower.....	SW.
25	N.	At Old Hunters' Camp on the east side of the Upper Yellowstone.	Noon ...	7,910	65	Clear	S.
25	9	Near Bridger's Lake	Sunset..	7,950	58	Showery...	E.
26	9	......do...............	Sunrise.	7,950	23	Clear	N.
26	10	Two Ocean Pass.................	Noon ...	8,061	60	...do	SW.
26	10	......do...............	Sunset..	8,061	51	...do	SW.
27	10	......do...............	Sunrise.	8,061	23	...do	NE.
27	N.	Continental Divide..............	10 a. m...	*10,100	45	...do	NE.
27	N.	Barlow Valley	1 p. m...	8,400	81	...do	SW.
27	11	Branch of Barlow River........	Sunset..	*8,600	60	...do	N.
28	11	......do...............	Sunrise.	*8,600	21	...do	N.
28	N.	Summit of pass from branch of Yellowstone to one of Heart Lake.	Noon ...	8,481	75	...do	SW.
28	12	Head of Heart Lake.............	Sunset..	7,475	60	...do	S.
29	12	......do...............	Sunrise.	7,475	23	...do	N.
29	N.	Summit of Mount Sheridan.....	11 a. m...	10,386	60	...do	S.
29	12	Head of Heart Lake..........	Sunset..	7,475	55	Cloudy.....	N.
30	12	......do...............	Sunrise.	7,475	32	Snowy......	N.
30	N.	Head of the thumb of the Yellowstone Lake.	Noon ...	7,738	31	Snow squalls	SW.
30	13	Bridge Creek, near Natural Bridge.	Sunset..	7,906	41	...do	SW.
31	13	......do...............	Sunrise.	7,906	19	Clear	W.
31	14	Mud Volcano on Yellowstone River.	Noon ...	7,725	60	Cloudy......	W.
31	14	......do...............	Sunset..	7,725	51	...do	W.
Sep. 1	14	......do...............	Sunrise.	7,725	31	Hazy	SW
1	N.	Pelican Creek................	Noon ...	7,800	58	...do	W.
1	15	Foot of Mount Chittenden	Sunset..	7,850	48	...do	W.
2	15	......do...............	Sunrise.	7,850	32	Snow squalls	NW
2	N.	Summit of Mount Chittenden...	9 a. m...	10,190	31	...do.	NW.
2	N	Pelican Creek................	Noon ...	8,000	48	...do.	NW.

54 Ab

Weather record, kept by P. W. Norris, &c.—Continued.

Date.	Camp.	Location.	Time.	Elevation.	Ther.	Weather.	Wind.
1881. Sept. 2	16	Camp Lovely, in pass to the East Fork of the Yellowstone River.	Sunset..	*8, 241	55	Clear	W.
3	16	......do.........................	Sunrise..	*8, 241	14	....do.	W.
3	N.	East Fork Valley................	Noon ...	7, 180	55	Cloudy.......	SE.
3	17	Three miles up Miller's Creek...	Sunset..	7, 190	61	....do.	SE.
4	17	......do.........................	Sunrise..	7, 190	50	....do.	SE.
4	N.	Head of Miller's Valley..........	11 a. m .	*7, 350	48	....do.	NW.
4	18	Old camp, one mile from Hoodoo Mountain.	Sunset..	*8, 490	35	Severe snow storm.	NE.
5	18	......do.........................	Sunrise.	*8, 490	30	...do.	NE.
5	18	......do.........................	Noon ...	*8, 400	35	...do.	NE.
5	18	......do.........................	Sunset..	*8, 490	36	...do.	NE.
6	18	......do.........................	Sunrise.	*8, 490	19	...do.	E.
6	N.	Summit of Hoodoo Mountain....	Noon...	*10, 700	21	Fogs..........	NE.
6	19	Old camp, one mile from Hoodoo Mountain.	Sunset..	8, 490	50	Clear	W.
7	19	......do.........................	Sunrise .	8, 490	18	Snow squalls	E.
7	N.	East Fork of Yellowstone Valley	Noon ...	6, 825	40	Clear	S.
7	20	Game keeper's cabin.............	Sunset..	6, 410	24	...do.	S.
8	20	......do.........................	Sunrise..	6, 410	22	...do.	NW.
8	N.	Cook City or Clarke's Fork Mines	Noon...	7, 590	36	Cloudy	NW.
8	21	Miller's Camp in the mines.......	Sunset..	8, 4255	39	...do.	NW.
9	21	......do.........................	Sunrise .	8, 42	13	Severe snow storms.	N.
9	N.	Soda Butte.....................	Noon....	6, 500	26	...do.	N.
9	22	Game keeper's cabin.............	Sunset..	6, 410	26	Clear	SE.
10	22	......do.........................	Sunrise.	6, 410	16	...do.	SE.
10	N.	Forks of the Yellowstone........	Noon....	6, 000	36	...do.	SW.
10	23	Mammoth Hot Springs...........	Sunset..	6, 450	65	...do.	SW.

Meteorological record for the season kept at the Mammoth Hot Springs.

KEY.—S. R., sunrise; M., noon, S. S., sunset; Cl., clear; Cd., cloudy. No wind gauge.

[Latitude 44° 59′ north; longitude 110° 42′ west; elevation, 6,450 feet.]

	January, 1881.							February, 1881.				
	Temperature.			Wind.	Snow or rain.	Sky.		Temperature.			Wind.	Snow or rain.	Sky.
Date.	S. R.	M.	S. S.				Date.	S. R.	M.	S. S.			
1	24	36	26	NW.	....	Cd.	1	30	36	38	S.	R.	Cd.
2	12	26	18	N.	....	Cd.	2	39	41	42	SE.	R.	Cd.
3	12	26	18	E.	....	Cd.	3	43	44	44	S.	R.	Cd.
4	24	32	30	SE.	S.	Cd.	4	39	43	40	S.	R.	Cd.
5	18	44	32	SE.	....	Cl.	5	32	51	36	E.	....	Cl.
6	10	30	26	S.	S.	Cd.	6	29	50	39	....	....	Cl.
7	6	4	2	N.	S.	Cd.	7	20	38	28	NW.	S.	Cd.
8	14	6	0	N.	S.	Cd.	8	19	32	24	SE.	....	Cd.
9	4	10	12	SE.	....	Cl.	9	8	30	22	NE.	....	Cd.
10	16	20	22	S.	....	Cd.	10	8	26	20	NE.	S.	Cd.
11	28	34	36	SE.	S.	Cd.	11	6	26	18	NE.	S.	Cd.
12	34	34	36	SE.	S.	Cd.	12	0	17	20	SE.	S.	Cd.
13	10	22	18	W.	....	Cl.	13	14	6	12	N.	S.	Cd.
14	18	32	34	SE.	S.	Cl.	14	4	14	2	W.	....	Cl.
15	28	50	40	SE.	....	Cl.	15	2	16	16	SE.	....	Cl.
16	4	28	24	SE.	....	Cl.	16	12	22	26	SE.	S.	Cd.
17	1	27	25	SE.	....	Cl.	17	16	42	26	SE.	....	Cd.
18	20	32	30	NE.	....	Cl.	18	9	29	20	SE.	....	Cl.
19	30	48	30	NW.	....	Cd.	19	19	38	26	SE.	R. & S.	Cd.
20	12	28	20	NW.	....	Cl.	20	9	24	22	SE.	....	Cd.
21	18	28	26	NE.	....	Cl.	21	28	33	30	SE.	....	Cd.
22	8	22	24	E.	....	Cl.	22	32	39	36	W.	....	Cl.
23	22	26	24	SE.	....	Cd.	23	32	40	34	S.	....	Cl.
24	18	38	20	SE.	....	Cl.	24	32	42	38	S.	....	Cl.
25	0	24	4	NE.	S.	Cd.	25	34	32	34	SE.	S.	Cd.
26	6	16	18	E.	....	Cd.	26	26	39	30	SE.	....	Cl.
27	22	32	35	SE.	....	Cd.	27	28	36	38	SE.	S.	Cd.
28	22	30	34	SE.	S.	Cd.	28	36	42	41	SE.	R.	Cd.
29	28	36	32	S.	S.	Cd.							
30	30	34	36	SE.	S.	Cd.							
31	28	40	38	SE.		Cl.							
	19	29	25	(Mean 24.)				22	33	29	(Mean 28.)		

	March, 1881.							April, 1881.				
1	32	36	34	SE.	....	Cl.	1	36	66	66	SE.	....	Cl.
2	32	36	28	SE.	....	Cl.	2	36	53	41	SE.	....	Cl.
3	36	38	32	SE.	....	Cl.	3	30	66	50	SE.	....	Cl.
4	30	42	36	SE.	....	Cl.	4	34	66	54	SE.	....	Cl.
5	23	44	35	SE.	....	Cl.	5	40	58	54	SE.	....	Cl.
6	37	38	30	N.	....	Cd.	6	44	60	40	SE.	R.	Cd.
7	2	44	34	SE.	....	Cl.	7	24	35	30	NW.	....	Cd.
8	18	40	32	SE.	....	Cl.	8	22	38	38	NW.	....	Cd.
9	18	56	40	S.	....		9	24	32	34	NW.	S. & R.	Cd.
10	41	48	41	S.	....	Cd.	10	20	48	28	NW.	R.	Cd.
11	29	43	30	N.	....	Cl.	11	21	48	30	NW.	....	Cd.
12	22	32	22	R.	....	Cl.	12	18	42	36	NW.	....	Cl.
13	18	40	29	S.	....	Cl.	13	22	42	34	NE.	....	Cl.
14	12	38	28	S.	....	Cl.	14	34	48	46	NE.	....	Cl.
15	6	48	28	SE.	....	Cl.	15	40	57	52	NE.	....	Cl.
16	11	46	32	SW.	....	Cl.	16	42	62	56	NE.	....	Cl.
17	14	42	36	SE.	....	Cl.	17	42	54	50	SE.	....	Cl.
18	25	38	29	N.	....	Cl.	18	44	50	45	SE.	....	Cl.
19	26	52	32	SW.	....	Cl.	19	43	54	50	SE.	....	Cd.
20	32	44	44	SE.	....	Cl.	20	45	62	50	SE.	R.	Cd.
21	22	50	42	SE.	....	Cl.	21	36	62	50	SE.	R.	Cl.
22	26	55	43	SW.	....	Cl.	22	40	49	40	SE.	....	Cl.
23	30	50	54	SW.	....	Cl.	23	32	44	40	SE.	....	Cd.
24	28	50	30	SW.	....	Cl.	24	38	50	48	SE.	R. & S.	Cd.
25	32	48	45	SW.	....	Cl.	25	40	48	42	SE.	....	Cl.
26	40	48	42	NE.	....	Cl.	26	35	42	42	SE.	....	Cl.
27	40	48	42	NE.	....	Cl.	27	37	50	47	SE.	....	Cl.
28	25	60	46	NE.	....	Cl.	28	32	48	46	SE.	R.	Cd.
29	32	66	50	SE.	....	Cl.	29	40	58	55	SE.	....	Cl.
30	35	66	53	W.	....	Cl.	30	40	56	50	SE.	....	Cl.
31	36	50	43	SE.	....	Cl.							
	27	47	37	(Mean 37.)				34	51	44	(Mean 43.)		

Meteorological record for the season, &c.—Continued.

May, 1881.

Date	Temperature S. R.	Temperature M.	Temperature S. S.	Wind	Snow or rain	Sky
1	40	56	50	S.	....	Cl.
2	40	60	50	SE.	....	Cl.
3	32	50	40	SW.	....	Cl.
4	40	60	56	S.	....	Cl.
5	40	60	56	S.	....	Cl.
6	35	55	50	S.	....	Cd.
7	45	60	56	S.	....	Cl.
8	48	65	60	SE.	....	Cl.
9	45	66	60	SE.	....	Cl.
10	40	70	65	SE.	....	Cl.
11	40	60	58	SE.	....	Cl.
12	35	56	50	SE.	....	Cl.
13	35	45	40	SE.	....	Cd.
14	37	40	40	SE.	....	Cd.
15	35	48	45	SE.	....	Cd.
16	40	50	45	SE.	....	Cl.
17	45	60	57	SE.	....	Cl.
18	50	65	60	SE.	....	Cl.
19	50	66	60	SE.	....	Cl.
20	52	60	58	SE.	....	Cl.
21	50	62	60	SE.	....	Cl.
22	50	65	60	SE.	....	Cl.
23	50	65	60	SE.	....	Cl.
24	50	65	60	SE.	....	Cl.
25	45	60	58	SE.	....	Cl.
26	48	63	60	SE.	....	Cl.
27	50	65	60	SE.	....	Ol.
28	55	70	65	SE.	....	Cl.
29	50	65	62	SE.	....	Cl.
30	52	67	60	SE.	....	Cl.
31	54	68	62	SE.		CL
	45	60	56	(Mean 54.)		

June, 1881.

Date	Temperature S. R.	Temperature M.	Temperature S. S.	Wind	Snow or rain	Sky
1	50	70	62	SE.	....	Cl.
2	48	83	74	SE.	....	Cl.
3	48	74	70	NE.	....	Cl.
4	42	65	60	SE.	....	Cl.
5	45	68	60	SE.	R.	Cd.
6	41	68	50	S.	....	Cd.
7	38	64	48	S.	....	Cd.
8	46	60	48	SE.	R.	Cd.
9	46	48	48	SE.	R.	Cd.
10	40	55	38	SE.	R.	Cd.
11	40	50	38	SE.	R.	Cd.
12	44	58	50	SE.	R.	Cd.
13	44	66	55	SE.	R.	Cd.
14	52	58	58	SE.	R.	Cd.
15	50	56	58	SE.	R.	Cd.
16	50	58	50	SW.	R.	Cd.
17	40	58	50	E.	....	Cl.
18	48	68	52	SE.	....	Cl.
19	55	70	53	SE.	....	Cl.
20	50	60	55	SE.	....	Cl.
21	45	60	55	SE.	....	Cl.
22	50	52	53	N.	....	Cl.
23	45	50	45	NW.	....	Cd.
24	50	80	45	S.	R.	R.
25	60	72	65	SE.	R.	R.
26	59	74	66	SE.	R.	R.
27	65	80	70	SE.	R.	R.
28	70	86	70	SE.	....	Cl.
29	70	83	70	SE.	....	Cl.
30	70	85	70	SE.	....	Cl.
	50	66	56	(Mean 57.)		

July, 1881.

Date	Temperature S. R.	Temperature M.	Temperature S. S.	Wind (*)	Snow or rain (*)	Sky (*)
1	58	96	84			
2	70	88	84			
3	60	78	72			
4	55	75	70			
5	50	80	76			
6	68	83	78			
7	62	63	48			
8	33	62	60			
9	50	56	58			
10	47	68	55			
11	50	60	58			
12	53	78	74			
13	58	85	76			
14	60	80	74			
15	54	76	68			
16	56	76	60			
17	58	86	80			
18	68	90	82			
19	66	80	60			
20	54	64	59			
21	50	76	60			
22	50	82	70			
23	52	84	80			
24	52	80	58			
25	50	80	80			
26	54	74	68			
27	60	78	62			
28	53	82	70			
29	56	80	74			
30	54	84	80			
31	64	74	68			
	55	77	69	(Mean 67.)		

August, 1881.

Date	Temperature S. R.	Temperature M.	Temperature S. S.	Wind (*)	Snow or rain (*)	Sky (*)
1	44	72	65			
2	46	80	72			
3	60	90	82			
4	60	92	65			
5	52	95	72			
6	60	94	87			
7	72	80	66			
8	60	76	74			
9	50	68	55			
10	60	74	70			
11	50	78	60			
12	46	88	74			
13	50	88	74			
14	60	74	70			
15	50	76	70			
16	52	75	70			
17	45	74	70			
18	48	80	65			
19	46	78	64			
20	47	85	60			
21	50	82	60			
22	50	85	80			
23	40	72	70			
24	50	86	58			
25	46	74	60			
26	54	86	74			
27	48	72	64			
28	40	76	54			
29	42	78	62			
30	40	64	60			
31	34	68	60			
	50	79	66	(Mean 65.)		

* No record of wind, rain, or sky.—C. M. S.

Meteorological record for the season, &c.—Continued.

	September, 1881.						October, 1881.					
	Temperature.			Wind.	Snow or rain.	Sky.		Temperature.			Wind.	Snow or rain.	Sky.
Date.	S. R.	M.	S. S.				Date.	S. R.	M.	S. S.			
1	50	62	56	(*)	(*)	(*)	1	40	50	48	SW.	....	....
2	40	66	48	....	....	....	2	20	68	64	S.	....	....
3	28	74	60	....	....	....	3	34	61	42	S.	....	....
4	48	48	50	....	....	....	4	35	63	46	SE.	....	....
5	34	46	28	....	....	....	5	38	68	50	E.	....	....
6	30	58	58	....	....	....	6	38	41	40	E.	....	....
7	34	46	42	....	....	....	7	32	38	42	NE.	....	....
8	50	70	60	....	....	....	8	31	51	39	E.	....	....
9	40	60	44	....	....	....	9	32	64	54	E.	....	....
10	30	68	46	....	....	....	10	39	68	58	SE.	....	....
11	44	74	64	....	....	....	11	34	40	32	N.	....	....
12	40	80	74	....	....	....	12	10	35	18	SE.	....	....
13	40	80	68	....	....	....	13	6	44	34	N.	....	....
14	40	78	62	....	....	....	14	12	24	30	SE.	....	....
15	34	86	70	....	....	....	15	9	30	22	NE.	....	....
16	40	84	72	....	....	....	16	18	34	25	E.	....	....
17	50	64	42	....	....	....	17	26	40	30	SE.	....	....
18	38	74	62	....	....	....	18	31	42	30	SE.	....	....
19	38	60	58	....	....	....	19	36	58	40	SE.	....	....
20	34	64	60	....	....	Cd.	20	32	54	40	W.	....	CL
21	40	60	58	....	....	....	21	34	47	42	....	....	CL
22	40	58	54	....	....	....	22	32	51	40	N.	....	CL
23	40	45	40	....	....	....	23	25	60	40	SE.	....	CL
24	30	48	40	....	S.	....	24	26	64	40	SE.	....	CL
25	40	56	35	....	S.	....	25	28	55	44	SE.	....	Cd.
26	28	48	32	....	S.	Cd.	26	32	48	42	SE.	....	Cd.
27	28	50	35	....	....	CL	27	30	50	40	SE.	....	CL
28	28	45	30	....	S.	Cd.	28	30	48	41	SE.	S.	Cd.
29	25	50	36	....	S.	Cd.	29	31	44	40	SE.	....	Cd.
30	28	40	35	....	S.	Cd.	30	34	40	32	SE.	R.	Cd.
							31	28	30	34	NW.	....	Cd.
	36	61	50	(Mean 48.)				29	49	39	(Mean 39.)		

	November, 1881.					
	Temperature.			Wind.	Sky.	Remarks.
Date.	S. R.	M.	S. S.			
1	30	35	31	NW.	Cd.	Rainy.
2	28	34	30	NW.	Cd.	
3	25	31	28	SE.	Cd.	Snow.
4	28	50	34	SE.	Cd.	Squally.
5	30	34	35	SE.	CL	
6	24	35	32	SE.	CL	
7	28	28	28	SE.	CL	
8	34	35	32	SE.	CL	
9	21	34	30	N.	CL	Windy.
10	20	31	24	N.	CL	Windy.
11	18	30	25	N.	Cd.	Snow squalls.
12	30	30	34	N.	Cd.	Snow squalls.
13	28	35	30	SE.	CL	
14	30	43	35	NE.	CL	
15	30	40	25	SE.	CL	
16	32	46	30	SE.	CL	
17	34	50	41	W.	Cd.	Rain.
18	34	46	38	W.	Cd.	Rain.
19	30	46	32	SW.	Cd.	Rain.
20	32	44	31	SW.	CL	
21	30	42	34	SW.	CL	
22	30	36	30	SE.	CL	
23	13	30	25	SE.	Cd.	
24	16	28	20	SE.	CL	
25	12	30	17	NE.	Cd.	Snow.
26	14	30	20	SE.	Cd.	Snow.
27	9	33	22	SE.	Cd.	Snow.
28	14	40	35	....	CL	
29	12	40	30	....	CL	
30	12	36	30	S.	CL	
	23	30	26	(Mean 29.)		

SULPHUR.

The demand for this mineral, for the purpose of preventing and curing the skin and hoof diseases of the sheep, increases, as does the animal, grazing upon the grassy slopes and terraced foot-hills of these mountain regions, where they are proving very profitable to their owners; and, as no refining of the substance is necessary for this and similar purposes, all thus needed by ranchmen could be readily obtained in the National Park, if they are allowed to do so, which has not been done further than to test its fitness and invite propositions. At the suggestion of the Hon. John Sherman, while we were visiting Sulphur Mountain during the past season, several excavations were made in the sulphur deposits of that and other localities, in order to learn something of their depth and quality. The uniform result was the finding of sulphur somewhat mixed with geyserite and other substances, in strata, or banding to where we were forced to desist by scalding hot sulphur water, or the stifling fumes arising from the deposit, at depths ranging from 3 to 6 feet from the surface. Specimens of these have been forwarded, with those of obsidian, geyserite, &c., to the National Museum for exhibition, as well as to obtain an opinion regarding their practical value. Although in this first search for beds of sulphur no heavy deposits cold enough to be worked were found, still I deem it far from conclusive evidence that none such exist, which may yet be found and profitably worked, if it be considered best to allow its being done. Hence, I suggest the propriety of allowing the search to be made by some responsible person or company, under a lease, allowing the mining and sale thereof of a limited quantity, and for a restricted length of time, and under such regulations as may be thought necessary and proper. While I do not in this desire to represent that any great revenue will immediately accrue to assist in the protection and improvement of the park, I see little danger of loss or injury in exploring some of its nearly countless sulphur deposits, but a certainty of obtaining many specimens of the fragile but beautiful sulphur crystals, and perhaps beds of commercial value, or knowledge of scientific interest.

PAINT-POTS.

This is a provincialism, or local phrase for the dwindled remnants of salses or mud geysers, which are difficult to describe or comprehend otherwise than by actual view of them.

Having in detail described the various kinds of geysers in my last year's report, I here only need to add that from the choking of the supply pipe, or fissure, to the regular intermittent Geyser, or from the bursting out of new ones, many of them dwindle into salses, with only an occasional eruption of their seething, foaming, muddy contents, and still dwindling in power, while increasing in their density and coloring, as well as the fetid smell, and nauseous, often noxious gasses escaping therefrom in spasmodic, hissing or gurgling throes or eruptions, become what are called paint pots. These are sometimes in gulches or basins commingled with or bordering the other kinds of geysers, but usually in more or less detached localities, each of which generally exhibits a preponderance of red, yellow, or other coloring characteristic of the predominant iron, sulphur, or other mineral substances of the basin, but in many of them are found closely and irregularly intermingled pools or pots of seething nauseous paint-like substances of nearly every color and shade of coloring known to the arts, and with a fineness of material and brilliancy of tinting seldom equalled in the productions of man. Although so brilliant, the colors of these paints are not permanent, but soon fade, and as the deposits are so numerous, accessible, and constantly accumulating, it is a question for scientific research to learn if the addition of lead or other minerals in proper proportions may not render these mineral paints practically valuable. There is direct evidence that the Indians used this paint liberally in adorning or besmearing their persons, their weapons, and their lodges. They also used a much more durable variety of red and yellow paint found in bands, layers, or detached masses, in the cliffs, a notable deposit of which was discovered by myself during the past season in the face of the almost vertical walls of a yawning, impassible earthquake fissue nearly opposite the mouth of Hellroaring Creek, which has evidently been visited by Indians in modern times.

INSTRUCTIONS TO WYMAN.

CAMP AT FORKS OF THE FIRE HOLE RIVER,
Yellowstone National Park, September 27, 1881.

C. H. WYMAN:

SIR: You are hereby instructed to proceed with George Rowland, and the necessary saddle, pack animals, outfit and provisions to the Lower, Midway, and Upper Geyser Basins, for the purpose of preventing vandalism of geyser cones and other objects of natural interest, and in general attend to the enforcement of the laws, rules, and regulations for the protection and management of the Yellowstone National Park.

For the prompt and full performance of this and other duties, you are hereby appointed an agent of the government, with full power of seizure of vandalized articles, and the outfits of those persons committing depredations, at your discretion, in accordance with article seven of the printed rules and regulations of the Superintendent of the Park and the Secretary of the Interior for the management thereof, published May 4, 1881, a copy of which is hereunto attached. *(See appendix marked B.) You are also to use due diligence in keeping a record of the weather, making and recording observations of the periods and altitudes of the various geyser eruptions, and especially the Excelsior in the Midway Basin.

Weather permitting, you are expected to remain ten or twelve days, returning via the Norris Geyser Basin, there spending at least one day and two nights, carefully noting the geyser eruptions, and, upon reaching headquarters at the Mammoth Hot Springs, make a detailed report in writing.

P. W. NORRIS,
Superintendent Yellowstone National Park.

MAMMOTH HOT SPRINGS.
Yellowstone National Park, October 10, 1881.

P. W. NORRIS,
Superintendent of the Yellowstone National Park:

SIR: In compliance with your attached instructions of September 27, I proceeded through the Lower to the Midway Geyser Basin, carefully noting geyser eruptions, until the non-arrival of Rowland necessitated my descending the main Fire Hole River to the Marshall Hotel at night. Returned early upon the morning of the 28th, and Rowland having arrived at noon we made our camp upon the road across the Fire Hole River from the Excelsior Geyser, judging it the nearest safe place for viewing its eruptions, as well as the movements of tourists. A terribly swollen knee, from the effects of a horse kick while in the great cañon of the Gibbon, had not only thus delayed Rowland's arrival, but also, despite his earnest efforts, continued to seriously curtail his proposed observations of geyser eruptions in the Upper Basin while I was thus engaged in the Midway one. Although the attached report contains the main features of these eruptions, I may properly add that the subterranean rumblings and earth tremblings were often so fearful as to prevent sleep—so great the cloud ascending from the Excelsior Geyser, and so dense and widespread the descending spray, as to obscure the sun at mid-day, and the united mists and fogs as to saturate garments like the spray from a cataract, and often render the nights so pitchy dark as to prevent accurate observations.

Most of the rocks, hurled hundreds of feet above the column of water, fall in the foaming pond, but many are strewn over surrounding acres. This monster geyser now seems settling down to regular business, with less powerful but more frequent eruptions than during the summer, but its eruptions fully double the volume of water in the Fire Hole River, here nearly 100 yards wide, 2 or 3 feet deep, here very rapid, rendering it too hot to ford for a long distance.

Owing to Rowland's lameness, and the dense fogs in the valleys, the eruptions of the adjacent geysers, as well as those of the Lower Basin and the Geyser Meadows, were not properly noted; and, although no concert of eruptions was observable, all were unusually active and powerful. Thus also, in the Upper Basin, as noted in the occasional visits of Rowland, as well as during our two days' continuous observations there. While Old Faithful was fully sustaining her proverbial reputation for reliability, the Grand, Beehive, Castle, Splendid, and others geysers, seemed struggling to rival it; in fact, all the evidence indicates greater power and activity than during my first visit in 1875, or at any intervening period.

The recent severe snow storms tend alike to clear the park of the tourists now in it, and restrict the number of future arrivals this fall, as well as the danger of forest fires and vandalism.

En route to the Norris Geyser Basin we had a distant view of geysers in eruption in the Monument Basin, nearly amid the clouds, and others in the cañon of the Gibbon, and the Paint Pots, the appearance of all of which, as well as in the Norris Basin, indicates unusual activity. In fact, there seems no room to question the marked increase of power and activity of the internal forces throughout the Fire Hole regions.

Most respectfully, yours,

C. H. WYMAN.

Record of the eruptions of the Excelsior Geyser in the Midway Basin, Yellowstone National Park.

Date.	Time of eruption.	Duration of eruption in minutes.	Height of the column of water in feet.	Remarks.
1880. Sept. 27	8.00 a. m.	5	100	Witnessed the last eruption from a distance.
27	3.30 p. m.	7	75	
27	5.30 p. m.	7	100	
27	7.15 p. m.	6	90	
28	9.00 a. m.	5	60	Heavy fog in the morning, clear until sunset, and thence dense mists from the Excelsior Geyser, and fogs from the foaming, hot Fire Hole River
28	10.30 a. m.	7	75	
28	11.48 a. m.	7	75	
28	3.00 p. m.	5	100	
28	5.20 p. m.	6	100	
28	7.30 p. m.	7	125	
29	9.30 a. m.	7	60	
29	3.30 p. m.	5	60	Heavy snow squalls, shutting off all observation after 7.30 p. m.
29	5.00 p. m.	5	70	
29	7.20 p. m.	7	75	
30	9.00 a. m.	5	50	Heavy clouds and mists much of the day.
30	3.00 p. m.	7	100	
30	5.20 p. m.	5	125	
30	7.15 p. m.	5	75	Mists too dense for observation at night.
30	9.30 p. m.	6	75	
Oct. 1	6.15 a. m.	5	80	Cloudy and nearly dark all day.
1	8.05 a. m.	10	150	
1	10.10 a. m.	15	100	
1	12.55 p. m.	10	200	
1	3.50 p. m.	10	250	
1	5.40 p. m.	10	225	
1	7.10 p. m.	5	75	Too dense fogs and mists to continue observations.
1	9.00 p. m.	5	75	
2	12.15 a. m.	5	75	
2	3.30 a. m.	5	75	Clear, but a very heavy wind down the valley, allowing approach upon the windward side, disclosing the fact that heavy masses of the horizontally-banded wall-rock were fractured and falling into the foaming cauldron, which was all that could be observed, save an occasional rush eruption.
2	6.45 a. m.	5	75	
2	8.15 a. m.	5	75	
2	10.10 a. m.	5	75	
2	12.15 p. m.	4	80	

Record of the eruptions of the Excelsior Geyser in the Midway Basin, &c.—Continued.

Date.	Time of eruption.	Duration of eruption in minutes.	Height of the column of water in feet.	Remarks.
1890.				
Dec. 2	2.15 p. m	5	50	
2	4.15 p. m	7	200	
2	5.30 p. m	5	75	
2	7.00 p. m	5	50	
2	9.05 p. m	5	50	
2	11.15 p. m	5	60	
3	6.30 a. m	5	100	
3	8.00 a. m	10	150	Countless rocks, of many pounds weight, hurled like a rocket high above the column of water, some of which fell in and across the river, which is here 100 yards wide, and during much of the day was a foaming flood of hot water.
3	10.10 a. m	10	300	
3	12.30 p. m	10	75	
3	3.00 p. m	10	250	
3	4.30 p. m	7	75	
3	5.45 p. m	5	80	
3	7.25 p. m	6	75	
3	9.20 p. m	5	75	
3	11.30 p. m	5	75	
4	6.00 a. m	5	75	
4	7.30 a. m	5	75	Broke camp and went to the Upper Basin at 9 a. m.
4	9.00 a. m	7	75	
4	10.20 a. m	10	150	
4	11.45 a. m	5	150	
6	3.00 p. m	5	75	Returned through mist and snow squalls; weather quite cold.
6	5.25 p. m	7	100	
6	7.19 p. m	6	80	
6	9.00 p. m	7	120	
6	10.40 p. m	5	75	
7	3.45 a. m	6	80	Clear and cold, but dense fogs along the river for miles.
7	5.20 a. m	7	125	
7	6.45 a. m	5	100	
7	9.05 a. m	7	130	Left the basin for the Norris Geyser.

ERUPTIONS OF GEYSERS IN THE UPPER BASIN.

Old Faithful—This typical geyser during our visit seemed to be in greatest activity and power, having hourly eruptions of five minutes' duration, and columns of water 175 feet high.

GRAND.

Date.	Time of eruption.	Duration of eruption in minutes.	Height of the column of water in feet.	Remarks.
1891.				
Oct. 4	9.45 a. m	20	200	Observed by Rowland. The column of water at all of these eruptions was vertical and of remarkable symmetry and beauty.
4	5.10 p. m	25	200	
5	3.25 p. m	20	200	
6	9.15 a. m	20	200	
6	4.20 p. m	20	200	

SPLENDID.

Date.	Time of eruption.	Duration of eruption in minutes.	Height of the column of water in feet.	Remarks.
1880. Oct. 4	7.15 a. m			Eruptions uniformly much like those of Old Faithful, but the form of the column of water less vertical and more spreading.
4	9 a. m			
4	11 a. m			
4	2.30 p. m			
4	6.30 p. m			
5	6 a. m			
5	8.20 a. m			
5	11.20 a. m			
5	1.15 p. m			
5	3.45 p. m			
5	6.30 p. m			
6	6 a. m			
6	8.30 a. m			
6	11 a. m			
6	1.20 p. m			

CASTLE.

Date.	Time of eruption.	Duration.	Height.	Remarks.
Oct. 4	3 p. m	25	75	There was a constant agitation and several small eruptions.
6	9.45 a. m	30	100	

BEEHIVE.

Date.	Time of eruption.	Duration.	Height.	Remarks.
Oct. 4	9.45 p. m	5	175	Column of water always vertical, and of great symmetry and beauty.
5	2.15 p. m	5	200	
6	8.40 p. m	5	180	

GIANT.

Date.	Time of eruption.	Duration.	Height.	Remarks.
Oct. 5	5 p. m	25	250	The accompanying earth-trembling was terrible.

The Lion, Lioness, Grotto, Fan, Riverside, Saw-mill, and other geysers had eruptions during the night, which we failed to properly observe, but, from the noise of their spouting, all were in full force and activity.

LOWER GEYSER BASIN.

Fountain.—Usually had an eruption each forenoon, those observed being of from 10 to 15 minutes' duration, with water column from 60 to 90 feet high, and very spreading. Rowland's lameness and the dense fogs prevented extended observations in the Lower Basin, as well as in the Geyser Meadows.

NORRIS GEYSER BASIN.

Monarch.

Date.	Time of eruption.	Duration of eruption in minutes.	Height of the column of water in feet.	Remarks.
Oct. 8	6.20 a. m	20	100	The eruptions are simultaneously through three orifices—2 by 12, 2½ by 11, and 5 by 6 feet, respectively, their combined flow producing for the time a large sized stream of hot water.
9	6.30 a. m	25	125	

New Crater.—Exhibits two kinds of eruptions—one of them, each half hour, 50 feet high, and another about 100 feet high daily.

Minute Man.—Eruptions 25 or 30 feet high each minute, with little variation.

Emerald.—Evidently has an occasional eruption, although none were observed.

Vixen.—Eruption from 40 to 50 feet high, each two or three hours.

Constant, Twins, Triplets, and many others in the Porcelain Vale, seem in nearly constant eruption, so that the spray and fogs greatly obscure the sun's rays by day, and render the nights dark, damp, and unpleasant.

Report of weather in the Geyser Basins.

MIDWAY BASIN.

Date.	Thermometer.			Remarks.
	Sunrise.	Noon.	Sunset.	
1881.				
Sept. 27..	32	50	38	Cloudy.
28..	38	49	42	Clear; heavy mist from the Excelsior Geyser
29..	40	55	32	Snow-squalls.
30..	26	52	30	Heavy clouds and mist.
Oct. 1..	36	50	32	Do.
2..	32	60	44	Clear, but windy.
3..	34	61	40	Clear, but windy; dense mist at night.
4..	26	....	....	

UPPER BASIN.

Date.	Sunrise.	Noon.	Sunset.	Remarks.
Oct. 4..	....	64	46	Dense mists from geysers.
5..	25	68	42	Clear morning; thunder-shower at 2 p. m.
6..	33	38	....	Snow-squalls and blinding mists.

MIDWAY BASIN.

Date.	Sunrise.	Noon.	Sunset.	Remarks.
Oct. 6..	....	....	30	Snow-squalls and blinding mists.
7..	33	....	....	Clear, but very windy. Went to the Norris Geyser Basin.

NORRIS BASIN.

Date.	Sunrise.	Noon.	Sunset.	Remarks.
Oct. 7..	....	....	32	Clear and lovely.
8..	18	50	40	Clear day. Left for headquarters at 7.30 a. m., arrived at 12 m.
9..	16	....	....	

GEYSERS.

The theories regarding these and other kinds of hot springs in the park were so fully treated of in my report of last year, and the records of their eruption, notably during the latter part of this season, in the foregoing trustworthy report of Wyman, leaves but little necessary to show that, with the exception of the local changes at the Mammoth Hot Springs and of the Safety-Valve Basin in the Grand Cañon, there is evidently a far greater development of power than ever before witnessed throughout the entire Fire-Hole regions. But as to the cause or causes, probable duration, or future tendencies, we only know that they are at variance with the accepted and apparently correct theory of their dwindling character, with one marked exception. This is in the Midway Basin of the Fire Hole River, where the evidence is conclusive of not only spasmodic, but continuous increase of power.

The following description is from Hayden's Report of 1871, pp. 114, 115:

About three miles up the Fire-Hole from Camp Reunion we meet with a small but quite interesting group of springs on both sides of the stream. There is a vast accumulation of silica, forming a hill 50 feet above the level of the river. Upon the summit is one of the largest springs yet seen, nearly circular 150 feet in diameter; boils up in the center, but overflows with such uniformity on all sides as to admit of the formation of no real rim, but forming a succession of little ornamental steps, from 1 to 3 inches in height, just as water would congeal from cold in flowing down a gentle declivity. There was the same transparent clearness, the same brilliancy of coloring to the water; but the hot steam and the thinness of the rim prevented me from approaching it near enough to ascertain its temperature or observe its depth, except at one edge, where it was 180°. It is certainly one of the grandest hot springs ever seen by human eye. But

Fig. 8.—Boulder Geyser, 1871.

the most formidable one of all is near the margin of the river. It seems to have broke out close by the river, to have continually enlarged its orifice by the breaking down of its sides. It evidently commenced on the east side, and the continual wear of the under side of the crust on the west side has caused the margin to fall in, until an aperture at least 250 feet in diameter has been formed, with walls or sides 20 to 30 feet high, showing the lamina of deposition perfectly. The water is intensely agitated all the time, boiling like a caldron, from which a vast column of steam is ever arising, filling the orifice. As the passing breeze sweeps it away for a moment one looks down into this terrible, seething pit with terror. All around the sides are large masses of the siliceous crust that have fallen from the rim. An immense column of water flows out of this caldron into the river. As it pours over the marginal slope, it descends by numerous small channels, with a large number of smaller ones spreading over a broad surface, and the marvelous beauty of the strikingly vivid coloring far surpasses anything of the kind we have seen in this land of wondrous beauty; every possible shade of color, from the vivid scarlet to a bright rose, and every shade of yellow to delicate cream, mingled with vivid green from minute vegetation. Some of the channels were lined with a very fine, delicate, yellow, silky material, which vibrates at every movement of the water. Mr. Thomas Moran, the distinguished artist, obtained sketches of these beautiful springs, and from his well-known reputation as a colorist, we look for a painting that will convey some conception to the mind of the exquisite variety of colors around this spring. There was one most beautiful funnel-shaped spring, 20 feet in diameter at the top, but tapering down, lined inside and outside with the most delicate decorations. Indeed, to one looking down into its clear depths, it seemed like a fairy palace. The same jelly like substance or pulp to which I have before alluded covers a large area with the various shades of light red and green. The surface yields to the tread like a cushion. It is about 2 inches in thickness, and, although seldom so tenacious as to hold together, yet it may be taken up in quite large masses, and when it becomes dry it is blown about by the wind like fragments of variegated lichens.

The above, cut from the Hayden report of 1872, and the description thereof in that of 1871, are here republished, both for their accuracy and as a datum from which to trace subsequent and future developments. This clearly proves the comparatively recent outburst of the yawning pool of hot water, in border parlance heretofore called "Hell's Half Acre," which during the past season has fully justified the name and greatly exceeded the dimensions. Although noted for the deep ultra-marine blue, ever-agitated waters, so characteristic of the true geyser when not in eruption, there was neither evidence nor indications of recent eruptions until late in August, 1878. I then distinctly heard its spoutings when near Old Faithful, 6 miles distant, but arrived too late to witness them, though not its effects upon the Fire Hole River, which was so swollen as to float out some of our bridges over rivulet branches below it.

Crossing the river above the geyser and hitching my horse, with bewildering astonishment I beheld the outlet at least tripled in size, and a furious torrent of hot water escaping from the pool, which was shrouded in steam, greatly hiding its spasmodic foamings. The pool was considerably enlarged, its immediate borders swept entirely clear of all movable fragments of rock, enough of which had been hurled or forced back to form a ridge from knee to breast high at a distance of from 20 to 50 feet from the ragged edge of the yawning chasm. Perhaps no published statement of mine in reference to the Wonder Land has ever more severely tested the credulity of friends or of the public; and even General Crook and Secretary Schurz, to whom I pointed out the decreasing proofs of this eruption, seemed to receive it with annoying evidences of distrust. The volume of steam arising from this pool continued to increase until, on reaching the Lookout lower border of the valley, late in November, 1880, it appeared so great as to cause me to visit it the next day, hopeful of seeing an eruption or evidences of a recent one. This I failed to find, but not a volume of steam which then shrouded all near it, as it did the whole of the lower valley before the next morning. In order to make the Mammoth Hot Springs, 40 miles distant, that day, I started early, and with the thermometer but little above zero groped my way through this fog, which chilled to the marrow, to the Lookout Terrace, 3 miles from the Forks of the Fire Holes and 8 from the geyser, and emerged therefrom by ascending above it into a broad and brilliant scene of beauty seldom witnessed by human vision. From the foaming half-acre caldron an enormous column of steam and vapor constantly arose, at first vertically, then swayed by a moderate but steady southern wind northerly, increasing with the altitude, until intermingling with or forming a cloud at the proper elevation, from which a nearly imperceptible descending vapor, carried northerly, covered and loaded to pendency the southern branches of the dark pine and fir fringes to the terrace slopes and craggy cliffs of the Madison Plateau, to its great cañon beyond the Gibbon, fully 15 miles from this earthly Gehenna.

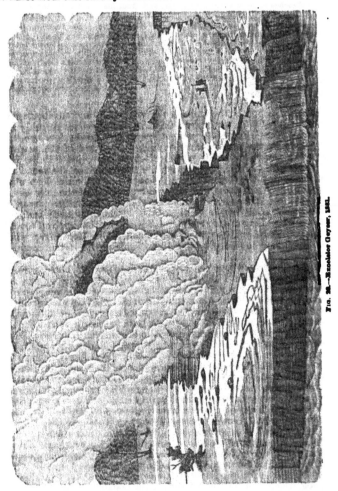

Fig. 28.—Excelsior Geyser, 1881.

Beneath this unique cloud-awning the low and seemingly distant rays of a cold, cloudless sunrising, in struggling through this vapor-laden atmosphere, formed a variety of tints and reflections from the inimitably beautiful festoons of frost formation, while commingled with a dark green background of foliage, of somber cliffs and snowy mountains—a brilliancy of blended wavy shades and halos enchantingly beautiful. This was my parting view of that geyser last year; and before my return this season, great changes had occurred. From the statements of G. W. Marshall, at the Forks of the Fire Holes, February was ushered in by dense fogs and fearful rumblings and earth tremblings, which he ultimately traced to regular eruptions, daily, or rather nightly, commencing about 10 o'clock p. m., gradually recurring later, until by July 1 they were after daylight; and this eruption is now about 10 a. m., showing a loss of twelve hours in nine months. During much of the summer this eruption was simply incredible, elevating to heights of from 100 to 300 feet sufficient water to render the rapid Fire Hole River, nearly 100 yards wide, a foaming torrent of steaming hot water, and hurling rocks of from 1 to 100 pounds weight, like those from an exploded mine, over surrounding acres. By far the finest landmark that I ever beheld in all my mountain wanderings was the immense column of steam, even when the geyser was not in eruption, always arising from this monster, which was ever plainly visible to where, at the proper elevation, it formed a cloud that floated away in a long line to the leeward in the clearest summer's day, and was never to be mistaken for any other wherever seen, which was upon all the surrounding mountains, including the Rocky and Shoshone ranges, portions of which that I visited were fully 100 miles distant. In September the eruptions branched into one about 4 o'clock p. m., and soon after to others, until it now seems to be settling down to regular business as a two or three hour geyser, so immeasurably excelling any other, ancient or modern, known to history, that I find but one name fitting, and herein christen it the "Excelsior" until scientists, if able, shall invent a more appropriate one. This pool is now 400 paces in circumference.

The Fire Hole River is down a declivity of some 20 or 30 feet from where the outlet beside the horseman is shown in the Hayden view (Fig. 27), Wyman's camp being across the river, still eastward—and many rocks were hurled into or across it, and also to the great spring, with the steam cloud in the background, as well as another, sixty paces to the north of the geyser, whose brilliantly colored outlet is shown as joining that of the geyser upon the brink of the declivity to the river, in the above view from my sketch (Fig. 28), which was taken at a period of less activity between the regular daily eruptions early in the season than observed at any subsequent period.

REPORT OF GAMEKEEPER.

MAMMOTH HOT SPRINGS,
YELLOWSTONE NATIONAL PARK,
September 30, 1881.

SIR: I hereby respectfully submit the following report of my operations as gamekeeper of the park, for the protection of its animals, since furnishing my report of November 25, 1880, from the gamekeeper's cabin, near the confluence of the Soda Butte and the East Fork of the Yellowstone River. I there remained, sometimes having George Rowland or Adam Miller for a comrade, but often alone, during the entire winter, the early part of which was so severe that there were no mountain hunters—the Clarke's Fork miners twenty miles distant one way, and the boys at the headquarters nearly forty the other, being the nearest, and in fact the only men in these regions. The snowfall was unusually great, and remained very deep high in the mountains, but the winds and hot vapors from the Fire Hole Basin at the foot of Mount Norris kept the snow pretty clear along its western slopes, where there were abundance of mountain sheep, and some elk, all winter. Elk to the number of about 400 wintered in small bands in the valleys of the East Fork and Soda Butte, where the snow was about knee-deep. The Slough Creek and Hellroaring bands of bison did not venture near the cabin until February, nor did those of Amethyst Mountain at all; and the most of the deer and antelope descended into the lower Yellowstone Valley early in the winter.

The most of the Clarke's Fork miners seemed disposed to kill only what game they needed for food, and preserve the rest from slaughter for their hides only, and hence I returned to the headquarters in the spring, which opened very early and continued warm and pleasant. This allowed me to visit many other portions of the park, sometimes on snow-shoes and sometimes with saddle and pack-horses. I found that very few of the deer or antelope wintered anywhere in the park; that a small band of bison wintered on Alum Creek, and another on the South Fork of the Madison; that there were elk in nearly all of the warm valleys, and moose around the Shoshone and the fingers of the Yellowstone lakes; big-horn sheep on all the mountain slopes; wolverine, marten, and various kinds of foxes, who do not leave the park in winter, nor do the bears of all kinds, as they hibernate. During the remainder of the season I have been active in the various duties of killing what game was necessary for our various parties of laborers, and protecting the rest from wanton slaughter by some of the tourists and a band of Bannock Indians on the North Madison. I also guided the party of Governor Hoyt and Colonel Mason from the Two Ocean Pass to the Fire Holes, and accompanied you in the long and arduous exploration of the Sierra Shoshone, and the Rocky Mountain, from Turbid Lake to Mount Sheridan; and in a final tour of the main roads and trails of the park close my services and resign my position as gamekeeper of the park to resume private enterprises now requiring my personal attention. The unfortunate breakage of my thermometer when it could not be replaced prevented my keeping other than a record of fair and stormy days, winds and rain and snow-fall during last winter, a synopsis of which is hereunto attached.

In conclusion, I may justly add that my relations with yourself, with your men, and with nearly all of the visitors to the park, as well as the surrounding miners and hunters have always been most cordial; but, as stated in my report of last year, I do not think that any one man appointed by the honorable Secretary, and specifically designated as a gamekeeper, is what is needed or can prove effective for certain necessary purposes, but a small and reliable police force of men, employed when needed, during good behavior, and dischargeable for cause by the superintendent of the park, is what is really the most practicable way of seeing that the game is protected from wanton slaughter, the forests from careless use of fire, and the enforcement of all the other laws, rules, and regulations for the protection and improvement of the park.

Most respectfully, yours,

                                        HARRY YOUNT,
                                            Gamekeeper.

P. W. NORRIS,
   Superintendent of the Yellowstone National Park.

OBSERVATIONS OF WEATHER.

November.—From the 26th to the 30th, inclusive, snowy.

December.—During this month, one day was rainy, two hazy, six clear, cold, and windy, and twenty-two snowy.

January.—The 13th, 16th, 17th, 18th, 20th, 21st, 22d, 24th, and 25th, nine days, were clear; the remainder of the month snowy, and mainly very cold.

February.—The 2d and 3d, two days, rainy; 14th, one day, was clear; the 8th, snowy; the 9th, squally, and twenty-three days snowy.

March.—Twenty-four days were clear, and mostly mild, and some warm; one day rainy, two snowy, and four cloudy.

April.—The 1st, 4th, 5th and 7th were clear, the 2d, 3d, and 6th rainy, and the snow so soft that traveling with my Norwegian snow shoes 14 feet long, was hard work, and leaving them at the middle fall of the Gardiner, went thence through the cañon to the boys at headquarters, they keeping the weather records correctly thereafter.

INTRODUCTION TO ROADS, BRIDLE-PATHS, AND TRAILS.

In preceding reports I have followed the usual custom of calling all traveled routes either roads or trails, but it having become, as it will continue, necessary to mention mountain, fire-hole, cliff, and cañon trails for footmen only, as well as those in common use for saddle and pack animals, the latter are herein tabled as bridle-paths, the former as trails; while the lodge-pole or Indian and game trails only are thus designated whenever mentioned in the body of this report. I have, also, in some of my preceding reports, stated that, as none of our roads, bridle-paths, or trails had ever been measured, the tables of them were at best only approximations, and the distances therein shown are more probably over than under estimated. This view the odometer measurements of Capt. W. S.

Stanton, Corps of Engineers, and of First Lieut. E. Z. Steever, Third Cavalry, made during July and August of the past season, have proven correct, and it is one of the amusing incidents in connection with these peculiar regions that while prominent judges, senators, governors, and other officers of the government were making me the subject of their raillery upon the annoying length of my estimated miles, other officers were by actual measure proving many of them far too short. This is especially noticeable in the direct or Mammoth Hot Spring road, estimated when made, in 1878, as 50 miles in length, and which was nearly correct at that time, but it having been materially shortened by changing the road from the cañon to the plateau of the Madison, a cut-off through the earthquake region and somewhat elsewhere, it is now found to be less than 37 miles long, which is only about one-half of the Mount Wabash route, and can never be essentially shortened. The tables of distances, as received from Captain Stanton and Lieutenant Steever, were well arranged and computed, evincing accurate odometer measurements, and are accepted and used as such; but owing to the subsequent construction of new roads and bridle-paths, or changes in old ones, as well as from their want of knowledge of the names of many places which it is believed essential to mention, these tables are thus amended; but all portions of them have been accepted which were proper to use, and are credited and indicated by a *.

SYNOPSIS OF ROADS, BRIDLE-PATHS, AND TRAILS IN THE YELLOWSTONE NATIONAL PARK.

	Between points.	Total.
Road towards Bozeman.	*Miles.*	*Miles.*
* From headquarters at the Mammoth Hot Springs to northern boundary line of Wyoming	....	1.99
Northern boundary line of the National Park, below the mouth of the Gardiner River	5.00	6.99
Direct road to the Forks of the Fire-Hole River.		
* From headquarters at the Mammoth Hot Springs to Terrace Pass	....	1.98
* Swan Lake	3.21	5.16
* Crossing of Middle Fork of Gardiner River	2.33	7.67
Willow Park, upper end	3.50	10.97
* Obsidian Cliffs and Beaver Lake	1.27	12.34
* Green Creek	1.40	13.74
* Lake of the Woods	.76	14.50
* Hot Springs	1.68	16.18
* Norris Fork Crossing	4.17	20.35
* Norris Geyser Basin	.71	21.06
* Geyser Creek and Forks of the Paint-Pot trail	3.13	24.19
* Head of Cañon of the Gibbon and foot-bridge on trail to Monument Geysers	.73	24.91
* Falls of the Gibbon River	3.75	28.66
* Cañon Creek	.50	29.35
Earthquake Cliffs	3.00	32.35
* Lookout Terrace	1.80	33.75
* Marshall's Hotel, at the Forks of the Fire Hole River	2.43	36.18
Road from Forks of the Fire Hole River to foot of the Yellowstone Lake.		
From Marshall's Hotel to forks of the road near Prospect Point	....	1.00
* Hot Springs	2.08	3.08
* Rock Fork	2.86	5.94
Willow Creek	2.00	7.94
Foot of the grade up the Madison Divide	2.00	9.94
Upper end of Mary's Lake	1.91	11.85
* Sulphur Lakes and Hot Springs	1.12	12.97
Alum Creek Camp	2.00	14.97
Sage Creek Crossing	2.00	16.97
Fork of the road to the falls near the Yellowstone River	5.00	21.97
Mad Geysers	2.00	23.97
Grizzly Creek	2.00	25.97
* Foot of the Yellowstone Lake	3.75	29.72

55 Ab

Roads, bridle-paths, and trails in the Yellowstone National Park—Continued.

	Between points.	Total.
Branch road to the Great Falls of the Yellowstone.	*Miles.*	*Miles.*
From Forks of the Fire Hole River to forks of the lake road to the Great Falls, as above		
Sulphur Mountain		
*Alum Creek		
*Upper Falls of the Yellowstone, bridle-path		
*Crystal Falls and Grotto Pool, bridle-path		
*Lower (Great) Falls of the Yellowstone		
Road to Tower Falls.		
*Headquarters at the Mammoth Hot Springs to bridge over the Gardiner River		
*Bridge over the East Fork of the Gardiner River		
*Upper Falls to East Fork of the Gardiner River		
*Black Tail Deer Creek		
Lava Beds		
*Dry Cañon, or Devil's Cut		
*Pleasant Valley		
*Forks of the Yellowstone		
*Tower Falls		
Geyser Basin road.		
*Marshall's Hotel to forks of road at Prospect Point		
*Old Camp Reunion		
Fountain Geyser in the Lower Geyser Basin		
*Excelsior Geyser, in the Midway Geyser Basin		
*Old Faithful, in the Upper Geyser Basin		
Madison Plateau road.		
Marshall's Hotel to Forest Spring		
*Marshall's Park		
*Lookout Cliffs		
Riverside Station and Forks of Kirkwood or Lower Madison Cañon road to Virginia City		
Bridge over South Madison River		
Madison Cañon road.		
Marshall's Hotel to forks of road to the Mammoth Hot Springs		
Mouth of the Gibbon River		
Foot of the Madison Cañon		
Riverside Station		
Queen's Laundry road.		
Marshall's Hotel to crossing Laundry Creek		
Twin Mounds		
Queen's laundry and bath-house		
A bridle-path 3 miles long extends from there to the Madison Plateau road, and another is partially completed via Twin Buttes and Fairy Falls to the Midway Geyser Basin		
Middle Fork of the Gardiner bridle-path.		
Headquarters at the Mammoth Hot Springs to the West Gardiner		
Falls of the Middle Gardiner		
Sheepeater Cliffs		
Road to the Geysers		
Painted Cliff bridle path.		
Meadow Camp to head of Grand Cañon		
Safety Valve Pulsating Geyser		
Yellowstone River at Painted Cliffs		
Paint Pots bridle-path.		
Mouth of Geyser Creek to the Paint Pots		
Geyser Gorge		
Earthquake Gorge		
Rocky Fork Crossing		
Mary's Lake Road, near Yellowstone Creek		
Mount Washburn bridle path.		
*Tower Falls to Forks of Trail		
*To Summit of Mount Washburn		
Cascade Creek		
*Great Falls of the Yellowstone		

Roads, bridle-paths, and trails in the Yellowstone National Park—Continued.

	Between points.	Total.
Grand Cañon bridle-path.	*Miles.*	*Miles.*
* Tower Falls to Forks of Trail............................	....	1.87
Antelope Creek	4.00	5.87
Rowland's Pass of Mount Washburn	2.00	7.87
Glade Creek	3.47	10.34
* Mud Geyser	1.00	11.34
* Hot Sulphur Springs	.83	12.17
* Meadow Camp and fork of Painted Cliffs bridle-path Trail.	1.50	13.76
Brink of the Grand Cañon	1.00	14.76
* Lookout, Paint, and forks of trail into the cañon below the falls.	2.19	16.95
* Great Falls of the Yellowstone	.74	17.69
Shoshone Lake bridle-path.		
* Old Faithful, in the Upper Geyser Basin, to Kepler's Cascades	....	1.94
* Leech Lake	3.72	4.66
Norris Pass, Continental Divide	3.00	7.66
DeLacey Creek, Pacific waters	.97	8.63
* Two-Ocean Pond, on Continental Divide	3.50	12.13
* Hot Spring, at head of thumb of the Yellowstone Lake.....	2.00	14.13
* Hot Spring, on Lake Shore	3.02	17.14
* Hot Spring Creek	4.00	21.14
* Natural Bridge	7.44	28.58
* Outlet of Yellowstone Lake	4.68	33.26
Miners' bridle-path.		
* Baronette's Bridge, at forks of the Yellowstone River, to Duck Lake.	....	1.76
* Amethyst Creek	8.30	10.06
* Crossing, East Fork of Yellowstone River................	2.16	12.22
Gamekeeper's Cabin	.50	12.72
* Soda Butte, medicinal springs...........................	2.65	15.37
Trout Lake	2.00	17.37
* Round Prairie	3.00	20.37
North line of Wyoming....................................	3.84	24.21
* Clarke's Forks Run Camp, near northeast corner of the park	3.14	27.30
Hoodoo or Goblin Mountain bridle-path.		
Gamekeeper's cabin, on the Soda Butte, to Hot Sulphur Springs.	....	.2
Ford of Cache Creek	1	3
Alum Springs and return..................................	4	7
Calfee Creek	4	11
Miller's Creek	2	13
Mountain Terrace..	8	21
Old Camp	5	26
Goblin Labyrinths	2	28
Monument on Hoodoo Mountain	1	29
Fossil Forest bridle-path.		
Summit of Amethyst Mountain	....	3
Gamekeeper's cabin to foot of Mountain	3	6
Orange Creek	5	11
Sulphur Hills..	4	15
Forks of Pelican Creek	8	23
Indian Pond at Concretion Cove of the Yellowstone Lake...	5	28
Lower Ford of Pelican Creek	3	31
Foot of the Yellowstone Lake	3	34
Passamaria or Stinkingwater bridle-path.		
Concretion Cove to Turbid Lake	....	3
Town's Pass of the Sierra Shoshone Range	7	10
Confluence of the Jones and Stinkingwater Fork of the Passamaria River	12	22
Nez Percé bridle-path.		
Indian Pond to Pelican Valley	....	2
Ford of Pelican Creek	3	6
Nez Percé Ford of the Yellowstone.......................	6	12
Alum Creek bridle-path.		
From the Great Falls of the Yellowstone, via Crystal Falls and Grotto Pool and the Upper Falls, to the mouth of Alum Creek...............	4	4

Roads, bridle-paths, and trails in the ...... *Nation...*

Branch road to the Great ...

From Forks of the Fire Hole River ... . the numerous act
above............................ ... .ners.................
Sulphur Mountain ....ut of the mountain
*Alum Creek............................ ....eet high..........
*Upper Falls of the Yellowstone ....gn, at the head of the
*Crystal Falls and Grotto Pool, betw ...
*Lower (Great) Falls of the Yello ... ... Sheepeater arrow-cove

*Headquarters at the Mam... ....at *Gardiner River.*
*Bridge over the East Fork ... .n along the eastern declivity,
*Upper Falls to East Fork ... .nalia, and like which, allows ...
*Black Tail Deer Creek ....ail rock.
Lava Beds..........................
*Dry Cañon, or Devil's Cut ... ... *Geyser Trail*
*Pleasant Valley ....e Gibbon, which ascends nearl
*Forks of the Yellow... ... ...he ...rtions of which are exceedin...
*Tower Falls......... ... .a ...al ....
... ...umbling geyser cones are alike ...
*Marshall's Hotel to f... ...ly beautiful.
*Old Camp Reunion
Fountain Geyse... ... ... of the Great Falls of the Yellowston
*Excelsior Geys...
*Old Faithfu ... ...amping ground above, and descend...
... ... to the pole-bordered outlook at the ...

Marshall's ... ... River below the Lower Falls of the Yellow
*Marshall's P...
*Lookou... ... ...g Run from the rustic bridge nearly to it
Riverside ... ...tivity beneath Lookout Point, in a winding
City... ... ...which cannot now be ascended, along it, as
Bridge over... ... ...this side, but can be reached upon the other,

... ... detached fragments of rock, which attain
... ...the river
Mar... ... ...here are several others to fossil forests, cliffs
M... ... ...which will be fully noted in the forthcoming g...
Fou... ...
Riv... ...

...ION OF DISTANCES, ROADS, BRIDL...
WITHIN THE PARK.

ROADS.

... ...orth line of the Park, towards Bozeman, ...
... ...to the Forks of the Fire Hole Rivers.......
... ...Forks of the Fire Hole Rivers to the foot ...
...out ....
...ad from Sage Creek to Alum Creek.............
...alls road, about.........
...Basin road ....
... ...Plateau ....
... ...a Cañon ....
... ...Laundry...........................

BRIDLE-PATHS.

...ate Gardiner..........................
...nted Cliffs...........................
... ...Pots..........................
...ent Washburn..........................
...Cañon from the Forks, about...............
... ...about ....
... ...in...........................

	Miles.
10. Passamaria	22.00
11. Nez Percé Ford	12.00
12. Alum Creek	4.00
	213.00

TRAILS.

	Miles.
1. Terrace Mountain	6.00
2. Falls of the East Gardiner	1.00
3. Monument Geyser	1.00
4. To head of Great Falls of the Yellowstone, about 200 yards.	
5. To river below the Great Falls of the Yellowstone, 200 yards.	
	8.00

RAILROADS.

Two railroads have entered Montana, the Northern Pacific being now completed to the vicinity of Miles City, at the mouth of Tongue River, upon the Yellowstone, about 300 miles below its Gate of the Mountains, which they promise to reach during 1882, and soon thereafter run a branch up the tolerably smooth open valley of the Yellowstone to the mouth of the Gardiner, ascending it to the great Hot Medicinal Spring, where application has been made by desirable parties for the establishment of a sanitarium, one mile below the Mammoth Hot Springs and about sixty miles from their main line. The Utah Northern Railroad is completed from Ogden to Silver Bow, near Butte, and is now engaged in surveying the route of a branch by way of Ruby Valley, Virginia City, and the Upper Madison, to the Forks of the Fire Holes, a distance of about 140 or 150 miles from the main line at Dillon. With little doubt, one or both of these roads will enter the Park within two or three years hereafter, and ultimately a connection by the latter, through the valleys and cañoned branches of the Madison and the Gallatin, skirt the western border of the Park from the Forks of the Fire Holes to Bozeman, on the line of the Northern Pacific Railroad.

Should the mining developments of these mountain regions equal present indications, a railroad will reach the Park from the east via Clarke's Forks Mines or the Two Ocean Pass, or both of them, within a few years hereafter. The approach of these railroads—notably the Utah Northern—materially facilitates reaching the Park, which each road as they near it, will increase accessibility, and will soon invite a healthy competition for the patronage of tourists in making a cheap, rapid, and easy visit to the Wonder Land; planning it as the turning point, as well as the main region of attraction, in a season's ramble for health and enjoyment.

Should these anticipations be realized a visit to the Park will become national in character and popular with our people, so that ere long the flush of shame will tinge the cheeks of Americans who are obliged to acknowledge that they loiter along the antiquated paths to pigmy haunts of other lands, before seeking health, pleasure, and the soul expanding delights of a season's ramble amid the peerless snow and cliff encircled marvels of their own.

There is now assurance of increased facilities for conveyance of tourists from Bozeman, nearly 80 miles through Trail Pass, and up the Yellowstone Valley to the headquarters of the Park at the Mammoth Hot Springs, and from Virginia City some 95 miles via the old Henry's Lake route, or 90 miles by the new one up the Madison to Riverside, which was constructed during the past season by Judge Kirkwood for the spirited citizens of that town, to the Forks of the Fire Hole River, and also by the practical use of the old route via Henry's Fork and Lake, which the odometer measurements of Lieutenant Steever during the past season make 103 miles from the Forks of the Fire Hole River to Beaver Cañon, and practically about the same distance to Camas Station, both upon the Utah Northern Railroad, in the Snake River Valley, below the mountains. Believing it to be a necessity, it is now my purpose to issue a guide-book of the Park, containing a map, illustrations, and descriptions of various objects of interest, routes of approach, list of articles necessary for camp outfit and provisions, approximate time, and cost of a tour of the Wonder Land, in time for the use of next season's tourists thereto.

CONDENSED SUMMARY OF THE SEASON'S EXPLORATIONS' WORK—RECOMMENDATIONS.

For the purpose of concisely showing what has been accomplished in the Park during the past season, as well as what is considered essential to be done therein during the next, the following synopsis of each is added:

SYNOPSIS OF THE PAST SEASON'S OPERATIONS.

The following explorations have been made: Nearly all of the Madison or Mary's Lake Divide, with several brimstone basins, and also passes to Violet Creek, to the Norris Fork of the Gibbon, and to the Paint Pots bordering the Gibbon Meadows, of a nearer route to the Hoodoo region, and additional Labyrinths of Goblins upon the Passamaria and elsewhere of an open lovely pass connecting the Pelican Valley with that of the East Fork of the Yellowstone. The first general exploration of the Sierra Shoshone range, or eastern border of the Park, which is known to have ever been made by white men, including a very low and direct pass from the Passamaria Cañon to the Yellowstone Lake. An examination was also made of the main Rocky Mountain portion of the southern border of the Park from the Two Ocean Pass via Phelps's Pass, and various unknown fountain heads of the Snake River branch of the Columbia, Mount Sheridan and Heart and Riddle Lakes to the Thumb of the Yellowstone, including the discovery of some fine valleys and passes.

IMPROVEMENTS MADE.

Buildings constructed.—Hopeful of a saw-mill and cheaper lumber, the only buildings constructed during the past season were:
A small, earth-covered vault or detached fire-proof store-room for the safety of much of our provision, tools, and camp outfit at our headquarters.
A double-roomed earth-roofed bath house at the matchless Queen's Laundry, near the forks of the Fire Hole Rivers, together with wooden troughs for conveying water thereto, for the free use of the public. A line of wooden troughs for the purpose of conducting the Terrace-building waters to and successful recoating and building up of the extinct pulsatory Geyser Cone, called Devil's Thumb, at the Mammoth Hot Springs.
Bridges Constructed.—One amid the spray at the head of the Upper Falls of the east fork of the Gardiner River. A bridge over the main Blacktail Creek near its forks, and another over Elk Creek near the Dry Cañon. Three bridges in the valley of the East Fork of the Fire Hole, two upon Alum Creek; two upon Sage Creek and two upon Hot Spring Creek, all upon the new road to the Yellowstone Lake, and several others upon the Shoshone Bridle Path across the Continental divide

to the said lake. Also two foot bridges across the Fire Hole Rivers near their forks, and two over the main Fire Hole Rivers in the Upper Geyser basin. While none of these bridges are very large or costly, all are necessary and serviceable.

Roads.—One road was constructed from near the bridges of the Gardiner, through the East Fork Cañon, *via* the Dry Cañon and forks of the Yellowstone, to Tower Falls—distance, 20 miles.

A road from the forks of the Fire Hole River *via* the East Fork, Mary's Lake, and Mud Geyser, to the foot of the Yellowstone Lake, 30 miles.

Branch of the latter road from Sage Creek by Sulphur Mountain to the mouth of Alum Creek, 4 miles.

                                                                    Miles.
Aggregate of roads constructed..54

Bridle-paths opened as follows:

                                                                    Miles.
Paint Pot, length.. 11
Passamaria... 22
Painted Cliffs.. 3
Hoodoo or Goblin Land.. 29

    Aggregate of bridle paths constructed................................. 65

Trails constructed:

                                                                    Miles.
Terrace Mountain... 7
East Gardiner Falls.. 1
Monnment Geyser Basin.. 1

    Aggregate of trails constructed 9

The ladders and benches at the Crystal Falls and Grotto Pool, as well as the pole railings to the various points of observation around the different falls, although rude, are convenient and safe for the use of visitors, until a supply of lumber will allow of the construction of better ones. These improvements have been made in addition to the constant care and labor requisite for the removal of falling timber, repairs of bridges, grades, and causeways, and important additions to the latter, notably at Terrace Mountain, Obsidian Cliffs, and Cañon Creek, and a ceaseless vigilance in the prevention of needless forest fires, and wanton vandalism of natural curiosities.

It is believed that the discoveries of the weapons, utensils, and implements, as well as the stone-heap driveways for game, of the present race of Indians or of some unknown prior occupants of these regions, as herein

Fig. 28.

illustrated, possess peculiar interest, as well as encouragement for further research; and this is equally true regarding the records, narratives, and traces of early white men in the Park, herein referred to. Nor can it be doubted that the permanent exhibition in the National Museum in Washington of the beautiful pulsating Geyser Cone, from a sequined gorge, and a large collection of geodes, concretions, amethysts, and fragments of fossil timber, obsidian, and other natural objects of interest from various portions of the Park, now in the National Museum, will

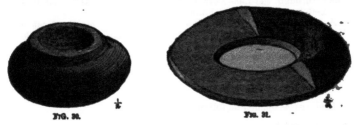

FIG. 30.   FIG. 31.

there greatly assist in disseminating a knowledge, an appreciation, and a desire to visit the enchanting scenery and matchless marvels of the distant Wonder Land. Figs. 29, 30, 31 exhibit curiously-formed water-worn concretions from the Yellowstone Lake, as described in my report of 1880, pp. 16, 17.

IMPROVEMENTS CONSIDERED IMPORTANT TO BE MADE DURING THE COMING SEASON.

Bridges.—As heretofore mentioned, it will be necessary to bridge the Yellowstone twice in order to avoid constructing several smaller bridges over branches, and heavy expensive grades in reaching the Great Falls from Alum Creek. A bridge between the mouth of this stream and that of Tower Creek nearly opposite, at a point where the river is fully 300 feet wide and very deep, but has a sluggish current, gravelly bottom, and fine approaches upon both sides, and another at the narrowest place upon the Yellowstone River below the lake, which is something less than 70 feet between the rocky abutments just above the Upper Falls, where there are good approaches, if a bridge be built high above the dashing waters near the brink. A bridge at this point would render accessible far the most open, elevated, and commanding views of the falls and adjacent rapids, as well as the most desirable site for a hotel, application for a leasehold of which by desirable parties is now pending. Several bridges of considerable magnitude, and a number of heavy grades will be necessary in the construction of a road from the Great Falls to that of Tower Creek, where one very high and costly bridge or expensive rock excavation, and probably both, are unavoidable to reach the forks of the Yellowstone, and complete the circuit of roads to the leading wonders of the Park. For reasons heretofore shown, it is very important that the old miner's bridge at the forks of the Yellowstone should be legalized as a toll-bridge, purchased, or else a new one constructed where there are more favorable approaches, as well as another over the East Fork of the Yellowstone near the mouth of the Soda Butte, at that end of the Park, and very long, heavy, and expensive grades or bridges, or both, on the Madison Plateau or Cañon route at the other.

Although not indispensable it is very desirable to construct bridges over the Fire Hole Rivers near their forks, and upon the main fork above, and below the Upper Geyser basin, and also just above the midway Geysers as soon as the necessary lumber can be obtained from a mill within the Park. A road from the Excelsior Geyser via the Twin Buttes to the Queen's Laundry, and thence to the forks of the Fire Holes with a bridle-path branch to the Fairy Falls, will be very valuable for its cost, as allowing tourists a choice of routes or a circuitous one upon each side of the river in a trip to the Upper Geyser basin. The desirability of the middle Gardiner Cañon route and of a bridle path to connect with the Two Ocean route to Wind River, the construction of troughs and scaffolding to carry the terrace building waters from the Devil's Thumb to the Liberty Cap for its preservation, and the necessity of a supply of cold water from the McCartney Creek or the West Gardiner in wooden troughs or iron pipes, have been heretofore treated of. Two other matters are of practical importance:

First. The cutting down of at least the dry timber along the main roads and bridle paths to a width sufficient to prevent the annoying obstructions constantly occurring along them.

Second. The removal of the uniformly low but troublesome stumps along the wagon roads, the necessity for both of which will, I am confident, be endorsed by all who have been jolted, or delayed by them. Nor can I believe that the prominent personages who have visited the Park, will consider my views as above expressed in reference to the necessity of additional legislation, registered guides, and an ample police force, far fetched, unnecessary, or impracticable.

SUGGESTIONS REGARDING LEASEHOLDS IN THE PARK.

The clause in the act setting apart the Yellowstone National Park which refers to revenues from leaseholds for hotel sites and from other sources therein, to be expended in its improvement, renders it evident that it was not the purpose of Congress in dedicating this heritage of wonders as a matchless health and pleasure resort for the enjoyment of our people, to thereby legalize a perpetual drain upon their treasury, a cardinal feature which in the entire management of the Park has been neither overlooked nor forgotten.

But it is also evident that leaseholds cannot be effected to parties possessing the requisite capital and ability to construct and properly manage hotels, which should be adequate to the wants of the public and creditable to the Park, until permanently clear of Indians, and the construction of roads alike necessary for the convenience of visitors, and for the conveyance of a portable steam saw-mill to the proper localities for the manufacture of material for bridge and building purposes.

Hence the undeviating policy has been to encourage and assist in making treaties with the four Indian tribes owning or frequenting any portion of the Park, to cede and forever abandon it as well as the adjacent regions, and with the construction of only such buildings as were absolutely necessary for the safety and convenience of the government officers, employés, and property, crowding the exploration of routes, and the construction of roads, bridle-paths or trails to the leading points of interest throughout the Park; meanwhile making only temporary leases for hotel purposes, but carefully selecting sites and securing propositions for permanent ones.

Upon the accompanying map of the Park may be found in distinct colors the various Fire Hole regions, at which or at other leading points of interest differently colored, the sites properly marked and numbered, as selected for 10 hotels, 2 sanitariums, and 1 for a steamboat harbor and landing at the foot of the Yellowstone Lake, being No. 6 of these hotel sites.

Temporary leases have been made for sites of the hotels at the foot of the Fire Holes and at the Mammoth Hot Springs, for which as well as for 3 additional sites for hotels, for both of the sanitariums and for the steamboat wharf, written propositions for permanent leaseholds are now pending, as well as for the establishment of a portable steam saw-mill and zoological garden.

The settled policy of the department has been to grant no title to any portion of the soil, nor licenses to persons or companies for road roads or bridges, but rather to make and manage all the improvements of a general nature, such as roads, bridges, bridle-paths and trails, leaving to private enterprise those of a local or private nature, such as hotels, &c., upon leaseholds, under proper restrictions as to time (which, for the purpose of securing a better class of structures, I suggest should be for any period not exceeding 30 years), for a prescribed portion of the frontage for buildings and rear extension for pasturage and for purposes at each of these selected sites, leaving the remainder for public use or future leaseholds.

The portable steam saw-mill, together with a sticker planer and other attachments necessary for the proper manufacture of lumber and shingles, should be constructed and managed by private enterprise, under a judicious arrangement as to price, and option of the government as to the place, time, and quantity desired for buildings, bridges, &c., allowing a generous stumpage to the owners of the mill upon any additional quantity which they may wish to manufacture for their own use or for sale to others for the purpose of constructing hotels or other necessary improvements within the Park.

An examination of the accompanying map of the Park, showing the lines of our various roads, bridle-paths and trails, and relative distances, and perusal of the above statements regarding them, it is believed will show a gratifying progress towards the completion of a circle of roads and a net work of bridle-paths and trails to the main and the minor routes of ingress as well as points of interest throughout the Park, and afford the assurance that appropriations for these purposes need not be perpetual, but that a point is nearly reached when, as above shown, responsible parties will secure leaseholds and make improvements which, without producing great immediate revenues, will soon add to the attractions and enjoyments of the Park, and ultimately at least assist materially in rendering it self-sustaining.

REMARKS ON THE MAP OF THE PARK.

The accompanying map, containing as it does the latest explorations and improvements, is believed to be far the most complete and accurate which has been made of the Park, and will be found reliable in all essential particulars. But as it is intended for practical use in the Park, it is upon a scale so small as to preclude showing many cliffs, cañons, and even some mountains throughout the Park, while the Two Ocean Pass, being outside its limits, is not shown, and the terrible cliffs and yawning cañons beyond the Sierra Shoshone range are mainly omitted in order to show the route of exploration along various creeks in that region. With care it is believed the route of this year's explorations can be traced along a fine continuous line, where, apart from roads or bridle-paths, and save No. 10 at the Two Ocean Pass, each of the 23 camps can be found by their numbers and guidons marked upon the map.

CONCLUSION.

In conclusion, I feel that I cannot in justice fail to express my thanks for the uniform kindness and assistance which I have ever received from yourself as well as from the other officers of the department over which you so ably preside, and it is hoped that any defects in the arrangement or the language of this report may be attributed to the fact that the writer thereof is more experienced in handling the weapons and the utensils of border warfare and life than the pen; but an earnest effort has, by a fair and full statement of facts, been made to show to Congress and the people of the United States, that the slender appropriations which have been made for the protection and improvement of the distant nearly unknown Wonder Land have not been misappropriated or misspent.

My own personal assistants in the Park know full well how thoroughly I appreciate their faithful and earnest services, and need no further recognition than that already made in different portions of this report. Without their cheerful and constant co-operation, my task in exploring and improving the Park, would have been indeed a hard one, and well-nigh impossible.

Very respectfully, yours,

P. W. NORRIS,
Superintendent of the Yellowstone National Park.

APPENDIX A.

ACT OF DEDICATION.

AN ACT to set apart a certain tract of land lying near the headwaters of the Yellowstone River as a public park.

Be it enacted by the Senate and House of Representatives of the United States of America in Congress assembled, That the tract of land in the Territories of Montana and Wyoming lying near the headwaters of the Yellowstone River, and described as follows, to wit: commencing at the junction of Gardiner's River with the Yellowstone River and running east to the meridian passing ten miles to the eastward of the most eastern point of Yellowstone Lake; thence south along the said meridian to the parallel of latitude passing ten miles south of the most southern point of Yellowstone Lake; thence west along said parallel to the meridian passing fifteen miles west of the most western point of Madison Lake; thence north along said meridian to the latitude of the junction of the Yellowstone and Gardiner's Rivers; thence east to the place of beginning, is hereby reserved and withdrawn from settlement, occupancy, or sale under the laws of the United States, and dedicated and set apart as a public park or pleasure ground for the benefit and enjoyment of the people; and all persons who shall locate, settle upon, or occupy the same or any part thereof, except as hereinafter provided, shall be considered trespassers and removed therefrom.

Sec. 2. That said public park shall be under the exclusive control of the Secretary of the Interior, whose duty it shall be, as soon as practicable, to make and publish such rules and regulations as he may deem necessary or proper for the care and management of the same. Such regulations shall provide for the preservation from injury or spoliation of all timber, mineral deposits, natural curiosities, or wonders within said park, and their retention in their natural condition.

The Secretary may, in his discretion, grant leases for building purposes, for terms not exceeding ten years, of small parcels of ground, at such places in said park as shall require the erection of buildings for the accommodation of visitors; all of the proceeds of said leases, and all other revenues that may be derived from any source connected with said park, to be expended under his direction in the management of the same and the construction of roads and bridle-paths therein. He shall provide against the wanton destruction of the fish and game found within said park and against their capture or destruction for the purpose of merchandise or profit. He shall also cause all persons trespassing upon the same after the passage of this act to be removed therefrom, and generally shall be authorized to take all such measures as shall be necessary or proper to fully carry out the objects and purposes of this act.

Approved March 1, 1872.

APPENDIX B.

RULES AND REGULATIONS OF THE YELLOWSTONE NATIONAL PARK.

DEPARTMENT OF THE INTERIOR,
Washington, D. C., May 4, 1881.

1. The cutting or spoliation of timber within the Park is strictly forbidden by law. Also the removing of mineral deposits, natural curiosities or wonders, or the displacement of the same from their natural condition.

2. Permission to use the necessary timber for purposes of fuel and such temporary buildings as may be required for shelter and like uses, and for the collection of such specimens of natural curiosities as can be removed without injury to the natural features or beauty of the grounds, must be obtained from the Superintendent; and must be subject at all times to his supervision and control.

3. Fires shall only be kindled when actually necessary, and shall be immediately extinguished when no longer required. Under no circumstances must they be left burning when the place where they have been kindled shall be vacated by the party requiring their use.

4. Hunting, trapping, and fishing, except for purposes of procuring food for visitors or actual residents, are prohibited by law; and no sales of game or fish taken inside the Park shall be made for purposes of profit within its boundaries or elsewhere.

5. No person will be permitted to reside permanently within the Park without permission from the Department of the Interior; and any person residing therein, except under lease, as provided in section 2475 of the Revised Statutes, shall vacate the premises within thirty days after being notified in writing so to do by the person in charge; notice to be served upon him in person or left at his place of residence.

6. *The sale of intoxicating liquors is strictly prohibited.*

7. All persons trespassing within the domain of said Park, or violating any of the foregoing rules, will be summarily removed therefrom by the Superintendent and his authorized employés, who are, by direction of the Secretary of the Interior, specially designated to carry into effect all necessary regulations for the protection and preservation of the Park, as required by the statute; which expressly provides that the same "shall be under the exclusive control of the Secretary of the Interior, whose duty it shall be to make and publish such rules and regulations as he shall deem necessary or proper;" and who, "generally, shall be authorized to take all such measures as shall be necessary or proper to fully carry out the object and purposes of this act."

Resistance to the authority of the Superintendent, or repetition of any offense against the foregoing regulations, shall subject the outfits of such offenders and all prohibited articles to seizure, at the discretion of the Superintendent or his assistant in charge.

P. W. NORRIS,
Superintendent.

Approved:
S. J. KIRKWOOD,
Secretary.

REPORT OF THE ARCHITECT OF THE UNITED STATES CAPITOL.

ARCHITECT'S OFFICE, UNITED STATES CAPITOL,
Washington, D. C., October 1, 1881.

SIR: I have the honor to submit the following report, showing the progress made on the various public works, in charge of the Architect of the Capitol, since the date of the last annual report from this office.

THE CAPITOL.

Congress having removed the restrictions, relating to the elevator in the south wing, referred to in my last, the work of constructing the elevator is now nearly completed.

It is located at the south end of the eastern corridor. This position was chosen because it was considered more convenient of access to those who are compelled to use the elevator, being near the main carriage entrance; besides, it connects with both the ladies' retiring room in the gallery and the rooms in the basement, where it is likely the bathing rooms may be placed. It is also more convenient of approach to the post-office and refectory. It is recommended that the bathing rooms be moved from their present location to the rooms just mentioned, at the foot of the elevator, which are comparatively light and can be well ventilated, while the rooms now used for that purpose are dark interior rooms, with no windows or other means of adequate ventilation. If this change should be made, the refectory could be extended so as to give a private room for members, as is the case in the Senate.

As provided in the act approved May 3, 1881, the gallery of the old Hall of Representatives and rooms connected with it have been made fire-proof, by taking out all the wooden joist and flooring, and substituting iron beams and brick arches.

The rooms thus fire-proofed have not as yet been fitted up for the House documentary library, as provided by law, as the Speaker of the last Congress, owing to the late day of the session at which the law was passed, did not consider that he had the power to select rooms to place the stationery and files, now stored in the rooms adjacent to the old Hall, and in consequence the stationery and files must remain in the rooms they formerly did, until the Speaker selects rooms in the basement of the south wing for their reception. In connection with the library I will state, that rooms in the cellar story have been shelved, in which there are stored about 40,000 deplicate volumes, taken from the House library, the gallery of the old Hall of Representatives, and the rooms adjoining.

By direction of the Committee on Public Buildings and Grounds of the Senate, the rooms in the loft of the northern part of the central building have been fire-proofed to store books belonging to the Senate documentary library. The wooden stairs leading to this loft have been taken out, and those of iron supplied. One of the rooms of this library is about to be fitted up for a committee room.

The body of the Senate Chamber has been painted and regilded and many rooms and corridors repainted. The iron panels have been taken from the ceiling of the Senate Chamber and glass used instead. Additional sky-lights have been placed in the Senate roof, by which the north gallery is as light as that of the south.

Mr. Costaggini has painted in fresco on the belt of the rotunda the "Settlement of New England," "Oglethorp and the Indians," and "Lexington." He has also completed "Penn and the Indians," left unfinished by Mr. Brumidi, and he is now engaged on the "Reading the Declaration of Independence." It is proper to state here, that Mr. Brumidi made the designs for these sections only in small size and Mr. Costaggini has had to make the full-sized cartoons.

In relation to the working of the heating and ventilating apparatus of the Hall of Representatives, rearranged under the commission named by law, Mr. Lannan, the chief engineer of the heating department, says in his report: ·

In submitting the following tabulated statement of the working of this apparatus, showing the result of observations made during the legislative days of the months of January and February, 1881, I have the honor to state that these observations for temperature, velocity, relative humidity, number of persons in Hall, &c., were taken at 2 p. m. each day—this being considered the best time for an average. The direction, force of wind, and state of weather being furnished each day by the United States Sginal Office from observations taken by them at the same hour. Your special attention is called to the following facts: the uniform temperature at which we are able to keep the Hall during the sessions. From the table you will see, that in no case has it

varied more than one degree during the ordinary sessions (
temperature from the duct in basement to louvers on roof
when the gas is lighted over ceiling.

The relative humidity, while yet below the standard, sho
servations heretofore taken. The relation between revolut
air in duct is very much improved. This I account for by
ceiving duct and construction of the perpendicular shaft a
improvements were made, the velocity of air in duct varied
and force of wind. The volume of air has also increased ab
ume of air carried to the Hall per minute for each person, i
removed from Hall through louvers on roof, is in excess
shows that the machinery is up to its work.

In all tests the drafts at gallery and Hall doors was outw
cases shown otherwise on table.

The registering thermometers, used for obtaining the ma:
peratures of Hall, and all instruments used in making tl
quality and of the most improved pattern, and great care
these tests reliable.

I also submit one set of observations taken during nig
1881), with all gas jets over ceiling lighted, by which it v
over 6,000 cubic feet more air expelled at the louvers than
This excess is attributed to expansion of the air when it res
contact with the gas jets, as may be seen by the temperat
'oft, the former being 69°, the latter 106°.

Revolutions of fan ....
Velocity of air in duct.......................................:..
Volume of air in duct in cubic feet...........................
Velocity at louvers on roof.......................:............
Volume at louvers on roof in cubic feet........... ....
Temperature outside ....
Temperature in duct ....
Temperature in Hall ....
Temperature at louvers.......................................
Draft at gallery and Hall doors about balanced.

These results must be regarded as highly satisf;
show that the temperature in the Hall is very '
perfect control, and that the air is rapidly change
drafts, except only when the Hall is overcrowded. '
air delivered in the Hall averaged during the mor
during the month of February 67 cubic feet per 1
in the Hall. Mr. Lannan's tabulated statement i

Of the electric lighting apparatus, Mr. Rogers, '
as follows:

The dynamo-electric machines continue to work well fc
Capitol. By substituting them for galvanic batteries th
year in acids, zinc, &c., and the large apparatus heretofore
may now be used for other purposes. These machines have
instead of forty-eight circuits, at first necessary for lightin
tives, only three are now employed, and consequently the
turning it on and ignition, escapes in the same reduced
hitherto diffused in the ceiling only one-sixteenth now e
advantage of which to the ventilation, and also in view of poss

I have examined carefully almost every system of electri
rimented continually to render some one practicable for li{
sentatives, but find that the "voltaic arc," though cheaper
ticable for legislative halls on account of its unsteadiness, whi
systems cost a great deal more than gas—certainly under t
cumstances twice as much.

The electro-thermometers, employed by the engineers be
perature in the Hall of Representatives above, have not '
the oxidation of the mercury in the very small columns used
others to be constructed with larger columns of mercury,
rendered practicable by an aero-thermometer in combinati
instead of the ordinary hermetical seal. The lighting depa
overhauled, and will be in readiness with new platinum
Congress convenes.

Four portable fire-engines, at a cost of $1,200, have been
in each wing of the building.

CAPITOL GROUNDS.

The progress made in the improvement of these grounds will be seen by the following report of F. H. Cobb, engineer:

"I have the honor to report that the improvement of the Capitol grounds, according to the plans adopted by Congress in 1874, has been carried forward during the year as rapidly as the appropriation would allow.

"When the work at present in progress is completed the main features of that plan, so far as it relates to the grounds alone, will have been executed. There still remain certain details to be provided for, as will be seen in the estimate for the coming year.

"The completion of the lawns and approaches on the west side bring into greater prominence the want of symmetry existing between the old plan and the new.

"When the upright marble walls and central approaches shall be substituted, with their broad landing places and stairways, carrying the steps far out into the west lawn, the wide walks which now converge towards the center will be in harmony with them. At present the narrow and steep central steps, being out of proportion both to the new plan and the Capitol building, present a cramped and undignified appearance. They are also difficult of ascent, and dangerous in the winter months. There is about 50 feet of elevation to overcome, and whatever plan is eventually carried into execution must of necessity follow these general principles, so that the walks now finished will be in their proper position.

"Owing to the uncertainty respecting the terraces, the lawns immediately surrounding them have been left unchanged, and to a certain extent uncared for.

"The severity of the past winter being almost unprecedented in this climate, a number of the choice plants and trees were injured, but as far as possible they have been replaced.

"The general condition of the shrubbery is satisfactory. The long continued dry weather of the present summer has affected the growth to some extent, but artificial watering is resorted to so far as practicable. Just here it may be said that much complaint has been made of the use of Potomac water during the day, claiming that it deprived the citizens of Capitol Hill of their ordinary supply. While this use of the water on the grounds undoubtedly diminishes the pressure to a limited extent, its influence is generally overestimated.

"The grounds occupy a space equal to more than eight squares, and the maximum amount of water used at one time during the day has not exceeded ten ordinary hydrants.

"There is probably no equally improved part of the city of the same area where less water is used. But in order to quiet the clamor the use of water for irrigating purposes has at present been discontinued during the middle of the day.

"The intense cold of the winter caused some injury to the roads, and slight injury to the walk pavements. The latter are made of Portland cement and sand, in blocks from 2 to 3 feet square and 4 inches thick, cut entirely free from each other, so that injury to one does not affect the other. It was first adopted as a substitute for stone on account of its cheapness and the ease with which it could be adapted to curves and winding grades, its durability, and general good appearance. Time serves to confirm the wisdom of the choice. That laid five years ago seems in perfect condition, and the frost of last winter has not done it material injury. Some blocks were upheaved, but most of them returned to their positions. No greater injury was done to this than to stone flagging under similar conditions; and the imperfections appearing have been promptly repaired by the contractor, according to the terms of his contract.

"The asphalt road pavement suffered to a greater extent. The intense cold caused it to crack badly in the east park. I have not been able to discover any principle governing the occurrence of these defects, except in general it can be said that those parts tamped with hot pestles are more subject to injury than that compressed with rollers; but it would be the part of caution hereafter to divide large areas, so as to afford opportunities for contraction. The base of cement concrete appears to be uninjured.

"The 15 per cent. reservation for three years, paving on all contracts finished in 1877, being due, was paid after the paving had been satisfactorily repaired.

"No new road pavement was laid last year or is to be undertaken this year; 3,318 square yards of artificial stone footwalk have been laid; 2,834 square yards of this was plain and 484 square yards mosaic. With what is now in progress, this will virtually complete the walks upon the grounds.

"The summer-house on the north side referred to in the last report has been completed, and affords a much needed resting place for pedestrians. The work is substantially done, and the permanent vines and shrubbery are growing rapidly.

"The southwest and southeast sides of the park have been inclosed with stone coping and wall similar in design to that upon the remainder of the grounds. The material is black granite from Maine. The incompleted portion of the east side is now under contract, and will be finished this season.

"Large granite piers, to be surmounted with bronze lamps, and a wall similar to that built on the northwest entrance, is now being erected at the southwest entrance from Maryland avenue.

"The walk entrance from Pennsylvania avenue has been completed except a small amount of coping as far east as the plaza. This is all that can be done here until the new arrangement of terrace is decided on. The corresponding entrance from Maryland avenue is being completed in a similar manner. The improvements at this point will be completed during the present season.

"Quite a large amount of shrubbery has been purchased during the year, as will be seen by reference to the statement of expenditures.

"It will be necessary to purchase this fall from 1,500 to 2,000 yards of manure to fertilize the lawns.

"The office, sheds, and shops on the rented ground at North B street and Delaware avenue have been moved to the premises belonging to the United States at South Capitol and B streets.

"The watchmen employed on the grounds have been faithful to their trust, and prevented many depredations being committed, as well as preserving good order. I would recommend that they be required to wear uniforms while on duty, and be appointed special police of the Metropolitan force.

"There has been expended $24, 570.81 for labor of men, including $1,245.50 for horses and carts.

"It has been my endeavor to make all connected with this department feel a personal interest in their work. To this end the most deserving have been recommended from time to time as worthy of the most time and pay. The result has been satisfactory, and at no previous time has more work been performed with the same expenditure of money."

In relation to the proposed terrace I invite especial attention to the letter of Mr. F. Law Olmsted, which is herewith appended.

EXTENSION OF COURT-HOUSE.

Work on this extension was commenced immediately on the approval of the plans, and bids for the sandstone work, the bricks and bricklaying were invited by public advertisement, the following awards being made to the lowest bidders, namely: Sandstone work to Richard Rothwell, for $17,299; the bricks to Charles I. Davis, for $6.70 per thousand; and the brick-work, including lime and sand, to Charles W. King, for $3.45 per thousand.

While this work has been somewhat delayed on account of the strikes among some of the workmen employed by the contractors, and by the difficulty in procuring the necessary rolled-iron beams, it is now making satisfactory progress.

In connection with this building, I will state that during the storm on the evening of June 27 last the entire northern portion of the roof was blown off, and considerable damage done to other portions of the roof.

To prevent injury to the public records thus exposed and interruption to the courts, it was considered necessary to replace and repair these roofs at once, depending on Congress to provide means for the expense thus incurred. These repairs, together with some others caused by the storm, were at once made at a cost of $1,830.70, for which amount an appropriation should be obtained.

EXTENSION TO THE PUBLIC PRINTING OFFICE.

The extension of this building is now ready for roofing, and is expected to be completed by the commencement of the next session of Congress.

Considerable difficulty was encountered in excavating for the cellar, as the ground was so exceptionally wet that a drain to the main sewer on North Capitol street had to be constructed.

On the land at the west of the main building, recently purchased by the government, has been constructed a brick stable. This structure will accommodate twenty horses, and has attached to one side and end sheds for sheltering wagons. The upper story is now used for forage, and a portion may possibly be used for storing material connected with the Printing Office.

PLANS FOR PUBLIC SCHOOLS.

In conformity with the requirements of the provision in the bill making appropriation for the District of Columbia for the present fiscal year, I have made the plan for the high-school building, for two District school buildings, and for two school buildings for the county. These have been approved by the trustees, and the buildings, I am informed, are being erected.

BOTANICAL GARDEN.

At the request of the Joint Committee on Library I have continued in charge of the repairs and improvements of this place, and would state that since the last report all the damage caused by the flood of 1879 has been repaired. As quite extensive alterations were necessary to accommodate the lawns and walks to the new grade of the Tiber sewer, advantage was taken at this time to change the central walk, raising it some 2 feet and narrowing it. The old Seneca flag was relaid, bordered with bluestone edging. Suitable steps were provided at the cross-walks and where the main walks cross the sewer. All the footways south of this, immediately surrounding the buildings, have been concreted with asphalt in the best manner.

56 Ab

The walk leading from the center of the main building to the Bartholdi fountain has been paved with artificial stone. During the present season it is proposed to finish all the footways surrounding this fountain and regrade the lawns. Much of this has already been done, and the remainder will be completed before cold weather. The walks are already outlined with Seneca bluestone edging, and will be paved with asphaltic concrete.

It was found necessary to pave the bowl of the fountain to prevent filtration. This was done with Neuchatel mastic, and it appears to be entirely water-tight. The pipes to the lamps surrounding the bowl of the fountain, as well as those on the fountain itself, have been connected with the main on Pennsylvania avenue. These are arranged for electric lighting from a battery in the main building.

A large amount of painting and reglazing has been done, the tin roofs of many of the propagating houses being replaced with glass, while the metal roofs of all the buildings have been painted. The houses on the south side of Maryland avenue have also been painted. No new buildings have been erected, except an orchid house of iron construction. The sashes and iron frames for the ventilator to the conservatory have not yet been received, owing to the destruction of the factory of the contractors, Lord & Burham, at Ironton-on-the-Hudson.

Statement showing amounts expended from June 30, 1880, to June 30, 1881.

CAPITOL EXTENSION.

For amount of pay-rolls of mechanics, labor, &c	$30,301 13
For amount paid for painting material	2,502 55
For amount paid for salary of Architect	4,500 00
For amount paid for plumbing and steam-fitting material	1,422 70
For amount paid for hardware and iron	1,514 30
For amount paid for disbursing agent	1,000 00
For amount paid for lumber	968 55
For amount paid for material for covering fly-doors, &c	340 52
For amount paid for marble and granite	570 10
For amount paid for freight and express charges	285 16
For amount paid for winding clocks, repairing, &c., in center building	100 00
For amount paid for stationery	233 97
For amount paid for forage	129 43
For amount paid for rent of carpenters' and smiths' shop	120 00
For amount paid for labor not on pay-rolls, paid by voucher	547 93
For amount paid for fresco painter	2,500 00
For amount paid for nickel plating	27 00
For amount paid for cement, lime, bricks, &c	621 40
For amount paid for brushes, soap, sponge, &c., and for cleaning floors	556 55
For amount paid for fuel for shops	9 75
For amount paid for grate-bars and castings	680 00
For amount paid for tile	30 50
For amount paid for galvanized-iron work for skylights	73 50
For amount paid for fire extinguishers	80 00
For amount to be returned to the Treasury, as being unavailable for elevator	7,000 00
	57,000 00
Amount appropriated June 16, 1880	57,000

HEATING APPARATUS, SENATE.

For amount paid for repairs to machinery	3,895 11
For amount paid for steam and water-pipe fittings	2,210 00
For amount paid for vacuum-pump	65 00
For amount paid for steam-traps	57 00
For amount paid for glass	42 54
For amount paid for hardware	39 00
For amount paid for fire-bricks	13 50

For amount paid for mason work	$220 26
For amount paid for brass castings.......................................	352 04
For amount paid for laboring work	476 00
For amount paid for transportation	108 56
For amount paid for tin and galvanized-iron work.....................	799 90

	10,000 00
Amount appropriated June 16, 1880..	10,000 00

HEATING APPARATUS, HOUSE OF REPRESENTATIVES.

For amount paid for hardware and tools	517 00
For amount paid for transportation	23 00
For amount paid for laboring work	10 00
For amount paid for pipe-cutting machine	450 00

	1,000 00
Amount appropriated June 16, 1880	1,000 00

LIGHTING CAPITOL AND GROUNDS.

For amount paid for pay-rolls, superintendent of meters, and lamp-lighters.	4,192 69
For amount paid for gas consumed......................................	21,753 80
For amount paid for gas-burners, chandeliers, and globes...............	283 83
For amount paid for regulators	118 00
For amount paid for wire, zinc, and chemicals for electric battery.......	1,814 95
For amount paid for lamps, posts, and lanterns.........................	1,125 37
For amount paid for freight	6 73
For amount paid for matches, &c...	118 70
For amount paid for repairs to meter.....................................	5 00
For amount to be returned to the Treasury..............................	2,580 93

	32,000 00
Amount appropriated June 16, 1880......................................	32,000 00

CAPITOL GROUNDS.

For amount paid for bluestone steps for Pennsylvania avenue walk	676 99
For amount paid for bluestone steps for summer-house...................	250 76
For amount paid for Ohio stone coping and wall	1,459 36
For amount paid for granite coping and wall at First and B streets south-east..	3,996 50
For amount paid for granite coping and wall at First and B streets south-west..	8,206 80
For amount paid for bronze lanterns	65 58
For amount paid for bronze drinking fountain...........................	228 50
For amount paid for park lamps	253 02
For amount paid for bluestone seats and drinking fountain..............	847 86
For amount paid for iron grates for Maryland avenue walk	297 40
For amount paid for bronze work and chimes for summer-house	264 20
For amount paid for iron gates for summer-house	180 00
For amount paid for cement, lime, and sand............................	332 11
For amount paid for building stone	31 75
For amount paid for brick	491 47
For amount paid for lumber	237 42
For amount paid for roofing tile and slate for summer-house	374 01
For amount paid for freight and hauling..................................	55 51
For amount paid for hardware and tools	443 63
For amount paid for plumbing material..................................	230 98
For amount paid for soil..	460 50
For amount paid for sodding and seed..................................	40 91
For amount paid for shrubbery and plants..............................	968 03
For amount paid for manure and other fertilizers.......................	238 10
For amount paid for services of men paid by vouchers..................	897 53
For amount paid for services of men paid by pay-roll...................	24,570 81
For amount paid for services and expenses of F. L. Olmsted	2,133 50
For amount paid for services of draughtsman...........................	104 73
For amount paid for miscellaneous bills.................................	158 13

For amount paid for repairing North B street............
For amount paid for removing old material ....
For amount paid for granite curb........ ....
For amount paid for granite coping at entrance of B an
   streets........... ...   .
For amount paid for office rent, coal, stationery, and rep
For amount paid for rent of carpenters' shop............
For amount pafd for roofing tool house..................
For amount paid for artificial stone pavement...........
For amount paid for mosaic pavement. ....
Balance cash on hand.......... ....

Amount appropriated June 16, 1880........ ....

PAYMENT OF RETAINED PERCENT.

Paid to George W. Riggs, September 28, 1890............
Paid to Cranford & Hoffman, August 24, 1880............
Paid to W. H. Groat, June 30, 1881.....................
Balance on hand........................ ....

                              ι

Amount appropriated June 16, 1880..................... ...

ENLARGING COURT-HOUSE, WASHINGT'

For amount of pay-rolls.............. ....
For amount paid for plumbing....Δ....... ....
For amount paid for sewers........................ ....
For amount paid for excavation........ ....
For amount paid for building stone.....................
For amount paid for cellar walls......................
For amount paid for cement..... ....
For amount paid for iron beams..   ....
For amount paid for advertising................. ....
For amount paid for bricks....... ....
For amount paid for transportation............ ....
For amount paid for cut stone........................ ...
Amount available July 1, 1881..........................

Amount appropriated February 23, 1881.................

EXTENSION OF THE GOVERNMENT PRINTI

For amount of pay-rolls.................. ....
For amount paid for lime, sand, and cement.............
For amount paid for building stone.....................
For amount paid for laying stone.......................
For amount paid for tin roofing.......................
For amount paid for laying bricks...... ....
For amount paid for excavation.................. ....
For amount paid for bricks................... ....
For amount paid for carting............. ....
For amount paid for concreting.......................... .
For amount paid for plastering............... ... .
For amount paid for labor not on pay-rolls, paid by vouch
For amount paid for surveying ....
For amount paid for plumbing material..................
For amount paid for cut-stone work......................
For amount paid for sewer ....
For amount paid for painting............................

For amount paid for iron work for stalls...............................	$399 20
For amount paid for lumber..	622 56
Amount available July 1, 1881..	32,694 82
	40,000 00
Amount appropriated June 16, 1880...................................	40,000 00

Very respectfully submitted.

EDWARD CLARK,
Architect United States Capitol.

Hon. S. J. KIRKWOOD,
Secretary of the Interior.

REPORT OF THE BOARD OF VISITORS OF THE GOVERNMENT HOSPITAL FOR THE INSANE.

GOVERNMENT HOSPITAL FOR THE INSANE,
Near Washington, D. C., October 1, 1881.

SIR: In accordance with the law establishing this hospital, the Board of Visitors have the honor to submit their twenty-sixth annual report.

The following tables give a synopsis of the movements of the population and operations of the hospital during the year ending June 30, 1881:

Summary.

	Males.	Females.	Totals.
Remaining June 30, 1880..	691	206	897
Admitted during the year ending June 30, 1881..................	161	62	223
Whole number under treatment	852	268	1,120
Recovered	62	10	72
Improved	27	9	36
Unimproved		6	6
Died	63	18	81
Total discharged and died.......................................	152	43	195
Remaining June 30, 1881..	700	225	925

Admissions and discharges.

		Males.		Females.		Totals.	
REMAINING JUNE 30, 1880.							
Army................................ {	White..	453		3			
	Colored..	11	464	......	3	467	
Navy .... {	White...	42					
	Colored..	1	43			43	
Marine Hospital service .... {	White...	7					
	Colored..	1	8			8	
Civil life .... {	White...	132		146			
	Colored..	44	176	57	203	379	
			691		206		897

Admissions and discharges—Continued.

		Males.		Females.		Totals.	
ADMITTED DURING THE YEAR 1880–'81.							
Army	White...	58		1		61	
	Colored..	2	60	......	1		
Navy	White ..	10				11	
	Colored..	1	11				
Marine Hospital Service	White...	4				7	
	Colored..	3	7				
Civil life	White...	63		43		144	
	Colored..	20	83	18	61		
			161		62		223
UNDER TREATMENT DURING THE YEAR.							
Army	White...	511		4		528	
	Colored..	13	524	......	4		
Navy	White...	52				54	
	Colored..	2	54				
Marine Hospital Service	White...	11				15	
	Colored..	4	15				
Civil life	White...	195		189		523	
	Colored..	64	259	75	264		
			852		268		1,120
DISCHARGED DURING THE YEAR—*Recovered.*							
Army	White...	25		1		28	
	Colored..	2	27	......	1		
Navy	White...	7				7	
	Colored..	......	7				
Marine Hospital Service	White...	......				1	
	Colored..	1	1				
Civil life	White...	17		5		36	
	Colored..	10	27	4	9		
			62		10		72
DISCHARGED DURING THE YEAR—*Improved.*							
Army	White...	7				8	
	Colored..	1	8				
Navy	White...						
	Colored..						
Marine Hospital Service	White.	2				2	
	Colored..	......	2				
Civil life	White...	16		6		26	
	Colored..	1	17	3	9		
			27		9		36
DISCHARGED DURING THE YEAR—*Unimproved.*							
Army	White						
	Colored..						
Navy	White...						
	Colored..						
Marine Hospital Service	White						
	Colored..						
Civil life	White...			5			
	Colored..			1	6		6
DECEASED DURING THE YEAR.							
Army	White...	44				44	
	Colored..	......	44				
Navy	White...	3				3	
	Colored..	......	3				
Marine Hospital Service	White...	1				2	
	Colored..	1	2				
Civil life	White...	9		12		32	
	Colored..	5	14	6	18		
			63		18		81

Admissions and discharges—Continued.

		Males.		Females.		Totals.	
REMAINING JUNE 30, 1881.							
Army {	White...	435		3			
	Colored..	10	445	......	3	448	
Navy {	White...	42			3		
	Colored..	2	44			44	
Marine Hospital Service {	White...	8					
	Colored..	2	10			10	
Civil life {	White..	153		161			
	Colored..	48	201	61	222	423	
			700		225		925

NOTE 1.—Of the 423 from civil life remaining at the end of the year 383 were indigent residents of the District of Columbia, 21 were indigent non-residents, and 2 were non-resident criminals.
NOTE 2.—There were 10 less persons than cases under treatment in the course of the year by reason of 8 readmissions and two transfers from "independent" to "indigent."

Monthly changes of population.

Date.	Admitted.			Discharged.			Died.			Total discharg'd, including deaths.
	Male.	Female.	Total.	Male.	Female.	Total.	Male.	Female.	Total.	
July, 1880	15	4	19	13	3	16	4	1	5	21
August, 1880	13	5	18	5	5	10	3	0	3	13
September, 1880	9	6	15	9	2	11	6	3	9	20
October, 1880	12	6	18	15	1	16	6	4	10	26
November, 1880	11	3	14	6	1	7	6	0	6	13
December, 1880	11	4	15	2	2	4	4	2	6	10
January, 1881	10	5	15	6	2	8	7	1	8	16
February, 1881	17	6	23	1	1	2	4	2	6	8
March, 1881	11	7	18	5	0	5	4	1	5	10
April, 1881	12	2	14	13	0	13	10	2	12	25
May, 1881	18	5	23	7	3	10	7	2	9	19
June, 1881	22	9	31	7	5	12	2	0	2	14
	161	62	223	89	25	114	63	18	81	195

Physical condition of those who died.

Apoplexy	1	Old age	1
Apoplexy (epileptic)	10	Organic disease of brain	18
Asphyxia (accidental)	1	Organic disease of brain and spinal	
Bright's disease	2	cord	3
Burn (self-inflicted)	1	Osteo-sarcoma (of thigh)	1
Cancer (of pancreas)	1	Paresis	11
Cardiac disease	4	Peritonitis, acute	1
Cirrhosis of liver, with cholesteræmia.	1	Pernicious fever	1
Diarrhœa	5	Phthisis pulmonalis	12
Erysipelas	1	Pulmonary oedema	1
Exhaustion of acute mania	1	Typo-malarial fever	1
Exhaustion of chronic mania	1		
Fracture of neck of femur	1	Total	81
Intussusception (intestinal)	1		

Duration of the mental disease of those who died.

Less than three months	4	Ten years	2
Three to six months	3	Eleven years	1
Six months to one year	1	Twelve years	4
One year	11	Thirteen years	4

Duration of the mental disease of those who died—Continued.

Two years	15	Fourteen years	2
Three years	8	Fifteen years	3
Four years	1	Sixteen years	1
Five years	4	Seventeen years	3
Six years	6	Twenty years	1
Seven years	3		
Eight years	2	Total	81
Nine years	2		

Duration of disease on admission.

		Males.		Females.		Totals.	
LESS THAN SIX MONTHS.							
Army	White 23 / Colored 2	25		1 /	1	26	
Navy	White 7 / Colored	7				7	
Marine Hospital Service	White 1 / Colored 2	3				3	
Civil life	White 29 / Colored 13	42	77	11 / 6	17	59	95
LESS THAN ONE YEAR.							
Army	White 11 / Colored	11				11	
Navy	White 1 / Colored	1				1	
Marine Hospital Service	White 2 / Colored	2				2	
Civil life	White 2 / Colored	2	16	4 / 3	7	9	23
ONE TO TWO YEARS.							
Army	White 17 / Colored	17				17	
Navy	White 3 / Colored	3				3	
Marine Hospital Service	White 1 / Colored 1	2				2	
Civil life	White 17 / Colored 4	21	43	8 / 3	11	32	54
OVER TWO YEARS.							
Army	White 1 / Colored	1				1	
Navy	White / Colored						
Marine Hospital Service	White / Colored						
Civil life	White 5 / Colored	5	6	5 / 3	8	13	14
OVER THREE YEARS.							
Army	White 1 / Colored	1				1	
Navy	White / Colored						
Marine Hospital Service	White / Colored						
Civil life	White 3 / Colored 1	4	5			4	5

Duration of disease on admission—Continued.

		Males.		Females.		Total.	
OVER FOUR YEARS.							
Army	{ White ... { Colored ..						
Navy	{ White ... { Colored ..						
Marine Hospital Service	{ White ... { Colored ..						
Civil life	{ White ... { Colored ..			6 2	8	8	8 8
FIVE TO TEN YEARS.							
Army	{ White ... { Colored ..	2	2			2	
Navy	{ White ... { Colored ..						
Marine Hospital Service	{ White ... { Colored ..						
Civil life	{ White ... { Colored ..	4 2	6	7 1	8	8 14	16
TEN TO TWENTY YEARS.							
Army	{ White ... { Colored ..	2	3			3	
Navy	{ White ... { Colored ..						
Marine Hospital Service	{ White ... { Colored ..						
Civil life	{ White ... { Colored ..		3	2	2	2	5
OVER TWENTY YEARS.							
Army	{ White ... { Colored ..						
Navy	{ White ... { Colored ..						
Marine Hospital Service	{ White ... { Colored ..						
Civil life	{ White ... { Colored ..	2 1	3			3	3 223

Table showing the nativity, as far as could be ascertained, of the 5,163 cases treated.

NATIVE BORN.		FOREIGN BORN.	
District of Columbia	560	Ireland	1,071
New York	385	Germany	715
Maryland	364	England	127
Virginia	367	France	51
Pennsylvania	274	Canada	44
Ohio	137	Scotland	38
Massachusetts	121	Switzerland	15
Maine	58	Italy	22
Illinois	49	Denmark	14
Connecticut	44	Norway	10
New Hampshire	49	Sweden	12

Table showing the nativity, &c.—Continued.

NATIVE BORN.		FOREIGN BORN.	
Indiana	40	Poland	11
Kentucky	37	Russia	6
Michigan	30	Austria	5
New Jersey	36	Nova Scotia	5
Tennessee	25	Spain	4
Wisconsin	20	Holland	6
Vermont	24	Wales	4
Missouri	21	Portugal	3
Rhode Island	15	Hungary	4
Delaware	14	Mexico	3
North Carolina	18	Saxony	4
Alabama	7	Malta	3
South Carolina	9	Cyprus	1
Iowa	4	Belgium	3
Georgia	9	Buenos Ayres	1
Mississippi	9	Costa Rica	1
Louisiana	5	Bavaria	2
West Virginia	6	Sicily	1
Kansas	2	British Columbia	1
Florida	2	British Possessions	1
Texas	4	East Indies (British)	2
California	3	West Indies (British)	4
Choctaw Nation	2	West Indies, Hayti	1
Colorado	1	New Brunswick	1
Arkansas	1	Cuba	2
		Sandwich Islands	1
Total	2,752	China	1
		Coast of Africa	2
		Total	2,386

Native born	2,752
Foreign born	2,386
Unknown	265
Total	5,163

FORM OF DISEASE IN THOSE ADMITTED.

	Total last year.	Admitted during year.	Total.		Total last year.	Admitted during year.	Total.
Mania, acute	1,828	50	1,878	Kleptomania	3		3
Mania, chronic	750	5	516	Nymphomania	3		3
Melancholia	578	6	63	Imbecility	39	4	6
Dementia	1,283	4	1,283	Opium eaters	11		11
Dementia, senile	54	2	56	Not insane	4		6
Paresis	55	10	65				
Dipsomania	341	10	351	Total	4,940	223	5,163
Typhomania (Bell's disease)	2		2				

COMPLICATIONS OF THOSE ADMITTED.

Epilepsy	268	17	285	Period city	186	9	195
Apoplexy	2		2	Puerperal state	29	1	30
Paralysis	108	11	119	Catalepsy	7	1	8
Suicidal disposition	130	19	149	Neuralgia	31	1	32
Homicidal disposition	45	5	50	Post febrile condition	41	3	44

As far as could be ascertained, the volunteers of the Army and Navy under treatment during the year ending June 30, 1881, entered the service from the following States:

	Army.	Navy.	Total.		Army.	Navy.	Total.
New York	48	....	48	Maine	7	....	7
Ohio	28	....	28	Nebraska	2	....	2
Pennsylvania	20	....	20	Delaware	1	....	1
Indiana	22	....	22	Minnesota	1	....	1
Michigan	11	....	11	Iowa	3	....	3
Illinois	16	....	16	North Carolina	1	....	1
Wisconsin	12	....	12	California	1	....	1
Missouri	4	....	4	New Mexico	1	....	1
Connecticut	8	....	8	Kentucky	1	....	1
New Hampshire	5	....	5	West Virginia	2	....	2
Vermont	1	....	1	Unknown	5	1	6
Maryland	7	....	7				
Massachusetts	18	....	18	Total	220	1	221
New Jersey	5	....	5				

Tabular statement of the time of life at which the 5,163 persons treated since the opening of the Institution became insane.

Under 10 years	83
Between 10 and 15 years	55
15 and 20 years	363
20 and 25 years	943
25 and 30 years	1,038
30 and 35 years	909
35 and 40 years	600
40 and 45 years	397
45 and 50 years	273
50 and 60 years	254
60 and 70 years	143
70 and 80 years	50
80 and 90 years	7
Unknown	64
Not insane	4
Total	5,163

Private patients.

			Total.
There were at the beginning of the year	6 males,	9 females	15
Received during the year	7 males,	4 females	11
Whole number under treatment	13 males,	13 females	26
Discharged during the year	4 males,	5 females	9
Remaining at the end of the year	9 males,	8 females	17

The number of admissions, which was 223, is almost identical with that of the two previous years, but the number remaining at the close of the year, 925, as well as the number under treatment during the year, 1,120, exceeds that of any previous report. As the hospital becomes a permanent home for the most of those who do not recover, it is to be expected that the number of inmates will slowly increase. The daily average number under treatment was 890. Rather more than one-third of the discharges, including deaths, have been recoveries, and the deaths, 81 in number, have been a little more than 7 per cent. of the whole number treated.

Throughout the year the hospital has enjoyed an immunity from epidemic disease or extensive disaster, which while it is not different from its usual record is none the less a subject for congratulation and thankfulness. In a community of nearly 1,000 insane persons the possibilities of accident or outbreak are many and are a source of daily anxiety to the officers in charge; indeed, when we take into account the crowded condition of the house, it is a matter of surprise that so little really serious trouble has hitherto occurred in our hospital.

The recently-erected buildings for special classes have afforded great relief to our overcrowded wards, and another year's test of their practical working has only confirmed the opinion that in some such provision for the quiet classes will be found a satisfactory solution to the great social problem of the care of the chronic insane. Startling events of almost daily occurrence show that it is unsafe to have them at large in the community; humanity protests that they shall not be left neglected in almshouses; what is wanted for them is care in comfortable but inexpensive homes connected with our present curative establishments for the insane.

So many requests have been received for information about the new buildings from those interested in the erection of similar structures elsewhere, that we have inserted in this report the ground plan and elevation of the relief building, so-called, which we think will convey the information desired. This is a building, with outer and interior walls of brick, constructed and furnished at a time when both labor and material were exceptionally low, and the whole expenditure did not exceed $250 per patient for the number now occupying it. Allowing that this would be an unsafe figure on which to base an estimate at present prices, as it certainly would, still it is demonstrable that accommodations which are all that are needed for the comfortable care of the mild cases of insanity can be provided at an expense for furnished buildings of less than $500 per patient.

When it shall become the settled policy of the States to care for all their insane, taking them out of the town and county almshouses, placing them in homes connected with the existing hospitals, and giving them workshops and tillage lands, it will be a greater advance in their treatment than any that has been made since the earnest philanthropy of Miss Dix first called attention to the condition of this unfortunate class and created so many of our present hospitals; which was a noble charity and meant for all, but practically it has been found that the liberal and expensive provision for the cure of insanity, admirable and necessary as it is for a part, has proved so great a tax that no State has thus far been willing to provide such elaborate asylums for the whole.

The following is the table of farm and garden products, with their estimated value:

Asparagus, 1,990 bunches, at 6 cents ....
Apples, 76 bushels, at 75 cents ....
Apricots, ½ bushel, at $5 ....
Beans (lima), 219 bushels, at $1 ....
Beans (string), 80½ bushels, at 75 cents ....
Beef (fresh), 3,336 pounds, at 7½ cents ....
Beets, 683 bushels, at 50 cents ....
Beets, 1,050 bunches, at 4 cents ....
Beets (greens), 71 barrels, at $1 ....
Blackberries, 275 quarts, at 10 cents ....
Cabbages, 12,681 heads, at 8 cents ....
Cabbages, 74 barrels, at $1 ....
Carrots, 2,328 bunches, at 3 cents ....
Celery, 7,991 heads, at 4 cents ....
Chickens, 21+ dozens, at $4 ....
Cucumbers, 2,654, at 1 cent ....
Cherries, 54 bushels, at $3 ....
Currants, 170 quarts, at 15 cents ....
Corn (green), 970 dozen ears, at 12 cents ....
Cantaloupes, 1,228, at 5 cents ....
Ducks, 10+ dozens, at $5 ....
Eggs, 2,957+ dozens, at 16 cents ....
Egg plants, 2,973, at 3 cents ....

Figs, 109 quarts, at 20 cents	$21 80
Geese, 26, at $1	26 00
Gooseberries, 470 quarts, at 15 cents	70 50
Grapes, 16,800 pounds, at 5 cents	840 00
Honey, 15 pounds, at 12 cents	1 80
Kale, 190 barrels, at $1.50	285 00
Lettuce, 8,632 heads, at 2 cents	172 64
Leeks, 29,193 heads, at 1 cent	291 93
Milk, 43,753 gallons, at 25 cents	10,938 25
Onions, 53 bushels, at $1	53 00
Onions, 2,474 bunches, at 5 cents	123 70
Onions (sets), 4 bushels, at $8	32 00
Oyster plants, 1,785 bunches, at 6 cents	107 10
Parsley, 4,991 bunches, at 3 cents	149 73
Parsnips, 305 bushels, at $1	305 00
Peppers, 2 bushels, at $1	2 00
Pease, 189 bushels, at $1	189 00
Pears, 20¼ bushels, at $3	60 75
Pork, 22,376 pounds, at 7 cents	1,566 32
Pigeons, 65, at 25 cents	16 25
Potatoes (Irish), 165⅓ bushels, at 75 cents	124 12
Potatoes (sweet), 672 bushels, at 50 cents	336 00
Pumpkins, 50 cart-loads, at $2	100 00
Peaches, 62¼ bushels, at $1.25	77 81
Quinces, 64 bushels, at $3	192 00
Raddishes, 1,023 bunches, at 3 cents	30 69
Radish (horse), 522 pounds, at 8 cents	41 76
Rhubarb, 653 pounds, at 3 cents	19 59
Raspberries, 144 quarts, at 20 cents	28 80
Strawberries, 3,880 quarts, at 12½ cents	485 00
Spinach, 44 barrels, at $1	44 00
Squash (summer), 3,784, at 2 cents	75 68
Squash (turban), 389 pounds, at 3 cents	11 67
Squash (turban), 41 barrels, at $3.50	143 50
Turkeys, 2, at $1.50	3 00
Turnips, 223 bushels, at 50 cents	111 50
Tomatoes, 1,051¾ bushels, at 50 cents	525 87
Veal, 286 pounds, at 8 cents	22 88
Watermelons, 22, at 6 cents	1 32
Total	21,389 49

The following are the products that were consumed on the farm, and consequently are not a part of the profits:

Corn (shelled), 400 bushels, at 60 cents	$240 00
Corn (fodder, green), 12 acres, at $35	420 00
Corn (fodder, dry), 25 tons, at $15	375 00
Grass pasturage	800 00
Grass (green), 8 acres, at $30	240 00
Hay, 250 tons, at $20	5,000 00
Mangel-wurzel, 112 tons, at $15	1,680 00
Rye (green), 5 acres, at $30	150 00
Rutabaga, 173 bushels, at 45 cents	77 85
Straw (rye), 15 tons, at $15	225 00
Total	9,207 85

The farm is now moderately remunerative and affords employment to many of our inmates. On the whole its production is satisfactory. The forage crops are large and are consumed on the place. The fruit crop is increasing and adds a pleasant variety to the table in its season. The vegetable garden can usually be relied on throughout most of the year for the same purpose. The amount of milk produced last year was 43,753 gallons, giving a daily consumption of about 120 gallons. With proper shelter for the herd it is probable that the production can be carried up to 150 gallons daily, which will afford a liberal supply of this best nutriment for the aged and infirm who constitute so large a proportion of the insane. What we consider the advantages of the farm,

in addition to its products, are, that it offers varied ████████ ███
otherwise so satisfactorily afforded, gives space for walks ███ ████
tion to a large proportion of the inmates, and is the most ████████ ██
all possible surroundings for so extensive a pile of buil████. ██ ███
torrid heat of the summers of this latitude it is restful and ████████
to come from the stifling pavements of the city upon our ████ ████
and feel the wind blowing from the river. The pleasing ████ ██
country fields and woods is a relief to the necessarily ████████ ██
of the insane, and, while such ample grounds show a most ████ ██
vision of the government for her insane, they are none too █████ ███
will the variety afforded by a few hundred acres seem too great to ████
who must perforce find in them the limit of their world.

The estimates of appropriations for the fiscal year ending June ██,
1883, are as follows:

1. For the support, clothing, and treatment in the Govern████ ███
pital for the Insane, of the insane of the Army, Navy, Marine ████
and the Revenue Cutter Service, and of all persons who have █████
insane since their entry into the military or naval service of the █████
States, and who are indigent, and of the indigent insane of the D█████
of Columbia, $202,500.

It is estimated that during the fiscal year ending June 30, 1883, ███
hospital will be called upon to provide for an average ████████ ██ ██
less than 900 of the indigent insane belonging to the above █████ ███
that the cost per patient will be $225; this includes all the ████████
of the hospital except those for special repairs and improvem█████. ██
the number of patients under treatment at the close of the last █████
year was 925, and is still increasing, it is possible that the above ██
prove an underestimate in numbers and consequently in amount.

It is asked that the provision which has been made for some year██ ██
continued; that not exceeding $1,000 of the appropriation for █████
may be expended to defray the expenses of the removal of ████████
their friends; also, that the permission which is now granted to the ███
unteer Soldiers' Homes be extended to the Government Hospital for ██
Insane, viz, to dispose of hospital products and articles ████████
by the inmates for the benefit of the hospital.

2. For general repairs and improvements, $10,000.

This annual expenditure is necessary to prevent deterioration in ██
hospital, and is true economy in the proper care of the building██ ██
grounds; it is the amount usually estimated, and is the same as ██
appropriation for the current year.

3. For special improvements, viz, a supply of pure water, ████████
accommodations for hay, stock, and farm implements; a ████████
kitchen and cooking apparatus, with scullery; fire-walls, ███████ ██
tions; a mortuary building; in all, $38,500.

No special improvement has been asked in this estimate that has not
been considered essential to the continued welfare of the hospital, and
certainly there is none more so than a full supply of pure water for all
purposes of the inmates. It is a cruel wrong to longer delay giving the
insane the use of the water from the Upper Potomac, which the United
States Government has so munificently supplied to the city of Washington and the departments here. It is not a difficult work. Our present arrangements for pumping and water service are ample; it only
needs suitable depositing reservoirs with a 6-inch iron pipe laid for
about three-fourths of a mile across the bed of the river, most of the
distance in shallow water, and it is believed that the sum asked will be
sufficient to complete the work. A little excellent water for drinking

is obtained from springs near the hospital, but this is a scanty supply at best and liable at any time to be greatly diminished, if not entirely cut off, by the summer's drought. The water for all other uses is pumped from the Anacostia at a point where it ebbs and flows by the hospital grounds. This stream takes the wash of East and South Washington; its flats have long been a favorite dumping-ground for the dredgings from the channel of the Potomac, and we believe it is endangering the health of our inmates to continue its use; every severe storm leaves it for days unfit for anything but a fertilizer. Surely the poisonous mud of this sluggish creek, with its annual increment of defilement, is unfit to be the water-supply for a great hospital of dependent sufferers who are allowed no option in the selection of a home. That there may be no delay in the completion of this very necessary work, it is asked that $25,000 of the appropriation for special improvements be made immediately available.

Another pressing want is room for the storage of hay and the proper care of the stock. More than 100 tons of hay is now standing in stacks exposed to the weather, simply because we have no room for it in the barn. A piggery was built last year, and with that exception no farm building has been added since 1874; meantime, the milk produced on the farm, every quart of which is needed for the proper sustenance of our great household, has increased from 15,925 gallons in 1875, to 43,753 gallons in 1881, the herd of milch cows being nearly doubled, with no additional provision for their shelter other than a few sheds, which afford but very indifferent winter protection. The thrifty farmer provides warm quarters for his stock and thereby reduces his expenditure for their food. It is economy for the hospital, whose dairy farm supplies so important an element of the daily food of its inmates, to take the best possible care of its neat cattle, and $5,000 is asked for these very necessary farm buildings.

The hospital has quite outgrown its old culinary arrangements, and some new provision will have to be made. The present kitchen is in the basement of the center building, directly under the executive offices, which enjoy a more than tropic heat in summer in consequence; the odor of cooking is less localized and extends through the whole building. In the best modern hospitals the kitchen is placed either in the highest story of the building or in a detached structure, thus avoiding all discomfort to the wards from heat and odor. The arrangements of this hospital do not admit of locating the kitchen in the top of the house, and indeed, unless the ground rent is a serious item as in cities, it would seem to be better in all cases, in view of the greater security from fire, to place it in a distinct building. Such detached building should be made fireproof, of one story, with skylights and ventilators directly over the cooking apparatus, making the whole room light and airy. The scullery should be an adjoining room, having all convenient arrangements for the preparation of vegetables and washing of dishes. The kitchen itself should be specially fitted with all the necessary apparatus for the cooking of food on a large scale, as well as such approved appliances as may be needed for making special dishes for the sick. Much of the apparatus in our present kitchen is comparatively new and excellent, and it is thought that $4,000 will enable us to erect the building and purchase all the additional apparatus which the increased accommodations have rendered necessary.

Several destructive fires have occurred in hospitals for the insane during the past year in different parts of the country; this has led us to make a careful re-examination of our own hospital for all sources of danger in this direction. In addition to the ample provisions in other respects, which have already been made, we recommend the construction of fire-proof walls of brick, with iron doors, between the different sections of the hospital building, so that should a fire unfortunately occur it could be confined to the section in which it originated. It will not be a difficult matter to arrange for such walls; some slight changes in a few rooms will be necessary, but these changes will be improvements rather than otherwise, and for the sum asked, $3,500, it is thought that the whole work can be accomplished. Within walls where every year more than a thousand insane persons are provided for, no safeguard against so terrible a calamity as fire should be omitted.

So far as it is possible all the surroundings of the insane should be pleasant, and all depressing scenes and associations should be avoided. The want of a suitable mortuary building has long been felt, and $1,000 is asked for this purpose. The fitness of things seems to demand a proper provision for the dead outside the wards of the living; no well-appointed hospital is without this.

4. For the erection of a distinct hospital building for the female insane, $250,000; for expenditure in the fiscal year ending June 30, 1883, $125,000.

The time has come when some new provision will have to be made for the female insane in this hospital. Accommodations for 150 women are now crowded with 230, and the number is steadily increasing. In making new arrangements it is very important that they should be the best known. The experience in Philadelphia, in New York, and in Michigan, has clearly established the decided advantage of providing for the care of the two sexes in distinct hospital buildings, having separate inclosures for each. Nowhere is the importance of such distinct provision for the female insane more clearly shown than at the Government Hospital for Insane. The male patients being in excess in point of numbers, the weaker party, as is usual in such cases, goes to the wall. In the matter of unrestricted liberty of the grounds, it is impossible to do justice to either sex so long as both share the same inclosures. All the space of the present buildings would only afford comfortable accommodations for the number of male patients now under treatment, if the rooms designed for day rooms and amusement rooms were no longer used as dormitories. With that change and a new building with all the modern improvements, built on a distinct site for the females, the United States could fairly claim to have made here a model provision for the indigent insane. The new building should be for 300 patients, and admit of extensions to provide for 100 additional, without marring the architectural portions or the unity of design. Such a structure, of brick, fireproof, complete in all its appointments, and embodying the best ideas of modern science in regard to the comfort and the cure of the insane can be completed for the sum named. The present steam, water, and gas supply, as well as the present bakery and laundry, would be available for both departments, and the whole would remain under one executive head. That there may be no delay in the erection of this very necessary building, the amount for expenditure in the fiscal year ending June 30, 1883, is asked immediately available.

Three citizens of Washington, each prominent in his sphere, who had in former years been members of the Board of Visitors, have passed away since the date of the last annual report. In view of the long and faithful service which each one of these gentlemen rendered to the hospital, it is deemed but proper that the resolutions of respect passed by the Board at their annual meeting should have a record here, and they accordingly inserted.

DR. WILLIAM GUNTON.

Whereas this Board, since the date of its last annual meeting, has been called to mourn the loss of Dr. WILLIAM GUNTON, who for fifteen years held an honored place among its members, and who during a large portion of that time was called to preside over its deliberations : Therefore be it

Resolved, That with profound respect for his memory, we hereby testify and record our admiration for the high intellectual qualities, the rare business sagacity, the unremitting industry, and the spotless integrity with which he adorned his long, laborious, and useful career in the presence of this community, and which, as they followed him in the diligent and faithful performance of every duty and trust, were especially manifest to those of us whose privilege it was to consult with him for the interests of this Hospital, and for the welfare of its afflicted inmates, who ever found in him a friend as sympathetic in feeling as he was wise in counsel.

Resolved, That while we can but deplore the loss of one who made his career as full of useful activities and honorable labors as it was full of years, we desire at the same time to add to these sincere regrets the gratulations and thanksgivings which are most due for the spectacle of a finished life, as harmonious and symmetrical in its well-ordered proportions as it was remarkable for the length of days accorded to it by the favor of Divine Providence.

Resolved, That these resolutions be entered on the minutes of the Board, and that a copy of them be sent to the family of the deceased.

HON. RICHARD WALLACH.

Whereas the Hon. RICHARD WALLACH, for many years a member of this Board, has departed this life since the date of the last annual meeting : Therefore be it

Resolved, That with sincere admiration for the mental endowments and engaging social qualities with which he adorned every sphere of life, and which were never seen to better advantage than when they called him to high and responsible public trusts, we desire here to record our special and grateful recollection of the intelligence, fidelity, and zeal which he brought to the discharge of the philanthropic labors devolved upon him as a member of this Board during the entire period of his connection with it, and by which he has justly won for himself a name and place among the friends and benefactors of this institution.

Resolved, That this resolution be entered on the minutes of the Board, and that a copy of it be sent to the family of the deceased.

HON. HENRY D. COOKE.

Whereas the Hon. HENRY D. COOKE, for many years a member of this Board, has been called away from this life since the date of our last annual meeting : Therefore be it

Resolved, That we hereby place on record the tribute due to the commanding abilities, the high public spirit, and the patriotic enthusiasm which in a difficult crisis of our country were evinced by services as useful as they were brilliant, and which, as they followed him in the performance of the duties assumed towards this institution, made him no less diligent than faithful in the discharge of the public trust with which he here identified his name, and with which his memory is now gratefully associated.

Resolved, That this resolution be placed on the minutes of the Board, and that a copy of it be sent to the family of the deceased.

Our acknowledgments are due to Washington amateurs for a number of dramatic and musical entertainments during the past winter, which were much enjoyed by our household, also to the Marine Band, under Professor Sousa, for an outdoor concert during the summer, which was quite an unusual treat. Amusements continue to be a prominent feature in the treatment of the insane, both here and elsewhere.

The medical staff of the hospital has been increased by the addition of a physician to the night watch, thus giving a medical officer always on duty at all hours of the day and night. Dr. A. O. Patterson, of Washington, D. C., who has for some months past performed this important night service in an acceptable manner, has been appointed to the position. We believe the result will show this step to have been a wise and important one, and that a night service which makes the medical service of a hospital continuous for the twenty-four hours will be found advantageous in all large establishments for the insane.

57 Ab

During a temporary absence of Dr. Witmer in Europe, Dr. M. S. Seip, senior assistant of the State Hospital at Danville, Pa., has rendered us valuable assistance.

The other officers of the staff remain as before, and have continued to perform their respective duties in a faithful and acceptable manner.

Again commending to Congress the interests of this great hospital, the importance of which can hardly be over-estimated or its responsibilities ignored,

We are, very respectfully, your obedient servants,

JOS. K. BARNES,
President of the Board.
W. W. GODDING,
Secretary ex-officio.

Hon. S. J. KIRKWOOD,
Secretary of the Interior.

REPORT OF THE FREEDMEN'S HOSPITAL AND ASYLUM.

FREEDMEN'S HOSPITAL,
Washington, D. C., September 30, 1881.

SIR: I have the honor to present the annual report of the Freedmen's Hospital and Asylum for the fiscal year ending June 30, 1881.

The Freedmen's Hospital was established by the military authority of the District of Columbia in the year 1862, and was located at the junction of Thirteenth and S streets, northwest. It was created for the support and medical treatment of disabled and sick colored persons from contraband camps, and was supported by military funds. In August, 1865, the hospital was formally turned over to the Commissioner of the Bureau of Refugees, Freedmen, and Abandoned Lands, and was supported from the funds of that bureau. While in the hands of the Commissioner, the Colored Orphans' Home and Asylum was attached to the hospital, and the name Freedmen's Hospital and Asylum was adopted. When the Freedmen's Bureau was about to be discontinued, in 1870, Congress made its first separate appropriation of $84,000 for the independent support of this hospital and asylum. Since that time Congress has made an annual appropriation for its support, but the amount has been gradually diminishing till this year it is only $41,800.

No assistance from this hospital is now rendered to the Colored Orphans' Home and Asylum, as that institution receives a separate appropriation from Congress.

Although the name of the hospital remains the same, the character of its inmates has very much changed.

The asylum has been dropped entirely, and only 52 of the original patients for whom the hospital was established now remain in it. The rest have either died or been discharged, and their places have been filled by others resident and non-resident of the District of Columbia, so that the original character of the institution has been lost to view, and it has been gradually merged into a general hospital for the reception of all persons needing hospital treatment, without regard to sex, color, nationality, or even residence, and for the treatment of all kinds of diseases except those of a contagious nature. At the present time the Commissioners of the District of Columbia are sending large numbers of the sick, poor, and destitute of the District to this institution for treatment and support. Of the 932 admissions this year, 360 were recommended by the police. *No law exists which determines who shall* be admitted to or excluded from the Freedmen's Hospital and Asylum. The color line has been ignored, and a decidedly impartial course has been pursued in the treatment of the white and colored patients.

As evidence that the patients are well cared for here, I cite the fact that most of them, white and colored, when cured leave the hospital with reluctance, and most of those who have once been treated here, when again overtaken by accident or disease, apply a second, third, fourth, and even a fifth time for admission. Indeed, the reputation of this institution is such that it is difficult to persuade persons applying for hospital accommodations to go to other places.

The whole number of patients in hospital during the past year was 1,160, viz:

	White.			Colored.			Grand total.
	Males	Females	Total	Males	Females	Total	
Remaining June 30, 1880	29	4	33	101	94	195	228
Admitted	283	60	293	280	266	546	841
Born	4	....		28	19	47	51
Transient							40
Totals	237	60	297	308	287	595	932
Totals in hospital	266	64	330	409	381	790	1,160
Discharged	222	53	275	223	238	461	736
Died	17	3	20	86	51	137	157
Still born				2	....	2	2
Transient							40
Totals	239	56	295	311	289	600	935
Remaining June 30, 1881	27	8	35	98	92	190	225

Of those discharged, 660 were cured, and 76 were discharged relieved.

A large dispensary has been supported during the year for the benefit of the numerous poor who are constantly applying to this hospital for aid. Of these, the names of 2,134 have been entered in the book for out-patients, and over 3,000 prescriptions have been made and put up for them.

The nativity of the patients admitted to hospital was as follows:

Virginia	395	Alabama	2
Maryland	174	Indiana	2
District of Columbia	162	Ohio	2
Ireland	50	Turkey	2
Germany	34	West Virginia	2
Pennsylvania	27	Africa	1
New York	25	Florida	1
England	16	Holland	1
North Carolina	9	Louisiana	1
South Carolina	8	Montana	1
Massachusetts	5	Mississippi	1
Canada	4	New Hampshire	1
Georgia	4	New Jersey	1
Connecticut	3	New Mexico	1
Illinois	3	Poland	1
Kentucky	3	Scotland	1
Maine	3	Sweden	1
Vermont	3	Tennessee	1
Switzerland	3	Unknown	8

The diseases and conditions for which the patients were admitted to hospital and treated in dispensary were as follows:

Disease, &c.	Hospital.	Dispensary.	Disease, &c.	Hospital.	Dispensary.
Fracture of skull	2	1	Anæmia		4
Fracture of nasal bones	1		Marasmus	1	
Fracture of clavicle	2		Cataract	3	1
Fracture of acromion	1		Ophthalmia	1	
Fracture of rib	1		Iritis	1	
Fracture of humerus	1		Staphyloma	1	
Fracture of radius	2	1	Opacity of cornea	3	
Fracture of forearm	1		Conjunctivitis	6	5
Fracture of finger		1	Keratitis	1	
Fracture of femur	2	1	Amaurosis	1	
Fracture of leg	4		Malignant disease of eye	1	1
Compound fracture of tibia and fibula	1		Prurites		1
Dislocation of thumb		2	Eczema	3	6
Gunshot wounds	4	3	Herpes	1	1
Contused wounds	1		Herpes zoster	2	1
Incised wounds	4	13	Urticaria	1	8
Contusions	6	24	Ecthyma		2
Abrasions	1		Lichen		3
Sprains	1	8	Tyriasis		4
Inflammation of wrist-joint	1		Tinea capitis	1	6
Inflammation of elbow-joint	1		Rupia		1
Inflammation of knee-joint	1	1	Intermittent fever	65	26
Synovitis	1	1	Remittent fever	7	1
Periostitis	1	1	Typhoid fever	7	1
Frost-bite	16	10	Congestive chill	3	
Man-bite	1		Varicella	1	2
Coxalgia			Scarlatina		1
Caries	9	3	Rubeola	6	3
Exostosis		1	Erysipelas	3	
Bunion		1	Phlegmonous erysipelas	1	
Chilblains		5	Diphtheria		12
Anchylosis of wrist		1	Catarrh		13
Traumatic tetanus	2		Croup		2
Osteo-sarcoma	1		Laryngitis		2
Mollities ossium		1	Acute bronchitis	14	7
Ulcers	7	5	Chronic bronchitis	16	5
Chronic ulcer	10	15	Pneumonia	3	
Varicose ulcers	3		Pleuro-pneumonia	3	
Varicose veins	1	1	Typhoid pneumonia	4	17
Senile gangrene	1		Pleurisy	1	
Abscess	10	26	Gangrene of lungs	7	11
Burns	1		Asthma	80	8
Paraphimosis		2	Phthisis pulmonalis	10	3
Poison		2	Hæmoptysis	3	2
Boils		4	Scrofula	2	1
Burns	8	10	Pertussis		1
Whitlow	3		Dyspnœa		10
Cancer	8	1	Pleurodynia		1
Carcinoma	1	2	Emphysema	1	
Tumors	3	8	Functional disease of heart		1
Keloid tumors		2	Hypertrophy of heart		1
Ovarian tumors	2		Valvular disease of heart	3	1
Foreign body in throat	1		Pericarditis	1	
Syphilis	59	39	Aneurism of the aorta	1	
Secondary syphilis	8	27	Aneurism of external iliac artery	1	
Tertiary syphilis	1	4	Mumps		6
Gonorrhœa	9	67	Goitre		1
Orchitis	3	7	Odontalgia		32
Bubo	1	5	Stomatitis	1	3
Incontinence of urine	1		Hæmatemesis		
Retention of urine	1	2	Hepatic dropsy	3	
Chronic cystitis	1	6	General dropsy	5	
Hæmaturia	3	2	Ascites	4	
Stricture of urethra	2	3	Albuminuria	30	1
Nephralgia	1		Hydrocele	3	
Gravel	1		Cephalalgia	3	20
Uræmia			Convulsions		4
Spermatorrhœa			Insanity	5	
Acute rheumatism	34	83	Insomnia		3
Chronic rheumatism	41	31	Softening of brain	4	
Syphilitic rheumatism	2		Chronic meningitis	1	
Lumbago	1	17	Chronic cerebro-spinal meningitis	1	
Sciatica	3	1	Chorea	2	
Delirium tremens			Epilepsy	12	7
Alcoholism		13	Neurasthenia		10
			Paralysis	24	6

Disease, &c.	Hospital.	Dispensary.	Disease, &c.	Hospital.	Dispensary.
Vertigo		1	Haemorrhoids	6	6
Apoplexy	2	1	Fistula in ano	1	1
Neuralgia	4	21	Worms		24
Coup de soleil	1		Cardiac dropsy	1	
Vesico-vaginal fistula	1		Renal dropsy		1
Abortion	2	2	Endometritis	1	2
Amenorrhoea	1	24	Congestion of uterus	1	3
Leucorrhoea	3	20	Subinvolution of uterus	1	2
Dysmenorrhoea	1	1	Hypertrophy of uterus	2	1
Menorrhagia	2	16	Ulceration of uterus	1	
Tonsillitis	8	83	Fibrous tumor of uterus	4	
Pharyngitis		4	Ulcerated os uteri	1	
Inflammation of submaxillary gland		3	Ulceration of vagina	1	
Dyspepsia	4	64	Cellulitis		1
Gastralgia	1	13	Prolapsus uteri	1	4
Constipation	3	101	Hysteria	2	20
Colic		24	Phlegmasia dolens		1
Acute gastritis	1		Mammitis		1
Chronic gastritis	3	2	Pregnancy	60	21
Cholera morbus	1	4	Suffering from parturition	7	
Enteritis		7	Premature labor		1
Acute diarrhoea	12	44	Born	51	
Chronic diarrhoea	9		Infancy	15	
Dysentery		10	Dentition		2
Hypertrophy of liver	2	1	Senile debility	9	
Chronic hepatitis	1	36	General debility	6	30
Jaundice	1	2	Kleptomania	1	
Peritonitis	4		Dementia	1	
Tubercular peritonitis	1		Curvature of spine	1	
Hernia	6	5	Teeth extracted		254

The following table shows the number of cases of each disease which resulted fatally:

Disease.	White.	Colored.	Total.	Disease.	White.	Colored.	Total.
Phthisis pulmonalis	3	44	47	Pleuro-pneumonia		1	1
Senile debility	2	13	15	Typhoid-pneumonia		1	1
Apoplexy	2	8	10	Congestive chill		1	1
Albuminuria		7	7	Cancer of stomach		1	1
Marasmus	3	4	7	Encephaloid cancer of right labium		1	1
Diarrhoea		1	1	Scirrhus of liver		1	1
Chronic diarrhoea	4	3	7	Scirrhus of parotid gland		1	1
Paralysis		2	2	Ovarian tumor		1	1
General paralysis		4	4	Fibrous tumor of uterus		1	1
Cardiac dropsy		2	2	Anthrax		1	1
General dropsy		2	2	Senile gangrene	1	2	2
Hepatic dropsy	1	3	4	Fracture of base of skull		1	1
Congenital debility	1	1	2	Convulsions	1	2	2
Uraemia		4	4	Epileptic convulsions		1	1
Traumatic tetanus		2	2	Chronic meningitis	1	1	1
Peritonitis		2	2	Chronic cerebro-spinal meningitis		1	1
Tubercular peritonitis		2	2	Diphtheria		1	1
Valvular disease of heart		4	4	Typhoid fever		1	1
Rheumatism of heart		1	1	Psoas abscess		1	1
Hypertrophy of heart		1	1	Acute lumbar abscess		1	1
Aneurism of the aorta		1	1	Cystitis and nephritis		1	1
Ossification of tricuspid valve		1	1	Erysipelas		1	1
Chronic bronchitis		1	1	Phlegmonous erysipelas		1	1
Softening of brain		1	1				
Pneumonia		2	2	Total	20	137	157

The severity of the cases admitted to hospital may be inferred from the fact that 18 died during the first four days after admission. A glance at the table of diseases which proved fatal will show that most of the

The diseases and conditions for which the patients were admitted to hospital and treated in dispensary were as follows:

Disease, &c.	Hospital	Dispensary	Disease, &c.	Hospital	Dispensary
Fracture of skull	2	1	Anæmia		
Fracture of nasal bones	2		Marasmus		
Fracture of clavicle	2		Cataract		
Fracture of scromion	1		Ophthalmia		
Fracture of rib	1		Iritis		
Fracture of humerus	2	1	Staphyloma		
Fracture of radius	1		Opacity of cornea		
Fracture of forearm	1		Conjunctivitis		
Fracture of finger		1	Keratitis		
Fracture of femur	2		Amaurosis		
Fracture of leg	4		Malignant disease of eye		
Compound fracture of tibia and fibula	1		Pruritus		
Dislocation of thumb		2	Eczema		
Gunshot wounds	4	3	Herpes		
Contused wounds	1		Herpes zoster		
Incised wounds	4	13	Urticaria		
Contusions	6	34	Ecthyma		
Abrasions	1		Lichen		
Sprains	1	8	Tyriasis		
Inflammation of wrist-joint	1		Tinea capitis		
Inflammation of elbow-joint	1		Rupia		
Inflammation of knee-joint	1		Intermittent fever		
Synovitis	1		Remittent fever		
Periostitis	16	10	Typhoid fever		
Frost-bite	1		Congestive chill		
Man-bite	1		Varicella		
Coxalgia	9		Scarlatina		
Caries		1	Rubeola		
Exostosis		1	Erysipelas		
Bunion		1	Phlegmonous erysipelas		
Chilblains		1	Diphtheria		
Anchylosis of wrist		1	Catarrh		
Traumatic tetanus	2		Croup		
Osteo-sarcoma	1		Laryngitis		
Mollities ossium		1	Acute bronchitis		
Ulcers		15	Chronic bronchitis		
Chronic ulcer	10		Pneumonia		
Varicose ulcers			Pleuro-pneumonia		
Varicose veins		1	Typhoid pneumonia		
Senile gangrene			Pleurisy		
Abscess	10	26	Gangrene of lungs		
Bursæ	1		Asthma		
Paraphimosis			Phthisis pulmonalis		
Poison			Hæmoptysis		
Boils		10	Scrofula		
Burns			Pertussis		
Whitlow			Dyspnœa		
Cancer			Pleurodynia		
Carcinoma			Emphysema		
Tumors			Functional disease of heart		
Keloid tumors			Hypertrophy of heart		
Ovarian tumors	2		Valvular disease of heart		
Foreign body in throat		1	Pericarditis		
Syphilis		28	Aneurism of the aorta		
Secondary syphilis		27	Aneurism of external iliac artery		
Tertiary syphilis		4	Mumps		
Gonorrhœa		47	Goitre		
Orchitis		7	Odontalgia		
Bubo		5	Stomatitis		
Incontinence of urine		4	Hæmatemesis		
Retention of urine		6	Hepatic dropsy		
Chronic cystitis		2	General dropsy		
Hæmaturia		3	Ascites		
Stricture of urethra		2	Albuminuria		
Nephralgia			Hydrocele		
Gravel		1	Cephalalgia		
Uræmia			Convulsions		
Spermatorrhœa			Insanity		
Acute rheumatism	14	23	Insomnia		
Chronic rheumatism	61	81	Softening of brain		
Syphilitic rheumatism			Chronic meningitis		
Lumbago		17	Chronic cerebro-spinal meningitis		
Sciatica	1		Chorea		
Delirium tremens	1		Epilepsy		
Alcoholism		13	Neurasthenia		
			Paralysis		

Disease, &c.	Hospital	Dispensary	Disease, &c.	Hospital	Dispensary
Vertigo		1	Haemorrhoids	6	6
Apoplexy	2	1	Fistula in ano	1	1
Neuralgia	4	21	Worms		26
Coup de soleil	1		Cardiac dropsy	1	
Vesico-vaginal fistula	1		Renal dropsy		
Abortion	2	2	Endometritis	1	
Amenorrhoea	1	24	Congestion of uterus	1	1
Leucorrhoea	3	20	Subinvolution of uterus	1	
Dysmenorrhoea	1	1	Hypertrophy of uterus	2	1
Menorrhagia	2	16	Ulceration of uterus	1	
Tonsillitis	3	88	Fibrous tumor of uterus	4	
Pharyngitis		4	Ulcerated os uteri	1	
Inflammation of submaxillary gland		2	Ulceration of vagina	1	
Dyspepsia	4	64	Cellulitis		1
Gastralgia	1	12	Prolapsus uteri	1	4
Constipation	2	101	Hysteria	2	36
Colic		24	Phlegmasia dolens		2
Acute gastritis	1		Mammitis		1
Chronic gastritis	2	2	Pregnancy	69	21
Cholera morbus	1	4	Suffering from parturition	7	
Enteritis		7	Premature labor		1
Acute diarrhoea	12	44	Born	51	
Chronic diarrhoea	9		Infancy	15	
Dysentery		10	Dentition		2
Hypertrophy of liver	2	1	Senile debility	9	
Chronic hepatitis	1	36	General debility	6	30
Jaundice	1	2	Kleptomania	1	
Peritonitis	4		Dementia	1	
Tubercular peritonitis	1		Curvature of spine	1	
Hernia	6	5	Teeth extracted		254

The following table shows the number of cases of each disease which resulted fatally:

Disease	White	Colored	Total	Disease	White	Colored	Total
Phthisis pulmonalis	3	44	47	Pleuro-pneumonia		1	1
Senile debility	2	13	15	Typhoid-pneumonia		1	1
Apoplexy	2	8	10	Congestive chill		1	1
Albuminuria		7	7	Cancer of stomach		2	2
Marasmus	3	4	7	Encephaloid cancer of right labium		1	1
Diarrhoea		1	1	Scirrhus of liver		1	1
Chronic diarrhoea	4	3	7	Scirrhus of parotid gland		1	1
Paralysis		2	2	Ovarian tumor		1	1
General paralysis		4	4	Fibrous tumor of uterus		1	1
Cardiac dropsy		2	2	Anthrax		1	1
General dropsy	1	3	4	Senile gangrene	1	2	2
Hepatic dropsy	1	1	2	Fracture of base of skull		1	1
Congenital debility		4	4	Convulsions	1	2	2
Uraemia		2	2	Epileptic convulsions		1	1
Traumatic tetanus		2	2	Chronic meningitis	1	1	1
Peritonitis		2	2	Chronic cerebro-spinal meningitis		1	1
Tubercular peritonitis		2	2	Diphtheria		1	1
Valvular disease of heart		4	4	Typhoid fever		1	1
Rheumatism of heart		1	1	Psoas abscess		1	1
Hypertrophy of heart		1	1	Acute lumbar abscess		1	1
Aneurism of the aorta		1	1	Cystitis and nephritis		1	1
Ossification of tricuspid valve		1	1	Erysipelas		1	1
Chronic bronchitis		1	1	Phlegmonous erysipelas		1	1
Softening of brain		1	1				
Pneumonia		2	2	Total	20	137	157

The severity of the cases admitted to hospital may be inferred from the fact that 18 died during the first four days after admission. A glance at the table of diseases which proved fatal will show that most of the

the month of April, but the pupil was immediately removed to his home, which fortunately was in Washington, and no spread of the disease followed. A number of cases of mumps occurred during the spring months, which presented no unusual features, and all the patients in due time recovered.

One of our students was afflicted during the year with persistent neuralgia, which affected different portions of his system. Toward the close of the winter term a fistula developed itself, an operation for which was successfully performed, after which the patient's general health was very greatly improved.

Alice Huhn, of Wilmington, Del., and a beneficiary of the State from which she came, died in April last at the age of fifteen. She had been connected with the institution only five months, and was in feeble health when she entered. Severe attacks of scarlet fever and paralysis occasioned her deafness some years ago, and from the general effects of these diseases she never recovered. The immediate cause of her death was pneumonia.

A few days after the opening of our current academic year, Mr. J. F. Haskins, of Ohio, a member of the freshmen class of our college, became ill with what proved to be typhoid fever. There is reason to believe that the seeds of the disease were in his system before his return here from his home.

The attending physician was hopeful of his recovery, but on the fourteenth day of the fever his strength rapidly failed, and a fatal termination of the disease was reached on the 25th of October.

The following extract from the records of the faculty will show how highly he was esteemed by his instructors :

James Finley Haskins was a young man of much beauty of character, and one whose virtues it is the wish of the faculty to commend to the emulation of all the young men under their care. Sensitive to the opinions of his associates, he was yet firm in his purposes; and while modest and unassuming he was self-reliant, and yielded his opinion but to reason. His cheerful good nature and manly bearing were untainted by weakness, and made every associate a friend; while his perseverance and painstaking thirst for knowledge, and his serious, eager attention and intelligent comprehension rendered his intercourse with his teachers one of the pleasantest of their lives. Indeed, in him were exhibited the virtues of a gentleman and a student in such degree as to arouse in them the warmest feelings of admiration and friendship, and lead them to anticipate for him a life of great usefulness. Their greatest sorrow in his death is that the wholesome example of his daily life is now no longer to be one of the restraining and ennobling influences of the college life, and that the world's good work will have one the less of earnest and serious workers.

CASUALTIES.

Since the date of our last report, two students in our college have met with fatal accidents.

In November last, John M. Brown, of Franklin, Ind., then a member of our advanced preparatory class, was killed on the play-ground by the falling of a heavy timber, used to support what is known as a revolving swing. This apparatus, intended to be used by no more than four boys, was, in a moment of recklessness, loaded down with twice that number of full-grown young men. The weight of all these coming suddenly on one side of the upright post, snapped it at the ground, and in falling it struck young Brown behind the left ear, causing instant death.

In attestation of the high esteem in which Mr. Brown was held by his instructors, the following minute was adopted by the faculty:

The faculty of the National Deaf-Mute College desire to place on record their high appreciation of the character and standing of the late John Miner Brown as a student of this institution, and their sense of the great loss which has befallen the college in his sudden death.

Disease, &c.	Hospital	Dispensary	Disease, &c.	Hospital	Dispensary
Vertigo		1	Haemorrhoids	6	6
Apoplexy	2	1	Fistula in ano	1	1
Neuralgia	4	21	Worms		24
Coup de soleil	1		Cardiac dropsy	1	
Vesico-vaginal fistula	1		Renal dropsy		1
Abortion	2	2	Endometritis	1	2
Amenorrhoea	1	24	Congestion of uterus	1	2
Leucorrhoea	3	20	Subinvolution of uterus	1	2
Dysmenorrhoea	1	1	Hypertrophy of uterus	2	1
Menorrhagia	2	16	Ulceration of uterus	1	
Tonsillitis	8	83	Fibrous tumor of uterus	4	
Pharyngitis		4	Ulcerated os uteri	1	
Inflammation of submaxillary gland		3	Ulceration of vagina	1	
Dyspepsia	4	64	Cellulitis		1
Gastralgia	1	13	Prolapsus uteri	1	4
Constipation	2	101	Hysteria	2	2
Colic		24	Phlegmasia dolens		1
Acute gastritis	1		Mammitis		1
Chronic gastritis	3	2	Pregnancy	60	21
Cholera morbus	1	4	Suffering from parturition	7	
Enteritis		7	Premature labor		1
Acute diarrhoea	13	44	Born	51	
Chronic diarrhoea	9		Infancy	15	
Dysentery		10	Dentition		2
Hypertrophy of liver	2	1	Senile debility	8	
Chronic hepatitis	1	36	General debility	6	20
Jaundice	1	2	Kleptomania	1	
Peritonitis	4		Dementia	1	
Tubercular peritonitis	1		Curvature of spine	1	
Hernia	6	5	Teeth extracted		254

The following table shows the number of cases of each disease which resulted fatally :

Disease	White	Colored	Total	Disease	White	Colored	Total
Phthisis pulmonalis	3	44	47	Pleuro-pneumonia		1	1
Senile debility	2	13	15	Typhoid-pneumonia		1	1
Apoplexy	2	8	10	Congestive chill		1	1
Albuminuria		7	7	Cancer of stomach		1	1
Marasmus	3	4	7	Encephaloid cancer of right labium		1	1
Diarrhoea		1	1	Scirrhus of liver		1	1
Chronic diarrhoea	4	3	7	Scirrhus of parotid gland		1	1
Paralysis		2	2	Ovarian tumor		1	1
General paralysis		4	4	Fibrous tumor of uterus		1	1
Cardiac dropsy		2	2	Anthrax		1	1
General dropsy	1	3	4	Senile gangrene	1	2	2
Hepatic dropsy	1	1	2	Fracture of base of skull		1	1
Congenital debility		4	4	Convulsions	1	2	3
Uraemia		2	2	Epileptic convulsions		2	2
Traumatic tetanus		2	2	Chronic meningitis	1	1	1
Peritonitis	2	3	2	Chronic cerebro-spinal meningitis		1	1
Tubercular peritonitis		2	2	Diphtheria		1	1
Valvular disease of heart		4	4	Typhoid fever		1	1
Rheumatism of heart		1	1	Psoas abscess		1	1
Hypertrophy of heart		1	1	Acute lumbar abscess		1	1
Aneurism of the aorta		1	1	Cystitis and nephritis		1	1
Ossification of tricuspid valve		1	1	Erysipelas		1	1
Chronic bronchitis		1	1	Phlegmonous erysipelas		1	1
Softening of brain		1	1				
Pneumonia		2	2	Total	30	127	157

The severity of the cases admitted to hospital may be inferred from the fact that 18 died during the first four days after admission. A glance at the table of diseases which proved fatal will show that most of the

the board of management, but he was on all occasions ready to give counsel when appealed to, and his advice was highly appreciated by associate officers.

The loss to any community of such a man as Mr. Eggrs is known have been is, in many points of view, irreparable, and the managers of this institution desire to join their fellow-citizens in mourning departure of one whose death is so universally deplored.

HON. WILLIAM STICKNEY.

On the 13th of October, after an illness of only four days, Hon. William Stickney, secretary of the board, was removed by death.

This sad event was a great grief to all connected with the institute for Mr. Stickney's genial manners and cordial manifestations of interest in the welfare of officers and pupils had endeared him as a friend to with whom he came in contact.

On the day of his burial, the ordinary exercises of the institution was suspended in order that the officers and older pupils might have an opportunity of attending the funeral services.

The flag flew at half-mast, and the chapel bell was tolled while funeral procession was moving to the cemetery.

At a meeting of the board of directors, held on Saturday, October at the office of Hon. William W. Corcoran, it was resolved that the board attend Mr. Stickney's funeral in a body, and the following minute was on motion of Hon. William McKee Dunn, unanimously adopted:

In the death of the honorable William Stickney, late secretary of the board institution committed to our charge sustains a loss the extent and magnitude of which is not easy to estimate.

Connected by near family ties with the distinguished founder of the institution late Hon. Amos Kendall, Mr. Stickney was naturally the adviser and assistant of Kendall in his early efforts towards its establishment.

Mr. Stickney's name appears as one of the corporate and provisional directors in act of Congress under which the institution was organized in 1857. He was chosen first secretary of the board, and continued to fill that office up to the time of his death. In this position, as well as that of auditor of accounts, he has performed valuable service for nearly a quarter of a century. His interest in the development of the institution was warmly manifested at every point of its progress, and by his wise counsel he has contributed largely to its success.

As a personal loss his death will be deeply felt by his associates in this board, his name will ever be held in respectful and affectionate remembrance.

To his widow, bending under the weight of a double sorrow, the president and members of the board desire to offer their heartfelt sympathy, and to express the hope in her grievous trial she may have from the source of all comfort that peace which world can neither give nor take away.

THE LATE PRESIDENT OF THE UNITED STATES.

In the tragic event of last summer, which laid a burden of sorrow the heart of the nation and called for the sympathy of the civilized world, the officers, students, and pupils of this institution had reason for grief, to which it is proper, as a matter of history, that allusion should be made in this report.

The law incorporating the institution provides that the President the United States, for the time being, shall *ex officio* fill the office patron. In this capacity he presides at the public anniversaries, affixes his signature to our collegiate diplomas.

Representing in these acts the government which has bestowed so generous benefactions on the institution, the patron, whoever he may be, is regarded with especial interest and respect by all who here look up to him as their official head.

The decease of the President of the United States, under any circumstances, would consequently be an occasion of mourning at Kendall

Green. But in the death of James A. Garfield this institution loses a friend to whom much of its prosperity and progress is due, and whose open advocacy of its interests in Congress and elsewhere has gone far toward securing for it the position of permanence it now enjoys.

General Garfield's first visit to the institution was made in the winter of 1865-'66, when the collegiate department had been in operation but a single year. Its students numbered no more than twelve. One of these was a senior pursuing a scientific course, four were freshmen, and the remainder formed a class of still lower grade. The college for deaf-mutes was looked upon at that time as a mere experiment. In many quarters it was spoken of openly with derision. But General Garfield, himself a practical teacher, was warm in his indorsement of the under-taking, and his magnetic encouragement served to inspire both officers and students with a determination that the college *should succeed.*

Maintaining his interest in the progress of the college, General Garfield, in the Spring of 1868, showed his confidence in its scholarship by requesting its earliest graduate, Mr. Melville Ballard, to make a transaction from the French of an important pamphlet, "*Le Bilan de l'Empire*," in which some very unfavorable criticisms of the financial management of the second empire were given to the world.

Some months after the completion of the translation, Mr. Ballard received the following:

DEAR SIR: Just before I was leaving Washington last summer, I received your very successful translation of "*Le Bilan de l'Empire.*" I should have acknowledged it at once but from the fact that I had to leave the city. My long delay in acknowledging your great kindness can only be accounted for by the recital of a series of accidents and *contretemps* which I have not now time to recount.

I take pleasure in forwarding to you a copy of Napoleon's Cæsar (in French) as a slight testimonial of my appreciation of your scholarship and kindness in making the translation.

With kindest regards, I am, very truly, yours,

. ⋅ J. A. GARFIELD.

This volume was handsomely bound, and Mr. Ballard's name had been stamped on the outside.

During the years 1868-'69 and '70, the progress of the institution, especially the development of the collegiate department, encountered serious and persistent opposition in Congress. This hostility was so vigorously continued as to jeopardize, on one or two occasions, the very existence of the institution. General Garfield never failed to give the weight of his influence in favor of continuing the aid of the government, and on the 21st of June, 1870, when a very important appropriation was under consideration in the House, he made a speech earnestly advocating the liberal support of the institution in its collegiate character, and urged the propriety of action on the part of Congress in the following language:

Nearly every State in the Union has its school for the deaf and dumb, where they are taken through the preliminaries of education, and are elevated from the condition of being irresponsible persons, which is the condition of the uneducated deaf and dumb, for in the eye of the common law they are not held responsible even for murder. They are not considered persons. But by the benevolent institutions of the United States and other countries which have paid attention to this matter, they have been lifted up into the full responsibility of citizenship and the full obligation to obey the laws. Now, here is an institution in the city of Washington that carries the education of the deaf and dumb to the highest point necessary to fit the students who go there to be the teachers of that class. We have here an institution which, according to the laws and regulations now governing it, we have ourselves a part in the work of controlling, which allows students coming from all the deaf and dumb institutions in the various States of the Union, after they have got in those institutions all the advancement they are capable of getting there, to come here and complete the course of study which will fit them to be teachers of the deaf and dumb. The result is that one institution here, as it were in the center, supplies, or can supply, all the schools for the deaf and dumb in the United States with thoroughly educated teachers, fully quali- fied for the work; and I know of no single thing which this Congress can do that will have more beneficial results to the whole body of the people than to have one institu- tution officially kept up to supply teachers for the various deaf and dumb institutions throughout the country.

The pending appropriation, which was for the completion of the main central building containing a chapel, lecture room, refectories, kitchen, &c., was passed by a decided vote, and from that time to the present no serious opposition to the support and development of the institution has arisen in either house of Congress.

On Sunday, the 29th of January, 1871, the building alluded to above was dedicated to its uses by the President of the United States, after appropriate public exercises. On this occasion General Garfield spoke as the representative of the lower house of Congress, closing his ad- dress as follows:

Several gentlemen have spoken of this movement as a work of charity; in my judg- ment, it is a work of very enlightened selfishness on the part of Congress. Mr. Presi- dent, to you is confided the honor of presiding over the thirty-eight millions of men and women who compose the body of this great republic. The source of all its great- ness lies behind the material evidences of its prosperity, lies in the heads and hearts, the brain, the muscle, and the will of the people over whom you preside. Anything therefore, that affects their welfare, their force, their efficiency, touches the very essence of the national life. It is well known that only that portion of the popula- tion between the ages of twenty and sixty is self-supporting. Of these thirty-eight millions, eighteen millions are outside those limits. In other words, eighteen millions of the population over whom you preside must be supported by the other twenty millions. From these twenty millions must be subtracted the infirm, and all those that for any reason are unable to support themselves. Now the students of this insti- tution represent more than twenty thousand of the population of the United States, most of whom, by the influence of institutions like this, have been lifted up from the lowest plane of intellectual life to the dignity and value of intelligent citizens.

* * * * * * *

One of the best things connected with their education is that that they have a lively sense of gratitude to the government for what it has done for them. These young men cannot fail to become good citizens. They cannot fail to be true to their country, when they remember what it has done for them. I say, therefore, it is en- lightened selfishness rather than charity to take this class of our fellow-men and make them capable of doing a great work for the country. I am happy to send this message to them to-day into their silence.

* * * * * * *

The House of Representatives has been proverbial for its economy in regard to ex- penses of this kind, but I am happy to say that from the beginning of this work the House has stood up nobly and generously to the support of this institution. And what these students have to-day contributed, and what they are sure to do in the future will be a most complete vindication of the wisdom of the House, the Senate, and the Executive united in this great work.

During the following year, General Garfield spent part of a day in the college with a party of friends. One who was at that time a student writes of this visit as follows:

I do not recollect who any of the gentlemen accompanying him were, but General Garfield's personality and actions impressed themselves upon me with the utmost dis- tinctness. The classes were assembled at the blackboards, and a couple of hours were spent in an informal endeavor to ascertain, I suppose, the grade of our acquire- ments. In all this General Garfield led. He went about from rank to rank, question- ing and allowing himself to be questioned. There was nothing of the cold examiner about him. He made us feel that he was no merely critical outsider, but a student with us and of us at heart. His blue eyes shone with a scholar's enthusiasm. Of one he asked the history and derivation of the word *dollar;* of myself a like sketch of the word *pariah;* to another he gave an algebraic problem; of still another he asked the nature and use of logarithms.

Near the close, he pointed to a well known print of Aurora, which represents the goddess standing tiptoe upon a broad leaf in mid-air and drinking from a morning glory at dawn, and asked a student why the artist was justified in portraying a human form standing upon an unsupported leaf.

In the summer of 1872 a measure of great consequence to the institution was pending before Congress. It was an application for $70,000 to secure the whole of the fine domain known as Kendall Green as the permanent home of the institution. This measure having been once unfavorably acted upon by the House Committee on Appropriations, of which General Garfield was then chairman, was approved when it came a second time before the committee, in the shape of a Senate amendment to the sundry civil appropriation bill. And it is safe to say that the appropriation would not have been made but for the favorable attitude of General Garfield.

During the summer of 1874, and in the winter of 1874–75, General Garfield being still chairman of the Committee on Appropriations, provision was made by Congress for commencing and continuing the construction of the main college building.

An appropriation for the completion of the college edifice was made in March 1877, and the building was occupied the following winter.

On the public anniversary of 1878, held on the 1st day of May, General Garfield again represented the lower house of Congress, and spoke as follows:

Mr. PRESIDENT, AND LADIES AND GENTLEMEN: Your exercises have been already sufficient for all your desires; I am sure, and I will only detain you to say how much I am gratified to see the completion of this enterprise, which has been struggling up for so many years, and has reached a point at last where I think almost anybody will rejoice at its further progress. I believe I said on this stage, nine years ago, that nothing impressed me more during the later days of the war, when I first came to this city, than seeing the great marble columns being set up on the east, west, north, and south fronts of yonder Capitol, while the sound of battle was echoing across the Potomac and shaking the very windows of the Executive Mansion. It was a touching exhibition of unshakable faith in the final triumph and permanency of the Union. While fighting with all their might to maintain its existence, the American people were quietly setting up these noble columns as symbols of their faith that there would forever be a great capital of a great nation here, beside the beautiful Potomac; and step by step, as the struggle went on and the restoration of the Union became certain, the determination seemed to be crystallized in the American mind that there should not be another rebellion like it; and as they had strengthened and adorned our marble Capitol, so also they set up new pillars of justice and freedom, the living temple of our liberties, to be its perpetual glory and support. By the same inspiration our work of education, national in its spirit, earnest and determined in its character, has been pursued during the last fifteen years more than in any other period, because our people saw that the safety of the nation required it.

I am rejoiced to know that this institution cherishes the ideas I have been trying to set forth. These afflicted young men were only recently regarded as an almost helpless and useless portion of our common humanity. The effort of their country to set them in a place where they should have an equal chance in the race of life is most worthy; and here first, I believe, on the earth, certainly first in America, the deaf-mutes find an opportunity to enjoy college rights and privileges equal to those enjoyed by others who are not so afflicted. And that is great. It is the great glory of our republic that she has done it; and at a time when it costs something to do it.

This institution is one of the three that the United States supports. The one to educate her sons for the Navy, the other for the Army, both of these for the safety of the nation in time of war, and for her safeguard against war; and the third, this institution, in which the government reaches out its hand to make you the equal of all her other citizens not afflicted as you are. What is the meaning of all this? The lesson it teaches is the increased value to Americans of training. That, in my judgment, is the best lesson of our century. We are coming to understand that, whether you want a man for war or for peace—for whatever purpose you need him—a trained man is better than an untrained man. However great your untrained man may be, he would be greater and more efficient if he had been trained. College training is not meant to give you facts, but to teach you how to handle facts when you enter the many-sided life of our country.

People waste a great deal of time thinking whether they had better study Latin or Greek, or this or that science. I sum up all I have to say on the subject by calling attention to the remark of a distinguished French scholar; when asked if it were necessary to have a knowledge of the ancient languages, he said, "O, no; it is not necessary to know Latin, but it is necessary to have forgotten it." That is, either be a man who now knows it, or be one who has forgotten it, but saved the training it gave.

Thanking you, Mr. President, and ladies and gentlemen, for your kind attention to this discursive talk, I bid you good day. [Applause.]

The final visit of General Garfield to the institution was on the occasion of our last presentation exercises, in May of the present year. On that day it was a source of genuine pride and pleasure to all connected with the institution that we were permitted to welcome a tried and valued friend of many years as our official *head*, for this implied his election by the free choice of his fellow-citizens to the highest office in their gift; and in this humble seat of learning there was further reason for rejoicing that the suffrages of the nation had so honored one whose devotion to letters had been life-long, who was a student and a teacher before he occupied the more elevated but not more ennobling positions of general, lawyer, legislator, and President.

The part taken by General Garfield in the exercises of presentation day will be found further on in this report.

One who was formerly a student in the college, and is now a member of the faculty, writes of his appearance on that day as follows:

He came in half an hour late, being unavoidably detained, the faculty and specially invited guests of course awaiting his arrival before proceeding to the platform. The circumstance lent a tinge of humility, when he did enter, to the habitual ease and dignity of his manner, and as he passed around the room, exchanging a grasp of the hand and a word with each whom he knew—erect, commanding, buoyant, frank—he seemed to me what indeed he was, the manliest of men. As such he remains, and forever will remain, in my mind—an exemplar of those noblest characteristics of person, mind, and spirit to which the record of his life now forms an incitement; and as such I am sure he has impressed himself upon very many of my fellow-students.

It would perhaps be out of place in this report to recount the occasions when General Garfield lent the charm of his presence to social gatherings at Kendall Green. It is sufficient to say that they were numerous, and that the memory of them will be ever green in the minds of those who were thus permitted to enjoy his companionship.

Since the preparation of this report was begun, a letter has been received by the president of the institution from the executive committee of an association of deaf-mutes in Christiania, Norway, tendering their sympathizing greetings to the students of our college, and through them to the deaf-mutes of America, on the occasion of the death of James A. Garfield, *the friend of deaf-mutes.*

Since the name of our lamented patron is *thus* honored on the far-off shores of Norway, and he is there already known and recognized as the friend of those whom "the hand of God hath touched," we venture to to ask, without fear of criticism, that this brief history of his connection with this institution be allowed a place in the official record.

COURSES OF INSTRUCTION.

The work of instruction in the several departments of the institution has proceeded with no essential changes, the courses of instruction remaining substantially the same as described in former reports.

With the academic year just entered upon, a change of some importance has been made in classification by the removal of what has been known as the lower preparatory class of the college to the primary department, where it will have the name of the advanced class.

The presence of a class of so low a grade in the college organization has been a matter of regret, and has only been permitted because hitherto it has seemed impossible for the larger part of the State institutions to prepare their pupils for admission to our advanced preparatory class.

This difficulty has been, however, to a great extent overcome; and this year, much to our satisfaction, *eleven* young men presented themselves for admission who were found on examination to be sufficiently advanced to join our advanced preparatory class, hereafter to be termed the introductory.

Five young men seeking admission to the college, being unable to sustain examinations for admission to the introductory class, but showing good intelligence and coming to us well recommended, have been assigned to the advanced class of the primary department, where it is hoped they may, within a reasonable period, complete their preparation for college.

LECTURES.

Lectures have been delivered during the year by the professors and instructors in the two departments as follows, viz:

To the students of the collegiate department:

The Freedom of the Sea—President Gallaudet.

Michael Angelo and Raphael—Professor Porter.

Views of the Centennial, the Far West, the Holy Land, given with the lantern—Professor Chickering.

The Waters of the Ocean; their effect upon the History of the World—Professor Gordon.

Suwarrow, the Russian Type of Character—Assistant Professor Hotchkiss.

Concord Village and its Literati—Assistant Professor Draper.

To the pupils of the primary department:

Two lectures descriptive of a tour in Europe, through England, Belgium, France, Italy, and Switzerland, made, in the summer of 1880, by Mr. Denison.

On the *Conquest of Mexico by Cortez*, and the *Invincible Armada*, by Mr. Ballard.

On *Gettysburg*, and the *Character of Washington*, by Mr. Kiesel.

EXERCISES OF PRESENTATION DAY.

The exercises of the regular public anniversary of our collegiate department took place on the 4th day of May. The late President of the United States, in his capacity as patron of the institution, occupied the chair. The exercises were opened with prayer by the Rev. Frederick D. Power, pastor of the Vermont Avenue Christian Church, Washington, D. C

The candidates for degrees presented essays as follows:

Dissertation: Our Country's Progress—Jeremiah P. Kelley, Minnesota.

Dissertation: John Wycliffe—Frank Wiley Shaw, Ohio.

Oration: Civil Service Reform in Great Britain—Richard L'Hommedieu Long, Ohio.

Dissertation: The Earth as Transformed by Man—Theodore Adams Kiesel, Delaware.

Oration: Scientific Associations—Isaac Newton Hammer, Tennessee.

Oration: Money; its use and abuse—Albert Henry Schory, Ohio.

Mr. Kelley was excused from the delivery of his essay on account of ill health.

Messrs. Schory, Hammer, Long, and Kelley were presented by the president of the college to the board of directors as candidates for the degree of bachelor of arts, and Messrs. Kiesel and Shaw for the degree of bachelor of philosophy.

The honorary degree of master of arts was conferred upon Mr. C.

Kierkegaarde-Ekborhu, principal of the Royal Institution for Deaf-Mutes at Bollnäs, Sweden, in recognition of his distinguished services as an instructor of deaf-mutes in Sweden.

The same degree was conferred on W. L. Hill, of Athol, Mass., editor of the Athol Transcript and a graduate of this college of the class of 1872.

In presenting the candidates for degrees, the president of the college spoke as follows:

MR. PRESIDENT, AND GENTLEMEN OF THE BOARD OF DIRECTORS: It is my duty on this occasion to present to you as candidates for degrees these young gentlemen, who have thus far sustained satisfactory examinations in an extended course of collegiate study. I may be permitted to take advantage of this occasion, ordinarily one of mere formality, to express in behalf of the faculty and the students of this college the gratification which we feel in being permitted to make the presentation to-day to you, Mr. President, as our official head, and as the representative of the government that sustains our work, and to speak of the pleasure we experience in having the presence, in the capacity of patron, of one who has been a friend of the college for many years.

Not a few here present will remember that when the college was in its infancy when it was jeered at by some and regarded as a doubtful experiment by many, you were its earnest friend. Many of us recall the fact with pleasure that, when the building in which we are now assembled was dedicated ten years ago, you were with us as representing the House of Representatives, and that, although the college had then barely emerged from the condition of an experiment, we had the comfort of your kind and encouraging words. And we are happy to remember that only three years since, when, as the result of that liberality of Congress which has ever been manifested to this institution, we could announce the fact that our buildings were finished, our grounds were paid for, and that no debt rested upon the institution, again had we your presence, with words of congratulation, at a time when we were permitted to feel that our institution was measurably completed. And so, Mr. President, we have reason for our gratification that in our new official head we may address an old friend.

In behalf of the young men presented to-day as candidates for the honors of the college, I am sure I can promise they will at least strive to pay the debt of gratitude they owe the nation in lives made sweeter and purer, broader and stronger, by reason of the education that has been given to them in the capital of the nation.

President Garfield replied:

I understand, sir, that you are "presenting" these young men to the country. Not long ago they were hardly a force or a power to their country. What your institution has done for them has made each of them a great power; and that increased power you to-day give to the country. Therein is the secret and beneficence of education.

It was supposed to be a wise saying that one who could make two blades of grass grow where only one was growing before was a benefactor. The man or institution that can multiply the power of a boy by three, four, five, ten, or, as you are doing, perhaps a hundred, is doing a vastly higher thing than the increase of blades of grass, and this institution, which takes a class of the community that the common law, before it had been warmed by the sweet charities of modern life, did not regard as citizens—for I believe that by the common law a deaf-mute was not considered a responsible person—I say this kind of educational work may almost be said to take these unfortunate people and create them into the full image of high, broad, and responsible citizenship. Therefore you do, Mr. President, present these young gentlemen to the country in a much wider sense than colleges usually present their graduating class.

I would like to say another thing: that during these many years of public service I have loved to look upon this as a neutral ground, where, from all our political bickerings and differences, we come under the white flag of truce that should be raised over every school-house and college in the land. I am glad to say that, in spite of all the differences of party opinion, we have worked together in trying to make this institution worthy of our capital and our people. I am glad to believe that this progress will be unimpeded by any changes that may happen at the capital, and unchanged by the vicissitudes that may happen to the country.

At the close of President Garfield's speech, the president of the college presented the excuses of the Secretary of the Interior, who was prevented from being present by the pressure of his official duties, and introduced Hon. Samuel J. Randall, as a friend and supporter of the college in Congress, who spoke as follows:

LADIES AND GENTLEMEN: By reason of the enforced absence of the Secretary of the Interior, I have just been asked to say a few words. I have been very much struck with this exhibition, as I do not doubt you also have been. More than twenty-five years ago it was my habit to visit a similar institution in my own city, and I am impressed with the very great advance which has been made in that period of time in this power of communicating thoughts by signs, not only in the accuracy with which it is done, but also in the rapidity with which these communications are made in following an address.

Now, I have always thought that when we educated a child we placed within the reach of that child happiness for the future. How much greater, my friends, is that accomplishment when we place within the hands of these deaf-mutes this power of communication, this power of education; and in that connection let me say to you to-day that the addresses I have listened to here, in research, in accuracy of reasoning and logic, and in the force of presentation and expression, have rarely, in my experience, been equaled on any such occasion.

It has been kindly stated to you that I have been a friend of this institution. Now I want to say that it is a great source of satisfaction to tell you to-day that, in all my public connection with appropriations from the Treasury, I never sought to strike at either science or charity. This institution combines both. Where is the heart or the head that would throw any obstacle in the way of the usefulness of such an establishment as this? Where is the heart or the mind that would not promote to the uttermost of its power such an institution in its full measure of usefulness?

I wish that I had not so suddenly been called upon to speak on this most interesting question of the education of deaf-mutes. There has been shown to-day, as you have witnessed, a development that is wonderful. It is almost, Mr. President, a triumph over nature.

The exercises of the day were concluded with the benediction by the Rev. Thomas Gallaudet, D. D., rector of St. Ann's Church for Deaf-Mutes, New York.

At the close of the academic year in June, degrees were conferred in accordance with the recommendations of presentation day.

COMPLETION OF THE GYMNASIUM BUILDING.

The gymnasium, work upon which was in progress at the date of our last report, was completed in July. It contains on the ground floor a swimming-pool 40 feet by 26, and 6 feet deep at one end, sloping upward to a depth of 3 feet at the other, and a bowling-alley. The entire second floor is occupied by a hall for gymnastic exercises, 63 feet by 48 on the floor, and 32 feet high. The swimming-pool is surrounded on three sides by dressing-rooms, and is well lighted by windows opening to the east, south, and west.

The apparatus for heating the building by steam, constructed by William E. Wood & Co., of Baltimore, is so arranged that the water passing into the pool can be warmed when its natural temperature is lower than is desirable.

It is proposed to have the swimming-pool in use during three months of the academic year, viz, six weeks at the beginning and six weeks at the end of the year.

The bowling-alley is fitted up with two tables, each 58 feet long.

The gymnasium hall is furnished with apparatus designed by Dr. D. A. Sargent, the director of the Harvard University Gymnasium, and manufactured and set up under his personal supervision. This apparatus includes, besides several ordinary appurtenances of a gymnasium, a number of weight-lifting machines, designed to accomplish special muscular development.

Under the system of physical culture pursued by Dr. Sargent, these machines are found to be of great value in strengthening particular muscles and sets of muscles, and by an adjustment of the weights, which is easily effected, they may be suited to the different degrees of strength which are found to exist in different persons.

Dr. Sargent's system will be followed in our college under the direction of Mr. John J. Chickering, a recent graduate of Amherst College.

58 Ab

The interest manifested by our students in the gymnasium is very great, and we have reason to anticipate a marked improvement in their physical standard.

The work on the gymnasium has been completed in an entirely satisfactory manner by the contractor, Mr. Henry Conradis, of Washington, under the supervision of Mr. J. G. Meyers, who has for several years acted in the capacity of supervising architect for the institution.

The plans of the building were prepared by Frederick Clark Withers, esq., of New York City, from whose designs our chapel and college building were constructed.

The entire cost of the building, including heating apparatus, gas fixtures, lightning rods, apparatus, furniture, cost of plans, specifications, and superintending, and the introduction of water and gas, falls a little below $14,600.

RECEIPTS AND EXPENDITURES.

The receipts and expenditures for the year now under review will appear from the following detailed statements:

I.—SUPPORT OF THE INSTITUTION.

Receipts.

Balance from old acccount	$1,231 0
Received from Treasury of the United States	53,500 0
Received for board and tuition	2,300 7
Received from manual-labor fund	314 0
Received for books and stationery sold	440 4
Received for work done in shop	137 1
Received from sale of live stock	430 3
Received from sale of gas	113 9
Received for damage to grounds	4 75
Received from pupils from shoe repairs and clothing	31 7
Received from sale of milk and sugar	214 2
Received from sale of wheat	236 8
Received from sale of old metals	56 6
Received from sale of ashes, soap-grease, &c	14 96
Received from sale of old carpets and stove	6 5
Received from sale of lumber	3 7
Received from sale of old billiard table	30 5
Received from sale of old stone	25 5
	59,071 9

Disbursements.

Expended for salaries and wages	$39,886 12
Expended for groceries	2,513 77
Expended for meats	3,803 85
Expended for potatoes	584 70
Expended for incidental and household expenses, marketing, &c	2,295 00
Expended for butter and eggs	2,902 21
Expended for fuel	2,467 37
Expended for bread	1,037 73
Expended for repairs on buildings	2,778 9
Expended for furniture	764 61
Expended for live stock	414 00
Expended for expenses of directors' meetings	114 00
Expended for books and stationery	637 37
Expended for seed	41 30
Expended for lumber	556 08
Expended for printing	130 65
Expended for ice	216 39
Expended for drugs and chemicals	333 21
Expended for carriage and wagon repairs	200 85
Expended for entertainment of pupils	30 00
Expended for illustrative apparatus	50 00
Expended for blacksmithing	118 18
Expended for harness and repairs	264 35

Expended for hardware	$564 12
Expended for rent of telephones	152 86
Expended for flour and feed	907 35
Expended for dry goods and shoes	311 36
Expended for medical and surgical attendance	730 00
Expended for manure	215 45
Expended for gas	904 80
Expended for paints	491 11
Expended for flowers, plants, &c.	31 62
Expended for funeral expenses	150 00
Expended for shoe repairs and clothing	51 30
Expended for board and care of pupil at institution for feeble-minded children	300 00
Expended for lightning-rods	101 90
Expended for gravel for repair of roads	26 80
Expended for tuition refunded	131 76
Expended for new steam radiators	351 93
Expended for portrait of Rev. T. H. Gallaudet, LL.D., founder of deaf-mute instruction in America	395 00
Expended for expenses of the president in attending international convention at Milan, in September, 1880	500 00
Balance unexpended	964 47
	59,071 99

II.—BUILDINGS AND GROUNDS.

Receipts.

Received from Treasury of the United States	$7,500 00

Disbursements.

Expended for plans, &c., for gymnasium	$397 08
Expended on contract with H. Conradis for erection of gymnasium	4,500 00
Expended for compensation of supervising architect	100 00
Expended for concrete roadway (1,768 yards)	1,806 40
Expended for grading, sodding, &c	224 35
Expended for gas and water pipes and laying same	290 00
Balance unexpended	182 17
	7,500 00

ESTIMATES FOR NEXT YEAR.

The following estimates for the service of the fiscal year ending June 30, 1883, have already been submitted.

For the support of the institution, including salaries and incidental expenses, and $500 for books and illustrative apparatus, and $2,500 for general repairs, $55,000.

For the completion of the farm-barn, the erection of two dwelling-houses for professors, and for the inclosure and improvement of the grounds of the institution, $15,000.

For the farm-barn	$2,000 00
For the dwelling-houses	10,000 00
For the inclosure and improvement of grounds	3,000 00
	15,000 00

The first estimate is greater by $1,500 than the amount appropriated for this year and for the last year. This small increase is thought to be necessary to meet the increased cost of fuel and of many articles of food, also to provide for the small increase in the number of our pupils that is almost certain to occur.

The need for the erection of a suitable farm-barn was fully set forth in our last annual report, and the last Congress appropriated just one-half the amount asked for to complete it. The item now submitted will, it is believed, be sufficient to finish the work already provided for in part.

Two of our instructors, each of whom have growing families, are living in the institution, occupying room much needed for the use of students and pupils.

By the erection of the cottages proposed, these instructors will be provided with suitable quarters, and the apartments they vacate will be available for their legitimate purposes.

No appropriation was made by the last Congress for the inclosure and improvement of grounds, and the necessity for the proposed appropriation, which was explained at length in our last report, is very pressing.

EDUCATION OF THE BLIND.

Appended to this report will be found a statement from F. D. Morrison, superintendent of the Maryland Institution for the Blind, as to the number of United States beneficiaries in that institution during the past year, and as to the progress they have made. The blind children are in the Maryland institution under the provisions of section 4869 of the Revised Statutes, and with the approval of the president of this institution, as required by law.

All of which is respectfully submitted by order of the board of directors.

E. M. GALLAUDET,
President.

Hon. S. J. KIRKWOOD,
Secretary of the Interior.

REPORT OF THE UNITED STATES INSPECTOR OF GAS AND METERS.

OFFICE U. S. INSPECTOR OF GAS AND METERS,
Washington, D. C., September 1, 1881.

SIR: I have the honor herewith to submit the annual report of this office, showing its operations for the fiscal year ending June 30, 1881.

At its commencement will be found condensed tables giving the illuminating power and purity of the gas furnished by the gas companies during the year.

Full monthly statements will be found in Tables A and B. In the remaining tables, lettered C, D, E, F, and G, the monthly inspection of meters, complaint meters, the pressure of the gas, and the receipts and expenditures are fully stated.

Very respectfully, your obedient servant,

S. CALVERT FORD,
Inspector of Gas and Meters.

Hon. S. J. KIRKWOOD,
Secretary of the Interior.

ILLUMINATING POWER AND PURITY.

The illuminating power and purity of the gas supplied by the Washington Gas Light Company from July 1, 1880, to June 30, 1881, are as follows:

Average illuminating power during the year ....candles.. 16.72
Highest illuminating power during the year ....do.... 19.3
Lowest illuminating power during the year ....do.... 14.4
Average quantity of ammonia in 100 cubic feet during the year ....grain.. .7
Highest quantity of ammonia in 100 cubic feet during the year.......grains.. 3.22
Lowest quantity of ammonia in 100 cubic feet during the year.........grain.. .5
Average quantity of sulphur in 100 cubic feet during the year.........grains.. 9.71
Highest quantity of sulphur in 100 cubic feet during the year.............do.... 26.82
    est quantity of sulphur in 100 cubic feet during the year. ....do.... 3.43

The quality of the gas supplied by the Washington Gas Light Company during the past year, has been uniformly good, and in accordance with the requirements of the act of Congress regulating gas works in this District.

Complaints have fallen off considerably regarding poor light, and stoppages produced mainly from the presence of naphthaline in the service pipes, have become much less frequent.

The gas contained.but a small quantity of sulphur (an impurity which no method yet devised in a commercial way, has enabled engineers to free gas from entirely).

The quantity of ammonia present was slight, and on two occasions the gas was absolutely free from it.

This impurity is now utilized, forming the base of ammonia sulphate, a salt which is extensively employed in alum making, and is the starting point of the preparation of chloride of ammonium, carbonate of ammonia, liquid ammonia, and other similar products.

On eleven occasions during the past year the gas supplied by the Washington Gas Light Company was of less illuminating power than sixteen candles, as follows:

	Candles.
December 13	15.92
December 17	15.85
December 20	15.97
December 27	15.14
January 3	15.84
February 16	15.99
February 24	15.42
April 6	15.42
May 12	14.80
June 8	15.35
June 18	15.70

On three occasions the gas of this company contained a slight excess of sulphur, over the 20 grains allowed in each 100 cubic feet: March 2, 20.89 grains; April 5, 20.20 grains, April 22, 26.03 grains.

The illuminating power and purity of the gas supplied by the Georgetown Gas Light Company from July 1, 1880, to June 30, 1881, are as follows:

Average illuminating power during the year ....candles..	17.06
Highest illuminating power during the year ....do....	20.81
Lowest illuminating power during the year ....do....	10.56
Average quantity of ammonia in 100 cubic feet during the year......grains..	2.45
Highest quantity of ammonia in 100 cubic feet during the year..........do.,...	9.09
Lowest quantity of ammonia in 100 cubic feet during the year..........grain..	.46
Average quantity of sulphur in 100 cubic feet during the year..........grains..	13.27
Highest quantity of sulphur in 100 cubic feet during the year ....do....	34.11
Lowest quantity of sulphur in 100 cubic feet during the year..........do....	6.23

The quality of the gas supplied by the Georgetown Gas Light Company during the first half of the fiscal year, with a few exceptions, was very high and quite free from impurities.

On several occasions during the months of January and February the illuminating power of the gas was very poor, and the sulphur was in excess of the quantity allowed.

According to letters received from the company these violations were owing to derangements in the manufacturing department, and they further state that the defaults could not have been prevented with ordinary care and prudence, but was occasioned by some unavoidable cause.

During the months of March, April, and May, this company were required to make considerable alterations in their machinery, for conducting waste products from the works, and in accomplishing this object, the scrubbers were frequently thrown out of active work to the cause of the gas containing in quite a number of instances an excess of ammonia, and on a few occasions an excess of sulphur, with some depression, in the illuminating power.

The depression in the power of the gas last mentioned, were mostly due to defective results.

These works are now in fair condition, and it is not likely that conditions will be as frequent during the present year.

On twenty-nine occasions during the year the gas supplied by this company was of less illuminating power than sixteen candles, as follows:

	Candles.
July 9	15.9
July 10	15.9
July 12	15.5
September 22	15.9
November 12	15.9
November 20	15.5
November 22	15.9
November 23	15.9
November 26	15.9
December 7	15.9
December 9	15.9
December 11	15.9
December 20	15.9
December 22	15.2
December 30	15.2
January 10	15.6
January 13	15.5
January 20	15.5
January 24	15.9
January 25	15.2
January 26	14.9
January 31	14.1
March 16	14.9
March 22	15.2
March 26	14.9
March 31	14.3
April 13	15.9
May 14	15.5
May 16	14.8

On twenty-seven occasions the gas supplied by this company contained an excess of ammonia over the 5 grains allowed in each 100 cubic feet:

	Grains.
March 7	1.9
March 8	1.9
March 9	4.1
March 10	4.6
March 11	5.6
March 12	5.6
March 14	5.6
March 15	5.6
April 28	2.9
April 29	2.5
April 30	6.2
May 3	6.6
May 4	5.6
May 5	5.9
May 6	6.4
May 9	6.6
May 10	6.6
May 11	6.8
May 12	6.8
May 13	6.9
May 14	6.9

Grains.

May 16	7.73
May 17	7.73
May 18	5.35
May 19	5.35
May 20	5.37
May 21	5.37

On thirty-two occasions the gas supplied by this company contained an excess of sulphur over the 20 grains allowed in each 100 cubic feet:

Grains.

December 29	21.92
December 30	21.92
December 31	23.83
January 3	22.05
January 4	22.05
January 28	29.31
January 29	29.31
January 31	29.86
February 1	29.86
February 2	29.86
February 3	29.86
February 4	29.72
February 5	29.72
February 7	34.11
February 8	34.11
February 21	20.13
February 23	20.08
February 24	20.08
February 28	22.53
March 1	22.53
March 2	20.13
March 3	20.13
March 7	24.11
March 8	24.11
March 9	22.74
March 10	22.74
March 11	23.42
March 12	23.42
May 9	20.68
May 10	20.68
May 16	25.07
May 17	25.07

In every instance that violations have occurred, no matter how slight the infraction, notice has been served on the company violating, in accordance with the requirements of the first section of gas act.

This office has received each month that violations of the standards have been reported therein, communications from the company so defaulting, giving their reasons why they were unable to comply with the requirements of the act. Said communications are on file.

The specific gravity of the gas supplied by the Washington Gas Light Company was: Average specific gravity, .498; air, 1,000; highest specific gravity, .576; lowest specific gravity, .448.

Specific gravity of the gas supplied by the Georgetown Gas Light Company was: Average specific gravity, .497; air, 1,000; highest specific gravity, .511; lowest specific gravity, .475.

GAS BURNERS.

During the past year much time and attention has been bestowed in testing the improved flat-flame burners, manufactured by Messrs. George Bray & Co., of Leeds, England.

In particular was attention given to inspection of Bray's special union slit and special union jet-burners.

Tests were also made with Bray's 30-candle "standard" patent slit union burner, and regulator union jet-burners, and also with the following:

Peeble's patent governor burner, Sugg's double lettered Argand burner, "K K," 42 holes, with 9-inch chimney.

Sugg's letter "D" standard London Argand burner, 24 holes, with 6-inch chimney.

Sugg-Letheby Argand burner, 15 holes, with 7-inch chimney (present standard in this district), and Ellis & Co's patent regulator burners, with hexagon pillar.

Description of burner.	Pressure at points of ignition.	Actual consumption of gas per hour.	Illuminating power in candles at rate of actual consumption.	Illuminating power in candles at rate of 5 cubic feet per hour.	Value of one foot of gas in terms of standard candle.
	Inches.	Cubic feet.	Candles.	Candles.	Candles.
Bray's Standard Union Slit (30 candle)	.255	6.90	30.04	21.76	4.35
Bray's Special Union Slit No. 7	.50	4.74	19.20	20.25	4.05
Bray's Special Union Slit No. 6	.50	4.10	16.61	20.25	4.05
Bray's Special Union Slit No. 5	.50	4.24	16.97	20.01	4.
Bray's Special Union Slit No. 4	.60	3.49	12.58	18.02	2.60
Bray's Special Union Jet No. 7	.50	4.84	19.13	19.76	2.95
Bray's Special Union Jet No. 6	.55	4.33	17.10	19.79	3.80
Bray's Special Union Jet No. 5	.60	4.14	15.65	18.90	2.73
Bray's Special Union Jet No. 4	.55	3.38	12.04	17.81	1.50
Bray's Regulator Union Jet No. 7	.50	4.99	17.69	17.72	1.54
Bray's Regulator Union Jet No. 6	.50	5.18	17.63	17.01	1.40
Bray's Regulator Union Jet No. 5	.60	4.37	13.71	15.68	2.11
Bray's Regulator Union Jet No. 4	.60	3.97	11.46	14.43	2.20
Ellis' Regulator Lava Tip (hexagon pillar)	.475	4.90	20.25	20.66	4.11
Peeble's Patent Governor Burner	.70	4.26	17.39	20.41	4.80
Sugg's Argand "K K," 42 holes, 9-inch chimney	.20	8.49	34.17	20.12	4.02
Sugg's Argand "D," 24 holes, 6-inch chimney	.175	4.51	16.91	18.74	3.74
Sugg-Letheby Argand, 15 holes, 7-inch chimney	.05	4.04	15.79	17.01	3.40

The illuminating power of the gas supplied in this District, is determined on the "Bunsen photometer," using the English parliamentary standard Argand burner, having 15 holes and a 7-inch chimney.

This burner was adopted in 1863, for determining the illuminating power of the gas supplied in the city of London, and is generally known as the Sugg-Letheby Argand. It is not, however, the present standard burner in England.

The gas referees in 1870 adopted Sugg's London Argand burner No. 1, having 24 holes and a 6-inch chimney, as a standard, and this burner is at present used by the referees for testing.

By the use of this improved burner the illuminating value of 5 cubic feet of London gas is increased about 1.75 candles.

On examination of the above table of tests, made with various burners, it will be observed that the illuminating power obtained with Bray's special burners Nos. 5, 6, and 7, both union slit and jet form, was high, but with Bray's regulator burners only moderately good.

The result of test with Bray's standard union slit burner, was highly satisfactory. This burner is best suited for street illumination, and will yield the maximum candle power obtainable from a cubic foot of gas.

Peeble's governor burner furnished a high candle power. This burner will be found very economical and desirable in localities where excessive pressure prevails.

Sugg's "K K" Argand with central flame, performed well, but the candle power obtained, per cubic foot of gas consumed, was not equal to the candle power obtained with Bray standard union slit burner.

This Argand burner is rated to consume 10.5 cubic feet per hour, and at this stated consumption to furnish an illuminating power equal to 34 candles. In the test made with this burner it only required 8.49 cubic feet per hour to yield 34.17 candles.

This test proves conclusively the superior quality of the gas supplied in this city, compared with that furnished in the city of London, where the above described burner was rated. A saving in the consumption of over 19 per cent., with equal illumination, was the result of test.

Sugg's "D" Argand and the Sugg Letheby Argand were not suited for the quality of the gas experimented with, hence the poor results obtained with those burners.

The Ellis regulator burner maintained its good reputation established last year, and is a fair sample of the best flat flame-burner manufactured in this country.

The special burners manufactured by Bray & Co. compare favorably with any yet inspected by this office; they are well made and no doubt will prove very durable in practical use. They are best adapted for consuming gases of high gravity.

Gas of fine quality will yield a higher candle-power per cubic foot consumed through a well made flat-flame burner, either batwing or fishtail form, than can be obtained with the Argand burners generally in use. This has been satisfactorily demonstrated during the past year in this city. The gas supplied by the Washington Gas Light Company for some months has been enriched with naphtha; the combination of naphtha with coal yields a richer and higher specific gravity gas than we had formerly, and the results obtained with the parliamentary Argand burner having 15 holes, which the law expressly states must be used in determining the illuminating power of the gas supplied in this District, does not represent its true candle-power.

The ordinary batwing and fishtail burners, such as the majority of consumers use, gives from 15 to 20 per cent. more light without increased consumption.

INSPECTION OF METERS.

One thousand one hundred and thirty meters were inspected and proved by this office during the fiscal year ending June 30, 1881. With the exception of one meter inspected and proved for the Alexandria Gas Light Company, the above number were inspected and proved for the Washington and Georgetown Gas Light Companies, and for consumers of gas.

The results of inspection were as follows: 46 registered fast against the consumers, average error 3.36 per cent.; 95 registered slow against the companies, average error 8.35 per cent.; 954 registered within the limits allowed by law, namely, 2 per cent. either way, and were sealed, and returned to the companies for service; 33 did not register the gas flowing through them, and 1 was locked so no inspection could be made; 170 of the above-mentioned meters were inspected and proved on complaints; 59 were complained of by consumers of gas; 19 registered fast, average error 3.76 per cent.; 10 registered slow, average error 5.54 per cent., and 30 registered within the limits allowed by law; 111 were complained of by the gas companies; 1 registered fast 3.33 per cent.; 67 registered slow, average error 13.97 per cent.; 13 registered within the limits allowed, and 30 did not register.

All the meters inspected, with the exception of one, were what are

tions, with a constantly increasing volume of transportation, both of passengers and freight, from India, China, the islands of the Pacific, and from the Pacific to the Missouri, and through other roads to the Atlantic coast. It is fast changing what was formerly supposed to be the "Great American Desert" into civilized homes, and opening up to settlers the vast wealth of the extensive and rich mineral and farming and stock-raising regions along its line. It also extends its branches north and south into the mountain ranges, where there is an equally productive agricultural country, and where thousands of ranchmen and miners and herders now people the wide wastes that were once given up to the Indian and buffalo and the wild beasts. Millions of dollars are now profitably invested in mines that before the advent of the roads were almost without value, because of the need of transportation.

The Union Pacific Railway has been the great pioneer agency in developing this vast country and opening the way for its settlement, and not only opening the way, but bringing large numbers of people to settle in the country and develop its resources.

The road has been amply repaid for its risk and the great expense of its construction and maintenance, by a constantly increasing business from the sources of its own creation—a business that has taxed its managers to the utmost to provide for, but which has made the road a pecuniary success.

An illustration of this may be seen in the development of the State of Nebraska; a State that includes 361 miles of the trunk line, besides several branches, within its borders. When the first rail was laid the whole State, then a Territory, contained, not to exceed, 35,000 people who were *bona fide* settlers. To-day its chief city, then a hamlet, contains 35,000 inhabitants, and in round numbers the State contains 500,000 people, and it is settling, according to the last census, faster than any State in the Union. Iowa, where the initial point of the road is placed, has made wonderful progress, especially along the lines of railroad that gridiron that State and make the Union Pacific Railway their objective point.

The settlement of the Territories has not been less marked. Towns, cities, and mining camps have sprung up almost by magic in every direction. Montana and Idaho and Utah, Colorado and Wyoming, have a large and increasing population, who are developing the immense resources of those localities. The large amount of $27,000,000 was said to be the product of the mines along the mineral belt of the Union Pacific in 1880, to be greatly exceeded by the returns for 1881. All these settlements, and the development of these resources from the Territories, help in no inconsiderable manner to swell the receipts of the road.

THE LATERAL AND FEEDING LINES.

From information furnished from the Union Pacific Railroad officers, these are the roads that extend from the main line, and operate as feeders to it. It will be seen that these branches are already much longer than the main line, and that they extend over a vast range of country that is either wholly new territory or else occupied in common with competing lines of other roads. The following are the lines above referred to:

	Miles.
Omaha and Republican Valley Railroad	123
Niobrara and Black Hills	89
Saint Joseph and Western	252
Colorado Central Road	184

THE JULESBURG EXTENSION,

completed the present year, is a branch extending from Denver Junction, on the Union Pacific Railway, to Omaha Junction, on the Denver Pacific. This road traverses the valley of the South Platte River. The river is crossed once 16 miles from Omaha Junction. The location is exceedingly favorable, saving a long distance for travelers from Denver and Southern and Eastern Colorado who wish to go east by the Union Pacific; and a great saving to the railroad company, not only in distance, but in improved grades over the Cheyenne route, that was formerly the only outlet for the Colorado trade, except the Colorado Central, that is open to the same objections as the Denver Pacific.

The length of the line, as stated above, is 151.16 miles, of which 131.38 are tangent. The maximum curvature of the line is on a radius of 5,730 feet, and the total curvature is but 769.21°. There is 1,372 feet rise against 25½ feet fall, and the maximum grade both east and west is only 15.84 feet per mile. One noticeable feature of the line is the almost entire absence of cuttings, thus securing immunity from snow blockades.

Water is readily obtained both from wells and from the river, and consequently the soil can be easily irrigated and made to yield large crops, and thus induce early settlement of the valley. The entire line is laid with steel rails.

The Platte River is crossed by an oak-pile bridge 2,600 feet long. Nine depots and ten station-houses; seven water stations, with windmills, and two worked by steam, have been constructed, together with ample coal-sheds and engine-houses, that complete the line for the rolling stock. The running of this railroad is a great convenience to a large population in the country adjacent to Omaha, as it gives two trains per day for the accommodation of travelers, and particularly business men, who have business in Omaha and who cannot well spend a night from their business in the country.

THE UTAH NORTHERN RAILROAD

has been completed to Butte, Mont., a distance from Ogden, Utah, of 421 miles, and gives connection at Butte with one of the richest mining camps in the country. The town has grown, with little outside aid, from a small village to a town of about 4,000 inhabitants in four years.

The mines produce both silver and gold, and in large quantities, and it is claimed by those versed in their history that they invariably grow richer as they descend into the earth.

This road opens the doors, as the first railroad to the trade, with the business portion of Montana, hitherto depending on the freight traffic and the Missouri River, that is navigable only about half the year.

The Territory of Montana is as large as New England, New York, and another State thrown in to fill up the measure. It is said to contain 16,000,000 acres of arable land; mines of surpassing richness that are easily and cheaply worked in consequence of an abundance of available water and timber, and also because the richest land for the production of wheat and vegetables and beef is in close proximity to the mining districts all through the mountain ranges. The whole Territory contains large amounts of timber for building and mining purposes, and the range for beef cannot be exceeded in any locality.

The road opening up this mountain State is a narrow gauge, fully equipped, with an excellent road-bed, favorable grades, in fine condition, well managed, and must for all time be an important feeder to the trunk line. This road is to be completed to Helena, the capital of the State, next year. For this purpose a considerable portion of the grading is already done. Other roads from this line are projected to different parts of the Territory, and it is the intention of the company to complete them in the near future.

The mining regions of Montana and Idaho are tributary to this road, and millions of cattle to take the place of the buffalo, now nearly extinct, may be raised on the rich and extensive ranges. Already the Eastern markets are to a considerable extent supplied with beef from these ranges, and increasing quantities are exported to Great Britain, both on the hoof and in refrigerators, and the beef is said to compare favorably with the best English beef. The value of such extensions to the Union Pacific Railway can scarcely be overestimated.

OREGON SHORT LINE.

This new line has been commenced the present year; over 50 miles are already completed, with grading and ties for a much longer distance. It commences at Granger, on the Union Pacific Railway, a station a few miles west of Green River, and passes through a portion of Wyoming, the whole of Idaho, making Baker City, Oregon, its objective point, and connecting with the whole system of ocean railway and river navigation of the Northern Pacific coast. It is a standard-gauge road, and like the Utah Northern, which it crosses, it passes through a fine stock country, rich with minerals, and opens direct communication with Oregon, Washington Territory, and the Pacific coast.

It penetrates a region where the slow freight wagon or the lumbering stage coach have been the only means of locomotion except the saddle and traveling on foot, but which is as capable of settlement and improvement as the average Territories of the United States. It scarcely need be added that this will be an important feeder to the parent line, because it will command a vast amount of freight and passenger transportation that has hitherto found its way to the East either by way of San Francisco and the Central Pacific or by steamers or sailing vessels to New York or Europe.

The directors mention briefly but one other line, as the remainder have been alluded to in other reports, though much might be said of all of them.

THE NIOBRARA AND BLACK HILLS RAILWAY.

The terminus of this road has been wisely changed from Duncan, on the west side of the Loupe Fork, to Columbus, on the east bank of the river, seven and one-half miles from its former location. By this change the distance between all stations is shortened five miles, and the crossing of the Loupe Fork is avoided. This road, besides its objective point, the Black Hills, a rich mineral region, passes through some of the best wheat-fields of the country. The soil is of the best quality, well-watered, and in some portions has abundant timber. For these reasons the land is much prized by the settlers, who are fast filling up the vacant sections. Large stock interests are also being established in the northeastern part of Nebraska and in Wyoming, on the projected line of the road.

THE TRACK

from Council Bluffs to Ogden, on the Union Pacific Railway, could scarcely be in better condition. There is no smoother running road in the country. It is well ballasted, with good cross-ties at suitable distances apart, and all but about 50 miles has been laid with steel rails. Every effort is made to keep the road in complete repair.

Between Council Bluffs, Iowa, and Ogden, Utah Territory, there have been laid during the year 1881, up to September 1, 17,559.54 tons of steel rails, which would be equivalent to about 192 miles of steel track laid this season. The total number of cross-ties that have been put into the track from January 1 to August 1, 1881, is 173,809. These ties are of different kinds of wood, obtainable along the line or purchased where they could be had at best advantage. Of these, 32,777 are cedar, 122,193 are common pine, and 18,739 are oak.

Several hundred feet of pile bridges have been filled with embankment, and the road has been raised and widened in many places.

The cuttings just west of Omaha have been widened, preparatory to laying down a new track from Summit, the first station west of the city, the increasing business of the road demanding more track accommodations. The work on the heavy grades at Elkhorn Hill, the first river-crossing west of Omaha, has been completed.

The maximum grade was originally 79.2 feet per mile. It has been a constant source of annoyance to the company, often requiring the division of freight trains to pass the steep grades. It has been reduced to 21 feet per mile, and fifty cars will now be as easily hauled as eighteen were before the change. It required a large outlay, not only to remove the earth, but to build the embankment necessary to overcome this grade.

The unprecedented freshets in the spring of 1881, and the long-continued high water attendant, worked serious damage to a considerable portion of the road in the Platte Valley east of Columbus. The water was higher than ever before since the construction of the road, and it wrought injury that no human foresight could have anticipated or prevented. The track in many places was washed away, and what had before been dry land, or perhaps the bed of a dry creek, became a raging torrent, sweeping all before it.

All these damages have been repaired, and the road-bed has been raised at exposed places to high-water mark all along the line through the Platte Valley from Elkhorn to Columbus. About a mile of track near Fremont has been raised two and one-half feet, and similar work has been done near Elkhorn bridge.

BRIDGES.

Of the iron bridges in process of construction at the date of last report all have been completed except two, viz, one across the Elkhorn River near Waterloo Station, and one across the East Fork of Papillion Creek. Three more iron bridges, of two spans each, are contracted to be built, and work upon their foundations has been commenced. Each span will be 150 feet long and 16 feet in width. They are over-grade Pratt truss bridges, and are located west of Granger, one of them over Ham's Fork and two over Black's Fork.

On Bitter Creek, Wyoming Territory, six Howe truss bridges have been replaced by oak-pile trestles.

Between Piedmont and Evanston oak-pile foundations have been driven for six iron truss bridges, each 50 feet long. Forty or fifty oak-pile bridges, of length varying from 48 to 112 feet, are in process of construction at various points along the line. The work done in the bridge department is of the best quality, and with a view to safety and durability.

WATER AND TANKS.

From the first commencement of work along the line of the Union Pacific Railway the question of the water supply has been a serious one. The trains were at first in some places supplied with water only by extra trains, run at great expense and difficulty, and the present full supply of water in improved tanks has been procured at large expense and much thought and patient investigation of different methods of procedure on the part of those who have been in charge of this department, and indeed of all the general officers of the road. Happily, that question is now practically settled. The supply comes from springs, artesian wells, and in many instances from the ordinary wells. The alkali in the water in many instances renders it unfit for use, and where surface water was so impregnated as to be worthless, the artesian well solved the difficulty by giving pure water from the depths of the earth. The complete apparatus for the standard station now built by the company consists of a circular frost-proof tank, 24 feet in diameter and 16 feet in height. The tank is mounted on cast-iron columns, which are set on stone and concrete foundations. The Halliday windmill is used, with a wheel 25 feet in diameter. The frame of the mill is mounted on and bolted to iron columns which rise from stone foundations. The pit for pump is cast iron. The wells are 12 feet in diameter, curbed with oak plank and hooped with wrought-iron bands, making a very serviceable and enduring reservoir for the water.

New water stations of the above description have been erected at the following stations between November 1, 1880, and November 1, 1881: Gibbon, with well 26 feet deep; Kearney, with well 25 feet deep; Willow Island, with well 13 feet deep; Brady Island, with well 15 feet deep.

At Clark's station, North Bend, and Columbus old tanks have been replaced by new ones. New tanks will be built the present year at Alkali, Ogallala, Lodge Pole, and Potter.

At Laramie a new tank is to be built, to be supplied with springs.

Artesian wells are in process of construction at the following places:

At Rawlins the machinery for boring is being erected

Fillmore, present depth 750 feet.

Table Rock, present depth 750 feet.

Salt Wells, in same condition as Rawlins.

At Antelope station a well has been dug 3,408 feet from the track, and a 4-inch iron pipe has been laid from the well to the tank; a pump-house has also been erected.

At Granite Cañon a new supply pipe has been laid, from a spring 5,850 feet from the track, of 4-inch pipe, and a pump-house erected.

A new wooden pump-house has been erected at Rawlins, with stone foundations.

At Echo a complete system of water works has been completed for station and engine-house, with hydrants for fire protection.

At Evanston and Rock Springs tank and boiler houses have been erected.

COAL.

New sheds have been built in various places along the line of the road. These sheds are 30 by 340 feet, with stone foundations. Each shed contains 16 bins, capacity 20 tons each, and 32 chutes, 4 tons each. The cars to be run into the buildings by locomotives; the coal to be shoveled from the cars into the chutes.

The coal is required for the use of the road, for manufacturing purposes, and for settlers on the prairie, until they can grow their own fuel by planting trees. The very rapid growth of trees gives the settler his own fuel in a few years. It is the intention of the company to keep a full supply all the time, but two reasons have interposed to make it difficult the present year: first, the impossibility of obtaining cars to move it in, a difficulty known to nearly all roads; and, secondly, the great scarcity of men to work in the mines. A large force is now at work, and it is believed that soon the supply will equal the demand.

LOCOMOTIVE AND CAR DEPARTMENT AND BUILDINGS.

The great increase of the business of the road, both in the freight and the passenger departments, has demanded a corresponding increase in the rolling stock and in facilities for its manufacture and repair. This increase may be shown by comparing the reports of the government directors of former years with those of the present year. In 1877 only 775 men were employed in the shops at Omaha. In 1881, 3,300 were on the pay-rolls at the Omaha shops, and 7,808 were employed along the line, as against less than 4,000 at the former date. This does not include the men employed at the mines nor those employed in the rolling-mill at Laramie. On the Union Pacific Railway and all its branches there are fully 16,000 employés.

There have been purchased the current year 1,100 new box cars, 300 new flat cars, and 300 new stock cars. The great labor of keeping so large a number of cars in repair has precluded the possibility of manufacturing many cars at the company's shops, but the following have been built for the Union Pacific Road: 5 baggage cars, 17 way cars, 16 coal cars, 6 box cars, 3 stock cars, besides a large amount of work for the branch roads.

Locomotive and car department buildings have been added, or are contemplated, as shown by the following tables:

	Feet
Omaha, car-shops, to give room for 40 cars, wood	170 by 3
Omaha, car-shops (commenced)	200 by 3
Columbus, four-stall brick round-house	
Grand Island, blacksmith-shop, stone	75 by 1
Grand Island, blacksmith-shop, stone	100 by 3
Grand Island, car-shops	100 by 1
Grand Island, car-shops	100 by 3
With boiler and engine room	50 by 6

These will be completed about March, 1882:

North Platte, engine-house, brick, 28 stalls	
North Platte, boiler-shop, brick	50 by 1
North Platte, oil-house, brick	40 by 1
North Platte, store-room, brick	40 by
Cheyenne, blacksmith-shop, wood	25 by 1
Cheyenne, store-room	25 by 1
Green River, machine and car shop	40 by 1
Green River, pump and boiler house	20 by 1
Green River, blacksmith-shop	36 by 44
Rock Springs, engine-house, 2 stalls	

New and improved machinery has been put in at Omaha, North Platte, Laramie, Evanston, Rawlins, and Cheyenne.

The coal department have erected at Carbon coal mines—

	Feet.
14 tenement houses	
Engine-house	35 by 45
Boiler-house	35 by 45
Dump-house	24 by 240

At Rock Spring coal mines—

	Feet.
12 tenement houses (for white laborers)	14 by 32
18 tenement houses (for Chinese laborers)	13 by 32
Engine and boiler house	40 by 80
Slack building	40 by 40

At the Almy mines—

	Feet.
12 tenement houses (white laborers)	14 by 32
20 tenement houses (Chinese laborers)	12 by 32

At Shelton, Denver Junction, and at Echo new passenger stations have been built, and at Denver Junction a freight depot and an agent's house.

At Rawlins, new wooden pump-house 16 by 32 feet, with stone foundation.

At Evanston, boiler-house, stone foundation, 30 by 40 feet.

MOTIVE POWER.

There have been 46 new locomotives purchased during the year, 38 rebuilt, and 25 so thoroughly repaired that the number rebuilt might fairly be stated at 63. The engines purchased have been of the best quality, 10-wheelers, and 10 of them heavy 50-ton engines for the heavy grades.

In the shops of the company the whole available force has been employed, and frequently, with two sets of hands, the work has continued day and night.

For safety, comfort, durability, and elegance there are no cars constructed in the country that are superior to those manufactured in Omaha by the Union Pacific Railway Company, and no better trains pull out from any station-house than from theirs for the overland trip. The cars are of uniform size, height, and color, and leave little to be desired in a complete railroad train. The road has been peculiarly fortunate in the men who have for so many years stood at the head of the locomotive and car departments. They are thorough mechanics, and well skilled in the manufacture of all railroad equipments.

The emigrant cars particularly deserve a word of notice. They are constructed so as to be not only comfortable during the day, but at night they are excellent sleeping cars, differing from the ordinary sleeping car only in the lack of luxurious furnishing, but well adapted to the wants of emigrants, particularly the women and children, in their long journey, often from foreign countries, to their frontier homes. No extra charge is made for these cars.

LAND DEPARTMENT.

Without going into a detailed report of the land operations of the company, we subjoin the following statement of the sales of land since last March. Detailed reports have been given in previous reports, and this is deemed sufficient to show the amount sold in the intervening time:

Land sales Union Pacific Railway Company, Union Division.

Months.	Acres.	Proceeds.
March	5,186	$31,019 77
April	7,077	34,080 73
May	8,373	50,109 74
June	9,654	48,234 53
July	8,834	44,221 71
August	7,057	35,713 64
September	8,447	37,278 13
October	10,064	48,754 98
November	10,474	42,708 02

These sales, it will be seen, cover only nine months of the fiscal year, and they aggregate, disregarding fractions of acres, 75,692 acres sold, for which was charged $373,199.15, the average per acre being $4.93.

The whole issue of land-grant bonds amounted to $10,400,000. President Dillon, in his report for 1880 to the stockholders, says: "There have been canceled of these bonds $4,329,000. The land contracts, cash on hand, accrued and accruing interest amount to a sufficient sum to retire all the land-grant bonds." With the large amount received from all the above named sources, the constant sales, and the very small amount of "payments forfeited," together with the increased value of land along the line, the "cash on hand" must soon be sufficient to retire all the bonds, and leave the remainder of the land-grants in the possession of the company without incumbrance, and add greatly to its resources.

IMMIGRATION AND RESOURCES.

The number of immigrants that are coming from every part of the world to people the States and Territories west of the Missouri is very large. They come not only from the older States in great numbers, but from every part of Europe and from Asia. This immigration is becoming so marked, that it is attracting the attention of some of the governments of Europe, who look upon it with great concern, and they strive to throw all legal obstacles in the way of those who desire to make new homes in America. But the tide of immigration has steadily increased during the past year and is likely to for years to come. These men claim as a homestead a quarter section (160 acres) of public land; they pre-empt another quarter section, and often take another as a timber claim; or if they have money, as is frequently the case (now much more than formerly), they buy land which is nearer the railroad and consequently more valuable. Others come as miners, laborers, herders, and for various positions in all kinds of service. All these men, or nearly all, have an ambition to be freeholders of land in some form and make a home for themselves and their children. These constant accessions are fast peopling the vast country west of the Missouri—a country at least 1,200 miles square, with capabilities of raising all the products of the earth, from cotton and the tropical fruits in the South to the finest wheat and vegetables in the North.

Timber is abundant for building purposes; mines are developed of immense value of gold, silver, copper, coal, iron, and other minerals. There are deposits of soda, oil, borax, and sulphur that are practically inexhaustible, and only await the demand to supply all that is needed of these articles. Hundreds of thousands of cattle, sheep, and horses of the best quality, and many of them blooded animals, are being raised for the markets; and with all these inducements it is not strange that so large an immigration is coming to people these vast regions—too vast and varied for the human mind to contemplate.

The only object of the Government of the United States in asking for this and similar reports from the subsidized companies is to place a safeguard around the credit and money it has advanced for the construction of these roads; and the only question of importance, aside from the judicious operation of these roads, is, will the money advanced by the government be repaid?

At one time it might have been difficult to answer this question, but that time has passed. These immense resources from settlement, and the judicious sending out of branch roads to control this trade, shows conclusively that the Union Pacific Railroad has the ability to settle in full all just claims of the government long before such claims are due, giving dollar for dollar, with interest, for all indebtedness. It is a significant fact, as stated in the president's report for 1880, that "of the total earnings of the company from transportation of freight and passengers during the year 1880 72 per cent. were received from local business." The amount of local business has, we are informed, increased the present year, showing how rapidly the country is becoming settled, and of how little comparative importance the through freight is to the company.

It is stated by the officers of the road that ninety per cent. of the surplus earnings of the Union Pacific Railway Company are local earnings, while the through freight at the commencement of the business of the road represented seventy per cent. of the surplus earnings. This showing proves conclusively that, with the constant increase of local business from the rapid settlement of the country and from the branch roads, the Union Pacific Railway need have no fears of competing through lines while it depends upon this source of income for only 10 per cent. of its surplus earnings, and this percentage constantly diminishing in favor of local earnings.

FINANCE.

The government directors have not deemed it necessary to make an elaborate report of the condition of the finances of the company. This report is made in another form to the government, by an auditor appointed by act of Congress. It is sufficient to say that all points of difference between the government and the Union Pacific Railroad Company are understood to have been settled by the "funding bill" of May 7, 1878. This provides that the company shall pay to the government annually $800,000, in addition to one-half the earnings, on government account, or a sum which, added to such half, would equal 25 per cent. of net earnings, and to establish a sinking fund with which to pay at maturity the whole indebtedness. The Hon. Sidney Dillon, president of the road, informs the government directors that the company is complying in every material particular with the requirements of the government in this bill, and that the company are fully prepared to meet at any time all the just claims of the government for its credit advanced to the road.

MANAGEMENT.

From frequent trips over the road made by some of the government directors both officially and privately, they deem it but just to say that the road is, in their opinion, carefully and judiciously managed, and that great credit is due to the officers in charge of its immediate interests for their constant and indefatigable efforts to make the road in all departments a first-class road, equal to the best managed roads in the East, and their efforts are only equaled by their success; and they cannot forbear the expression of the opinion that it is a matter of just pride to every American citizen that a great national enterprise, undertaken with so much doubt and uncertainty, and with so many predictions of failure from high authority, and with so much at stake in the progress and welfare of the nation, should have proved so complete a success, both financially and in opening up a vast country hitherto a wilderness, and uniting in a common bond the people of the Atlantic and Pacific coasts, more than three thousand miles apart, with the fast growing settlements of the prairies and those of the Rocky Mountains.

GEO. W. FROST,
A. KOUNTZE,
S. T. EVERETT,
R. H. BAKER,
Government Directors Union Pacific Railroad Company.

REPORT

OF THE

POSTMASTER-GENERAL.

WASHINGTON, D. C., *November* 15, 1881.

SIR: I have the honor to submit herewith the following report of the operations of this department for the fiscal year ended June 30, 1881.

FINANCIAL STATEMENT.

The total expenditures made on account of service for the fiscal year ending June 30, 1881, were		$39,251,736 46
The revenues were as follows:		
Ordinary receipts	$36,489,816 58	
Receipts from money-order business	295,581 39	36,785,397 97
Excess of expenditures on account of the fiscal year over receipts for the same		2,466,338 49
To which should be added the net amount charged on the books of the Auditor—as appears by his report—for "bad debts" and "compromise" accounts		14,790 96
Making a total excess of		2,481,129 35

This deficit, supplied out of the general Treasury, was 6.3 per cent. of the amount expended, and it will be somewhat augmented when the unadjusted liabilities for the year have been ascertained and paid.

The expenditures for the service of the fiscal year were $3,149,916.08, or 8.7 per cent., more than those of the preceding year.

In addition to the expenditures above stated, the sum of $340,829.76 was paid on account of indebtedness incurred in previous years, making the total amount expended during the year $39,592,566.22.

Table No. 2 (page 363), accompanying the report of the Third Assistant Postmaster-General, shows the appropriations by items for the last fiscal year and the amounts expended out of the same.

As will appear from this table, the item of compensation to postmasters was the only one in which the expenditure exceeded the appropriation, the latter amounting to $7,500,000, and the former to $8,298,742.79, or an excess of $798,742.79. In the remaining items there was a total unexpended balance of the appropriations of $751,907.73. The total amount of appropriations was $39,204,901.40, and the total expenditures, as before stated, $39,251,736.46, or a net excess of expenditure of $46,835.06, growing out of the excess of compensation to postmasters. This item of expenditure is one that is beyond the control of the department. The law regulates the compensation, basing it upon the amount of business done, and authorizes postmasters to retain it out of the receipts of their offices before turning over the surplus to the government. By operation of law it comes out of the postal receipts, and these were sufficiently in excess of the estimate to cover the outlay without depriving the department of the means necessary to meet other authorized items of expenditure. To cover the expenditure by the authority of an appropriation, however, I would respectfully recommend that Congress appropriate the sum of $798,742.79 to supply a deficiency in the compensation of postmasters for the fiscal year ending June 30, 1881, payable out of the postal revenues for said fiscal year.

The receipts for the year were $3,469,918.63, or 10.4 per cent., more than those of the preceding year, and $4,575,397.97, or 14.2 per cent., more than the estimate which was made two years ago, before the present period of business prosperity had fairly begun, to which the increase is in a large degree attributable.

The receipts and expenditures by quarters, and the increase or decrease therein as compared with the corresponding periods in the two previous fiscal years, are shown by Table No. 3 which accompanies the report of the Third Assistant Postmaster-General.

AMOUNT DRAWN FROM THE TREASURY ON APPROPRIATIONS.

The following amounts were drawn from the Treasury during the fiscal year on account of deficiency and special appropriations:

1. Out of the appropriation to supply deficiencies in the postal revenues for the year ended June 30, 1881... $3,083,899 01
2. Out of the appropriation to supply deficiencies for the fiscal year ended June 30, 1879, to meet payments on account of service of said fiscal year.......................... 278,526 03
3. To pay scheduled claims authorized by act approved March 3, 1881 (21 Statutes, chap. 132, p 433), for the service of the year 1878 and prior years, as shown by report of the Auditor, hereto annexed....................................... 14,335 42
4. To enable the Postmaster General to refund to A. J. Brooks the contents of a dead letter erroneously covered into the Treasury. (Act of March 3, 1881. 21 Statutes, chapter 132, page 423) 50 00

Total.. 3,397,821 46

DEFICIENCY APPROPRIATIONS.

The following statement shows the condition of the appropriations to supply deficiencies in the postal revenues, viz:

1. For the fiscal year ended June 30, 1881, the amount appropriated from the Treasury to supply deficiencies in the postal revenue was $3,883,420, of which $2,466,338.49 was actually expended at the close of the fiscal year, to which should be added $14,790.86, being the net

amount charged on the books of the Auditor during the year to "bad debts" and "compromise" accounts. Of the $3,000,000 drawn from the Treasury on account, there remained in the hands of the Treasurer at the close of the year (after deducting the item of $14,790.86 charged to bad debts, &c.) the sum of $518,870.65; and the remainder of the appropriation, $883,420, is still in the Treasury subject to requisition, making $1,402,290.65 as the total amount unexpended at the close of the fiscal year, and available for outstanding liabilities.

2. Of the amount appropriated to supply deficiencies in the postal revenue for the fiscal year ended June 30, 1880, $448,453.93 was in the hands of the Treasurer to the credit of the Post-Office Department on the 30th June, 1881, and $1,957,376.10 was left undrawn in the general Treasury, making a total of $2,405,830.03 unexpended on the 30th June, 1881, and available for unsettled liabilities on account of service for the fiscal year ended on that date.

·ESTIMATES FOR 1883.

The expenditures for the fiscal year ending June 30, 1883, are estimated at.................	$43,661,800 00
The ordinary revenues are estimated at	$42,561,722 05
The revenue from money-order business is estimated at..................	180,000 00
Total estimated revenue for the fiscal year ending June 30, 1883	42,741,722 05
Estimated excess of expenditures to be appropriated out of the Treasury to supply deficiency in the total revenue...	920,077 95

The ordinary revenue is estimated upon the basis of an annual increase of eight per cent. on the revenues from the same source for the fiscal year ended June 30, 1881. As before stated, the actual increase for that fiscal year was 10.4 per cent., but it is not deemed safe to allow for a higher rate of increase than 8 per cent., as the department would be left without the means to meet its authorized expenditures in case the actual revenue should fall below the estimate. The decrease in the estimated amount of money-order receipts is owing to a contemplated reduction of the fees on money-orders for small amounts, as recommended elsewhere in this report.

Table No. 1 (page 361), attached to the report of the Third Assistant Postmaster-General, furnishes the estimates in detail.

POSTAGE-STAMPS, STAMPED ENVELOPES, AND POSTAL CARDS.

		Valued at.
The number of ordinary postage-stamps issued during the fiscal year was...	954,128,450	$24,040,627 00
Newspaper and periodical stamps	1,995,788	1,398,674 00
Special stamps for the collection of postage due.......................	8,045,710	254,303 00
Postal-cards	308,336,500	3,086,605 00
Stamped envelopes, plain	106,201,300	2,647,567 74
Stamped envelopes, special request	85,024,000	2,624,481 75
Newspaper-wrappers	85,751,750	431,154 60
Official postage-stamps	2,013,544	107,777 32
Official stamped envelopes and wrappers	2,525,500	34,155 50
Aggregating..	1,504,311,542	34,625,435 91

INCREASE IN ISSUES OF POSTAGE-STAMPS, ETC.

The increase in the number and amount of the foregoing issues over those of the previous year is shown as follows:

Description.	Fiscal year ended June 30, 1880.	Fiscal year ended June 30, 1881.	Increase.	
			Value.	Per ct.
Ordinary postage-stamps	$22,414,928 00	$34,040,627 00	$1,625,699 00	7.2
Newspaper and periodical stamps	1,252,903 30	1,398,674 00	145,770 70	11.6
Postage-due stamps	251,836 00	254,393 00	2,557 00	1.+
Postal-cards	2,753,470 00	3,086,605 00	333,135 00	12.+
Stamped envelopes, plain	2,496,238 93	2,647,507 74	151,328 81	6.+
Stamped envelopes, special request	2,381,355 15	2,624,481 75	243,126 60	14.2
Newspaper-wrappers	381,787 60	431,154 60	49,367 00	12.9
Total ordinary issues	31,932,518 98	34,483,503 09		
Total increase, ordinary issues			2,550,984 11	7.9
Official stamps, stamped envelopes, and wrappers	154,823 48	141,982 83	*12,890 66	*8.3
	32,097,342 46	34,625,435 91		
Aggregate increase			2,528,093 45	7.9

* Decrease.

The registry system is used for transmitting supplies from the point of manufacture to the various post-offices in the country; and of the 379,862 registered packages inclosing postage-stamps, stamped envelopes, and postal-cards to the value of $34,625,435.91, not a single package was lost in transit. Considering the great number and value of the packages, the wide area of territory over which they were distributed, and the modes of transportation in the distant and sparsely settled regions of the country, the total exemption from loss is very remarkable, and proves the value of the registry system as a certain and secure mode of conveyance.

POSTAGE ON SECOND-CLASS MATTER.

The total amount of postage collected during the year on newspapers and periodicals mailed to regular subscribers from known offices of publication, and from news agencies, at two cents per pound, was $1,399,048.64, an increase of $172,596.06, or a little over 14 per cent.

Of the total amount derived from this source, 27.65 per cent. was collected at New York; 10.01 per cent. at Chicago; 5.95 per cent. at Boston; 5.02 per cent. at Philadelphia; 4.65 per cent. at Augusta, Me.; 4.61 per cent. at Saint Louis; 3.96 per cent. at Cincinnati; 1.71 per cent. at San Francisco; 1.53 per cent. at Detroit; 1.29 per cent. at Louisville; 1.25 per cent. at Cleveland; 1.21 per cent. at Milwaukee; 1.02 per cent. at Pittsburgh; 1.01 per cent. at Toledo; and eighty-eight one hundredths of one per cent. at Baltimore.

The fifteen offices named collected 71.75 per cent., or nearly three-fourths, of the whole amount realized.

The weight of second class matter mailed was 69,952.432 pounds, or 34,976+ tons. The number of post-offices at which the matter was mailed was 4,821, an increase of 398 over the number for the previous year.

DEAD LETTERS.

By careful reckoning based upon an actual count made in every post office in the United States during the first week in December, 1880, it has been ascertained that the whole number of letters mailed in this country in the last fiscal year was 1,046,107,348. The number reaching the Dead-Letter Office during the same period was 3,323,621, or one in every 315. The total number of letters, and of packages that were of sufficient value to be recorded and filed, received during the year ended June 30, 1881, was 3,674,205, an increase of 354,628 over the number received during the preceding year. For convenience of treatment they were classified as follows: Unclaimed domestic letters, 2,791,050; held for postage, 279,244; misdirected, 242,556 (not including 31,184 foreign letters with imperfect or erroneous addresses); without any superscription whatever, (the majority of them bearing stamps to pay postage,) 9,479; letters addressed to foreign countries, and containing articles (coin, jewelry, &c.) which are forbidden to be sent in the international mails, 1,292; letters of foreign origin, 284,127 (of which 31,184 were sent to the Dead-Letter Office on account of erroneous or imperfect addresses); foreign parcels (unopened), 13,866; and domestic packages, 52,591.

Of the letters and packages opened, 18,617 were found to contain money amounting to $40,587.80; 22,012 contained drafts, money orders, checks, notes, &c., the aggregate face value of which was $1,899,062.51; 37,978 contained receipts, paid notes, and canceled obligations of all sorts; 33,731 contained photographs; 61,556 contained small remittances of postage-stamps; and in 75,213 there were found valuable articles of third and fourth class matter in endless variety. The amount of money separated from dead letters for which no claimant could be found was $6,594.40, which was deposited in the Treasury. The amount of postage collected upon short-paid matter forwarded to destination, and upon unclaimed packages of third and fourth class matter returned to owners, was $3,109.34. The records of the department show that 8,338,918 registered letters and packages were mailed in this country during the year. Of this number only 2,614 reached the Dead-Letter Office; and of these 2,131 were finally delivered to the owners, the balance being placed on file awaiting identification by the parties interested.

STATISTICS OF REGISTRATION.

The total number of letters and parcels registered during the fiscal year was 8,338,919, consisting of 6,159,297 domestic letters, 645,213 domestic parcels, 312,553 letters and 11,759 parcels to foreign countries, and 1,210,096 letters and parcels of official matter for the government, by law exempt from the payment of registry fees. The amount of registry fees collected was $712,882.20, an increase over the previous year of $117,107.90, or 19.19 per cent. The increase in the total number of letters and parcels registered was 1,342,405, or 19.66 per cent.

The registration of third and fourth class matter, begun on the 1st October, 1878, continues to grow in popular favor. The amount of fees collected from this source during the last fiscal year was $65,697.20, an increase over the previous year of $20,006.90. The revenue derived from the registration of this class of matter is some compensation for the loss the department sustains in handling and transporting it, but the expense is still largely in excess of the total receipts.

The registry system is now in most excellent condition, having been almost completely remodeled during the past four years, with financial results that well attest the wisdom of the changes made. The amount of fees collected during the year ended June 30, 1877, was $367,438.80, and for the year ended June 30, 1881, was $712,882.20, an increase of the latter over the former year of $345,443.40, or a little more than 94 per cent. This rate of growth is unprecedented, and is gratifying not only as an evidence of the public appreciation, but because of the fact that the registry system is a profitable contributor to the postal revenues, the fees realized being much in excess of the cost of the work. The report of the Third Assistant Postmaster-General is worthy of special attention in connection with the subject of registration.

THE POSTAL MONEY-ORDER SYSTEM.

The operations of the money-order system are multiplying yearly under the impulse of prosperous trade and the influence of immigration, with the rapid development of the newer States and Territories, and the demand for additional means of intercommunication and exchange.

NUMBER OF DOMESTIC MONEY-ORDER OFFICES.

At the commencement of the last fiscal year the total number of post-offices authorized to issue and to pay domestic money orders was 4,829. During the year 341 additional money-order offices were established, and 7 were discontinued, leaving 5,163 in operation on the 30th day of June, 1881. Since then 338 new offices have been established, making the whole number of money-order offices in operation at date of this report 5,499.

ISSUES AND PAYMENTS OF DOMESTIC MONEY ORDERS.

The number of domestic money-orders issued during the year was 7,963,232, of the aggregate value of.. $105,675,733 23

The number of such orders paid during the same time was 7,627,716, amounting in value to.. $104,219,871 63

To which must be added the amount of orders repaid to remitters...... 704,981 96

Making the total amount of payments and repayments............................. 104,924,853 C.

The excess of issues over payments was 150,975 74

The total amount of fees paid by the public to postmasters for the issues of domestic orders was.. $81,732 73

The foregoing figures show an increase of $4,722,950.52, or 4.71 per cent., in the amount of orders issued; an increase of $4,758,870.83, or 4.75 per cent., in the amount of orders paid and repaid, and a gain of $50,279.95, or 5.49 per cent., in the amount of fees received over the like transactions of the previous year. The domestic money orders issued during the year averaged $13.71 each, the average being about 15 cents smaller than that of the previous year, and the average fee upon each was $12\frac{42}{100}$ cents, being $\frac{7}{10}$ of a cent less than the average fee for the year preceding.

As in previous years, in compliance with the request of the War Department to insure correct payment, money orders issued by the postmaster at Washington, D. C., to the Paymaster-General of the Army for the payment of claims against the United States for services rendered by colored soldiers of the late war have been transmitted through the office of the superintendent of the money-order system to the paying postmasters, instead of being mailed, as are other money orders, by the remitter directly to the beneficiaries. The amount of orders thus transmitted through the office of the superintendent during the past year was $14,512.45.

DUPLICATE MONEY ORDERS.

Duplicates of domestic money orders to the number of 18,391 were issued by the department during the last fiscal year. The number issued during the previous year was 20,647. Such orders are issued without additional charge. They are given in cases where the originals have been destroyed before payment, or lost in transmission, or from some unknown cause have failed to reach the payee, or when, through the operation of law, the originals have become invalid because not presented for payment until more than a year from date, or are invalidated by a second indorsement; also, to the remitters and in their favor in cases where the payment of the originals, drawn in favor of the proprietors or agents of fraudulent lotteries, or of persons engaged in conducting other schemes or devices for obtaining money through the mails by means of false or fraudulent pretenses, has been prohibited by the Postmaster-General in pursuance of the provisions of section 4041 of the Revised Statutes of the United States. A classified statement of the number of duplicates issued during the last fiscal year will appear in Table B, page 413, of the Appendix.

TRANSFER OF MONEY-ORDER FUNDS.

At many offices the amount of money orders payable is continuously or occasionally greater than the amount of orders issued. Postmasters at such offices are authorized to transfer funds from the postage to the money-order account for the purpose of meeting the demand for the payment of money orders. In cases where the postage funds are insufficient or not available for the purpose at offices east of the Rocky Mountains, postmasters are allowed each a credit to a designated amount with the postmaster at New York and instructed to draw upon him as the exigencies of the money-order business may require. In like cases in the Pacific States and Territories postmasters are supplied with funds by the postmaster at San Francisco, Cal., or the postmaster at Portland, Oreg. The drafts drawn by postmasters during the year against the credits allowed them, as stated, with the postmaster at New York, amounted to $9,654,220.34, while during the same period postmasters on the Pacific slope who required assistance to pay orders drawn upon their offices were furnished with funds to the amount of $263,702 by the postmaster at San Francisco, and to the amount of $25,936 by the postmaster at Portland, Oreg. The transfers made by postmasters from the postage to the money-order account amounted to $895,908.35, and the transfers made by them from the money order to the postage account to $431,403.28, leaving at the close of the year a balance in favor of the latter account of $464,505.07, which sum has been duly refunded by a deposit made September 27, 1881, in the Treasury for the postal service.

REMITTANCES OF SURPLUS MONEY-ORDER FUNDS.

During the past year the sum of $95,326,072.31 surplus money-order funds, i. e., funds which had accumulated from the excess of issues over payments at the remitting offices, was transmitted for deposit by postmasters to certain of the larger money-order offices designated as depositories.

LOST REMITTANCES.

Seventy-seven cases of alleged lost remittances of surplus money-order funds, amounting to $10,753, as shown in Table C, page 414, were under investigation during the year. Seventeen of these, involving the amount of $3,452, were cases undergoing investigation at the close of the previous year, and five, in which the amount involved was $517, were cases of loss alleged to have occurred during that year, but not reported to the department until after June 30, 1880. Allowances were granted during the year, after due investigation on account of losses of this kind, aggregating $167 to the credit of the postmasters by whom the remittances were made, which sum constitutes the item of "lost remittances" under the head of Revenues and Expenses of the Domestic Money-Order System, stated below. Claims for credit to the amount of $1,817 on account of the loss of nine of the alleged remittances were disallowed, and $2,334 of the losses reported were recovered by post-office inspectors in the service of the department, while in three instances, in which the amounts together aggregated the sum of $486, it was ascertained that the remittances had been delayed in transit and had finally reached their destination. Thus, as is minutely set forth in the aforementioned Table C, thirty-four of the total number of cases, aggregating $4,804, were disposed of during the year ended June 30, 1881, and forty-three, in which the claims together amounted to $5,949, remained unsettled at that date.

MONEY ORDERS ERRONEOUSLY PAID.

During the year claims were filed in thirty-six cases on account of alleged improper payment of money orders. The amount of all these claims was $767.07. Their number, compared with the total number of payments made during the year, s as 1 to 211,881.

Ninety-nine cases of alleged improperly paid money orders, amounting to $2,153.49, were investigated during the year. Sixty-three of them were cases of payments made during previous years, and of these twenty-two were not brought to the notice of the department until after June 30, 1880. In thirty-three instances the amounts, the total of which was $477.75, were recovered by post-office inspectors and paid over to the rightful owners; in seven cases, in which the orders altogether amounted to $84.15, the paying postmasters were, after due investigation, held responsible for the erroneous payments; in four, where erroneous payment was directly attributable to carelessness on the part of remitters, payees, or indorsees, they were required to sustain the loss, $124; in nine, the loss, $268.88 altogether, was assumed by the department, the paying postmaster having been found not at fault; and in eleven it was ascertained that the orders, amounting to $236.52, had been originally paid to the proper persons. Thirty-five claims, involving the payment of $962.19, were pending at the close of the year. Each of these cases of alleged improper payment will be found separately reported in the table marked D, page 417.

REVENUES AND EXPENSES OF THE MONEY-ORDER SYSTEM,

The receipts and expenditures of the domestic money-order system for the fiscal year ended June 30, 1881, are reported by the Auditor as follows:

RECEIPTS.

Fees on orders issued	$966,722 73
Premiums, &c.	1,049 16
	967,772 92

EXPENDITURES.

Commissions and clerk-hire	$607,190 19
Lost remittances	167 50
Bad debts	3,602 25
Incidental expenses	104,498 82
	715,458 29

Excess of receipts over expenditures, being gross revenue | 252,314 64

During the past year allowances for clerk-hire, amounting in the aggregate to $166,528.23, against $151,596.82 in 1879-'80, were made for certain of the larger offices out of the surplus of commissions accruing from the issue and payment of money orders at such offices, that is to say, in each case out of the excess over and above such amount of money-order commissions as accruing at his office and added to his fixed annual salary made the postmaster's entire compensation for the year $4,000, the limit fixed by law, except in the case of the postmaster at New York City. These allowances are included under the above head of "commissions and clerk-hire."

· The item of "incidental expenses" includes the cost of books, blanks, and printing furnished to the Money-Order Office of the Post-Office Department by the Public Printer for distribution to postmasters and for use by the latter in the transaction of their money-order business, viz, $68,406.23, which amount was paid during the year directly out of the proceeds of the money-order business. Of this sum, $19,406.97 was paid for material and work ordered from the Public Printer during the previous fiscal year.

CAUSE OF REDUCTION OF GROSS REVENUE.

The amount of gross revenue is found to be $5,260.44, or $2\frac{7}{10}$ per cent. less than the gross revenue for the year ended June 30th, 1880, notwithstanding the fact that a comparison of the receipts for one year with those of the other shows that the amount received during the last year is the larger by $48,681.35.

This falling off is attributable in part to a readjustment of allowances for clerk-hire, which for the year ended June 30, 1880, amounted to $16\frac{7}{10}$ per cent., and for the year ended June 30, 1881, to $17\frac{22}{100}$ per cent. of the total amount of fees received, respectively, during each of those years. In part it may be referred to an increase in the amount of "bad debts," under which head the Auditor this year reports $3,692.28, against $1,011.06 the previous year. In a larger measure it is due to heavier requisitions on the Public Printer, involving an expenditure, for books and blanks, of $25,240.48 over and above the amount paid for like supplies during the preceding year. This additional expenditure was necessary for the replenishment of exhausted stocks of books and blanks for the use of postmasters. The readjustment of allowances for clerk-hire was made, as usual, upon the basis of the number of transactions during the preceding year at the offices to which the allowances were apportioned.

In the appendix (page 413) will be found a tabular statement (A showing the number of money-order offices in operation, with the amount of orders issued, of orders paid, fees received, expenses, and revenue each year since the establishment of the system, November 1, 1864, to June 30, 1881.

INTERNATIONAL MONEY-ORDER BUSINESS—NEW CONVENTIONS.

The conventions for the exchange of money orders between the United States, on the one hand, and Switzerland, Great Britain and Ireland, the German Empire, Canada and Newfoundland, and France and Algeria, on the other, have remained in force, without alteration, since the close of the fiscal year ended June 30, 1880. A convention has recently been concluded for the establishment of a like system of exchange between the United States and the island of Jamaica, to go into operation on the 1st of January next, and negotiations for a similar purpose are now in progress between the United States and the British Australasian Colonies of Victoria, New South Wales, Tasmania, and New Zealand.

Prior to date of the last annual report certain modifications of the original money-order convention between the United States and the Kingdom of Italy had been agreed upon by the postal administrations of the two countries. A new convention embodying these modifications went into effect on the 1st of October, 1880, after having been ratified by the proper authorities. Its provisions greatly simplify the method, besides lessening the expense, of conducting the exchange of money orders between the two countries, and tend still further to secure uniformity of system in our entire international money-order correspondence.

By the terms of this new convention, a copy of which is hereto annexed, the rate of commission to be paid by the postal administration of each of the contracting countries, on orders issued within it, to the postal administration of the other, was lowered sufficiently to warrant a reduction, which has been made, of the charges for the issue of Italian orders in this country from two and a half to one and a half per cent. on the maximum amounts of the different divisions of the scale of fees for such orders.

On the 30th day of June, 1880, there were in the United States 185 Swiss, 1,193 British, 706 German, 435 Canadian, 143 Italian, and 1,193 French international money-order offices. At present 1,347 offices are authorized to transact British, German, Canadian, Italian, and French international money-order business, and 185 the Swiss business. It is intended that every office transacting one kind of international money-order business shall issue and pay international money orders of all kinds, upon the ratification of a proposed new convention with Switzerland, the terms of which will admit of the use of the same forms and methods in the transaction of Swiss as in the conduct of British, German, Canadian, Italian, and French international money-order business.

EXCHANGE OF MONEY ORDERS WITH SWITZERLAND.

The number of Swiss international orders issued in the United States during the year was 7,521, amounting to $145,749.94, of which amount $485.56 were repaid to the remitters; and the number paid in the United States was 3,630, amounting to $109,371.31. The fees received for the orders issued in the United States amounted to $4,106.90. These statements show, in comparison with the totals of similar transactions during the preceding year, an increase of $15,148.38, or nearly 12 per cent., in the issues; an increase of $30,710.23, or rather more than 39 per cent., in the payments; and an increase of $371.40, or nearly 10 per cent., in fees.

EXCHANGE OF MONEY ORDERS WITH GREAT BRITAIN.

The number of British international orders issued in the United States was 145,244, amounting to $2,001,989.65, of which amount $4,662.91 were repaid to the remitters; and the number paid in the United States was 21,169, amounting to $360,736.71. The fees received for the orders issued in the United States amounted to $58,225.10. By comparing these amounts with those representing the aggregate of British international money-order business transacted during the year ended June 30, 1880, there is shown an increase of $376,046.70, or about 23 per cent., in the issues; an increase of $22,646.26, or nearly 7 per cent., in the payments, and an increase of $11,236.20, or nearly 24 per cent., in fees.

EXCHANGE OF MONEY ORDERS WITH GERMANY.

The number of German international orders issued in the United States was 84,291, amounting to $1,395,725.83, of which amount $6,350.41 were repaid to the remitters; and the number paid in the United States was 28,007, amounting to $825,021.07. The fees received for the orders issued in the United States amounted to $24,904.60. Compared with the figures representing the business of the previous year, these amounts show an increase of $381,263.94, or nearly 38 per cent., in the issues, and an increase of $187,864.04, or a little over 29 per cent., in the payments, but a decrease of $895.75, or about 3½ per cent., in fees. This decrease is attributable to the adoption of a new scale of fees April 1, 1880.

EXCHANGE OF MONEY ORDERS WITH CANADA.

The number of Canadian international money orders issued in the United States was 40,008, amounting to $827,756.92, of which amount $3,826.94 were repaid to the remitters; and the number paid in the United States was 38,375, amounting to $611,163.69. The fees received for the orders issued in the United States amounted to $14,058.65. A comparison of this business with that of the preceding year exhibits an increase of $316,140.34, or nearly 62 per cent., in the issues; of $188,434.02, or nearly 45 per cent., in the payments, and of $2,485.45, or nearly 21½ per cent., in fees.

EXCHANGE OF MONEY ORDERS WITH ITALY.

The number of Italian international orders issued in the United States was 9,385, amounting to $239,673.95, of which amount $1,031.99 were repaid to the remitters; and the number paid in the United States was 528, amounting to $13,548.15. The fees received for the orders issued in the United States amounted to $4,497.90. As compared with the transactions of the previous year, these figures show an increase of $71,820.39, or nearly 43 per cent., in the issues; a decrease of $242.92, or about 1½ per cent., in the payments, and an increase of $15.65, or a little more than ½ of 1 per cent. in fees.

EXCHANGE OF MONEY ORDERS WITH FRANCE.

The number of French international orders issued in the United States was 4,649, amounting to $73,030.09, of which amount $817.14 were repaid to the remitters; and the number paid in the United States was 1,676, amounting to $38,380.22. The fees received for the orders issued in the United States amounted to $1,333.30. The system of exchange of money orders between the United States and France did not go into operation until the 1st of April, 1880.

REVENUE FROM INTERNATIONAL MONEY ORDERS.

The length of time required for the adjustment of the yearly accounts between the Auditor for this department and the proper accounting officers of the several foreign countries exchanging money orders with the United States precludes the incorporation herein of a report of the revenues derived from the transaction of international money-order business during the last year. A detailed statement, however, of the receipts, expenditures, and revenues for the year ended June 30, 1880, of the Swiss, British, German, Canadian, Italian, and French international money-order business will be found in the Auditor's report hereto annexed, page 685.

From this statement it appears that the revenue, for the year in question, from the Swiss international money-order business was $2,200.82; from the British, $22,987.10; from the German, $8,250.13; from the Canadian, $7,271.40; from the Italian, $2,656.88. In the transaction of French international money-order business during the three months ended June 30, 1880, a net loss of $99.58 was sustained consequent upon the outlay incident to the establishment of the system. The system of exchange of money-orders with France, as before stated, did not go into operation until the 1st of April, 1880, three months before the termination of the period embraced in the Auditor's statement of account which includes the above item of "net loss." Deducting this loss from the aggregate net revenue derived from the Swiss, British, German, Canadian, and Italian business, for the year ended June 30, 1880, there remained a balance of net revenue amounting to $43,266.75 from the exchange of money-orders with foreign countries during that year.

GENERAL FINANCIAL RESULTS OF THE MONEY-ORDER BUSINESS.

The gross number of domestic and international money orders issued in the United States during the last fiscal year was 7,954,330, of the aggregate value of $109,759,695.73. The fees thereon amounted to $1,073,859.20. The whole number of domestic and international money orders paid in the United States during the same period was 7,721,095, amounting to $106,178,092.80, to which should be added the amount of

60 Ab

... ... If deemed expedient, in the ... ... for example seven ... ... during which the amount of any money order would ... available to the owner thereof, and beyond which the amount of all orders unpaid would accrue to the United States.

POSTAL ORDERS FOR LESS THAN FIVE DOLLARS.

Although the money order fulfils every reasonable expectation of remitter and payee where the amount sent is considerable, a strong and growing demand has arisen, since the withdrawal of fractional currency from circulation, for some device by which amounts under five dollars could be transmitted by mail at less cost than at present. I desire to call special attention to the plan proposed by the superintendent, for the transmission of sums less than five dollars by means of an order of a new form, to be termed "Postal Order," in which the written application and the advice, which is the chief element of expense as well as of security, are to be dispensed with, so that these orders may be issued more expeditiously and at cheaper rates than money-orders. The details of this plan will be found in page 446, in the appendix to this report.

The chief and distinguishing features of the proposed postal orders, besides the absence of the application and the advice, are these, viz: as a complete safeguard against alteration of the amount to be paid, the figures which represent that amount are to be punched from three rows of figures upon the right of the order, as for example, if a postal order be issued for $2.34, the 2 is to be punched out of the first or dollars column, the 3 from the second or dimes column, and the 4 from the third or cents column. Again, no record is to be kept of the name of the remitter or of the payee, of a postal order which is to be payable to the bearer at a designated money-order office, at any time within three months from the month of issue. If presented after the expiration of three months from the last day of the month of issue it is to be cashed only upon payment of an additional fee, equal to the original fee, for every three months or portion of three months in excess of that period; it is to be sold to the public for a fee of three cents, and no duplicate can be issued of a postal order lost in the mails or otherwise.

As stated above, this postal order is to be confined to sums under $5; and is not intended as a substitute for money orders of like small amounts, but is to be issued concurrently with the ordinary money order, so that a remitter who desires to send a small sum by mail will have the option of purchasing a postal order, for 3 cents, of which, if it be lost, a duplicate cannot be issued, or a money order for the same amount, for 5 cents, for which, in case of loss, a duplicate is granted. In the one case the risk is taken by the remitter, if he chooses to do so; in the other case, the department assumes the entire responsibility for the transmission and payment of the amount to a designated payee.

orders be fixed at three cents for each transaction instead of the present rate of one-third of the fees received and one-fourth of one per cent. on the gross amount of orders paid. As the labor of issuing and of paying a small order is as great as that of issuing and paying a large one, it not infrequently happens that postmasters who issue and pay orders for small sums mainly, receive less compensation for the same amount of work than others who issue and pay orders chiefly of the higher denominations.

UNCLAIMED MONEY-ORDER FUNDS.

The amount of unclaimed money orders, domestic and foreign, at the close of the fiscal year ended June 30, 1881, is estimated by the Auditor as $1,250,000. (See Appendix, page 410.) At the end of the same year the approximate amount due by the United States to foreign countries on account of the exchange of money orders with them was $330,000, and the money-order system was liable at the same time for the payment to the Treasury for the service of the Post-Office Department of the amount of the revenue from the international money-order business for the fiscal year ended June 30, 1881, estimated at $50,000. But the total available amount of money-order funds in the sub-treasury at New York City on June 30, 1881, after deducting the amount due the postage account for transfers from the postage to the money-order account, and also the amount of the annual revenue for the last year, was $1,561,654.37. It is apparent, therefore, that the total unclaimed amount as estimated by the Auditor, $1,250,000, could not be turned over to the Treasury for the service of the Post-Office Department without detriment to the money-order system, because, in that event, there would remain in the hands of the assistant treasurer only $311,654.37, a sum insufficient by $68,345.63 to pay the indebtedness to foreign countries and the revenue from the international money-order business for the last fiscal year. The amount representing this deficit forms part of the sum of $1,427,-108.59, which at date of June 30, 1881, was in the hands of postmasters in the form of reserves to meet the payment of orders and in remittances in transit, this latter sum of $1,427,108.59 forming the larger portion of the working capital of the money-order system. There is

NO PROVISION OF LAW UNDER WHICH THIS UNCLAIMED MONEY CAN NOW BE DISPOSED OF.

It would seem to be expedient that a portion of it should be turned over to the Treasury for the service of the Post-Office Department. The superintendent of the money-order system suggests that it would be well to retain in the hands of the assistant treasurer, for the operations of the service, a sum equal to the amount of all unpaid money-orders during a period of five years next preceding the commencement of each fiscal year. It rarely happens that a money order more than five years' old is presented for payment. If deemed expedient, in the interest of payees of money-orders, a longer period, for example seven or ten years, might be fixed by Congress, during which the amount of any money order would be payable to the owner thereof, and beyond which the amount of all orders unpaid would accrue to the United States.

POSTAL ORDERS FOR LESS THAN FIVE DOLLARS.

Although the money order fulfills every reasonable expectation of remitter and payee where the amount sent is considerable, a strong and growing demand has arisen, since the withdrawal of fractional currency from circulation, for some device by which amounts under five dollars could be transmitted by mail at less cost than at present. I desire to call special attention to the plan proposed by the superintendent, for the transmission of sums less than five dollars by means of an order of a new form, to be termed "Postal Order," in which the written application and the advice, which is the chief element of expense as well as of security, are to be dispensed with, so that these orders may be issued more expeditiously and at cheaper rates than money-orders. The details of this plan will be found on page 403, in the appendix to this report.

The chief and distinguishing features of the proposed postal orders, besides the absence of the application and the advice, are these, viz: as a complete safeguard against alteration of the amount to be paid, the figures which represent that amount are to be punched from three rows of figures upon the right of the order, as, for example, if a postal order be issued for $2.84, the 2 is to be punched out of the first or dollars column, the 8 from the second or dimes column, and the 4 from the third or cents column. Again, no record is to be kept of the name of the remitter or of the payee of a postal order which is to be payable to the bearer at a designated money-order office, at any time within three months from the month of issue. If presented after the expiration of three months from the last day of the month of issue it is to be cashed only upon payment of an additional fee, equal to the original fee, for every three months or portion of three months in excess of that period; it is to be sold to the public for a fee of three cents, and no duplicate can be issued of a postal order lost in the mails or otherwise.

As stated above, this postal order is to be confined to sums under $5; and is not intended as a substitute for money orders of like small amounts, but is to be issued concurrently with the ordinary money order, so that a remitter who desires to send a small sum by mail will have the option of purchasing a postal order, for 3 cents, of which, if it be lost, a duplicate cannot be issued, or a money order for the same amount, for 5 cents, for which, in case of loss, a duplicate is granted. In the one case the risk is taken by the remitter, if he chooses to do so; in the other case, the department assumes the entire responsibility for the transmission and payment of the amount to a designated payee.

Postal orders are to be printed upon thin, bank-note paper, from engraved plates, with every precaution against counterfeiting, and are to be of such a size as to be conveniently transmitted in an ordinary letter-size envelope.

For making small remittances by mail the postal order would answer the purpose for which fractional currency was formerly largely used and for which coin is not suitable, while at the same time this order could not be conveniently employed as a circulating medium, because it would be issued, not, like fractional currency, for round sums, but for all possible amounts under $5, and would be invalid if not presented for payment within three months from the month of issue.

I am of the opinion that the superintendent's plan is entirely practicable and well calculated to meet the popular demand, and that appropriate legislation to carry out the project would be very acceptable to the public.

NEW BUILDING NEEDED FOR THE MONEY-ORDER SYSTEM IN WASHINGTON.

At the last session of Congress an act was passed authorizing the Postmaster-General "to take the necessary steps to rent a suitable building, or buildings, for the use of the money-order office of the Post-Office Department and of the money-order division of the Auditor of the Treasury for the Post-Office Department," provided "that the annual rental of such building or buildings shall not exceed $5,000, and the cost of the necessary furniture for the same shall not exceed $10,000, and that these expenses shall be paid out of the proceeds of the money-order business.

A committee, consisting of three officers of this department and two from the Treasury, were appointed by me in April last to inquire into the matter of renting a building, or buildings, for the purpose set forth in the act. This committee reported under date of June 4, 1881, that owing to the failure of Congress to make provision for watchmen and laborers to take proper care of such building, and to perform the manual labor required therein, and for the cost of fuel, gas, and other expenses of a miscellaneous character, the building contemplated in the act of Congress, even if rented, could not be made available for occupancy, and recommended that the renting of such building be delayed until after Congress shall have made, upon application therefor, provision for these necessary items of expense.

In a final report, made November 4, 1881, which will be found upon page 423 of the appendix, the committee state that no structure well suited to the requirements of the money-order service can be obtained within a convenient distance from this department, and recommend that Congress be asked to make an appropriation of $150,000 to defray the cost of a plain and substantial brick edifice of sufficient dimensions to meet those requirements, to be erected under the direction of the Supervising Architect of the Treasury, in some suitable locality in the immediate vicinity of the Post-Office Department.

I fully concur with the committee in this recommendation, and in view of the overcrowded condition of the general post-office building. respectfully urge that speedy action be taken by Congress in the premises.

The committee, furthermore, call attention to the fact that the net revenue arising from the transactions of the money-order system during the two fiscal years ended respectively June 30, 1880, and June 30. 1881, which has been duly deposited in the Treasury, for the service of the Post-Office Department, amounted, in the aggregate, to $225,981.13, a sum considerably in excess of the above estimate of the cost of a building which would, in the opinion of the committee, not only meet the present wants of the money-order system, but would accommodate its rapidly increasing business for at least ten years to come.

POSTAL SAVINGS DEPOSITORIES.

As early as 1871 a recommendation was made by one of my predecessors for the establishment of a system of savings depositories in connection with this department, and in several subsequent annual reports this recommendation has been renewed.

December 18, 1873, "A bill to establish and maintain a National Savings Depository as a branch of the Post-Office Department" was introduced in the House of Representatives by Hon. Horace Maynard, of Tennessee. From time to time since that date the measure has occupied the attention of Congress, and many bills have been introduced. but without securing definite action.

A system of post-office savings-banks went into operation in Great Britain September 16, 1861. At the close of its first complete year, the number of open accounts was 178,495, and the amount standing to the credit of depositors was £1,698,221, being an average of £9 10s. 3d. to each account. Since that time the institution has grown rapidly in popular favor, and on the 31st of December, 1879, the number of outstanding accounts had risen to 1,988,477, and the amount of the credit of depositors to £32,012,134, an average of £16 1s. 11¾d. to each. The interest paid to depositors is only two and one-half per centum, a rate so low as practically to exclude the post-office savings-banks from competition with other banking institutions, as the history of the rise and progress of savings institutions in Great Britain has demonstrated, the object of the government being to offer to the depositor security rather than profitable investment for his earnings, and to promote frugality, steady habits, and consequent thrift among the laboring classes.

My predecessor, in his last annual report, said that in the larger portion of the United States there are no savings depositories, and are not likely to be; and he expressed the opinion that, to the people of these parts, the use of the post-office for this purpose would be a real boon. That it would be an advantage to the patrons of the institution, that deposits would be available at any depository post-office in the country, "an important consideration with a people so migratory as ours." He further expressed the belief that the system would interfere little with the business of the savings-banks, but would rather absorb funds not now deposited in them. He thought that the patronage of the government would not be sensibly increased, since the system would be conducted by persons already in the public service, with no considerable addition to their number.

In these views I concur. It is my earnest conviction that a system of this description, if adopted, would inure more than almost any other measure of public importance to the benefit of the working people of the United States, and I commend it to the favorable consideration of Congress.

STATISTICS OF INLAND TRANSPORTATION.

On the 30th day of June, 1881, there were 5,156 contractors for transportation of mails on inland routes.

There were 2,129 special offices, each with a mail carrier whose pay must not exceed the net postal yield of the office.

There were in operation 11,592 routes (of which 1,194 were railroad routes, showing an increase of 76 routes of this class since the last annual report), aggregating in length 344.006 miles, and in annual cost $19,323-890; adding the compensation of railway post-office clerks, route-agents, mail-route messengers, local agents, and mail-messengers, amounting to $3,872,142, the total annual cost was $23,196,032.

The service was divided as follows:

Railroad routes: Length 91,569 miles; annual transportation,103,521,-229 miles; annual cost, $11,613,368 (including $1,364,107 for railway post-office car service), about 11.22 cents per mile.

Steamboat routes: Length, 21,138 miles; annual transportation, 5,046-507 miles; annual cost, $753,167, about 14.92 cents per mile.

"Star" routes, on which the mails are required to be conveyed "with celerity, certainty, and security:" Length, 231,299 miles; annual transportation, 79,557,296 miles; annual cost, $6,957,355, about 8.74 cents per mile.

There were 5,014 offices supplied by mail-messengers, at an annual cost of $763,341.

The railroad routes were increased in length 6,249 miles, and in cost $1,114,382.

The steamboat routes were decreased in length 2,182 miles, and in cost $134,054.

The "star" routes were decreased in length 3,949 miles, and in cost $364,144.

Since the last annual report, there was an increase in the total length of routes of 118 miles; in annual transportation, 9,888,036 miles; in annual cost, $616,184. Adding the increase in cost of railway post-office clerks, route-agents, mail-route messengers, local agents, and mail-messengers, amounting to $323,864, the total increase in cost was $940,048.

The founders of our government intended

THE POSTAL SERVICE TO BE SELF-SUPPORTING.

The guardianship of the postal revenues was assumed in order that the whole power and all the machinery of government might be employed to enforce the strictest accountability. That the people might have the greatest possible advantages from an institution peculiarly their own, at the least possible cost, all competition was forbidden. To preserve with sacred inviolability the communications intrusted to the mail, the sovereignty of the government was to be everywhere present.

For more than half a century the wisdom of the fathers of the Republic was unquestioned, and the Post-Office Department was administered in accordance with their theory. So well was this theory understood that the sole limitation placed by Congress upon the discretion of the Postmaster-General in regard to the transportation of the mails was that he should simply keep the expenses within the revenues. The act of 1792 says the Postmaster-General "shall provide for carrying the mail," and "shall defray the expense thereof, together with all other expenses arising on the collection and management of the revenue of the Post-Office" out of the current receipts of the service. He was to determine the manner and frequency of carrying the mail, but he was required to "have

DUE REGARD TO THE PRODUCTIVENESS" OF THE VARIOUS POST-ROADS.

That Congress might exercise some supervision over the extensions of post-roads the act of 1797 required the Postmaster-General "to report annually to Congress every post-road which shall not, after the second year from its establishment, have produced one-third of the expense of carrying the mail on the same." The act of 1814 excepted from the provisions of the act of 1797 post-roads necessary to furnish mail communications to county towns which had no mail; but the act of 1825 required the Postmaster-General to discontinue all post-roads which, after three successive years, failed to yield one-fourth the expense of carrying the mail on the same, provided they were not necessary to connect other profitable routes, or to supply county towns. Every enactment of Congress down to 1845 adhered to the original theory, and contemplated the management of the business of the Post-Office Department upon

BUSINESS PRINCIPLES.

The act of 1845 made the first reduction in letter postage; and, to provide for any deficiency which might result temporarily therefrom, Congress appropriated the sum of $450,000, which the act of appropriation said might be applied "under the direction of the Postmaster-General, to supply any deficiency in the regular revenues from postage in the same manner as the revenues of said department are now by law applied." The same act provided however, "that the amount of expenditures for the Post Office Department shall not in the entire aggregate, exclusive of salaries of officers, clerks, and messengers of the general Post-Office, and the contingent fund of the same, exceed the annual amount of four million five hundred thousand dollars." This restriction not only prevented any extravagance, because the total expenditures, including the items excluded by the above quoted proviso, ordinarily ranged from four millions to four millions and a half a year; but it evidenced the purpose of Congress not to depart from the theory that the postal service must be self-supporting.

The act of March 3, 1847, which appropriated annually the sum of $200,000 "in compensation for such mail service as may be performed for the several departments of the Government," was a recognition of the principle that the postal fund was a sacred one, and that the transportation even of the official mail of the government ought not to be a charge upon it. Every argument that has been made to abolish or restrict the franking privilege has been based upon the same broad principle.

From 1790—the earliest date at which the exact financial status of the Post-Office Department is given—down to 1838, the excess of expenditures over receipts occurred rarely, and the deficiency was always trifling. In 1838 railway mail service began; and the department from that time to this has been engaged in an unsuccessful struggle to adjust the pay for this class of service upon just and equitable rules. There was also, as one of the ablest Postmaster-Generals has said, about this time,

"A TOO RAPID EXPANSION OF THE SERVICE,"

which was "the first manifested tendency to a permanent excess of expenditure." This was, however, soon checked, and the department again brought upon a solid business basis. The reduction of the rates of letter postage, in 1845, caused some reduction of receipts; but with the exception of 1848, when the expenditures exceeded the receipts by $165,772, the balance at the close of each fiscal year, till 1852, was in favor of the department.

THE BEGINNING OF DEFICIENCIES.

The rates of letter postage were reduced by the act of March 3, 1851, from five to three cents. There were also reductions made for second and third-class matter. The effect of these reductions was a very much greater diminution of the revenues than was expected; at the same time it was found necessary to readjust the commissions of postmasters which sensibly increased the cost of collecting the revenues of the department. But there was at this date

A RADICAL DEPARTURE

from the theory which the founders of our government adopted, and which had up to that time been tenaciously adhered to. Section 7 of the act of March 3, 1851, provided "that no post-office now in existence shall be discontinued, nor shall the mail service on any mail route in any of the States or Territories be discontinued or diminished, in consequence of any diminution of the revenues that may result from this act; and it shall be the duty of the Postmaster-General to establish new post-offices, and place the mail service on any new mail routes established, or that may hereafter be established, in the same manner as though this act had not passed."

This did not repeal the act of 1825, requiring the Postmaster-General to discontinue all routes not producing after three years one-fourth the cost of maintaining them. It was not designed to repeal that law; it was a mere temporary provision; no post-office was to be discontinued, and the mail service was not to suffer because "of any diminution of the revenues that may result from this act." Nevertheless, the discontinuance of routes because they did not yield one-fourth the expense of maintaining them gradually ceased, and the law of 1825 in this particular became a dead letter.

The principle recognized in the act of 1847, that

THE GOVERNMENT'S MAILS

ought not to be a charge upon the postal fund, was still more positively recognized in the act of 1851. Not only was an annual appropriation of $500,000 made to pay "for the mail service performed for the two houses of Congress and the other departments and offices of the government," but the money appropriated by the act of 1847, which had not been drawn from the Treasury, was made available and the appropriation continued. By these two enactments Congress solemnly recognized the great principle underlying the establishment of the Post-Office Department that the revenues collected through postal charges are not to be used for any other purpose than that for which they are assessed and collected, namely, to afford the people the best possible postal facilities at the least possible cost. Not even the government, which assumed the control and administration of the postal fund, has an equitable right to charge it with the cost of performing its official mail service. However, from 1851 dates the policy which enlarged very much

THE SCOPE OF THE POST-OFFICE DEPARTMENT.

The opportunity which was then offered for increased expenditures of money in extending the mail service was a very favorable one. The recently acquired territory on the Pacific coast had, by the discovery of gold, assumed the utmost importance. The tide of emigration westward received a new impetus. The populous States east of the Mississippi River were separated from the new Eldorado by a vast stretch of uninhabited country and by what was then supposed to be an almost impassable range of mountains. The cost of supplying the rapidly-accumulating population on the Pacific coast with mails was necessarily great. What was practically a branch post-office department had to be established in San Francisco. The advertisement and letting of mail routes had to be delegated to a special agent of the department clothed with extraordinary power for this purpose. The great distance from the seat of government, and the delay in communicating with the department's agents, incident to a long sea voyage, crippled the efforts of the government in establishing a mail service. Private enterprise, always alert to seize opportunities which promise large returns upon small investments, was equal to this occasion, and

THE EXPRESS MAILS OF CALIFORNIA

were the result. The miners depended largely upon the private express companies, not only for their necessary supplies, but as safe mediums of transmitting their accumulations to friends or a place of safety. It was but natural that the general office of the express company at San Francisco should become the address of all the adventurers who flocked to the golden shores of the Pacific. The express company readily undertook the task of delivering letters thus accumulating at their office, because it was very profitable. They could charge what they pleased. This was the origin of what is known as Wells, Fargo & Co.'s postal service in California—an institution to which the people have become so accustomed that notwithstanding the acknowledged efficiency of the government service, they still very largely patronize it. The building of the Panama Railroad did not decrease the cost of transporting the mails to California. That company had a monopoly of transportation across the isthmus and regulated its own charges. For several years the government was at the mercy of the railroad company. Then followed other mail routes by way of Tehuantepec and across Mexico.

ADVENTURERS AND SCHEMERS

swarmed about the corridors of the Capitol and labored session after session of Congress for special contracts. The great overland routes were established, and vast sums were annually drawn from the Treasury for this costly branch of the service.

It is not my purpose to discuss the wisdom of the administration of the Post-Office Department during this period. It was an unusual occasion. It was undoubtedly the duty of the government to furnish to these outlying settlements the speediest and safest postal facilities possible. It must be remembered also that Congress assumed the entire responsibility of the

GREAT OVERLAND MAIL SERVICE,

and established the routes, and prescribed the service and the rates of compensation therefor. The only discretion left to the Postmaster-General was the determination, in the first instance, of the one most advantageous among the several routes suggested. And, moreover, the cost of operating these large and expensive routes was not made a charge upon the regular postal fund. The appropriation was at first specific, and the accounts kept separate in the Post-Office Department as well as in the Treasury. But little by little the departure from the long-established principle of the department grew more and more radical, and

THE ANNUAL DEFICIENCY

kept pace, till in the year 1860 the expenditures exceeded the receipts by more than ten and a half million of dollars. The people gradually became, in a manner, accustomed to the enormous expenditures of the department. The contractors, who grew rich at the expense of the government, found it comparatively easy, and probably very profitable, to defy a Postmaster-General disposed to economize and by degrees bring back the department to the honest business basis upon which our fathers had established it. It became the fashion to go to Congress and lobby through bills establishing routes and prescribing the pay for such and such service thereon. If the department attempted to hold contractors to a strict performance of their contracts, and to exact penalties for the non-performance of service, they resorted to Congress for relief, and seldom failed to obtain it.

THE INEVITABLE RESULT.

The result was of course inevitable. In this as in every other case, the departure once made from a wise and prudent practice, and every species of extravagance necessarily follows. It is not the immediate evil that is to be feared the most, but the train of other and still greater resultant evils. The condition of the department in 1860 had become alarming. The deficit was $10,652,542.59, and this enormous deficiency was, in spite of a late but honest effort, which was made toward the close of Buchanan's administration, to reform existing abuses and curb lavish expenditures.

THE SITUATION IN 1859.

Postmaster-General Holt, in his annual report for 1859, thus eloquently depicted the situation and earnestly recommended reform. He said:

This department cannot much longer occupy its present equivocal position. If not allowed to return to the principles on which it was constructed in its earlier and better days—the days alike of its independence, its efficiency, and its renown—borne down by the pressure of the existing course of legislation, it will ultimately become an established burden on the national revenues. The first step which would probably follow thereafter would be for Congress in creating and adjusting the principal post-routes to declare what should be the compensation of the contractors. This would open an almost illimitable field for mercenary intrigue and spoliation. An approach to the inauguration of this system has already been made, and the results are before the country. Since 1853 Congress has interposed and made extra allowances to contractors, amounting to $649,161.22, beyond what the department regarded them as entitled to receive under their contracts, and beyond what it was believed the postal service demanded or required. It has also fixed the compensation for the semi-weekly overland mail at $600,000 per annum, though the receipts from the route are but $27,229.94, and for the transportation of the California mails via the isthmus it paid annually $738,250, though the same service, less that from San Francisco to Astoria and San Diego, under a recent contract with the department is now performed at the rate of $351,000 per annum, with an arrangement for its further reduction. These are fair illustrations of the fruits which naturally, if not inevitably, follow from transferring the contract bureau of this department to the halls of Congress. Should this step be taken, the department being thus completely dependent and sustained by an exhaustless treasury, and having no longer the powerful motive to economy which has ever been the conservative element of its being, would be tempted to plunge deeper and deeper into schemes of extravagance and waste, until, it may well be apprehended, all the safeguards of its purity would finally disappear. With its army of postmasters and contractors, now numbering 36,000 and constantly increasing, with its twenty millions of disbursements, for they will soon reach and surpass that sum, and with its ramifications extending to every city and village and neighborhood in the Union, it could not fail to be seized upon by ambitious hands, and wielded for political power, until the very air of its being might become an atmosphere of political corruption. The gigantic system of internal improvements by the general government, which a few years since was overthrown by the voice of the American people, in the omnipresence of its complete development, could scarcely have a more potent instrument for exhausting the treasury and depraving the public morals.

The immediate

EFFECT OF THE WAR, UPON THE POSTAL REVENUES,

was largely to increase them. This is not surprising, because with a million of soldiers in the field, chiefly drawn from a class whose correspondence is in ordinary times quite limited, the volume of mail matter was thereby greatly increased. And, moreover, every business interest was stimulated to the utmost by the enormous expenditures of the government for war material and supplies. The general correspondence was, of course, proportionately increased and the postal revenues swollen. The cutting off of the mail service in the South and Southwest largely reduced the expenditures of the Post-Office Department, and although the expensive and unprofitable overland mails continued to be a heavy drain, the department at first slowly and then rapidly began to be lifted

OUT OF THE SLOUGH OF INSOLVENCY.

In 1863 the expenditures exceeded the receipts by $2,825,543.23. In 1864 the deficit was $206,532.42, but in 1865 the receipts had mounted above the expenditures $861,430.42.

A grand opportunity was offered, at the close of the rebellion, to have maintained the department upon the ancient basis of honest business principles to which the accident of war had brought it back. But, unfortunately, this opportunity was not embraced. The field for successful ventures upon the Treasury was restricted as the demand for war supplies ceased, and

THE POST-OFFICE DEPARTMENT ATTRACTED THE SPOILERS,

who had found occupation elsewhere during the war. The prosperity of the loyal States was at flood-tide. The million of brave men who returned to peaceful vocations carried into civil life the same courage and persistence which enabled them to crush the rebellion. Southern society was demoralized, southern industry was paralyzed, by the transition from an old to a new system. The South languished for a time, but the contagion of prosperity was resistless. Her cotton fields, as if quickened to renewed vigor by the blood shed in their heroic defense, blossomed with an increased yield of a staple for which the markets of the world were eager. The war taxation, continued in peace, filled the Treasury to overflowing. The people, flushed with victory, radiant with joy at the return of peace and the preservation of the Union, prosperous and contented, were not disposed to question the motives of their servants, or to grumble if expenditures were not reduced.

The time was auspicious and the opportunity favorable for extravagant expenditures by the Post-Office Department. The

FALSE AND VICIOUS THEORY

that the postal fund could be properly charged with subsidies for the development of commerce on the high seas, or the encouragement of private enterprise on land, had zealous advocates in the department and in Congress. The men who profited by the ill-judged liberality, the criminal waste of the public money, swarmed about the halls of legislation, and in the midst of the political excitement and confusion incident to the administration of Andrew Johnson, were enabled to lobby through many schemes which the sober judgment of the country has since pronounced unmitigated evils. It was during this period that the practice of

STRAW BIDDING

unblushingly prevailed, and increased largely the cost of the star mail service in the Western States and Territories. The combination of contractors, who then dominated the department and defied the law, not only robbed the government, but their evil influence is felt to this day. The extension of the mail service was unquestionably far in advance of the actual needs of the country. The enormous pay for fast daily service over many long star routes was in reality a subsidy or bounty to the proprietors of stage-lines. The excuse for these excessive expenditures was that the development of the country was accelerated and civilization advanced thereby. Admitting this to be true, for the sake of argument, it is questionable whether the good accomplished in the remote regions of the West compensated for the positive evil which resulted here from the

DEGRADATION OF OFFICIAL MORALS.

It is a fact, which cannot be denied, that the scandals attending the administration of the Post-Office Department during the past quarter of a century have been very serious in their consequences. The responsibility for this evil rests largely upon the legislative branch of the government, because the power to remedy it could have been exerted at any time.

RE-ESTABLISHMENT OF SOUTHERN MAIL SERVICE.

The re-establishment of mail service in the Southern States after the war increased considerably the expenditures of the department, and the revenues were not increased in the same proportion. There was a diminution of the receipts in 1866, and but a slight increase in 1867. The expenditures in 1867 exceeded the revenues by nearly four million dollars, or more than one-fifth of the total receipts. In 1876, a decade later, the deficiency had not diminished; the percentage still being the same. From that time, however, the increase of the revenues has been large, and in 1880 the deficiency was only ten per cent. of the revenues. This was accomplished by the natural growth of the country and not by any effort to economize.

THE POST-OFFICE SHOULD NOW BE SELF-SUSTAINING.

The country has reached that stage in the progress of its material development where, it seems to me, an effort ought to be made to bring the credit and debit sides of the department's balance sheet nearer together. All or nearly all the long and expensive star routes have been superseded by railroad service. The cost of the star service ought therefore to rapidly decrease in the Western States and Territories. A careful and impartial examination of the star service made during the past summer, satisfied the department that large reductions could be made without causing any inconvenience to the sections of country supplied thereby. In this connection I respectfully call attention to that portion of the very able report of the Second Assistant Postmaster-General which deals with the star service. He says:

New service has been established, and increased trips have been ordered on routes believed to require additional facilities, while routes believed to be useless have been discontinued, others reduced in trips, curtailed in distance, and diminished in expedition. The reduction of 3,949 miles in excess of the number embraced in the routes of 409 routes has been accomplished only by careful investigation touching the needs of the people in the section of country affected. A part, however, of the decrease is due to the extension of railroad routes, which superseded a portion of the star service. In certain instances it was ascertained that increased trips and expedited schedules had not been performed by contractors, after the orders and allowances therefor, and in but few instances have the people upon the routes made complaint. As far as can be ascertained the orders reducing this service have not caused embarrassment, and in a few cases, to those citizens directly interested in the routes, the first information that any increased trips or speed had been ordered was contained in the notices of discontinuance.

REDUCTION IN STAR AND STEAMBOAT SERVICE IN 1881.

The total reductions made during the last fiscal year in the star service was $655,628 per annum, but some of the orders did not take effect till the beginning of the present fiscal year. The net reduction, allowing for new and increased service, during the last fiscal year was $364,144. The aggregate reduction of the cost of steamboat service for the last fiscal year was $282,009, from which is to be deducted the cost of increased service, $30,653, making the net reduction $251,356. Thus far in the present fiscal year reductions amounting to $701,551 have been made in the star service. The steamboat service during the same time has been reduced $51,872. There have been increases in the cost of the star service to the extent of $164,597; and of steamboat service to the amount of $56,569. The net reductions from July 1 to October 31, in the star and steamboat service, are $532,257. These results may be summarized as follows:

Aggregate reductions in star service from March to June 30, 1881 .... $655,628
Aggregate reductions in star service from July 1 to October 31, 1881 701,551
Aggregate reductions in steamboat service from March to June 30, 1881 282,009
Aggregate reductions in steamboat service from July 1 to October 31, 1881 51,872
                                                                                    1,691,060

Aggregate increases of star service from March to June 30, 1881 .... $291,668 *
Aggregate increases of star service from July 1 to October 31, 1881 164,597
Aggregate increases of steamboat service from March to June 30, 1881 ... 30,653
Aggregate increases of steamboat service from July 1 to October 31, 1881 . 56,569
                                                                                    543,287

Net reduction of star and steamboat service.. 1,147,773

A minute investigation into alleged

ABUSES IN THE STAR ROUTE SERVICE

was instituted by direction of the late President, and is still being prosecuted. The Post-Office Department has co-operated, and will continue to co-operate, with the Department of Justice in this investigation. No one who has not been directly concerned in the matter can fully appreciate the magnitude of the undertaking, the mass of record evidence examined, the difficulties of a personal investigation in sparsely-settled territories, and the results attained by the patient and intelligent labors of the inspectors of this department. There can be no doubt, from the facts already ascertained, that the existing statutes leave the way open to great abuses, and that there is abundant ground for asking a judicial investigation of the transactions of the last few years.

The one serious difficulty in the way of bringing back the department to a self-sustaining basis is the

CONSTANTLY INCREASING COST OF THE RAILWAY MAIL SERVICE.

This increase during the past fiscal year was $487,446. I regret to say that there is a deficiency of $478,155 for this branch of the service for the fiscal year ended June 30, 1881, which must be provided for, and also that there must be an increased appropriation for the same service of $1,097,319 for the fiscal year ending June 30, 1882. The estimate for the fiscal year ending June 30, 1883, for the railway service is $10,655,000. There has recently been an unprecedented growth of railroads, and this accounts largely for the enormous increase of the cost of the railway service. There were up to June 30, 1881, 5,221.81 miles of new service on which the pay under the law was readjusted; and from July 1 to October 18 new service was established on 3,352 miles of new road. It is estimated that there will be between October 18, 1881, and June 30, 1882, 5,000 miles of new service to be added. These figures, however, do not represent the entire cost of the railway mail service. The pay for postal cars and special facilities for fast mail must be added. The cost of these two items for the fiscal year ended June 30, 1881, was as follows:

Railway post-office cars... $1,268,221 50
Special facilities for fast mails 348,748 69
                                                                                           ——————
Total 1,617,970 19

The actual payment for the railway mail service during the fiscal year, 1881, was therefore $11,411,120.90. The cost for the current fiscal year will be $12,006,601, and the estimates for 1883 are $13,181,601. The enormous growth of railroads in 1880 and 1881, and their anticipated increase of mileage in the near future, will account for a great proportion of the augmented cost of the service. But there are other causes which must also be taken into consideration. The increase in the weight of the mail transported by the trunk lines has been unparalleled and the maximum does not appear to have been reached. The legitimate function of the postal service is undoubtedly to transmit intelligence and diffuse knowledge. If this were the sole requirement of

61 Ab

the service now, the present cost of the railway mail service could not
be justified. But it is not; Congress saw fit a few years since to make

THE POST OFFICE DEPARTMENT A COMMON CARRIER OF MERCHANDISE.

And, moreover, it fixed the rates of transportation so low that the
mere cost of handling this class of mail matter, to say nothing of its
transportation, is unremunerative. The compensation the government
receives for the reception, transportation, and delivery of second, third,
and fourth class matter is far below the cost. The revenue derived from
letter postage and other sources is more than consumed by the losses
sustained on second, third, and fourth class matter. The transportation
on trunk lines of the mail thus increased in bulk and weight is not the
only problem the department has to solve. The reception and preparation for dispatching these classes of mail matter, their transportation to
the railroad depots, the loading into postal cars, and their distribution
in the cars, all seriously interfere with the dispatch, distribution, and delivery of the letter mail en route. The transportation of second class matter, which is composed of newspapers and periodicals is, of course, legitimate postal business. They disseminate intelligence among the people,
and Congress has accordingly provided by law for their distribution by
mail at a low rate, without regard to the cost of transportation. Third
and fourth class matter, being transient printed matter and merchandise, come under a different category. If it were probable that in the
course of time their transportation would become remunerative, or at
least self-sustaining, then it might perhaps be well to nurture it, but this
is not possible. The more this matter grows in bulk, the greater will be
the loss to the government. The rates for third and fourth class matter
are not only unremunerative, but the wisdom of requiring the government to become a carrier of merchandise is very questionable.

ADDITIONAL POSTAL CARS NEEDED.

Already, as I have said, the transportation of the mails, increased as
they are by second, third, and fourth class matter, has become a serious
problem for the department and railway trunk lines. An additional
postal car on the Hudson River Road is now demanded. It will not be
long before a like demand will have to be made of the Pennsylvania
Road. The principal trunk lines are already complaining, and doubtless with justice, that they are not adequately compensated for their
services. In the near future one of four things will have to be done.
first, either to increase largely the pay of these roads; or, second,
to increase the rates on third and fourth class matter; or, third, to
dispatch by fast-mail trains only first and second class matter; or,
fourth, to abandon the fourth class altogether.

I am satisfied that public sentiment and justice to the department demand a

REDUCTION OF THE COST OF THE RAILWAY MAIL SERVICE.

It is undoubtedly true that while some railroads may not be fully paid for the service they render, the great majority are overpaid. There is and always has been a disposition on the part of railroad corporations in dealing with the department to exact their own terms. The subject is a complex one, and while it demands immediate attention it should have a most careful consideration. There can be no doubt that if the pay for this branch of the postal service is adjusted upon a basis alike equitable and just to the department and the railroad companies, the result will be a very large saving. I am so strongly impressed with the necessity for this, and so confident that Congress will lose no time in giving the subject intelligent and prompt consideration, that I have thought it my duty to recommend a less appropriation for railway transportation than the superintendent of that branch of the service and the Second Assistant Postmaster-General have urged in their reports. I had hoped to be able to submit the outline of proposed legislation, which I believe would accomplish a great saving in the cost of the railway mail service, improve its efficiency, and be satisfactory to the country, the department, and the railroad companies. The sad events of the past summer rendered the accomplishment of this duty impossible. I desire, however, in this connection, to call attention to the very wise suggestions contained in the report of the Second Assistant Postmaster-General, page 101.

The public sentiment of the country demands the reduction of taxation, and Congress will doubtless undertake the task. This will only add another to the many existing reasons for the greatest possible economy in every branch of the postal service. A very considerable saving has, without any injury to the service or detriment to the public, been made in the star and steamboat mail service. I think it cannot be doubted that a corresponding reduction in the cost of the railway mail service is feasible. In addition to these two items of cost come the

SALARIES AND ALLOWANCES OF POSTMASTERS.

Some saving has already been effected in the matter of allowances to postmasters, and still more may be practicable. The salaries of postmasters in towns of ten thousand inhabitants and less are greater than the compensation for equally onerous and responsible duties paid by banks and express companies. A saving in this direction can be made without injustice to the office-holders or detriment to the postal service.

If these suggestions are deemed worthy of consideration, and Congress carries them out, the

REDUCTION OF LETTER POSTAGE

from three to two cents will be possible within three years. I believe this reduction could be accomplished without the proportionate diminution of receipts which followed the adoption of three-cent postage in 1851. The people have shown their appreciation of cheap postage. The introduction of the postal card, instead of diminishing the receipts, has on the whole largely increased them. Two-cent postage would, I believe, after one or two years' trial produce the same result. It is my deliberate judgment that two-cent postage is feasible in the near future. I would favor it even if the rates of postage on third and fourth class matter had to be increased. The great mass of the people are interested in cheap letter postage. The proportion of those benefited by the unremunerative rates on third and fourth class matter is comparatively small. Moreover, the people who are benefited could afford to pay more liberally for the advantages extended to them. The bulk and weight of third and fourth class matter adds so largely to the cost of transporting the mails that all the profit realized from letter postage is thereby absorbed. If these classes of matter contributed proportionately, two-cent postage would at once be assured. If the government is to be a common carrier, ought it to be compelled to lose money thereby? Ought the many who are interested in cheap letter postage be taxed for the benefit of the few who are concerned for low rates on third and fourth class matter?

MAIL SERVICE OTHER THAN RAILWAY.

The estimate of the Second Assistant Postmaster-General, for the item of star routes, $7,250,000 for the year 1883, it will be observed, is $650,000 less than the amount appropriated for the current year; for the steamboat service $800,000, or $125,000 less than the last appropriation; and for mail messengers $800,000, or $24,250 more than the current appropriation.

Sufficient service should be provided for all communities with a reasonable expenditure of public money, and appropriations corresponding with the estimates given above will, in my judgment, accomplish the object desired.

The recommendations of the Second Assistant Postmaster-General, presented in his report, relative to the extension of post routes after advertisement and award of service, and the repeal of the laws requiring the deposit of certified checks with proposals of bidders for carrying the mails, have my concurrence. Respecting the certified checks, it may be said that in some States, and in the Territories, many persons who desire to enter proposals for the transportation of the mails on star routes are restrained from bidding because of distant residence from national banks, and their inability to pay, besides traveling expenses to secure loans, exorbitant rates of interest for money during the time when the mail service is open to competition.

COST OF RAILWAY SERVICE.

The cost of the transportation of mails on railroad routes for the year ended June 30, 1881, was by the books of this department $9,908,991, and by the accounts of the Auditor $9,543,155. The appropriation for the same year was $9,315,000.

The appropriation for the year ending June 30, 1882, is $9,458,282. It will therefore be seen, as is elsewhere explained in detail, that the appropriation for this year will not be sufficient to cover the cost of the service, and that an additional appropriation will be required.

The amount estimated to be necessary for the fiscal year ending June 30, 1883, is placed at $10,655,000; this is $500,000 less than is estimated by the superintendent of railway mail service and recommended by the Second Assistant Postmaster-General. I have before in this report given at length my reasons for recommending a less appropriation for railway mail service than the superintendent of that branch of the service and the Second Assistant Postmaster-General recommend.

RAILWAY POST-OFFICE CARS.

The appropriation for the use of postal cars for the current fiscal year is $1,426,000, which is $176,000 more than was appropriated for 1881. The estimate for the year ending June 30, 1883, is placed at $1,526,000, which is $100,000 more than the sum appropriated for the current year.

SPECIAL FACILITIES.

Appropriations have been made each year since 1878 to enable the department to secure from railroad companies facilities for the transportation of mails for which compensation could not be made under the general law. The advantages secured to the public by this expenditure are very great and are specially valuable to the chief centers of population. The appropriation for this object for the current year is $425,000, and I recommend that $500,000 be appropriated for the fiscal year ending June 30, 1883.

ADDITIONAL POSTAL FACILITIES BETWEEN THE EAST AND THE WEST.

I desire to call attention to the fact that numerous petitions have been received from the Pacific Coast, from the city of New York, and from the Eastern States, asking for more speedy and frequent service between the two sections. In my opinion, the service should be extended so as to accord better with the volume of business transacted. The time between New York and San Francisco has recently been reduced twenty-four hours by the action of the Pennsylvania Railway Company in establishing the Chicago Limited Express, which leaves New York at 8 a. m., and arrives at Chicago the following day at 10 a. m., in time to make the overland connection. An effort will be made to have the mail arrive in San Francisco at 6 a. m. instead of at 1.30 p. m., as at present,

and to depart at 6 p. m. instead of 4 p. m. Additional facilities
also be asked from Mr. Vanderbilt, president of the northern li
Chicago, so as to give the same facilities to the Eastern States in ge
as are now possessed by the city of New York and the State of Pe
vania for communication with Chicago and points west. The pr
ness always shown by Mr. Vanderbilt in meeting the wishes of th
partment induces the belief that these negotiations will be succe
especially as it is not his habit to permit the country supplied t
lines to possess mail facilities inferior to those enjoyed by other sec

REORGANIZATION OF THE RAILWAY MAIL SERVICE.

By an order of the Postmaster-General (printed on page 317,
April 7, 1881, and taking effect on the 1st of May following, the
way mail service was completely reorganized and its efficiency g
promoted. It appears from the report of the general superinte
of this service (page 315) that the effect of the reorganization has
most salutary; that it has been accepted by the employés as an
ance that their advancement to the highest salary allowed by la
pended upon themselves, and that they now feel that to secure prom
they have only to earn it. In consideration of the fact that the
required of all employés of the railway mail service are similar in
acter, varying only in the amount of work assigned to each and the
necessary for its proper performance, I indorse the recommendat
the general superintendent that the appropriation for their payme
made in one gross sum of $3,480,000 for railway mail service clerk
that at the same time it be enacted that hereafter the railway mail se
clerks be divided into five classes, whose salaries shall not excee
annual sums of—

For the first class ....
For the second class ....
For the third class ....
For the fourth class ....
For the fifth class ....

This would involve no change in the service as reorganized unde
order of April 7, and would greatly simplify the accounts of the de
ment.

CHIEF HEAD CLERKS OF THE RAILWAY MAIL SERVICE.

The recommendation of the general superintendent of railway
service that an allowance be made to chief head clerks of railway
service for their necessary traveling expenses is worthy the seriou
tention of Congress. The duties of these officers are difficult and la
ous, requiring a high grade of executive ability, and it is hardly fair
when they are required to travel upon the business of the governm
they should suffer therefor a decrease of their salaries to the exte
the extra expense necessarily incurred.

PENSIONS IN THE RAILWAY MAIL SERVICE.

During the past fiscal year sixty-two railway accidents have been reported to this department, in which seven employés of the railway mail service lost their lives, six of them having been burned to death, fifteen were severely, and twenty-two slightly, injured. No provision has ever been made for the widows and orphans of men killed in this service, nor for the continuance of pay to men disabled by injuries received while in the line of duty. Should no better plan commend itself to the wisdom of Congress, I would recommend that the Postmaster-General be authorized, as suggested by the general superintendent of railway mail service, to pay to the widow or guardian of the minor children of employés of this service killed in railway accidents the salary of the deceased for a period not to exceed two years. I also recommend that authority be given by law to continue men disabled by such accidents upon full pay until recovery, not to exceed one year.

FOREIGN MAILS.

The total weight of mails dispatched during the year to countries and colonies of the Universal Postal Union (the Dominion of Canada excepted) was 794,392,727 grams, or 1,751,523 pounds. The weight of the letter mails was 154,652,944 grams, or 340,988 pounds, and of printed matter and samples of merchandise 639,739,783 grams, or 1,410,535 pounds, being an increased weight as compared with the preceding year of 68,807 pounds of letters and 229,115 pounds of printed matter and samples.

Of the letter mails dispatched, 155,835 pounds (45.70 per cent.) were sent to Great Britain and Ireland, 84,091 pounds (24.66 per cent.) to Germany, 75,110 pounds (22.02 per cent.) to other countries of Europe, and 25,952 pounds (7.61 per cent.) to Postal Union countries and colonies other than European.

Of the printed matter and samples dispatched, 670,688 pounds (47.55 per cent.) were sent to Great Britain and Ireland, 285,434 pounds (20.23 per cent.) to Germany, 261,200 pounds (18.52 per cent.) to other countries of Europe, and 193,213 pounds (13.70 per cent.) to other Postal Union countries and colonies.

Compared with the weights of the mails dispatched during the preceding year, there was an increase in the letter mails of 25.28 per cent., and in the printed matter and sample mails of 19.39 per cent.

A statement of the weights of mails dispatched to each Postal Union country and colony is appended (see pages 440).

The number of letters exchanged with foreign countries and colonies not embraced in the Universal Postal Union, exclusive of Canada, was 755,216, of which number 434,165 were sent to, and 321,051 received from such countries, a decrease compared with the previous fiscal year of 14,570 letters sent, and 788 letters received from non-union countries.

COST OF THE OCEAN MAIL SERVICE.

The sums reported for payment on account of the sea transportation of the United States mails dispatched to foreign countries during the fiscal year 1881, including 13,197 francs and 43 centimes ($2,547.10) credited to France in the quarterly accounts with the French postal administration, for the conveyance of United States mails by French contract packets from New York to Havre, amounted to $239,149.21, an increase, compared with the cost of same service in 1880, of $40,481.75. Of this amount, $189,673.73 was reported for the trans-Atlantic service; $13,683.14 for the trans-Pacific service, and $33,225.24 for services to and from the isthmus of Panama, Central America, and the South Pacific, to Mexico, to Cuba and Port Rico, to and from the West India Islands, to Brazil, the Argentine Republic, Paraguay and Uruguay, to Venezuela and Curaçoa, and to Canada and New Foundland. Particulars of these several services are appended (see page 439).

The additional sum of $13,355.83 was reported for payment on account of the Atlantic sea conveyance of the British and Australian closed mails from New York to Great Britain, for which credit was claimed in the quarterly accounts with the British office, making the total cost of sea transportation of mails during the year $252,505.04.

The aggregate amount of the quarterly balances, paid to this department, on settlements of postage accounts with other Postal Union administrations, was $108,196.51, and the aggregate amount of the quarterly balances paid by this department to other union administrations was $28,091.57.

The sums credited to this department, by Postal Union administrations, on account of the United States territorial and sea transit of foreign mails amounted to $115,181.45, and the sum credited by this department to union administrations on account of the foreign territorial and sea transit of United States mails amounted to $51,818.61.

ADMISSIONS TO THE UNIVERSAL POSTAL UNION.

The following countries and colonies have since the last report declared their adhesion to the universal postal union:

1. The British colonies of Grenada, St. Lucia, Tobago, and Turks Islands, admitted from February 1, 1881.
2. The Republic of Chili, admitted from April 1, 1881.
3. The Republic of Hayti, admitted from July 1, 1881.
4. The Republic of Paraguay, admitted from July 1, 1881.
5. The United States of Colombia, admitted on special conditions, from July 1, 1881.
6. The Republic of Guatemala, admitted from August 1, 1881.
7. The British colonies Barbadoes and St. Vincent, admitted from September 1, 1881.
8. The Sandwich Islands, admitted from January 1, 1882.
9. The Republic of Nicaragua, admitted from May 1, 1882.

The United States of Colombia, having ceded in 1849 to the Panama Railroad Company for a term of 99 years the exclusive right to transport mails across the isthmus of Panama, at certain rates fixed by that company, the government of that country no longer possesses complete sovereignty in postal matters so far as isthmus transportations are concerned. Consequently the United States of Colombia has been admitted to the Union with the reservation that special rates of transit of mails across the isthmus are to be applied in lieu of the Union territorial transit charges fixed by article 4 of the Convention of Paris.

The countries and colonies having organized postal services which have not yet adhered to the Postal Union are Bolivia in South America, Costa Rica in Central America, New Zealand and the British colonies in Australia. With these exceptions the territory of the Universal Postal Union may now be said to embrace the civilized world. It includes an area of over 50,000,000 square miles, with a population of about 800,000,000.

MODIFICATIONS OF POSTAL UNION ARRANGEMENTS AND DETAILS.

The administrations of the union, in order to establish uniformity of treatment for registered articles which may be insufficiently prepaid, or which do not fulfill the conditions of form required for admission to the mails at the lower rate, have adopted a proposition that registered articles, insufficiently prepaid or not fulfilling the conditions of form demanded by the category to which they belong, shall not be taxed at the charge of the addressee nor stopped in their circulation. Under this arrangement deficient postages may be reclaimed from the senders through the respective offices. This treatment is not to apply, however, to registered articles of the domestic service, which, by reason of reforwarding, pass into the international service.

The consent of this department has been given that the special arrangement of 13th November, 1880, with the postal administration of France, extending the limits of weight and dimensions for packets of samples of merchandise prescribed by article V of the Convention of Paris shall be so interpreted that the same shall be terminable at any time on a notice by either government of one year.

A clause has been added to the first paragraph of Article XVII of the regulations of detail and order for the execution of the Convention of Paris, of which the following is a translation:

The mechanical processes designated under the names of chromography, polygraphy, hectography, papyrography, velocigraphy, &c., are considered as easy to be recognised; but in order to enjoy the privilege of the reduced rate the reproductions obtained by means of these processes must be mailed at the post-office windows and in the minimum number of twenty perfectly identical copies.

Paragraph 7 of Article XXXII of the regulations of detail and order has been modified so as to read as follows:

7. The post-offices which the administration of the English colony of Hong-Kong maintains at Kiang-Chow, Canton, Swatow, Amoy, Foochow, Ningpo, Shanghai, and Hankow (China).

The following paragraph has been added to Article XX of the regulations of detail and order, to take effect January 1, 1882:

4. The correspondence of all kinds, ordinary or registered, which, bearing an incomplete or erroneous address, is returned to the senders for them to complete or rectify, is not considered, when re-entering the service with a completed or corrected address, as reforwarded correspondence, but as newly dispatched, and becomes in consequence subject to a new postage.

Articles IX and X of the regulations of detail and order have been modified as follows, to take effect January 1, 1882.

The two following sentences are inserted between paragraphs 2 and 3 of Article IX:

The return receipts for registered articles entered in table I of the letter bill are indicated by the letters A R placed opposite the articles to which they relate in the column of observations of said table.

Return receipts are entered in said table, either individually or collectively, according as the receipts are more or less numerous.

The first paragraph of Article X is amended to read as follows:

The registered articles, the return receipts relating thereto, and, if necessary, the special list specified in paragraph 3 of Article IX, are placed together in a separate packet, which must be suitably inclosed and sealed so as to preserve its contents.

The following new paragraph is added after paragraph 4:

"5. Return receipts in course of return are placed in an envelope by the office distributing the registered articles to which these receipts relate. These envelopes, bearing the inscription '*Avis de reception en retour, bureau de poste de * * * pays, * * *'* are subjected to the formalities of registration, and are forwarded to destination as other registered articles."

The postal administration of Japan having requested an abatement in its favor of the special United States territorial transit charge for articles of mail matter other than letters conveyed between San Francisco and the Atlantic seaboard, alleging that the rate of two francs per kilogram practically prohibits the use by Japan of the United States route for correspondence of this class mailed in Japan for European destination, I considered it expedient, in view of the comparatively small amount of such matter forwarded from Japan in transit through the United States, to accept a reduced transit charge thereon of one franc per kilogram.

Tabular statements are appended (page 441) giving detailed information with corrections to latest date—

1. Of the equivalents, according to which postage rates are levied in countries of the Universal Postal Union which have not the franc for a monetary unit, with the fees charged for registration and for return receipts.

2. Of the length of time for retaining in the offices of destination unclaimed correspondence addressed *poste restante*.

3. Of the regulations within the Postal Union respecting the return to the senders of letters of the international service.

4. Of the sur-taxes charged in certain union countries on correspondence addressed to the United States.

MODIFICATIONS OF POSTAL REGULATIONS AND DETAILS RESPECTING MAIL EXCHANGES WITH THE DOMINION OF CANADA, AND WITH COUNTRIES AND COLONIES NOT EMBRACED IN THE UNIVERSAL POSTAL UNION.

The special postal arrangement between the United States and Canada has been modified by the execution of additional articles, authorizing the reciprocal transmission in the mails between the two countries of insufficiently paid letters, on which at least one full rate of postage has been prepaid, and also empowering the Canada office to collect double rate of Canadian postage on newspapers, periodicals, and other printed matter published or originating in this country and posted in Canada for destinations in the United States, with the apparent purpose of evading the payment of the higher rates of United States domestic postage or the laws and regulations governing the treatment of such matter in the United States.

It having been found that large numbers of United States mail sacks, which for a long series of years had been sent with correspondence to Canada, had failed to be returned to the sending United States post-office, regulations were proposed by this department and agreed to by the Canada office, providing for the exclusive use by each country for its mails to the other of its own sacks, and the prompt return, empty, to the sending country of the sacks belonging to it.

My attention having been called to the frequent transmission in the mails from Canada to this country of Canadian reprints of American books, &c., published in Canada in violation of copyrights granted by the United States, an order has been issued, in conformity with the provision of the act of March 3, 1879, including all such publications received by mail from Canada in the classification of unmailable matter.

The provisions of the 3d paragraph of article 4 of the postal conventions concluded with the colonial governments of New South Wales, New Zealand, Queensland, and Victoria respectively, have been further modified by accepting a reduced United States sea transit charge on closed mails from said colonies forwarded from San Francisco to Panama of 9 cents per ounce for letter mails and 4 cents per pound for printed matter mails.

The arrangement concluded with the British colony of Victoria, Australia, for the redirection and forwarding of ordinary (unregistered) international letters from the United States to Victoria, or *vice versa*, on application of the senders without prepayment of postage, has been made to apply generally to the redirection and transmission upon the same conditions of all ordinary letters of whatever origin or place of first dispatch.

An arrangement has been concluded with the post department of New South Wales for the registration as far as Sydney in that colony of letters addressed to South Australia, North Australia, West Australia, and Tasmania.

A proposition of the post department of Queensland to amend article 3 of the postal convention with that colony by the substitution of 16 cents for 12 cents as the single rate of postage between the two countries has been declined by this department, but consent was given, as a temporary measure, to the levying by the Queensland office of an increased postage of 8 pence per single rate on letters forwarded to the United States by the San Francisco route, such increase having been represented as necessary to meet the cost of the transit charge on such letters between Brisbane and Sydney.

APPROPRIATION IN AID OF STEAMSHIP SERVICE TO NEW ZEALAND AND NEW SOUTH WALES.

The act of March 3, 1881, making appropriations for the service of the Post-Office Department, contained a proviso authorizing the Postmaster-General "to pay to the colonies of New Zealand and New South Wales so much of the cost of the overland transportation of the British closed mails to and from Australia as he may deem just, not to exceed one-half of said cost," and appropriated the sum of $40,000 for that purpose. In compliance with the terms of this act, I have ordered that the sum of $40,000, if not exceeding one-half of the cost of the overland charges paid to this department by the British post-office for the United States territorial transit of the British and Australian closed mails during the current fiscal year, be paid to the colonies of New Zealand and New South Wales from this appropriation. As the object of this legislation is understood to have been the granting of aid to the colonies of New Zealand and New South Wales in maintaining the present monthly mail-steamship service between Sydney and San Francisco, the propriety of continuing such aid during the next fiscal year is respectfully referred to Congress.

FOREIGN MAIL MATTERS REQUIRING LEGISLATION.

The existing law in regard to the treatment of letters irregularly received in the United States by vessels arriving from foreign ports is imperfect and difficult of execution on account of the changed conditions of international mail exchanges established under the Universal Postal Union Convention. Such letters are frequently received by vessels regularly employed in carrying mails from foreign ports, including those of Postal Union countries, and cannot be treated under the present law as ship letters, such treatment being restricted to letters brought by vessels not regularly employed in carrying the mails, and as they are not made up and dispatched by offices of exchange under the forms, regulations, and conditions prescribed by the Convention of Paris, they cannot be regarded as regular mails, and the department is often greatly embarrassed respecting their proper treatment. Additional legislation is needed prescribing a uniform treatment for such letters in harmony with existing postal arrangements.

The recommendations of my predecessors for legislative authority to carry into effect the provisions of article VI of the Paris Convention, and also for a modification of the provisions of section 17 of the act of March 3, 1879, are respectfully renewed.

IMPROVEMENT OF MAIL COMMUNICATIONS WITH MEXICO.

The comparatively recent growth of commercial mining and railway interests in Mexico, largely augmented by the capital and enterprise of citizens of the United States, together with the reduction of postage rates effected by the adhesion of Mexico to the Universal Postal Union, while contributing to an extensive increase of the mails exchanged with that country, have at the same time developed the necessity for increased mail facilities. Correspondence in relation to the subject, had with the Mexican post department, has shown that that government is ready to co-operate with this department in remedying any existing defects, and in effecting such necessary improvements of interior mail service on both sides as will secure more rapid and frequent exchanges of mails between the two countries. A considerable increase of frontier exchanges has been already effected, and by these and other border exchanges which are in process of arrangement, and will shortly go into operation, the larger and more populous districts of Mexico will be placed in more frequent communication by overland routes, via the frontier, with the United States.

Owing to the peculiar organization of the Mexican postal service, which commits to the several states the inauguration and modification of mail services within them, it has been found that arrangements by correspondence relative to this subject have been protracted and tedious, propositions of this character submitted to the central administration at Mexico requiring reference to the state organizations interested before definite conclusions in regard thereto could be reached. This difficulty, and the necessity for an early improvement, particularly in the overland mail communications, which shall be at once comprehensive and methodical, has suggested the advisability of effecting desired modifications by means of a commission to be sent from this department to Mexico for that purpose.

FOREIGN MAIL STATISTICS.

The estimated amount of mail matter exchanged during the year with foreign countries, based upon counts of such matter taken at the respective United States offices of exchange during the first seven days in October, 1880, and April 1881, is as follows:

Total number of letters	43,622,547
Total number of single rates	44,584,919
Total number of postal cards	2,063,912
Total number of packets, of newspapers, other printed matter, and business papers	33,302,186
Total number of packets of samples of merchandise	481,671
Total number of registered articles	531,360

The estimated amount of postages collected thereon in the United States is as follows:

On prepaid letters *sent*..	$1,086,363 68
On unpaid and insufficiently paid letters *received*....................................	107,058 06
On postal cards *sent*..	27,771 42
On newspapers, printed matter, samples, and business papers *sent*...................	334,748 38
On insufficiently paid newspapers, &c., *received*....................................	4,756 34
	1,560,697 90

The estimated amount of registration fees on registered articles sent to foreign countries is $37,698.50.

The estimated amount of unpaid postages are as follows:

On unpaid letters *sent*...	$15,883 60
On newspapers, &c., *sent*..	298 17
	16,181 77
On unpaid letters *received*...	$107,058 08
On unpaid newspapers *received*...	4,756 34
	111,814 41

For other details respecting these estimates see page 440 of the appendix.

POST-OFFICES ESTABLISHED AND POSTMASTERS APPOINTED.

The report of the First Assistant Postmaster-General shows the following:

Number of post-offices established during the year...................................	2,915
Number discontinued..	1,415
Increase..	1,500
Number in operation June 30, 1880..	43,012
Number in operation June 30, 1881..	44,512
Number filled by appointment of the President...	1,863
Number filled by appointment of the Postmaster-General................................	42,649

APPOINTMENTS WERE MADE DURING THE YEAR,

On resignations and commissions expired...	6,217
On removals..	958
On changes of names and sites	242
On deaths of postmasters	421
On establishment of new post-offices	2,915
Total appointments..	10,753
Number of cases acted on during the year	12,591

EMPLOYÉS OF THE RAILWAY MAIL SERVICE.

The number and aggregate compensation of railway post-office clerks, route agents, mail route messengers, and local agents in service during the year ended June 30, 1881, were:

1,298 railway post-office clerks...	$1,487,879
1,386 route agents	1,266,700
322 mail route messengers	196,741
176 local agents	157,720
	3,108,881

Disbursements on account of appropriation for post-office inspectors and mail depredations during the fiscal year ended June 30, 1881, salaries and expense allowance of post-office inspectors, attorneys' fees, rewards, &c., $143,608.85.

There are claims against this fund still unadjusted.

EMPLOYÉS IN THE POSTAL SERVICE.

The following table shows the number of employés in the Post-Office Department; also the number of postmasters, contractors, clerks in post-offices, railway post-office clerks, route agents, and other officers in the service June 30, 1880, and June 30, 1881:

Officers and employés.	June 30, 1880.	June 30, 1881.
DEPARTMENTAL OFFICERS AND EMPLOYÉS.		
Postmaster-General	1	1
Assistant Postmasters-General	3	3
Superintendent of money-order system	1	1
Superintendent of foreign mails	1	1
Superintendent of railway adjustment	....	1
Chief clerk to the Postmaster-General	1	1
Chiefs of divisions	6	8
Topographer for Post-Office Department	1	1
Disbursing officer and superintendent of building	1	1
Law clerk	1	1
Stenographer	1	1
Appointment clerk	1	1
Superintendent of blank agency	1	1
Chief clerks of bureaus	5	5
Clerks, messengers, watchmen, &c	424	437
	447	462
POSTMASTERS AND OTHER OFFICERS AND AGENTS.		
Postmasters	43,012	44,512
Contractors	5,862	5,150
Clerks in post-offices	5,519	5,200
Letter-carriers	2,688	2,861
Railway post-office clerks	1,206	1,298
Route agents	1,253	1,396
Mail route messengers	338	332
Local agents	150	176
Post-office inspectors and railway mail service superintendents	*56	77
	60,530	61,444

*Railway mail service superintendents not included last year.

THE FREE-DELIVERY SYSTEM.

The appropriation for this service was $2,500,000, an increase of $85,000 over that of the preceding year. The total cost of the service was $2,499,911.54, leaving an unexpended balance of $88.46. The increase in the cost of the service over that of the previous year was $136,218.40. This increase was owing to the extension of the service to additional cities as authorized by the act of February 21, 1879, and to the appointment of additional letter-carriers to improve its efficiency, where already in operation.

The service was extended during the year to Leadville, Colo., Mansfield, Ohio, Meriden, Conn., Richmond, Ind., and Zanesville, Ohio.

The operations of this branch of the service during the last fiscal year are presented in detail with the accompanying report of the First Assistant Postmaster-General. From the tabular statement included therein, it will be seen that there has been an increase during the year of more than 84,000,000 in the number of letters and other articles of mail matter delivered and collected by carriers, and of $204,833.25 in the receipts from local postage; those receipts exceeding the cost of the service by $779,658.25. This exhibit furnishes in itself a sufficient reason for the increase in the estimate of appropriation for free-delivery service over the estimate for the same purpose submitted in the last annual report of my predecessor. That, in cities covering so large an extent of territory as to render frequent communication by post between their residents a necessity, the employment of a sufficient number of carriers to insure efficiency in such a service results in large profit to the department, is a fact which has been amply demonstrated by experience.

It has been observed in connection with the establishment of street letter-boxes (from which collections are made by the postmaster or his clerks) at convenient points in towns where no letter-carriers are employed, that a marked increase in the number of letters posted for mailing has invariably followed—a proof that the furnishing of means whereby correspondence may be readily and conveniently deposited acts as an incentive to the writing of letters which would otherwise have remained unwritten.

The receipts for local postage at the larger post-offices have enabled the department to show, in several successive annual reports, that the free-delivery service, as a whole, has become a source of revenue instead of an item of expense; and I present herewith, in tabular form, a statement showing the remarkable increase during the past ten years, both in the operations of the service and in the receipts from local postage incident thereto:

Fiscal year ending June 30—	Letters, &c., delivered and collected by carriers.	Expenditures free-delivery service.	Receipts from local postage.	Deficiency.	Surplus.	Number of offices.
1872	311,847,397	$1,385,965 76	$907,351 93	$478,613 83		52
1873	374,915,664	1,422,495 48	1,113,251 21	310,244 27		53
1874	503,386,397	1,802,696 41	1,611,481 66	191,214 75		55
1875	574,201,474	1,880,041 99	1,947,559 54		$67,517 55	57
1876	631,787,473	1,981,186 51	2,065,561 73		84,375 22	55
1877	666,563,478	1,893,619 85	2,254,597 83		360,977 98	57
1878	715,782,150	1,824,166 96	2,452,251 51		628,084 55	57
1879	809,854,065	1,947,706 61	2,812,528 86		864,817 25	88
1880	932,121,343	2,362,692 14	3,068,797 14		705,104 08	104
1881	1,016,197,562	2,498,972 14	3,278,630 39		779,658 25	121

In the face of a record which shows that every dollar expended at points where an extensive local postal business is transacted returns so large a profit, it is difficult to perceive how an argument can be made against appropriation for the service at those points to any reasonable extant that may be asked. The increase in the receipts of the free-delivery offices during the past year has been 17 per cent.

I have felt no hesitation in pressing the claims of the free-delivery branch of the service with some urgency, for the reason that the advantages which I believe will result from an allowance sufficient to provide for an extension of its operations will not be confined to any particular city, nor to any section of the country, but will be shared by the business community and the general public in every portion of the land.

The successful operation of our postal service is a matter in which the entire nation is interested. I venture to hope that the utmost liberality will be exercised by Congress in its appropriations for that branch of the service, the revenues from which so largely aid in reducing the present deficiency.

COMPENSATION OF AUXILIARY LETTER-CARRIERS.

I recommend that section 3 of the act approved February 21, 1879, be so amended as to increase the annual compensation of auxiliary letter-carriers from $400 to $600 for their first year's service in that grade, and to $700 for such term as they may thereafter serve in the same capacity. This recommendation is made not only on the ground that such increased pay is no more than a fair compensation for the service performed, but because experience has shown the difficulty of obtaining for the inadequate sum now paid the services of persons who possess the educational and other desirable qualifications for appointment.

SUBSTITUTE LETTER-CARRIERS.

I have also to recommend such legislation as will authorize the appointment of substitute letter-carriers at post-offices where their employment is necessary, to be paid a nominal salary of $1 per annum and the *pro-rata* compensation of the carriers in whose places they may be called on to serve.

WORK OF THE TOPOGRAPHER'S OFFICE, POST-ROUTE MAPS, ETC.

During the past year new editions have been issued of all the maps hitherto prepared (23 in number, comprising 61 sheets).

Successive editions, at short intervals, have been, and always will be, required to show the numerous additions and changes of post-offices, and the course and frequency of the service on the several post-routes.

New maps to take the place of provisional copies are in course of preparation, and are well advanced. These embrace the Pacific States and the Territories, and the State of Florida (showing the Gulf and the mail connections of the West India Islands). A new set, in engraved form, of the maps of Virginia, West Virginia, North Carolina, and South Carolina is almost completed; also a map showing the river and side-connecting service of the Mississippi River between Saint Louis and New Orleans.

The work of this office necessarily increases with the extension of the

62 Ab

mail service. Maps for the use of the postal employés are in constant demand—more particularly for those of the railway mail service—as indispensable for the intelligent performance of their duties. For the more rapid production of revised editions of the maps, I have directed to be taken into consideration the advisability of having the printing (by lithography or otherwise) of these successive editions done within the walls of the department, so as to be under more constant and direct control.

As usual, the topographer has answered all inquiries in reference to mileage and telegraph accounts referred for his certificate.

Attention is again called to the desirability of the compilation and publication of an extended table of distances for use in the settlement of these accounts, the existing edition of the table having long been obsolete in many details. This shall be provided for as soon as arrangements can be perfected.

In the estimates for the next fiscal year I have requested for this bureau an amount the same as that allowed for the present year, taking into account the general increase of the work. As usual, this will cover the salaries of draughtsmen, clerks, and others employed in keeping up the special maps or diagrams for the department proper, as well as the miscellaneous expenses connected with the production, printing, and distribution of the post-route maps.

POST-OFFICE INSPECTORS.

It affords me gratification to call attention to the competent, faithful, and expeditious manner in which the arduous and varied duties imposed upon the post-office inspectors, who are the direct agents of the Postmaster-General in guarding the interests of the service, have been performed.

ARRESTS AND CONVICTIONS.

There were 461 arrests made during the year. Of this number 424 cases were prosecuted in the United States courts, and 37 in the courts of the several States in which the arrests were made. Of the former, 188 persons were convicted, 26 were acquitted, 3 escaped, 5 forfeited bail, 24 proceedings were dismissed, 1 was killed while resisting arrest, and 177 await trial; 30 highwaymen were arrested and prosecuted in United States courts. The arrests are classified as follows—

Subject to jurisdiction of United States courts:

Postmasters	4
Assistant postmasters	11
Clerks in post-offices	9
Postal clerks and route agents	9
Letter-carriers	8
Mail-carriers	18
Other employés	4
Highwaymen	30
Burglars	61
All others, for various offenses	23

Subject to jurisdiction of State courts:

Burglars	7
All others, for various offenses	30
	164

CASES ACTED UPON BY INSPECTORS.

The number of cases referred to inspectors for investigation during the year was 31,649, as follows:

Registered cases, Class A, 4,636.—The number of registered letters reported lost was 3,635; of which 1,307 contained money, and 2,328 contents were not specified. Of this number, 1,838 were reported as having been recovered and delivered to addresses, viz: 491 with valuable inclosures, and 1,347 with contents not specified. Of the 387 letters reported as having been rifled of their contents, investigation of 109 of the complaints showed the claim of valuable inclosures to be false. Only 13 registered letters were reported as having been tampered with, and investigation of 5 cases (the remaining 8 still under investigation) showed there had been no loss.

Registered packets reported lost 387, of which 268 were delivered. Eighty-six packets were reported rifled, of which reports 44 were found to be false.

The disbursements of moneys collected and recovered on account of lost and rifled registered letters and packets amounted, in 578 cases, to $13,657.90.

Attention is invited to the fact, that of the total number of complaints of registered letters and packages as lost, rifled, tampered with, and detained, viz, 4,636, 2,575 were recovered or satisfactorily accounted for, leaving only 2,061 still under investigation, or finally closed as lost, including losses by fire, highway robberies, and ordinary thefts. By comparing this number, 2,061, with the entire number of letters and packets registered during the year, viz, 8,300,000, the certainty and security of the registered mail is clearly demonstrated.

Ordinary cases, Class B, 23,782.—There were 16,562 ordinary letters reported lost, of which 12,108 were letters with valuable inclosures, and 4,454 contents not specified. Of this number, 1,737 were reported as delivered. The number of ordinary packets reported lost was 6,508, of which 451 were found to have been delivered. The disbursements of money recovered on account of lost ordinary letters amounted, in 77 cases, to $701.23.

Three hundred and twenty-three robberies of post-offices were reported during the year, and 92 offices were burned. Robberies of mail stages on the highway numbered 86. One hundred and thirty-five complaints of depredations were made by postmasters, of which 19 were found to have been groundless. Eleven mails were reported as burned in mail-cars, in railway accidents, or in post-offices, and 65 were reported as lost by mail-carriers, by floods, snow-blockades, or from other causes.

Miscellaneous cases, Class C, 3,231.—This class embraces a variety of cases not, strictly speaking, mail depredations, such as failing contractors, delinquent postmasters, change of postmasters, solvency of the sureties of postmasters at money-order offices, forgery of signatures to, and wrong payments of, money-orders, schemes to defraud by the use of the mails, and other offenses. The amount of money collected in this class of cases by inspectors during the year amounted to $22,701.71, of which amount $20,157.96 was from delinquent postmasters.

CASES REPORTED ON BY INSPECTORS DURING THE FISCAL YEAR ENDED JUNE 30, 1881.

Registered cases, including those referred in previous years 4,502
Ordinary cases, including those referred in previous years 11,221
Miscellaneous cases, including those referred in previous years................................. 4,247

Total... 19,971

PERMISSIBLE WRITING ON MAIL MATTER OF THE FOURTH CLASS.

The present law concerning permissible writing on mailable matter of the fourth class (which consists largely of samples of merchandise) or on the tags or labels attached thereto restricts such writing to the name and address of the sender, the number and names of the articles, and a single "mark, number, name, or letter, for purpose of identification." This restriction has given rise to much complaint from that large portion of the mercantile and manufacturing community who make use of the mails for the transmission of samples of their goods, and who claim that they are subjected to an onerous tax in being compelled to pay postage at letter rates on samples bearing only the ordinary marks required by commercial usage, and the absence of which renders samples valueless for the purposes they are intended to serve. In view of the fact that such marks contain nothing in the nature of a personal correspondence, and are essential to the complete exercise of the right to send samples of merchandise by mail, I therefore recommend such legislation as will provide a remedy for this apparent injustice, while securing the revenues of the department against loss through the abuse of the enlarged privileges which may be thereby granted.

EXPLOSIVE AND OTHER DANGEROUS ARTICLES IN THE MAILS.

The law excluding from the mails such articles as "from their form or nature are liable to destroy, deface, or otherwise damage the contents of the mail-bag, or harm the person of any one engaged in the postal service," provides no penalty for its violation; and as instances have occurred in which there have been deposited in the mails articles of so destructive and dangerous a nature as to imperil not only the safety of other mail matter, but the lives of postal employés and of the persons to whom those articles were directed, it seems desirable that such acts, whether resulting from culpable carelessness or prompted by malice or a spirit of wanton mischief, should be followed by punishment more or less severe, according to the circumstances of each case; and I therefore recommend the passage of a law providing suitable penalties for such offenses.

POSTAL LAWS AND REGULATIONS.

The edition of the Postal Laws and Regulations, compiled and published under the authority of the act of Congress of March 3, 1879, has been exhausted, and it has been found necessary to order a small number reprinted from the stereotype plates to supply new post-offices and employés of the service. The edition of Postal Laws and Regulations of 1879 was a great improvement upon any previous edition, and the experience since acquired in this connection has necessitated many changes. These, as well as all subsequent laws affecting the postal service (some of which are very important) ought to be incorporated into the text of a new edition. It is a matter of the utmost moment to the Post-Office Department that this revision be at once made.

The work involved should be performed by able and experienced officers of the department. The appropriation for printing and binding estimated for is sufficient to pay for printing the book; but the officers who may be selected by the Postmaster-General to compile, edit, and superintend its publication, including the preparation of an exhaustive index, should receive extra compensation for the work imposed upon them.

In the proper place and at the proper time I will ask for a small appropriation sufficient for the accomplishment of this work.

SALARIES OF THE ASSISTANT POSTMASTER-GENERALS.

Upon mature reflection I am convinced that it is my duty to recommend that the salaries of the three Assistant Postmaster-Generals be increased to $5,000 each per annum. Officers holding similar positions in other departments of the government, whose duties are certainly no more responsible and require no greater executive ability, have for many years received $5,000 each per annum, and it would be no more than an act of simple justice to place the officers of this department on an equality with them.

COMPENSATION OF POSTMASTERS AT THE LARGE OFFICES.

Attention is invited to the following statement:

Office.	Ordinary gross revenue.	Bond of postmaster.	Compensation of postmaster.	Money-order business.	
				Value of orders issued.	Value of orders paid.
Chicago, Ill	$1, 440, 072 94	$300, 000 00	$4, 000 00	$1, 764, 250 16	$7, 020, 692 98
Philadelphia, Pa	1, 294, 712 58	150, 000 00	4, 000 00	1, 000, 041 42	2, 637, 577 30
Boston, Mass	1, 221, 274 73	150, 000 00	4, 000 00	1, 088, 441 21	2, 642, 550 48
Saint Louis, Mo	675, 680 12	150, 000 00	4, 000 00	904, 384 46	4, 530, 092 57
Cincinnati, Ohio	540, 186 73	300, 000 00	4, 000 00	597, 116 50	2, 397, 089 07
San Francisco, Cal	468, 741 27	350, 000 00	4, 000 00	988, 402 75	2, 146, 290 33
Baltimore, Md	444, 303 61	200, 000 00	4, 000 00	433, 216 31	1, 515, 273 97
Total	6, 085, 072 04	1, 600, 000 00	28, 000 00	6, 835, 951 89	22, 829, 445 18
Total of all offices in the United States	34, 785, 397 97		6, 296, 743 79	100, 750, 695 73	106, 173, 092 89

In view of the facts thus presented I recommend that the compensation of the postmasters at Chicago, Philadelphia, Boston, and St. Louis be increased to $7,000, and that of the postmasters at Cincinnati, San Francisco, New Orleans, and Baltimore to $6,000 per annum.

It is as essential to the interests of the government as to those of private enterprise that its business be transacted by men equipped for their work by natural qualification and special training. Surely, the government cannot expect to secure the services of the men best qualified to do its work when it offers a salary affording little more than a bare support to officials who are clothed with the largest responsibilities.

A COMMISSION TO CONSIDER THE REORGANIZATION OF THE DEPARTMENT.

In April of the present year, a commission was appointed, consisting of four officers of the department, charged with the duty of examining into the status of the clerical force of the department, the manner of assignments to duty, the methods of transacting public business, &c., with a view to the instituting of such changes and readjustments as might result in simplifying the organization and improving the *personnel* of the employés.

Verbal and other reports have been made to me, from time to time, embodying practical suggestions, which have been adopted and are now in operation, greatly to the benefit of the discipline and efficiency of the working force. Other recommendations touching the compensation of clerks and kindred subjects have been utilized and applied in their proper connection.

CIVIL SERVICE REFORM.

Careful observation in this department and elsewhere has but confirmed my conviction of the great public benefit to be derived from conducting the public business on business principles. Some method of relief must be provided from the overwhelming pressure for appointment to clerkships and other subordinate positions, and from the equal pressure for the removal of capable and experienced assistants to make room for those who are not more competent. The public service is a public trust to which every citizen may properly aspire, and the public interest plainly demands that admission to it should not depend upon personal favor, because such favor cannot well be impartial, and because a system of appointment by mere influence may be readily perverted to the promotion of private interests and personal ambition. Appointment by influence naturally results in making the tenure of office depend not upon fidelity and efficiency in the discharge of official duty, but upon the assiduous cultivation of the favor of a patron. Such a tenure is incompatible with the self-respect of the incumbent, and the service must necessarily suffer from the decline of its *morale*. But the evil consequences cannot be limited to the public service; they affect all political action, the purity and vigor of the government, and the national character itself. The question, therefore, is one of far higher importance than that of the comparative fitness of clerks in the employment of the government, and really concerns the character and success of republican institutions.

The first step, in my judgment, toward the relief of the appointing officers and the promotion of the greater efficiency and economy of the civil service would be a method of minor appointment, which should be independent of personal or partisan influence. In some important government offices of which I have had personal knowledge, such a system is already in operation. In those offices minor appointments are determined solely by proper qualifications, ascertained by impartial tests open to all applicants upon equal terms. The great success which has attended this method of selection proves its practicability, while the good results, both in the service and in the character of the officers thus selected, demonstrate its value. The extension of this method under uniform conditions is earnestly to be desired, both to correct familiar evils in the public service itself and to remove the still graver evils which spring from them.

In my opinion, the same general principles should govern the selection and retention of employés in this department. The public is best served by honest, experienced, and competent officers, and changes, therefore, should be made carefully and only for reasons affecting official conduct. My views upon this subject are the result of prolonged official experience, and I am persuaded that the practical application of these principles would promote public morality, increase the economy and efficiency of the public service, and assuage the fury of party spirit, against which Washington warned the country as its chief peril.

THOMAS L. JAMES,
Postmaster-General.

The PRESIDENT.

PAPERS

REPORT OF THE POSTMASTER-GENERAL.

REPORT OF THE FIRST ASSISTANT POSTMASTER-GENERAL.

POST-OFFICE DEPARTMENT,
OFFICE OF FIRST ASSISTANT POSTMASTER-GENERAL,
Washington, D. C., November 14, 1881.

SIR: The business of this office during the past fiscal year was, in some respects, much larger, and in others, somewhat smaller, than for the previous year. While fewer post-offices were established, and more discontinued, yet in the matter of correspondence and in the management of the details of the business of the bureau, much additional clerical labor was made necessary.

*   *   *   *   *   *   *

Notwithstanding the number of allowances made for clerical assistance and for separating purposes at post-offices during the past fiscal year, there remain as many applications for allowances for one or the other of such purposes on file, which, though reasonable in character, could not be granted on account of the insufficiency of the appropriation. These applications are believed to be proper in every respect, and no reason is known why they should not be granted. I hope an effort will be made soon after the convening of Congress to procure an appropriation of at least $100,000 to enable the department to dispose of these requests in order that they may not remain on the files, without action, until the next fiscal year, and then become a charge upon that year's appropriation.

Allowances for rent of post-offices can be legally made only at offices of the first and second classes; postmasters at offices of the third and fourth classes pay their own rent.

Some change has recently been made in the manner of doing business in this division with a view to making it more efficient.

FREE DELIVERY DIVISION.

During the fiscal year the changes in the letter carrier force were 1,453. These changes involved the writing of the names of each carrier six times. They also involved the sending out of 2,906 blank bonds and oaths.

A record was kept monthly of the number of pieces of mail matter collected and delivered by the letter carriers at the several free delivery offices; also of the amount of postage on local matter at these offices.

There were 2,508 letters written and an indefinite number of circulars sent out during the year.

Force employed in this service: 1 superintendent, 2 clerks, 2 post-office inspectors, and 2,861 letter carriers.

*POSTAGE ON LOCAL MATTER.

The postage on local matter at the several free delivery offices amounted to $3,273,630.39, an increase over that of the preceding year of $204,833.25. It also exceeded the total cost of the service by $773,718.85. This increase in postage on local matter was 6.67 per cent., while the increase in the cost of the service was 5.76 per cent.

The average cost piece of handling matter was two and four-tenths-mills, a decrease of one-tenth of a mill as compared with last year. The average cost per carrier was $873.54, a decrease of $11.74 per carrier.

Aggregate result of free delivery service for the fiscal year ended June 30, 1881.

Statistics of free delivery.	Total.	Increase over last year.	Per cent. of increase.
Number of offices......................................	109		4.99
Number of carriers....................................	2,861	173	6.43
Mail letters delivered.................................	282,495,688	18,511,049	7.05
Mail postal cards delivered..........................	69,968,556	9,921,680	16.95
Local letters delivered...............................	70,733,206	4,486,179	6.71
Local postal cards delivered........................	43,886,158	4,877,544	12.90
Registered letters delivered.........................	2,195,300	319,854	17.70
Newspapers delivered................................	146,417,114	24,701,082	19.79
Letters collected......................................	284,756,945	4,390,755	1.52
Postal cards collected................................	85,792,125	6,512,805	8.21
Newspapers collected................................	54,075,476	11,062,945	25.99
Whole number of pieces handled..................	1,016,197,562	84,075,719	8.92
Pieces handled per carrier...........................	355,936	5,437	1.55
Total cost of service, including pay of post-office inspectors.....................................	$2,499,911 54	$136,218 40	5.76
Average cost per piece, in mills.....................	2.4	Decrease. 0.1	Decrease. .04
Average cost per carrier*............................	$873 54	$11 74	1.33
Amount of postage on local matter................	$3,273,630 39	Increase. $204,833 25	Increase. 6.67
Excess of postage on local matter over the total cost of service...................................	773,718 85	68,614 85	9.73

*Based on the aggregate ($2,498,972.14) paid carriers, including incidental expenses at the several offices, less $5,939.40 paid post-office inspectors.

These several cities represent, in a large degree, the business activity, enterprise, and commercial interests of the country, and include within their free delivery limits 10,000,000 inhabitants (about one-fifth of the population of the country), who are directly benefited by this service. Its benefits, however, are not confined to the population of these cities, as all who correspond with or receive letters from any of them are interested in the quick delivery of their letters at the point of destination, and also in the prompt collection and transmission of letters in reply.

The stimulus given to correspondence by the facilities afforded by this service has, no doubt, greatly increased the number of letters passing in the mails, and built up in the larger cities a local correspondence, which already yields a revenue from postage on local matter alone largely in excess of the cost of the service, and promises, with increased facilities, to yield a much larger revenue.

I desire to direct special attention to the importance of increasing the efficiency of the carrier service in the cities where it is now in operation, and its extension to other cities where the revenues of the offices at such points will justify. I firmly believe that such increase in the efficiency of this branch of the service will result in a gratifying increase of revenue to this department.

It is therefore earnestly recommended that the estimate of the cost of this service for the next fiscal year be appropriated to meet the reasonable wants of the public.

For full details of the operation of this service see tabular statement marked O, hereto appended.

LEASE DESK.

The following is a summary of the work pertaining to this desk, though the clerk in charge was variously employed during the fiscal year:

Number of leases for post-offices prepared during the year 41
Number of letters written 549
Number of cases referred to the chief post-office inspector, requesting information concerning the same.. 43
Number of post-office leases, including leases of stations in the large cities in operation June 30, 1881.. 290

In this connection I desire again to call attention to the necessity of Congressional action for the purpose of conferring upon the department the power to enter into contracts for the leasing of buildings for post-offices (of the first and second classes), and for stations. As heretofore said, this power is now exercised by implication, derived from the authority conferred to make allowances for the rent of buildings for post-office purposes, at offices of the first and second classes.

No embarrassment has yet arisen from the exercise of this implied power, but a due regard for the public interests seems to require that there should be express provisions of law for the guidance of the department in such matters.

LETTER-BOOK DESKS.

There were recorded by the two clerks in charge of these desks 19,697 letters during the year.

The number of reference papers and circulars directed and mailed by these clerks are estimated at 75,000 for the twelve months.

PRINCIPAL MESSENGER.

This employé receives and distributes all the mail and express matter for the bureau. The number of letters, papers, requisitions, and packages opened by him during the fiscal year amounted to 273,655.

Besides the principal messenger there are two assistant messengers whose time is entirely taken up in services incident to such positions.

The supervision of the blank agency division has recently been transferred from this office to that of the Postmaster-General, and the report, by its chief, of the clerical work performed therein during the past fiscal year and the recommendations he has made, looking to an improvement in the efficiency of the service, will be found in another place.

In closing this report, which from the general nature of the work performed in this bureau is necessarily somewhat brief, I can say the character of the duties assigned to this office require much attention, labor, and promptness, and so far as they involve the appointment of post-masters I am of the opinion that annually a better class of officers of this description is being obtained, notwithstanding the disadvantages the department labors under in the selection of such officers on account of the majority of them being so remote from the appointing power.

The number of postmasters not thoroughly competent to perform their duties is believed to be annually decreasing, and during the last fiscal year the department inspectors in their examinations into the solvency of the sureties of postmasters found fewer cases to report against than for some years previous.

Very respectfully,

FRANK HATTON,
First Assistant Postmaster-General.

Hon. THOMAS L. JAMES,
Postmaster-General.

A.—*Statement showing the number of Presidential post-offices in each State and Territory June 30, 1880, and June 30, 1881, with increase and decrease; also the number of post-offices of each class, together with the number of money-order post-offices and stations, by States and Territories, June 30, 1881.*

States and Territories.	Number of Presidential post-offices June 30, 1880.	Number of Presidential post-offices June 30, 1881.	Increase.	Decrease.	Number of post-offices of the first class.	Number of post-offices of the second class.	Number of post-offices of the third class.	Number of post-offices of the fourth class.	Number of money-order post-offices June 30, 1881.	Number of money-order post-office stations.
Alabama	16	18	2	....	1	3	14	1,196	63	......
Alaska								3		......
Arizona	4	6	2	....		3	3	107	6	......
Arkansas	9	9	..	....	1	3	5	950	71	......
California	50	51	1	....	3	14	34	841	123	4
Colorado	22	29	7	....	2	10	17	344	43	......
Connecticut	49	48	..	1	3	12	33	406	60	......
Dakota	8	11	3	....		6	5	423	22	......
Delaware	6	6	..	....		1	5	107	14	......
District of Columbia	1	1	..	....	1			4	1	1
Florida	7	7	..	....		2	5	361	28	......
Georgia	25	26	1	....	3	3	20	1,131	74	......
Idaho	2	2	..	....		1	1	110	13	......
Illinois	162	170	8	....	5	31	134	1,874	480	6
Indiana	74	78	4	....	5	13	60	1,606	239	......
Indian Territory								91	4	......
Iowa	101	107	6	....	4	21	82	1,405	356	1
Kansas	58	65	7	....	2	11	52	1,496	201	1
Kentucky	27	28	1	....	1	9	18	1,366	83	......
Louisiana	10	10	..	....	1	2	7	480	46	......
Maine	29	30	1	....	2	7	21	916	100	......
Maryland	15	16	1	....	1	2	13	696	51	......
Massachusetts	108	107	..	1	6	30	71	654	147	13
Michigan	86	91	5	....	3	28	60	1,384	273	......
Minnesota	40	41	1	....	2	7	32	973	137	......
Mississippi	18	19	1	....		3	16	733	72	......
Missouri	50	51	1	....	3	6	42	1,738	285	3
Montana	7	9	2	....		3	6	147	13	......
Nebraska	28	32	4	....	1	4	27	788	112	......
Nevada	11	10	..	1		6	4	111	12	......
New Hampshire	25	28	3	....		6	22	485	68	......
New Jersey	52	52	..	....	2	12	38	629	75	......
New Mexico	3	4	1	....		1	3	144	7	......
New York	189	192	3	....	10	39	143	2,702	375	17
North Carolina	18	15	3	....		3	12	1,492	88	......
Ohio	112	120	8	....	7	27	86	2,358	350	3
Oregon	9	9	..	....	1	2	6	364	43	......
Pennsylvania	126	137	11	....	3	32	102	3,369	363	5
Rhode Island	11	11	..	....	1	4	6	107	16	......
South Carolina	12	14	2	....	1	1	12	673	44	......
Tennessee	18	19	1	....	2	3	14	1,505	82	......
Texas	44	50	6	....	3	13	34	1,814	150	......
Utah	3	4	1	....		1	3	221	16	......
Vermont	20	22	2	....		6	16	475	83	......
Virginia	25	25	..	....	3	4	13	1,766	87	......
Washington	4	6	2	....		1	5	248	13	..
West Virginia	8	9	1	....		1	8	905	46	......
Wisconsin	60	64	4	....	1	18	45	1,304	204	......
Wyoming	3	4	1	....		2	2	81	10	......
Total	1,760	1,863	106	3	84	417	1,362	42,649	5,100	54

B.—*Total operations of the appointment division of the office of the First Assistant Postmaster-General for the year ended June 30, 1881; also statement of the number of post-offices in each State and Territory June 30, 1880, and June 30, 1881, with increase or decrease.*

States and Territories.	Post-offices.				Postmasters.				Whole number of post-offices June 30, 1880.	Whole number of post-offices June 30, 1881.	Increase.	Decrease.
	Established.	Discontinued.	Names and sites changed.	Appointments on change of names and sites.	Resigned and commissions expired.	Removed.	Deceased.	Total number of cases.				
Alabama	104	32	4	1	229	30	9	408	1,144	1,216	72	....
Alaska	1	....	....	....	1	1	..	3	2	3	1	....
Arizona	57	24	4	2	22	2	1	110	85	113	28	....
Arkansas	155	34	28	20	236	46	10	569	897	968	71	....
California	78	50	9	6	117	22	12	284	889	912	23	....
Colorado	93	51	17	3	131	9	3	304	351	393	42	....
Connecticut	5	4	3	....	43	2	2	60	453	454	1	....
Dakota	100	37	31	9	69	2	1	240	371	434	63	....
Delaware	3	1	....	....	7	1	..	12	111	113	2	....
District of Columbia	....	....	....	....	....	..	2	2	5	5	..	....
Florida	40	32	5	....	75	7	5	164	360	368	8	....
Georgia	122	33	8	4	200	8	10	381	1,068	1,157	89	....
Idaho	25	14	1	1	21	5	1	67	101	112	11	....
Illinois	58	26	16	4	239	48	22	409	2,012	3,044	32	....
Indiana	67	33	14	3	277	61	20	472	1,650	1,684	34	....
Indian Territory	17	12	2	1	21	2	..	54	86	91	5	....
Iowa	71	45	13	1	185	39	9	361	1,486	1,512	26	....
Kansas	196	82	37	36	286	36	10	627	1,507	1,551	44	....
Kentucky	107	40	23	5	252	14	10	446	1,347	1,414	67	....
Louisiana	43	25	10	3	105	17	3	203	472	490	18	....
Maine	18	2	6	....	78	8	13	120	930	946	16	....
Maryland	26	8	6	....	53	11	6	110	696	714	18	....
Massachusetts	8	1	2	....	50	6	7	83	754	761	7	....
Michigan	58	29	21	10	185	29	13	334	1,396	1,425	29	....
Minnesota	68	48	36	16	126	25	3	295	994	1,014	20	....
Mississippi	90	42	13	9	126	36	7	204	704	752	48	....
Missouri	127	77	46	20	302	51	22	625	1,729	1,780	50	....
Montana	38	30	6	2	31	7	1	113	148	156	8	....
Nebraska	80	28	41	19	151	20	3	322	768	820	52	....
Nevada	9	13	3	....	20	4	..	49	125	121	....	4
New Hampshire	9	5	1	1	22	7	4	48	459	463	4	....
New Jersey	15	7	7	5	53	20	11	112	683	691	8	....
New Mexico	50	16	3	1	50	5	1	125	114	148	34	....
New York	63	20	15	2	234	46	35	402	2,946	2,988	42	....
North Carolina	101	52	15	3	228	28	10	434	1,458	1,507	49	....
Ohio	98	36	24	7	277	59	29	518	2,416	2,473	57	....
Oregon	25	23	11	9	61	1	2	122	371	372	2	....
Pennsylvania	92	31	21	9	340	54	30	568	3,444	3,505	61	....
Rhode Island	3	1	....	....	12	..	1	19	116	118	2	....
South Carolina	84	33	8	3	94	6	13	238	641	692	51	....
Tennessee	154	35	14	1	282	37	19	531	1,405	1,524	119	....
Texas	147	127	22	6	312	34	18	660	1,344	1,364	20	....
Utah	18	7	2	1	28	8	1	64	214	225	11	....
Vermont	3	3	1	....	52	3	2	64	497	497	..	....
Virginia	109	40	17	6	218	64	13	441	1,722	1,791	69	....
Washington	41	30	7	1	36	6	2	112	233	254	21	....
West Virginia	45	30	11	3	135	20	12	242	889	914	25	....
Wisconsin	56	29	20	8	131	19	14	280	1,329	1,368	29	....
Wyoming	17	7	2	2	21	..	..	47	75	85	10	....
Total	2,915	1,415	665	243	6,217	956	421	12,591	43,012	44,512	1,504	4

C.—*Statement of the operations of the free-delivery*

Post-offices.	Carriers in service June 30, 1881.	Delivered.				Registered letters.	Newspapers, circulars, &c.
		Mail.		Local.			
		Letters.	Postal cards.	Letters.	Postal cards.		
Akron, Ohio	5	520,620	182,262	29,059	22,336	2,073	498,035
Albany, N. Y	30	2,563,559	499,914	283,579	270,993	9,287	1,467,200
Allegheny, Pa	11	1,068,900	249,448	160,702	126,616	7,130	1,061,422
Atlanta, Ga	8	1,377,429	429,390	101,073	128,066	24,505	1,062,458
Auburn, N. Y	6	494,188	146,656	80,820	22,969	2,436	373,718
Augusta, Ga	6	340,911	138,783	27,901	15,446	5,932	276,295
Baltimore, Md	81	6,192,205	1,360,348	1,273,587	1,212,472	43,491	3,345,610
Bangor, Me	4	287,059	69,704	22,152	10,985	3,278	182,268
Bloomington, Ill	3	468,564	180,744	28,937	54,668	4,487	398,070
Boston, Mass	200	13,635,615	8,831,269	5,945,880	3,489,581	76,240	9,290,848
Bridgeport, Conn	7	377,138	95,113	49,438	35,719	2,011	329,538
Brooklyn, N. Y	116	6,648,667	1,782,632	2,153,029	1,501,117	36,113	4,322,013
Buffalo, N. Y	37	4,498,854	690,535	583,270	545,558	35,278	3,097,697
Burlington, Iowa	7	817,049	156,307	55,812	45,318	7,158	535,713
Camden, N. J	8	489,629	183,129	60,768	49,380	2,275	443,717
Charleston, S. C	8	603,316	140,224	58,463	75,525	6,785	373,406
Chicago, Ill	199	26,376,858	5,307,869	5,449,388	3,424,242	261,109	9,153,531
Cincinnati, Ohio	81	8,048,176	1,515,854	1,743,582	1,332,300	57,509	3,388,436
Cleveland, Ohio	36	4,785,778	1,447,817	698,717	474,070	54,274	2,864,856
Columbus, Ohio	14	1,524,973	463,281	116,855	115,909	12,662	1,110,783
Covington, Ky	6	322,158	99,427	19,113	18,654	1,864	225,986
Dallas, Tex	5	273,149	71,080	10,257	11,274	1,126	165,737
Davenport, Iowa	8	791,548	177,770	54,232	89,007	4,415	554,907
Dayton, Ohio	12	1,332,945	425,587	168,956	131,452	10,400	794,621
Denver, Colo	10	1,529,908	331,055	186,572	133,932	2,667	831,346
Des Moines, Iowa	9	1,042,596	393,696	84,833	107,194	8,714	722,282
Detroit, Mich	34	5,740,193	1,189,067	743,864	333,372	55,938	2,580,942
Dubuque, Iowa	7	582,236	214,391	34,472	32,577	7,248	440,505
Easton, Pa	7	652,471	217,316	62,089	00,634	2,046	438,587
Elizabeth, N. J	6	526,950	127,329	88,854	38,314	1,696	497,651
Elmira, N. Y	7	870,951	234,087	54,415	41,139	6,659	464,943
Erie, Pa	7	1,101,686	92,932	86,480	42,418	1,449	661,449
Evansville, Ind	8	854,429	319,809	32,360	57,865	6,241	711,987
Fall River, Mass	6	612,518	61,692	47,276	41,420	664	543,979
Fort Wayne, Ind	7	838,397	118,542	100,330	83,006	4,511	742,606
Galveston, Tex	8	956,058	142,878	35,790	16,687	6,668	367,065
Grand Rapids, Mich	10	1,406,155	444,322	148,454	107,083	11,520	1,018,576
Harrisburgh, Pa	6	473,283	163,049	36,468	37,306	3,250	591,473
Hartford, Conn	11	1,133,309	280,726	369,454	258,368	8,755	1,303,482
Hoboken, N. J	4	301,456	89,830	23,441	31,848	1,892	134,296
Houston, Tex	5	810,108	57,770	24,039	10,132	2,834	192,896
Indianapolis, Ind	30	3,179,551	735,608	293,960	818,544	20,105	1,317,146
Jackson, Mich	5	464,833	176,933	28,902	24,129	2,109	498,546
Jersey City, N. J	22	1,213,471	303,334	155,869	175,666	5,657	664,943
Kansas City, Mo	19	3,292,181	900,675	274,776	187,973	31,294	1,471,075
La Fayette, Ind	5	401,146	150,196	39,126	20,176	2,648	363,829
Lancaster, Pa	9	589,454	156,508	39,250	38,710	2,253	402,502
Lawrence, Mass	5	784,539	102,071	80,230	89,627	1,612	730,268
Leadville, Colo	5	376,883	28,628	20,750	12,580	1,534	110,063
Leavenworth, Kans	5	453,712	87,072	21,722	20,724	2,450	427,399
Little Rock, Ark	5	482,251	103,294	70,094	63,585	4,993	256,592
Louisville, Ky	32	3,899,246	933,821	433,614	525,111	44,218	1,917,674
Lowell, Mass	10	911,895	180,555	103,690	78,880	2,542	499,830
Lynn, Mass	10	721,967	207,741	55,628	84,935	801	592,765
Macon, Ga	5	382,784	175,834	13,852	14,274	7,808	249,650
Manchester, N. H	7	574,399	160,133	29,835	51,577	2,649	535,232
Mansfield, Ohio	4	247,701	94,177	15,142	8,053	1,259	194,221
Memphis, Tenn	13	1,503,402	233,204	75,049	116,173	16,632	516,392
Meriden, Conn	5	102,787	23,197	19,595	9,519	572	74,563
Milwaukee, Wis	34	3,923,100	650,803	534,977	507,350	31,533	1,661,78?
Minneapolis, Minn	12	1,294,285	338,489	129,526	114,609	9,648	976,00?
Mobile, Ala	6	511,115	137,269	67,896	66,943	4,539	743,95?
Nashville, Tenn	12	1,430,937	413,926	100,017	119,980	25,319	1,141,42?
Newark, N. J	27	2,237,626	680,562	426,315	381,283	12,522	1,329,96?
New Bedford, Mass	8	685,760	107,616	67,348	42,621	1,231	436,98?
New Haven, Conn	19	1,270,776	247,724	186,463	142,652	4,290	1,096,68?
New Orleans, La	47	1,975,676	285,359	327,502	306,133	36,101	1,441,546
New York, N. Y	503	50,970,109	8,770,899	36,504,190	12,430,862	452,278	17,128,411
Norfolk, Va	7	737,385	190,139	68,129	86,949	2,521	448,709
Oakland, Cal	8	631,008	95,548	50,304	59,404	2,594	499,97?
Omaha, Nebr	10	1,087,112	217,341	127,068	107,014	9,180	892,8??
Oswego, N. Y	6	442,193	117,578	31,487	21,521	2,780	275,564

* Established August 15, 1880.   † Established September 1, 1880.

system for the fiscal year ended June 30, 1881.

Collected.			Pieces handled.		Cost of service (including incidental expenses).			Postage on local matter.
Letters.	Postal cards.	Newspapers, circulars, &c.	Aggregate.	Per carrier.	Aggregate.	Per piece, in mills.	Per carrier.	
222, 389	121, 348	166, 766	1, 836, 888	267, 577	$3, 350 00	1. 8	$670 00	$1, 324 36
1, 566, 284	513, 812	271, 587	7, 406, 215	246, 877	27, 117 00	3. 7	903 90	9, 360 55
678, 816	246, 070	195, 852	3, 794, 956	344, 096	9, 355 46	2. 4	850 50	6, 706 80
634, 690	309, 650	55, 273	4, 123, 543	515, 442	6, 328 96	1. 5	791 11	4, 445 76
329, 378	114, 604	83, 260	1, 648, 119	274, 686	4, 649 94	2. 8	774 90	2, 486 90
231, 137	91, 644	45, 040	1, 173, 080	195, 515	4, 404 00	3. 7	734 00	2, 060 25
8, 569, 779	2, 171, 489	397, 313	24, 511, 194	302, 607	72, 662 17	2. 9	897 08	47, 790 60
360, 656	133, 897	42, 848	1, 112, 344	278, 086	3, 420 96	3.	855 24	1, 247 89
235, 913	119, 998	79, 624	1, 572, 005	262, 001	5, 100 00	3. 2	850 00	1, 468 34
21, 350, 017	6, 329, 715	3, 999, 957	67, 889, 122	339, 445	177, 551 94	2. 6	887 76	232, 060 33
256, 201	73, 668	36, 068	1, 257, 294	179, 613	5, 514 58	4. 3	787 80	2, 666 88
5, 627, 762	2, 471, 254	906, 891	25, 449, 478	219, 392	90, 146 41	3. 9	854 71	122, 317 98
3, 366, 050	1, 382, 479	539, 169	14, 678, 849	396, 726	84, 981 70	2. 3	945 45	19, 343 23
511, 943	182, 594	85, 398	2, 397, 292	342, 185	5, 513 98	2. 3	787 70	2, 427 53
824, 806	105, 301	65, 749	1, 724, 854	215, 607	5, 913 54	3. 4	739 19	1, 989 35
447, 651	176, 824	82, 021	1, 064, 215	245, 527	6, 825 48	3. 4	853 18	3, 018 50
30, 543, 713	8, 684, 651	5, 421, 904	94, 622, 765	475, 491	168, 581 37	1. 7	897 89	183, 618 75
4, 906, 870	1, 812, 029	1, 409, 196	24, 216, 942	298, 975	73, 033 97	3.	901 65	60, 253 94
3, 290, 369	1, 415, 759	893, 417	15, 873, 057	440, 974	36, 074 35	2. 2	974 01	30, 968 75
892, 210	404, 227	158, 809	4, 799, 709	342, 836	11, 400 00	2. 3	816 29	5, 640 70
176, 250	62, 768	31, 866	958, 086	159, 681	4, 370 50	4. 5	728 48	764 32
237, 066	90, 63v	36, 416	896, 744	179, 349	4, 251 75	4. 7	850 35	982 76
257, 146	150, 065	58, 427	2, 187, 517	273, 440	6, 872 33	3. 1	859 04	3, 067 04
866, 584	403, 902	382, 947	4, 519, 894	376, 616	10, 550 87	2. 3	879 24	5, 230 92
645, 529	153, 021	107, 361	3, 922, 433	392, 243	8, 168 80	3	816 88	9, 188 15
697, 258	841, 569	188, 876	3, 594, 018	390, 324	6, 997 14	1. 9	777 46	3, 095 79
2, 511, 109	779, 957	428, 393	14, 362, 835	422, 436	32, 404 66	2. 2	963 20	19, 931 72
543, 022	238, 691	123, 750	3, 210, 962	315, 712	5, 450 00	2. 4	778 57	1, 871 17
456, 714	216, 847	345, 646	3, 477, 850	353, 907	6, 325 76	2. 3	908 68	3, 056 13
278, 644	111, 205	49, 808	1, 715, 741	285, 957	5, 231 20	3	871 87	3, 330 80
311, 345	144, 232	57, 620	3, 185, 890	312, 178	5, 785 92	2. 6	823 70	3, 373 72
302, 907	126, 691	38, 296	2, 494, 378	356, 340	6, 470 67	2. 6	924 38	3, 427 34
487, 288	235, 440	71, 275	2, 776, 690	347, 087	6, 611 94	2. 3	826 40	1, 995 60
244, 707	47, 900	43, 171	1, 642, 325	273, 721	5, 112 40	3. 1	853 07	3, 307 21
537, 609	139, 952	64, 729	2, 649, 682	378, 526	6, 249 30	2. 3	892 76	4, 129 21
503, 265	106, 335	89, 918	3, 316, 684	280, 585	5, 376 90	2. 3	672 12	1, 477 30
1, 226, 270	395, 201	176, 542	4, 937, 123	493, 712	7, 939 17	1. 6	793 92	4, 325 68
145, 262	88, 982	19, 408	1, 596, 475	266, 412	5, 104 86	3. 1	850 81	2, 391 55
912, 288	242, 479	227, 318	4, 736, 182	430, 562	9, 366 46	1. 9	851 68	12, 849 67
137, 204	65, 961	9, 400	795, 448	198, 862	3, 400 00	4. 2	850 00	977 68
115, 663	29, 119	12, 483	756, 064	151, 209	4, 735 45	6. 2	947 09	1, 420 29
1, 954, 570	966, 381	344, 799	9, 630, 684	321, 023	28, 661 74	2. 9	955 39	9, 064 64
228, 716	102, 028	32, 033	1, 554, 029	310, 806	3, 505 25	2. 2	701 05	1, 325 62
771, 718	305, 159	108, 278	3, 704, 095	166, 368	20, 539 56	5. 5	933 61	6, 689 62
1, 439, 248	547, 998	340, 661	8, 485, 876	446, 625	15, 085 17	1. 7	793 96	10, 734 47
253, 537	123, 350	51, 494	1, 405, 502	281, 100	4, 260 05	3	852 01	1, 378 80
191, 413	77, 230	17, 116	1, 514, 436	232, 406	4, 661 99	3	777 00	1, 342 72
800, 069	128, 416	92, 991	2, 798, 843	310, 983	7, 693 91	2. 7	854 77	2, 632 98
144, 697	22, 112	29, 161	746, 408	149, 281	4, 160 73	5. 5	532 15	1, 156 77
453, 927	90, 373	70, 905	1, 628, 295	325, 659	4, 414 53	2. 7	882 91	786 56
412, 570	164, 268	53, 355	1, 612, 992	322, 598	4, 262 00	2. 6	852 40	3, 276 19
2, 576, 060	1, 046, 118	534, 571	11, 910, 433	372, 201	30, 689 06	2. 5	930 02	20, 767 44
613, 498	153, 719	64, 159	2, 608, 756	260, 875	8, 515 74	3. 2	851 57	6, 283 44
466, 927	306, 745	98, 383	2, 437, 912	243, 791	7, 489 43	3	748 94	2, 774 18
533, 071	172, 836	86, 708	1, 476, 216	295, 243	3, 371 49	2. 2	674 30	982 58
284, 965	102, 065	34, 447	1, 796, 222	256, 603	5, 072 38	2. 8	724 62	1, 580 56
122, 800	51, 406	46, 647	781, 407	195, 352	2, 165 94	2. 7	541 48	741 50
662, 653	199, 328	123, 187	3, 446, 020	265, 078	11, 106 57	3. 2	854 35	2, 722 50
41, 919	15, 428	3, 258	290, 832	58, 166	2, 945 97	10. 1	589 19	1, 710 06
2, 063, 226	770, 885	407, 466	10, 541, 121	310, 033	28, 250 25	2. 6	830 89	17, 702 34
765, 006	259, 755	133, 530	4, 022, 033	335, 169	10, 354 32	2. 5	862 86	5, 859 27
581, 641	153, 841	304, 821	2, 572, 027	428, 671	5, 100 00	1. 9	850 00	2, 349 89
582, 812	229, 088	138, 024	4, 181, 525	348, 460	9, 524 30	2. 2	793 69	4, 549 10
1, 277, 316	536, 999	265, 180	7, 147, 766	264, 732	23, 008 97	3. 2	852 18	14, 520 58
373, 876	112, 205	47, 054	1, 874, 609	234, 326	6, 623 35	3. 5	827 92	1, 973 71
606, 297	169, 572	138, 009	4, 154, 646	218, 666	15, 482 47	3. 7	814 87	14, 190 68
2, 450, 338	693, 582	221, 669	8, 337, 906	177, 402	43, 843 33	5. 2	932 84	13, 091 97
95, 195, 415	21, 672, 536	12, 801, 283*	249, 986, 513	496, 991	429, 991 98	1. 7	854 77	1, 579, 777 86
842, 094	352, 624	134, 632	2, 872, 182	410, 312	5, 218 27	1. 8	745 47	2, 880 77
432, 371	101, 477	73, 219	1, 936, 897	242, 112	7, 060 57	3. 6	882 57	2, 054 40
412, 439	190, 409	80, 234	3, 129, 778	312, 978	8, 150 72	2. 6	815 07	4, 012 89
288, 806	109, 876	47, 003	1, 346, 810	224, 468	5, 111 90	3. 8	851 97	971 35

C.—*Statement of the operations of the free-delivery*

Post-offices.	Carriers in service June 30, 1881.	Delivered.				Registered letters.	Newspapers, circulars, &c.
		Mail.		Local.			
		Letters.	Postal cards.	Letters.	Postal cards.		
Paterson, N. J	8	727,203	120,206	70,147	63,552	2,645	756,878
Peoria, Ill	8	737,638	250,246	51,269	50,348	4,707	530,106
Petersburgh, Va	6	501,313	162,499	18,885	22,503	4,129	383,896
Philadelphia, Pa	309	19,783,274	5,792,312	12,365,922	6,624,885	144,431	16,564,001
Pittsburgh, Pa	36	2,881,859	738,421	648,596	434,709	20,602	1,818,758
Portland, Me	10	720,540	214,318	63,812	95,316	4,216	828,244
Portland, Oreg	5	257,316	33,741	32,958	14,595	3,167	214,481
Pottsville, Pa	4	284,768	92,925	30,258	11,477	1,224	491,552
Poughkeepsie, N. Y	7	658,440	118,533	61,726	43,420	2,453	545,919
Providence, R. I	26	1,563,233	899,388	333,797	206,442	5,711	1,164,442
Quincy, Ill	8	892,306	262,066	40,815	74,288	7,184	563,696
Reading, Pa	10	761,561	230,055	65,542	72,096	2,595	596,818
Richmond, Ind*	6	188,285	41,263	17,533	7,049	956	156,929
Richmond, Va	18	1,416,961	462,659	123,128	129,200	16,208	697,063
Rochester, N. Y	26	2,929,269	566,451	299,517	314,193	15,249	1,629,682
Sacramento City, Cal	5	354,602	53,170	25,700	20,491	1,906	265,929
Saint Joseph, Mo	9	1,073,629	302,627	118,962	83,230	13,123	846,616
Saint Louis, Mo	123	12,657,026	3,560,938	2,221,359	1,777,469	139,309	5,236,391
Saint Paul, Minn	14	1,605,732	364,595	134,227	114,447	26,909	1,215,642
Salem, Mass	6	379,975	119,356	37,329	44,933	882	432,180
San Francisco, Cal	67	4,818,187	530,480	1,943,916	1,124,950	58,963	3,835,972
Savannah, Ga	8	626,624	180,726	128,142	116,341	7,109	380,142
Springfield, Ill	6	509,363	202,476	30,556	24,972	2,748	476,448
Springfield, Mass	8	807,016	254,452	89,914	61,429	3,061	467,961
Springfield, Ohio	6	430,236	176,547	35,601	23,970	2,659	458,396
Syracuse, N. Y	20	2,129,164	426,511	260,484	243,265	8,836	1,228,391
Terre Haute, Ind	8	673,724	265,549	45,458	44,346	5,151	675,036
Toledo, Ohio	15	1,895,870	314,233	139,880	134,068	12,498	763,428
Topeka, Kans	5	780,744	174,073	75,437	58,031	5,155	571,275
Trenton, N. J	6	463,440	118,923	42,091	31,554	1,847	367,634
Troy, N. Y	16	2,366,987	605,734	430,603	246,581	4,948	1,268,378
Utica, N. Y	12	1,133,244	327,955	116,440	72,486	6,758	661,008
Washington, D. C	55	3,582,043	628,601	606,234	376,015	18,311	2,567,514
Wheeling, W. Va	8	607,501	242,709	48,605	47,830	8,428	516,128
Wilmington, Del	10	757,073	183,781	115,025	92,258	2,681	517,344
Worcester, Mass	12	802,877	217,956	107,441	134,307	2,663	637,889
Zanesville, Ohio†	5	235,304	97,877	16,854	12,494	2,653	267,129
Total	2,851	262,425,668	59,968,559	76,733,208	43,896,158	2,126,300	146,417,114

Amount paid post-office inspectors on free-delivery service ,...

---

* Established January 1, 1881.　　　† Established October 1, 1880.

system for the fiscal year ended June 30, 1881—Continued.

Collected.			Pieces handled.		Cost of service (including incidental expenses).			Postage on local matter.
Letters.	Postal cards.	Newspapers, circulars, &c.	Aggregate.	Per carrier.	Aggregate.	Per piece, in mills.	Per carrier.	
411,486	134,824	91,091	2,878,082	297,254	$6,874 08	2.6	$796 76	$2,735 05
580,008	200,926	180,825	2,485,298	310,602	7,002 30	2.8	875 29	2,386 82
270,550	144,519	30,680	1,537,608	256,282	4,654 49	8	775 75	793 56
20,471,043	11,865,117	9,773,430	113,384,415	366,980	279,891 00	2.6	905 79	396,626 28
2,095,129	752,700	512,812	9,901,657	275,046	83,305 50	3.3	922 37	22,515 50
875,179	837,281	211,686	8,350,592	335,059	8,536 60	2.5	853 96	4,861 41
452,738	99,805	44,273	1,158,158	230,632	4,520 50	2.9	904 10	1,921 95
171,306	75,150	80,274	1,248,024	312,006	3,407 98	2.7	851 99	951 99
681,680	134,495	110,908	2,857,574	338,796	5,962 48	2.5	851 78	2,008 40
1,494,612	445,647	204,522	5,816,794	228,722	24,941 81	4.3	959 30	18,957 57
881,180	172,991	29,803	2,442,819	305,352	6,679 61	2.7	834 95	1,866 82
356,964	181,197	87,123	2,348,911	234,391	8,515 14	3.6	851 51	2,519 92
182,630	55,642	43,731	647,006	107,835	1,877 82	2.9	312 80	831 22
815,702	333,841	108,876	4,096,672	227,704	13,905 86	3.4	772 55	4,399 16
1,295,286	454,214	273,602	7,717,566	296,060	23,251 31	3	868 51	10,957 44
296,802	48,051	82,580	1,079,293	215,858	4,750 00	4.4	950 00	1,415 70
744,407	278,568	152,987	3,615,151	401,682	7,186 00	1.9	792 80	4,037 34
8,476,348	3,013,392	2,731,959	39,796,501	323,565	116,423 17	2.9	946 58	72,132 99
1,165,457	395,968	196,233	5,219,205	372,800	11,528 16	2.2	823 42	5,517 12
276,643	108,509	58,148	1,452,965	242,161	5,131 06	3.5	855 18	1,868 43
7,432,682	1,407,165	1,299,519	21,432,774	319,591	59,780 94	2.8	891 33	61,327 63
455,005	192,847	148,825	2,206,856	283,856	5,928 87	2.6	741 08	7,445 98
228,592	104,888	58,954	1,633,997	272,533	4,916 09	3	819 35	1,486 62
496,737	180,013	96,485	2,850,108	293,763	6,827 68	2.9	853 46	4,177 09
186,890	75,767	29,508	1,400,658	233,443	4,711 94	3.3	785 32	2,006 62
970,300	415,258	243,516	5,944,229	297,211	15,247 73	2.5	762 38	8,412 38
632,714	322,377	230,697	2,885,054	360,632	6,387 10	2.2	798 30	2,101 30
1,466,236	415,818	249,338	4,891,349	326,123	12,853 58	2.6	856 91	4,856 99
514,888	134,650	37,928	2,847,181	469,436	4,307 18	1.8	861 44	2,880 78
348,167	61,489	39,273	1,510,217	251,703	5,140 07	3.4	856 68	3,835 35
2,632,177	500,010	649,480	8,195,896	512,244	13,326 96	1.6	833 56	11,513 83
814,860	324,732	202,882	3,663,032	305,253	10,229 58	2.7	852 46	3,497 73
2,698,543	768,080	553,547	11,733,888	212,342	46,530 60	1.9	846 01	22,331 27
556,405	223,589	85,478	2,426,773	303,349	5,816 78	2.4	727 10	2,161 98
287,427	161,106	46,429	2,273,122	227,312	8,576 22	3.7	857 62	4,045 05
436,596	165,388	64,973	2,554,087	196,468	10,089 05	3.9	772 28	5,136 61
161,681	80,346	64,840	939,188	187,838	2,635 86	2.8	827 17	838 64
394,759,945	85,798,125	54,075,476	1,016,197,562	355,906	2,493,972 14	2.4	873 54	3,272,690 20
					5,999 40			
					$2,499,911 54			

63 Ab

Statement of matter mailed in the U

Rank	States and Territories.	Number of letters mailed in plain envelopes upon which postage was paid by adhesive stamps. 1	Number of letters mailed in special-request stamped envelopes printed and furnished by the Post-Office Department upon orders received through postmasters. 2	Number of letters mailed in ordinary stamped envelopes. 3	Number of letters mailed in envelopes bearing business cards or return requests not printed by the Post-Office Department. 4
29	Alabama	2, 557, 268	1, 210, 716	2, 146, 716	1, 613, 092
49	Alaska Territory	8, 148	....	1, 404	....
44	Arizona Territory	645, 000	141, 394	223, 680	115, 634
34	Arkansas	2, 954, 952	654, 064	1, 576, 380	1, 129, 998
12	California	12, 092, 040	1, 403, 658	2, 382, 068	4, 627, 194
26	Colorado	5, 004, 220	1, 801, 545	1, 138, 600	2, 628, 544
33	Connecticut	11, 875, 084	4, 030, 832	1, 459, 328	5, 947, 124
37	Dakota Territory	2, 171, 312	351, 280	478, 304	713, 848
40	Delaware	1, 810, 444	308, 760	90, 480	472, 428
25	District of Columbia	3, 967, 716	122, 172	214, 032	1, 084, 382
39	Florida	1, 805, 760	163, 872	674, 960	416, 424
17	Georgia	5, 842, 250	2, 129, 808	2, 431, 208	3, 008, 888
46	Idaho Territory	438, 384	89, 034	173, 004	68, 684
3	Illinois	27, 514, 916	9, 432, 336	2, 975, 868	25, 435, 176
10	Indiana	13, 641, 836	2, 368, 844	1, 616, 420	6, 908, 536
48	Indian Territory	242, 632	34, 348	107, 692	33, 030
8	Iowa	14, 574, 768	3, 632, 656	3, 363, 608	7, 751, 720
16	Kansas	9, 375, 188	1, 649, 072	1, 901, 484	4, 384, 400
15	Kentucky	8, 863, 552	1, 715, 792	1, 312, 896	4, 776, 380
23	Louisiana	8, 634, 444	1, 317, 434	536, 484	3, 173, 748
9	Maine	7, 961, 824	2, 256, 516	593, 580	4, 348, 868
18	Maryland	36, 022, 584	3, 896, 448	2, 397, 540	12, 366, 136
5	Massachusetts	17, 283, 856	4, 835, 912	2, 541, 708	7, 366, 504
7	Michigan	8, 317, 452	3, 002, 560	1, 347, 372	4, 491, 562
20	Minnesota	3, 072, 056	956, 332	1, 040, 276	1, 671, 322
32	Mississippi	16, 021, 688	4, 647, 968	2, 304, 380	14, 332, 436
6	Missouri	760, 616	383, 884	712, 100	394, 448
42	Montana Territory	4, 950, 304	1, 024, 332	1, 158, 863	3, 857, 604
24	Nebraska	1, 075, 724	223, 948	362, 900	184, 240
41	Nevada	5, 223, 764	517, 888	386, 652	1, 267, 748
27	New Hampshire	13, 442, 594	1, 536, 148	1, 383, 964	4, 165, 172
14	New Jersey	597, 164	204, 580	397, 208	229, 844
43	New Mexico Territory	106, 158, 104	20, 791, 784	10, 947, 612	71, 300, 788
1	New York	4, 031, 300	1, 019, 300	1, 379, 640	1, 728, 332
28	North Carolina	26, 677, 872	8, 504, 496	3, 162, 172	21, 056, 504
4	Ohio	1, 824, 472	259, 532	857, 724	435, 948
30	Oregon	47, 967, 652	9, 568, 306	4, 548, 948	41, 353, 354
2	Pennsylvania	2, 840, 400	1, 149, 939	208, 244	1, 740, 544
32	Rhode Island	3, 580, 980	942, 136	344, 968	1, 543, 204
30	South Carolina	4, 812, 340	1, 188, 408	1, 692, 900	3, 175, 900
22	Tennessee	6, 326, 840	2, 851, 004	4, 234, 934	3, 530, 582
19	Texas	1, 322, 256	337, 448	507, 608	480, 324
38	Utah Territory	4, 483, 034	676, 988	327, 764	1, 304, 936
31	Vermont	8, 954, 764	2, 515, 968	2, 231, 268	2, 540, 924
21	Virginia	842, 876	60, 996	302, 512	61, 980
45	Washington Territory	2, 835, 560	563, 680	534, 234	804, 700
35	West Virginia	11, 750, 540	2, 431, 832	1, 860, 838	5, 493, 628
11	Wisconsin	468, 364	69, 836	107, 276	143, 780
47	Wyoming Territory	237, 900	11, 076	51, 376	31, 924
	Miscellaneous	13, 659, 932	5, 441, 644	4, 212, 676	7, 805, 200
	Railway mail service				
	Total	500, 747, 628	119, 984, 016	83, 069, 844	304, 424, 848
	Registered mail	6, 047, 652	....	....	....
	Grand total	500, 795, 280	119, 984, 016	83, 069, 844	304, 424, 848

Respectfully submitted,

Hon. THOMAS L. JAMES,
Postmaster General.

during the year ending December 31, 1880.

First-class mail.		Second-class mail.		Third-class mail.	Fourth-class mail.			
Total number of letters.	Number of postal cards.	Number of newspapers mailed to subscribers or news agents by publishers and news agents.	Number of magazines and other periodicals mailed to subscribers or news agents by publishers and news agents.	Number of packages of transient printed matter, books, circulars, &c.	Number of packages of merchandise, &c.	Number of pounds of merchandise, &c.	Total number of pieces of mail matter of all classes.	Rank.
6	**7**	**8**	**9**	**10**	**11**	**12**	**13**	
8, 891, 376	2, 574, 884	4, 037, 832	26, 700	1, 310, 660	70, 824	22, 760	16, 911, 776	29
6, 812	260	....	....	156	364	52	7, 592	49
1, 278, 420	77, 220	838, 136	8, 804	111, 644	15, 184	14, 820	2, 324, 408	44
6, 419, 296	1, 486, 836	8, 606, 356	23, 352	592, 748	49, 068	12, 177, 676	21, 177, 676	34
22, 563, 268	5, 187, 936	18, 110, 976	135, 420	5, 296, 564	361, 140	825, 728	51, 655, 204	12
10, 749, 024	2, 197, 780	6, 063, 772	9, 312	2, 240, 160	112, 216	109, 460	21, 872, 184	26
23, 780, 376	6, 506, 968	7, 808, 424	124, 716	12, 122, 552	596, 336	193, 336	50, 948, 372	13
4, 023, 708	718, 276	1, 674, 660	1, 692	329, 524	80, 836	34, 960	6, 778, 496	37
2, 384, 928	747, 656	1, 141, 348	19, 260	299, 936	85, 516	12, 116	4, 628, 644	40
15, 154, 620	1, 777, 672	5, 052, 008	30, 072	2, 058, 628	65, 872	31, 564	24, 138, 572	25
3, 071, 276	809, 952	1, 141, 452	420	413, 608	40, 352	23, 348	5, 477, 060	39
14, 607, 216	5, 496, 816	15, 355, 288	651, 396	3, 334, 968	222, 964	94, 536	39, 889, 588	17
825, 812	77, 428	374, 556	24	31, 460	10, 296	11, 700	1, 310, 576	46
68, 643, 328	24, 990, 264	87, 126, 444	4, 343, 460	37, 841, 232	1, 484, 648	585, 000	234, 461, 376	3
25, 574, 536	9, 611, 888	20, 490, 080	444, 000	4, 771, 624	229, 892	96, 956	61, 122, 020	10
465, 452	81, 796	115, 648	....	19, 396	3, 432	3, 224	685, 724	48
26, 984, 592	10, 141, 508	25, 261, 184	275, 868	4, 835, 116	330, 928	145, 132	69, 829, 196	8
15, 380, 908	5, 631, 184	13, 708, 924	97, 224	2, 159, 560	147, 316	105, 560	40, 120, 116	16
14, 581, 008	5, 433, 272	17, 443, 296	100, 656	3, 717, 168	158, 504	61, 776	41, 428, 904	15
13, 782, 184	2, 846, 428	6, 645, 132	24, 888	3, 994, 068	209, 248	80, 912	27, 691, 964	23
13, 215, 696	3, 742, 752	17, 962, 204	1, 627, 380	25, 374, 282	328, 224	132, 392	62, 230, 488	9
16, 475, 732	6, 271, 096	9, 886, 968	193, 512	6, 575, 296	455, 416	130, 792	39, 641, 284	18
69, 010, 604	22, 442, 940	88, 661, 792	3, 933, 624	42, 676, 348	1, 575, 652	674, 024	178, 900, 960	5
32, 938, 896	9, 886, 968	24, 442, 932	215, 172	7, 282, 368	486, 408	210, 600	73, 212, 744	7
16, 742, 440	4, 636, 268	13, 065, 260	145, 524	3, 157, 960	199, 368	92, 040	37, 946, 820	20
7, 285, 544	1, 875, 172	3, 834, 604	1, 932	592, 800	55, 796	36, 920	13, 125, 448	32
39, 702, 208	15, 891, 720	46, 128, 784	1, 865, 784	16, 513, 016	560, 768	243, 568	120, 662, 280	6
1, 576, 234	157, 560	866, 268	2, 652	113, 464	22, 880	28, 496	2, 739, 048	43
10, 291, 320	3, 433, 352	8, 974, 524	46, 548	2, 000, 492	125, 060	58, 760	24, 871, 296	24
1, 953, 884	167, 128	1, 383, 512	492	224, 796	24, 856	26, 884	3, 784, 688	41
7, 668, 548	2, 364, 804	7, 436, 416	198, 936	1, 076, 348	170, 404	83, 564	18, 045, 456	27
20, 783, 048	6, 216, 656	6, 403, 280	270, 224	8, 834, 228	317, 408	161, 356	42, 834, 848	14
1, 584, 700	182, 000	441, 584	1, 236	111, 072	15, 600	19, 812	2, 326, 192	42
211, 435, 640	60, 536, 840	172, 245, 528	9, 060, 780	150, 440, 316	6, 910, 956	2, 565, 160	610, 630, 060	1
6, 137, 012	2, 623, 556	6, 235, 372	30, 864	461, 364	78, 052	54, 132	17, 566, 200	28
61, 454, 052	24, 528, 192	72, 125, 560	6, 498, 216	28, 344, 940	1, 103, 752	460, 408	194, 064, 712	4
3, 636, 880	826, 708	4, 035, 096	146, 532	451, 204	58, 812	55, 952	8, 846, 232	36
106, 227, 340	30, 380, 168	71, 535, 464	7, 882, 364	65, 787, 124	2, 556, 268	731, 868	283, 378, 728	2
7, 174, 960	1, 762, 176	2, 230, 092	50, 868	2, 537, 028	144, 872	50, 892	13, 919, 996	32
7, 205, 278	2, 641, 996	4, 367, 400	8, 820	1, 853, 332	143, 676	48, 072	16, 226, 580	30
11, 262, 704	4, 265, 924	12, 620, 712	553, 008	2, 474, 888	133, 640	70, 148	31, 310, 956	22
18, 723, 016	5, 169, 892	12, 066, 756	21, 816	3, 263, 936	212, 732	179, 348	39, 438, 148	19
2, 796, 040	424, 892	2, 053, 272	22, 944	220, 584	32, 136	32, 956	5, 549, 868	38
7, 059, 668	2, 532, 296	4, 263, 844	223, 284	1, 482, 572	147, 004	64, 584	15, 707, 688	31
16, 674, 104	5, 304, 968	8, 639, 384	361, 056	3, 057, 756	422, 344	105, 612	34, 659, 672	21
1, 141, 452	143, 572	540, 816	636	83, 304	10, 036	10, 400	1, 909, 816	45
4, 912, 492	1, 885, 376	3, 742, 980	6, 948	518, 544	42, 692	23, 344	10, 829, 072	35
22, 765, 912	6, 516, 536	20, 143, 520	460, 632	5, 516, 524	344, 800	158, 080	55, 807, 924	11
880, 508	131, 144	176, 956	180	60, 892	15, 964	14, 508	1, 285, 704	47
335, 504	85, 020	146, 924	30	93, 860	4, 160	1, 612	664, 804	
31, 649, 044	11, 696, 724	29, 536	....	4, 584	2, 116, 972	137, 488	12, 220	45, 634, 948	
1, 046, 107, 348	324, 556, 440	812, 082, 000	40, 148, 792	468, 728, 312	21, 017, 880	8, 548, 848	2, 712, 509, 772	
7, 145, 528	....	....	....	....	....	497, 952	....	7, 843, 480	
1, 053, 252, 876	324, 556, 440	812, 082, 000	40, 148, 792	468, 728, 312	21, 515, 832	8, 548, 848	2, 720, 234, 252	

E. J. DALLAS,
JNO. JAMESON,
E. C. FOWLER,
Committee to supervise the official count of 1880.

POST-OFFICE DEPARTMENT,
Washington, D. C., May 19, 1881.

SIR: We have the honor to submit the following comparative statement showing the population of the several States and Territories, the number of letters mailed therein, and the average number mailed by each person.

Very respectfully,

E. J. DALLAS,
JNO. JAMESON,
E. C. FOWLER,
Committee.

Hon. THOMAS L. JAMES,
Postmaster-General.

Names of States and Territories.	Population by the census of 1880.		Letters by the official count of 1880.		Average number mailed by each person.
	Rank.	Number.	Number.	Rank.	
Alabama	17	1,262,794	8,891,376	27	7.04
Alaska	48	30,178	*6,812	49	.22
Arizona	45	40,441	1,278,620	44	31.61
Arkansas	25	802,564	6,419,296	34	7.90
California	35	194,649	10,749,024	25	55.22
Colorado	28	622,683	22,789,376	10	38.30
Connecticut	40	135,180	4,023,706	36	29.76
Dakota	38	146,654	2,384,928	40	16.38
Delaware	36	177,838	15,154,620	19	85.31
District of Columbia†	34	267,351	3,071,276	38	11.48
Florida	12	1,539,048	14,607,216	20	9.49
Georgia	47	32,611	825,812	47	25.32
Idaho	4	3,078,769	68,843,328	4	22.29
Illinois	6	1,978,362	25,574,536	9	12.97
Indiana	42	76,885	465,452	48	6.05
Indian Territory	10	1,624,620	28,984,592	8	17.84
Iowa	20	995,996	18,330,908	15	18.45
Kansas	8	1,648,708	14,581,008	21	8.84
Kentucky	22	940,103	13,782,184	22	14.66
Louisiana	27	648,945	13,215,896	23	20.36
Maine	23	934,632	16,475,732	18	17.62
Maryland	7	1,783,012	69,010,804	3	38.70
Massachusetts	9	1,636,831	32,928,896	7	20.12
Michigan	26	780,806	16,742,440	17	21.44
Minnesota	18	1,131,592	7,265,544	30	6.42
Mississippi	5	2,168,804	39,702,208	6	18.30
Missouri	46	39,157	1,576,224	43	40.25
Montana	30	452,433	10,291,320	26	22.74
Nebraska	44	62,265	1,963,884	41	31.54
Nevada	31	346,984	7,606,548	29	23.14
New Hampshire	19	1,190,963	20,783,048	13	18.37
New Jersey	41	118,430	1,584,700	42	13.38
New Mexico	1	5,083,810	211,435,640	1	41.56
New York	15	1,400,047	8,137,012	28	5.81
North Carolina	3	3,198,239	61,464,052	5	19.21
Ohio	37	174,767	3,636,880	37	20.81
Oregon	2	4,282,786	105,237,340	2	24.57
Pennsylvania	33	276,528	7,174,980	32	25.94
Rhode Island	21	995,622	7,205,276	31	7.22
South Carolina	12	1,542,463	11,262,784	24	7.30
Tennessee	11	1,592,574	18,722,016	14	11.75
Texas	39	143,906	2,796,040	39	19.42
Utah	32	332,286	7,058,688	33	21.24
Vermont	14	1,512,806	16,874,104	16	11.15
Virginia	43	75,120	1,141,452	45	15.19
Washington	29	618,443	4,912,492	35	7.94
West Virginia	16	1,315,480	21,765,912	11	17.30
Wisconsin	49	20,788	880,568	46	42.35
Wyoming					

* These letters were all mailed at Sitka to be sent out by ships.
† The official letters from all of the executive departments are included in this table.

REMARKS.—The whole number of letters mailed during the year was 1,053,352,876, or an average of 21 for each man, woman, and child in the United States. 31,649,644 letters mailed on the postal cars. 7,145,528 registered letters, and 235,504 letters reported by postmasters at small offices too late to appear in their proper order, are not included in this table.

POST-OFFICE DEPARTMENT,
Washington, D. C., May 19, 1881.

SIR: We have the honor to submit the following comparative statement showing the population of fifty of the principal cities in the United States, the number of letters mailed therein, and the average number mailed by each inhabitant.

Very respectfully,

E. J. DALLAS,
JNO. JAMESON,
E. C. FOWLER,
Committee.

Hon. THOMAS L. JAMES,
Postmaster-General.

Names of cities.	Population by the census of 1880.		Letters by the official count of 1880.		Average number mailed by each person.
	Rank.	Number.	Number.	Rank.	
Albany, N. Y	21	90, 903	4, 232, 592	22	46. 56
Allegheny, Pa	28	78, 681	1, 272, 024	41	16. 16
Atlanta, Ga	50	37, 421	2, 243, 540	34	60. 22
Baltimore, Md	7	332, 190	11, 083, 280	9	33. 36
Boston, Mass*	5	362, 535	38, 896, 860	3	34. 18
Brooklyn, N. Y	3	566, 689	19, 589, 596	5	34. 58
Buffalo, N. Y	13	155, 137	4, 738, 968	21	30. 54
Camden, N. J	43	41, 658	523, 328	50	12. 80
Charleston. S. C	35	49, 999	2, 009, 852	35	42. 19
Chicago, Ill	4	503, 304	32, 252, 636	4	64. 06
Cincinnati, Ohio	8	255, 708	14, 725, 100	8	57. 55
Cleveland, Ohio	11	160, 142	7, 144, 800	13	44. 61
Columbus, Ohio	32	51, 665	2, 936, 336	29	56. 83
Dayton, Ohio	46	38, 677	1, 424, 020	38	36. 84
Denver, Colo	48	35, 630	3, 495, 440	28	98. 10
Detroit, Mich	18	116, 342	6, 288, 180	15	53. 61
Fall River, Mass	36	49, 006	742, 716	47	15. 15
Hartford, Conn	41	42, 553	3, 654, 976	25	85. 89
Indianapolis, Ind	24	75, 074	3, 547, 284	27	47. 25
Jersey City, N. J	17	120, 728	1, 396, 096	39	11. 56
Kansas City, Mo	30	55, 813	5, 706, 272	16	102. 23
Lawrence, Mass	45	39, 178	940, 212	43	23, 99
Louisville, Ky	16	123, 645	5, 644, 860	17	45. 65
Lowell, Mass	27	59, 485	1, 296, 428	40	22. 01
Lynn, Mass	47	38, 284	835, 016	44	21. 81
Milwaukee, Wis	19	115, 578	4, 931, 992	20	42. 67
Minneapolis, Minn	37	46, 887	2, 549, 872	32	54. 38
Nashville, Tenn	39	43, 461	1, 876, 420	37	43. 17
Newark, N. J	15	135, 400	5, 309, 564	18	38. 92
New Haven, Conn	26	62, 882	7, 313, 280	12	116. 30
New Orleans, La	10	216, 140	10, 100, 110	10	46. 72
New York, N. Y	1	1, 206, 500	121, 840, 744	1	100. 98
Oakland, Cal	49	34, 556	801, 268	45	23. 18
Paterson, N. J	33	50, 887	700, 960	48	13. 77
Philadelphia, Pa	2	846, 964	52, 527, 800	2	62. 01
Pittsburgh, Pa	12	156, 381	6, 794, 320	14	43. 44
Providence, R. I	20	104, 850	3, 996, 668	23	38. 11
Reading, Pa	40	43, 280	797, 680	46	18. 43
Richmond, Va	25	63, 803	4, 992, 416	19	78. 09
Rochester, N. Y	22	89, 363	3, 571, 984	26	39. 98
Saint Louis, Mo	6	350, 522	16, 150, 680	6	46. 07
Saint Paul, Minn	44	41, 498	2, 760, 216	30	66. 54
San Francisco, Cal	9	233, 956	9, 220, 224	11	39. 41
Scranton, Pa	38	45, 850	654, 368	49	14. 27
Syracuse, N. Y	31	51, 791	2, 384, 460	33	46. 04
Toledo, Ohio	34	50, 143	2, 009, 592	36	40. 07
Troy, N. Y	29	56, 747	3, 712, 644	24	65. 42
Washington, D. C.†	14	147, 307	15, 135, 692	7	102. 74
Wilmington, Del	42	42, 499	1, 186, 512	42	27. 96
Worcester, Mass	28	58, 295	2, 616, 588	31	44. 88

* The letters mailed in Cambridge. Chelsea, and Somerville are included with Boston.
† The official letters emanating from all of the executive departments are included in this table.

Statement of matter mailed in one hundred of the principal cities

Rank in mail importance.	Name of post-office.	First-class mail.				
		Number of letters mailed in plain envelopes upon which postage was paid by adhesive stamps.	Number of letters mailed in special-request stamped envelopes printed and furnished by the Post-Office Department upon orders received through postmasters.	Number of letters mailed in ordinary stamped envelopes.	Number of letters mailed in envelopes bearing business cards or return requests not printed by the Post-Office Department.	Number of official letters mailed by officers and employés of the government.
		1	2	3	4	5
22	Albany, N. Y	1,854,216	519,324	133,484	1,631,760	93,808
67	Alleghenv, Pa	596,492	203,164	144,040	286,832	41,496
96	Altoona, Pa	225,316	20,020	6,864	117,468	10,088
28	Atlanta, Ga	664,924	266,760	210,444	832,728	265,684
65	Auburn, N. Y	400,200	163,800	48,932	195,884	26,780
63	Augusta, Ga	331,604	212,316	49,972	474,084	13,000
8	Baltimore, Md	3,979,040	2,026,284	262,548	4,644,068	171,340
88	Bay City, Mich	246,428	139,516	8,476	293,600	19,780
4	Boston, Mass	*16,564,028	5,098,428	2,149,106	13,782,392	769,904
50	Bridgeport, Conn	481,156	137,384	19,052	232,388	23,244
7	Brooklyn, N. Y	12,290,044	974,220	860,860	5,353,764	110,708
20	Buffalo, N. Y	826,664	1,040	16,276	167,856	11,492
83	Camden, N. J	657,540	517,452	118,612	679,120	37,122
42	Charleston, S. C	6,257,316	6,442,072	1,104,844	17,358,284	1,095,120
3	Chicago, Ill	3,800,180	1,641,536	412,568	8,803,704	547,111
6	Cincinnati, Ohio	2,145,052	1,773,980	277,264	2,708,368	340,136
12	Cleveland, Ohio	836,628	401,232	74,204	1,491,308	132,964
33	Columbus, Ohio	184,652	34,372	12,272	125,632	18,098
99	Covington, Ky	387,324	19,968	79,196	378,248	43,982
75	Davenport, Iowa	521,144	279,760	84,968	496,236	41,913
46	Dayton, Ohio	1,215,864	792,376	226,096	1,183,400	67,794
48	Denver, Colo	453,908	288,080	44,356	555,516	88,712
79	Des Moines, Iowa	1,762,852	1,769,664	596,744	2,055,560	113,360
13	Detroit, Mich	254,956	232,180	46,228	209,100	82,156
60	Dubuque, Iowa	297,700	17,524	9,568	78,988	5,512
97	Elizabeth, N. J	398,476	115,232	67,148	855,680	15,132
64	Elmira, N. Y	412,152	342,992	81,406	503,152	32,656
55	Erie, Pa	310,336	124,904	9,880	477,412	57,480
68	Evansville, Ind	427,544	108,784	48,776	146,712	18,906
94	Fall River, Mass	545,324	337,844	70,960	507,832	40,040
59	Fort Wayne, Ind	478,358	776,620	163,800	574,600	70,408
58	Galveston, Tex	720,096	528,268	270,972	723,944	45,864
52	Grand Rapids, Mich	608,556	157,404	104,000	503,308	32,500
51	Harrisburgh, Pa	1,125,540	671,892	840,184	1,354,964	162,398
31	Hartford, Conn	232,024	2,496	8,944	92,300	7,436
98	Hoboken, N. J	324,480	116,272	15,340	228,748	65,312
93	Holyoke, Mass	1,008,904	379,812	62,140	2,019,524	85,904
25	Indianapolis, Ind	875,472	35,840	16,016	448,188	20,540
57	Jersey City, N. J	1,867,632	841,152	131,924	2,710,812	154,752
21	Kansas City, Mo	327,444	52,884	19,032	229,112	16,016
49	Lancaster, Pa	675,896	96,384	21,580	183,120	11,232
84	Lawrence, Mass	1,422,200	961,012	163,228	3,010,384	88,036
14	Louisville, Ky	840,840	103,948	30,244	290,420	27,976
61	Lowell, Mass	536,848	126,828	26,728	131,404	13,208
79	Lynn, Mass	402,844	67,860	21,372	182,912	16,172
74	Manchester, N. H	518,336	432,692	161,729	805,584	54,028
45	Memphis, Tenn	1,309,828	684,268	186,264	2,578,368	173,264
18	Milwaukee, Wis	1,132,508	475,852	58,448	824,668	58,396
34	Minneapolis, Minn	537,524	402,740	389,532	564,304	26,920
54	Mobile, Ala	531,024	216,000	51,792	1,009,580	67,964
26	Nashville, Tenn	2,782,156	683,956	623,168	1,160,328	59,956
27	Newark, N. J	580,060	96,252	23,638	164,548	23,883
82	New Bedford, Mass	8,187,600	1,369,368	567,944	2,126,436	61,932
19	New Haven, Conn	2,491,580	1,371,240	1,682,760	4,421,248	132,363
15	New Orleans, La	91,208	812	3,952	25,376	30,420
100	Newport, Ky	53,820,256	10,990,564	6,176,924	50,217,804	626,296
1	New York, N. Y	426,764	320,736	58,448	294,008	22,412
56	Norfolk, Va	313,308	162,552	26,208	141,856	10,348
78	Norwich, Conn	640,224	54,236	44,304	39,520	22,964
71	Oakland, Cal	460,044	230,328	246,896	062,376	62,688
36	Omaha, Nebr	303,316	53,976	21,216	104,416	21,060
87	Oswego, N. Y					

* The matter mailed in Cambridge, Chelsea, and Semerville, are included in Boston.

of the United States during the year ending December 31, 1880.

First-class mail.		Second-class mail.		Third-class mail.	Fourth-class mail.			
Total number of letters.	Number of postal cards.	Number of newspapers mailed to subscribers or news agents by publishers and news agents.	Number of magazines and other periodicals mailed to subscribers or news agents by publishers and news agents.	Number of packages of transient printed matter, books, circulars, &c.	Number of packages of merchandise, &c.	Number of pounds of merchandise, &c.	Total number of pieces of mail matter of all classes.	Rank in mail importance.
6	7	8	9	10	11	12	13	
4,232,592	1,289,288	4,639,648	180	1,779,440	55,640	31,772	11,996,788	28
1,372,024	497,952	267,072	1,104	569,764	39,520	13,728	2,647,436	67
379,756	95,160	399,204	......	51,064	3,848	1,716	929,092	96
2,348,540	1,029,600	3,726,840	221,640	1,930,932	38,480	23,660	9,181,032	28
895,596	366,344	1,300,676	......	204,412	15,444	7,748	2,782,472	65
1,080,976	405,444	928,356	100,116	305,708	21,632	8,840	2,842,323	63
11,083,280	4,609,124	6,816,680	193,392	6,031,220	397,904	103,636	29,131,600	8
637,780	176,644	521,612	......	27,508	8,944	3,276	1,372,488	88
38,806,860	13,004,888	29,048,344	3,317,148	32,266,832	805,176	378,404	117,101,248	4
886,204	277,264	437,112	5,904	2,346,864	20,956	9,464	3,981,304	50
19,589,596	8,294,624	404,820	96,884	4,435,808	127,036	176,800	32,548,288	7
4,738,968	1,768,000	2,816,372	15,732	6,006,520	54,302	24,076	15,399,984	30
533,328	264,628	133,848	15,012	740,532	8,216	4,212	1,685,584	88
2,969,852	1,088,404	1,450,644	7,428	1,287,624	58,292	15,964	5,602,304	42
23,252,636	12,181,780	62,111,192	4,278,252	29,955,640	1,007,448	391,092	141,786,048	2
14,725,100	4,505,436	29,285,984	654,672	15,438,072	254,896	101,920	64,968,980	6
7,144,800	2,870,212	9,905,792	32,184	3,759,444	224,276	83,564	23,436,708	12
2,986,336	862,836	3,905,616	226,044	848,172	24,648	10,452	8,903,652	32
875,100	114,296	118,924	312	52,156	5,824	3,380	666,536	90
858,728	304,356	820,040	53,220	270,660	5,772	2,286	2,312,776	75
1,434,020	691,756	1,700,556	2,095,416	535,600	19,344	12,168	6,460,692	46
2,495,440	794,456	8,313,700	7,704	1,205,464	88,636	33,436	8,455,400	48
1,430,572	645,112	2,316,600	14,760	659,568	25,220	9,932	5,091,822	79
6,228,180	2,237,144	10,052,016	23,400	3,956,940	153,868	61,256	32,061,548	13
854,620	367,172	1,425,840	47,328	401,388	9,256	3,796	3,105,604	60
409,292	119,184	68,848	......	136,968	8,060	3,848	742,352	97
941,068	521,612	1,191,268	16,780	113,932	17,576	6,344	2,804,836	64
1,322,360	420,576	905,216	......	821,652	86,164	10,920	3,585,968	55
979,992	368,680	718,120	60,336	508,768	7,228	3,224	2,643,134	68
742,716	169,000	119,652	228	110,864	10,504	3,172	1,152,964	94
1,502,020	418,652	963,744	5,496	208,512	24,908	10,608	3,143,228	59
2,058,784	787,020	2,689,544	36	1,015,092	19,700	12,480	6,570,286	38
2,289,144	715,364	631,540	81,944	141,908	49,764	27,820	3,850,664	52
1,405,768	398,996	1,258,192	250,800	580,060	19,188	5,096	3,918,004	51
8,654,976	1,044,212	2,581,540	8,736	1,570,244	124,020	44,668	13,988,726	31
343,300	141,024	20,800	36	203,424	4,160	1,924	712,644	98
750,152	125,840	185,588	36	105,872	10,140	3,536	1,177,628	93
3,547,284	1,744,860	3,294,824	207,168	2,189,304	35,250	11,804	11,018,696	25
1,396,096	483,680	83,252	48	1,526,512	31,876	8,540	3,471,464	57
5,706,272	2,414,880	3,838,432	17,940	2,493,972	79,872	38,012	14,551,368	21
644,488	229,060	2,129,344	809,280	242,788	14,612	5,400	4,159,576	49
940,212	159,328	310,024	120	147,732	12,584	5,096	1,570,000	84
8,644,860	2,307,968	11,391,952	96,180	2,633,072	81,952	28,340	25,155,984	14
1,299,428	474,136	351,728	4,428	931,736	22,100	9,464	3,083,556	61
835,016	324,584	97,812	380	492,180	32,552	13,520	1,782,504	79
641,160	213,720	1,316,380	14,160	135,584	12,688	5,200	2,328,672	74
1,972,380	1,033,844	1,280,500	120	809,908	34,268	16,328	5,190,500	45
4,831,992	1,514,344	7,423,364	450,900	2,719,184	96,200	34,476	17,135,984	18
2,549,872	718,172	3,483,688	77,244	1,066,468	35,548	15,548	7,931,012	34
1,931,020	413,920	343,200	13,380	877,448	17,420	6,968	3,596,388	54
1,876,420	825,656	6,911,580	501,360	691,756	26,312	11,180	10,833,084	26
5,309,564	1,728,272	582,704	20,688	2,902,232	97,240	34,632	10,700,760	27
907,764	270,452	296,972	552	197,496	28,064	13,364	1,702,200	82
7,813,290	2,238,392	1,704,352	59,760	4,807,244	133,604	63,440	16,276,636	19
10,100,116	2,318,732	5,288,764	24,732	3,825,640	184,080	61,672	21,742,064	15
151,268	31,460	103,648	......	15,406	1,248	520	303,160	100
121,840,784	30,850,076	124,395,076	7,926,264	117,682,854	5,421,728	1,840,800	408,117,692	1
1,122,308	435,136	1,772,524	2,004	181,532	11,440	4,264	3,525,004	56
654,472	172,224	627,328	740	345,836	12,740	7,800	1,723,380	78
801,268	214,896	1,179,048	1,612	194,692	16,536	16,796	2,411,572	71
1,681,732	629,616	3,738,332	38,400	813,748	17,940	12,376	6,919,768	36
503,984	223,964	445,432	96	236,132	4,680	2,184	1,414,288	87

Statement of matter mailed in one hundred of the

Rank in mail importance.	Name of post-office.	First-class mail.				
		Number of letters mailed in plain envelopes upon which postage was paid by adhesive stamps.	Number of letters mailed in special-request stamped envelopes printed and furnished by the Post-Office Department upon orders received through postmasters.	Number of letters mailed in ordinary stamped envelopes.	Number of letters mailed in envelopes bearing business cards or return requests not printed by the Post-Office Department.	Number of official letters mailed by officers and employes of the government.
		1	2	3	4	5
91	Paterson, N. J	457,704	21,060	11,960	201,916	8,250
53	Peoria, Ill	395,460	242,424	56,420	344,604	34,372
92	Petersburgh, Va	236,756	106,704	62,556	118,300	23,972
2	Philadelphia, Pa	18,771,168	3,647,956	1,163,188	28,528,864	416,694
11	Pittsburgh, Pa	1,729,000	1,169,480	345,382	3,216,928	333,580
17	Portland, Me	743,704	508,456	38,688	977,600	192,868
80	Poughkeepsie, N. Y	574,444	94,016	32,292	198,380	16,120
30	Providence, R. I	1,798,628	710,944	140,296	1,306,812	39,966
73	Quincy, Ill	326,716	83,668	23,712	431,964	54,940
69	Reading, Pa	351,832	83,720	45,240	201,564	25,324
24	Richmond, Va	2,034,968	1,194,752	769,080	788,372	205,244
16	Rochester, N. Y	1,269,944	918,164	119,080	1,182,582	82,264
58	Sacramento, Cal	432,068	122,720	48,256	395,252	55,932
48	Saint Joseph, Mo	381,056	336,648	28,392	503,372	36,668
5	Saint Louis, Mo	4,101,864	2,364,128	659,620	8,495,604	529,464
29	Saint Paul, Minn	697,424	387,140	327,756	1,151,124	196,872
90	Salem, Mass	381,420	50,596	10,920	67,080	9,048
66	Salt Lake City, Utah	287,248	119,652	28,288	200,620	51,844
81	San Antonio, Tex	309,348	159,900	174,304	211,120	119,756
9	San Francisco, Cal	4,488,200	869,928	647,712	3,448,068	316,316
44	Savannah, Ga	852,176	736,060	574,652	893,048	90,940
85	Scranton, Pa	284,804	129,376	23,972	208,728	7,488
72	Springfield, Ill	504,088	62,960	70,148	150,904	34,368
35	Springfield, Mass	546,052	193,128	18,616	481,208	17,056
41	Springfield, Ohio	328,224	120,224	22,048	296,156	40,872
37	Syracuse, N. Y	905,580	604,240	52,624	748,072	73,944
89	Taunton, Mass	351,572	133,016	50,960	162,800	7,332
77	Terre Haute, Ind	404,924	131,820	40,872	305,344	28,532
23	Toledo, Ohio	490,256	670,540	67,132	702,208	79,456
76	Trenton, N. J	446,004	195,052	25,480	352,352	16,234
39	Troy, N. Y	1,306,396	843,700	455,624	1,071,148	35,776
47	Utica, N. Y	578,188	290,056	107,640	356,148	31,876
10	Washington, D. C	*3,649,932	132,964	213,512	1,604,096	9,535,148
95	Waterbury, Conn	291,148	116,480	10,920	191,972	10,296
62	Wheeling, W. Va	332,540	281,840	50,336	277,576	38,168
86	Wilkesbarre, Pa	280,072	117,780	45,240	236,080	15,288
70	Wilmington, Del	620,932	217,880	37,076	299,996	12,688
43	Worcester, Mass	1,237,444	415,324	87,960	835,692	40,788
	Total	198,746,384	66,870,284	25,671,932	207,302,876	19,238,742

*The official letters emanating from all the Executive Departments are included in this table.

To Hon. THOMAS L. JAMES,
Postmaster-General.

principal cities of the United States, &c.—Continued.

First-class mail.		Second-class mail.		Third-class mail.	Fourth-class mail.			
Total number of letters.	Number of postal cards.	Number of newspapers mailed to subscribers or news agents by publishers and news agents.	Number of magazines and other periodicals mailed to subscribers or news agents by publishers and news agents.	Number of packages of transient printed matter, books, circulars, &c.	Number of packages of merchandise, &c.	Number of pounds of merchandise, &c.	Total number of pieces of mail matter of all classes.	Rank in mail importance.
6	7	8	9	10	11	12	13	
700,960	203,060	103,324	....	238,922	8,944	3,484	1,255,210	91
1,078,280	454,324	1,592,604	2,172	660,920	21,944	4,160	3,805,214	53
548,288	336,024	196,484	588	134,888	15,028	8,060	1,233,300	92
52,527,300	13,871,520	27,616,940	5,634,312	50,180,624	1,795,664	462,004	151,626,890	2
6,794,320	1,982,896	6,404,580	716,340	7,555,496	99,112	43,888	23,552,244	11
2,461,316	706,940	3,759,652	48	10,990,304	81,380	27,300	17,999,640	17
915,252	228,696	421,096	2,496	163,904	16,796	4,836	1,748,240	80
3,396,668	3,043,368	1,322,880	50,484	1,590,992	83,980	27,040	9,109,872	30
822,900	441,116	667,056	72,108	235,924	13,624	4,316	2,352,828	73
797,690	350,268	1,158,820	2,352	301,600	16,016	5,720	2,635,736	69
4,962,416	1,222,920	2,933,476	288,000	1,317,108	274,664	27,248	11,008,584	24
3,971,984	1,384,292	3,807,128	638,592	9,050,028	262,080	102,544	18,714,104	16
1,064,348	173,628	1,585,220	26,364	504,920	79,092	87,204	3,421,472	58
1,376,076	631,644	1,375,452	4,812	594,984	23,400	9,828	4,006,368	48
16,156,680	7,617,532	29,197,272	1,751,232	12,091,560	297,752	116,272	67,100,028	5
2,760,216	756,028	4,502,628	36,624	1,040,312	58,552	19,032	9,154,460	29
519,064	340,236	193,232	1,572	202,644	9,412	4,160	1,266,150	90
786,682	105,352	1,692,028	22,944	108,628	8,840	9,516	2,694,444	66
974,428	155,116	510,588	9,672	39,936	25,480	17,732	1,715,230	81
9,220,234	8,059,784	10,395,788	98,556	3,302,832	136,240	104,052	26,213,424	9
3,063,876	943,488	1,415,440	14,780	165,412	68,016	19,812	6,801,092	44
664,368	190,944	429,200	36	240,292	17,264	5,408	1,552,184	83
692,348	250,536	850,400	226,012	251,784	5,408	1,924	2,409,368	72
1,254,060	530,104	1,723,956	507,060	3,256,500	61,360	27,976	7,325,040	25
797,524	256,880	1,355,900	3,280,800	588,744	58,448	30,264	6,308,296	41
2,384,440	870,272	2,324,244	72,192	1,164,592	64,116	28,288	6,878,876	37
706,690	196,880	140,296	276	309,556	7,540	5,096	1,302,728	89
651,402	531,492	453,232	17,568	307,372	7,852	3,640	2,239,008	77
4,603,692	3,255,304	4,734,912	58,820	1,263,184	65,676	30,576	11,382,488	23
1,495,113	384,024	582,452	45,600	324,376	9,308	3,588	2,290,872	76
2,715,644	997,776	691,288	22,296	1,057,680	60,684	26,728	6,542,368	39
1,362,608	550,108	2,135,952	75,044	504,868	33,120	11,752	4,664,100	47
15,135,668	1,778,980	5,052,008	30,072	2,057,172	65,416	31,512	24,114,340	10
566,816	109,148	378,300	204	91,624	13,884	5,772	1,127,076	95
260,460	320,996	1,402,648	36	330,512	10,816	4,056	3,045,468	62
604,460	196,506	501,488	8,160	92,664	12,688	6,604	1,505,068	86
1,128,512	353,652	705,276	19,260	212,680	23,064	8,736	2,504,444	70
2,616,568	1,048,184	816,868	3,420	1,209,416	50,336	23,452	5,741,792	43
512,981,234	164,146,912	496,706,132	35,880,240	382,622,014	14,314,400	5,282,432	1,606,602,022	

Respectfully submitted,

E. J. DALLAS,
JNO. JAMESON,
E. C. FOWLER,
Committee to supervise the official count of 1880.

REPORT OF THE SECOND ASSISTANT POSTMASTER-GENERAL.

POST-OFFICE DEPARTMENT,
OFFICE OF SECOND ASSISTANT POSTMASTER-GENERAL,
Washington, D. C., November 5, 1881.

SIR: The cost of inland transportation June 30, 1881, was:

For 1,194 railroad routes, aggregating 91,569 miles..........................	$11,613,368
For 126 steamboat routes, aggregating 21,138 miles	753,167
For 10,272 other routes, known as "star" routes, aggregating 231,299 miles.	6,957,355
Total cost...	19,323,890

Compared with the last annual statement, the railroad service shows an increase of 76 routes, of 6,249 miles, and of $1,114,382 in annual cost. The steamboat service shows a decrease of 5 routes, of 2,182 miles, and of $134,054 in annual cost. The "star" service shows an increase of 409 routes, a decrease of 3,949 miles, and of $364,144 in annual cost.

CONTRACTS.

Number of contracts drawn during the year ended June 30, 1881, 10,532.

RAILROAD SERVICE.

Cost for 1881, appropriation for 1882, and estimate for 1883.

The estimate submitted for railroad transportation for the current fiscal year was $10,288,482; the sum appropriated was $9,458,282. The cost of the service on the 30th June, 1881, aside from the cost on certain Pacific roads on which pay is withheld, as reported by the auditor, was $9,543,155, by the books of this office $9,908,991. And at the same date there were 5,221.81 miles of new service on which the rates were unadjusted, which will cost not less than $250,000, thus making the cost on that date, of the service for which actual payment must be made, $9,793,155. The appropriation was $9,315,000, which leaves yet to be provided for, a deficiency of $478,155 to cover the cost for that year. From July 1 to October 18, 1881, service has been established on 3,352 miles of new road, which will cost $125,000.

The readjustment, Table E, shows an increase of $1,287,446, from which $800,000 is deducted because included in the audited cost on 30th June, 1881, leaving a difference of $487,446 additional cost from July 1, 1881.

These sums will bring the cost to October 18 to about $10,405,601. And to this must yet be added the new service from October 18, 1881, to June 30, 1882, probably 5,000 miles at a cost of $150,000, and the total cost to June 30, 1882, will be $10,555,601. There will therefore be required for the current fiscal year an additional appropriation of $1,097,319.

In estimating for railroad transportation for 1883, it is noted that the regular weighing will fall in the Pacific section, where there are not so many routes; and that there will not be so large an increase shown in the weight of mails on the routes as there was in the eastern section, for which the pay has just been readjusted. It is believed that $600,000, in addition to the probable cost on the 30th June, 1882 (viz, $10,555,601), will be sufficient to cover the cost of the service for the fiscal year ending June 30, 1883. This will be about 5.68 per cent. increase (or about 17.94 per cent. increase over the insufficient appropriation of $9,458,282 for 1882), and will make the sum required $11,155,601.

ESTIMATE FOR RAILWAY POST-OFFICE CARS.

The appropriation for railway post-office cars for the current year is $1,426,000, which is $176,000 more than was provided for the preceding year.

The growth of the railroad system renders necessary the extension of the railway post-office system also.

It is believed that the increase for 1883 will not be as great as is provided for the current year, and the amount necessary for the year ending June 30, 1883, is placed at $1,526,000, which is but $100,000 more than the present appropriation.

SPECIAL FACILITIES.

For the year ending June 30, 1882, the amount appropriated for this item was $425,000. The reasons for the expenditure of this fund have been fully set forth in previous reports, upon which appropriations have been made for this object each year since 1878.

The running of special trains or trains by schedules, prescribed by the Post-Office Department, cannot be secured for the rates of compensation which can be paid for postal service under the general laws controlling the same.

To discontinue the advantages thus secured would result in delaying the delivery of postal matter to a very large number of people. I therefore recommend that the appropriation for this object for the year ending June 30, 1883, be placed at $500,000, which will maintain the present service and extend it to several great centres of population where needed.

PACIFIC ROADS.

In submitting the estimates of the cost of railroad transportation for the year ending June 30, 1882, a deduction of $700,000 was noted on account of amounts due certain railroads. This sum is less than was reported by the auditor on page 553 of the annual report; but the sum there given includes the cost of railway post-office cars, which is a separate item of appropriation. The Court of Claims has decided that the pay on certain leased lines should not be withheld; from this decision, however, an appeal has been taken, and the matter continues in the same condition as last year, with the exception that the law has been construed to cover a much larger number of roads than was formerly believed to be subject to its provisions.

By the books of this department the amount withheld for the year ending June 30, 1881, was, for transportation, $1,017,629.33. By the auditor's books the sum is $961,977.99.

RATES OF PAY TO RAILROADS.

The question of railroad transportation in its relation to the public, has received much attention from both the legislative and judicial authorities of the country; but up to this time the most that has been accomplished is the creation of commissions, through which like rates for like service over the same line are secured to the people. Though several attempts have been made, no substantial progress has resulted in the way of determining just and equitable rates of compensation for such service as a whole, nor has the power of the government to exercise supervision or control in the matter of the operation of railroads been defined.

It l.
least.
remen
last y
two p
conce
railro:
law h
obtain
This
compe
nies, l
obliga
franel
from t
immec
The
custor
space.
accon
and d
depar
the co
The
sation
may o
per ar
the ca
strikir
· ployec
mileag
and r
total l
facts a
of the
cost of
the qu
The
be fou
ing pr.
of the
ment
fining
each i
specif
expen
This v
road e
tion t
than t
I t
direct
due c
perfe

MAIL EQUIPMENTS.

By reference to tabular statement H it will be seen that the total number of mail-bags of every description, purchased during the year ended June 30, 1881, was 100,310, of which 8,301 were locked mail-bags and 92,009 were canvas-tie sacks, being altogether, an increase of 35,912 mail-bags, compared with the preceding year; that the number of mail-catchers purchased was 300, and that the total expense on account of mail-bags and mail-catchers, including their necessary appurtenances and repairs, amounted to $183,929.46.

The total number of mail-bags of every description repaired during the year was 413,004, and the cost of their repairs was $49,218.39, an increase of 49,652 in number and $7,028.48 in expense, compared with the preceding year.

The expense of $90,999.60, shown by tabular statement I to have been incurred for mail locks and keys, does not include any expense for mail locks and keys of the kinds now and heretofore used in the service, as there was none during the last fiscal year. It has sole reference to a new outfit for mail service of entirely new kinds, styles, and patterns of mail locks and keys, to take the place of all the old kinds now in the service, and soon to be discontinued as a necessity for the better security of the mails in future.

The full expense incurred during the last fiscal year, as exhibited by Table I, does not appear in the auditor's statement, for the reason that up to the close of the fiscal year the payments were not made. But the full expense will be shown in a future statement from his office, after all the liabilities incurred for locks and keys during that year shall have been actually paid. These locks and keys were ordered to be manufactured and furnished under new contracts, the terms of which are specifically stated in Table G.

The several amounts estimated (as specifically stated elsewhere) for mail-bags and mail-catchers, and for mail locks and keys, for the year ending June 30, 1883, cannot, in my judgment, sustain any reduction without risk of serious detriment to the service, more especially is it so respecting the items of expense for mail locks and keys, which is based on a calculation of the lowest certainty.

CLERICAL FORCE.

The recommendation in the report for 1880 for increase in the clerical force was justifiable, and is here respectfully renewed. In the estimate for the year ending June 30, 1883, the salary of the chief clerk is placed at $2,500; of the superintendent of railway adjustment; chief of division of inspection; and chief of division of mail equipments, $2,250. The critical discrimination, responsibility, and care demanded in the proper execution of their respective trusts renders the present compensation of these officials entirely inadequate. The additional fifteen clerks and one messenger asked for are needed for the following reasons: The territory assigned to many of the clerks charged with the correspondence and examination of post routes in the contract office is so large and the labor has so increased by the additional service established during recent years that it has been found necessary, in order that the work may be properly performed, to divide the sections; and the same necessities exist in the division of inspection. The division of railway adjustment and the division of mail equipment also require further aid. It is believed that the expense incurred in granting the addition to the clerical force of this office will be more than offset by the gain accruing from close application to details in expenditures, now rendered difficult by the insufficiency of previous appropriations.

It is the intention to assign the additional clerks to duties as follows: To the contract office, six; to the division of railway adjustment, two; to the division of mail equipments, four; and to the division of inspection, three; and one assistant messenger.

FINES AND DEDUCTIONS.

The amount of fines imposed upon contractors and deductions from their pay for failures and other delinquencies for the fiscal year ended June 30, 1881, was $542,866.79, and the amount remitted for the same period was $52,609.28, leaving the net amount of fines and deductions $490,257.51. While prosecuting inquiries relative to performance of star and steamboat service, it was ascertained that in certain cases postmasters had made false reports to the department of arrivals and departures of the mails, the effect being to save the contractors from fines and deductions imposed upon them for delinquencies under the provisions of section 3962 Revised Statutes. It will thus be observed that in this respect the appropriations for mail transportation are open to very grave assaults, and I recommend the enactment by Congress of a statute prescribing penalties to be imposed upon any postmaster or other employé of the postal service who shall for any purpose willfully make and render to the Post-Office Department any false report of arrivals and departures of mails. At present the difficulties of proof and conviction under section 5440 Revised Statutes are almost insurmountable, and offenders have gone unpunished, save in cases where the Postmaster-General has exercised the power of removal.

In concluding a year, a portion of which has been of more than usual interest, I desire to express my appreciation of the ability and fidelity shown by the chief clerk, chiefs of division, and gentlemen of this office in protecting the interests of the government.

Very respectfully,

RICH'D A. ELMER,
Second Assistant Postmaster-General.

Hon. THOMAS L. JAMES,
Postmaster-General.

Cost of inland transportation and incidental items for 1880 and 1881; appropriation for 1882, with estimate of amounts necessary to be appropriated for 1883; cost, appropriation, and estimate for mail equipments; also, percentage of increase and decrease.

64 Ab

Object	Cost for 1880.	Cost for 1881.	Per cent. increase or decrease in cost for 1881 as to cost for 1880.		Appropriation for 1882.	Per cent. increase or decrease in appropriation for 1882 as to cost for 1881.		Estimate for 1883.	Per cent. increase or decrease as to appropriation for 1882.	
			Increase.	Decrease.		Increase.	Decrease.		Increase.	Decrease.
Inland transportation, railroad routes	$9,237,945	$10,249,261	10.95		$9,488,283		7.42	$11,155,000	17.57	
Railway post-office car service	1,261,041	1,364,107	8.17		1,425,000	4.54		1,525,000	7.01	
Necessary and special facilities on trunk lines	150,000	340,740	133.17		425,000	21.52		500,000	17.65	
Inland transportation, steamboat routes	897,221	753,187		15.11	925,000	22.81		800,000		13.51
Inland transportation, "star" routes	7,221,460	6,967,365		4.97	7,900,000	13.55		7,250,000		8.22
Railway post-office clerks	1,438,100	1,497,560	7.94		1,650,000	4.20		1,650,000	6.45	
Route agents	1,138,130	1,296,790	11.23		1,275,000	.65		1,875,000	7.84	
Mail-route messengers	205,540	196,741		4.74	235,000	19.45		280,000	19.15	
Local agents	127,220	157,720	23.92		150,000		4.89	175,000	16.67	
Mail messengers	607,296	763,341	9.47		775,750	1.63		800,000	3.12	
Mail locks and keys	14,723	100,000	578.98		25,000		75.00	25,000		
Mail bags and mail catchers	144,802	138,629	25.46		200,000	8.74		200,000		
Miscellaneous items in the office of the Second Assistant Postmaster-General					1,000			2,000	100.00	
Total					24,876,082			25,723,000	5.90	

N. B.—The above estimates are based upon contract prices and annual salaries, irrespective of fines and deductions; hence the apparent discrepancy between this table and the Auditor's statement.

RICHD A. ELMER,
Second Assistant Postmaster-General.

A.—*Table of mail-service in operation June 30, 1881.*

[The entire service and pay are set down to the State under which the route is numbered, and not divided among the States into which the routes may extend.]

States and Territories.	Length of routes.	Celerity, certainty and security.		By steamboat.		By railroad.	Annual pay for transportation.	Annual pay for railway post-office cars.	Total annual pay for rail-road service.	Total annual transportation by celerity, certainty and security.	Total annual transportation by steamboat.	Total annual transportation by railroad.	Total annual transportation.	Total annual cost.
	Miles.	Miles.	Dollars.	Miles.	Dollars.	Miles.	Dollars.	Dollars.	Dollars.	Miles.	Miles.	Miles.	Miles.	Dollars.
Maine	5,736	3,615	90,029	979	3,327	1,142	129,902	13,879	143,781	1,797,799	118,092	1,238,971	3,154,862	237,137
New Hampshire	1,948	1,163	35,043	65	2,650	720	64,440	65,891	65,891	614,198	11,960	919,646	1,545,804	103,584
Vermont	2,350	1,508	48,537			851	86,137	9,532	95,669	904,225	57,928	3,786,861	4,751,014	338,659
Massachusetts	3,151	1,173	66,069	102	10,655	1,876	280,270	31,665	261,935	116,599	49,880	395,688	562,167	44,073
Rhode Island	452	166	12,054	105	11,448	181	17,447	3,129	177,462	499,536		2,274,829	2,766,365	909,348
Connecticut	1,859	789	31,896			1,070	147,296	30,169		1,461,539	113,643	10,023,392	12,546,916	1,722,029
New York	12,758	6,374	252,040	173	8,450	6,211	1,179,698	281,841	1,461,539	451,178		2,571,282	3,022,460	258,730
New Jersey	2,293	857	29,089			1,436	197,691	31,950	229,641	4,183,321	85,224	7,145,004	11,963,550	972,592
Pennsylvania	14,823	9,429	285,280	80	5,500	5,304	621,256	80,556	701,812	91,510		253,569	345,079	24,303
Delaware	457	188	5,507			269	18,796		18,796	261,644	277,368	2,327,626	3,682,226	338,950
Maryland	3,825	1,861	62,884	756	14,431	1,208	216,400	45,244	261,644	296,629	443,534	2,442,813	5,092,469	472,952
Virginia	12,371	8,605	135,607	1,315	46,627	2,251	231,056	59,543		1,330,550	125,892	966,229	1,823,071	115,243
West Virginia	5,805	5,255	63,043	246	15,800	804	32,212	4,183	36,395	2,676,022	149,344	1,213,142	4,038,508	247,882
North Carolina	10,885	9,057	105,435	498	16,364	1,330	111,117	12,966	124,083	945,484	9,992	1,372,876	2,328,292	170,154
South Carolina	4,838	3,508	48,343	51	881	1,279	107,830	12,600	120,930	1,773,966	52,502	2,636,682	4,444,100	874,628
Georgia	9,948	6,102	87,390	288	4,600	3,562	242,741	38,888	282,629	842,421	718,480	463,882	2,024,783	180,889
Florida	8,419	3,217	58,659	4,509	90,969	687	29,158	1,913	31,071	2,561,930	137,176	1,948,066	4,642,772	341,615
Alabama	11,390	8,580	131,389	725	17,327	2,085	172,430	20,469	192,899	1,686,391	79,092	916,224	2,681,707	215,389
Mississippi	7,306	5,621	95,301	470	8,492	1,215	102,939	8,607	111,546	2,474,166	84,699	1,189,400	3,748,265	298,561
Tennessee	9,188	7,767	142,415	358	9,035	1,063	109,171	7,940	117,111	2,409,408	347,360	2,282,778	5,040,540	386,226
Kentucky	9,960	7,080	105,909	862	40,800	2,018	215,988	23,579	239,517	2,674,792	192,878	11,631,983	14,499,653	1,454,501
Ohio	13,831	6,338	138,154	261	25,840	7,234	1,102,798	187,714	1,290,507	1,614,392		4,925,907	5,940,359	440,411
Indiana	7,878	4,611	79,815			3,267	340,346	40,350	380,696	1,810,164		7,225,460	9,035,624	1,158,225
Illinois	12,442	4,944	104,191			7,498	924,255	129,779	1,054,034	1,552,756	248,543	4,438,733	6,240,082	447,574
Michigan	9,385	4,654	89,681	788	17,520	3,943	328,929	11,444	340,373	1,641,778		3,164,164	4,805,942	387,385
Wisconsin	8,713	5,485	82,504			3,228	379,254	25,527	304,781	1,137,058		3,392,175	4,529,233	322,825
Minnesota	8,960	4,900	72,817			4,060	342,881	7,127	250,008	2,125,864		3,778,322	5,904,186	516,497
Iowa	11,848	6,806	108,073			5,042	386,421	21,973	408,394	3,922,416	285,480	6,179,570	9,987,466	596,697
Missouri	15,065	9,931	161,683	684	21,800	5,050	603,775	75,735	679,510	3,527,007	451,413	353,480	3,531,906	384,014
Arkansas	10,850	8,402	228,556	1,904	133,272	544	31,502		31,502	1,002,089	476,840	629,715	2,108,504	322,488
Louisiana	7,131	4,273	140,811	2,129	113,844	729	64,572	4,161		5,835,099	22,320	1,586,768	8,446,180	951,230
Texas	21,043	17,410	600,088	465	4,800	3,168	250,432		250,432	994,752		934,752	165,365
Indiana	3,138	3,138	165,365			3,763	307,274	27,632	394,906	3,100,918		3,576,682	5,696,599	583,000
Kansas	14,937	11,165	188,094										
Nebraska	9,356	7,042	145,774			3,316	460,354	55,892	516,346	3,043,434		1,505,332	3,553,715	662,080

Dakota Territory	5,195	4,893	194,947			943	6,778	6,773	1,481,198		194,513	1,561,928	201,799
Montana Territory	8,398	3,966	340,679						1,438,789			1,438,789	240,579
Wyoming Territory	1,393	1,363	62,168						448,907			448,907	62,168
Colorado	5,623	4,221	350,433			1,404			1,713,681			2,530,523	445,315
New Mexico Territory	2,140	1,906	153,278			354	52,963	52,963	595,660		1,117,943	670,928	133,277
Arizona Territory	3,518	2,460	230,477			467			961,969		145,843	1,342,658	222,477
Utah Territory	2,093	2,095	217,467			728	31,259	31,259	1,345,458		343,887	1,688,528	243,659
Idaho Territory	4,029	1,439	194,564						997,438		633,743	997,438	164,504
Washington Territory	4,981	4,220	44,080	55,459		310	11,980	11,980	823,634	192,653	194,413	992,489	111,304
Oregon	2,769	2,533	274,629	13,477		429	24,818	24,818	1,466,983	134,160	265,679	1,966,965	311,924
Nevada			199,943			257	13,818	13,818	1,095,982		147,907	1,211,869	195,964
California	13,341	6,819	595,124	42,498	63,799	3,797	435,448	435,448	3,484,582	500,628	2,068,839	5,962,098	1,134,481
Total	344,008	281,200	6,957,355	759,167	1,364,107	91,660	10,248,261	11,612,986	78,657,396	5,044,807	103,621,229	158,125,032	19,325,899
Railway post-office clerks													1,467,500
Route agents													1,206,780
Mail-route messengers													194,741
Local agents													157,720
Mail messengers													768,341
Aggregate													23,196,032

NOTE.—This table shows contract prices and annual salaries, irrespective of fines and deductions, hence the apparent discrepancy between this table and the Auditor's statement.

REPORT OF THE GENERAL SUPERINTENDENT OF RAIL-WAY MAIL SERVICE.

POST OFFICE DEPARTMENT,
OFFICE GENERAL SUPERINTENDENT RAILWAY MAIL SERVICE,
Washington, D. C., November 5, 1881.

SIR: At the close of the fiscal year ended June 30, 1881, there were engaged under my supervision in the distribution and dispatch of the mails upon railroad and steamboat lines, in addition to the three assistant superintendents, 3,177

EMPLOYÉS OF THE RAILWAY MAIL SERVICE

with salaries aggregating at the rate of $3,108,801, or an average of $978.53 per annum for each employé. In fact, however, the salaries of these employés ranged from $1 per annum, paid to officers of steamboats as a nominal compensation for taking the oath required of all persons who handle the mails, to $1,400, the highest salary allowed by the law, paid to chief head clerks in charge of the distribution upon one or more important lines of railroad. For a statement of the number and grades of railway post-office clerks reference is made to Table K, attached to the report of the Second Assistant Postmaster-General. A comparative statement of the number of and amount paid for all classes of employés of the service is found in Table A appended to this report. Although the duties performed by and required of all employés are similar in character, varying only in the amount of work assigned to each and the study necessary for its proper performance, the

APPROPRIATIONS FOR THEIR PAYMENT

are made by Congress under four different heads, viz, railway postal clerks, route agents, mail-route messengers, and local agents. The law fixes the salaries of railway postal clerks at not more than $1,400 a year each to the head clerks, and not more than $1,200 each to the other clerks. Route agents shall be paid not less than $900 each and not more than $1,200. Mail-route messengers are paid less than $900 per year, their salaries being ascertained by multiplying the number of miles of their daily run by ten, the product being the amount of their annual salaries in dollars. The first mention in law of the two grades of employés last named is in the act of July 11, 1870 (Post Office appropriation), which appropriated—

For transportation of the mail inland, including pay of mail messengers, route agents, mail-route agents, *local agents*, postal railway clerks, and baggage-masters, thirteen million five hundred and six thousand eight hundred and ninety-three dollars.

The act of March 3, 1871, making appropriations for the service of the Post Office Department for the fiscal year ending June 30, 1872, appropriated—

For pay of route agents, seven hundred and eighty-six thousand five hundred and sixty-nine dollars.

For pay of *mail-route messengers*, fifty-nine thousand and forty-four dollars.

For pay of *local agents*, forty-nine thousand and forty-four dollars.

For pay of railway post-office clerks, five hundred and eighty-five thousand three hundred and thirty-eight dollars.

Since that time the appropriations for the employés of the railway mail service have followed the language of the act last above quoted, of course changing yearly the amount appropriated.

No good reason exists for continuing this manner of making appropriations. It involves keeping a record in this office of four appropriations, and to avoid exceeding any of these appropriations or crippling the service by a reduction of the number of employés, it almost always becomes necessary to transfer employés from one designation to another near the close of the fiscal year without changing their compensation or assignment to duty.

It would seem to be time that the

GROWTH AND DEVELOPMENT OF THIS SERVICE

should be recognized by law, and that proper provision be made for the classification and payment of its employés, under a system which would protect the government against extravagant expenditure of the public money, and at the same time prevent any injury to the vast public and private interests involved in the prompt distribution and speedy transportation of the mails, which might arise from limiting the number of employés, or in any other manner depriving the Postmaster-General of discretionary powers to meet the emergencies which constantly confront him.

STUDY REQUIRED OF EMPLOYÉS.

All employés of this service are required to study the post-offices of the division to which they are assigned by States and counties, to keep themselves informed of all connections made by other lines with those upon which they work, to note the establishment and discontinuance of post-offices, to inform themselves upon the postal laws and regulations, and upon all orders affecting this service issued by the Postmaster-General or by the general and division superintendents, and they are subjected to frequent examinations upon these points. Repeated failures to pass satisfactory examinations are followed by retirement from the service, for it is against public policy to permit the mails to be distributed by incompetent or negligent persons. For a report of these

"CASE EXAMINATIONS"

see Table F, appended to this report. These examinations are conducted by employés of the grade of head clerk, assigned to duty under section 713 Postal Laws and Regulations, edition of 1879, as

CHIEF HEAD CLERKS.

The knowledge and experience demanded for the discharge of the duties of a chief head clerk are such as to task severely the powers of the most competent men in the service. They must be thoroughly familiar with the time-tables and connections of all the railroads in their divisions and of all the more important lines in the United States; they must understand the distribution of the mail so as to be able to decide what direction should be given to mail matter for all post-offices within their divisions and those adjoining; they must bear in mind all the changes which occur daily in the operation of star routes as well as of railroads; they must know by heart all the post-offices in the divisions to which they belong, which vary in number from four to seven thousand, so as to name the county in which each office is found; and, above all, they must possess sufficient executive ability to obtain the most effective work possible from the employés under their charge. To maintain proper supervision of the work committed to their charge and to conduct examinations, it is necessary for them to travel constantly, and yet the utmost salary allowed by law is $1,400 per annum, out of which all of their expenses must come. In no other branch of the public service are officers of so high a grade of intelligence and efficiency so poorly paid. I therefore respectfully recommend that authority be given for the appointment of not to exceed thirty-two chief head clerks of railway mail service at a salary of $1,400 per year and an allowance of $3 per day for expenses when actually traveling upon business of the department, to be paid out of the appropriation for transportation by railroad.

REORGANIZATION OF THE SERVICE.

Upon the 1st of May, 1881, the service was entirely reorganized by the following order of the Postmaster-General:

ORDER OF THE POSTMASTER-GENERAL.

POST OFFICE DEPARTMENT,
Washington, D. C., April 7, 1881.

ORDER NO. 47.

The following regulations for the government of the officers and employés of the railway mail service will hereafter be observed:

1. *Organization of working crews.*—Hereafter the working crews in all offices on railway post-office lines will be composed as follows: Upon a line where but one employé is necessary to perform the service he will be of a grade not to exceed $1,000 per annum. On lines that require two employés to an office there will be one at $1,300 per annum and one at $1,150 per annum. On lines that require three employés to an office there will be one at $1,300 per annum, one at $1,150 per annum, and one at $1,000 per annum. On lines that require four employés there will be one at $1,300 per annum, one at $1,150 per annum, one at $1,000 per annum, and one at $900 per annum. If more than four employés are required to an office such additional employés will be of a grade not to exceed $900 per annum, except on lines where there are two offices on the same train, one for letters and the other for papers. On such lines the crews will be composed of one employé at $1,300 per annum, two at $1,150 per annum, one at $1,000 per annum, one at $900 per annum, and all additional employés of a grade not to exceed $900 per annum.

2. *"Short stops" or "helpers."*—Except in case of emergencies, as hereinafter provided, no employé or local mail agent above the grade of $900 per annum will be assigned to duty as a "short stop" or "helper" on any railway post-office line, and "short stops" or "helpers" on route-agent lines will be of a grade not to exceed $900 per annum.

3. *Providing for emergencies.*—To meet emergencies, superintendents can make any assignments of employés and local mail agents in their respective divisions which may seem to them necessary for the benefit of the service, but not for a longer period than ten consecutive days; and such assignment must be at once reported to the general superintendent, for the information of the department, and, if necessary, for the readjustment of the grade and salary of employés so assigned, in accordance with this order.

4. *New appointments.*—All new appointments of employés and local mail agents will be for a probationary period of six months, and at a salary not exceeding $900 per annum. If, at the expiration of six months, such employés' records are satisfactory, the appointments will be made permanent.

5. *Assignment of employés.*—Whenever it shall appear that an employé is unable to perform the duties assigned to his grade his division superintendent will at once report the facts to the general superintendent, with a recommendation for a reduction or retirement of such employé, but in no event will an employé be allowed to receive the salary of a higher grade than is by this order assigned to the duties actually performed by him, except when ordered by the division superintendent to perform lower duties in an emergency.

6. *Reassignment of employés.*—Division superintendents are instructed to reorganize their working crews, and reassign employés in accordance with this order. Where there are more employés of the higher grades now in the service than will be needed under the reassignment they will assign the most efficient to duty in accordance with their grades, under the order, and will report the least efficient to the general superintendent for reduction to a lower grade or retirement.

7. *Details of employés from one route to another.*—This order will not interfere with the present practice of detailing employés and local mail agents from one route to another, but employés so detailed must be assigned to duty in accordance with the provisions of this order.

8. *Details of employés for clerical duty.*—No more employés will be detailed for clerical duty than the exigency of the service absolutely requires. No employé will be assigned to assist a chief head clerk except in special cases, and then the grade of the employé so assigned must not exceed $1,000 per annum.

9. *Salaries of mail-route messengers.*—This order does not change the mode of adjusting and determining the salaries of mail-route messengers, which will continue to be based upon the number of miles of daily service performed.

10. *Date at which this order takes effect.*—This order will take effect upon and after the 1st day of May, 1881. Division superintendents will report at once to the general superintendent any changes which this order may require to be made at that time in the grades of employés.　　　　　　　　　　THOMAS L. JAMES,

Postmaster-General.

Although this order seemed at first harsh to those employés whose salaries were thereby reduced, or whose retirement became necessary, its general effect upon the service has been most salutary. While it insists upon the duties being properly performed, it also secures, at the same time, the right to promotion when earned by faithful and intelligent service. It has always been my aim, and the aim of my predecessors in charge of this branch of the postal service, to impress upon all employés the assurance that their advancement to the highest salary allowed by law depended solely upon themselves and their ability to perform the duties assigned to them, and that their superiors were not only willing but anxious to recognize and advance true merit wherever found. The order above quoted was issued for the purpose of making this policy more clearly apparent, and while its beneficial results can already be seen in the increased efficiency of the service, I am confident that the test of another year will remove any doubts that may exist in the minds of any persons as to the wisdom of this reorganization of the service. Indeed, I have already been informed by many of the employés that they liked this order, and believed in it, that they felt now that when they had earned and were entitled to a promotion they could obtain it.

ESTIMATES FOR 1883.

I would therefore renew the recommendation made by my immediate predecessor in his report for the fiscal year ended June 30, 1878, and repeated by myself in the reports for 1879 and 1880, that the appropriation for the payment of the railway mail-service clerks for the fiscal year ending June 30, 1883, be made in gross for the sum of $3,480,000, and that it be enacted that hereafter the railway mail-service clerks be divided into five classes, whose salaries shall not exceed: For the first class, $800 per annum each; for the second class, $900; for the third class, $1,000; for the fourth class, $1,200; and for the fifth class, $1,400. This would involve no change in the service as organized under the Postmaster-General's order above quoted, and would greatly simplify the accounts of the department.

In the old form the estimates for 1883 are as follows:

For railway post-office clerks	$1,650,000
For route agents	1,375,000
For mail-route messengers	280,000
For local agents	175,000
Total	3,480,000

This is an estimated increase over the appropriation for the current year of $100,000 for postal clerks, $100,000 for route agents, $45,000 for mail-route messengers, and $25,000 for local agents, or a total for all employés of $270,000. This increase is the lowest possible estimate, and will be barely sufficient to meet the demands of the country for the extension of postal service upon new lines of railroad now building and in contemplation.

MORE LOCAL AGENTS NEEDED.

The welfare of the service and the safety of the registered mails demand an increase in the number of local agents. Applications are on file in this office from all the division superintendents for the appointment of local agents at railroad junctions to receive and receipt for registered matter and to superintend the transfer of registered and ordinary mail matter, so as to save the delay incident to having registered matter pass through the local post-offices, and to insure the transfer of ordinary matter so as to make close connections. There is no branch of the service more important than this, for the advantages of close distribution upon the cars are lost if connections are missed for the want of an agent to see that transfers are properly made and that mails are not neglected by the employés of railroad companies.

INCREASE OF RAILROAD SERVICE.

During the fiscal year ended June 30, 1881, 6,380 miles of new railroad service were recognized under the law, and since the close of the fiscal year to the 18th of October, 1881, there have been recognized 3,352 additional. This is the greatest increase reported in any one year since 1872, as will be seen by reference to Table B, hereto appended. The number of miles of annual railroad service in 1881 was 103,521,229, of which 70,684,211 were performed under the charge of railway mail service clerks (see Table L, appended to the report of the Second Assistant Postmaster-General), and the remainder, 32,837,018 miles, represents the transportation of closed pouches in baggage and express cars under charge of the employés of railroad companies. It will be seen from Table B that the increase in railroad service during the fiscal year ended June 30, 1881, over the preceding year was 7.32 per cent. in miles of route and 7.27 per cent. in miles of annual service.

MAIL DISTRIBUTED, ERRORS MADE, ETC.

There were employed in the distribution of the mail in transit, during the past fiscal year, 504 cars and 1,371 apartments in cars. In these the railway mail service clerks handled and distributed 1,803,983,720 letters and 1,049,296,350 pieces of other matter, or a total of all classes of ordinary matter of 2,853,280,070, besides 12,028,765 registered packages and pouches, being an increase over the preceding year of 194,796,850 pieces, or 7.32 per cent. of ordinary matter, and 325,483 packages and pouches, or 2.78 per cent. of registered matter. In the distribution of this matter 787,505 errors were made, or one in every 3,624 pieces handled, against one in every 3,482 pieces handled during the preceding year. The percentage of correct distribution in 1881 was 99.97.

During the same time 454,349 errors in distribution were checked by the employés of this service against post-offices. For a detailed statement, by divisions, of work performed and errors checked see Tables C, D, and E, appended to this report.

CASUALTIES.

Appended hereto (Table G) is a statement of the casualties of the fiscal year, from which it will be seen that the railway mail service is no less dangerous than are its duties difficult and imperative. During the past year 62 accidents are reported, in which 7 employés of this service lost their lives, 6 of them having been burned to death, 15 were severely and 22 slightly injured. No provision has ever been made for the widows and orphans of men killed in this service, nor for the continuance of pay to men disabled while in the line of duty. I earnestly recommend that the Postmaster-General be authorized to pay to the widow, or guardian of the minor children, of men killed in this service, the salary of the deceased, such payment not to continue longer than two years. I also recommend that men disabled in the service be continued on full pay until recovery, not to exceed one year.

RAILWAY POST-OFFICE SERVICE.

During the past fiscal year railway post-office service was established on the following lines:

Detroit and Chicago, 284 miles, 50-foot cars.
Omaha and Hastings, 151 miles 40-foot cars.
Vanceborough and Bangor, additional line, 114 miles, 40-foot cars.

On the Saint Louis and Atchison Railway post-office 60-foot cars have been substituted for the 40-foot cars formerly in use. There are many other lines on which railway post-office service should be established, and the communities and business interests that would be benefited thereby are very anxious to have such service put on. I have recommended an appropriation of $1,526,000 for railway post-office car service for 1883, being an increase of $100,000 over the appropriation for the present fiscal year. I should not feel so free to recommend this increase in the service but for the fact that wherever such service has been established the receipts have grown more rapidly than the expenditures, showing that the service is a source of profit to the department.

FAST MAILS AND SPECIAL FACILITIES.

The appropriation for special facilities for fast mails for the fiscal year ended June 30, 1881, was $350,000. The wisdom of Congress in making this appropriation has been fully vindicated by the results of its judicious disbursement by the Postmaster-General. During the past fiscal year the fast mail service has been extended from West Philadelphia, Pa., to Washington, D. C., Richmond, Va., Atlanta, Ga., New Orleans, La., and Charleston, S. C., with connections to Savannah, Ga., and Jacksonville, Fla. In former years the service between the States northward and Florida has been slow, tedious, and very unsatisfactory, but with the improvements already made, and those contemplated, I am confident there can be no cause for complaint in the future.

The time has been materially shortened from New York, N. Y., to Atlanta, Ga., and New Orleans, La., and the southern fast mail has, upon the whole, proved a success. Yet the immense traffic on the railroads, due to the "business boom," has required so many trains to be placed on the roads that the fast mail has frequently been delayed. I do not wish to be understood as intimating that the time of the fast mail is too short. On the contrary, I believe the speed can and will be increased with safety as the roads are improved and the employés become accustomed to fast schedules, for I hold that, with a good track, motive power, and rolling stock, there is no more danger at 40 miles an hour than at 20. In fact, more accidents are reported to accommodation trains than to fast mail and express trains.

On the first day of the last fiscal year there was a fast mail established on the Pennsylvania Railroad, between New York, N. Y., and Columbus, Ohio, leaving New York at 8.30 p. m., after the close of business, receiving all the important business mail of the day, and by fast running overtaking at Columbus, Ohio, the regular fast express that left New York two hours and a half earlier. At Columbus the postal cars attached to this train are separated, one going to Cincinnati, Ohio, on the regular fast express, and the other two going to Saint Louis, Mo., via Indianapolis, Ind., on the regular express and passenger train, arriving at Saint Louis in time to make connections with all morning outward trains.

There is a similar train on the New York Central and Hudson River Railroad and Lake Shore and Michigan Southern Railway. This train leaves New York at 8.50 p. m., receives at Albany the eastern mail that left Boston at 6 p. m., and overtakes at Cleveland, Ohio, the fast passenger train that left New York at 6 p. m. At Cleveland this train makes connections for the southwest, and at Toledo, Ohio, both northwestern and southwestern connections are made. The postal cars are transferred at Cleveland to the regular train for Chicago, where they arrive at 6 a. m., in time for early city delivery, and connect with all outward trains. This service has been very satisfactory and beneficial to business men and other patrons of the postal service.

There has also been established a fast-mail service on the New York Central and Hudson River Railroad, leaving the Grand Central depot, New York, at 4.35 a. m., making very fast time to Poughkeepsie, arriving at Albany at 9 a. m. At Albany the postal car is transferred to the regular express for Rochester. This gives an early service that was much desired and accomplished all that was expected of it.

The 5 a. m. fast-mail service from New York to Springfield, Mass., has been continued.

Without the appropriation for special facilities it would have been impossible for the Postmaster-General to have established and maintained this service, or any part of it.

ESTIMATES FOR SPECIAL FACILITIES FOR 1883.

The estimate for special facilities for 1883 is $500,000, being $75.000 more than for 1882. In my opinion, certainly during five months of the year, the fast-mail service should be extended to Jacksonville Fla., and during the whole of the year to New Orleans, La. There is also need of a fast-mail service between New York, N. Y., and Boston, Mass., leaving each city late at night, after the close of business, and arriving at the other city early in the morning, in time to have the city mail delivered by the first carriers. There should also be a later departure than 6 p. m., from Boston to connect at Albany, N. Y., with the fast mail. This (6 p. m.) is the latest departure that it has hitherto been possible to secure. If a train could leave at 7 p. m. a large amount of important mail could be forwarded several hours earlier.

If the postal car which leaves the Grand Central depot, New York, at 4.35 a. m., and runs to Rochester could be run through to Chicago, arriving there the following day about 10 a. m., in time to make connections with all outward bound railway post-office and route-agent lines, it would advance all mail for offices west of Chicago from twelve to twenty-four hours.

There are other places that are desirous of fast-mail service, and it should be provided as soon as possible. It can be demonstrated from the annual reports of the Postmaster-General, for the past twenty years, that fast mails and frequent service on railroads between important cities, and through populous sections of country, are a source of revenue far greater than the outlay for such service. The estimate for special facilities is below rather than above the amount actually required, and I therefore earnestly request that the full amount be appropriated.

ADDITIONAL ROUTE-AGENT SERVICE NEEDED.

What are known as accommodation trains are run on nearly all the railroads leading out of the principal cities of the United States. These trains usually have a run of about 100 miles or less, arriving at the city in the morning soon after the commencement of business and departing about 4 or 5 p. m. Route agent service should be put upon all these trains which run through populous sections. It would be a great accommodation to the people living along the line of road and a source of revenue to the department. Such additional facilities induce a large number of letters to be mailed, and letters are the chief source of the postal revenues. The regular mail trains that must be provided would then, as now, carry the second, third, and fourth class matter, which constitute nine-tenths of the weight of the mail upon which the compensation of railroads is based, and upon which the postage barely pays for transportation, so that a route-agent service upon accommodation trains will increase the expenditure but slightly, while the number of letters will be greatly increased by the facilities afforded to business men in the country to write to their city correspondents in the morning and receive a reply in the evening. The records of the department show that every increase of frequency of mail exchanges in populous sections has been followed by an increase of revenue far greater than the expenditure. Exchanges in closed pouches will not meet the wants of the people who need exchanges between intermediate points, for this can only be performed by route agents. The cost of transporting the mail would be the same in pouches as in route-agent lines, the only additional expense being the salaries of the route agents, and this would be more than made up by the increased revenues.

COST OF RAILROAD SERVICE.

The cost per mile of railroad service, including postal cars and fast mails, has not increased with the weight of mails, as will be seen by the following statement:

In 1854 there were 14,440 miles of railroad routes, and 15,433,380 miles of annual service, at an average cost per mile of annual service of 9.6 cents. The weight of the mails at that time was unknown, and the rate of payment was fixed by the Postmaster-General, under the acts of 1839 and 1845. In 1867 there were 34,015 miles of railroad routes, and 32,437,900 miles of annual service, at an average cost per mile of 11.75 cents. In that year the mails were weighed for the first time, and the average daily weight of mail sent from New York City by rail was 20,031 pounds, or 10 tons. In 1873 there were 63,457 miles of railroad routes, and 50,340,420 miles of annual service, at an average cost per mile of 11.05 cents. In that year the average daily mail from New York City by rail was 100,311 pounds, or 54 tons. In 1877 there were 74,546 miles of railroad routes, and 85,358,710 miles of annual service, at an average cost of 10.5 cents per mile. In that year the average daily weight of mail from New York City by rail was 123,107 pounds, or 61 tons. In 1881 there were 91,569 miles of railroad routes and 103,521,229 miles of annual service, at an average cost of 10.44 cents per mile. In this year the daily weight of mail sent from New York City by rail was 170,336 pounds, or 85 tons. It will thus be seen that while the weight of mail carried out of New York has increased from 10 to 85 tons, or more than eight-fold, the average cost per mile of service is actually one cent and a third less in 1881 than it was in 1867, and only forty-eight one-hundredths of a cent more than in 1854. The increase in the weight of mail all over the country has been in proportion to that sent from New York, and these figures have been taken only because they were more readily accessible.

IMPROVEMENT SUGGESTED IN THROUGH REGISTERED POUCHES.

The introduction of through registered pouches has added greatly to the safety of the registered mail, and has relieved employés of the trouble and responsibility of receipting separately for each package of registered matter. The present style of pouches does not, however, afford the protection and security to registered matter which would be obtained by the substitution therefor of substantial packing trunks. The original cost of such trunks is far greater than of the pouches, yet their greater durability and the increased protection which they afford to the mail would, in the end, compensate for the outlay. For more than a year six trunks have been in use between New York, N. Y., and San Francisco, Cal., and experience has proved them to be far superior to pouches for the transportation of large quantities of registered matter between important offices. I would therefore respectfully recommend that authority be given to purchase, out of the appropriation for mail bags, two hundred of these trunks for use between the principal offices in lieu of pouches.

CEDAR KEY AND KEY WEST, FLA.

It has not been the practice of this office to make recommendations in regard to the appropriations for, or the management of, steamboat service, yet I desire to call your attention to the unsatisfactory state of the service between Cedar Key and Key West, Fla. Although this service is very expensive, it is far from what it should be. The boats ought to make close connection with the cars at Cedar Key, but they often fail to connect even when the train is held back for them for hours. The boats are due to arrive in the morning and depart at night, but it has often happened that the boat due in the morning had not arrived when it was due to depart. I recommend that some action be taken to obtain faster and better boats for this service, and that the schedule be arranged so that unbroken mail communication can be secured between interior points and Key West, which is a city of 12,000 people, and entitled to better service than it now has. With this service performed by a fast steamer, making regular connections at Cedar Key, it could be extended to Havana, Cuba, with advantage to the business interests of this country, and with but slight additional cost.

CONCLUSION.

In concluding this report I desire to express my personal obligation to the officers and employés of this service for the intelligence, zeal, faithfulness, and energy with which they have discharged the difficult, responsible, and often dangerous duties intrusted to their care. The safety of the mails in transit and the prompt delivery of letters at their destinations demonstrate far better than any words of mine can do the fidelity and efficiency of these gentlemen. It is not laudation but a simple statement of facts to say that no civil service in the world can show their superiors.

I have the honor to be, very respectfully, your obedient servant,

W. B. THOMPSON,
General Superintendent.

Hon. R. A. ELMER,
Second Assistant Postmaster-General.

TABLE A.—*Statement for the years 1870 to 1881, inclusive, showing the number of railway post-office clerks, route agents, mail-route messengers, and local agents employed; total amount paid to each class; and the percentage of increase and decrease in number of employés and annual expenditure.*

Year.	Number of railway post-office clerks in service at end of each fiscal year.	Increase in railway post-office clerks.	Increase, per cent.	Total amount paid railway post-office clerks.	Increase in amount paid railway post-office clerks.	Decrease in amount paid railway post-office clerks.	Increase, per cent.	Decrease, per cent.	Number of route agents in service at end of each fiscal year.	Increase in route agents.	Decrease in route agents.	Increase, per cent.	Decrease, per cent.	Total amount paid route agents.	Increase in amount paid route agents.	Decrease in amount paid route agents.	Increase, per cent.	Decrease, per cent.	Number of mail-route messengers in service at end of each fiscal year.
1870	275			$442,600 00					887					$574,800 00					78
1871	513	138	26.6	640,600 00	$198,000 00		44.73		854	97		18.85		671,280 00	$96,680 00		16.83		103
1872	518	129	25.15	851,600 00	173,200 00		26.96		764	80		8.91		737,820 00	66,540 00		8.91		146
1873	628	110	17.12	911,000 00	172,400 00		2.35		785	76		13.25		828,240 00	90,420 00		13.25		171
1874	762	98	13.02	1,056,000 00	117,400 00		12.45		985	51		8.45		885,680 00	68,440 00		8.26		211
1875	801	51	6.00	1,165,000 00	105,400 00 18		6.16		996	39		4.73		946,380 52		$259 48			225
1876	1,042	141	15.65	1,122,766 30	66,159 08			06.01	1,017	48		2.72		950,690 61	43,701 45		4.88		268
1877	1,051	90	0.85	1,223,589 41	14,723 30		1.20		1,065	78		7.82		993,361 51	19,506 88		4.07		246
1878	1,061	10	0.54	1,238,889 71	105,101 43		8.23		1,123	10			10	1,035,685 99	34,150 40		3.55		341
1879	1,081	20		1,241,394 14	20,069 21		1.90		1,252	119		9.50		1,077,675 00	42,090 00		7.23		247
1880	1,200	115	9.54	1,367,463 25	86,150 00		6.73		1,386	124		9.67		1,118,685 00	96,990 72				288
1881	1,238	67	6.73	1,465,275 52	96,150 07	$189 70								1,241,406 41	124,721 78		10.05		283

Year.	Increase in mail-route messengers.	Decrease in mail-route messengers.	Total amount paid mail-route messengers.	Increase, per cent.	Decrease, per cent.	Increase in amount paid mail-route messengers.	Decrease in amount paid mail-route messengers.	Increase, per cent.	Decrease, per cent.	Number of local mail agents in service at end of each fiscal year.	Increase in local mail agents.	Decrease in local mail agents.	Increase, per cent.	Decrease, per cent.	Total amount paid local mail agents.	Increase in amount paid local mail agents.	Decrease in amount paid local mail agents.	Increase, per cent.	Decrease, per cent.
1870	25		$45,710 00							66					$44,220 00				
1871	43		61,910 00	35.44		$16,200 00		33.05		82	16		24.24		56,430 00	$12,200 00		26.39	
1872	43		89,910 00	45.38		23,000 00		41.75		95	13		15.85		66,216 00	10,786 00		18.45	
1873	40		106,740 00	18.72		16,830 00		17.12		110	15		15.70		82,896 00	12,680 00		18.76	
1874	14		136,540 00	27.92		29,800 00		23.20		124	14		12.73		94,710 00	11,814 00		14.25	
1875		20	129,989 37		4.99		$6,540 85		4.99	137	13		9.6		98,980 70				4.6
1876	91		147,595 27	13.19		17,182 92		13.24		134		1			101,818 87	11,833 57		13.15	
1877		7	147,675 64	0.55		444 34			2.63	134					105,718 70	8,905 43		3.84	
1878			154,341 93	4.52		6,718 93		4.56		134					109,041 64	3,322 91		3.54	
1879	16		171,391 03	10.55		16,685 78		10.66		156	16		10.66		112,177 88	3,345 91		2.71	
1880	98		174,374 89	2.08		3,449 00			00.73	166	28		14.77		116,452 79	13,771 43		10.33	
1881				10.91		21,449 52				176					133,196 22		$4,729 30		

TABLE B.—*Statement for the years 1870 to 1881, inclusive, of steamboat and railroad routes, miles of annual service on the same, also miles of railway post-office service and miles of annual service thereon, together with the increase and decrease and decrease per cent.*

Year.	Miles of steamboat routes.	Increase of miles of steamboat routes.	Decrease of miles of steamboat routes.	Increase, per cent.	Decrease, per cent.	Miles of annual service on steamboat routes.	Increase in miles of annual service on steamboat routes.	Decrease in miles of annual service on steamboat routes.	Increase, per cent.	Decrease, per cent.	Miles of railroad service.	Increase of miles of railroad service.	Decrease of miles of railroad service.	Increase, per cent.	Decrease, per cent.	Miles of annual service on railroad routes.	Increase in miles of annual service on railroad routes.	Decrease in miles of annual service on railroad routes.	Increase, per cent.	Decrease, per cent.
1870	20,695					4,122,365					43,727					47,551,970				
1871	20,834		281		1.74	4,684,778	562,908		13.64		49,584	6,107		13.99		55,557,048	2,005,078		16.83	
1872	18,860		1,474		7.25	4,308,438				8.27	57,911	4,077		16.21		55,491,749	2,701		12.48	
1873	18,762		2,846		11.12	3,947,785					63,457	5,546		8.49		65,621,445	2,129,696		5.01	
1874	18,634		2,905			3,976,725	190,940		3.32		67,734	4,277		6.74		72,460,545	6,839,100		10.42	
1875	15,788				15.27	3,933,833				9.01	70,083	2,349		2.47		75,154,910	2,694,365		2.72	
1876	14,983				5.73	3,704,338	333,705		14.53		74,548	2,265		3.04		77,741,172	2,586,262		3.80	
1877	17,655	1,872		18.83		4,038,238	561,902		9.98		74,544	2,196		3.45		83,358,710	6,761,685		9.92	
1878	18,673	887		2.18		4,629,298	462,176		10.18		77,119	2,573		3.72		92,120,395	972,597		1.06	
1879	21,240	3,158		17.59		4,091,474					85,320	5,873		3.25		93,092,992	3,404,471		1.53	
1880	22,320	2,060		8.92		5,052,588					91,569	6,249		7.82		96,497,463	7,023,766		7.27	
1881	21,138		2,183		9.36	5,046,507	577,064	622,031		10.97						103,521,229				

Year.	Miles of route on post-office service.	Miles of route on railway post-office service which there is railway post-office service.	Increase of miles of route of railway post-office service.	Decrease of miles of route of railway post-office service.	Increase, per cent.	Decrease, per cent.	Miles of annual service by railway post-office.	Increase of miles of annual service by railway post-office.	Decrease of miles of annual service by railway post-office.	Increase, per cent.	Decrease, per cent.	Total miles of railroad and steamboat routes.	Increase of miles of railroad and steamboat routes.	Decrease of miles of railroad and steamboat routes.	Increase, per cent.	Decrease, per cent.	Miles of annual service on railroad and steamboat routes.	Increase of miles of railroad and steamboat routes.	Decrease of miles of railroad and steamboat routes.	Increase, per cent.	Decrease, per cent.
1870	6,509,000	8,253										64,422					51,674,335				
1871	10,072,340	11,206	2,956		35.83		8,677,540	3,074,210		54.96		70,168	5,746		8.92		60,241,826	8,567,471		16.58	
1872	12,747,625	12,254	2,908		25.95		9,234,314	456,775		5.26		76,171	6,603		8.41		66,580,296	6,388,439		10.58	
1873	14,639,763	14,896	749		5.30		9,483,139			3.66		82,219	6,048		7.96		73,540,270	6,970,040		4.14	
1874	15,204,865	16,414	1,548		10.41		9,952,130	383,130		12.23		86,308	6,140		7.96		78,574,490	6,574,490		10.03	
1875	15,923,660	16,932	518		8.16		9,770,138			2.82		85,671					81,231,243	2,331,343		3.86	
1876	16,925,910	17,713	781		4.61		9,998,133			11.27		85,131					87,962,745	1,922,745		2.36	
1877	17,040,210	17,761	48		.27		9,916,180	1,798,135		11.37		89,191					98,740,480	7,424,778		8.52	
1878	19,963,610	16,980		781		4.80	1,086,500	1,098,500		14.44		101,281					96,184,690	1,421,585		1.48	
1879	21,745,710	17,340	860		2.13		3,013,490					104,040					102,185,001			2.89	
1880	23,140,340	20,140	2,800		13.90		3,044,569	65,700			23.57	114,707					105,897,766	6,407,786		6.38	
1881	22,457,000	20,116		24		6.11															

TABLE C.—*Statement of mail distributed en route on the cars by employés of the railway mail service during the fiscal year ended June 30, 1881.*

Division.	Number of letter packages distributed.	Whole number of letters distributed.	Number of sacks of second, third, and fourth class matter distributed.	Whole number of pieces of second, third, and fourth class matter distributed.	Whole number of letters and pieces of other mail distributed.	Number of packages, pouches, and cases of registered mail matter.
First	4,900,610	196,024,400	533,521	80,028,150	276,052,550	1,028,898
Second	5,827,629	233,105,160	867,425	130,113,750	363,218,910	1,951,350
Third	1,881,002	75,240,060	816,184	47,427,600	122,667,660	44,253
Fourth	2,357,786	94,311,440	370,247	55,537,060	149,848,490	1,229,610
Fifth	7,715,726	308,629,040	1,426,837	214,025,550	522,654,590	1,817,153
Sixth	10,917,871	400,694,840	1,475,889	221,387,890	622,072,190	2,622,605
Seventh	5,906,432	236,257,280	943,664	141,549,600	377,806,889	1,866,542
Eighth	1,420,109	56,804,360	197,863	29,679,450	86,482,810	511,445
Ninth	5,072,928	202,917,120	868,679	129,561,850	332,466,970	959,778
Total	45,099,593	1,603,963,720	6,998,809	1,049,298,880	2,853,280,076	12,028,785

Whole number of pieces of mail handled in 1881 2,853,280,076
Whole number of pieces of mail handled in 1880 2,658,482,230

Increase 194,798,880

Percentage of increase, 7.32+.

Packages, pouches, and cases of registered matter handled in 1881 12,028,765
Packages, pouches, and cases of registered matter handled in 1880 11,703,282

Increase 325,483
Percentage of increase, 2.78+.

TABLE D.—*Statement of errors made by employés of the railway mail service during the fiscal year ended June 30, 1881.*

Division.	Number of incorrect slips returned.	Number of errors on incorrect slips.	Missent.				Misdirected.			Number of errors checked against other employés.
			Number of packages.	Number of pouches.	Number of sacks.	Number of registered packages.	Number of packages.	Number of pouches.	Number of sacks.	
First	19,984	31,748	942	387	102	80	86	42	20	44,019
Second	35,141	63,570	657	379	122	43	95	26	16	108,262
Third	14,984	25,262	247	1	2	......	83	3	2	53,050
Fourth	29,640	51,887	665	145	66	56	67	45	86	113,540
Fifth	102,673	201,234	921	92	145	*64	342	29	92	452,588
Sixth	78,289	144,168	1,218	210	104	34	382	60	136	227,034
Seventh	63,112	129,342	1,984	391	296	*104	61	8	22	397,719
Eighth	2,610	3,451	75	......	2	......	14	......	1	35,521
Ninth	58,864	136,748	933	965	188	50	130	13	36	70,836
Total	405,298	787,505	7,642	2,470	1,030	414	1,130	233	348	1,438,809

RECAPITULATION.

Number of letters and pieces of paper mail distributed during the year 2,853,280,076
Number of errors made in the distribution of the same 787,505
Number of letters and pieces of paper mail distributed to each error, 1881 3,624
Number of letters and pieces of paper mail distributed to each error, 1880 3,482
Percentage of correct distribution, 1881 .... 99.97
Percentage of correct distribution, 1880 .... 88.97+

*Including 15 pouches.

REPORT OF THE THIRD ASSISTANT POSTMASTER-GENERAL.

POST-OFFICE DEPARTMENT,
OFFICE OF THE THIRD ASSISTANT POSTMASTER-GENERAL,
Washington, D. C., November 10, 1881.

SIR: I have the honor to submit the following report, showing the operations of this office for the fiscal year ending June 30, 1881, and to call attention particularly to the accompanying tables, numbered from 1 to 21, inclusive, viz:

No. 1. Explanation of estimates of appropriation for the office of the Third Assistant Postmaster-General for the fiscal year ending June 30, 1883.

No. 2. Statement showing appropriations for the Post-Office Department for the fiscal year ending June 30, 1881, and the expenditures made, by items, out of such appropriations up to September 30, 1881.

No. 3. Statement exhibiting the receipts and expenditures under appropriate heads, by quarters, for the fiscal year ending June 30, 1881, compared with the fiscal years ending June 30, 1880, and June 30, 1879.

No. 4. Statement showing receipts and disbursements at Treasury depositories during the fiscal year ending June 30, 1881.

No. 5. Statement showing receipts and disbursements at depository post-offices on account of the fiscal year ending June 30, 1881.

Nos. 6 and 7. Statements showing the number and value of postage-stamps, stamped envelopes, newspaper wrappers, and postal cards issued during the year ending June 30, 1881.

No. 8. Statement showing the number and value of official postage-stamps issued to each of the executive departments during the year ending June 30, 1881.

No. 9. Statement showing the issue of postage-stamps, &c., by denominations, during the year ending June 30, 1881.

No. 10. Statement showing the increase in the issues of postage-stamps, stamped envelopes, and postal cards for the fiscal year ending June 30, 1881, over those of the preceding year.

No. 11. Cost of procuring supplies in the office of the Third Assistant Postmaster-General from July 1, 1877, to June 30, 1881, as compared with the cost of the same supplies during the preceding four years.

No. 12. Statement showing disposition of dead mail matter treated in the division of dead letters during the year ending June 30, 1881.

No. 13. Statement showing the disposition of mail matter opened in the division of dead letters during the year ending June 30, 1881.

No. 14. Statement showing the amount, classification, and disposition of unmailable matter received at the dead-letter office during the fiscal year ending June 30, 1881.

No. 15. Statement showing the number of dead foreign letters received and disposed of during the fiscal year ending June 30, 1881.

No. 16. Statement showing amount of dead matter returned to and received from each foreign country.

No. 17. Statement showing the number, classification, and disposition of dead registered letters during the year ending June 30, 1881.

No. 18. Statement showing the number of registered letters and parcels transmitted through the mails from each State and Territory in the United States during the year ending June 30, 1881.

No. 19. Statement showing the number and value of registered packages forwarded during the fiscal year ending June 30, 1881, for the Post-Office and Treasury Departments.

No. 20. Statement showing increase of registered letters and parcels upon which fees were collected at the twenty-five leading cities of the country during the fiscal year ending June 30, 1881.

No. 21. Statement showing the operations of the registered-letter system at the cities of New York, Philadelphia, Chicago, Saint Louis, and Washington, during the year ending June 30, 1881.

FINANCIAL STATEMENT.

The receipts and expenditures of the department during the fiscal year ending June 30, 1881, were as follows:

Receipts:

Letter postage, paid in money	$100,809 23
Box-rents and branch offices	1,499,449 87
Fines and penalties	15,751 44
Sales of postage-stamps, stamped envelopes, newspaper wrappers, and postal-cards	34,835,745 10
Dead letters	6,584 40
Revenue from money-order business	295,581 39
Miscellaneous	31,476 54
Total	36,785,397 97
The total expenditures for the service of the year were	39,251,736 46
Excess of expenditures	2,466,338 49
To this should be added the net amount charged on the books of the Auditor during the year to "bad debts" and "compromise" accounts.	14,790 86
Making a total excess of expenditures over receipts for the service of the fiscal year of	2,481,129 35

This deficit was 6.3 per cent. of the entire expenditures, and will be somewhat increased when all the liabilities of the year are adjusted and paid. Exclusive of these unadjusted liabilities, the expenditures for the year were $3,149,916.08, or 8.7 per cent., more than those of the preceding year.

In addition to the above expenditures the sum of $340,829.76 was paid on account of indebtedness incurred in previous years, making the total amount expended during the year $39,592,566.22.

Table No. 2 which accompanies this report shows the appropriations by items for the service of the last fiscal year, and the amounts expended out of the same. These expenditures came within the appropriations in all the items except that of "compensation of postmasters," in which there was an excess of expenditure over the amount appropriated of $798,742.79, to cover which a deficiency appropriation should he made by Congress, payable out of the postal revenues for the year ending June 30, 1881. In regard to this excess, it is proper to state that expenditures for compensation of postmasters, no matter what may be the amount appropriated by Congress, are practically beyond the control of the department, inasmuch as the law regulates the rate of compensation by the amount of business transacted, and gives to postmasters the right to retain the same out of the revenues of their offices.

The receipts for the year were $3,469,918.63, or 10.4 per cent., more than the receipts of the preceding year, and $4,575,397.97, or 14.2 per cent., more than the estimates therefor. This great increase is attributable, of course, mainly to the business prosperity of the country, the extent of the same not being foreseen when the estimates were made. The principal item of increase was the sales of postage-stamps, stamped envelopes, and postal cards, the total amount of which was $3,341,624.95 greater than that for the year 1880, and $6,690,670.11 greater than that for 1879.

65 Ab

Table No. 3 which accompanies this report shows the receipts and expenditures by quarters, and the increase or decrease of the same as compared with previous years.

AMOUNTS DRAWN FROM THE TREASURY.

In addition to the receipts stated above, there were drawn from the Treasury, on account of special and deficiency appropriations, the following amounts:

Out of the appropriation to supply deficiencies in the revenues for the year ending June 30, 1881	$3,000,000 00
Out of the appropriation to supply deficiencies in the revenues for the year ending June 30, 1879	279,556 03
To pay scheduled claims authorized by act approved March 3, 1881, (Statutes, chap. 132, p. 433, pamphlet edition,) for the service of the year 1878, and prior years, as appears by the report of the Auditor	18,315 43
To enable the Postmaster-General to refund to A. J. Brooks the contents of a dead letter erroneously covered into the Treasury (act of March 3, 1881, chap. 132, page 423, pamphlet edition)	50 00
Total	3,297,921 46

CONDITION OF DEFICIENCY APPROPRIATIONS.

The following statement shows the condition of the appropriations from the general Treasury to supply deficiencies in the postal revenues, viz:

1. For the fiscal year ending June 30, 1881, the amount appropriated from the Treasury to supply deficiencies in the postal revenue was $3,883,420, of which the sum of $3,000,000 was drawn and placed in the hands of the Treasurer to the credit of the Post-Office Department. Of the amount thus drawn, $2,466,338.49 was actually expended up to the close of the fiscal year, and $14,790.86 was charged on the books of the Auditor as the net amount lost during the year by "bad debts" and compromise accounts, leaving available in the hands of the Treasurer $518,870.65. The remainder of the appropriation—$883,420—is still in the general Treasury, subject to requisition. Of the appropriation for deficiencies, therefore, the entire amount unexpended at the close of the year, and available for its outstanding liabilities, was $1,402,290.65.

2. For the fiscal year ending June 30, 1880, the amount appropriated to supply deficiencies in the postal revenue was $5,457,376.10, of which $1,957,376.10 remained undrawn in the general Treasury at the close of the fiscal year ending June 30, 1881. There remained also in the hands of the Treasurer, at the same time, to the credit of the Post-Office Department, the sum of $448,453.93. The total amount unexpended, therefore, out of the appropriation for the year ending June 30, 1880, and available for its outstanding liabilities, is $2,405,830.03.

TRANSACTIONS AT DEPOSITORIES.

The receipts and disbursements at Treasury and post-office depositories during the last fiscal year may be briefly stated as follows:

At Treasury depositories:	
Balance subject to draft June 30, 1880	$2,335,648 94
Deduct amount of error discovered in balance since last statement, and rectified by counter entry	123 36
	2,335,525 62
Outstanding warrants, June 30, 1880	164,864 39
Aggregate receipts during the year ending June 30, 1881	15,055,084 64
Total	17,555,474 65
Amount of warrants paid during the year	13,842,231 67
Balance at depositories June 30, 1881	3,713,242 98
Outstanding warrants June 30, 1881	61,337 60
Balance subject to draft June 30, 1881	3,651,905 38

Transactions at these depositories, in detail, with amount of increase or decrease, as compared with previous years, are shown in table No. 4 accompanying this report.

At post-office depositories:

Balance subject to draft June 30, 1880...................................	747,084 07
Deduct credit balance June 30, 1880................................	2,618 68
	744,465 39
Aggregate receipts during the year ended June 30, 1881......	9,278,005 61
Total	10,022,471 00
Disbursements during the year......:.................... $7,256,476 52	
Transferred to other depositories....................... 2,080,938 05	
	9,337,414 57
	685,056 43
Add amount credit balances	122 26
Amount subject to draft June 30, 1881..................................	685,178 69

Table No. 5 submitted with this report exhibits the receipts and disbursements at the different post-office depositories in detail.

CONTRACTS ENTERED AND ACCOUNTS KEPT.

During the year there were 5,307 contracts for mail service received from the Second Assistant Postmaster-General, and 15,274 orders of the Postmaster-General (of which 7,637 were double) recognizing mail service not under contract, curtailing or extending service or modifying previous orders, being a decrease of 2,163 contracts and an increase of 920 orders, as compared with the previous year. These contracts and orders were entered upon the books of the division of finance for reference when passing upon reports from the Auditor for the payment of mail contractors and other creditors of the department. The number of such reports received and adjusted during the year was 42,047, an increase of 2,341 over the previous year.

Accounts were kept with the Treasury, 9 sub-treasuries, and 39 designated depositories, involving the sum of $15,055,084.64, against which 14,713 warrants were issued.

Accounts were also kept with 110 post-office depositories, involving the sum of $10,022,471, of which $3,794,586.48 arose from the proceeds of the depository offices themselves, $5,436,513.26 from deposits by other offices, and $46,905.87 from collection drafts. Against the accumulations in the depository offices 27,334 drafts were issued, amounting to $5,694,642.70. In addition to the amount paid out by draft, the sum of $1,561,833.82 was paid to route agents, railway post-office clerks, mail-messengers and letter-carriers by the postmasters authorized to make such payments, the accounts for which were rendered monthly to this office.

APPROPRIATIONS, EXPENDITURES, AND ESTIMATES FOR SERVICE OF OFFICE.

The appropriations for the service of this office during the last fiscal year amounted to $935,420, and the expenditures to $887,553.09, leaving an unexpended balance of $47,866.91, or 5.3 + per cent. of the appropriations.

The estimated amount of expenditures required for the service of this office for the fiscal year ending June 30, 1883, is $1,044,800, a decrease of $29,600, or 2.8 + per cent., from the aggregate appropriations for the current fiscal year. A detailed explanation of the items is attached to the table of estimates accompanying this report.

The decrease of estimates from the appropriations in the face of a contemplated large increase in the quantity of supplies required, results from new contracts entered into during the year for the manufacture of postage-stamps and postal cards. Stamps which cost 9.98 cents per thousand under the old contract running from 1877 to 1881, are now obtained at 9.19 cents per thousand. The cost under the contract which preceded the last one, and which ran from 1873 to 1877, was 14.99 cents per thousand. Postal cards which under the last contract cost 69.56 cents per thousand, are now furnished at 54.43 cents per thousand. From 1873 (when postal cards were first introduced) to 1877 the cost was $1.39⅞ per thousand.

The present decrease in the cost of supplies is the more gratifying because it follows in the line of a steady declension of prices during the past four years. The annexed table exhibits the comparative cost of supplies for this office for the past four years, with that of the four years ending June 30, 1877. It will be observed that the total number of articles—postage-stamps, stamped envelopes, postal cards, registered package and office envelopes—furnished during the four years ending June 30, 1877, was 4,051,301,066, costing $3,159,552.18. The number of articles furnished during the four years ending June 30, 1881, was 5,361,650,551, at a cost of $3,042,019.28, showing an increase of 1,310,349,485, or 32.3 per cent., in the number of articles, and a *decrease* of $117,532.90, or 3.7 per cent., in cost. The relative saving in cost during the past four years may therefore be placed at 36 per cent

The sum of $1,629,216.29, or 53.5 per cent. of the total expenditures, was for stamped envelopes and wrappers, and this sum was refunded to the government, as by law the cost of manufacturing the envelopes and wrappers is added to the postage value in fixing the schedule of prices to the public. The net cost of supplies for the past four years was therefore $1,412,802.99.

Supplies in the office of the Third Assistant Postmaster-General.

Articles.	Four years ending June 30, 1877.		Four years ending June 30, 1881.	
	Number furnished.	Cost.	Number furnished.	Cost.
Postage-stamps............	2, 789, 554, 265	$483, 622 77	3, 418, 674, 501	$339, 934 71
Postal cards..............	519, 525, 500	724, 686 14	1, 003, 514, 000	704, 029 11
Stamped envelopes and wrappers....	633, 584, 249	1, 605, 858 78	804, 194, 325	1, 629, 216 29
Registered package, post-office, dead-letter, and official envelopes.......	108, 687, 052	345, 384 49	135, 267, 725	368, 839 17
Total.....................	4, 051, 301, 066	3, 159, 552 18	5, 361, 650, 551	3, 042, 019 28

COMPARISON.

Articles.	Increase in number furnished.	Decrease in cost.	Percentage of increase in number furnished.	Percentage of decrease in cost.
Postage-stamps........................	629, 120, 236	$143, 688 06	22 5	29 7
Postal cards..........................	483, 988, 500	20, 657 03	93. 1	2 9
Stamped envelopes and wrappers..............	170, 660, 076	*23, 357 51	26. 9	*1 4
Registered package, post-office, dead-letter, and official envelopes........	26, 580, 673	*23, 454 68	34. 4	*6. 7
Total............................	1, 310, 349, 485	117, 532 90	32. 3	3. 7

* Increase.

POSTAGE-STAMPS, STAMPED ENVELOPES, POSTAL CARDS, ETC.

The work performed by the stamp division of this office during the year may be summarized as follows: The number of ordinary postage-stamps issued for sale to the public was 954,128,450, valued at $24,040,627; of newspaper and periodical stamps, 1,995,788, valued at $1,398,674; of stamped envelopes, plain, 106,291,300, valued at $2,647,567.74; of stamped envelopes, bearing a return request, 85,024,000, valued at $2,624,481.75; of newspaper wrappers, 35,751,750, valued at $431,154.60; of special stamps for the collection of insufficiently prepaid postage, 8,045,710, valued at $254,393; of postal cards, 308,536,500, valued at $3,086,605; of official postage stamps issued to executive departments for official use, 2,012,544, valued at $107,777.32; and of official stamped envelopes and wrappers, 2,525,500, valued at $34,155.50; making a total number of 1,504,311,542, and a total value of $34,625,435.91.

The increase in value of these several issues over those of the preceding year is as follows: Of ordinary postage-stamps, $1,625,699, or 7.2 per cent.; of newspaper and periodical stamps, $145,770.70, or 11.6 per cent.; of stamped envelopes, plain, $151,328.81, or 6 + per cent.; of stamped envelopes bearing a return request, $243,126.60, or 10.2 per cent.; of newspaper wrappers, $49,367, or 12.9 per cent.; of postage-due stamps, $2,557, or 1 + per cent.; of postal cards, $333,135, or 12 + per cent.; and of official stamped envelopes and wrappers, $19,531.10, or 133.5 + per cent. There was a decrease in the value of official postage stamps of $32,421.76, or 23.1 + per cent.

The total increase in the value of all the issues was $2,538,093.45, or 7.9 + per cent.

In addition to the foregoing articles there were issued for official use 7,389,300 registered-package envelopes, 98,800 tag envelopes for registered packages, 20,055,350 post-office envelopes, 1,255,000 envelopes for returning dead letters, and 885,500 departmental envelopes for the use of the several bureaus of this department. There were also issued 7,711 books used by postmasters in the collection of postage on second-class or newspaper and periodical matter.

In sending out the foregoing supplies the following number of requisitions was filled:

For ordinary postage-stamps	128,502
For postage-due stamps	8,846
For newspaper and periodical stamps	10,091
For stamped envelopes, plain	60,462
For stamped envelopes bearing a return request	69,153
For postal cards	71,420
For official postage-stamps and stamped envelopes	33
For registered-package envelopes	52,103
For tag envelopes for registered packages	56
For post-office envelopes	23,259
For newspaper and periodical receipt-books	7,013
Total	430,868

In the following table a comparison is m:
stamp division in the same particulars dur

Articles.

Ordinary postage-stamps...................................
Postage-due stamps......................................
Newspapers and periodical stamps..........................
Stamped envelopes, plain..................................
Stamped envelopes, printed................................
Postal cards..
Official postage-stamps and stamped envelopes...............
Registered-package envelopes..............................
Tag envelopes ....
Post-office envelopes.....................................
Newspaper and periodical receipt-books ....

     Total....................................

NOTE.—A net increase of 6.8 + per cent.

The following number of packages was n
ing requisitions received during the year :

Of ordinary postage-stamps.........................
Of postage-due stamps.............................
Of newspaper and periodical stamps...............
Of stamped envelopes, plain ....
Of stamped envelopes, printed ....
Of postal cards...................................
Of official postage-stamps........................
Of official stamped envelopes....................
Of registered-package envelopes ....
Of post-office envelopes...........................
Of newspaper and periodical receipt-books ....
Of tag envelopes for registered packages ....

     Total.................................

For the first time in the history of the st:
registered packages of stamps, stamped e
report.

In inviting attention to the tabular state
report, it may be well to explain that the c
second quarter of 1881 was not caused by
for either postage-stamps or stamped env
indicate. On the contrary, there was a g1
classes of articles during that period; but c
large demands made on the department d
year, the appropriations for their manufact
ing exhausted long before the new appropri
to avoid either the total suspension of the
stamped envelopes before the close of the
ciencies, it was found necessary, in filling re
of May and June, to restrict their issue to v(
that all requisitions received might be fillec
sued, the department was enabled to sup
these articles for immediate use; to keep 1
ated; and to show an unexpended balance
of $97,000 for the manufacture of postage-
$444,020 appropriated for the manufactur
newspaper wrappers.

POSTAGE COLLECTED ON SECOND-CLASS MATTER.

The weight of newspaper and periodical matter mailed during the year from regular offices of publication or from news agencies was 69,952,432 pounds (34,976+ tons), the postage on which was $1,399,048.64. This is an increase of $172,596.06, or 14.07 per cent., over the amount of postage collected on such matter during the preceding year.

The whole number of post-offices engaged in the collection of postage on second-class matter was 4,821, being 398 more than during the previous year.

The following is a comparative statement showing the weight of second-class matter mailed, and the amount of postage collected thereon, at fifteen of the principal post-offices in the United States:

Post-office at—	Weight of second-class matter mailed during the fiscal year ended—		Increase in weight of second-class matter mailed during the year ended June 30, 1881.	Amount of postage collected on second-class matter during the year ended—		Amount of increase during the fiscal year ending June 30, 1881.	Per cent. of increase over preceding year.	Per cent. of total amount collected in the United States.
	June 30, 1880.	June 30, 1881.		June 30, 1880.	June 30, 1881.			
	Pounds.	*Pounds.*	*Pounds.*					
New York, N.Y.	17,326,455	19,340,898	2,014,443	$346,529 10	$386,817 96	$40,288 86	11.6	27.65—
Chicago, Ill	5,775,760	7,003,925	1,228,165	115,515 20	140,078 50	24,563 30	21.2	10.01+
Boston, Mass	3,753,016	4,163,075	410,059	75,060 32	83,261 50	8,201 18	10.9	5.95
Philadelphia, Pa	3,169,614	3,509,202	339,588	63,392 28	70,184 04	6,791 76	10.7	5.02
Augusta, Me	2,216,901	3,251,388	1,034,487	44,338 02	65,027 76	20,689 74	46.6	4.65
Saint Louis, Mo	2,697,319	3,223,492	526,173	53,946 38	64,469 84	10,523 46	19.5	4.61
Cincinnati, Ohio	2,593,799	2,774,289	180,490	51,875 96	55,485 78	3,609 80	6.9	3.96
San Francisco, Cal	1,180,764	1,197,029	16,265	23,615 28	23,940 58	325 30	1.3	1.71
Detroit, Mich	950,446	1,069,023	118,577	19,008 92	21,380 46	2,371 54	12.4	1.52
Louisville, Ky	763,840	904,042	140,202	15,276 80	18,080 84	2,804 04	18.3	1.29
Cleveland, Ohio	770,294	878,119	107,825	15,405 88	17,562 38	2,156 50	13.9	1.25
Milwaukee, Wis	779,805	848,461	68,656	15,596 10	16,969 22	1,373 12	8.8	1.21
Pittsburgh, Pa	622,792	715,519	92,727	12,455 84	14,310 88	1,854 54	14.9	1.02
Toledo, Ohio	585,084	704,063	118,979	11,701 68	14,061 26	2,379 58	20.3	1.01
Baltimore, Md	592,546	614,091	21,545	11,850 92	12,281 82	430 90	3.6	.88
Total	43,776,435	50,196,616	6,418,181	875,566 70	1,008,982 82	133,363 62	14.6	71.75

DEAD LETTERS.

The whole number of letters and parcels handled, including 45,433 remaining on hand at the close of the previous year, was 3,719,638, an excess of about 11 per cent. over 1879–1880. The number of ordinary unclaimed letters was 2,791,050, an increase of 230,648, or 9 per cent.; misdirected letters 242,556, an increase of 40,657, or 20 per cent.; parcels of merchandise 52,591, an increase of 6,927, or 15 per cent.; foreign letters 284,127, an increase of 76,908, or 34 per cent.; letters originating in the United States by foreign countries as unclaimed 125,760, an increase of 15,537, or 14 per cent. The number of held-for-postage letters was less than the previous year, being 279,244 as against 284,503, a decrease of 5,259, or 2 per cent. This is due to a modification of the treatment of such letters at some of the post-offices, a notice of the cause of detention being sent direct by the postmaster instead of through the dead-letter-office. The number of letters without superscription (and upon these the postage is usually paid by stamps) was 9,479, an increase of 312. The failure to address a letter is always, of course, purely accidental, and it is an interesting fact that such letters prove to contain a larger ratio of valuable inclosures than any other class of letters opened in the dead-letter-office. To illustrate the steady increase of this class of correspondence, I will state the number received during each of the previous five years: In 1876 there were 6,945; in 1877, 7,020; 1878, 7,587; 1879, 7,944; and in 1880, 9,167. The inclosures are mainly drafts, notes, and money-orders, and the writers are almost invariably men engaged in active business pursuits.

The total number of registered letters and parcels received during the year was 9,086, but of these 6,472 were mailed abroad, and being unclaimed in the United States are required to be returned to the country of origin through the dead-letter-office. Of the remainder (2,614 domestic), 2,131 were restored to the owners, and the balance placed on file. When it is remembered that there were 8,368,918 registered articles mailed in this country during the same period, the security that registration affords will become apparent. No higher commendation of the system could be made to the patrons of the mails than the publication of these facts.

Of the domestic misdirected letters received (242,556), 39,627 were forwarded to their proper destination, the deficiency in address having been supplied by experts in this office. The number of misdirected letters of foreign origin was 31,184, and on 3,884 of these the correct address was supplied and the letters delivered.

One of the most gratifying facts observed in the opening of letters and packages in the dead-letter office is the decrease of obscene matter found, thus proving that the United States mails are used less each year in disseminating immorality. Not one obscene book has been received during the year, and to find an indecent photograph is a rare occurrence. Of the 3,500 prints of all sorts which reached the office during the two months following last St. Valentine's Day, not one could have been declared unmailable under the law.

STATISTICS OF REGISTRATION.

The total number of letters and parcels forwarded by registered mail during the year was 8,338,918. Of this number 6,159,297 were domestic letters; 645,213 were domestic parcels; 312,553 were letters to foreign countries; 11,759 were parcels of third and fourth class matter to foreign countries; and 1,210,096 were letters and parcels forwarded for the government, which by law are exempt from payment of registry fees.

The amount in fees collected during the year was $712,882.20, being an increase over the amount for the previous year of $117,107.90, or 19.19 per cent. The increase in the total number of letters and parcels registered was 1,342,405, or 19.66 per cent. The increase in the number of letters registered for the public was nearly 18 per cent.; of third and fourth class packages for the public, nearly 44 per cent.; and of letters and parcels for the government, a little over 16 per cent.

Statistics more in detail will be found in tables numbered 18 to 21, hereto annexed.

LOSSES.

During the year 3,722 letters and parcels were reported to the chief post-office inspector as having been lost, and 614 as having been tampered with. Of these 2,575 were recovered or satisfactorily accounted for, leaving 2,061 still unsettled. Further investigation will undoubtedly lead to recovery in a large proportion of these cases. The losses occurred by fire, burglary, highway robbery, and theft by employés. Too much credit cannot be given the post-office inspectors for the zeal ¹ efficiency with which they have pursued depredations upon the registered mails; and to their efforts in this direction is due much of the security for which the registry system is justly celebrated.

Credit is also due to the assistant superintendent of the railway mail service detailed to this office for suggesting valuable improvements, and for his fidelity in carrying out the work intrusted to his care.

THE THROUGH-POUCH SYSTEM.

The system of exchanging through pouches between the larger offices on the great arteries of communication was extended to 52 offices during the year, at the close of which it was in operation at 125 offices.

THROUGH-POUCH EXCHANGES WITH CANADA.

In June last, after some preliminary negotiations, formal arrangements were entered into with the Post-Office Department of Canada for direct exchanges of through registered pouches between Buffalo, N. Y., and the principal post-offices in the province of Ontario. The arrangement is now in successful operation, and negotiations are very nearly concluded for through exchanges with the eastern portion of the Dominion of Canada.

NEW REGISTERED LOCK.

A long-felt want has at last been supplied in securing a suitable lock for through pouches. This lock is under contract and will be put in use about the first of January next. It is fitted with a combination of numbers, the order of which is changed by turning the key. The pouch will be billed at the dispatching office under a given number corresponding with the lock, and receipted for under this number from point to point until it reaches the office of destination. Improper interference will be readily detected by a disagreement between the number on the lock and that on the bill, and the responsibility readily located. It frequently happens that through pouches are compelled to lie over in transit at intermediate through-pouch offices; and in case of such temporary detention it becomes necessary, with the use of the present ordinary lock, to require the postmaster to open the pouch, check off, certify, and record its contents. This imposes a vast deal of clerical labor which will be saved by the use of the new lock, avoiding as it does the necessity of opening pouches between terminal offices. In the mode of construction the new lock is much superior in all respects to the old one.

BRASS-LOCK REGISTRY EXCHANGE SYSTEM.

The "brass-lock registry exchange system," established two years since and explained in my report of last year, has proven completely successful, and is rapidly being put in operation on all the important lines of star service in the country. It corresponds to the through-pouch system on the railroads, to which it is an adjunct, and is governed by somewhat similar regulations. Not only does it greatly add to the security of registered matter, but it greatly facilitates its transmission and saves much labor in rehandling. Prior to the establishment of the system registered matter was rebilled and recorded at each intermediate post-office on the line in order to fasten responsibility in case of loss. It not unfrequently happened that the registered mail was so large that it could not be handled in time for the first outgoing mail, and was permitted to lie over to be sent on a subsequent day. On one important star route a post-office inspector reported constant detentions of regis-

tered matter, varying from ten to fifteen days, when the schedu
for the trip was only fifteen hours.

The delay in rehandling registered matter at intermediate offi
frequently pleaded by contractors in extenuation of failure to mak
ule time, and as a reason for the remittance of fines imposed f
failure.

In this connection I beg to renew the following recommendation
from my report of last year, viz :

It is believed that additional security would be given to registered matter-
routes if the contractors for carrying the mails on them were made accoun
losses directly traceable to the carelessness or other fault of their agents. Mo
losses of registered matter occur on star routes, and many of them are doubtla
by the delinquency of mail contractors. Of course, in every such case the da
and the public are without pecuniary redress. There is no good reason why
ral rule of law, that the principal is responsible for the acts of his agent, sh
apply to cases of this kind. If it did, there can be but little doubt that t
would soon cease. Nor would this be the only benefit secured, for as contracto
be compelled, for their own protection, to engage only reliable persons to perf
work, the general service of carrying the mails on star routes would probab
proved. It is respectfully suggested that in all contracts hereafter to be ent
for carrying the mails a clause be inserted providing for the accountability f
of registered matter in the manner here referred to.

THE MANIFOLD PROCESS FOR REGISTRY FORMS.

The use of the manifold process for registry forms, introduced
the previous year and explained in my last report, has been exte
an additional number of the larger offices, resulting in a saving
time and labor. It is in contemplation to adapt the process in t
its forms to all through-pouch offices.

REGISTERED-PACKAGE TAG ENVELOPES.

Much difficulty was experienced in preparing for transmission
ages too large for inclosure in the regular registered-package en
This envelope, besides giving the address, contains also the reg
number and the record of transit made by officers and employés
whose hands the package passes. Usually it was applied in the
of a wrapper to large parcels, but even this was not practicable
of irregularly shaped packages. Various expedients were cons
with the view to a remedy, resulting, finally, in the adoption of
known as the registered-package tag envelope, which is simply t
envelope made of tough manila paper, and of sufficient size to
the registry bill and return registry receipt. The envelope is o
the top, midway across which it is furnished with eyelets, through
it is fastened with twine to the package, serving as a tag. On
contains the address and registered number and the other direc
tions and space for the record of transit. It avoids the wrapp
packages and the clumsy adjustment of the regular registered
envelopes and their removal for preservation at receiving offices.
device has proved completely successful, reports having been re
from the principal post-offices commending it as a saving of
twine, clerical labor, and time.

REGISTRATION OF THIRD AND FOURTH CLASS MATTER.

On the 1st October, 1878, an important feature was added to th
ice by the extension of the registry system to third and fourth
matter, it having previously been confined to letters or matter c
able with first-class rates of postage. This step was taken afte
deliberation, and in the face of opposition from many whose p
and experience in the postal service entitled their opinions to

weight. It was apprehended that insuperable difficulties would be encountered in handling bulky matter in the registered mails, an apprehension that results show to have been unfounded.

The act of March 3, 1855, establishing the registry system, confined its provisions to "*valuable letters* posted for transmission in the mails," but the act of June 8, 1872, which still prevails, provides that "for the greater security of *valuable mail matter* the Postmaster-General may establish a uniform system of registration." It was clearly the intention of the law, in substituting the term "*valuable mail matter*" for "*valuable letters*," that the benefits of the system should be extended to all classes of matter entitled to admission in the mails. Aside from the evident contemplation of the law, strong practical reasons existed for taking the step. Registration adds nothing to the weight of mails, and nothing, consequently, to the cost of transportation. Its burdens are purely of a clerical character, resting upon postal officers and employés, in the giving and taking receipts and making of necessary records.

The fees received from the registry service are greatly in excess of the cost of conducting it, thus offering an inducement for adding to the volume of business. Since the law compels the admission into the mails of samples and small articles of merchandise at scarcely remunerative rates of postage, it would seem to be only the duty of the department to throw around this class of matter the security afforded by registration, the more especially since it can be done at a considerable profit. Moreover, not only does registration largely lessen the liability to losses, but it diminishes the ground for complaint when chances are taken in the ordinary mails to save the payment of the registry fee. But superior to all other considerations is the public convenience, which is greatly promoted by a safe and regular means of transmitting small articles of value to remote points not reached by ordinary means of public conveyance.

The measure has succeeded beyond the most sanguine expectations. All difficulties in the way of carrying it into practical effect have been surmounted. Complaints as to the loss of packages in the ordinary mails have greatly diminished. Evidences of the popular appreciation of the step are of the most undoubted character.

The registry fees collected from this source during the last fiscal year amounted to $65,697.20, an increase over the previous year of nearly 44 per cent., as against an increase of about 18 per cent. in the amount collected on registered letters. The statistics of the last year show that one out of every 33 parcels of merchandise mailed was registered, while the registration of letters was only one out of every 104 mailed. These proportions are remarkable, considering that the registration of letters has been in operation for over twenty-five years, and of third and fourth class matter only three years.

Not least among the benefits to the public from this measure was the reduction to which it led in the rates of the express companies.

RETROSPECTIVE.

During the past four years the advancement of the registry service has been the object of special solicitude to this office. The machinery of the system has been thoroughly revised, and it has been much simplified in all its details, greatly lessening the work and at the same time adding to the security. Every effort has been made to commend the system to the public confidence, and to make it what it should be—one of the most conspicuous and useful features of the postal service.

Among the principal changes to be noted are the extension of the system to third and fourth class matter; the development of the through-pouch system, and the establishment of its adjunct, the brass-lock system, on star routes; the sending of matter direct, and the abolition of distributing offices; the discontinuance of the return registered-letter bill, which in effect was a duplicate of the registered-letter bill; the combination of records at both dispatching and receiving offices; the employment of card forms, or official postal cards, for the registry bill and the registry-return receipt, leading to the adoption of the card form for various official purposes in this and other departments of the government; the use of the manifold process for official forms and records; the adoption of the tag envelope for packages of third and fourth class matter; and a complete and thorough revision of the standing regulations governing the registry system.

The generous confidence with which the efforts to improve the service have been met by the public is shown in an unprecedented increase of business during the last four years. The amount of registry fees collected during the fiscal year ending June 30, 1877, was $367,438.80, and during the year ending June 30, 1881, the amount derived from the same source was $712,882.20, an increase in the latter over the former year of $345,443.40, or a little more than 94 per cent.

The increase is the more extraordinary in view of the fact that the registry system has been in existence for more than twenty-five years.

In reporting the registry business of his office for the year ending June 3, 1879, the postmaster at New York, who now presides over the Post-Office Department, referred to the efficiency of the registry system in the following language:

The extension of the registry system on October 1, 1878, to include third and fourth class matter, has been the great event of the year.

From the beginning it was regarded by the public with great favor, and the amount of such matter registered has steadily increased and will continue. * * *

Of the 69,644 parcels of third and fourth class matter sent registered from this office, there have been but five complaints of loss, and these are on stage routes in the far western Territories, and may prove after investigation to be delays through carelessness. It speaks well for the efficiency of the registry system that such an immense amount of heavy matter can be suddenly thrown into it, and the only effect be that of showing the perfection of the system. There have been scarcely any complaints of losses of contents of any of the parcels sent, and most of those investigated show mistakes on the part of the sender. A larger amount of sample and merchandise parcels, formerly sent in ordinary mail, now go forward registered; consequently there is a great diminution in the ordinary mail complaints respecting such parcels. It could not well be otherwise, as the registered matter being inspected before it is registered, all imperfections as to address, insecure wrapping, &c., are corrected by the sender, the evidence of their being mailed is positive, and the parcels are carefully secured before dispatch. This cannot be obtained where they are dropped into the ordinary mails.

FILES, RECORDS, AND MAILS.

The number of letters and other inclosures received, opened, and examined in this office during the year was 1,130,470. Among these were 1,144 that contained money, and 4,230 that contained stamps, stamped envelopes, and postal cards returned by postmasters for redemption. Of the letters received 31,862 were briefed and recorded, and filed after final action had been taken on them. The number of letters written in the office, copied, enveloped, and mailed, was 11,381.

I have the honor to be, very respectfully, &c.,

A. D. HAZEN,
Third Assistant Postmaster-General.

Hon. THOMAS L. JAMES,
Postmaster-General.

POSTAL ORDERS FOR THE TRANSMISSION BY MAIL OF SUMS OF MONEY LESS THAN FIVE DOLLARS.

POST-OFFICE DEPARTMENT,
OFFICE OF SUPERINTENDENT OF MONEY-ORDER SYSTEM,
Washington, D. O., November 7, 1881.

SIR: Since the withdrawal of fractional paper currency from circulation, there has been a somewhat general demand upon the Post-Office Department to provide some means for making remittances of small sums through the mails, which shall be cheaper and simpler than the present money order and advice; and numerous plans, more or less crude and impracticable, or inexpedient, have been submitted to it, from time to time, the details of which have, nevertheless, received careful and thorough consideration.

It is not to be questioned that the transfer of small sums by mail, even at comparatively cheap rates, can be effected with less risk of loss to the public by the money order and advice now in use than by any postal-note or postal-order device that has yet been proposed; but it is believed that a simpler method, involving less expense to the department, and therefore less cost to the public, even though it afford a less degree of security than the money order, would, if put into operation in connection with the present money-order system, meet a public want, and that it would be largely employed, especially by publishers of newspapers and extensive dealers in articles of small value.

In the consideration of this question, which has engaged the attention of this office for some months, the effort has been to devise a means for making small remittances which should afford the greatest practical safety for the least possible expense. I early became convinced that the advice which, in the present money order, is the principal element of expense as well as of security, would have to be dispensed with; that the written application, the preparation of which devolves upon the remitter, must, in order to simplify the process of purchasing, be done away with; and that the amount of clerical labor required must be reduced to a minimum in order to further lessen the cost to the department.

The advice in the present money-order system is intended to prevent erroneous and fraudulent payment, by putting the postmaster drawn on in possession of all the particulars of the remittance before the order—which does not contain either the name of the remitter or that of the payee—is presented for payment. It furthermore serves as a safeguard against the alteration of the amount as well as the counterfeiting of the order. A device intended for remittances which is not to embrace an advice must, therefore, to afford reasonable security, provide in an absolutely effectual manner against alteration of the amount of the order, and in the process of manufacture should be made to contain efficient checks against counterfeiting.

The public could not with reason expect the same degree of security for remittances made by postal orders, without advice, and at slight expense to the remitter, as for those made by money orders, and it has been thought that a scheme which would as far as practicable insure against alteration of the amount and counterfeiting of the order, and would provide for payment to the bearer at a designated money-order office, would fill all the requirements of the popular demand.

With this preliminary explanation I have the honor to submit a design for a postal order to be issued concurrently with money orders, the several distinctive features of which I beg leave to describe hereunder:

NEW YORK, N.Y.
No. 26398.

Stamp of issuing office.

Amount, $ _____

FEE 3 CENTS.

Date of Issue, _____

Office drawn upon.

Stamp of paying office.

Postal Order
for sums less than five dollars.

To the Postmaster of the Money-Order Office at _____

Pay to Bearer, at any time within Three Months from the last day of the month of issue,

the sum of _____

Dolls.	Cents.

_____ Postmaster.

Received the above. _____

[Signature of the person who obtains payment.]

A duplicate cannot be issued of this postal order if lost in the mails or otherwise.

After the expiration of three months from the last day of the month of issue, this order will be payable only on payment by the holder of a fee of 3 cents, and if more than three months have elapsed since the said expiration, the holder will be required to pay an additional fee of 3 cents for every further period of three months which has so elapsed, and for every portion of any such period of three months over and above every complete period.

After once paying this order, by whomsoever presented, the Post-Office Department will not consider any further claim.

NEW YORK, N.Y.
No. 26398.

Dolls.	Dimes.	Cents.
1	1	1
2	2	2
3	3	3
4	4	4
	5	5
	6	6
	7	7
0	8	8
	9	9
	0	0
Hunds.	Tens.	Units.

1. No written application is to be required from the remitter.

2. The postal order is to be issued for sums less than five dollars.

3. It is to be made payable at a particular money-order office.

4. It is to be issued without advice.

5. The orders are to be numbered consecutively for each office of issue.

6. The stub in the book of forms is the only record of issue to be kept in the post-office.

7. The orders are to be payable to bearer.

8. A duplicate cannot be issued of a postal order lost in the mails or otherwise.

9. The orders are to be payable at any time within three months from the month of issue. If presented after the expiration of three months from the last day of the month of issue, they are to be cashed only upon payment of an additional fee, equal to the original fee, for every three months, or fraction of three months in excess of such period.

10. The orders are to be printed in sheets, upon thin bank-note paper, from engraved plates, and are to be separated from each other and from the stubs by perforated lines. The sheets are to be bound in book form.

The comparatively small sums for which postal orders of this description would be issued would offer but slight temptation to theft.

The issue of orders without advice and without the written application, and the dispensing with registers of orders issued and of orders paid, will much lessen the cost of the service to the department, and correspondingly reduce the fees to be charged the public.

The provision that postal orders shall be payable to bearer will tend to further economy by lessening the costliness of the process of paying, inasmuch as it will relieve the paying postmaster of all responsibility as to requiring the identification of the applicant for payment. It is believed that this feature will be especially acceptable to extensive business houses in the larger cities, upon which, it is anticipated, the greater proportion of postal orders for small amounts will be drawn, because it will obviate the inconvenience of either personal application at the post-office for payment of small sums or of the formal appointment of an agent or attorney to collect such sums in the name of the firm.

The postmaster who is called upon to issue a postal order is first to write upon the stub the amount in figures, the date of issue, and the name of the office drawn upon. He is then to write the name of the office drawn upon and the amount in figures in the order, sign the latter, stamp it with his money-order stamp, and punch, with a conductor's punch or ordinary hand-punch, from the figures on the right those which represent the amount of the order; as, for example, if the order be for $3.47, the 3 from the dollars or hundreds column, the 4 from the dimes or tens column, and the 7 from the cents or units column. The order is then complete and ready to be handed to the applicant upon payment of the amount and fee.

I beg leave to invite attention to the fact that the punching from the order of the figures which go to make up the amount entirely precludes the possibility of the alteration of the amount.

The postmaster to whom a postal order is presented for payment is to require the receipt of the holder. He must see that the amount written in the body of the order and the amount represented by the figures which have been punched out agree.

The accounts of issued and paid postal orders may be embraced in the postmaster's weekly statement of money-order transactions, the summary of the week's business being made to include the postal-order as well as the money-order business.

Careful estimates, so far as they could be made, regarding the several elements of cost, lead me to believe that, if postal orders of this description be issued concurrently with money-orders, and the maximum amount of the latter be increased to $100, the fee to be charged the public for a postal order need not exceed 3 cents. It is proposed that a commission of 1 cent shall be allowed to the postmaster for every order issued, and of three quarters of a cent for every order paid, and the cost of engraving and printing has been estimated at three-quarters of a cent for each order; so that a margin of one-half of a cent on each order is left to cover the cost of distribution and of the clerical labor of supervision in the department and in the auditor's office, and to provide for miscellaneous items of expense.

I venture to express the opinion that while it would be unwise for the government, having due regard to the safety of the post-office establishment as well as of the public, to amend the conditions under which money orders are issued beyond the readjustment of the scale of commissions, as recommended by this office last year and again urged hereinafter, it would be both desirable and practicable to issue, in connection with money orders, "postal orders," under the conditions above set forth, which would afford additional facilities for the rapid transmission of very small sums at a reduced cost to the public both of time and money.

I am not prepared to deny that the introduction of the proposed postal orders will be attended by some additional risk to those who may avail themselves of the facilities which they will afford. The scheme, however, is one devised to meet a popular demand, and the risk would be incurred, not by the department, but by those who would take advantage of the postal order as a simpler method of remittance, this order supplying for that purpose the place of the old fractional currency. It would always be open to the public, provided the two systems were in concurrent operation, to obtain the greater and almost absolute security of the money order by the payment of the slightly-increased fee which its use would involve.

It has been urged, as I had the honor to state in my letter of October 27, 1880, to the Postmaster-General, published upon pages 399–409 of his annual report for that year, that the present fee of 10 cents on money orders of small amounts, particularly on those not exceeding $5, is too high and ought to be reduced in the interest of public convenience.

During the five years ended June 30, 1880, the gross revenue derived from the transactions of the money-order system averaged a fraction over 12.7 cents upon each order issued, and the expenses a little over 12.6 cents, leaving a margin of one mill as a net profit upon each order. As shown in my letter of last year, nearly one-half of the orders issued in the United States are for sums less than $5; so that any diminution of the fees charged for such orders must necessarily result, other conditions remaining as at present, in a loss to the system. This office then suggested, and it is still of the opinion, that this charge might be lessened without causing direct loss to the department by extending the maximum amount for which an order can be issued from $50 to $100, with an increase of the fee for each additional amount of $10 in excess of $50, and by slightly decreasing the commissions allowed to postmasters for the issue and payment of orders. The gain from the increased fees for orders of the larger amounts would, it is believed, counterbalance in great measure, if it would not entirely offset, the loss incurred by the diminution of the fees for small orders.

Under existing law (Revised Statutes, section 4047), all postmasters at money-order offices are allowed—

As compensation for issuing and paying money orders, not exceeding one-third of the whole amount of the fees collected on orders issued, and one-fourth of one per centum on the gross amount of orders paid at their respective offices, provided such compensation, together with the postmaster's salary, shall not exceed four thousand dollars per annum, except in the case of the postmaster at New York City.

But the Postmaster-General is authorized (section 970, Postal Laws and Regulations of 1879) to allow to "postmasters whose total compensation from all sources amounts to $4,000 per annum," "a fixed sum for the necessary clerical force actually employed in" their money-order business.

This office has uniformly held to the opinion that the commissions accruing to postmasters "as compensation for issuing and paying money orders" are not to be considered in the nature of a perquisite or a gratuity but that they ought to be disbursed to the clerk or clerks whose time, either wholly or in part, is occupied in the transaction of the money-order business. But some postmasters whose salary is less than $4,000 per annum have claimed that they, individually, are entitled by law to receive an amount from money-order commissions sufficient to make the aggregate compensation $4,000 per annum, without rendering any clerical service therefor. The commissions accruing by law primarily to the postmaster, it has been difficult to control the final disposal thereof, in accordance with what seems to be the intent of the law.

Under date of December 18, 1880, in compliance with the Postmaster-General's order, No. 52, of September 7, 1880, I transmitted to him, with an explanatory letter, the draft of a bill entitled "A bill to modify the postal money-order system," the provisions of the first section of which were intended to change the scale of commissions charged for domestic money orders, and to increase the maximum limit of an order to $100, in accordance with the suggestion hereinbefore made. The provisions of the second section were devised with a view to settle the vexed question of the ownership of money-order commissions, by not allowing to postmasters at first-class offices any compensation for their money-order business, and by permitting them to employ under the authority of the Postmaster-General, the clerical force requisite for the transaction of that business. It furthermore—

1. Fixed the compensation for the clerical labor employed in the money-order business, at all other money-order post-offices, at three cents for each transaction, to wit, three cents for each domestic or international money order issued, paid, or repaid, and three cents for each certificate of deposit issued in acknowledgment of the receipt of surplus money-order funds.

2. It required the postmaster who claimed credit on account of any expenditure in payment for clerical service in the money-order business of his office to furnish a voucher duly receipted by the person by whom the labor was performed and to whom the money was paid.

3. It provided that the compensation for money-order service at post-offices where no allowance is made to the postmaster out of postal funds for an assistant or clerk may be paid to the postmaster; and

4. "That the salaries of postmasters, as fixed by law, shall be deemed and taken to be full compensation, except as above provided, for the responsibility and risk incurred, and for the personal services rendered by them as custodians of the money-order and other funds of the Post-Office Department."

The change in the method of compensating postmasters from the

66 Ab

present rate, one-third of the fees received for orders issued, and one-fourth of one per centum on the gross amount of orders paid, to that proposed, of 3 cents for each transaction, is deemed particularly desirable in the interest of justice, as well as for the sake of simplicity, because the labor of issuing or paying an order of small amount is as great as that involved in issuing and paying one of large amount.

The draft of the bill in question was incorporated in a communication from the Postmaster-General, dated January 5, 1881, in response to Senate resolution of June 15, 1880, in regard to changes of laws affecting the Post-Office Department, and with suggestions on various topics from other officers of the department, was printed in pamphlet form, under the title of Ex. Doc. No. 16, Forty-sixth Congress, third session.

This bill (H. R. 6775) was introduced in the House on January 10, 1881, by Mr. Money, of the Committee on the Post-Office and Post-Roads, with the unanimous approval of the committee, as I am informed; but owing to the briefness of the session and the pressure of other legislative business, it failed to become a law. I beg leave to suggest, for your consideration, the propriety and expediency of recommending legislation to substantially the same effect this year.

In the same pamphlet to which reference is made above (Ex. Doc. No. 16) is published the draft of a bill entitled "A bill to provide for the disposal of the amounts of money orders remaining five years unpaid," which was submitted by this office to the Postmaster-General on December 31, 1880, and by him to the Senate, in response to the Senate resolution of June 15, 1880, but which likewise failed to receive consideration, owing to the shortness of the last session of Congress and the press of other business before that body.

At the close of the fiscal year ended June 30, 1881, the amount of money-order funds in the sub-treasury at New York, N. Y., to the credit of the Postmaster-General, was..................................... $2,321,740 83

Of which sum there was due to the postage account on account of transfers from the postage to the money-order account... $464,505 07

And the amount of the annual gross revenue from the money-order business for that year, which must by law be deposited in the Treasury for the service of the Post-Office Department.. 295,581 39
                                                                          —————
                                                                          760,086 46

Leaving the whole amount of available funds in the sub-treasury. 1,561,654 37

According to an estimate made by the Auditor of the Treasury for this department, which will be found in the appendix, the amount of unclaimed money orders, domestic and foreign, at the close of the fiscal year ended June 30, 1881, was $1,250,000. There was also due at that time from the United States to certain foreign countries, on account of the exchange of money orders with them, the amount of about $330,000, and the money-order system was liable, at the same time, for the payment to the service of the Post-Office Department of the total revenue from the international money-order business for the last year, estimated at $50,000. It is apparent that if the department should be called upon to pay over the amount of every unclaimed money order, the accumulated fund in the subtreasury, after deducting therefrom the amount of the indebtedness to foreign countries and the amount of the international revenue for the last fiscal year, would be insufficient for the purpose, and that a portion, to wit, $68,345.63, would have to be made up out of the amount of $1,427,108.59, which at the close of the year, as reported by the Auditor, was in the hands of postmasters in the form of reserves to enable them to meet the payment of orders, and in remittances in transit, this last-mentioned sum, $1,427,108.59, representing at date of June 30, 1881, the larger portion of the working capital of the money-order system.

It is important, therefore, in the consideration of the question as to what amount might be turned over to the Treasury for the service of the Post-Office Department, without detriment to the money-order system, that provision should be made for the retention, not only of a sum equal to the amount required from year to year for working capital, but of a sufficient amount in addition to meet any unforeseen or unusual demand upon the money-order funds, such as might be occasioned by delay in remittances of surplus money-order funds from distant points.

After mature consideration I am of opinion that it would be expedient to retain in the hands of the assistant treasurer at New York City, to the credit of the Postmaster-General, for the exigencies of the money-order service as well as for its current operations, a sum equal, at least, to the amount of all unpaid money orders during a period of five years next preceding the commencement of each fiscal year. Especially would I favor this course in view of the fact that this department is constantly indebted to foreign postal administrations in large sums which must be promptly paid. The current of the international money-order business with each of the foreign postal administrations with which an exchange of money orders is maintained is continually in favor of those countries, the amount of the orders issued in the United States exceeding by very large sums the amount of orders issued abroad for payment in the United States. As a consequence, the excess of the issues in the United States over those abroad for payment here must be remitted at short intervals to the creditor departments to reimburse them for the payment of orders of United States origin. And while it is true that the money is received in this country for the issue of the orders, it might be necessary to make heavy remittances before funds received at distant offices could reach the general depository, the New York post-office, or the sub-treasury, and be available for the purchase of bills of exchange.

It rarely happens that a money order more than five years old is presented for payment; but if deemed expedient in the interests of payees of money orders, a longer period, for example, seven or ten years, might be fixed by Congress, during which the amount of any money order would be payable to the owner thereof, and beyond which the amount of all orders unpaid would accrue to the United States.

I am, respectfully, your obedient servant,

C. F. MACDONALD,
Superintendent Money-Order System.

Hon. T. L. JAMES,
Postmaster-General.

OFFICE OF THE AUDITOR OF THE TREASURY
FOR THE POST-OFFICE DEPARTMENT,
Washington, November 5, 1881.

SIR: In reply to your letter of this date, I have the honor to state the approximate amount of unclaimed domestic and foreign money orders at the close of the fiscal year ended June 30, 1881, as $1,250,000.

Very respectfully,

J. H. ELA,
Auditor.

Hon. C. F. MACDONALD,
Superintendent Money-Order System, Washington, D. C.

REPORT OF THE TOPOGRAPHER OF THE POST-OFFICE DEPARTMENT.

POST-OFFICE DEPARTMENT, TOPOGRAPHER'S OFFICE,
Washington, D. C., October 22, 1881.

SIR: I have the honor to submit this report of the work of the Topographer's Office during the past year (ending September 30, 1881), having previously, in compliance with order, presented estimate of appropriation required for the fiscal year ending June 30, 1883, for the general expenses of this office.

Hitherto this estimate has been made annually for a specific total amount, to include the salaries of all the employés of this office, along with the miscellaneous expenses in "the preparation and publication of post-route maps, &c.;" that is, for the work of engraving, lithographing, photo-lithographing, printing and other work, and for the purchase of materials required in the production of the maps. But on this occasion, in compliance with your instructions, a new departure is made, the salaries, specifically indicated, being kept separate for insertion in the general (legislative, executive, and judicial) appropriation bill, and the other miscellaneous expenses to form an item in the proper place in the contingent expenses of the Post-Office Department in the same bill. This arrangement will make more clear the use of the appropriation asked for from Congress.

During this past year the regular duty of "keeping up" the exhibit of the mail service on the numerous maps and diagrams used by the officers and clerks in the several bureaus, and the furnishing the geographical data for the different branches of the department, has been accomplished to the full capacity of the force employed.

For the continuous (daily) use of the officers and corresponding clerks of the contract office, 118 large maps or diagrams have been "kept up," showing the changes in the service at least once a month. There are also kept up, under the same conditions, two sets of 46 maps for use in the appointment office, one set (23 maps) for the office of the general superintendent of railway mail service, and one set (23 maps) for reference in this (topographer's) office. In addition to this constant assistance to these offices, there have been brought up at longer intervals than a month, 184 maps for use in the under-named offices: Finance, money-order, post-office inspectors, dead-letter, assistant attorney-general for Post-Office Department, and for the office of the Sixth Auditor of the Treasury Department (located in post-office building).

In procuring data for the original construction and additions to the post-route maps, 254 letters of inquiry have been addressed to engineers and other officers of railroads, in most cases with inclosure of a special tracing made in this office to facilitate their returning the exact lines for transference to our maps. With the same view, 3,298 circular queries have been sent to postmasters to get the locations of their post-offices, where inadequately furnished by the data presented to and reported from the appointment office, or to get more precise definition of sites and adjacent topography.

The miscellaneous correspondence—exclusive of the above circulars—consisted of 2,979 letters written by the topographer on matters appropriate to his work. The number of letters received—exclusive of these returned circular queries—was 3,154.

Seven thousand nine hundred and seventy-nine sheets of post-route maps, colored to exhibit the post-offices and the frequency of service on the several post-routes, have been distributed during the year. Of these, a large proportion has been, as in former years, sent to the larger post-offices in the several States and Territories, either for the first time, or to replace (by new editions) those hitherto supplied, but rendered obsolete by the great additions to and changes in the service. But the largest distribution has been to the officers, clerks, and other agents of the railway mail service, the maps (with the latest information carefully transcribed) being furnished on requisitions from the general superintendent and division superintendents for their office use, and for distribution to employés in that special service. Thirty-nine per cent. of all the maps thus prepared and distributed in various quarters have been backed, mounted on rollers, or bound for portable use. A detailed statement of this distribution of maps during the past year is appended (marked A), with a side comparison with the numbers for the two preceding years. Apart from the distribution to the railway mail service, there has not been the increase in the past year expected in the total number of maps issued, owing to the more numerous calls for maps to be brought up to the very latest date, and the consequent great number of additions and changes required to be made *by hand* on the sheets, and, in a measure, to the restricted appropriation allowed. It is hoped, however, that during the current year, and with arrangements contemplated, these numbers will increase.

The post-route maps are much sought after by the other governmental departments; their large scale, clearness of matter, without superfluity of detail, rendering them acceptable for reference and for special exhibition and demarkation of district divisions, &c. Maps have been sent during the past year, in compliance with request, to the following:

Treasury Department, Office of the Secretary;
Treasury Department, Director of the Mint;
Treasury Department, Bureau of Statistics;
Treasury Department, United States Coast and Geodetic Survey Office;
War Department, Chief Engineer, United States Army;
War Department, Paymaster-General;
War Department, Signal Office;
Department of the Interior, General Land Office;
Department of the Interior, Pension Office;
Department of the Interior, Auditor of Railroad Accounts;
Department of the Interior, Census Bureau;
Department of the Interior, United States Geological Survey;
Department of Agriculture;
Library of Congress.

A set of the post-route maps, suitably bound in atlas form, accompanied by a few (selected) specimen books of report and record, has been sent, by your order, as a contribution to the United States exhibit at the (third) International Congress of Geography, meeting this year, in September last, at Venice, Italy.

The calls for certificates of distances, required in the settlement of mileage accounts by officers of the public service and in the adjustment of telegraphic rates for government messages, have been promptly answered. In this duty 198 letters have been answered, covering 359 queries.

A new and thoroughly revised edition of the "Distance Tables," required in these compilations, has, for a long time, been much wanted. The present (first) edition, printed in 8vo, 151 pp., was compiled under my care, by order of the Postmaster-General, "for the regulation and adjustment of telegraphic rates for government messages," and was issued August 16, 1873. I have had the honor to call attention, in several reports to your predecessors, to this want and to the insufficiency of the personal force of this office to provide for it. From careful and independent estimates by myself and my principal assistant, it would appear that to revise or compile anew and extend these tables will require the steady work of two careful clerks for at least six months. In default of such revised tables, the various calls, by letters and telegrams, have been promptly answered as presented.

During the past year, the preparation and publication—with successive editions to keep pace with the constant progress of the postal service—of the series of post-route maps have been continued under my supervision. New editions have been issued of all the maps hitherto prepared (23 in number, covered by 61 sheets). Successive editions, at short intervals, have been (and always will be) required to show the numerous additions and changes of post-offices, and the course and frequency of service on the several post-routes.

New maps, to take the place of provisional copies, are in course of preparation and are well advanced, of the Pacific States and the Territories, and of the State of Florida (showing the Gulf and West India Islands mail connections): a new set, in engraved form, of the maps of Virginia, West Virginia, North Carolina and South Carolina, is almost completed; also a map showing the river and side connecting service of the Mississippi River between Saint Louis and New Orleans.

Much of the time of the employés of this office is absorbed in making the constant additions and alterations to the maps *by hand*, it having hitherto been found impracticable to bring out more than three or four new *printed* editions of each map annually, under present arrangements.

Careful consideration has recently been given to the advisability of having within the department's walls an establishment for printing (from lithographic stones) these successive editions, with a view to economy and more rapid production of prints of maps by doing away with so much hand-work (additions) to the printed sheets. On this subject I shall have the honor to report, when the data have been presented to and viewed by your committee examining the workings in this respect.

The *personnel* of this office now consists of—

The topographer.
7 draughtsmen (1 acting as principal assistant).
2 corresponding clerks (1 acting as general aid).
21 map-colorists and copyists (ladies).
2 map-mounters.
1 messenger.
2 watchmen (day and night, for building occupied for office).

The salaries of all these, with the exception of the topographer (who is the only officer of this bureau recognized by law), have hitherto been paid out of the specific annual appropriation "for the preparation and publication of post-route maps," &c.; but, as mentioned in the previous part of this report, it is proposed to transfer the items and estimate for these salaries to the general (legislative, executive, and judicial) appropriation bill.

In making that estimate, while the total amount allowed by Congress for this bureau for the current fiscal year has not been exceeded, an increase of one in the number of draughtsmen is estimated for; this is, indeed, requisite at the present time to keep up our current work.

I take pleasure in testifying to the general faithful and steady work of the employés of this office, particularly mentioning the efficient help

I have from the principal assistant, Mr. Charles E. Gorham, and from the two corresponding clerks, Mr. W. B. Todd (acting also as general aid) and Miss R. Howard.

I sincerely hope that the estimate submitted for the appropriation for the work of this office for next fiscal year may be sustained by the committee of Congress, being the same in amount as that allowed for the present year.

Very respectfully, your obedient servant,

W. L. NICHOLSON,
Topographer Post-Office Department.

Hon. THOMAS L. JAMES,
Postmaster-General.

Detailed statement of distribution of post-route maps during the year ending September 30, 1881.

	During year ending September 30, 1881.	During year ending September 30, 1880.	During year ending September 30, 1879.
Maps furnished (number of sheets):			
To officers and clerks of the Post-Office Department at Washington......	909	908	544
To postmasters	999	914	823
To railway mail service (besides special tracings and diagrams)	2,042	1,542	1,152
To post-office inspectors	165	166	130
To officers of other governmental departments of the United States	687	1,239	897
To Senators and Members of House of Representatives	903	687	903
To committees of Congress..	100	160	262
To miscellaneous: including educational and scientific institutions, libraries, and geographical publishers	523	2,216	1,300
To State authorities and State libraries...................................	223	195	188
To foreign governments	209	32	21
Number of sheets sold during year..	1,239	873	708
Total..	7,979	8,915	6,982

OPERATIONS OF THE BLANK AGENCY.

POST-OFFICE DEPARTMENT,
OFFICE OF THE CHIEF CLERK, BLANK AGENCY,
Washington, D. C., October 15, 1881.

SIR: I have the honor to report that the work of this agency for the past year has increased over that of any former one, as will be seen by the tabular statements herewith returned.

The principal part of departmental supplies, particularly blanks, paper, twine, marking and canceling stamps, letter balances and scales, to enable postmasters to make up uniformly and forward mails, to rate and cause to be prepaid accurately all registered letters and packages, to record and report the same, as well as to account in detail all official business to the Postmaster-General and his assistants and the Sixth Auditor of the Treasury, are sent out from this agency and accounted for on the records of this office.

Of these supplies there were forwarded the past year various articles, as follows:

Blanks for statements and accounts of postmasters	36,301,000
Facing slips for making up packages for the mail	41,942,400
Books for record of post-office business	84,820
Jute twine ....pounds..	393,901
Hemp twine ....do....	105,022
Of paper 20 by 25 inches ....reams..	11,021
Of paper 26 by 40 inches ....do....	624
Marking and rating stamps of all kinds	6,092
Type for use of same ....pieces..	17,985
Letter balances and scales	2,429

The total expenditure for these articles is stated at $241,500.00.

The number of post-offices at the commencement of the last fiscal year was 42,955, to which were added during the year 1,557 new offices, making a total of 44,512 in operation on the 30th of June last.

Of this number there were entitled to be supplied with letter balances or scales such only as the gross receipts of which amounted to $75 and upwards per annum, and entitled to be supplied with marking and canceling stamps such as yielded gross receipts of $50 and upwards per annum, leaving at least 10,000 minor offices not to supplied with balances or scales, and a larger number not supplied with balances or scales or marking stamps of any kind whatever.

This has been the policy heretofore adopted from the small importance of the class of offices yielding less receipts than $50 per annum, and from the small consideration given the fact that the non-conformity of these minor offices with the general mailing system, from their want of material supplied to other offices by the department, tends directly to the imperfection and injury of the whole system.

It may not be improper to consider the question whether the policy ought not now to be changed, or may not be modified to the interest of the department and to the public advantage.

The class of unsupplied postmasters are at present obliged to adopt any convenient plan of postmarking letters and of canceling postage-stamps, either autographical or mechanical, which untoward circumstances may suggest or permit. Also, for the want of letter scales they are put to the device of determining the weight of letters and packets of all classes, and of registered matter, and the rate of postage prescribed, without the aid of any official method or the employment of exact means to the proper ends. They are most apt to forego the personal expense of scales for their assistance, and are generally too unpracticed and inexpert to guess correctly the weight and rate of each package and the postage due in many cases.

Errors are constantly committed and revenue is uncollected under this system. It is not deemed possible, with due diligence by postmasters, that it could be otherwise. Matter mailed at the minor offices is postmarked unintelligibly, is canceled imperfectly, and underrated constantly for the want of the department stamps and scales, so that many thousands of postage-stamps, considerable in value, are sought for and made account of by unscrupulous persons in cleaning the face and using them again.

This, then, is a certain loss of revenue to the department, and has been estimated to amount to hundreds of thousands of dollars per annum. The exact amount it would be difficult to estimate, but certainly it is so considerable as to superinduce the expenditure of means to correct the loss and restore the revenue.

The more extended supply of canceling stamps to be used with an indelible ink, specific to that purpose, would go far towards preventing further loss, and would tend to destroy the trade and practice of washing postage-stamps.

For the complete and perfect use of marking and canceling stamps the flexible pad, for stamping, should also be supplied to every office. It has the advantage of convenience of method, celerity of action, and preserves the instrument from injury to an extent that may be reckoned a reimbursement of its cost.

It would also seem important to secure an indelible ink for canceling postage-stamps that would render the obliteration effectual. Such an article, it is believed, can be obtained at a reasonable cost and supplied to postmasters to the public advantage.

People within the delivery of many minor offices are frequently not well-enough informed to nearly approximate the rate of postage due upon different letters and packets, and the exigency is necessarily referred to the postmaster, who finds himself equally deficient in the means of supplying it.

If it be suggested that postmasters should supply themselves with scales, stamps, ink, and pads at the small yearly cost involved, and thus volunteer to remedy and assist in remedying the evils and deficiency complained of, it may be answered that the cost would be still less to the government than the officer, and more to the general than the individual advantage, and would be of more importance to the public than to the officer whose credit would be exalted at private expense while discharging an unprofitable public duty.

It would seem in almost every view that it is the department's interest to extend its supplies to these minor offices.

The department requires *all* mail matter, excepting periodical publications, mailed at *any* post-office, to bear a postmark, with the name of the office and an abbreviation of the name of the State; and on written matter the date of deposit; and letters from other offices for delivery or redistribution to other offices, to be postmarked on the reverse side, with the date, and, when possible, the hour received. It is required that the postage-stamps or stamped envelopes of *all* mail matter at *any* post-office be canceled by the use of black printing ink, whenever that material can be obtained, and, if otherwise, by several heavy crosses or parallel lines upon each stamp with a pen dipped in good, black writing ink. The use of the postmarking stamp, as a canceling instrument, is positively prohibited by reasons stated. (See sections 377, 379, pages 103, 104, Laws and Regulations, 1879.)

The provisions for executing these requirements in all post-offices, excepting the minor ones now here considered, are nearly perfect, without the loss of revenue, and in the most expeditious and economical manner. But the ten thousand village, hamlet, and wayside postmasters are still left to follow their own unskillful and unassisted methods of postmarking, stamping, and weighing the mail, by which the revenue is reduced, and errors and inconveniences tolerated which are likely to become aggravated complaints against the postal service.

To correct these errors is deemed of importance sufficient to employ considerable time, labor, and expense. For this purpose circulars are addressed to postmasters reminding them that all stamps must be effectually canceled, and all letters and parcels plainly marked and postmarked previous to mailing. In cases of underrating the weight and postage of registered matter, the postmaster is required to remit the deficiency of postage and registration fee immediately to the (department) general office in uncanceled *postage-due stamps*, to be destroyed in an effort intended to recover a part of the revenue liable to be lost.

The amount thus collected from small offices unsupplied with scales to determine the weight of registered packages is estimated at $200 per month, which, besides the cost of collecting, may be considered an unpleasing penalty to enforce against postmasters who execute their office according to the ways and means supplied them, and greatly more to the accommodation of the public than to their own private advantage.

It may not be insignificant to state the fact that not less than 5,000 requests by letter from these offices are yearly referred to this agency, stating that having been required to pay additional postage on underrated matter, and having no means of weighing mail matter, the postmaster would be obliged to the department for a pair of small scales—thus showing the importunity as well as the necessity for extending these supplies to the smaller offices.

The increased expense, it is believed, will not be considerable in view of the profit to be derived. It will tend to complete a uniformity in the despatch, carriage, and delivery of matter not now wholly perfect. It will save all the revenue of the department. It will prevent errors and delay in correspondence. It will extend conveniences of public importance, and do that justice to a class of offices heretofore withheld. An estimate of $50,000, it is believed, will be sufficient for the next year to extend the system properly.

In view of these facts and representations, it is suggested that all post-offices apparently permanent in location, or all those yielding yearly receipts of $10, be supplied with a complete outfit of scales for weighing, stamps for marking and canceling, indelible ink for obliterating postage, and pads for necessary use, to be accounted for like other public property of the government, and to be turned over to the successor in office.

Respectfully,
                       D. W. RHODES,
                       Superintendent Blank Agency.

JOHN R. VAN WORMER, Esq.,
     Chief Clerk, Post-Office Department.

REPORT OF THE AUDITOR OF THE TREASURY FOR THE POST-OFFICE DEPARTMENT.

OFFICE OF THE AUDITOR OF THE TREASURY
     FOR THE POST-OFFICE DEPARTMENT,
         Washington, November 16, 1881.

SIR: I have the honor to submit herewith the annual report of the receipts and expenditures of the Post-Office Department, as shown by the accounts of this office, for the fiscal year ended June 30, 1881.

REVENUE ACCOUNT OF THE POST-OFFICE DEPARTMENT.

Fiscal year 1881:

The revenue of the department for the fiscal year ended June 30, 1881, was		$36,785,397 97
The amount placed with the Treasurer for the service of the department for the fiscal year, being grants in aid of the revenue, under the second section of the act approved June 11, 1880 (Statutes, chapter 206, page 179, pamphlet edition), was		3,000,000 00
Aggregate of revenue and grants		39,785,397 97
The expenditures for the service of the fiscal year were		39,251,736 46
Excess of receipts		533,661 51
Amount of balances due by postmasters charged to "bad debts" and "compromise" accounts	$16,215 70	
Amount of balances due postmasters credited to "suspense" account	1,424 84	14,790 86
Balance available for service of 1881		518,870 65

Fiscal year 1880:
The balance available for the service of 1880 at the close of the last
annual report was.. $719,029 82
Amount paid during last fiscal year.. 270,575 89

Balance available for the service of 1880........................ 448,453 93

Fiscal year 1879:
The amount placed with the Treasurer, since last annual report, for
the service of 1879, being grants in aid of the revenue, under the second section of the act approved June 17, 1878 (Statutes, vol. 20,
page 143), was 279,556 03
The excess of expenditures, as per last annual report, was. $228,344 44
Amount paid during last fiscal year...................... 50,816 64
                                                                    279,161 08

Balance unexpended for service of 1879........................ 394 95

Fiscal year 1878:
Amount credited to postmasters for disbursements on account of 1878. 466 06

Fiscal year 1878 and prior years (scheduled claims):
The amount placed with the Treasurer under the act approved March
3, 1861 (Statutes, chap. 132, page 433, pamphlet edition), was...... 18,315 43
Amount paid during last fiscal year 18,211 58

Balance available for 1878 and prior years................ .... 103 85

Fiscal year 1877 and prior years (scheduled claims):
The balance available at the close of last annual report was........... 10,891 30
Amount paid during last fiscal year.. 709 59

Balance available for 1877 and prior years..................... 10,181 71

Fiscal year 1867:
The amount placed with the Treasurer under the act approved March
3, 1861, to enable the Postmaster-General to refund the contents of a
dead letter erroneously covered into the Treasury (Statutes, chap.
132, page 423, pamphlet edition), was.................................... 50 00
Amount paid to A. J. Brooks under the act........................... 50 00

SUMMARY OF REVENUES AND EXPENDITURES.

Revenue of 1881.. $36,785,397 97
Grants from Treasury, 1881 .... $3,000,000 00
Grants from Treasury, 1879 .... 279,556 03
Grants from Treasury, 1878 and prior years............. 18,315 43
Grants from Treasury, 1867............................. 50 00
                                                         3,297,921 46

Total receipts... 40,083,319 43

Expenditures for 1881 .... 39,251,736 46
Expenditures for 1880 .... 270,575 89
Expenditures for 1879 .... 50,816 64
Expenditures for 1878 .... 466 06
Expenditures for 1878 and prior years................. 18,211 58
Expenditures for 1877 and prior years................. 709 59
Expenditures for 1867................................. 50 00

Total expenditures 39,592,566 22

                                                                    490,753 21
Net amount charged to "bad debts" and "compromise" accounts dur-
ing the fiscal year.. 14,790 86

Excess of receipts 475,962 35

The balance standing to the credit of the general
enue account at the close of the fiscal year ended .
30, 1880, was.................................
Excess of receipts during last fiscal year...........

Balance to the credit of the revenue account at th'
year ended June 30, 1881 ....
Due by late postmasters { accounts in suit...........
                         { accounts not in suit......

DEFICIENCY ACCO

The amount appropriated from the general Treasur;
cies in the revenues of the Post-Office Departmen
ended June 30, 1881, was.........................
The actual deficiency at the close of the fiscal year

Balance available for 1881 ....~....
Amount held by the Treasurer subject to warrant..
Amount in general Treasury subject to requisition.

POSTMASTERS' QUARTERLY AC

The net revenues of the department fro
gate revenues at post-offices for the fiscal
of postmasters and clerks and the conting

For the quarter ended September 30, 1880.........
For the quarter ended December 31, 1880..........
For the quarter ended March 31, 1881..............
For the quarter ended June 30, 1881 ....

Total ....^...........

The number of quarterly returns of post;
on which the above sum was found due th

For the quarter ended September 30, 1880 ....
For the quarter ended December 31, 1880..........
For the quarter ended March 31, 1881 ....
For the quarter ended June 30, 1881...............

Total ....^.....

STAMPS SOLD

The amount of stamps, stamped envelo;
and periodical stamps, and postal cards so

For the quarter ended September 30, 1880.........
For the quarter ended December 31, 1880..........
For the quarter ended March 31, 1881.............
For the quarter ended June 30, 1881 ....

Total ....

The amount of official stamps furnishe
included in the above amount of stamps a

For the State Department ....
For the War Department ....
For the Interior Department......................
For the Department of Agriculture ....

Total official stamps........................

Total ordinary stamps sold ....

LETTER POSTAGES.

The amount of postages paid in money was.......................... $100,809 23
Included in the above amount are the following sums paid by foreign countries in the settlement of their accounts:

Kingdom of Great Britain and Ireland......................	$73,484 54	
Dominion of Canada..	2,064 33	
Colony of New South Wales	1,732 00	
Colony of Queensland	56 92	
Colony of British Guiana..................................	4 60	
Kingdom of Spain	869 22	
Republic of Switzerland...................................	49 43	
Empire of Brazil..	28 80	
Republic of Mexico	1,240 25	
Empire of Japan	1,061 27	
Kingdom of Netherlands	14 07	
Kingdom of Norway..	17 22	
		80,622 45
Total collected by postmasters		20,186 78

The following balances were paid and charged to the appropriations
for—

BALANCES DUE FOREIGN COUNTRIES.

Service of 1881:

Kingdom of Italy..	$1,682 01	
Republic of France......................................	1,270 20	
Kingdom of Belgium	4,360 49	
Empire of Germany......................................	2,670 72	
Kingdom of Sweden	559 21	
Kingdom of Denmark	1,361 47	
Argentine Republic......................................	77 12	
International Bureau—Postal Union	752 53	
Total, 1881..		$12,733 75

Service of previous years:

Kingdom of Italy..	1,682 01	
Republic of France......................................	3,933 75	
Kingdom of Belgium	4,360 49	
Empire of Germany......................................	2,670 73	
Kingdom of Sweden	559 21	
Kingdom of Denmark	1,361 47	
Colony of St. Thomas	918 61	
Argentine Republic......................................	192 80	
Total, previous years...............................		15,679 07
Aggregate amount paid		28,412 82

MAIL TRANSPORTATION.

The amount charged to "transportation accrued" and placed to the
credit of mail contractors and others for mail transportation during the
fiscal year was:

For the regular supply of mail routes	$20,647,099 65
For the supply of "special" offices	40,159 07
For the supply of "mail messenger" offices	•729,196 48
For the salaries of postal railway clerks, route, and other agents	3,039,113 97
For the salaries and per diem of the assistant superintendents of the railway mail service..	39,127 19
Total	24,494,696 36

FOREIGN MAIL TRANSPORTATION.

New York, Great Britain and Ireland and countries beyond, via Great Britain...........................	$131,384 84	
New York, Great Britain and Ireland and Germany and countries beyond................................	50,272 89	
Philadelphia, Great Britain and Ireland..................	2,712 99	
Boston, Great Britain and Ireland.......................	756 50	
Post-Office Department of Canada, English mail.........	703 23	
New York, Baltimore, Philadelphia, Boston, Key West, New Orleans, and San Francisco, West Indies, Central and South America, Mexico, &c...............	32,962 55	
New York and Newfoundland............................	35 40	
Boston and Nova Scotia................................	157 97	
Baltimore and Bremen.................................	13 64	
Upper Pacific coast, local mail.........................	404 98	
San Francisco, China, Japan, Farther India, Australia, and South Sea Islands.............................	13,992 88	
Expenses of government mail agent at Aspinwall........	940 00	
Expenses of government mail agent at Panama.........	1,426 00	
Expenses of government mail agent at Shanghai, China..	2,113 85	
		$237,897 39
		24,732,595 75
The amount credited to "transportation accrued" and charged to mail contractors for over-credits, being for "fines and deductions," was..		489,478 83
Net amount to the credit of mail contractors........................		24,243,116 92
The amount paid during the year was................................., ...		23,048,754 29
Excess of "transportation accrued"...................................		1,194,362 63

PACIFIC RAILROAD ACCOUNT.

Included in the above excess of transportation accrued are the following balances accrued for the transportation of the mails over Pacific Railroads, certified to the Register of the Treasury under instructions of the Secretary, dated May 19, 1879, and August 28, 1880. The items are not charged as expenditures of the Post-Office Department (see Statutes, vol. 20, page 420):

Regular service, 1881:		
Union Pacific Railway Company......................	$559,292 89	
Central Pacific Railroad Company....................	386,397 17	
Sioux City and Pacific Railroad Company.............	16,193 67	
		$961,883 73
Use of postal cars, 1881:		
Union Pacific Railway Company......................	61,101 21	
Central Pacific Railroad Company....................	38,852 02	
		99,953 23
Total of certified for 1881..........................		1,061,836 96
Regular service of previous years:		
Union Pacific Railway Company......................	33,846 14	
Central Pacific Railroad Company....................	3,356 26	
Sioux City and Pacific Railroad Company.............	1,650 29	
Total certified for previous years....................		38,852 69
Aggregate amount certified during the fiscal year...............		$1,100,689 65

STATEMENT OF THE CONDITION OF THE ACCOUNTS OF LATE POST-MASTERS.

Balance due the United States brought forward from last report.........	$424,637 30	
Balance due the United States on account of postmasters becoming late during the fiscal year......................................	345,578 36	
		770,215 66

Amount collected during the year............................ $242,330 90
Amount charged to "suspense"............................... 1,179 15
Amount charged to bad and compromise debts............. 16,215 70
                                                                          ───────────
                                                                          $259,625 75

Balance remaining due United States......................... 510,690 91
Of which there is in suit..................................... 257,306 06
Not in suit... 253,384 85
                                                                          ───────────
                                                                          510,690 91

Balance due late postmasters brought forward from last report......... 56,308 26
Amount becoming due during the fiscal year........................... 43,725 57
                                                                          ───────────
                                                                          100,033 83
Amount paid during the year.. 13,968 86
                                                                          ───────────
Balance remaining due late postmasters............................... 86,064 97

Amount in suit June 30, 1879.. 246,250 39
Amount submitted for suit during the fiscal year..................... 51,065 51
                                                                          ───────────
                                                                          297,315 90
Of which there was collected during the year.............. 32,035 69
Amount otherwise settled................................... 7,974 15
                                                                          ───────────
                                                                          40,009 84
                                                                          ───────────
Balance remaining in suit.. 257,306 06

Amount of costs and interest collected by suit....................... 2,709 52

MONEY-ORDER ACCOUNT.

Statement of the net revenue derived from the domestic money-order transactions for the year ended June 30, 1881, and of the international money-order transactions for the year ended June 30, 1880.

Revenue accrued on domestic transactions, 1881......................... $252,314 64
Revenue accrued on Canadian international transactions, 1880........... 7,271 40
Revenue accrued on British international transactions, 1880............. 22,987 10
Revenue accrued on German international transactions, 1880............. 8,250 13
Revenue accrued on Swiss international transactions, 1880.............. 2,200 82
Revenue accrued on Italian international transactions, 1880............. 2,656 88
                                                                          ───────────
                                                                          295,680 97
Loss on French international transactions, 1880...................... 99 58
                                                                          ───────────
Total revenue... 295,581 39

The following tables, numbered from 1 to 17, inclusive, exhibit more in detail the financial transactions of the Department for the fiscal year.

No. 1.—*Statement exhibiting quarterly the receipts of the Post-Office Department, under their several heads, for the fiscal year ended June 30, 1881.*

Accounts.	Quarter ended September 30, 1880.	Quarter ended December 31, 1880.	Quarter ended March 31, 1881.	Quarter ended June 30, 1881.	Aggregate.
Letter postage	$1,632 18	$852 55	$2,605 26	$24,718 14	$109,809 22
Box-rents and branch offices...	364,352 49	368,971 95	377,895 20	426,230 23	1,490,449 87
Fines and penalties............	830 60	3,739 77	8,610 49	2,570 58	15,751 44
Postage-stamps, stamped envelopes, and wrappers, and postal cards.............	7,977,019 13	8,790,575 66	9,052,960 61	9,015,189 70	34,835,745 10
Dead letters...................	927 50	238 30		5,418 60	6,584 40
Revenue from money order business................				295,581 39	295,581 39
Miscellaneous..................	6,825 86	6,392 62	8,690 29	9,567 77	31,476 54
Total......................	8,351,587 76	9,170,774 85	9,451,761 95	9,511,279 41	36,785,397 97

No. 2.—*Statement exhibiting quarterly the expenditures of the Post-Office Department, under their several heads, for the fiscal year ended June 30, 1881.*

Appropriations.	Quarter ended September 30, 1880.	Quarter ended December 31, 1880.	Quarter ended March 31, 1881.	Quarter ended June 30, 1881.	Total expenditures on account of 1881.	Expended on account of previous years.	Aggregate expenditures.
Compensation of postmasters	$1,906,053 33	$2,044,700 78	$2,129,644 64	$2,128,344 04	$8,208,742 79	94,445 54	$8,303,188 33
Compensation of clerks for post-offices	909,542 20	906,348 57	914,209 48	946,655 97	3,676,756 22	3,778 22	3,680,534 54
Compensation of letter-carriers, and incidental expenses							
Wrapping-paper	608,577 83	625,374 02	629,840 55	656,119 15	2,469,911 54	21,759 58	2,521,671 12
Twine	12,222 47	11,797 96	659 89	221 21	24,900 10		24,900 10
Postmarking and canceling stamps	37,838 00	19,651 88	23,446 85	3,666 70	24,003 88		64,003 88
Letter balances	6,418 75	2,931 75	3,028 20	1,794 80	13,499 80		13,499 80
Rent, light and fuel for post-offices	6,030 60	1,552 60	3,103 60	310 80	7,997 80		7,997 80
Stationery	96,950 97	55,850 28	94,505 09	105,970 55	352,714 80	973 56	353,688 42
Furniture for post-office	12,431 43	13,290 89	13,577 53	10,708 90	49,238 43	297 90	49,449 40
Miscellaneous, office of First Assistant Postmaster-General	4,179 97	4,981 10	5,709 52	4,476 28	13,296 87	3,235 16	22,633 08
Inland mail transportation, railroad	25,882 49	28,849 72	18,004 42	10,472 52	80,989 15	9,679 90	90,669 05
Inland mail transportation, star	2,170,349 65	2,400,552 08	2,263,901 62	2,708,351 81	9,543,155 88	201,924 80	9,745,079 98
Inland mail transportation, steamboat	1,873,444 01	1,830,445 61	1,785,674 17	1,730,878 29	7,170,624 10	32,776 82	7,203,400 92
Transportation by railway post-office cars	241,444 01	198,502 15	178,796 84	219,354 51	828,097 51	1,316 68	827,414 84
Compensation of railway post-office clerks	301,153 07	316,317 71	327,346 11	322,394 61	1,288,221 50		1,288,221 50
Compensation of route agents	386,219 14	367,950 49	387,961 87	364,154 03	1,406,275 52	571 88	1,406,846 90
Compensation of mail-route messengers	301,228 59	309,838 40	314,315 78	316,031 60	1,241,400 41	983 79	1,242,383 20
Compensation of local agents	51,550 29	48,882 13	47,173 17	48,650 28	196,274 90	63 75	196,338 65
Compensation of mail messengers	30,629 75	31,700 87	31,722 25	39,162 95	133,195 22	350 00	133,545 22
Mail locks and keys	173,717 03	180,641 35	184,501 44	186,124 49	724,984 21	4,214 27	729,198 48
Mail bags and catchers	58,094 78	45,159 34	61,534 45	16,092 03	188,879 99	11,841 01	10,441 00
Post-route maps	8,683 60	17,975 88	12,314 70	4,751 15	43,725 40		45,725 40
Mail depredations and post-office inspectors	34,370 88	34,116 48	34,884 74	37,121 55	140,543 68	2,425 00	142,968 68
Fees to United States marshals, clerks, and counsel	259 15	870 92	900 12	1,135 63	3,065 22	943 46	4,008 68
Postage-stamps	39,980 94	26,431 91	26,411 27	4,426 18	96,630 30		96,630 30
Distribution of postage-stamps	1,810 98	1,591 50	1,969 69	1,992 75	7,204 51		7,204 51
Stamped envelopes and newspaper wrappers	196,846 86	115,816 98	114,219 30	27,585 33	443,967 43	249 00	444,216 43
Distribution of stamped envelopes and newspaper wrappers							
Paper wrappers	3,673 56	3,738 00	3,762 05	3,727 73	15,150 34	34 43	15,184 77
Distribution of postal cards	91,678 66	55,693 01	52,651 00	15,740 61	215,700 97		215,700 57
... envelopes, locks, and seals	1,580 50	1,641 97	1,728 40	1,483 64	6,434 57		6,434 57
... and 1-cent letter envelopes							
Ship, steamboat, and way letters	18,625 08	23,293 12	31,065 24	27,293 17	100,249 50		100,249 50
Engraving, printing, and binding drafts and ...	222 08	281 04	129 52	297 76	990 96		990 96
Advertising	441 50	435 83	347 50		1,224 83	419 10	1,224 93
Miscellaneous, office of Postmaster-General	16,184 49	11,787 77	8,407 80	8,615 16	90,905 01		40,376 11
	409 20	243 05	118 90	109 90	940 00		940 30

Foreign mail transportation	52,898 44	59,651 08	71,258 46	40,653 38	224,461 36	11,833 74	236,295 12
Balance due foreign countries	19 53	3,408 72	6,356 20	2,982 31	12,733 75	13,679 07	26,412 82
Postmarking-machines	6,000 00				6,000 00		6,000 00
Refund of dead-letter inclosure to A. J. Brooks							
Stamps for Postal Union correspondence						50 00	50 00
Totals	9,737,554 23	9,853,789 89	9,711,343 32	9,974,050 02	39,251,726 46	340,829 76	39,592,566 22

*Included in the item of amount paid for the "Inland mail transportation, railroads," second quarter, 1881, is the sum of $304,583 24, paid for the service of previous quarter.

67 Ab

No. 3.—*Statement by States o*

Number.	States and Territories.	Letter postage.	Waste paper and twine.
1	Maine	$3 64	$281 28
2	New Hampshire	2 15	188 43
3	Vermont	8 85	172 68
4	Massachusetts	2 40	1,439 18
5	Rhode Island	39	186 51
6	Connecticut	2 93	355 61
7	New York	14,584 75	5,464 34
8	New Jersey	4 33	289 77
9	Pennsylvania	2,630 51	1,516 07
10	Delaware	15	19 94
11	Maryland	4 36	112 89
12	Virginia	4 16	139 13
13	West Virginia	2 75	62 95
14	North Carolina	7 02	86 61
15	South Carolina	3 92	29 41
16	Georgia	5 98	188 66
17	Florida	1 83	20 09
18	Ohio	47 87	2,228 86
19	Michigan	14 81	814 04
20	Indiana	4 89	712 65
21	Illinois	43 33	2,883 83
22	Wisconsin	26 67	440 35
23	Iowa	5 80	586 72
24	Missouri	25 87	776 25
25	Kentucky	5 60	447 54
26	Tennessee	8 07	119 37
27	Alabama	10 61	102 19
28	Mississippi	5 11	58 47
29	Arkansas	4 06	44 49
30	Louisiana	4 83	112 82
31	Texas	28 22	210 08
32	California	11 31	395 15
33	Oregon	1 99	71 76
34	Minnesota	51 54	299 20
35	Kansas	18 14	255 69
36	Nebraska	8 12	86 66
37	Nevada	21	22 29
38	Colorado	4 85	300 01
39	Utah	10 12	77 46
40	New Mexico	3	8 45
41	Washington	8 01	3 87
42	Dakota	2 10	54 03
43	Arizona	18	29 71
44	Idaho	4 06	19 67
45	Wyoming	1 78	7 88
46	Montana	2 78	26 14
47	Alaska		75
48	District of Columbia		570 27
		17,623 51	22,320 23
	Deduct miscellaneous items		
	Add miscellaneous items	83,185 72	
		100,809 23	22,320 23

of the United States for the fiscal year ended June 30, 1881.

Compensation of post-masters.	Clerks for offices, rent, light, and fuel, and incidental expenses of post-offices.	Compensation of letter-carriers.	Compensation of route-agents, postal railway clerks, mail messengers, and supply of special offices.	Transportation by States.	Total expenditures.	Excess of expenditures over receipts.	Excess of receipts over expenditures.	Number.
$180,653 77	$49,632 20	$11,957 56	$48,956 73	$236,609 34	$527,809 60	....	$54,642 71	1
1,1,115 35	20,032 42	5,072 38	19,409 11	104,326 43	271,955 69	$602 40	60,030 71	2
116,677 97	14,894 77	....	16,042 28	144,781 48	204,506 50	....	....	3
J2,541 22	329,656 88	234,983 58	283,721 88	844,696 67	1,565,600 23	....	919,091 56	4
41,661 85	31,331 22	24,941 84	10,258 52	44,421 39	152,614 82	....	129,345 62	5
177,149 25	69,831 61	83,311 48	52,693 64	233,809 18	566,795 16	....	164,577 54	6
777,499 71	1,125,478 96	674,792 93	391,140 09	1,796,753 01	4,763,664 69	....	2,011,475 43	7
195,918 99	47,985 53	69,607 32	35,359 88	291,327 71	640,199 43	....	108,234 06	8
636,423 94	379,565 32	356,938 34	318,710 53	960,241 70	2,675,879 83	....	653,403 85	0
23,192 74	5,850 39	8,576 22	9,361 38	24,303 20	73,283 93	....	14,950 81	10
96,676 61	82,408 23	72,662 17	60,853 97	382,976 08	675,577 06	29,084 98	....	11
182,043 68	48,856 30	23,778 64	66,861 81	541,993 06	863,523 49	320,309 33	....	12
73,900 81	13,218 55	5,816 78	14,357 98	115,615 80	222,909 92	27,028 77	....	13
115,360 79	18,786 71	....	30,267 38	283,332 81	447,747 69	164,448 78	....	14
77,940 66	13,327 15	6,825 48	30,923 54	186,161 15	315,177 98	77,461 51	....	15
136,096 76	46,086 06	20,033 02	98,696 47	405,771 87	706,684 18	238,902 71	....	16
50,607 90	9,030 37	....	16,706 57	182,364 77	258,799 61	138,146 70	....	17
515,361 54	237,269 04	155,776 51	523,330 96	1,467,148 98	2,898,887 03	506,516 02	....	18
376,344 83	92,868 73	43,853 02	109,514 44	435,600 67	1,078,250 60	....	192,371 21	19
315,090 73	92,801 56	54,047 45	111,689 31	454,172 08	1,028,701 15	43,136 70	....	20
583,542 24	418,947 06	202,279 37	874,563 94	1,106,817 03	2,686,149 63	....	294,448 81	21
271,918 34	71,176 27	28,250 25	65,033 77	383,069 82	820,048 45	....	48,701 82	22
409,022 35	71,552 38	24,833 40	118,609 69	528,072 76	1,152,090 58	7,654 07	....	23
287,752 58	181,154 51	138,644 34	227,664 15	969,675 69	1,804,891 27	303,429 17	....	24
159,607 09	46,528 66	35,059 65	50,344 87	406,575 30	698,176 41	135,816 93	....	25
126,501 90	48,680 43	20,630 87	73,641 58	284,986 67	534,441 45	90,111 31	....	26
110,063 77	25,561 54	5,100 00	28,336 44	346,730 97	515,792 77	217,698 83	....	27
109,138 25	13,452 87	....	16,721 45	223,860 63	363,173 00	126,905 03	....	28
103,311 90	17,608 59	4,262 00	23,632 17	635,224 61	784,129 27	540,309 56	....	29
73,936 88	50,879 60	43,843 33	28,362 64	342,934 13	548,946 60	165,352 10	....	30
234,024 60	67,607 61	14,364 19	49,708 97	1,037,778 00	1,434,482 37	749,238 64	....	31
223,651 34	138,374 31	71,600 48	89,372 05	1,091,801 39	1,614,799 57	569,708 24	....	32
53,477 35	11,123 87	4,520 50	13,792 06	311,287 80	391,201 58	213,460 94	....	33
183,312 81	48,397 35	21,882 48	71,631 24	320,318 84	615,542 76	37,731 15	....	34
256,550 59	42,340 68	8,721 71	81,954 82	601,725 21	991,301 41	346,769 89	....	35
128,925 83	25,638 58	8,150 72	64,613 49	665,763 52	807,072 14	543,852 53	....	36
41,423 43	11,557 93	....	2,792 00	226,143 84	281,916 12	192,432 40	....	37
105,609 21	49,879 39	18,929 53	33,283 51	520,125 52	727,307 16	300,767 41	....	38
41,293 29	11,766 11	....	13,815 29	255,946 51	322,821 20	220,115 52	....	39
23,041 41	1,889 75	....	7,184 51	189,443 00	221,556 67	169,804 54	....	40
27,720 33	2,523 00	....	5,004 46	110,076 35	143,824 14	85,005 16	....	41
60,427 94	9,319 15	....	6,778 02	250,472 31	326,997 42	193,072 75	....	42
21,853 51	2,682 50	....	163 44	356,930 38	381,629 83	327,342 65	....	43
17,184 27	1,507 00	....	2,583 04	177,182 42	198,460 73	161,470 69	....	44
16,831 15	4,207 50	....	60 26	148,352 80	169,452 11	129,027 92	....	45
32,341 53	5,729 44	....	5 22	206,245 49	304,321 68	242,978 51	....	46
200 82	....	....	....	....	200 82	....	132 54	47
4,425 26	121,737 21	46,530 60	115,287 60	....	267,980 67	61,189 77	....	48
N,292,682 35	4,239,821 14	2,493,978 14	3,813,387 50	20,429,019 36	39,268,888 49	7,702,783 71	4,651,406 77	
10,505 98	34,887 07	27,692 98	4,915 98	209,826 27	201,656 22	201,656 22	240,812 88	
8,303,188 83	4,274,708 21	2,521,671 12	3,808,471 52	20,159,193 09	39,067,232 27	7,501,127 49	4,802,219 65	

No. 3.—*Statement by States of the postal receipts and expenditures, &c.*—**Continued.**

Items of expenditure of a general nature not embraced above.		Items of receipt of a general nature not embraced above.	
Amount paid for foreign mails and expenses of government agents....	$236, 325 12	Receipts on account of dead letters.	$6, 584 40
Balances paid foreign countries......	28, 412 82	Receipts on account of fines and penalties	15, 751 44
Ship, steamboat, and way letters	990 95	Receipts on account of miscellaneous...........................	9, 156 31
Wrapping-paper	24, 900 10	Revenue from money-order business	295, 581 39
Twine	84, 603 38	Excess of "transportation accrued "	1, 194, 382 63
Post-route maps......................	43, 725 40	Total excess of expenditures over receipts	2, 807, 168 25
Advertising..........................	27, 934 08		
Mail bags and catchers...............	146, 505 21		
Salary and expenses of assistant superintendents of the railway mail service	39, 127 19		
Mail locks and keys	10, 941 50		
Postmarking and canceling stamps..	13, 499 50		
Mail depredations and post-office inspectors.............................	146, 977 31		
Letter-balances	7, 997 80		
Expenses of postage-stamps, stamped envelopes, wrappers, and cards ...	785, 371 14		
Dead-letter, official, and registered-package envelopes.................	100, 249 50		
Sundry and miscellaneous payments.	22, 135 58		
Excess of expenditures brought down	2, 608, 907 84		
	4, 328, 604 42		4, 328, 604 42

No. 4.—*Statement showing the condition of the account, with each item of the appropriation, for the service of the Post-Office Department for the fiscal year ended June 30, 1881.*

Title of appropriations.	Amount appropriated, including special acts and deficiencies.	Expended.	Balance unexpended.	Excess of expenditures.
Compensation of postmasters	$7,500,000 00	$8,298,742 79	....	$798,742 79
Compensation of clerks for post-offices....	3,680,000 00	3,676,756 22	$3,243 78	....
Compensation of letter-carriers and incidental expenses	2,500,000 00	2,499,911 54	88 46	....
Wrapping-paper	25,000 00	24,900 10	99 90	....
Twine	84,756 00	84,603 38	152 62	....
Postmarking and canceling stamps	13,500 00	13,499 50	50	....
Letter-balances	8,000 00	7,997 80	2 20	....
Rent, light, and fuel for post-offices	425,000 00	382,714 86	42,285 14	....
Stationery	50,000 00	49,238 45	761 55	....
Furniture for post-offices	20,000 00	19,296 87	703 13	....
Miscellaneous, office of First Assistant Postmaster-General	85,000 00	80,989 15	4,010 85	....
Inland mail transportation, railroad	9,665,000 00	9,543,155 36	121,844 64	....
Inland mail transportation, star	7,375,000 00	7,170,624 10	204,375 90	....
Inland mail transportation, steamboat	900,000 00	826,097 51	73,902 49	....
Transportation by postal cars	1,366,000 00	1,268,221 50	97,778 50	....
Compensation of railway post-office clerks.	1,470,000 00	1,466,275 52	3,724 48	....
Compensation of route-agents.	1,245,000 00	1,241,400 41	3,599 59	....
Compensation of mail-route messengers...	200,000 00	196,274 90	3,725 10	....
Compensation of local agents	135,000 00	133,195 22	1,804 78	....
Compensation of mail-messengers	725,000 00	724,984 21	15 79	....
Mail locks and keys	100,000 00	....	100,000 00	....
Mail bags and catchers	185,000 00	183,879 59	1,120 41	....
Post-route maps	43,725 40	43,725 40	....	....
Mail depredations and post-office inspectors	150,000 00	143,608 85	6,391 15	....
Postage-stamps	97,000 00	96,630 30	369 70	....
Distribution of postage-stamps	8,100 00	7,204 51	895 49	....
Stamped envelopes and newspaper wrappers	444,020 00	443,967 42	52 58	....
Distribution of stamped envelopes and newspaper wrappers	16,000 00	15,150 34	849 66	....
Postal cards	237,000 00	215,700 57	21,299 43	....
Distribution of postal cards	7,300 00	6,434 57	865 43	....
Office dead letter and registered envelopes, locks, and seals	120,000 00	100,249 50	19,750 50	....
Ship, steamboat, and way letters	4,500 00	990 95	3,509 05	....
Engraving, printing, and binding drafts and warrants	1,500 00	1,224 93	275 07	....
Advertising	40,000 00	39,955 01	44 99	....
Miscellaneous, office of Postmaster-General	1,500 00	940 00	560 00	....
Foreign mail transportation	225,000 00	224,461 38	538 62	....
Balances due foreign countries	45,000 00	12,733 75	32,266 25	....
Post-marking machines	6,000 00	6,000 00	....	....
Stamps for Postal Union correspondence	1,000 00	....	1,000 00	....
Total	39,204,901 40	39,251,736 46	751,907 73	798,742 79

In conclusion, I would invite your attention to the present overcrowded condition of the rooms allotted to this office, and the urgent necessity for increased accommodations.

My predecessor, in his last two annual reports to the Postmaster-General, referred to the vast accumulation of accounts current, and other papers in the files of this office, which are not now necessary for reference, having long since been audited, and the items therein contained transferred to permanent records. He recommended that authority be obtained from Congress for the sale or destruction of such files, over ten years old, and I renew that recommendation.

I have the honor to be, very respectfully,

J. H. ELA,
Auditor.

Hon. THOMAS L. JAMES,
Postmaster-General.

REPORT

OF THE

COMMISSIONER OF AGRICULTURE.

DEPARTMENT OF AGRICULTURE,
Washington, D. C., November 25, 1881.

To THE PRESIDENT:

I respectfully submit the annual report of the Department of Agriculture for the year 1881.

When I entered upon my duties as Commissioner, July 1 of the current year, I found the work for the season, both regular and special, elaborately laid out by my predecessor. Provision had been made for investigating the agricultural condition of the Pacific coast; for continuing the work on the artesian well in Colorado; for proceeding with the experiment in the cultivation of the tea plant; for concluding the investigation into the manufacture of sugar from sorghum; for observations on the existence of pluro-pneumonia and other contagious diseases of animals, both in this country and in those English ports to which American cattle are exported; for continued examinations into the necessities and opportunities of American forestry; for tests of textile fibers, both animal and vegetable; for a scientific investigation of the habits of insects injurious to vegetation, and of the best methods of destroying them; and for the usual work of the various divisions of the department for which appropriations had been made by Congress.

I have endeavored to conduct all experiments in which I found the department engaged, with an ardent desire to bring them to legitimate conclusions, in the spirit of an investigator and not in the spirit of an advocate.

The process of manufacturing sugar from sorghum has been conducted by the best skill I could obtain in the country, under the eye of experienced chemists, and with ample and somewhat expensive machinery, run by an accomplished and faithful engineer.

The crop was gathered with the greatest possible economy of time, labor, and expense, and the work was carried on with as much expedition as the season would allow. The result of this work will be found under the appropriate head of this communication and in the elaborate report of the chemist of the department.

The expenses of the attempt to cultivate the tea plant in South Carolina have been somewhat curtailed, without, however, interfering with the proposed experiment. In the management of this enterprise, I have been governed largely by the opinions of the accomplished and experienced horticulturist of the department, Mr. Saunders, and by a proper regard for economy in the expenditure of the money appropriated for this purpose.

A thoroughly scientific and practical commission, appointed with great care and provided with instructions obtained from Major Powell, has examined the artesian well now in process of construction, and has explored, under the rules of structural geology, a large portion of the arid regions in which these wells may be valuable.

A veterinary surgeon has been sent to England to confer with the Privy Council upon the exact condition of American cattle landed in her markets; and agents and experts have been employed to ascertain all facts relating to the existence of contagious diseases in this country, in accordance with appropriations for this purpose. And while these various commissions and agents have been employed in prosecuting the work assigned them, the work of the various divisions of the department has been prosecuted with diligence and fidelity by those into whose hands it has been committed.

During the last three months I have considered it my duty to visit various important agricultural sections of the country on occasions where I could not only witness the exhibited results of the farmers' industry, but could also obtain an opinion of the general condition of agriculture and the popular expectations of the department. I have been especially desirous of ascertaining the sources whence the department obtained its statistics and crop returns, and the estimate put upon these reports by those interested in them.

It seemed to me important to learn how far the distribution of seed by the department had improved our old crops and introduced new ones. I have been anxious to learn what breed of domesticated animals had been introduced wisely and increased judiciously and profitably, with due regard to quality and market. For these observations, I have visited New England, Illinois, Wisconsin, Pennsylvania, Virginia, South Carolina, Maryland, and Georgia, and have been liberally furnished with all possible means for pursuing my work.

That the American soil is producing vast crops, at the hands of diligent and intelligent cultivators, the returns of the markets constantly bear witness; and I can add my own testimony to the energy and skill with which this work is performed, even under the discouragements of drought and flood and frost. I have found the agricultural mind of the country active in its desire to obtain the best knowledge, and to examine and test all the best methods; and I have been especially impressed with the vast opportunities which this department possesses for aiding the development of our vast resources, and for accumulating and distributing information upon that great cluster of industries upon the successful prosecution of which the prosperity and power of our country depends. That in agriculture we have still great room for improvement every one must be aware who realizes that a large proportion of our staple crops is as yet, as it were, a spontaneous production of the earth, and that exhausted soils are abandoned for more fertile regions as the best method of farming.

That our manufacturers have but just commenced their career (important as they are) must be evident to him who remembers that fifty years ago they had hardly an existence, and that a producing and consuming population increases here at the rate of a million or more a year. That much may yet be done to systematize and organize the producing and transporting business of our country no one can doubt who has studied, even carelessly, these great economic questions. And I am confident that an enlarged and well endowed and well arranged department, devoted to industrial investigations, will commend itself to those who are engaged in the work of legislation, upon which the policy and practical operation of our government depend.

By surveys of the great unexplored mineral wealth of the southern slopes of the Alleghanies; by more careful examination of the farming lands of the government; by supplying recorded data of our manufacturing and mechanical productions; by obtaining more accurate knowledge of our agricultural resources and capabilities; by securing all the possible fruits of industrial education, and recording all the conditions of labor; by pursuing our scientific investigations, in which the Agricultural Department has been so long engaged, with increased zeal and endowment, the Government of the United States may take its stand among the most enterprising and prosperous of those nations in which departments are provided and supported for every purpose which can possibly increase the national wealth and intelligence and stimulate the national enterprise.

In setting forth these views, I do not overestimate the value and importance of a department devoted to agriculture and the industries that stand around it and depend upon it for existence, nor do I exaggerate the picture of that organization which will ultimately be established in accordance with the legislative wisdom of the land, guided by the demands of an intelligent and prosperous people, who will spare no effort to make this country equally distinguished for prosperity and that cultivation which always attends the march of industry.

For the purpose of bringing the department into immediate conference with the various institutions organized to develop the agriculture of the country, I have called delegate conventions, composed of representatives of the State societies and the colleges founded on the land grant of Congress, to meet at Washington in January next, and have assigned to each convention one of the following topics for consideration, viz: Agricultural education, as promoted by societies and conveyed by colleges; Animal Industry; Horticulture; Cereals and Grasses. I have also called a convention of cotton planters, which met at Atlanta November 2. in connection with the admirable industrial exposition there, and considered the cotton culture and general agriculture of the cotton States. During my visit to Atlanta my attention was called to a most remarkable exhibit of the crops, woods, mineral products, &c., of a section of our country south of the latitude of Washington, furnished by many railroads in that section, as an illustration of the resources which abound there. I have not seen in this country a more valuable representative and illustrative exhibition of our natural wealth, and, impressed with the idea that the examination of these products would impress the mind of all, native and foreign, who might see them, I have requested the parties having them in charge to bestow them upon the Agricultural Department for proper arrangement and public observation. I am happy to say that several of the roads which have made the collections have complied with my request, and I hope to be able to exhibit in the department this most important display of some portions of that industry, to develop which the department itself was organized.

Of the work of the various divisions in the department, I submit the following concise statements:

DIVISION OF GARDENS AND GROUNDS.

The distributions during the year have embraced over 100,000 plants of various kinds. Large quantities of the hardiest varieties of the foreign grape have been sent to Texas, Florida, and others of the Southern States, with good promise of success.

The distribution of tea plants has also been continued, and preparations are in progress for a more liberal supply of tea seeds, so that the efforts to further the introduction of this important crop may be maintained.

The purposes of the experimental grounds can never be fully realized until facilities are secured for extending the work in various suitable localities. The department is constantly subject to demands from California, Florida, and similar climatic sections for plants of semi-tropical countries. The most important, perhaps, of these requests are those for oranges and lemons, and for other species of the citrus family. In the climate of Washington the propagation of semi-tropical plants is necessarily confined to glass structures; and although several thousands are annually produced, the number is totally inadequate to meet the wants of correspondents or make an impression upon the progress of this branch of culture. With a propagating establishment in an orange-growing climate, operations could be conducted on an extensive scale, similar to that practiced in regard to peaches, apples, and other hardy fruit trees in the Northern States, and to an extent more in accordance with the requirements of the country.

Propagation would not be confined to the orange family; many other semi-tropical plants require attention. The pine-apple, banana, guava, chocolate, cinnamon, coffee, tea, pepper, ginger, arrowroot, and many fiber-producing and starch-yielding plants might be mentioned as being altogether worthy of careful experimental culture or for propagation.

But the value of such an establishment is not confined to the propagation of plants only. There are numerous questions of much moment which can be answered only from the results of well-directed and closely-conducted tests. The facts, as well as the principles involved in the systematic rotatation of crops, rest in comparative obscurity; but little is known about it, except that it is a practice absolutely essential to profitable culture. The same remarks apply in regard to the value of changing seeds from one soil and climate to another soil and climate. It is well known that results follow such changes, sometimes favorably and sometimes unfavorably; but how far these are influenced by soil alone, by climate alone, or their combination, has not reached a decision of practical applicability.

All of our cultivated plants have run into numerous varieties, many of them comparatively worthless, and many others of local value only, or of limited special utility; it is therefore a matter of much importance to acquire a thorough and exact knowledge, as far as practicable, of their respective values, and this can only be secured by comparative tests where all are cultivated under similar conditions in similar climates.

The results of such tests will also indicate the line of operations to be pursued in improving by crossing or by hybridizing varieties combining special values; this is a most important work, and if properly conducted cannot fail in reaching results of great value. But to reach these results will require several operative points, carefully selected so as to embrace distinct regions for purposes of interchange of crops, &c.

The subject is one of immense importance and might be elaborated in extensive detail. What has been said above merely outlines some of the work which may occupy attention on experimental grounds.

BOTANICAL DIVISION.

During the year past the botanist has continued the work of his division as thoroughly as circumstances would permit.

His attention has been largely employed in the necessary investigations for the proper classification of the plants in the herbarium.

Extensive additions have been made during the year, chiefly of plants from California and the Western Territories. A valuable collection of the plants of Southeastern Texas and the adjacent parts of Mexico has also been procured.

These plants, however, still remain in the original packages, on account of the withdrawal of the customary assistance which has been employed in the preparation and mounting of the specimens.

The work of describing and delineating grasses for the annual report has been continued. More extended and practical results might be anticipated with respect of the cultivation of our native grasses, by observations and investigations in the field, which are not at present provided for.

During the past two or three years botanical investigation in different parts of our country, and especially in the new States and Territories, has been unusually active; many new species have been discovered and a better knowledge of many others has been obtained. All that is valuable in the collection of these investigators should be procured at the earliest opportunity and added to the herbarium, in order that the department may have the means of answering any inquiries respecting the vegetable productions of the country.

The herbarium contains a representation of about nine-tenths of all the plants at present known as natives. A portion of this number, however, are imperfect specimens, which require replacement as soon as good and characteristic specimens can be procured.

The value of the herbarium is not limited to its uses in connection with this department. Inquiries sometimes occur from the Patent Office and other departments relative to plants which have medicinal or economic properties. Within a few years a considerable number of California plants have gradually assumed importance as standard medical remedies, and others for various economic properties, and it is certain that as our vegetation becomes better known still other valuable additions to the arts and sciences will be obtained from that source.

MICROSCOPICAL DIVISION.

During the past year the microscopist has made many investigations relating to plant and animal diseases, with a view of providing remedies. Fruits, vegetables, and food adulteration, including butter and oleomargarine, milk, "poisoned cheese," diseases of wheat, orange-tree rust, pear-leaf rust, yellows of peach, and diseases of the foliage of various trees, have engaged his attention. He has also made many specimens of microscopical slides, illustrating animal diseases. He has discovered new and effectual methods of distinguishing the fats of various animals and vegetables from each other promptly and decisively, by which means butter and oleomargarine are distinguished at once from each other.

For several years past many correspondents have urged upon the department the necessity of publishing information on the edible mushroom of the United States. To this end the microscopist has prepared for publication a series of twelve typical plates in natural colors, with a full and instructive statement of their character, habits, and habitats, together with the most reliable and improved methods of preparing mushrooms for the table.

His microscopical investigations have also comprised the search for trichinæ in the swine flesh of the Washington markets—an animal parasite found in the muscles of animals, and sometimes in man, producing death by its presence—but in no case has a trace of their presence been found in the flesh of swine sold in this city, although found in specimens sent from distant parts for microscopical investigation.

Microscopical investigations have also been made for other divisions of this department.

CHEMICAL DIVISION.

Since the completion of the work reported in the annual report of the department for the year 1880, the following investigations and analyses have been accomplished in the chemical division:

Analyses of 57 marls, 47 ores, &c., 2 mineral waters, 9 soils, 11 fertilizers, 1 medicinal plant, 4 sumacs for tannin, and 9 miscellaneous analyses, making in all 140.

Besides the above, there have been made 1,858 analyses of saccharine juices, sirups, and sugars; the greater part of these being the expressed juices from thirty-eight varieties of sorghum, and eight varieties of maize, grown upon the department grounds.

A portion of the force of the division has been occupied in making sirup on a small scale from sorghum and maize, and a report of these operations, together with the report of the numerous analyses of the cane juices, carried on in the laboratory, will be submitted as soon as it is possible to complete final averages, tabular statements, &c., which work is being prosecuted as rapidly as is possible with the force engaged.

Several other investigations of much importance are in progress, among which may be mentioned the analyses of grasses and various feeding materials, which are being carried out with a view to determine, as accurately as possible by the modes of analysis at present in use, the actual nutritive value of all the agricultural food-materials in the different conditions in which they are sold and fed. For this purpose, a large and representative collection of samples has been made and carefully prepared for analysis.

Again, extensive work on the question of analysis of commercial fertilizers is progressing. The importance of the adoption of a uniform method of fertilizer analysis by all the official chemists of the country can scarcely be overestimated. The subject has already occupied nearly the entire time of three conventions of agricultural chemists, held in Washington and Boston in 1880, and in Cincinnati in 1881. The method adopted at the latter meeting, and at present in use, is only provisional.

Among other subjects that have been awaiting attention, is an examination of certain lands which injuriously affect the growth of the cotton plant and orange tree. The same has been earnestly requested of the department for a long time, as has, also, a series of exhaustive analyses of our cereals, more especially of corn and wheat, connected in the latter case with experiments as to their milling properties and the bread-making qualities of the flour obtained therefrom.

ENTOMOLOGICAL DIVISION.

The principal work of the past year in this division has been in relation to the scale-insects or bark lice (family *Coccidae*) which so seriously affect most kinds of fruit trees. It grew out of the special investigation of the insects affecting the orange begun by Professor Riley in 1878, as it was found that the chief enemies of citrus fruits were scale-insects. So little attention had been given to this family in the United States, however, that the investigations naturally broadened so as to include all scale-insects affecting cultivated plants, and the forthcoming report of the entomologist for the year 1880 is chiefly devoted to the consideration of these insects. It contains a general review of their characters; important discoveries as to their habits and mode of development; a consideration of the most available means of destroying them; a special report on the parasitic checks; and descriptions of many new species. Various other insects of economic importance are likewise treated of in that report, especially such as affect the sugar-cane and corn.

The increased appropriation given to this division by the last Congress has afforded the means for greater activity in the more practical field work of the division, and special agents are engaged thereat in various parts of the country. Particular attention is being paid to the insects injuriously affecting the chief staples, as corn, wheat, rice, sugar-cane, and also to those affecting fruit trees and vegetables.

The United States Entomological Commission, which has done excellent work under the Interior Department, is, by late action of Congress, now connected with this department—a connection eminently appropriate. The commission is at work on its third report; a revised and enlarged edition of Professor Riley's report on the cotton worm is also being prepared, and a bulletin on forest-tree insects by Dr. Packard is in press and nearly ready for distribution.

The special investigation of the insects affecting the cotton crop is being actively carried on, particularly in its more practical bearings, and most valuable discoveries have been made in mechanical details and principles that lessen the cost of protecting the crop and simplify the necessary machinery.

Recognizing the importance to our Western farmers of acquiring data upon which to predicate as to the probable action of the Rocky Mountain locust in 1882, I have had an agent specially engaged under the direction of the entomologist to gather such data in the permanent breeding grounds of this pest, lying for the most part in the thinly settled regions of the Northwest. Remembering the incalculable loss and suffering which this insect entailed between the years 1873 and 1877— losses which largely helped to prolong the commercial depression of that period—this information seems to me of sufficient moment to warrant annual observations of a more extended nature. There is an increasing interest manifested in the work of this division, quite out of proportion even to the rapid increase in agricultural production, and largely due to the greater attention now paid to applied science in our educational institutions and to increased facilities for intercommunication. The correspondence of the division is so large, and the requests for special information from all parts of the country so numerous, as to absorb too much of the time of the division; an increased clerical force and assistance are imperative. In order to relieve the division of much repetition in the replies, the entomologist will soon begin to prepare a series of well-illustrated bulletins, each treating of one of the more important of the insects injurious to our agriculture, and of such convenient form and size as to be cheaply and readily mailed. A bibliography of economic entomology, which has been commenced, will also facilitate this labor, as it will contain a digest of whatever has been published up to the present time, and a critical synopsis of remedies duly classified.

SEED DISTRIBUTION.

Tabular statement showing the quantity and kind of seeds issued from the seed division, Department of Agriculture, under the general and special appropriation act from July 1, 1880, to June 30, 1881, inclusive.

Description of seeds.	Varieties.	Senators and Members of Congress.	Agricultural societies.	Statistical correspondents.	Granges.	Special farmers.	Miscellaneous applicants.	Special distribution to sufferers by drought and grasshoppers.	Grand total.
		Papers.	*Papers.*	*Papers.*	*Papers.*	*Papers.*	*Papers.*	*Papers.*	
Vegetable	105	676,753	847	108,258	13,023	....	27,748	499,293	1,325,922
Flower	97	121,933	35	100	85	....	13,032	84	135,269
Sunflower	1	277	8	....	10	....	....	....	295
Tobacco	5	80,721	314	14,940	16,265	....	2,945	14	115,199
Herbs	10	10	....	....	....	....	128	....	138
Tree	4	266	14	2,088	....	....	1,194	22	3,568
Borage	1	....	....	....	....	....	12	....	12
FIELD SEEDS.		*Quarts.*	*Quarts.*	*Quarts.*	*Quarts.*	*Quarts.*	*Quarts.*	*Quarts.*	
Wheat	13	77,946	53	16,626	672	9,372	5,011	6,806	116,487
Oats	3	18,889	62	8,940	1,508	....	328	20,645	50,372
Field corn	8	11,209	68	3,906	3,278	....	779	13,282	32,522
Buckwheat	1	63	16	....	2,815	....	285	13,597	16,776
Potatoes	3	7,907	8	4,792	16	....	354	....	13,077
Grass	5	9,387	28	36	34	....	836	8	10,329
Clover	3	1,621	18	16	198	....	423	14	2,290
Sugar beet	2	75	154	6	20	....	485	....	740
Sorghum	12	7,987	230	16	4,294	....	2,060	64	14,651
Doura	1	....	....	....	8	....	87	7	102
Pea-nuts	1	229	20	....	6,796	....	13	....	7,058
Rice	1	90	4	10	1,781	....	258	....	2,143
Mangel-wurzel	1	....	16	4	84	....	49	6	159
Broom corn	1	21	....	....	....	....	32	....	53
Cotton	4	23,524	4	8	6,415	....	725	....	30,676
Jute ....papers	1	42	8	....	....	....	862	2	914
Total	283	1,038,950	1,907	159,746	57,303	9,372	57,634	553,860	1,878,773

Statement showing the quantity and kind of seeds issued by the Department of Agriculture to States and Territories ravaged by grasshoppers, under special appropriation by Congress of $20,000.

	Vegetable.	Flower.	Tobacco.	Tree.	Borage.	Grass.	Clover.	Jute.
	Papers.	Papers.	Papers.	Papers.	Papers.	Quarts.	Quarts.	Quarts.
Kansas	225,094	21	6	14	......	......	6	1
Colorado	36,752	7	......	2	......	4	......	......
Dakota	41,323	8	......	......	......	......	1	......
Nebraska	196,124	48	8	10	12	4	7	1
Totals	499,293	84	14	26	12	8	14	2

	Doura.	Wheat.	Oats.	Buckwheat.	Sorghum.	Mangel-wurzel.	Field corn.	Grand total.
	Quarts.	Quarts.	Quarts.	Quarts.	Quarts.	Quarts.	Quarts.	
Kansas	4	2,587	6,921	4,428	21	......	3,894	242,997
Colorado	......	618	2,128	1,344	......	......	1,166	42,021
Dakota	......	292	302	1,396	2	......	1,996	45,320
Nebraska	3	3,309	11,294	5,429	41	6	6,226	223,522
Totals	7	6,806	20,645	13,507	64	6	13,282	553,860

STATISTICAL DIVISION.

The statistical division of the department, with a working force quite too small for the broad field which it is designed to occupy, has continued during the past year its plan of crop reporting which was inaugurated early in the history of the department.

It has also collated current records of official boards, commercial organizations, and voluntary associations which hold relationship with agriculture, or with the distribution and sale of its products. As heretofore, it has attempted to supply the public demand for such information in systematic form, through published reports; the commercial and agricultural press; and in response to requests of departments, boards, societies, and individual publicists.

This is a work of constantly enlarging importance, in a field that is continental, with population rapidly increasing and production swelling in still higher ratio. It is a work demanded by the producer who would know where to find the best markets and highest prices; by the consumer who would seek abundance at a cost within his means, and without extortionate exactions of the carrier and the middlemen; and by the legitimate dealer who seeks protection, as does the farmer, against the piratical course of the reckless speculator. It becomes a necessity—an imperative duty, when opportune falsehood is able in a single day to wrench millions from the grasp of producers—that the government should forewarn and forearm the multitudes which represent its foundation industry.

This protection the statistical division of the department, if properly equipped and administered, can effectually accord.

To command public confidence and respect, to accomplish results commensurate in any good degree with the importance of the work to be done, enlarged means and facilities are an imperative necessity. The provision hitherto made for this branch of the department service has exceeded that accorded by a State legislature to its board of agriculture for a similar, though more limited purpose, yet the difference bears no proportion to the relative breadth of territory occupied. The record of current production and of the meteorological and economic fluctuations which constantly modify it throughout thirty-eight States and ten Territories, is of sufficient importance to call for ample means and unremitting endeavor.

The time has arrived when the crop-reporting system should be made more thorough and accurate and its results should be communicated to the public at the earliest possible moment. A synopsis of such results, furnished to the press by telegraph, should command general publication throughout the country in advance of the full printed report forwarded by mail. The co-operation of statistical authorities of States tending to uniformity, and inspiring increased public confidence, may be a possible consummation, as it is one greatly to be desired if practicable.

In several States this service, modeled upon the plan of the department, through manifest and profitable efficiency, has gained a strong local hold upon the confidence and regard of farmers and legislators.

While this system has thus been adopted in several States, and is already in operation in some European countries, its methods may possibly be improved, and its work may certainly be rendered more thorough by fuller information, and ampler elaboration and test of accuracy, thus leading to more uniformly reliable results. Its voluntary work, by thousands of public spirited farmers, should receive all practicable consideration and acknowledgment, and no reasonable expense should be spared to complete requisite data, and facilitate consolidation and embodiment in accurate results.

The marketing of surplus production in Europe, which is yearly assuming increased importance, makes it necessary to obtain prompt and trustworthy information of current crop reports of the world, and especially of European countries.

This department has already done something in this direction, yet more remains to be done in obtaining systematically and frequently the condition of foreign crops and results of foreign harvests.

While the changing area in special crops, their current condition in the growing season, and their harvest outcome hold prominent place, the whole field of statistical investigation in scientific and practical agriculture may be explored.

The relations of labor to proprietorship and production, the prices of lands and products, the peculiar adaptation of industries to localities, the rate of development of new and promising industries, and indeed the collection and co-ordination of all facts representing the status or the progress of agriculture come properly within the province of this branch of the department reserve.

FORESTRY.

The vast and increasing importance of the subject of forestry has led to the establishment of a distinct division in the department, to be exclusively devoted to such investigations of the subject as will tend to the fullest development of the resources of the country in that respect; the discovery of the best methods of management, and the preservation of our wasting forests, and the maintenance, in all its bearings, of the universal interest involved in that industry.

In furtherance of this design an agent of the department is now on a visit to different countries of Europe for the purpose of investigating the organization, working, and previous condition of experimental forest stations, schools of forestry, private tree-planting, and the aid afforded by governments to the business of forestry.

ARTESIAN WELLS.

By an act of Congress approved June 16, 1880, it was provided:

That with a view to the reclamation of the arid and waste lands lying in certain Western States and Territories, the Commissioner of Agriculture is hereby authorized to contract for the sinking of two artesian wells on the plains east of the Rocky Mountains; said wells are to be sunk at such places as the Commissioner of Agriculture shall designate. * * * The sum of $20,000 is hereby appropriated to carry out the objects of this provision; the same to be disbursed under such rules and regulations as the Commissioner of Agriculture shall prescribe.

Acting under this provision my predecessor in office proceeded to make an examination of the arid country lying on the eastern slope of the Rocky Mountains in Colorado, and selected for the first trial well the arid plain a few miles from the Arkansas River, adjoining the military reservation of Fort Lyon.

On my accession to office an examination showed that on June 30 this well had been bored to the depth of 450 feet, at an expense of $18,353.55.

By an act of Congress approved March 3, 1881, an appropriation of $10,000 was made "For the reclamation of the arid and waste lands lying in certain Western States and Territories."

Realizing that the success of the well at Fort Lyon was not commensurate with its cost, and believing that the continuance of the work would absorb the additional appropriation, without practical result, I concluded to have an intelligent scientific survey made of the country to be benefited, and an examination made of the well at Fort Lyon. After conference with Prof. J. W. Powell, Director of the United States Geological Survey, I appointed Prof. C. A. White and Prof. Samuel

68 Ab

Aughey, both eminent geologists, with instructions to visit the well at Fort Lyon, and to explore the eastern slope of the Rocky Mountains with a view to determine proper sites for the location of wells in future, should such be the pleasure of Congress.

Hon. Horace Beach, of Wisconsin, a gentleman of large experience in sinking wells, was subsequently added to the commission. These gentlemen took the field in the latter part of August and prosecuted their labors as long as the season would allow. A preliminary report of this commission accompanies this (Appendix A).

Acting upon the information contained in the report of these gentlemen, that the well was not located in a section of country geologically promising success, I have suspended work upon it for the present.

AGRICULTURE OF THE PACIFIC SLOPE.

By act of Congress approved March 3, 1881, an appropriation was made of $5,000, "to enable the Commissioner of Agriculture to procure and publish data touching the agricultural needs of that portion of the United States lying west of the Rocky Mountains."

To carry out this provision, I appointed Prof. E. W. Hilgard, of the State Agricultural College of California, Hon. Robert W. Furnas, of Nebraska, and Hon. T. C. Jones, of Ohio, commissioners, with instructions to investigate and report upon the cultivation of the grape on the Pacific coast, and especially the inducements offered by the soil and climate of New Mexico for vine culture in reference to supplying the market with valuable grapes, wines, and raisins; to report upon the animal industries of that section, and to examine and report upon the agricultural methods prevailing, and the general management of land for horticultural as well as agricultural purposes.

This commission took the field in the latter part of August, and I shall have the pleasure of laying their report before Congress early in January.

EXAMINATION OF WOOLS AND ANIMAL FIBERS.

The work of examination of wools during the past year has been almost exclusively devoted to the continuation of the measurement of the fineness of the fibers, and the mathematical calculations necessary to the presentation of the results in such form that they may be readily understood by all interested in the woolen industries, in every part of the world, whether they be producers, dealers, or manufacturers.

It is difficult, by a written description, to make one, unacquainted with the methods necessarily involved in the accurate execution of this work, comprehend the amount of tedious and patient labor required, but an approximate idea of it may be obtained from the fact that it has been necessary to make with the microscope at least 75,000 individual measurements of fibers, the immediate results of which, to secure the accuracy desired, were of necessity relative, so that each one had to be reduced by calculation to the absolute standard. We have thus measured in all about 600 samples of wool of different qualities, making altogether about 2,100.

An interesting feature of our work is found in the fact that through the courtesy of Mr. William G. Markham, secretary of the National Association of Wool Growers, we have been able to make measurements of wools from Germany, graded by one of high authority on the subject of the German system of classification, so that we are able to present authoritative figures for the comparison of the fineness of our own wools with the celebrated products of the old world.

In this comparison we find that many of our manufacturers are at fault, when they complain that it is impossible to obtain in this country wools of the fineness required in the best work. It enables us to confidently affirm that it is possible to produce in the United States as fine wools as can be produced in any other part of the world; and further, that the fineness of the products of the Saxony and Spanish merinos have not deteriorated since their introduction to this country, wherever the maintenance of this quality has been kept in view by the breeders.

Examination of the felting properties of the wools has not yet been begun, because our time has thus far been fully occupied with the work connected with the measurements of fineness, and of the tensile strength and of some of the mechanical difficulties involved, requiring the construction of special apparatus, both to facilitate and hasten the operations, as well as to insure perfect accuracy in the results.

This apparatus is now in course of construction, and will in a very short time be put into actual operation. It is expected that this branch of our investigation will give exceptionally interesting data, upon which to base estimates of the commercial and manufacturing value of the wools brought to our markets. In the measurements of the tensile strength, ductility, and elasticity more progress has been made.

A large number of samples have been prepared for examination of the minute structure of the fiber, as modified by the breed and the conditions to which the animals producing the fiber may have been subject. The limited observations that we have made in this direction indicate that it will prove an important field of inquiry, and that the results that are possible may have a bearing upon the determinations of the purity of any given breed under consideration.

Our report upon this inquiry will be accompanied by drawings, illustrating the peculiarities to which we refer. A large amount of labor is still necessary for the completion of the investigation as contemplated by the act of Congress ordering it. The work is being pushed forward with all due diligence and rapidity, and it is hoped that provision will not only be made for its entire completion, but that we may be enabled to extend our researches to wools of other sections of the country, and produced under different conditions of breeding, feeding, management, and climate.

I would suggest that an examination of cotton fibers, produced under different conditions of variety, culture, soil, and climate, should be undertaken and prosecuted in a similar manner, and there can be no doubt that, if the suggestion be adopted, the results obtained will be of quite as great value to the cotton industry as those we have already obtained are to the woolen industry.

The results of the proposed examination of cottons would make additions of an entirely new character to the literature of the fiber, for we know of no investigations looking to the determination of the tensile strength, at least. And there is just now a very favorable opportunity for securing the material for examination in the International Cotton Exposition being held in Atlanta, Ga., where samples from all parts of the world will be obtainable.

GRAPE CULTURE AND WINE-MAKING.

During the past year there has been in course of preparation a report upon the culture of the vine, and the manufacture of wine in Europe, having for its object an exposition of the more important principles upon which this great industry is based, and upon which success in its prosecution depends.

The work is governed by the idea, that for wine-making in this country it is better for those desiring to enter upon this branch of agricultural industry to begin with inexpensive methods and arrangements, to produce large crops of wines of medium quality, which may be early sent to market and sold at low prices, and thus made to yield quick and profitable returns, rather than from the first to attempt to produce wines of high grade to rival those of the more celebrated qualities of the old world. The latter is believed, with our new vineyards, comparatively new varieties, and general want of knowledge and experience on the subject, to be practically impossible, and that it may therefore be accepted as a general rule that it is better to devote all possible energy to the production of good, healthy table wines for the present, and wait for the larger experience this will afford and the accession of new varieties to lead to the production of wines of higher grades.

With this end in view it has been the endeavor in the preparation of this report to present those principles of vineyard and cellar management, as may be applied, with the greatest measure of economy and the greatest probability of yielding profitable results. It is hoped that this report will be completed and ready for publication early in February next.

MANUFACTURE OF SUGAR FROM SORGHUM.

Congress at its last session appropriated the sum of $25,000 for expenses of machinery and apparatus, labor, &c., to continue experiments in the manufacture of sugar from sorghum and other sugar-producing plants, the appropriation to be made immediately available. My predecessor had purchased the machinery and other apparatus, appointed several additional chemists, and made contracts with parties residing near the city to raise the sorghum cane for experiment.   Upon assuming the duties of the office I found growing 135 acres of sorghum cane, consisting of 52 varieties.   One of the farms on which this cane had been planted was within the city limits, the other two were located some distance beyond the boundary.   Having engaged the services of an expert in sugar-making, who had been highly recommended for the position, operations were commenced at the mill on September 26, and continued with slight interruptions until the latter part of October, at which time the supply of cane became exhausted.   Forty-two acres of the 135 planted in sorghum were overtaken by the frost before sufficiently ripe for use, and the crop was so badly damaged as to be regarded as unfit for experiment.

The following condensed statement gives the results of the operations for the season:

Statement showing amount of sorghum cane raised, amount manufactured into sugar and sirup, and to cost of raising and manufacturing.

Acres of cane passed through crushing-mill	93.5
Yield of cane per acre in pounds	4,903
Pounds of cane crushed	458,444
Gallons of juice obtained after defecation	26,794
Pounds of sirup obtained	34,985
Gallons of sirup obtained	2,977
Pounds of sugar obtained	165

The expenses of raising the cane were as follows:

Rent of land	$1,854	00
Labor and superintendence	3,474	22
Tools and implements	347	13
Hire of teams and hauling cane to mill	914	10
Total	6,589	45

Expense of converting the cane raised into sirup and sugar:

Paid for labor and running mill	$1,342	11
Coal and wood	325	48
Total	1,667	59

Of the sirup made there has been sold 2,328 gallons, at 33 cents per gallon, and the money covered into the Treasury.

TEA CULTURE.

f Congress an item was included in the agricult-
roviding $10,000 for experiments in connection
nfacture of tea.

duties of my office as Commissioner, I insti-
tion of the condition of this enterprise both

financially and economically. The disposition of the appropriation I found to be as follows:

Surveying	$225 00
Furniture	116 00
Iron safe	365 00
Wagon and harness	252 00
Salaries, labor, and expense account	3,377 11
Total	4,335 11

In order to ascertain the precise condition and value of the experiment being carried on in South Carolina, I directed, on July 9, Mr. William Saunders, the horticulturist of the department, to proceed to Summerville and to examine the premises and report upon the work. His statement, which will be found in full in Appendix B, sets forth that the 200 acres of land selected for the experiment are most of them covered with a heavy forest growth, the soil being "poor, hungry sand," of a character "to support only the scantiest kind of vegetation." Of this, about 15 acres had been cleared and was under a primitive cultivation. On these acres operations were commenced in January last; a space was prepared for sowing the tea seed, and preparation was made for covering the plants, which when young suffer severely on being exposed to the sun. The plants were growing well and constituted the entire tea crop of the farm. Mr. Saunders reported that "with regard to the future prospects of the enterprise, if continued in the line of the present scheme and under the present system, it may be said that there is not much room for encouragement." The poverty of the soil and the character of the climate, in which frosts sometimes occur, seem to be unfavorable to the production of strong, highly-flavored teas, as had already been proved by an experiment in McIntosh, Ga.

As to the future management of the tea farm [says Mr. Saunders], following the conviction that no experiment which can be made in the culture of tea at this place will warrant a continuation of the undertaking, it may be suggested that expenses be cut down to the lowest figures admissible; that all operations of clearing the ground of stumps and trees be stopped at once; that until further notice the mule team be employed in deep plowing, harrowing, and putting in thorough condition for planting about 6 acres of the best portion of the cleared land, which can be used for the formation of a nursery of tea plants if desired; that the expensive superintendence be modified, so that $300 per month will not be paid for the management of $60 worth of labor during the same period of time, as at present, and that all labor cease, except so much as may be found necessary to look after the young plants.

Acting on this advice, I have disposed of all the animals except one horse; have removed a large portion of the outfit to Washington, and have employed one person, whose duty it is to look after the growing plants, of which a few thousand have been distributed by the department. In concluding his report, Mr. Saunders says:

In a general way it may be stated that since July 1, 1880, $15,000 have been appropriated by Congress for the encouragement of tea culture. So far as is visible to the ordinary observer, the only practical, palpable result of expenditures from this fund is to be found and what has been done on this farm.

CONTAGIOUS DISEASES OF DOMESTICATED ANIMALS.

On assuming control of the Department of Agriculture I found that my predecessor had provided for a continuation of the investigation of contagious diseases of domesticated animals by assigning to duty those previously employed and the appointment of an additional number of veterinary surgeons. This additional force seems to have been made necessary by the increased duties imposed by Congress in making an appropriation for the purpose of determining the extent to which the disease known as contagious pleuro-pneumonia exists in the States heretofore reported as infected with the malady. Agents for this purpose had been appointed in the following-named States: New York, New Jersey, Pennsylvania, and Maryland. Two surgeons had been appointed in New Jersey, one of whom had been directed to make examinations also in Delaware.

The agent in Maryland had been directed to extend his investigations into the District of Columbia, and such counties on the eastern border of Virginia as he might be able to visit. As these agents were engaged in an active prosecution of the investigation, it was thought best to continue them until the work was completed, or at least until satisfactory evidence was obtained as to the prevalence or non-existence of this destructive disease in the territory above named.

Notwithstanding the many disadvantages under which these agents have labored, being without either State or governmental authority for making inspections, their reports indicate the existence of contagious pleuro-pneumonia among cattle in the above-named States and in the District of Columbia. While but comparatively few acute cases of the disease were discovered, many chronic cases and numbers of infected stables, premises, &c., were found in a majority of the localities visited.

The reports of these veterinary surgeons will be submitted in detail hereafter.

In addition to further experiments for the purpose of more accurately determining the nature of the diseases known as swine plague and fowl cholera, Dr. D. E. Salmon had been instructed to institute and carry out as thorough an inquiry as possible into the nature and peculiar characteristics of the fatal disease among cattle known as Spanish fever. This inquiry was regarded as necessary for the purpose of more definitely determining the nature of the virus or infecting principle of the disease —the part of the body in which this virus multiplies, and the manner in which it is excreted and conveyed to healthy animals.

To properly understand this disease it would seem necessary to know how an animal, apparently healthy, can be the means of so widely disseminating so fatal a malady, and why those actually affected with it in its most destructive type are unable to transmit it to other animals.

Another equally important point to be determined is, as to how the virus of this disease can become acclimated and resist a temperature much lower than was formerly possible, and to what extent this acclimation may continue, and consequently what danger there may be of the Northern States becoming permanently infected in the future. These points once clearly and definitely established, much more effective measures for the prevention of the disease may be devised than are now possible.

The past season has been rather an unfavorable one for the successful prosecution of this investigation, owing to the fact that the disease has prevailed to a much less extent than in former years. Dr. Salmon has, however, made some important discoveries in regard to the transmission of the malady, having already successfully inoculated several He is still engaged on this branch of his work, and as soon as the results of his experiments are more definitely determined, a detailed report of his investigation will be transmitted for the consideration of Congress.

Dr. H. J. Detmers was instructed to continue his experiments with the disease known as swine plague, with special reference to ascertaining what agents seem to offer the best results when used as prophylactics. He was advised to put to a practical test, on a large scale, the subjects selected for experiment. By studying the disease in large herds, and watching closely the effects of the agents used, it was thought that a cheap, simple, and efficient preventive of this destructive disease might be discovered and a lasting benefit thus conferred on the farming community and the nation generally. A full report of the results of his experiments will be submitted hereafter.

In addition to the above-named diseases, which require still further experiments to definitely determine all their peculiar characteristics, there are many other destructive contagious maladies which, as yet, have received no consideration at the hands of this department.

The most important, because the most fatal and destructive, of these diseases is that of anthrax or charbon. Many classes of our domesticated animals are subject to this disease, and perhaps the annual losses from this malady are heavier than from any other single disease now prevalent among our farm animals. While the investigations referred to were going on in this country, Dr. Lyman, a veterinary surgeon who had been employed for that purpose, was pursuing his investigations in England with regard to the alleged existence of pleuro-pneumonia and foot and mouth disease among cattle landed in that country from the United States. He was accompanied by Professor Whitney, the accomplished microscopist, and the results of his scientific inquiry and of his conferences with the privy council are interesting and valuable. He was instructed by my predecessor to continue the investigations undertaken by the department in England the previous year. In an interview with the privy council Dr. Lyman requested that an examination of portions of diseased lungs taken from the cattle condemned last year might be made by the veterinary surgeon of the council and himself unitedly, at the same time assuring them that no pleuro-pneumonia had been found West, and that this department had employed competent officers to inspect all suspected districts along the Atlantic coast. As the result of the examination, the British veterinary surgeon, Dr. Brown, expressed the opinion that there need be no occasion for alarm in the future with regard to condemning cattle, and that "if the United States was entirely free from pleuro-pneumonia no condemnations would be made upon lungs presenting the appearances only of those that were condemned last year." It appears that out of 32,000 animals imported into English ports, outside of Liverpool, in six months ending June 25, 1881, only 35 had been condemned even under the suspicion of having contagious pleuro-pneumonia. And Dr. Lyman remarks that—

As a result of my conference with the authorities of Great Britain upon this subject, I think it may safely be stated that the impressions which they held regarding the health, in this respect, of our western herds, have been materially changed, and that lungs, having a certain appearance, heretofore condemned as being of contagious pleuro-pneumonia, will not be so considered in the future.

Between January 1 and May 31, 1881, large numbers of American cattle landing at London, Liverpool, and Glasgow were considered as having foot-and-mouth disease. Careful investigation shows that the disease, if it existed, was caused by infection communicated to the cattle after they were shipped from American ports, and is to be attributed to exposure to the virus imported into England from France, and spread abroad from Deptford market, where it was first discovered. It is considered possible that the disease may be imparted to American cattle by the use of the head-ropes, which are often taken from diseased European animals and used on board American vessels employed in the cattle trade, and also by taking on board these vessels articles for shipment from wharves where diseased cattle have been landed. If this theory is true, legislation will be required to remedy the evil. Dr. Lyman reports that during his stay in Great Britain no diseased hogs were landed from the United States. He quotes from the report of the veterinary department of the privy council for the year 1879 a statement showing that out of 279 portions of swine flesh taken from American hogs that had been condemned and slaughtered on account of swine fever, only three were found to contain living trichinæ. The British report, after giving as a reason why the direct importation of American pork was not prohibited, that "such a measure would have damaged the trade without producing any satisfactory results," continues: "Besides, trichinosis among swine is known to exist in Germany, and it probably exists in other exporting countries, so that nothing short of prohibition of swine flesh in all forms from all foreign sources would have been effectual." "In view of the recent total embargo placed by some of the foreign governments upon the imports of our hog products on account of the alleged existence in them of trichinæ," it is recommended that measures be taken to ascertain more definitely what percentage of American hogs are thus diseased, the geographical distribution of the disease in this country, and all other information which may

aid in devising such means as shall decre
ence in American pork products.

With regard to the transportation of cat
I am happy to say that American cattle, i
" arrive at their destination with fewer br
generally than do those from some of the i

The losses of cattle on ship-board from
1880, exceeded 5 per cent. In the corres
losses were about 2¼ per cent.

SUGAR FROM BI

Under the act of Congress appropriati
tion of experiments in connection with tl
beets, and for the cultivation of beets for t
contracted for improved English and Frei
the beet, which were to be loaned to the D
at Wilmington, Del. I have carried out
and in addition thereto have contracted f
seed of the sugar beet for distribution to :
to grow the beet for sugar-making purpos

DISBURSING OFI

The following table exhibits in a conde
made by Congress for this department,
pended balance for the fiscal year ending

Object of appropriation.
Salaries ....
Collecting statistics ....
Purchase of seeds ....
Experimental garden ....
Museum and herbarium ....
Furniture, cases, and repairs ....
Library ....
Laboratory ....
Contingent expenses ....
Postage ....
Improvement of grounds ....
Printing and binding ....
Report on forestry ....
Investigating the history and habits of insects ....
Investigating the diseases of swine, &c ....
Examinations of wools and animal fibers ....
Machinery, &c., for experiments in the manufacture of sugar.
Data respecting the needs of arid regions ....
Reclamation of arid and waste lands ....

Very respectfully,

C

INDEX.

D.

E.

69 Ab